Summary of Contents

Professional MFC with Visual C++ 6

Mike Blaszczak

Wrox Press Ltd. ®

Professional MFC with Visual C++ 6

Reprinted May 2001

Published by Wrox Press Ltd,
Arden House, 1102 Warwick Road, Acocks Green, Birmingham B27 6BH, UK.
Printed in Canada
3 4 5 6 TRI 04 03 02 01

ISBN 1-861000-15-4

Trademark Acknowledgements

Credits

Author
Mike Blaszczak

Additional Material
Craig McQueen
Kenn Scribner

Technical Editors
Adrian Young
Andrew Tracey
Robin Smith

Managing Editor
Victoria Hudgson

Development Editor
John Franklin

Index
Catherine Alexander

Technical Reviewers
Christophe Nasarre
Kenn Scribner
Marc Simkin
Stephen Danielson
Curt Krone
Bryon Vargas
Craig McQueen
Julian Templeman
Jim Brzowski

Design/Layout
Mark Burdett
Tom Bartlett
William Fallon
John McNulty

Cover
Chris Morris

Technical Diagrams
David Boyce

Dedication

All of my friends have contributed something to who I am today. People who made the most substantial contributions include, in no particular order, Mike Engstrom, Sean Flynn, Mike Faulkner, Bob Loescher, and Frank Yerrace. Joey Madden, the bartender down at Scarlett O'Hara's, helped out too. I won't mention Bob's name because he never got me a sandwich, but I'll certainly mention my parents who gave me lots of sandwiches and a couple of computers. Now, through a funny twist of fate, I tell *them* what kind of computer to buy.

Liz has exhibited a tremendous amount of patience with me during the daunting fourth revision of this very difficult writing assignment. Somehow, she's convinced me that making the keys go down all night and weekend is heroic.

Even when I'm not writing books, the waitresses and bartenders at TGI Friday's in Kirkland, Washington, exhibit an amazing amount of patience with me.

And to everyone with whom I've ever worked: while you were putting up with my dopey humor and persistent grumbling, I'm sure I learned something from you in one way or another.

About The Author

Mike Blaszczak lobbied his high-school principal until he was allowed to graduate six months early. In 1988, he moved to Hartford, Connecticut and attended the University of Hartford part-time. Disgruntled by the lack of an advanced placement curriculum at the school, he quit taking classes and concentrated on working hard and making money. After working – and traveling extensively – for a small consulting firm in Bloomfield, Connecticut, he took a position in Microsoft's Consulting Services organization in March of 1992. In November of 1993, Mike joined the Microsoft development team in Redmond, Washington, working on the Microsoft Foundation Classes. Mike accepted a promotion (which is Latin for 'lateral move') to Program Manager and was, for a time, responsible for managing the development, documentation and delivery of the Microsoft Foundation Classes and the C Run-time Libraries. Mike decided eventually that playing with code was much more fun than playing with people, so he laterally removed himself back to the development team. After a stint as the lead for both the MFC and ATL development teams, Mike has moved on to work in Microsoft's Hardware division.

A veteran of Microsoft for more than seven years, Mike has previously been published in Byte Magazine, Microsoft Systems Journal, Computer Buyer's World Magazine, Visual C++ Developers' Journal, and in books published by Que and Microsoft Press. Mike squandered the money he should have spent on a vowel for his last name by buying fast cars and motorcycles. He's responsible for telling all his friends about the rules of ice hockey, is still trying to find the perfect set of bass guitar strings, and trying to keep the floor in the garage tidy.

You can contact Mike via e-mail at `mikeblas@msn.com`. Mail sent care of The Goose Pub and Eatery may be answered, but is *not* guaranteed to reach the author.

Foreword

I hope you'll enjoy using this book. I doubt that anyone will actually read it cover-to-cover (except the people Wrox pays to try and correct my mistakes), so I've said "using" instead of "reading". I anticipate that you'll read a few chapters and then only refer back to the book as you find it necessary – when you get stuck as you try your own stunts with Visual C++ and the Microsoft Foundation Classes.

This is the fourth edition of this book, and the level of work still required to revise it and improve it is still daunting. While this revision didn't kill me (like writing the original edition did), writing the software the book discusses with one hand and writing the book with the other is about as much as I can do in a day. I'm trying to spend more time at the rink, and the track, and with other – you know – *people*.

Whining aside, throughout the book, I've tried to stick to the 'Why's and 'How's of MFC rather than blurting out the 'What's that most other books offer. I've tried to use my page count to talk to you, assuming that you'd have the initiative to run off and look at the samples from the Wrox web site, or find the appropriate items in the Visual C++ online help system on your own. Certainly, there's some overlap between this book and the product's help contents – but that's because both describe the same product. My charge is to breathe more continuity and insight into the material than the online references do. Just the same, this book should augment the product's documentation and not replace it. I hope I've succeeded in reaching these goals. If I have, you should feel more confident that you understand *why* MFC works the way it does – and therefore be able to fend for yourself when a challenging aspect of your project presents itself.

The best advice I have to offer you as you move forward with the product is this: don't be afraid. If you think you need to try something, try it. If you need to trace through MFC or the C Run-time libraries, do so. If you get stuck, think about it. Try to minimize the problem. Carefully apply scientific method to prove your hypothesis. There are no places where black magic is at work, here – you can observe and repeat everything that's happening. By being patient and doing a little investigation, you'll usually surprise yourself by quickly finding the way through what might have initially seemed impenetrable.

I'll probably make an attempt at a fifth edition, somewhere down the line. But I need your feedback before I do so – what things would you change? What do you wish I would cover? What do you think deserves more attention? More importantly, what left you stumped even though I covered it? What could use more detail? I can't address every aspect of the product – that would be like publishing a book of every oil painting that possibly could be painted. If you write, you might have to wait a little while before I have time to respond. I do my best to carefully consider and eventually answer every note I receive.

Thank you and have fun!

Table of Contents

Chapter 2: The Wizards and The Gallery   57

Table of Contents

Chapter 6: User Interface Issues   **305**

Chapter 7: Advanced User Interface Programming 349

Chapter 8: Using the Windows Common Controls   415

Chapter 9: Utility and Exception Classes

505

Chapter 10: Writing Multithreaded Applications with MFC   595

Chapter 11: Creating Dynamic-link Libraries 657

Chapter 13: Writing OLE Containers — 775

Chapter 18: Internet Server Programming   1013

Appendix D: The Foundation Classes Headers and Libraries

Appendix E: A History of MFC

Appendix F: Integrating ATL and MFC

MFC Quick Index

Index

Introduction

Welcome

Welcome to *Professional MFC with Visual C++ 6.0*, a revision of *Professional MFC with Visual C++ 5.0*. Mike has taken note of corrections and feedback received from the readers of previous editions, and combined them with material on the new MFC classes, to make this the ultimate technique reference for MFC 6.0. This book has been designed to give you, the Windows developer, an edge when you develop applications using some of the interesting and powerful features that MFC has to offer.

Who Should Read this Book

This book was written with the advanced developer in mind. You should already have some experience of Windows programming, and you should feel comfortable reading C++ code. This book is not suitable for those developers who don't understand C++, who have not previously developed software in Windows, or who are interested in a reference manual warmed up and served stale.

It goes without saying that you should be an adept Windows user. Nobody who develops software for Windows needs to be told, in painstaking detail, that they can exit a dialog box in three different ways, or that the mouse can be used to drag-and-drop a file to a new location. I will point out the less obvious, potent tricks available via the Visual C++ user interface, but this book will mostly discuss programming techniques using the application framework.

If your experience of Windows programming isn't vast, you may learn a thing or two about the Windows architecture during our tour through the Microsoft Foundation Classes; if you're not the kind of C++ guru who often quotes passages from Bjarne Stroustrup books, you may learn some finer points about the C++ programming language. However, what we're really here for is to learn how to develop real world applications for Windows, using one of the finest compilers and class libraries available today.

What's Covered in this Book

This book focuses on the use of the Microsoft Foundation Classes to develop software. Of course, 'software' is a very broad term – some readers are doubtless interested in writing low-level technical applications that might not even have a user interface, while others will be interested in coding form-oriented applications that do little more than data validation and formatting before they hand the information off to a database server.

While we won't be writing database servers, we *will* write a few utilities, some DLLs, an ActiveX control and even an OLE document server, as well as examining Microsoft's Open Database Connectivity (ODBC), Data Access Objects (DAO) strategies. At the very end of the book, we'll take a look at what the Microsoft Foundation Classes provide to make programming for the Internet easier.

This book will give a detailed discussion of the majority of classes present in Microsoft's application framework library. While it will point out what parameters are required for the member functions of those classes, it will concentrate more on describing what utility the classes really provide. It should be obvious that a class named CWnd will probably provide the functionality inherent in a window, but it may not be obvious when some class derivatives are more appropriate than others, exactly how objects of that class are created and destroyed, or what interaction that class has with others in the framework.

I should say that there are a few things this book doesn't do. It isn't an exercise in marketing hype, because although I do work at Microsoft, and while I may be tremendously excited about my group's product, I don't intend to gloss over issues that are problems, or be shy about showing workarounds that are faster than the way things were intended to be.

I'm not going to beat the glossy features of Visual C++ to death. I am sure that you can impress yourself with the power and utility of the tools provided with Visual C++ 6.0 in your own time, or with some other book. Instead, I will spend the space between these covers discussing the details that come up when your work with the Visual C++ AppWizards is complete; the real code that will make your program the best selling application, the fastest utility, or the most flexible embedded object in town.

Why Use the Microsoft Foundation Classes?

In addition to some more specialized tools, Microsoft's Visual C++ package encompasses a C/C++ compiler, a resource editor, a debugger, and the Microsoft Foundation Class library. This class library provides a collection of C++ classes that take most of the drudgery out of writing software for Windows.

The most compelling reason to use MFC is the vast amount of functionality that the classes can realize. Since the classes are targeted at the features your application needs – such as status bars, the implementations required for multiple document windows, and support for context-sensitive help – using MFC saves you coding time that you can use to implement other features in your application.

For some features, like colored dialog box backgrounds or menu management, the functionality is pretty basic. However, for other features, such as support for OLE, ODBC or DAO, MFC provides an astonishing amount of pre-implemented, ready-to-use functionality.

Visual C++ and the Microsoft Foundation Classes enjoy a symbiotic relationship. The Microsoft Visual Studio, which you will learn about in Chapter 1, provides you with the ability to manipulate your MFC code as it evolves – you can add classes, manage their member variables and functions, and even enable MFC features through this medium.

Within minutes of installing Visual C++, you can be compiling and running your first MFC program. As we examine the tools and the foundation classes throughout this book, you will learn how all of the features in the environment come together with the features of MFC, giving you tremendous power to develop your application.

What You Need to Use this Book

First and foremost, you'll need a PC. You should have a 32-bit operating system installed on your machine; Visual C++ 6.0 requires that you run under Windows 95 (or newer), or Windows NT 4.0 (or newer).

You'll need a CD-ROM drive, 24MB of RAM and between 235 and 263 MB of free disk space after installing the operating system (less, if you only want a minimal installation). To run faster, you should get more memory and you should invest in more disk space. See Appendix A for more information.

As Visual C++ supports multiple development targets, the code you'll learn to write here can be rebuilt to run natively on the Macintosh, as well as machines with Alpha or MIPS CPUs. The work needed to do this is beyond the scope of this book (although you should be able to follow along if you're using Visual C++ on those platforms), and I will be making no special effort to ensure that the material here blankets all Visual C++ platforms. The cross-platform features of Visual C++ are designed to be used by developers who have existing Windows-based code for the Intel processors and wish to port it to a different CPU platform.

Contacting the Author

I sleep almost constantly. If I'm not sleeping, I'm either busy at work or playing pool. As you can see, I'm a busy guy, but if you have questions about the material covered in this book, or if you have a problem with the example applications, please don't hesitate to e-mail me – my address is mikeblas@msn.com.

Please tell me what version of Visual C++ you have installed, what operating system you are using, and what's going wrong. "I get a out of memory error," is not what I mean. Do you get the problem from Visual C++, the AppWizard, the ODBC driver, or from Solitaire? The more specific the information you give me, the more eager I will be to help you.

If you have a problem with something you're writing, or have a question about how something in Visual C++ works, please *don't* contact me. Microsoft has gone to great trouble to provide product support services, and support engineers are available by telephone and on CompuServe. You should contact these engineers when you have a problem with the product in general; it is their job to help you.

Conventions Used

We use a number of different styles of text and layout in the book to help differentiate between different kinds of information. Here are examples of the styles we use and an explanation of what they mean:

> **These boxes hold important, not-to-be forgotten, mission critical details, which are directly relevant to the surrounding text.**

Background information, asides and references appear in text like this.

> ➤ **Important Words** are in a bold font.
> ➤ Words that appear on the screen, such as menu options, are in a similar font to the one used on screen, for example, the File menu.
> ➤ Keys that you press on the keyboard, like *Ctrl* and *Enter*, are in italics.
> ➤ All filenames are in this style: Videos.mdb.
> ➤ Function names look like this: sizeof().
> ➤ Code that is new, important, or relevant to the current discussion will be presented like this:

```
int main()
{
    cout << "Welcome to the book";
    return 0;
}
```

> ➤ Code you've seen before, or isn't directly relevant to the matter at hand, looks like this:

```
int main()
{
    cout << " Welcome to the book";
    return 0;
}
```

The Wrox Press Web Site

Our desire to see you succeed doesn't stop once you've purchased a Wrox Press book. We believe that you've entered into a partnership with us, and as such, it's our responsibility to provide you with the latest information available to us to help you succeed. To that end, we maintain two identical web sites:

For Europe: http://www.wrox.co.uk/
For the US: http://www.wrox.com/

The Wrox Press web site provides:

> ➢ Extensive information on our latest titles
> ➢ A wealth of links to relevant web sites around the world
> ➢ Errata sheets for current Wrox Press titles
> ➢ Useful tools, add-ins and tips
> ➢ Source code for the examples in the book

We recommend that you use a version 3.0 (or later) web browser. If you have any suggestions regarding the Wrox Press web site, then please e-mail the Webmaster at webmaster@wrox.com. The web site is as much your resource as it is ours.

Source Code

All the relevant code for the examples in the book can be downloaded from our web site (see above). All source code is free and can be found via the web page for this book.

Errors

While we have made every effort to make sure the information contained within this book is accurate, we're only human. If you're having difficulty with some aspect of the book, or have found a genuine error, then please check the errata sheet for this book on our web site.

If the answer to your problem isn't there, please feel free to fill out the form at the bottom of the web page with your question and we'll do our best to sort it out for you.

Tell Us What You Think

We've tried to make this book as accurate and enjoyable for you as possible, but what really matters is what the book actually does for you. Please let us know your views, whether positive or negative, either by returning the reply card in the back of the book or by contacting us at Wrox Press using either of the following methods:

e-mail: feedback@wrox.com
Internet: http://www.wrox.com

The Microsoft Visual Studio

Learning about a new development environment is often a daunting task. When you move away from familiar tools towards new ones, the new tools often seem awkward compared to your old favorites. You might become frustrated at the perceived lack of productivity, because you're not sure how to complete a simple task and it may take a while for you to find out the most efficient way to do the job.

Some people call this attachment to a tool the 'baby duck' syndrome. You are at ease with the first compiler, utility, editor or development method that you learned, just as the newborn duckling adopts the first duck that it sees as its mother. Instead of traumatically tearing you away from your mother compiler as you learn about Visual C++, I hope to show you that this new partner has many of the old, familiar and comfortable traits, as well as a lot of exciting new features designed to make your life easier.

In this chapter, we'll cover:

- ➤ The Microsoft Visual Studio
- ➤ Handling Visual C++ projects
- ➤ Creating and editing resources
- ➤ An overview of the MFC libraries

Microsoft Visual Studio

To provide you, the developer, with a more efficient workspace, Microsoft Visual Studio integrates tools for creating, editing, compiling and testing software under a single user interface. This means that you can, for example, set or clear breakpoints using the same interface that allows you to edit your source code. When you build your project, the IDE (integrated development environment) traps any errors which the compiler detects and lets you jump to the exact line number containing the error, even if the file is not already open!

Microsoft Visual Studio is actually bigger than it looks. For example, you can put a Java compiler and an automated testing tool inside the same IDE and use them, with impressive integration, with all your C++ projects and source code. However, no matter how much you're looking forward to the joys of Java, we'll just concentrate on C++ and MFC in this book.

The three major types of file that Windows developers commonly manipulate are project files, source code files and resource scripts. Throughout this chapter, you'll see the special features provided by Microsoft Visual Studio to handle these different file types.

The Project Workspace

Traditionally, one of the most complicated, and indeed most subtle, parts of building and maintaining a Windows application was maintaining the application's build process. However, in Visual C++, the build process can be maintained automatically by Visual Studio; any changes that you make to your project from within Visual Studio are automatically conferred on your project's description file, without any need for further intervention on your part.

In Visual C++ 6.0, the build information is maintained in project (.dsp) files. However, the Visual C++ developer's attention is usually focused on the project workspace (.dsw) file. Workspace files are responsible for storing all the information used to coordinate between all the other files that make up a project, including the source code files and the related project files.

If you're working to build a system – i.e. a collection of executables that work together, instead of just a single program that operates alone – you may find your workspace contains multiple projects. You can imagine that it's a very popular idea to put both your executable program and all of the DLLs that you need to build yourself within the same workspace. With such an arrangement, you can issue a single command and build all of the projects in the workspace.

You can create a new project by using the New... command in the File menu and activating the Projects tab in the resulting New dialog. When you create a new project, you also get a workspace for free. (With a deal like this, I'm not sure how Microsoft can stay in business.) You can, of course, create a blank workspace and insert projects into it later. Alternatively, you can add additional projects to the workspace you got for free when creating your initial project.

If you want to use an existing project or workspace, you can load it into Visual Studio by using the Open Workspace... item in the File menu.

When you open the project workspace file, Visual Studio will set itself up with all of the information stored in the file. This obviously means that it will load the file, but it also means that the Studio will open and position the windows exactly as they were when the file was last saved. It'll try to leave you on the same help topic that you were looking at before, and make sure all of your breakpoints are right where you left them.

State information for your Visual Studio session is stored in the options (.opt) file, which will bear the same name as your project. If there is no .opt file with the project files, Visual Studio will create it.

Makefiles

Previous versions of the Visual C++ development environment would always generate .mak files automatically. This version of the old-fashioned makefile could be fed to the command-line utility Nmake to build the project. In the Visual C++ 6.0 environment, you'll need to ask the environment to produce the makefile for you explicitly, by using the Export Makefile... command in the Project menu. If you find that the makefile is vital to your survival, you can set an option so that it is exported on every save of the project by checking the relevant box on the Build tab of the Options dialog. Use the Tools | Options... menu item to display this dialog.

If you're going to be sharing your project in a version control system, you'll probably want to check in the .dsw and .dsp files but not bother to check in the .opt file. You *may* wish to check in the .mak file, but it's just as easy to have developers who wish to use it generate it themselves. On the other hand, you might want to check it just to help guarantee that it is consistent for everyone on your team.

Project Workspace Window

One of the windows available to you in the Visual Studio is the Project Workspace window.

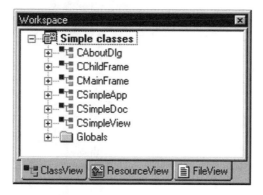

> You might notice that the menu bars in screenshots of the IDE in this book might
> not look like those on your own system. As a matter of personal preference, I use
> 'Screen Reader Compatible' menus in the studio. You can set your own installation
> to use this same look by marking the Use screen reader compatible menus box in the
> Workspace tab of the Options dialog, reachable from the Options... command of the
> Tools menu.

This window gives you access to many key project management features. If it's hidden, you can
display it using the Workspace item in the View menu, or toggle the window's visibility using the
related toolbar button. Like many other windows in the Visual Studio, the Project Workspace
window is dockable. You can let it float around on your desktop as you work, you can dock it to an
edge of your workspace, or you can close it altogether and open it only when you really need it. You
can set these options from the context menu that appears when you right-click on it.

Since the Project Workspace is the focal point of your work with projects in the Visual Studio, you'll
probably want to keep the window open whenever you can. The window can have up to three tabs in
it; each tab activates a different view of information in, or related to, your project. I'll leave the
ResourceView until our complete discussion of resources later in the chapter. For now, I'll
concentrate on the other two tabs that present information about your source code: FileView and
ClassView.

The FileView

When you have a project open, you can see
the files in the project by clicking the
FileView tab. An active FileView (with the
Project Workspace window undocked) is
shown here:

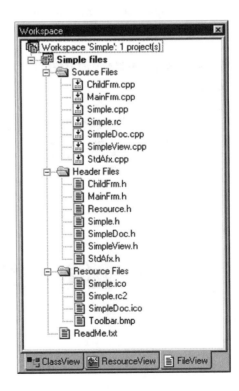

You'll note that the files in the project are represented in a hierarchical list. You can expand and collapse this list just like other tree view control in Windows. There are three levels of 'container' icons in the FileView:

Icon	Meaning
	This represents the workspace. There can only be one workspace open at a time, so you'll only ever see one of these icons.
	This represents the project. A workspace can contain multiple projects, so you may have more than one of these icons grouping the files for that project.
	This represents a logical grouping of files. You may have as many folders as you choose. These folders can be used to organize your files exactly how you choose.

Folders are a great way of organizing your files in FileView. You can add new folders by right-clicking on a project or folder icon and selecting New Folder... from the context menu. If you use the New Folder... command, you'll be offered the opportunity to add a new folder to the list that you see in the FileView window. If you use the New Mulder... command, you can invent yet another wildly successful television show based on superstition and pseudo-science. New Folder... results in this very simple dialog:

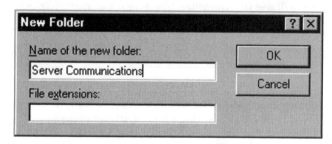

When you add a new folder, you give the folder a name and can choose to give the folder a list of file extensions. If you choose to give a folder a list of extensions, any new files added to the project that have the same extension will automatically appear under that folder. Once you've created a folder, you can drag-and-drop other files from your project into it. The folder will be created, by default, in whatever folder you have selected in the FileView window. If you don't have anything selected over there, the folder will be created at the topmost level within your project. Whether your folder has files in it or not, you can drag the folder to live anywhere within your project.

You can remove a file from FileView by selecting its icon and tapping the *Delete* key. Note that this doesn't delete the file – it just removes it from the project. You can add files to a project in a number of ways, such as selecting the Project | Add To Project | Files... menu item, or selecting Add Files to Project... from the context menu that appears when you right-click on the name of the project in the FileView window.

You only need to add files to your project when you create them yourself. If you use one of the Wizards, which we'll examine later, to create a class (or a whole project!) that resides in a brand-new file, you'll find that the Wizard will take care of adding everything to your project for you. If you add a file to your project manually, you'll need to add everything to your project – adding a given .cpp file to your project, for example, doesn't automatically add the related .h files to your project.

Obviously, you will always add your C++ source code files to the project, but you should only add object files or library files when they are not otherwise built by your project. Library files that come as part of the Win32 SDK or the Visual C++ development suite should be added to the Object/Library Modules list in the Link tab in the Project Settings dialog. However, you should add libraries to your project files list if you plan to modify them during your development effort. Libraries that have been added to your project will be checked to see if they are newer than your linked executable during the new build, whereas libraries in the linker's option screen won't be checked for updates.

Back in the FileView, you can double-click on a file to have the Visual Studio instantly load and open that file, and you can drag-and-drop files between folders and into and out of this window to alter the content of the project. Three different icons can be shown next to the name of a file in FileView:

Icon	Meaning
🗋	Visual C++ will use this file when building the currently selected configuration
🗋	Visual C++ won't use this file when building the currently selected configuration
🗎	The indicated file can't be used directly when building a defined configuration

The last icon indicates that the file is a part of the project, but not an active part of the build process. Header files have this icon next to them because they are not compiled directly, even if they are used in the build process. Documentation files which are a part of the project may have this icon next to them, since they are indeed part of the project, but Visual C++ will never use them as source when building the project.

While it may seem like a fruitless exercise to place such files into a project, it's really not a bad idea. Since Visual C++ can offer source code version management from within the IDE, the encapsulation of non-source code files in a project is quite appealing. Visual Studio's Active Document support also makes it possible to edit DocObjects such as Word documents from within the IDE.

FileView Tricks

Like most windows in the Microsoft Visual Studio, you can use the right mouse button, a *Shift+F10* keystroke, or the context menu key on your keyboard (if it has one), to bring up a context-sensitive floating menu. This menu provides you with some shortcuts to get some things done faster.

Throughout the book, I'll be politically incorrect and say 'right mouse button' and 'left mouse button'. If you're right-handed, you won't even notice. If you're left-handed and you've tweaked the Windows Control Panel to switch the buttons so that the primary mouse button is really the right mouse button, you'll know I actually mean 'left mouse button' when I say 'right mouse button' and vice versa. In a way, it makes sense; if I was reading this to you, I'd be facing you and then my right really would be your left.

In the FileView, the context menu has an O<u>p</u>en command, which is just the same as double-clicking on the file. It has a <u>C</u>ompile command, which compiles the file (if that's possible). It also has a <u>S</u>ettings... command that takes you to the Project Settings dialog, showing the settings for the file you've selected.

Finally, it has a Pr<u>o</u>perties command, which takes you to a property page window like this:

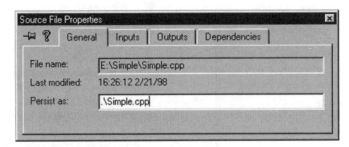

The different tabs each provide some piece of interesting information about the file you've selected. The General tab, visible above, shows the file name and the last modified date for the selected file. For the selected file, the Inputs, Outputs, and Dependencies tabs show which files contribute to the build step, which files come out of the build step, and which other files in the project are dependencies of the selected file. These tabs can help you verify the build process for the specific file you've selected.

Updating Project Dependencies

When you modify a file in your project, Visual Studio will automatically scan the file for its dependencies. It will make note of which files are dependent on changes in which other files, and will use this information to build the project most efficiently. Visual Studio will notice #include directives in source files and header files, and act accordingly. It also recognizes cursor, bitmap, and icon dependencies for .rc files. Unfortunately, it's easy to confuse the dependency analyzer; for example, file inclusions that are removed by conditional compilation directives are not noticed.

The ClassView

The Project Workspace window also features a ClassView tab. The ClassView for a project called `Simple` (which you will come across in Chapter 2) is shown here:

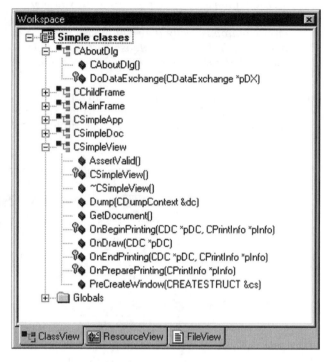

As you can see, this tab allows you to see a hierarchical view of the classes in your application. The view can be expanded to show the member functions and variables in your classes and, just like with the FileView, you can create folders to organize your classes.

You can double-click on entries in this tab to see their definitions. Double-clicking on **CSimpleApp**, for example, would open `Simple.h` and put the cursor on the definition for the `CSimpleApp` class. The view covers only the classes defined in files that are part of your project. It won't normally display classes from MFC. If you're interested in seeing absolutely every class your application references, you should read about the source browser in the next chapter.

You'll notice that the items in the view are shown next to one or two tiny icons, which describe the item.

ClassView Icon	Meaning
▪ᶠᶜ	The item is a class.
◆	The item is a function. If this icon appears alone, the function is `public`.
◆	The item is a variable or data member. If this icon appears alone, the item is `public`.

ClassView Icon	Meaning
🔒	The item is `private`. Shown to the left of the 'function' or 'data member' icon above.
🔑	The item is `protected`. Shown to the left of the 'function' or 'data member' icon above.
⊶○	The item is a COM interface.
⊸◆	The item is a COM method.
🖭	The item is a COM property.

Like the FileView, you can right-click (or press *Shift+F10* or the *Menu* key, if you have a Windows-compatible keyboard) to get a menu of other interesting tricks. The ClassView has a couple of menu choices here that connect you to the more powerful source browser. The References... command in the context menu, for instance, takes you to the Definitions and References window and lets you jump to lines of code that reference the class you've selected. You can similarly use the Base Classes... and Derived Classes... commands to move off to the browser to find information about the base class or any derived classes, respectively.

The ClassView window uses a quick, fuzzy parser. It's easy to fool it; if you have functions that are declared in a macro, for example, the window will not see them. You'll also find that the window doesn't preprocess your code before building the list of items that it displays, so the view will always include things which you might have excluded from your current build by using preprocessor directives. Namespaces and templates are also good ways to confuse the ClassView.

Adding Functions

The most impressive commands in the pop-up context menu are the choices that let you edit and augment your classes. If you right-click on a class, the two modification commands are Add Member Function... and Add Member Variable.... The Add Member Function... command brings up a dialog like the one shown below:

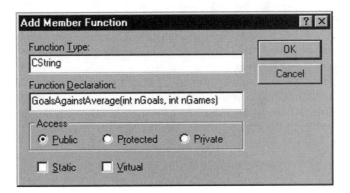

The box is quite straightforward; you can supply the return type for your new function in the Function Type edit box, and provide the declaration for the function in the Function Declaration box. You can specify additional keywords, like `inline`, in the Function Type edit box without any problem. After a bit of experience, you'll notice that these dialogs do very little syntax or context checking. You'll find that you're allowed to type almost anything you want in either of the boxes – very little syntax checking is done on them whatsoever.

Adding Variables

You can use the Add Member Variable... command in ClassView's context menu to reach this dialog box, which is very similar to the Add Member Function box:

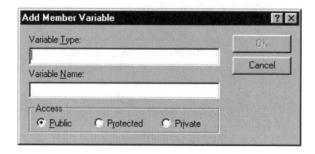

To use the box, just specify the Variable Type you want by typing it in the edit box. Specify the declaration for the variable in the Variable Name box. Like the function box, you can specify any additional attributes you need in the Variable Type box. You're very likely to specify asterisks or ampersands here to define pointers or references. While the box is quick and handy, I don't think I'd ever use it for complicated declarations; building an entry for a member pointer to a member function is probably right out.

You should try to be careful with the leeway afforded by both of these dialogs, as the dialog will let you enter data that can break your code. Your project will never be trashed, but you might just end up with a new function that has a bogus declaration. Hopefully, a future version of Visual C++ will address these issues without taking away any flexibility. The need to add comments to your code may also sway you towards adding class members manually.

Project Configurations

Microsoft Visual Studio projects support the notion of multiple project configurations, by which I mean that a single project file can manage the production of several different builds of the same code. The source files used will essentially be the same, but settings such as compiler options or preprocessor directives will differ between configurations.

If you're familiar with older versions of Visual C++, by the way, you'll recognize the configuration feature here as being quite similar to the targets feature from previous versions.

For example, you might have three source modules that produce your application. Usually, you'll want to compile these modules for debugging on Intel platforms, but sometimes you might build a release version of the same code for distribution to your users and, occasionally, you'll make release builds for DEC Alpha machines. These three scenarios define three different configurations for your project, which you might name Win32 Release, Win32 Debug and DEC Alpha Release.

Even though you might have an executable that's closely related to several other executables in the global scope of your project, you can't build more than one different executable without using different projects. That is, if a system you're developing consists of a Client.exe application and a Server.exe application, each with several C++ modules in common but otherwise completely different, you must build each executable with a different project or with a different subproject. However, you can build the debug and release builds, or indeed the builds for different target CPU platforms, using different configurations within the same project.

Think of it this way; a configuration is a set of options for the tools to build a single executable or library. A project (or subproject) actually produces some interesting output, such as an executable, a dynamic-link library, or a static library.

The second drop-down list in the Build toolbar enumerates all of the configurations that your current project can build. The currently selected configuration in that box is the configuration that will be built by default when you use the Build or Rebuild All commands in the Build menu. To change the configuration, just select a new one. Note that the configuration selected in this control will become the default configuration for the .mak file when you export the makefile.

The full Build toolbar is not displayed by default when you install Visual C++, but you can easily display it by right-clicking on an inactive area of a toolbar and selecting its name from the context menu.

You can add and remove build targets by selecting the Configurations... item in the Build menu, which brings up the dialog box shown here:

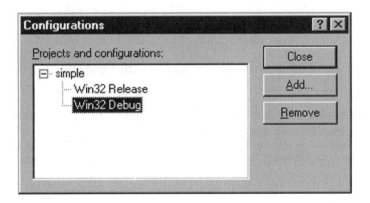

Managing Complex Projects

Microsoft Visual Studio is very proficient at handling complicated projects. It allows you to include more than one project in a workspace, and it lets you define the dependencies between the projects, so that one project can be a subproject of another.

Multiple Projects

Having multiple projects stored in one workspace file is quite handy for situations where the project involves multiple (but very related) executables. If you were working to implement the system comprising `Client.exe` and `Server.exe` that I mentioned before, you would probably want a project for each executable within the same workspace.

You might follow steps like these to get your project workspace configured correctly:

1. Use the <u>N</u>ew... command in the <u>F</u>ile menu to create a new project and workspace.

2. Select the appropriate project type.

3. Name the project appropriately. The name should be one of the two projects you wish to combine.

4. Once the workspace is created, you can insert the other project by using <u>F</u>ile | <u>N</u>ew... to create a new project. This time, make sure that the <u>A</u>dd to current workspace option is selected.

After doing this, you'll find you can use the resulting project workspace to manipulate all of your source code conveniently. When it comes to building your project, you'll often want to use the Batch Build... command in the <u>B</u>uild menu to get everything rebuilt completely. If you want to insert into your workspace a project that already exists, you can use the <u>P</u>roject | <u>I</u>nsert Project into Workspace... menu item.

Subprojects

In this case, there is an implicit build dependency between the top project and the subproject. If you have a project that relies on a dynamic-link library that you also build, you can make the DLL project a subproject of your application project. If you do this, the Visual Studio will know your executable is dependent on having the DLL built, so that when you build a parent project, the build mechanism will notice the dependency and automatically build the subproject as well.

You can tell Visual Studio about the dependencies of a project when it is being added to a workspace by checking the <u>D</u>ependency of box and selecting a project in the workspace. You can also tell Visual Studio about dependencies between the projects once the additional projects are added to your workspace. You can use the D<u>e</u>pendencies... command in the <u>P</u>roject menu to do this, which produces the following dialog:

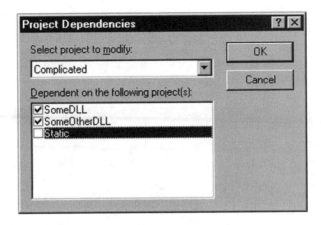

Once there, you can use the Select project to modify drop-down to pick one of the projects or subprojects in your workspace. Then you can use the check boxes in the Dependent on the following project(s) list to indicate which other projects will support the project selected in the drop-down. In the figure above, SomeDLL and SomeOtherDLL are subprojects of Complicated, so they will be built, if necessary, whenever Complicated is built.

You can make any number of projects and subordinate projects in your application. You can also wire them up any way you'd like, as long as you don't try to make a circular dependency. An important fact to remember is that any project can be a subproject for more than one project. Maybe things got *really* complicated for you, and you have a SomeApplication project which has SomeDLL and SomeDLL2 projects. But maybe you also have a static library of neat functions called HandyCode; that project can be a subproject for the DLLs *and* the application project without a problem.

By the way, if you're familiar with previous versions of Visual C++, this section might have surprised you a little. In Visual C++ Version 2.*x* and older, projects were .mak files, period. You couldn't do any of these fancy things unless you made your own external makefile. As we mentioned, in the new Visual Studio, the **project workspace** (that .dsw file that keeps popping up) is what you're really working with. You can still have the convenience of a makefile – just use the Export Makefile... command in the Project menu.

Project Settings

Now that you've seen how to create projects, subprojects and configurations, you're probably wondering how you can set compile and link options from within Visual Studio. The answer is through the Project Settings dialog, which is the nerve center for this sort of activity.

From this dialog you can provide the behind-the-scenes build tools with different command-line options, select different libraries or implementation models, change the internationalization strategies for your application or even influence the way builds are completed by adding custom build steps. Not only does it allow you to alter the settings for an entire project, but also for a particular configuration or even individual files.

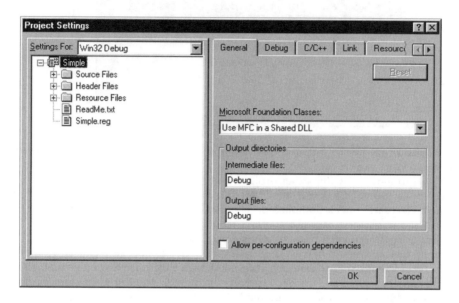

You can bring up this dialog by clicking the Settings... item in the Project menu or by pressing *Alt+F7*. As you can see, the dialog consists of a tree view control on the left. This shows you all the files contained in the various configurations of all the files in your current workspace. The project folders can be expanded to show the individual files. The elements highlighted on the left determine the information displayed in the tabs on the right. There are a large number of tabs offering a huge quantity of options, so we'll just cover the most important ones here.

If you have other packages, such as Microsoft J++, installed in the Visual Studio, you will also see other tabs appropriate for those packages in the dialog and your view of the world won't perfectly match what we've shown here.

At the top of the Project Settings dialog, you'll notice a drop down control labeled Settings For. This drop down allows you to select the configurations for which you'll be modifying settings. Note that this box contains a special choice labeled All Configurations, which actually will let you change the build settings for all configurations of your project. You can alter the settings for the selected builds simply by filling in the right-hand side of the screen. When All Configurations is selected, the box will use a tri-state control or appropriate text to indicate how the settings of a particular attribute might be different across the different configurations in the project.

The General Options

The General options for the project allow you to change the way that MFC is used by your project and set the compiler to output files into a different directory for each build target. For example, the objects resulting from a Win32 release build might go into a directory named Release, while the objects from a Win32 debug build might land in a directory named Debug.

C/C++ Language Options

The C/C++ tab can be used to change compiler options. While only a few compiler options are available when this option is first selected, the Category drop-down list box provides eight screens of options that you can set! Thankfully, the defaults are adequate for most applications, and the project files that are produced by the AppWizard are also automatically set up by Visual C++.

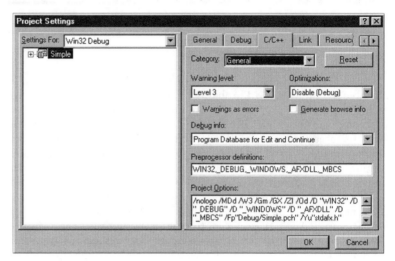

Link Options

You may be surprised to learn that the Link tab contains the options for the linker (or maybe you won't!). Like the C++ tab, the Link tab has a Category drop-down to give you access to several more pages' worth of settings.

Most of the tabs in the Project Settings dialog have a Reset button. This lets you return the content of the dialog to its state when the project was first created, without forcing you to use Cancel to leave the dialog. Be careful when experimenting – changing options can make your project unbuildable, or can dramatically increase your compile and link time! The different tabs in the Settings dialogs provide for a vast array of different ways to alter the linking of your application. While many of those changes are useful in some special circumstances, the vast majority of MFC applications you write will be fine with the settings provided by the AppWizard. I've only described the settings that are commonly used by MFC programmers.

Converting Projects

If you have an application built for Win16 using Visual C++ 1.5x, you can begin converting the project by simply opening the existing project makefile under Visual Studio by using the Open Workspace menu option in the File menu. When you attempt this, the Visual Studio will show a warning message before the conversion is actually performed. As the message warns, it's a good idea to save the project with a new name in case there are problems with the conversion. Further to this, if you overwrite the old file, you will no longer be able to use it with Visual C++ 1.5x.

Visual C++ will produce a project file based on the rules and file lists that were defined in the old project

If you are converting an application that uses MFC and restricts calls to the Windows APIs in a portable manner, you will probably be able to convert your application to run directly under Win32 with this simple step. MFC hides the implementation details of Windows so that your code will take advantage of MFC's portability to bridge the gap between Win16 and Win32. Unfortunately, some MFC features are unique to Win16 and can preclude your project from recompiling without any manual intervention. The most commonly used Win16-specific feature to cause this problem is support for Visual Basic Custom Controls (OCXs). Applications that require OCXs can't be run under Win32, because their use is not supported by the Win32 architecture.

You can also walk up to your old pre-Visual C++ 6.0 projects and open them outright with the new Visual Studio. Again, if you want to continue using the project from the older package, you should save the converted file to a different name; the conversions are not backwards-compatible. Remember that you'll have to export your project's .mak file explicitly before it is updated by the new project manager.

Source Code Files

Having looked at projects in all their glory, maybe you want to know a little something about source files. When you open a writeable source file with Visual C++, it will be opened in a window, allowing you to edit it. If the file is read-only, you can edit it but you are not allowed to save the file to the same file name. In this way, Visual C++ helps support version control systems that mark files that you have not checked out with the read-only attribute.

*It is also possible to set a compatibility option (*Protect read-only files from editing*) on the* Compatibility *tab of the* Options *dialog to prevent read-only files being edited at all.*

If you have the appropriate options selected, Visual C++ will also add color to your source code in the editor window. This may seem like a silly idea if you have never used it before, but it comes in handy when you are browsing through the source code. For example, comments are colored differently than other code, which allows you to identify incorrectly formatted blocks of code quickly. You may never again improperly close a string literal, as the editor will draw attention to your endless string with the appropriate use of color.

The Options dialog box has an Editor tab, as shown below, which allows you to change the text editor's general settings:

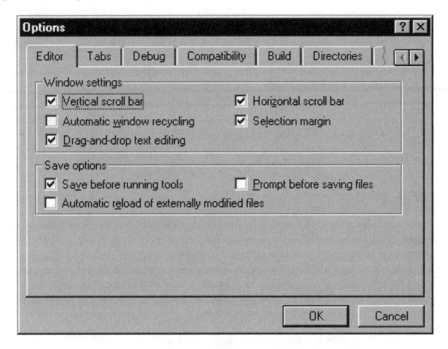

These settings are global; that is, any changes will be used for any file you edit and not just the current project or current file. You can adjust some extra features of the editor with the Tabs tab; this tab offers the ability to set not only tab spacing, but also the rules that the editor will apply to automatic indentation if you have that option enabled.

If you want to change the color scheme given to your text, you can do so by selecting the Format tab. The controls in that tab will allow you to select different color settings for features throughout the Visual Studio. The Format tab also allows you to change the font used in each of the Visual Studio windows. This is useful if you want a smaller font to see more code on the screen, or if you want a larger font to let others view your code on a projector during a presentation. If you have a background in APL, you might want to change the font in the Visual C++ source editing window to one of the symbols-only fonts, to help abate your uneasy feelings about C++.

The Workspace tab gives you the option of docking the different windows that make up the Visual C++ IDE. If a window's name is checked in this tab, it will act as a pane within the main frame window in the IDE. The pane can be resized and docked to different edges of the window. This allows you to position the window so that you can see it at any time. If a window does not have its name checked in this window, it behaves like a document window, acting as an MDI child window within the Visual Studio interface.

Resource Scripts

Every executable image for Windows – be it an application or a dynamic link library – can have resources. Windows resources come in several flavors, but they are all essentially non-code objects that an application requires to run successfully; an application's dialog boxes, for example. They are created using the Visual Studio and stored in the application's executable. Other resource types include string tables, accelerator tables, menus, version information, bitmaps, icons and cursors. If you are so inclined, you can also store arbitrary binary information as a resource in your application.

Resources are defined in a plain-text resource script, which is converted to a binary representation at compile time, and then merged into the executable image of the application. Visual Studio hides the mechanics of this process, allowing you to edit your resources visually, so you may never have to concern yourself with the exact syntax of the resource compiler's input scripts.

ResourceView

If you have your project open, you can see its resources by activating the ResourceView tab in the Project Workspace window. You can open resource scripts directly using the Open... command in the File menu. You can also create a new resource script from scratch using the New... command in the File menu; choose Resource Script when you receive the prompt for the type of file that you wish to create. When you use the AppWizard to build a new application, as we'll see in the next chapter, an appropriate resource script will be generated for you. You are free to edit it, but remember that changes you make might require changes in the source code of your program.

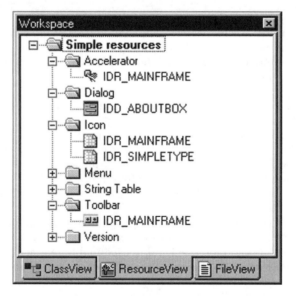

When you open a resource script, Visual C++ presents you with a window like that shown above. The conventional file extension for resource scripts is .rc. Visual C++ displays each of the resources in the file, grouping them by their type.

Creating New Resources

If you wish to add resources to your file, you'll need to use the Resource... command in the Insert... menu. This will obviously be the case if you create a new resource script; it will have no resources in it by default.

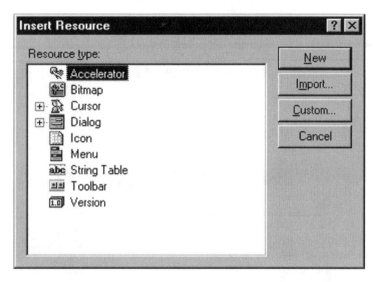

You may notice that the dialog provides a Custom... button. This allows you to type the name of your own resources, thus allowing you to create your own **custom resource** types.

The most common use for custom resources is to embed initialized data in your application. If you have a large amount of text that is unsuitable for a string table resource, you may wish to make your own custom resource to hold the information. Many multimedia applications use custom resources to embed waveform files as binary images, avoiding the need to distribute a separate (and more easily copied!) .wav file.

Importing Resources

You can use the Open... item in the File menu to steal a resource from an executable image, like a .exe or a .dll. This is a great way to swipe bitmaps, icons, and even whole dialog boxes from other applications. You'll need to decide exactly what the moral ramifications of this are, but the feature can be a lifesaver for the times when you can't come up with the artwork or layout yourself.

By the way, you can also use the resource editor for in-place editing of resources in an executable image. This means that you can open an executable file for which you don't have the source code and change, delete, add, or replace the resources in that executable. This feature only works if you're running Visual C++ under Windows NT, simply because Windows 95/98 doesn't implement the API required to pull off these tricks, although you can open the resources as read-only under either operating systems.

Resource Templates

When you're coding a large project, and especially when you are working on a big team, you'll be interested in techniques to make sure the work you do matches the work of the other developers. You'll find that one of the most important areas in which to have consistency is the layout of controls within a dialog box.

To aid your efforts, the Visual Studio supports the notion of **resource templates**. A resource template is a binary file that lives in your `\Microsoft Visual Studio\Common\MSDev98\Template` directory. You can create a new template by choosing Resource Template from the dialog brought up by the File | New... command. When you have added and edited the resources you want, your resource template is saved in the `\Microsoft Visual Studio\Common\MSDev98\Template` directory with the extension `.rct`, for the Studio to use later.

When you've created such a file, you'll see the resources it contains added to the Insert Resource dialog box, like this:

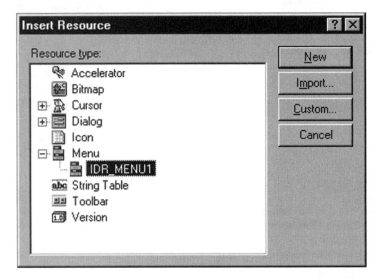

By double-clicking the resource (in this case, IDR_MENU1), you can insert a new menu that takes its look from the template. If you were presented with the above dialog, you could still insert a normal, blank menu by selecting the Menu item.

Resources that you add based on a template are yours to rumple, wrinkle and modify as you see fit. Changes to the newly inserted resources only appear in your own script, not in the resource template.

Resource templates are quite handy, but for now, there's one catch; you need to be very careful to make sure each template you register has a different name from other templates that your users might have. That is, if you have two dialog templates in different resource templates that are both named IDD_PERSONAL_INFO, they'll both show up in the list with the same name, and with no way of telling them apart. Hopefully, a future release of the Visual Studio will solve this problem.

Identifying Resources

You'll notice that each resource is identified by a cute icon and a name. The names you see are actually preprocessor symbols defined for you by the resource file editor. Both the resource script and the compiled source code will include a header file. This header file (called `Resource.h` by default in Visual C++, although it may have any name) contains C preprocessor-style `#define` directives that create preprocessor symbols for each resource. Any of your `*.cpp` files may reference the header, and your application's resource script will certainly do so.

This technique is employed because resources used within a program are almost always identified by a number called the **resource ID**. Since programs often have tens of resources (and complicated applications may have hundreds), it's very hard to maintain the resources using only their number. If the ID of the resource changes in the script, it must also change in the program. This is exactly the type of problem preprocessor constants created with the `#define` directive are designed to solve.

It is therefore convenient that the name shown next to the cute icon is actually the symbol associated with a resource of the type indicated in the hierarchy. You can name resources anything you'd like, and it's a great idea to pick something meaningful. Without knowing another whisper about MFC or Visual C++, you can guess that:

```
CDialog pDialog = new CDialog(IDD_ORDERENTRY);
```

probably creates a dialog which allows the user to perform order entry, while statements like:

```
CDialog pDialog = new CDialog(3014);
CDialog pDialog = new CDialog(IDD_DIALOG37);
```

could be loading any old dialog box.

When you create a dialog or any other resource, Visual C++ will assign it a name that follows a few simple rules. The beginning of the name will be composed of `ID` and one other letter. That letter will describe what sort of resource is being identified, and will be followed by an underscore (_) character. It is at that point that the real name of the resource begins. Visual C++ simply names the resource and appends a monotonically increasing number. For some resources (such as accelerator tables, where you'll only ever have one object of that type) this naming convention is acceptable. However, you'll probably want to change the name after the underscore to something more meaningful.

The different letters used to identify each resource type are described in this table:

Letter	Resource Type
R	Accelerator Table
C	Cursor
I	Icon

Table Continued on Following Page

Letter	Resource Type
D	Dialog
R	Menu
R	Toolbar
B	Bitmap
S	String

If you look at a standard resource script, you'll see that version information resources are the exception that proves the rule. Rather than conforming to the naming style, they are named VS_VERSION_INFO. This is just fine; version resources are never directly loaded or modified, so it's probably better that they just stay as they are.

> **You may notice that string tables don't have a resource ID, while the individual strings in the string table do. Only one string table may exist per resource script, and only one resource file may be bound into an executable.**

Managing Resource IDs

As you create resources, Visual C++ will create new resource IDs for you. You can divorce yourself from the worry surrounding the numbers that are associated with each ID to concentrate on the real programming issues at hand. If you'd like to see the resources in use at any given time, you can use the Resource Symbols... choice in the View menu. This menu command shows the Resource Symbols dialog, shown here for your reference:

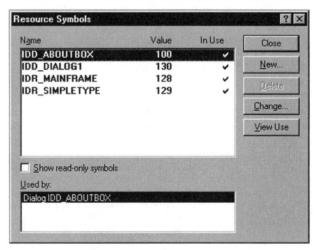

The list box at the top of the dialog shows the symbols in use, ordering them by name. It also shows the corresponding ID for each symbol, and a check mark will appear if that symbol is actually being used by some resource. If you wish to change a symbol, you can do so using the Change... button in the dialog. The resulting dialog walks you through the procedure of modifying the value associated with an ID.

The bottom half of the Resource Symbols window contains a Used By list. This list shows which resources actually use the symbol in question. The View Use button makes it easy for you to see and edit the resource that is using the ID you have selected.

If you check the Show read-only symbols option in the dialog box, it will show the read-only symbols in the same list box as the other IDs, but they will appear in a lighter font. Some read-only symbols are provided by MFC for internal use within an application, these are all prefixed with the letters AFX_. Other read-only symbols are used for global constants, like IDOK or IDCANCEL, which are always #defined to the same values for all Windows applications. Still more are used within your application when you won't be referencing a resource by its ID. This is typically true for static text in dialog boxes, which are usually named IDC_STATIC.

The header file associated with your resource script is named Resource.h by default. If you wish to change this name, you can use the Resource Includes... command in Visual Studio's View menu. This command also allows you to enumerate any header files or directives you wish to have included when the resource script is compiled. Additional headers are not maintained by any of the Visual C++ resource editors, so they can be convenient places to store symbols that you wish to remain constant throughout your development effort.

Let's examine in detail how creating, drawing, positioning and moving each general resource type is handled with Visual C++.

Dialog Boxes

Dialog boxes are possibly the most common resource found in applications and dynamic link libraries. Editing dialogs with Visual C++ is easy, and quite fun. The figure below shows a newly created dialog, as Visual C++ would display it:

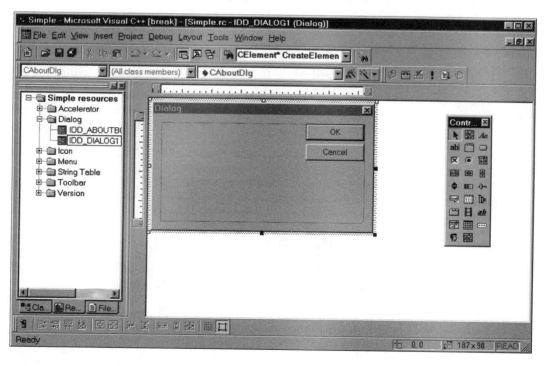

The Controls window, visible to the right of the dialog that's being edited, is like any other Visual C++ toolbar; you can drag it to the edge of the window and dock it there. This will resize the active window and the toolbar will always make its appearance at that location until this request is revoked. Dockable toolbars also allow you to customize your environment and, as a feature of MFC itself, you can add them to any application. We'll examine this feature of MFC during Chapter 4.

Most types of Windows control are represented on the Controls toolbar. If you don't recognize the exact kind of tool that will be drawn when you use one of the buttons, you can hold your mouse cursor over it for a second or two and a small caption will be displayed for the button, telling you exactly what kind of control the button will draw. These **tooltips** can also be added to your own applications using MFC. We'll examine how to add tooltips to our applications when we cover toolbars in Chapter 4.

> **If you're an old hand at Visual C++, you'll remember that the Rich Edit control is a relative newcomer to the controls toolbar. Make sure you check the documentation for `AfxInitRichEdit()` before tossing this control on a dialog in your MFC application!**

Adding and Editing Controls

Editing dialogs is a snap. If you want to draw a new control, just select the control in the toolbox and click the left mouse button on the dialog to insert the control with the default size, or drag the control from the toolbox to the dialog and drop it. Alternatively, you can add controls of any size by drawing them onto the dialog by clicking and dragging to opposite corners of a bounding rectangle. Once the control is drawn, you can always resize it by first clicking on it to activate its grab handles, and then dragging these handles to give the control the size and shape you'd like. You can position an existing control just by dragging it with the mouse.

Combo boxes are the only controls that are a little tricky. They really have two sizes; their standard size, and their size when the user has dropped the list down. While you are working with a combo box in the dialog editor window, you can click on the drop-down button to have the editor show you the size of the box when its list is dropped down. If you click the button again, the editor will show you the size of the box as if it were inactive.

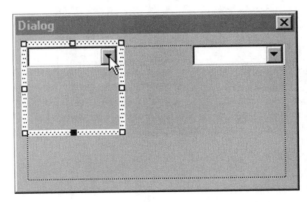

The box on the left will be just a little bigger than half the height of the window when it is dropped down, but exactly the same size as the control on the right while it isn't dropped down.

Guidelines and Rulers

When you begin editing a dialog box, you'll immediately notice there are a few extra doodads floating about in the dialog aside from your controls. If you wish, you can use the Guide Settings... command in the Layout menu to make a grid, which will help you align your controls. The border of the dialog editor window will contain rulers and margins, and the dialog box will contain thin blue lines that mark a border inside of the dialog. You can drag the blue border around using the mouse. If the border bumps into any controls, it will drag those controls with it. This is a great way to get some controls aligned at an edge of the window. This all works, no matter what controls are selected already. If you need to move the border without the controls moving, you can hold the *Alt* key down while dragging the border.

The guide comes into play when you move the controls. You can't drag a control past the guide, enforcing the border established by the control. If you need to move a couple of controls outside of the borders, you'll find that you can hold down the *Alt* key to let the control hop the border.

Control Properties

You can edit the specific properties of a control by right-clicking on the control and selecting Properties from the context menu. Note that, by default, you can't double-click controls to see their properties, as you could in earlier versions of Visual C++. If you want to be able to double-click on controls to see their properties, you can adjust the behavior of the IDE by visiting the Compatibility tab in the Options dialog, which you can reach by using the Options... command in the Tools menu, and unchecking Double-click in dialog editor edits code (MFC only). Alternatively, you can hold down the *Alt* key and then double-click on the control.

Requesting the control's properties will bring up a floating Properties dialog. Depending on what kind of control you're editing, the dialog may have many different tabs. For example, the dialog for combo boxes has four tabs; one for general settings, one for list items and two for style settings.

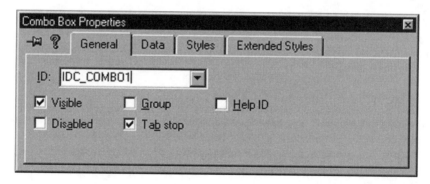

The General tab for any control will always provide you with the ability to change the ID of the control. You can enter a numeric value (for example, 302 or 101), or a symbolic value (such as IDE_FIRSTNAME or IDL_STATES), which will be associated with a numeric value in the header file for your resources. You can also enter a symbol and assign it a particular numeric value by typing the symbol, an equals sign then the value (for example, IDE_FIRSTNAME = 302).

Since dialogs are themselves windows, they also have properties, which you can display and edit in the same way as the properties for controls.

As you get more comfortable with your dialog, and as it becomes fully populated, you may wish to test it. Before you embed it into the rest of the code in your application, you can use the T̲est command in the L̲ayout menu or press *Ctrl+t*. This will let your dialog behave as if it were running in your application, allowing you to use the *Tab* key to move from control to control, and use the keyboard to access the buttons. To exit test mode, press the *Esc* key, or click on either the OK or Cancel button, if they are present, or use the close button in the title bar.

If you're planning on modifying the properties of many different controls in one sitting, you might want to 'pin down' the floating properties dialog. Simply click the push-pin button at the top left of the dialog and the dialog won't automatically close when you select another resource or control.

Control Tab Order

Windows is designed to still be very usable even if you don't have a mouse. Power users (you know, guys like me) who type very fast actually disdain the mouse as a way to control an application. I keep my hands on the keyboard, and I know lots of different keystroke combinations, shortcuts, and tricks to get the focus where I'm going or select the object of my desire.

One of the more important aspects of the keyboard-oriented user interface in a dialog box is the **tabbing order**. The tabbing order is the order in which controls receive focus as the user uses the *Tab* key to move from one control to the next. The tabbing order should always follow a natural, right-to-left and top-to-bottom flow in your controls – unless a very logically grouped block controls causes the order to sway slightly.

After testing your dialog, if you notice that the tabbing order in your dialog is off, you can use the Tab O̲rder command in the L̲ayout menu. You will notice that each control is then given a number at its top left corner. This number indicates the order in which the *Tab* key will take the user through the controls. You can reset the order by clicking on each control in the order you wish the controls to appear in tab sequence. You can exit tab ordering mode by striking the *Enter* key.

The L̲ayout menu technique is handy when you initially set up the dialog. However, if you need to change the order of a couple of controls in a dialog that already exists, you'll probably find that method cumbersome. If you wish to change the tab order for a subset of controls in a dialog, you can follow a few simple steps:

1. In the L̲ayout menu, select the Tab O̲rder command.

2. Select the control where the tab order will begin. You should select the last control that is already correctly tabbed; that is, select the control before the first control that tabs incorrectly. To do this, you must hold down the *Ctrl* key and click the control. Otherwise, you will immediately change the tab order for the control you click!

3. Click the controls in the order you want the *Tab* key to follow.

4. Press the *Enter* key to exit tab order mode.

You can save your changes to dialog resources at any time by using the S̲ave command in the F̲ile menu as usual, but remember you are saving the entire resource file and that changes to any other dialogs or resources will be saved at the same time.

Control Layouts

Dialogs provide your application with an interface to the world. If your dialogs are poorly drawn, you'll find they put off users. To facilitate the creation of clean, crisp dialogs, you can use the commands in the Layout menu to make sure that your controls align and are all the same size.

Many of the commands in this menu are only active if you have more than one control selected, or if you have a certain type of control selected.

> You can select more than one control by holding down the *Ctrl* key while clicking on various controls, or you can select multiple controls by clicking on the background of your dialog and dragging the mouse so that the selection rectangle completely encompasses the controls you're interested in.

The Center In Dialog command allows you to center a control or group of controls horizontally or vertically in the dialog. If you center one control, it is centered in the client area of the dialog, but if you center a group of controls, the controls are moved so their relative position is the same, but the rectangle that bounds them all is centered. This command is a momentary action; if you change the size of the dialog, you must use this command to center the controls again.

The Arrange Buttons command is only available if you have a push button, check box, or radio button control selected. The command deposits the selected buttons at the bottom of the dialog and centers them along that edge of the dialog if you select the Bottom command. If you select the Right command, the buttons are placed near the top of the dialog at the right edge. Since these are the two most common locations for buttons in a dialog, it makes it easy for you to place the OK and Cancel buttons in standard places.

The Make Same Size command allows you to make all of the selected controls the same size as the most recently selected control and, consequently, is only available when you've selected more than one control in your dialog. The most recently selected control will have opaque grab handles, while the other selected controls will have hollow handles.

The dominant or primary control, which is the one with opaque handles, will be measured and used as a reference for the other controls. If you use the Height item from the Make Same Size menu, the primary control's height will be used as the height for the other controls. The Width command operates in a similar manner for the width of the controls, while the Both command makes all of the select controls the same size in both dimensions, based on the dominant control.

The Align Controls command is only available when more than one control is selected, and includes choices which provide the programmer with the ability to make controls appear aligned along one edge. The Left, Right, Top, and Bottom commands that are available from this menu use the named edge of the dominant control to align the other selected controls.

The dominant control won't move, and all other selected controls will be moved so that their named edge lines up with the dominant control's named edge. The last two commands in the menu, Vert. Center and Horiz. Center, allow you to align controls to the vertical center or horizontal center (respectively) of the dominant control. Each control will be moved so that its center is aligned with the dominant control's center.

The Size To Content command works on single or multiple controls. It snaps the control's vertical and horizontal sizes to align with its contents. The command only works on controls that have text assigned to them, such as static text and button-style controls, and therefore has no effect on combo boxes, list boxes or edit text fields. The command is convenient for making sure that static text doesn't take up more space than it should and, in particular, that it doesn't spill unused space into some adjacent control.

Note that the Size To Content command is *not* available when the dialog box itself is selected – it only works on individual controls.

The Space Evenly command requires that you have at least three controls selected. This command will space the selected controls evenly from top to bottom or from left to right. The dominant control has no meaning for this command. Instead, the controls are simply spaced evenly over the area that they occupy. For instance, if you space the controls evenly Down, the controls will be moved so that they are spaced evenly between the controls closest to the top and the bottom of the dialog. The northernmost and southernmost controls won't move, only the remainder.

The menu also features a Flip command, which will flip the contents of a dialog from right to left. The flip operation includes switching justification for controls – for example, a flipped edit control that previously justified its text to the left edge of the control will justify its text to the right side of the control instead.

You may have already noticed that the commands from the Layout menu are also available through the Layout toolbar. You should also note that when the right mouse button is clicked over a feature of your dialog or one of your dialog controls, it brings up a pop-up menu that allows you to manipulate the item, navigate to the ClassWizard or bring up the properties page for the control.

String Tables

String tables allow your application to hold strings of textual characters within a resource. For several reasons, this is usually better than holding strings within literals or initialized memory areas in your program. First, it allows Windows to perform slightly better at its memory management. All of the strings in your application, when stored as resources, are guaranteed to be read-only. This means that Windows can discard them completely, instead of them taking up space in the swap file. It also means that Windows can discard all of your strings at once.

Perhaps the most important advantage of this technique is that you can more readily localize your application if you've put all of its prompts and text into a string table. This allows you to change the text in your application by changing the version of the string table your resource script loads, rather than editing individual strings within your code. You can easily hand the string table file off to someone who is fluent in other languages to utilize their translation skills, even while you continue to work on your application. We'll discuss this topic further in Appendix B.

Besides, I find that code like:

```
AfxMessageBox(IDS_UTILDISK_PROMPT, IDS_SETUPTITLE)
```

is much easier to read than:

```
AfxMessageBox("Legen Sie die Dienstprogrammdiskette in das
                              Laufwerk A: ein", "Setup");
```

Some features offered by MFC, such as tooltips and micro help (that is, the status bar messages which you see as you highlight different items in a menu), are dependent on the text they use being available in a string table. Often, the ID of a string resource must match the ID of a menu command, dialog box, button or other control to make these features work. I'll point out these situations as they arise.

As with other resources, you can start editing string tables by clicking on an existing table in an opened resource file, or by creating a new one from the Insert Resource dialog (Resource... on the Insert menu).

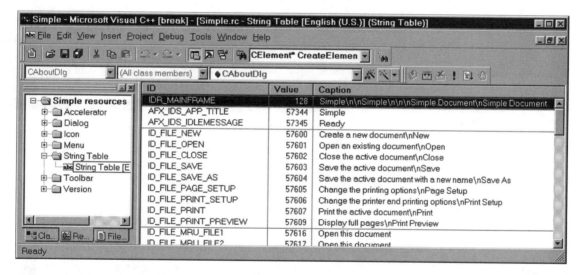

The string table editor window allows you to view, add, and remove strings from the string table in your resource script. If you are looking for an existing string, you can use the Find... command in the Edit menu to do so.

To add a string to your table, just tap the *Insert* key, but if you want to edit an existing string, double-click on it, or right-click on it and choose Properties from the context menu. After any of these operations, you will be presented with a property dialog, which allows you to change the string's ID within the table and to provide the text for the string, up to 255 characters in length. If you need to store a string longer than this, you'll need to create a custom resource type and use it directly.

> If you need to add a special character to a string, you can do so using the backslash
> escape character. You can enter newline or tab characters using \n or \t respectively,
> or you can enter \ddd for any ASCII character, where ddd specifies the three digit
> octal sequence representing the character you wish to add. To place a backslash in a
> string resource, you must use two backslashes in a row.

Accelerator Tables

String tables and accelerator tables are probably the two simplest resources in Windows. An
application can use an accelerator table to translate a key (or a key combination) pressed by the user
into a WM_COMMAND message, which is understood as a specific command ID.

You can create a new accelerator table for your application using the New button in the Insert
Resource dialog. If you wish to edit an existing accelerator table, you can double-click on its entry in
the ResourceView. The resulting accelerator table editor window is shown below. You can add a new
entry in the accelerator table by pressing *Insert*.

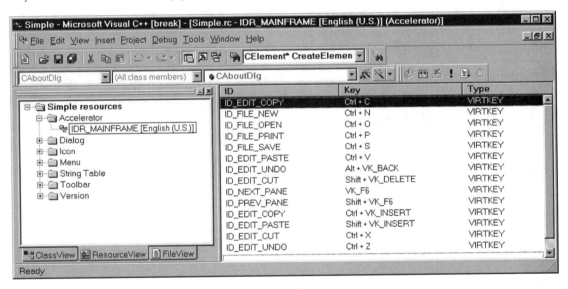

The left column of the window shows the ID of the entry, while the middle column allows you to see
the keystroke associated with the entry. The rightmost column, called Type, indicates the type of the
mapping, which must be either **ASCII** or **VIRTKEY**. VIRTKEY means that the keystroke is defined
by describing it, allowing for descriptions of non-character keystrokes like numeric keypad entries or
function keys. ASCII means that the keystroke is described by the ASCII code it generates.

By double-clicking on an entry in the accelerator table, you can have Visual C++ display the properties dialog for that entry. The dialog will show only one tab, allowing you to set any of the attributes of the entry. The dialog also features a button marked Next Key Typed. If you press this button, the dialog will set the properties of the entry to match the next keystroke you make. This allows you to create or change entries easily, without mucking around with silly codes or settings.

Accelerators are commonly associated with menu items. In the next section, when we examine menu resources, we'll see how to associate a menu item with a keyboard accelerator.

Menus

Menus are possibly the most obvious part of your application's user interface. Menus accept direct commands from the user and let the user effectively browse through the features of your application at a glance.

You can open a menu editor window in Visual C++ by using the Insert Resource dialog (Resource... on the Insert menu) to create a new instance, or by double-clicking on an existing menu resource in ResourceView. The menu editor window is shown below, where you will see a partially built menu:

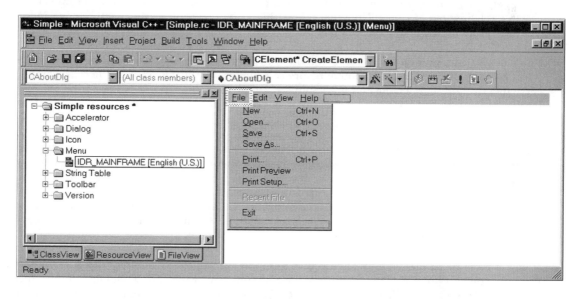

You can add menu items to your menu by double-clicking the blank menu item at the end of each menu. Visual C++ will pop up a properties dialog that allows you to assign the menu item to an ID. This ID will be sent to your application as part of the wParam element in a WM_COMMAND message when the user selects your menu item. The properties dialog contains several check boxes that affect the style of your menu item.

When the Separator check box is marked the menu item in question will be a menu separator and it won't accept an ID, caption, prompt or any other settings.

If the Checked check box is checked, the menu item will be initially displayed with a check mark to its immediate left. This attribute can be programmatically queried, set or reset by your application at run time.

The menu item will be a Pop-Up menu if the box with the same name is marked. If the menu item is on the menu bar, this setting will allow it to have child menus. If the menu item is itself an entry within another pop-up, the menu starts another branch of a cascading menu. If this box is checked, the item won't have an ID or a prompt.

The Grayed option will cause the menu item to be initially grayed and inactive. This attribute can be interrogated or assigned programmatically.

Checking the Inactive option will make the item inactive initially. Note that this won't gray the menu item. This setting can also be adjusted programmatically.

When the Help box is checked, the menu item will be right justified. This is traditionally used to offset help menus from other commands on the menu, making them easier to find. However, this practice is falling out of vogue. Note that this setting won't be visible in the menu editor window; it will only make itself apparent at runtime.

You can also set a prompt for your menu item in the Prompt edit field. This will be shown in the status bar if the user highlights the item before selecting it. The string you enter here is stored as an entry in a string resource table and is given the same ID as the menu item being edited. If you set the ID of a menu item to the ID of a preexisting string resource, Visual C++ will populate the Prompt field with the content of the string entry.

You enter the name of your menu item in the Caption edit field, and you can indicate a mnemonic key for it using the ampersand (&). To insert a menu with a visible ampersand, use two; Hockey && Beer, for example. You can also insert a tab escape sequence in the Caption field to indicate to the user that the menu item has an accelerator. For example, if ALT+S was the accelerator for your menu's Salad entry, it would be appropriate to have a caption of Salad\tALT+S. To make sure that the accelerator table entry is correctly associated with your menu item, you must use the same ID for both the menu item and the accelerator.

If you're designing a menu that will be shown as a pop-up, you can check the View As Popup item in the context menu (from clicking the right mouse button). This will cause the menu editor to display your menu as a pop-up. When the View As Popup item is not checked, your menu will be displayed as a conventional menu bar.

Icons, Bitmaps and Cursors

Most resource elements in a non-console Windows application are purely graphical, with your resource script containing icons, bitmaps and cursors. As with other resources, you can open any of these types of graphical elements either by creating a new resource with the Resource... command in the Insert menu, or by double-clicking on an existing resource entry in ResourceView. If you wish, you can use the Open... command in the File menu to open an existing .jpg, .gif, .ico, .dib, .bmp or .cur file. You can then use the Edit menu to copy and paste the content of that graphic into your own application's resource script.

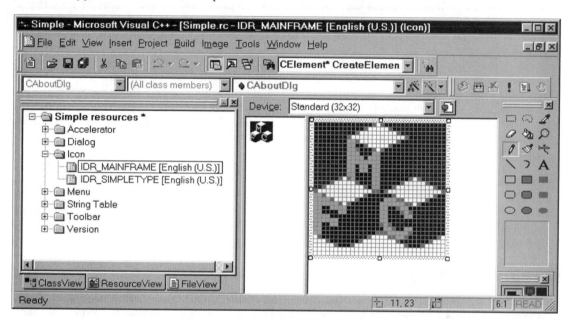

As they perform very similar functions, the icon, bitmap and cursor editors all have very similar user interfaces. Each of the editors provides a grid and life-size display of your graphic resource side-by-side. You can use the enlarged grid to edit your resource pixel-by-pixel, while the life-size display allows you to see how the resource would be displayed normally on your screen.

These editors share the same toolbars, but each may provide different colors or patterns depending on the color depth of the resource you're editing. The color toolbar allows you to select a foreground color to be used when drawing with the primary mouse button, and a background color for the secondary mouse button.

The cursor editor also features the ability to set the **hotspot** for the cursor. This is the point which is considered to be the activation point of the cursor – the exact point within the cursor's image which will be returned when the user clicks or positions the cursor.

The graphics toolbar allows you to choose from a variety of different drawing tools, from straight lines to spline curves and simple closed or open shapes. You can also fill regions of your graphic with the paint can.

Through its display driver architecture, Windows supports a myriad of display devices. You can run Windows on anything from a standard monochrome VGA system to a high-powered, accelerated, super-high resolution, enhanced graphics adapter. Some vendors even provide graphics boards that can drive more than one monitor simultaneously, effectively allowing you to have twice the desktop! Since all of these different displays have very different attributes, sizes, resolutions and color depths, it is sometimes difficult to ensure that your program will provide the same display on a variety of different platforms. For instance, a 32 by 32 pixel button might be just the right size for a standard VGA system, but it may appear infinitesimal on a high-resolution 1280x1024 pixel display.

To this end, Windows provides the ability to manage different resolutions of the same graphical resource. The icon and the cursor editor windows have drop-down list boxes that allow you to choose the image size and resolution you wish to render. Your program can load the same resource ID, but different icons would be loaded at runtime, depending on the target of the drawing operation. Always consider changing all of the resolutions of a given graphical resource so that your program looks nice no matter what kind of display your user has, or no matter where the icon is displayed in the application.

Graphical resources are different from other resource types because they don't actually store their data in the resource script file. Instead, the resource script file includes a command that references the actual bitmap, icon or cursor by file name. This means that you must be aware of the individual graphic files that will show up in your project's directory as you work to add graphic resources to your application.

Version Resources

Version resources are stored in executable files to provide identification information about the file. The version resource consists of both binary and textual information that describe the executable file.

You may insert a version resource in exactly the same way as any other resource. If you have an existing version resource that you'd like to edit, you can double-click on it. The resulting version information editor window is shown on the next page:

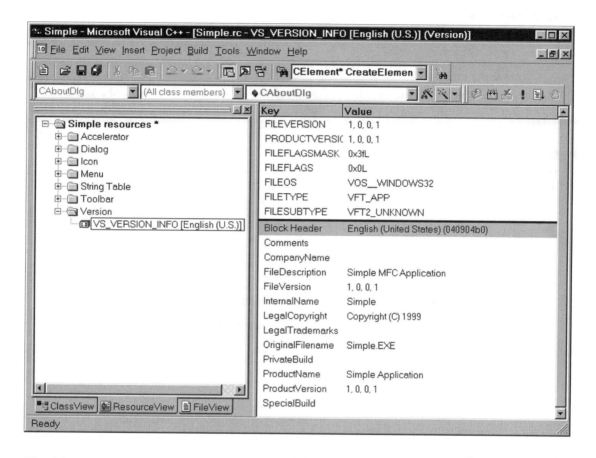

The information is divided into two parts; the version information for the file, and the textual information. Your installation program, or even third-party installation management or software license metering programs, may look at the version resource using the appropriate Win32 APIs. This information may be used to decide when to overwrite your program file with a newer version, or to allow a user to make sure they have the most current build number. The legal types among you might even consider the copyright information quite important.

Version Information

The fields in the versioning part of the resource break down like this:

FILEVERSION

The FILEVERSION field contains the version number for your executable file. It is composed of four 16-bit integers separated by commas. You are free to use these fields for whatever you wish, but most developers, by convention, use the first two integers to indicate the major and minor release numbers of their product. You may find it appropriate to use the third or fourth integer to indicate the build number, beta release number, or patch number of your file.

PRODUCTVERSION

Like the FILEVERSION field, the PRODUCTVERSION field indicates a version number represented by four 16-bit integers separated by commas. The PRODUCTVERSION is different from the FILEVERSION because the PRODUCTVERSION indicates the version of your *product*, not the version of this particular file. An entire product may span several .exes and .dlls, each of which may be updated independently. If this is version 2.0.0.35 of a particular DLL, and it is a part of release 2.0 of your product, you would set this field to 2,0,0,0 and set the FILEVERSION field to 2,0,0,35.

FILEFLAGSMASK

The FILEFLAGSMASK field indicates which bits in the FILEFLAGS field are valid, by which I mean that this field should indicate the bits which FILEFLAGS could possibly have set. For Windows NT/2000, Windows 95/98 and Win32s applications, this should be 0x0000003F.

FILEFLAGS

The FILEFLAGS field contains a flag describing the purpose of the file's build. The following table describes the valid flag settings for this field:

Flag	Description
VS_FF_DEBUG	A debug build
VS_FF_PRERELEASE	A work-in-progress

FILEOS

The FILEOS field specifies the operating system that the file was targeted for. You may specify one of these values:

Value	Description
VOS_DOS	DOS specifically.
VOS_NT	Windows NT specifically.
VOS__WINDOWS16	Any operating system providing an implementation of the Win16 API.
VOS__WINDOWS32	Any operating system providing an implementation of the Win32 API.
VOS_DOS_WINDOWS16	DOS running under a Win16 operating system.
VOS_DOS_WINDOWS32	DOS running under a Win32 operating system.

Value	Description
VOS_NT_WINDOWS32	Win32 under Windows NT. *Not* any other implementation of Win32.
VOS_UNKNOWN	Some other operating system.

FILETYPE

The FILETYPE field specifies the type of the file and should contain one of these values:

Value	Description
VFT_UNKNOWN	Some unidentified file type.
VFT_APP	An application.
VFT_DLL	A dynamic-link library.
VFT_DRV	A device driver. This requires a FILESUBTYPE flag to be set.
VFT_FONT	A font. This file requires that the FILESUBTYPE field be set.
VFT_VXD	A virtual device driver.
VFT_STATIC_LIB	A static link library.

FILESUBTYPE

If the FILETYPE field contains VFT_DRV, this field may be one of the following values:

Values	Description
VFT2_DRV_SOUND	A sound-device driver
VFT2_DRV_INSTALLABLE	An installable device driver
VFT2_DRV_NETWORK	A network device driver
VFT2_DRV_MOUSE	A mouse driver
VFT2_UNKNOWN	Some other type of file not listed here
VFT2_DRV_COMM	A communications device driver
VFT2_DRV_PRINTER	A printer device driver
VFT2_DRV_SYSTEM	A system driver (such as a DMA or timer driver)
VFT2_DRV_KEYBOARD	A keyboard device driver
VFT2_DRV_LANGUAGE	A language driver
VFT2_DRV_DISPLAY	A display device driver

If the FILETYPE field contains VFT_FONT, the FILESUBTYPE field should contain one of these values:

Value	Description
VFT2_FONT_RASTER	A raster font
VFT2_FONT_VECTOR	A vector font
VFT2_FONT_TRUETYPE	A TrueType font

For fields like FILEFLAGS, where the field is based on a combination of flags, you may double-click the field and use a property page to edit its value. Other fields, such as FILEOS, where the field is exactly one flag from a list, may be edited by clicking on the value in the file version resource editor window and selecting the appropriate choice from a drop-down list box.

> *Note that you can't affect the* VS_FF_DEBUG *flag in the* FILEFLAGS *property page because Visual C++ automatically sets or clears this flag during resource compilation by using an* #ifdef *directive.*

The flags used in these files are defined as preprocessor macros in the file Winver.h, which can be found in the Include subdirectory of your Visual C++ installation.

Textual Information

The fields in the string block of the resource are as follows (note that some of the strings are required, while others are optional):

Field	Requirement Criteria	Description
Comments	Optional	This catch-all field can contain any comment that you see fit. This information may be displayed by a diagnostic utility, such as a post-mortem crash analyzer.
CompanyName	Required	The name of the company that produced the compiled file, 'Tarzan's Software Company', or 'King Of The Jungle Systems, Inc.', for instance.
FileDescription	Required	A description of the file's purpose. '64-bit Accelerated Display Driver', or 'Mortgage Analysis Tool', for example.

Field	Requirement Criteria	Description
FileVersion	Required	Specifies a version of the file in text. This should mimic the **FILEVERSION** field in the binary part of the resource, but neither the system nor the resource compiler will verify this. Since the resource is a string, it may contain characters other than numbers; for instance '3.00 Release Candidate 2' or '1.00 Golden Build' are both valid.
InternalName	Required	Internal name of the file, if it has one. For DLLs, this file should indicate the name of the module. If there isn't an internal name assigned to the file, you should place the original file name here, without the extension.
LegalCopyright	Optional	Should be used to hold all copyright notices that apply to the file. While this string is optional, it does become a part of the binary version of the executable and can be used to indicate copyright ownership.
LegalTrademarks	Optional	Should be used to identify all trademarks used within the file. This string is optional, but it can be used to identify registered trademarks, legal symbols, disclaimers and so on.
OriginalFilename	Optional	Contains the as-distributed name of the file, without a path. This can be checked against the current name of the file to see if the user has renamed the file.
PrivateBuild	Should be present only if the **VS_FF_ PRIVATEBUILD** flag is set in the **FILEFLAGS** field of the binary half of the resource	Should be used to provide information describing a private build of the file. A `SpecialBuild` may see the light of day, but `PrivateBuild`s are strictly used internally to the organization that develops the software in question.
ProductName	Required	Names the product.

Table Continued on Following Page

Field	Requirement Criteria	Description
ProductVersion	Required	Provides a textual representation of the product version with which the file is distributed. This should match the ProductVersion field in the binary data portion of the resource, but is not checked by the system or resource compiler.
SpecialBuild	Should be present if the VS_FF_ SPECIALBUILD flag is set in the FILEFLAGS field	Should describe any deviation between this file and standard versions of the file. If you produce a special build of your application to solve a particular problem for one customer, or make a change as an experiment for one specific user, it's a good idea to use this field to mark your file so that it is recognizable as a randomly deviant thing-file from Planet X and not the real McCoy.

The PrivateBuild and SpecialBuild flags are intended to allow developers to mark one-off builds of their products. These flags might be used for special test builds, for example, which might be used to reproduce a particular problem or test a particular fix, but aren't intended for redistribution.

You can include more than one string block in your version resource. This is necessary when you have internationalized your application, as you should provide national language copies of the string resources in the version block for each country to which you'll be shipping. To add a new string block, use the New Version Info Block command in the Insert menu. You can use the Delete Version Info Block command in the same menu to delete an unused string block. You can double-click a string field to edit its contents.

Custom Resources

Windows supports the inclusion of custom binary resources in a resource script, which allows you to place, within a resource, any arbitrary binary data you wish to have available at runtime. The advantage of placing data in a custom resource over placing it in any of the identifiable types we've talked about so far is that the format of the custom resource is exactly that – custom. You specify the bits to be stored and made available to your application when you load the resource.

Most often, custom resources are used for situations where you have medium-sized data that you don't want to carry around as a separate file. By embedding it within your own executable image, you can be certain that the data is always available.

You'll need to decide carefully the format for your custom resource data. Since it's just binary data, you'll need to find some structure for it, however simple.

The Visual C++ Compiler

For the developer, compiling is the bane of existence. The middle part of the coding cycle can be made unmercifully painful by long waits for slow compilers, awkward tools, or unintegrated environments. Visual C++ tries to take some of the tedium out of the development process by allowing the developer to rebuild their project with a single menu command or mouse click.

When you're ready to rebuild your application in Visual Studio, you can use the Build command in the Build menu. Visual C++ will check the dates and time stamps of all files in your project and rebuild only the files that are out of date. You can force Visual C++ to rebuild every object file as well as the target executable or dynamic link library by using the Rebuild All command.

> *Note that building with any of these commands saves any files that you may have open at that time.*

As your project builds, you will see the output of the build process as it is generated in the output window:

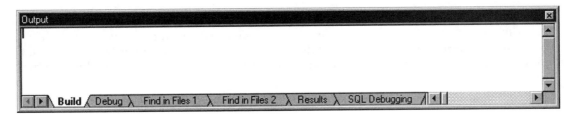

If you suddenly realize that something is woefully wrong (say, you are concerned that tax rates are too high, you left your oven on, or you forgot to make one last change to your sources before building) you can use the Stop Build command.

> *Just to remind you of your days building at the command line, you can also stop the build using the shortcut key for the* Stop Build *command,* Ctrl+Break.

If the build encounters an error, you can double-click on the line of the error and Visual C++ will open the source file with the error, place your cursor on the line of the error and let you begin fixing the problem. You may also press *F1* when the flashing insertion point is on an error number to get help about the error message from Visual C++ online help.

When developing software, it's quite normal to encounter dozens of errors at a time. Conveniently, Visual Studio can help you with them by allowing you to press *F4* to move from one error to the next. The error text is kept synchronized in the build window, and Visual C++ will always open the file if it's not already open. *Shift+F4* allows you to move to the site of the previous error.

Compiling on the Command Line

While the integration and facility of the project management in Visual C++ is quite impressive, there might be instances when building from the command line has more utility. Visual C++ project files are very similar to carefully formatted scripts for the Nmake utility, Microsoft's version of the standard Make program, but if you need to compile from the command line, you will need to export the .mak file.

If you're going to directly modify a Visual C++ produced .mak file, you should be careful about how you do it, but if you do make a mistake, you can always go back to the .dsw file and use it to export a new makefile.

Once you've properly set up the environment to include the location of the tools in your PATH= environment variable, the libraries in your LIB= environment variable, and the headers in your INCLUDE= environment variable, you can run a build for a project named Sample by making the project's directory current and typing the following command in a Windows NT/2000 Command window or Windows 95/98 DOS Window:

```
nmake /f sample.mak
```

This will kick off a build for the default target. At the command line, the default target isn't the same as that defined in the IDE, as you can't set the default target for command line builds. You can force a given build type to be done by naming the target of your desire on the command-line. For example:

```
nmake /f sample.mak CFG="Sample — Win32 Debug"
```

The exact string you can provide with the CFG option is dependent on the names of the targets you specified in the project. You can see a list of acceptable targets by providing the CFG option with no setting, like this:

```
nmake /f sample.mak CFG
```

The Nmake script will then enumerate the targets it knows how to build.

The C++ compiler and all of the other Windows programming tools with which you are familiar are also available at the command-line. The available command line tools are listed in the following table:

Tool	Command
C/C++ Compiler	Cl
Librarian	Lib
Linker	Link
Maintenance Utility	Nmake
Resource Compiler	Rc
Interface Definition Language Compiler	Midl

You can use these tools to compile an older project. You may also wish to use them when you know you are planning something special; for example, you might craftily use C1 to invoke the C preprocessor to massage a file that you will use later as an input file to some other tool.

Without exception throughout this book, we'll be working with projects that can be built within the Visual Studio. You are more than welcome to try building the programs from the command line to enhance your understanding of the underlying tools and their options. Since this book will concentrate on the Microsoft Foundation Classes, we won't be spending that much time on the underlying build tools or their special capabilities.

Edit and Continue

Most developers work very incrementally – that is, they write some code, build it, test it, and write some more. Each iteration of the process finds the developer adding more code, and hopefully more stability, to their application. The process can be frustrating, particularly when a build takes a long time. You might do a build that takes six minutes and then, in order to test it, you have to start the debugger and wait patiently for the program to reach a state where code debugging can actually start. And what do you know! When you hit your breakpoint, you quickly realize that you meant to code:

```
int nLen = strlen(pstrString) + 1;
```

instead of:

```
int nLen = strlen(pstrString);
```

Few things (besides a drunken Boston Bruins fan) could be more aggravating! Visual C++ 6.0 features a very innovative technology called **Edit and Continue** that rescues you from such torment.

When your program is stopped in the debugger, you can simply change the offending line of code. Visual C++ will notice the changes and attempt to compile the different code into your program while it is stopped. It isn't always possible; you might add significant code, muck around with destructors, or code some syntax errors. The technique is ideal for simple changes, like the one-off error above, but it is also able to accommodate surprisingly advanced and involved changes.

But, if it is possible for the environment to accommodate your changes, you'll end up compiling them right back into your live code. Only the changes you make will be compiled, and the whole process will take a fraction of the time a complete restart and rebuild would. Then, you're on your way!

Statement Completion

A developer has a lot to remember; the tens of hundreds of APIs in Windows, all of the interesting functions in the C++ runtime libraries, and the functions and classes within MFC add up to more information than you can write on the back of an envelope. This swamp of information has most developers continually switching their focus from the editor back to the online help to find parameter types and names, structure member names and so on.

In the newest release of Visual C++, you'll notice some impressive features that work right as you type. The editor sees what you're doing and can pop-up help for your function, or let you know the members of a structure or class you're about to use. With a single keystroke, you can select the name of one of those members and have the editor insert it immediately before you type anything else.

While these features provide an immense amount of convenience, they do slow down editing just a tad. It's normally not noticeable, but if you have a slow or busy machine you can always disable the features and simply use them on demand.

The Foundation Classes

Ironically, although we've been compelled to mention them along the way, we have yet to point out the most impressive part of the Visual C++ environment – the Microsoft Foundation Classes (MFC). The Foundation Class libraries are installed when you do a minimal installation, and if you do a typical installation you get the source code as well. If you do a custom install, their installation is at your discretion. The CD-based install option sets up Visual C++ to expect to find the MFC files on your CD-ROM drive; however, you're still at liberty to use MFC in your projects.

There are three distinct groups of MFC files in addition to sample programs: MFC source code, library files, and header files. The sample programs are self-explanatory; they each demonstrate some aspect of MFC in a simple program.

> *In addition to the sample programs that ship with Visual C++, there is sample code provided for this book, which can be downloaded from the Wrox web site. Both should provide you with a wealth of information about the operation of the Microsoft Foundation Classes. See the section entitled* Source Code, *in the* Introduction, *for more information about the samples in this book.*

MFC Source Code

Complete source code for the Microsoft Foundation Classes is shipped with Visual C++. This serves several very useful purposes.

Tracing Through the Frameworks

Since source code is shipped with the libraries, you can build debug versions of your MFC applications and simply trace through the code in the frameworks whenever you need to. This is very useful when you're trying to understand why a call to MFC has failed, or why your code is not executed within the context, or at the time, that you expected it to be.

Sample Code

You might consider the MFC source code itself as sample code. If you browse through this, you can see some of the techniques that real Microsoft programmers use to put together professional tools. The code provides the groundwork for functionality that your application might use directly, or might subclass in other classes.

Help with Subclassing

You are strongly encouraged to review the implementation of classes that you use in your application, particularly if you subclass them. This can provide tremendous insight to you when you are developing additional code in your application; you might be able to completely reuse the difficult code from the frameworks and re-implement only the functionally different code in your application. When you become *au fait* with this technique, you will be realizing the intrinsic reusability in object-oriented development to its fullest potential.

For more information on subclassing, see Chapter 7.

Avoiding Roadblocks

While it's very unlikely, you may find problems in the frameworks that hamper your design. You may also find, dare I say it, outright bugs. Using the source code, you can track down these problems. If it becomes absolutely necessary to your success, you may even see fit to recompile the libraries.

The MFC source code is all stored in the `Mfc\Src` *subdirectory of your Visual C++ installation directory. If you accepted the default of* `C:\Program Files`, *you can find the MFC source stored in* `C:\Program Files\Microsoft Visual Studio\vc98\Mfc\Src`.

However, Microsoft strongly discourages this practice, as it makes the use of a consistent version of Visual C++ throughout an organization very difficult. For example, when you build private copies of the libraries, you should never give them the same names as stock builds of the libraries. If you do, things will become far too confusing to recover from!

A note from the author:

"Yeah, I work at Microsoft, but not every bug in every product we ship is my fault. Only some of them. If you think you've found a problem with MFC, your best bet is to get in touch with product support services; they're best equipped to handle problems you report. However, if you want to write with questions about the code from this book specifically, or questions you have about MFC, I'll do my best to reply to you."

Header Files

The header files for the Microsoft Foundation Classes are stored in the `Mfc\Include` directory under your Visual C++ directory. This directory contains all of the header files that you'll ever need; there are more than three dozen, but your MFC programs will only ever directly reference a handful. If you need to know what the header files do, they are all described in Appendix D.

While browsing around in the `Mfc\Include` directory, you'll also notice lots of `.inl` files. These contain implementations for small MFC functions that are declared `inline`. MFC is built in such a way that the inline functions are not inlined for debug builds, but are made so in release builds. This eases debugging without exacting a performance hit when the application is built for final distribution. If you're on the prowl for source code to a particular MFC function implementation, make sure you look at these `.inl` files too.

Any file that has a name ending in an underscore is something that MFC will include for you if you nab the correct file. You should consider these underline-extended files as private to MFC; including them directly will be more trouble than it's worth.

You'll note, by the way, that these files all begin with the letters Afx. *Many of the functions and constants in MFC include these letters, too. They represent a part of MFC's heritage. Originally called 'Application Frameworks', AFX stuck around in many symbols and file names in MFC. The 'A' stands for 'Application' and the 'F' stands for 'Frameworks'. The 'X' doesn't stand for anything.*

The headers are the only part of MFC with which you will notice your involvement. Based on the type of build you perform, the headers will automatically cause the inclusion of the appropriate library at link time. You can see how the mechanism works by examining Afx.h, starting at about line 30.

MFC Libraries

The Microsoft Foundation Classes are provided in library as well as source form. The libraries that you link to when you build an MFC application include the standard Windows API libraries, as well as any additional special-purpose libraries that you need, such as those for OLE support.

There are several different ways to use MFC. The first is to statically-link MFC directly into the application or the DLL you're writing, and contributes directly to the on-disk executable image size. While the size penalty for this can be very large, depending on how much of MFC's functionality you use, the benefits are that you don't need to install any additional files when you redistribute your application or library. Your load time is also decreased, because Windows won't need to go searching for a DLL to resolve function references at runtime.

The second version of MFC is built into a dynamic link library. When you build a DLL or an application that uses MFC in a shared DLL, you'll find that the executable file size is significantly reduced. Your executable's startup time might be slightly lengthened – because you'll need to get the DLL that contains MFC loaded and initialized for your process – but if you're building a system of several programs that all use MFC, you'll find that this extra time is actually negligible in light of the memory savings you gain. Since each process using MFC isn't going to have the same statically-linked MFC code in its own address space, but will instead share a common copy of the MFC code, dynamically linking to MFC is the preferred approach when you're expecting to concurrently run many MFC-based applications.

If you're writing a DLL that needs to pass MFC objects from your DLL back to applications that are calling your DLL, you'll need to use the DLL build of MFC – and those applications will need to use a DLL-based build of MFC, too. A DLL written with this model is called an **MFC Extension DLL**. If your calling application doesn't use MFC, or if you don't expect to pass MFC-based objects back and forth between your DLL and your application, you can use MFC in a special DLL-based build that doesn't allow you to share objects between the DLL and the application, but does afford you the benefits of the dynamic linking model. Such a DLL is called a **regular DLL**.

We'll focus on the different MFC DLL models in Chapter 11, but for now let's examine the different MFC library files that allow you to build these different application and DLL types.

Since not all applications built to use the shared DLL build of MFC will use each and every feature of MFC, the classes in the DLL are split by functionality over three DLLs, but only for debug builds of the library. The main MFC functions are in a large, primary DLL, while OLE and ODBC support classes are each split into separate DLLs; and of course, both debug and non-debug builds are available. The files, found in `Mfc\Lib` for any non-CD based installation, are enumerated in the following table:

Files	Description
Mfc42.lib	Release build of core MFC classes for shared DLL use
Mfc42d.lib	Debug build of core MFC classes for shared DLL use
Mfcd42d.lib	Debug build of MFC database classes for shared DLL use
Mfco42d.lib	Debug build of MFC OLE support classes for shared DLL use
Mfcn42d.lib	Debug build of MFC network support classes for shared DLL use
Mfcs42.lib	Static helper library for release shared DLL use
Mfcs42d.lib	Static helper library for debug shared DLL use

If you're familiar with older versions of MFC, you'll notice that MFC 4.0 and newer no longer have function-specific libraries for the release build. That is, previous versions of MFC didn't put their release build in a single huge DLL; they split the library into different DLLs, just as the current debug build of MFC does. The idea behind this change is to facilitate debugging while optimizing load time for release applications. When you build your release version, you want the application to run as quickly as possible. Loading up to four DLLs for each application is a bit more expensive than loading just one DLL, even if it is much larger. However, working with the debugger is more convenient if the libraries are split into pieces.

The above table mentions a couple of **static helper libraries**. These libraries are statically linked to your application, even when you link to MFC in a DLL. The static libraries provide code and data that lives in each application that uses MFC, and help MFC to track information that's local to each module that is using MFC's shared implementation. The size of the statically-linked data is not very large.

Windows NT supports national language versions of applications by providing access to the Unicode character set. As Unicode imposes special rules for the handling of strings, there are separate versions of the libraries that utilize wide, Unicode-compatible string access. These are listed in the following table:

File	Description
Mfc42u.lib	Release, Unicode build of core MFC classes for shared DLL use
Mfc42ud.lib	Debug, Unicode build of core MFC classes for shared DLL use
Mfcd42u.lib	Release, Unicode build of MFC database classes for shared DLL use

Table Continued on Following Page

File	Description
Mfcd42ud.lib	Debug, Unicode build of MFC database classes for shared DLL use
Mfcn42ud.lib	Debug, Unicode build of MFC network support classes for shared DLL use
Mfco42ud.lib	Debug, Unicode build of MFC OLE support classes for shared DLL use
Mfcs42u.lib	Static Unicode helper library for release shared DLL use
Mfcs42ud.lib	Static Unicode helper library for debug shared DLL use

The static versions of MFC are provided in versions compatible with Unicode and ANSI character sets, as well as being made available for debug and release builds. The normal static builds have afxc in their name, while the statically-linkable versions of MFC for use in a regular DLL have afxd in their name. This table shows the libraries containing different static and regular DLL-compatible versions of MFC:

File	Description
Nafxcw.lib	ANSI version of statically linkable release build MFC classes
Nafxcwd.lib	ANSI version of statically linkable debug build MFC classes
Nafxdw.lib	ANSI version of statically-linkable regular DLL release build MFC classes
Nafxdwd.lib	ANSI version of statically-linkable regular DLL debug build MFC classes
Uafxcw.lib	Unicode version of statically linkable release build MFC classes
Uafxcwd.lib	Unicode version of statically linkable debug build MFC classes
Uafxdw.lib	Unicode version of statically-linkable regular DLL release build MFC classes
Uafxdwd.lib	Unicode version of statically-linkable regular DLL debug build MFC classes
Eafxis.lib	Internet Server API classes for release builds that use MFC in a shared DLL
Eafxisd.lib	Internet Server API classes for debug builds that use MFC in a shared DLL
Naxfis.lib	Internet Server API classes for release builds that use MFC in a static library, or don't use MFC at all
Nafxisd.lib	Internet Server API classes for debug builds that use MFC in a static library, or don't use MFC at all

You'll find an additional special library named `Mfcuia32.lib` in the `Microsoft Visual Studio\vc98\Lib` directory. This library provides access to a common user interface for OLE in ANSI and Unicode applications. This library is so-named because it was previously a component of MFC; but now it's actually a part of the operating system. The library gives your OLE-aware application the ability to react to special situations with a user interface that meets the OLE user interface standard.

Run-time Libraries

Visual C++ also includes several megabytes of library files and standard `.obj` files which you must link with to reuse. Since file names are stuffed into the DOS 8.3 character format, the connection between their names and functionality is sometimes cryptic. If you want to determine what a particular library file does, you will find a description of each of the libraries and objects shipped with Visual C++ in Appendix D.

You will rarely, if ever, have to directly involve yourself with these files, because the MFC headers will select the correct libraries for you. MFC's header files include special directives to the compiler so that it emits records the linker uses to find particular libraries. When you process `Afx.h`, for example, MFC directs the compiler to tell the linker to get the MFC library that's appropriate for the application build you're performing. When you reference `Afxwin.h`, there are more directives that have the linker get the most important Windows system libraries.

If you make a change to your program that requires functions that are not supported by the libraries that are automatically referenced, you will need to explicitly add a library, or an object file, to the list of files that the linker considers for your project.

MFC Version Compatibility

The version of MFC installed with Visual C++ 6 is 6.0. With few exceptions, previous versions of MFC are upwardly compatible with MFC 6.0. Code written for previous 32-bit versions of MFC 3.*x* with Visual C++ 2.*x* can largely be compiled with Visual C++ 6 and run against MFC 6.0 headers and libraries. Porting code that uses MFC 4.2*x* from Visual C++ 4.2 or Visual C++ 5.0 can be done with without difficulty. The notable exceptions to this ease of portability are code for 16-bit versions of MFC that supported Visual Basic Custom Controls (OCXs), and code from 32-bit versions that subclassed painting for toolbar and status bar windows.

Summary

In this chapter, we've taken a whirlwind tour through Visual C++. We've seen how to get the best from the Visual Studio, and learned a little bit about the MFC libraries. I recommend that you take some time to play with Visual C++ before continuing. See how it works and get a feel for it. Intentionally write some bogus code to make sure you understand how to navigate from error to error. Tap *F1* to see the online help for your errors. Look through the online documentation and understand how it works so that you can get help with the environment as we move through the classes.

In our next chapter, we'll examine how to go about building an application using the AppWizard and ClassWizard. We'll also see how the development environment's source browser provides us with a convenient way to navigate through even the largest projects.

The Wizards and The Gallery

Many aspects of software development are simply repetitive grunt work. Whilst building the mundane and basic code doesn't take an incredible amount of thought or insight, it can be very worrying, simply because it's so easy to make silly mistakes. Even experts who've lived through the process several times become afraid of it, because they're forced to reexamine things they haven't thought about recently.

Microsoft has addressed this problem with several **Wizards**, in addition to some other tools, that make your life easier by leading you through otherwise confusing or time-consuming tasks. All these tools are designed to help you avoid tedious coding, increase code reusability and reduce code maintenance by organizing it into easily identifiable entities.

In this chapter, we'll be looking at:

 ➢ The MFC AppWizard
 ➢ The MFC ClassWizard
 ➢ The Visual C++ source code browser
 ➢ The Components and Controls Gallery

The MFC AppWizards

"A journey of a thousand miles must begin with a single step."

Lao Tzu, Tao Te Ching

He wasn't a programmer, but Windows developers have learned that Lao Tzu was right. Truer words have never been written, and modern developers might even offer the corollary that the first few steps often seem to be the most tedious. Setting up a Windows program involves getting the same, error-free code in place for almost every application. From the smartest spreadsheet to the tiniest one-time utility, the great bulk of Windows applications share these basic features:

> ➢ A message pump
> ➢ A message handling function
> ➢ Application initialization code
> ➢ Application shutdown code

More advanced programs, like those used on desktops in the corporate world, also share many more advanced features:

> ➢ Status bars
> ➢ Toolbars
> ➢ Context-sensitive online help

It has been said that lots of other features can be thought of as absolutely necessary in a competitive application just because it seems like everybody else has them. And some might even be required for Microsoft's compatibility logo programs:

> ➢ MDI support
> ➢ OLE support
> ➢ Floating toolbars
> ➢ Tabbed dialogs

And, if most programmers think that these things are too tedious to write by themselves, they certainly don't want to worry about the mundane constructs that drive most programs:

> ➢ Error handling and reporting
> ➢ Project build management

All of these features, from those that are technically necessary to those that help you keep up with developers who are competing with you, are provided in MFC classes that can be derived from and customized in your applications. Unfortunately, those classes must still be hooked up and built with commands issued to the compiler and linker. Even though the complex compiler and linker options that you need to use are tidily hidden in the project file for your application, they don't go away in Visual C++.

To avoid all of this drudgery, Visual C++ provides several **AppWizard**s. This manifestation of Microsoft's Wizard technology allows you to create a project, including a project file, source code files, a resource script and a module definition file. In a few short clicks, you have an application with a few basic (and not so basic) features that you can begin to shape into The Next Great Software Product.

An AppWizard is simply any of the entries in the list offered to a developer when they ask Visual Studio for a new project. The choices in the list each offer a different, dialog-based way to pick a few options before creating a project based on those options. There are several MFC AppWizards; you can use them to create different types of DLL and EXE projects, as well as MFC-based OLE Controls. In this book, whenever I refer to AppWizard without qualifying it with the word *custom*, or by some other means, I really mean either **MFC AppWizard (exe)** or **MFC AppWizard (dll)**. The ControlWizard is just like a regular AppWizard, save that it produces projects suited for the development of ActiveX controls instead of complete applications. It should be clear from the context which Wizard I mean.

Starting an AppWizard

When using Visual C++, you'll normally begin your projects by using New... from the File menu to bring up the New dialog box. If you click on the Projects tab in that box, your view of the world will resemble what's shown here:

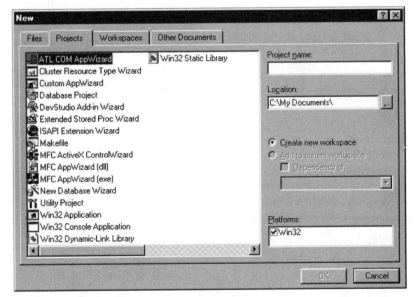

The list view control that dominates this window offers a list of possible project types that you can create – each one of the choices is implemented by an individual AppWizard. The two choices which include the words MFC AppWizard in their name together form (surprise!) the **MFC AppWizard**. We'll be discussing how to use the second of these options, MFC AppWizard (exe), to create an MFC-based executable project later in this chapter, but first we'll take a quick look at all the possible project types.

If you're porting an application from another development platform, you'll probably want to use one of the project types that doesn't *mention AppWizard – like the* Makefile *project type, the* Win32 Application *type, or the* Win32 Console Application *type. Since you'll have your existing code, you won't need the program files that it would generate – but you'll still benefit from the project and support files those Wizard types will create for you.*

Project Type	Description
ATL COM AppWizard	The ATL COM AppWizard helps you create ATL-based projects. ATL is Microsoft's Active Template Library, and is a complementary library to MFC. ATL is ideal for creating small, lightweight COM objects and ActiveX Controls.
Custom AppWizard	This is an AppWizard that lets you develop an AppWizard project of your own. You can define your own steps and build your own screens to pump out your favorite kind of application (or non-executable project) with the same kind of cookie-cutter ease as the regular AppWizard.
Database Project	A database project usually contains no interesting files – it simply encapsulates a connection to a data source and provides a rudimentary user interface for viewing and editing some data in that data source. You can, if you'd like, add sub-projects to your database project and use them to actually implement code that will work with the particular database connection.
Microsoft Visual Studio Add-in Wizard	Visual C++ version 5.0 and onwards expose a very rich extensible set of interfaces. By writing a Microsoft Visual Studio Add-In, you can take advantage of these additional interfaces to automate common tasks. Your Add-In is able to interact with the Microsoft Visual Studio environment very closely – it may even provide a toolbar and receive notifications of events within the studio.
Extended Stored Proc Wizard	An extended stored procedure is a special DLL that allows your SQL Server applications to execute server-side code on demand.
ISAPI Extension Wizard	MFC, in versions 4.1 and newer, supports the implementation of modules that can be used to extend Internet web servers, including Microsoft's Internet Information Server. This kind of project is very special, and is described in great detail in Chapter 18.
Makefile	Back when dinosaurs roamed the Earth, developers built applications from the command-line. Sometimes, you still might have to do this if the 'custom build step' feature of the IDE can't accommodate the special needs of your project. Alternatively, you might have to start using a command-line makefile to absorb an old project as you begin converting it. A Makefile project lets you set up your own makefile.
MFC ActiveX ControlWizard	The ControlWizard helps you build an ActiveX control. Controls are flexible, insertable, reusable COM objects that support Automation. You'll learn lots about the ActiveX control architecture in Chapter 15.
MFC AppWizard (dll)	This project type doesn't produce an application at all, but instead allows you to choose a few options to help create a dynamic-link library. AppWizard will create the necessary files for you, including a .def file and a project file. We discuss creating DLLs in Chapter 11.

Project Type	Description
MFC AppWizard (exe)	This Wizard produces a basic MFC application that will result in an executable (.exe). This can be tuned to include support for a range of optional extras, as we'll see shortly.
Utility Project	A Utility Project is a project that doesn't generate any known output files, though you can export a makefile. Utility Projects are useful tools for getting the IDE to build very complicated projects. You have to create your own set of custom build rules for a utility project.
Win32 Application	This will create a simple project with the options set to allow you to write a graphical user interface application from scratch, using your own code. This code can be based around the Microsoft Foundation Classes or the standard Win32 API. Unlike the Wizard-based projects above, you can't perform any customization of the project before it's created.
Win32 Console Application	The Win32 Console Application Wizard creates a project that helps you build a Windows console application. A console application is a Windows application that normally presents a character-mode user interface in a command prompt-like window. We discuss console applications in Appendix C.
Win32 Dynamic-Link Library	This creates a project that can be used to build a DLL. The resulting DLL project may have very few features – from no files at all (aside from the project itself) to a very simple DLL stub that you can grow into a useful project. This Wizard differs from the MFC AppWizard (dll) choice in that the DLLs produced by this Wizard never use MFC.
Win32 Static Library	This option creates the necessary project file required to build a static library. The project file automates the construction of the modules for the library and will run the librarian utility to actually create the .lib file.

The list of project types you see when you examine the New dialog yourself might not exactly match the list I have here. For example, Database Project is only available if you have the Enterprise Edition of Visual C++. If you've installed some third-party software that extends Visual Studio, you might have even more project types in your list. The Extended Stored Proc Wizard, installed by the Microsoft SQL Server developer tools package, is an example of a **custom AppWizard**.

You can create your own custom AppWizards with the help of the Custom AppWizard project type. Some versions of Visual C++ ship with their own special custom AppWizards, as I've mentioned. It's certainly very possible that the management within your organization has added custom application Wizards to your development environment to help you with the specific problems that are prevalent at your company. There's tons of information about such Wizards in Microsoft's online help – I'm afraid they're a little beyond the scope of this book.

We're Off to Choose the Wizard!

As I mentioned, starting your project from scratch essentially means that you're about to choose a Wizard to get your project file setup and your application built. You can, if you want to, always construct projects by hand – or use one of the bare-naked Wizard styles to create only the most minimal of project setups with no included source code.

Collectively, the AppWizards offer you lots of choices. Making the right choice now will help you get your development tasks started smoothly. If you choose the wrong Wizard, you'll end up with a project type that's not a great match for your goal. Not every single development task is completely targeted by a Wizard, so you will have to do *some* work. (And that's why you get paid the big bucks, champ!)

Before you select a Wizard, you'll want to think about your program's overall architecture as well as its fundamental user interface. Since this is a book on MFC, we'll focus on the MFC AppWizards, here.

Making a Graphical User Interface Application

Let's examine how AppWizard helps us create MFC applications. If you'd like to follow along, make sure you select the MFC AppWizard (exe) file type (I called my application `Simple`). When you press OK in the New dialog, you will be whisked away to the first of AppWizard's cue cards. AppWizard will use these dialogs to gain some information from you about the application you wish to create.

The first page of options you'll be offered relates to the fundamental structure of your application; will your application support a single document interface, a multiple document interface, or will it display only a dialog box as its sole user interface? Here, you can see the first step in the path to creating a new MFC project using AppWizard:

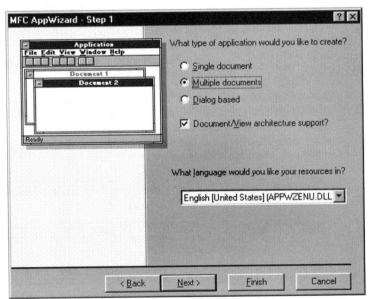

To create our simple SDI application, I chose the **Single document** button. An MDI application would have a slightly different architecture – it would readily allow more than one document open at a time, and allow multiple views of both the same or alternate documents open at a time. Applications like WordPad and Notepad are SDI applications, while applications like Word and Excel and the Visual Studio IDE itself qualify as MDI applications.

To facilitate the design of applications that manipulate and display file-based data, MFC supports a concept called the **document/view architecture**. Most applications are appropriate for the document/view architecture, but some aren't. If you're not manipulating data that lives in a file, for example, or porting an application written without MFC, you might want to eschew the document/view architecture for your own infrastructure. You can generate an application that doesn't have document/view plumbing wired-up by making sure the Document/View architecture support? box is not checked.

If you select a Dialog based application, your application will contain only a dialog – no menus, and no document/view architecture. The Calculator applet that ships with Windows is an example of a dialog-based application – even though it does add a menu. Since a dialog-based application never has the document/view code hooked-up, the Document/View architecture support? button will be disabled whenever the Dialog based button is marked.

> In Chapters 3 and 4, we'll examine the MFC classes that help you write dialog-based and SDI-based applications. The document/view architecture, including reasons for its application and avoidance, are discussed in depth in Chapter 4.

In the first step of the AppWizard, you can also indicate a language base for your resource files. Using a particular human language resource doesn't preclude you from migrating your application to a different locale later in the development cycle. For the time being, let's create a single document interface application with the US English resources file. (*Si vous avez le goût de l'aventure, vous pouvez même créer une application en français.*) The internationalized version of Visual C++ ships with additional language DLLs, or you may obtain them from Microsoft as they become available.

You can proceed to the next page of options by pressing the Next> button. If, at any time, you make a mistake or wish to review the options you've selected, you can page through the dialogs using the Next> and <Back buttons. You can also use the Finish button to skip all of the remaining questions and accept all the default options. The first Step dialog doesn't show the number of steps on the way to creating your application, because that's dependent on the type of application; dialog applications have fewer options and take fewer steps than applications using the document/view metaphor.

The balance of the steps you'll follow in the AppWizard depend on exactly what options you've selected. The remaining sections in this chapter discuss the path you'll follow when you're writing an SDI or MDI application that has document/view support. At the end of the chapter, I'll discuss the differences in the Wizard's user interface when you've selected a dialog-based application, or when you've turned off document/view support. In the meantime, let's go to the second step!

Selecting Database Support

The second step in creating an application with AppWizard provides the opportunity to include database support. MFC supports database access through OLE DB, ODBC and DAO (but not yet ADO). If your application focuses around database interaction – that is, you envisage your application's main user interface revolving around a form that shows, edits, and stores database records – you should make sure you add database support by selecting one of these options now.

If you intend to have database support in your application, but don't wish to use MFC's provisions for database access (e.g. you wish to code directly to your database vendor's API, or you wish to use classes or code that you've already written to work with ODBC), you won't need to specify any database requirements to AppWizard. Simply mark the None button and move on to the next step of the Wizard.

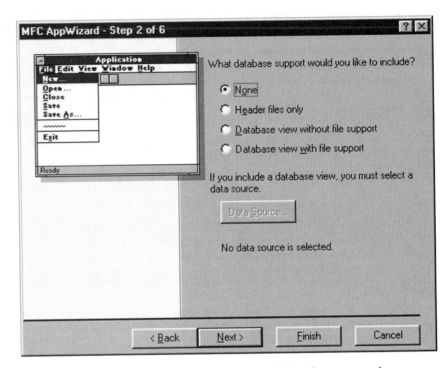

If you select the Header files only option, the generated project will include references to the appropriate database classes and the necessary definitions from the Afxdb.h and Afxdao.h header files. No other work will be done for you; you will be on your own to implement the database features of your application. If your application uses a database but doesn't provide a form-style user interface at its very core, you'll find that it's easier to code the brunt of that architecture manually, after using the Wizard to incorporate the database-specific MFC header files in your project.

If you choose the Database view without file support or Database view with file support options, you'll be obliged to press the Data Source... button to select a data source for your application. AppWizard assumes that you'll be writing an application that will access only one data source, and will create a view that includes code to browse, read and write information to and from that data source.

Since MFC can use ODBC to perform the data access, you can use any installed ODBC driver to provide your application with a path to the data. With the appropriate driver, you can have your application work against the data in Excel spreadsheets right there on your machine, or an Oracle database server across campus on your company's network.

Complex Database Support

If you're planning to develop an elaborate application which references many databases, or works with many different tables, you're probably better off selecting Header files only in the Step 2 dialog and writing your own database interface code. Once your project is created, you can always add additional data sources and queries using the ClassWizard. If you chose any other option for a more complicated application, you would end up deleting the code provided by AppWizard, as it's only directly applicable to a browsing application.

If you're planning an elaborate application, you may wish to create another AppWizard-generated project. In this case, however, select one of the other database options and set it up for one of the data sources you intend to use. You can then pillage the simple browse-and-edit code from this dummy application and move it into your own creation to save time in development. Or, you can use ClassWizard to add the database support classes you need piece-by-piece to your application. ClassWizard allows you to customize your new classes for the database source, just as AppWizard does, so you won't lose many steps.

The Database view without file support means that your application will treat the set of database records your application manipulates as a document. When the user chooses the Save command in your File menu, MFC will only write any changes to the record to the database. If you chose Database view with file support, your application will not only be able to read data from and write data to the data source, but will also include code that provides a file-like representation of the data. This means that you could also save the data to a file, or ship it off to some in-memory storage facility. You might decide to have your application's documents actually comprise a hybrid of database records and information you store in files for the user. For such an application, the Database view with file support option would be the way to go.

If you're planning on adding OLE server support (which we'll investigate in the next section) to your application, *and* you want to have database support, you must select the Database view with file support option. Your application will need to provide a persistent version of its state by writing to a storage, which MFC perceives no differently than a normal disk file.

I chose None for the level of database support that I needed in the Simple application.

Adding Compound Document Support

The third AppWizard step, illustrated below, allows you to specify the level of compound document support you require in your application. If you don't provide support for Automation, or even compound documents, your application will be smaller. However, you may wish to improve the interoperability of your application by turning on some of these options.

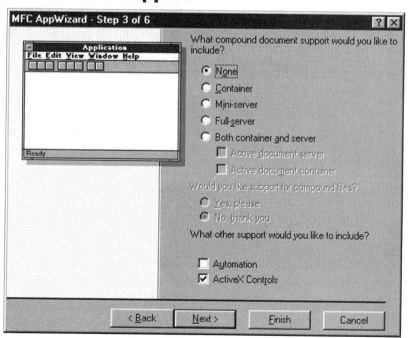

Writing a **container** means that your application will be capable of hosting other insertable OLE objects. For example, your users may wish to embed objects created with the Microsoft Equation Editor, or they may wish to drop entire Excel charts into your application. Selecting this option changes a few base classes in your application from their defaults, and also includes a few extra classes. The exact nature of these changes is discussed in Chapter 13.

OLE Servers

A **mini-server** is an OLE server application that can't exist as a stand-alone application; that is, the application was written simply to service an OLE object. It has no other function besides managing an object, and it operates as an embedded object in another application. Due to this inherent limitation, mini-server applications only run when the user decides to edit the served object in another application.

As mini-server applications can't be used to work with files and only store their data parasitically in another application, they generally don't have conventional File menus. One example of a mini-server application is the Microsoft Equation Editor that we mentioned before. You can save equations that you've embedded in your Word document by saving the document, but the Equation Editor doesn't allow you to work with them outside of that document's environment.

By contrast, **full-servers** are useful as applications even when they aren't supporting an embedded object. They expose embedded objects, but can be used directly by the user to edit full files. Examples of commercial full-server applications include Excel and Word.

The final choice, Both container and server, includes support that allows your application both to provide objects to other applications, and to host embedded objects serviced by other servers or mini-servers. This type of application, as produced by AppWizard, is always a full-server.

> If you include database support in your application and you want your application to provide OLE container, mini-server or full-server functionality, you must provide file serialization support in your application. We'll look at that in Chapter 4.

OLE requires that applications be able to render their documents as binary images. If your database application doesn't provide compound file support, it won't be able to render data for consumption by OLE. AppWizard will warn you if you've selected features that are incompatible.

Extra OLE Stuff

This dialog step also allows you to hook up support for ActiveX control containment. If you check the ActiveX controls box, your application will contain a couple of extra lines of code to allow your application to hold ActiveX controls in its windows and dialogs. We'll talk in great detail about this feature of MFC in Chapter 16.

If you've requested any level of compound document server support in your project, you'll notice that the Step 3 dialog enables a checkbox labeled ActiveX document server. If you mark this box, the AppWizard will produce a tiny bit of extra code that allows your application to serve as an ActiveX document. ActiveX documents are very similar to normal embedded objects, but have very different rules for activation. You'll learn more about this project feature in Chapter 15.

If you request Automation in your application by checking the appropriate box, MFC will hook it up by including some related classes and providing a type library for your application. We'll discuss these changes in detail in Chapter 15.

You don't need to enable any compound document support (that is, you don't need to select any level of container or server support) to use these last two options. To keep our application simple for this early part of the book, I asked for no compound document support whatsoever.

Embellishing Your User Interface

The fourth step presented by AppWizard allows you to tailor the user interface in your application. The dialog for this step allows you to select several different features for your application:

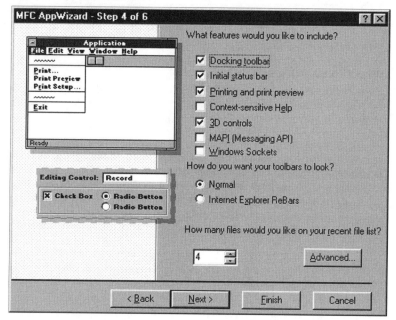

Docking Toolbar

Like Word or Excel (or even the Microsoft Visual Studio IDE itself), you can let your application have multiple toolbars that the user can 'dock' to any edge of the window, or have 'floating' in the client area of your application. If you select the Docking toolbar option, your application will get a docking toolbar that features buttons which can execute commands within your applications. With the toolbar option turned on, you'll notice that some controls in the center of the dialog become enabled.

Those controls, under the How do you want your toolbars to look? heading, let you change the implementation class and appearance of your toolbars. The Normal toolbar choice uses toolbars based on MFC's CToolbar class. The toolbar will include some default commands and buttons, but you can easily alter these. I'll cover the functionality provided by CToolbar in Chapter 4. CToolbar makes a bar that has individual buttons for each command.

If you chose Internet Explorer ReBars, you'll end up using a class called CReBar. We'll examine that one in Chapter 4, too. It makes a user interface that looks more like the thicker bars of Internet Explorer, and has a flat appearance and is normally just a bit larger in size.

Initial Status Bar

The Initial status bar option will endow your application with a status bar at the bottom of its main window. AppWizard will wire up an instance of CStatusBar, the main frame window will organize the positioning of the bar and the application framework will help to manage its content at runtime. I'll examine the CStatusBar class in more detail in Chapter 4.

Printing and Print Preview

The application produced by AppWizard will make use of the document/view architecture that we'll examine in Chapter 4. This architecture inherently supports printing and print preview. If you carefully write your application's screen painting code, you can make use of these features with almost no additional effort. If you don't enable the Printing and print preview option, the corresponding functionality can be added manually with some work at a later date.

Context-sensitive Help

If you select this option, your application will include support for Context-sensitive Help. Not only will handlers be hooked up for Help menu entries and the *F1* key, but AppWizard will actually write a minimal help file to help you get started in implementing your own.

> Help for your application is built outside of the integrated development environment. You need an editor that can handle the .rtf (Rich Text File) file format — such as Word for Windows, WordPerfect for Windows, or another third party tool. If you're using Word for Windows, you'll find that Microsoft Visual Studio can open Word as a document object server and allow you to edit your help file directly within the Microsoft Visual Studio environment.
>
> For the time being, the Visual C++ development environment doesn't provide direct support for the generation of projects that use HTML Help for their online references. Perhaps this will be addressed in a future edition of the development system.

To assist you when you build your help file, AppWizard also generates a help project file (with a .hpj extension) and a batch file called MakeHelp.bat, which builds your help file for you.

3D Controls

If this box is checked, AppWizard will generate code that formerly turned-on three-dimensional features in your application's user interface. In older operating environments, this feature gave the dialogs generated by your application gray backgrounds and your controls a 'chiseled' appearance.

This option creates a dependency on the Ctl3d32.dll dynamic-link library to implement a three-dimensional appearance into your application. A 32-bit version of this DLL is shipped with Visual C++, but you may be familiar with the 16-bit version if you've ever written an application that utilized it in Windows for Workgroups, or even in stock Windows. And it's those ancient versions of Windows at which this option is aimed at; the only 32-bit platforms which require Ctl3d32.dll, or where this option will have any noticeable effect, are on Windows NT 3.1 and Windows NT 3.50! You can probably expect that this option (and the associated code, in MFC) to soon be removed from the product.

As you adjust the options for your application, AppWizard will update the visual samples in the left of the AppWizard window to reflect the effects of your selection on the main window of your application.

MFC provides support for a most-recently-used (MRU) file list in the File menu of your application. Whenever users of your application open a file, its name will be added to a list in the File menu. If that list becomes full, the oldest file name on the list will be removed. You can set the number of items of that list by changing the field near the bottom of the Step 4 dialog.

Additional User Interface Considerations

There are a couple of additional options in this step. They won't strongly affect the user interface of your application, but they'll add some code to your application that will later affect your decisions about its feature set.

The first option is the inclusion of **MAPI, M**essaging **A**pplication **P**rogramming **I**nterface support, represented by the MAPI (Messaging API) checkbox in this step. If it's checked, AppWizard will give the application's main menu a Send... command in its File menu. This menu item will be hooked up to code that serializes the document to a file and then mails that file with MAPI. The implementation of this code is just a default command handler for this message. We'll talk about what gets serialized (and what *serialization* means) in Chapter 4, when we examine the document/view architecture.

The second of the two options involves support for the Windows Sockets library. Checking this option causes the generated application to have a reference to `Afxsock.h`. This gains access to the `CSocket` and `CAsyncSocket` classes which wrap the Windows Sockets API. These classes are useful for peer-to-peer and client/server network communication.

For the simple application that I occasionally reference for the remainder of this chapter, I accepted only the default options in all of the screens. While we'll walk through the rest of the screens, you could, if you were in a rush, press the Finish button to skip the rest of the prompts.

Adding Advanced Features

The Advanced... button in Step 4 leads to the dialog shown here:

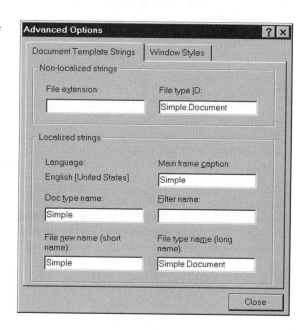

The Advanced Options dialog's Document Template Strings tab, shown above, allows you to adjust the settings for your application's documents. As these features of your application are indeed advanced, I will be covering them fully when we examine MFC's document architecture in more detail during Chapter 4. For now, though, and for the sake of completeness, I'll give you a quick overview.

Most of the options affect the way your application is named in a variety of situations. The File extension edit control specifies the file extension that you'd like to use. In Visual C++ 6.0 and MFC 6.0, you're free to use an extension that's longer than three characters. You can name the file extension as it will appear in your application's Open dialog box by entering your description in the Filter name field. If your application ever prompts the user for the type of new file that they'd like to open, MFC will use the text you place in the File new name (short name) field. If files managed by your application are COM-creatable, COM will identify them with the naming information that you provide in the File type name (long name) field.

The File type ID field identifies the file type to Windows if your application is an OLE server, while the Main frame caption field lets you set the initial caption for the main window of your application; whatever you'd like is just fine as far as the AppWizard and MFC are concerned. MFC will modify the caption in appropriate situations – by adding the title of the opened file to it, for example – as per the Microsoft Windows application user interface style guidelines, which can be found at http://msdn.microsoft.com/UI/.

The Window Styles tab, snappily depicted opposite, allows you to adjust the style of your main window (and the MDI child window frame if you're writing an MDI application). The check boxes in the Main frame styles group box correspond to the different window style bits that your main window can accept. Changing the style bits will let you determine the initial state of your main window, as well as affecting its functionality.

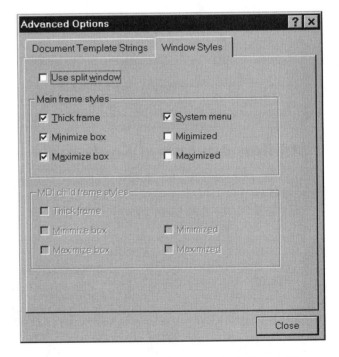

For example, when your window is active, the user can't resize it if it doesn't have a thick frame. If you make the initial state minimized, but don't provide a maximize box, a thick frame, or a system menu, then your application will always run as a button in the task bar. I'll discuss the specifics of your main frame window's attributes in Chapter 3.

The MDI child frame styles group has controls that help you set the options for the MDI child windows your application will create. If you're creating an SDI or dialog-based application, these controls will be disabled. The options here are almost the same as those for the main frame; they allow you to dictate the initial style of windows created as MDI children in your application.

The Use split window option allows you to request that your application uses a CSplitterWnd class for its windows. We'll cover splitter windows in detail during Chapter 6, and MDI windows in Chapter 4. A CSplitterWnd basically allows the user to split the content of a window, either horizontally or vertically, to create two independently editable panes. You can use this feature in both SDI and MDI applications.

Miscellaneous Options

Step 5 involves setting three options that finalize the implementation of your project. The first option in the Step 5 dialog allows you to choose the style of the project you'd like to implement; you can request a traditional MFC Standard user interface, which shows a single view in your MDI or SDI application. The AppWizard in all versions of Visual C++ has been able to generate an application with this kind of user interface.

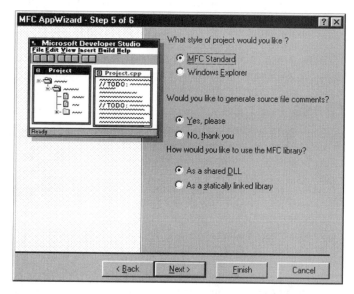

Visual C++ 6.0, however, provides for Windows Explorer-based applications. Such an application features two separate views vertically, in a static splitter window. While the application style affords some flexibility, the left hand view normally shows some navigable overview of items or objects – like the directory structure in a file system. The right-hand view shows details related to the item on the left-hand view that is currently selected, and will update and refresh to reflect that selection.

Almost any application that allows the user to browse a list or tree of entities and quickly see the details of those entities can be written using the explorer-style user interface. These "explorer-style" applications, shown opposite, are so named because they strongly resemble Microsoft Windows' own Explorer windows.

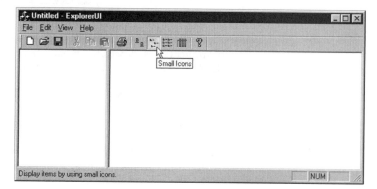

The Step 5 dialog box has controls that give you a couple more choices. One set of buttons allows you to enable or disable the inclusion of source code comments. If you request that comments are to be generated and placed in your source, AppWizard will clearly mark your application in places where you will be required to write code, or where special situations arise.

The third choice in the dialog, allows you to choose how your application links to the MFC implementation libraries. If you statically link MFC to your application, it will load very quickly and won't require any additional non-system dynamic-link libraries in order to execute. Statically linked applications generally use less memory than dynamically linked applications, but there are some exceptions; I'll spell out the specific differences in Chapter 11.

If you know that your application will be run at the same time as other MFC-based applications you've written, you might try to ensure that those applications use a shared implementation of MFC. Doing so will guarantee that only one copy of MFC is in memory at any one time, potentially reducing the working set for all involved applications. More information about the libraries involved in this step can be found in the section of Appendix D that names and describes the libraries shipped with Visual C++. We'll also explain some subtle aspects of the shared DLL implementation of MFC when we discuss coding DLLs with MFC in Chapter 11.

Class Names

The sixth AppWizard step allows you to change the class names which will appear in your application. The defaults picked by AppWizard are based on the name of your application, so they should be adequate for most tastes, although some long application names can be truncated to awkward, or even embarrassing, class names. This dialog lets you change those names, as well as the file names for the implementations of the classes bearing them:

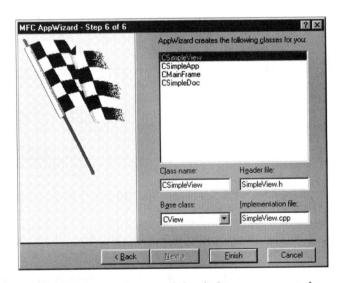

If you select the different derived class names in the list box at the top of the dialog you can see the relevant file names and base classes in the edit controls at the bottom of the window. AppWizard will implement each of your application's classes, with each being derived from a class implemented in MFC. The name of each MFC class is shown in the Base Class field at the bottom of the dialog.

With the exception of your application's view class (or classes), you can't change the base classes MFC will use. For any view class your application uses, you can select one of the eight base classes implemented by MFC. These classes, which we'll cover in great detail during our discussion of the document/view architecture in Chapter 4, each provide a slightly different user interface for your application. Most applications that deal with graphically presented data or heavily formatted text will use a CScrollView, while applications that deal with plain text will probably use a CEditView.

> You can't change the name of the application's base implementation file, although you *can* change the names of the implementation and definition files used by all the other classes. You can't make two classes use the same files.

One More Step

The final step in creating an application using AppWizard is simply to confirm the choices you've already made by pressing the Finish button. The dialog, which presents the information about your application, is shown next:

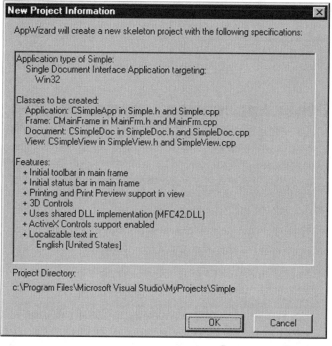

Once you've reviewed the options and names you've selected, you can click the OK button to generate your application. If you've noticed something that bothers you, then you can click the Cancel button to return to the Step 6 dialog. From there, you can use the <Back and Next> buttons to move to the option you wish to fix before using the Finish button to see your updated project information.

AppWizard will generate all of these files for you:

> ➤ A .cpp implementation file for your application's document class, if any
> ➤ A .cpp implementation file for your application's view class, if any
> ➤ A .cpp implementation file for your application's frame window class
> ➤ A .cpp implementation file for your application
> ➤ Supporting header files, with the .h extension
> ➤ A resource script, and other resource files such as icons and toolbar layout with the .rc extension
> ➤ A module definition file, with the .def extension, if one is required
> ➤ A Visual C++ project file, with the .dsw and .dsp extensions
> ➤ A Readme.txt file describing what changes or additional work may be necessary

In Visual C++6, as in Visual C++5, makefiles are no longer produced by the environment automatically. You can use the Export Makefile... *command in the* Project *menu to explicitly export your project's makefile. To have the IDE automatically export a makefile for all of your projects, you can mark the* Export makefile when saving project file *checkbox on the* Build *tab of the* Options *menu, reachable with the* Options... *command in the* Tools *menu.*

If you've requested context-sensitive help, AppWizard will also generate a `hlp` directory and a simple help file to get you started. If you chose to have Automation in your application, you will also have a basic `.odl` file, which contains information for your application's type library. When AppWizard has finished writing these files, you can immediately use the Build command in the Build menu to compile and link your application.

Other Application Interfaces

As we mentioned in the first step, you can use AppWizard to create a variety of different applications. You will notice that the series of steps that you are taken through for one type of application is not the same as for another. SDI and MDI applications vary only slightly – SDI applications don't allow you to adjust any of the parameters that pertain to the features of MDI applications. There are no child frame windows in an SDI interface, so you can't adjust their parameters.

If you choose to not use the document/view architecture (by clearing the Document/View architecture support? box in the very first step) you'll find that some of the choices you're provided in the remainder of the wizard are very limited.

First, you'll only be able to request the Header files only level of database support. The other database support features require the document/view architecture. You'll not be able to request any level of OLE support, including OLE automation, but you may request that your application be a container for ActiveX Controls. ActiveX Controls can be held by an MFC application whether the application uses the document/view architecture or not.

Since MFC's support for printing and print preview and MAPI are based on the document/view architecture, you won't be able to turn those options on in the fourth step of the AppWizard. The Advanced... button, also available on the fourth step of the Wizard, will still lead to a dialog that allows you to change the styles of the frame window you've created, but it won't allow you to make settings related to file extensions or OLE. Finally, the Windows Explorer application type isn't available when you create an application that doesn't use the document/view architecture.

If you choose to make an application which is based around a dialog box, you'll automatically have no document/view support. As such, you'll have even fewer options when you create your application with the Wizard. You can't use MFC's OLE support in a dialog-based application, since that support is tightly bound to the document/view architecture. It's not to say a dialog-based application can't use or serve COM objects – but it can't participate in object embedding or containment.

Furthermore, when creating a dialog-based application, the AppWizard won't help you add any level of database support at all, although you *can* add it manually once AppWizard has finished its work. This exclusion is a little bit more arbitrary, since it is possible to use MFC's database classes in a dialog-based application – it's just not possible to use the document/view database classes (like `CRecordView`). We'll examine the constructs and classes (including `CRecordView`) you'll use to make a database application in Chapter 12.

As it creates a dialog-based application, AppWizard will offer you an abbreviated version of the user interface options dialog and the miscellaneous options dialog, before confirming the class names it will use when creating your application.

Other Application Styles

You might remember that the first dialog you saw when you used the <u>N</u>ew... command in <u>F</u>ile menu within the IDE listed many project types – but here we've only discussed the options you'll have when you select MFC AppWizard (exe)!

In Chapter 11, which is on DLLs, I'll mention the AppWizard for MFC DLLs, but we won't cover it in such great detail. That's because this book is about MFC; while the AppWizard provides a starting point for your program, it's really far more important to understand what MFC is doing for you, and to understand what the AppWizard's generated code means, than it is to understand the user interface provided by the AppWizards.

> *The MFC ActiveX ControlWizard is interesting, but deals greatly with OLE and ActiveX, and that subject is covered in many other books including: Chapter 23 of* Beginning Visual C++6 *by Ivor Horton, Wrox Press (ISBN 186100088x);* Beginning MFC COM Programming *by Julian Templeman, Wrox Press (ISBN 1874416877); and* Professional Visual C++ 5: ActiveX/COM Control Programming *by Sing Li and Panos Economopoulos, Wrox Press (ISBN 1861000375). Note that the latter two references use Visual C++ 5.0; as far as the ActiveX ControlWizard is concerned, there is very little difference between Visual C++ 5.0 and Visual C++ 6.0.*

One other AppWizard project style deserves note: the Win32 Console Application project type. This AppWizard lets you make a character-based program that can be run from the command-line in an existing console window, such as a DOS box. Or, when run from the Explorer or another part of the shell, the application will create a new console window. Since console applications are very appropriate for some tasks, the Win32 Console Application AppWizard now contains support for MFC-based applications as well as plain Win32 applications. I'll discuss this AppWizard in Appendix C.

Choose Carefully!

Perhaps AppWizard's biggest shortcoming is that it's an application generator and not an application manager. AppWizard can save you a tremendous amount of time when you first begin your project, but once you begin modifying the AppWizard-produced code, you can't use AppWizard to go back and add in features that you forgot earlier. As such, it's important to select the options correctly on your first trip through the AppWizard.

While it's nowhere near as comfortable as using AppWizard, you can revamp your application's design by manually adding code to realize new features. This isn't necessarily difficult; to alter the name of your data source in a database application, for instance, you only need to amend one parameter in a function call generated by AppWizard. To add support for compound documents, you may only need to change the base classes of the major component classes of your application. And, hopefully, by the time you've worked your way through this book, you'll be so familiar with MFC that it will seem like second nature to make any change you'd like to your Wizard-produced code.

However, if you're backed into a corner and need to add functionality that you didn't request from AppWizard but don't know where to find the source code you need, then all may not be lost. If you rerun AppWizard and create a new project with the same options as your existing one, you can then use AppWizard yet again to generate a third project with the options you wanted to have. By running a comparison program (like the WinDiff program supplied with Visual C++), you can discover all the differences between the two applications. Armed with this information, you can more readily adapt your application to include those features.

Alternatively, if you've not modified your current project much, you might create only one new project and directly compare it to the fresh project from AppWizard.

Either approach sounds a lot grittier than it really is — it's easy to do and it can save you a great amount of time if you do it carefully.

These caveats aside, Visual C++ certainly doesn't leave you high and dry for development assistance after you've begun your application. As we'll examine in this chapter, you can use ClassWizard to conveniently manipulate the classes involved in your program.

Compiling Your Application

The code generated by AppWizard forms a completely functional application, so now that we've seen how to create a complete product, it's time to take a little diversion to look at some of the options for building.

You can use the Build button (or the Build option in the Build menu) any time you'd like to create an executable for an application. The AppWizard-generated project will, by default, build a debug application for you. If you don't want this type of build, you can use the drop-down list box in the Build toolbar to change the build target to a Win32 Release build.

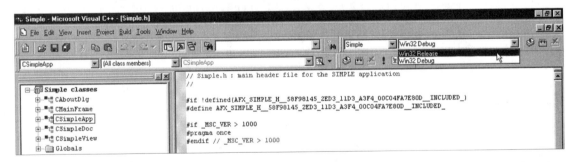

The project settings will place files generated by the build into a subdirectory named Debug if you're building for debug, or Release if you're building for a release target. You can adjust these directory names using the edit fields in the Output Directories group box in the General tab of the Project Settings dialog.

After a build, you can take a peek at the output directory for your project. Here, you'll find the .obj files that were created during the build process. You'll also find the .exe that you built, if your build was successful.

Precompiled Headers

You'll also find a .pch file in your build's output directory if you chose to use **precompiled headers**. By default, an AppWizard-produced application will use Precompiled Headers in the Category dropdown box in the C/C++ tab of the Project Settings dialog.

The preprocessor is a part of any C or C++ compiler that runs on your source code. The resulting code is stored temporarily on your drive before given to the compiler itself, which then translates it from C or C++ to object files the linker will eat. The preprocessor resolves all of the preprocessor directives, such as #include, and conditional compilation directives, like #ifdef and #else. You can spot a preprocessor directive a mile away because it will always begin with a hash mark (#).

As it writes the temporary file, the preprocessor also expands any macros that you've defined. For example, if you've coded something like this:

```
#define BUFFER_SIZE 1024
char szMyBuffer[BUFFER_SIZE];
```

the preprocessor will produce this output:

```
char szMyBuffer[1024];
```

Even if the macro makes a syntax error, the precompiler doesn't care – it simply does the substitution. It's up to the compiler itself to check syntax and generate an error. Of course, if the syntax is within the use of the preprocessor directive itself, the preprocessor *does* issue the error. Consider this case:

```
#define
#define BUFFER_SIZE "really big"
char szMyBuffer[BUFFER_SIZE];
```

The first line would cause the preprocessor to make an error – the syntax of the #define directive itself is in error. The second line is parsed by the precompiler without hesitation, as its syntax is clearly valid. The third line is expanded using the BUFFER_SIZE macro. The preprocessor would generate this output:

```
char szMyBuffer["really big"];
```

and, neglecting that first line, complete without warning or error. It's up to the compiler to notice that the string literal doesn't belong there and issue an error.

The preprocessor is also responsible for removing comments from your source code. It converts them to white space.

Because MFC applications absorb a very large header chain, including all of the MFC includes and the infamous Windows.h file, it's not unusual for the preprocessor to suck down nearly two megabytes of header files. As you can imagine, even though the preprocessor has been efficiently engineered, it takes a while to read and parse such a large volume of data.

The volume of headers digested by the preprocessor is multiplied because most programs aren't built from single source files. Instead, they're built from collections of smaller source files. Each of those smaller source files will repeatedly include most of the same files, and the compiler will be obliged to preprocess them again and again within the same build.

To attack this problem, the Microsoft Visual C++ compiler offers a feature called precompiled headers.

Precompiled Header Files

Precompiled headers provide the ability to compile a set of header files just once. After the precompiler has run on a particular source file, everything the precompiler has done is saved in a special binary file. That binary file represents all of the work the precompiler has done, and can be loaded immediately by a subsequent invocation of the precompiler all in one swoop — that second invocation doesn't need to do any parsing whatsoever.

As produced by the AppWizard, any type of MFC project will use precompiled headers. All of the precompiled header settings are visible on the C++ tab of the Project Settings dialog box. Just select Precompiled Headers in the Category: drop down list of the dialog. Remember that you can expand the tree control and examine the settings in use for individual files within your project. File-specific settings are very important when coming to understand precompiled headers.

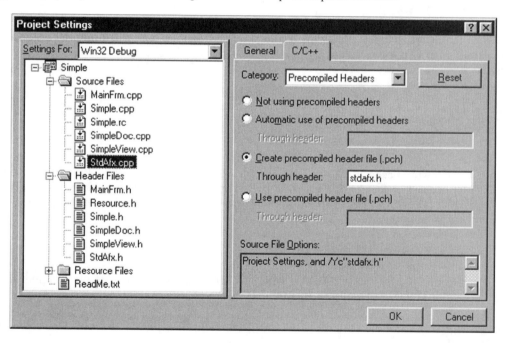

Note that the above dialog shows the use of the Project Settings dialog to modify the build options for just one file within the project. While the dialog opens with All Files selected, you can click on the tree view on the left-hand side of the window and select individual files – or use the *Shift* key to select multiple files.

The precompiled headers for the project are all managed through a file called `StdAfx.cpp`, which you can see selected in the dialog box shown above. The settings on the right-hand side of the dialog indicate that the compiler will create a precompiled header file when `StdAfx.cpp` is compiled because the Create precompiled header file option is marked. Also note that the Through header: edit control contains the file name `Stdafx.h`.

The Create precompiled header file option in the dialog corresponds to the `/Yc` option on the compiler's command line. The name in the Through header: edit control identifies the file name, and that file name immediately follows the `/Yc` option on the command line.

The build system realizes that `StdAfx.cpp` will create a precompiled header that is used by the rest of the files in the project, so it will build `StdAfx.cpp` before any other files in the project. The preprocessor will open `StdAfx.cpp` and begin processing it. As the preprocessor reads the file, it will build its table of symbols and macros just as if the preprocessor was running normally.

The preprocessor is watching, though, for the `Stdafx.h` file to be included. If it doesn't find it, it will issue an error complaining about the lack of that file. The output might look like this if the compiler wanted to find `Fooey.h` and couldn't:

```
Compiling...
StdAfx.cpp
e:\projects\simple\stdafx.cpp(11) : error C2857: '#include' statement specified with the /Ycfooey.h
command-line option was not found in the source file
Error executing cl.exe.
```

When the compiler does find the file, it pauses. It takes everything that it's preprocessed and writes it out to a disk file. By default, the produced file will have the same name as the "through" file, but will have the extension `.pch`. You can change the name of the generated file with the `/Fp` on the command line, but not from within the IDE. For an AppWizard-generated project, the default precompiled header will have the name of the project with the extension of `*.pch`. For our sample application, the file will be named `Simple.pch`.

You can expect the `.pch` file to be pretty big, as it contains all of the symbols and information the compiler would have encountered in the regular headers. Even though Visual C++ is writing the file in a very efficient binary format, the file still grows very quickly. For an MFC program, the `.pch` file is nominally more than four megabytes!

After everything is written to the `.pch` file, the compiler finishes compiling the `StdAfx.cpp` file and produces a `Stdafx.obj` file. Because a file name was specified in the Through header: edit control, declarations in the `StdAfx.cpp` file which appear after the reference to the named header file won't be reflected in the precompiled header file. For this reason, the `StdAfx.cpp` file that AppWizard gives your project includes nothing more than a reference to the `StdAfx.h` file.

On the other hand, if *no* file name was specified in the Through header: edit control, the compiler would continue preprocessing until `StdAfx.cpp` had been read completely, would then write the `.pch` file, before creating the `.obj` file containing the code from the source file. The `.pch` file would take its name from the name of the `.cpp` file used for the compilation.

When `StdAfx.cpp` is compiled, the compiler produces two files: `Stdafx.pch` and `Stdafx.obj`. `Stdafx.obj` contains no code, but might be pretty big because it will contain debug information that defines all the structures found in the headers that were built. In a build that has no debugging information, the file is miniscule simply because `StdAfx.cpp` declares no actual code or data. Here's the `StdAfx.cpp` file for the `Simple` project in its entirety:

```
// stdafx.cpp : source file that includes
//          just the standard includes
//    Simple.pch will be the pre-compiled header
//    stdafx.obj will contain the pre-compiled
//          type information

#include "stdafx.h"
```

Let me stress again that anything in the `*.cpp` file after the `#include` directive that references the file named in the **Through header:** edit is not written to the precompiled header file. The balance of the `.cpp` file can be used to generate code, and that code will be put into the `Stdafx.obj` file, which is consumed by the linker.

The other source files in the project, `Simple.cpp`, `MainFrm.cpp`, `ChildFrm.cpp`, `SimpleDoc.cpp`, and `SimpleView.cpp` will all use the precompiled header as they're being built. The file settings for each of those files mark the **Use precompiled header** file option, like this:

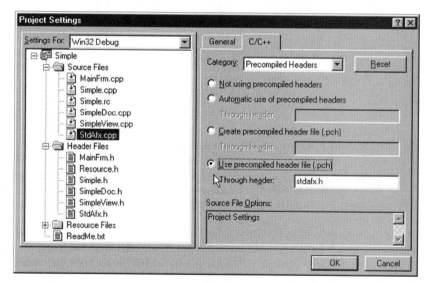

The compiler knows the actual precompiled header will be named `Simple.pch` because the compiler uses the same naming rules for consuming precompiled files as it does for generating them; the compiler knows the binary file has the `.pch` extension. The **Use precompiled header file (.pch)** option in this dialog corresponds to the `/Yu` option on the compiler's command line. And again, the **Through header:** control contains the name of the file given to the compiler immediately after the `/Yu` option.

As the compiler processes any file that uses a precompiled header, it will first read the precompiled information from the `.pch` file. It will then scan the source file until it sees a reference to the file identified in the **Through header:** edit control in the settings dialog. *Anything* in the file before an `#include` directive that references the "through" header is completely ignored. The compiler never sees it, and the preprocessor just reads it to see if it's a reference to the precompiled header – nothing more.

And when I say the preprocessor ignores it, I really mean that it is ignored! If a `*.cpp` file starts this way, and the compiler is instructed to use the `StdAfx.pch` file, the program will compile just fine!

```
This text is ignored
I can type anything I want here.
Hockey is best!
#define SOME_SYMBOL 37
#include "stdafx.h"
```

There are no syntax errors; even though the English sentences make no sense to the preprocessor or compiler, they're completely ignored! Of particular note is the fact that the `#define` is ignored, too. The preprocessor doesn't even consider it.

Once the binary information is loaded from the `.pch` file, the compilation of the other files continues as normal; the code is built, and a `.obj` file is emitted. No new information is emitted to the `.pch` file.

Adding Additional Headers

If you need to make use of additional headers, you can do so by simply adding them to your source files *after* the reference to `Stdafx.h`, or by adding them directly to your `Stdafx.h` file. In the former approach the compiler will read the precompiled header information and then process the additional headers as normal. If you have a header file that's referenced by a small percentage of the modules in your project, this technique is very beneficial. This process won't enlarge your `.pch` file unnecessarily; nor will it cause your builds to be slow.

If you have a header file that's used by several of your modules, you can save the time required to reprocess it during each build by simply editing `Stdafx.h` to include that header. If the majority of your modules reference this file, you will achieve great savings in compile time. Appendix D has a list of MFC headers along with their *raison du disk space*.

Precompiled headers, like any other sharp tool, deserve to be used carefully. When using `.pch` files, remember that the savings is in the ability to compile a large amount of headers just once. If you make your build recreate the `.pch` file every time you change a header, you're completely defeating the purpose of precompiled headers!

ClassWizard

While we've complained at some length about the tedium of building a Windows application, we haven't yet started on the troubles involved in maintaining C++ code, even outside of the context of a Windows application.

While C++ realizes great benefits, it exacerbates some of the problems inherent in C. For example, most developers structure their programs so that class definitions appear in header files, making them accessible to any other module which needs them. Then, the actual implementations of the classes are contained in `.cpp` files.

Splitting the implementation and declaration files is highly desirable, as it supports the reusability of code while also allowing the greatest level of coding flexibility. However, it does require that you edit two separate files for any fundamental change in the structure of your classes.

To simplify matters, Visual C++ provides **ClassWizard** to add and maintain classes in your application. Make sure you've got a project workspace open in Microsoft Visual Studio (ClassWizard won't work without an open project), then choose ClassWizard... from the View menu or hit *Ctrl+W*.

ClassWizard's main dialog box has several tabs, as shown opposite. For now, we can focus our attention on the Message Maps tab, which is active by default. You can see from the controls shown here that this tab will grant us the ability to manipulate how the window classes in our application react to messages sent by Windows.

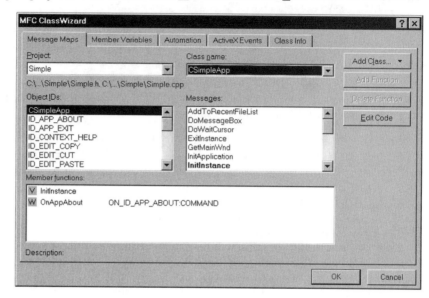

Creating a New Class

When you press the Add Class... button, you're offered a cascading menu with two choices. You can select New... to create a brand-new class from scratch, or From a type library... to create a class that will help you use a COM object from another application.

We'll talk about the other options and features of the ClassWizard dialogs later. (The COM wrapper classes won't come up in conversation until Chapter 13!) For now, let's choose the New... option to add a simple class to our application using this dialog:

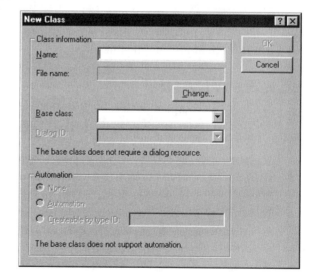

The <u>N</u>ame edit box lets you specify the name for your new class. ClassWizard will then guess at file names for the header and implementation files of your new class. You can imagine that, if we created a new class named `CCafeMenu`, we'd produce a new header file called `CafeMenu.h` and an implementation file called `CafeMenu.cpp`. If you don't like those names, you can press the <u>C</u>hange... button to get to a dialog that will allow you to change the name of the files that implement the class. Remember that you're using Win32; you can use long file names if that's soothing to you, but you might still have problems with other utilities you like to use if they don't support long file names. In the <u>B</u>ase class drop-down, we can select the MFC class from which our new class will derive its functionality.

Unfortunately, ClassWizard doesn't support non-MFC classes. This limitation has two facets; first, you can't derive a second class from a class you've made with ClassWizard, even if your intended base class derives from MFC. Second, you can't derive from your own arbitrary classes.

Once you've settled on a name for your class, your header file and your implementation file, you can press the OK button to have ClassWizard create the class for you. ClassWizard will even have Visual C++ automatically add the implementation file and the header file to your project. These operations take place on the project that is currently open – that's why you can't use ClassWizard unless you have an open project. However, you don't have to make a clean build on your project before you can begin using ClassWizard.

If you go ahead and create a `CCafeMenu` class based on `CDocument`, the header file `CafeMenu.h` will contain some code that looks vaguely like this:

```
class CCafeMenu : public CDocument
{
    // other stuff automatically generated
    // by ClassWizard!
};
```

ClassWizard will help you create these classes and will automatically add the files to your project, but you still have to write software! You still need to design and code the member functions for the class, decide what to override and what not to override, and (last but not least) work out just how you are going to accomplish the high-level task you're using the classes to implement. That's what the rest of this book is about.

The .clw File

To keep track of the classes and their relationships in your project, ClassWizard maintains a file with the extension `.clw` in your project directory. This file, which is just an ASCII file with formatting similar to that of a Windows `.ini` file, contains information that ClassWizard uses when helping out with your project.

> The file is named using your project name and the `.clw` extension; for our example it would be `Simple.clw`.

The contents of this file are best left alone, but there may be some situations when you are compelled to manage it. An example of when you might want to do this is when using base classes MFC provides but doesn't allow you to create using ClassWizard, say `CStatusBar` (not `CStatusBarCtrl`). You can still convince ClassWizard to help you maintain your code, but you may have to add some text to the `.clw` file to enable that to happen. If the file becomes corrupted, you can regenerate the `.clw` file for your project; delete the `.clw` file from your project directory, then open ClassWizard. As the `.clw` isn't available, Microsoft Visual Studio reports this with the following dialog:

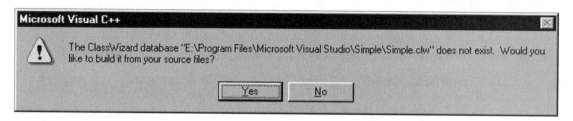

Clicking Yes here takes you to another dialog, which allows you to select all the files (`.cpp` and `.h`) in the project, which Microsoft Visual Studio will use to generate a new `.clw` file.

Examining much more of ClassWizard would force us to take a look at functionality that we haven't yet explained, so we're only scratching the surface here. ClassWizard provides far more utility than simply adding classes to your application. Rest assured that we'll revisit ClassWizard throughout this book, whenever it's appropriate.

I'll make suggestions about using ClassWizard to update features of your application as we work through examples. I'll also explain shortcuts provided by ClassWizard as we examine the classes in MFC which benefit from ClassWizard's functionality. ClassWizard makes a big impact when we work with ActiveX and Automation, delve into data exchange between database records, or data exchange between memory and dialog box fields.

The Browser

Due to the nature of C++ programs, the individual component parts of a single class can be difficult to track down. Sometimes, you spend so long carving member functions into the bark of trees that you lose sight of the forest. This is, perhaps, even more evident with C++ applications than with C programs. In C++, classes and their implementations can hide the functionality, definitions and code related to a program. You may be executing yards of code that you weren't even aware of each time you create an object. You can use the **browser** (a map of your favorite National Forest) any time you're editing the source code of an application in the code editor.

The information that the browser uses to keep track of the various components is created when the code is compiled. You can enable or disable the generation of browser information by checking the Build browse info file box in the Browse Info tab of the Project Settings dialog box.

You'll also find that some settings on the C/C++ tab will affect browsing. Select this tab and make sure Listing Files or General is selected in the Category combo box. The Generate browse info option must be checked for browse information to be produced.

To produce browse information, you'll need to make sure the option in the Browse Info tab is set. You can turn the Generate browse info option for the compiler on or off for individual files in your project to have them contribute or refrain from contributing to the browse information generated for the entire project. If you have a very large project, you might want to turn off browse information for some of the source files in your project to save disk space or save time while building your project.

Browser Files

If you look in the project and output directories after you have built a project with browse information enabled, you'll notice files with two extensions: .sbr and .bsc. .sbr files (named for 'Source Browser') are created for each module in your build. They contain information about the way that module was compiled. The .bsc file is the complete, merged database directly referenced by the browser. If the .bsc file isn't present, you won't be able to use the source code browser.

You've probably also noticed that the .sbr files have a length of zero. When the project build process runs the Bscmake utility, which actually creates the browse information, it erases the content of .sbr files that it processes. The empty file serves as a flag to remind the utility that the file doesn't need to be reprocessed. If the build recompiles a module, the .sbr file will have new information in it, and Bscmake will then update the .bsc file to contain the revised information.

If you're interested in using the browser against MFC, you should make sure that you have MFC browser information available when you're using the IDE. You can find the .bsc file for MFC itself on the distribution CD-ROM (\Microsoft Visual Studio\Vc98\Mfc\Src\Mfc.bsc). You'll want to copy the file to your Mfc\Src directory on your hard drive.

Browsing

Once browse information is ready for your application, you can place the cursor on any identifier in your source code and press *Alt+F12* (or select Source Browser... from the Tools menu) to bring up a list of available options:

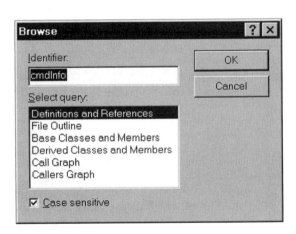

Selecting one of the items in the list will display particular information about the item in the Identifier box. This works for classes, variables, locals, globals, structures and even preprocessor macros, as well as any symbols that were defined within your source code. You can even use the * wildcard to search for a pattern. For example, searching on Creat* will yield information about Create() and CreateEx() functions, as well as functions with names like CreateCaret() or CreateCompatibleDC(). This is a useful ability when you're not sure of the exact spelling of a symbol's name, but need to find information on it.

Remember that some preprocessor symbols (like _DEBUG) are defined on the compiler command line, and others (like __FILE__) are predefined by the preprocessor and can't be found by the source code browser. However, you should also note that the browse information includes the headers for MFC itself, so you can readily look up information about any class in your application.

The Select query list box allows you to direct the browser to perform one of six different operations:

Operation	Description
Definitions	This indicates where symbols are defined and referenced. This option finds the and References symbol that you specify. You can then jump to its definition or to references.
File Outline	This is perhaps the most exciting browser option. Here, you're presented with information about all of the symbols encountered while your application was being compiled. You can filter the list by any combination of class, function, data, macro or type.
Base Classes	This option displays all of the classes from which the selected class inherits and Members attributes. When this hierarchy is displayed, you can navigate up and down it to see information on the functions and data local to the class in question.
Derived Classes	This option is the counterpart of Base Classes and Members. Instead of showing and Members the classes from which the selected class inherits attributes, the Derived Classes and Members option shows all of the classes that inherit attributes from the selected class.
Call Graph	This query shows a hierarchy of calls performed by the named function. This option lists the functions that the selected browse target calls.
Callers Graph	This query is a counterpart to the Call Graph option. Instead of finding the called functions, this query results in a list of functions that call the target function.

The box also lets you dictate the case-sensitivity of your query. The Case sensitive box is checked by default – after all, C++ *is* a case-sensitive language.

Each of these operations produces a pop-up window that, like a property dialog, can be pinned down to keep it active, even when you shift focus away from it. This dialog, with the special controls provided by the File Outline operation, is shown below:

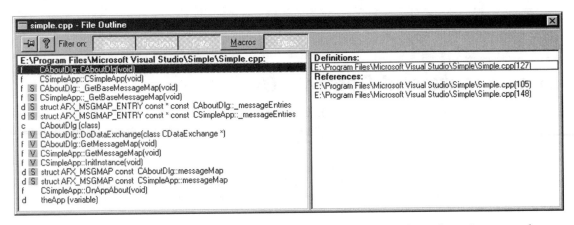

The window is divided into two resizable panes. The left shows the list of matching functions, the outline of calls, or the inheritance, depending on the type of query. The right side shows a terse list of references and definitions. You can double-click on any element in either pane, and you can double-click on an entry on either side of the window to open the source code pertaining to that entry. Single-clicking on the left side window updates the right-hand pane with the references and definitions you've selected in the left-hand window.

Shortcuts

You can also make use of the browser without having to bring up the browse window. Right-clicking on an identifier in your code gives you access to a couple of menu items (Go To Definition Of... and Go To Reference To...) that use the browser information to help you navigate through your code. Selecting one of these menu items will do exactly what it says it does.

If you elect to go to a reference of a symbol, you can then use *Ctrl+(Num+)* (that is, the control key and the plus key on the numeric keypad) to jump to subsequent references of that symbol. This can be a wonderfully handy feature when you need to comb your source after changing the definition of a function or macro in order to fix any references to that definition. If you step too far, you can use *Ctrl+(Num-)* to go to the previous reference.

If you ask the browser to take you to a definition where the request may be ambiguous because the name of the symbol you're searching for has multiple definitions, you'll be presented with a dialog box. The one here shows what happened when we searched on InitInstance:

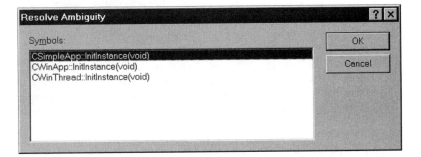

Simply select the definition context that makes the most sense to you and the Visual C++ browser will take you there.

Components and Controls Gallery

Every program written for a computer shares many common aspects with other programs. To help take away the tedium of rewriting that common code, most programmers make use of libraries that implement functions or classes that can be used over and over again.

That's a great solution, but those routines are quite static; it's difficult to reuse them when you need to modify their behavior significantly. To this end, the Microsoft Visual Studio provides the **Components and Controls Gallery**. It implements a container for special features that let you extend the attributes of your application with a few mouse clicks.

You can reach the Components and Controls Gallery by using the Components and Controls... item in the Add To Project cascading menu under Project. Your efforts will be rewarded with the main Components and Controls Gallery dialog, which looks like this:

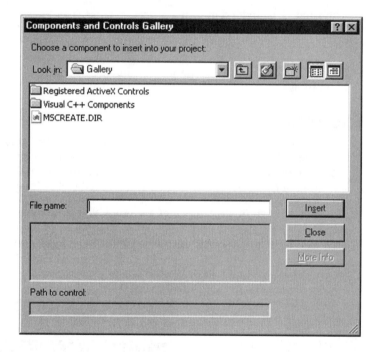

The centerpiece of this dialog is a list view control that allows you to select the component or control you'd like to add to your project. You can directly choose an available control or component here, or you can navigate to a different file or directory and select a component or control. You should only need to use the navigation features of the dialog if you need to work with a control or component that isn't properly or fully installed on your machine.

The Registered ActiveX Controls folder contains ActiveX controls that you've installed on your system. Visual C++ installs a little more than a dozen controls, but if you've written any of your own, or if you have a recent version of Visual Basic, or any other development tool that provides lots of ActiveX controls, then you'll see them in this tab. Look for full coverage of ActiveX Controls in Chapters 15 and 16.

The Microsoft Visual Studio Components folder includes lots of neat things that you can add into your project. The components included here are more capable than just simple classes that you can add. They can actually add particular pieces of code to the right place in existing classes, or they may also add resources. For example, the Clipboard assistant adds code to one of the `CView`-derived classes in your project. If you don't have a `CView`-derived class, it will show an error message. The Progress Dialog component adds a complete dialog class and all its associated resources. Alternatively, the component may not add anything directly to your project; the GUID Generator creates a GUID that it copies to the clipboard.

There are a lot of components that we aren't going to discuss here. Instead of confusing you with their technical details before you've read far enough to understand MFC, I'm deferring the analysis of the most important components until we reach the appropriate points in our discussions of the whole setup.

Summary

In this chapter, we've learned a lot about Visual C++'s built-in AppWizard, which produces predefined code and makes it easy to begin writing your applications. We've examined some of the features offered by ClassWizard, and we've taken a look at the browser; both of these are tools designed to help you maintain your application after AppWizard has finished its work.

As some features of ClassWizard and the Components and Controls Gallery bind very tightly to features in the Microsoft Foundation Classes, we haven't examined them as yet. Instead, we'll draw attention to these features and shortcuts throughout the book, when we examine those parts of the framework that benefit from the support that they give.

While we won't be mentioning the browser very frequently throughout the rest of the book, please don't underestimate its utility. It can help you wade through thousands of lines of source code in seconds, so becoming familiar with it will be very important as you use the Microsoft Foundation Classes more and more extensively. Remember that you have the source code to MFC, so the browser will also let you look up definitions and references within it!

In the next chapter, we'll actually begin our in-depth discussion of the features of the Microsoft Foundation Classes by examining the code produced by AppWizard. Get your thinking cap on and make sure you have plenty of your favorite caffeinated beverage on hand.

3

The Application Architecture Hierarchy

So far, I've helped you examine some of the major user interface components of the Microsoft Visual Studio environment, and discussed some of the features in Visual C++. We've also looked at some general MFC features, as well as the time saving Wizards that help you get your MFC applications off the ground. You should now be ready to move on to the subject of real application programming. To promote the concept of application development, the Microsoft Foundation Classes implement an application framework, composed of classes in the application architecture hierarchy.

In this chapter, we will:

> Cement our understanding of AppWizard

> Examine the overall structure of MFC

> Begin examining the inner workings of MFC application framework classes

> Take a look at some of the features of the Microsoft Visual Studio that help you *after* you have created your project

The Application Framework

Like any other set of class libraries, the Microsoft Foundation Classes provide reusable code in the form of pre-written C++ classes. When you're writing programs that use a class library, you can apply the classes to the specific problems your application needs to solve. For most class libraries, this means that they include abstractions of commonly applied programming idioms. For example, they might provide several classes to perform input and output operations on files, or to manage data structures like maps, linked lists or sparse arrays.

Class libraries designed for Windows might add to this functionality with code to wrap common Windows APIs or data structures, such as `::CreateWindow()` or device contexts.

The Microsoft Foundation Class libraries do provide such utility classes, but they also implement an application framework. Above and beyond the functionality normally presented by simple class libraries, this framework offers a backbone for your application, allowing you to concentrate on coding the application's real functionality. The application framework built into MFC manifests itself in classes and data structures designed to help in the creation of an application and its most fundamental features.

The application framework is responsible for helping your application to initialize, for running your application (by providing it with the capability to respond to messages sent by Windows at runtime), and for gracefully terminating your application when it has completed its course. It also provides a fertile bed for the implementation of OLE, as well as other large-scale application features such as print preview.

Generating an Application with AppWizard

To provide some fodder for our discussion of MFC's application framework, let's continue working with the sample that was discussed in the previous chapter, which was named `Simple`. You don't have to be a member of the American Association of Psychics to guess why I gave it that name.

If you like, you can download `Simple` from the Wrox web site, or you can regenerate it yourself. Since most applications you write will start out with a visit to AppWizard, it would probably be appropriate for you to practice a little now. You can create the application by using all the AppWizard defaults with the exception that you should use the single-document interface setting in Step 1, instead of the default multiple-document interface.

If you do choose to follow the examples, it's a good idea to give your application the same name as mine. If you use a different name, AppWizard will choose different names for the classes in your application, which might hamper your reading of the code snippets provided here.

It's often said that AppWizard allows you to tap a great deal of functionality from MFC, which is, of course, true. Sometimes, I can't imagine programming without AppWizard. The only thing I dislike more than setting compiler options is warm beer. And maybe taxes. And cleaning the bathtub. And when the rental agent gets me a bulky full-size car when I specifically requested a nimble little compact to get me around a crowded, unfamiliar city a lot quicker. AppWizard saves me grief by churning out correctly working skeleton code and a project with all the compiler options properly set.

However, the point I'm trying to make here is that you should never over-estimate the functionality supplied by AppWizard; once you've used it to break the ground for your application, AppWizard isn't going to do much more work for you. That's one of the reasons my coverage of AppWizard in previous chapters was so superficial. What you do with Visual C++ is done by you with a little help from ClassWizard, and not by AppWizard.

Understanding the Generated Code

As you already know, when you generate an application with AppWizard, it produces code that implements an application around the options that you've requested. But what's really happening in the application? To understand exactly what's going on, let's examine some of the classes that are generated by AppWizard for your application.

Your natural inclination might be to go to the directory where you've created your sample project and issue a `dir` command; but, if you haven't already done so, you should really begin to acquaint yourself with the Microsoft Visual Studio from here on in. You can examine the components of your new application by opening the project file and viewing the files and their dependencies in Visual C++. To see all of the files involved in your project just open the Project Workspace window and activate the FileView tab. You can use the ClassView tab to see the classes in the project, too.

> *Remember that you can double-click on files in the* FileView *tab of the Project Workspace to open them in the editor window, or double-click on class names in the* ClassView *tab to see the definitions of the classes.*

The application framework classes in MFC are almost never used directly. Instead, your application will gain functionality by deriving new classes from those supplied by MFC. This allows MFC to provide the backbone of your application unobtrusively, while allowing you wide flexibility to override the functionality provided by Windows and MFC.

MFC provides three major classes from which you will derive the most basic functionality for your application: `CWinApp`, `CDocument` and `CView`. These provide a minimal user interface and no real application functionality, but they do give you a framework upon which you can hang the real meat of your application. When you create an application with AppWizard, it hooks up derivatives of these classes to your creation, depending on the options you selected.

File Name	MFC Base Class	Derived Class	Functionality
`Simple.cpp`	`CWinApp`	`CSimpleApp`	Core application, message dispatch, command-line processing
`SimpleDoc.cpp`	`CDocument`	`CSimpleDoc`	Document implementation
`SimpleView.cpp`	`CView`	`CSimpleView`	View implementation
`MainFrm.cpp`	`CFrameWnd`	`CMainFrame`	Main SDI window

By default, AppWizard produces the derivatives of these core classes and names them after the application. The table shown above lists the files and classes created by AppWizard when you make a single-document application named `Simple`. In this chapter, I'll examine the functionality behind `CWinApp`, while in subsequent chapters I'll look at `CDocument`, `CView` and `CFrameWnd`.

The Wizard will also generate header files and a project file for you. You'll receive a resource file as well, which includes some bitmaps for your application's toolbar, a dialog template for your About box, and an icon for your application. It'll also have your application's main menu, a toolbar description resource, some version information, and a small string table. The project file, as produced by the Wizard, is ready to build!

There's no good abbreviation for 'assassin', so you'll probably want to make sure that your class names make sense and are convenient to you before you leave AppWizard. Also, make sure you watch out for long file names; AppWizard will create them without much fanfare, and if you have *any* tools that only accept 8.3-format file names, you'll save time by avoiding long names from the start.

CDocument and CView

If you imagine the CWinApp-derived class in your application as a furnace, you can think of the CDocument- and CView-derived classes as the fuel and fire. An instance of a CWinApp derivative will always exist while your application is running, and will create and destroy CView and CDocument classes. The furnace exists before the fire is lit and after the fire goes out, just as your CWinApp class will exist before and after the classes that provide other functionality in the application are created or destroyed.

Loosely, an instance of CDocument is used to manage the information that your application will handle. If you're writing a spreadsheet application, your CDocument class will be responsible for loading and saving spreadsheets, as well as holding the in-memory representation of the spreadsheet while the file is open. If you're writing a communications program, maybe you'll use CDocument to encapsulate all the terminal settings you need to save between sessions.

An instance of CView, on the other hand, will provide the user with a way to see the information that your CDocument is managing. The view is also charged with accepting input from the user and reflecting it back to the document. For example, a CView instance in your spreadsheet might display the data it retrieved from its related CDocument. It's the document that contains the actual spreadsheet data. When the user clicks on the window created by the CView and starts typing some data, the CView handles the input messages – but asks the CDocument object to handle the updates to the data held in memory. Similarly, your communications program might need to use a CView to show the data that you're transmitting and receiving, using the session settings represented by the CDocument in your application.

The CDocument and CView classes implement MFC's version of the document/view architecture. Not every application will make full use of a CDocument and CView class, but every true MFC application is based upon at least one CWinApp-derived class. Some applications will feature complicated, intricate relationships between the three classes, while others will just use a CDialog to display a dialog box as their user interface, without applying CView and CDocument to the problems of information presentation and management. In fact, that's exactly what happens when you ask AppWizard to produce a dialog-based application for you.

The issues you might face when designing with the document/view architecture are complicated, so they have their own chapter: 4. For the time being, in this chapter, let's concern ourselves with the part of the application framework that directly holds up our application – that's CWinApp.

The Components of CWinApp

It turns out that CWinApp is not a root class in MFC. It's actually a derivative of several other important classes; you can see the hierarchy that contributes to CWinApp in this figure:

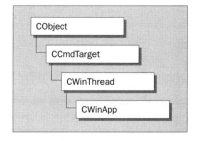

CWinApp has functionality built into it from CObject, CCmdTarget and CWinThread. As soon as we pull back the covers on CWinApp, we'll need to take a look at how these other classes work. To describe the functionality built into MFC and provided in the CWinApp class, let's climb up the class inheritance tree, starting with CWinApp itself and moving up to each of its parent classes until we reach the top.

CWinApp

In the Simple application, you'll find a Simple.cpp file that contains the implementation for the application's CWinApp-derived class, which is declared in Simple.h and named CSimpleApp. These two files were produced by AppWizard and are now your responsibility. You will be modifying them, either indirectly using ClassWizard or directly with the editor (or both), as you evolve the minimal application produced by AppWizard into a fully-fledged application.

You should be able to find code near the beginning of Simple.h that looks something like this:

```
class CSimpleApp : public CWinApp
{
public:
    CSimpleApp();

// Overrides
    // ClassWizard generated virtual function overrides
    //{{AFX_VIRTUAL(CSimpleApp)
    public:
    virtual BOOL InitInstance();
    //}}AFX_VIRTUAL

// Implementation

    //{{AFX_MSG(CSimpleApp)
    afx_msg void OnAppAbout();
        // NOTE - the ClassWizard will add and remove member functions here.
        //     DO NOT EDIT what you see in these blocks of generated code !
    //}}AFX_MSG
    DECLARE_MESSAGE_MAP()
};
```

The first line of the code is where all the action is happening. We declare that our CSimpleApp class will derive from CWinApp. This grants our application all of the functionality already available in CWinApp as defined in MFC. AppWizard then provides a declaration for a constructor for the class.

The comment lines give ClassWizard landmarks that it can easily find when you use it to modify your code. Any code between the comments is fair game for ClassWizard to change at any time, and any code outside the comments is yours and yours alone.

As you work with MFC more and more, you'll learn that the coding method of 'derive and run', at its most abstract level, is very common. You'll frequently derive your own classes from MFC classes before adding, modifying and removing functionality using overridable functions. The key to programming this way is to understand what MFC is doing for you and how you can build a symbiotic relationship with it. This will allow your code and code from MFC to work together, making the whole application greater than the sum of its parts.

CWinThread

The Win32 API, supported by Windows NT, Windows 95, and Windows 98, implements preemptive multitasking through the use of threads.

When it starts, a program has exactly one thread, known as its **primary thread**. The program can create more threads and use them to help manage processor time while the program works on different tasks. Whether we're talking about the primary thread or one of these explicitly-created secondary threads, MFC wraps the thread in the CWinThread class.

Threads are a deep subject. Mercifully, you don't need to know much about them unless you're actually using them. Sitting around in your application with your one primary thread doesn't feel very different to writing an application for Win16 systems. If you're interested in using threads more aggressively, have a peek at Chapter 10, where I'll discuss the CWinThread class and MFC functions which support it.

For now, it's important to know that the primary thread for your application is represented by the '*is-a*' relationship between CWinThread and CWinApp. That is, since CWinApp derives from CWinThread, a CWinApp 'is a' CWinThread. The CWinApp's primary thread is buried in the functionality inherited by CWinApp from CWinThread.

Locating Threads

Even if you're not actively stitching up threads in your application, it's helpful to know that you can access the thread you're currently running by calling the AfxGetThread() function. This returns a pointer to the CWinThread object related to the current thread. If you call AfxGetThread() from your application's primary thread, the pointer you get will reference the CWinThread object represented by your applications CWinApp-derived object.

> **AfxGetThread()** is a global MFC function implemented by the MFC libraries; it's not a member function of a class.

To find the primary thread of your application, you can call MFC's `AfxGetApp()` API function to get a pointer to the current application's `CWinApp` object. Since `CWinApp` inherits from `CWinThread`, a pointer to the currently executing `CWinApp` is also a pointer to the primary thread of the running application, but it isn't necessarily a pointer to the currently running thread!

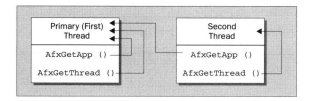

Threads and You

A couple more notes about threads. First, you might notice that the Code Generation category of the C/C++ tab in the Project Settings dialog has a Use run-time library control that lets you choose multithreaded or single-threaded run-time library builds. You might be interested in single-threaded libraries for some very special reason, but there's almost never a reason to use this library variant with MFC. MFC libraries always expect to be linked to the multithreaded version of the run-time libraries. Unless you rebuild MFC yourself, always use a multithreaded version of the libraries.

CCmdTarget

`CCmdTarget` is one of the most fundamental classes in MFC. Every window and 'OLE' class in MFC derives functionality from `CCmdTarget`, which means that more than half of the classes in MFC are based, at least indirectly, on `CCmdTarget`. To this end, it's imperative to have a good understanding of how `CCmdTarget` works and what it brings to your application.

As an experienced Windows programmer, you know that Windows programs don't actually run. Instead, they just respond. A Windows program doesn't hold the attention of the processor for very long. It receives a message from Windows, does some work, and returns control back to Windows again. This technique, called **event-driven programming**, was a radical departure from traditional programming methods. It fits Windows very well, but it can make programs a little hard to understand at first glance. The reason for this lies with the way Windows C-based programs are normally structured.

If you're used to writing standard C code for your Windows programs, you've probably become accustomed to the idea of writing a message handling function for some of your application's windows. This function probably took the form of deeply nested `if` statements, or maybe a `switch` statement that included a `case` for each message that the program needed to handle. In some instances, your code would span dozens of pages because you handled almost every message Windows had to offer. In other programs (or even in the message handling function for other windows within the same program), you might handle only two or three messages and pass the work back to Windows because the default behavior implemented by Windows was adequate for your needs. Such a construct might look like this:

```
switch (uMessage)
{
    case WM_COMMAND:
        switch (wParam)
        {
```

Continued on Following Page

97

```
        case ID_M_FILEOPEN:
            bHandleFileOpen(hWnd);
            break;
        case ID_M_FILECLOSE:
            bHandleFileClose(hWnd);
            break;
    }
    break;

case WM_PAINT:
    bComplexPaintRoutine(hWnd);
    break;

case WM_GETMINMAXINFO:
    bCalcSize(lParam);
    break;

default:
    return DefWindowProc(hWnd, uMessage, wParam, lParam);
}
```

This code could go on forever. It might be split across different modules (for example, the `bComplexPaintRoutine()` function in our above example might exist in a different module), or it might even come from a library. Sharing code between two windows was also rather difficult, since the code in each `case` block was often dependent on the state of the window in question. In this example, things can easily get ugly when nested `switch` statements are required to discern the meaning of the different parameters that the message might be carrying. The simple handler for `WM_COMMAND` in the above code makes my point; imagine if the function above was from a real application, with several controls and many different menu items!

To extend the object-oriented philosophy to C++ requires some amount of work. A direct translation would certainly be functional, but rather inappropriate because it's bad practice to use massive `switch` statements and awkward global functions when C++ neatly provides the idea of inheritance within the scope of the language. On the other hand, it's absolutely necessary to have some way to tightly relate the receipt of a Windows message to the execution of some identifiable function within the instance of a C++ object.

Commands for Classes

To help solve the fundamental message handling problem, MFC implements a class called `CCmdTarget`. You can think of any Windows message as a command to the application. This analogy may be very direct; if the user selects a menu item, they are instructing the application to do something very identifiable as a command, such as 'print this page' or 'check the spelling'.

Regardless of the source of the command, *any* window can be thought of as a target for commands. They may also be interested in receiving commands more programmatically (i.e. from sources other than Windows), say through OLE Automation. This is equally true for applications, which is why MFC derives the `CWinApp` class from `CCmdTarget`. It is `CCmdTarget`, along with `CWinApp`, which enables message processing to work in an MFC application.

The trick is to allow Windows to get the message across to the application, while allowing the underlying C++ language to unobtrusively provide all the features that made it famous. MFC could have implemented the message dispatching mechanism using `virtual` functions, but this would have made the message dispatch process very expensive. Every class of any window type in an application would have a huge `virtual` function dispatch table associated with it. Even modest windows might have tens of `virtual` function pointers in their message dispatch table. Since they're virtual, a function pointer ends up in the `vtable` for each function, at the cost of four bytes each per windowing class in your application. For a relatively complicated application with thirty or forty window classes (since the general category of 'window classes' includes controls in dialogs or forms), a solution relying on `virtual` functions could quickly burn up tens of thousands of bytes of memory.

A **vtable**, by the way, is a compiler-produced data structure that holds pointers to each of the virtual functions in a class. The vtable exists in memory once, no matter how many instance are created of the class owning the functions. The compiler uses the table to decide where to call when you code a call to a virtual member function of a class through a pointer to an object of the class.

Perhaps even more importantly, the virtual function approach is very rigid. As extra messages are added to the Windows operating system, the need for more and more virtual functions (and more and more wastful vtable bytes!) would be required in MFC. The libraries would need to be revised for each message added to the system. Worse yet, MFC wouldn't be able to efficiently or conveniently handle registered or user-defined messages!

About Message Maps

Instead of this memory overhead, MFC provides a much better way to associate Windows and user messages with the functions that handle them. The MFC feature that provides the association is called the **message map**. By implementing message maps the way it does, MFC avoids the problems associated with those brutishly large vtables.

Message maps are far more intuitive than the difficult `switch` statements that we've all been using for years, like helpless sheep. They make it obvious that a given message is handled by a certain function within an MFC class, because that information is provided directly from the message map. They make it apparent that a particular function is responsible for the response to a particular message by very clearly declaring that intent in a central location.

Any MFC class that is derived from `CCmdTarget` (including `CCmdTarget` itself) can accept a message map. `CSimpleApp`, as I've pointed out, eventually derives this functionality from `CCmdTarget`, so it can handle command notifications and messages. `CWnd`, MFC's window class, also derives from `CCmdTarget`, so it too can process messages. Obviously, `CWinApp`'s message handling capabilities take a back seat to its ability to govern the execution of your application, while the whole point of `CWnd`'s existence is simply to handle messages as they're sent to Windows.

To declare a message map for your class, you make use of some special macros, namely `BEGIN_MESSAGE_MAP()` and `END_MESSAGE_MAP()`. Within these delimiters, you can use several other macros to indicate exactly what messages you will map. `CCmdTarget` takes care of implementing the message map searching and linking code, while `CWinThread` actually has the code that pumps messages and gets them routed to the appropriate handler in the corresponding `CCmdTarget`-derived object.

How are Message Maps Created?

If you look at the `Simple.cpp` file that AppWizard created for you, you'll find code that looks like this:

```
/////////////////////////////////////////////////////////////////////////////
// CSimpleApp

BEGIN_MESSAGE_MAP(CSimpleApp, CWinApp)
    //{{AFX_MSG_MAP(CSimpleApp)
    ON_COMMAND(ID_APP_ABOUT, OnAppAbout)
        // NOTE - the ClassWizard will add and remove mapping macros here.
        //    DO NOT EDIT what you see in these blocks of generated code!
    //}}AFX_MSG_MAP
    // Standard file based document commands
    ON_COMMAND(ID_FILE_NEW, CWinApp::OnFileNew)
    ON_COMMAND(ID_FILE_OPEN, CWinApp::OnFileOpen)
    // Standard print setup command
    ON_COMMAND(ID_FILE_PRINT_SETUP, CWinApp::OnFilePrintSetup)
END_MESSAGE_MAP()
```

The scary DO NOT EDIT comment explains the ClassWizard comments I mentioned before. Actually, you *can* edit the code between the comments, but you're taking your life in your own hands. If you do modify the code yourself, and do so without great care and attention, a possible result might be that ClassWizard chokes on your change and requires you to regenerate the `.clw` file for your application and remove your changes so that ClassWizard can understand your project. Another bad outcome may be that ClassWizard completely overwrites your change with regenerated code.

Finally, if you provide a syntactically correct but semantically wrong prototype for one of the message handlers, you'll find that your application will begin to exhibit very poor behaviour – even if it manages to compile. Because of a couple of naughty casts used in MFC's message map macros, you can get away with having a bad prototype and not getting an error message out of the compiler at compile time. That's bad news, since the improperly prototyped function will trash the stack frame when called and either corrupt some of your local data or cause a crash. And because of the optimization the compiler does, it's quite possible you won't notice these symptoms until you've compared a release build to a debug build.

In the face of a mistake, ClassWizard will usually notice that something seems fishy and simply refuse to allow you to edit your class.

If you do change these code blocks, you're safer if you only use the same syntax constructs that ClassWizard employs. As you become more and more familiar with ClassWizard, you'll probably become more comfortable with changing their content. However, as soon as you've made your change, it's prudent to check that ClassWizard still functions correctly. I'm afraid I can't responsibly offer suggestions for editing the ClassWizard-provided code, because even tiny changes to the implementation of ClassWizard might have sweeping effects on any rules that I might try to describe. As your experience with the tools grows, you can learn when to change the ClassWizard-provided code yourself. Until then, your best bet is to place any of your modifications outside of the comments that delimit ClassWizard's domain.

Targeting the Messages

The `BEGIN_MESSAGE_MAP()` macro at the top of this code fragment indicates that we've declared a message map for our application object. If you're thinking it seems a bit odd for an application to be receiving messages, then you're right; Windows only sends messages to Windows, not to applications.

> *You could argue that applications always receive messages because they're responsible for emptying the message queue, and in a way that's true. They're actually just pumping the messages, though – they have a loop that gets the next message, figures out which window procedure needs to handle it, and then have Windows call that procedure to actually handle the message. In Chapter 10, which discusses threads in detail, we'll examine the notion of a thread itself being the direct recipient of a message. That is, it's possible to send a message directly to a thread and not to a particular window owned by the thread. We'll discuss the semantics of window-bound messages here, and the semantics of thread-based messages in Chapter 10.*

However, MFC bends the semantic notion of messages going mostly to windows to actually allow other objects in your application to receive messages. In particular, MFC provides for allowing the routing of any `WM_COMMAND` messages that aren't handled by an active window to be sent to a document or to the application, thus letting you handle some messages on an application-wide or file-wide basis. The application produced by AppWizard handles `WM_COMMAND` messages with the wParams of `ID_FILE_NEW`, `ID_FILE_OPEN` and `ID_FILE_PRINT_SETUP` at the application level.

As MFC receives messages, it tries to distribute them to a target that will handle them; this process starts when the MFC message pump receives the message. MFC keeps an internal map of windows created by the class library, which relates a window handle to a pointer to an existing `CWnd`-derived object. This map is scanned for the window handle that is targeted by the message being dispatched.

If MFC receives a message for a window that it isn't trying to associate with a C++ object somewhere in your application, it will call the default message handling procedure for that window. MFC tries to subclass every window it can see so that it can properly route messages that it might receive. That is, MFC tries to watch the creation of every window it can. If it sees a window being built, it steps in and replaces the window procedure associated with that new window with its own. Of course, it remembers the original window procedure so that it can be called later.

We'll examine the general use of the term in detail soon, but MFC's inherent practice of **subclassing** is the only way that Windows uses to let developers add functionality to a window without actually rewriting the window procedure itself.

So, if MFC doesn't recognize the window identified as the target of a message it's about to process, MFC immediately calls the old window procedure of the window. MFC thereby allows the code that implements the window directly (or any other code that had already been subclassing the window) to handle the message.

If a matching window *is* found, MFC tries to find a handler for the message in the message map of the MFC window object. If no entry is found, the search progresses to the next base class until it reaches the root base class of the window object. If the final base class doesn't handle the message, MFC lets `::DefWindowProc()` deal with it. In this scheme, most messages are handled by `CWnd`; if `CWnd` doesn't handle the message, MFC considers asking `CCmdTarget`. As `CCmdTarget` has almost no message map entries, the messages usually end up being sent to `::DefWindowProc()`. If you've written your own class for the window, or if you're using one of MFC's classes, the handlers of those classes are offered a crack at the message first.

If the message is actually a command message (that is, a WM_COMMAND message), then MFC will try to route the message artificially; MFC's special routing doesn't happen for messages that aren't command messages. MFC provides for this routing because it's reasonable and useful. For instance, you might need to handle command messages generated by buttons or menus in almost any window involved in your application. MFC doesn't route other messages this way, simply because it's inappropriate to do so. Any other system message handled by a window needs to be handled by *that* window; such a message affects the interaction of the window with the rest of the system, not with the user.

MFC handles WM_COMMAND messages in a special way, and doesn't target a particular C++ object for the window, as it does for system messages (like WM_PAINT or WM_CLOSE). For WM_COMMAND MFC instead considers a whole list of windows that might be candidates for handling the messages. MFC also handles WM_NOTIFY messages sent to some windows with special code by offering them to the immediate parent window as well; this is a process called **message reflection**. We'll examine message reflection and the various WM_NOTIFY messages that the common controls send in Chapter 8.

There are a couple of other messages which MFC handles with particular care so that it can properly manage any extra features of the framework. For example, MFC needs to know when the application's main window is becoming active or inactive so that it can properly handle any state changes necessary for active OLE objects within that window. MFC handles these messages to effect functionality, which is a different notion than the routing I've been talking about. MFC routes all messages to try to find someone to handle them – but it's quite possible that MFC itself will supply the message map that finally handles the message. No matter what MFC is about to do with a given message, you'll always have the opportunity to get your hands around the message and do something else with it.

Let me underline the difference between system and command messages; Windows itself is completely responsible for targeting system messages. When a message is sent, the sender directs it to a particular window. The target window is provided to MFC when MFC begins processing the message, and MFC tries to pass the message directly to the code that implements that window, or more accurately, the code that implements the C++ class which was instantiated to manage that on-screen window. The vast majority of windows displayed by an application actually *don't* have C++ objects for them, and MFC ends up handling their messages by calling the window procedure owned by the Windows API to affect the default behavior of the window.

For example, even though you might place or retrieve text from an edit control on a dialog box in an application, you really don't respond to any of the messages that the edit control retruns. As such, you probably won't even create a C++ class to handle the messages sent to the edit window. MFC realizes that, and routes all of the messages sent to the edit directly to Windows – which has the window procedure that actually responds to those messages to implement the control. However, because of the aggressive subclassing work that MFC does, should you decide to handle the message sent to the edit, you can do so with great facility!

MFC's reliance on the natural Windows-provided target doesn't mean you can guarantee that a message will be handled globally by your application simply by coding a handler for it in the message map of your application. If you wish to handle a message at the application level, investigate overriding the CWinApp::PreTranslateMessage() function in your application's CWinApp-derived class. We'll be looking at the PreTranslateMessage() function in a little more depth towards the end of the chapter. As its name implies, PreTranslateMessage() allows you to snoop the application's message queue and handle messages yourself before MFC takes a crack at them.

The Command Routing Mechanism

When a WM_COMMAND message is received, MFC's command routing code is executed. After checking the window directly targeted by the message, MFC will then examine some other windows to see if they'd be interested in handling it. The command dispatch order for messages is slightly different for multiple-document interface applications than it is for single-document interface applications. The following table shows the classes in each type of application, listing the base classes in the order in which the message maps are scanned. Again, if a system message is sent by Windows directly to the frame window (such as a WM_MOVE, for example), the lesser windows don't receive it because no command routing is performed for system messages. However, such messages are still offered to Windows along the class hierarchy for the class of object that directly received the message.

SDI Applications with Doc/View		MDI Applications with Doc/View	
Functionality	**MFC Base Class Name**	**Functionality**	**MFC Base Class Name**
View	CView	View	CView
DocTemplate	CSingleDocTemplate	DocTemplate	CMultiDocTemplate
Document	CDocument	Document	CDocument
SDI Main Frame	CFrameWnd	MDI Child Frame	CMDIChildWnd
Application	CWinApp	MDI Main Frame	CMDIFrameWnd
		Application	CWinApp

SDI Applications without Doc/View		MDI Applications without Doc/View	
Functionality	**MFC Base Class Name**	**Functionality**	**MFC Base Class Name**
View-like Window	CWnd	View-like Window	CWnd
SDI Main Frame	CFrameWnd	MDI Child Frame	CMDIChildWnd
Application	CWinApp	MDI Main Frame	CMDIFrameWnd
		Application	CWinApp

In the tables above, you'll immediately note that the MDI and SDI application models still use an instance of a CWnd-derived class in a way that's strikingly similar to the way a CView-derived class might be used by a regular document/view architecture application! While the use of an extra window in the client area of an application might initially sound simply insane, the architecture is actually quite intentional. As we'll learn in Chapter 5, the view always lives inside a frame window. If a frame window didn't have an extra client-area window inside of it, your application would do all of its drawing inside the client area of the frame. That becomes a little awkward as the *usable* client area changes shape and size – such as when the frame window adds or removes a toolbar or status bar. We'll examine these issues in detail in Chapter 5.

Of course, the window behaves just like a CView-derived window, but it's really a CWnd-derived window. You're still working without the document/view architecture, even though one of the greatest single benefits of the architecture can be realized by the extra CWnd-derived window you're given for the client area.

Back to message targeting; if an MDI application is running and the view receives a WM_PAINT message, for example, then MFC tries to get the CWnd-derived class in your application to handle the message. If your class doesn't handle the message, MFC offers the message to the parent class (CWnd itself, which handles few interesting messages) as implemented by MFC. Since WM_PAINT is a system message and not a command message, it isn't routed.

On the other hand, if a frame window receives a WM_COMMAND message with the code ID_FILE_OPEN, as if a user had clicked on the Open... command in the File menu, then MFC will first offer the message to the CView-derived object in the running application. If the view doesn't handle it, it will be offered to MFC's implementation of CView, and then to MFC's implementations of CWnd and CCmdTarget, since they're the ancestor classes of CView. If no handler is found in any of these base class maps, the framework will route the message to the next command target – in this case, the CDocument-derived object.

You'll notice that I didn't include CWinThread in this chart – it's something of a special case. Exactly which CWinThread object gets checked if CWinApp ends up not handling the command depends upon the thread that owns the targeted window. The tables show what happens if your primary thread owns the window that was to receive the message. If you've created a subordinate thread, CWinApp is still checked, but it's checked in the context of the subordinate thread. If a frame window in your application was created by a subordinate thread, messages that aren't handled by the frame window class will be offered to the CWinApp object, but the call to the message handler will be made by the secondary thread, not by the primary thread normally associated with the CWinApp. There's more on threaded programming and thread window ownership in Chapter 10. If you're not very interested in threads, the above chart serves perfectly. If you're using threads, you can imagine that the tables are replicated for the windows your additional threads own with special case handling added for the different CWinThread objects you have floating about.

The two parameters associated with BEGIN_MESSAGE_MAP(), as shown in the code fragment below, tell the macro that we're defining the message map for the CSimpleApp class, and that this class is a derivative of the CWinApp class. This code from Simple.cpp is actually allocating and filling the data structure that defines the message map. It's also necessary to put a DECLARE_MESSAGE_MAP() macro in the declaration for the class in Simple.h, so that any symbols named by the BEGIN_MESSAGE_MAP() macro will be properly declared for the class in question.

```
/////////////////////////////////////////////////////////////////////
// CSimpleApp

BEGIN_MESSAGE_MAP(CSimpleApp, CWinApp)
    //{{AFX_MSG_MAP(CSimpleApp)
    ON_COMMAND(ID_APP_ABOUT, OnAppAbout)
        // NOTE — the ClassWizard will add and remove mapping macros here.
        //    DO NOT EDIT what you see in these blocks of generated code!
    //}}AFX_MSG_MAP
    // Standard file based document commands
    ON_COMMAND(ID_FILE_NEW, CWinApp::OnFileNew)
    ON_COMMAND(ID_FILE_OPEN, CWinApp::OnFileOpen)
    // Standard print setup command
    ON_COMMAND(ID_FILE_PRINT_SETUP, CWinApp::OnFilePrintSetup)
END_MESSAGE_MAP()
```

The innards of the BEGIN_MESSAGE_MAP() and DECLARE_MESSAGE_MAP() macros are defined in the Afxwin.h header file, which you can find by looking in the \Microsoft Visual Studio\Vc98\Mfc\Include directory, assuming that you've done your installation with the default name. If not, you can always find the files by looking for this directory on the distribution CD-ROM. The declaration for the DECLARE_MESSAGE_MAP() macro looks like this:

```
#define DECLARE_MESSAGE_MAP() \
private: \
    static const AFX_MSGMAP_ENTRY _messageEntries[]; \
protected: \
    static AFX_DATA const AFX_MSGMAP messageMap; \
    static const AFX_MSGMAP* PASCAL _GetBaseMessageMap(); \
    virtual const AFX_MSGMAP* GetMessageMap() const; \
```

You can see that, as its name suggests, this macro just provides some declarations; for this reason, it's only used in the class declaration, and not in the implementation. First, it declares a private array of AFX_MSGMAP_ENTRY structures. This array will contain the actual message map entries and will be searched by the message pump functions. Then the macro declares an AFX_MSGMAP structure for the class.

AFX_MSGMAP is actually a structure of two pointers, one to the _messageEntries array of the class and the other to the GetMessageMap() function of the base class. The macro also declares an overridable GetMessageMap() function and a static _GetBaseMessageMap() function.

Notice in particular, that all of the declarations for the message map implementation are static, with the only exception of the GetMessageMap() function. This means that only one copy of the declaration will exist no matter how many times the class is instantiated. The static qualifier for the functions means that they can be called even when no instantiation of the object exists.

These are germane to the message map architecture; they're a prerequisite, even when the class doesn't actually exist. The fact that only one message map exists for each class, no matter how many times it is instantiated, is important for memory considerations; there's no reason to replicate the class data for each and every object of the class in the running application.

You should also be aware that the data structures are const, since they're initialized once and then not changed throughout the execution of the program. An MFC window can't look at when a message was issued and then decide from that to handle a different message (or to handle a message with a different function) dynamically. Certainly, it's possible to switch around message maps on the fly by overriding the GetMessageMap() function and returning a pointer to your own AFX_MSGMAP_ENTRY array depending on what your mood is, but why bother? You can implement such dynamic code by writing an override for OnWndMsg() or PreTranslateMessage() in your own class.

The BEGIN_MESSAGE_MAP() Macro

Now that we've identified exactly what we're dealing with, let's have a look at what goes on under the hood. The macros that take care of the actual definition of the data structures and functions declared by DECLARE_MESSAGE_MAP() are BEGIN_MESSAGE_MAP() and END_MESSAGE_MAP(). Let's go through the expansion of BEGIN_MESSAGE_MAP().

There are three main activities taking place, all declaring the message map information for the class. The data structures involved don't normally see the light of day and are used directly by functions provided by MFC, but by understanding the mechanism at hand you can gain some valuable insights into the way MFC works. At the very least, understanding how these macros work is invaluable information for those times when you have a problem with your message map declaration and you get a few pages of odd compiler errors.

```
#define BEGIN_MESSAGE_MAP(theClass, baseClass) \
    const AFX_MSGMAP* PASCAL theClass::_GetBaseMessageMap() \
        { return &baseClass::messageMap; } \
    const AFX_MSGMAP* theClass::GetMessageMap() const \
        { return &theClass::messageMap; } \
    AFX_COMDAT AFX_DATADEF const AFX_MSGMAP theClass::messageMap = \
    { &theClass::_GetBaseMessageMap, &theClass::_messageEntries[0] }; \
    AFX_COMDAT const AFX_MSGMAP_ENTRY theClass::_messageEntries[] = \
    { \
```

The first parameter to the BEGIN_MESSAGE_MAP() macro is theClass. This is the name of the class for which the message map is being declared, and it's used 'right from the off' to scope the name of the _GetBaseMessageMap() function. This returns the address of the message map for the base class, identified by the second parameter to the macro: baseClass. The GetMessageMap function is declared in similar fashion:

```
#define BEGIN_MESSAGE_MAP(theClass, baseClass) \
    const AFX_MSGMAP* PASCAL theClass::_GetBaseMessageMap() \
        { return &baseClass::messageMap; } \
    const AFX_MSGMAP* theClass::GetMessageMap() const \
        { return &theClass::messageMap; } \
    AFX_COMDAT AFX_DATADEF const AFX_MSGMAP theClass::messageMap = \
    { &theClass::_GetBaseMessageMap, &theClass::_messageEntries[0] }; \
    AFX_COMDAT const AFX_MSGMAP_ENTRY theClass::_messageEntries[] = \
    { \
```

Instead of returning the address of the messageMap entry for baseClass, this returns it for theClass. The functions are necessary because MFC will use them internally to get the message maps of the class and the parent class – which handle how a message is to be dispatched.

BEGIN_MESSAGE_MAP() also declares the message map array, as you can see in the last line of the macro. The macro leaves the declaration of the array set up for subsequent initializers, which are supplied by the different message map entry macros you'll use (or that you'll ask ClassWizard to supply) in your map. The open bracket at the end of the macro dangles until you supply another macro to close the map.

The declarations, by the way, are pretty noisy. Of course, MFC needs to use all of its own types to define the map. Other modifiers are present in the declaration because MFC fights inflation at every turn by trying to assure that all of its data is properly aligned and declared – thus affording the linker every opportunity at throwing away things which are unused. AFX_COMDAT is a symbol which invokes the compiler's __declspec() modifier to make it all happen.

Inside the Message Map

What is actually stored in an `AFX_MSGMAP_ENTRY` structure? As it turns out, the `AFX_MSGMAP_ENTRY` structures have six members, as illustrated by this code snippet:

```
struct AFX_MSGMAP_ENTRY
{
    UINT nMessage;     // Windows message
    UINT nCode;        // control code or WM_NOTIFY code
    UINT nID;          // control ID (or 0 for Windows messages)
    UINT nLastID;      // used for entries specifying a range of control id's
    UINT nSig;         // signature type (action) or pointer to message #
    AFX_PMSG pfn;      // routine to call (or special value)
};
```

The `nMessage` member is the actual Windows message ID number that the message map entry describes. The value is usually equal to one of the `Windows.h` preprocessor symbols, such as `WM_PAINT` or `WM_CLOSE`. It indicates the message ID to be handled by the entry. It's this member that keys the searches that MFC performs when trying to find the handler for the message. In some instances, such as message map entries for user-registered Windows messages, it may be a special value that MFC uses to indicate special flavors of Windows messages.

Since many messages are related to a particular menu item or control, the `nID` member is provided to record the ID of the particular control, menu item or child window that the message map entry covers. It's sometimes convenient to use one function to handle a range of controls and you can indicate this desire in a message map by using the `nLastID` member. Normally, this member is equal to the `nID` member when the message map is to handle exactly one control ID. If you're handling a range of IDs with one message map function, you can set the `nID` member to the lower inclusive bound of the range and `nLastID` to the highest. Differing `nLastID` and `nID` members are used by the `ON_COMMAND_RANGE()` and `ON_NOTIFY_RANGE()` message map entry macros, which allow your class to declare the desire to handle messages generated by controls with IDs in any given range.

The final member, `pfn`, contains a pointer to the function that handles the message. The rules for declaring the function are a little different for each message being handled. ClassWizard will normally set up these functions for you, or you can check the on-line help to see exactly which parameters the function will require.

`nSig` is used to store a signature that describes the function referenced by `pfn`. For every type of message handling function, there exists an enumerated constant for `nSig` that describes the function type. These function types are listed in the following table:

`nSig` value	Message Function		Typical Message
	Return Type	Parameter List	
AfxSig_bb	BOOL	(BOOL)	WM_NCACTIVATE
AfxSig_bD	BOOL	(CDC*)	WM_ERASEBKGND
AfxSig_bHELPINFO	BOOL	(HELPINFO*)	WM_HELP
AfxSig_bNMHDRpl	BOOL	(NMHDR*, LRESULT*)	notifications

Table Continued on Following Page

nSig value	Message Function		Typical Message
	Return Type	Parameter List	
AfxSig_bpv	BOOL	(void*)	(unused)
AfxSig_bv	BOOL	(void)	WM_QUERYOPEN
AfxSig_bw	BOOL	(UINT)	ON_COMMAND_EX handlers
AfxSig_bwsp	BOOL	(UINT, short, CPoint)	WM_MOUSEWHEEL
AfxSig_bWww	BOOL	(CWnd*, UINT, UINT)	WM_SETCURSOR
AfxSig_cmdui	void	(CCmdUI*)	update command UI handlers
AfxSig_cmduiw	void	(CCmdUI*, UINT)	update command UI handlers
AfxSig_hDw	HBRUSH	(CDC*, UINT)	WM_CTLCOLOR
AfxSig_hDWw	HBRUSH	(CDC*, CWnd*, UINT)	WM_CTLCOLOR
AfxSig_hv	HANDLE	(void)	WM_QUERYDRAGICON
AfxSig_iis	int	(int, LPTSTR)	WM_COMPAREITEM
AfxSig_is	int	(LPTSTR)	WM_NCCREATE
AfxSig_iwWw	int	(UINT, CWnd*, UINT)	WM_CHARTOITEM
AfxSig_iWww	int	(CWnd*, UINT, UINT)	WM_MOUSEACTIVATE
AfxSig_iww	int	(UINT, UINT)	WM_CHARTOITEM
AfxSig_lwl	LRESULT	(WPARAM, LPARAM)	generic WM_ handlers
AfxSig_lwwM	LRESULT	(UINT, UINT, CMenu*)	WM_MENUCHAR
AfxSig_vb	void	(BOOL)	WM_ENABLE
AfxSig_vbh	void	(BOOL, HANDLE)	WM_ACTIVATEAPP
AfxSig_vbw	void	(BOOL, UINT)	WM_SHOWWINDOW
AfxSig_vbWW	void	(BOOL, CWnd*, CWnd*)	WM_MDIACTIVATE
AfxSig_vCALC	void	(BOOL, NCCALCSIZE_PARAMS*)	WM_NCCALCSIZE
AfxSig_vD	void	(CDC*)	WM_ICONERASEBKGND
AfxSig_vh	void	(HANDLE)	WM_DROPFILES
AfxSig_vhh	void	(HANDLE, HANDLE)	WM_CHANGECBCHAIN
AfxSig_vM	void	(CMenu*)	WM_INITMENU

nSig value	Message Function		Typical Message
	Return Type	**Parameter List**	
AfxSig_vMwb	void	(CMenu*, UINT, BOOL)	WM_INITMENUPOPUP
AfxSig_vNMHDRpl	void	(NMHDR*, LRESULT*)	notifications
AfxSig_vOWNER	void	(int, LPTSTR)	owner-draw messages
AfxSig_vPOS	void	(WINDOWPOS*)	WM_WINDOWPOSCHANGING
AfxSig_vpv	void	(void*)	(unused)
AfxSig_vs	void	(LPTSTR)	WM_WININICHANGED
AfxSig_vv	void	(void)	WM_PAINT
AfxSig_vvii	void	(int, int)	WM_MOVE
AfxSig_vw	void	(UINT)	WM_TIMER
AfxSig_vW	void	(CWnd*)	WM_KILLFOCUS
AfxSig_vWp	void	(CWnd*, CPoint)	WM_CONTEXTMENU
AfxSig_vWh	void	(CWnd*, HANDLE)	WM_PAINTCLIPBOARD
AfxSig_vwii	void	(UINT, int, int)	WM_SIZE
AfxSig_vwl	void	(UINT, LPARAM)	WM_SYSCOMMAND
AfxSig_vwNMHDRpl	void	(UINT, NMHDR*, LRESULT*)	notifications
AfxSig_vwp	void	(UINT, CPoint)	WM_NCMOUSEMOVE
AfxSig_vws	void	(UINT, LPCTSTR)	WM_SETTINGCHANGE
AfxSig_vwSIZING	void	(UINT, LPRECT)	WM_SIZING
AfxSig_vww	void	(UINT, UINT)	WM_SPOOLERSTATUS
AfxSig_vwW	void	(UINT, CWnd*)	WM_ENTERIDLE
AfxSig_vwWb	void	(UINT, CWnd*, BOOL)	WM_ACTIVATE
AfxSig_vwwh	void	(UINT, UINT, HANDLE)	WM_MENUSELECT
AfxSig_vwww	void	(UINT, UINT, UINT)	WM_KEYDOWN
AfxSig_vWww	void	(CWnd*, UINT, UINT)	WM_VSCROLLCLIPBOARD
AfxSig_vwwW	void	(UINT, UINT, CWnd*)	WM_VSCROLL
AfxSig_vwwx	void	(UINT, UINT)	scrolling messages
AfxSig_wp	UINT	(CPoint)	WM_NCHITTEST
AfxSig_wv	UINT	(void)	WM_GETDLGCODE

In addition to all of these message identifiers, MFC uses two more special values for the `nSig` member. First, the value of `nSig` for the last entry in the message map will contain `AfxSig_end`. This lets the loops that check for matches in the message map know where the message map ends. If you browse the `Afxmsg_.h` file (which can be found in your `\Microsoft Visual Studio\Vc98\Mfc\Include` directory), you can see that each signature is often used only once or twice. Since MFC must be prepared to call each type of function, the slightest difference in the message's parameters requires a completely new signature.

The other special value that may appear in `nSig` is a pointer to the message number. This happens when you write a message handler for a registered, user-defined Windows message. The `nMessage` value for such messages is always set to `0xC000`, while the `nSig` member points to the actual message number returned by `::RegisterWindowMessage()`.

Once MFC has identified a target entry for the message, it uses the `nSig` value in a large `switch` statement to place a type-safe call to the handler function. It's imperative that your implementation of the handler is correctly typed – if it isn't, MFC won't place the call and your function will never execute. Unfortunately, it's impossible for MFC or the compiler to generate an error message for these situations; since the C++ language supports function overloading, there's no way to know if the function prototype was intentional or accidental.

The Message Passing Architecture

The message passing architecture is one of the mechanisms that makes it much easier to port MFC applications than 'standard' C or C++ applications from Win16 to Win32. Since MFC is responsible for calling the member functions that implement a window's message handlers, it can hide all of the work required to unpack the message parameters from the Windows `wParam` and `lParam` parameters to the message handler function.

It's not only the work that gets hidden; all the platform differences are hidden too. Messages that are unpacked differently in Win32 than in Win16 don't affect the implementation of the message handler function like they would in standard C or non-MFC C++ applications, because MFC handles the packing and unpacking based on the signature of the message in the message map.

If you make a mistake when declaring message map functions by hand, you'll probably get an error message about a particular line of code requiring a cast from a member of a non-`CWnd` derived type to a member of a `CWnd`-related class. This simply means that the compiler has found a typing problem – you've either used the wrong return value type, or parameters that don't match the prototype generated by the map macro entry you used.

Filling the Holes

While the structures used to define a message map might seem to be terribly complicated, things aren't as bad as they look because we've been studying their implementation rather than their actual use. Coding with them is pretty simple, mainly because of the macros I've dissected here, but also because the Visual C++ development environment provides two potent tools to make things go a little easier.

The message map for the `CSimpleApp` object, which is shown below, uses several macros and never mentions an `AfxSig_` value. The macros it uses, which are supplied by MFC in the `Afxmsg_.h` file, define all of the entries for an `AFX_MSGMAP_ENTRY` structure. This organization is used to allow you to concentrate upon the message handling function, instead of playing with the signatures and pointers required to initialize the structure.

```
BEGIN_MESSAGE_MAP(CSimpleApp, CWinApp)
    //{{AFX_MSG_MAP(CSimpleApp)
    ON_COMMAND(ID_APP_ABOUT, OnAppAbout)
        // NOTE - the ClassWizard will add and remove mapping macros here.
        //    DO NOT EDIT what you see in these blocks of generated code!
    //}}AFX_MSG_MAP
    // Standard file based document commands
    ON_COMMAND(ID_FILE_NEW, CWinApp::OnFileNew)
    ON_COMMAND(ID_FILE_OPEN, CWinApp::OnFileOpen)
    // Standard print setup command
    ON_COMMAND(ID_FILE_PRINT_SETUP, CWinApp::OnFilePrintSetup)
END_MESSAGE_MAP()
```

You'll notice that this message map only has `ON_COMMAND()` entries. This is because MFC sends `WM_COMMAND` messages along to the C++ application object, but doesn't forward any other messages to the application object. This is exactly what we discovered when we investigated the rules MFC follows when routing messages earlier in this chapter.

Windows Messages

The `Afxmsg_.h` header includes macros that allow you to declare message map entries conveniently. For the bulk of Windows messages, you can simply add the appropriate message map macro with no parameter. The names of the message handling member functions for *predefined* Windows messages never change, so the macros accept no parameters. You can simply prefix `ON_` to the name of the Windows message you're interested in trapping. For example:

```
ON_WM_PAINT()
ON_WM_KEYDOWN()
ON_WM_CLOSE()
```

and so on. The messages are handled by functions with similar names; `ON_WM_PAINT()` calls `OnPaint()`, while `ON_WM_KEYDOWN()` will call `OnKeyDown()` when the message is received.

Some messages are not serviced by macros in this way. For example, you may be doing some owner-draw painting work and need to trap the `WM_SETFONT` message to identify the font that your control will be painting with. Since there's no `ON_WM_SETFONT()` macro, you can use the MFC-supplied `ON_MESSAGE()` macro. If your `WM_SETFONT` message handler message was named `OnSetFont()`, the message map entry to declare this handler looks like this:

```
ON_MESSAGE(WM_SETFONT, OnSetFont)
```

The prototype for the `OnSetFont()` function would be:

```
afx_msg LRESULT OnSetFont(WPARAM wParam, LPARAM lParam);
```

A more common use for the ON_MESSAGE() macro is coding a handler for a user-defined message. The parameters and return type for the handler's prototype should be as shown above for OnSetFont(). If you want to send yourself a message, for example, you might give the message an ID based on the WM_USER constant, which is a range of messages that you're allowed to use without conflicting with other applications. If your message is WM_USER+37, for example, you can code this message map entry:

```
ON_MESSAGE(WM_USER+37, OnMyMessage)
```

and write this member function:

```
afx_msg LRESULT OnMyMessage(WPARAM wParam, LPARAM lParam);
```

In your implementation of OnMyMessage(), you'll find that the wParam and lParam parameters receive the wParam and lParam parameters carried with the message.

The Windows ::RegisterWindowMessage() API allows your application to register a Windows message. ::RegisterWindowMessage() takes a string parameter and returns the ID of the message. If two applications register a message with the same identifying string, they're guaranteed to get the same message identification number. Otherwise, the number is unique and can safely be used by the application to communicate with itself.

To use the message, you'll obviously need to save the return value from the API. It's quite safe simply to declare a global variable to hold the message ID, like this:

```
static UINT uGameStart = ::RegisterWindowMessage(_T("DropThePuck"));
```

Once the message is registered, you can use the variable that contains its registered value in a macro that's very similar to the ON_MESSAGE() macro we just saw. ON_REGISTERED_MESSAGE() might look like this, for example:

```
ON_REGISTERED_MESSAGE(uGameStart, OnGameStart)
```

The first parameter is the UINT variable where I stored the return value from ::RegisterWindowMessage(); the second names the function which will handle the message for me. The prototype for the function will be the same as that for an ON_MESSAGE()-related handler:

```
afx_msg LRESULT OnGameStart (WPARAM wParam, LPARAM lParam);
```

> **It's important to prototype your message handler member functions correctly, as the C++ language provides no way for MFC to decide that you've prototyped them incorrectly. Be careful not to mismatch a prototype for a message handler. Usually, you'll get some pretty goofy symptoms — like incorrect parameters when you least expect them, or crashes that happen only in release builds. Your code will be so buggy that your houseplants will all die.**

Command Messages

Map entries for command messages are a little different. Since they could be performing almost any function, the message map entry doesn't name the handling function for you. Instead, it accepts a function name as a parameter. WM_COMMAND messages are also identified by the wParam of the command message they're handling, so this information is also supplied as a parameter. The message map for the application object in Simple.cpp contains these lines:

```
ON_COMMAND(ID_FILE_NEW, CWinApp::OnFileNew)
ON_COMMAND(ID_FILE_OPEN, CWinApp::OnFileOpen)
```

These macros make two message map entries. Each one is for a WM_COMMAND message; if WM_COMMAND is received with wParam set to ID_FILE_NEW, the CWinApp::OnFileNew() function is called. For a wParam of ID_FILE_OPEN, CWinApp::OnOpenFile is called.

You may have also noticed some more of those //{{AFX_MSG_MAP(CSimpleApp) comments in the message map shown earlier. As usual, they indicate that ClassWizard has been around. The macros between the two comments are known to and are modifiable by the ClassWizard, while macros outside of the comment blocks are not. When you use ClassWizard's **Message Maps** tab, shown below, you can have ClassWizard manage message handling functions for you automatically.

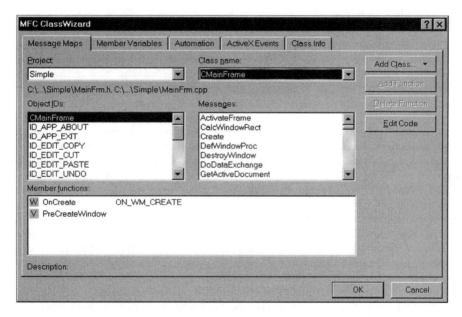

I've now mentioned the two most common flavors of messages handled by a message map: command messages and Windows messages. There are other types of command notification that are handled by MFC, such as user interface update notifications and Automation calls. Since this is just an overview of the message map architecture, I'll save the coverage of other specific message handling applications until we see material where those features are of interest.

The END_MESSAGE_MAP() Macro

One of the more entertaining ways of generating a few pages of wacky compiler errors is to forget the END_MESSAGE_MAP() macro. The definition of that macro is shown below:

```
#define END_MESSAGE_MAP() \
     {0, 0, 0, 0, AfxSig_end, (AFX_PMSG)0 } \
  }; \
```

The macro declares a special, easily identifiable, out-of-bounds AFX_MSGMAP_ENTRY , which lets any function trying to search a map know that it's not going to find anything else. It also provides the closing brace and semicolon for the structure definition started by BEGIN_MESSAGE_MAP(), which is why a missing END_MESSAGE_MAP() macro causes such havoc; the structure is never closed, and the compiler tries to interpret any code subsequent to the last message map entry in the source file as a part of the structure. You can see the AfxSig_end signature I talked about earlier being used here as well.

Now we know how message maps are declared and filled, let's go on to look at how MFC actually uses them.

Unfolding the Map

CCmdTarget also contains some of the code that's required to dispatch messages. It implements a function called OnWndMsg(),which is responsible for reading the message map and calling the correct member function to handle the message. The code finds the message map for the CCmdTarget-derived object that's handling the message by calling the GetMessageMap() function which was implemented by the BEGIN_MESSAGE_MAP() macro.

These mechanisms take us a long way towards replacing the use of those difficult switch statements. So far, we know how the procedure goes in some detail; a Windows message is received by the MFC message pump. The pump dispatches the message to the target window procedure, which is also implemented by MFC. This procedure searches out the target C++ object and begins looking through that object's message map for a handler. On finding one, the procedure will then call that function.

But what if the search doesn't find a message map entry that claims to handle the message we wish to dispatch? It might not find an entry simply because we don't want to handle the message, but the entry might also be absent because we know that the message is handled by the base of our class and we wish to allow the base class to do the processing just as if we were inheriting functionality from our base class.

Since the BEGIN_MESSAGE_MAP() macro also knows the name of our base class, it creates a link backward, up the chain, so that the search can spin off the given class' message map to look through the message map of the base class. If the very top of the message map chain is found – in other words, if the link to the parent class is NULL, as it is in the implementation of CCmdTarget – then the search has failed. If the message is not found after all pertinent classes and maps have been checked, the message handler calls the appropriate default window procedure to let Windows handle the message instead.

This brings up the important issue of **multiple inheritance** – that is, declaring a class to inherit functionality from more than one base class. **MFC does not support multiple inheritance**. This is simply because the notion of command dispatching becomes too vague if one class inherits from two different classes and both want to handle a message. The macros we've discussed here provide no provision for the use of multiple inheritance. You *can,* if you're very motivated, override some of the message map management functions MFC uses under the covers (such as GetMessageMap()) in order to add multiple inheritance capabilities to your programs. You'll have to look elsewhere for documentation on this, though; I'm afraid it's beyond the scope of this book.

There's No Sense of Obligation

MFC has been designed to hide all the internal workings of message maps and how command routing works, and to be honest you don't *really* need to know very much about what we've been discussing. You can use MFC forever without worrying about exactly what's going on. Who cares?

Nobody cares, of course – until something breaks. (I got *really* interested in water pumps when my car started smelling like burnt antifreeze.) Maybe you tried some funny business, like intercepting messages before they really needed to get processed. Maybe you've hacked together your own message maps without using ClassWizard and broken something by incorrectly declaring the base classes or message map members. Maybe you crashed your motorcycle in a nearby state park and came back to work even though you had mild amnesia. Maybe it smells like antifreeze every time you run your app.

Knowing how the mechanism actually works will help you in your role as an MFC programmer. It can help you think of ways to structure hierarchies of command-handling classes efficiently (so that the most frequent messages are handled high in the message map, for example). Or it can provide you with some insight as to why MFC seems to be throwing ASSERTs when you do things in a certain order, perhaps circumventing the natural way messages were meant to be handled in your application.

For now, our coverage of CCmdTarget is complete. Earlier, we alluded to the fact that commands might take the form of Automation dispatches. We'll revisit how CCmdTarget takes care of these special calls in our look at MFC OLE classes. Let's move to the next level up the hierarchy and have a look at the granddaddy of all classes, CObject.

CObject

CObject is the root of all MFC classes (well, *almost* all of them), but although it's really fundamental, it provides surprisingly little functionality. CObject's four major roles in life are memory management, debugging, serialization and run-time type information. Let's take a look at each of these features so that we can understand some of the most intimate features of every MFC class.

Memory Management

Since almost every class in MFC can eventually be derived from CObject, it follows that you can point at almost any MFC class using a pointer to CObject. This has the side-effect of causing the C++ new and delete operators to use the MFC-supplied new and delete operators related to the CObject data type, effectively routing all requests for class memory through one central point in MFC.

In debug builds of MFC, the central handling of memory management is extremely valuable because it helps MFC to track memory use. If, when your program exits from a debugging session, you have objects that you have not deleted, MFC can offer diagnostic messages to warn you of the memory leaks. Release builds of the library include an implementation of these operators that are designed to be more efficient rather than aware of leaks.

Specifically, debug versions of the MFC implementations of new and delete put markers in the heap to aid the process of memory management. These markers include information to describe leaks, but you can also use the line:

```
#define new DEBUG_NEW
```

within each module of your application before you use the new operator to get more precise information. This step will cause your program to use DEBUG_NEW, a special version of the MFC new operator, which will also record line number and file name information for each allocation as it occurs. With this #define in place, any memory leak dumps will also include line number and source module name information for the allocation that caused the leak, thus helping you to pinpoint problems in your code.

> In the release build, **DEBUG_NEW** reverts back to the normal **new** operator. Also note that, as of MFC 4.0, it uses the heap management from the C run-time library.

Furthermore, it's worth pointing out that you can't mix debug and non-debug versions of MFC in the same process. If you allocate some memory in one module and that memory is allocated by the debug memory allocator, it turns out it will be a different size to what the release-mode memory release code expects. That's true for two reasons. First, a debug version of a C++ object will probably have extra member functions, and maybe even extra member data, when compared to a release-build object. The debug allocator simply allocates more memory to accommodate the larger object, and the release-mode allocator won't expect that larger size. Second, the debug allocator will stamp the memory with some extra data to describe it in support of the debugging features we've just reviewed. Again, the release-mode version of the memory routines won't expect that extra size, and will get sick. Obviously, I've described allocating memory with the debug code and freeing memory with the release code – but the same problems apply the other way, with the debug memory routines expecting larger block sizes than they're actually offered.

About Placement Syntax

The #define mentioned above is a double-whammy. Your code has the macro we examined before:

```
#define new DEBUG_NEW
```

but the MFC headers contain this macro, if you're building for debug:

```
#define DEBUG_NEW new(THIS_FILE, __LINE__)
```

Taken together, those two defines mean that a simple call to the operator `new`:

```
LPBYTE pMemory = new BYTE[1024];
```

ends up expanding to this call:

```
LPBYTE pMemory = new(THIS_FILE, __LINE__) BYTE[1024];
```

which is pretty awkward. But it really works; it's called **placement syntax**. The original idea for placement syntax was to override `operator new()` so that it would construct an object at a specific address, supplied to the `operator new()` implementation as an extra parameter. Placement syntax has been mottled over the years to mean any syntax for `operator new()` or `operator delete()` that takes some extra parameters.

The ANSI C++ Standard Committee finally got their act together in 1998 and ratified the standard. The standard spells out some interesting requirements for placement syntax. The most interesting is that any use of placement syntax new requires a placement syntax `delete` operator that accepts the exact same parameters. The above invocation of `operator new()` ends up calling a function with this prototype:

```
void* operator new(size_t size, char* pstrFile, int nLine);
```

The matching `operator delete()` for such a new would look like this:

```
void operator delete(void* pMemory, char* pstrFile, int nLine);
```

Of course, for MFC's purposes, `operator delete()` doesn't need to do anything with the `nLine` and `pstrFile` parameters – and won't. While you can't legally directly invoke the placement `delete` operator, the declaration *must* be there, and must delete the memory referenced by `pMemory`. However, the compiler will invoke the operator if the object being allocated throws an exception while being constructed. If the compiler can't find a placement syntax `delete` operator that matches the placement syntax new operator used for the failed construction, the compiler won't bother to delete the memory used by the object's construction.

MFC supplies placement `delete` operators for each of the placement new operators it provides to assure that memory allocated to objects that throw during their destructors can be cleaned up. And the VC++ 6.0 compiler is the first Microsoft compiler to actually implement the placement syntax semantics per the standard. In previous releases, the compiler didn't support placement syntax `delete` and never cleaned up memory when the constructor threw and placement syntax new was used. Since MFC only forces placement syntax new in debug builds, the problem was largely harmless – while many developers figured objects that threw in their constructors were actually leaking, they were only leaking in debug builds because those debug builds used placement syntax new.

MFC's use of a macro to invoke placement syntax new for debugging information also causes a problem for developers who want to provide their own placement syntax new. Since a user-defined placement syntax new operator still uses the word "new", the preprocessor will muddle it with MFC's definition of the new macro. And that will end up causing some annoying syntax errors. The only real workaround is to avoid the use of DEBUG_NEW in situations where your own placement syntax new is required.

Debugging Support

As you debug code you've written in C++, you often want an object to present information about its status. Using a debugger, you can usually get this information by evaluating a pointer or reference to the object and then expanding information about the members of the object. But having access to state information at runtime can also be very useful. If, for instance, you code defensively and have traps in your application to notice problems which indicate that the integrity of your application (or its data) has become questionable, you may wish to dump the contents of some objects to a diagnostic file. Such information can be invaluable when performing post-mortem debugging.

MFC suggests a standardized approach to this technique by providing a Dump() function in debug versions of CObject. This function is always declared in debug builds; you can implement it at your own discretion. However, it doesn't exist in release builds of MFC, so you shouldn't implement it in those circumstances. A declaration for an example class called CClient, which implements a Dump() function, could look like this:

```
class CClient : public CObject
{
public:
#ifdef _DEBUG
    virtual void Dump(CDumpContext& dc) const;
#endif
    CString m_sCompanyName;
    CString m_sContactFirstName;
    CString m_sContactLastName;
    // other members or data...
};
```

We might actually implement the CClient::Dump() function like this:

```
#ifdef _DEBUG
void CClient::Dump(CDumpContext& dc) const
{
    // Call base class dumper first
    CObject::Dump(dc);

    // Now, dump everything that CClient implements itself.
    dc << "Company name: " << m_sCompanyName << "\n"
        << "Last Name: " << m_sContactLastName << "\n"
        << "First Name: " << m_sContactFirstName << "\n";
}
#endif
```

Notice that the declaration and implementation of Dump() are enclosed in #ifdef directives to prevent them from being included in release builds.

Dump() can be called any time you wish. You should design the function so that it does eventually return to its caller, although it doesn't return any value.

The single parameter to Dump() is a reference to a **dump context**. This context, as we'll learn, contains information about the target of the dump and the level of detail desired in the dump. If MFC decides to call the Dump() member of one of your objects, it'll provide a dump context for you automatically. The dump context managed by MFC on behalf of your application is always named afxDump.

Shallow Snapshots

Dump() is intended to produce a **shallow snapshot** of an object's status. You may have your Dump() function produce whatever output you see fit but, by convention, it's most often used to present the member variables stored in the dumped object. If your member data is complex (or downright meaningless to humans) you might wish to decode the data or to produce more meaningful information.

The notion of a 'shallow' snapshot means that the object should only dump information in members that *aren't* inherited from its base class. For example, if our CClient class is derived from a CPerson class, we should let the CPerson class handle the dumping of information it implements (such as the person's name or birthday) while the CClient::Dump() function should output the things unique to the CClient class (such as the client's contact name, for example).

To this end, the dc parameter passed to the Dump() function should be propagated throughout subsequent calls to Dump() in the base classes. Note that the base class call should be made before the given class performs its dump functionality. This lets the output progress in a logical manner, from the highest base class to the class initiating the dump. The dc parameter that's passed to the Dump() function should also be propagated to any subsequent calls made to sub-object implementations.

The dump context *can* provide information to your Dump() implementation that indicates what level of dumping should be performed. You can call CDumpContext::GetDepth() to find a depth which allows your program to decide to dump more or less information. You might, for example, implement a class called CClientList that keeps a list of CClient objects as data members. The CClientList::Dump() implementation might check the value returned from GetDepth() – if the value is 0, the code might dump only the immediate member variables, while any other value would cause the code to call Dump() recursively on each CClient element in the list as well. You should always implement your Dump() routines to dump the data implemented by your own class. If GetDepth() returns something larger than zero, consider dumping the content of objects your class owns; otherwise, stick to the simple data types. Never should your class dump members actually managed by your base – it should call the base class to do that.

You'll need to set the dump depth yourself by calling CDumpContext::SetDepth() during your program's initialization. The depth is zero by default.

The C++ Insertion Operator

You can see that Dump() uses the C++ insertion operator (<<) to generate its output. The dc parameter that is passed to Dump() is a reference to a CDumpContext class. This class is very similar to the CArchive class, which we shall examine later. The insertion operator for this class is implemented for the following data types:

CObject*	BYTE	double	LPCWSTR
CObject&	WORD	float	LPCSTR
LPCTSTR	DWORD	LONG	SIZE
void*	int	UINT	POINT
RECT&	CString&		

If you need to produce output based on any other data type, you're on your own where type conversions are involved, but you may be able to get by with a simple cast. For instance, you can't dump the value of a pointer to a specific data type, but you can cast the pointer to a `void*` before dumping it. In this context the data type doesn't really matter, since the information will be translated as a simple address for output to the dump device; that is, your dump output will contain the value of the pointer, not what it references.

Where Do Trace Messages Go When it Rains?

I'm not sure where butterflies go when it rains but, whether it's rainy or not, trace messages are sent to a dump context. The dump context is normally hooked up by MFC to point at the debug output monitor for your process. If you're running your program under the Visual C++ debugger, the debug output will appear in the **Debug** pane of the Output Window. The results of `Dump()` calls show up here, as do any extra messages you write using MFC's `TRACE()` macros. Let's investigate `TRACE()` macros first, and then go on to talk about the dump context.

`TRACE()` macros are provided by MFC to let you write text to the debug device. They disappear when you compile for a release build, but are present in a debug build. If you wanted to, you could code some diagnostic output in the event of a failure, something like this:

```
DWORD dwRetVal;
dwRetVal = ImportantFunction();
if (dwRetVal != NO_ERROR)
{
    TRACE1("ImportantFunction() failed and returned %d\n", dwRetVal);
    // some error handling code that you need...
}
```

The `TRACE()` macro accepts one string parameter and a variable list of additional parameters. The string you give to `TRACE()` can contain %-sign escapes just like a formatting string supplied to `printf()` might; you can use %d to print decimal numbers, %s to print strings, and so on. `TRACE()` supports all formats except for floating point numbers. You can also use `TRACE0()`, `TRACE1()`, `TRACE2()`, or `TRACE3()` if you know that you'll be supplying zero, one, two, or three parameters to the formatting string, respectively. The only real difference between the numbered `TRACEn()` macros and the generic `TRACE()` macro is that the latter's first parameter *must* be an LPCSTR type. That is, if you're building your application for Unicode, `TRACE()` will allow you to supply Unicode strings and handle Unicode parameters, while the numbered `TRACEn()` macros won't. The numbered macros require an ANSI formatting string as their first parameter regardless of the build type – and can always process both Unicode and ANSI parameters. You can read about more Unicode programming issues and the LPCSTR type itself in Appendix B.

The code in this fragment compiles and works properly, regardless of the build type.

```
#ifdef _UNICODE
    TRACE(_T("Some message here. %d items.\n"), nItems);
    TRACE1("Some other message. %d people, %d seats.\n", nAttendees, nSeats);
    TRACE0("A one-liner.\n");
#else //not _UNICODE
    TRACE(_T("Some message here. %d items.\n"), nItems);
    TRACE1("Some other message. %d people, %d seats.\n", nAttendees, nSeats);
    TRACE0("A one-liner.\n");
#endif
```

As an MFC user – that is, as a developer – you have the ability to use the **MFC Tracer** tool to turn tracing, as a whole, on or off. The tool also provides you with the more granular ability to choose whether or not you want to see the various kinds of trace messages that are built into MFC. Looking at the **Debug** Output Window to follow along with what's going on is a great way to find problems – particularly those that deal with message routing or command handling.

You should find a menu item that runs **MFC Tracer** in the **Microsoft Visual C++ 6.0 Tools** tear off in the **Microsoft Visual C++ 6.0** menu under the **Start** button. If you ever get separated from your parents, you should find a security guard and wait by the door, but if you get separated from the Tracer utility, you should look around in the `Microsoft Visual Studio\Common\Tools` directory for a file named `Tracer.exe`.

All of these messages – that is, messages generated by `TRACE()` calls inside of MFC itself, calls you make to `TRACE()`, and data you pass to the `CDumpContext` object you find inside your `Dump()` implementation – are sent to MFC's dump context. The global `afxDump` object that MFC uses is declared in a module called `Dumpinit.cpp` in the `\Microsoft Visual Studio\Vc98\Mfc\Src` directory. You can review this file to see some instructions for replacing `afxDump`, which you should do if you want trace output to go to a disk file, for example.

Those instructions simply involve modifying the `m_pFile` member of the `afxDump` object that MFC is maintaining. In your `InitInstance()`, you might want to write code like this:

```
BOOL CRedirApp::InitInstance()
{
    TRACE0("Redirecting afxDump output to REDIR.BUG\n");

#ifdef _DEBUG
    CStdioFile* pFile = NULL;
    ASSERT(afxDump.m_pFile == NULL);
    try
    {
        pFile = new CStdioFile(_T("REDIR.BUG"),
            CFile::modeCreate | CFile::modeNoTruncate
                | CFile::typeText | CFile::modeWrite);
    }
    catch (CException* pEx)
    {
        TCHAR sz[1024];
        TRACE0("Redirection failed! ");
        if (pEx->GetErrorMessage(sz, 1024))
            TRACE1("%s\n", sz);
        else
            TRACE0("Cause unknown!\n");
        pEx->Delete();
    }

    if (pFile != NULL)
    {
        afxDump.m_pFile = pFile;
        afxDump.m_pFile->SeekToEnd();
    }
#endif

    // More work here
```

As you can see, I protect the code in #ifdef conditionals so that the code isn't shown to the compiler in non-debug builds. In release builds, the afxDump symbol isn't declared, and the code wouldn't compile if I didn't take this precaution. Note that I'm very careful to use a try/catch construct to handle any exceptions that the code might throw.

> *You can read more about the CStdioFile object and the exceptions that I use in Chapter 9.*

Once the file object has been opened, I simply assign its address to the m_pFile member of the afxDump object. From that point on, MFC will write output to the file object instead of the debugger.

Since I've created a new object in code that I'm adding to InitInstance(), I should code something in ExitInstance() to close the file. Code to do so would look like this:

```
int CRedirApp::ExitInstance()
{
#ifdef _DEBUG
    if (afxDump.m_pFile != NULL)
    {
        afxDump.Flush();
        afxDump.m_pFile->Close();

        delete afxDump.m_pFile;
        afxDump.m_pFile = NULL;
    }
#endif

    return CWinApp::ExitInstance();
}
```

The Redir sample on the Wrox web site has all of this code in one convenient spot for you. The Redir sample also has some code to handle mouse click messages in the view – that code just generates some debug output to make the application a little more interesting. You'll notice when you run the sample that only output generated with MFC's own TRACE() macros are sent to the file. Output generated by Windows itself, or by the C Runtime Libraries, will not be sent to the file.

Validity Tests

To further help development and debugging, MFC also implements a validity check in CObject. Classes that derive from CObject can implement a function named AssertValid(). If your class inherits from CObject, you might implement your AssertValid() function like this:

```
class CYourClass : public CObject
{
protected:
    // whatever it is your class has
public:
    // whatever it is your class does

#ifdef _DEBUG
    virtual void AssertValid() const;
#endif
};
```

Like the other debugging features of MFC, AssertValid() should only be implemented when you're building a debug version of your application. When you compile your application for release, and when you use the release build version of MFC, AssertValid() is not implemented or called. This sacrifices the diagnostics generated by the validity assertions for higher execution speed and smaller code size.

Like the CObject::Dump() function, your implementation of AssertValid() should perform a shallow check, by which I mean that it should only perform validity checks on the variables, state or features of the class it's implemented for. It should call the base class implementation of AssertValid() before its own validation is performed. If the validity of member data in a given class is dependent on the member data of an ancestor of the class, of course, then you should make an appropriate test in the more derived class to make sure that interdependency is valid.

The validation tests should be done with the ASSERT() macro. This will generate an error message box identifying the file and line number containing the ASSERT() that failed. There's more on the features of this box in the section called 'About Asserts in MFC' later in this chapter. The AssertValid() function would then look something like:

```
#ifdef _DEBUG
void CYourClass::AssertValid()
{
    // Check out the base class
    CObject::AssertValid();

    // Check out this class' own data
    ASSERT(this_member > 0 && this_member< 100); // range check
    ASSERT(that_member != NULL);                  // initialization check
}
#endif //_DEBUG
```

The ASSERT_VALID() macro is used to call the AssertValid() function. The macro needs a pointer to the class instance that is to be validated. Release builds of this macro don't generate code, so you don't have to protect it with #ifdefs; you only need to use conditionals around the implementation and declaration of your AssertValid() functions.

When writing your own code, you might decide to call AssertValid() on objects you handle. You might simply test the validity of your own object, like this:

```
void CMyClass::DoSomething()
{
    ASSERT_VALID(this);
    // Do your work here...
```

Or, you might make the call on an object one of your functions receives in a method, like this:

```
void CMyClass::ChangeThat(CThat* pThat)
{
    ASSERT_VALID(pThat);
    // Do the work here...
```

Again, note that I don't call AssertValid() directly; instead, I use the ASSERT_VALID() macro to make the call indirectly. The ASSERT_VALID() macro is handy because it disappears in non-debug builds, thus saving you from coding the conditional pre-compiler directives you'd need to have around calls to AssertValid().

About Assertions in MFC

I've mentioned the ASSERT() macro a few times in this chapter without really explaining what it does. Well, MFC is written very defensively, wrapping a number of safety checks around both the Windows API and the functions that MFC implements itself. Most of the checks in MFC center around ASSERT(). This macro, in debug builds of both MFC and your applications, is designed to accept a Boolean expression. The macro performs a test of the expression; if it evaluates to be non-zero, the function takes no action. If the expression evaluates to zero (in other words, if the expression is FALSE), the macro produces a dialog like this one:

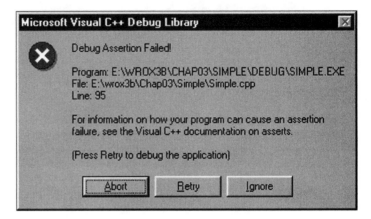

The box features three buttons. <u>A</u>bort lets you bail out of your application on the spot. You can press <u>I</u>gnore to let the application return from the ASSERT() call and carry on. If you press <u>R</u>etry, though, you'll be tossed back into the debugger and allowed to trace through your code to see what caused the assertion.

Tracing Assertions

The <u>R</u>etry choice in the assertion dialog box will either switch to the debugger, if you are running the application from there, or start up a new instance of Microsoft Visual Studio and load in the source code. Pressing this button will cause the debugger to execute a software breakpoint instruction, which will, in turn, cause the debugger to react as if a breakpoint were set deep in the MFC code.

The code which brings up the assertion dialog will be displayed and structured so that you can easily trace the function calls that actually generated the assert. Use the Step Out command in the <u>D</u>ebug menu to do to this or, if you find it more convenient, press *Shift+F11* or the Step Out button in the debug toolbar. The first thing that I usually look for when bouncing back into the application is the call stack; this will show me which function called which other function and with what parameters. It almost always provides enough clues to help me diagnose the problem.

Some naive programmers use assignments in ASSERT() statements to do work. They might code things like this:

```
// allocate a new box car
ASSERT(NULL != (pNewCar = new CBoxCar));
// add it to the train
ASSERT(TRUE == (pMyTrain->AddCar(pNewCar)));
```

This code will work just fine in debug builds, but will mysteriously fail miserably in release builds. The reason? The problem is that the ASSERT() macro has no effect in release mode builds. Not only does it not generate failure messages, it doesn't even evaluate the expression passed to it. After this code has been executed, pNewCar doesn't point at a new CBoxCar, nor has the AddCar() function been called! Watch out for things like this; it's a tempting trap to fall into, especially when you want to show off your cool 'assign and validate' trick.

If you *do* want to use 'assign and validate' tricks, use the VERIFY() macro instead of ASSERT(). This performs the same task as ASSERT() in the debug build, but in the release build the expression is still evaluated – it's just that the release build doesn't do anything with a value of zero.

To drive the point home, let's examine the MFC implementation of the ASSERT() macro:

```
#ifdef _DEBUG

// ...other code deleted for brevity...
#define ASSERT(f) \
    do \
    { \
    if (!(f) && AfxAssertFailedLine(THIS_FILE, __LINE__)) \
        AfxDebugBreak(); \
    } while (0)

// ...other code deleted for brevity...
#else    // _DEBUG

// ...other code deleted for brevity...
#define ASSERT(f)          ((void)0)

// ...other code deleted for brevity...
#endif
```

As you can see, the definition of the ASSERT() macro is dependent on the presence of the _DEBUG preprocessor symbol. If the symbol is present, the macro expands to a tiny do/while loop that really serves no purpose other than making the code emitted by the ASSERT() macro appear effectively like a single function statement. If the expression given to the macro evaluates to zero, the application will call AfxAssertFailedLine(). This function puts up a message box that explains the cause of the assertion and allows the user to halt the application, ignore the error, or bring it up in the debugger.

In a build without the _DEBUG symbol, the ASSERT() macro evaluates to zero, which the compiler will discard as it has no semantic meaning in the operation of the program. The expression supplied to the macro does *not* become part of the code emitted by the compiler for the application. But it also means that the expression inside the ASSERT() macro is not evaluated in a release build of your application. In the next section, about debug builds, I'll examine some foolish ASSERT() usage that can get you into real trouble.

Commenting Your Code

If the failed assertion came from your code, you know better than anyone else what the assertion means. I suggest that you carefully comment your assertions, so that even months later you can remember what happened. However, if the assertion occurs in MFC, it might take a little while longer to figure out what happened. MFC assertions are all about defensive programming – they protect the work that MFC performs internally by checking that the objects, pointers and values are valid for that particular operation.

Understanding Debug Builds

I've tossed about a couple of phrases in this chapter that deserve some more attention. The terms **debug build** and **release build** are very important because they strongly affect the way your application behaves. I should first point out, though, that builds are exactly what you make them. The terms, formally, really mean nothing very specific – debug builds are used by developers and should never be widely redistributed to customers, while release builds are essential for performance tuning and are always provided to customers.

By convention, these terms, when applied to an MFC project, mean some more specific things; but even these are only loosely defined. To enable all the debugging support I've just discussed, the preprocessor symbol _DEBUG must be defined when the MFC headers are processed by the compiler. If you're making a release build, you shouldn't define the _DEBUG symbol; define the _NDEBUG symbol instead.

When you've defined the _DEBUG symbol, the MFC header files automatically instruct the linker to use a special version of MFC that has been built with the debugging support I've discussed in this section. If, for example, you leak an MFC object in such a build, MFC will provide dump information about this object. The additional debugging code makes the MFC libraries considerably larger, and building with the _DEBUG symbol set will therefore make your own program much, much larger.

It's imperative to understand that the compiler doesn't do anything special for debug builds. The compiler itself doesn't really understand what a debug build or a release build is; it knows to provide you with symbolic information when you ask it to, and the compiler might process more special code when it sees the _DEBUG preprocessor symbol go by. But the compiler doesn't automatically produce code to initialize uninitialized variables in debug builds, and doesn't do any other extra work itself either. It still only does exactly what you tell it to do. It's really the AppWizard that defines exactly what 'debug build' means, and the AppWizard might change that definition over time. It certainly uses different options depending on exactly what kind of project you're building.

The symbolic information that the compiler and linker provide lets the debugger know, at runtime, what source code was used to build what parts of the object code you're actually debugging. Information about each symbol and data type your program uses is also produced, and makes a substantial contribution to your application's executable image size. This information is normally discarded in release builds, but if you should need to, you can modify the parameters offered to the compiler so that it emits symbolic information for your program even when you've otherwise requested a release build. You might choose to do this if you need to fix a problem that appears in release builds of your program, but not in debug builds.

Such problems, while frustrating and elusive, are nearly always the fault of the programmer. In a release build, the compiler is normally instructed to optimize the code it produces very aggressively, while in a debug build it's usually instructed to perform no optimization whatsoever. It's possible that a bug in the compiler is causing it to produce bad code, but this situation is very rare. On the other hand, since the compiler is using heavily optimized code and the libraries used in a release build do very little checking of parameters, non-debug builds may seem to behave a little differently in borderline cases – and those borderline cases are almost always caused by questionable coding practices by the user of the library. In a build with the _DEBUG flag set, assertions are used to trap parameters or variables that have questionable values.

Writing code that works in a debug build but not in a release build is really pretty easy to do. You might forget, for example, that the ASSERT() macro doesn't emit any code in a release build and code something like this:

```
LPTSTR pstrSport;
ASSERT((pstrSport = (LPTSTR) malloc(100)) != NULL);
_tcscpy(pstrSport, _T("Hockey"));
```

While this'll be just fine in a debug build, you'll get into deep trouble in a release build; the value of pstrSport isn't initialized, since the highlighted line causes the compiler to emit no code at all when _DEBUG isn't defined! There are subtler ways to get in trouble, so you should take care to build and test release versions of your code occasionally, even when your final ship date is still far in the future.

Even subtler problems can crop up when the problem you've caused involves dynamically allocated memory or objects. Perhaps, in the debug build, the versions of the memory allocation routines you use don't notice a problem that you've caused by writing to memory you don't own. The retail version of the memory manager might expose the problem you've caused, as its more efficient routines end up using slightly different rules for allocating and releasing memory.

You can use the Configurations... command in the Build menu of the IDE to add a new build configuration to your project workspace. In the resulting dialog, pressing the Add... button takes you to this dialog, which allows you to name the new configuration you will create:

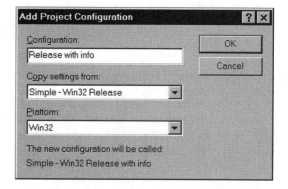

You can see that I named the configuration Release with info, which is easy enough for me to remember. You can choose your own name, of course. It's easiest to select the release configuration of your application in the Copy settings from drop down list. The Platform drop down will, of course, be the target platform — you'll only need to worry about this if your project targets multiple platforms. Once you click OK to dismiss the Add Project Configuration dialog, you'll be back to the Configurations dialog. Once you've checked your new configuration is in the tree control, you can click Close to dismiss this dialog as well.

To get debug information into your newly-created configuration, you've only got to perform a couple more steps, and both involve the Project Settings dialog. Select your new configuration in the Settings For drop down list, and click on the C/C++ tab. Make sure Program Database is selected in the Debug info drop-down. This change forces the compiler to provide debugging information that lets the debugger know what data types and source code your program is executing.

Finally, you can click in the Link tab in the Project Settings dialog. Here, check the Generate debug info box in the General category of this tab. While asking the compiler to produce debug information gets the data into your .obj files, you still need to ask the linker to get the final, runtime debugging information that the debugger will actually use.

Other Debug Runtime Changes

It's possible that the operating system may realize that you've run your program under a debugger and decide to initialize memory that you request, or automatically clean up unclosed handles that your program would otherwise leak. But remember that the compiler is really doing its best to do *exactly* what you tell it to do — even if what you tell it to do is wrong. When I ride my motorcycle, it does exactly what I tell it to do as well. Incidents of mechanical failure do arise, but they're very rare; crashing a motorcycle is far more frequently caused by a problem with the rider.

127

This said, let's turn our focus back to features that exist in your application whether you've built for debugging or not.

Serialization

Programmers commonly find it necessary to make objects **persistent** in some way; that is, to initialize them from storage or to write them to storage for recovery at a later date. If you design your application to use objects to represent data or states internally within your application, you'll probably find that serialization is a very convenient method for writing and reading data files for your application to and from disk.

Serialization is implemented for most MFC classes, and is done so by the `CObject::Serialize()` function. MFC implements serialization for objects that will normally be persisted. The declaration for `Serialize()` looks like this:

```
virtual void Serialize(CArchive& ar);
```

To realize the serialization functionality in an object, you must first derive it from `CObject`. This derives the serialization functions for your object from the base code in `CObject`. You can then invoke the MFC-supplied `DECLARE_SERIAL()` macro in the declaration of your class. This macro provides prototypes for the serialization functions, as well as a special extraction operator implementation for your class. That extraction operator is *not* used to serialize the data in your class; instead, it's provided so that MFC can properly recover the class name and the raw class data from the persistent stream when your application is running.

The IMPLEMENT_SERIAL() Macro

Having done this, you must use the `IMPLEMENT_SERIAL()` macro in your implementation file. Like the other `IMPLEMENT_` and `DECLARE_` macros, the `IMPLEMENT_SERIAL()` needs to be part of the implementation of your class, while the `DECLARE_SERIAL()` macro needs to be a part of your class definition. You'll probably want to put the `IMPLEMENT_SERIAL()` macro in your `.cpp` implementation file and the `DECLARE_SERIAL()` invocation in the header file that declares your class.

The `DECLARE_SERIAL()` macro only accepts the name of your class as a parameter, but the `IMPLEMENT_SERIAL()` macro is a little more complicated. It takes three parameters: the name of the class you are declaring to be serializable, the name of its base class and a **schema number**. The schema number is a stamp that can be used to identify the version of the object that created the serialized information. The schema is a `UINT`, and you can use any value valid for the range of `UINT`s, except `-1`, as this is used internally by MFC.

A declaration for a serializable class might look like this:

```
class CClient : public CObject
{
public:
    // declare serial based on our parent class - in this case, CObject
    DECLARE_SERIAL(CClient)
    void Serialize(CArchive& ar);
```

```
private:
    CString    m_Address;
    long       m_IDnumber;
    CString    m_Name;

    // maybe other stuff here...
};
```

The Serialize() Function

The last step is to implement a `Serialize()` function. The parameter passed to `Serialize()`, a reference to a `CArchive` object, provides a context for the function. By calling `Serialize()`, you're preparing the `CArchive` object for reading from or writing to the implemented object, allowing it to save or restore its state. You must override `Serialize()` for each class that you intend to serialize. The overridden `Serialize()` must first call the `Serialize()` function of its base class. By convention, this is done before you serialize the data in your class.

You can use `CArchive::IsLoading()` or `CArchive::IsStoring()` to determine whether the archive is loading or storing. A serialization implementation might look like this:

```
#define CCLIENT_SCHEME    0x100

// Note — no semicolon for IMPLEMENT_SERIAL
IMPLEMENT_SERIAL(CClient, CObject, CCLIENT_SCHEME)

void CClient::Serialize(CArchive& ar)
{
    // Call base class function first
    // Base class is CObject for us...
    CObject::Serialize(ar);

    // Now do the stuff for our specific class
    if(ar.IsStoring())
    {
        ar << m_Name << m_IDnumber;
        ar << m_Address;
    }
    else
    {
        ar >> m_Name >> m_IDnumber;
        ar >> m_Address;
    }
}
```

Here, I've defined an additional macro that carries the schema number for my serialization. If you're pedantic about programming style, you might want to have this symbol around. Since the value isn't used anywhere else in the application outside of the `IMPLEMENT_SERIAL()` invocation, the extra symbol is of dubious value and probably doesn't amount to much more than eye candy.

Chapter 4 examines in detail the use of serialization to load and store data for a `CDocument` object in a realistic application. However, each class contained by that document implements a function like the one shown here. Since every serializable object has its own serialization code, any higher level object can be delegated to by the serialization code in the contained objects.

The extraction and insertion operators for CArchive allow you to serialize objects simply by using the appropriate operator. If CClient contained an instance of some class named CProposal, the Serialize() implementation of CClient would serialize proposal objects by calling the Serialize() member function of the class. Assuming m_pProposal points at an object of a CObject-derived class, this code is just fine:

```
if (ar.IsStoring())
    ar << (CObject*)m_pProposal;
else
    ar >> (CObject*&)m_pProposal;
```

We have to cast down to CObject in order to match the operator that MFC expects to use. The second cast goes to a reference to a pointer to a CObject, and has the framework both allocate the in-memory storage for the object *and* serialize the object.

The extraction and insertion operators for the CArchive class also support these data types:

CObject*	WORD	COleDateTime
LONG	double	COleDateTimeSpan
DWORD	float	COleVariant
BYTE	int	COleCurrency
short	char	CString&

For other data types, you'll need either to write your own overload, develop a macro that uses implemented types to correctly (and portably!) read from and write to the unsupported types, or perform a cast that effectively utilizes the existing overloads.

To drive home the example, let's imagine that CClient has three members: a pointer to a m_pProposal, an integer, and a double. A properly coded Serialize() member for the class might look like this:

```
void CClient::Serialize(CArchive& ar)
{
    m_pProposal->Serialize(ar);
    if (ar.IsStoring())
    {
        ar << m_dMyDouble;
        ar << m_dMyInteger;
    }
    else
    {
        ar >> m_dMyDouble;
        ar >> m_dMyInteger;
    }
}
```

Note that I call `Serialize()` directly on the `m_pProposal` object outside of the test for `IsStoring()`. This is simply because `CProposal::Serialize()` will have its own check for `IsStoring()` – I can pass along the `CArchive` object to get the necessary work done, and that's all there is to it. By calling `Serialize()` on the `m_pProposal` object, I'm indicating that I already have an allocated object, pointed to by `m_pProposal`. Serializing it simply stores it or loads it – it doesn't actually create or destroy the object. If I want the serialization code to also create the object, I'd use the insertion and extraction operators on the `CObject` pointer directly, as in the code fragment before this one.

The VERSIONABLE_SCHEMA Macro

As I have already indicated, you can use a schema number in the `IMPLEMENT_SERIAL()` macro to indicate the version of the data you are reading or writing. If the schema number of the file you are trying to read doesn't match that supplied in the macro, then MFC asserts. This obviously precludes you from reading in earlier versions of your data.

If you're planning to provide backward compatibility in your application so that it can read information written by previous versions, you should use the macro `VERSIONABLE_SCHEMA`, which you do by ORing it with the schema number in the `IMPLEMENT_SERIAL()` macro. You would then need to get the schema number of the data being read in within the `Serialize()` function. To retrieve the schema number, use the `GetObjectSchema()` function of the archive object, which returns the schema number of the object. If I apply schema-checking code to `CClient`, the serialization code then becomes:

```
IMPLEMENT_SERIAL(CClient, CObject, VERSIONABLE_SCHEMA|0x200)

void CClient::Serialize(CArchive& ar)
{
    // call base class function first - base class is CObject for us...
    CObject::Serialize(ar);

    // now do the stuff for our specific class
    if(ar.IsStoring())
    {
        ar << m_Title << m_Name << m_IDnumber;
        ar << m_Address;
        ar << m_CurrentDebt;
    }
    else
    {
        UINT nVersion = ar.GetObjectSchema();
        switch (nVersion)
        {
          case -1:
             // Unknown version number so don't know how to load
             break;
          case 0x100:
             // Old version...
             ar >> m_Name >> m_IDnumber;
             ar >> m_Address;
             // Give new members some default values
             m_Title = "";
             m_CurrentDebt = 0.0;
             break;
```

```
        case 0x200:
            // New version...
            ar >> m_Title >> m_Name >> m_IDnumber;
            ar >> m_Address;
            ar >> m_CurrentDebt;
            break;
        default:
            // Even newer version? But still don't
            // know how to handle
            break;
    }
}
}
```

In the default *case, you might want to inform your user that the file format being read isn't recognized.*

Storing the data is the same as always; MFC takes care of recording the schema number of the object for us. As you can see, I store the major version number in the high byte, and the minor version in the low byte of the UINT called nVersion. As such, I'm using the number 0x0200 to represent version 2.0 of my file format. This nifty little mechanism (also used by Windows itself) makes it trivial to store the version number, and very easy to compare one version number with another.

When I read the serialized data, on the other hand, I'm obliged to check and see what's going on. For this example, I'm assuming that *all* versions of my application have m_Name, m_IDnumber and m_Address. Version 2.0 of my application added m_Title and m_CurrentDebt. I can check the version number first and see if it indicates that the data stream will have those values. The important thing to remember is that you'll need to do something reasonable if the values aren't there. In my example, I've chosen to initialize the values with some sensible defaults, which are presumably appropriate for my application.

There would be other alternatives, depending on what my application was up to. For example, I might set a flag that says the data came from an old file. If I wanted to, I could use that flag when writing, so the user would be able to write an old file and maintain compatibility with folks who haven't upgraded yet.

Unfortunately, the VERSIONABLE_SCHEMA mechanism in MFC has been broken for some time. Even in MFC 6.0, which is in the Visual C++ 6.0 box, the mechanism doesn't provide for the graceful degradation of all objects stored in the archive. That is, the objects that read a file format should be able to handle older or newer file formats and do something reasonable in reaction to having too much data or not enough. As such, if you want to implement a robust mechanism that allows you to keep your objects serialized in a very version-compatible manner, you'll need to do so by implementing some of your own code. The shortcoming in MFC's design in this area is that only a single object knows the schema that was used to write it. If you're serializing more than one object, you'll need to decorate each and every one carefully with its own schema, and decide what to do in each and every object's Serialize() implementation, based on the schema found when retrieving data from the archive.

Run-time Type Information

The Microsoft Foundation Classes implement **run-time type information** through the CObject class. Run-time type information provides your code with the ability to discern the type of an object at run-time, given a pointer to any class in the hierarchy of that object. This can be very useful when handling different derived classes with the same code, and it can also be used as a validation check, making sure that code that receives a pointer to an object actually receives a pointer to the correct object type.

This mechanism is *not* ANSI-standard C++. In fact, in Visual C++, this information is provided by MFC's CObject class and not by the C++ compiler itself. That means that if you don't use MFC or don't base your objects on some CObject-derived class, you'll find that those objects don't support MFC's brand of run-time type information.

Of course, CObject's run-time type information is not the only type of run-time type information support provided by Visual C++. As of version 4.0, the compiler also supports ANSI standard C++ run-time type information. ANSI run-time type information is not normally generated, so if you want to use it you need to check the Enable Run-Time Type Information (RTTI) *checkbox, which turns on the* /GR *compiler option. The setting can be found under the* C++ Language *category on the* C/C++ *tab of the* Project Settings *dialog. MFC itself is built with C++ run-time type information, so you can use ANSI C++ RTTI against any class MFC provides for you. I'll contrast ANSI and MFC type information it at the end of this section.*

Implementing the MFC Run-time Type Information Option

Providing a class with run-time type information is optional; if you don't need it, you can derive a class from CObject without including it. If you wish to endow a class in your code with run-time type information, you should use the DECLARE_DYNAMIC() macro like this:

```
DECLARE_DYNAMIC(CClassName)
```

CClassName is, of course, the name of the class that you are declaring. If you want to use its features, you should place a call to the macro in the class declaration, just as I did with DECLARE_SERIAL() earlier in the chapter. DECLARE_DYNAMIC() declares a small data structure and an associated function, which are used by other run-time type information constructs. To complete the installation of run-time type information in your class, you also need to use the:

```
IMPLEMENT_DYNAMIC(CClassName, CBaseClassName)
```

macro somewhere in the implementation file for your class. As with the DECLARE_MESSAGE_MAP() and IMPLEMENT_MESSAGE_MAP() macros we saw earlier, you should only compile the IMPLEMENT_DYNAMIC() macro once in your application for any given class. As a result, it's common practice to use DECLARE_ macros in the header that will declare your class, and invoke the IMPLEMENT_ macros in the actual .cpp file that implements the class.

> Note that the macro pairs **DECLARE_DYNCREATE()** and **IMPLEMENT_DYNCREATE()**, **DECLARE_SERIAL()** and **IMPLEMENT_SERIAL()** also generate the run-time type information (RTTI). The table overleaf gives details of what each of the macro pairs can achieve:

Macro Pair	Run-time Type Information	Dynamically Creatable	Capable of Serialization
none (plain CObject)	no	no	no
*_DYNAMIC()	yes	no	no
*_DYNCREATE()	yes	yes	no
*_SERIAL()	yes	yes	yes

Deriving Derivatives

Once you've used these macros to enable run-time class information for your class, you can determine whether a given object belongs to or is derived from a specified class. For example, you might implement an application that has a simple class hierarchy consisting of the base class CClient. From this, you might derive some specialized types of clients; maybe you have CInsuranceClients, CBrokerageClients, CPlanningClients and CVentureCapitalClients. Most likely, since these classes all represent clients, you'll derive each from CClient.

However, if you wish to write a single function that performs some operation on different types of CClient-derived objects, you may wish to know exactly what type of CClient you are handling. You might code a routine such as this:

```
double CClient::ServiceCost(CClient *pcClient)
{
    double dCharge = 0.0;

    if (pcClient->IsKindOf(RUNTIME_CLASS(CPlanningClient)))
    {
        CPlanningClient* pPlanningClient;
        pPlanningClient = (CPlanningClient *) pcClient;
        dCharge += pPlanningClient->EvaluateEstateValue();
    }
    dCharge += pcClient->AssessFee();
}
```

This simple function, which calculates the cost of a service for a given client, accepts a pointer to an object of type CClient. Semantically, this may actually be a pointer to a plain CClient object, or it may be a pointer to any of the CClient types I've discussed. If I'm doing work for a CPlanningClient, I might want to opportunistically add a fee based on the value of the client's actual portfolio. Since I can only refer to the data needed to calculate the fee if pcClient is pointing at a CPlanningClient object, I need to check what kind of client I'm working with.

Of course, I'm using this example just to get my point across. In a real application, you'd hope to encapsulate the computation code into the actual objects themselves – CPlanningClient and CClient should have an AssessFee() that handles the extra work. Realistically, such an ideal design isn't always possible, so you might need RTTI to bail yourself out.

The IsKindOf() Function

The condition in the `if` statement performs this check for us; it uses the `IsKindOf()` function from `CObject` to do it. The function accepts a pointer to a run-time type information structure. Since I want to perform the check against a constant class type, I can use the `RUNTIME_CLASS()` macro. If the object that `pcClient` points to is an instance of the same class as (or an instance of a subclass of) the object I'm checking for, the `IsKindOf()` function returns `TRUE`.

`RUNTIME_CLASS()` returns a pointer to the `CRuntimeClass` structure that describes a given class. I'll describe `CRuntimeClass` in the next section.

Only if the `IsKindOf()` test is `TRUE` is it safe to make the cast of `pcClient` from a pointer to a `CClient` to a pointer to `CPlanningClient`. If you wish, you can safeguard your functions which accept pointers to classes in your code by using the `IsKindOf()` function in an `ASSERT()` macro. For instance, I may decide to protect our `ServiceCost()` function by using a construct like this:

```
ASSERT(pcClient->IsKindOf(RUNTIME_CLASS(CClient)));
```

You should notice particularly that I check for the root class in the `ASSERT`. If the `ServiceCost()` function was passed a pointer to some unusable class of object, or even to some arbitrary memory, the `IsKindOf()` function would be able to trap this problem and trigger the `ASSERT()` macro – assuming, of course, that you don't generate an access violation first. If `IsKindOf()` is `NULL`, for instance, you'll get an access violation before you get an assertion.

Since the check is enclosed in an `ASSERT()` macro, it only affects debug builds of your application. Internally, MFC uses this technique to make applications easier to debug. If you pass the wrong class of object to an MFC function, you're almost guaranteed to trip an `ASSERT()` dialog box. This is one of the main contributors to the large size of MFC's debug builds. Not only does each `ASSERT()` generate more code, but it may also generate some error text to identify the exact line number and file name where the assertion occurred.

> Every member of the hierarchy here needs to have **DECLARE_DYNAMIC()** and **IMPLEMENT_DYNAMIC()** macro invocations in its definition. If I was interested in simply seeing run-time type information for **CClient** (to do a simple sanity check for the parameters of the function, for instance), I might only use the macros for the root class. A pointer to any derivative of that class would return **TRUE** for **IsKindOf(RUNTIME_CLASS(CClient))**, but I couldn't perform a specific check for any subclass of **CClient**.

About CRuntimeClass

I mentioned the `CRuntimeClass` structure a few lines ago, but I didn't provide much detail about it. `CRuntimeClass` is provided by MFC to identify a particular class at runtime without actually naming the class. `CRuntimeClass` is similar to, but much more powerful than, the `type_info` class suggested by the ANSI C++ Standards Committee. On the other hand, once you've asked the compiler to provide ANSI type information, you need do nothing else while `CObject` requires that you add a couple of macros to your declaration and implementation in order to assure the type information is available.

You can get a pointer to the CRuntimeClass that describes a particular class by using the RUNTIME_CLASS() macro. We'll use this macro in many places throughout our investigation of MFC. The heaviest use of the structure comes in the creation of a document template; the document template constructor takes pointers to the runtime class information for the view, the document, and the frame window type that the document template will be associating.

Given the pointer to a particular CRuntimeClass object, the most interesting task you can perform is the creation of an object of the class. The code:

```
CRuntimeClass* pClass = RUNTIME_CLASS(CMyObject);
CMyObject* pObject = (pClass->m_pfnCreateObject)();
```

results in the creation of a CMyObject instance. The highlighted line ends up allocating the memory needed by the object and then calling the default constructor for the object. There's no way to use this mechanism to call any other constructor – and that offers some insight into the real reason that so many MFC classes have a two-step construction mechanism. The syntax of the highlighted line looks a little goofy, by the way, because it's dereferencing a pointer to a function; if you're not familiar with pointers to functions, check a good book on C or C++.

The technique of using m_pfnCreateObject to instantiate a new object seems rather convoluted. After all, this code:

```
CMyObject* pObject = new CMyObject;
```

seems much more direct. Of course, it *is* more direct, but it's also very limited; what if you wanted to write a function that could create an object and get it to do some work, but didn't know the exact class of object to be created until runtime?

If you need to write such a function, you can accept a pointer to a CRuntimeClass object, and that object will describe the class you'd like to have your function create. Your function might return a pointer to the new object, and will probably manipulate pointers to the object too. Generally speaking, you'll apply this technique to base classes. That is, in these examples, maybe CMyObject serves as a base class for CMySpecialObject and CMySimpleObject and CMyAmazingObject. I know I can use a pointer to CMyObject, though, since it's a safe cast away from the other related classes.

Careful Casting

As we've seen, run-time type information is used by many programmers to identify the type of an object at runtime. (Water ballet: it's ballet in the water.) Run-time type information lets you make sure that polymorphic classes that you're referencing via pointers really are objects of the type you expect to handle.

You've seen how to access the run-time type information that's built into any CObject-derived class that has used the DECLARE_DYNCREATE() macro and can be accessed with the IsKindOf() function, but there are also some convenient macros which use the same information to make safe type casting much easier.

STATIC_DOWNCAST()

The STATIC_DOWNCAST() macro allows you to cast a pointer to an object of one type to a pointer to an object of a related type. In non-debug builds, this macro will simply perform the cast you request. In debug builds, the macro will ASSERT() if the pointer is NULL or if the cast is illegal.

You might cast a CView pointer to a pointer to a CScrollView by coding something like this:

```
// Got CView* pView from somewhere else
CScrollView* pScroll;
pScroll = STATIC_DOWNCAST(CScrollView, pView);
```

If, in a debug build, pView points at something that isn't a CScrollView, then the code will make an assertion message. If pView points at something that *is* a CScrollView, the pointer will be cast properly and the code will execute quietly.

The STATIC_DOWNCAST() macro is similar to the static_cast<> operator introduced by the ANSI C++ standard document, but differs in a couple of key areas. First, STATIC_DOWNCAST() works only on classes derived from the MFC class CObject which have runtime type information, while static_cast<> works on any data type you can find. Furthermore, in debug builds, STATIC_DOWNCAST() will cause an ASSERT message to be posted in a _DEBUG build when used with an invalid cast, while static_cast<> fails only at compile time.

The word **downcast** means that the cast forces the type of the pointer down the class hierarchy to a deeper level of inheritance.

DYNAMIC_DOWNCAST()

The DYNAMIC_DOWNCAST() macro, on the other hand, behaves the same way in both debug and release builds. If the cast is legal, it will be made and nobody will notice. If the input pointer is NULL or the cast isn't legal, the macro will return NULL.

This is a useful macro for situations where your cast will be performed against a parameter that might legally be NULL, or might legally be a pointer to a different type of object.

DYNAMIC_DOWNCAST() has essentially the same effect as the standard ANSI C++ operator dynamic_cast<>, save for a couple of differences which, as you might expect, are similar to those between STATIC_DOWNCAST() and static_cast<>. For example, DYNAMIC_DOWNCAST() only works with CObject-derived classes that have runtime type information, while the dynamic_cast<> operator works for any old type – including reference types.

ASSERT_KINDOF()

The ASSERT_KINDOF() macro is useful for asserting that a pointer to an object is actually a pointer to an object of the correct type. You might use this macro to check pointers to functions that you've implemented. Maybe you've written a function that accepts a pointer to a CView object, for instance. You could use the IsKindOf() function I described before to make sure this pointer is really a pointer to an object of a type you can handle. That code would look like this:

```
ASSERT(pMyView->IsKindOf(RUNTIME_CLASS(CView)));
```

It's a lot easier (and a lot more readable) to use the ASSERT_KINDOF() macro. The above line of code becomes simply:

```
ASSERT_KINDOF(CView, pMyView);
```

As you can see, the first parameter is the class name and the second parameter is a pointer to the object that you'd like to test. Like all ASSERT() macros, the ASSERT_KINDOF() macro has no effect in release builds; it's removed from your code and takes up no space.

Real Run-time Type Information Support

If you've read much about C++, you probably know that a standard defining the C++ language supports the implementation of run-time type information. Despite this, throughout the chapter I've prattled on only about MFC's support for run-time type information, which might appear a bit narrow-minded. I'll try to justify my decision.

MFC uses its own brand of run-time type information for two reasons. First, the heritage of MFC involves Microsoft's compilers. Version 4.0 of Visual C++ was the first version of the development system to ship a compiler supporting the standard for RTTI in the C++ language. Since lots of code was (and is) written using MFC, Microsoft isn't interested in breaking it all by adopting a different method of type information management.

The second reason is that run-time type information, as suggested by the standard in its present state, isn't really a great form of class *identification*. You can use the C++ typeid() operator (which is part of the ANSI standard for the C++ language, and implemented by Visual C++) to get type information that describes a class. That information actually ends up being the name of the class – you can get the compiler to give you the internal 'decorated' representation of the name, or the real, source code class name. The typeid() operator returns a reference to an object of type type_info – which is the data type that the ANSI C++ standard suggests the typeid() function ends up returning. A type_info object has barely enough information in it to describe the type of a particular object. This simple program:

```
#include <iostream.h>
#include <typeinfo.h>

class CMyClass
{
public:
    CMyClass() { };
    ~CMyClass() { };
};

void main()
{
    const type_info& ti = typeid(CMyClass);
    cout << ti.name() << "\n";
    cout << ti.raw_name() << "\n";

    return;
}
```

would generate this output:

```
class CMyClass
.?AVCMyClass@@
```

The strings aren't very useful; MFC can't use this information to identify serialized data for particular types efficiently, like it could with the CRuntimeClass information. Also, the strings aren't compatible across platforms, which would ruin portability for people who want to read files compiled with Visual C++ on platforms other than Intel. Unfortunately, until the standard provides for such a mechanism, MFC will continue to use its own. If the language ever provides for runtime class information that MFC can use, the MFC development team will examine the standard and consider embracing it if it provides a clear benefit over the existing mechanism.

Your Own Classes and CObject

If you create your own classes in an MFC application, you should try to find a natural point in the MFC hierarchy from which to 'hang' the new class you're creating. When you create an application with AppWizard, it will derive your application-specific classes from the most appropriate MFC classes, effectively adding them to the hierarchy. When you create your own classes, or indeed class hierarchies, you should decide carefully which base class to use for your new class or classes.

If you don't use an MFC base class, you forgo all of the functionality provided by CObject – quite a substantial loss. (Well, this isn't strictly true because not *all* MFC classes are themselves derived from CObject in the first place, but most of the time, CObject is lurking somewhere in the class' genealogy.) If you use an inappropriate MFC class, you might have a hard time re-implementing functionality that you could have had for free if you had used a more appropriate one. This exercise will lead to nothing more than frustration as you force-fit the pieces of your application together. However, be warned; deriving your class in this way will mean that the code is largely unusable outside of MFC and can unnecessarily bloat the size of your class and make it more complicated than it need be.

As we examine more advanced applications through the balance of this book, I'll talk about the important considerations you'll need to make when choosing a base class from those implemented by MFC. Many MFC classes are designed to be used only as base classes; for example, as I've already mentioned, you'll always use the CWinApp class through inheritance. Many MFC classes (from little ones like CObject to monsters like CWinApp) are not *technically* abstract base classes but are of no practical use without some added functionality.

The Big Picture: A New Life

Now that you understand what CWinApp is doing for your application, how does it really work? Back at the beginning of the chapter, I drew your attention to Simple.h, which contains the class definition for CSimpleApp. Somehow, an instance of this class must be created so that your code will actually run. For the class truly to mimic reality and only exist when the application is running, it needs somehow to create itself automatically before your application is run, and exit only after the ride has completely come to a halt.

How can this be done? Simple: create a global instance of CSimpleApp. You'll find a declaration for an object called theApp in Simple.cpp. The declaration produced by AppWizard in Simple.cpp looks something like this:

```
/////////////////////////////////////////////////////////////////////////////
// The one and only CSimpleApp object

CSimpleApp theApp;
```

When your application loads, it comes into memory with all the globals declared in an initialized data segment. The actual values are stored in the executable image. The C++ language dictates that the first thing to happen is the construction of static objects. MFC has some internal, private, static objects, and their constructors are run first because they were specially declared to initialize first in MFC's source code. After MFC's static objects are initialized, the constructor for CSimpleApp runs.

It's worth pointing out how MFC forces its static objects to initialize early. It uses a #pragma called init_seg to cause the compiler to initialize some of its objects early. The sytax of the pragma is pretty simple. After the compiler sees the pragma, anything after it is initialized using the rules predicated by the pragma. For example, to have a static instance of CFoo initialize before *anything* else in the module, you might code:

```
#pragma init_seg(compiler)
CFoo myFoo;
```

The parameter to init_seg may be compiler, as we've used above. compiler objects initialize first, then lib and user objects.

Anyway, the constructor in your AppWizard-produced application does nothing by default. There are two reasons why it's best to leave the constructor without any code, or at least with as little code as possible:

> First, it's bad programming style to do any serious work in a global constructor. Of course, if you have some member variables in your CWinApp-derived class, it would be a great idea to initialize them here, but running off and allocating memory, or hitting a database or communications library (even to initialize them) is probably a bad idea; such work is best suited to CWinApp::InitInstance(). Even if the code throws an exception as it fails, there's nobody around to properly handle the exception and explain to the user what has gone wrong.

> The second reason is that the code you've written yourself isn't really running yet. Remember, the constructor for your static CWinApp object executes even before what you're used to thinking of as WinMain() is called!

Of course, I know you didn't code a WinMain(), but MFC supplied one for you, which it had to do because every GUI Windows program requires a WinMain(). The C Runtime Libraries actually provide the real implementation of your program's entry point, though. It's responsible for intializing the runtimes and then calling the function named WinMain(). Once WinMain() returns, the runtimes resume control and undo their initialization.

Some might balk at my assertion that constructors that throw exceptions are a bad idea, but it's true; they really are. The C++ Standard Committee has only recently nailed down the rules that pertain to an object that throws an exception as it's being constructed. This code, for example:

```
CFoo* pFoo = new CFoo(37);
```

where the `CFoo(int)` constructor ends up throwing an exception, has some interesting side-effects. Most notably, since `CFoo`'s constructor threw an exception, the memory that was allocated by the `new` operator isn't referenced by `pFoo` because the assignment doesn't happen until the call to `new` returns. Since the constructor throws an exception, the function never returns.

The ANSI committee mandated what happens in this case, and the newer compilers support the proper cleanup proposed by the committee. (For non-placement invocations of `operator new()`, Visual C++ 5.0 conforms to the standard and, as we investigated earlier in this chapter, VC++ 6.0 supports the standard's specification even for placement syntax usage.) Again, while a 'pure' object-oriented design is an amusing thing to pursue, developers really need to make sure that their language robustly supports such constructs before embarking on the trip.

This talk of constructors segues nicely into a related subject: **static objects**. (Well, it's actually a pretty crummy segue, but it'll be best for both of us if you concentrate on learning and try to refrain from commenting on my writing style.) In your MFC applications, you should be careful about declaring static objects. The C++ language doesn't guarantee any order for construction of the objects, although it *does* guarantee that they'll be constructed before the entry point for your application is called.

> *That the language guarantees no initialization order can be a problem; you may find that executing certain code in static constructors will make MFC unstable, or make your application unusable. For example, if code in one of your static constructors uses some features of MFC, you'll find that those calls will fail if MFC hasn't yet initialized itself, or if the CWinApp controlling your application hasn't yet been constructed. If you're dependent on a particular initiation order, it's completely up to you to enforce and maintain that order. I strongly recommend, at the very least, coding some ASSERTs that bring any problems to your attention immediately.*

The `CWinApp` class is designed to be constructed first. If you have other static MFC objects in your application, you'll find that they'll make calls to MFC when MFC isn't initialized. If they work, that's fine; if they don't work, they might end up trying to terminate an application that doesn't exist, or try to report an `ASSERT()` against an unknown application instance. Many classes won't have a problem. The collection classes, for example, aren't going to cause you much trouble if they're lying about globally. You'll also find no problem making static instances of `CString`, unless you need to make the `CString` use string resources. On the other hand, you'll almost *never* get away with using advanced user interface classes, like `CStatusBar`, or any of the database classes – these will get you into deep, deep trouble very quickly.

If you really need to fool with these kinds of things, you should spend some time with the source code for the C run-time libraries. It's on the product CD, and you can trace through it if you're using a debug build of the library and you've let the development environment know where it is. The interesting code is in files like `Crt0dat.c`, where you'll find routines like `_cinit()` and `_initterm()`. These implementation details are likely to change, so be careful. If the C run-time source scares you, you can hook up other methods of guaranteeing static object initialization. For example, you might use global ordinal variables that are manipulated by the constructors of the involved objects.

The WinMain() Function

MFC's `WinMain()` implementation is only called when all global static constructors are complete. Like all other `WinMain()` implementations, its responsibility is to get the program running. After setting up some internal variables, as well as getting MFC initialized, it calls the `CWinApp::InitApplication()` member function, which is a legacy of 16-bit MFC. You should override the default implementation of `InitApplication()`, which normally does nothing, with the code you need to initialize your application when it will be running as the first instance of itself. Remember to call `CWinApp::InitApplication()`, as MFC has some work to do as well.

In 16-bit versions of MFC, `InitApplication()` was called once when the program was first loaded. The same code would then be used to handle all instances of the application so subsequent instances didn't need to do any global re-initialization. In Win32 systems, this doesn't happen. Every application runs as if it is the only instance. Win32 programmers will realize that this means the `hPrevInstance` parameter to their `WinMain()` function is always `NULL`. (In fact, MFC's `WinMain()` doesn't even bother to check the value of `hPrevInstance`.) You'll find some code in Chapter 10 that suggests a mechanism for detecting a previously running instance of your program.

If you have old code that's hanging around inside your `InitApplication()` function, it's fine to leave it there. Remember though, that putting code into `InitApplication()` is really no different to putting code into `InitInstance()` – it's just that `InitApplication()` is called first.

You'll find notes in the Microsoft documentation that states the `InitApplication()` function is obsolete. Unfortuantely, the documentation tells only half of the truth as the meaning of the function has changed over the years but its value and usability have not. In the old, Win16-days, `InitApplication()` was intended to initialize an instance of your application. That is, it was called the first time your application was started, but not called when a subsequent instance of your application was started when one instance already existed in memory. Now, `InitApplication()` is *always* called each time your application is started.

InitInstance()

If you supply an `InitApplication()` function for your `CWinApp` class and it returns `FALSE`, your application will terminate, effectively canceling the load of your application. If you don't supply an `InitApplication()` routine, or if that routine returns `TRUE`, the MFC-supplied `WinMain()` will continue by calling `CWinApp::InitInstance()`. Again, the default implementation of this function does nothing but return `TRUE`, to let initialization progress successfully.

You can add an override for this function in your derived class (which is `CSimpleApp::InitInstance()` in our example) to perform any per-instance initialization your application needs. It's far more common to add code to this function than to `InitApplication()`. For example, you can allocate memory that each instance of your application needs, or you may need to load DLLs such as the one for SQL Server.

In our application, `CSimpleApp::InitInstance()` does several things. One of the first initialization tasks it completes is calling either `Enable3dControls()` or `Enable3dControlsStatic()` (depending on whether you are using statically or dynamically linked MFC) to turn on three-dimensional effects in the application's user interface. Then it makes a `LoadStdProfileSettings()` call to initialize the `.ini` file settings that MFC automatically manages for the application. These settings usually include the most recently used file list in the application's main File menu, but they can also extend to toolbar status information runs, allowing the user to preserve toolbar docking status between sessions.

MFC will maintain a handful of standard settings for you. Specifically, MFC will write out the most recently used file list and the number of pages the user has visible in the print preview for the application. When your application calls `CWinApp::ExitInstance()`, MFC calls `CWinApp::SaveStdProfileSettings()` to save that state. `SaveStdProfileSettings()` is, obviously, the inverse of the `LoadStdProfileSettings()` function I mentioned in the previous paragraph.

.INI Files and Registry Entries

Applications often store information that pertains to their global state – perhaps their configuration or options settings, or information about the last thing they did before the user shut them down. Back when dinosaurs (Dinosaur: a huge lizard with a 16-bit brain) roamed the Earth, this information was stored in `.ini` (short for 'initialization') files.

Applications had two choices. Either they could store information in a `.ini` file with their own name, privately tucking away their data (this was called a **private profile**), or they could store information in one of the Windows system initialization files, most notably `Win.ini` (this was called a **public profile**).

In Win32 systems, you can more efficiently write and read information to and from the **system registry**. The registry is a very well-organized data store with a hierarchical structure. On Windows NT, the registry is securable; you can make sure that nobody else can see your data. Even on Windows 95/98, the registry settings are easily made user-dependent. The settings you write for one user don't necessarily overwrite the settings that you might store for another.

To facilitate the development of applications that need to do this, MFC's `CWinApp` class has a couple of members that can come to your rescue. There's an `m_pszRegistryKey` member that holds a pointer to a copy of your application's registry key name. By default, this pointer is actually `NULL`.

Although it's `public`, you shouldn't change the `m_pszRegistryKey` member directly. Instead, you should use the `SetRegistryKey()` member of the `CWinApp` class to set the variable. Even then, you can't use this function to change your application's registry key *repeatedly*. `SetRegistryKey()` comes in two flavors: one that takes a `LPCTSTR` and another that takes a `UINT`. It will come as no surprise that the `LPCTSTR` version takes a pointer to the string you want to use. The `UINT` version, on the other hand, takes the ID of a string resource for use as the registry key.

You can store and retrieve data from the registry, or from your application's private profile, by using some `CWinApp` methods. There are six in all: two for binary blocks of data, two for integers and two for strings. One of each data type handles setting the value, while the other handles retrieving it. This is all pretty obvious from the function names:

```
BOOL GetProfileBinary(LPCTSTR lpszSection,
                LPCTSTR lpszEntry,
                LPBYTE* ppData,
                UINT* pBytes);

BOOL WriteProfileBinary(LPCTSTR lpszSection,
                LPCTSTR lpszEntry,
                LPBYTE pData,
                UINT nBytes);

UINT CWinApp::GetProfileInt(LPCTSTR lpszSection,
                    LPCTSTR lpszEntry,
                    int     nDefault);
```

Continued on Following Page

```
BOOL CWinApp::WriteProfileInt(LPCTSTR lpszSection,
                             LPCTSTR lpszEntry,
                             int     nValue);

CString CWinApp::GetProfileString(LPCTSTR lpszSection,
                                  LPCTSTR lpszEntry,
                                  LPCTSTR lpszDefault = NULL);

BOOL CWinApp::WriteProfileString(LPCTSTR lpszSection,
                                 LPCTSTR lpszEntry,
                                 LPCTSTR lpszValue);
```

The Get...() functions take a default parameter which will be returned if the value isn't found in the registry/file. If the default value *is* returned, it's also written to the registry/file. It's therefore a good idea to use a value that's either very meaningful or very recognizable for this parameter. If a value is found at the position specified by the other parameters, it is returned by the function.

The Write...() functions don't take a default, and they just return TRUE to indicate success or FALSE to indicate failure. If the function returns FALSE, there was a catastrophic error — at the very least, some mean user has taken privileges away from your application's .ini file or the registry keys it expected to write to, or maybe the user is absolutely, completely and totally out of disk space. On the other hand, if the function returns TRUE, you're home free.

The other parameters are a little more complicated. Remember that through these functions, MFC has to support both the registry and .ini files. If your m_pszRegistryKey pointer is still NULL, MFC will go after a .ini file. If your m_pszRegistryKey isn't NULL, calls to the above functions will touch registry keys instead.

In the former case, MFC will use the m_pszProfileName for the actual file. It will then use the lpszSection parameter for the section name and lpszEntry for the key name. So, if I make this call:

```
free(m_pszProfileName);
m_pszProfileName = _tcsdup(_T("MyTerm"));
WriteProfileString(_T("PROTOCOLS"), _T("CHECKSUM"), _T("CRC"));
```

the file named Myterm.ini in the Windows directory will contain this text:

[PROTOCOLS]
CHECKSUM=CRC

The _T() macro, which might be foreign to you, is described in Appendix B. If you want the .ini file to appear in any other directory, you must supply the full path in the m_pszProfileName variable. By default, m_pszProfileName is set to the name of the executable during CWinApp initialization.

Note that I called free() on the current m_pszProfileName member before assigning it. I do this because MFC, during its initialization, dynamically allocates memory for the m_pszProfileName member. MFC will later free that memory, so I allocate a copy of my string with _tcsdup() to avoid having MFC get sick as it shuts down. As described in Appendix B, _tcsdup() is a version of strdup() that works with TCHAR strings.

In the latter case, when you're working with the registry, m_pszRegistryKey should be set to, say, "WroxSoft", or whatever your company name is. MFC still pays attention to m_pszProfileName; it should still be something identifiable and concise (one or two words), but you don't have to worry about the normal DOS filename conventions. You could still set m_pszProfileName to "MyTerm", or you could use something like "My Terminal Program". If you make the same WriteProfileString() call, like this:

```
WriteProfileString(_T("PROTOCOLS"), _T("CHECKSUM"), _T("CRC"));
```

You'll end up creating a registry key like this:

    HKEY_CURRENT_USER\Software\WroxSoft\MyTerm\PROTOCOLS

and giving it a value named "CHECKSUM" with the data "CRC". The HKEY_CURRENT_USER\Software part of the key is automatically generated by MFC. Note that this is just a shade different from the way the .ini file version works; you might have expected something like this from the parameters I've described:

    HKEY_CURRENT_USER\Software\MyTerm\Protocols

but that's not the way MFC works. Since the key is written to the HKEY_CURRENT_USER root of the registry though, the setting will naturally be local to a single user. If someone else logs onto the system, their own user name will keep their settings for the program local to their sessions even if some other user runs the same program on the same machine.

I'm sorry if this section has been a bit of a struggle – just be thankful you're reading it and not writing it! The information is here in this chapter for two reasons. Firstly, these functions are a part of CWinApp and therefore a part of your application's framework. Secondly, it's inevitable that at some point you'll want to think about allowing your application to store persistent information outside of its documents and other user files. If you want to be a good Win32 citizen, you'll probably want to place a call to SetRegistryKey() in your application's InitInstance() implementation to make sure everything is targeted properly to the registry. On the other hand, if you want to make your application's configuration for one user speak for all users, or to facilitate some aspects of backup, you might think of using .ini files instead.

> *The other option is to use the HKEY_LOCAL_MACHINE hive for storage that is global to the users of the application. In this case, you would have to use the registry functions of the API. MFC only supports writing and reading strings and integers from and to registry keys – if you need to read or write any other data types, you'll need to call the registry APIs directly.*

Parsing the Command Line

After dealing with the profile settings, InitInstance() will create a **document template**, which is used to help the application manage its user interface and the data the user will work with while using the application. I'll describe document templates in Chapter 4, which discusses the document/view architecture. Once the template is out of the way, MFC gets to work parsing the command line. Your application receives a copy of the command line via a member variable in the CWinApp object. This member, m_lpCmdLine, is a pointer to the whole command line for your application. The string referenced by this parameter is *not* broken into separate arguments; it's exactly what the user provided on the command line.

If you need to examine the command line using the traditional C approach, by using `argc` and `argv`, you can do so by referencing `__argc` and `__argv`. These are global variables made available by the run-time libraries; they are *not* parameters to any function or members of any MFC class.

By convention, Windows applications support different command line options for advanced features; applications might support special options to facilitate drag-and-drop printing, DDE activation, or OLE functions. You can have MFC parse your command line and help with those features by using the `CCommandLineInfo` class. You'll need to tuck a `CCommandLineInfo` instance into your `CWinApp` object and call `CWinApp::ParseCommandLine()`, passing the `CCommandLineInfo` instance as your application starts – right from within your `InitInstance()` function. As you might hope, the AppWizard-generated code already does this for you.

You can use `CCommandLineInfo` in conjunction with your own parsing of the `__argv` or `m_lpCmdLine` strings, or you can derive your own class from `CCommandLineInfo`. You only need to override one `CCommandLineInfo` member function: `ParseParam()`. MFC will repeatedly call this function with each command-line parameter it finds; you can analyze the parameter yourself and set whatever flags you'd like, or you can call the base class implementation of the function to get the default behavior.

`ParseParam()` is pretty simple, though there are two overrides. Here are the definitions:

```
virtual void CCommandLineInfo::ParseParam(const TCHAR* lpszParam,
                                          BOOL     bFlag,
                                          BOOL     bLast);
#ifdef _UNICODE
virtual void CCommandLineInfo::ParseParam(const char* lpszParam,
                                          BOOL     bFlag,
                                          BOOL     bLast);
#endif
```

The first parameter, as you might guess, is a pointer to the parameter in question. Note that a `const TCHAR*` version is available in both Unicode and ANSI builds. The second override is present only in Unicode builds, and accepts a pointer to an ANSI string. Thus the parameter name you supply the function must be an ANSI string in ANSI builds, but can be a Unicode string or an ANSI string in a Unicode build.

If the parsing routine has noticed an option flag on it, that is, the argument began with a forward slash (/) or a minus (-), the character is stripped and `bFlag` is TRUE. If the passed flag is the last on the command line, `bLast` is TRUE. The default implementation of `ParseParam()` works with these options:

Option	Effect	**CCommandLineInfo Member Variable**
(no option)	New document	`m_nShellCommand = FileNew`
<filename>	Opens file	`m_strFileName = <filename>`
/p <filename>	Print file to the default printer	`m_nShellCommand = FilePrint` `m_strFileName = <filename>`

Option	Effect	CCommandLineInfo Member Variable
/pt <filename> <printer> <driver> <port>	Print file to a specific printer	m_nShellCommand = FilePrintTo m_strFileName = <filename> m_strPrinterName = <printer> m_strDriverName = <driver> m_strPortName = <port>
/dde	Begin serving a DDE session	m_nShellCommand = FileDDE
/automation	Start the application as an Automation server	m_bShowSplash = FALSE m_bRunAutomated = TRUE
/embedding	Start the application and prepare to serve an OLE object embedded in another application	m_bShowSplash = FALSE m_bRunEmbedded = TRUE
/unregister or /unregserver	Unregister entries that the application has made in the registry and delete any .ini files the application may have created	m_nShellCommand = AppUnregister

The implementation sets appropriate member variables of the CCommandLineInfo structure, as described above, to ensure that the rest of your application knows what's going on.

The default implementation of ParseParam() ends up calling ParseParamFlag() and ParseParamNotFlag(). ParseParamFlag() is called when the parameter does have a slash or minus sign, and ParseParamNotFlag() is called when the parameter isn't identifiable as a flag. You might find it slightly more convenient to override ParseParamFlag() or ParseParamNotFlag() if you're only interested in one type of command line argument.

Reacting to the Command Line

You're free to do whatever you want in your ParseParam() function. Normally, you'll just look at the parameter passed and set some flags in your application object or in your CCommandLineInfo-derived object so you can remember what options or modes the user specified later in your program, when it really matters. If you set flags in your CWinApp object, you can access them at any time by using AfxGetApp() to gain a pointer to a CWinApp; you'll need to cast it to a pointer to your application object. If you store flags in your CCommandLineInfo object, you'll probably want to make your CCommandLineInfo object global to make sure you can get at it from anywhere in your application. If you're a little more object-oriented than I am, you can make your CCommandLineInfo a member of your CWinApp and write a function to return the state of the options in the CCommandLineInfo object.

During your application's execution, you can react to your own parameters any way you'd like to. MFC, on the other hand, will implement much of its default handling for the application by calling ProcessShellCommand() from the application's InitInstance(). This function takes a reference to the CCommandLineInfo-derived object that contains information from the parsed command line. The whole section of code looks like this:

```
// ...other parts of the function

// Parse command line for standard shell commands, DDE, file open
CCommandLineInfo cmdInfo;
ParseCommandLine(cmdInfo);

// Dispatch commands specified on the command line
if (!ProcessShellCommand(cmdInfo))
    return FALSE;

// ...other parts of the function
```

`ProcessShellCommand()` has a look at the `m_nShellCommand` member of the command line and decides what to do. If `m_nShellCommand` is `FileOpen`, the function calls `OpenDocumentFile()`, passing the `m_strFileName` member of the referenced `CCommandLineInfo` object.

If `m_nShellCommand` is `FileNew`, MFC calls your `OnFileNew()` handler to create the new file. If `m_nShellCommand` indicates one of the printing commands, MFC opens the document and then performs the printing by sending an `ID_FILE_PRINT_DIRECT` command message to the main window of the application. This ends up printing the opened document because MFC implements a handler for this command that does the work for you.

Understanding this whole mechanism is important because you might want to tweak the way your application responds to the user. Even if you aren't interested in having your own command-line parameters, you might not always want a new file automatically created for your user when the application opens. To avoid this, make sure that `cmdInfo.m_nShellCommand` is not set to `FileNew` when your `InitInstance()` calls `ProcessShellCommand()`. The least invasive way to do this is simply to code:

```
if (cmdInfo.m_nShellCommand == CCommandLineInfo::FileNew)
    cmdInfo.m_nShellCommand = CCommandLineInfo::FileNothing;
```

before your call to `ProcessShellCommand()`. However, this code should only be used in an MDI application. SDI applications need the window produced by `CCommandLineInfo::FileNew`.

The `CWinApp` object, by the way, also carries an `m_nCmdShow` member, which is used as a parameter to a call to `ShowWindow()` later in AppWizard's default implementation of `InitInstance()`. The call to `ShowWindow()` is made on the main window of your application. This code exists there to make sure your application sizes itself appropriately for the work you've asked it to do on the command line. For example, if the application is serving an embedded OLE object or working to print a file, the user interface of the application should not be shown. `ProcessShellCommand()` implements this feature by setting m_nCmdShow to SW_HIDE.

Where's My WinMain()?

If you're an experienced Windows programmer, you might be interested in finding other things that are normally passed to your `WinMain()` function. As you know, MFC implements `WinMain()` for you, so you don't have to worry about it; however, it also makes the `WinMain()` parameters available to you. Like the command-line pointer, these values are managed as member variables of `CWinApp`. A typical `WinMain()` prototype might look like this:

```
int WINAPI WinMain(HINSTANCE  hInstance,
                   HINSTANCE  hPrevInstance,
                   LPSTR      lpCmdLine,
                   int        nCmdShow);
```

The `hInstance` parameter provides a handle to the executing instance of the application. It's pretty common for non-MFC Windows programs to save this value in a global variable so it can be used later to reference the currently running instance of the executable image. In an MFC application, the value is available as `m_hInstance` in the `CWinApp` object for the application. You can always get the value by calling `AfxGetInstanceHandle()`, which is a global function available anywhere.

As I mentioned in the discussion of the `InitApplication()` member, the `hPrevInstance` parameter is obsolete; it is always `NULL` in a Win32 application. If you're a Win16 programmer, you might miss the ability to use `hPrevInstance` to detect a previous instance of your application. Since the parameter is obsolete, you'll need to cook up some other method to find another instance of yourself. You might consider cognitive therapy, or you can check out the slick and lightweight approach I offer in Chapter 10, where I discuss multithreading.

`nCmdShow` (available as `CWinApp::m_nCmdShow`) is a parameter which indicates to the program how it is to present itself initially. The value is appropriate for passing to the `CWnd::ShowWindow()` function.

With all of this done, your application's main message loop is running and it's ready to interact with your user; this activity happens in `CWinApp::Run()`. The default implementation of this overridable function defers to the `CWinThread::Run()` implementation, which contains the **message pump** for your application.

MFC's Message Pump

The `CWinThread::Run()` function lets an application run. Our `Simple` application is structured to have a single thread, so only one `CWinThread` object (and therefore only one Windows thread) exists through the life of the application. The `CWinThread` object that exists in `Simple` is exactly the same object as the application's `CWinApp`-derived object, called `theApp`.

Like all message pumps, the `Run()` function implements a loop that dispatches messages that Windows places in the thread's (in this case, the application's) message queue. For normal messages, the function does some simple tracing for debug builds. You can use the MFC Tracer application in the Tools menu to modify the level of information provided by MFC's tracing facilities. The Main message pump, Main message dispatch and WM_COMMAND dispatch check boxes in the MFC Trace Options dialog will cause the `Run()` function to emit a diagnostic message to the debugger for every Windows message that is received and dispatched. I encourage you to try this, because it will help you realize just how busy MFC is.

PreTranslateMessage()

The business that `Run()` implements continues as the function then offers the message to the application by calling `CWinApp::PreTranslateMessage()`. This overridable function, which accepts a pointer to a `MSG` structure and returns a `BOOL`, allows you to let your application 'snoop' through the messages before they're actually translated and dispatched. If your `PreTranslateMessage()` function returns `TRUE`, the message is neither translated nor dispatched by the message loop. If your `PreTranslateMessage()` function returns `FALSE`, the Windows `TranslateMessage()` and `DispatchMessage()` APIs are called to handle the message normally.

Most applications don't override the `PreTranslateMessage()` function, but it can be valuable when you need to avoid processing messages to implement some special functionality. This can arise when your application has a complicated window hierarchy, when you subclass windows, or when you implement hooks for special features in your application, like special application-wide hot keys.

> *Note that the* `PreTranslateMessage()` *function may only be overridden in your application's class or in a* CWnd-*derived class that your application implements. While the* CWinThread *class also implements this function as* virtual, *you can't actually override it because you don't implement a derived version of* CWinThread; *it is internal to the* CWinApp *implementation. If you use additional* CWinThread *instances to manage secondary threads throughout your application, you'll then be able to derive your own* CWinThread-*based class and override the* CWinThread::PreTranslateMessage() *function in your derived classes.*

MFC Idle State

MFC implements an artificial 'idle' mode for your application. If your thread's message queue becomes empty, and the virtual `CWinThread::IsIdleMessage()` function returns `TRUE`, MFC enters an idle state. It repeatedly calls `OnIdle()` until it returns `FALSE` or a message arrives in the queue. The `CWinApp::OnIdle()` function is overridable and acts as a callback for idle states.

While most applications don't implement it, the function provides an excellent place to implement code that performs some seemingly 'background' task. This alternative can be appealing if you find that your need for background processing doesn't easily translate to the Win32 multithreading architecture. Of course, this type of background processing is not preemptive; if you truly need preemptive multitasking, you should implement it with Windows threads. That is to say, if the work you need to do is in any way time-critical, you shouldn't do it in an override of `OnIdle()`.

The MFC idle state is also used to update your application's user interface. MFC will offer your application a chance to update the disabled or enabled status of menu items or controls when it's in an idle state. The MFC idle state really is nothing different than Windows telling the application that it is in an idle state. While a GUI-based application executes under Windows, it continually receives and reacts to messages. If the user goes away to lunch, they probably aren't touching the mouse or pressing buttons on the keyboard, and the desktop where the application is running becomes relatively dormant; nobody's asking the application to move its window, or to repaint or process a menu command, or to redraw the mouse cursor. Sometimes, there are just no messages to be processed and that means the application has gone idle. Having no messages to process at a particular point in time is quite different than the application being entirely *done*, however.

It's possible that your application will never enter an idle state. That could happen if you have very frequent WM_TIMER messages. For example, if your OnTimer() handler takes longer to process than the interval between WM_TIMER messages, you'll find that your application never becomes idle, because it never has any spare time between the processing of the timer messages! Needless to say, an application working this way is a sure sign of a very poor design. Another symptom of such a design will be that MFC never has a chance to clear the temporary object map, and could start using lots more memory than it really should. If you find yourself in a situation where you're doing too much processing to ever be idle, you might want to force a call to OnIdle() yourself in order to let MFC get to its housekeeping. You might want to call OnIdle() on me, too; that way I might eventually get around to cleaning my kitchen.

Application Termination

The message loop in CWinApp::Run() executes this way until the time comes for the application to terminate. This happens when the application receives a WM_QUIT message, posted by the Windows ::PostQuitMessage() API. MFC keeps an eye on the windows being destroyed by handling WM_POSTNCDESTROY for all the CWnd-derived classes. If a WM_POSTNCDESTROY message is received for the window that's identified by m_pMainWnd in the current CWinThread object, MFC will call AfxPostQuitMessage(). AfxPostQuitMessage() does just a stitch of housekeeping before turning around and callling the regular ::PostQuitMessage() API.

When CWinApp::Run() is ready to terminate, it will call CWinApp::ExitInstance(), which helps shut down your application. Unfortunately, this means you can't use CWinApp::Run() as a secondary message pump — if you need to push messages around someplace else in your application, you'll need to write your own pump.

When the Run() function encounters a WM_QUIT message, it calls CWinApp::ExitInstance() and then returns to the caller. The implementation you provide in your override of CWinApp::ExitInstance() should shut down your application, undoing any initialization that you've done in your InitInstance() function.

CWinApp::ExitInstance() returns an integer. When the function is done, the return value it generates is returned by MFC's WinMain() to the operating system as a status code. Before WinMain() returns control to the operating system, destructors for any static objects in your application begin to run, including the destructor for your theApp object. Again, you probably won't perform any work inside this function, since no corresponding work is done in your constructor. If you need shutdown code, use the CWinApp::ExitInstance() function.

> While **CWinApp::InitInstance()** has a corresponding **ExitInstance()** function, **CWinApp::InitApplication()** has no corresponding **ExitApplication()** function.

In this section, I've blamed all of the work the application gets done on CWinApp. It's CWinApp that you'll actually derive your own class from in order to set up your application's functionality after AppWizard has made the basic project for your application. As I explained earlier, CWinApp actually derives from CWinThread, which helps out with the implementation of the application's message pump, startup and shutdown functions. CWinThread's involvement doesn't concern you unless you're actually using CWinThread directly, and I'll address the specifics of CWinThread's implementation and use in Chapter 10, which is devoted to multithreaded programming.

Summary

In this chapter, we've taken a very close look at the functionality provided by MFC that has been designed to be the guts of your application. We've seen how messages are dispatched to your application and we've taken a look at the fundamental support that MFC will provide as you design your own classes. In the latter part of the chapter we also took a quick look at how MFC applications are initialized.

In the next three chapters, we'll move deeper into the class library by examining further how your application can manage file data and present its user interface to the world.

The Document/View Architecture

Everyone would agree that computers are tools for manipulating information. However, good programmers know that one of the most important aspects of application design is the way in which processed information is presented to and manipulated by the user. MFC provides many individual classes to help the programmer with the task of developing a user interface, but it also addresses the user interface issue at the architectural level, providing a number of classes which work together to produce a whole that is greater than the sum of its parts – the **document/view architecture**.

The document/view architecture embodies techniques for storing and loading information, as well as for presenting that information to the user. The architecture doesn't make any assumptions about the way the information is presented, the way it is stored, or the way it's used – it just provides a mechanism for presenting and storing the information. The framework that MFC provides has lots of user interface functionality built into it, and relieves the programmer of duties involved in implementing the most fundamental user interface aspects of their application. It provides file and window management user interfaces, including prompting and error-handling code.

In this chapter, we'll cover:

> Document templates

> Frames

> Documents

> Views

> The interaction between documents and views

> The surrounding MFC-supported user interface features, such as tool tips and the status bar

We'll also discuss situations when the document/view architecture isn't appropriate, and examine the support the Visual C++ product provides for writing applications that *don't* use the document/view architecture.

Documents and Views

If you have any experience of writing full-blown applications, you may have come to the realization that there's a natural break between the code that manages an application's data and the code that's required to present it to the user. Of course, both of these areas of code are dependent on each other, but that interdependence usually manifests itself in only a few, very identifiable ways.

In the document/view model, the class that manages the data is called the **document**. The document should completely encapsulate the data that the application manipulates. In MFC, a document is represented by a document class. It may store the data in memory, relying on member variables to contain it, or it may retrieve the data on demand from a disk file, using member variables only to hold the name and handle of the open data file. The document class should be designed to have functions which abstract that data, while the interface which the document object exposes should provide ways to request records, points, sets, or any other logical groups of information which the rendering code can digest.

The code that renders the data for the user is called the **view**. MFC represents a view with one of a number of view classes. The view code is used to draw the data on an output device – perhaps a printer, or a window in the display. The view must have some way of knowing which document it is associated with. That association allows the view to invoke the functions in its document to request information as it renders the display.

In fact, the view is also responsible for interacting with the user. Since the view is the window that the user manipulates directly with the mouse and keyboard, the view may implement a two-way interface between the document and the user. If the user sees data drawn in the view, they might click on it, drag it, select it, or use menus in the view's frame to perform actions on it. The view can have code to react to these input events, and will also maintain and implement transient user interface features like selection markers, scrolling, and highlighting. The view implements code to respond to input events in the user interface, but the code isn't essential; the view might be only responsible for presenting information if the application wishes to present a 'browse-only' interface.

To support the notion of the view providing both the output of information from the document and accepting input from the user, an obligation or **contract** exists between the view and the document. The document needs to provide a way for the view to access the document's encapsulated data. If the user executes commands or performs input with the keyboard or mouse, the view calls functions on the document to notify it of the changes. If a document class exists that doesn't provide a way to manipulate the data it owns, it isn't fulfilling its side of the contract – much like a carpenter who never finishes the job, or a hockey player who gets drunk and throws a fire extinguisher through the window.

Strictly speaking, no other interfaces, expectations or obligations exist between a document and a view. A view can perform whatever rendering method the developer wants it to. At any time, it may display some, all, or none of a document's data, and the view can even completely ignore notification by a document that the information has been altered if that's what the programmer wants.

The document/view architecture isn't appropriate for all applications – we'll examine when it is and isn't appropriate to use the document/view architecture later in this chapter. You might have already noticed that dialog-only applications created by the AppWizard have neither a document nor a view, but still use the rest of MFC for their features. Starting in Visual C++ 6.0, the wizard also allows you to get an MDI or SDI application which doesn't support the document/view architecture.

As we complete our discussion of the document/view architecture, don't be confused by the term *document* and assume that it only means a file that contains words, paragraphs and text formatting information. While you might very well be writing an application which handles text documents, paragraphs or pages, like a word processor or a document management system, the term *document* doesn't mean that the document/view architecture is limited to such applications. You may, for instance, have your document class render information that more closely represents report cards, stock trades, terminal emulator sessions, box scores for hockey games, or even spreadsheets.

Document/View Designs

Any AppWizard-produced MFC applications that support SDI or MDI will use the document/view architecture unless you specifically request otherwise. The application is designed in such a way that an instance of the application's document class is created for each file that the application loads. The application will then use an instance of a view class to let the user interact with the application and the data in the document.

Note that more than one instance of a particular view may be associated with a given document and that you may even associate instances of different views to the same document. This is the inherent power of the document/view architecture; as the user works with the application, they create and destroy instances of the file and user interface management code (and data) that defines their perception of the data with which they work.

A user-friendly application gives views of the application's data that are intuitive to the user. It would be hard to imagine how cold it is in central Tennessee based on tabular temperature data from the entire United States, but the common 'blue is cold, orange is hot' weather graphs that appear in newspapers make it easy to guess what range of temperatures a traveler might expect with a quick glance at the right part of a map of the nation. The tabular data still has value, though – it's an easy way to enter the data in the first place, and it's the only way you might ever find out what kind of coat to wear if you weren't completely sure where Tennessee was.

Single document interface applications produced using AppWizard only ever use one document and one view type, and only ever instantiate one of each of these classes. Of course, this is only true of the AppWizard-generated code; once the AppWizard has churned out your application, you're free to hack away at it if you decide that it's convenient to use multiple instances of each different view or document.

Multiple document interface applications will make use of at least one document/view pair, but they may make use of additional documents and views in different combinations to enable the user to work with other files or to represent their data in a myriad of different ways.

The figure below shows which classes may support a simple SDI application implemented around MFC.

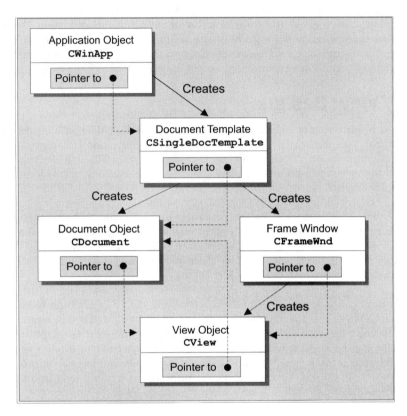

In AppWizard-generated SDI applications, the frame window itself is implemented by the CMainFrame class. In this case, AppWizard will define this class for you in MainFrm.h and implement it in MainFrm.cpp. The CMainFrame class derives most of its functionality from CFrameWnd, which is MFC's wrapper for a simple frame window. The class isn't responsible for very much in the single document interface application; if you've decorated your frame window with a menu, a status bar, or dockable toolbars, the CMainFrame class will handle the creation and initialization of those objects.

The Layout of an MDI Application

The layout of a multiple document interface application is a little more complicated. There's still a main frame, which holds the menu, toolbar and status bars, but you should be aware that in the MDI variant build, this CMainFrame class derives from MFC's CMDIFrameWnd class rather than CFrameWnd. CMDIFrameWnd has the same visual characteristics as a CFrameWnd, but it also implements the MDI frame protocol that Windows expects in an MDI application.

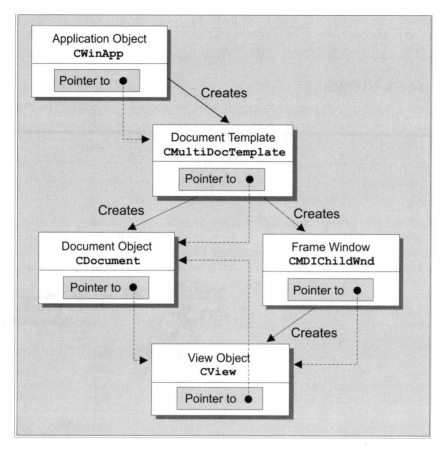

The child windows that crop up in the figure are also frame windows; CMDIChildWnd instances, to be specific. This MFC class provides the child windows that a Windows MDI application uses in its client area. The framework will create a class called CMDIChildWnd, which will be instantiated as frame windows which are children of the MDI frame serving as the application's main window. Each instance of CMDIChildWnd will contain a each view the application creates, just as the CMainFrame wrapped the single view in the SDI application. The wrapped view may be of any type and can refer to any open document that the application is currently managing.

Your charge as a developer of MFC applications is to decide exactly what kinds of documents and views you'll implement, and how they'll interact with the basic framework provided by MFC's implementation of the single document or multiple document interfaces. Your code alters and enhances the way the generic documents and views interact and behave. By tuning things to work the way you want them to, and by stealing functionality from other parts of MFC, you will eventually develop the skeleton provided by MFC and AppWizard into an application that does exactly what you need.

Conventional Windows applications written in C would modify the way that Windows' own classes worked; such code would paint, draw or store something at the direction of input messages (or combinations of input messages) to your application windows. Fortunately, by using MFC, your work has been promoted to a slightly higher plane of existence.

You're now adding more involved features to more advanced classes. These classes, which we'll learn about throughout this book, also support the ability to intercept those basic Windows messages and, when appropriate, do work at a much lower level.

The Different Views

While applications with a wide range of features and usability requirements may be structured around this architecture, their exact applications and user interfaces may differ quite significantly. Conceivably, a program that generally deals with text would have in its view a user interface like an edit control, while an application which does painting or drawing work might paint directly onto its window, adding scroll bars to allow the user to see a picture that is larger than the window. The details of implementing two such diverse applications are distinct, but each can still rely on the underlying functionality of the document/view architecture in MFC.

As a matter of fact, these applications can make use of relatively high-level, predefined classes in the Microsoft Foundation Classes framework. CView is the base class for many different view classes in MFC. By default, your AppWizard application will base its views on CView, but the dialog in the final step of creating your application with AppWizard allows you to change the base class for your application's view class. You can make one of several selections; stick with CView or use CScrollView, CEditView, CHtmlView, CRichEditView, CFormView, CTreeView or CListView:

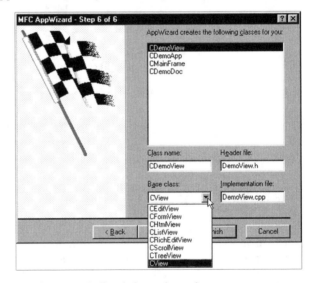

If you're creating a database application, you won't have such flexibility when choosing your view type. MFC will ask you to use a CRecordView, which is a class derived from CFormView and includes a little extra code to provide for database connectivity, something that will be discussed further in Chapter 12.

CView

The basic CView class implements all of the functionality that we'll describe, in this chapter, as being important for view classes. CView has the code to interact with the document in the application to do all of the rendering and user interface work you've heard about. CView has member functions that implement intra-document drag-and-drop, and accessor functions that allow the view to discover information about the frame it's being displayed in and the document that owns it. As such, CView's most important asset is that it's the base class for every other MFC-provided view you'll meet in life.

CView has two very important overridables; OnInitialUpdate() and OnDraw(). OnDraw() is called when the view needs to be painted. Essentially, it's MFC's mechanism for responding to WM_PAINT messages sent to the view. MFC does some preparation before the painting, which in CView consists of nothing more than preparing a CDC object to allow you to paint. In more interesting CView descendants, the preparation might include offsetting origins within the device context to effect scrolling.

> *We'll find out more about the CDC class and device contexts when we give them the full treatment in Chapter 6.*

OnInitialUpdate() is called the first time the view updates itself – which *isn't* the same as the painting the view for the first time. When a document changes, it notifies views attached to it that it has changed, and asks the views to update themselves. This mechanism has MFC call OnInitialUpdate() the first time, and OnUpdate() on subsequent occasions. The MFC-supplied implementation of OnUpdate() does nothing more than invalidate the window with a call to Invalidate(). That call forces the window to completely repaint. Windows will eventually send a WM_PAINT message to the window, which in turn causes OnDraw() to be called. The MFC-provided implementation of OnInitialUpdate() just turns around and calls OnUpdate().

Both OnInitialUpdate() and OnUpdate() are overrideable. You might want to override OnInitialUpdate() to measure things that only need to be measured once when your document is first opened, such as the size of the screen or the font you'll use, for example. You can do your measurements – retrieve device capabilities, or measure your default font, for example – and squirrel away the results so that you don't have to calculate everything again and again in your OnDraw() code. On the other hand, it might be a bad idea to measure your window size in OnInitialUpdate() because, at the time the function is called, the window may not have yet been sized.

It's not necessary to call the base class implementation if you override either of these functions, as long as you've invalidated which ever part of the window you want to repaint yourself. When MFC invalidates the window in the base class implementations, it invalidates the *whole* window. As such, calling the base class implementation will cause your application to repaint the entire client area of the view – not just the smaller area you might have found to require an update. Painting more than you need to can cause your application to seem a little less crisp in the hands of your users.

CScrollView

CScrollView, a derived class of CView, adds the ability to scroll the logical view window through the limited physical area of the on-screen window. The view controls the scroll bars, adjusting their presence, range and granularity. The scrollbars automatically provide their current position to the painting code in the view, allowing it to compensate for the adjusted logical position of the display.

A CScrollView learns about changes to the scrolling position of the window both when the user performs the scrolling and when an application forces the view content to scroll. MFC calls OnScroll() and OnScrollBy() when a scrolling operation takes place. Normally, applications don't react to these calls and instead learn about their scrolled position when it's time to paint – that is, during their handling of the OnDraw() call.

CEditView and CRichEditView

CEditView uses a Windows edit control to realize a text-edit view with scrolling and search-and-replace capabilities. Documents that support CEditViews don't often actually hold the text – it's usually contained in the view, which means that they're something of an exception in the world of document/view applications. Most applications you'll write will have a minimum amount of data stored in the view and keep everything of interest in the document. Any view based on a control, such as CRichEditView and CEditView, will have a copy of the data in the view class.

The CRichEditView is very similar to the CEditView, except that it uses the Windows rich text edit control, which is one of the 32-bit Windows common controls. We'll examine this and the other common controls in Chapter 8.

As far as the view is concerned, you can assume that the CRichEditView and CEditView are just the same; they display textual data to the user. If your application uses a CRichEditView, though, you'll be able to use all of the extra (and impressive) formatting, layout, coloring and font management features that it provides.

CFormView and CRecordView

CFormViews encapsulate a trick that's familiar to most experienced Windows programmers who have worked with form-oriented applications. The CFormView takes a dialog template and draws the dialog in the client area of the view. This allows you to create views that have embedded forms, without doing any work to create, destroy or manage the user interface.

If you've elected to have database support in your application, the AppWizard also lets you use a CRecordView class. This is a special flavor of the CFormView class that's wired to a CRecordset class, uniting MFC's support for data validation in dialog boxes within the CFormView to the ODBC support provided through the CRecordset class.

CTreeView and CListView

The CTreeView class allows your application to represent hierarchical data in the form of a tree control, while the CListView class lets you display information in a free-form control that can be managed by the user. The tree control and the list control are relatively new Windows common controls, and we'll examine both of them in Chapter 8.

The tree control is very similar to the display in the FileView and ClassView tabs of the Project Workspace window in the Microsoft Visual Studio. The list control is exactly the control that Windows uses in the Explorer to show files in a particular directory.

CHtmlView

The CHtmlView class, new to MFC in Visual C++ 6.0, is another control-based view type. It provides you with the ability to show the user a simple HTML-based interface. CHtmlView contains an instance of the Microsoft Web Browser ActiveX Control, and hooks it up to properly interact with your application's frame window and menus. The class features methods which allow you to browse history, navigate to other pages, or set various options on the user interface of the control. The view also provides several overridable functions that allow you to react to notifications the contained ActiveX control manages.

Types of Document

Documents also come in a few different types, with a variety of functionality. Since documents aren't responsible for any user interface features in your application, it's not always obvious which document is present in a given type of application. Most applications are based on the CDocument class, but those that support compound documents will base them on a CDocument-derivative. The exact type of derivative depends on what level of support the application will provide.

If you elect to provide simple compound document container support, your application's document class will be based on COleDocument. This is a direct derivative of CDocument which *only* adds container support. Selecting any other level of compound document support in the AppWizard (full-server, mini-server or both container and server support) produces an application document class derived from COleServerDoc, which is a further subclass of COleDocument. We'll take a look at these more advanced classes in the chapters on OLE towards the end of the book. For now, we'll concentrate on the fundamentals of the document/view architecture.

Document/View Consciousness

Perhaps the most important line of communication that occurs between a document and any of its associated views is the notion of **consciousness** – the document should 'know' which views are rendering it, and a view needs to have access to its document to retrieve or make changes to the existing information. The methods by which a view can learn about the document it's managing, or by which a view and document notify each other about update and refresh requests, are well-defined. When you're developing a document based on the Microsoft Foundation Classes, these features are designed around the classes provided by MFC for these purposes.

It's up to you to implement the code which stores data in your document, handles serialization for your document and provides the data in your document to your view. You'll need to consider carefully how this mechanism will work; your document may be servicing more than one view at a time, so it may need some way to tell the view what information is being provided. Your document may be supplying information to more than one *type* of view as well, so you'll need to make the interface flexible.

What are Document Templates?

The first thing we need to concern ourselves with is how MFC keeps track of the documents and views that are floating around in the application, and which documents and views are related to one another. The run-time class information that we described in the previous chapter is important when we are considering these relationships, since MFC wants to relate one dynamically instantiated class with other dynamically instantiated classes.

As the document/view architecture is the crux of your application, MFC must be able to create and destroy objects from the document/view implementation classes. As your application may handle more than one type of document/view relationship, MFC must have some way of knowing which document, view and display classes you implement and how to create them. After all, while one document may support many different types of views, associating other views with that same document might be nonsensical.

CSingleDocTemplate

To learn how these associations are described and maintained, have a peek at the code in Simple, the tiny example application that we've seen in previous chapters. In Simple.cpp, you'll find some source like this:

```
CSingleDocTemplate* pDocTemplate;
pDocTemplate = new CSingleDocTemplate(
    IDR_MAINFRAME,
    RUNTIME_CLASS(CSimpleDoc),
    RUNTIME_CLASS(CMainFrame),          // main SDI frame window
    RUNTIME_CLASS(CSimpleView));
AddDocTemplate(pDocTemplate);
```

This is from the CSimpleApp::InitInstance() function. The code dynamically allocates a new CSingleDocTemplate object, the constructor for which takes four parameters.

The first parameter is a resource ID, and we'll discuss the significance of this a little later. The second, third and fourth parameters associated with the CSingleDocTemplate() constructor are pointers to run-time class information. The RUNTIME_CLASS() macro generates a pointer to the run-time class information for the application's document, main frame and view classes. These pointers are all passed to the CSingleDocTemplate constructor, which stores the pointers so that it can create instances of the objects as needed, in order to put together a complete document/view team.

The CSingleDocTemplate object lives as long as the application does. You can find the code that allocates CSingleDocTemplates for your application in the InitInstance() override provided by AppWizard for your application, but you'll never have to write code which deletes the document template objects if you use AddDocTemplate() on the template, because the CWinApp destructor will clean up for you. Once AddDocTemplate() is called for a given document template object, MFC uses the object internally and destroys any added document templates as the application's CWinApp object is destroyed.

The CSingleDocTemplate object that we've created gives MFC everything it needs to know to handle all situations the document, view, and frame triumvirate will encounter during the lifetime of the application. If the user invokes the New command in the File menu of the running application, for example, MFC needs to create a document, a view, and a frame, and get them working with each other. Prompts, icons and menus associated with the frame come from the resource ID passed to the document template, and given the run-time class information for each of the classes you'd like to use for the frame, view, and document, MFC can create them at will.

Let me underscore exactly how the document template fits into the architecture of the application as it initializes by walking through the steps an application takes as it starts up:

1. The application loads.

2. Your CWinApp constructor is called.

3. MFC gets initialized.

4. Your CWinApp::InitInstance() function is called.

5. You can create and register a document template in that function.

6. InitInstance() processes anything on the command line for the application's invocation. If nothing was there, the function will create a new, untitled document by default.

A document isn't actually created until very late in the game. If the user hasn't put a file name on the command-line, the application actually *won't* initialize the document it creates. Otherwise, the application creates a new document and tries to load its state from the named file.

Frame Windows

We're here to learn about documents and views, so you probably expected to see information about them, but I keep mentioning frames. That's because while it's certainly true that the view your application implements is a window, it isn't a pop-up or a frame window. Rather, it's a borderless child window which doesn't have a menu bar or title bar of its own, so it must be contained by some sort of frame window. MFC places the view window that you create into the client area of the frame window identified in the document template constructor.

When they're developing a Windows application, most programmers wouldn't take the extra step of separating the client area of their application from the frame window. Instead, they would just create a big ol' WS_OVERLAPPED-style window and paint right in its client area. To make MFC a little more modular, it's implemented to make a distinction between the two types of frame window that you might use – a single document or a multiple document interface frame window. Furthermore, the view window can be placed into a frame, or inside an activated OLE object, or even into a frame inside of an activated OLE object. If you've implemented your application by placing all the drawing code into the frame window, you'll be hard-pressed to dice things up in such a way that allows you to use the same code for the OLE window architecture that you used for your standalone application architecture. More on this later, but for now it's enough to say that the frame window is the one that receives all the menu and window frame messages, while the view window directly receives all the keyboard and mouse messages.

Window frame messages are messages that only windows with frames receive – messages about resizing, maximizing, minimizing, moving, and so on. The frame window also receives lots of non-client area messages, since it's responsible for implementing the non-client area of your application.

Views play a special secret role in their relationship to frames; they help lay out your client area nicely. An MFC application almost always has a bunch of toolbars and a status bar. Those windows can appear and disappear at the user's whim. If you're used to writing C/SDK applications from scratch, you're also probably accustomed to drawing directly on the client area of your application's main window. That works just fine, until you decide it's time to add decorations (like toolbars or status bars) to the client area of your window. The problem is simply that those decorations must be a part of the client area, and will change its shape and size.

For example, you can assume that the top-left corner of your frame's client area is at point (0,0), but only if you don't have a toolbar. If you have a toolbar, then the client area's *useable* top-left corner actually changes and becomes offset by the size of the toolbar. By placing a borderless window into the client area, your application can always assume that the top-left corner of the client area it will use for drawing is at the point (0,0).

Of course, it's possible to solve the offset problem with a little math as you're drawing, or using the device context origin and mapping functions to effectively displace the logical coordinates. But that's tedious, and error-prone, and difficult to manage dynamically. An extra window is a small price to pay for the convenience of avoiding likely bugs and certain complexity.

The Document Template Resources

As we mentioned, the first parameter to the CSingleDocTemplate constructor is a resource ID. It tells the frame used by the template what kind of resources it needs to have on hand to complete the link. This ID identifies the resources used to supply the frame with an accelerator table, menu and icon. The frame window your application uses should have the same resource ID for each resource type it wishes to use.

If you examine Simple.rc, you'll find that there's an accelerator table, a toolbar bitmap, a menu and an icon. Each resource is identified by the ID IDR_MAINFRAME, the ID passed to the CSingleDocTemplate constructor. Having exactly the same frame window resource ID is far more convenient than requiring the constructor for CSingleDocTemplate to take six or seven parameters.

The resource ID is also the ID of an entry in your application's string table. The identified string has a very special format; it's really seven strings in one, with the strings separated by newline (\n) characters, like this:

```
Simple\n\nSimple\n\n\nSimple.Document\nSimple Document
```

The String Resource

The substrings identify seven things about your application and, specifically, about the document implemented by your application. The first substring provides a **window title** for the application's main window when the document type you'll be handling is active. The second substring is a basis for the name of the default document; MFC will append a number to it for each opened document. For example, the third document opened against a given document template would be named Booklet3 if the second string contained Booklet. Some references call this a **document name**. If this string is blank, MFC always uses untitled as the document name.

The third substring is the name of the **document type**. If your application supports more than one document type, when the user selects the New command in the File menu they will be provided with a list of document types to choose from. The sort of list box that could appear is shown below:

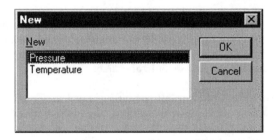

If you specify an empty string for this entry, the document type that you're registering is *not* exposed in the New dialog box.

You can use this as a technique to hide document types that you don't want the user to create directly. Since the document type name isn't used in any other situation, leaving the name blank won't cause you any nasty side-effects.

The fourth string provides a description of the document type and a wildcard filename filter used to match document files of the type you're registering. The string is added to the List Files Of Type: combo box in the File | Open... dialog box for your application. You might want to set the string to Exchanger Maps (*.hxg), for instance, if you have a document which maps heat exchangers and has the file extension .hxg. The text in this string is used only for the benefit of the user – it doesn't actually determine the wildcards used to find files in the File | Open... dialog.

 The fifth string, on the other hand, specifies the extension for any files stored by the document type in question. If you don't specify an extension here, the window will default to the first in the list of filters. Your extension name should include a leading period, but not an asterisk (*). For instance, .xyz is correct, but xyz and *.xyz are not.

The sixth string element identifies the document type for the registration database. This string is used by the File Manager, Explorer, the registry and COM to register your document type. It isn't shown to the user unless they examine the Associate dialog box in File Manager, or the file association information in Explorer, or snoop through the registry itself.

The seventh and final string element is the name of the document as stored in the Windows registry. Assuming that you're implementing compound document support, this string is used in the registry (and by OLE itself) to identify the type of document that your application implements. This string is shown to users when they use the Insert | Object... command in Excel or Word, for example, to embed an object serviced by your application in the host application's document. You should make this string as short and as meaningful as possible, in order to get the idea over to the user with the minimum of fuss.

Breaking Down the String Resource

Since the string resource is the crux of the document registration process, and since you can alter many of your application's more subtle features using the string resource registered by your application, you should carefully check what you place in the string. As you've seen (and to save you flicking back and forth), the default string produced by the AppWizard for the Simple example looks like this:

```
Simple\n\nSimple\n\n\nSimple.Document\nSimple Document
```

This gives the application a window title of Simple, a File | New type name of Simple, an OLE internal name of Simple.Document and an external name of Simple Document.

The CDocTemplate class from which CSingleDocTemplate and CMultiDocTemplate are derived features a function called GetDocString(). This function, which accepts a reference to a CString object and an index, allows you to query the values of the registered string resource.

```
virtual BOOL GetDocString(CString& rString,
                          enum     DocStringIndex index) const;
```

The second parameter, the index, is expressed as a private enum of the CDocTemplate class. Valid values are shown in the table below:

Value	Meaning
CDocTemplate::windowTitle	Text for the application window's title bar. Only important for SDI applications.
CDocTemplate::docName	Root for the default document name.
CDocTemplate::fileNewName	Name of the document for the File | New box.
CDocTemplate::filterName	Text for the File | Open dialog's File Type drop-down list box.
CDocTemplate::filterExt	Wildcard filename filter matching files for this document type.
CDocTemplate::regFileTypeId	Registry database internal name, used by OLE and the File Manager.
CDocTemplate::regFileTypeName	Registry database document name. Used by all OLE applications and exposed to the user.

There's no corresponding CDocTemplate::SetDocString() function. You can't change the attributes of a document template once it's been created.

As we've explained here, the string resource dictates many subtle aspects of your application, and the default string resource produced by the AppWizard gives your application a healthy but basic user interface. In Chapter 2, we described some of the fields in the Document Template Strings tab of AppWizard's Advanced Options window.

The fields in this tab of the dialog box all correspond directly to substrings in the document template string resource. If you know what your application will look like when you're done, you can start off by changing the appropriate strings in the Advanced Options dialog:

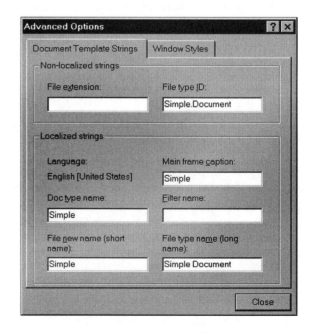

However, as you add features, you'll certainly need to make adjustments to the string resource. To perform these adjustments, you must edit the string resource directly, using the string table editor. If you make a mistake, MFC will either blindly put the wrong string in the wrong part of your user interface, or will generate an **Assert Failed** error message at runtime. When you change the document template resource string, it's a good idea to test your application immediately to make sure that no other features have been adversely affected.

Stock View Resources

As I outlined when I introduced the .rc file, there are a number of other resources in your application that are identified by the resource ID in your document template. These resources are all associated with the document type that your application is currently editing. For the SDI AppWizard application, the ID that's used for the default document template string resource, and all of the other resources associated with the template, is called IDR_MAINFRAME.

AppWizard gives your application's main frame a menu that's also identified by IDR_MAINFRAME. In single document interface applications, this means that your menu depends on what kind of document is active – while it's a little difficult to make an SDI application activate more than one document at a time, the application can certainly support multiple document types which are activated at different times. For multiple document interface applications, it means that each individual document type will have its own type of menu. Of course, if you don't want this, you can just create each template type to point at the same menu resource.

The frame will also have an icon with the same identifier as the other resources, which means that the icon will be used to represent that SDI application. The named icon will be used when the application is minimized, for example. For multiple document interface applications, the icon ends up being that of minimized MDI child windows. The icon used for the application in this case comes from another source, which we'll discuss in a moment.

Your application may also feature a dialog named after that same template resource ID. Such applications are rare; they generally have a dialog as the core interface for viewing their documents. We'll see more situations when this happens as we investigate classes like CFormView during our study of MFC's support for ODBC and data access.

The toolbar resource provided by the AppWizard is used to build the default toolbar for the frame window. While the toolbar seems to be composed of several buttons, the buttons are actually sections of a single bitmap. We'll discuss the CToolBar class, used to make toolbars in MFC, nearer the end of this chapter.

Since the frame implements a window with a menu, it may also provide an accelerator table. This table provides translations between keystrokes and WM_COMMAND messages, which should be sent when the keystroke is detected. The framework takes care of searching for the accelerator table and translating and dispatching the messages generated when a key is pressed as appropriate. The default accelerator table produced by the AppWizard has accelerators for the standard user interface elements in the menu, which are also produced by AppWizard.

You should feel free to modify any of these resources to suit the needs of your application. However, you may need to change more than the resource to keep things working. Make sure that you read up on the classes which make use of the resources before you change them so that your application will stay healthy.

The Document Template Lifecycle

CSingleDocTemplate is a lightweight class – it requires very little memory. While a thousand of anything (except bottles of beer) is bad, you shouldn't worry about keeping document template classes lying about, even if you have dozens of them.

> *In MFC versions for Win16 platforms, creating document templates was problematic because the template would always create and register a menu. In Win32, though, the negative effect of this practice is reduced because Win32 can handle system resources much more adeptly than Win16.*

CSingleDocTemplate and CMultiDocTemplate, the subjects of the next section, are used heavily by the application frameworks. After setting them up and getting them started, you'll never need to meddle with them again.

> **Your application should register all of the document templates that it will use in its derived version of the `CWinApp::InitInstance` function. By making them `public` members of your application object, you can access them later on when you need to juggle documents and views.**

Regarding the use of document templates, one of the best pieces of advice I can give you is to let MFC do the work. That is, you should ask MFC's code in the document template object to create the view and document you need, and hook up all of the associations. You should hardly ever need to run around and directly create your own views, documents and frames. Have a document template do the work!

Multiple Document Interface Applications

When you're writing an MDI application, the features of CDocTemplate become far more important than they are in single document applications. In an SDI application, you'll generally only work with one document/view/frame set, but in an MDI application, you're far more likely to have different sets of views and documents working together.

The most important step to take in your multiple document interface application is to use the CMultiDocTemplate class to register your document templates, instead of CSingleDocTemplate. This doesn't stop you, though, from using the AddDocTemplate() function to do the actual registration.

This code fragment is from the InitInstance() member function of a CWinApp-derived object from an application with an MDI interface:

```
CMultiDocTemplate* pDocTemplate;
pDocTemplate = new CMultiDocTemplate(
        IDR_MYMDITYPE,
        RUNTIME_CLASS(CMyMDIDoc),
        RUNTIME_CLASS(CChildFrame), // custom MDI child frame
        RUNTIME_CLASS(CMyMDIView));
```

```
AddDocTemplate(pDocTemplate);

// create main MDI Frame window
CMainFrame* pMainFrame = new CMainFrame;
if (!pMainFrame->LoadFrame(IDR_MAINFRAME))
    return FALSE;
m_pMainWnd = pMainFrame;
```

If you compare this with the code we examined for an SDI application, you'll see that one of the differences is the use of `CMultiDocTemplate` instead of `CSingleDocTemplate`. These two classes have the same interface, but differ internally. The exposed functionality for both classes is provided by their common base class, `CDocTemplate`.

Semantically speaking, the use of `CMultiDocTemplate` is a little different to that of `CSingleDocTemplate`. The frame window associated with a `CMultiDocTemplate` is actually a child window of the real frame window. In an MDI application, the frame window will be derived from the `CMDIFrameWnd`, while each child window class will be derived from `CMDIChildWnd`, rather than `CFrameWnd`.

The AppWizard expects that you will tweak both the main MDI frame window and the MDI child window to make them work in your application. To this end, by default, it creates for you a class derived from `CMDIChildWnd`, called `CChildFrame`. You can see this class mentioned in the code fragment above. So, to set up the document template, the `CMultiDocTemplate` constructor call produced by AppWizard passes a reference to the run-time class information for `CChildFrame` as the third parameter.

You may also notice that additional code is called after the `AddDocTemplate()` function. This code creates an instance of the `CMainFrame` class, a derivative of `CMDIFrameWnd`, before calling the `LoadFrame()` member function. If this function is successful, it assigns a pointer to the newly created `CMainFrame` object to the `m_pMainWnd` member variable of `CWinApp`.

As it happens, the `m_pMainWnd` member variable is actually inherited from `CWinThread`, the parent class of `CWinApp`. By assigning a pointer to the frame window, the application ensures that its primary thread controls its primary window. For single document interface applications, this work is normally done by the innards of the `CSingleDocTemplate` class.

This may seem a little confusing at first if you're used to thinking in terms of SDI applications, but remember that the frame window class that you need to associate with a document and a view when you create the document template is the frame associated with the view window, not the frame for the application. In a multiple document interface application, an individual child window is created for each view.

Frame Window Styles

`CFrameWnd::LoadFrame()` is used to load the Windows frame window and associated resources, and to attach the frame window to the `CFrameWnd` object. It takes four parameters:

- ➢ The resource ID
- ➢ The window style
- ➢ A pointer to the window's parent

> ➢ A pointer to the information store concerning your customization of the window's features

Only one of these parameters (the first) is required; it's the ID of the icon, string and accelerator resources the frame window will use. The LoadFrame() function creates the frame window and uses the resource ID to get the resources loaded. The string resource is only used for the title of the frame window, so it doesn't contain any substrings.

By default, the second parameter is set to WS_OVERLAPPEDWINDOW | FWS_ADDTOTITLE. The WS_OVERLAPPEDWINDOW style flag makes the frame into a sizable, movable window, with a system menu and minimize/maximize buttons. The MFC-specific FWS_ADDTOTITLE flag makes sure that the active document name is also displayed in the title bar. If you don't want MFC to manage the title of the frame window, you can prevent this functionality by not setting this flag in the value you give for the second parameter.

You can affect the order in which the document name and the window title appear in the title bar with the FWS_PREFIXTITLE flag. By default (without specifying the flag), the document name appears *after* the window title. However, if you OR FWS_PREFIXTITLE with the other style flags and pass it as the second parameter of LoadFrame(), the document name will appear *before* the window title.

As an example of how this works, if Myfile.doc was opened in a window titled **Super Editor** with FWS_PREFIXTITLE set, you would see **Myfile.doc – Super Editor** in the title bar. On the other hand, without FWS_PREFIXTITLE, you'd see **Super Editor – Myfile.doc**. This flag exists only to keep MFC compatible with future operating systems that might use a different title convention, and to assist with the localization of applications in countries where the having the file name before the application name is more natural. Needless to say, this flag has no meaning if FWS_ADDTOTITLE isn't set. The correct setting of the FWS_ bits is a matter of preference and localization.

The MFC CFrameWnd implementation also handles a FWS_SNAPTOBARS style bit. This style bit is used to resize the window according to its contents. Its name is derived primarily from how it is used internally to implement dockable toolbars.

You will generally provide the second parameter to change the way that your application's frame window behaves. You can use any WS_ style from Windows; the composite style WS_OVERLAPPEDWINDOW includes:

```
WS_OVERLAPPED
WS_CAPTION
WS_SYSMENU
WS_THICKFRAME
WS_MINIMIZEBOX
WS_MAXIMIZEBOX
```

If you don't want your window to have one of the corresponding features, simply construct a list of the style bits that you *do* want using the C++ bit-wise OR operator (|). Of course, you can use other logical operators to get your work done if you like.

For instance, if you didn't want `WS_CAPTION`, you could logically AND the value with the inverse of `WS_CAPTION`, like this:

```
dwDefaultStyle &= ~WS_CAPTION;
```

You should set these Windows style bits depending on the results you're trying to obtain. I frequently meet people (like my friend, Robert R. Loscher) who wonder how to get their code to circumvent some feature of Windows – to be non-resizable or non-movable, for instance. Don't try to give your window this kind of behavior by 'eating' the messages involved. If you play along with Windows and simply remove the feature from your window style, you'll be much more successful.

The third parameter to `LoadFrame()` is a pointer to the `CWnd` which acts as the parent for the frame. The default value for the third parameter is `NULL`, which is convenient since almost all frame windows will be created as top level windows with no parent. The most notable exceptions are the MDI child frame windows implemented by `CMDIChildWnd`... a class supplied by MFC derived from `CFrameWnd`.

Finally, the fourth parameter is yet another way for you to affect the way your frame will behave. The parameter is a pointer to a `CCreateContext` object that maintains pointers to the frame, document, document template and view that the new window will manage. By providing your own `CCreateContext`, you can change the way a particular window will behave with respect to the document/view architecture. By default, the parameter is `NULL` – and you don't have to fool with it, if you don't want to.

`CCreateContext` is a `struct` provided by MFC to encapsulate some of the information a frame usually needs as it is being created. If you pulled it from the MFC headers and prettied it up, the declaration for `CCreateContext` would look like this:

```
struct CCreateContext
{
    CCreateContext();

    CRuntimeClass* m_pNewViewClass;
    CDocument* m_pCurrentDoc;
    CDocTemplate* m_pNewDocTemplate;
    CView* m_pLastView;
    CFrameWnd* m_pCurrentFrame;
};
```

The constructor is trivial; it just calls `memset()` to zero all the members of the class. This structure is not normal (in MFC, at least) for that reason – most other MFC structures and classes that represent simple values don't initialize their elements in the constructor.

As you can see, all the members provide information that a newly created frame might need to fit in with all of its friends. As fate has it, most of the members of `CCreateContext` aren't used by MFC – or, at best, are used with vigor only in very specific circumstances. The `m_pCurrentFrame` member falls into the former category; it's completely unused by MFC `m_pNewDocTemplate` will let you know which `CDocumentTemplate` was responsible for creating the frame and document and view. While MFC assures that member is initialized, it doesn't make use of it.

The m_pLastView member is used by MFC when creating a CPreviewView, which is the undocumented MFC class that implements Print Preview. m_pLastView is used by the CPreviewView class to remember the view which had focus before the preview operation took place. The preview view will use the printing routines in the view referenced by m_pLastView, and will return control of the application to m_pLastView after the preview operation is done. Printing support in views is covered in some detail in the section called 'Printing' later in this chapter. (The section isn't for several pages, so I gave it a name that should be easy to remember.)

The m_pNewViewClass and m_pCurrentDoc members do very light work in the creation of a new frame, but very important work – very much like a middle manager. When the frame creates itself, it will *normally* create a view window to live inside of it. The frame window creates a new instance of the class specified by m_pNewViewClass, and then creates a window using that object. It then tells the document referenced by m_pCurrentDoc that the document owns a brand new bouncing baby view, and the creation is done.

Again, let me stress that the creation of a view *normally* happens as the frame which owns the view is created, just like I'll *normally* have a couple of beers at a hockey game. Certainly, I can go to a hockey game and not have a few brews, but it doesn't happen very often. In fact, it's kind of weird. But it really can happen. If you don't want to have a new view created, you can set m_pNewViewClass to NULL and m_pCurrentDoc will be ignored. And, remember – new view creation stops after the end of the second intermission.

When you create a CCreateContext, you should initialize as much of it as you can – someone, somewhere, may be expecting the information to arrive. m_pNewViewClass is the crucial member; make sure it's set NULL if you don't want a view to be created by the frame. If you want a view to be created, the member should be set to point at the CRuntimeClass that describes the view. (We visited CRuntimeClass and its pals back in Chapter 3, in the section called 'About CruntimeClass'.) You'll also want the m_pCurrentDoc to point at the document you've currently got created – you must create a document before you create a frame to go with it.

CCreateContext is tremendously useful when working with splitter windows. Even though it often doesn't use the class members itself, MFC always sends a pointer to the structure you pass to any frame or view created by the framework. You can find the pointer in the lpCreateParams member of the CREATESTRUCT sent with the WM_CREATE message. Your OnCreate() member can grab the structure there and use it to initialize member variables of the structure.

CDocTemplate::CreateNewFrame()

When your application needs to create a new view based on one of the document templates it has registered, it should call the CreateNewFrame() member function of the document template it needs. The creation of a document given a template is already handled by the application framework for two of the occasions when it's needed – during the processing of the New and Open... commands in your application's File menu.

While it might not seem quite intuitive to call CreateNewFrame() when you really want a new view, you need to do it this way. Why? Because every view needs a frame window. Views are not pop-up windows – they're borderless, caption-less child windows without menus. The frame is necessary to hold the view in place and give it a user interface.

The `CreateNewFrame()` function takes two parameters, the first of which is a parameter to the document to be created. If the parameter is NULL and the run-time class (referenced when the CDocTemplate object was created) is available, a new document is created. If the parameter is not NULL, the function assumes you wish to associate a new view with an existing document. The second parameter is unused by MFC. In `CreateNewFrame()`, the second parameter is a pointer to a CFrameWnd and is used to initialize the m_pCurrentFrame member of a CCreateContext structure that's passed around during the creation of the new window. But no code in MFC actually references the value, so it's meaningless – unless you write an OnCreate() override that makes some use of it.

You may need to implement some feature of your application that doesn't use the functionality provided by MFC for the construction of a new document/view from a template – if your application has an import feature, for instance. Since an import feature is different from the <u>O</u>pen... and <u>N</u>ew commands in your <u>F</u>ile menu, you will need to create your own code to do it. You'll also need to implement a function to take care of actually importing the information from the foreign file and creating or storing the data in the document.

Code for this might go something like:

```
void CMyApp::OnImport()
{
    CString strFromFile;

    // Find a file name from the user
    if (!GetImportFile(strFromFile))
        return;

    // Create a new frame and a new document from scratch
    m_pNewFrame = m_pDocument->CreateNewFrame(NULL, NULL);
    if (m_pNewFrame == NULL)
    {
        // Complain politely to the user
    }
    else
    {
        // Ready to go!
        if (!(m_pNewFrame->DoImport(strFromFile)))
        {
            // Complain nicely again
        }
    }
}
```

In this little hypothetical example, I call DoImport() as a member of the new frame. It could be a member of the new document, of course; there are no hard restrictions on what I can and can't do once I've created everything.

What Does it Really Mean?

As you can see by examining the constructor calls, a document template contains the necessary information to create a new instance of a document. The framework knows what type of view will be controlling the document, and what kind of document the view needs for support. The template also contains a few more tidbits of information, by way of the resources.

In particular, the document string resource is used to determine various specific qualities of the user interface that the document will manage.

These data items of the CDocTemplate-derived classes go a long way towards helping you understand why document templates are necessary. The other slice of the pie comes from the member functions implemented by the CDocTemplate classes. We've looked at one of the most important, CDocTemplate::CreateNewFrame(), which can be used by your code to create new frames from a given document template, but CDocTemplate::InitialUpdateFrame() is equally significant. It's responsible for updating a frame for the first time, allowing proper initialization and making the frame known to MFC.

Document templates are generally used by MFC itself, and infrequently by your own application code. In some circumstances, you'll want to maintain a pointer to the document templates that you created as your application is initialized; then, you'll have the objects for later use. You might need them for any of the calls we've talked about, or you might want to use them while initializing a CCreateContext object, as we described a couple of sections ago. You may even want to poke around with the list of document templates that MFC manages for you.

If you're going with the flow – that is, letting MFC manage your document templates for you, you should register them with MFC (by using CWinApp::AddDocTemplate()) to buy into the functionality that MFC will provide. That functionality includes automatic management of all the document, view, and frame classes associated with your template, management of file types for file loading and saving routines, and appropriate management of OLE registration information if you make your application OLE-aware.

If you choose not to register your template, you should remember to delete it in the destructor for your application object. MFC can only delete the document templates it knows about when it destroys the application.

Using the document template methodology implies that every combination of a document, view and frame needs a new document template. Some programmers approach MFC as if they can dynamically create and destroy views, documents and frames at their leisure. This *can* be done, but it forces the programmer to code like a salmon; you spend your time thrashing against the current, just to get a little bit of productive work completed – it's really not worth the effort!

In the 'Tricks with Templates' section, which closes the chapter, we discuss and solve some of the more interesting document/view architectural approaches that aren't part of the mainstream 'one document, one view' support realized by the AppWizard's code. Rather than jump straight to it, though, I suggest you read your way towards the section – the balance of the chapter contains useful information about documents and views which you'll need to understand just why the tricks are so appealing.

Documents

Now that your document template is lined up, you're ready to think about the creation, serialization and content of your document. While you read this section, keep in mind that your document *doesn't* provide a user interface. Its primary responsibilities in life are to provide a data repository for the view and to store and load the actual file format that your application will use.

About the Document Metaphor

Again, while you're reading the word 'document' over and over again in this chapter, remember that it's just a place holder for the information your application will be managing. Your application may implement a spreadsheet or an endless piece of paper for use in a drawing program. Your document doesn't need to be logically divided into paragraphs or sentences, but having a plan for where page breaks and margins may be set up will give you an edge when it comes to implementing printing support in your application.

When the user opens a file in your application, they are really creating a new instance of a document. The frameworks use the document template to decide what needs to be done as the document is created; the creation of a new document will always result in the creation of a new view window and may result in the creation of a new frame for that window.

Think carefully about the questions that inevitably arise from this state of affairs:

> How do I represent data in my document?

> How do I efficiently let the views know about that data?

> How do I efficiently let views know about changes in that data?

> How do I make the data in the document persistent?

Apart from the actual process of notifying your view, the document implementation in MFC provides little help with answering these questions. You need to think about the problem and come up with a solution; this is real programming. If you use an inefficient data structure, you'll end up with lots of problems for the other three issues. If you have a natural way to let your views know that something has changed, you can be assured of efficient painting and printing.

Data Storage

We've established that the document class or classes of your application are responsible for storing the data that your application is managing. This means the class should be used both to manage data in memory, making it available to the view as necessary, and to load and store that data in your application's disk file format.

If you spend a bit of time thinking about the design of your document, you will realize that you can derive great benefit from storing format information in your document using member variables. Since MFC can manage your documents, and your documents can manage your in-memory data, you'll win automatic management of separate instances of your data. MFC will create a new instance of your document class for each open file, so if you store everything in that class, you needn't worry about creating a new copy of the format information for each file. The purists will tell you that, in C++, you have little excuse for using global variables anyway.

However, the real benefit comes in the area of **serialization**. If your document can manage everything it needs, then when the time comes to load or save the data in your application, it can just serialize itself to a file using the tools provided by MFC. These tools cover reading existing files, writing new files and rewriting old files. The foundation classes provide an implementation for the New, Save As..., Save and Open... commands in your File menu, and any AppWizard-produced program has these features wired-up correctly.

The most recently-used file list, if you've enabled it, also makes use of the MFC-provided file saving and file loading code.

Like any other technique, serialization has a down side; you've little control over the actual format used when writing the file to disk. MFC writes out information it needs to recreate the objects serialized – data that describes their size in memory, and – before actually writing any content to disk. If you're not too concerned with your file format and are prepared to use the abstraction of serialization, go right ahead.

But if you need to read or write data in a predetermined format, you'll probably want to invent your own save and load mechanisms. In a few pages, we'll look at virtual functions like OnSaveDocument() which you can override as you hook-up your own code that still works with the document/view architecture but avoids the use of MFC's CArchive class and its inherent formatting.

A Note About Serialization

More often than not, the serialization code provided for documents doesn't just serialize the object. You may, for example, write some identifying information to your file so that you can read it back when the file is reloaded. When your loading code runs, you can check for this information and make a decision about how to proceed. This may be as simple as using the VERSIONABLE_SCHEMA() macro that we discussed in Chapter 3, or as elaborate as activating some sort of file conversion and translation mechanism.

The CArchive object reference passed to your document's serialization code is nothing more than a file abstraction. You may wish to provide some code that tries to identify the type of the file being opened, or code that marks the very beginning of your serialization code's file, and then checks for this mark and reacts appropriately. For example, you might look for a particular file signature and then execute the code that handles the file format identified by that file signature, to allow your application to handle different file formats transparently. If you're implementing things strictly in C++, you can use the insertion and extraction operators as usual to present and check for this special data in your file. If you're trying to read a file format which might not be read using the insertion and extraction operators, you're welcome to use Read() and Write().

A simple implementation may look like this:

```
void CMyDocument::Serialize(CArchive &ar)
{
    DWORD dwMagicID;

    if (ar.IsStoring())
    {
        dwMagicID = MY_MAGIC_NUMBER;
        ar << dwMagicID;    // remember!
        // store the rest of the documents data
    }
    else
    {
        ar >> dwMagicID;
        if (dwMagicID == MY_MAGIC_NUMBER)
        {
            // great!  it's our file...
            // process it accordingly!
        }
```

```
        else
        {
            // uh oh, it's not ours. Make a decision based
            // on what's really in dwMagicID, or do some other
            // work to decide what's happening
        }
    }
}
```

If your application's CDocument includes its own objects, you'll be able to get the serialization code to recreate them as they're read. One of the problems with reading data into those objects using some other code is that you'll probably need to create the objects yourself and initialize the data using some other method. In other words, stick with the serialization routines. It's easy to call them for contained objects, too – just do it someplace in your own serialization code:

```
void CMyDocument::Serialize(CArchive &ar)
{
    DWORD dwMagicID;

    if (ar.IsStoring())
    {
        // code as before
    }
    else
    {
        // code as before
    }

    m_InsideObject.Serialize(ar);
    m_AnotherObject.Serialize(ar);
    m_SomethingElse.Serialize(ar);
}
```

Note that the calls are outside the IsStoring() test; the objects contain their own tests in their Serialize() functions, so you don't need to worry about doing them yourself. It doesn't matter whether your calls to the Serialize() functions are before or after the code to explicitly serialize your data members.

You should remember as your applications evolve that reading and writing from a stream is an ordered operation. If you change the orders of the calls to Serialize() or to the insertion operator, you'll change the format of your underlying file.

The Dirty Flag

Documents predominately manage information, but they also provide an opportunity to reach data in permanent storage, be that an OLE object, a set of database records or a disk file. As the user does work against a document, it's inevitable that at some time or another they'll change some feature of the document and forget to save it. Since this could easily result in them losing their work, the foundation classes provide a method for a document to remember that it is 'dirty' and to know when to warn the user before the document is destroyed and the changes are lost forever.

The primary feature of this mechanism is the **dirty bit**. Each document has a flag that reminds the document that it has been changed. If it's set, the dirty bit indicates that the document has been changed and not saved. The dirty bit is reset whenever a document is loaded, created or saved.

You can set the flag by calling `SetModifiedFlag()` and passing it TRUE as a parameter. Since this is a frequent call, the function supports a default parameter of TRUE, so you can omit the parameter when you are marking a document. If you wish to reset the flag, explicitly supply FALSE to the function.

You can query the dirty flag by calling `IsModified()`. This function returns FALSE when the flag is clear, and TRUE when the flag is set. The flag itself, a BOOL named m_bModified, is actually managed as a member variable of CDocument, which in some cases you might have access to directly, since it's declared as `protected`.

The framework will set the flag for you when you change an OLE object that your document contains, but other than that you're on your own. On the other hand, the framework does *clear* the flag for you during the default handling of `OnOpenDocument()` and `OnSaveDocument()`. If you override either of these functions, you should take care to manage the flag correctly, so that you can use it when prompting the user before overwriting or destroying an unsaved document.

OnSaveDocument()

`CDocument::OnSaveDocument()` is called to save the data in your document. This function takes one parameter: a constant string pointer to the name of the file to be saved. Your code is responsible for writing the data in your document to its persistent storage medium. AppWizard doesn't produce an override for this virtual function in your application-specific CDocument descendent. Instead, the default implementation opens the specified file by name, calls `Serialize()` against a CArchive tied to that file, closes the file and then marks the document as clean.

The framework invokes `OnSaveDocument()` when a user of your application selects either the File | Save or File | Save As... menu items, or when the user saves a file in response to a request from the dialog that can appear when either the document or application is closed.

When they're saving a file that hasn't been previously saved, or when they use Save As..., the user is greeted with the standard File Save dialog which asks the user for a filename. However it's saved, the document's filename is passed as the parameter to `OnSaveDocument()` so that the save code can work correctly.

While MFC makes the `OnSaveDocument()` function virtual, you won't need to override it in most situations. However, if you're interested in doing some special work just before saving your code, you can override it. You might wish to override `SaveModified()` or `DoSave()`, too, if you aren't actually writing your document data to a file but storing it in a database instead. It's `DoSave()` that prompts for a file name.

One situation when you would be interested in overriding the `OnSaveDocument()` function is when you're handling your own file format explicitly and not using the MFC-provided serialization mechanism. If you were handling your own file format, you'd open the file right in your implementation of `OnSaveDocument()` and not implement a `Serialize()` member at all. Overriding `OnSaveDocument()` is also a good idea in applications where you're not interested in actually serializing anything. For instance, if you're writing an application that acts as a front-end to a database, you might not actually be opening a file. For such applications, you could override this function to do whatever work interests you.

OnNewDocument()

`CDocument::OnNewDocument()` is called by the document template when it creates a new document of a specific type. This creation can happen during the act of opening an existing template, or during the framework's default response to the <u>N</u>ew command in the <u>F</u>ile menu.

The default implementation of this function takes care of cleaning out the content of the existing document instance by calling `DeleteContents()` against the document. This function, which is described shortly, should delete any memory that has been dynamically allocated by the document for storage, resetting the document to an empty state. There are few reasons, if any, ever to override this function, as MFC overrides it internally to provide OLE support for descendants of `CDocument`.

OnCloseDocument()

The `CDocument::OnCloseDocument()` function is called when the user wishes to close a document opened in an existing application. Remember that this is different to closing a view window – the user might have more than one view opened against a document. The function will not be called if the user is closing a view window and other views are open against the same document.

The default implementation of the `OnCloseDocument()` member function, as supplied by MFC, closes all of the frames (and therefore, the views, too) associated with the document and then the document itself. It calls `DeleteContents()` and deletes the document if the `m_bAutoDelete` member variable is `TRUE`. Again, you'll rarely be interested in overriding this function. You should only supply an override if you need to do some special work when a document is destroyed.

Appropriate overrides for this function will almost always involve you having to do some work before the resources associated with the document are destroyed. You might, for example, release memory or close connections to other computers or database resources. You'll almost always want to call the default implementation in your overriding function because it does a great deal of work to close and delete any open views properly.

ReportSaveLoadException()

Things sometimes go wrong, and more often than not they do so when files are being read or written. The user might run out of disk space, give a bad path name, specify a drive that doesn't exist or run into any number of other traps.

To facilitate error reporting in `CDocument` file handling functions, the class provides an overridable `CDocument::ReportSaveLoadException()` function. It takes four parameters:

> ➢ A pointer to the path name and file name of the document that was being manipulated
> ➢ A pointer to the exception thrown when the problem was encountered
> ➢ A flag, set to `TRUE` if the error occurred due to a problem while saving a file or to `FALSE` if the problem occurred while loading
> ➢ An integer that identifies the default error message

In the default implementation, the last parameter to `ReportSaveLoadException()` (the integer identifying the error message) is only used if the generated exception doesn't clearly identify the error condition that caused the trap.

If a CArchiveException or CFileException is thrown, the default implementation of ReportSaveLoadException() will automatically select an error message to identify the problem to the user. In any other circumstance, the default error message will be used.

The code in CArchiveException and CFileException, which provides an error message for the problem that caused the exception to be thrown, is built in to all CException-derived classes. MFC throws CException-derived objects to describe error situations encountered in the library. Thus, the error message code is available whenever you catch an exception while using MFC, even if your involvement with MFC is outside of the file management routines in CDocument. We'll cover exceptions and MFC's file management classes in greater detail in Chapter 9.

The integer passed to ReportSaveLoadException() should identify a string resource that contains the appropriate error message, even if the cause of the error is identified by the exception parameter. The standard error messages are provided by MFC. If you ask AppWizard for an application that uses MFC statically, these will become part of your executable via an #include directive in your resource file. If you use a shared version of MFC, the strings actually reside in the MFC DLL. You can override this function to develop any more specific error messages that your application might need to produce.

The ReportSaveLoadException() function is called by the default implementations of OnOpenDocument() and OnSaveDocument() in the CDocument class. If you override either of these functions and your code runs into an error, you'll want to make sure you call the ReportSaveLoadException() function.

OnOpenDocument()

The OnOpenDocument() member of the CDocument class is called to open a document. It takes a single parameter – a pointer to the name of the file to be opened. The function opens the file, calling DeleteContents() against the document to set its initial state and ensure that any data previously stored in the document is deleted. The default implementation of OnOpenDocument() proceeds by turning on the wait cursor and attempting to load the document's data.

Once it has been opened, the file is converted to a CArchive, and a reference to that archive is passed in the call to the Serialize() function of the document. If the serialization throws an exception, the OnOpenDocument() function handles it by turning off the wait cursor, cleaning up both the file and any CArchive objects, then calling the ReportSaveLoadException() function before finally returning FALSE to the caller.

Unfortunately, the serialization procedure introduces a fistful of things that we're not going to discuss in this chapter but will, instead, leave for elsewhere in the book. CArchive is a class in MFC that implements a storage mechanism that abstracts the differences between disk files, memory files, communications devices, and OLE storage and stream objects. CDocument uses CArchive for two reasons. First, your application needs to be coded so that it can abstractly write or read its data to or from any of those storage mechanisms. Second, all MFC CObject-derived objects are based on a very similar storage mechanism. Since CDocument is ultimately derived from CObject, MFC uses that same mechanism. You might write CObject-derived classes of your own and use those to store data in your document, or you might write classes that are actually collections of your own structures or objects to manage the data in your document conveniently. All such collection classes, as well as CArchive and its less abstract friend CFile, in addition to strategies relating to designing classes with CObject, are discussed in Chapter 9.

If everything goes okay, the function closes the file and cleans up the CArchive as before, but returns TRUE without further incident. Note that the OnOpenDocument() function will leave the document's dirty flag set if the load fails, but will clear the dirty flag of the document if the load is successful.

If you're writing a database application, or some other application that doesn't use files for storage, you'll probably override this function to do whatever is necessary to begin working with the data that your application will handle. Otherwise, the default implementation will be fine for most occasions.

DeleteContents()

In single document interface programs, several features of the CDocument class replace the content of the current document entirely. For example, when you open a new document, the default implementation of CDocument::OnOpenDocument() deletes the contents of the current document before attempting to serialize the new document's data. The OnCloseDocument() function deletes the document contents to free its memory, and OnNewDocument() erases the contents of the document (if the user confirms the new operation) in preparation for the insertion of new data into the document.

To perform this deletion, your document class should implement a DeleteContents() function that overrides the CDocument::DeleteContents() function. The default version of this function, which is of type void and takes no parameters, does nothing. Your implementation should free any memory the document has allocated, and perhaps reset the state of any member variables in the document to indicate that the document is indeed empty.

In the Paintobj example application, the DeleteContents() function just rips through the m_Objects array, which holds all of the objects you've drawn, deleting each element. Since this array represents the complete content of the document, that's all that needs to be done.

Views

The second part of the document/view architecture is built with the view classes. These classes all provide a frameless window that is used to convey information represented in the document to the user. The view will also recognize commands initiated by the mouse or keyboard, enabling the user to interact with the view.

Remember that a view is unique because it provides a window that is dependent on a frame *and* a document. Although a view doesn't exist alone, your frame windows will provide very little functionality to your application by comparison. They'll just handle menu commands and do a little window management, particularly if the frame is an MDI frame window..

With a few exceptions, all views contain no persistent data. Your applications should be designed to store any pertinent information in the document, making it easy for the document to handle the storage and retrieval of information. You should remember to extend this requirement to any information that you wish to be persistent across consecutive invocations of your application − if the docking state of toolbars or modes of operation in your application are specific to the file loaded, and not to the application on a global level, you may want to store them with the document. You'll have to find another place for global settings − you may use an initialization file that you load yourself in CWinApp::InitInstance(), or you can tuck them away in the registry.

MFC provides a few predefined view classes from which your application will derive its own class to implement application-specific functionality. One of the more important choices you'll make while designing your application is which class will provide most of the functionality you need. If you choose correctly, you'll get a lot of functionality for free, leaving you to concentrate on implementing the features unique to your application. Let's take a look at the specifics of the view classes and see how they'll affect the way that your view, and the application as a whole, is implemented.

CScrollView

If you've thought of using a regular CView, it probably means that you're doing the drawing for your application yourself. However, if the image you'll be rendering will be larger than the area of the visible window, you'll need to make sure your application can cope when the data demands more real estate than you have to offer.

You can allow the user to view and edit the extra data in one of three ways:

> ➢ Intercept the WM_GETMINMAXINFO message and force a certain size using SetWindowPos() calls

> ➢ Make your application automatically scale its content to the size of the visible window

> ➢ Have your application subclass CScrollView instead of CView for its view classes

The first approach would have the effect of forcing your application to stick to a certain size. You might further enforce nonsizeability (look it up, smart guy) by writing code to remove the Size command from the system menu, or by changing the main frame's style so that it doesn't have a thick, sizable border.

The second method (also known as **automatic scaling**) is appropriate when the level of detail in the client area of the window doesn't really matter. Applications that only display information and don't let the user edit it are the only real candidates for this option, since small windows make it very difficult for the user to select accurately any objects that they contain.

The third approach (using CScrollView) is by far the most comfortable for the majority users in most applications. CScrollView is derived from CView and adds scroll bars to the normal interface. These scroll bars will allow the user to 'pan' the window over the underlying data, an effect that's a bit like working with a cross-stitch hoop on a large piece of fabric. You can scroll the hoop over other parts of the fabric, stretching them taut when you're interested in working with them, but letting the other pieces fall out of interest's way, collecting in your lap. The window is the hoop – the user can only view and interact with the parts of the document that are rendered inside it.

The Catch

As with all miracle cures, there's a catch. The scrollbars must know how big the entire document is, and the view must know the current position of the scrollbars so that the logical depiction of the view appears correctly scrolled when the view is drawn.

The view can set its scrollable size by calling the SetScrollSizes() function, which takes an integer representing a **mapping mode** and up to three SIZE structures.

This initializes the view so that it knows the size of the underlying document. If, during the life of the view, the size of the document changes, you should call `SetScrollSizes()` again to adjust the range of the scroll bars.

> **A mapping mode specifies the parameters Windows will use to translate logical coordinates to the coordinates used by physical devices, like a video display or printer.**

Two convenient places for your application to call the `SetScrollSizes()` function are the `OnUpdate()` and `OnInitialUpdate()` members of your view. This guarantees that the scrollbars will be re-scaled each time the document forces the view to update itself.

The biggest challenge you'll face in your plan to call `SetScrollSizes()` is efficiency. Depending on exactly what your application is doing, you might face a situation where measuring the extension of the visible objects on your document is very expensive – perhaps nearly as expensive as drawing the whole darn thing in the first place. You might wish to code a bit of cache in your document so that you can measure the size of your visual representation just once and then hang on to the result for as long as possible. If something is deleted or added to the document, you may be able to adjust the cached size instead of measuring everything in sight all over again.

Using SetScrollSizes()

The second parameter to `SetScrollSizes()`, a `SIZE` structure, indicates the maximum size of the scroll bars. The `SIZE` structure has just two integer members that specify the width and height of a rectangle; the `cx` member indicates the maximum horizontal size, while the `cy` member indicates the maximum vertical size. Although the members are integers, they should only be set to positive values. If your document uses x coordinates from -100 to +200, the `cx` value you report back to MFC should be 300.

You should implement a function in your document that provides the current logical size of the document. This function should either return meaningful numbers that the view can convert to the mapping mode using a simple scaling factor, or it should return a usable `SIZE` structure.

Your document may also benefit from an 'is empty' function. If the document is empty, you shouldn't set the scroll sizes to (0,0); instead, you should choose some reasonable minimum. Code something like this should do nicely for most situations:

```
CMyDocument* pMyDoc = GetDocument();
if (pMyDoc->IsEmpty())
{
    // we're empty, so use some reasonable size
    SetScrollSizes(MM_TEXT, CSize(100, 100));
}
else
{
    // we're full, so use the actual size
    SetScrollSizes(MM_TEXT, GetDocument()->GetMyDocumentSize());
}
```

The two additional (optional) parameters to `SetScrollSizes()` dictate other scrollbar characteristics. The third parameter, a reference to a `SIZE`, dictates how far the scrollbars in the view window will scroll when the user presses the *PgUp* or *PgDn* keys, or clicks the mouse in the scrollbar shaft.

The fourth parameter, which is also a reference to a `SIZE`, dictates by how much the scroll bars will move the window when the user presses the arrow keys or clicks the arrows at the end of the scroll bar. When you don't supply these parameters, MFC makes the view scroll one-tenth of the total document size when the user scrolls by pages, and one-tenth of the page size when they scroll by lines.

So far, we've conveniently ignored the first parameter to `SetScrollSizes()`, but now it's time to face facts. The first parameter indicates the mapping mode for the coordinates provided in each `SIZE` parameter. For most applications, this is conveniently `MM_TEXT`, which dictates that each coordinate unit is exactly equal to one pixel on the device which is rendering the image to the user. If you fancy yourself as a very advanced programmer, you may wish to consider using alternate mapping modes, a technique that can either confound or compound your efforts at writing drawing code.

OnPrepareDC()

To implement the actual scrolling, `CScrollView` implements an override for the `CView::OnPrepareDC()` function. This function is called by the view to create and initialize the device context that is passed to the `OnDraw()` function.

> **Whether you're using `CView`, `CScrollView` or any other view class, it's in the view's `OnDraw()` function that all of your actual rendering should take place.**

The default implementation of `OnPrepareDC()` will use the mapping mode you've specified with your call to `SetScrollSizes()` to calculate new logical origins for the drawing so that it will appear to be properly scrolled with the scrollbars.

This means that the mapping mode parameter that you pass to `SetScrollSizes()` must match the mapping mode with which you plan to draw; you can't just change to a more convenient mode in your `OnDraw()` implementation. The scrolling code has computed a displacement for your drawing so that the scrolling will appear to have shifted any new drawing you try to do. If you change mapping modes, the displacement will be similarly affected and things will not line up as they should.

If you want, you can override the behavior of `OnPrepareDC()` to do whatever additional work your `OnDraw()` function might need, but it's a good idea to call the base class implementation of `OnPrepareDC()` before you do any of your own work. The MFC code behind this function uses the `SetViewportOrg()` member of `CDC` to alter the initial logical position of the window before the drawing code executes.

When your view actually paints, you can draw without worrying about the actual position of the scrollbars. However, although you can treat your drawing this simply, it will probably make things a tad slow – you'll waste a lot of time painting objects or text which are outside the field of view. You can improve your code by calling the `GetUpdateRect()` function, implemented by the `CWnd` class, to retrieve the coordinate rectangle to be updated. Only drawing items within or which cross this rectangle will make your drawing code much more efficient.

You can find the exact position of the scrollbars by calling the `GetScrollPosition()` function. This returns a `CPoint` that depicts the status of the scroll bars in logical units. The `GetDeviceScrollPosition()` function works the same way, but returns the position in device units. Neither function requires parameters.

While discussing printing and the other code that renders visual aspects of views, we'll inevitably encounter different coordinate systems. Views normally render in **physical coordinates**, unless you've changed the rules by calling `SetMapMode()`. Physical coordinates relate to a particular device, and simply indicate where the device would draw by itself, without any help from Windows. Using device coordinates is the simplest way to draw, but it doesn't allow very much control over the way the real physical image is scaled. If you draw a line of 72 pixels, for example, you might see a line that's an inch long on your monitor, but only six hundredths of an inch long on your printer!

The relationship between device coordinates and physical coordinates is available as a ratio from the device driver – just call `CDC:GetDeviceCaps()` and ask for `LOGPIXELSX` or `LOGPIXELSY` to find the number of logical pixels per physical inch. A call to `SetMapMode()` can establish a different logical relationship between logical coordinates and physical coordinates. If you establish that ratio with the value you get back from `GetDeviceCaps()`, you can assure that anything you draw will be the same size on whatever device the user has selected for you at runtime.

Blue Jeans Views: Scale-to-Fit

Of course, MFC is always ready with some way to make things a bit simpler, although in this case it does sacrifice some functionality. The `CScrollView` class implements a mode called **scale-to-fit**. A `CScrollView` class, in such a mode, doesn't show scroll bars. Instead, the logical view is stretched or compressed to fit precisely in the client area of the containing window. If you wish to initialize this mode, you can call `CScrollView`'s `SetScaleToFitSize()` function.

The `SetScaleToFitSize()` function takes one parameter: a `SIZE` indicating the total size of the document, which is similar to the second parameter for `SetScrollSizes()`. If you wish to use the scale-to-fit mode, you don't need to call `SetScrollSizes()`. However, by calling both these functions at the right times, you can move a view back and forth between scale-to-fit mode and scrolling mode.

Control-based Views

A large subset of the MFC view classes (`CEditView`, `CRichEditView`, `CTreeView`, `CListView` and `CHtmlView`) all work by containing a Windows control. That is, the client area of the view window is actually filled by a control. The control does all the work for you, and you don't need to worry about painting anything in the area of your view.

In fact, it turns out that MFC is pulling a nifty implementation trick; the view window itself really *is* the control! When the view is created, it creates an instance of the control in question and manages that window as the view. A view really is just a child window that doesn't have a border and interacts with a user – and therefore shares a lot in common with a control. The extras that make the control into a usable view are simply C++ functions added to the class. It's just that the underlying window is an instance of a different Windows window class than for a "plain" view.

Anyway, if you need to access the control directly, you can do so by making a call to the appropriate member function of the derived class.

I'll mention the particular function names in later sections, but the idea is that a member function will return a reference to the control window inside of the view. You can then manipulate it directly as you see fit.

With the exception of CHtmlView, all of the control-based view classes in MFC derive from the CCtrlView class – CHtmlView derives from CFormView. On its own, it's not very interesting; it just puts together the framework for the control classes, while the derived classes do all of the necessary work. If you need to cook up a class based on your own control or combination of controls, CCtrlView is a great base class to use.

One of the most important aspects of using CCtrlView-based classes is learning how to adjust the style bits in the control. Before the window is created, MFC will call the PreCreateWindow() member of your view. It will pass a reference to a CREATESTRUCT structure that it has initialized with the default class name and attributes for your window.

You can override PreCreateWindow() to tweak the style bits or even use your own class name for the new window. You should always call the base class implementation of the function first, though, before you do any tweaking. Base class implementations of PreCreateWindow() always initialize the CREATESTRUCT with appropriate values but, more importantly, they will always make sure the particular type of window you want to create has been made available to your process. MFC defers loading control libraries and registering window classes until PreCreateWindow(), so you must call it to make sure Windows is ready to create your window. The whole process might look like this:

```
BOOL CTreeVuView::PreCreateWindow(CREATESTRUCT& cs)
{
    if (!CTreeView::PreCreateWindow(cs))
        return FALSE;

    cs.style |= TVS_HASLINES | TVS_LINESATROOT;
    return TRUE;
}
```

The notion of overriding PreCreateWindow() is especially important for CCtrlView-based windows because there's just no other good way to modify the style bits for the window as it's used in the view. We'll examine the meaning of all the style bits in Chapter 8, when we consider programming with controls.

Message Reflection

Control windows, including windows created by the new common controls, can fire off notification messages to their parent to let the application know about things that are happening to the control. Controls send notifications when the item selected in the control changes, or when the control needs to retrieve data from the application.

Since the notification messages are normally sent to the parent window that owns the control, the developer is faced with a problem. For example, to implement a CListView-derived class that handles notifications, you'd have to actually put the notification code in the frame window that owns the view. Clearly, splitting the code for the view across different classes isn't nice – you'd like to be able to keep the code bound to the view class.

To facilitate such an architecture, MFC 4.0 introduced the concept of message reflection. This simple change to the message routing code in MFC causes notification messages and command messages not handled by the parent window (if that window is known to MFC) to be passed back down to the control window class itself.

MFC discerns between message map entries for messages directly handled by a window and messages handled by a window via reflection. When you select the Message Maps tab of ClassWizard and look at the Messages list, you'll see an equals sign (=) before messages which are handled via reflection:

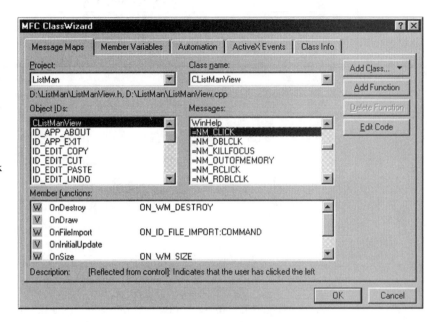

The macros added to your message map by ClassWizard for reflected messages have slightly different names than the other message map macros we've examined. Here are the reflection message map entries that MFC supports

```
ON_CONTROL_REFLECT(wNotifyCode, memberFxn)

ON_CONTROL_REFLECT_EX(wNotifyCode, memberFxn)

ON_NOTIFY_REFLECT(wNotifyCode, memberFxn)

ON_NOTIFY_REFLECT_EX(wNotifyCode, memberFxn)

ON_UPDATE_COMMAND_UI_REFLECT(memberFxn)
```

Except for the ON_UPDATE_COMMAND_UI_REFLECT() message, all the macros accept the notification code and the name of the member function which will handle the notification. The notification code is the code that the control sends which identifies the particular message – for example, tree view controls send messages identified by constants which begin with TVN_.

Besides the notifications, there are also a number of control-oriented messages that are reflected by MFC. These are shown here:

Message	Message map macro
WM_CTLCOLOR	ON_WM_CTLCOLOR_REFLECT()
WM_DRAWITEM	ON_WM_DRAWITEM_REFLECT()
WM_MEASUREITEM	ON_WM_MEASUREITEM_REFLECT()
WM_DELETEITEM	ON_WM_DELETEITEM_REFLECT()
WM_CHARTOITEM	ON_WM_CHARTOITEM_REFLECT()
WM_VKEYTOITEM	ON_WM_VKEYTOITEM_REFLECT()
WM_COMPAREITEM	ON_WM_COMPAREITEM_REFLECT()
WM_HSCROLL	ON_WM_HSCROLL_REFLECT()
WM_VSCROLL	ON_WM_VSCROLL_REFLECT()
WM_PARENTNOTIFY	ON_WM_PARENTNOTIFY_REFLECT()
WM_NOTIFY	ON_NOTIFY_REFLECT()
WM_COMMAND	ON_COMMAND_REFLECT()

The WM_CTLCOLOR message I list above isn't a real message; it's a fabrication invented by MFC that, for the purposes of our discussion here, is enough like a message that differences don't matter. We'll examine the differences in Chapter 7.

The messages above are reflected because they're generally needed by controls. There are a couple of other reflected messages that are indirectly granted to the control using the same message identifier. If the message isn't handled by the parent, the default handler for the message reflects the message back to the control, using the same message ID number. This is done for all messages which are involved in implementing owner-drawn controls; WM_COMPAREITEM, WM_DRAWITEM, WM_MEASUREITEM and WM_DELETEITEM are the messages in this category, as well as the registered drag list messages which common controls send when their content is being dragged.

When you let your view handle notifications for these last reflected messages, you don't need to use special message map entries because the reflected message has the same identifier as the original, unlike the other reflected messages, which use different message IDs.

CEditView

If you're planning an application that allows you to edit a bunch of text, you may wish to make use of CEditView. This is a view window that places an edit control in the client area of the frame window holding the view. The edit view is a fully-featured Windows edit control, and though it can't handle font or color formatting for individual characters, it does provide the ability to readily accept or show text for input.

If your application demands font management or coloring in its user interface, you can use `CRichEditView` instead. This class is similar to `CEditView`, but it has many extra features to support the use of fonts and colors. A `CRichEditView` can do everything that a `CEditView` can, plus much more. For economy of space here, assume that whenever we refer to `CEditView` in this section, we mean both `CEditView` and `CRichEditView`. We'll point out any differences as they arise. We describe the extra features of `CRichEditView` in the last subsection of this chapter, and examine them in more detail in Chapter 8.

Since `CEditView` is a `CView`-derived class, it includes code to perform printing and print preview, as well as find-and-replace. The class also includes implementations of the commands commonly found on the Edit menu: Cut, Copy, Paste, Clear, Undo, Select All, and Repeat.

While the edit view implements handlers for these functions, it doesn't implement a menu, so you're responsible for making sure your menu contains commands to allow the user the functionality they require. You also need to make sure that when the menu is activated, it produces the correct command ID. AppWizard-generated applications include a menu that offers most of these commands, depending on the options you've selected. The table below shows the commands implemented by the `CEditView` class:

Typical Menu Name	Typical Command Name	Command ID
File	Print	ID_FILE_PRINT
Edit	Cut	ID_EDIT_CUT
Edit	Copy	ID_EDIT_COPY
Edit	Paste	ID_EDIT_PASTE
Edit	Clear	ID_EDIT_CLEAR
Edit	Undo	ID_EDIT_UNDO
Edit	Select All	ID_EDIT_SELECT_ALL
Edit	Find	ID_EDIT_FIND
Edit	Replace	ID_EDIT_REPLACE
Edit	Repeat	ID_EDIT_REPEAT

`CEditView` handles these commands using normal message maps. When you derive your own class from `CEditView`, you can provide your own message map to override any of the default handlers. As usual, you're also welcome to handle any other messages that you need to process, adding your own message map for your edit control. You can do this by using the ClassWizard or by directly editing the message map yourself.

Accessing CEditView Data

Data storage in `CEditView`s can be interesting because the edit control represented by a `CEditView` actually holds the current copy of the data in the view, rather than letting the data remain in the document. If it helps, you can think of the `CEditView` class as a wrapper for the edit control.

`CEditView` provides the member function `GetEditCtrl()` to return a reference to the `CEdit` instance used in the view. (The `CRichEditView` provides similar functionality via a function named `GetRichEditCtrl()`.) Using this reference, you can perform any operation you want on the edit control, but you should be aware that some operations may change the status of the control, and so confuse the `CEditView`. For example, you shouldn't call `SetTabStops()` directly on the `CEdit` because this will throw off some of the math that `CEditView` needs to do when it's printing.

One useful application of `GetEditCtrl()` is to change the text in the edit control, or you may wish to use the `SetWindowText()` function to set the text directly. Directly calling `SetWindowText()` will overwrite any existing data in the control, but is very simple. With the call to `GetEditCtrl()`, you might code:

```
CEdit& refEdit = GetEditCtrl();
refEdit.SetWindowText("Some initial text here!");
```

Calling `SetWindowText()` directly means just that:

```
SetWindowText("Some initial text here!");
```

While a call to `SetWindowText()` has the same effect against either the `CEditView` or the reference to the `CEdit` it can produce, there are many member functions which `CEdit` implements that `CEditView` doesn't, simply because the `CEdit` is so readily accessible.

If you need to examine or add to the text held in the control, rather than directly modify it, you can call the `GetHandle()` member function to get a handle to the memory used to hold the edited text. This code substitutes all minus signs (–) in the edit control with plus signs (+).

```
CEdit& pEdit = GetEditCtrl();
LPTSTR lpstrCharacter;
HLOCAL hMemory;

hMemory = pEdit.GetHandle();
lpstrCharacter = (LPTSTR) ::LocalLock(hMemory);
ASSERT(lpstrCharacter != NULL);

while (*lpstrCharacter != _T('\0'))
{
    if (*lpstrCharacter == _T('-'))
        *lpstrCharacter = _T('+');

    lpstrCharacter = _tcsinc(lpstrCharacter);
}
```

```
// Release the memory we took
// and force the window to update
::LocalUnlock(hMemory);
pEdit.Invalidate();
```

Note that this code fragment won't work on Windows 95, Windows 98, or Win32s, although it will run fine on Windows NT. Those operating systems aren't interested in allowing you access to the memory handles in their edit controls. If you make a call to `GetHandle()` on an operating system that doesn't support it, the `hMemory` retrieved will be bogus, the call to `::LocalLock()` will fail, and the `ASSERT()` in the code above will trip.

We'll examine more features of the CEdit class, along with the other MFC wrappers for Windows controls, during the next chapter – where we examine most of the windows controls individually. You'll find this interesting reading if you're planning an application around CEditViews, as the controls provide many other cool functions and messages to manipulate the text of the control.

Solving the Data Management Problem

Now, since all the control-based views are managing the data they display to the user (instead of having the document manage the data), you'll need to deviate from the normal approach when it comes time for the document to do some work with the data. Normally, when you create a document/view based application the document strictly manages the persistent data for the application.

But when you use a control-based view, the view itself manages all the data that it's showing. That's simply because Windows controls (with a few exceptions) are designed to own the data that they draw.

You can solve the data management problem in one of two ways. First, you might have the view represent data from a member variable in the document. Any time the document knows the member changes, it asks the view to redraw itself. Or, you can simply have the document relegate control of the data the view owns and just carry on. If the document is loading or saving, it will ask its initial view to load or store the data. Maybe this means that the view directly touches the archive, or maybe it means that the document manipulates the archive and has the view immediately load itself from that data as it goes by.

For almost all cases, having the view step in and take the data from the document is preferable. Letting the view own some data bends the rules a little, but in the long run it makes things easier. Certainly it would be nice to have a perfectly squared-up object oriented design. But such a design loses its appeal when you realize how much work you'll have to go through to work around the underlying system architecture.

Your CDocument::Serialize() function will have to find some way to cause an associated view to serialize itself. The CEditView class has members to do serialization to handle exactly this problem. You can use a serialization implementation like this one to handle the storage of data from the edit control in the view:

```
void CMyDocument::Serialize(CArchive& ar)
{
    m_viewEdit->Serialize(ar);

    if (ar.IsLoading())
    {
        // do your own loading work here
    }
    else
    {
        // do your own saving work here
    }
}
```

Note that the call to CEditView::Serialize() takes place outside of the conditional that's usually seen in these situations.

As `CEditView::Serialize()` takes the reference to the `CArchive` object for the serialization context, it can make its own decision about saving or loading modes and act appropriately. We've shown the call to `Serialize()` before the conditional here, but you could place it inside or after the conditional, depending on how you want your data file to be structured.

Further, we're simply using a member variable to remember where our view lives. You might need to enumerate the views associated with your document to get to the view itself. If that's the case for your application, you'll want to find the section called 'Enumerating Views' later in this chapter.

You may have also noticed a member of `CEditView` called `SerializeRaw()`. This function serializes the text in a `CEditView`, while the `Serialize()` code writes the size of the text data as extra binary information to the archive. It's appropriate to use `Serialize()` when you're writing other non-textual information from your document, and to use `SerializeRaw()` when you want to produce a plain text file that your users can later manipulate with other programs or commands.

Using Multiple CEditViews

If you're planning on allowing those who use your application to create multiple `CEditViews` for the same document, things become pretty complicated pretty quickly. With this feature in mind, you'll need to find some way to let any edit view notify the document that the text has been updated, as well as providing a mechanism for the document to pass that data to the other views, so they can be updated properly.

You can do this by having the view call `UpdateAllViews()` in its controlling document. In response, the document should refresh all other views under its control. Obviously, this can be a rather time-consuming practice, so you'll need to design the process carefully.

CRichEditView

The relatively recent advent of the rich edit common control was one of the more eagerly-received additions to Windows. The control allows you to present to the user an edit box that can understand the Microsoft Rich Text format. This file format is a plain-text language that allows you to express both text and the formatting information for that text. Though it isn't very complicated, the format is robust and powerful. It is, however, hard to implement completely.

Furthermore, the Rich Edit control can inherently handle more text than the regular Windows edit controls can. In Windows 95/98, a regular edit control is limited to less than 40 kilobytes of text, while a Rich Edit control can handle almost as much text as you have in memory regardless of which operating system you're using.

As I mentioned earlier, the programmatic interface to a rich edit control is mostly just like a regular edit control. The only difference is this ability to handle the rich text format, as well as all the fancy formatting that goes with it. You should use a rich edit control (or rich edit view) in situations where varying the font, color, size, or formatting of your text very carefully is important. You should use a regular edit control (or regular edit view) when you just need to display some text that all uses the same font and color. You might think of using a regular edit control (or edit view) in situations where you would use Windows' Notepad, and using a rich edit control in situations where you would have used your favorite word processing package.

The ability to handle the rich text format affords the rich edit control flexibility beyond simply handling colors and fonts. It can also accommodate embedded pictures and OLE objects.

A side effect of the control's OLE containment support is that you'll need to enable OLE container support for your application if you're going to use a rich edit control – that is, if you've selected CRichEditView as your view's base class in Step 6 of AppWizard. If you use the final step in AppWizard to request a rich edit view, you'll get a warning message like this before the Wizard creates your application:

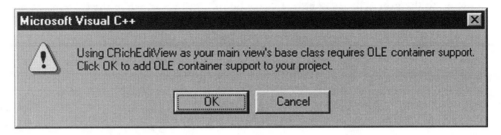

The change that AppWizard will make is very, very important; it will use a CRichEditDoc instead of a plain CDocument class to support your CRichEditView. This document type has an incredible amount of support for the edit control. It includes all of MFC's OLE support to deal with the control's OLE features, and also adds-in support for serializing the data the control contains.

Serialization

CRichEditView serializes data *very* differently when compared to the regular CEditView. I mentioned in the previous section that you could call Serialize() or SerializeRaw() against a CEditView to get the data from the view in different ways. You might think of using similar calls against your CRichEditView instance, but you'll have little luck with it. The data structure that's maintained by the rich edit control isn't trivial, so the CRichEditView interacts carefully with the CRichEditDoc class to perform serialization. The implementation of that interaction manifests itself as a single function call in your Serialize() implementation. It would look like this:

```
void CEditorsDoc::Serialize(CArchive& ar)
{
   if (ar.IsStoring())
   {
      // TODO: add storing code here
   }
   else
   {
      // TODO: add loading code here
   }

   CRichEditDoc::Serialize(ar);
}
```

The call to the base class serialization implementation is very important. It's this call that gets both the text and any embedded objects in the control serialized.

Your application *must* serialize the content of the CRichEditDoc class *after* any other data you serialize in your document, because the view class reads data until the end of the file rather than until any specific number of bytes have been read. If you were to have your document serialize other information after calling the CRichEditDoc::Serialize() function, the load-side code provided by CRichEditDoc would suck up the data you'd written to the file without remorse – it just continues reading until the file ends.

There's more information on the rich edit control (and the other 32-bit common controls) in Chapter 8.

A Different Architecture

CRichEditView and CRichEditDoc are unique because they share the burden of managing the data presented to the user. The CRichEditView holds all the text, while the CRichEditDoc holds information about any OLE objects inserted in the control. There's a one-to-one correspondence between the CRichEditView object and the CRichEditDoc object, and you can't have more than one CRichEditView attached to a CRichEditDoc.

We've already talked about the GetDocument() call that CView classes support, but using CRichEditDoc's GetView() function, you can navigate in the other direction – from the document to the view. This is only reasonable and possible in this case because the CRichEditDoc is engaged in an exclusive relationship with the view.

The document class exposes little other functionality. It has a public BOOL data member named m_bRTF which you can set to specify whether you want the document to save formatting information in the serialized data. If it is set to FALSE, the stream generated is just plain text with no formatting; if TRUE, the stream is formatted as a .rtf file. This setting is closely related to the GetStreamFormat() function, which returns SF_TEXT if m_bRTF is FALSE or SF_RTF if it's TRUE.

CRichEditDoc also offers a CreateClientItem() function. This function allows you to programmatically insert an OLE object into the control. The function is similar to the COleDocument member function of the same name; please refer to Chapter 13 for notes on how to use it.

CRichEditView on the other hand, has many more member functions, but there's *almost* a one-to-one correspondence with the member functions of CRichEditCtrl, so we'll examine them together in Chapter 8 when we look at the common controls in depth.

CTreeView and CListView

The CTreeView and CListView classes work just like all the other CCtrlView classes. These classes are quite stripped, however. They don't have any special functions like the edit control view classes.

You'll be very likely to override the PreCreateWindow() member of your list or tree view. The controls are quite complicated and, as such, have lots of interesting style bits you can fiddle with to make the window work exactly the way you want it to. You'll probably also want to implement the OnInitialUpdate() function of your tree or list view object in order to populate it.

If what the user does to the control during its lifetime really matters to you, you should carefully code responses to all of the notification messages that the control sends. Just let your view talk to the document as the user manipulates it, and let the document always reflect the state of the control. If the user saves the document, make the settings they changed persistent, along with the data. You might want to save the widths of columns or the positions of icons in a list view control, or information about what levels were expanded in a tree view control.

Finally, and like the other control-based views, you can use the `CListView::GetListCtrl()` and `CTreeView::GetTreeCtrl()` functions to gain references to the `CListCtrl` and `CTreeCtrl` objects C++ side of the view.

Once again, I've intentionally not discussed any details about the controls themselves, as we'll cover them in detail in Chapter 8.

CHtmlView

MFC 6.0 added a new and exciting view class, `CHtmlView`. While `CHtmlView` shares many of the control-based view aspects we've seen so far, it is somewhat different in that it is the only MFC view to wrap an ActiveX control rather than an intrinsic Windows control, like the edit or tree controls we've just seen. You'll see more about wrapping ActiveX controls in Chapter 15.

`CHtmlView` was created to provide you with easy access to the Microsoft Internet Explorer Web Browser ActiveX control (referred to as **MSIE**), and it shares many of the control's capabilities. For example, you can easily navigate to any URL by simply providing the URL to the view. The view, in turn, passes the URL to MSIE. MSIE then queries the URL and begins the Internet data transfer process. The view can receive notifications from the control for interesting events, such as the moment when the URL responds. And, of course, `CHtmlView` and MSIE provide you access to the very powerful HTML document object model **Dynamic HTML**, or **DHTML**. DHTML coverage, unfortunately, is beyond the scope of this chapter, even this book, but I'll show you how to access the DHTML information within MSIE. There are now a plethora of books and articles available to show you what to do with DHTML once you gain access to the document.

To begin, `CHtmlView` derives from `CFormView` rather than `CCtrlView`. This underscores the main difference between this view and the other control-based views. `CHtmlView` really wraps an ActiveX control rather than one of the basic Windows controls you've been used to using. That doesn't mean the view is any more difficult to use. It's just that the notifications and parameters are used slightly differently. I should also note you need to make sure MSIE is properly installed on any client system that intends to use your application. Since `CHtmlView` doesn't use a standard Windows control, you can't simply execute your application and know it will run properly on any given client system.

When you create the view class using AppWizard, you'll find `PreCreateWindow()` has already been overridden for you, as has `OnInitialUpdate()`. If you need to modify any general view style bits, you can modify the `CREATESTRUCT` parameter passed into `PreCreateWindow()`, as with any view. Unlike the other control-based views, however, you don't typically tailor `CHtmlView`'s operation here. Instead, you change the *parameters* MSIE offers through `CHtmlView`. We'll see how this is done in a bit and discuss ActiveX control parameter mutators in detail in Chapter 15. `CHtmlView` handles the really interesting initialization for you when it activates the MSIE control and hooks it up, so you needn't concern yourself with the details at this time. You will be interested in changing the code you'll find in `OnInitialUpdate()`, though. It's here you'll see the URL to where the control will initially navigate:

```
// TODO: This code navigates to a popular spot on the web.
// change the code to go where you'd like.
Navigate2(_T("http://www.microsoft.com/visualc/"),NULL,NULL);
```

CHtmlView uses its Navigate2() method to supply MSIE with an initial URL. Any URL here will do, though it's best if the URL is valid. Your users will probably dislike navigating to some unseemly URL or receive a navigation error just as the application initializes. A good way to make sure the initial application's displayed content is precisely what you intend is to include the HTML in your application as a resource, then navigate to the stored content you provide.

Adding HTML as a resource is a simple matter. Once you create the HTML you want to display, you use the Insert | Resource menu item to activate the resource dialog:

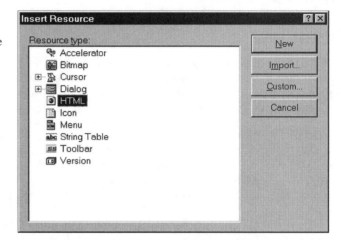

When you select the HTML resource type and click the Import button, you'll be asked to select the HTML file you wish to insert into your applications resources:

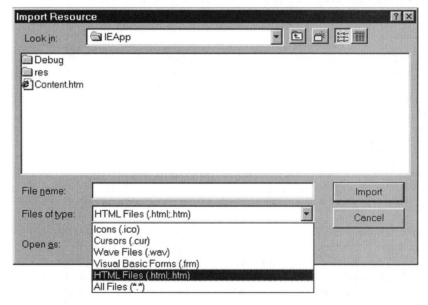

Microsoft Visual Studio will load the HTML file, include it in your application's resources, and provide it the default resource identifier IDR_HTML1 (at least for the first HTML document). Feel free to change the resource ID if you like.

Now that we have some basic HTML content loaded as a resource, we can use CHtmlView's LoadFromResource() method to retrieve the HTML content when OnInitialUpdate() is executed. We'll change the navigation code we saw previously to this:

```
// Load initial HTML content from resource.
LoadFromResource(IDR_HTML1);
```

This is exactly what I've done with the IEApp example. When you run the example, you'll be able to type in a URL into a combo box stuffed in a **rebar** control (like Internet Explorer). The application begins its life with "Hello, World!" displayed in its content area; it got this HTML from the application's resource memory. If you type a URL into the combo box, or if you pick one from its list control, MSIE is handed the URL using Navigate2() as we've seen previously.

CHtmlView also wraps other useful MSIE functionality. For example, you have all of the common Web browser functions you'd expect, such as GoForward(), GoBack(), GoHome() and, of course, Stop(). CHtmlView automatically connects MSIE to your frame window, but you can change the size using the control's property methods SetLeft(), SetTop(), or SetHeight(). But probably the most interesting aspect of using CHtmlView is it provides you with MSIE events by simply overriding some of CHtmlView's virtual event methods. For example, if you're interested in determining whether a given URL navigation was successful, you can override OnNavigateComplete2(). OnNavigateComplete2() provides you with the URL that was actually navigated, be it a textual URL, a UNC (Universal Naming Code) file name, or a **PIDL** (which we came across when discussing the Windows Shell in Chapter 7). When OnNavigateComplete2() fires, you know the navigation command was successful and to which URL the browser actually navigated. Of course, if the URL doesn't exist, OnNavigateComplete2() won't be fired.

Finally, as I mentioned, you have access to the DHTML document MSIE is currently displaying. If you use the CHtmlView's GetHtmlDocument() method, MSIE will hand to you an IDispatch pointer you can query for IHTMLDocument2, which is the granddaddy DHTML interface (you'll certainly see this interface used in any good DHTML reference you find). I discuss COM interface pointers and IUnknown's QueryInterface() method in more detail in Chapter 13. There is one thing to note here, however. If you haven't navigated to some URL, there will be no document, and hence GetHtmlDocument() will return a NULL pointer.

CFormView and CRecordView

CFormView and CRecordView are two other special derivatives of the CView class. CRecordView is a subclass of CFormView which is, itself, derived from CView via CScrollView. The big news for CFormView is that it implements a form view – a view based on a form. Plenty of applications are written, particularly in the corporate environment, where the interface for the application is an electronic re-implementation of a form.

It's easy to imagine a claims-processing application at an insurance company that simply mimics the familiar paperwork for processing a claim. The application presents a user interface that the user understands, while the underlying application breathes new life into the process by providing a front-end to a database or statistical package.

The idea behind CFormView is to provide a method to present a form window that can be used as the primary interface for an application.

There are two ways to go about this; the first is to painstakingly code `CreateWindow()` calls that create Windows controls for your main window. Since it won't be a WYSIWYG process, positioning and sizing the windows, creating them in the right order and figuring out all of the parameters to `CreateWindow()` for each call is likely to send your blood pressure through the roof.

The other, preferable approach is to create a dialog template that has all of the controls you need for your form. You can use Microsoft Visual Studio's dialog editor to create the template you want, positioning and sizing the controls with the facilities described in Chapter 1.

When you create your `CFormView` or `CRecordView`, the client area of the view will be created using your dialog template – that is, the dialog will be created and placed in the client area of the view, effectively wrapping the frame window, toolbars, status bar and menus your application uses as its user interface. Since your view is actually a modeless instantiation of your dialog template, you must create your dialog without a border or a caption. You can select all of these settings in the property page of the dialog box as you edit it.

> If the frame window is sized to be too small to show the whole dialog, the view will automatically grow scrollbars to allow your users to move the visible area of the view around on the underlying form.
>
> If you want the frame to fit the view, you can use code like that shown in the **SNAPVW** sample which ships with the Visual C++ product. Code in the **OnSize()** member of the view in the sample measures the view and sizes the frame to match.

As the view is created, the framework creates your dialog box based on the dialog ID you've provided to the `CFormView` or `CRecordView`. When you create a `CFormView`-derived dialog, you'll need to pass the ID of the dialog you wish to place in the view as a parameter to the constructor. The constructor is overloaded, and it can accept either a string name for the resource, or an integer ID. You'll need to write code in the constructor for your derived version of the `CFormView` class to make sure you pass the ID of the dialog to the constructor of `CFormView` in a format it was expecting.

If you ask ClassWizard or AppWizard for a `CFormView`-based view, you can see that the template ID is provided to the `CFormView` constructor in an initializer list:

```
CSampleFormView::CSampleFormView()
   : CFormView(CSampleFormView::IDD)
{ // real work here... }
```

Back in the header file, the Wizards have declared an enum local to the `CSampleFormView` class that defines the `IDD` value to match the resource associated with the view.

As you can probably guess from these descriptions, `CRecordView` is very much like `CFormView`. The thing that sets `CRecordView` apart from the other classes, though, is its ability to handle `CRecordset` data. `CRecordset`s are used to wrap the recordsets that are produced by the ODBC wrappers in MFC. You can use a `CRecordView` to avoid having to code your own user interface to let your users page through records produced by a database query.

CRecordView automatically places fields returned in a CRecordset in corresponding fields of a dialog-based view, and also provides facilities to format and edit the data as it's moved to and from the recordset.

> MFC also provides equivalent **CDaoRecordView** and **CDaoRecordset** classes. We'll examine all these classes in much more detail during our treatment of the database-related classes in Chapter 12.

Rendering Your View

Eventually, the time comes to have your view actually do some work – it needs to paint the data from the document it represents. If you've implemented CFormView, CListView, CRichEditView, CTreeView, CRecordView, CEditView or CHtmlView, the class intrinsically contains the code that it needs to paint itself. You don't need to worry about any of the fundamentals. In some special instances, you may wish to fool around with OnEraseBkgnd() methods or suchlike, but these cases are rare and they are as easy as handling the appropriate WM_ message with an MFC message handler function.

As a Windows programmer, you're undoubtedly aware that painting is one of an application's most basic functions – it's a response to one of the many Windows messages that fly around applications like horseflies at the Kentucky Derby. As far as the user is concerned, painting is easily the most important response your application ever makes. MFC inherently provides support for two different rendering modes: printing to a printer and painting to the screen. Your view needs to implement code that is appropriate to both of these.

The tips, suggestions and code that we'll discuss in this section are aimed squarely at the CView and CScrollView classes, since they're the only ones in which you're forced to implement your own painting and printing.

OnDraw()

MFC provides an implementation for the OnDraw() member function in every view class type. It is called as a result of the processing of the WM_PAINT message. In response to WM_PAINT, MFC calls OnDraw() after calling the OnPrepareDC() function to initialize the device context. For CScrollViews, MFC does the scaling or scrolling calculations necessary to make the view work. For other view types, such as CEditView, and CFormView, OnPrepareDC() does no work. In plain old CViews, the function does nothing more than check to see if the number of pages to be printed is known. If it isn't, it assumes that only one page will be printed. On the other hand, if you're implementing a CScrollView class, it's particularly important to call the base class implementation of OnPrepareDC() in any overriding code.

The OnPrepareDC() function is of most relevance to device context initialization in classes based on CScrollView. You can override this function to do any device context initialization you like – preparing fonts, brushes, pens, background colors and mapping modes are all very common uses, but when MFC is preparing to print your view, the call takes on special meaning, which we'll come to shortly.

If you're writing code for another view class, like `CEditView` or `CFormView`, you'll never need to change the way your drawing is done to the screen, since the base class handles this work for you adequately.

OnPaint()

If you need to, you can add code to handle `WM_PAINT` messages directly. This is useful if you're interested in preempting the call to `OnPrepareDC()`, or if you're interested in doing your own processing first. Only view classes in MFC implement `OnDraw()`, so if you use other classes you *must* provide an `OnPaint()` function to handle `WM_PAINT`.

> To summarize, **OnPaint()** is called first, since that's what directly handles the **WM_PAINT** message. In turn, MFC's default implementation of **OnPaint()** calls **OnPrepareDC()**, before passing that **CDC** object to your **OnDraw()** function. If you override any of these functions, you should make sure you keep the chain of control in this order.

OnInitialUpdate()

Painting can become very complicated – you'll often find that you need to do tricky calculations to lay out and scale whatever it is you need to draw. You might need to do work to calculate offsets if you're scrolling, and anything you draw needs to be measured to calculate the location of anything next to it.

You can greatly speed up your code if you cache the information that you need to do painting. For instance, if you're drawing text, you might create a font and keep it around throughout the life of your window, instead of creating it each time Windows requests that you repaint the content. In order to perform positioning calculations later, you'll probably need to measure the font to get its text metrics. It's very convenient to store this sort of information in a member variable of your view class so that you can readily access it from your `OnPaint()` or `OnDraw()` code.

For these reasons, the first time you repaint your window, you'll probably need to do some amount of special initialization work. To this end, the Microsoft Foundation Classes provide an `OnInitialUpdate()` member function in their view classes. This function is called after the window associated with the view has been created but before it becomes visible.

> You can also call the function yourself indirectly by calling the undocumented **SendInitialUpdate()** member of **CDocument**, which will call the **OnInitialUpdate()** function of each view associated with the document.

If you allow your users to change things that affect the way you'll paint, such as the font they're using, you can always modify the member variables directly and invalidate the client area of your window. This can be done by calling `InvalidateRect()`, just like you would in a standard C Windows programming application.

Enumerating Views

Some functions of your application may need to iterate through all of the views associated with a given document and perform some operation on them. For example, if you've written a drawing program, you may wish to provide a menu item that turns on a grid when a user selects it. Furthermore, if this function affects all views of a particular drawing, you might actually implement the function in the document rather than within a view. You can associate the menu item with this `OnTurnGridsOn()` function using a message map entry, and then attach it to a function that looks like this:

```
void CYourDocument::OnTurnGridsOn()
{
    POSITION pos = GetFirstViewPosition();
    while (pos != NULL)
    {
        CYourView* pView = (CYourView*)GetNextView(pos);
        pView->SetGridMode(TRUE);
    }
}
```

When the function is called, it creates a variable of type `POSITION` named `pos`, and with a call to `GetFirstViewPosition()` initializes it to the first element of an internal list of views for that document. `POSITION`s are used to store the current position in a **list**, which I'll cover in Chapter 9. If there aren't any views associated with the document, the loop in the function will not run, because `pos` will be `NULL`. Otherwise, for each iteration of the loop, the `pos` variable is passed to the `GetNextView()` function.

The function I've coded here simply calls my hypothetical `SetGridMode()` function on each of the views – presumably, the views in the drawing program actually implement the grid, so they're the ones that need to do the work. It's probably more appropriate to implement this particular command at the level of the document, though, since the document knows all of the views it owns. And that makes the implementation of this command handler and example of a situation where we'd enjoy great use of MFC's command routing. Since neither the view nor the frame would handle the message, and the document is architecturally our most appealing spot anyway, it's quite convenient!

GetNextView()

`GetNextView()` returns a pointer to the view, incrementing `pos` to the next view at the same time. If there are no other views, `pos` will be set to `NULL` and the loop (and the function) will exit. The pointer returned is used to call `SetGridMode()`.

Note that, in this function, we've shamelessly cast the return value of `GetNextView()` to a pointer to a `CYourView` object. This is dangerous in situations where an application implements different types of view classes. `GetNextView()` returns a pointer to a generic `CView` object. If the pointer returned isn't actually pointing to a `CYourView`, the dereference and call to `SetGridMode()` will have unpredictable and undesirable results. You may wish to use run-time type information in the view classes and an `ASSERT()` to protect your code, or actually to test the run-time type information to make sure the returned view pointer is meaningful.

Managing Views

The association and interaction between the document and view instances in your application is its lifeline. This relationship guarantees that the user is able to visualize the data in any way they want, even if that means multiple windows on the same data. The foundation classes notify your document when the list of views associated with a document changes, enabling your application to react in any way that it sees fit.

AddView() and RemoveView()

AddView() and RemoveView() are called to add a new association between an existing document and an existing, but unattached, view. Both of these functions take a single parameter that provides a pointer to the view object that is being added or removed. The default implementation of these functions simply adds or removes the view from the list of views each document manages.

You can't override these functions since they're not virtual, but you *can* override the OnChangedViewList() function. Before we move on, however, we should note that AddView() is very important when you're interested in constructing or altering the document/view classes that live in your application. You might call AddView() in handlers for commands in your window's menu so that the user can add different types of views to the currently open document.

OnChangedViewList()

When the view list for a document changes, the application framework calls the OnChangedViewList() function for that document instance. The default implementation of this member function closes the document by calling OnCloseDocument() if there are no more views associated with the document.

OnChangedViewList() is called by the default implementation of the AddView() and RemoveView() functions. Your application-specific document class implementation can override this function if it's interested in staying active even when no views are open against the document. You might wish to have this functionality if your document instance is persistent through the life of your application, rather than only leaving it loaded while your application runs. By overriding this function, you'll be notified whenever the list of views in your application changes.

You don't have to manage a list of views yourself, because the CDocument code does this for you.

UpdateAllViews()

By the time you get around to letting your document interact with your view, you'll be interested in changing its content. If you do this, you'll be obliged to get the views associated with your document to update, reflecting any changes that you've made.

MFC provides you with CDocument::UpdateAllViews() to get this done. The framework will rip through the list of views associated with the document instance and call their OnUpdate() functions. You can even pass UpdateAllViews() a few parameters which may speed up the painting.

```
void UpdateAllViews(CView*   pSender,
                    LPARAM   lHint = 0L,
                    CObject* pHint = NULL);
```

The first parameter is a pointer to the view which requested the update – since the view accepts input from the user, you can just pass the `this` pointer to the function. `UpdateAllViews()` always does exactly what its name implies – it updates all of the views associated with a document. If you just want to update a single view, you should do it directly by calling its `Invalidate()` function. The parameter is only a way for you to tell your painting code that a particular view was responsible for affecting the change to the document.

A typical invocation of `UpdateAllViews()` might look like this:

```
void CMyView::DoSomething()
{
    CMyDocument *pDoc = GetDocument();
    pDoc->ChangeDocument(UsingSomeInformation);
    pDoc->UpdateAllViews(this);
}
```

Note that only one parameter is passed to `UpdateAllViews()` here. If you want, you can pass a long integer as a second parameter; this in turn is passed to the `OnUpdate()` function of each view to optimize your painting or updating code. You can also pass a third parameter – a pointer to any `CObject`-derived class. Like the long integer, this parameter is optional and its meaning is completely up to you. If you don't offer these parameters, they default to `0L` and `NULL`, respectively.

Of course, if you only want to update one view or a subset of views, you can do so by combining the code we described above with a call to the `OnUpdate()` functions associated with individual views. Simply remove the call to `UpdateAllViews()` and substitute it with calls to `OnUpdate()` on the individual view objects that you want to have updated.

Printing

During the process of writing code for Windows applications in C, it's common for developers to experience problems when the time comes to plow through the printing code. It just isn't much fun to feel you're repeating all the work you did when you were drawing on the screen. Fortunately, the Microsoft Foundation Classes go a long way towards helping you avoid the drudgery of re-implementing everything in sight when you're ready to send things to the printer. Let's take a look at the way this code, all provided by the `CView` classes, has been implemented.

Note that the AppWizard will have generated printing code for you if the Printing and Print Preview box was checked on Step 4 of the project creation dialog. If you need to add code for printing post-AppWizard, you'll need to set up Print, Print Preview and Print Setup. The Print command is usually hooked to the `OnFilePrint()` function in `CView`. If you wish to implement print previews, you'll also need to hook up the appropriate command to the `OnFilePrintPreview()` function of your view. Views provided by MFC supply these functions, so you can call the base-class implementations directly if you don't need to override them for your own purposes.

Other functions you'll need to override in your `CView` class, if you didn't ask for printing support from AppWizard, are `OnPreparePrinting()`, `OnBeginPrinting()` and `OnEndPrinting()`.

By way of example, the `Hexview` sample provided with this book supports printing. The program lets you open a file and display its contents in hexadecimal. As you'll see, managing a file's page count is probably the trickiest part of printing. `Hexview` is also important in Chapter 9, where we showcase the various utility classes provided by MFC.

OnFilePrint()

OnFilePrint() is the first view class member function that's called when the user decides to start a print job. (CView::OnFilePrint() isn't documented – it seems to be an oversight in the documentation. There's certainly nothing secret about the function.) Normally, you won't override this function unless you have some very special printing work to do. The MFC-supplied implementation of OnFilePrint() creates a CPrintInfo object and initializes it before calling OnPreparePrinting(), which is therefore called before the framework even displays the printing parameters dialog. It can display any dialog that you're interested in processing before showing the user the standard printing dialog. For example, you might prompt the user for more information on exactly what to print through this added dialog.

OnFilePrint() passes a pointer to the active CPrintInfo object when it calls OnPreparePrinting(), and the latter is free to modify it to express preferences or settings for the print job. Perhaps the most important member of CPrintInfo is m_bPreview, which is a BOOL that's TRUE when the printing job is working to do a print preview, and FALSE when the code will execute for a regular printing job. The framework tests this flag frequently during the execution of the printing process, and we'll describe how the flag affects the operation of the framework's printing functions in a moment.

> Any code you implement in the printing process, particularly in overrides of the standard printing functions, should examine the **m_bPreview** flag and act accordingly.

During the print job, CPrintInfo also reflects the current page number the job is processing; the page number is stored as an integer in m_nCurPage. You can find the range of pages in a given print job by calling CPrintInfo::GetFromPage() and CPrintInfo::GetToPage(). Note that these numbers reflect the page numbers the user requested to be printed; the actual number of pages in the entire document is given by CPrintInfo::GetMinPage() and CPrintInfo::GetMaxPage(). When MFC starts your printing job, the minimum and maximum pages are set to 1 and 0xFFFF, respectively.

After the call to OnPreparePrinting(), the default OnFilePrint() implementation creates a CDC object which will be used for the duration of the print job. The device context is simply a copy of the one stored in the CPrintInfo object; the OnPreparePrinting() call is responsible for implementing code to create and initialize the device context.

OnPreparePrinting() and DoPreparePrinting()

What kinds of things should OnPreparePrinting() actually do? As we've discussed, the function is called by OnFilePrint() when the printing job starts. The function call is an overridable one, and in fact your view class *must* implement an override if it is to support printing. The override should do two things, the first of which is to use the SetMaxPage() and SetMinPage() members of the CPrintInfo object to set the maximum and minimum print page numbers, based on the information in the document.

You should set up your document so that it has public member variables (or accessor functions) which either the view or OnPreparePrinting() can use to calculate the number of pages in the document.

A simple (and perhaps naïve) OnPreparePrinting() function might assume a constant number of lines per page and look something like this:

```
BOOL CPrintView::OnPreparePrinting(CPrintInfo* pInfo)
{
    CPrintDoc* pDoc = GetDocument();
    pInfo->SetMaxPage(pDoc->m_nLineCount / 60);

    return DoPreparePrinting(pInfo);
}
```

The second thing your OnPreparePrinting() override needs to do is also shown above – call DoPreparePrinting(). When printing, the most important work that DoPreparePrinting() performs is the display of the print options dialog box. That dialog box (shown here) allows the user to select a printer and specify the details of their print job:

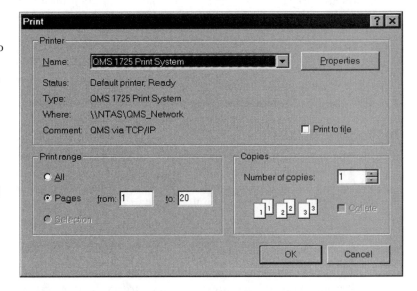

The window shown above, one of the common dialogs provided by Windows, creates a device context based on the user's selection of printing options, including their printer selection. A pointer to the dialog's class, a CPrintDialog, is maintained as a member of the CPrintInfo object and may be accessed as m_pPD. If pInfo is a pointer to the CPrintInfo, and the dialog processed successfully, the device context created is at pInfo->m_pPD->m_pd.hDC.

The dialog and the device context are deleted by the destructor for the CPrintInfo object; this destructor runs when the OnFilePrint() function returns, since the CPrintInfo is local to that function.

OnBeginPrinting()

OnBeginPrinting() is called once for your print job, just after OnPreparePrinting(). You can use the function, which is passed a pointer to a CDC object and a pointer to a CPrintInfo object, to create any objects that you're going to need for all pages in your print job. You may also wish to use this function to handle any printing you need to do yourself – if you want to completely avoid the printing support that MFC provides and do everything yourself, this function is the place to do it. As a part of the initialization that MFC performs in this function, the print job is started – MFC calls StartDoc() to let Windows know that a new document is on its way to the spooler.

After `OnBeginPrinting()` has been called, `OnFilePrint()` creates a `CPrintingDialog`. The dialog is initialized with the from-page and to-page variables in the `CPrintInfo` structure, and is updated as the `OnFilePrint()` function loops over all the requested pages. For each page, the loop calls `OnPrepareDC()` to do any per-page initialization required by the device context during the print job.

If the `m_bContinuePrinting` member of the `CPrintInfo` structure is still `TRUE`, the loop executes `StartPage()` and `EndPage()` control operations against the printing device context to control the print job. These calls bracket a call to `OnPrint()` for each page of the document. The function also prepares the `m_rectDraw` member in the print information class so that it reflects the logical size of the page. Your `OnPrint()` function can save time by using this member instead of measuring the size of each page as it is printed.

If you wish to abort your print job, you can have any of your printing functions reset the `m_bContinuePrinting` member of the `CPrintInfo` structure to `FALSE`. The next iteration of the loop on `OnFilePrint()` will end the print job, cleaning up as it goes. Otherwise, the loop continues as we've outlined here, updating the printing dialog to inform the user of its progress.

OnPrepareDC()

Inside the page-by-page loop run by `OnFilePrint()`, a call is made to `OnPrepareDC()` for each page. This enables you to set up the printing device context with any mapping modes, fonts and anything else you'll need to complete the task. The function is passed a pointer to the `CDC` that's handling printing, as well as a pointer to the `CPrintInfo` that's controlling the print job

> Note that `OnPrepareDC()` is also called during drawing operations to the screen.
> If you're drawing on the screen and not printing, the `CDC` will return `FALSE` from
> its `IsPrinting()` member function. The pointer to the `CPrintInfo` is also `NULL`
> during non-printing contexts, so take care not to dereference that pointer if
> `IsPrinting()` returns `FALSE` when working in the `OnPrepareDC()` function.

You can improve your printing performance if you avoid repeating unnecessary work. Developers often fall into the trap of completely reinitializing the printing device context for every call to `OnPrint()`, that is, once per page. There are some instances when this is a good idea, such as when you're doing an incredible amount of work with different GDI objects during your print job, but generally you should try to move some of that work to `OnBeginPrinting()`.

When `OnBeginPrinting()` is called, the context of the print job is already known – the device context for the printer is already set up and passed to the function. You can create any fonts you'll need to use here, and it's a good idea to measure them here, too. These operations are quite expensive, so if you only do them once for your entire print job, you can save a surprising amount of time. Avoiding work you don't need to do is a great way of saving time.

> *Dean McCrory, formerly the long-time lead developer on the Microsoft Foundation
> Classes at Microsoft, is well known for tautologies such as this: "It's an easy problem to
> solve, once you've worked it out." Dean is perhaps the Yogi Berra of object-oriented
> programming.*

OnPrint()

OnPrint() receives two parameters – a pointer to the CDC object that's being used as the output device for the print job, and a pointer to the CPrintInfo object that's controlling the print job. Odd though it may seem, you don't actually need to implement an OnPrint() function if you don't want to. The default implementation falls through OnDraw(), passing the printer DC instead of a display DC. If you're using similar code for drawing to the screen and printer, you can use OnDraw() for both purposes.

> Once again, you can use CDC::IsPrinting() to determine whether the device context is to be used for a printing operation or a screen display operation.

If you *do* override OnPrint(), you can use it to do whatever work you need to, that is draw to the printer device context and select whatever objects you need to complete the print job.

Note that OnPrint() is granted a lot more information than OnDraw(). OnDraw() only receives the device context, but OnPrint() receives information about the print job as well, via the pointer to the CPrintInfo passed to it. This architecture forces you to print one page at a time. Make sure you consider the notion of page-by-page access when you're spending time on the design of your CDocument class and its internal data structures.

Sometimes you can't handle printing one page at a time because of your data structure, or because of the complexity of your pagination code. Sometimes, it's difficult to structure things so they work right – but you'll really need to do so. It's not that MFC requires you to print one page at a time, it's that your printer does!

OnEndPrinting()

When the loop in OnFilePrint() is complete, the framework makes a call to OnEndPrinting(). Note that OnEndPrinting() is called regardless of whether the loop ended due to an error, or because it completed the print job.

Since the function is passed a pointer to the CDC that's used to do the printing, you can close the print job with a status report or a final summary page. The function is also passed a pointer to the CPrintInfo object that controlled the job, so you can check the m_bPreview flag in order to find out whether you're printing or previewing.

Printing using CHtmlView

If you're using CHtmlView as your view class, you needn't be too concerned with the printing mechanisms I've just discussed. CHtmlView and MSIE handle the printing chores for you automatically. In fact, the normal CView printing overrides aren't even inserted into the AppWizard-generated view class code.

Print Preview

As a creature comfort for your users, you can elect to provide a print preview mode that shows the user how their file will look on paper before it's actually printed. Most popular programs support this, and it's something of a Windows standard for baseline functionality.

One of the basic premises of MFC is that there are very few differences between printing and print preview. We outlined most of them in the previous sections when we discussed the printing functions and the occasional test for m_bPreview in the default implementations of those functions. However, MFC implements two more functions that only have special meaning to a print preview.

When a print preview is active, the regular printing functions in your application are called as usual. The difference is that they actually render into a CPreviewDC instead of a plain old CDC.

Initializing the Print Preview Operation

When the user asks for a print preview, the first function called in your application is OnPrintPreview(). This function is called by the Print Preview command in your application's File menu, essentially replacing the OnFilePrint() command that your application would otherwise call. This function calls back to the OnBeginPrinting(), OnPrepareDC() and OnPrint() functions as usual, except that the CPrintInfo object passed in a preview context has the m_bPreview flag set to TRUE.

Shutting Down the Print Preview Operation

Like OnEndPrinting(), OnEndPrintPreview() is a virtual function that you can use in order to wrap up your print preview. Since you're unlikely to want to change much about print previewing, you'll hardly ever override this function. If you do, make absolutely sure that you eventually call the base class implementation of the function; otherwise, you'll be restricting MFC from cleaning up some of the many objects it created during the preview process.

A Note About WYSIWYG

Many Windows users expect to get from their printer exactly what they see on their screen. You can hardly blame them – an application which provides complete control over the printer and shows on-screen exactly what you can expect to see on paper really would provide the ultimate print preview feature.

Unfortunately, it's quite a challenge to get this kind of result. Using TrueType fonts helps a great deal, but the Control Panel allows users to change the way TrueType fonts are handled by offering printer font substitutes, and to change the download parameters for those fonts. You can compensate for some of these things, but it's a lot of work.

If you're truly after 'what-you-see-is-what-you-get' printing, having your printing and screen drawing routines share the same code is a tremendous asset.

A Note about CHtmlView

CHtmlView doesn't support print preview. If you create a new application using the Visual Studio AppWizard that contains both a CHtmlView-derived view and print preview, the print preview request will be ignored and the code I just discussed won't be inserted.

Updating Your Document

Since the view provides the bulk of the user interface, the view will need to update the document whenever the user changes any data stored in it. Unfortunately, there are times when the user doesn't interact with the view to work with a document but, instead, uses the frame window to get something done.

The frame window almost always handles any menu commands the user might issue (since the frame often owns the menu), while the view window handles any mouse or direct keyboard input. There are several functions offered by MFC that support this exercise, so let's examine how they're used and the situations that make them important.

GetDocument()

All the MFC view classes implement a function called GetDocument(), which returns a pointer to the CDocument that is associated with the view. Even the bare-bones CView class has a GetDocument() member that gets you a pointer to the associated document. Due to the strong typing rules in C++, you'll need to cast the result of your GetDocument() call to the specific document type your application implements. If you've used AppWizard or ClassWizard to produce your CView-derived class, you'll find that the class has a member function that returns the document type associated with the view class in question when the class was created.

It's a good idea to exercise a little defensive programming and use the run-time class information in CDocument to make sure the document type is one that you're prepared to deal with. Your painting code might do something like this:

```
void CMyAmazingView::OnDraw(CDC* pDC)
{
    CMyCoolDocument*    pDocument;

    // get a pointer to our document
    // cast it so we can use it
    pDocument = static_cast<CMyCoolDocument*>(GetDocument());
    ASSERT_KINDOF(pDocument->IsKindOf(RUNTIME_CLASS(CMyCoolDocument)));

    // ... do some work ...
    pDocument->DoSomeWorkSpecificToMyDocumentType();
    // ... your work never ends ...
}
```

Remember that a given view is only ever associated with one document, but a document might have many views associated with it. Since the GetDocument() function is a member of the CView class, it's most often used from within the code of a member function of that class. However, you may want to find the active view from some other code, so MFC provides a GetActiveDocument() and a GetActiveView() function in the CFrameWnd class.

While the GetActiveDocument() function helps you reach the active document from your frame window, it's a little more difficult to reach the active document from your CWinApp-derived class. You can get a pointer to the frame window of your application by checking the m_pMainWnd member of your application's CWinThread object – the pointer references your application's frame window if it is not NULL, and you can then call the GetActiveDocument() or GetActiveView() members of the referenced object.

Altogether, the code might look like this:

```
void CYourApp::DoSomething()
{
    CFrameWnd* pFrame = DYNAMIC_DOWNCAST(CFrameWnd, m_pMainWnd);
    if (pFrame == NULL)
    {
        // There is no main window, or it isn't a CFrameWnd-derived object
    }
    else
    {
        CDocument* pDoc = pFrame->GetActiveDocument();
        CYourDocument* pActiveDocument = DYNAMIC_DOWNCAST(CYourDocument, pDoc);
        CView* pView = pFrame->GetActiveView();
        CYourView* pActiveView = DYNAMIC_DOWNCAST(CYourView, pView);
        // pActiveDocument or pActiveView may be NULL!
    }
}
```

You'll notice that I've used the DYNAMIC_DOWNCAST() macro to help enforce type safety. This macro is similar to the dynamic_cast<> operator available in C++, but DYNAMIC_DOWNCAST() uses the type information built into the CObject class by MFC. You can learn more about the macro and the type information afforded by CObject in Chapter 9. If the casts fail because of a bad type relationship, you'll find that the pointer resulting from DYNAMIC_DOWNCAST() is NULL, so you must react to this situation appropriately. If you don't need to access members specific to your derived classes, you can forgo the DYNAMIC_DOWNCAST() and simply reference the bare CView or CDocument objects – but they can still be NULL, too, if no view, document, or frame is available.

Drag-and-drop Support

The view associated with your document manages a window. If you like, you can enable the window to be a drag-and-drop client. Users can then drag files, text or other objects from other applications and drop them over the client area of the window, expecting that the application will perform some action on the files or information dropped to the application.

This support can come at one of two levels (or one of three, if you're in marketing and count 'none' as a level of support). The more advanced support for drag-and-drop is only available in applications that support OLE, as the drag-and-drop is motivated through the use of objects. OnDragEnter(), OnDragLeave() and OnDragOver() are all member functions of CView (and COleDropTarget).

>   *Treatment of these functions is cloaked in OLE terminology and rules, so let's save it*
>   *for Chapters 13 and 14, where we'll investigate the whole OLE story.*

On the other hand, simple drag-and-drop registration for files is directly supported by Windows, via simple messages. Files most often come from Explorer (or the File Manager), but may be drawn from any application that's a drag-and-drop file source.

'Dropped' objects are presented to the application when the user selects the files and drags them to the window of the accepting application. You know you're dragging a file or files because the cursor changes depending on your actions; by holding down a key on the keyboard you can achieve varied effects while you're dragging and dropping. For instance, holding *Shift* while dragging files within Explorer means they're to be moved, but holding *Ctrl* down instructs that they're to be copied.

DragAcceptFiles()

To implement this simple form of drag-and-drop, the first thing you should do is code a call to DragAcceptFiles() to register your window as a drop target. You can't perform this call in your window's constructor because the constructor is called when an object of the *class* is created, not when the *window* is created. Fortunately though, view windows afford the OnInitialUpdate() function, which is a good place to make this call.

Alternatively, you can make the call to DragAcceptFiles() in a handler for the WM_CREATE message. If you need to disable the acceptance of dragged files to your application's window, you can call DragAcceptFiles() with FALSE as a parameter. At a later date, you can call the function again with a TRUE parameter (the default, so you can leave it out) to turn the feature back on.

Note that DragAcceptFiles() needs to be called for each window that will accept dragged files. You may find things are simpler in your application if you do DragAcceptFiles() against the highest level window which will be supporting drag-and-drop; this will ensure that your child windows accept dragged files, too.

Accepting WM_DROPFILES Messages

At any rate, once you've got DragAcceptFiles() turned on, your window will receive WM_DROPFILES messages when the user drops files over it. Your response to the WM_DROPFILES message is wrapped by the MFC OnDropFiles() function, which has a prototype like this:

```
void CWnd::OnDropFiles(HDROP hDropInfo);
```

The default implementation of this function in a frame window calls OpenDocumentFile() in your application's CWinApp object to try and open each dropped file as a document for your application. In a plain CWnd, the default implementation of OnDropFiles() does nothing.

The hDropInfo parameter to OnDropFiles() contains a handle to some data that describes the files dragged to your application. Your implementation can override the existing one, but at the very least it must call the Windows ::DragFinish() API against the hDropInfo handle. This frees the memory allocated by Windows to contain the drop information. A typical OnDropFiles() implementation might work something like this:

```
void CMyScrollView::OnDropFiles(HDROP hDropInfo)
{
    // find the number of files we're working with
    UINT nFiles = ::DragQueryFile(hDropInfo, (UINT)-1, NULL, 0);

    for (UINT iFile = 0; iFile < nFiles; iFile++)
    {
        TCHAR szFileName[_MAX_PATH];
        ::DragQueryFile(hDropInfo, iFile, szFileName, _MAX_PATH);

        DoSomethingWithFileName(szFileName);
    }

    ::DragFinish(hDropInfo);
}
```

Calling `DragQueryFile()` can have one of two effects. If the second parameter is -1, the third and fourth parameters are meaningless and the function returns the number of files in the dragged bunch. There is, of course, no restriction on the number of files that a user can drag. The same code must cope with one hundred files as well as it does with just one.

In the example above, the number of files is squirreled away to be used as a counter for a loop that will process each file in turn. In its body, the loop passes the index of the file of interest to `DragQueryFile()` as the second parameter. Invoking the function in this way requires the third parameter to be a pointer to a buffer and the fourth parameter to be the number of characters in that buffer. The function will copy the name of the file corresponding with the index to the buffer. Once `DragQueryFile()` returns, we can do whatever we wish with the file name. Here, we run off and call some function that presumably does some work with the retrieved file name.

In my bogus little code fragment above, I just call an imaginary `DoSomethingWithFileName()` function. You might want to call some more meaningful function, like `CWinApp::OpenDocumentFile()` to open all of the files you've been passed.

DragFinish()

Finally, `OnDropFiles()` calls `DragFinish()`. Like most other things in Windows, forgetting to free memory that Windows has so kindly provided won't result in an error message, but forgetting to call `DragFinish()` will undoubtedly cause unpredictable behavior.

How Documents and Views Interact

The design of your document and view, like any other coding effort, is destined to be an iterative process; don't fret if all seems lost halfway towards getting printing to work. However, you can save yourself some real problems by learning to anticipate what will happen as you design your document and view. In particular, your document needs to provide data in a few different formats before it can function properly in your application.

You should be prepared to have your document render data in whatever form is convenient for your view, but on the other hand, you should make sure that your document is capable of readily presenting data to the view on a page-by-page basis. This allows your `OnPrint()` function convenient access to the data it needs to draw its content one page at a time. In general, you should strive to have your view retrieve and set persistent data within your document rather than having your view manage data itself.

Your document and view will always notify each other of updates – that's the purpose of the `UpdateAllViews()` function calls. When your view needs to update something in the document based on an action the user has taken, you should have the view perform it in a few simple steps.

Managing Document/View Interdependence

As your views and documents grow up together, they'll become more and more interdependent and so you need to manage their relationships very carefully. If your goal for the use of MFC and C++ is strictly related to the ability to reuse code and reapply previous solutions, you'll be disappointed if you make every bit of data in your document and view public.

Doing so will undermine your ability to reuse functionality in either class, since you'll be worried about dependencies created by the direct access of public variables. Changes in the implementation will become impossible as you lose track of all the unregulated dependencies you've allowed.

On the other hand, jumping through academic and idealistic hoops by making sure that everything interesting is done by some function, is sometimes something of a Holy Grail. In extreme cases, the same functionality can be a little less efficient and rather annoying to implement. Of course, that performance and implementation difficulty might not be an appropriate tradeoff in light of concerns about maintenance. You'll need to find a comfortable compromise that suits your own needs. If your experience comes to match mine, you'll probably find that the right design has almost everything privately managed and exposed via assessor functions and a very few exception cases directly available as public data.

Some Document/View Strategies

Throughout this chapter, I've endeavored to provide all the background you need to understand how the document/view architecture is implemented in MFC, and how you might use it in real applications. Because there's such a vast amount of material to cover, the explanations of related concepts are not necessarily in close proximity to each other. Further, because no book can describe every situation you'll ever run into, you might find that this chapter is a little hefty – you'll need to read it and understand it before you feel very secure about solving any application architecture problem you might confront.

In the form of a summary, to ease the pain a bit, let me provide some overall notes about writing programs with the document/view architecture. This section of the chapter won't offer much detail because the gizzards of the architecture are described elsewhere in this chapter (or in this book). Here are seven rules I try to stick to:

1. You control your own destiny.

If you want to use the document/view architecture, you can. If you don't want to, you don't have to, but you'll benefit strongly from having it around if only because it helps your application manage its frame window – particularly in MDI applications. Writing an OLE server that also works as a standalone application and doesn't use the document/view architecture is nearly unthinkable, but it can be done. The next section in this chapter describes how to avoid the document/view architecture. The approaches range from ripping document/view constructs out of your application to having them, but ignoring them. It really is all up to you.

2. Plan for serialization.

If you choose to use your document for data storage, make sure that you understand how data will be stored and retrieved. If your application can always keep all of its document data in memory, this is trivial; just `Serialize()` things. If not, you'll need to make sure that you've carefully designed your document so that it can provide on-the-fly chunks of arbitrary data to the view as it is needed. Either way, you'll need to have a firm understanding of data structures, file structures, and algorithms. While MFC is a powerful framework, it doesn't excuse you from knowing how to write computer software.

3. Plan for access patterns.

   Spend some time thinking about how your view needs to get data from your document. Then spend some more time thinking about how you might build a data structure within your document so that those access patterns are inherently supported – and fast! Is that data structure easily serializable?

4. Think about ownership.

   In general, your document will own the data you'll display and your view will take care of displaying it. However, your view may have some data of its own, and that data is probably unrelated to what's in your document. In the `Paintobj` sample which comes with this book, for example, the document manages a list of shapes that the view then draws. The view, though, manages information about the currently selected shape and understands how to draw the shape in two different modes: selected and unselected. The view manages that selection state – and deciding where to store information about that isn't as obvious a decision as you might think.

   If, instead of a simple drawing program, I had actually written an elaborate CAD program, zillions of settings and selections might actually become a part of the information stored with each drawing in its document file. You *might* make such data owned by each view; maybe I want to open a CAD drawing and see one view in metric and one view in standard measurement units. In that situation, the document object contains data that represents the object and provides persistent storage for the elaborate settings that the application supports.

5. Decide about multiple views early.

   If your application provides for the use of multiple views, you need to bake those needs into the implementations of both your view and your document. What if one view has some data selected when the user switches to the other view and deletes that same data? What if the user tries to paste or drag-and-drop data from one view to the other when the views are of the same document? These situations are not handled automatically by MFC, because MFC has given you complete freedom to manage the data structures and user interface that your application will implement. But that also means that you're responsible for detecting and remedying these situations. Before you decide that your application will support multiple editable views of the same document, be sure that you can afford the time it will take to find and solve these problems.

6. Modality is your friend.

   Modeless dialogs that allow your user to modify the content of your document can complicate your application's design to a very surprising degree – particularly if your application supports multiple views. You can avoid the resulting updating problems by making sure the dialog manages no data whatsoever about the view and its underlying document. That is, the dialog should fire off commands to the view and document without keeping any information about their respective states. Having the dialog communicate directly with the document isn't always a realistic goal, and you might need to discover some other mechanism for managing changes; one way to avoid all these problems is to make dialogs which modify your view (and therefore the content of your document) modal. Modeless toolbars or palettes aren't targeted by this advice – they just let the user choose a tool or command; they don't modify the document and certainly don't contain any information from the document within themselves.

7. Think about additional documents and views.

Does your application warrant more than one document type, or more than one view type? Simple applications usually don't; they're quite capable of displaying what they need to display with one mode. If you need to display the same data in different ways, you need multiple views. If you need to work with data from different sources, particularly if the data is in different formats, you might want to create a separate document for each format. Remember that having multiple views doesn't mean that the user needs to open them all at the same time, and doesn't even mean that the user needs to open each manually when they start working with a file – you can write code to do this automatically. (See the section on 'Two Views Automatically' later on in this chapter.) And remember that having multiple documents doesn't mean that the user needs to open two different files, either. If there's a hard link between a file of one type and a file of another type, why not pursue that link for the user when they open one file or the other?

While I've mentioned several common scenarios and briefly described how they might be implemented using the document/view architecture, it's just impossible to address every conceivable situation. I hope that the above guidelines and suggestions provide you with enough food for thought when you start considering the design of your own application. That said, please remember that even these rules are really just speculation. Every design is different, every new group of users is more challenging than the last, so you might have other issues to solve that I don't know about and, therefore, can't offer responsible guidance. However, do take my advice that the document/view architecture is much more flexible than it might seem when you first start using it.

Document/View — When Not to Use It

The Microsoft Foundation Classes are designed to address the issues faced by most developers in most of their projects. It therefore follows that the majority will find them useful, but they may not fit every situation perfectly. Some of these situations require you to abandon the idea of using the document/view architecture.

Such situations frequently occur when you are immersed in systems-oriented programming; perhaps you're writing software that monitors some piece of data acquisition hardware and records the data generated by it. In a situation like that, you're probably not interested in using document/view to solve your problems, because you're not storing any data directly in the application; you're simply hanging on to it as it goes by.

Occasions when a full document/view based implementation causes more trouble than it's worth are almost always dictated by situations where your application doesn't manage any file-oriented data. These applications defeat the purpose of the document because they have no data to maintain. The notion of the user interacting with a view that, in turn, manages some amount of data becomes weak since the data is not there to be managed. Since the view is dependent on the document for its functionality, you'll find that your view will have a disproportionately large amount of code, while your document has almost none.

In all candor, you may wish to avoid MFC completely for projects such as these, restricting yourself to stock C++. If you only produce a dialog or two, or you don't need any of the other MFC-provided functionality, you might be able to write your application with less overhead without the class libraries.

As useful as the MFC features might be, you'll find that their presence is too cumbersome when they genuinely aren't needed.

On the other hand, you'll probably draw the most benefit from a solution that embellishes the application by continuing to use the Foundation Classes for other features and either avoids the document/view architecture completely, or bends it to accommodate the needs of the particular application.

Avoiding the Document/View Architecture

As you may have guessed from the cover, the techniques demonstrated in this book are highly MFC-centric. For the most part, the examples take the high road and demonstrate the use of the document/view architecture in appropriate situations. In the real world, the circumstances surrounding the needs of your application may warrant you considering other approaches.

You're completely free to roll your own application from scratch, using MFC as little or as much as you like; remember that the heart of Visual C++ is a C++ compiler. You might not be interested in the class library at all, or you might use every single feature of MFC; at either extreme, however, you can still compile C++ code into a Windows application.

For instances where you're just interested in writing C++ code, you're on your own (as least as far as this book is concerned). You can readily apply your knowledge of C++ to the Windows API, and maybe you'll even come up with a class library of your own, especially as there are plenty of books on plain C and C++ Windows programming. However, I'd like to spend a bit of time looking at applications that don't use the document/view architecture. Just as there are many ways to stress test a weld in a nuclear reactor, there are many ways to avoid the document/view architecture in your MFC program.

One approach would be to write your own application using some basic features of MFC's architecture, avoiding features that you know you won't want. This approach is usually the most productive because your application still has the embellishments that MFC provides, but avoids use of the class library in situations where the gains are outweighed by the disadvantages.

Another approach is exemplified by the AppWizard when you create an application with a dialog user interface, or when requesting the newly available Document/View architecture support? checkbox in AppWizard's very first step. Such an application has a CWinApp class and uses MFC for everything it does, but it manages without the document/view architecture. As you might guess, the trick lies within the InitInstance() function of the application's main window. Let's first examine how a Dialog-only application works, and then turn our attention to a frame-based application that doesn't use the Document/View architecture.

Dialog-only Applications

If you generate a dialog-only application, your InitInstance() routine will contain code something like this:

```
CTestDlg dlg;
m_pMainWnd = &dlg;
int nResponse = dlg.DoModal();
...
return FALSE ;
```

We'll get on to exactly how the CDialog class works (including the DoModal() function) in the next chapter, but for now, the point is this; if you create a CDialog instance, you end up with a C++ object that represents a dialog. You still haven't gotten around to creating a window; as we've learned, C++ objects are different than Windows objects. Your application needs a main window, and since CDialog derives from CWnd, it will do quite nicely; and so the code above takes the address of the dialog object and assigns it to m_pMainWnd. When the actual Window for the CDialog C++ object is created by the call to DoModal(), a pointer to the representative C++ object is already stored in the m_pMainWnd member of the CWinApp that is running.

In the case of a dialog-only application, the InitInstance() function never ends up entering the application's formal message pump – the InitInstance() function returns FALSE so that MFC shuts the application down and leaves memory. The application lives as long as the dialog is up because the DoModal() function blocks further execution until the dialog is dismissed by the user.

If you were assigning a pointer to a real frame window to the m_pMainWnd member, you'd have to return TRUE to make sure MFC began processing the messages your application would need to receive as it ran. We'll see that in the code that AppWizard produces for a frame-based application. As it stands for a dialog based application, though, creating a dialog and entering the DoModal() function for the dialog is enough to run the dialog box. Since the dialog box is modal, it's pumps its own messages by definition!

Remember that, since your application doesn't implement the document/view architecture, it will forgo some of the functionality that MFC implements. You can't expect to be able to print things easily, since views are closely married to the printing functionality, and you don't have any.

Frame-based Applications

If you use AppWizard to create your application and you remove the mark from the Document/View architecture support? checkbox, you'll end up with an application that creates a CFrameWnd-derived object and shows it to the user. This application initializes a little bit more like the applications we've been studying so far, but doesn't initialize any document/view features. In fact, AppWizard won't emit a CDocument or a CView-derived class.

Since there's no document class to register, there are no templates to create. The InitInstance(), then, is substantially simpler. You'll end up with that CFrameWnd-derived class and an extra CWnd-derived class named CChildView. Thought it derives from CWnd, CChildView actually bears some comments indicating that it's a "view".

And the comments aren't completely inaccurate. The extra CWnd-derived class doesn't derive from CView, so it isn't quite as weighty or capable as the CView-derived classes we've examined in this chapter. But it still serves a very useful purpose; visually, it lives in the client area of the application's view just like a CView-derived object would.

Getting such a view isn't really so bad, since it's not carrying the weight of CView. Your CFrameWnd-derived window will still support docking toolbars and a status bar, and they still take area out of the client area of your frame. As such, you'd have to carefully write painting code that detected the presence of and measured those extra adornments before offsetting all the coordinates in your painting code. Instead, having the extra CWnd-derived child window allows you to always assume that the top-left of the usable painting area is at (0,0), and that the size of the window itself contains all the area you can draw in. No extra math is necessary!

The `InitInstance()` implementation supplied by the Wizard starts out with familiar enough code. We'll first enable control containment and then set the registry key to be used by the `CWinApp`-supplied registry functions:

```
BOOL CNoDocApp::InitInstance()
{
    AfxEnableControlContainer();
    SetRegistryKey(_T("Local AppWizard-Generated Applications"));
```

That done, we'll create a new instance of our `CFrameWnd`-derived object. It will become the main window, so we'll assign it to `m_pMainWnd`, like this:

```
    CMDIFrameWnd* pFrame = new CMainFrame;
    m_pMainWnd = pFrame;
```

Then, we'll call `CFrameWnd::LoadFrame()` to get the window created and assign it a menu and a title. We'll still supply the name of a resource where MFC will get this information, but the resource doesn't have as many interesting features as the document string we described earlier in the chapter. If the load fails (for example if the resources can't be found), the code immediately returns `FALSE` and terminates the application.

```
    if (!pFrame->LoadFrame(IDR_MAINFRAME))
        return FALSE;

    HINSTANCE hInst = AfxGetResourceHandle();
    m_hMDIMenu  = ::LoadMenu(hInst, MAKEINTRESOURCE(IDR_PTYPE));
    // if this is an MDI application, we'll call LoadAccelerators(), too
    m_hMDIAccel = ::LoadAccelerators(hInst, MAKEINTRESOURCE(IDR_PTYPE));
```

Finally, now that the window is ready, we can run off and get it painted:

```
    pFrame->ShowWindow(m_nCmdShow);
    pFrame->UpdateWindow();
    return TRUE;
}
```

There are a few subtle changes throughout the application – for example, the creation of the frame window also creates that special child window. But the architecture for the windows you see is the same for their counterparts in a document/view-based application. It's just that you don't have the document or the view, or any of the features they would otherwise bring you.

Again, since you're not using the document/view architecture, you won't have implicit support for any of the things you might have already learned to take for granted by MFC. You can use any MFC feature that you want to re-implement similar functionality in your application, of course. Since you don't have a document, for example, you don't get code that opens or saves files. You can start writing your own by using `CFileDialog`, though, to prompt the user for a name. And you can still store that name in a `CString` and use `CFile` (or its friends) to create and write to the file. But printing, scrolling, and serialization are your own problem.

Such a spartan approach might seem foreboding, but it's quite appropriate for applications that, in fact, have no data to serialize. It's also a great starting point for applications you're porting from plain SDK code to use MFC.

Playing Along with the Document/View Architecture

Another easy way to avoid the document/view architecture is just to roll with the punches. Accept the minimal implementations of the CDocument and CView-derived classes that the AppWizard provides and implement your application as normal responses to Windows messages by writing message handlers in your CView derivative.

The advantage of this approach is its simplicity. You're not abusing MFC in any way; you're just not conforming to the status quo demanded by document/view applications. Since your code doesn't need the storage facilities of CDocument, it won't need to rely on any of the interaction functions that so closely connect a CDocument to a CView. This method is most obviously applied to a single document interface application. If you're implementing a multiple document interface application, you'll still need to pay attention to the instance data in each CView, so your code must be aware of the window or which data set it is working with.

You may be concerned that having a CDocument lying around will waste memory, but if you don't implement any additional code or data members in your CDocument-derived class, you can expect that it will take less than a kilobyte of extra memory at runtime, and incur a one-time code cost of less than twenty-four kilobytes. These numbers hold true even if your application has full OLE support, but only applies to optimized, release-mode builds of your application.

The existence of a dormant CDocument class at runtime incurs an infinitesimal penalty for execution speed, simply because it's just another target to which messages may be sent. (You can't just remove the message handling maps – you must at least have empty ones.) The penalties for having, but not really using the classes that support document/view are as nothing compared to the time you might spend refitting your application to work with MFC, while avoiding the document/view architecture altogether.

Tricks with Document Templates

When I was young, I continually peppered my older brother with questions about my universe. Not quite content with knowing the height of the house, I wanted to figure out how high the sky was. After all, I might hit it with something someday. And, if it came crashing down, how fast would it be going? My brother, far more interested in mowing the lawn to get gas money to go downtown to see Eric Clapton, quickly tired of my questions and began dodging them. His most effective tactic was probably telling me, "That depends on your point of view."

No matter how many times you've seen Eric Clapton, the way your application works really does depend on your point of view. If your users have to do a lot of work to get to a view of the data they're interested in, they'll quickly get frustrated. If the views you offer don't represent information in the way your users perceive as intuitive, your application will be seen as awkward, since they'll have to spend too much time thinking about how things should work instead of actually getting work done.

Out-of-the-box applications that the AppWizard produces are too good not to use as basis for most of your applications. Even after some modification, MFC will react to your changes in ways that are generally seen by the user as conducive to getting things done. If you register several different document templates, you'll get the extra dialog box we saw earlier on to allow the user to choose their document type after doing a File | New. And once you've noticed this opportunity, you'll soon pick up on some other instances where you might want to deviate from the mainstream.

Multiple Templates

You're always allowed to use more than one template when you're running an MFC document/view application. Generally, your application will create any necessary templates as it handles `CWinApp::InitInstance()`. If your application initially came from the AppWizard, you'll find that the function has been coded to create and register a template for the document/view pair that your application uses by default.

If you ever need to use documents or views in any other combination, you should add code to create templates for those document/view pairs as well. This will make it much easier for you to create instances of the pairs at the user's request.

The `CDocTemplate`-derived object you create is just that – an object – and as such, you'll need to maintain a pointer to it after you use `new` to create it. It's a good idea to keep these pointers as instance data to your application's `CWinApp`-derived class. If you do, you can reference them at any time you need to create a new view or template.

While writing a spreadsheet application, for example, you might register a document template that relates your chart view to your spreadsheet document, and also register a different template to relate your textual spreadsheet view to your document. Code to do the registrations would look like this:

```
BOOL CSheetApp::InitInstance()
{
    // ... other work ...
    m_pSheetTempl = new CMultiDocTemplate( IDR_SHEETTYPE,
                                           RUNTIME_CLASS(CSheetDoc),
                                           RUNTIME_CLASS(CChildFrame),
                                           RUNTIME_CLASS(CSheetView) );
    AddDocTemplate(m_pSheetTempl);

    m_pGraphTempl = new CMultiDocTemplate( IDR_GRAPHTYPE,
                                           RUNTIME_CLASS(CSheetDoc),
                                           RUNTIME_CLASS(CChildFrame),
                                           RUNTIME_CLASS(CGraphView) );
    AddDocTemplate(m_pGraphTempl);
    // ... more work ...
}
```

Now, the `m_pGraphTempl` and `m_pSheetTempl` are accessible from anywhere in the application – a simple call to `AfxGetApp()` gets a pointer to the application, and that pointer leads to the template pointer members.

Enumerating Document Templates

Each template you register with the framework using `CWinApp::AddDocTemplate()` is kept in a linked list. MFC uses this list to find templates when the user asks to create a new document or a new view, or indeed performs any operation that requires the application to find an appropriate document template. If more than one document template exists when `CWinApp::OnFileNew()` is called, the framework presents a list box allowing the user to select the template for the type of document they wish to create.

The linked list is managed by an internal instance of a class called `CDocManager`. This class is an implementation feature of MFC and as such is undocumented. Understanding how it works, though, can be quite handy.

An instance of the class is created by the `CWinApp`-derived object in your application, and this holds a pointer to the object. It destroys the object just before your application exits, in `CWinApp`'s destructor. The pointer is stored in `m_pDocManager`, which you can use at any time to gain access to the document manager.

The list of document templates itself is stored in the manager's public `m_TemplateList` member. You can walk the list using code like this:

```
void CYourWinApp::DoSomethingWithEveryTemplate()
{
    CDocManager* pManager = AfxGetApp()->m_pDocManager;
    if (pManager == NULL)
        return;

    POSITION pos = pManager->GetFirstDocTemplatePosition();
    while (pos != NULL)
    {
        // get the next template
        CDocTemplate* pTemplate = pManager->GetNextDocTemplate(pos);

        // we can now do work with each pointer
        DoSomething(pTemplate);
    }
}
```

One of the more interesting things you can do with the list of templates is to derive a list of all active documents. This involves a nested loop; for each template you find, you can loop through the documents that the template has created. To do that, you might use some code like this:

```
void CYourWinApp::DoSomethingWithEveryDocument()
{
    CDocManager* pManager = AfxGetApp()->m_pDocManager;
    if (pManager == NULL)
        return;

    POSITION posTemplate = pManager->GetFirstDocTemplatePosition();
    while (posTemplate != NULL)
    {
        // get the next template
        CDocTemplate* pTemplate = pManager->GetNextDocTemplate(posTemplate);

        POSITION posDoc = pTemplate->GetFirstDocPosition();
        while (posDoc != NULL)
        {
            CYourDocument* pThisOne = (CYourDocument*)GetNextDoc(posDoc);

            // do some work with each document
            pThisOne->SomeFunctionCall();
        }
    }
}
```

In both of these code fragments, you'll notice that I retrieve a pointer to the manager by first getting a pointer to the application object with a call to `AfxGetApp()`. Then I interrogate the `m_pDocManager` member for the pointer to the template manager. This is a little silly here; the above code fragments are member functions in `CYourWinApp`, so they're presumably members of the very object which I'm finding with the call to `AfxGetApp()`. I could have accessed the `m_pDocManager` member directly! By creating this inefficiency on purpose, though, I've demonstrated the use of `AfxGetApp()` to retrieve information about the running application object. But more importantly, I've provided code you could use in any function of any object in your application.

The code fragments above make use of the `CDocManager` member functions `GetFirstDocTemplatePosition()` and `GetNextDocTemplate()`. The second of these is the one that does the real work by getting a pointer to the next document in the list.

We'll talk about lists and the `POSITION` type in Chapter 9.

There's some casting going on in the code fragments because I need to promote the pointers to plain `CDocument` objects to pointers to my special `CYourDocument` class. It might be a good idea to do `IsKindOf()` tests here, or use MFC's `DYNAMIC_DOWNCAST()` macro to make sure you get what you really wanted. We described these run-time type information tricks back in Chapter 3.

AddDocTemplate()

If you use `AddDocTemplate()` to add your new template to the list that MFC manages for you, you needn't worry about `delete`ing the template when your application closes. In some circumstances, however, you may wish to have the template hidden from the user, and it's then that you'll need to make sure your template is `deleted`. Doing this in the destructor of your application's `CWinApp` object is too good an opportunity to miss.

Have no fear about keeping templates around as long as you need them – they're very lightweight. By the same ticket, though, a thousand of just about anything is bad for you, so try to keep things sensible; adding your tenth or twentieth template should cause you no grief.

Adding a New Item to your Window Menu

Many applications based around the multiple document interface need an alternate way to create a view for an existing document aside from actually opening a document file. Commonly, this functionality is placed on the Window menu of the application. You might implement a New command to let the user create an extra instance of the currently active window – AppWizard-produced applications allow for this functionality by default; MFC's `CMDIFrame` class implements an `OnWindowNew()` function that does just this job.

However, you may be interested in finding a way to get a new window of a *different* view type on the active document. You can readily implement *this* functionality using the `CreateNewFrame()` function provided by the `CDocTemplate` class. You should create a template for the document/view pair you want and tuck it away in your `CWinApp` class, ready for work later on.

Maybe you want to create a new 'listing' view, based on a 'listing' template. The code to handle the menu choice to create such a window would go something like this:

```
void CYourFrameWindow::OnNewListingWindow()
{
    CMDIChildWnd* pActiveChild = MDIGetActive();
    CDocument* pDocument;
    if (pActiveChild == NULL ||
                (pDocument = pActiveChild->GetActiveDocument()) == NULL)
    {
        // something's really wrong; fail gracefully
    }

    CDocObjectTemplate* pListTemplate;
    CYourApp* pApp = static_cast<CYourApp*>(AfxGetapp());
    pListTemplate = pApp->m_pListTemplate;

    CFrameWnd* pFrame =
            pApp->pListTemplate->CreateNewFrame(pDocument, pActiveChild);
    if (pFrame == NULL)
    {
        return;
        // command failed... notify the user about it
    }

    pApp->pListTemplate->InitialUpdateFrame(pFrame, pDocument);
}
```

The curveball in the code above is the attainment of a pointer to the template that will be used to create the new document. Some of the highlighted code grabs a pointer to the application object and then references a member of the application object, assuming it contains a pointer to the template that will be use to create the new view and frame. That code in turn is based on the assumption that you'll create the template in your application's initialization and store it away in your application object. In fact, that's quite a valid approach; as we've mentioned elsewhere, it's a good idea to squirrel away pointers to specific document template objects you might need in your application object. I'm assuming here that m_pListTemplate is a member of CYourApp, and has been initialized to point to the template you'll use to create the new view you want from the command you're implementing.

You should pay special attention to the InitialUpdateFrame() call. This function calls CreateNewFrame() to create the frame window and makes sure the associated view gets its OnInitialUpdate() call so that it is correctly painted. If you don't make this call, your application will be wandering around with an orphaned window until the application is called off.

Two Views Automatically

Using a variation of this technique, you can get MFC to create two views automatically where only one was requested before. This might be of interest if your application requires the user to see the data in more than one slant. If you're interested in this technique, you should present both views as soon as possible.

You can realize this functionality by moving the code we've outlined in the previous section to the OnFileNew() handler. Call the default handler for OnFileNew() to get the main document created, and then use the code above after that function returns.

Since the new view will be the active one, this will immediately create a new view on the document that has already been created.

You may wish to move the code shown above to a member function of your document so that you can call it when it's needed – you might be interested in calling it whenever the user opens a file as well, for example. The TwoVus sample shows how to get this done.

Changing Views in an SDI Application

If you implement a single document application, pushing around different views might not seem so intuitive. The trick is to use the SetActiveView() member of the frame window. This causes the frame to adopt another view as its currently active one; you'll also need to make a call to RecalcLayout() to have the frame align the view and set its size within the client area of the window. The frame is responsible for managing toolbars and status bars, so it might decide to give the active view less of the frame's client area than it should.

To get RecalcLayout() to work, the active view needs to have its ID set to AFX_IDW_PANE_FIRST. Here's a hint to the layout code. You'll need to retrieve the ID from the newly active view and pass it to the previously active view. So, if you have two CView pointers, pViewOld and pViewNew, you could swap the IDs like this:

```
int nOldID;
nOldID = pViewNew->GetDlgCtrlID();
ASSERT(nOldID != AFX_IDW_PANE_FIRST);
pViewNew->SetDlgCtrlID(AFX_IDW_PANE_FIRST);
pViewOld->SetDlgCtrlID(nOldID);
```

You can query the active view of the frame by calling GetActiveView(), while the new view will have to be added to your document with CDocument::AddView() and the old view should be removed using CDocument::RemoveView().

How MFC Reacts to Multiple Templates

Elsewhere in the chapter, I talked at some length about how creating a new CDocTemplate instance was often paired with the idea of registering that template type with MFC. MFC uses the list of registered document templates in several different ways.

Creating New Files

When you use the New command in the File menu, for example, MFC looks at the list of document types maintained in the CDocManager. If there's more than one, MFC will pop up the New dialog box which allows the user to decide what kind of file they'd like to begin working with. The names entered in the box are the fileNewName strings from the resource strings in each of the registered document templates.

When the user selects a file, MFC will call the OpenDocumentFile() function of that template to get the new file created. Note that this aspect of the OnFileNew() handler also comes into play if your application's InitInstance() function calls ProcessShellCommand() to give your application a blank document to get the user started. If you have more than one document template registered, the function will also end up displaying the New dialog.

This is bad, since your application might not have any other part of its user interface drawn just yet.

You can easily avoid this. Set the `CCommandLineInfo` object's `m_nShellCommand` member so that it doesn't contain the `FileNew` flag; setting it to `CCommandLineInfo::FileNothing` will do the trick, and will stop your application from opening an empty file. If you still want one, you can grab a pointer to the template from which you wish to create a new opened document and call its `OpenDocumentFile()` member directly.

Saving Files

When you use the <u>S</u>ave command in the <u>F</u>ile menu, MFC will use the file name that you used to open the file. If the file is new and hasn't been opened before, or you've used the Save <u>A</u>s command to save the file with a new name, MFC will examine the document template associated with the file to see what file extension should be used to save it. That file extension, and the generic All files (*.*) extension, will appear in the Save As dialog's Save file as type: drop-down.

At this point, your user can specify their own file extension or select one of the entries in the drop-down. No matter what they do, though, the file will be saved by the document in question. This brings to light an important issue about the design of your application; if you plan to use the Save As dialog box as a way to let your user change the format of a file, you'll need to do some careful planning and a little extra work.

Let's say, for example, that you've implemented an application that displays and edits graphical images. You can let the user open any kind of file they see fit. You can look at the first few bytes of the file to figure out what format it's in, and then hand the rest of the bytes off to the appropriate code to handle the issue of decoding the file and displaying it.

When the time comes to save the file, you'll have a spot of trouble. MFC inherently provides no mechanism to communicate what Save file as type choice the user made. To support such a design, you'll need to make a user interface that lets the user know and choose, very explicitly, what type the file is and how it will be saved. Alternatively, you can implement your own Save As dialog that *will* check to see what the user specified as a save-as type and react appropriately. It isn't that much work; just create a handler for `ID_FILE_SAVE_AS` and take a look at Chapter 5 of this book for information on the `CFileDialog` class, which will let you use the Windows common file dialog to prompt the user for the file name.

Opening Files

When the user asks to use the <u>O</u>pen command in the <u>F</u>ile menu, they'll be prompted with a common file dialog box that offers a list of files and a list of file extensions built from the list of document templates known to the application. Be aware, though, that MFC isn't 'aware' of the extension filter selection the user makes; it works entirely by looking at the extension itself and comparing it with the files available.

MFC walks the list of document templates, comparing the extension on the filename the user specified with the extension that the path has registered and trying to find a good match. If it doesn't find one, it puts up an error stating that it can't figure out how to open the file. If the file is already open, it has the application make the window that holds the file active.

The matching process is based on a few simple rules. Exact matches between a template's registered extension and the extension specified in the file are always a direct hit.

However, if no exact match is found, MFC will try to use a close match. This means that MFC might try to open a file by sending it to the serialization code of a document that actually knows nothing about the file type in question.

All of this work gets started in the `CWinApp::OpenDocumentFile()` function. If you don't like the way it works, you can override it in your application instance. The default implementation (and almost certainly yours, too) calls the homonymous `OpenDocumentFile()` member of one of the templates your application has registered; this is the function we were discussing previously. If the function is called in the context of creating a new file, the filename parameter passed to it is `NULL`. When the file being opened exists, the parameter to `OpenDocumentFile()` points to its path name.

The only hairiness in the process of opening a file arises in situations where more than one registered template can handle the extension of the file being opened. In this case, the first template to have been registered gets the call. If you need to depend on this feature, you might be best off overriding `CWinApp::OpenDocumentFile()` to guarantee you get what you want.

The Most-Recently-Used List

The Microsoft Foundation Classes are also kind enough to provide a most-recently-used file list, or MRU for short. This list appears in the bottom part of the File menu and allows your users to have a convenient spot to retrieve the names of files with which they have previously worked.

MFC manages the MRU behind the scenes – you don't have to lift a finger. You might remember that AppWizard prompts you for the number of MRU entries you'd like to keep. It turns out that the number you request is passed to a call to `LoadStdProfileSettings()` during the `InitInstance()` of your application. `LoadStdProfileSettings()` reads the MRU files from your application's area in the registry or from your application's private `.ini` file. (For more information on this, see the section called '.ini Files and Registry Entries' in Chapter 3.)

You can call `LoadStdProfileSettings()` with 0 as a parameter to make your application manage no MRU. If you *do* choose to manage an MRU, MFC will create a `CRecentFileList` and hold it in your application. You can access the list at any time by referencing the `m_pRecentFileList` member of your `CWinApp` object. If you didn't create an MRU, `m_pRecentFileList` will be `NULL`. If you're not positive that a list has been created, you should check `m_pRecentFileList` to make sure it isn't `NULL` before you begin playing with it.

Under the implementation line, outside of the interface publicly exposed and documented by MFC, the libraries manipulate the recent file list by calling its `Add()` and `Remove()` members. When the user selects a menu item that actually turns out to be an MRU member, MFC retrieves the file name from the list and calls `CWinApp::OpenDocumentFile()` to get it opened. If the opening call fails, MFC will automatically remove the filename entry from the MRU. When you open a file successfully via the Open command in the File menu, MFC automatically adds the new file name to the list and removes any extra file names that would take the list over the limit specified by the call to `LoadStdProfileSettings()` back when the list was initialized.

If you ever dynamically doctor your application's menus, you may need to call the `CRecentFileList::UpdateMenu()` function to get the menu redrawn or recreated correctly.

What Frames are For

We've covered what documents and views are all about, but we can't forget that a view almost always lives in a frame window.

> The only times a view isn't created in a *real* frame window are when it's active as an embedded OLE object or within a splitter window. As an embedded OLE object, it still has a frame, but one very different from the kind we'll talk about here. Within a splitter window, the splitter window acts as the view's parent, and the splitter is actually a child of the frame.

As we've mentioned before, a CFrameWnd instance is usually created by SDI applications, while a CMDIFrameWnd is used by MDI applications. Of course, if you've written a dialog-based application, the dialog is the main window and your application doesn't have any frame window at all.

Due to the way command dispatching works, you'll find that the frame window often acts as a backstop for choices in your command window, by which I mean that any command from a menu which isn't handled by your view will be offered to your frame window.

You should implement handlers that are ready for any frame message, regardless of which view is being shown to the user. If you have menu choices that should react in different ways for different views, you can implement handlers in both the frame and the view classes. The view handler will be executed if the view object is active; otherwise, the frame's handler will be called.

Frames act as the main window for the thread which controls your process. If you call AfxGetMainWnd() at any point in your program, you can retrieve a pointer to the CWnd which is your thread's main window. You'll need to cast that pointer to the appropriate type if you need to access any CFrameWnd or CMDIFrameWnd specific members.

Status Bars and Toolbars

A frame window is responsible for one or two more things than just making sure your application has a menu and a sizable frame. It also serves as an anchor for your window's toolbar and status bar. As yet, we haven't examined these classes, but since they're so often paired with a frame window, let's have a look at what they do.

If your application has a status bar or a toolbar, you'll find code in your main frame window which creates instances of CStatusBar or CToolBar. As you might guess, CStatusBar creates a status bar and CToolBar handles a toolbar. In most applications, the creation of these windows is handled in the OnCreate() member of the application's frame window.

If you're working with an AppWizard-produced application (Paintobj for example) the status bar in your application will be called m_wndStatusBar and your first toolbar will be called m_wndToolBar. Note that it's your 'first' toolbar that receives this name. Your frame is completely capable of handling more than one toolbar; MFC will lay out as many toolbars as you'd like.

By the way, CStatusBar and CToolBar classes are dependent on a frame window. Using them in other types of window (like dialogs) is beyond the scope of this book. Suffice it to say that these classes aren't really dependent on the document/view architecture, but that they do rely on the frame window associated with the document and view classes, in order to lay themselves out in your application's user interface; furthermore, they keep the view informed of the available drawing area.

CStatusBar

A CStatusBar object can live with your frame window object to give a border area at the bottom of the frame window, where the application can display context sensitive help or other status information. If your status bar is hooked up with a regular MFC application, you'll see this help almost instantly – just highlight a menu item and you'll be treated to the one line description of that menu command.

As well as a line of text, the status bar can also handle some on/off indicators. The bar, as it appears in the example, is shown below for your reference:

The text that is left-aligned in the status bar is where fly-by help (or any other status information you'd like to show) will appear. In the example, we've used the leftmost recessed pane to display the coordinates of the mouse pointer. The other three are the indicators; they show the state of the *Caps Lock*, *Num Lock* and *Scroll Lock* keys on the keyboard. This feature is hooked up automatically by MFC and it monitors the key presses and updates them as necessary. If you want to set up your own indicators, you'll have to handle them yourself.

Creating the Status Bar

Creating your status bar window couldn't be much easier. The AppWizard gave the frame window a CStatusBar member named m_wndStatusBar (see Mainfrm.h for a working example). To create the window, call the Create() member of this object, passing it a pointer to the frame window which will own it. This call, taken from the example, looks like this:

```
if (!m_wndStatusBar.Create(this) ||
    !m_wndStatusBar.SetIndicators(indicators,
                              sizeof(indicators)/sizeof(UINT)))
{
    TRACE0("Failed to create status bar\n");
    return -1;      // fail to create
}
```

If the call to Create() was successful, the code also calls SetIndicators(). This function takes a pointer to an array of integers, which identify the string resources to be used in the indicator panes when active. If the indicator is inactive, nothing will be displayed.

When you're using C++, you should remember that the compiler produces code which stops evaluating the if statement as soon as its result is known. This means that if the first call fails, the second call isn't even made – the argument will be TRUE, regardless. If either call fails, the code drops a trace message for the debugger and then returns –1 from the frame window's WM_CREATE message handler.

Returning a non-zero value from this function tells MFC that the creation of the window failed, and MFC won't continue without a frame.

The `indicators` array from `MainFrm.cpp` in the example looks like this:

```
static UINT BASED_CODE indicators[] =
{
    ID_SEPARATOR,            // status line indicator
    0,                       // mouse position indicator
    ID_INDICATOR_CAPS,
    ID_INDICATOR_NUM,
    ID_INDICATOR_SCRL,
};
```

The first element and the last three elements of the array were added automatically by AppWizard. `ID_SEPARATOR` tells the status bar that we want to keep the text area of the status bar as just that – a text area. The framework uses this area to provide fly-by hints for toolbar buttons and menu items.

The fly-by help is stored in a string resource with the same ID as its associated menu item, containing the text that the status bar should display when it's previewed. You should note that the properties window for the menu and toolbar editors in Visual C++ gives you a field where you can edit this string without having to fool around with the string editor as a separate step.

The last three elements in the array are recognized by MFC and are actually handled by the default implementation of `CFrameWnd`. In addition to these indicators, MFC can also inherently handle a few others, including an `ID_INDICATOR_KANA` indicator. If you're in Japan and you've knocked your keyboard into Katakana mode, you'll see this indicator appear.

Adding a Pane

The `Paintobj` example uses an extra pane to display the cursor position, which is why we have that zero in the `indicators` array. There's no string resource that matches zero, so nothing will be displayed in the pane to begin with. The code to initialize this pane, found in `CMainFrame::OnCreate()`, starts out with a call to `GetPaneInfo()`, which collects information about the relevant pane of the status bar:

```
m_wndStatusBar.GetPaneInfo(1, uID, uStyle, nWidth);
```

We also call `GetDC()` on the status bar to get the drawing context the status bar will use, because we need to get information about the font which was selected in the device context before making a call to `DrawText()`, like this:

```
pDC = m_wndStatusBar.GetDC();
pDC->SelectObject(m_wndStatusBar.GetFont());
pDC->DrawText(_T("X=9999, Y=9999"), -1, rectArea,
                                    DT_SINGLELINE | DT_CALCRECT);
```

The purpose of the exercise is to measure the maximum amount of text which we'll be using in the status bar. Therefore, by using the `DT_CALCRECT` flag for `DrawText()`, we've requested that `DrawText()` doesn't actually draw the text, but just calculates the size of the text as it would appear with the selected font.

Once we've got this information, we just tidy up the DC and set the pane's width based on the rectangle that we received from DrawText():

```
m_wndStatusBar.ReleaseDC(pDC);
m_wndStatusBar.SetPaneInfo(1, uID, uStyle, rectArea.Width());
```

Now we know that the pane will be large enough to hold the text that we're likely to put into it, we can move on to actually setting the pane's text. Back in the application's view code, we need to set the pane's text to reflect the current position of the mouse. To make this easy, and because the pane and toolbar are protected members of the frame, we've written two functions: ClearPositionText() and SetPositionText().

SetPositionText() is trivial:

```
void CMainFrame::SetPositionText(CPoint& point)
{
    CString strPosition;
    strPosition.Format("X=%d, Y=%d", point.x, point.y);
    m_wndStatusBar.SetPaneText(1, strPosition);
}
```

The function just calls Format() to convert the point passed to it to a readable value. We give this string to the SetPaneText() member of m_wndStatusBar and let MFC take care of the rest. ClearPositionText() is even easier, as it doesn't have to do any formatting. It just passes a NULL to SetPaneText() to cause MFC to clear the pane.

Taking the approach above is something of the long way around. The benefit realized in exchange for the extra work is that we can be sure that the pane is exactly wide enough to show our text. If we provided a string resource in the indicators array (instead of passing a zero), we'd be able to let MFC set the size for us when it handled the indicators array. Without ever making a call to SetPaneInfo(), though, we'd not know how wide our text could be before it was clipped.

CToolBar

If you've asked the AppWizard to give your application a toolbar, you'll find the code which creates it in the OnCreate() function of your frame as well. If you've always wanted a toolbar but were too shy to ask AppWizard to provide one, you could add similar code after declaring the CToolBar member in your frame window. The creation code for a toolbar looks like this; you just pass the toolbar resource ID to the LoadToolBar() function:

```
if (!m_wndToolBar.CreateEx(this, TBSTYLE_FLAT,
    WS_CHILD | WS_VISIBLE | CBRS_TOP | CBRS_GRIPPER |
    CBRS_TOOLTIPS | CBRS_FLYBY | CBRS_SIZE_DYNAMIC) ||
    !m_wndToolBar.LoadToolBar(IDR_MAINFRAME))
{
    TRACE0("Failed to create toolbar\n");
    return -1;      // fail to create
}
```

> As we saw in the first chapter, the toolbar resource editor provides you with a very convenient way of managing your toolbars. The editor helps you by making the default grid settings fit the standard 15x16 format and it shows how the toolbar will be laid out, with spacing and all. You can also add one button at a time to the toolbar and alter the size of the buttons.

The `CreateEx()` function takes three parameters. The first is a pointer to the parent window. Since the above code lives in the `OnCreate()` handler of the frame window, the `this` pointer references the frame and that will be the parent of the toolbar. The second parameter provides styles for the toolbar control itself. Here, we're passing `TBSTYLE_FLAT`. That results in a user interface similar to most modern applications, including Office and The Visual Studio IDE itself. The buttons will be flush with the toolbar – and, in fact, won't show an edge at all. Without this style (that is, if zero was passed for the second parameter), you'd have a user interface very similar to old applications; the buttons on the control will show an edge.

The third parameter is a combination of window styles for the control and for MFC. You can specify which edges of the control have borders, using the following symbols:

```
CBRS_BORDER_TOP
CBRS_BORDER_BOTTOM
CBRS_BORDER_LEFT
CBRS_BORDER_RIGHT
```

You can specify any or all of these symbols (by ORing them together) in that third parameter to the `CreateEx()` function, or you can pass them along to the `SetBarStyle()` function.

The code above also makes use of `CBRS_SIZE_DYNAMIC`, which allows the toolbar to size itself in width (if docked horizontally) or height (if docked vertically) to exactly fit the buttons within. `CBRS_GRIPPER` gives the toolbar a gripper – just a few lines that have a three-dimensional textured effect – to make the toolbar appear that it can be grabbed. `CBRS_GRIPPER` is normally only used if `TBSTYLE_FLAT` is present. `CBRS_FLYBY` means that the bar supports **fly-by help**, which is the one-sentence text in the status bar that gives you a little advice about what a button might do. Finally, `CBRS_TOOLTIPS` enables tooltip help for the control.

You might find it interesting to note that buttons also have some simple styles, which you can manipulate using the `GetButtonStyle()` and `SetButtonStyle()` members of `CToolBar`:

Button Style	Description
TBBS_CHECKED	The button is checked (that is, down)
TBBS_INDETERMINATE	The button is indeterminate
TBBS_DISABLED	The button is disabled (up and grayed)
TBBS_PRESSED	The button is currently pressed by the mouse

Table Continued on Following Page

Button Style	Description
TBBS_BUTTON	Standard pushbutton
TBBS_SEPARATOR	Spacing gap between buttons; this style is used alone and doesn't actually create a control
TBBS_CHECKBOX	Automatic check box button
TBBS_GROUP	Added to a button, this style indicates the start of a new group of buttons
TBBS_CHECKGROUP	Added to a button, this style indicates the start of a new group of check box buttons

You can also use TBBS_CHECKBOX to make a button toggle, by which I mean that it moves from off to on with one press and on to off with the next. This won't make your button look like a check box from a dialog, it just stays released until it is pressed, and stays depressed until it is released.

Docking

Toolbars can be docked, that is, they can be dragged by the user to snap into a position on any edge of the frame window. If you want to implement docking support in your toolbar, you'll need to make a few extra calls. Again, stolen from the example application, your calls will look something like this:

```
m_wndToolBar.EnableDocking(CBRS_ALIGN_ANY);
EnableDocking(CBRS_ALIGN_ANY);
DockControlBar(&m_wndToolBar);
```

The EnableDocking() call that is made against the toolbar takes a set of flags that let the bar know where it should dock. CBRS_ALIGN_ANY allows the toolbar to dock to any edge of the window. The other options are:

```
CBRS_ALIGN_TOP
CBRS_ALIGN_RIGHT
CBRS_ALIGN_LEFT
CBRS_ALIGN_BOTTOM
```

You can, of course, combine these options with the bit-wise OR operator to get any combination you'd like:

```
CBRS_ALIGN_ANY = CBRS_ALIGN_TOP | CBRS_ALIGN_RIGHT |
                 CBRS_ALIGN_LEFT | CBRS_ALIGN_BOTTOM;
```

The second EnableDocking() call isn't redundant – the frame window has the same function to tell it that a toolbar should be allowed to dock. In the example, we have passed CBRS_ALIGN_ANY, but you could pass any combination of the CBRS_ALIGN flags. A given toolbar will only dock when the toolbar and the frame share alignment bits.

I know what you're wondering. Yes, you can make a toolbar that never docks. Either make its alignment flags incompatible with those in the frame, or pass a FALSE for its EnableDocking() parameter.

The third call, to `DockControlBar()`, forces the control bar to dock. MFC will try to dock against the top, left, right and bottom of the window, in that order. You can use these constants in an optional second parameter to force the bar to dock to a particular side:

```
AFX_IDW_DOCKBAR_TOP
AFX_IDW_DOCKBAR_BOTTOM
AFX_IDW_DOCKBAR_LEFT
AFX_IDW_DOCKBAR_RIGHT
```

FloatControlBar()

If you want, you can call `FloatControlBar()` and pass to it the address of the control bar you wish to float. The function has a second, mandatory parameter; the screen coordinate where the upper left corner of the toolbar should appear. Essentially, this means that the following call would float the 'shapes' toolbar to the top left of your desktop:

```
FloatControlBar(&m_wndShapeBar, CPoint(0,0));
```

Note that, if the user docks your toolbar to the left or right edge of the window, then MFC will draw the buttons and the window vertically. You shouldn't make any left-to-right dependencies in your buttons unless you disable left- and right-edge docking.

Tool Tips

MFC's toolbars come equipped to help the user by displaying **tool tips**. Sometimes called 'balloon help', tool tips indicate to your user what each toolbar button does. If the user parks the mouse cursor near a button, then after a few seconds MFC will automatically display a tiny window which describes, in a couple of words, the effect of the button. Normally, this feature is not enabled on your toolbars. If you call `SetBarStyle()` to set the appropriate style, or pass the appropriate style bits to the `Create()` function, you can enable the feature. The call that AppWizard produces looks like this:

```
m_wndToolBar.SetBarStyle(m_wndToolBar.GetBarStyle() |
    CBRS_TOOLTIPS | CBRS_FLYBY);
```

It just sets the style based on the current style, plus `CBRS_TOOLTIPS` and `CBRS_FLYBY`. `CBRS_TOOLTIPS` turns on tool tips, while `CBRS_FLYBY` causes the bar to display fly-by help, just like menus do. It's useful to have both − fly-by help is usually around a little longer than tool tips, but is only visible when (and if) your control bar is visible.

MFC uses the same string resource for the tool tips as for the fly by help, and can be applied by simply concatenating the two string resources together. If the fly-by help string is this:

    Save a file

with the additional tool tip, it would be:

    Save a file\nSave

Remember to limit your tool tip help to just one or two words – it's awkward and distracting for the user to see a huge pop-up.

Applications with ReBars

If you ask AppWizard, in step four, to create an application that uses rebars instead of providing a normal user interface, your wish will be granted – your application will support rebars. Rebars are a user-interface element that supports inherent docking and convenient resizing. They're a little different than MFC's normal toolbars in that they resize themselves, offer a very flat appearance, and occupy the width of their container. The controls themselves allow docking handled controls side-by-side, and the underlying rebar lives under the control placed into it.

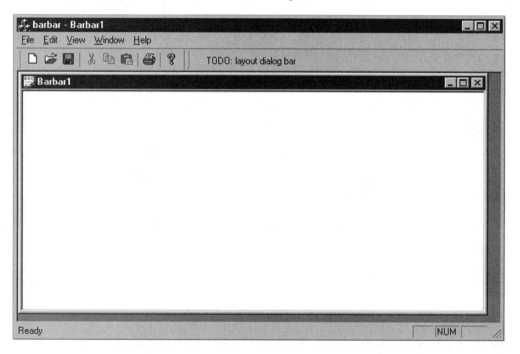

When you ask for a rebar in your application, the architecture of the application changes only very slightly. Obviously, you'll get a CReBar instance as a member of your main frame window. The OnCreate() implementation supplied by the Wizard will still create toolbar and status bar windows (if you ask the Wizard for them).

But then it does something interesting; it tells the rebar instance about the other controls:

```
if (!m_wndReBar.Create(this) ||
               !m_wndReBar.AddBar(&m_wndToolBar) ||
               !m_wndReBar.AddBar(&m_wndDlgBar))
{
    TRACE0("Failed to create rebar\n");
    return -1;       // fail to create
}
```

The calls to AddBar() ask the rebar to begin containing the toolbar a dialog bar as individual bars within the rebar window. That's all there is to it!

Summary

Documents and views provide very fertile ground for growing your application. If you choose to write your application to this scheme, you'll make the most of a great deal of functionality already implemented in the Microsoft Foundation Class libraries. This functionality makes it easy for your application to present the same data in different ways, as well as to load and save your application. Remember, though, that there are many identifiable instances when you might not want to use this architecture. It's important to consider these situations carefully before you run off, blindly placing your faith in the document/view model.

The most important thing to keep in mind when you're using the document/view architecture is an understanding of how your document and view interact. You need to carefully implement your document classes, so they can provide data to your views efficiently, as well as readily accept information about changes from the user through the view class. Even more importantly, you need to think about how your document and view working together will be greater than the sum of their parts. Forming a symbiotic relationship between the document and view is what will really make your applications impressive.

Using Dialogs and Controls in MFC

Microsoft Windows is an operating system based around a convenient and consistent user interface. Each program running under Windows that needs to interact with the user stakes out its user interface within a window – or a few windows. Those windows can have many features within them – other windows nested inside, even – but anything the application shows to the user, and anything the user does to the application, must happen within a window drawn by the application. Features of your application that are only occasionally needed can be placed in subordinate dialog boxes that are displayed on demand and disappear when no longer needed.

Aside from things that the application paints from scratch by itself, the content of application windows is made up of two distinct groups of elements: **dialogs** and **controls**. It is these elements that make up the subject of this chapter.

In this chapter, we'll cover:

- ➤ The different types of dialog
- ➤ The difference between modal and modeless dialogs
- ➤ The range of controls that you can use in your dialogs
- ➤ The ins and outs of Dialog Data Exchange
- ➤ A run through of the common dialogs offered by the Windows API

User Interfaces; The Windows Way

It's a little difficult to write robust applications if you're strictly following a model where everything the application does is handled from within one window. For example, if the user requests the document to be printed, the program will quite naturally want to ask the user about the print job. Which pages? What format? Draft or proof quality? Which printer to send it to? Forcing a user interface into the main window of your application for an action that may only be occasionally completed is foolhardy at best. You'll quickly run out of valuable screen real estate, your user will become distracted and annoyed, and your application's main window will look like a road traffic accident.

To solve these problems, Windows gives you the ability to create **dialog boxes**. Dialog boxes are special windows that carry on a dialog with the user, hence the catchy name! Unfortunately, because the technique of using subordinate windows for temporarily necessary user interface features wasn't declared an industry standard by three certain companies, there's no cute three-letter acronym to identify the technique.

The approach of using a main window for the main features of an application and using dialog boxes to implement subordinate features is so natural that you'll almost always have at least one dialog in your application somewhere. If you're working on the most spartan of applications, you might fit everything into one window – or maybe even on a single dialog with no underlying "main" window. (On the other hand, if you're working on the most tartan of applications, you'll have few dialogs and lots of plaid bitmaps.)

Since dialogs are always created to ask or tell the user something, you'll need to find some mechanism within them for communicating simple facts or questions. Windows gives you a little help here by providing a set of controls which you can use to decorate your dialog box. Controls can present the user with a list, enable the user to set some binary option, or can communicate a simple command like 'Go Ahead', 'Print', or 'Add Record'.

The Microsoft Foundation Classes provide several classes that let you write code to handle dialog boxes and the controls that live within them. This chapter will examine those controls and show you how to draw and use dialog boxes within your application.

Drawing Your Dialog

The first trick to drawing a dialog box is to go someplace quiet. Start by thinking about what's going to be interesting to your user when they're using your dialog, and try to find some way for them to find the information they want conveniently. They should be able to understand what your dialog needs and how it works just by just by seeing it – the Windows user interface provides enough consistency to let users worry more about the information in the dialog rather than the use of the dialog itself. You should also provide some way for the user to panic and get back to the application's main window without suffering any consequences from their aborted command. How many times have you been forced to 'guess' an answer to a modal dialog box when the information that you require to make a decision is held in another part of the application? Don't let your own applications suffer from the same handicap.

Dialog boxes, in my opinion, fall into a number of distinct categories, including:

> Requesters
> Notification dialogs
> Modifiers

Let's paw through these different types and discuss them. Hopefully, they'll give you some ideas for the architecture of your own applications.

Requesters

Some dialogs are brought into the world just to request information. If you tell an application that you want a sandwich, it's likely to respond with a question – hot or cold? Dialogs that request information directly will always be dismissed in one of two ways; either the user panics, or they make a choice and continue the operation. If the user suddenly realizes that their cholesterol is way too high and they'd rather have a salad instead, they'll need some way to back out of the sandwich dialog and go and choose the kind of salad that suits their fancy from the application's main window. You can see a typical requester dialog here:

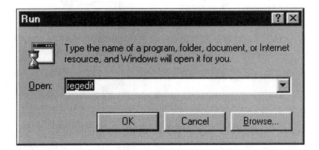

Most dialogs will have a button marked Cancel. The Cancel button should back the user out of the dialog by closing it, throwing away any changes the user has made, and returning them to the window which brought up the dialog. Most users expect that the *Esc* key will be shorthand for the Cancel button; an association which is available for free by assuring that your application uses the identifier IDCANCEL for the dialog's button.

Requester dialogs will also have a button labeled OK. This invites the user to accept the dialog in its current state. The **current state** simply means that the user has made all the changes they require to controls in the dialog box, and is ready for the application to accept the dialog's current settings. You can make sure that your dialog box accepts *Enter* as a shortcut for the OK button by making the OK button the default push button, and by providing it an identifier named IDOK.

The settings within the dialog may be parameters for a command, indicate a mode the user would like to enter, or dictate a new status for the application or one of the objects the application manages for the user. Pressing the OK button indicates that the user wants to accept any changes they've made and have them applied to their application.

Notifications

On the other hand, your application might also use a dialog box to *tell* the user something. You might use the `AfxMessageBox()` function to create a dialog that tells the user about an error, or gives the user information about something that just happened, such as a print job being completed. Since notification dialogs are so popular, the `AfxMessageBox()` function (and its pal, `CWnd::MessageBox()`) lets you get away without drawing a dialog box all by yourself and, instead, takes care of the most common needs of the user.

Alternatively, you might provide the user with a more complicated, custom dialog that tells them about the status of some part of their application. Maybe you need to convey this type of information, without affording the user the ability to make changes to that status. Typically, in dialogs like this, the controls that populate the dialog are disabled – or just static text that the user reads before dismissing. This lets the user see what's really going on, but clearly shows them that they can't make any changes. A typical notification dialog is shown here:

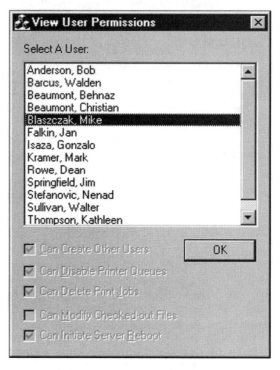

In such a dialog, the user isn't able to change anything. They're only offered the chance to acknowledge the dialog box. Instead of having Cancel and OK buttons, notification dialog boxes often have only an OK button. Note, though, that the use of a button called Close in place of OK button has come into vogue of late. Whatever the button's title, it will invariably act like an OK button, dismissing the dialog box and uneventfully returning the user to the window that created the dialog.

In certain circumstances, a requester and a notification dialog box can be combined. One user might not be allowed to change data in the dialog, but should be allowed to see what's going on, while others might have the authority to change it. Such an application could use the same dialog template with some controls enabled and some not, depending on security criteria. Of course, it's a good idea to provide some mechanism for the dialog to explain to the user what mode the dialog is in – and, more importantly, *why* it is in that mode.

Modifiers

Some dialog boxes are really a combination of requesters and notifications. They tell the user what's going on right now and offer them the ability to change it. This kind of dialog, known as a modifier, is often used to present 'options' to the user; should measurements be made inches or centimeters? What are the current margin sizes in that particular unit of measurement? Modifiers accept information and, like requester dialogs, also carefully check the user's input to make sure that it is valid and reasonable.

Sometimes, certain settings within the dialog are incompatible with others that can be obtained within the same dialog. You might wish to disallow the ability to use metric measurements when the user has selected a paper size based on inches, for example. It is the responsibility of your application to make sure it receives the information that it requires; you should make sure that it is capable of informing the user when the information it has been offered is unacceptable. You should also offer the user a way to change the information or to abort the operation in question.

Developing a Dialog

Once you're confident that you know what your users are after, you should sit down with your machine (that is, your computer, not your motorcycle) and draw your dialog box. As you design your box, you might follow the rules put forth by the current Windows User Interface Style Guidelines book, or you might follow some rules that you've developed in-house. Whichever you choose, your users will feel that it is important to have your application offer a consistent and understandable design in your application's user interface.

As we discussed in Chapter 1, you do your dialog design right within the Microsoft Visual Studio, using the resource editor built into the integrated development environment. Or, you can steal resources from other executables, or even import Visual Basic *.FRM files. You'll need to identify your dialog with a resource ID, which the dialog editor will manage for you in a header file. You'll also need to make sure any module of your application which needs to access the dialog (or to any other resources) uses the #include directive to get those resources into the symbol list used by your application.

Instantiating Your Dialog

Your dialog template is binary data that lives in your application's executable image, but isn't actually used until you create a window that requires it. You can create multiple instances of any such window, requesting either a **modal** or a **modeless** interface.

A modal dialog requires the user to respond before the application continues. While a modal dialog is up, other windows in the application are effectively disabled, and the user must dismiss the dialog box before they can return focus to the application itself. A modeless dialog allows the user to do other work with the application. The user can activate the other windows of the application and later return to the dialog as they see fit. Of course, if a subsequent modal dialog is created, it disables any modeless dialogs, along with any other windows in the application.

MFC makes presenting your dialog to the user a two-step process. While it sounds like marketing spin, it is really true; the two-step process used by MFC is actually easier than the regular one-step process normally used by the Windows API. A fundamental idea behind many of the MFC's classes is that their lifetimes bracket those of the physical objects they represent. This is true for dialog windows and any controls you might *dynamically* create for your dialog. If the dialog is created and then creates controls from its resource template, though, Windows will create the controls before MFC has a chance to wrap them. In such cases (which we'll examine in detail later in this chapter), you'll carefully need to connect a C++ object instance to the control window, and disconnect it later.

CDialog

MFC provides a class called CDialog for basic dialog operations. CDialog class derives from CWnd, which in turn is derived from CCmdTarget, so MFC knows that the dialogs are command targets which can send and receive messages, and that they are also windows that have titles, borders and styles. CDialog isn't an incredibly useful class on its own; you'll normally derive your own class from CDialog to manage a particular dialog box template in your application. Your new class will be different from the bare CDialog class in several ways:

> Your class will know what dialog resource template is associated with it

> Since your class knows what dialog template will be used, it may have member variables that reflect the state of controls in that template

> You might add specialized code to initialize, reset, validate, or process information available in the dialog box

> You'll add a message map and message handlers so that your dialog can react to the user

When you're ready to create an instance of your dialog, be it modal or modeless, you'll first need to create an instance of the class for your dialog. You can create the class with one of three constructors. The first two versions of the CDialog constructor are similar; they both take parameters that indicate which template the dialog will be associated with, as well as a pointer to the parent of the dialog window.

The first version of the constructor takes the *name* of the template and the optional pointer to the parent window, like this:

```
CDialog(LPCTSTR lpszTemplateName,
        CWnd*   pParentWnd = NULL);
```

The second version takes the *integer ID* of the template instead of the template's string name, like this:

```
CDialog(UINT  nIDTemplate,
        CWnd* pParentWnd = NULL);
```

Remember that the template's name, as you see it in your source code, is usually a preprocessor symbol defined to be equal to the ID number of the resource. Don't be confused; the preprocessor symbol may look like a string name, but it isn't! You can further confuse matters by having preprocessor symbols that are defined to be string names themselves. Most modern programs just use IDs, since they're more efficient at runtime than the string names. MFC doesn't mind, but the Windows API does.

It's a good idea to use the third constructor when you're not interested in creating the dialog from a static template resource from your application's executable image, but instead create it from a resource data structure that you've built in memory. This approach to creating a dialog box is rare, but since Windows provides the `CreateDialogIndirect()` API, the Microsoft Foundation Classes provide support for it by allowing you to create your `CDialog` class using a constructor with no parameters, thus not loading any particular dialog template. You can then make a call to the `CreateIndirect()` member of `CDialog` with a pointer to the `DLGTEMPLATE` structure that you'd normally use in the Windows API `CreateDialogIndirect()` function.

`CDialog::CreateIndirect()` actually creates an instance of the dialog window. If you want to initialize the `CDialog` object with information about the template and then create the dialog instance later, you can use `InitModalIndirect()`.

If you use ClassWizard to add a `CDialog`-based class to your application, or work with an application that has dialog classes supplied by AppWizard, you'll notice that the Wizard has produced an overridden constructor that looks like this:

```
CAboutDlg::CAboutDlg() : CDialog(CAboutDlg::IDD)
{
    //{{AFX_DATA_INIT(CAboutDlg)
    //}}AFX_DATA_INIT
}
```

The constructor uses the initializer list syntax to call the base-class constructor and pass it a constant that identifies the ID of the resource you want to use with your dialog. ClassWizard has added an `enum` local to your new class, which you see used as the parameter to the base-class constructor. The base class simply holds on to the ID in a member variable so that calls to window construction functions later on will create the window from the appropriate template. Given this additional constructor, you can make an instance of your `CDialog`-derived class simply by declaring it with the default constructor. In this example:

```
CAboutDlg dlg;
```

creates an instance of the C++ dialog class named `dlg`.

Now that we have beaten the constructors to death, we've completed the first step – constructing an object of the class. Let's move on to creating the dialogs themselves. As the modal and modeless methods are different, we'll cover them in two separate sections, starting with a discussion of modal dialogs.

Modal Dialogs

Once you've created an instance of `CDialog`, you can create a modal instance of the box by calling the `DoModal()` member function of the `CDialog` class. This function takes no parameters; it just creates the dialog box from the template that was passed when the class was initialized. The function returns when the user dismisses the dialog, returning a code that the user specified when they dismissed the dialog box.

It's very common to use the return value of `DoModal()` to reflect the actions of the user to the code that created the dialog. By default, MFC will return `IDOK` from `DoModal()` if the user presses the OK button or taps the *Enter* key while the dialog is displayed, and `IDCANCEL` if the user presses the Cancel button or taps the *Esc* key.

If you want to hook up a dialog that allows the user to cancel their changes, you can do so by checking the return code. When DoModal() returns, you can tell whether the user approved or dismissed your dialog by examining the return code of DoModal(),which reflects the value passed to EndDialog() in the dialog's message handlers. Here's how such an approach might pan out:

```cpp
void CMyView::OnRespondToSomeMenu()
{
    CAskQuestionsDlg MyDlg;

    int nDisposition = MyDlg.DoModal();
    if (nDisposition == IDOK)
    {
        // The user said OK, so the dialog is useful and
        // we should do some work to get the job done.
        DoSomeWork(MyDlg.m_SomeMember);
    }
    else
    {
        // Do nothing, probably; the user didn't want to
        // continue. If your dialog can return more than
        // IDOK and IDCANCEL, though, you'll need to
        // test for those other possibilities here.
        // You might want to test for a return of -1,
        // which indicates that MFC or Windows couldn't
        // display the dialog.
    }
}
```

Since we coded an instance of CAskQuestionsDlg as a local in this function, the object lives as long as the function is executing, but the dialog is only actually on screen during the execution of the MyDlg.DoModal() function. When DoModal() returns, the dialog window is gone, but the C++ object still exists. The C++ object provides a brilliantly simple way for your dialog to hand back more information to the code calling the dialog. Returning lots of information from a dialog was always a tedious venture in C programming, since there's nothing in that language to really tie your dialog instance to any particular code.

With the MFC CDialog wrapper class around your dialog, you have any information the dialog box managed right at your fingertips. Note that Bill Gates' 'Information At Your Fingertips' vision extends beyond having easy access to dialog data, even once a dialog window has been closed.

In the function code above, you can continue to use any information you've placed in member variables of your CDialog class; since the member variables are part of your CDialog class object, they stick around until you destroy it. You could use the object to create another instance of the dialog, or, as we did here, to examine the member variables in the dialog after it runs to see what they contain. This implies that any dialog code you write is likely to store information about the work it has done in its member variables, making it easy for the consumer of the dialog's features to use the information collected by the dialog.

Of course, if you're just implementing a notification dialog, it might not collect any information at all. Alternatively, the dialog may be able to tell the application everything it needs to know, simply by providing different return values from the DoModal() function.

Some developers find that it is convenient to invent structures or classes that describe various groups of settings managed by an application. Instances of such objects can be added to your application's `CDocument`-derived class. You can then invoke a dialog box that takes a pointer or reference to that object and uses it to initialize or copy the settings the user makes for your application. A strategy involving such objects can help you serialize the information that the dialogs represent, instead of exchanging the values back and forth on a piecemeal basis. You can call the `Serialize()` member of the `CDialog` object contained in your document when it's time to serialize the document. (Serialization is the act of making an object's data persistent. We talked about serializing documents in Chapter 4.)

We'll examine some cool ways to manage the instance data in your `CDialog` classes a little later in this chapter. You can bet that MFC has a few tricks to make even the most elaborate dialogs easy and painless.

Modeless Dialogs

In many circumstances, you might want to implement your program to offer the user more than one window. It might need to show the user some information that's continually updating, while reserving the rest of the space on the main window for the real meat of the application. Alternatively, you may need to offer the user a convenient way to set or change options while they continue to work with the information in the window. While popping up a modal dialog is very simple for both the application developer and the user, it interrupts the user's thought pattern and distracts their focus. They must move their eyes and thoughts (and maybe even their mouse pointer) over to the new dialog, make a decision, and then dismiss the box once they're done.

In contrast, a modeless dialog hangs around and doesn't need to be dismissed; the user can put focus on the application's main window to get some work done and hop over to the modeless dialog whenever they need to tweak the options, settings or values that it offers.

Coding a Modeless Box

Modeless dialogs differ from their modal counterparts in three important ways. First, the semantics of it not being modal change the way that you should think about how your dialog is implemented. Rather than running your dialog and returning all the information necessary, you'll need to find some way to present the information that the dialog is collecting to the parts of your application which need it. How will the application know your dialog has changed something? When will it update?

Second, the creation code for your modeless dialog will be slightly different. It will be much more like a regular pop-up window; create the dialog, run away, and destroy it later. Of course, the notion of the MFC C++ `CDialog` object outliving the dialog window doesn't change – your dialog class will probably not be local to one function.

A relatively common use of modeless dialogs has the application creating the dialog in response to a menu command and destroying it in response to another. The dialog remains active to provide its services between the user hitting those two commands.

This means that you'll probably use the new operator to build an instance of your CDialog-derived class. You can then tuck the pointer to the object away someplace convenient and return to it later, perhaps to access the values it has collected, but certainly to destroy it and free the memory it was using. While dialog boxes often collect information that affects the mode a program operates in, they just as often collect data that will become a part of the data a program actually maintains in its document. We'll examine a couple of interesting ways to establish communication between a document and a dialog later in the chapter.

Third, the modeless dialog must override some of the features of the CDialog class. By default, CDialog has handlers for the OK and Cancel push buttons. These buttons call the Windows ::EndDialog() API to dismiss the dialog. While a call to ::EndDialog() is an acceptable way for modal dialogs to die, the correct technique to end a modeless dialog is to call ::DestroyWindow() on the dialog's handle. This means that your handler for any user action which needs to dismiss the dialog should call ::DestroyWindow() and not ::EndDialog(). Note that CDialog has its own implementation of DestroyWindow() which it inherits from the CWnd class – you should call this function, not the Windows API version.

The Dynamic Lifestyle of CDialog

It's a great deal more convenient to use a modeless CDialog by allocating it and destroying it dynamically, but this can result in problems when it comes to deleting the dialog box. In particular, how will you remember to release the memory you've dynamically allocated when the dialog box is done? To make things a bit easier, you might want to try overriding the PostNcDestroy() member in your modeless CDialog-derived implementation class and doing a delete this there.

Be warned that the technique of deleting a C++ dialog object when the dialog window is closed can have some unwanted side-effects. Deleting the dialog as the window closes can ease the clean up of the C++ class you're using for your dialog, but it will also mean that the C++ object for your dialog dies almost immediately once the user closes the window. Since the C++ object is gone, so has all of its data. You can't, therefore, rely on the convenience of member variables to retrieve data from your dialog.

On other hand, your dialog implementation might notify the rest of the application about changes to the data the dialog maintains on-the-fly through a callback mechanism. Maybe, for example, the application grants the dialog a pointer to itself, and the dialog calls member functions — including CDocument::UpdateAllViews() and CDocument::SetModifiedFlag() – as the user changes the information the dialog displays. This on-the-fly approach is interesting for some applications – particularly with modeless dialog boxes – but doesn't make it very easy to implement code that cancels the dialog box and reverts the changes that the user made before the dialog box came up.

By the way, coding delete this sounds pretty dubious and, unless you treat it with respect, it certainly can be. The object won't receive any other messages after it handles WM_NCDESTROY, which is responsible for the call to PostNcDestroy(), so it's safe as far as MFC is concerned. But once delete this executes, you can't touch any members of your object anymore because they're all gone.

The requirements of your implementation will dictate exactly what path you'll need to take. If you do data exchange (which we'll get to a little later in this chapter) to some other more permanent class, you'll find that destroying the C++ class is really inconsequential. On the other hand, you might find that you really need to have your class around for much longer to retrieve data from it in an organized manner.

The `Dialogs` example application implements a modeless dialog in a class called `CMyModeless`. You can find the code for this class in `Modeless.cpp`, while its declaration resides in `Modeless.h`. My implementation doesn't do any data exchange, so I coded an override for the `OnCancel()` and `PostNcDestroy()` functions. The functions are trivial; they implement the hints that we identified in this section.

A Modeless CDialog

When you're using one menu item to show the dialog and another to destroy it, as in the `Dialogs` sample, the most effective way to proceed is to add a `CDialog` pointer to the class data in your frame window and initialize the pointer to `NULL` in your constructor. If the user asks the application to display the dialog, then create the `CDialog` object and hold its pointer in the member variable.

You can then test for the existence of the dialog by checking to see if the member variable is `NULL`. Of course, when the user requests that the dialog be closed, you should close it, `delete` the object and then reset the member variable to `NULL`.

So, let's address the second issue first by presenting a code fragment that creates an instance of the `CDialog`, holding a pointer to it in the instance data of the running frame window. The subsequent function destroys the dialog and sets the `m_pDialog` member to `NULL` so that anyone who stops by can see that the store is closed.

Since the two functions are invoked in response to the **Modeless** and **UnModeless** push buttons in the example's main dialog, the functions are called `OnModeless()` and `OnUnmodeless()`. You can find these in the `Dialogs` example application – they're in the file `Maindlg.cpp`:

```
void CMainDialog::OnModeless()
{
    ASSERT(m_pdlgModeless == NULL);

    // get a new CMyModeless instance
    m_pdlgModeless = new CMyModeless;

    // create it as a child of our own bad selves
    m_pdlgModeless->Create(IDD_MODELESS, this);

    // update the UI
    UpdateButtons();
}

void CMainDialog::OnUnmodeless()
{
    ASSERT(m_pdlgModeless != NULL);

    // kill the window and clear our pointer
    m_pdlgModeless->DestroyWindow();
    m_pdlgModeless = NULL;

    // update our UI
    UpdateButtons();
}
```

The user interface of the example, spartan as it is, allows you to create or close the modeless dialog from the main dialog of the application. This is a very typical use of modal dialogs – you can have a way for the user to close the dialog directly, and some option for the user to show or hide the dialog in the menus of the application's main window.

From the point of view of the main window, things are easy. If the user presses the <u>Modeless</u> button, the button allocates the new instance of CMyModeless and calls Create() on it. It holds the pointer to the class in m_pdlgModeless and then calls UpdateButtons() so that the buttons on the main dialog are disabled or enabled correctly. On the way back, OnUnmodeless() just calls DestroyWindow() and sets m_pdlgModeless before calling UpdateButtons().

The other problem we are faced with is that of knowing how to update the user interface of the main window when the user dismisses the dialog. There's an extra function in the sample that we haven't bothered with until now – UpdateButtons(). That function just tests the m_pdlgModeless member variable to enable or disable the buttons in the main dialog if the dialog already displayed. It looks like this:

```
void CMainDialog::UpdateButtons()
{
    BOOL bAlreadyUp = (m_pdlgModeless != NULL) && !m_pdlgModeless->m_bDeleted;
    GetDlgItem(IDC_MODELESS)->EnableWindow(!bAlreadyUp);
    GetDlgItem(IDC_UNMODELESS)->EnableWindow(bAlreadyUp);
}
```

You might also notice that we just use GetDlgItem() *in this function and don't bother casting the* CWnd *returned to a* CButton. *We don't need any functionality specific to* CButton; EnableWindow() *is a plain ol'* CWnd *member, so we can just let the sleeping type lie. Of course, it might have been a good exercise in defensive programming to get the pointer back and* ASSERT() *on it not being* NULL, *but life can sometimes seem so dull!*

The mechanism in UpdateButtons() takes care of everything for the user interface from the main window. However, if the user closes the modeless dialog by pressing its <u>Done</u> button, then the main window needs to be notified somehow, so that it can update the user interface and store a NULL in the m_pdlgModeless member variable.

After a little thought, you may think that handling WM_SETFOCUS in the main dialog would be a good solution. Since the main window is the dialog's parent, the focus would return to the main window after the dialog was terminated. The handler could check the m_hWnd member of the dialog; if the window has been destroyed, this member will be NULL. If the window still exists (for example, if the user has used *Alt+Tab* to get away to some other application, and has then returned without destroying the modeless dialog), the m_hWnd member would still be non-NULL.

However, testing in reaction to WM_SETFOCUS doesn't work; the focus comes back *before* the dialog is actually destroyed. When the focus returns, Windows is still tearing down the window, because it turns out that changing focus back is one of the first things that happens as the window is destroyed. So, another mechanism is required.

The easiest way to solve these problems is to maintain a simple public BOOL member variable in the modeless dialog class. This member is set to TRUE when we handle the <u>Done</u> push button; if it is set, the WM_SETFOCUS handler knows that the dialog is on its way down.

Things might not work out so well in your application – for instance, maybe you need to do too much testing for it to be practical for your user interface to handle the focus' return. Alternate solutions to this problem involve setting up your own callback to pass between the modeless box and the controlling window of your application. Thankfully, there's another way to get around this trickery; see the section entitled 'Another Modeless Paradigm'.

Data Transfer Issues

Communicating the changes and commands your user issues from a dialog box can be complicated – the solution you'll choose really depends on exactly how your program manages data, and the features that your dialog needs to provide. Your application might use the member variables within the modeless dialog class as storage for the data that it's managing. The dialog could then be given a member function which copies the data from the application – perhaps straight from the application's active document – back to the member variables the dialog maintains.

On the other hand, you may have to plan the retrieval of data back into the dialog if your program is also managing it elsewhere. This approach would require you to write a couple of functions that would help get the information in and out of storage. The object containing the data must have some function that accepts the changes that the user has made. The dialog requires a function to force a refresh (and perhaps accept the data from the caller) if the program changes the data asynchronously while the dialog is active. This is all well and good if the data that your dialog needs to show is stored in one convenient location, but the practice breaks down if it is spread far and wide.

There are two ways to address the problem of data exchange between the application and a dialog, the first of which is not to allow the data that your dialog handles to become spread out in the first place! The other technique would be to hide the collection mechanism required to hunt the data down. You might tuck it away in the one single function that provides the data to the dialog, but, since code in other parts of your application will need some way to get a hold of the data, you'll probably have to use other methods to achieve this. The idea here is simply to have the dialog use the same data-access functions your application's views might use to touch data within the document. There's nothing wrong with an object other than a view calling methods on a CDocument-derived object.

If the dialog you've created actually displays or changes data in the program's document, you might want to alter the constructor for your dialog class slightly, so that it accepts a pointer to your document. You can then have the constructor store the pointer to your document in a member variable, and then reference it during the life of the dialog whenever you need to. The management of a document pointer in the dialog is a useful approach for both modal and modeless dialog boxes. It's a better idea than trying to find a pointer to the document dynamically, because MFC only provides a way to get the active document – and the active document might not be the document you've logically associated with your displayed dialog in your application's user interface.

Exactly how you engineer the relationship between your document and any modeless dialogs that are available to the user will dictate the tone of your user interface. If, for example, you create your modeless dialog, offer it a pointer to a document, and have the dialog store that pointer, you're binding the dialog to the document which was displayed at the time the dialog was shown. That's fine – as long as something reasonable happens when the user activates another document. (If the user can't activate a different document, as in most SDI applications, the point is moot, of course.) Users are confused by commands and controls that change things they can't see. You might want to code your application so it hides whatever modeless dialog you have when a different view or document becomes active.

On the other hand, if you let your modeless dialog dynamically seek out which document is active, the application can allow the user to keep the dialog conveniently in place, and still provide the functionality the modeless box offers them.

Another Modeless Paradigm

Now, the notion of creating and destroying the dialog class instance is handy, but it also means that your class will need to reinitialize the content of the dialog box each time it's recreated. This might be inconvenient if the data the dialog requires isn't easy to find, calculate or create.

As a result, you may want to eschew the notion of a disposable CDialog object. Instead, create the object as soon as your window is created, and destroy it when the window is destroyed. Initialize it once and use some other method to see if the dialog window has been instantiated or not. You might want to create a BOOL member variable that is set to TRUE when you create the dialog, and FALSE after you destroy it. Alternatively, you can check the m_hWnd member of your dialog class with a call to the ::IsWindow() API to see if it's managing a window. Since MFC just wraps around Windows API functions (with varying degrees of added functionality in between), the class must maintain a handle to the dialog's window, whenever it's been created.

> By the way, if you're ever attending one of my presentations and you hear me say 'paradigm', please yell out, "Twenty cents!" It will soothe me, and the rest of the presentation will be of much higher quality. Not only will I be less nervous, but I'll also be reminded to refrain from using silly words like 'paradigm', 'leverage' and 'non-issue'. I'll also avoid using 'opportunity' when I really mean 'nearly fatal problem'.

The technique of creating the dialog once, using it all day and destroying it when you're finished can simplify your code somewhat. You're keeping the C++ object around a little longer than you need, though, and this may mean that you're wasting memory. In today's world, where most folks have plenty of memory, you might be tempted just to create all the dialog objects you can all at once.

Modeless Constructor Tricks

I lied! We didn't really beat the CDialog constructors to death. If you're interested in using a CDialog to create a modeless dialog without using a template *or* any of the in-memory DLGTEMPLATE structures, you can; use the parameterless constructor.

The parameterless CDialog constructor we reviewed earlier is also handy if you're creating the dialog from a template that's not loaded at initialization. Before actually creating the dialog window, you can use the CreateIndirect() function to let the C++ dialog object know where the appropriate template is.

Code that gets a template, modifies it and then uses CreateIndirect() might go something like this:

```
CDialog    MyDialog;
HGLOBAL    hResource;

// Get the resource handle from MFC
HINSTANCE hInst = AfxGetInstanceHandle();
hResource = ::LoadResource(hInst, FindResource(hInst,
                   reinterpret_cast<LPCTSTR>(IDD_MYDIALOG), RT_DIALOG));
if (hResource != NULL)
{
    LPDLGTEMPLATE lpTemplate =
                   static_cast<DLGTEMPLATE*>(LockResource(hResource));
```

```
        // lpTemplate points at the template
        // Party on it! When the party is over,
        // call CreateIndirect()
        MyDialog.CreateIndirect(lpTemplate);
    }

    // Later, when ready to display the dialog
    // and if initialization really worked...
    MyDialog.ShowWindow(SW_SHOW);
```

If the dialog template you're using to create the dialog has the WS_VISIBLE style, the call to CreateIndirect() will immediately show the window. Of course, ShowWindow() returns immediately without waiting for the user to dismiss the dialog box — it is, after all, modeless.

The DLGTEMPLATE Structure

Now, we didn't show any code which actually fools with the DLGTEMPLATE structure because this isn't something that most applications do. Code that does this kind of work is fraught with pointer arithmetic and alignment tomfoolery. Applications that do this are usually those that allow users a great deal of customization, or the ability to design their own screens on the fly. If you're dying to get under the hood this deeply, you can find examples of this kind of work in various Microsoft references, such as the Microsoft Developer Network CD.

Your Dialog Classes

The art of using dialogs in MFC manifests itself when you consider how to implement the actual dialog class. What will it send to the dialog instance? What will it bring back? Most of this will come from controls in your dialog, and we'll need to look at how those controls work when we're using MFC dialog classes.

In the meantime, you can use your CDialog-derived class to handle any messages your dialog might need. ClassWizard lets you create new classes, so you might wish to use this feature to set up a header file and implementation file appropriate for your class. Clicking the Add Class button on any page in ClassWizard will bring you to the dialog shown below. This allows you to add a class of your own; base it on CDialog to create a dialog and supply any class name and file names that you like:

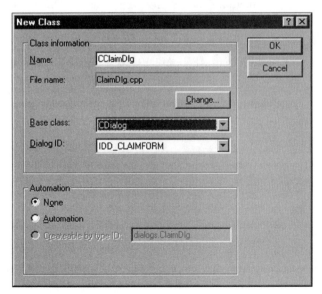

Whether you create the dialog with ClassWizard or not, you can use ClassWizard to manage message map functions for the window. If you need to do some initialization work on member variables in your dialog class, you can do this in your class constructor, but since the dialog window is created after the class, it isn't available while your constructor runs. You'll have to do work on initializing the controls and features in your dialog while processing a message that it handles, such as WM_INITDIALOG.

Let's now move on to examine the class library support for controls.

Working with Controls in Your Dialog

MFC doesn't automatically create instances of control classes for the controls in your dialog box. This is because it would take too long, and would slow down the presentation in your application's dialog. Since you don't always reference every control in your dialog, creating such class instances would be a waste of your time.

You can get MFC to create and manage a C++ object for some controls in your dialog box at your discretion. You can find information about this during the discussion on ClassWizard a little later in this chapter.

So, you'll need to create your own instance of a control class each time you need to reference one. This isn't all that hard, thanks to the fact that all control classes in MFC derive (sooner or later) from MFC's CWnd class. CWnd lets you quickly attach an instance of the object to a window handle, use the object, and then detach the object. Since the controls are windows in their own right, using CWnd-derived classes makes sense. The trick is to get the control class you're using associated with a CWnd object representing the control you wish to juggle.

If you've done much work with dialogs in the regular C Windows API, you're doubtless old friends with a function called ::GetDlgItem(). This workhorse of the dialog procedure takes a handle to the dialog, an integer that identifies a control within it and returns a handle to the control's own window.

It turns out that MFC implements a GetDlgItem() function of its own, as a member of the CWnd class. The MFC version of the function returns a pointer to a CWnd instead of a handle to a window. You can then cast this CWnd pointer to a pointer at any control class you'd like. If you're trying to get a grip on some edit control for example, you might write some code that works like this:

```
CEdit* pFirstNameEdit;
pFirstNameEdit = (CEdit*)GetDlgItem(ID_E_FIRSTNAME);
```

Once you've developed a pointer to the class, you can use the class to do work with your control. MFC hides all of the tomfoolery normally associated with control work, which means that you'll rarely, if ever, need to send a message to your control directly. (The obvious situation where you'll need to send a message directly is the eventuality that MFC doesn't provide a wrapper function for a particular control's feature for you.) All of the messages you'd normally send have been hidden away inside MFC functions that are members of the control's representative class. This doesn't represent a sizable performance hit; in your release build, these functions are defined as inline members of the class, and just fire off the messages you really need.

All that's left for us to examine are the different control classes that the class libraries implement for you.

Edit Controls

You might remember that I mentioned the CEdit class in our coverage of the CEditView class back in Chapter 4. The framework creates an edit control window to handle user input and the display of text in the CEditView object – in fact, it turns out that the CEditView *is* actually a CEdit, but has the additional CView-derived classes that help it lay out and size itself in a frame, and interact with a document. But when you use a CEditView, most of your work is done directly with the view, so you don't often need to fiddle with the CEdit control directly.

ES_MULTILINE

Your edit control can exhibit several different styles, the most potent of which is ES_MULTILINE. The presence of ES_MULTILINE differentiates between multi-line edit controls (which have the style) and single-line edits (which don't). Note that this style has no bearing on the height of the control; you can make a single-line control as tall as you like, or a multi-line control as short as you please. The style does, however, change the effect or meaning of many other style flags.

The styles that most directly interact with ES_MULTILINE are ES_AUTOVSCROLL and ES_AUTOHSCROLL.

ES_AUTOVSCROLL

This style (if the control is an ES_MULTILINE) will cause the control to show as many lines of text as possible, and vertically scroll the text automatically when the user presses *Enter*. If ES_AUTOVSCROLL isn't specified, the control will be filled with as many lines as possible. It will also not react to *Enter* in the same fashion, now only beeping in response.

ES_AUTOHSCROLL

If you add this style to an ES_MULTILINE control, the control will pan horizontally over the text as the user moves the insertion point right or left. If the user wants to start a new line, they must press *Enter*. If ES_AUTOHSCROLL isn't provided, the control wraps text that it holds. The user can still press *Enter* to create a new line if they wish.

If you have a multi-line edit control, and if the control has the ES_WANTRETURN style, you can let the user break lines in the control by pressing *Enter*. If the control doesn't have this style, then when the user presses *Enter*, the default push button in the dialog box is activated.

> *If the user wishes to start a new line when the control doesn't have the* ES_WANTRETURN *style applied, they should use Ctrl+Enter. You should also note that strings from a multi-line edit control have a carriage return-newline pair* ($\r\n$).

Controls that have ES_MULTILINE can have scroll bars automatically added and removed if the text is of variable size. The control also automatically scrolls text when the user actuates the bars.

ES_UPPERCASE and ES_LOWERCASE

You might want to use a couple of edit controls to receive a username and password. If your username must be upper case, you can use the ES_UPPERCASE style to make sure the control maps every character in it to upper case. If you're developing a system for humble poets, like e. e. cummings, you might want to use the ES_LOWERCASE style to force entries to lower case. Without either of these styles the control will, by default, not change the case of characters as they are typed.

ES_PASSWORD

The password control in your logon dialog can use the ES_PASSWORD style to ensure the password isn't shown on screen. An edit control with this style doesn't show any text, but echoes the user's input with an asterisk. You can use the SetPasswordChar() function to change the character that is echoed to the user for each character entry. The function takes a single TCHAR type parameter that indicates the character. You can find the current password character with a call to GetPasswordChar(), which returns a TCHAR.

ES_NOHIDESEL

When an edit control has the focus, it shows the selection to the user. That is, if the user has some text highlighted in the control, the edit control darkens the background of the selected text to highlight the selection. This selection is kept internally in the control, but the visual effect of the selection is removed when the user removes focus from the control. This effect of removing the selection highlight can be negated by adding the ES_NOHIDESEL style to the control.

The ES_NOHIDESEL style is quite esoteric – in your programming life you'll use it rarely, if ever. One of the rare instances where it's appropriate is in a window that features both an edit control and a subordinate find or find/replace dialog box. In such a situation, the edit control should have ES_NOHIDESEL so that the user can see the selection in the control even when they've given focus to the find/replace dialog box.

ES_OEMCONVERT

If you write code that might be internationalized or run on uncommon platforms, you should carefully consider adding the ES_OEMCONVERT style to any edit control you create. This style takes text that the user enters in the control and folds back and forth between OEM and ANSI character sets. If an edit control doesn't have this style, the text is assumed to be either ANSI or Unicode characters, which might mean the user can't enter characters that their localized operating system might support. Using this style ensures that the user will get what they expect from your program, particularly when they enter file names that always use the OEM character set. If you don't have this flag, the operating system may incorrectly convert text that the user enters.

ES_RIGHT, ES_LEFT and ES_CENTER

By default, text in an edit control is aligned to the left edge of the rectangle that the control occupies. The ES_RIGHT style changes this to align text to the right. Similarly, the control may have the ES_LEFT or ES_CENTER style.

Note that ES_RIGHT, ES_LEFT and ES_CENTER affect *all* of the text within an edit control – you can't use these styles to make some subset of the control's content align differently from the rest. If your application needs to control the text formatting like this, you should consider using a rich text edit control, which is covered in Chapter 8, where we look at the Windows Common Controls.

Don't confuse ES_RIGHT with the extended style WS_EX_RTLREADING. ES_RIGHT causes the text to be aligned right. WS_EX_RTLREADING causes the edit control to layout its text in a way that's compatible with versions of Windows localized for the Middle East — such as the Arabic countries — which use right-to-left or bi-directional text layouts.

ES_READONLY

You may wish to prevent a user from changing text in an edit control, particularly if you're using the control in a notification dialog. If you do, make sure the ES_READONLY style is set. This prevents the user from entering or editing text in the edit control. You can change this style with a call to SetReadOnly(). The function takes a BOOL that is defaulted to TRUE, which makes the control read-only. Using an edit control with the ES_READONLY style is better than just showing the user text in a static control, because the user can highlight the text in the edit control and copy it to another place, and can also scroll through larger amounts of text.

LimitText()

Further, you may also wish to limit the amount of text the user can place in your edit control. If you're not always carefully engineering code that reads the text from the edit control to deal with even the longest strings provided by the user, limiting the text allowed in the control in the first place is an adequate way to make sure you'll not someday run into problems.

To put an upper limit on the number of characters allowed in a control, call the LimitText() member function of the control and pass it the number of characters you'll want as a maximum. The control will accept up to that number of characters; if the user attempts to type or paste more characters than the limit, the control will beep and ignore the keystroke or command.

Edit Control Methods

The MFC CEdit class has lots of different functions that can be used to retrieve, set, or manipulate its content. For example, you can call SetWindowText() or GetWindowText() against an instance of CEdit to set or query the text in the control. SetWindowText() takes a pointer to the new text, while GetWindowText() takes a pointer to a string which it will fill with the content of the control.

Managing the Selection

The control maintains an insertion position and a selection. You can change these with the SetSel() function which takes two parameters, each of which is an int. The first integer indicates the start of the highlighted selection and the second indicates the end. If you wish to mark all of the text as selected, you can pass 0 for the first integer, and -1 as the second. If you wish no text to be marked as selected, you can pass -1 as the first integer. In this case, the value of the second integer is ignored.

You can query the current selection by using a call to GetSel(). This function takes references to two integers, corresponding to the parameters passed to SetSel().

By the way, there is an overloaded version of this function that accepts a DWORD instead of two integers. This version of the function is convenient for developers who are familiar with the EM_SETSEL message that the CEdit::SetText() function wraps. This messages takes its input from two integers packed into a single DWORD.

The selection is as useful to you as a programmer as it is to the user. You can replace the current selection with some text by calling ReplaceSel(). This function takes a pointer to a string which will replace the selected text in the control. Text not selected is left unchanged. If the selection is empty – if just an insertion point is present – ReplaceSel() will insert the provided text at the selection point.

Edit Notifications

As the user works with your edit control, you may receive one of several notifications. The most important are EN_CHANGE and EN_UPDATE. **Notifications**, by the way, are special messages that Windows will send to the owner of a control; in most cases, a control is owned by the dialog box in which it lives. Windows will send a WM_COMMAND message with EN_CHANGE to indicate that a control is sending that notification. Along with the message comes the ID of the control sending it. As you'd expect, MFC unpacks the information sent with the message so you don't need to worry about it directly.

EN_UPDATE

This notification is sent when the user takes some action that changes the content of the control. That action may be a single key press, or it might be the action of pasting or cutting the content of the control. You can trap the notification using an MFC message handler by using the ON_EN_UPDATE() macro in your message map.

EN_CHANGE

This notification is sent after EN_UPDATE, when the user has changed the control. EN_UPDATE is sent after the text of the control has changed but before Windows has painted it. The EN_CHANGE notification is sent after Windows has done the painting.

You can make your application appear to operate a little more responsively if you're careful to use EN_CHANGE instead of EN_UPDATE where appropriate, otherwise your code will run before the user sees their changes on the screen. You can use ON_EN_CHANGE() to make message map entries for the change notification. Of course, you can use ClassWizard to create an entry for either ON_EN_ message.

> **Unlike some other controls, edit controls always send their notification messages. You don't need to set an ES_NOTIFY style. Don't even try; there is no such duck.**

The Rich Edit Control

Windows implements a large group of controls known as the Common Controls. This group includes a very powerful edit control called the **rich edit control**. It's so named because it handles the rich text format, sometimes called RTF for short. From Visual C++ 5.0 onwards, you can draw a rich edit control directly on any dialog you like. If you do so, however, you'll need to initialize the rich edit control before creating your dialog box – you'll need to call AfxInitRichEdit() before displaying the box.

This extra call is necessary because the common controls are implemented in a separate dynamic link library that needs to be initialized at runtime. Since the rich edit control is terribly expensive on memory use at runtime, the initialization of the control is something you'll need to do as a separate step if you know you're going to be using it.

> *We give the rich edit control and all of the other common controls very detailed treatment in their own chapter – Chapter 8.*

List Controls

MFC libraries have classes which support both list and combo boxes. CListBox and CComboBox provide you with the ability to wrap list and combo boxes. You can add these controls to your dialog using the dialog editor, and optionally populate them with several choices as they are initialized. They're very similar in nature, so we'll treat both of them together; both CListBox and CComboBox implement AddString() and InsertString() functions.

AddString()

AddString() tosses the string into the box and lets the box position it, based on the sorting rules for that box. This function takes a single parameter; a pointer to the string you'd like to add to the list box.

InsertString()

On the other hand, InsertString() takes two parameters: an integer specifying which spot in the list box will receive the string, and a pointer to the string to be inserted in the box.

The string that was in that position previously (and all of the strings after it) is moved down one position. If you want to use InsertString() to add a string as the last entry of a list box (thereby displacing no other strings), pass -1 as the integer parameter.

Both InsertString() and AddString() return an integer indicating the position of the newly added string. With a combo box, they may return CB_ERR if there was an error in the insertion procedure, or CB_ERRSPACE if the box has run out of space. The corresponding errors when they are used with a list box are LB_ERR and LB_ERRSPACE respectively. If you are using Windows NT, you'll practically never see the latter message, but in any version of Windows, you can generate the former by using a bogus index for InsertString(). Always check for both error conditions!

The indexes which come back from a call to InsertString() or AddString() are valid until you change the box again. If you add another string, the list box may reorder other items – if you explicitly insert an item before another item, or if you add a string to a sorted box, the list box may reorder some of the items in the box. Or, you might delete a string from the box and that may reorder the strings in the box. In either case, indexes which you previously received from InsertString() or AddString() are now invalid.

Unless you do a bunch of extra programming – making an owner-drawn control – you'll find that you'll need to add each string you want to a list control or combo box. There's no way to add an array of strings to a control, aside from repeatedly adding each individual string. It's not hard to write the code, but it really isn't all that efficient. Unfortunately, that's life with Windows – there's really no other way to get the job done!

Tidying Boxes

The indexes you pass to and receive from and all list and combo box functions are zero-based, i.e. the first or 'top most' element in a list box is always element zero, and the last is identified by an index one less than the number of items in the box. You can call the parameterless GetCount() member function to find out how many items a box holds; an empty box returns zero from this function.

Once your box is stuffed with data, you can use DeleteString() to remove individual strings from it. DeleteString() takes a single parameter: the index of the item to remove. After the DeleteString() function completes, it compacts the box by moving the other items up a notch to fill the space vacated by the removed item. If you'd like to completely annihilate the contents of your box, call ResetContent() against it. This purges the box of all its content in one fell swoop.

GetItemData() and SetItemData()

In many situations, it's convenient to associate some amount of data with each item in a list or combo box. For example, you might have a list box that enumerates every employee in your company by name. It would be wonderful to have their employee numbers stored in the box, but out of view of anyone using the box. You can do this using the GetItemData() and SetItemData() functions, which are members of both the CListBox and CComboBox classes.

An Application of SetItemData()

Once you have inserted the employee's name, you can call SetItemData() to associate a DWORD value with that entry in the list box, so that when you call GetItemData(), you can retrieve that DWORD. SetItemData() takes a zero-based index integer to the item to be set, and the DWORD value you'd like to set.

> Note that SetItemData() *will return* LB_ERR *or* CB_ERR *(for list boxes and combo boxes respectively) if you give it an index which is out of bounds.*

GetItemData() only takes the index integer and returns a DWORD. It will return LB_ERR or CB_ERR if the index doesn't exist, so you might want to make sure you never use these values for your associated data. Both macros are defined to be equal to –1. Code to load the list box, in your WM_INITDIALOG handler, might look like this:

```
void CMyDialog::OnInitDialog()
{
    DWORD     dwEmployeeNumber;
    CString   strEmployeeName;
    int       nIndex;

    // Get a pointer to a list box object
    CListBox* pBox = static_cast<CListBox*>(GetDlgItem(IDC_EMPLOYEELIST));

    // Initialize our imaginary data retrieval calls
    GetEmployees();

    // Make an imaginary call to retrieve data records one by one
    while (GetNextEmployee(&dwEmployeeNumber, strEmployeeName))
    {
        // Add the string, remembering where we put it
        nIndex = pBox->AddString(strEmployeeName);
        if (nIndex == LB_ERR || nIndex == LB_ERRSPACE)
        {
            break;
```

```
        // And probably make an error message!
    }

    // Store the extra data in the list box
    pBox->SetItemData(nIndex, dwEmployeeNumber);
}

return;
}
```

Remember that the list or combo box will blindly manage the data and keep it associated with the string. This is true even if the string changes position in the box, which means that the value you've associated with a string is associated with that string, not with the particular index of the strings in the box.

GetItemDataPtr() and SetItemDataPtr()

The box has no idea what the item data really means, so you can, for instance, keep pointers in the DWORD value. You can have each element in the list box maintain a pointer to some object or some data buffer which maintains a great deal of information for your application.

You might find it more convenient to use the GetItemDataPtr() and SetItemDataPtr() if you're throwing pointers around. These functions return and accept LPVOID pointers, so you can usually avoid any weird casts or annoying 'possible data loss' error messages. If you need to set the item data for a particular item in a list box to point at a CHockeyPlayer object, you might code this using the SetItemData() function:

```
CHockeyPlayer* pPlayer = GetPlayer();
CListBox* pBox = static_cast<CListBox*>(GetDlgItem(IDC_MY_LIST));
pBox->SetItemData(nIndex, (DWORD) pPlayer);
```

Code which uses SetItemDataPtr() is a little neater because you can avoid the cast:

```
CHockeyPlayer* pPlayer = GetPlayer();
CListBox* pBox = static_cast<CListBox*>(GetDlgItem(IDC_MY_LIST));
pBox->SetItemDataPtr(nIndex, pPlayer);
```

Remember that if you allocate storage for this data, the list box won't free it for you automatically when it's destroyed! You'll need to work through each item in the list box to delete the memory you allocated. Windows will send a WM_DELETEITEM message to the owner of the control when you delete an item from the control with CListBox::DeleteString(), but will *not* send such a message when you call ResetContent() or destroy the window! Because of the goofy way Windows works, you should probably take the safe road and carefully release any memory you've allocated for the item data yourself.

GetCurSel()

If the user clicks on your single-selection box, you can find out what they've selected by calling the GetCurSel() function. (If you've got a multiple selection box, you've got a little more work to do – see the multiple selection section a few pages from here.) This returns the index of the currently selected item in the box. If there's nothing selected in a combo box, the function returns CB_ERR, while if it's called against a list box in the same condition, the function returns LB_ERR.

You can use this index in a call to `GetItemData()` or `GetItemDataPtr()` to retrieve the per-item data that you may have stored. Alternatively, you can call `GetText()` to retrieve text for the entry. `GetText()` can be used against any entry in the list box; it takes an integer parameter providing the index of the item to be retrieved. For the combo box the function to use is `GetLBText()`.

Handling Box Events

Typically, you'll set up `WM_COMMAND` message handlers in your dialog box to handle events that your list and combo boxes wish to tell you about. The most popular events to trap are `LBN_SELCHANGE` and `CBN_SELCHANGE`, which tell your application that the user has changed the selection in the list or combo box respectively.

The user is likely to change the selection quite frequently (particularly if they're using the arrow keys to move the selection!), so don't do anything too costly in response to these messages.

It's also pretty common to respond to `LBN_DBLCLK` or `CBN_DBLCLK`. If the control is the only list in your dialog, you can assume it is a shortcut for clicking the default push button of the dialog box. You can have ClassWizard add these handlers for you, or you can use the `ON_LBN_DBLCLK()` or `ON_LBN_SELCHANGE()` message map entries yourself to add handlers for the messages.

> *Of course, the same message map macros exist for combo boxes; they just have _CBN_ in their name, instead of _LBN_.*

Note that if you are interested in receiving these notification messages, your control must have the `LBS_NOTIFY` style. Windows doesn't send notification messages for controls without the appropriate style.

> *While I've used the term 'string' throughout this section, list and combo boxes can be used to contain things other than strings. If you want them to contain numbers, for example, you need only convert them to a string before adding them to the box. You can also use owner-drawn list or combo boxes to hold any graphical items you'd like. Owner-drawn boxes help you by handling hit testing and measurement of the user's mouse activity, but you'll need to measure the items you're adding and do all of the painting yourself. You can read about owner-drawn list boxes in Chapter 7.*

Setting Box Size and Preference

You should size your list or combo box to show a reasonable amount of data. Of course, the notion of what constitutes a reasonable amount of data varies from application to application, and almost always from list box to list box as well. If the user is just picking an entry from a list, a very small control is appropriate, but if the user has a very large number of choices, it's usually a good idea to use a large control.

For list boxes, this aspect of the control's appearance can be affected by the presence of the `LBS_NOINTEGRALHEIGHT` style. If this style bit isn't present, the control will size itself to fit an exact number of list box entries, while remaining within the size of the control's bounding rectangle. If the style is present, the list box will always size itself to fit in the bounding rectangle, even if it means only partially showing an entry at the bottom edge of the control.

The figure opposite demonstrates the effect of the LBS_NOINTEGRALHEIGHT style; the list box on the right has LBS_NOINTEGRALHEIGHT, while the box on the left doesn't:

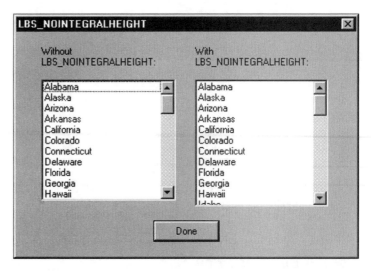

Both boxes are the same size in the dialog definition, but the box with the LBS_NOINTEGRALHEIGHT style sizes itself to be exactly the size specified in the resource script for the dialog. The box without LBS_NOINTEGRALHEIGHT snaps its size to fit a whole number of visible entries.

If you're interested in any special layout functionality for your box, you can use SetTopIndex() to dictate which item in your list box will be displayed first. This doesn't change the order of the list box; it just scrolls the contents so that the item you select is the first to be displayed in the box. You can identify the item to be displayed as the first visible entry by passing its index as the sole parameter to the SetTopIndex() function. If you'd like to see which item is currently in first spot, you can call GetTopIndex().

Horizontal Scrolling

When your application contains a list box that has WS_VSCROLL, Windows will measure the box and the items that are in it. Based on that total size, Windows will automatically maintain a scroll bar so that the user can move through the content of the box and see more elements than would normally fit in the space that the box uses on the screen. Sadly, Windows doesn't provide automatic measurement for list boxes that have WS_HSCROLL.

If you add WS_HSCROLL to your list box by checking the Horizontal Scroll checkbox on the Styles tab for the control's properties, or by assuring that the control has WS_HSCROLL when it is created, the box won't automatically measure all of the items in the box. Instead, you'll need to call the CListBox::SetHorizontalExtent() function to let the box know how wide items you're adding to the box actually are. SetHorizontalExtent() takes only an integer as a parameter – the integer indicates the maximum width of an item in pixels.

If you've created a box which will display only strings, you can use the DrawText() member of CDC to find the width of a particular string. Just call DrawText() with the DT_CALCRECT flag set in the nFormat parameter. You'll want to get the DC by calling GetWindowDC() on the dialog box, and you'll also need to get the font the list control will be using by calling GetFont() on the list box. Select the font you receive into the device context before doing the measurement.

Given a pointer to a CDialog-derived object named pDlg, a pointer to a CListBox object named pListBox, and a CString with the string to be measured in strYourString, the whole operation might look something like this:

```
CDC* pDC = pDlg->GetWindowDC();
CFont* pOldFont;
CFont* pListFont = pListBox->GetFont();
pOldFont = pDC->SelectObject(pListFont);
CRect rect;
pDC->DrawText(strYourString, &rect, DT_CALCRECT | DT_SINGLELINE);
pDC->SelectObject(pOldFont);
pDlg->ReleaseDC(pDC);
```

Once this code executes, you can call rect.Width() to retrieve the calculated width. This is the value you should pass to the SetHorizontalExtent() function. If you end up dynamically removing items from the box, you'll find that the horizontal scroll bar is displayed even when everything in the box has been deleted. You can call ShowScrollBar(FALSE) to turn off the bars.

Combo Box Specifics

Combo boxes have one big difference from list boxes; the edit control inside of a combo box may allow the user to change the content of the box. Combo boxes are ideal when you'd like your user to choose an item from a list of predefined choices, and also to allow the user to enter their own entry if they don't like the choices already available in the list.

For example, if the user can select one font from a list of dozens, you may wish to provide them with a combo box populated with all of the fonts on the system. The box can drop down when the user needs to make a selection, but otherwise takes up very little real estate because it only shows the user the font that is currently selected.

CBS_DROPDOWN

A combo box such as the one I just described is known as a **drop-down**, and it has the CBS_DROPDOWN style. A drop-down is useful when you wish to allow the user to type the name of their selection.

CBS_DROPDOWNLIST

If you are coding for a similar situation, but one where the user can't type a new entry, you should use a CBS_DROPDOWNLIST. This type of combo box doesn't allow the user to enter or change text in the edit control part of the combo; they're limited to the established text – the choices within the list box part of the control.

CBS_SIMPLE

The rarest type of combo box is CBS_SIMPLE. It usually only finds a home in file-oriented dialog boxes, where the user might want to see a list of available files in the current directory, but may need to explicitly type the name of a directory or wildcard file name. CBS_SIMPLE is like CBS_DROPDOWN in that the user can change content of the edit control at will, but is different in that the drop-down part of the box (the list box part) is always visible.

A CBS_SIMPLE box doesn't have a down-arrow allowing the user to drop or retract the list box. This means that CBS_SIMPLE combo boxes always take up more screen space than boxes with one of the previous two styles.

Conducting the Box Actions

From the programmer's point of view, combo boxes present a combination of the interfaces available in `CEdit` and `CListBox` controls. For instance, you can use `GetCurSel()` to find the currently selected list box item, or `GetCount()` to find the number of items in the drop-down. Adding and removing items in the drop-down can be done with the `AddString()` and `InsertString()` functions that I described earlier.

When you're working with a combo box, you can also perform operations on the edit control; you might want to get the text of the control using `GetWindowText()`, or change the highlight over the text in the control using `SetEditSel()`. Combo boxes have the same `Clear()`, `Cut()`, `Copy()`, and `Paste()` functions found in the `CEdit` class.

Combo boxes will send back a notify message when the user drops down their list box. They will also send many of the same notifications that edit controls can send; for example, you'll find that your combo box sends `CBN_EDITCHANGE` and `CBN_EDITUPDATE` notification messages.

You can trap combo box notification messages by hooking up the appropriate functions using ClassWizard, or by writing your own message map entries with the appropriate message map macros.

Exactly what functions make sense depends on the exact style of your control. Calling `GetWindowText()` against a `CBS_SIMPLE` box is more meaningful than calling it against a `CBS_DROPDOWNLIST` box. This is because the simple box might have text the user entered from scratch, while the `CBS_DROPDOWNLIST` box will never have text which came from the user directly. However, MFC doesn't preclude your use of silly functions against combo boxes of a given type; you're free to do what you like.

Tab Stops

List boxes are often used to show choices that are from some multiple-column data source. You can represent columnar data in a list box by using tab characters to separate each item in the list. The list box needs to have the `LBS_USETABSTOPS` style so that it can properly draw the items using the tabs.

You can set the exact position of the tabs by using the `CListBox::SetTabStops()` function. You can use one of two different overloads of the function to set an array of tab stops; with the other you can pass one tab stop position and have the control automatically space tab stops at a given frequency throughout the control.

The only drawback with tab stops is that of having to measure exactly where they should be. All dialog measurements are done in **dialog units**. Dialog units are not pixels; they're based on the font that's in use within the dialog box, which can be quite a nuisance. While it does make things a little easier when you want to change the font in a dialog, it makes it difficult to measure the dialog box or its elements.

Changing fonts is easier because the dialog resizes all of its contents depending on the selected font, which frees you from manually measuring and resizing things.

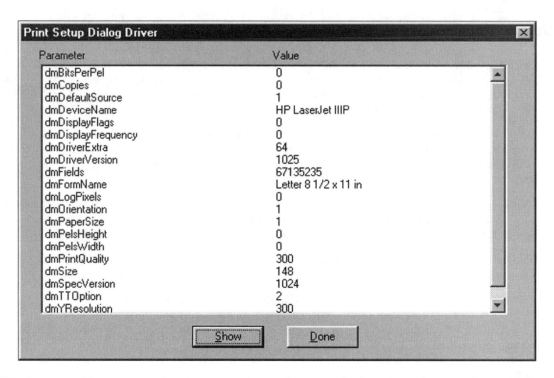

Windows provides a ::GetDialogBaseUnits() function which exposes the ratio that is used to convert dialog units to pixels. Unfortunately, the values returned from this function won't work for every dialog – some say they don't work for most. The cause of such disdain is the fact that the ::GetDialogBaseUnits() API returns information that describes the coordinate conversion in a dialog box that's actually based on the default system font. You can use the CDialog::MapDialogRect() member to map a rectangle to correctly scaled points without regard to the dialog's selected font.

The Dialogs example makes use of the tabbed dialog box, shown above, to display the results returned from a print setup box. You can find the code that does the measurement and calls the SetTabStops() member of CListBox in the OnInitDialog() handler for the CPreSetupDlg class.

Multiple Selection List Boxes

There may come a time in your application when you want to provide a list box that is capable of allowing multiple selections. A list box that has the LBS_MULTIPLESEL style lets users use the *Ctrl* and *Shift* keys to select more than one item.

The obvious change for the programmer when using a multiple selection box is that the notion of a current selection is gone, and therefore the meaning of the GetCurSel() function for such controls changes. Since GetCurSel() can only return a single index for one selected item, you'll need to use a different interface to query the state of the box. Instead, your work should start with a call to GetSelCount(). This function will return the number of currently selected items in the list box. If it returns 0, you know that nothing in the box is selected and you'll need to do something else with your time.

The more interesting case, however, is when `GetSelCount()` returns a non-zero value. To find out exactly what elements are selected, you'll need to call `CListBox::GetSelItems()`. This function takes an integer, indicating the maximum number of selections for which information should be returned, and a pointer to an array of `int`s where that information can be stored. You can allocate this array statically, or you can allocate it dynamically like this:

```
int nSelected = pBox->GetSelCount();
if (nSelected > 0)
{
    int *pArray = new int[nSelected];
    pBox->GetSelItems(nSelected, pArray);

    // Now, do work on each item in the array
    int nIndex;
    for (nIndex = 0; nIndex < nSelected; nIndex++)
    {
        CString str;
        pBox->GetText(pArray[nIndex], str);
        // Do something with str...
    }

    delete [] pArray;
}
```

Once you're finished locating the items in the box, you're free to use the regular `GetText()`, `GetItemDataPtr()` or `GetItemData()` calls to work with the items you're interested in. It certainly takes a bit more work to get the job done when you're using a multiple selection list box, but users are highly appreciative.

> Because the multiple selection user-interface just doesn't make sense for combo boxes, all of these features and functions are only available in `CListBox`.

Note that where multiple-selection list boxes are found, tri-state controls aren't often that far behind. For example, if your dialog allows the user to select an item in the list box, and then displays information about the selection elsewhere in the box, you should use tri-state controls to reflect the status of the selection. If you have a list of employees and a Full Time check box, for instance, the user may select several full-time employees and several part-time employees. For these situations, the Full Time check box should be set to its indeterminate state.

A Note about Initial Lists

You may have noticed that the property pages for list and combo box controls in the dialog editor window of Microsoft Visual Studio offers you the ability to enter initial list choices. Right-click on the control while you are editing the dialog and look for the edit control marked E_nter listbox items.

Most programmers populate their list and combo boxes in the `WM_INITDIALOG` handler for their dialog box. You can code all of the `AddString()` or `InsertString()` calls you need for this function there, but you might wish to take advantage of this simpler method provided by the dialog box editor and MFC.

> Note that the **E̲nter list choices** strings will only be added to list boxes and combo boxes that are created with the **CDialog** class in an MFC application. The data won't be placed into the controls if you're not using MFC to create the dialog at run time.

Anything you enter in the dialog becomes a part of a custom resource type maintained by the IDE in your resource file. This resource, given the user type DLGINIT and an identifier equal to the resource ID of the dialog to which it corresponds, contains the text you entered into the Properties window to initially populate the control. The resource includes the ID of the control and the message that should be sent to insert the data in the control.

ExecuteDlgInit()

As it creates the dialog box object, MFC calls an undocumented member of CWnd called ExecuteDlgInit(). This function is responsible for parsing the information in the resource and firing off the messages necessary to populate the controls with the data in the resource. The resource takes up very little memory and stores the information more conveniently and efficiently than you could if you simply coded AddString() calls in your WM_INITDIALOG handler.

The default implementation of OnInitDialog() in CDialog calls ExecuteDialogInit(). If you override the OnInitDialog() function with your own WM_INITDIALOG handler, MFC won't have the chance to read the dialog initialization resource information into memory and perform the required initialization. If you suddenly find that your dialogs don't have their list or combo boxes initialized, this is probably the first thing you should check! If you add your OnInitDialog() handler using ClassWizard, it will automatically make the call to the base class for you, which means that you can avoid this pitfall.

Button Controls

Microsoft Windows provides a myriad of button-style controls. Obviously, push buttons fall into the button class that Windows maintains. However, you may not know that Windows also considers check boxes and radio buttons to be of the same window class. Check boxes and radio buttons differ in their exact window style bits (as far as Windows is concerned) but they also accept different messages and have many different style bits too! Let's examine the different button types and see what features MFC provides for each one.

Push Buttons

You'll rarely need to manipulate a push button in a dialog directly. In the few instances that you do, it's usually just as easy to use the raw CWnd object returned by GetDlgItem(). You can use this function to set the text on the button, or to enable and disable the button.

For advanced applications, you may need to make a push button the default push button for the window. You should cast the CWnd pointer from GetDlgItem() to a CButton pointer, before you can use the SetButtonStyle() and GetButtonStyle() functions to retrieve or set style bits associated with the push button. Clearly, a push button *must* have the BS_PUSHBUTTON style applied, but the only other push button-specific style that can be applied to the button is BS_DEFPUSHBUTTON. A button with the BS_DEFPUSHBUTTON style has a heavy black border. When the user presses *Enter* and another control that doesn't need the *Enter* key has focus the default push button is activated.

When they are activated, push buttons send a WM_COMMAND message to their parent window. For this reason, you'll never need to make your own subclass of CButton. The exceptions that prove this rule are owner-draw push buttons, where you're likely to be interested in handling all aspects of the button's ability to render itself.

To react to the user when they push your button, use ClassWizard to add a handler for the command message your button sends to the application. By default, the CDialog class in MFC provides a handler for OK and Cancel buttons which close down the dialog and return status codes IDOK or IDCANCEL respectively.

Radio Buttons

The reason you rarely need to use a CButton object when you manipulate push buttons is that push buttons don't have an inherent state. Aside from their style, which you rarely need to change anyway, push buttons don't offer you feedback until the user comes along and pounds them.

Radio buttons, on the other hand, *do* show some state to the user. They are used in groups to show a set of mutually exclusive choices. For example, you might use two radio buttons in a group box to let the user select portrait or landscape mode, or you may have a list of five radio buttons letting the user indicate their preference between coach, economy, executive, tourist or first class.

On the other hand, having a list of 50 radio buttons (that is, one for each state in The United States), which lets the user choose the state destination of their package, is silly. Not only would you actually have to use 51 buttons (because of the District of Columbia), but you'd also senselessly waste screen real estate and make it rather awkward for your user to get anything done with your application in the first place.

Grouping Radio Buttons

So that they can see which radio buttons work together when they are choosing an option, the buttons of a functional group are almost always placed in a group box. As well as providing a visual cue for the user, the group box is used as a marker by Windows. If you have some radio buttons in a group box and they are not behaving as you'd expect, it's quite likely that you've somehow declared one or more of the buttons as having a tab order outside of the group box. You can remedy this using the tabbing order feature of the dialog box editor.

Once things are set up correctly and the user activates a button, if the buttons in the group have the BS_AUTORADIOBUTTON style, Windows will automatically clear all other buttons in the group. If you don't have BS_AUTORADIOBUTTON set, you'll need to respond to the WM_COMMAND message that each button in the group fires when it is set. You can respond to this message by unchecking all other buttons in the group and checking the one that has generated the message.

Unless the button has the BS_LEFTTEXT style, radio buttons always draw their text to the right of the button's indicator circle.

Style and Status

You can retrieve and set the BS_AUTORADIOBUTTON and BS_LEFTTEXT styles using the GetButtonStyle() and SetButtonStyle() member functions of the CButton class. You should be aware that, since BS_LEFTTEXT changes the appearance of the button, you should almost always pass TRUE as the second parameter to SetButtonStyle() so that the button correctly repaints with its new look. Of course, the buttons are created with the styles you specify in the dialog template. You don't usually need to change their styles at run time.

You'll also need to use a `CButton` pointer to access the checked status of the button. You can use `GetCheck()` to see if the button is marked. To initialize your buttons, you can use the `SetCheck()` function.

You should study the design of your dialog box and how it relates to the `WS_GROUP` style bit. This style makes a logical group out of the controls if you set the style bits on your radio buttons properly – the first control in a group box should have the `WS_GROUP` style, and the rest shouldn't. You should also know that if all the controls in the group are `BS_AUTORADIOBUTTON`s, the framework can very conveniently let you query the selection option in the dialog. If you'd like, MFC can return a single integer, indicating which control from the group is selected.

> *This functionality is provided by the* `DDX_Radio()` *function, covered in more detail a little later with the rest of the dialog data exchange functions.*

It's imperative to use the `WS_GROUP` flag properly when you're working with radio buttons on your dialog. If you design a dialog that has more than one bunch of logically associated radio buttons, you'll want to make sure you've used `WS_GROUP` to tell Windows and MFC which radio buttons form which groups. Consider this dialog:

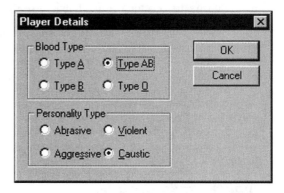

And, while you're busy thinking about the dialog, I'll be going through your stuff. The dialog's **Type A** and **Abrasive** controls have the `WS_GROUP` style. That's absolutely necessary, otherwise Windows would think that buttons in the **Personality Type** group box were in the same group as the **Blood Type** group box. The user would notice this when they selected a personality type; such an action would cause buttons in the **Blood Type** box to be reset, and vice versa. Further, the tab order of the items with the `WS_GROUP` style is important, too; otherwise using the tab key or the arrow keys to exercise the keyboard interface to the dialog will fail.

Check Boxes

The last flavor of button control is the check box. Check boxes are used to request or indicate discrete settings that are either on or off. In this case, *discrete* means that the setting of each check box in a dialog isn't necessarily related to any other setting. While you should use radio buttons when only one choice from a small list is valid, you can use check boxes to indicate choices which are selected or not selected, independently of other selections.

Style and Status

Check boxes must always have the `BS_CHECKBOX` style set, although some may have the `BS_3STATE` style, which indicates they will allow an indeterminate state as well. This state fills the check box with a hatched pattern, rather than blanking it out or filling it with a check mark. This isn't to indicate that the control has a third state, but that the control's state is indeterminate. If you're using the check marks to allow users to modify selections which affect many objects, each element of the selection may not have the same setting. Since it's impossible to conveniently show which elements have which settings, the box can just show its indeterminate state.

SetCheck() and GetCheck()

You can call the CButton::SetCheck() function on the button object to set its state, supplying a single integer as a parameter. If the parameter is zero, the button is cleared; passing 1 will set the button and place a mark in the box. If the button has the BS_3STATE style, you can also pass 2 to set the control to its indeterminate state. The states are also provided by the preprocessor symbols BST_UNCHECKED, BST_CHECKED, and BST_INDETERMINATE. If you're more comfortable using the symbols, by all means – go ahead!

Similarly, the CButton::GetCheck() function allows you to query the state of the button. The values returned from this parameterless function are the same as those passed to the SetCheck() function.

Aside from changing its text, the only way to modify the appearance of a check box is to use the BS_LEFTTEXT style. Normally, the check box is to the left of the button. If this style is set, the box will paint itself with its label text at the left side of its bounding rectangle, and the check box will be at the right side of the text.

You should use a check box to imply that some attribute does or doesn't apply to a given situation. For example, you might use one to indicate whether or not a file is read-only. However, if an attribute doesn't have an intuitive opposite, you're better off using a pair of radio buttons. If you're about to print, you might offer the user a Draft radio button and a Letter Quality radio button. This tells the user exactly what they're going to get.

Static Controls

Without a doubt, your dialogs will contain a number of controls that act as labels for other controls, as markers for different groups of controls, or that simply decorate it with an icon. Note that group boxes are actually a button style. The rectangular markers to which I'm referring are exactly that; rectangles drawn around other controls. Unlike radio buttons, such a rectangle has no semantic meaning and can't be a tab stop.

Each of these controls is a little different, but MFC groups them all together under the heading of **static controls**. The MFC CStatic class allows you to get or retrieve the text associated with a static control, or change the icon associated with it.

There are only a few occasions when this class is actually useful; it is provided primarily for accessing icons in the controls that handle them. While you can create instances of this class that reference static text in your dialog, it's just as easy to use the raw CWnd class to retrieve or set the text in such a control.

If you are using an icon-based static control, you can use the CStatic::GetIcon() function to retrieve an HICON to the icon that the control is showing. The GetIcon() function accepts no parameters. The CStatic::SetIcon() function sets the icon that the control will use. It accepts a handle to the icon that you'd like to display as an HICON. The function also returns the handle to the icon that the control was using previously.

Note that when the dialog editor creates static controls it gives them an ID of IDC_STATIC by default. This value is #defined to be -1, which is acceptable to Windows and convenient for you as a programmer. This is helpful, as you don't need to think of IDs or ID names for each static control when you're not extremely likely to reference them anyway. However, if you want to manipulate the static control at any time while your program is running, you *must* give the control a unique ID of its own, so that Windows can determine exactly which control you're talking about.

Dialog Data Exchange

Perhaps the most annoying part of writing code for Windows involves getting information back from dialog boxes. If your application uses dialog boxes to return even a little information from the user, you'll need to write some code to examine each control of interest and provide some means of returning data.

The problem of managing the data associated with controls is made even more evident when you need to restrict the values acceptable to your application. If you only want to allow a certain range of values or a certain string length, you'll need to do more work to check the values you get back. That work involves edits and writing code to set the focus to the controls causing the error, before finally showing the user an error message – all without letting that bogus value back into the program.

To help you develop this kind of code (which has a home in almost every application), the Microsoft Foundation Classes provide **dialog data exchange** and **dialog data validation**. For short, and for naming most of the functions and macros involved in the processes, **DDX** refers to dialog data exchange and **DDV** refers to dialog data validation.

Dialog data exchange encapsulates macros that help you move information between variables in your program and the controls in your dialog box. Dialog data validation provides functions that allow you to check for valid data in your dialog, and even provides stock error messages for out-of-bounds values.

The `Dialogs` example application, which supports this chapter, uses the dialog data validation and dialog data exchange code quite aggressively when it displays its Employee Information dialog box. The code in `Employee.cpp` and `Employee.h` shows how the dialog moves data around. You can find a tiny bit of code near the end of the `Maindlg.cpp` file that takes care of displaying the dialog.

Since the C++ dialog object will outlast the Windows on-screen dialog object, the C++ dialog object provides an ideal place to put information that the dialog returns, creates or uses. Each dialog control you'll need to work with can be mimicked by a member variable of the class that can then be altered by the changes the user makes, or be used as a source of information to initialize the control when the dialog appears.

For instance, you can put code in the constructor for your dialog class to initialize these variables so that when the dialog window is actually created, MFC can handle copying the data to the controls as they are created and displayed in the window. Once the dialog has been displayed, you can get the most recent values from all the controls by letting MFC copy them back to the member variables of the C++ object.

Data Exchange Code in Practice

In the example application, you'll find code that swaps data back and forth between the dialog's controls and the member variables of the class implementing the dialog. Look around in the `Employee.cpp` file for a function named `DoDataExchange()`. This function takes a pointer to an object called `CDataExchange`.

For your reference, the code is reproduced here:

```
void CEmployeeDlg::DoDataExchange(CDataExchange* pDX)
{
    CDialog::DoDataExchange(pDX);
    //{{AFX_DATA_MAP(CEmployeeDlg)
    DDX_Control(pDX, IDC_JOBS, m_opqekrk);
    DDX_Text(pDX, IDC_FIRSTNAME, m_strFirstName);
    DDV_MaxChars(pDX, m_strFirstName, 30);
    DDX_Text(pDX, IDC_LASTNAME, m_strLastName);
    DDV_MaxChars(pDX, m_strLastName, 30);
    DDX_Text(pDX, IDC_SALARY, m_uSalary);
    DDV_MinMaxUInt(pDX, m_uSalary, 0, 150000);
    DDX_Check(pDX, IDC_CATS, m_bCatAllergy);
    DDX_Check(pDX, IDC_DOGS, m_bDogAllergy);
    DDX_Check(pDX, IDC_LACTOSE, m_bLactoseAllergy);
    DDX_Check(pDX, IDC_PENICILLIN, m_bPenicillinAllergy);
    DDX_Radio(pDX, IDC_USD, m_nPaymentMethod);
    //}}AFX_DATA_MAP
}
```

Let's examine what these calls do. The calls you'll normally make from your DoDataExchange() routine fall into two categories: data exchange (functions which begin with DDX_), and data validation (functions which begin with DDV_).

DDX_ Routines

The data exchange function calls are all highlighted above; DDX_ stands for **dialog data exchange**. You can see that there are several types of dialog data exchange functions, but they all have roughly the same format. They take the pointer to the CDataExchange context object that's passed to the function, as well as the integer ID of the control and the name of the member variable that will be exchanging the data.

If you're experienced with the C++ language, you might wonder why MFC doesn't implement these functions as many overloads of a single function name. The implementation as it stands, with functions having several different names, makes the type of exchange intended by the developer completely unambiguous.

Don't jump to conclusions from the small set of functions we've seen above; in fact, some of the DDX_ function names *are* overloaded to allow a range of types for member variable targets. For instance, there are several flavors of DDX_Text which accept integers of various sizes; this is simply because you might have a text field which accepts text, but actually manipulates a variable of a particular integer type. C++ will allow you to use the data type you feel most appropriate for the expected range of values. The name of the DDX_ function is actually intended to show what control type the function handles, rather than the defined data type.

On the following page is a list of the different DDX_ functions provided by MFC, as well as the data type of their member variable parameter:

Exchange Function Name	Member Variable Parameter Type
DDX_CBIndex()	int
DDX_CBString()	CString
DDX_CBStringExact()	CString
DDX_Check()	int
DDX_Control()	CWnd
DDX_LBIndex()	int
DDX_LBString()	CString
DDX_LBStringExact()	CString
DDX_Radio()	int
DDX_Scroll()	int
DDX_Text()	UINT
DDX_Text()	BYTE
DDX_Text()	int
DDX_Text()	LONG
DDX_Text()	DWORD
DDX_Text()	CString
DDX_Text()	COleDateTime
DDX_Text()	COleCurrency
DDX_Text()	float
DDX_Text()	double

As a crafty programmer, you're wondering what the standard implementations of these functions do, and perhaps in particular, what the deal is with the CDataExchange context object. After all, NATO and the European Union both guarantee that developers are free to create data types and process information with any format they see fit.

If you want to create your own data exchange functions, there's no reason why you shouldn't. Read on and we'll describe the rules you should follow to make sure that your application remains a well-behaved citizen of the world.

Ye Olde CDataExchange Objecte

The pDX pointer, which is tossed about to each and every data exchange call, including your application's own DoDataExchange() function on start up, provides some important contextual information. This allows the individual data exchange functions to get their work done.

The most pertinent piece of information contained in CDataExchange is a flag called m_bSaveAndValidate, which is available as a public member variable. It dictates the direction in which the exchange is occurring:

When m_bSaveAndValidate is TRUE, the data exchange and data validation function calls should be validating (and saving) the data by reading it from the dialog box controls and writing it in the member variables of the class.

When m_bSaveAndValidate is FALSE, you should assume that the dialog data exchange is to take the data from the member variables and apply them to the controls in the dialog. Exchanges in this direction don't need to perform validation; the data in the member variables is assumed to be well-formatted and quite valid.

PrepareEditCtrl() and PrepareCtrl()

The CDataExchange class also implements and exposes two important functions: PrepareCtrl() and PrepareEditCtrl(). The DDX_ routine you create should call one of these two functions before it does anything else. If you're dealing with an edit control, call PrepareEditCtrl(), but if you're dealing with any other type of control, call PrepareCtrl().

Either function sets up the control and the data exchange context so that your data exchange context will be ready to act with the control. PrepareEditCtrl() sets a flag in the data exchange context so that it will know that the exchanging control is an edit. This flag is stored in m_bEditLastControl; TRUE in this member indicates that the control being edited was indeed an edit control. Before doing this work, PrepareEditCtrl() calls PrepareCtrl().

PrepareCtrl() simply validates the control; if the ID passed doesn't exist, is zero or -1 (the value associated with IDC_STATIC), the function causes an ASSERT. If the function was passed a reasonable ID, it gets the hWnd of the control and stores it in the m_hWndLastControl member of the CDataExchange object, while also returning it as the result of the function.

Setting the Boundaries

You should get your custom DDX_ code to use this SDK-level window handle to work with the control in question, rather than allowing the code to create a temporary CWnd object. The reason for this restriction is that your DDX_ code, or other functions it may call, can throw exceptions that may cause your CWnd to leak a window object. Additionally, dynamically creating a CWnd for a particular window handle is an expensive process that you'd best avoid repeating while you are validating or performing data exchange on controls in the dialog.

If your code is indeed copying information from the control to the member data (i.e. if m_bSaveAndValidate is TRUE), you should perform whatever action is necessary to copy the data from the control. You'd be wise, at this point, to perform a sanity check on the value returned. Make sure that it isn't out of extreme bounds in terms of the control or data type requested – if it is, ASSERT(). This isn't the same as actually validating the data that the control returns; what you're doing here is ascertaining that the data value is valid for the control, not for the exact context of information returned from the user.

If the data value is to be moved from the member variable to the control (i.e. if m_bSaveAndValidate is FALSE) your code can use the member variable itself as a source for the information the control needs.

DDX_TextWithFormat()

You should be aware that if your code is retrieving numeric data from a text control, you can use the MFC function `DDX_TextWithFormat()` to aid the conversion of the string to useable numeric data. The `Dlgdata.cpp` file in the `Microsoft Visual Studio\vc98\mfc\src` directory after a default installation (`vc98\mfc\src` directory on the CD, if you've decided not to install MFC source) for the dialog data exchange routines. Here, you can review the exact features of the `DDX_TextWithFormat()` function and how it is used and implemented.

Just like every other `DDX_` function, `DDX_TextWithFormat()` accepts a pointer to a `CDataExchange` object and a control ID. The next parameter is an `sscanf()`-style formatting string, informing the function how to format or parse the data expected from the string. The subsequent parameter is an ID for a string resource in your code (or within MFC) that will be used to show a message to the user if the conversion procedure fails.

This parameter must be supplied; there is no default. MFC doesn't check for special values like 0, and it uses internal messages appropriate for the type of conversion. These messages, listed below, are also available to you:

Resource ID	Message box text
AFX_IDP_PARSE_INT	Please enter an integer
AFX_IDP_PARSE_REAL	Please enter a number
AFX_IDP_PARSE_INT_RANGE	Please enter an integer between %1 and %2
AFX_IDP_PARSE_REAL_RANGE	Please enter a number between %1 and %2
AFX_IDP_PARSE_STRING_SIZE	Please enter no more than %1 characters
AFX_IDP_PARSE_RADIO_BUTTON	Please select a button
AFX_IDP_PARSE_BYTE	Please enter an integer between 0 and 255
AFX_IDP_PARSE_UINT	Please enter a positive integer
AFX_IDP_PARSE_DATETIME	Please enter a date and/or time
AFX_IDP_PARSE_CURRENCY	Please enter a currency

I would encourage you to use these predefined strings where appropriate, as MFC will internationalize them to whatever country is suitable, providing that you've requested such AppWizard support in your application. On the other hand, there's no substitute for a message that's correct, even if it's in the wrong language!

Once these parameters have been provided, you can specify a predefined list of variables to receive the results of the conversion. Alternatively, they may act as a source for the routine that will provide a character representation of the data in question. A typical invocation of `DDX_TextWithFormat()` might look something like this one, stolen from an overloading of `DDX_Text()` that handles `BYTE` values:

```
DDX_TextWithFormat(pDX, nIDC, _T("%u"), AFX_IDP_PARSE_INT, &n);
```

The `AFX_IDP_PARSE_INT` preprocessor symbol identifies an MFC-provided string resource which serves as an error message if the function fails, in which case the string entry is 'Please enter an integer'.

Note that the supported formatting strings are relatively simple; you can use %u, %d, %lu and %ld without fear, but you can't pass any length, precision or formatting flags. Neither do these functions support floating point formatting or parsing, since they use `wsprintf()` for output and a simple reimplementation of `sscanf()` to get their work done.

If your requirements fall into any of these categories, you'll need to roll your own code for the conversions. Also remember that the strings need to be of type `TCHAR` for Unicode/ANSI compatibility. The easiest way to accomplish this is to encase your string literals in an invocation of the `_T()` macro. Using this macro will ensure that your string literals are promoted to wide character strings for Unicode builds of your program.

Invoking Fail()

Remember that the code you write to retrieve your data from a control might fail because the data is incorrectly formatted, or because it is out of bounds for the data type you are trying to retrieve. If this is the case, you should display an error message to the user and call the `Fail()` member of the `CDataExchange` object passed to your routine.

Remember that your `DDX_` code should simply try to convert the data. The possibility of the data being out of bounds or inappropriate for any application should be left to the `DDV_` function, or the code in the `DoDataExchange()` function specific to the dialog. Only throw a `Fail()` or display a message box if the user has provided data that doesn't fit between the extreme bounds of acceptability for the data value.

DDX_HexText()

The example application features a function called `DDX_HexText()` which lets you exchange hexadecimal numbers using edit controls in your dialog box. We declare the function as a global so that it can be used anywhere in the module. The declaration for the function is:

```
void AFXAPI DDX_HexText(CDataExchange *pDX, int nIDC, unsigned long &value)
```

The function is more than a few lines long, so we don't want to go into all of its gritty features here. Suffice to say that it does some math to convert each character found in the edit control identified by `nIDC` into an integer. The third parameter references the integer which will supply or receive the value, depending on the direction of the transfer. If the function is initializing the control, we simply use the following piece of code:

```
if (pDX->m_bSaveAndValidate)
{
    // Other stuff...
}
else
{
    // We're initializing the control...
    wsprintf(szFormat, _T("%8.8lX"), ul);
    ::SetWindowText(hWndCtrl, szFormat);
}
```

By the way, you might see code that eschews the use of CStrings *in* DDX_ *and* DDV_ *functions. In older versions of MFC (which worked with compilers that didn't understand C++ exceptions) exceptions thrown when a* CString *was lying about could leak memory. You could safeguard against this by painstakingly freeing the memory owned by the* CString *with an explicit call. This is no longer a problem; you can safely have a* CString *(or any other object!) lying about when an exception is thrown, without worrying about it leaking memory.*

All we need to do if m_bSaveAndValidate is FALSE is get a ::SetWindowText() fired off.

Using the Windows API

If you take a look, you'll find that MFC's code uses the Windows ::SetWindowText() API instead of using the MFC CWnd::SetWindowText() function, so that we don't have to ask MFC to create a temporary CWnd object for us. Since MFC works this way, I follow suit in the sample application. This results in a function that is just a fraction faster; if you have a kajillion fields to validate, your users will appreciate these savings.

m_bSaveAndValidate, if you've forgotten, is a member of the CDataExchange *object referenced by the* pDX *parameter given to your validation function from the* DoDataExchange() *function. And a kajillion, if you don't have a scientific dictionary handy, is an integer well over a few dozen.*

Taking the data value from the control and making an integer out of it is, of course, a little more tedious – that's the bulk of the function. Essentially, the implementation in DDX_HexText() just accomplishes safe character referencing, converting the string the user supplied into an integer. We have to be careful with the validation; the user could have typed any old string of characters, so if we see something we don't like, we call the Fail() member of CDataExchange, just like this:

```
if (bFailed)
{
    AfxMessageBox(_T("Please enter an eight-digit hexidecimal quantity."));
    pDX->Fail();
}
```

Any code after the call to Fail() won't be executed. Fail() pitches an exception back to MFC so that the libraries know about the failure, but it's important to display an error message of your own here, before you have MFC throw the exception.

Note that I used a string constant for clarity, but you should probably use a string resource to make localization of your program easier.

In case you're wondering, I don't use a C run-time library function to do the conversion because I want a lot more control over the conversion and error checking than the run-time functions would afford. atoi() would, for example, simply return zero in the event of an error and not give us any way to know that there really was an error and not simply a problem.

Data Validation Code with DDV_

In your `DoDataExchange()` routine, you can call one of the `DDV_` functions MFC provides. The call will ensure that MFC provide some form of data validation on the value returned for you. The data validation function will check the appropriate specification against the actual data and inform the user with a message box if there's a problem.

From the `Employee.cpp` file in this chapter's example, the `DoDataExchange()` function below is shown with its data validation calls highlighted:

```
void CEmployeeDlg::DoDataExchange(CDataExchange* pDX)
{
    CDialog::DoDataExchange(pDX);
    //{{AFX_DATA_MAP(CEmployeeDlg)
    DDX_Control(pDX, IDC_JOBS, m_opqekrk);
    DDX_Text(pDX, IDC_FIRSTNAME, m_strFirstName);
    DDV_MaxChars(pDX, m_strFirstName, 30);
    DDX_Text(pDX, IDC_LASTNAME, m_strLastName);
    DDV_MaxChars(pDX, m_strLastName, 30);
    DDX_Text(pDX, IDC_SALARY, m_uSalary);
    DDV_MinMaxUInt(pDX, m_uSalary, 0, 150000);
    DDX_Check(pDX, IDC_CATS, m_bCatAllergy);
    DDX_Check(pDX, IDC_DOGS, m_bDogAllergy);
    DDX_Check(pDX, IDC_LACTOSE, m_bLactoseAllergy);
    DDX_Check(pDX, IDC_PENICILLIN, m_bPenicillinAllergy);
    DDX_Radio(pDX, IDC_USD, m_nPaymentMethod);
    //}}AFX_DATA_MAP
}
```

> The groups of **DDX_** and **DDV_** functions that handle the controls in your application can be in any order, but you must use **DDX_** to retrieve the data for a particular control before calling **DDV_** against that control. You can order the pairs of calls in any way that you see fit, but for a given control the **DDX_** call must come first.

You should be aware that the `DDV_` functions are meaningless unless the `DoDataExchange()` function has been called to copy data from the window to the control. The purpose of the call is reflected by the `m_bSaveAndValidate` member of the `CDataExchange`. If `m_bSaveAndValidate` is `TRUE`, data is being taken from the controls and placed back into the member data and the `DDV_` functions have effect. When you are implementing your own `DDV_` function, you should first check the `m_bSaveAndValidate` flag; if it is `FALSE`, just `return` without incident.

You should also note that the `DDX_` function will set up a state in the `CDataExchange` object to assure that any error raised by the `DDV_` function can be blamed on the appropriate control. This means that your `DDX_` function should be immediately followed by the related `DDV_` functions, but you can (if you're crafty) poke the appropriate state back into the `CDataExchange`'s window handle and edit the relevant flag members.

The `DDV_` functions that are provided by MFC don't test to see whether the control has been disabled or hidden. They will always go after data in controls, even when others in your dialog box dictate that some controls are meaningless or out of scope.

> *If you were to design a dialog box where a check box enables or disables a large group of controls, you'd need to put an* if *statement around the dialog data exchange and validation calls for that group of controls. Unfortunately, this also means that your code can no longer be managed by ClassWizard; the rogue* if *is enough to send the simple parser in ClassWizard running for the hills. There's no real way around this; you'll have to forgo using ClassWizard to maintain that part of your exchange and validation function.*

DDV_ Messages

The `DDV_` functions implemented by MFC will post an appropriate error message to the user if a problem occurs when they are conducting range validations, such as in the `DDV_MinMaxUInt()` call above. The message will explain to the user that the field must contain a value within the range specified by the parameters to the function. Again, to play along with the status quo, any custom `DDV_` functions you decide to implement should post a similar error message.

The implementation of your own `DDV_` functions is quite similar, in a general sense, to the implementation of your own `DDX_` functions. As I've mentioned before, you shouldn't do any work in your `DDV_` functions if `m_bSaveAndValidate` is `FALSE`. If your validation fails, simply post an error message to the user and call the `Fail()` member of the `CDataExchange` object passed to your validation function.

Using ClassWizard

The dialog data exchange and validation functions that MFC provides are just lovely. Sadly though, you'll still have to write code for your own special types and even for some more common ones, like money, or Roman numerals, or dates. (A vast amount of data entry in modern systems is done in Roman numerals.) Happily, you have an architecture that poses very few restrictions and lets you get on with it, although that means you're left to manage the member variables you'll need to make everything work. Left to your own devices, you'd also have to add the appropriate function calls to do the exchange and validation steps – and remembering all of these parameters is a little tedious.

Fortunately, ClassWizard comes to the rescue! If you wish, you can have ClassWizard create almost all of the code that you need to get your dialog off the ground. This probably isn't a surprise; if you looked carefully at the code fragments in the previous sections, you will have noticed those tell-tale `//{{AFX_DATA_MAP...` comments, a sure sign that ClassWizard is staking out its territory.

Implementation

To have ClassWizard help you implement data exchange and validation, follow these steps:

1. Draw your dialog resource using the dialog resource editor window, remembering that the first step in adding a dialog to your application is to sit down and think about how it should be designed!

2. Once the dialog is added, click on the **Add Class** button in any of the tabs in the ClassWizard window.

3. When the dialog is shown, make sure you choose a `CDialog` derived class in the **Base class** drop-down.

4. When you finish, you'll see another drop-down, labeled Dialog ID. This lists the dialog resources that you've not associated with any other class in your application.

5. Choose your new dialog resource ID in that dialog.

6. Choose the header file and implementation file names that you want.

7. Press OK to indicate that you've finished. ClassWizard will create the appropriate files with the names you requested and then add them to your project.

Once you've done all this, you'll be able to find the class you've created in the Class name drop-down of the Member Variables tab in ClassWizard, shown next:

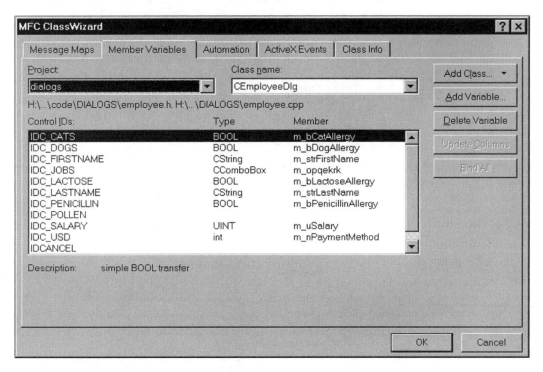

Select your dialog's class name here and ClassWizard will use the list box central to the Member Variables tab to enumerate the control IDs found in the resource associated with the dialog.

Have no fear; if you change the dialog box resource and revisit this dialog, the list will be updated to show any controls that you add, or remove any that you delete.

If you have a control on your dialog that isn't listed in the Control IDs *list box, you should make sure that you've included the proper styles on your control. Note that controls with hard-coded integer IDs and controls with IDs of* IDC_STATIC *won't be listed in the box.*

Adding Member Variables

Pressing the Add Variable... button results in the Add Member Variable dialog, where you can choose a member variable name to shadow your control. The suggestion of m_ in the name is just that – a suggestion. Most people use m_ as a prefix to member variables to identify them as such, but if you don't want to do this, you can just backspace over the characters in the box.

If you're after a control in your dialog which will let you perform data exchange, you should pick Value in the Category drop-down. You'll also need to pick an appropriate data type in the Variable type drop-down. The type of variable you choose will directly affect the way that validation is completed for your control. If you pick a string, you can only perform a length validation on it. If you choose a numeric value, ClassWizard will generate code that can check the entered value against a predefined range.

When you close the Add Member Variable dialog, the changes you make will be reflected in the Control IDs list box. When any given control is selected, ClassWizard may add extra fields to the Member Variables tab to show the data validation that will take place. It is here that you can type the maximum and minimum acceptable values for numeric types, or enter a maximum length for string types. If you don't want to have ClassWizard produce validation code for your control, just leave these fields blank.

Implementing the Code by Hand

If, instead of using ClassWizard, you'd like to have a way to reference the control and write code yourself, you can select Control in the Category drop-down. ClassWizard will then automatically select an appropriate MFC control class from the Variable type drop-down. For some controls, there's only one appropriate type, but for others, you'll see that you can do the exchange against a control type or a simple data type appropriate for holding to the control's value. If you find it convenient, you can do exchanges between a simple data type and a control class for the same control.

Asking ClassWizard to perform data exchange with a control class member will create an instance of the MFC class that wraps the control you've selected in your dialog's C++ class. ClassWizard will produce a special call to the DDX_Control() function in the DoDataExchange() implementation for your class, which will ensure that the data value maintained in the wrapping C++ class is current. While handling most other messages or notification functions in your class, you're free to use the MFC class to manipulate the control in any way you like.

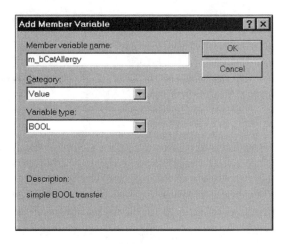

I say *most* other functions because you can't fool with the control object before it has been initialized – the object won't be valid until after the DoDataExchange() function has been called for the very first time. You can only safely assume this is done if the default implementation of CDialog::OnInitDialog() has been called.

If you make an inappropriate change in the Member Variables tab, you'll have to actually delete the member you don't want with the Delete Variable button before adding the variable you want the right way around.

ClassWizard - Hazard Warning

When modifying your code, you should try and stay out of ClassWizard's way or you'll run the risk of ClassWizard becoming confused by (and perhaps even inoperable with) your project. I've mentioned it in a few places before, but it really is best to stay away from the curly bracket comments that ClassWizard adds to your code to mark its territory.

Outside of this restriction, you shouldn't hesitate to modify the way `DoDataExchange()` works. If you need to alter the way that your fields are managed, you should feel free to change the implementation of `DoDataExchange()`.

One of the most common reasons to do this is when you want to perform a **cross-edit** – assuring that the value of one control is correct when compared to the state or value of others.

Performing Cross-Edits

The functionality provided by the `DDV_` routines is restricted to single values in individual controls. If you need to check that one field is correct in relation to the value of another, you'll need to write this code yourself. For example, you might wish to restrict the value of Salary to a maximum of $30,000 if the Programmer button is marked in the Job Title box of an employee information dialog, while you might wish to allow salaries of up to $150,000 if the Department Head button is checked.

The most efficient way to perform cross-edits is to work with the values once they have been placed in the member variables of the dialog class. Just check the values that you've already retrieved and call `DDV_` against the variable affected in the cross-edit.

So, to enforce this hypothetical cross-edit, we might do something like this:

```
DDX_Text(pDX, IDC_SALARY, m_uSalary);
// Maybe more DDX_ and DDV_ calls here...
//}} AFX_DATA_MAP

// After the close bracket, we're out of ClassWizard's way.
// To set up the context for error handling, we need to call
// PrepareEditCtrl() on the faulting control:

pDX->PrepareEditCtrl(IDC_SALARY);
if (m_title == ID_PROGRAMMER)
    DDV_MinMaxLong(pDX, m_uSalary, 18500, 30000);
else
{
    // Must be an ID_DEPARTMENT_HEAD
    DDV_MinMaxLong(pDX, m_uSalary, 75000, 150000);
}
```

While this approach works just fine for most edits, you might be disappointed to find that the error message produced is a little too generic. `DDV_MinMaxLong()` will construct a message that indicates the entered value must be between the specific upper and lower bounds.

While, strictly speaking, the generated message makes sense, it doesn't really give the user enough information. Your user might not be able to understand why salaries are suddenly restricted to between $18,500 and $30,000. It would be a great help to have more information, or more specifically, to know that the salary must be in that range for programmers.

Custom Messaging

To code your own error message, you'll need to implement your own version of `DDV_MinMaxLong()`. This isn't as hard as it sounds, since you only really need a check on the value for the range and complain if there's a problem. The special work required involves your custom error message. Instead of coding the `DDV_MinMaxLong()` calls as we did before, you can use calls to your own function, like this:

```
pDX->PrepareEditCtrl(IDC_SALARY);
if (m_title == ID_PROGRAMMER)
{
    DDV_Salary(pDX, m_uSalary, 18500, 30000, "Programmer");
}
else
{
    // Must be an ID_DEPARTMENT_HEAD
    DDV_Salary(pDX, m_uSalary, 75000, 150000, "Department Head");
}
```

As you can see, this is almost the same code. The actual `DDV_Salary()` routine would look like this:

```
void AFXAPI DDV_Salary(CDataExchange* pDX, LONG value,
                                   LONG min, LONG max, LPCSTR psErr)
{
    if (!pDX->m_SaveAndValidate)
    {
        if (value < min || value > max)
        {
            CString strTemp;
            strTemp.Format(_T("Salaries for %s employees "
                "must be between %ld and %ld"), pstrEmpType, min, max);

            AfxMessageBox(strTemp, MB_ICONEXCLAMATION);
            pDX->Fail();
        }
    }
}
```

The code simply prepares a message and calls `AfxMessageBox()` to have it displayed. After the user clears the dialog box, we code a call to `pDX->Fail()`. This function, a member of the `CDataExchange` object described in the previous section, is responsible for throwing the exception that indicates the failure of the data exchange function. This cleans up the data exchange object and sets the focus to the control that's blamed for the exception.

Refining DDV_Salary()

There are a couple of pretty obvious ways to improve the function we wrote above. First, you should probably use string resources to handle your strings. We didn't do it here in an attempt to make things look a little simpler, again.

Another thing would be to take advantage of the help context parameter that `AfxMessageBox()` accepts. The optional third parameter, which wasn't specified, could be a constant that identifies a help context. This context could be hooked up to identify a topic in the application's help file, which could help the user understand what the message box really means.

Further Reading

When you're thinking about adding your own cross-edits and, in particular, your own `DDV_` functions, don't hesitate to look through the MFC source code for details and examples of the right way to do it. You can find all of the `DDX_` and `DDV_` functions in the `Dlgdata.cpp` file in your `Microsoft Visual Studio\vc98\mfc\src` directory.

You can find more dialog data exchange code and dialog data validation code in the `Dialogs` example. The `Commons.cpp` file performs many cross-edits in the `CPreFontDlg::DoDataExchange()` function. The `CPreColorDlg::DoDataExchange()` function also makes use of its own dialog data exchange and validation functions.

To push around hexadecimal color reference numbers, we wrote a `DDX_HexText()` exchange function, which can do data exchange for hexadecimal integers. The file also includes a `DDV_MinMaxGreater()` function which does a special cross-edit for forms with multiple fields, showing minimum and maximum entries. The function ensures that the minimum number is less than or equal to the maximum.

About Live Edits

At this time, MFC doesn't support live edits, i.e. the ability to react to each individual keystroke that the user makes in an edit control. Neither does it support the notion of a 'picture edit' or 'masked edit' control which might work from a formatting picture (such as using '###-##-####' for a Social Security number, or '##/##/####' for a date).

> *As the use of picture formats is a technique used by programmers who frequent lesser languages than C++, such as COBOL or Basic, you should try to refrain from talking about how useful they are in public.*

While these features may be added to MFC sometime in the future, you could have a go at implementing them yourself – although it can be tricky to do so. You'll need to subclass the control window which is supporting the edit control and find a way to react appropriately in response to every message the control receives. This can be a substantial number of messages, leading to quite a few combination problems.

It's relatively simple to reject a given set of characters, say, tossing out everything apart from numbers. However, implementing 'real' picture edit controls is very difficult, even for situations where the control only needs to accept one type of data from the user.

Using Common Dialogs

Windows provides support for using standard dialogs that are referred to as **common dialogs**. These are supplied by the operating system itself and help your application query the user for information that almost every application requires. For example, most applications in Windows need to obtain a font selection from the user, so Windows offers a common font selection dialog box that enumerates the fonts available on the system.

This approach to accepting file names or font descriptions can save the developer a great deal of time. Writing a font dialog is a pretty serious investment, even though it seems pretty simple at first. Even a typical File Save dialog has to cope with lots of tricky situations, such as allowing the user the ability to browse network drives, change directories or even to ask for help.

MFC wraps the common dialogs supported by Windows, so let's have a peek at each style of dialog and examine a typical application of each one.

File Save and Save As

Any application that deals with files will probably make use of the `CFileDialog` class. This is used by MFC in the internal implementation of the `CWinApp::OnFileOpen()`, `CDocument::OnFileSave()` and `CDocument::OnFileSaveAs()` functions. However, you're welcome to create instances of `CFileDialog` for your own needs; when you're offering to import a file, for example.

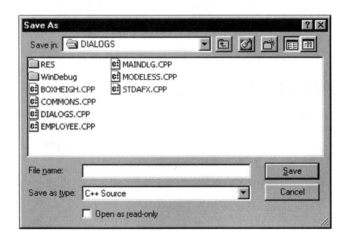

The constructor has the following declaration:

```
CFileDialog::CFileDialog(BOOL    bOpenFileDialog,
                         LPCTSTR lpszDefExt = NULL,
                         LPCTSTR lpszFileName = NULL,
                         DWORD   dwFlags = OFN_HIDEREADONLY | OFN_OVERWRITEPROMPT,
                         LPCTSTR lpszFilter = NULL,
                         CWnd*   pParentWnd = NULL);
```

Let's go through the parameter list, one at a time.

BOOL bOpenFileDialog

You can create a Save As dialog by building a `CFileDialog` instance and passing the constructor FALSE as the first parameter. Passing TRUE creates a File Open dialog (which we'll mention in the next section). The constructor for the class takes most of the parameters you'll need for a typical File Save dialog.

LPCTSTR lpszDefExt

The second parameter is a pointer to the default filename extension for the file to be opened. If the user doesn't specify a file extension, this parameter is automatically appended to the file name that is returned. Like all other parameters to the constructor, this parameter is optional. By default, it is NULL, indicating that no extension should be appended.

LPCTSTR lpszFileName

The third parameter is an initial file name used to edit the file name box. This parameter is useful if you are implementing a Save As dialog, where you'll probably want to offer the user a file name by default. This parameter's default value is NULL, indicating that the default file name will be NULL.

DWORD dwFlags

The fourth parameter is a flag which will be placed in the OPENFILENAME structure of the class. This structure has a field named Flags, which subtly alters the way the box works. The default set of flags is illustrated in the following table:

Flag	Meaning
OFN_ALLOWMULTISELECT	This allows the user to make multiple selections in the File name list box. If you specify this and your user makes multiple selections in the box, the returned file name will contain all of the files selected in one string. If you're using Windows NT 3.51, each file name will be separated by a space, and may be quoted if it contains a space. If you're using Windows 95/98, Windows NT 4.0 or newer, you'll find that each file name is separated by a null, and the list of files ends in a null. You're best off using the GetNextPathName() member of the dialog class to enumerate the selected files.
OFN_CREATEPROMPT	If present, this flag forces the dialog box code to prompt the user before it creates the file, if the dialog finds that the file identified by the user doesn't already exist. (This flag implies the OFN_PATHMUSTEXIST and OFN_FILEMUSTEXIST flags.)
OFN_ENABLEHOOK	This allows you to specify a function which receives all messages processed by the dialog before the Windows code for the dialog receives them. Use the lpfnHook member to specify a pointer to your message-handling function – which must be callable without a this pointer.
OFN_ENABLETEMPLATE	Use this flag if you want to customize your dialog using your own dialog box template. You should supply a pointer to the template's name (or its resource ID) in the lpTemplateName field, and the handle of the module where the file is stored in the hInstance field.

Table Continued on Following Page

Flag	Meaning
OFN_ENABLETEMPLATEHANDLE	This indicates that hInstance identifies a data block which contains a preloaded dialog box template. The handle references global memory with template data in it.
OFN_FILEMUSTEXIST	This specifies that the user can only type names of existing files in the File Name entry field. If this flag is specified and the user enters an invalid name, the dialog box procedure displays a warning in a message box. If this flag is specified, the OFN_PATHMUSTEXIST flag is also used.
OFN_HIDEREADONLY	This hides the Read Only check box. Use it if you don't want to let the user create a read-only file.
OFN_NOCHANGEDIR	This forces the dialog box to maintain the current directory across calls to the dialog. If the user navigates to a new directory or changes the current drive and this flag is not set, the current directory and drive for your process will change. Specifying this flag guarantees that the current directory won't change for your application while the dialog is displayed. The user will still be allowed to change directories to suit their needs.
OFN_NONETWORKBUTTON	This hides and disables the Network button present in the dialog if you've not specified the button OFN_EXPLORER style. It denies the user access to a subdialog that will let them create connections to network drives. If you've specified OFN_EXPLORER, you'll find that the user's ability to browse the network isn't affected – they can still get to their Network Neighborhood group by navigating first to the My Computer group.
OFN_NOREADONLYRETURN	This specifies that the returned file doesn't have the Read Only check box checked, and is not in a write-protected directory. Use this flag for File Save dialogs where you'll need to be absolutely sure that the returned file is writeable.
OFN_NOTESTFILECREATE	This flag dictates that the file is not created before the dialog box is closed. The flag should be specified if the application could potentially save the file on a network share that allows file creation, but not file modification. When an application specifies this flag, the library doesn't check for write protection, a full disk, an open drive door or network protection. Applications using this flag must perform file operations carefully because a file can't be reopened once it has been closed.

Flag	Meaning
OFN_OVERWRITEPROMPT	This causes the Save As... dialog box to generate a message box if the selected file already exists. The user must confirm whether to overwrite the file. Use this flag when you want to protect your users from accidentally overwriting other files when saving their work.
OFN_PATHMUSTEXIST	This specifies that the user can only type valid paths and filenames. If this flag is used and the user types an invalid path or filename in the File Name entry field, the dialog box function displays a warning in a message box and the dialog won't return control to the caller. This relieves your application from validating the path name. In File Save dialogs, you'll usually want to set this flag to restrict your user to directories which already exist, when choosing a spot for their new file.
OFN_READONLY	This causes the Read Only check box to be checked initially when the dialog box is created. After the dialog is displayed, this flag indicates the state of the Read Only check box.
OFN_SHAREAWARE	This allows the user to connect to a server dynamically and select a file without worrying about using Explorer. If you allow the user to connect to network files in this way, the box will make proper use of the sharing access flags when it is opening the file for your application.
OFN_SHOWHELP	Shows a Help button in the box.

> There are many other useful flags. While the example application demonstrates most of them, you should have a look at the Windows SDK documentation to see the full set of choices. You should also be aware that you can pass any combination of flags you'd like for this parameter, using a bit-wise OR operator to hook them together.

The OPENFILENAME structure is kept as a public member of the CFileDialog class. You can access it with the name m_ofn. Most of its members are managed by class functions, but you can directly manipulate its members if you reference the SDK documentation for the class. Another important member of the OPENFILENAME structure allows you to change the title used for the dialog; the lpstrTitle member allows you to specify a pointer to your own string.

LPCTSTR lpszFilter

You can use the fifth parameter to specify a filter for your file. The filters are predefined groups of files that your users might look for. If your application helps the user test cigars and stores files with an extension of .bct, for example, you might wish to show the user Bogart Cigar Tester files (*.BCT) in the ...type drop-down list in the files dialog. This allows the user to conveniently make a choice in the drop-down to get the files which most frequently pique their interest.

The string that you pass as the fifth parameter is actually composed of pairs of strings: file filter descriptions and wildcards for the filters. You should separate each entry in the filter with the pipe character (|). Customarily, you should offer the user the ability to choose from a list of all files with a *.* mask.

So, a typical string for the fifth parameter might look like this:

```
_T("Bogart Cigar Tester Files (*.bct)|*.bct|All Files|*.*||")
```

Note that the string ends in two consecutive vertical bars, and that you could provide as many filters as you'd like; you're not limited to two. The user is welcome to override the mask you've provided, something that they can do at any time.

Your file dialog will provide filters as a convenience to the user. They're not a requirement for the use of the file common dialogs, but they *do* help the user understand what file types and file extensions your application would like to work with.

CWnd* pParentWnd

The final parameter to the function is a pointer to the CWnd object that will act as a parent for the dialog.

The Dialogs example provides code in the Commons.cpp file to test-drive different common dialog boxes. The CPreFileDlg allows you to supply strings for the various fields of the dialog and tweak its many options. It is a great test-bed for the file dialog; you can alter various features and take each version for a test-drive.

File Open

If you use the same CFileDialog class as the **File Save** and **Save As** dialogs, you can create dialogs that allow the user to open files. You'll simply pass TRUE instead of FALSE as the first parameter to the structure. Syntactically, everything else is the same.

However, using a CFileDialog as for opening files does imply some semantic differences which are usually expressed by the use of different flags. You would never, for example, offer OFN_OVERWRITEPROMPT for a **File Open** dialog; opening an existing file never overwrites anything. On the other hand, you'll probably be certain to specify OFN_PATHMUSTEXIST to make sure the user gives you a valid file name. You may also want to specify the OFN_NOREADONLYRETURN to make sure the returned file is not write-protected.

Aside from these subtle differences, the use of the CFileDialog class is just the same when you're saving files as it is when you're opening files for read operations. The example application offers a pair of radio buttons so that you can specify the mode in which your test dialog will operate.

Print

The `CPrintDialog` offers you a user interface to the standard Windows Print and Print Setup dialog boxes. The Print Setup dialog is used to allow the user access to the printer and printing options before their print job begins. They can use this dialog (shown below) to choose the printer they're targeting with their job. The dialog may offer additional printer-specific options and printer-provided setup dialogs, depending on the exact printer the user selects. The dialog almost always offers printer-specific features through the Properties push button. While the printing dialog is common, the specific features of each printer supported by Windows are presented by a dialog box owned by the printer driver. You don't need to worry about the implementation of these dialogs, nor about bringing up the Properties dialog when you're using the common printing dialog. Information collected by the common dialog and any printer-specific dialog is available via the `GetDevMode()` member of the dialog class.

Here's a glimpse of the common Print Setup dialog:

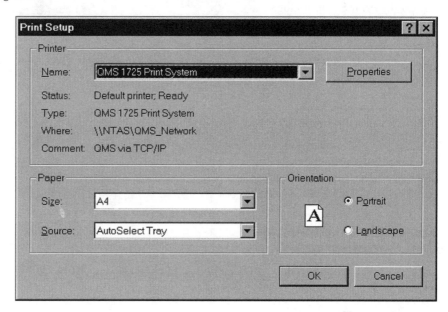

The user can access more advanced features of their printer's setup by using the Properties button. This shows a device-driver dependent dialog, where the user can adjust features specific to the selected printer.

The Print Setup dialog may be used before the user even plans to print their document; it might be used to define a default output printer for the application as a default, or as the default for the open document.

On the other hand, the Print dialog is used immediately before the user starts printing. It allows the user to specify the range of the document to be printed, as well as last-minute options, such as a copy count. Note that the dialog also offers the **Properties** push button which can take the user back to the same dialog they could get to from the **Print Setup** dialog. An example **Print** dialog is shown below:

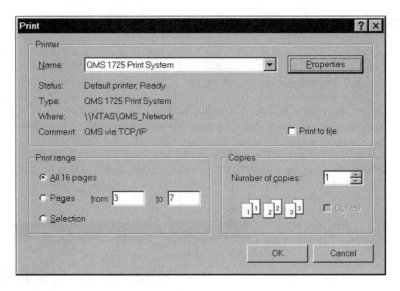

The `CPrintDialog` class in the Microsoft Foundation Classes library provides an interface to both of these dialogs. You can create a `CPrintDialog` object using the dialog's constructor, shown here:

```
CPrintDialog::CPrintDialog(BOOL  bPrintSetupOnly,
                    DWORD dwFlags = PD_ALLPAGES
                                  | PD_USEDEVMODECOPIES
                                  | PD_NOPAGENUMS
                                  | PD_HIDEPRINTTOFILE
                                  | PD_NOSELECTION,
                    CWnd* pParentWnd = NULL);
```

BOOL bPrintSetupOnly

The first parameter specifies whether the class will generate a setup dialog (if the parameter is TRUE) or a printing dialog (if the parameter is FALSE).

DWORD dwFlags

The `dwFlags` parameter provides access to the `m_pd.Flags` member, which directly affects the way the print dialog is displayed to the user. The default parameter, which performs a bit-wise OR on several different flags, gives the dialog a reasonable appearance for most simple applications. The `Flags` you specify here are ORed against the flags that MFC needs to set internally; you can directly manipulate `m_pd.Flags` if you need to realize any special functionality.

`PD_ALLPAGES` forces the dialog initially to select the **All** range for printing. The `PD_NOPAGENUMS` flag causes the dialog to hide the edit controls which allow the user to specify distinct page numbers. This combination of options effectively forces the user to print the entire document. If you're ready to allow page-by-page printing on demand, you should remove the `PD_NOPAGENUMS` flags from the value passed for the `dwFlags` parameter.

You can have the dialog initially select the page range radio button by specifying PD_PAGENUMS flag instead of PD_ALLPAGES, or you can have the dialog initially activate the selection radio buttons by specifying the PD_SELECTION flag. You should consider the PD_SELECTION, PD_PAGENUMS and PD_ALLPAGES flags to be mutually exclusive.

The PD_USEDEVMODECOPIES causes the Print dialog to disable the multiple copies features of the control if the device driver for the selected printer inherently supports multiple copies. You should specify this flag if you are not prepared to write code that handles printing multiple copies on printers which don't inherently give that support.

By specifying the PD_HIDEPRINTTOFILE flag, the constructor requests that Windows not show the Print to File check box. If it was visible, this check box would allow the user to have the printer driver redirect its output to a file for later printing, rather than sending it directly to the printer.

CWnd* pParentWnd

The last parameter, pParentWnd, offers a parent for the printing dialog.

Once you've called DoModal() and the user has successfully cleared CPrintDialog, the dialog is ready to provide information about the selections the user has made. The most important bit of information to come back is the device context that will let you talk to the printer the user has selected. You can retrieve a pointer to that DC by calling GetPrinterDC().

This function returns the device context for the printer that the user specified. You can use this device context in subsequent printing operations and be assured that the operations will hit the printer the user selected exactly. You might want to hang on to the device context to use it later, when you are browsing fonts, and so on.

However, when you're done with that device context you must call the DeleteDC() function on it. And you must do so even if you've not actually used the DC! The DC is created for you by the dialog, as long as the user presses OK in the box and you've kept the PD_RETURNDC flag in the Flags member of m_pd.

In the next section, I'll mention how to pass the printer's device context to the font selection dialog box, so that the dialog enumerates fonts on the printer for the user.

> It's also useful to call **CPrintDialog::GetDefaults()** to retrieve information about the default printer, without displaying the dialog box first. This function takes no parameters and simply returns a **BOOL** indicating its success. It populates the **m_pd** member of **CPrintDialog** with information about the defaults for the printer.

Whether you've used the dialog for printer setup or for printing, you can retrieve individual bits of information from the dialog by calling the various members of the class. For example, you can call GetFromPage() and GetToPage() to retrieve the page range of the print run as requested by the user through the print dialog.

293

When you use the dialog for setup, you can call `GetDevMode()` to return the `DEVMODE` structure for the printer device. Alternatively, call `GetPortName()` to learn about the port name which should serve as the target for your printing operations.

If you requested printing support from AppWizard when you created your application, the `CWinApp` override in your application makes calls to the `CWinApp::DoPrintDialog()` function. This will present the user with the printing dialog, as appropriate, and you won't need to worry about doing the work yourself.

Further Print Reference

A call to the printing dialog is coded in the demo through the `CPrePrintDlg` class in `Commons.cpp`. Like the other boxes in the `Dialogs` example, `CPrePrintDlg` offers you the ability to mess with the most important members of the `CPrintDialog` class. You can use the example to see several reasonable ways to call the dialog, as well as testing the dialog to learn how it can be called within your own application.

You can see an example of the setup dialog if you use the `CPreSetupDlg` instance in the `Commons.cpp` file. This dialog differs a little from the others in the `Dialogs` example, as it is intended to retrieve information and not offer much in the way of user prompts. The values that the print setup version of `CPrintDialog` manifests are all returned through an SDK `DEVMODE` structure This is returned from the `CPrintDialog` by calling `CPrintDialog::GetDevMode()`.

This `DEVMODE` structure is allocated by the SDK implementation of the dialog, so you'll have to call `GlobalFree()` against a pointer to the structure to avoid a memory leak when you are finished.

Font Browser

If your application allows users to change the font used in any of its output, you can save time by using the font chooser common dialog. This is shown here, where you'll see the familiar Windows user interface:

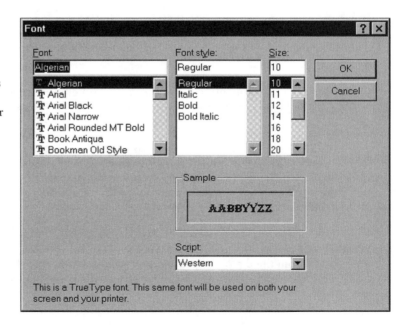

The dialog has provisions to let the user select any font installed on the system. Once they have chosen the font, the user can then select from sizes, styles and any general effects available for that font. To facilitate the choice, the user can take a peek at an example line of text.

CFontDialog and CHOOSEFONT

Like the other common dialogs, MFC support for this class comes in the form of a class which wraps the Windows API associated with the dialog. The class that supports the font browser is CFontDialog. You can instantiate the class and call the DoModal() member of the resulting object. Like most other modal dialogs, this function will return IDOK if the user has made a selection and pressed the OK button. Otherwise, if the user has aborted the font selection process by pressing the Cancel button, it will return IDCANCEL.

Many specifics of the appearance of the dialog are controlled by a member of the CFontDialog called m_cf. This member is a structure of the SDK type CHOOSEFONT. Let's visit some of the more important members of the structure, but bear in mind that CFontDialog, like the other MFC classes which wrap common dialogs, uses a combination of direct access to the CHOOSEFONT structure in the class and its own member functions to get its work done.

Like the controlling structure for most of the other common dialog wrapping classes, the structure is partially initialized by the constructor for the class. One of the more important fields in this controlling structure is m_cf.Flags. This integer can accept several different flag values, all of which are documented in the online Windows SDK reference that ships with Visual C++:

Flag	Meaning
CF_ANSIONLY	This specifies that CFontDialog should allow only the selection of fonts using the Windows character set. (If this flag is specified, the user won't be able to select a font that contains only symbols.)
CF_APPLY	This specifies that CFontDialog should enable the Apply button.
CF_BOTH	This causes the dialog box to list the available printer and screen fonts. The hDC member identifies the device context(or information context) associated with the printer.
CF_EFFECTS	This specifies that CFontDialog should enable strikeout, underline and color effects. If this flag is specified, the lfStrikeOut, lfUnderline and rgbColors members of the LOGFONT pointed to by lpLogFont can be set before calling and can be used after the user closes the dialog box.
CF_ENABLEHOOK	This enables the hook function specified in the lpfnHook member of this structure.
CF_ENABLETEMPLATE	This indicates that the hInstance member identifies a data block that contains a dialog box template identified by the lpTemplateName member.

Table Continued on Following Page

Flag	Meaning
CF_ENABLETEMPLATEHANDLE	This indicates that the hInstance member identifies a data block that contains a preloaded dialog box template. The system ignores the lpTemplateName member if this flag is specified.
CF_FIXEDPITCHONLY	This specifies that CFontDialog should select only fixed-pitch fonts.
CF_FORCEFONTEXIST	This specifies that CFontDialog should indicate an error condition if the user attempts to select a font or style that doesn't exist.
CF_INITTOLOGFONTSTRUCT	This specifies that CFontDialog should use the LOGFONT structure, indicated by the lpLogFont member, to initialize the dialog box controls.
CF_LIMITSIZE	This specifies that CFontDialog should select only font sizes within the range specified by the nSizeMin and nSizeMax members.
CF_NOFACESEL	This specifies that CFontDialog shouldn't make an initial face name selection because there is no one single face name that applies to the text selection. Set this flag if the text selection contains multiple face names.
CF_NOOEMFONTS	See the CF_NOVECTORFONTS description below.
CF_NOSIMULATIONS	This specifies that CFontDialog shouldn't allow graphics device interface (GDI) font simulations.
CF_NOSIZESEL	This specifies that CFontDialog shouldn't make an initial size selection because there is no one single size that applies to the text selection. Set this flag if the text selection contains multiple sizes.
CF_NOSTYLESEL	This specifies that CFontDialog shouldn't make an initial style selection because there is no one single style that applies to the text selection. Set this flag if the text selection contains multiple styles.
CF_NOVECTORFONTS	This specifies that CFontDialog shouldn't allow vector font selections.
CF_PRINTERFONTS	This causes the dialog box to list only the fonts supported by the printer associated with the device context (or information context) identified by the hDC member.
CF_SCALABLEONLY	This specifies that CFontDialog should allow only the selection of scaleable fonts. Scaleable fonts include vector fonts, scaleable printer fonts, TrueType fonts and fonts scaled by other technologies.

Flag	Meaning
CF_SCREENFONTS	This causes the dialog box to list only the screen fonts supported by the system.
CF_SHOWHELP	This causes the dialog box to show the **Help** button. The hwndOwner member must not be NULL if this option is specified.
CF_TTONLY	This specifies that CFontDialog should only enumerate and allow the selection of TrueType fonts.
CF_USESTYLE	This specifies that lpszStyle member points to a buffer that contains style data that CFontDialog should use to initialize the **Font Style** selection. When the user closes the dialog box, the style data for the user's selection is copied to this buffer.
CF_WYSIWYG	This specifies that CFontDialog should allow only the selection of fonts available on both the printer and the display. If this flag is specified, the CF_BOTH and CF_SCALABLEONLY flags should also be specified.

Some of the more important flags allow you to restrict the specific kinds of fonts that will appear in the font box. For example:

Font Flag	Restriction
CF_FIXEDPITCHONLY	Possibly in conjunction with CF_TTONLY – restricts the choice to fixed-width fonts.
CF_NOSIMULATIONS	Limits user to real fonts – restricts dynamically-generated GDI fonts from being present in the list.
CF_TTONLY	You are restricted to only TrueType fonts.
CF_WYSIWYG	Prints using the font selected. This will guarantee that the font the user selects will be available both on the printer and on the screen. Assures match between the displayed rendering of application's data and the printed rendering.

Since fonts are often very important when you are working with the printer, you may wish to implement an invocation of CFontDialog that enumerates only printer fonts, instead of screen fonts. To realize this functionality, you'll have to set the CF_PRINTERFONTS bit in m_cf.Flags. You will also need a handle to a device context for the printer which has the fonts that you wish to enumerate.

If an unrestricted range of font sizes is inappropriate for your application, you can use the nSizeMin and nSizeMax members of m_cf to limit choices in the dialog to a range you specify. If either of these members is set to zero, the limit is ineffective. You must set both limits to achieve a bounded set of font sizes, but you can just set the lower limit to restrict your user from using fonts that are too small. Set nSizeMin to the appropriate limit and nSizeMax to 0 achieve this. Note that you can't perform a similar job on the upper limit.

Once your call to `CFontDialog::DoModal()` has returned, you can call `CFontDialog::GetCurrentFont()` to copy a `LOGFONT` structure which describes the font the user has selected. You'll need to use your own `LOGFONT` structure to hold the information retrieved before using `CFont`'s `CreateFontIndirect()` function to create a font object and get some work done.

Code to create a font object after the user's work with the dialog might go along these lines:

```
CFontDialog dlg;
if (dlg.DoModal() == IDOK)
{
    LOGFONT lf;
    CFont chosenFont;
    dlg.GetCurrentFont(&lf);

    chosenFont.CreateFontIndirect(lf);
    // chosenFont can now be used in your painting code
    // to update the display
}
else
{
    // User canceled; nothing to do!
}
```

Back to Base!

The only chasm left to jump is the management of your `CFont` object. Since it's a C++ object that wraps a Windows resource, you'll need to find a way to make sure the font is destroyed when your application is finished with it. You'll also need to find a way to communicate the font information back to your application's painting code in its `CView` implementation.

Depending on the exact implementation of your application, you might try to solve this problem in one of two ways. Maybe you'll hand the initialized `CFont` object back to the `CView` object for which the dialog is changing the font. The `CView` would then be responsible for deleting it, as well as the previous font.

Allowing the `CView` in your application to manage fonts is probably more applicable to situations where your application has more than one font in a given view, or when it manages more than one view. For instances where you only have one view or only manage one font, you might wish to store the font information in the instance data of the document to which it relates.

Of course, these are just suggestions. You might find it convenient to keep everything in your `CDocument` class; you'll just need to find a way to separate one font from another. Whatever approach you take, you'll probably adopt one that strongly favors performance – keeping initialized `CFont` objects in your view or document and then using and changing them as necessary is probably the most reasonable method. Recreating fonts each time you need to paint can result in sluggish painting and bad user response.

There are other members of the CFontDialog class that can retrieve information about the selected font. You might wish to call GetFaceName(), GetStyleName() or GetSize() to retrieve specific information about the selected font. IsItalic(), IsBold() and IsUnderline() can give you information about the escapements and styles associated with the font. The only member function that exposes information which is not available through the LOGFONT structure concerns any color that the user may have selected. You can obtain this information through the CFontDialog::GetColor() member function.

You can simplify your use of the CFontDialog class by using the class constructor to initialize the exact features of the dialog you would like to utilize. The CFontDialog constructor prototype is as follows:

```
CFontDialog::CFontDialog(LPLOGFONT lplfInitial = NULL,
                         DWORD     dwFlags = CF_EFFECTS | CF_SCREENFONTS,
                         CDC*      pdcPrinter = NULL,
                         CWnd*     pParentWnd = NULL );
```

LPLOGFONT lplfInitial

The first parameter provides a pointer to a LOGFONT structure that will be used to initialize the selection in the dialog box. The description is passed from this structure, but not returned to it. You must still use the CFontDialog::GetCurrentFont() function to retrieve the selected font when the dialog is done.

DWORD dwFlags

The second parameter provides you access to the m_cf.Flags member. By default, MFC will have the dialog choose from screen fonts and offer controls to change the font effects. This allows the user to strikeout or underline the chosen font.

CDC* pdcPrinter

The third parameter, a pointer to an MFC device context class, allows you to specify which printer context is to be used for finding fonts. This applies if you're using the CF_PRINTERFONTS or CF_BOTH flags to offer the user printer fonts.

CWnd* pParentWnd

The final parameter simply specifies the parent window to be used by the font dialog.

The example application, Dialogs, implements a driver for the font chooser common dialog. The driver dialog features interesting cross-edit and custom data validation code in its DoDataExchange() function. The dialog provides a useful way for you to experiment with the font common dialog to see how it works. It's a good idea to play with the printer and font setting flags to make sure they bring back the requisite set of fonts.

Color Chooser

Most applications that support graphics (like the Paintobj example in Chapter 4), and even some that support text, have a use for color. Users enjoy the ability to render things to their own taste by changing the color or pattern of the display. While you could always allow the user the ability to select a color from a small, predefined list, most people have displays capable of showing a staggering number of colors.

MFC provide access to the color common dialog with the `CColorDialog` box. You can create an instance of this class to display the color dialog. Doing so is quite simple, as this code demonstrates:

```
pDocument = static_cast<CMyDocClass*>(GetDocument());
CColorDialog dlg;
dlg.SetCurrentColor(pDocument->GetColor());

if (dlg.DoModal() == IDOK)
{
    COLORREF color = dlg.GetColor();
    // The user accepted the new color,
    // so update the document with it
    pDocument->SetColor(color);
    pDocument->UpdateAllViews(NULL);
}
```

The selected color value can be retrieved using the `GetColor()` member of `CColorDialog`. This function returns a `COLORREF`, which describes the color the user ended up selecting.

You may modify the appearance of the dialog, using the `m_cc` member of the `CColorDialog` instance you've created. This member contains an initialized `CHOOSECOLOR` structure, which is defined (and perhaps better described) in the Windows SDK documentation. The structure contains several interesting fields to help the dialog do its job. These utilitarian fields are all initialized by MFC when you create the `CColorDialog` object. Some of the fields, such as `rgbResult`, are made available by MFC through member functions of `CColorDialog`.

Once you've retrieved a `COLORREF` from the color chooser dialog, you can use the value in many calls in the MFC `CDC` class. For example, you can call `CDC::SetBkColor()` or `CDC::SetTextColor()` to change the colors used when drawing text. You can use `COLORREF` values in calls that create `CPen` and `CBrush` objects too.

The most interesting member of `COLORREF` is `m_cc.Flags`, which can be set to a combination of several values to provide your dialog the look and feel that you like. You might bit-wise OR together a combination of `CC_FULLOPEN`, `CC_PREVENTFULLOPEN` and `CC_SHOWHELP` to tailor the look of your box.

`CC_FULLOPEN` causes the dialog to appear in its fully opened state, i.e. it shows the custom color part of the box. If you don't specify the `CC_FULLOPEN` flag, the dialog will open and allow the user to press the **Define Custom Colors** button to show the extended part of the box. You can disable the **Define Custom Colors** button by passing the `CC_PREVENTFULLOPEN` flag.

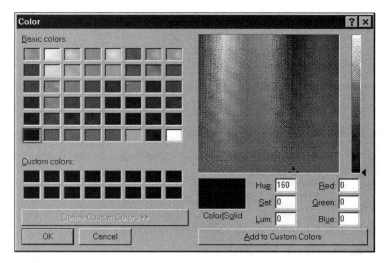

Note that the framework implicitly provides support for some of the flags that the SDK manages. For example, CC_RGBINIT is turned on by calling the SetCurrentColor() member of the C++ class.

For this reason, you should always bit-wise OR any additional flags you specify with the current value of the Flags member, which implies that you should code something like this to add the CC_SHOWHELP flag:

```
dlg.m_cc.Flags |= CC_SHOWHELP;
```

If you just blindly assign the values, you'll end up overwriting other flags that MFC may have set on your behalf; you may end up destroying effects that you've otherwise requested.

The code fragment given above uses the CColorDialog::SetCurrentColor() function to let the dialog know what the currently selected color is. This allows the dialog to initialize its user interface, indicating the appropriate settings for the current color. If you don't make this call, the dialog initially displays white as the selected color.

Custom Colors

As I mentioned before, the user can mix their own custom colors if the standard list of colors in the dialog doesn't appeal. These colors can be retrieved by calling the CColorDialog::GetSavedCustomColors() function. This function actually retrieves a pointer to an array of sixteen COLORREF values. The array is stored in the application's state data by MFC, so the settings are application-global. Note that they're *not* persisted by MFC in the registry or a .ini file unless you go out of your way to add such code to your application. If you like, you can use the lpCustColors member of the CHOOSECOLOR structure in m_cc to initialize the list yourself.

You can simplify your use of the CColorDialog class by using the MFC constructor to pass initial values to the dialog. The constructor's prototype looks like this:

```
CColorDialog::CColorDialog(COLORREF clrInit = 0,
                           DWORD    dwFlags = 0,
                           CWnd*    pParentWnd = NULL);
```

The first parameter is the color value which will be initially selected in the box; the parameter ends up being passed through the m_cc.rgbResult member. If the clrInit parameter is not zero, the CC_RGBINIT mask is set in m_cc.Flags to indicate that the dialog implementation should initialize itself with this value.

The dwFlags parameter allows you to access the m_cc.Flags member directly through the constructor. Anything you supply through this value is copied to the m_cc.Flags member by logically ORing the parameter with whatever values MFC needs to set, which are based on the options or function calls you've made. The third parameter, a pointer to a parent window, simply indicates the parent of the dialog.

The example application allows you to work with the color chooser dialog in a test environment. The supporting code, which appears as CPreColorDlg in Commons.cpp, shows you how to manipulate the fields and functions. This code should give you some ideas about how to incorporate a working color chooser into your application, as well as providing you with a test bed to experiment with.

Summary

Throughout this chapter, while explaining how dialogs and controls work, I've spent some time soapboxing about how applications should work. I've discussed things that I find intuitive and have made generalizations about things that have worked for me in the past. Please take this chapter for what it's worth; an experienced and ornery Windows programmer divulging what he knows about the way applications work.

Please don't decide not to implement something, or change your techniques, because of something I've said here. I've tried to convey ideas that will help you understand how applications really work and let you know what professionals do when their backs are against the wall. This book isn't a religious document about dialog box design, but rather a scroll that prospective MFC developers can digest before beginning the trek along their long, long road. Balance your innovation with careful thought about what users will consider intuitive and what is efficient.

6

User Interface Issues

No matter how complex the programming or how useful the tool, if your user can't conveniently use your application, all your effort in writing it has been wasted. Whether you're following the tried-and-tested line or pushing forward a radically new design strategy, if the user finds your application difficult to use, or if it clashes with the commonly accepted shortcuts, it's a failure. This chapter will illustrate some of the techniques that you can employ to get a successful front end on to your application, to give it a fighting chance in the world of competitive software. Along the way, we'll cover:

> Property sheets and wizards
> Splitter windows
> Painting Issues
> GDI usage with MFC

Developing Applications

Developing applications is easy enough in itself. Most decent Windows programmers can crank out simple applications in a few days. For example, I've just written a little C++ application that helps me manage my compact disc collection. I have a SQL Server database that manages the tables and makes the database available to the other two systems on the microscopic network in my bedroom.

While I was watching football all day Sunday, I developed all of the application's user interface and laid out most of the SQL statements to browse the six tables in my database. The database, by the way, encompasses artists, their albums and the songs on each of them. It knows which record company distributes the recording and which label does the marketing. It remembers the catalog code that the title was released with, so I can discern priceless first pressings from crummy knock-offs sent out by mass-marketing record clubs. Over a few beers while Monday Night Football was on, I cranked out the code to generate two or three different reports.

Besides impressing my friends with my original Japanese copy of Pink Floyd's *A Saucerful of Secrets*, or a quadraphonic copy of Frank Zappa's *Apostrophe*, I like to mention the database when I do presentations. I find it amusing to point out that it's a database full of records.

Even when working with the application I wrote myself, I often wish there were slightly easier ways to get common tasks done. If I could enter records a little faster, or had a more fluid way to find existing albums and edit their track lists, I could have more fun maintaining my collection. That's ironic, as I developed the application myself, for myself! Even though I knew what I wanted the program to do, I wasn't completely sure of the most fluid way to do it until I actually had started using the application.

The Problems with Application Development

The point I'm getting around to here is that the reason it takes months or even years to develop real business applications is that nobody is ever happy. The sales people want price increases to be handled in a slightly different way, and the accountants go nuts when they find out that interest was calculated at the end of the month and not the beginning. Me, I'm happy to print out my record collection on the second or the twenty-ninth of the month; I don't care how difficult it is to produce the report, or when it finally reaches my coffee table.

For large-scale applications, nailing down details about calculation methods and formatting can take months. Once all of these details have been ironed out, the real rub is getting the application past the users. They invariably complain. This results in indignation from the programming staff who have the attitude that users should feel pretty darned lucky that programmers gave the application *any* user interface in the first place.

Realistically, whether you're shipping to 15 million Windows users or to 37 account representatives on the nineteenth floor, you need to pay careful attention to the way your application is used. Different people approach computers and the tasks performed with applications in different ways. To serve these diverse approaches, Windows and its applications have developed different solutions to the user interface problem.

Unfortunately, this means that the full weight of the problem lies squarely on the shoulders of the programmer. You must jump through hoops and walk the high wire, all in the name of pleasing your users by providing them with the features that they demand, even if that means putting negative balances in red and past-due payments in blue.

The MFC Solution

To come to the aid of the developer once again, MFC provides several classes that wrap up user interface items and make them easy to apply. We covered the raw controls that MFC supports in Windows, but MFC also supports more advanced composite user interface elements. The purpose of this chapter is to investigate those different classes and the techniques for using them so you know what's in your arsenal when the time comes to implement your user interface. We'll be building on the information about the `CToolbar` and `CStatusBar` classes and the different ways to change how your Windows application handles the user interface by subclassing, which we looked at in Chapter 4.

We'll start off by taking a peek at the incredible amount of functionality provided by the MFC property sheet classes. These allow your application to concisely and conveniently give the user access to any number of dialog boxes full of settings and options.

Using Property Sheets

It's not uncommon to find that a single dialog box is not enough to accommodate the controls your application uses to represent its collection of options, settings and modes to the user. Many applications address this problem by logically grouping their controls into different dialog boxes. For example, a program that displays graphical images might have different dialogs for settings about the image compression method. It may have options that affect the actual display of the image, choices that change the user interface of the application itself, and selections that dictate how the program in question will manipulate memory as it runs.

Access to the option dialogs in this program might be represented by different menu choices, each of which leads to individual dialogs that handle the appropriate group of options, as shown here:

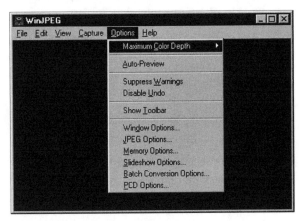

Such a design forces the user to navigate to one option dialog, change it, dismiss it, then use the menu to get to another. Since users typically manipulate many different options settings in their applications at any one time, you can see that this approach is less than efficient. Worse yet, the application isn't quite so discoverable – the user needs to hunt for the dialog that might hold the option that interests them.

However, Windows applications now often have **property pages**. Without wishing to sound too Microsoft-centric, the first time I saw these in action was in Microsoft Word for Windows. As Visual C++ users, we've been using these dialogs all along; the Options dialog, reached from the Options... command in the Tools menu, provides access to almost every global option in Visual C++:

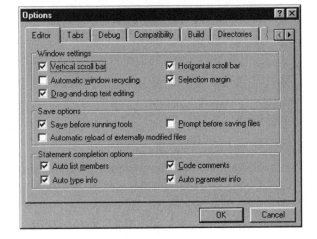

Each cluster of controls is logically grouped together to determine the settings for a particular group of features. The entire dialog above implements a **property sheet** containing property pages. A property page is one dialog full of information shown by activating a tab within a property sheet. A property sheet is the frame, the OK and Cancel buttons, and, as we'll learn later, an optional extra Apply button. The user can click on the named tabs in the window to activate them. The window redraws itself, showing the dialog associated with the tab in the client area. The tabs are also redrawn to render the three-dimensional effect of the selected tab, making it appear to be on top of the others. Some also call the dialog a **tabbed dialog** because of the tabs used to activate each page. We'll call them **property sheets** because this is the term used in Windows' own documentation. The property sheet name makes sense because a property sheet is almost invariably shown when the user selects the Properties menu item after right-clicking on a particular object in the user interface of an application.

The property sheet above sets all of the tabs side by side, all on one line. As there are so many tabs, the sheet adds small scrollbar arrows to allow the user to move left and right among the contents of the control. However, this is not the only way of dealing with multiple tabs. Stacking tabs, as shown opposite, can also be used:

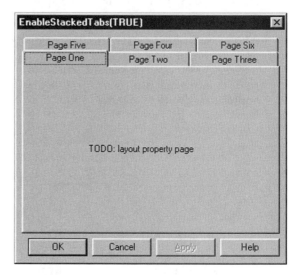

Stacking tabs are the default, but if you have too many tabs things can get messy this way, as the tabs will be stacked higher and higher, forming several rows. When things get too wide you can call `CPropertySheet::EnableStackedTabs()` passing `FALSE` to produce a property sheet with scrolling controls. Each property page is managed by the MFC `CPropertyPage` class, while the containing property sheet is handled by the `CPropertySheet` class. Let's take a look at how these classes are used and what they can do.

> *Versions of MFC older than 4.0 also had implementations of classes called* `CPropertyPage` *and* `CPropertySheet`*. These versions of the classes were different in that they implemented the tabs and painted themselves, while the* `CPropertyPage` *and* `CPropertySheet` *classes in MFC 4.0 and later are actually just wrappers for Windows common controls. This should only matter to you if you've done lots of painting in your own class based on one of these classes.*

I'll repeat this in the chapter on common controls, but it bears mentioning here – tab controls are not the same as property sheets. Windows uses a tab control to implement a property sheet, and makes the tab control available to you to do your own thing. A property sheet has a lot of built-in functionality above and beyond a bunch of tabs that you can use to perform selections.

Okay, enough background – let's chat about the features!

Creating Property Pages

Since a property page is really just a special dialog box, you can draw it using the dialog box editor in Visual C++. You will, however, need to follow some rules to make sure that MFC can handle the definition of your dialog. You should also take heed of some special considerations so that your dialog has a reasonable and consistent user interface during its special life as a property page.

MFC will use the caption of your dialog as the caption for the tab on the completed property sheet. Therefore, you should choose your caption carefully so that it reflects the meaning of the controls in the tab. Note that most applications use one word or very short two-word combinations for their tab captions, while most stand-alone dialog boxes have much more descriptive captions. Memory Usage Settings might be appropriate for a dialog box caption, but Memory is a more appropriate choice for the same controls in a property page.

Remember that your property page will be displayed inside another dialog box that provides the navigation user interface. Your dialog can't convey information via its caption bar and shouldn't implement OK or Cancel push buttons.

Setting the Properties

When the dialog is selected in the editor window, you can view the properties for it in three ways; by right-clicking on the dialog itself, by going to Properties in the View menu, or by pressing *Alt+Enter*. Your dialog should have a Thin Border and have its Style set to Child. This enables MFC to lay out and paint the dialog correctly as a child window of the property sheet. You'll need to make sure the dialog has the Title bar checkbox set so that the editor will retain the title you provide. Believe it or not, MFC will also want the dialog to be disabled by default, so you should make sure that the dialog's Disabled checkbox is checked. MFC needs this setting so that Windows won't send the dialog messages while its tab is inactive. A correctly set property page style box is shown here:

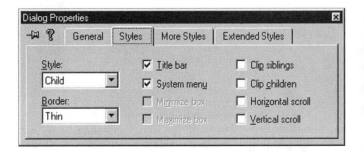

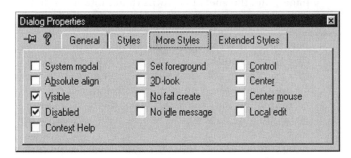

Your property pages will be shown one at a time in the same frame, so before the property sheet is created, MFC will measure all the pages you've added to the sheet and make it large enough to fit all of the pages within it. For this reason, you should try to ensure that your dialogs are pretty much the same size, otherwise some will show up surrounded by a tremendous amount of white space.

You should pay particular attention to the location of the first control in your dialog box. The user will be treated to an annoying 'jiggle' if the controls in each page of your sheet are lined up irregularly.

The features of the Microsoft Visual Studio dialog editor are really handy for creating new property sheets. If you expand the template list when you add a new dialog resource to your project, you can get a dialog box in one of three standard styles (they have names beginning IDD_PROPPAGE_) for use in a property sheet. The resource will also have appropriate settings for margins, which will help you place the controls on your sheet. Finally, the settings for the style of the dialog box (which I outlined above) will be made automatically for you when you use the template.

Once you've drawn the dialog, you can press *Ctrl+W* in the dialog editor to bring up ClassWizard; this will automatically detect that you've generated a new resource and will bring up the Adding a Class dialog. Select Create a new class, the default option, click the OK button and you'll see the following dialog:

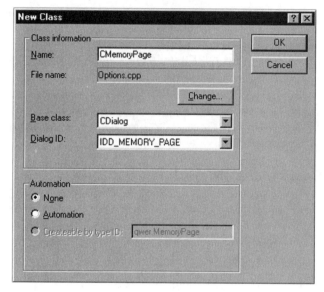

The dialog allows you to name your class and decide which files will be used to store its definition and implementation. If you like, you can put each object you create (each of your property pages and the property sheet that displays them) into individual files. I personally prefer to put all of the related pages, and the sheet that owns them, into a single file. That way, I have only one file to remember when I want to use the sheet.

For the Tabbed sample application, I've placed my CMemoryPage class into files named Options.h and Options.cpp. I will use these files for all of the pages, as well as the CPropertySheet class when we get around to creating it. If I have any property pages which have complicated code, I might put them into a file of their own to help reduce the number of files to recompile during builds and make the task of editing and tracing through the code a lot easier. Arranging the code in this way is just a technique for convenience and by no means a requirement.

After adding other property page dialogs to the project and using the ClassWizard to create MFC classes for them, I'll use the ClassWizard to create a property sheet to tie all of my property pages together.

Building a Property Sheet

The MFC CPropertySheet class contains all the code you need to manage a property sheet, but the sheet will probably need some extra code to cover your specific demands. Using the ClassWizard, you can add a CPropertySheet class to your project by selecting CPropertySheet in the Base class drop-down list box in ClassWizard's Create New Class dialog box.

In keeping with conveniently locating the option handling code in a single source file, it's a good idea to make sure that the CPropertySheet class is added to the Options.h and Options.cpp files. Since we want to access the property sheet from a menu item, we'll use the #include directive in the frame window implementation to grab Options.h, allowing us to refer to the CPropertySheet-derived class to display the property sheet. In the Mainfrm.cpp file, we'll respond to the invocation of the **Options...** menu command with code as follows:

```
void CMainFrame::OnViewOptions()
{
    COptionSheet dlgOptions(_T("Tabbed Options"), this);

    CMemoryPage pageMemory;
    CWindowPage pageWindow;
    CCompressionPage pageCompress;

    dlgOptions.AddPage(&pageCompress);
    dlgOptions.AddPage(&pageWindow);
    dlgOptions.AddPage(&pageMemory);

    dlgOptions.DoModal();
}
```

This code fragment comes from the Tabbed sample, too. The **Options...** command in the sample's **View** menu brings up a property sheet, which allows you to set some of the options related to the display in the application. Some of the sheets are, unfortunately, just for show.

We created the CPropertySheet-derived COptionSheet object first, passing its caption and a pointer to its parent window, neglecting to provide the constructor with its optional third parameter, which would be an integer identifying the page which should be activated by default when the sheet comes up. When the parameter isn't specified, the default value of zero is used, indicating that the first page should be made active.

AddPage()

Once the COptionSheet object is created, we can start calling its AddPage() member to add the sheets. The order in which we make these calls is the order (from left to right) in which the page tabs will be shown to the user. The CPropertySheet object will maintain pointers to the added pages, but you'll need to make sure that the page objects stay around until the property sheet window is destroyed. In the code snippet above, my property pages hang around as local objects on the stack. This is a clear and natural approach that is workable for any modal property sheet.

You can see that I painstakingly drew three dialog boxes and used ClassWizard to hook them up to classes named CMemoryPage, CWindowPage, and CCompressionPage. Once I've used ClassWizard to add declarations for those classes into my source file, I'm free to create instances of the individual pages. The page classes by themselves are useless — before you can even see them, they need to be tossed into a CPropertySheet, like we've done here.

If you want, it's quite acceptable to create the pages in the constructor of the CPropertySheet-derived COptionSheet class and have them as members of the property sheet. Leaving the pages as members of the sheet keeps the implementation of the sheet out of your way as you work to create the sheet for the user. The technique I use above in the OnViewOptions() code sample, which has local instances of the property pages, is equivalent in functionality to this, but it's not so smooth for ensuring good encapsulation. On the other hand, it can make the dynamic management of property pages just a bit easier.

In the above code fragment, we called DoModal() to display the property sheet dialog. We could have called Create() to make a modeless property sheet, which would force the issue of the life-spans of the local CPropertyPage objects because they'd be destroyed off the stack as the function returned. For modeless property sheets, the easiest approach to proper object lifecycle management is to allow the sheet object to manage the property pages as member data.

Whether your sheet is modal or modeless, your property page objects *must* outlive your property sheet object. If you use CPropertySheet::DoModal(), you will keep your pages alive long enough, because the DoModal() call doesn't return until the property sheet has been destroyed. On the other hand, if you're creating a modeless sheet by calling Create(), you'll want to be sure that you don't destroy your property page objects until the property sheet has been destroyed.

Page Management Functions

Once you've used CPropertySheet::AddPage() to get all of your pages into your property sheet, you can use any of several CPropertySheet members to query the sheet about the pages within.

For instance, you might call SetActivePage() to set which page is active within the sheet. There are two SetActivePage() overloads. One accepts an integer, which is a zero-based index of the page you wish to make active. The other accepts a pointer to a CPropertyPage object, which similarly indicates the page you wish to make active. The pointer must be to a CPropertyPage that has already been added to the sheet.

You can call GetActivePage() to find a pointer to the currently active page object, which you can then use in a later call to the CPropertyPage* overload of SetActivePage() to make a particular page active again. Given a pointer to a page, you can find the page's index by calling GetPageIndex(). This function accepts the pointer to the page and returns the index.

Setting the active page does *not* change the ordering of the pages on the sheet. Changing the active page deactivates the currently active page and makes another page active instead.

Data Exchange in Property Sheets

I talked about data exchange in dialog boxes in Chapter 5. The idea there was to use MFC's DoDataExchange() function to move data back and forth between controls and member variables in the dialog box. For property sheets, the practice is the same but the patients are different.

Since the property sheet is comprised of many different dialog boxes, you'll need to perform your data exchange operations with each of those dialog boxes, which means implementing DoDataExchange() functions for each of the property pages. These DoDataExchange() functions will copy values from controls in the respective property page to member variables in the property page object, and vice versa.

Normally, the code that you've written to present the dialog to the user can retrieve data from the individual property page objects that it created. Usually, this retrieval will only happen if the user accepted the changes that they made in the property sheet when they pressed the OK button. Put simply, this means that most applications will only copy data back from the property page members if the DoModal() function returns IDOK. If the user cancels the changes, you need do nothing.

The premise of a more interactive attribute application extends our code fragment like this:

```
void CMainFrame::OnViewOptions()
{
    COptionSheet dlgOptions(_T("Tabbed Options"), this);

    CMemoryPage MemoryPage;
    CWindowPage WindowPage;
    CCompressionPage CompressPage;

    dlgOptions.AddPage(&CompressPage);
    dlgOptions.AddPage(&WindowPage);
    dlgOptions.AddPage(&MemoryPage);

    CTabbedDoc* pDoc =
                    static_cast<CTabbedDoc*>((GetActiveView()->GetDocument()));

    MemoryPage.m_nMaxBuffer = pDoc->m_nMaxBuffer;
    MemoryPage.m_nMinBuffer = pDoc->m_nMinBuffer;
    CompressPage.m_nGamma = pDoc->m_nGamma;
    CompressPage.m_nMaxDelta = pDoc->m_nMaxDelta;
    CompressPage.m_nMinDelta = pDoc->m_nMinDelta;
    WindowPage.m_bShowScroll = pDoc->m_bShowScroll;
    WindowPage.m_bSnapSize = pDoc->m_bSnapSize;
    WindowPage.m_bWindowPos = pDoc->m_bWindowPos;

    if (dlgOptions.DoModal() == IDOK)
    {
        // Pull values back from pages into document
        pDoc->m_nMaxBuffer = MemoryPage.m_nMaxBuffer;
        pDoc->m_nMinBuffer = MemoryPage.m_nMinBuffer;
        pDoc->m_nGamma = CompressPage.m_nGamma;
        pDoc->m_nMinDelta = CompressPage.m_nMinDelta;
        pDoc->m_nMaxDelta = CompressPage.m_nMaxDelta;
        pDoc->m_bShowScroll = WindowPage.m_bShowScroll;
        pDoc->m_bSnapSize = WindowPage.m_bSnapSize;
        pDoc->m_bWindowPos = WindowPage.m_bWindowPos;
    }
}
```

Here, we've copied the settings back from the dialogs to members of our document. And I've done it pretty abrasively too; I just moved data from the members of the property sheet to the document directly. And such an approach implies that the members are public and directly exposed – or at least, that the main frame class is a friend of the document.

If this approach makes your encapsulation bone ache, you can approach the issue in a couple of other ways – but anything else will require some amount of interdependency between your frame class and your document class. If that's acceptable, you can make an extra member in either side of the class to exchange a structure containing all the data you wish to pass around and then hold the data in that structure as well.

With either approach, the copy operation is performed only if the user has accepted the changes. The real DDX_ operations occur in DoDataExchange() within the individual page; it follows the same direction as the DDX_ code you saw in the previous chapter, so it's not replicated here.

In some applications the user's changes will always be accepted and the code will immediately apply the changes to the appropriate aspect of the document being edited. In such cases, you may be interested in receiving the changes right away; perhaps the change is very expensive to implement and is difficult or impossible to undo. If so, you may want to have the `DoDataExchange()` code in each of your property pages perform their data exchange directly with the data in the document. So instead of letting ClassWizard insert code like this:

```
DDX_Text(pDX, IDC_MYFIELD, m_nMyField);
```

you can actually code something like this by hand:

```
DDX_Text(pDX, IDC_MYFIELD, pDoc->m_nMyField);
```

Calling `DDX_` and referencing a member variable in the document rather than the object itself tells MFC to toss the resulting data straight back into the document. Such a direct approach isn't always practical, as it will change your document's data without any editing and will leave the document's members changed even if data validation fails. As such, you'll find that it's usually easier to write a few lines of code to copy the data members of the property page back to the document individually in an `OnOK()` override of your `CPropertyPage` class. Then you also have the option of invoking functions to set the document's dirty flag, or asking the document to refresh the views associated with it.

Performing Special Validation

While `CPropertySheets` do support `DoDataExchange()`, you may wish to perform validation on the values in your property page before the user activates a different page. To do so, you can either add `DDV_` functions to the `DoDataExchange()` of the page, or write an override for the `OnKillActive()` function of the `CPropertyPage`. If your implementation of this function returns `TRUE`, MFC will assume that everything is okay. If you return `FALSE`, MFC will disallow the transfer.

MFC calls `OnKillActive()` when the user moves to a different page, or when they dismiss the entire sheet by pressing OK. The `OnKillActive()` is called before `OnOK()` when the user presses the OK button. Returning `FALSE` prevents the action from happening. In fact, returning `FALSE` from `OnKillActive()` causes MFC to do nothing. If you want to post an error message, sound a beep, or format the user's hard drive so they know they've made a mistake, it's up to you to write that code and get it executed. The default implementation of `OnKillActive()` is shown below for your reference (you can find it in `Microsoft Visual Studio\vc98\mfc\src\Dlgprop.cpp`):

```
BOOL CPropertyPage::OnKillActive()
{
    ASSERT_VALID(this);

    // Override this to perform validation;
    //    return FALSE and this page will remain active...
    if (!UpdateData(TRUE))
    {
        TRACE0("UpdateData failed during page deactivation\n");
        // UpdateData will set focus to correct item
        return FALSE;
    }
    return TRUE;
}
```

Calling `UpdateData()` causes MFC to run the `DoDataExchange()` code which brings the user-supplied data back from the controls into your member variables.

OnSetActive()

`OnKillActive()` has a sister function named `OnSetActive()` which, as you might have guessed, is called just before the page becomes active. You can use the event to prevent a page from becoming active by returning `FALSE` from this function. Normally, MFC uses `OnSetActive()` to load the dialog box template that contains the page, before populating that page with data.

If you override `OnKillActive()` or `OnSetActive()`, you should call the `CPropertyPage()` implementation of the function as a part of your override. You can perform any additional validation in these functions which is inappropriate for `DoDataExchange()`, although in truth there's really very little difference between doing your validation in one of the activation notification functions and within `DoDataExchange()` itself.

In actual fact, `OnKillActive()` and `OnSetActive()` both end up calling `UpdateData()`, which will call your implementation of `DoDataExchange()`. You can use the activation functions as an easy way to segregate the simple data exchange routines from those that actually carry out complex, cross-field validation. Your activation notification handlers might call `DoDataExchange()` immediately, before completing cross-field validation and returning the status of the transfer to MFC.

Using an Apply or Help Button

You might wish to provide your users with the ability to make their property page settings effective immediately, especially if you create a modeless property sheet. If you provide the ability to immediately apply changes, your `OnKillActive()` or `DoDataExchange()` function should call code outside of the property sheet which will copy the information from the page back to the appropriate place in the objects outside. One convenient way to implement the notification that kicks off the application of the new values is to supply your property sheet with the address of a function or a pointer to an object that can be called to initiate the application of the properties. Pass the pointer to the constructor of your `CPropertySheet`-derived class and keep it around as a member variable throughout the life of the object.

While this mechanism probably seems a little awkward, the only other method for having the property page inform its owner of changes would be to declare the property page as a friend of the parent class. This would allow the property page to call members of the parent to effect the changes directly. The disadvantage of the friend approach is that the parent class and the property sheet class become a little too interdependent. Instead of a generic callback, the two classes have a troubling shadow action.

The Apply Button and SetModified()

Normally, the Apply button in the property sheet is disabled. You can enable it by calling `SetModified()` from any one of your property pages. `SetModified()` takes a single Boolean parameter which should be `TRUE` if you want an indication that the page has been modified and is therefore 'dirty'. After the first `TRUE` call to `SetModified()`, the sheet will enable the Apply button, showing that pending changes can be applied. Note that once the Apply button is enabled, it will remain enabled no matter which page is being shown. The Apply button is intended to indicate that *any* change to the property page will be applied to the object, not just changes to the currently shown property sheet.

You can call `SetModified(TRUE)` when any of the controls in your page record changes; perhaps you would call it in response to an `EN_CHANGE` message being sent to edit controls as their content is changed.

When the user presses the **Apply** button, the `OnKillActive()` and `DoDataExchange()` members of *only* the visible page will be called. The `CPropertySheet` code manages a modified flag for each page in the sheet, calling `SetModified(FALSE)` in response to the button pressed. The privacy of each page's modified flag ensures that each page retains its own state for the modified button.

In the `Tabbed` sample, for each of the pages for the **Text Options** dialog, I've added a handler for the `EN_CHANGE` message for both the edit boxes on the page. The message map points both messages to appropriate handlers; the `OnChangeText()` and `OnChangeHeight()` members simply set the modified flag to `TRUE`.

```
BEGIN_MESSAGE_MAP(CLine3Page, CPropertyPage)
    //{{AFX_MSG_MAP(CLine3Page)
    ON_EN_CHANGE(IDC_TEXT, OnChangeText)
    ON_EN_CHANGE(IDC_HEIGHT, OnChangeHeight)
    //}}AFX_MSG_MAP
END_MESSAGE_MAP()
```

The default implementation of the `OnApply()` function is used (as it contains all the functionality that we need) by simply calling `OnOK()`, which is where the 'hard' work is done:

```
void CLine3Page::OnOK()
{
    CWnd* pMain = AfxGetApp()->m_pMainWnd;
    pMain->SendMessage(WM_USER, 0, 0);
    SetModified(FALSE);
}
```

After obtaining a pointer to the window frame, I use `SendMessage()` to send a `WM_USER` message to the frame. My reason for using `SendMessage()` instead of `PostMessage()` is that I don't want the function to return until the message has been processed. Finally, I reset the modified flag. The last task is to add the message handler to the frame:

```
BEGIN_MESSAGE_MAP(CMainFrame, CFrameWnd)
    ON_MESSAGE(WM_USER, Exchanger)
    //{{AFX_MSG_MAP(CMainFrame)
    ON_WM_CREATE()
    ON_COMMAND(ID_VIEW_OPTIONS, OnViewOptions)
    ON_COMMAND(ID_VIEW_TEXTSETTINGS, OnViewTextSettings)
    //}}AFX_MSG_MAP
END_MESSAGE_MAP()
```

The message handler simply maps the `Exchanger()` function, which assigns the new values for the page objects to those in the document and updates all the views.

Property Pages as Wizards

Yet another trend in Windows software involves **Wizards**. Certainly, being an astute user of Microsoft Visual Studio, you're familiar with cue-card style software that walks you through a task. Microsoft Visual Studio's AppWizard is similar to the Wizards you'll find in other Microsoft applications like the Office suite.

To state the obvious, Wizards (apart from ClassWizard) allow your application to present a series of steps to the user. The steps are all presented in the same dialog, and the user can move between them using buttons that are always present in the frame of the Wizard window.

If you need to add a Wizard to your own application, you'll be relieved to hear that the features of Windows built into the property sheet classes allow you to concentrate on writing the Wizard itself, rather than its user interface. It might not sound obvious at first, but it's the `CPropertySheet` and `CPropertyPage` classes that allow you to implement the familiar Wizard user interface.

You should start by deciding how the steps of your Wizard will fit together. Do you have only a few steps, or do you need more? If the choices the user makes actually dictate the number of steps, you should plan on asking those questions in the first or second step of the Wizard.

Once you have the story line of your Wizard planned, you should draw a dialog resource to reflect each of the steps you want. You *don't* need to add navigation buttons to your dialog templates, because they'll be provided by the Wizard window at runtime in much the same way as the property sheet dialog supplied the Apply, Help, OK, and Cancel buttons for your property sheet.

As you draw the dialogs that you'll use for the step pages in your Wizard, you're governed by the same rules as when you drew property pages. As before, each of the pages in your Wizard should be the same size, so that the user doesn't notice any annoying window movement while switching from page to page. The dialogs involved in your Wizard can have any style you like. You need to make sure each page has the Caption property set and uses its caption to identify itself in the title bar of the dialog where it lives.

Once you've created all of the objects that wrap your dialog templates, you can go ahead and create a `CPropertySheet` instance. Use the `CPropertySheet::AddPage()` function to add individual pages to your Wizard, just as we did before with normal property pages. Before calling `DoModal()` against the `CPropertySheet` object, you'll need to call `SetWizardMode()` against the property sheet object. Calling the `SetWizardMode()` function will direct MFC to add the appropriate style bits to the property sheet as it is created, so that it turns out to be a Wizard dialog and not a property sheet dialog.

That's really all there is to it. As the user moves from step to step in your Wizard, you'll receive the same `OnKillActive()` and `OnSetActive()` notifications you would receive while working with a property page. When the user presses the <Back and Next> buttons in the Wizard, it's as if they were moving from the current to the previous or next tab in a property sheet. If you don't want to allow them to move, you can return `FALSE` from your `OnKillActive()` override, as we explained for property sheets.

By default, MFC only provides <Back, Next> and Cancel buttons, which obviously isn't enough. At the very least, you need a Finish button to accept the options selected in your Wizard, and you may want to disable the <Back button on the first step and the Next> button on the last step. You can manipulate which buttons are available by using the `SetWizardButtons()` member of `CPropertySheet`.

`SetWizardButtons()` takes a single parameter indicating which buttons are to be shown. This flag can be a combination of the following four ORed together:

Flag	Description
PSWIZB_BACK	Shows the <Back button. If it is not included, the button is shown disabled.
PSWIZB_NEXT	Shows the Next> button. If it is not included and neither of the FINISH flags is included, the button is shown as disabled.
PSWIZB_FINISH	Replaces the Next> button with a Finish button.
PSWIZB_DISABLEDFINISH	Replaces the Next> button with a disabled Finish button.

> The **PSWIZB_FINISH** and **PSWIZB_DISABLEDFINISH** flags have precedence over the **PSWIZB_NEXT** flag.

However, you can't use SetWizardButtons() before you call DoModal(), so you must add OnSetActive() overrides to all the pages, and not just to the first and last steps; this is because the settings are persistent from one step to the next. Therefore, on the first page, you might have:

```
BOOL CStep1Page::OnSetActive()
{
    CPropertySheet* Parent = static_cast<CPropertySheet*>(GetParent());
    Parent->SetWizardButtons(PSWIZB_NEXT);

    return CPropertyPage::OnSetActive();
}
```

while on the second and penultimate pages:

```
BOOL CStep2Page::OnSetActive()
{
    CPropertySheet* Parent = static_cast<CPropertySheet*>(GetParent());
    Parent->SetWizardButtons(PSWIZB_BACK|PSWIZB_NEXT);

    return CPropertyPage::OnSetActive();
}
```

and on the final page:

```
BOOL CStep6Page::OnSetActive()
{
    CPropertySheet* Parent = static_cast<CPropertySheet*>(GetParent());
    Parent->SetWizardButtons(PSWIZB_BACK|PSWIZB_FINISH);

    return CPropertyPage::OnSetActive();
}
```

Finally, instead of IDOK, a wizard returns either IDCANCEL or ID_WIZFINISH when DoModal() returns.

The Wizard97 User Interface

With the release of Internet Explorer 5.0, Microsoft updated the system DLL that implements the Wizard-based user interface. If you're targeting systems that have this update installed, you can make use of the newest Wizard features – called **Wizard97**. This feature should really only be used with Windows 98 and Windows 2000.

I'll not include a sample for the Wizard97 user interface because the WIZARD97 sample, which ships with Visual C++ 6, is quite adequate for demonstrating the changes that were made. From this screen shot, the differences should be quite obvious:

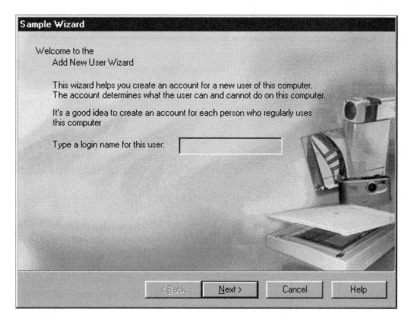

The dialog, from the first step of the WIZARD97 sample, shows a very nice background bitmap. The layout of the interior of the wizard is still the same – it still comes from your own dialog box. However, the Wizard makes it easy to clip your background to the area above the stock buttons. Two classes introduced with MFC 6.0, CPropertySheetEx and CPropertyPageEx, support dialogs such as these. CPropertySheetEx provides support for the expanded PROPSHEETHEADER structure (introduced in Windows 98 and Windows 2000) that allows a 'watermark' background bitmap and CPropertyPageEx provides support for the expanded PROPSHEETPAGE structure that can produce a deeper header area to accommodate both a title and a subtitle.

The Wizard97 sample derives its own class – named CWizard97Sheet — from the MFC-supplied CPropertySheetEx class. The sample uses the constructor of that class to load all of the pages using the regular AddPage() calls. But, most importantly, it also sets the PSH_WIZARD97 flag on the m_psh.dwFlags member of the class. Windows won't show any of the Wizard97 user interface features if this flag isn't set.

The constructor also takes a couple of extra parameters – a handle to a bitmap for the **watermark**, and a handle to a bitmap to be used as the header. The first page, shown above, uses only a watermark. The top section of the bitmap is bare, and the center of it holds the watermark bitmap. The watermark is much like a watermark on a piece of typing paper or an official document. It appears on the background of the dialog, and controls are drawn as if they're over the watermark design. The second page is shown here.

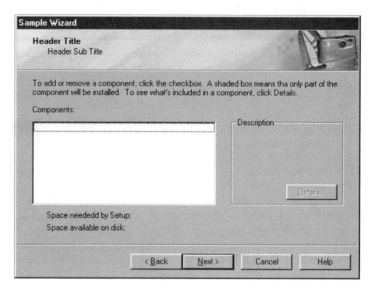

It actually uses a header bitmap to make the page pretty. As you can see, the header is true to its name; it's drawn at the top of the wizard page and the balance of the page shows just the dialog resource for the page. You may have noticed a spelling mistake or two in the above screen shot. To make sure this book is accurate, I haven't retouched the screenshot to fix the errors inherent in the sample!

The first page of the Wizard is represented by the class `CIntroPage`, defined in the sample's `INTROPG.H` header. The constructor for that class sets the flag `PSP_HIDEHEADER` in the `m_psp.dwFlags` member of the `CPropertyPageEx` class. The intent of this flag is quite obvious; it hides the header. By default, the class shows the header on the balance of the pages. Headers are shown by default unless you've specified the `PSP_HIDEHEADER` flag. Watermarks aren't shown unless you do show the `PSH_USEWATERMARK`.

That's really all there is to it – the new user interface is obtained just by asking for the updated style. You can copy the code from the product's `WIZARD97` sample to get code to make the classes easy to use for yourself.

Painting Your User Interface

With the exception of special system or driver-level programs, Windows applications will always display information to the user in the application's window. We took a look at the `CView` class and its derivatives in Chapter 4, describing `CScrollView` as one of the most common view-oriented classes for use in applications that paint their own user interface. But how do you get that painting done?

When you handle the `CView::OnDraw()` function, you're passed a pointer to a `CDC` object, which is the wrapper for a Windows **device context** (or **DC**) data structure. The device context contains everything Windows needs to communicate with the device driver responsible for a graphic output device. Among a few other things, it remembers what font, color, pen, bitmap, pattern, orientation and mapping mode you're using to draw with.

You might have noticed that certain drawing tools in Windows are referred to as **logical**; logical fonts, for example. A font is logical when it's created, because Windows creates a font of some known, measurable size. Windows doesn't know how many pixels make up each character until that font is actually selected into a device context. That's the point at which it becomes a physical font, and the process by which it does so is called **realization**.

Windows Object-oriented Programming

Back when Windows programming first became a curiosity, people were impressed because Windows was touted as a system that encouraged **object-oriented programming**. Of course, Windows didn't inherently offer classes or objects that you could use over again, like C++ or Object COBOL. What Windows *did* have were these drawing objects: fonts, pens, brushes, and so on. You could use one of these objects for different effects in your application's output, just like a real artist might use real brushes and pens to draw a masterpiece.

Right now, MFC doesn't provide any extra code to select or deselect objects in the device context automatically. Whenever you make use of a new drawing object, you'll need to select it into the device context. The selection function, usually `SelectObject()`, will return the object that was previously selected in the device context. Once you're done drawing with a given object, it's a good idea to deselect the object and destroy it. Some people call this the Windows **sandwich model**; the work you do is sandwiched by code that requisitions and frees Windows' resources.

The Sandwich Model

For instance, you might draw a line in the window hWnd using C code like this:

```
HDC   hDC;
HPEN hOldPen;
HPEN hDrawPen;

hDC = GetDC(hWnd);
hDrawPen = CreatePen(PS_SOLID, 1, RGB(0, 0, 0));
hOldPen = (HPEN) SelectObject(hDC, hDrawPen);

MoveTo(hDC, 0, 0);
LineTo(hDC, 50, 50);

SelectObject(hDC, hOldPen);
DeleteObject(hDrawPen);RleaseDC(hDC);
```

The fragment uses hDrawPen to actually do the drawing. The pen is created by the call to CreatePen(), and we provide a pen type (which might indicate whether the pen is used to draw a dashed or dotted line), a width and a color reference for the pen. Note that this API doesn't take an hDC; the pen could be used in any device context in town. The device is responsible for deciding what the pen really looks like. For example, you might have a device context for a plotter that doesn't have a black pen mounted. At the time the device selects the pen, it will decide for itself what to do; maybe it will first draw with a blue pen, then redraw the same line with a green pen to give the effect of a black line.

The sandwich metaphor applies here to the use of the hOldPen and hDrawPen objects. The pen we'll use for drawing is created and selected into the device context before any drawing work commences. Once the drawing work is done, we make sure the previous pen is put back into the context and the object we used for our drawing is destroyed.

The code in MFC that does the same job is slightly simpler, but it has much the same flavor. The most notable difference is that every function that takes a handle to the device context is instead referenced as a member function of the CDC object with which we're painting. So in MFC, this is what you get:

```
CClientDC clientDC;
CPen* pOldPen;
CPen  penDraw;

penDraw.CreatePen(PS_SOLID, 1, RGB(0, 0, 0));
pOldPen = clientDC.SelectObject(&DrawPen);

clientDC.MoveTo(0, 0);
clientDC.LineTo(50, 50);

clientDC.SelectObject(pOldPen);
```

You should be aware that the MFC code doesn't explicitly call DeleteObject() on the DrawPen. Since CPen is a C++ object, the destructor in the CPen object will call DeleteObject() for us. CreatePen() is something only pens need to do, so this function is a member function of the CPen object. Before CreatePen() is called on CPen(), the object is uninitialized and unusable. CPen has a constructor which takes the same parameters as CPen::CreatePen(), so you can declare and initialize the DrawPen in one easy step if you like:

```
CPen DrawPen(PS_SOLID, 1, RGB(0, 0, 0));
```

Letting the C++ object destroy and delete the underlying physical object is a great saving for people like me who often forget to, uh... Well, anyway, you can get in trouble if you let a C++ object destroy itself before you're done using the Windows object that it was wrapping. If, in the above example, I kept DrawPen selected in the device context I was using, I'd get in trouble when the function that I coded reached completion. The DrawPen object would go out of scope and be destroyed, causing MFC to delete the object that Windows would still need to use when painting with that device context.

All drawing objects in MFC (including pens, fonts, and brushes) commonly derive from the CGdiObject class. Carefully writing your code so that CGdiObject-derived classes are around as long as you need them is just as important as making sure that any other MFC-wrapped Windows object is always available.

SelectObject() and Data Typing

As you make the transition from drawing with Windows objects (which you're probably familiar with if you have any experience with the Windows SDK) to using MFC's classes, the biggest concern you'll have is data typing. You should have noticed that the MFC fragment shows the old pen to be a pointer to a CPen object, while the pen with which we're drawing is a CPen object. This is just for convenience, as SelectObject() returns a pointer to the selected object after building it internally. Behind the scenes, all of the MFC wrappers for CDC use normal Windows API calls and data types to get their work done.

When you call SelectObject(), the code selects the object you've passed into the device context that the CDC object represents. The SelectObject() code receives the handle to the GDI object from Windows for the previously selected object. It then constructs a C++ object from that handle, initializing the object before it's returned to you from the `SelectObject()` code. MFC owns this object and it is automatically freed when it's no longer needed.

MFC also performs the destruction of temporary C++ objects, like those returned from `SelectObject()`, during the processing of the next message in the thread's message queue. The deletion of MFC's temporary objects is *not* related to the deletion of the same Windows objects. If you call `SelectObject()`, the object referenced by the returned pointer will be deleted. The underlying Windows object will *not* be deleted. You can't squirrel away a pointer to any object returned from `SelectObject()` for use after the current message has been completely processed. The next time a stored pointer is referenced (during the processing of a subsequent Windows message), the memory will undoubtedly be invalid and the reference will generate an error.

If you look at the documentation for `SelectObject()`, you might be a little overwhelmed by the number of overloaded versions of this function that are made available to you. A different version of `SelectObject()` exists for every kind of graphics object that can be selected into a device context. The type returned is a pointer to the type selected, so `SelectObject()` on a `CPen` returns a pointer to a `CPen`, and so on.

To make sure the C++ language nets the correct overload for you, you must make sure that the type passed to your call of `SelectObject()` is unambiguous and correct. Whatever type you pass `SelectObject()` is the type you should expect in return. So, using `SelectObject()` on a pointer to a `CFont` returns a pointer to a `CFont` wrapping the old GDI font.

For the rare cases when it's necessary, you can use the generic `CGdiObject` class when you need to work with any GDI object without worrying exactly what it's for. This might be appropriate for instances when you're manually dissecting the content of a Windows metafile but, in my opinion, you should only use it as a last resort. Instead, you'll more often use the type-specific classes for the bulk of your work. We'll describe the different specific types later in this section.

The CDC Class and Device Contexts

To be specific, the `CDC` class is designed to let you do general purpose drawing when you need to work with a window in response to a paint message, or to implement your `OnDraw()` functionality. It turns out that `CDC` really has two device contexts: one for drawing and one for handling queries. The handle to the drawing DC is available in m_hDC, while the handle to the attribute query DC is available in the m_hAttribDC member of your DC object. For any basic work you do with `CDC`, these device contexts are exactly equivalent; you don't need to worry about using them directly yourself, and you can get them to do your work simply by using `CDC` member functions.

By the way, you can't get a metafile DC to tell you anything interesting, because the metafile is just a record of actions carried out against a device context. The actions are recorded in much the same way you'd make the calls yourself. Since the calls aren't actually completed, none of the objects you've used to do your drawing are actually realized. Using fonts is an extreme example, but one that's easy to understand.

If you have a beautiful, state-of-the art display adapter and you select an ornate font into it, Windows, TrueType, GDI and your display driver will all work together to draw the font as accurately as possible. However, if you obtain a device context to a dot-matrix printer and try to use the same font, you'll probably find that the printer driver (depending on its configuration) throws up its hands in disgust. The printer driver will probably select a device font that doesn't even remotely resemble the ornate font you requested, either in size or appearance. Selecting a 36-point font into a display device context would mean that subsequent calls to measure the text metrics would return a very different set of numbers than the exact same font selected into a printer device context.

Since the metafile device context doesn't know what device it will be using when it finally gets around to doing some drawing, it can't possibly support the same query functions you're used to using against real live device contexts. (I'll explain exactly what metafiles are and what they're used for a little later on in this chapter.)

CDC Functions

Functions implemented in the CDC class allow you to perform drawing tasks or to set the way that drawing is actually performed.

The vast majority of functions in CDC fall into the first category – those that actually do drawing and there are dozens of them. One thing almost all have in common is the notion of a **current point**. The current point in a device context is where drawing will happen if you don't specify a different point. The MoveTo() function moves the current point for the device context without performing any drawing. You might later call LineTo() to draw a line from the current point to the point you pass to the LineTo() function.

So, you might draw a line from the point (x1,y1) to (x2,y2) with these two calls:

```
pDC->MoveTo(x1, y1);
pDC->LineTo(x2, y2);
```

After the call to LineTo(), the current point is moved to the endpoint of the line. So, an immediately subsequent call to LineTo() would draw starting at (x2,y2).

Other member functions of CDC draw shapes that are more complicated. You can draw rectangles using the Rectangle() member function and ellipses using the Ellipse() member function, as well as many others. If the normal compliment of sided objects isn't good enough for you, you can use the Polygon() member function to draw regular and irregular polygons from collections of points you supply.

Using a Coordinate System

The most important of the drawing mode functions involves the coordinate system, which will be used for drawing in the device context. The coordinate system used is set by any of several **mapping modes**. These will dictate how Windows should map the coordinates that you specify in your drawing calls to the pixels that your output device can handle.

The MM_TEXT Drawing Mode

Normally, the drawing mode is MM_TEXT. This means that the coordinates you specify in your drawing functions will directly correspond to single display units on your output device. For printers, this means that one printer element of resolution is used. For display devices, one coordinate unit corresponds to one pixel. The top left of the screen (or the client area of the window, if the numbers are client coordinates) is (0,0) and higher *y* coordinates move down, while higher *x* coordinates move right.

In some instances, though, it might be nice to be able to alter this. For example, CScrollView implements scrolling by changing the top-left coordinate of the window; you can duplicate this behavior by calling the SetViewportOrg() of your CDC object.

> **MM_TEXT** is very convenient, since most programmers don't need to have any coordinate translation done and are quite content to visualize their graphics calculations in terms of pixels.

Other Mapping Modes

You might recall that CScrollView can also zoom your document to be large enough (or small enough) to fit the view window. CScrollView performs its zooming magic by setting the mapping mode to MM_ANISOTROPIC with a call to SetMapMode(). This allows CScrollView to set the logical mapping of *x* and *y* coordinates independently, adjusting the scrolling in different ratios along the two axes. You can set the mapping mode to MM_ISOTROPIC if you need to have a one-to-one correspondence between the mappings on the *x* and *y* axes.

There are a handful of other mapping modes which are useful in specialized situations. MM_HIENGLISH and MM_LOENGLISH provide mapping modes that map to imperial linear measurements, while MM_HIMETRIC and MM_LOMETRIC provide mapping modes that map to metric measurements. You can also use MM_TWIPS if you're doing any work that is heavily oriented towards text processing. **Twips** are a twentieth of a point, or 1/1440 of an inch.

There's no reason for me to spend time here enumerating all of the CDC members, as they're extensively documented in the Visual C++ online documentation. If that isn't enough for you, look for functions of the exact same name in any Windows programming book, or the Windows API references. The CDC class implements a relatively pure mapping to the Windows device context object; there's nothing extra happening when you call MFC's implementation of a drawing function, compared to calling the Windows API directly.

Of course, the parameter list of the Windows API always needs an HDC, but the CDC member function just works on the device context represented by the CDC object. Remember that MFC sometimes provides overloaded implementations of GDI functions, which means that you can use CSize, CPoint or CRect objects in place of the SIZE, POINT or RECT structures, respectively, or in the case of the last two, for explicitly passing two or four integers.

Metafiles

While CDC will serve most of your basic painting needs, you'll sometimes need to do things that are a little more advanced. Windows supports the option of 'recording' the activity against a device context into a special block of memory called a **metafile**, which contains the steps used to draw something. Those steps can be replayed against a device over and over, or they can be replayed after scaling, clipping or translation. They might even be replayed to a completely different device than the creator of the metafile device context originally expected!

Metafiles are often used to paint things that require a lot of work quickly, since the complex calculations that are necessary to perform painting can slow down the painting process significantly. However, once the points are plotted, they can be stored in a metafile and then be rapidly redrawn to order. Metafiles are often used by OLE objects; OLE might ask an object to render itself into a metafile so that the application containing the object can rapidly redraw, or even save the object's appearance. Thus, it can be redrawn without actually loading the code to do the drawing.

We'll consider OLE in much more detail in Chapter 13, including their special usage of metafiles.

The Disadvantages of Using Metafiles

The big rub with metafiles is that many of the convenient attribute query calls that work against a normal device context don't work against a metafile. For instance, you can't query the mapping mode of a metafile DC. Additionally, you can't use GetTextMetrics() to see how your text maps into the metafile because you don't know exactly what kind of device the metafile will play into. These limitations can trip you up when you implement complex painting code.

If you're working with a metafile device context then you should make use of the CMetaFileDC class, because it discriminates between the attribute and output DC. The metafile DC will use the m_hDC when you implement some output to the device context, such as drawing text or painting lines, and the attribute DC when you perform a query call against the device context that would normally fail against a metafile device context.

For example, given a CMetaFileDC, a call to GetTextMetrics() will return information from the m_hAttribDC that has been initialized to contain information compatible with the current settings in the output DC.

Any calls which you make to change the output DC are applied to both the m_hAttribDC and the m_hDC device contexts, assuring that the attribute DC and the output DC stay synchronized. For this reason, you shouldn't call Windows device context APIs directly when you require an MFC device context object; the change will drive the MFC object out of sync.

Note that the trick of using two DCs to handle different calls only works if MFC has a chance to initialize both device contexts; that is, if you create the metafile DC yourself. If your code possesses a handle to a metafile device context, MFC can't initialize the information cached in the attribute DC to be compatible with it. So, things will be just as bad as they were before, which implies that there's no adequate solution to this problem.

I've spent some time here waving my arms about the use of metafile device contexts. You can probably close your eyes and imagine a handsome young guy in a hockey jersey and a pair of jeans ranting about how some crazy technical facet of Windows programming works. (Or maybe I'm a pretty crummy writer and you're just wishing it would end.)

When to Use Metafiles

Metafiles are actually seldom used in Windows programming; the most common application for them is OLE. In OLE, as we'll learn in a later chapter, one program might ask another to render itself. This rendering might be a blind, brash dump of the other program's bits, or it might be a way for one program to ask the other for a visual representation of itself. This is normally done via a metafile; the program making the request supplies a metafile device context to the other program, and that program draws into the DC. Through the magic of OLE, the metafile can be stored and replayed, even when the program that originally rendered it isn't around.

When you create a CMetafileDC, you pass it the name of a file. If you pass NULL as the file name, MFC will create an in-memory file for your metafile; otherwise, you'll create a real-life disk file. When you paint into that CMetafileDC using all the regular calls, Windows simply writes a little bit of information into the metafile about what you've done. These metafile records can be used to recreate your steps at some other time.

When you're done painting into the metafile, you can call `CMetafileDC::Close()`. The `Close()` method returns an `HMETAFILE`, which is a handle to the metafile you've created. You should call the Windows API `::DeleteMetaFile()` if you're done with the metafile and want it to be erased. You can call `::CopyMetaFile()` if you want to make a copy of a metafile, or move it from disk to memory.

Later on, you can take the file and replay it using the `PlayMetafile()` method, which is a member of the `CDC` class. You don't need a `CMetafileDC` to play a metafile, only to create one.

CFont

The `CFont` class provides you with a way to manage fonts in your code in the C++ style. Whenever you need to draw text on the screen, you should create a font that will give your application the look it deserves. Fonts are terribly complicated, which unfortunately means that Windows needs lots of information to describe one; it isn't quite as easy as just naming the font and picking a size.

If you're letting a user choose their own font for any part of your application, you can get the information to create the font that the user requested with the `CFontDialog` described in Chapter 5. `CFontDialog` has a member called `m_cf`, and this `CHOOSEFONT` structure has a member called `lpLogFont` which, in turn, is a pointer to a `LOGFONT` structure. You can pass this same pointer to `CFont`'s `CreateFontIndirect()` function to have the object initialize itself with the font your user requests.

Creating Your Own Fonts

You can, of course, set up a `LOGFONT` structure all by yourself to create a font. `CFont::CreateFontIndirect()` uses a Windows API of the same name to do all its work. This API will ignore values in the structure that are zero and use an appropriate default value for them. In other words, when you're about to create a font, it's a great idea to start with a `LOGFONT` and then call `memset()` on it to set all of the elements to zero. Then, you can explicitly set the values you really need.

Leaving values as zero and accepting the default isn't always about being lazy. Some values *need* to be zero; for example, `LOGFONT`'s `lfItalic` member is zero if you don't want an italic font and nonzero if you do. So, a typical font initialization might go something like this:

```
CFont CMyFont;
LOGFONT lf;

memset ((void*)&lf, 0, sizeof(lf));
lf.lfHeight = 32;
_tcscpy(lf.lfFaceName, _T("Times"));
CMyFont.CreateFontIndirect(&lf);
```

Once we've called `CreateFontIndirect()`, we're done with the `LOGFONT` structure and can allow it to be destroyed. You should note that the height of the created font is 32 logical units, not 32 points. You can create a font with a given point size using code like this:

```
lf.lfHeight = -MulDiv(32, GetDeviceCaps(hDC, LOGPIXELSY), 72);
```

A point to note here is that the return value from `MulDiv()` is negated; this makes the font set its own size to the number or logical size of the font's characters. A positive value checks for a size of the character *cell*, which is slightly larger than the character size, as the latter doesn't include internal leading space. The code calls GetDeviceCaps() on a device context which you'll use for painting. This will reveal how many logical units the device maps to an inch; since there are 72 points per inch, the division is done to convert units.

CreateFont()

If you've got lots of time, you can call CreateFont() instead of CreateFontIndirect(). CreateFont() is for people with no deadlines because it takes fourteen parameters, all of which must be specified. In most circumstances, it's far easier to use CreateFontIndirect() and your own LOGFONT structure.

Once the CFont is created, it can be selected into any device context you're using to paint. When it's destroyed, the CFont object will delete the Windows font object. Windows doesn't like it if you destroy a GDI object that is selected into a device context. So if you're going to keep your font around longer than it takes you to handle your drawing code then you should make sure the CFont object doesn't get destroyed while the font is actively selected in a device context.

When to Create Fonts

You should be aware that creating a font is a comparatively expensive process. Instead of creating and destroying your fonts while your application is processing its OnPaint() or OnDraw() function, I advise you to create them at program start-up and delete them when your program ends.

Remember that typography is a very complex art; fonts possess dozens of attributes. The Windows font mapper tries to use reasonable rules to return a font that is installed on your system and which matches the parameters you request. Most folks don't need to worry about exactly how fonts look, but if you do, I suggest that you review the LOGFONT and CreateFont() documentation in the Windows API references to make sure your code will do exactly what you need.

CPen

Any time you ask a device context object to draw a line, it will use the currently selected pen. LineTo(), which draws a straight line, is the simplest member of CDC, but other members, like Ellipse() or Rectangle(), will draw the outline of the shape with the currently selected pen before filling the inside of the shape with the currently selected brush.

Pens have a few attributes that affect the way they draw. The first is width; pens have a width in pixels or logical units, which describes the breadth of the line they draw. The pen can also have several patterns; solid pens draw a solid line, dotted pens draw a dotted line, and so on, but you should know that these styles are only applicable to pens that have a width of 1. You can also define a pen style, which draws lines with a custom, specified pattern.

Pens may also have attributes that specify how they draw the ends and corners of lines. The ends might be drawn square, flat or rounded, while corners between two lines might be rounded, beveled or mitered. All of these attributes, including the break style, are represented by various constants. For example, PS_DASHDOT specifies a dash-dot line, while PS_JOIN_BEVEL assures that joined lines are beveled at their meeting point. The final attribute that you can set is the color of the line that the pen draws.

Creating a CPen Object

You can create an MFC CPen object simply by declaring the object; the default constructor doesn't initialize the pen. On the other hand, you may want to create a pen, passing it the styles, width and color that you need.

If you've created the CPen without any parameters to its constructor, you can call CreatePen() on the object to initialize it. Overloads of this function take the same parameters as the second and third constructors.

The three constructors for CPen use the following syntax:

```
CPen();


CPen(int      nPenStyle,
     int      nWidth,
     COLORREF crColor);

CPen(int      nPenStyle,
     int      nWidth,
     const    LOGBRUSH* pLogBrush,
     int      nStyleCount=0,
     const    DWORD* lpStyle=NULL);
```

Once the object is created, you may select it into the CDC where you're actually doing your drawing by using the CDC::SelectObject() function. When you select a CPen object, a pointer to a CPen object describing the previously selected GDI pen is returned.

The pen objects that the GDI provides have a normal array of dashed styles. If you're running under Windows NT, you can, however, create a pen with the PS_USERSTYLE type if you'd like to have your own pattern. (Unfortunately, the style isn't available for Windows 95 or Windows 98.) The third CPen constructor (and an overload of CreatePen()) accepts a count of style words and a pointer to an array of DWORDs. The nStyleCount parameter simply specifies how many words are in the array. Each subsequent value in the array alternates between specifying the length of a solid portion of the line and blank portion of the line, starting with a solid portion. Code that looks like this for example:

```
DWORD dwBreaks[] = { 20, 5, 3, 5 };
CBrush brush(RGB(127, 127, 127));    // Grey
LOGBRUSH brushDescr;
brush.GetObject(&brushDescr);
CPen penDoubleDashed(PS_USERSTYLE, 1, &brushDescr,
                              sizeof(dwBreaks)/sizeof(DWORD), dwBreaks);
```

would create a pen that draws a line with 20 units of solid space, five units of blank space, three units of solid space, and five units of blank space. As the pen draws, it will reuse this pattern over and over again for the length of the line it is drawing.

CBitmap

Bitmaps are rectangular clips of raster data that Windows can display as a picture in any window. You can create a bitmap object by creating an instance of the CBitmap class and initializing the content of it.

Most of the time, you'll simply load a bitmap from your application's resources. Once the CBitmap object is created, just call its LoadBitmap() function, passing either the resource name or the resource ID. Once the bitmap resource is loaded, you can use the bitmap for painting or for creating a brush. CBrush can be initialized with a bitmap to define how it will look, but you'll need an eight-by-eight bitmap to do this on Windows 95 and 98 – on Windows NT, a bitmap of any size can be used.

You can select your CBitmap into a device context. You should notice, however, that to paint your bitmap you need to transfer the bits from one device context to another. This enables the bits in the image to actually appear in the window that you're painting. You should create a memory device context that is compatible with the target device context, and then select the bitmap before transferring it from the bitmap image stored in memory to the output bitmap you wish to use. The whole exercise looks like this:

```
void CMyView::OnDraw(CDC* pDC)
{
    CBitmap bmSmile;
    bmSmile.LoadBitmap(IDB_SMILE);

    CDC dcCompatible;
    dcCompatible.CreateCompatibleDC(pDC);

    CBitmap* pOld = dcCompatible.SelectObject(&bmSmile);

    BITMAP bmInfo;
    bmSmile.GetObject(sizeof(bmInfo), &bmInfo);

    pDC->BitBlt(0, 0, bmInfo.bmWidth, bmInfo.bmHeight,
                                    &dcCompatible, 0, 0, SRCCOPY);

    dcCompatible.SelectObject(pOld);
}
```

To be clear in this example, I've doctored things a little bit. It's slow to reload and recreate the bitmap every time you handle a paint message. In real life, it might be better to load the bitmap during the constructor for the CView object and hang on to it for the life of the view.

The call to GetObject() on bmSmile is used to retrieve a BITMAP structure from the graphics object.

Most Windows GDI objects support some sort of GetObject() call to obtain more information about their description. For most objects, you'll get an intuitive structure back to describe the object. For an HBITMAP, you get a BITMAP structure back to describe the size and depth of the bitmap object. Given an HFONT, you'll get a LOGFONT back. Similarly, an HPEN gets a LOGPEN and a HBRUSH returns a LOGBRUSH. All of these structures are well documented, so I won't tear into their members here.

The exception to the structure rule is the act of offering an HPALETTE to the GetObject() call. You'll get back a WORD that tells you how many entries are in the palette.

For us here, the BITMAP structure we get back is terribly interesting because it will give us the size of the bitmap in pixels as well as the number of bits in each pixel. We can use this information when we call BitBlt() screen DC to get it displayed.

If you're not already a Windows programmer, you might be wondering why you need two device contexts and need to select the bitmap into a different bitmap before copying it. It turns out that the bitmap in a device context represents the bits that are on the actual device! If you get a screen device context, you can copy the bitmap from the device context and store it somewhere else – perhaps to build a BMP file as a screen capture, or to copy the content of a window to the printer.

BitBlt()

CDC::BitBlt() is an incredibly versatile function. The first four parameters it takes are the origin and width that you'll copy to. These four numbers describe positions and sizes within the destination bitmap. The fifth parameter is a pointer to the CDC object that will act as the source bitmap, and the sixth and seventh are offsets into that bitmap, from where the information will be copied. If you overstep the bounds of the bitmap with bad parameters, you'll undoubtedly have very odd results; Windows will spray trash all over your output window.

Raster Operations

The last parameter to BitBlt() is the raster operation which BitBlt() will use to perform the move. A **raster operation** is an integer which indicates what operation BitBlt() should perform on the pixels in the bitmap as it moves them. You can write tremendously complicated raster operations to filter out background colors, add borders to the bitmap object, or even invert the object. Since we just want to move the bitmap from one place to another, we simply copy the bitmap, pixel for pixel, over to the target device.

Have a look at the Windows SDK documentation for information on the more complicated raster operations that are available. Many of these operations are dependent on other GDI objects that are selected in the source or destination bitmap. The raster operation might fill background space with the current brush, or color certain pixels with the selected pen. In the meantime, you can get by with using SRCCOPY to copy bitmaps on a one-shot basis. The SRCXOR operation can be used to toggle the bitmap image; the first SRCXOR will draw the image, while the second will 'undraw' it.

Altering Specific Bits of a Bitmap

If you're writing an image processing application, you might be interested in directly dabbling with the bits in the bitmap. You can call SetBitmapBits() to change bits or GetBitmapBits() to retrieve bits in the bitmap.

If you want to load or save a bitmap, you should use the CreateBitmapIndirect() function. This function takes a pointer to the BITMAP structure containing all of the information you'd like to be in the bitmap (with the exception of the actual picture bits). Once CreateBitmapIndirect() is done, you can call SetBitmapBits() to initialize the actual picture.

The CreateBitmap() function takes the width and height of the desired bitmap as its first two parameters. The third parameter is the number of color planes in the bitmap – this value will always be 1. The fourth parameter is the number of bits per pixel. This number indicates how many bits will be used to represent each pixel on the display device. If the display is set to use 16-bit color, for example, this value would be 16 to indicate that each pixel needs two bytes of storage.

Taken altogether, the process of creating a bitmap and accessing the bits for a monochrome bitmap might look like this:

```
CBitmap bmp;
bmp.CreateBitmap(100, 50, 1, 1, NULL);
void* pbBits = new BYTE[(100 * 50) / 8];    // One bit per pixel

// "draw" in bpBits
bmp.SetBitmapBits((100 * 50 / 8), pbBits);
```

As the name implies, a monochrome bitmap has only one color, plus black. As such, a single bit is adequate to represent the state of any pixel. The bitmap will pack as many pixels as possible into a byte and, so the bitmap actually stores eight pixels in a byte, the size of the bitmap is given by the width times the height, divided by the number of bits per pixel. Since we've created a bitmap of 100 by 50 pixels in the call to `CreateBitmap()`, we need to allocate one byte for every eight pixels, which is why the call to `new()` has some division in it.

If you need to find the number of pixels in a bitmap, you can call `GetObject()` on the bitmap and look at the `bmBitsPixel` member of the returned `BITMAP` structure. If you want to know how many bits per pixel a given device uses, you can call `GetDeviceCaps()` on a DC related to the device. Asking the `GetDeviceCaps()` function for the `BITSPIXEL` attribute will get you the number you need.

CBrush

Brushes are used during drawing operations to fill any solid area drawn by your application. If you call a CDC function which draws a solid object, such as `Ellipse()` or `Rectangle()`, the shape will be filled with the brush currently selected in the device context. Generally, there are four sorts of brushes:

> **Hatched** – paints a diagonal, horizontal, vertical or cross-hatched pattern, using the color specified for the brush. This can be useful when you wish to paint an object that is disabled or unavailable.

> **Patterned** – you can specify your own fill pattern for the brush. The pattern is expressed as a bitmap that's a group of eight pixels by eight. The brush paints through the pattern, effectively allowing you to define your own hatching pattern.

> **Solid** – paints a solid color.

> **Null** – a brush that doesn't paint at all. A null brush is actually a Windows stock object. While it sounds a little silly to have a brush that doesn't paint anything, you can select a null brush into your device context when you're using functions that need a brush, but you don't want to use one. If you call `Rectangle()`, for instance, it will use the currently selected brush to fill the rectangle. If you want a hollow rectangle, make sure a null brush is selected.

Nothing in the descriptions above, by the way, mentions **dithering**. Dithering is the technique of making a new color by drawing pixels in a pattern of different, existing colors. Even if you request a solid brush, you may have a dithered brush if the device can't represent the exact color you've requested.

The MFC CBrush object can be constructed without any parameters, resulting in a C++ brush object which you can initialize with a call to `CreateSolidBrush()`, `CreatePatternBrush()` or

CreateHatchBrush() on the object. These three functions take the COLORREF and pattern or bitmap information required to build the brush. Alternatively, CBrush supplies additional constructors, similar to the CreateSolidBrush(), CreatePatternBrush() and CreateHatchBrush() functions, conveniently letting you construct the CBrush you need in one step.

Once initialized, your CBrush object can be selected into a CDC through SelectObject(). The CDC::SelectObject() overload will return a pointer to a CBrush object which describes the brush previously selected into the device context.

CPalette

Display cards used by systems that run Microsoft Windows are typically limited by the memory they use to display information. When you draw information on the screen, the 'drawing' actually takes place in a frame regeneration buffer, which lives on the display card. The card needs a sliver of memory to store each and every pixel on the display. The greater the color depth your display is running at, the larger that sliver of memory has to be.

Color Depth and the Palette

The **color depth** is the number of colors your system can display concurrently. Even if you only have enough memory to show 640 by 480 pixels of 256 colors, your display card can actually select those colors from a **palette** that is much larger. Instead of the color number (stored for each pixel) actually being an absolute color value to be displayed, this number is really an index into the palette. This allows a small 8-bit number to index the 24-bit numbers that appear in the palette for each color entry.

Of course, since memory is getting very cheap, most display cards are capable of having impressive resolution and color depth. Even my laptop can display 1024 by 768 pixels at a color depth of 16 bits per pixel. On such a machine, there's really little need to manage the color palette. If you're writing code that needs to work well in any video mode, or you're targeting less capable machines for your customers, you may need to manage the palette yourself.

Normally, Windows will manage the palette for you. It will set up a palette with the 20 colors normally used by the system and the window manager, and then use the balance of the colors available on the device (if any) to draw any colors that correspond to selected graphic objects, such as pens or brushes. However, if you're doing advanced image management, such as writing code to display stored image files or to transmit images by modem, you may wish to be in complete control of the palette entries.

If you set up the palette yourself, you're guaranteed to match the color values you need exactly. If you don't set your own palette entries, Windows will try to find the best match in the current palette for any colors you request.

Creating a Palette

CPalette wraps up the Windows palette APIs for MFC applications. You can create a CPalette object and later initialize it with a call to CPalette::CreatePalette(). This function accepts a pointer to a LOGPALETTE structure, which is defined by the Windows API as a collection of PALETTEENTRY structures. These in turn are just a collection of red, green and blue color values, and some flags that are designed to tell Windows how to handle the palette entries.

You can get a list of palette entries for a particular range of the palette by calling `GetPaletteEntries()`. This function takes the range of entry numbers you're interested in using and copies the appropriate `PALETTEENTRY` values back to a buffer you've created and passed to the function. You can change these and call `SetPaletteEntries()` to place them back into the palette.

By calling `GetNearestPaletteIndex()`, you can look up a color supported by a palette (and a device). The function returns the index of the `PALETTEENTRY` that is the closest match to the `COLORREF` you passed to it.

Once you've created a `CPalette` with the entries you'd like, you can pass the palette to `CDC::SelectPalette()`. This will make Windows allow your application to draw with the palette you've created.

> **Be aware that this can affect other applications, since you might map colors that aren't used by any other applications, or you might delete colors that other applications do use. In some circumstances, selecting a palette can cause *your* application to paint correctly, while other applications will operate incorrect color mappings. Windows will always ensure that the active application paints correctly.**

You can switch colors in your application immediately by calling `AnimatePalette()`. This function gets its name from the way some animation techniques map unused palette entries to the window background color. They can then rotate different colors through masks in the bitmap to effectively make the bitmap appear as if it were moving.

Selecting a palette through a `SelectPalette()` call will result in the old palette being returned to you. You should be careful to select this palette back into your device context when you're done painting, so that Windows can correctly map colors for other applications.

CRgn

While you're drawing, it's sometimes convenient to apply a mask to the shapes you're creating. You may want to ask Windows to clip your drawing so that it's only inside a certain area, and doesn't overwrite other things you've drawn.

Regions

Windows does this work using regions. A **region** is simply the space defined by a rectangle, a polygon, an ellipse, or any combination of these shapes. Internally, Windows manages regions using a complicated data structure, together with some clever algorithms. You can access this code by creating a region and working with it in whatever way you see fit.

You can create a region by first creating an MFC `CRgn` object and then calling `CreateRectRgn()` against it. Regions based on different shapes can be created with `CreateEllipticRgn()` or `CreatePolygonRgn()`. These functions also have versions which accept pointers to their data, so that you can `CreateRectRgnIndirect()` instead of passing all four integers to `CreateRectRgn()`.

If you prefer, you can create a rectangle region with rounded corners by calling
`CreateRoundRectRgn()`.

Combining Multiple Regions

Once you've created a region using one of these functions, you can combine it with others that you've
created in the same way. To make a region from two rectangles, you should create another CRgn
object and initialize it by calling the `CreateRectRgn()` with the other rectangle, before calling
`CombineRgn()`on the two regions, like this:

```
CRgn rgnOne;
CRgn rgnTwo;

rgnOne.CreateRectRgn(10, 10, 50, 50);
rgnTwo.CreateRectRgn(100, 100, 125, 125);
rgnOne.CombineRgn(&rgnOne, &rgnTwo, RGN_OR);
```

After the `CombineRgn()` call, rgnOne will contain the unified region and rgnTwo will be
untouched. The third parameter to `CombineRgn()` dictates how the regions will be combined.
RGN_OR signifies that the resulting regions should be a union of the two basic regions, while
RGN_AND would signify that it should be the intersection between them. In the example given above,
the combined region would be empty if I used RGN_AND, since there's no common area between
rgnOne and rgnTwo.

RGN_XOR would combine the two and provide a region containing points in one, but not both, of the
source regions. The RGN_DIFF combination mode is unlike the others because it's not commutative.
The area in the second region is removed from the area in the first, and the resulting region is
returned.

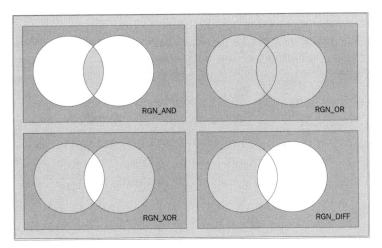

We didn't test or even save the return code from `CombineRgn()`, but if you took time to examine it,
you should note that it was a COMPLEXREGION (a region built from more than one simple shape) as
opposed to a SIMPLEREGION, which is composed of a region from a single shape.

We mentioned that RGN_AND in the above example would cause `CombineRgn()` to develop an
empty region; this would cause `CombineRgn()` to return NULLREGION. Windows does, however,

allow regions to be disjointed; the two shapes that you combine to form a region don't need to be adjacent or overlapping, as the example demonstrates.

As odd as it might sound, regions can be selected into the device context. The region can be selected as a **clipping region** using CDC::SelectClipRgn(). Any subsequent painting will be clipped by the region selected, which means that the output is limited to the region you specify. Unlike other selection functions, SelectClipRgn() doesn't return a handle to the old region. Windows makes a copy of the region you pass, so you can delete it immediately. However, SelectClipRgn() does return an integer indicating the type of the resulting region.

Using Regions for Hit Testing

Hit testing is the notion of getting a point from the user – usually where a mouse click has happened – and trying to find an object (or a part of an object) on the screen. When you click on a top-level window, Windows takes the mouse coordinates of that click and hit tests the window to determine where on the window you've clicked. Did you click on the title bar to move the window, or did you click on the edge to resize it?

It turns out that regions are very useful for hit testing. The PtInRegion() function accepts two integers defining a point, or a CPoint object. The function will return TRUE if the point is within the region, or FALSE if not. You can create a region for any object that you have floating about on the screen and then call PtInRegion() to see if the user has clicked on that object. If the item is indeed hit, you can call InvertRgn() to have Windows invert the area on the screen corresponding to the region your object occupies, informing the user that it has been selected. If the user deselects the object, you can call InvertRgn() again to make sure that it's redrawn correctly.

You can find the smallest rectangle bounding a region by calling GetRgnBox() against it. A complex region might be incredibly detailed, which means that Windows has to spend some time testing the region for a hit. Internally, Windows stores a region as a collection of rectangles – and as you can imagine, checking through a long list of rectangles to find out if they combine or disjoin to cover or uncover a given point is necessarily going to be a pricey operation. You might want to GetRgnBox() and test against the rectangle for a cheaper use of resources.

You can displace a region using OffsetRgn(). This function takes *x* and *y* axis displacements for the region, which may be negative, and moves the region as required. FillRgn() draws the region and fills it with paint. Since regions may be closed or irregular polygons, the rules for FillRgn() are quite complicated. You should check with the Windows documentation to make sure that things will work to your plan. PaintRgn() is similar to FillRgn(), but it uses the currently selected brush instead of accepting a parameter of a pointer to a CBrush object to be used to paint the region.

Stock Objects

Some painting operations are very common, such as painting things white, drawing black lines, or drawing some text with the system font. Windows provides a great many **stock objects**, available via a simple API call, to make sure that the GDI objects necessary for these common painting operations are readily available without having to be defined by the programmer.

MFC also makes these objects available, and does so perhaps a little more conveniently than the Windows API. You could call the Windows ::GetStockObject() API to get a handle to a stock object and then use it later in a ::SelectObject() call. MFC provides a shortcut in its

`CDC::SelectStockObject()` call, as the `SelectStockObject()` takes the same parameters as `::GetStockObject()` – symbols from `Windows.h` which identify each stock object. For example, `SYSTEM_FONT` is the Windows system font, `BLACK_PEN` is a black pen, `WHITE_BRUSH` is a white brush, and so on.

One point to remember is that these stock objects are always exactly what they say they are; that is, a `WHITE_BRUSH` is always a white brush. Windows doesn't, for example, automatically make a brush the same color as the background of a window; you should call the `::GetSysColor()` API to find out the color value for the current settings. These are the different stock objects you can use:

Stock Object	Description
ANSI_FIXED_FONT	An ANSI fixed system font
ANSI_VAR_FONT	An ANSI variable system font
BLACK_BRUSH	A black brush
BLACK_PEN	A black pen
DEFAULT_PALETTE	A default color palette
DEVICE_DEFAULT_FONT	A device-dependent font
DKGRAY_BRUSH	A dark gray brush
GRAY_BRUSH	A gray brush
HOLLOW_BRUSH	A hollow brush
LTGRAY_BRUSH	A light gray brush
NULL_BRUSH	A null brush
NULL_PEN	A null pen
OEM_FIXED_FONT	An OEM-dependent fixed font
SYSTEM_FIXED_FONT	The fixed-width system font used in Windows prior to version 3.0
SYSTEM_FONT	The system font
WHITE_BRUSH	A white brush
WHITE_PEN	A white pen

Remember that a `SelectStockObject()` will return a pointer to a `CGdiObject`. You'll have to cast this pointer to the type you want to store away. C++ can't tell which kind of function you want, even when informed of the manifest preprocessor constant, so the `SelectStockObject()` function doesn't offer overloads for different object types.

If you want to use a stock white brush, for example, you'll want to cast the return from SelectStockObject(), like this:

```
void CMyView::OnDraw(CDC* pDC)
{
    CBrush* pOldBrush = static_cast<CBrush*>(pDC->SelectStockObject(WHITE_BRUSH));
    CPen* pOldPen = static_cast<CPen*>(pDC->SelectStockObject(BLACK_PEN));

    // Do some drawing...

    pDC->SelectObject(pOldPen);
    pDC->SelectObject(pOldBrush);
}
```

The calls to SelectStockObject() require casts, but the calls to SelectObject() don't.

Splitter Windows

Until now, we've only talked about applications that present one main window for their user interface. For some applications it's interesting to have two related sections of the application's document visible in the application. Applications that can potentially render vast ranges of information to the user are common candidates for this sort of user interface. Excel, for example, allows you to split your view of a spreadsheet and independently scroll over each half of the window, or over a different portion of the sheet.

Some of our applications, like PaintObj from Chapter 4, could easily contain more information than could possibly fit on one screen. Even though we allow scrolling, the user might be interested in seeing information from different parts of the document at the same time. By allowing the user to split their view of the window, we can get more stuff under their nose in the same amount of space. Best of all, the user can see information from the same document that isn't spatially contiguous, even when there's no hope of all of it (and everything in between) fitting on their screen.

Unfortunately, painting this kind of window is a real chore. You have to run the paint code twice, essentially fooling it into believing that the window is smaller than it really is, and transposing the coordinates painted into each half of the split. As you would expect, it's a mathematician's dream but a programmer's nightmare.

Of course, I wouldn't have brought this problem up if MFC didn't provide some solution! That solution turns out to be the CSplitterWnd class. CSplitterWnd is a special window class provided by MFC to live inside your application's frame window. Before we discuss how to incorporate a splitter window into the design of our application, let's quickly review the different types of splitter that are available.

The Different Kinds of Splitters

First off, the term **splitter** tends to get used for both the CSplitterWnd class and the windows it represents, so try not to get confused – it should be clear what's intended from the context. With that out of the way, let's take some time to think a little about the way a CSplitterWnd is used within your application, and the semantic rules that must be true for the class to make any sense.

When the user splits a window, they might decide to add another pane either horizontally or vertically. This means that the splitter will have to request that another view be created to fill the area to the right of, or below the divider. A user can also further divide a window, requiring three new views to be created immediately. This will fill the area to the right of, beneath, and to the bottom right of the existing window, giving a quartering effect.

The CSplitterWnd class is capable of doing all of this work since, as it is created, it records contextual information about the document template. This lets the splitter know what document and which view class will be referenced by the new view windows. You can develop code to have the splitter generate different views for each pane in the window, or alternatively you can let it generate a new instance of the same view type used in the original window. I'll show you both of these approaches during the rest of this chapter.

You should first decide how you'd like the user to approach the splitter window in your application. You'll have two general choices: a **dynamic splitter**, or a **static splitter**.

Dynamic Splitters

Dynamic splitters allow the user to split the window at their leisure. The figure here shows an application with a dynamic splitter, just after it's been started. The application has small boxes, one above the vertical scrollbar and one to the left of the horizontal scrollbar. These can be dragged to split the window in one direction or the other:

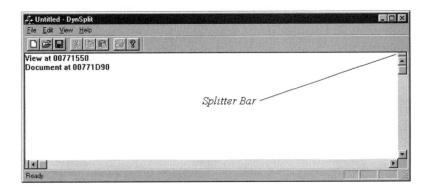

After dragging the box above the vertical bar down a little, the window splits and automatically creates another view:

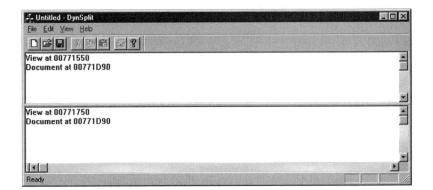

To set up this kind of splitter, you'll need to declare an instance of `CSplitterWnd` in your application's frame window; for SDI applications produced using AppWizard, this will be in the `CMainFrame` class.

To initialize a dynamic splitter window, you create it when the framework wants to create a client area of the frame window. Normally, the frame window will simply create the view and have it inserted into the client area of the frame, but instead you can have the splitter create and insert itself into the frame. The splitter will initialize a single view to populate itself, and will create more views when the user splits the window's content.

In the screenshots above, you'll notice that the client area of the windows showing pointer values for both the view object and the document object being shown. The extra view created by the split window is based on the same document as the original view. The new view is attached to the document after it is created. The original view remains – it's just cropped to allow room for the new view.

To get your frame to create the splitter, install an override of the `OnCreateClient()` function. For a dynamic splitter in an SDI application, the function just needs something like this:

```
BOOL CMainFrame::OnCreateClient(LPCREATESTRUCT lpcs, CCreateContext* pContext)
{
    return m_wndSplitter.Create(this, 2, 2, CSize(1, 1), pContext);
}
```

The `CSplitterWnd::Create()` function accepts a few parameters. The first is a pointer to the parent window of the splitter, which must be the frame. Your next two parameters are the maximum number of rows and columns that the splitter will support. You can force it to disallow horizontal splits by passing 1 for the maximum number of rows, or, to avoid vertical splits, by passing 1 for the maximum number of columns. Such a window won't have a split box on the appropriate side of the window.

Multiple Dynamic Splitters

Dynamic splitters in MFC are unable to support more than two rows and two columns. If you try to pass numbers larger than two to the `Create()` function, you'll trip a landslide of `ASSERT()` messages in your debug build.

The value of `CSize()` that was passed to the function will cause the splitter to enforce lower size limit for the panes it creates. A size of 1 x 1, as we used above, effectively makes the splitter allow any window size. If, because of its content, your view has problems painting in terribly small windows, you may want to enforce a lower limit on your splitter by passing a larger `CSize` to the creation function.

MFC won't allow your user to create a pane smaller than your passed `CSize`. It will snap the pane shut when the user lets go of the mouse while dragging a new size. Debug builds of MFC will cough up an appropriate warning like:

```
Warning: split too small to create new pane.
Warning: split too small to fit in a new pane.
```

So, given the way all this works, with the splitter creating all of the views, how does the splitter know what view to create? How can it hook it up to the right document?

You can see from our sample OnCreateClient() function that the pContext parameter gets passed on to the Create() function in CSplitterWnd. This points at the contextual information that tells the CSplitterWnd code what should handle the creation of the new view and its subsequent attachment to a document.

MDI Applications

In an MDI application, CMDIChildWnd acts as the frame for views, so you'll need first to create a CMDIChildWnd subclass in your application. You can easily do this by using the ClassWizard to declare a class with your own name, based upon CMDIChildWnd. Add a CSplitterWnd instance to the protected data in that new class and create a handler for the OnCreateClient() to do the creation for the dynamic splitter window, like this:

```
BOOL CChildFrame::OnCreateClient(LPCREATESTRUCT lpcs,
                                              CCreateContext* pContext)
{
    return m_wndSplitter.Create(this, 2, 2, CSize(1, 1), pContext);
}
```

In older versions of Visual C++, code generated by AppWizard for an application's InitInstance() registered a document template based directly on CMDIChildWnd. However, since Visual C++ 4.0, the AppWizard has created code that makes a class based on CMDIChildWnd, and it's *this* class that is used in the document template. AppWizard names the class CChildFrame, since instances of the class will represent windows that are children of the CMainFrame class that creates the application's main frame window.

Whenever an MDI child window is created, the OnCreateClient() member will create the client area of the window by calling the Create() function in the splitter window instance within the application. It's the CSplitterWnd::Create() function that, in turn, creates a view to work against the application's default document.

You can register any type of template you'd like in the application's startup code. If you want, you can register an additional CMultiDocTemplate object that manages the same view and document types as your splitter-enabled document template, but that doesn't include splitters itself.

Using Different Views in Dynamic Panes

The code snippet from CChildFrame::OnCreateClient() shown above will result in a splitter that contains two instances of CView, registered in the document template which created the frame. You can use a different view in the extra panes of your splitter, which allows you to convey information in a different manner side-by-side with information in another view. I've implemented this functionality in the XSplit application shown here:

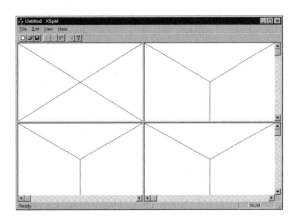

When the user creates new panes in a dynamic splitter window, MFC calls the CreateView() function of the CSplitterWnd class to perform the creation. Normally, this code runs off and creates the required view, based on the context information passed through the pContext parameter. If pContext is NULL, the function does a little bit of querying to figure out what view is active and tries to create the same one.

You'll need to derive your own class from CSplitterWnd if you want to have different views in the panes of your application's dynamic splitter window. You'll also have to override the CreateView() function, creating the view of your choice. Fortunately, the overriding code is simple – just pass the call along to CSplitterWnd::CreateView(), naming the RUNTIME_CLASS of the view class you wish to create for the splitter.

The code to perform this task isn't very impressive:

```
BOOL CMySplitter::CreateView(int row, int col, CRuntimeClass* pViewClass,
                             SIZE sizeInit, CCreateContext* pContext)
{
    if (row == 0 && col == 0)
    {
        return CSplitterWnd::CreateView(row, col, pViewClass,
                                                sizeInit, pContext);
    }
    else
    {
        return CSplitterWnd::CreateView(row, col, RUNTIME_CLASS(CYView),
                                                sizeInit, pContext);
    }
}
```

Here, we check to see if the view is being created at row 0 and column 0 in the splitter. If it is, that means the splitter is being initialized right now, and we'll create a view object of the class requested; in other words, the first view created will be the one that was asked for. However, if the view is being created at a position other than the very first, we'll return the RUNTIME_CLASS() of the CYView class.

Using a CRuntimeClass Object

In fact, this isn't completely obvious from the code, because the calls to CreateView() supply a pointer to a CRuntimeClass object. As you might remember, CRuntimeClass describes the runtime type information for a class. Given this pointer, the code inside of CreateView() can accomplish the construction of whatever object the runtime type information describes.

The above code fragment is a part of the XSplit sample available from the Wrox web site; you can find the code in MySplit.cpp. This sample manages two views: CXView and CYView. It doesn't manage any data, but denotes CYView by drawing a 'Y' in its client area, and CXView by drawing an 'X'. (Feel free to reuse these amazingly functional classes in your own applications.) If you set a breakpoint on the CMySplitterWnd::CreateView() function and play with the application, you'll learn some important facts about the splitter window class. Most notably, you'll find out that the splitter will destroy views that are no longer visible and recreate them later. This effectively means that the life of a splitter and its views might be described by the following table:

User Action	Splitter Response
Start the application (`CFrameWnd` creates the `CSplitterWnd` within it)	Create a view at (0,0).
Drag the horizontal splitter box down	Create a view at (1,0).
Drag the vertical splitter box over	Create a view at (0,1). Also create a view at (1,1), as there are four panes now.
Drag the horizontal splitter box up, erasing the split	Destroy the panes at (0,0) and (1,0).
Drag the horizontal splitter down again, recreating the split	Create a view at (1,0) again, and then create the view at (1,1) as we have four panes again.

If you try this out, then you'll end up with four 'Y' views. You can fix this by ensuring that only row 1 or column 1 is ever deleted.

You can see that the splitter window does a lot of work to juggle the logical row and column position of the views in the splitter. Behind the scenes it's also doing a bunch of math to lay out each view window in the client area of the splitter correctly.

Using Splitters with More than One Document

Everything we've described about splitter windows (and the code to demonstrate it in the XSplit sample), clearly applies to situations where your new view will reference the same document as the existing views. But what if you want another document in there too? For multiple document scenarios you'll need to create the splitter and actually give it a different creation context. You have to let it know that it must instantiate new documents and views, as well as moving the view window to the correct coordinates so that it fits with the rest of the window. Believe it or not, this last part is harder than the whole of the rest of the process put together!

You can avoid doing all of this work by ditching the call to `CSplitterWnd::CreateView()`. The trick is to develop your own creation context to pass along to the `CreateView()` function, while letting it know just what needs to be done.

The `pContext` parameter is a pointer to a `CCreateContext` object. This object records which frame, object and document should be used for the newly created document/view pair. In this fragment, we build our own `CCreateContext` object called `ctxMine`. The object is initialized to have the view, document and template information we want to create in the new splitter pane:

```
BOOL CYourSplitter::CreateView(int row, int col, CRuntimeClass* pViewClass,
                               SIZE sizeInit, CCreateContext* pContext)
{
    CCreateContext   ctxMine;

    // If there is no active view, we can't work this way...
    CView* pOldView = static_cast<CView*>(GetActivePane());
    ASSERT(pOldView == NULL);
    // You should test pOldView here and do something reasonable
```

```
    // Find out where the old view is
    ctxMine.m_pLastView = pOldView;
    ctxMine.m_pCurrentDoc = pOldView->GetDocument();
    ctxMine.m_pNewDocTemplate = m_pCurrentDoc->GetDocTemplate();

    // Pass call along
    return CSplitterWnd::CreateView(row, col, pOldView->GetRuntimeClass(),
                                        sizeInit, &ctxMine);
}
```

MFC uses the information in the `CCreateContext` object to create properly and attach the new view window to an existing document and frame window. The view creation code in MFC needs to know about the template as well as the objects involved so that it can properly create the new view and get it communicating with the existing objects.

Static Splitters

Static splitters are used in applications where dynamic splitters are inadequate or inappropriate. They can be used when your application needs to show more than two split rows or two split columns.

If you're interested in having your window split (no matter what the column or row count), but don't want to allow the user to select how and where the splits should occur, then you should use a static splitter instead of a dynamic splitter. This is because it's easier to code what you need than it is to write code to negate the actions of MFC.

Static splitters still use the `CSplitterWnd` class, but require a slightly different creation mechanism. You'll still put a `CCreateContext` instance in the `CFrameWnd` or `CMDIChildWnd` derivative of your application, but your override of the `OnCreateClient()` function will contain quite different code.

Creating a Static Splitter

To begin with, you should call `CSplitterWnd::CreateStatic()` instead of `CSplitterWnd::Create()`. The `CreateStatic()` function still creates and wires up the splitter, but you'll need to create the individual panes yourself. If you don't, MFC will toss more `ASSERT`s than you can shake a stick at and your application will crash. To create the panes, call `CreateView()` on the `CSplitterWnd` object you're using. You'll need to make one `CSplitterWnd` call for each splitter pane you add.

Code to create a static splitter with five rows and three columns, from the `StaSplit` sample, looks like this:

```
BOOL CMainFrame::OnCreateClient( LPCREATESTRUCT /*lpcs*/,
    CCreateContext* pContext)
{
    CRect rect;
    GetClientRect(rect);
    CString str;
    str.Format(_T("View at 12345678\r\nDocument at 12345678"));
    dc.DrawText(str, rect, DT_CALCRECT);

    BOOL bRet;
    int nRow;
```

```
        int nCol;

        if(!m_wndSplitter.CreateStatic(this, 5, 3))
            return FALSE;

    for (nRow = 0; nRow < 5; nRow++)
        for (nCol = 0; nCol < 3; nCol++)
        {
            bRet = m_wndSplitter.CreateView(nRow, nCol,
                RUNTIME_CLASS(CStaSplitView),
                rect.Size(), pContext);
            if (bRet ==  FALSE)
                return FALSE;
        }

    return TRUE;
}
```

The code preceding the loop, which calls `DrawText()`, just estimates how big some text will be. It doesn't actually draw any text – the `DT_CALCRECT` flag causes the function to return the rectangle needed to contain the text. Since the `OnDraw()` function implemented by the view will draw text that looks very similar, measuring this text lets us have a reasonable initial size for the splitter panes that is sure to show the text we're planning to draw.

If we were interested in having different views in each pane, we could code the function to pass different `RUNTIME_CLASS()` information for each `CreateView()` call.

I've outlined ways to add a splitter window to your application manually in this chapter mainly because a splitter window is most often an afterthought. If you're starting from scratch, you can check the Use Splitter Window *in your application's* MDI Child Frame *or* Frame Window *page. You can reach this checkbox by pressing the* Advanced... *button in step four of the AppWizard. The AppWizard always sets up a dynamic splitter, though – so if you're after a static splitter, you'll probably find it just as easy to create an application without a splitter window and then manually add the code yourself afterwards.*

Splitters and Performance

Splitters make it easy to chop up the client area of your frame or MDI children to make them hold more than one view. However, this means that your view's painting code will be called many more times than before the split.

Your view window will necessarily be smaller than it was before you adopted a splitter window, so you need to make sure your view doesn't do any drawing that it doesn't need to – namely, beyond the bounds of the window. This will help assure the greatest possible performance from your application. This is by far and away the most important consideration for applications that paint their views repeatedly in the different panes of a splitter window.

The likelihood that one view will change when another visible view must update its content for the same document is also much greater when you're working with splitter windows. You should think about the different views in your application and try to assure that your `UpdateAllViews()` or `UpdateView()` calls pass enough information to the updating view, thus ensuring that it can do the smallest amount of repainting required.

Summary

Through this chapter, I've tried to indicate the scope of functionality provided to allow you to implement your user interface, either by API wrappers (as in the case of device contexts), or less directly (as with `CSplitterView`). All of these functions follow the Microsoft line, giving an interface that has a standard look-and-feel. Of course, what you draw in the client area of your window is entirely up to you. In the next chapter, I'll show how you can deviate from this path, if that suits your purpose better.

7

Advanced User Interface Programming

MFC does a lot of work to make sure your applications have a rich, standard "look and feel" for their users. Sometimes though, this general standard isn't what you want. For instance, you may want the window title to be centered, rather than left-justified; you may want to have user-configurable menus; or perhaps you would like to use a different font in your dialogs. MFC doesn't support any of these things directly, so to implement features like those described, you need to do a little bit of your own work.

In this chapter, we'll cover:

- ➢ Dialogs and how to handle them in your application
- ➢ Context menus and handling command messages dynamically
- ➢ Subclassing controls and using owner-draw controls

Caveat

Before we go any further, a bit of a warning is in order:

Don't change or deviate from existing user interfaces too radically.

If your application doesn't fit in with other applications on the desktop, your users might not like it. If they don't like it, they won't use it. If they won't use it, you've wasted your effort. Microsoft has spent a lot of time and money on usability tests, so you can use this investment yourself by following the user interface guidelines described by Microsoft.

This isn't to say that you shouldn't change the appearance of the interface, because, let's face it, not even Microsoft gets it right every time. Furthermore, you know your users and you know best when determining how they will perceive your application; you may decide to make your product a little bit different from everyone else's.

About CWnd

Throughout our coverage of the MFC classes so far, we've neglected any deep analysis of an important MFC-supplied class: CWnd. MFC uses CWnd as a basis for all window-based classes. CWnd, which is derived from CCmdTarget, is the parent class for almost every class that manipulates a window, including borderless windows like CView and controls like CButton and CEdit. CWnd is also the parent of CFrameWnd, which represents a window containing menus and borders, and CDialog, which creates dialog boxes. Indeed, CWnd controls every aspect of window manipulation in MFC, right down to the tiniest control window associated with a push button – the kind of thing that's returned from a CDialog::GetDlgItem() call.

Back in my first years at school, I somehow found out you could subtract a large number from a smaller number and end up with a negative number. My math teacher, interested in protecting her curriculum, insisted that negative numbers just didn't exist and that I couldn't subtract twelve from eight to get negative four. I was angry: I knew it was possible. I even smuggled my brother's expensive Hewlett-Packard calculator into school to prove it! I've done something of the same so far in the book; to simplify the discussion of other MFC features, I've neglected the fact that CWnd exists and is very usable.

Before you fire off angry e-mails at me, please understand that until now we haven't needed to do anything with CWnd directly, and so we've never discussed it. Aside from converting a pointer to CWnd to the specific Windows control wrapper class we needed, the CWnd hasn't been of specific interest, just like negative numbers really weren't that important to the average first grader back in that math class. After all, it would turn out to be more than twelve years before I would try to balance my checkbook.

So, let's take this time to pull the facts out of the shadows. It's important to know that CWnd:

> Encapsulates all of the features of a window
> Provides an m_hWnd member variable which holds the handle of a window after it's created, or NULL if the window hasn't been created or has since been destroyed
> Wraps the functions in the Windows API which manipulate windows
> Abstracts the Windows HWND data type
> Counts MoveWindow(), SetWindowPos(), ShowWindow() and GetDC() among its huge list of member functions
> Has members which react to window messages, providing default behavior for the CWnd-derived classes your application uses
> Allows you to supply non-virtual members which respond to messages yourself and usurp the default behavior

You'll only use CWnd directly if you're trying to pull cool stunts with existing MFC classes which derive from CWnd, or if you're working to add your own window classes to your application. Let's take a look at some of the things you can play with.

System Level Messages

Beyond the normal window messages, CWnd also has handlers for system-level messages which Windows sends to applications. This notifies Windows that the system palette has changed, for example, or that important settings in the Windows system registry have been altered. By implementing functions to process these messages for the main window of your application, you allow your application to react appropriately when the user changes the time and date format, system time or color settings for the system.

If your application needs to know the current time, or the current default system font, or the current system-wide colorsettings, it will find those settings with calls to GetSystemmetrics(), GetSysColor(), or SystemParametersInfo(). But the user can update those settings with the Control Panel at any time. If you cache settings returned from those APIs, you'll need to know when they change. That's easy; just watch for WM_SETTINGCHANGE messages, which are broadcast to all top-level windows active at the time any change is made.

A **top-level** window is one which exists at the top of the window hierarchy – regardless of where it lives in the C++ hierarchy of classes which implement windows in your applications. A top-level window has no parent, neither is it a child of the desktop window. Your application's main window is almost always a top-level window, and dialog boxes are sometimes top-level windows, too. You'll therefore want to add your WM_SETTINGCHANGE handler to your application's main frame window implementation.

CWnd's Interaction with CCmdTarget

Perhaps the most interesting feature of CWnd is its interaction with CCmdTarget. As you'll recall from our discussion in Chapter 3, CWnd implements the mechanism for discovering which active window object will handle any given Windows message sent to the application. If the message turns out to be a WM_COMMAND message, code in CCmdTarget may finish the job by routing the message to other windows – or even to non-windowed objects, like we described in Chapter 4. But CWnd does all of the work for plain system messages like WM_PAINT or WM_CLOSE. While the classes work together to do the dispatch work, CWnd contains the default message procedure, which will eventually be called to take care of the messages.

If the handler for the Windows message wasn't found while searching the message map for classes which were the actual target of the message, or if the message handler eventually routed control for handling the message to a class which didn't want to do anything interesting with the message, then MFC will end up calling CWnd::Default(), which is the default message handling function. Default() doesn't do anything but call CWnd::DefWindowProc(), which is a virtual function that, in turn, calls the appropriate message handler that's either built into Windows, or previously supplied by the window before it was subclassed. We'll describe what "subclassing" means and how it is done in the next section.

`Default()` doesn't take any parameters. Instead, it references the parameters for the current message that MFC has squirreled away in the `m_msgCur` member of the thread object handling the message. It would actually take a bit of extra work, for each and every message the thread processed, to reassemble the `lParam` and `wParam` parameters based on the message, before sending them along to the default handler. Since the vast majority of messages that an application processes aren't actually handled by the application but are instead given to Windows to allow it to implement the default behavior, repackaging the messages would have an undesirable impact on the efficiency of any application.

You can write a handler to intercept messages that affect your application in a general sense. For example, you may want to set up a global application state whenever your main frame is activated. In that situation, it could be efficient to handle `WM_TIMER` messages in `CWnd::PreTranslateMessage()` so you can provide code to handle background printing or communications tasks.

While the real task in ice hockey is to control your assignment by forechecking or backchecking, the real task of `CWnd::DefWindowProc()` is to provide a way for MFC applications to subclass the windows that they own.

Don't confuse `CWnd::DefWindowProc()` with `::DefWindowProc()`. The first is a member function which MFC supports; the second is a Windows API function that does something reasonable (and in many cases, necessary), in response to a Windows message that wasn't otherwise handled by the application.

In an MFC application, `CWnd::DefWindowProc()` may call the `::DefWindowProc()` API if no part of the application is interested in handling the message at hand. This section may appear a little wordy, but it's important not to get the two functions mixed up. To help, I'll pedantically write `CWnd::DefWindowProc()` to make sure you know when I'm talking about the MFC member function and not the Windows API with the same name.

Subclassing

Subclassing, in the context of Windows programming, describes the notion of providing an extra message handling routine for a particular instance of a window. That extra message processing function is called in lieu of the normal message handling function – often, the latter is a part of Windows itself. The new message handler can delegate messages it isn't interested in to the original handler. In this way, you can use subclassing to make slight modifications to the functionality of a window.

Of course, subclassing can take on a meaning more closely related to its original and true object-oriented definition; it might also mean writing your own derived classes when you're dispatching messages. Thankfully, you don't need to mess around with callbacks or default functions. You just declare your message map appropriately and get on with it.

Subclassing is useful when you know that some part of Windows has the user interface you want, but the Windows implementation doesn't quite do everything you'd like it to – a technique which parallels C++ subclassing in MFC. You should subclass a MFC class when you know it covers most of the task you set, but some of its functionality needs expanding or, sometimes, eliminating.

Comparing MFC to Windows

Windows subclassing and C++ subclassing are conceptually similar, but implemented in two very different ways. C++ subclassing is very formal; you have to make all of the proper declarations and carefully implement code that the compiler agrees with. On the other hand, Windows subclassing lets you declare a function that will be called each time a message is sent to the window you've subclassed. You can react to the message by passing it to the original window procedure where it will be handled normally, or you can have your function do all the work.

Protecting Controls

A typical (and common) situation where subclassing is an extremely appropriate technique is in the development of special controls. We alluded to this earlier, in Chapter 5, when we discussed the 'live' validation of characters typed into edit controls. Normally, an edit control notifies its parent after the user has typed a character and the control is just about to accept, or has just accepted, that character. Unfortunately, this is often way too late. The content of the control has already been changed and you're going to be hard pressed to determine how the typed character affected the content of the control. This makes it difficult, if not impossible, to use the messages provided by Windows to interactively and immediately put range checks or content checks on an edit control.

It would be wonderful if you could intercept the Windows WM_CHAR, WM_KEYDOWN or WM_KEYUP messages to snag the keys offered to the control before the control itself sees them. If you see a character you don't like, you simply wouldn't offer it to the edit control. It's a type of subclassing which provides the capability of seeing messages destined for a window before the window actually sees them.

The task of protecting a Windows edit control in this manner can be separated into two distinct parts. The first is subclassing the control in a way which MFC likes, and the second is writing the code to do the character validation. Since the code to do the character validation isn't that hard, you can look at the EditNab sample to see how it's really done – the code you're after is in the Nabber.cpp file. Here, we validate social security numbers; these nine-digit pieces of Americana identify each person who pays taxes in the United States and are normally divided into three-, two- and four-digit groups. Typical numbers might be 123-55-8734 or 765-51-0953.

The other part of our subclassing problem, the notion of letting MFC sink its teeth into every message the application ends up handling, is one that's common to any subclassing problem you'll face.

The SubclassWindow() Function

You may remember from our discussion of CCmdTarget that MFC knows the whereabouts of all windows by way of a map. Using this map, MFC can translate the window handle associated with any message, to a pointer to a CWnd object which represents the target of that message. If it finds a message handler in that CWnd object, CCmdTarget will call the function. On the other hand, if CCmdTarget can't find a match, it calls the CWnd::DefWindowProc() function. In turn, this function normally calls the Windows ::DefWindowProc() API to handle the message in a way that Windows will really dig.

What we need to do is to step in and let MFC know our code should handle *every* message sent to the window and not let DefWindowProc() (neither the CWnd member nor the Windows API function) get the message unless we say so. The gateway to this kingdom is the SubclassWindow() function, a member of the CWnd class.

If MFC creates a window for you by constructing a CWnd-derived object and then calls one of its create functions (like Create() or CreateEx() or DoModal() – depending on what's appropriate for your situation and the window type you're creating), it implicitly subclasses the window during the creation process. MFC handles every message sent to the window until you either disassociate the C++ object from the window, or until the window is destroyed.

But if you have an existing CWnd object that doesn't reference a window, you can use SubclassWindow() which takes a window handle as its only parameter. Calling SubclassWindow() against a given window attaches the CWnd object to the window handle, subclassing the existing window procedure. You may subclass an existing edit control in a dialog with code like this:

```
BOOL CEditNabDlg::OnInitDialog()
{
    // Initialization bits & pieces

    // Grab a pointer to the edit control
    CWnd* pEdit;
    pEdit = GetDlgItem(IDC_SSN);
    ASSERT(pEdit != NULL);

    // Make the control use the system fixed-width font
    // because with numbers and dashes, it will look nicer
    HFONT hFont = static_cast<HFONT>(::GetStockObject(SYSTEM_FIXED_FONT));
    CFont* pFont = CFont::FromHandle(hFont);
    pEdit->SetFont(pFont);

    // Subclass the edit control so it's connected to our CNabbedEdit class
    m_Nabbed.SubclassWindow(pEdit->m_hWnd);

    return TRUE;  // return TRUE  unless you set the focus to a control
}
```

Note that in this case we don't save the control's original font when we change it with the call to SetFont(). Since we know we're the only users of the control, and we have no need to use the original font, we end up changing it once and for all, without regard for restoring its original setting.

From the point when this code is executed, the messages sent or posted to the IDC_SSN control are offered first to the m_Nabbed object, an instance of CNabbedEdit. This is a class that derives (in the C++ sense) from the MFC CEdit class. Since, after the SubclassWindow() call, the CNabbedEdit class becomes a living, breathing MFC window, it will start to receive messages via the CCmdTarget instance inside the CEdit class. You can perform the edits using ClassWizard to create message map entries for WM_CHAR, and to code whatever validation you need in response to those messages.

In the Nabbed sample's NabDlg.h file, you can see that an object of the CNabbedEdit class is a member object of the application's dialog class. When the dialog is constructed, the CNabbedEdit object is also constructed. The CNabbedEdit object in that new CDialog-derived object does absolutely nothing until we let both Windows and MFC know we intend to use it to subclass one of the controls on the dialog. When the dialog initializes, the SubclassWindow() call is made against the social security number edit control. The EditNab sample doesn't have to do anything to undo the subclassing, because the subclassing is disconnected when the dialog window is closed.

It would certainly be possible, within the bounds of the C++ language, to use a local instance of the CNabbedEdit class and call SubclassWindow() on that. This almost certainly isn't an acceptable approach, since the CNabbedEdit instance has to outlive the control which it subclasses. Declaring a subclassing MFC class locally to a function is almost worthless because there are very few functions which continue to run while messages are being dispatched. The subclassing code would never be installed while messages were being received.

Finally, let me point out that there's an interesting situation where subclassing can implicitly occur. You'll recall that we investigated the DDX_Control() routine back in Chapter 5. DDX_Control() ties an instance of a CWnd-derived class to a window instance, normally a dialog box. The function will subclass the window for the lifetime of the dialog box.

This is where we leave the discussion on subclassing – we shall be returning to it later in this chapter.

Painting in Dialogs

Dialog boxes receive WM_PAINT messages just like any other window. However, you'll infrequently perform any processing in response to these messages, since controls are capable of painting themselves. If you want to alter the way a control paints itself, you'll end up subclassing the control within the dialog and handling the message yourself.

If you do anything in response to a WM_PAINT, you should be aware that dialog boxes work a little differently than regular windows do. The coordinate system in a dialog box is dynamically set up by Windows, based on the font in use within the dialog. Windows does this dynamic computation so that the dialog box will automatically adjust itself to whatever display resolution and system font is installed and active on the machine where the dialog ends up being created.

When working with a dialog box, developers need to refer to a special coordinate system called **dialog units**. When Windows creates a dialog box, it expects the coordinates describing each control in the dialog template to be in dialog units. It converts these numbers to screen and window coordinates on the fly as it creates the dialog. If you paint, move, or dynamically create controls in the dialog yourself, you will need to understand dialog units before you can use them properly. Of course, Windows offers a couple of API functions to help you.

The ::GetDialogBaseUnits() API returns a DWORD which contains the horizontal base unit in the low word and the vertical base unit in the high word. Given these two numbers, you'll need to do a little math to convert from dialog units to screen or client coordinates. In the following example, I use GetWindowRect() to find the window position of a given control and then do the math to get the real coordinates:

```
RECT rectWindow;
RECT rectConverted;
DWORD DBU = ::GetDialogBaseUnits();

CWnd* pEditControl = GetDlgItem(IDE_EDIT1);
pEditControl->GetWindowRect(&rectWindow);
ScreenToClient(&rectWindow);
rectConverted.left = (rectWindow.left * LOWORD(DBU)) /4;
rectConverted.top = (rectWindow.top * HIWORD(DBU)) /8;
rectConverted.right = (rectWindow.right * LOWORD(DBU)) /4;
rectConverted.bottom = (rectWindow.bottom * HIWORD(DBU)) /8;
```

Division by four and eight is required because Windows defines a horizontal dialog unit as being equal to four horizontal base units, and a vertical dialog unit as eight vertical base units.

If your dialog box is based on the system font, then `::GetDialogBaseUnits()` and the above code will work and will return the correct values based on your input. If your dialog box uses a different font (which it probably does), you'll have to figure the dialog base units out by yourself! You can do this by measuring a string of a few characters to determine the width of an average character, and then do the same division.

Solving Non-System Font Problems

The horizontal base unit is equal to the average width, in pixels, of the characters in the dialog's font. The vertical base unit is equal to the height, in pixels, of the dialog font. Based on this information, you can just take these metrics of the font in your dialog and perform the necessary calculations upon them instead of using the values returned from the `::GetDialogBaseUnits()` API.

The easiest way to get this information is to call `GetObject()` on the font that the dialog is using. You can ask the dialog for the `HFONT` currently being used by calling `GetFont()` on the window. (This function actually returns a pointer to a `CFont` object, but has an `HFONT()` operator defined.) So, maybe in your `WM_INITDIALOG` handler, you can initialize your own `DWORD` of dialog base unit information.

Assuming that we have a `DWORD` member variable, named `m_DBU`, in the dialog box class, the code might go something like this:

```
void CMyDialog::OnInitDialog()
{
    //...call the base class, other code, too...
    HFONT hfMine = GetFont();
    LOGFONT lf;
    ::GetObject(hfMine, sizeof(lf), &lf);
    m_DBU = MAKELONG(lf.lfHeight, lf.lfWidth);
    //...maybe more code...
}
```

After this code has run, you can go ahead and use `m_DBU`, just as if it were the real `DWORD` returned from `::GetDialogBaseUnits()`, working with the same ratios which were mentioned before.

Here, I used the Windows `GetObject()` API directly, since we're just playing with the `HFONT` and don't really need any of the extra functionality that MFC provides after wrapping the data structures. We call `GetObject()` on the `HFONT` to find the `LOGFONT` structure containing the information we need: the `lfHeight` and `lfWidth` of the font. With this code in tow, you can run off and convert all of the coordinates you need and paint away!

You can also use the `CDialog::MapDialogRect()` function to convert a whole rectangle at a time. `MapDialogRect()` will use whatever font you've established for the dialog, converting from dialog units to pixels.

Coloring Your Controls

You don't need to be Ted Turner to see value in adding a little bit of color to your dialog boxes. Many applications warrant the use of color in dialogs to draw attention to error conditions or controls that have more meaning than others do – according to the particular mode or situation.

Since Windows will draw all of the controls in your application, you'll need to work carefully with Windows to get the colors of controls within your dialog changed. Windows will send your dialog messages from the WM_CTLCOLOR family to let your application know that it's preparing to paint a particular control. Back in 16-bit versions of Windows, there was simply a single message, named WM_CTLCOLOR, which would notify your application that something was about to be repainted. Win32, on the other hand, sends a different kind of message for each kind of control which is being painted. Here's a table that shows the messages you'll receive for each kind of control:

Message	Controls
WM_CTLCOLORBTN	Buttons, including check boxes and radio buttons.
WM_CTLCOLORDLG	The dialog box itself – this message is used when Windows wants to erase the dialog's background.
WM_CTLCOLOREDIT	Edit controls.
WM_CTLCOLORLISTBOX	List box and list view controls.
WM_CTLCOLORMSGBOX	Message boxes. This message allows you to set the color of text in, and the background of, a message box created with the ::MessageBox() API or the AfxMessageBox() function.
WM_CTLCOLORSCROLLBAR	Scroll bar controls.
WM_CTLCOLORSTATIC	Static text controls.

Notice that some controls don't have WM_CTLCOLOR messages; for example, you can't change the color used in an up-down control or a progress control. You can trap any of these messages individually with the appropriate ON_MESSAGE() MFC message map entry. Normally, you'll write an OnCtlColor() handler for your window. When MFC calls your OnCtlColor() handler, it's actually doing so in response to any of several messages: WM_CTLCOLORBTN, WM_CTLCOLOREDIT, WM_CTLCOLORLISTBOX, WM_CTLCOLORMSGBOX, WM_CTLCOLORSCROLLBAR, or WM_CTLCOLORSTATIC. All of these messages have very similar effects, but MFC bundles them into one override so that older code from Win16 days doesn't need to be modified; Win16 had only one WM_CTLCOLOR message.

The prototype for OnCtlColor() looks like this:

```
HBRUSH OnCtlColor(CDC*  pDC,
                  CWnd* pWnd,
                  UINT  nCtlColor);
```

OnCtlColor(), the CDialog member which handles WM_CTLCOLOR messages, receives three parameters: a pointer to a CDC, a pointer to a CWnd, and a UINT that indicates which type of window is to be painted. You can identify the window which is about to be painted by checking the value of nCtlColor against one of the constants in the table below:

nCtlColor Value	Meaning
CTLCOLOR_BTN	Button controls, including push buttons, radio buttons, check boxes and the drop-down button that might appear in a combo box
CTLCOLOR_DLG	The dialog box itself
CTLCOLOR_EDIT	Edit controls, including the edit control that might appear as a part of a combo box
CTLCOLOR_LISTBOX	A list box control, including the list box which might appear when a combo box becomes active
CTLCOLOR_MSGBOX	Message boxes
CTLCOLOR_SCROLLBAR	Scroll bar controls
CTLCOLOR_STATIC	Static text controls

Obviously, each constant indicates which type of control is being handled by a particular WM_CTLCOLOR message. You can figure out *exactly* which control in your dialog is being painted by checking the CWnd object in your dialog. One way to use the CWnd to find a control would be to get the control of your dreams and compare the m_hWnd members of each object. If you want to handle WM_CTLCOLOR for an edit control named IDC_EDITONE, for example, you might code something like this:

```
HBRUSH CColorCtlDlg::OnCtlColor(CDC* pDC, CWnd* pWnd, UINT nCtlColor)
{
    HBRUSH hbr = CDialog::OnCtlColor(pDC, pWnd, nCtlColor);

    CWnd* pEditCtrl;
    pEditCtrl = GetDlgItem(IDC_EDITONE);
    if (pEditCtrl->m_hWnd == pWnd->m_hWnd)
    {
        // Handle it!
        // Set hbr to something...
    }
    return hbr;
}
```

This will work just fine, but it's a little inefficient because it creates a temporary CWnd object which it doesn't really need. A better approach would be to use the GetDlgCtrlID() member of CWnd to get the ID of the control referenced by pWnd. You could then perform a simple integer comparison for each control that made you curious using code like this:

```
HBRUSH CColorCtlDlg::OnCtlColor(CDC* pDC, CWnd* pWnd, UINT nCtlColor)
{
    HBRUSH hbr = CDialog::OnCtlColor(pDC, pWnd, nCtlColor);

    int nCtrl = pWnd->GetDlgCtrlID();
    if (nCtrl == IDC_EDITONE)
    {
        // Handle it!
        // Set hbr to something...
    }
    return hbr;
}
```

The CDC object provides a pointer to a device context which is owned by Windows. You must treat the device context you receive very carefully. Since it is owned by Windows, any foolish tricks you pull can directly affect the stability of your application. Windows keeps the device context local to your application, so you won't be able to crash the whole of Windows if you make a mistake. But you will notice that your application can get awfully sick if you do something like delete a brush or select a bad bitmap.

Once you've determined that a WM_CTLCOLOR message for a control is of interest to you, you will need to react to the message by setting drawing attributes in the device context you've received to paint the control correctly. If the control you're working with features text, you can make calls to SetTextColor() and SetBkColor() to change the color of the text and the text background the control will use. In your OnCtlColor() function, you can change the text colors without worrying about saving the values previously selected in the device context, i.e. you can safely ignore the values returned from SetTextColor() and SetBkColor() in your device context. Such freedom is yours, because Windows will always do WM_CTLCOLOR processing for every control in the dialog. Each time Windows paints a control, it will reset the color values and doesn't rely on values kept current in the device context.

Transparency and Controls

If you haven't come across it yet, you might want to learn about the SetBkMode() function. This member of CDC lets you tell Windows how to paint the background of text painted with calls to ExtTextOut(), TextOut(), or DrawText(). The text background mode can be either OPAQUE or TRANSPARENT. If the background mode is OPAQUE, the text output functions will use the background color set by SetBkColor() to draw the background of the text. If the background mode is TRANSPARENT, calls to the text output functions will result in text that's drawn with the text color on whatever background happens to be specified at the time. You can set the background mode with a call to SetBkMode(), and pass the TRANSPARENT or OPAQUE constants defined by Windows.

The background (or face) of the control will be painted by Windows using the brush which your OnCtlColor() function returns. If you are not interested in changing the colors, you can return the value from the base-class implementation of OnCtlColor() – a technique you'll see evident in the flow of control in our code snippets above. If you *are* interested in meddling with the brush, however, you'll need to return an HBRUSH for a brush which your code owns.

Unfortunately, Windows doesn't accept an MFC CBrush structure, and MFC provides no automatic conversion between what is returned by your implementation of OnCtlColor() and what Windows requires. In these circumstances, you return either an HBRUSH you've cooked up using direct SDK calls, or the m_hObject member of a CBrush object you're managing.

The CBrush destructor *will* delete the m_hBrush object, as the CBrush object goes out of scope. That means that if you make the CBrush object local to your OnCtlColor() implementation, you'll meet with disaster – the HBRUSH you return from the CBrush object will be deleted before it goes back to Windows. Windows will find itself trying to paint with a deleted brush, which isn't effective at all!

In fact, if the return from your OnCtlColor() function is a bogus brush, Windows will assume your application ignored the WM_CTLCOLOR message and will perform *all* of the default processing for you. If you only want to change the foreground color of text in a control, you'll need to call the base class implementation of OnCtlColor() *before* you call SetTextColor(). If you make the call to SetTextColor() first, the default implementation will effectively undo your change. In this case, you simply return the brush you received from the default implementation. If you are interested in changing the brush, then you'll have your own brush ready to return, but you will still want to call the base class implementation to set the foreground and background color if you're not going to do it yourself.

To implement an OnCtlColor() handler correctly, you'll need to make CBrush objects members of your CDialog-derived class. In your OnInitDialog() function, you may wish to initialize the brushes by calling the appropriate CBrush member function – CreateSolidBrush(), for example. If you need to change the color you're using to paint in response to OnCtlColor(), you call the DeleteObject() member of the CBrush object before calling initialization functions like CreateSolidBrush() against it.

The ColorCtl sample application shows how to write a decent OnCtlColor() handler. The handler implements color changes for a few different controls in the application's dialog – some of the controls are always changed to the same color, while others are changed to a selectable color. The sample also features a control which lets you set the text background mode for the list box in the dialog, demonstrating the use of SetBkMode(). This sample should provide a great basis for your work with WM_CTLCOLOR.

Remember that WM_CTLCOLOR is sent to your application as Windows responds to WM_ERASEBKGND and WM_PAINT messages – that is, WM_CTLCOLOR isn't sent to your application unless some painting is being done. If you need to programmatically change a control from one color to another, you'll probably want to call the Invalidate() member of CWnd against your dialog, or against a particular control within it, in order to generate a paint message and effect the color change that you've planned.

You need to make your handling of WM_CTLCOLOR as efficient as possible, because one WM_CTLCOLOR message is sent for each control in your dialog box, and one more is sent for the dialog itself. If your WM_CTLCOLOR processing takes too long, you'll notice your dialog box paints very slowly – controls in the dialog will seem to fill in gradually rather than appearing immediately when the dialog box is shown.

When WM_CTLCOLOR Won't Do

The WM_CTLCOLOR messages give your application a chance to change the color scheme for a control without changing the global color settings for all of Windows. You can handle WM_CTLCOLOR if you want some text in your dialog to be a different color than what's set in Control Panel. WM_CTLCOLOR, though, isn't capable of changing the color of individual items within a list box or combo box, though it can change the color of *all* items in these controls in one go, as well as change the background color for these controls.

If you need to change the colors of individual items, you'll want to implement an owner-draw control, or perhaps handle all painting for the control by subclassing it. I'll explain how to perform subclassing in more detail and implement owner-draw controls with MFC later on in this chapter.

Modifying Common Dialogs

We've already talked about the various common dialogs that Windows lets us use in place of rewriting common functions for each of our applications, but sometimes the common dialog boxes fall just a wee bit short of what we really need. We might want to use the File Open dialog handler, but have it produce a dialog with a completely different appearance. We might want to use the Font dialog, but provide our own complex rules for deciding which fonts are shown and which aren't.

Thankfully, Windows provides us with a convenient way to get at the code that populates these boxes and readily allows us to hook our code into the dialogs.

The Windows Common Dialog Templates

If you want to start off with the Windows version of the dialog, you should have a look at the \vc98\Include directory. Here, you'll find files that contain the templates Windows uses for the various common dialogs, as well as the header appropriate for accessing the symbols in the templates. Even if you only need to make the tiniest of modifications, you'll find it easier to start by copying one of these templates to your application's own resource file.

> *Think carefully before making changes that aren't absolutely necessary for your cause. Your users might hate it if you've made what they perceive to be gratuitous changes to the dialog – you could be ruining their familiarity with the existing and established dialogs, and making it a little more difficult for them to use the software you've written.*

You must then copy the Dlgs.h header file to get the manifest constants for the control IDs. You can see the specific file for each of the dialogs you'll want to use in this table:

Template Filename	Dialog Box
Color.dlg	Color
Fileopen.dlg	Open (single selection)
Fileopen.dlg	Open (multiple selection)
Findtext.dlg	Find
Findtext.dlg	Replace
Font.dlg	Font
Prnsetup.dlg	Print
Prnsetup.dlg	Print Setup

Once you've set up the dialog in your project, you can get to work on hooking up your code. I imported the `Fileopen.dlg` file for the `IDD_MYSAVE` and `IDD_MYOPEN` resource in the `Stdboxes` sample. If you aren't adding or removing any controls, you can just point the appropriate MFC common dialog wrapper to the template you've added. Do this by adjusting the `hInstance` and `lpTemplateName` fields of the controlling structure in the common dialog object. For `CFontDialog`, the tweak would look like this:

```
// :
// maybe other initialization
// :

dlgFont.m_cf.hInstance = AfxGetResourceHandle();
dlgFont.m_cf.lpTemplateName = MAKEINTRESOURCE(IDD_MYFONTTEMPLATE);
dlgFont.m_cf.Flags |= CF_ENABLETEMPLATE;

// :
// run off and use it!
// :
```

You'll want to modify the `m_cf` members before you actually create the dialog – putting this code in the constructor for your `CFontDialog`-derived class would be a swell idea. The `Myopen.cpp` and `Mysave.cpp` files in the `Stdboxes` sample demonstrate the same setup code, though it uses the `CFileDialog` class to get its work done.

By setting the `CF_ENABLETEMPLATE` bit in `m_cf.Flags`, we can instruct the Windows code to use our template and resource handle rather than its own. You'll have to use the Windows `MAKEINTRESOURCE()` macro to convert the integer ID of your resource to a resource designation; if your resource is identified by a name and not an integer with a manifest constant, you need not use it. The `AfxGetResourceHandle()` function returns the handle of the module containing the resources of your program.

Explorer Style Boxes

The File Open and File Save dialog boxes created by `StdBoxes`, using the code in `Myopen.cpp`, look like an old Windows application. That is, they're based on the standard dialog boxes that were in Windows NT 3.51, and those boxes don't look very different from the boxes that came in 16-bit versions of Windows. Windows 95/98, and Windows NT 4.0 employ a user interface based around the Windows Explorer. The Explorer provides more interesting file dialog boxes, which look like this:

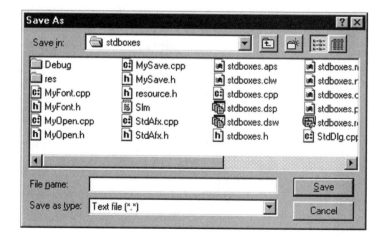

If you create a **File Open** or **File Save** dialog using MFC's `CFileDialog` class, you can request that your dialog use either the new Explorer style or the traditional MFC dialog style. The `CFileDialog`, as discussed in Chapter 5, has a member structure called m_ofn, which contains lots of parameters that describe the operation of the dialog. One of the bits that can be set in the `Flags` member of that structure is `OFN_EXPLORER`. MFC initializes this bit to be set, so your applications get the new dialog by default, but you can set it or clear it at your will.

If you're porting an older program to Win32 and your program already supplies a customized dialog box template, you'll probably want to clear the `OFN_EXPLORER` style so the box continues to work properly. Then, when you get the chance, you can fix your code so it works correctly with the new dialog style, and can begin to look and work like all other applications. If you're writing a new application, you'll probably want to keep the `OFN_EXPLORER` style.

In the context of customizing a **File Open** or a **File Save** dialog box, the `OFN_EXPLORER` flag has a very special meaning. If you specify the `OFN_EXPLORER` bit, Windows will use the template you supply to *add* to the dialog box – the dialog template you supply won't completely replace the stock dialog built into Windows. If you've still got some applications you're porting and you want it to enjoy the benefits of the Explorer-style dialogs, make sure that you have the `OFN_EXPLORER` bit set.

The most important thing to know when creating a dialog template to hold the new controls for your customized box is you *must* use special style bits on your resource, otherwise the creation of the dialog will fail. Your dialog must have these following styles set:

Style Bit	What to do in the Dialog Editor	Meaning
WS_CHILD	Select **Child** in the **Style:** drop-down list on the **Styles** tab	Your new dialog will be created by Windows as a child of the normal dialog box
DS_CONTROL	Mark the **Control** box in the **More Styles** tab	This style facilitates seamlessly integrated keyboard control for your dialog and the rest of the controls in the stock dialog
DS_3DLOOK	Mark the **3D-look** box in the **More Styles** tab	Provides your controls with the same 'chiseled' three-dimensional appearance as the stock controls
WS_CLIPSIBLINGS	Mark the **Clip siblings** box on the **Styles** tab	Causes your dialog to paint outside areas of the window in use by controls that already exist in the stock dialog box

All these styles really only affect the way the controls in your dialog box appear. Given these styles, they'll draw neatly and have an appearance similar to that of the other controls in the dialog. You don't have to be particular about borders or captions in your add-on dialog box because Windows will strip those styles from your dialog as it is created. You can't use the dialog template to create a border or a caption for your extra controls.

The WS_CHILD style is the most important of these styles. It means exactly what it implies. Windows will create a common file dialog box with the appropriate controls, and the controls on the dialog will be child windows of the dialog box. Windows will then attempt to create your additional dialog box. If successful, it will make your dialog box a child of the original common dialog box. Your controls are a child of that secondary dialog box window.

Windows will enlarge the common dialog box by adding the populated height of your box to the bottom of the common window, and the populated width of your box to the right edge of the existing common window. Once that work is done, the dialog is displayed. StdBoxes displays this enhanced dialog, for example (can *you* spot the difference?):

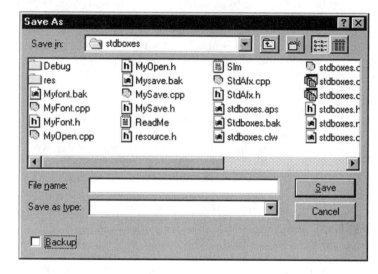

The IDD_EXPLORERSAVE dialog template, in the StdBoxes sample, is really only a little higher and wider than the Backup button itself. By carefully sizing the button, you can make sure your custom dialog box looks nice.

When the code for the customized Save dialog in the sample initializes the CFileDialog template to display this customized box (found in the Mysave.cpp source file), it simply tells Windows that the OFN_EXPLORER flag bit is needed, along with the OFN_ENABLETEMPLATE bit. With those two bits set, the supplied dialog box resource will extend (and not replace) the existing controls on the common dialog.

Changing Behavior

Changing the behavior of a given common dialog is easily done by subclassing the MFC class that handles that dialog. You can allow the base class to handle most of the work, just stepping in with your own overrides of virtual functions and message handlers when the time is appropriate. Later in the chapter, in the section titled 'The Gentle Art of Subclassing', you can read a detailed comparison of Windows-style subclassing and C++ subclassing.

The StdBoxes sample application has a Font dialog box which only lists fonts that have face names beginning with the letter *M*. The box in this code, called CMyFont, subclasses the MFC-provided CFontDialog. To get the box to list only fonts that begin with the letter *M*, I took a terribly lazy (but strangely forceful) approach – calling the CFontDialog code to fill the box, and then deleting all the entries from the box, except those beginning with the letter *M*.

This code is pretty simple – you can find it in the `OnInitDialog()` handler in the `MyFont.cpp` file within the `StdBoxes` sample:

```
BOOL CMyFont::OnInitDialog()
{
    CFontDialog::OnInitDialog();
    CComboBox* pBox = static_cast<CComboBox*>(GetDlgItem(IDC_FONTLIST));

    int nIndex;
    CString strBuffer;

    for (nIndex = pBox->GetCount()-1; nIndex >= 0; nIndex--)
    {
        pBox->GetLBText(nIndex, strBuffer);
        if (strBuffer.GetLength() > 0)
            if (strBuffer[0] != _T('m') && strBuffer[0] != _T('M'))
            {
                pBox->DeleteString(nIndex);
            }
    }

    return TRUE;   // return TRUE unless you set the focus to a control
                   // EXCEPTION: OCX Property Pages should return FALSE
}
```

Just as with the file dialog, I had to import the definition for the font dialog from the `Include` directory. I named the dialog box instead of keeping its integer ID around, because ClassWizard doesn't like dialogs with plain integer IDs – it must see a manifest constant.

I used ClassWizard to add the dialog to the project and created `CMyFont`, basing the class on `CDialog`. Next, I went back to the code and made sure that anything referencing `CDialog` was changed to `CFontDialog`. Most importantly, the declaration of the class in `MyFont.h` had to be fixed so the `CMyFont` class derived from `CFontDialog` and not `CDialog`. This shows up everywhere. Remember to search through your header file as well as your implementation file (even the `CDialog` references) for invocations of MFC macros like `BEGIN_MESSAGE_MAP()`.

The Class Constructor

As a consequence of these actions, the constructor for the class has been tweaked as well. MFC normally sets up the constructor so that the subclass passes everything it needs to the normal `CDialog` constructor. Our code needs to create `CFontDialog` instead, and that has a very different constructor. For example, you could tweak the code from ClassWizard so it looks like this:

```
CMyFontDialog::CMyFontDialog(CWnd* pParent /*=NULL*/)
    : CFontDialog()
{
    //{{AFX_DATA_INIT(CMyFontDialog)
        // NOTE: the ClassWizard will add member initialization here
    //}}AFX_DATA_INIT
}
```

The most important change that we made here was to make the initializer call the `CFontDialog` constructor, not that of `CDialog`. For this little sample, we're not interested in constructor parameters. It would have been pretty easy to change the code so it accepted all the parameters that `CFontDialog` takes; we would just need to pass them along to the `CFontDialog` constructor. In the sample, I chose to alter the constructor to accept the additional parameters.

The OnInitDialog() Function

With all of this done, the only remaining task is to write the handler for `OnInitDialog()`. When we add this function with ClassWizard, the Wizard may produce code which calls the `CDialog` implementation of `OnInitDialog()`. Of course, this default implementation doesn't do anything for our font dialogs – we want to call `CFontDialog::OnInitDialog()`. This function will work just fine against our dialog template because we were careful to import the dialog template from the Windows header file. Since all of the child control IDs are correct, the code in `CFontDialog`'s `OnInitDialog()` implementation (and the Windows code which it calls to get some work done) will be fine.

We can override more functions if we want to, which we'll cover in the next section. For now, the code in the application will work just fine, allowing us to step in and serve our own needs by tweaking what we want in the `OnInitDialog()` function. We call the 'real' implementation of `OnInitDialog()` first, to make sure it does all the work it needs to and doesn't undo anything we initiated.

You should notice that ClassWizard will, by default, set up an empty `DoDataExchange()` function for you. For most cases, where you subclass a common dialog, you'll find that you don't need to use a `DoDataExchange()` function. The overriding function is harmless, but you can delete it if you see fit.

MFC OLE Functionality

Finally, try to keep this section in mind when we come to talk about OLE, as MFC grants you a good deal of OLE functionality. Some of this arrives in the implementation of dialogs which offer parts of a standardized user interface for OLE functions. We won't discuss those here because, like those negative numbers, we don't need to know anything about OLE yet. While these dialogs *are* common for all applications, they aren't truly Windows common dialogs – they're part of the OLE common user interface. The point is that this same technique of overriding the functionality that the class normally provides can also be applied to those OLE dialogs. This will be important later. Just look forward to it!

Adding Controls

You may decide you want to tweak a common dialog box by adding an extra control. For instance, imagine you want to add a check box to the standard file save dialog which allows you to create a backup file if the box is checked, and to avoid the generation of the `.bak` file if the box isn't.

To start such an endeavor, you'd only need to do a little more work than was described in the previous section. Get going by importing the dialog template from the header file and adding it to your own project before editing the template to create your check box, naming it as you see fit.

When you generate the C++ class for your dialog with ClassWizard, go back and add a member variable to the class which will be used to reflect the state of your check box. You might, as your design flair dictates, add a function which returns the state. This is an alternative to letting users of your dialog box romp around in the member variables of your class. In other words, you might think it more appropriate to have a function named `GetBackupFlag()` that returns a `BOOL` to indicate the state of the flag, than to allow folks to touch `m_bBackupFlag` directly.

To set the flag that reflects the state of the control correctly, you can create an override for OnOK() in your subclass. Here, check the state of your check box first, set the member variable of your C++ class, then call the default MFC and Windows handlers for the messages to dismiss the visible dialog and absorb the rest of the information collected by the box. The sample application does this in the Mysave.cpp file, where I implement a CMySave class that behaves just as I've suggested in this section.

More Advanced Techniques

Windows provides for the need to 'hook' any message the standard dialog may pass around. This is enabled by setting the OFN_ENABLEHOOK flag in the Flags member of the m_ofn structure of the controlling dialog. Through the magic of MFC and C++, we don't need to fool around with this sort of function. Once you've created the C++ class for your customized common dialog box, MFC takes ownership of everything that happens. Your subclass effectively acts as its own hook procedure. If you don't handle a message, it will be passed along to the default MFC or Windows implementations, or both. In fact, you *mustn't* specify your own hook function using OFN_ENABLEHOOK because MFC needs the hook in order to manage your class' relationship with the dialog and the control windows it creates.

For the cases where you do derive your own version of one of the common dialog classes, make sure you call the base class implementation of any of the functions you override. Otherwise, you'll make Windows angry by not letting it see the messages it needs to see. Of course, you might have a need to completely override the functionality that the default implementation provides. In these situations, test your code carefully; you might be overlooking a scenario where Windows finds itself in a strange state because you didn't pass a message to it!

> *Remember that the common dialog boxes are an asset because they are just that – common. This means users are used to seeing the same* File Open *or* Font *dialog boxes in every application they use. If you change your dialogs so substantially that they're very different from the norm, you're probably safe – safe, that is, as long as you're willing to buy off the fact that you're now responsible for documenting and explaining the different dialogs, and that your users are responsible for learning how they work.*

> *But, irony of ironies, if you change the dialogs subtly, you'll probably annoy your users more than the wholesale redesign. They'll see your dialog box and expect the standard dialog box actions. They'll be disappointed when their favorite keyboard or mouse shortcuts don't work!*

Cool Painting Tricks

Sometimes, you may feel the client area of your window just isn't big enough to express yourself to the world. While MFC offers status bars and toolbars, you may want to tweak the way your application draws its frame window, caption and borders. You can present information to your user in the borders around your window's caption by subtly changing the way your application paints them.

If you're interested in simply changing these features of your application, you should think carefully about how to do so. Most of the time, you can alter the style bits of the window to achieve the effect you want. You can tweak the style bits or class information of your window by overriding the `PreCreateWindow()` function. MFC calls `PreCreateWindow()` on any `CWnd` object being created just before it calls the Windows `::CreateWindow()` API for that window. The `PreCreateWindow()` function is passed a reference to a structure of type `CREATESTRUCT`, which contains a bunch of information that Windows will offer to the target window as it is created. Your override of the `PreCreateWindow()` function can doctor the contents of this structure to change the style, menu, title or other features of the window.

You can modify the style via bit-wise manipulation of the style member of this structure. To ensure your window has a caption, you could write:

```
cs.style |= WS_CAPTION;
```

To make sure the window *doesn't* have a caption, you can knock out the caption bit by using the bit-wise AND operator against the compliment of the caption flag, like this:

```
cs.style &= ~WS_CAPTION;
```

You can find out about all of the other interesting `CREATESTRUCT` fields by having a peek at the online references, although modifying the `style` member is by far the most popular for modifying the type of window created.

The default implementation of `PreCreateWindow()` checks for a `NULL` window class name and substitutes the appropriate default. For example, if you're creating a frame window, the MFC standard class name for a frame window is used. You'll usually call `PreCreateWindow()` in the base class before you modify any of the `CREATESTRUCT` members.

When PreCreateWindow() isn't Enough

Sometimes, overriding `PreCreateWindow()` isn't enough. It's nice to be able to change the color or text in your caption bar, or even handle the painting of the borders on your window yourself. This ensures that you get exactly what you need from your user interface.

You shouldn't really completely tear down the user interface that Windows has made standard over the years. You can often get enough information into the non-client areas of your window to draw immediate attention to the things that the user must be informed about. You could put the time into the caption bar, for instance, or paint a red, yellow and green stoplight there to indicate intuitively the overall status of the application.

Responding to WM_NCPAINT Messages

Tweaks to your application's caption bar and window frame can be brought about by your code if you write a response to the `WM_NCPAINT` message. This message is sent by Windows to your application at the point when it is required to draw its non-client area. By default, Windows paints the standard window features based on the style bits specified at the time the painting is done. However, by handling the message yourself, you can paint whatever you like. You may also need to trap `WM_NCACTIVATE`, to make sure your painting code reacts correctly when the window is activated or deactivated.

Be careful with code that touches the non-client area of your application's windows, because the user interface standards in Windows are changing. Major changes in the size, shape and format of standard Windows buttons, system menus, borders and captions occurred for the Windows 95 and NT 4.0 operating systems. If you are considering porting code to older versions of Windows, such as Windows NT 3.51, for instance, you have to make sure that the changes you might make to the user interface are compatible with that system. You might want to provide differing code for each operating system, or you might decide to allow any unrecognized operating system version to handle its own non-client area painting.

With Windows 98, more changes have been introduced. In fact, the sample we're about to examine can help you paint a fade from one side of the title bar to the other. That's great, but it turns out the capability to have faded caption bars is already a feature of Windows 98, but has to be specifically coded in Windows 95/NT 4.0 to have the same effect. Further changes to the user interface are included in Windows 2000.

To test and see whether you have the new user interface, your application should call the Windows `GetVersionEx()` API. If `GetVersionEx()` returns Version 4.0 or better, you know that your user has the new shell user interface. If the version isn't one you specifically recognize, you may wish to abort your customization in order to assure the user's stability and give your application some more longevity.

Coding a Handler for WM_NCPAINT

If you still decide to do this work in spite of all the caveats, you'll need to code a handler for `WM_NCPAINT`. The `EditNab` sample has such a handler in `Caption.cpp`, which makes use of the standard handler for the message in Windows by calling `CDialog::OnNcPaint()`. If this was a regular pop-up window, we would call `CWnd::OnNcPaint()` or `CFrameWnd::OnNcPaint()`, just to get the base class to help you with the message.

In the sample, we implement a `PaintCaption()` function which draws the caption, depending on the setting of radio buttons in the dialog. We call `PaintCaption()` after calling the `OnNcPaint()` message to draw the caption, thereby erasing the work carried out by Windows. The code looks like this:

```
void CCaptioner::OnNcPaint()
{
    CDialog::OnNcPaint();
    BOOL bActive;

    if (GetActiveWindow() == this)
        bActive = TRUE;
    else
        bActive = FALSE;

    PaintCaption(bActive);
}
```

The code in `PaintCaption()` itself is pretty simple, but looks a bit confusing. It has to do lots of measuring to figure out the size and location of the caption. Calculations to find these rectangles rely on lots of calls to the Windows `::GetSystemMetrics()` API:

```cpp
void CCaptioner::PaintCaption(BOOL bActive)
{
    int nFrameHeight = ::GetSystemMetrics(SM_CYDLGFRAME);
    int nFrameWidth = ::GetSystemMetrics(SM_CXDLGFRAME);
    int nMarkerHeight = ::GetSystemMetrics(SM_CYSIZE);
    int nMarkerWidth = ::GetSystemMetrics(SM_CXSIZE);

    COLORREF rgbTextBackground;
    COLORREF rgbTextForeground;

    if (bActive == TRUE)
    {
        rgbTextForeground = ::GetSysColor(COLOR_CAPTIONTEXT);
        rgbTextBackground = ::GetSysColor(COLOR_ACTIVECAPTION);
    }
    else
    {
        rgbTextForeground = ::GetSysColor(COLOR_INACTIVECAPTIONTEXT);
        rgbTextBackground = ::GetSysColor(COLOR_INACTIVECAPTION);
    }

    CString strCaption;
    GetWindowText(strCaption);

    int nStartTop;
    int nStartLeft;
    CRect rectCaption;
    CRect rectWindow;

    GetWindowRect(&rectWindow);
    rectCaption.left = nFrameWidth + 1;
    rectCaption.right = rectWindow.Width() - nMarkerWidth - nFrameWidth;
    rectCaption.top = nFrameHeight+1;
    rectCaption.bottom = nFrameHeight + nMarkerHeight;

    CWindowDC dc(this);

    CFont* pOld;
    NONCLIENTMETRICS ncm;
    ncm.cbSize = sizeof(NONCLIENTMETRICS);
    ::SystemParametersInfo(SPI_GETNONCLIENTMETRICS, 0, &ncm, 0);
    CFont* pNew = new CFont;
    BOOL bMustDelete = TRUE;
    if (!pNew->CreateFontIndirect(&ncm.lfCaptionFont))
    {
        delete pNew;
        pNew = GetFont();
        bMustDelete = FALSE;
    }

    pOld = static_cast<CFont*>(dc.SelectObject(pNew));

    CSize szText = dc.GetTextExtent(strCaption);
    if (szText.cy <= nMarkerHeight)
        nStartTop = rectCaption.top + (nMarkerHeight - szText.cy)/2;
    else
        nStartTop = rectCaption.top;
```

```
    if (m_nAlignment == 0)
        nStartLeft = rectCaption.left;
    else if (m_nAlignment == 1)
        nStartLeft = rectCaption.right - szText.cx;
    else
        nStartLeft = rectCaption.Width()/2 - szText.cx/2;

    COLORREF rgbOldText = dc.SetTextColor(rgbTextForeground);
    COLORREF rgbOldBack = dc.SetBkColor(rgbTextBackground);
    int nOldMode = dc.SetBkMode(OPAQUE);

    dc.ExtTextOut(nStartLeft, nStartTop, ETO_CLIPPED | ETO_OPAQUE,
                                    &rectCaption, strCaption, 0);

    dc.SelectObject(pOld);
    dc.SetTextColor(rgbOldText);
    dc.SetBkColor(rgbOldBack);
    dc.SetBkMode(nOldMode);

    if (bMustDelete)
        delete pNew;
    return;
}
```

You'll have to change some of these calls if you're making this code work in a pop-up window, since they have a different border size from that of dialogs. If you screw up the code for the measurements, or forget to call the default message handler in the base class, then you could end up with a weird-looking window caption – perhaps one that's not quite centered or justified. Or you may find yourself with a window which has its sizing buttons partially overwritten by the opaque rectangle used as a background for the text drawn in the caption area.

Finally, this code demonstrates that fooling around with non-client features is a real chore. The code works fine, if you don't have a secondary color defined for your title bar – that is, if you don't have a fade in your window captions. The code to measure the colors and paint the fade is a little more substantial, so I've not shown it here so I don't distract you from the subclassing mechanism at hand. Believe it or not, even I will leave something as an exercise for the reader!

PaintCaption() takes a BOOL which is TRUE if the window is active and FALSE if it isn't. Of course, the caption changes color when the window becomes active or becomes inactive, so the painting code needs to know which color to use in each event. You'll note that the sample *doesn't* hook-up a notification to repaint the caption when the window becomes active or inactive – that isn't necessary, because Windows itself will invalidate our non-client area. That invalidation will cause a WM_NCPAINT message to be sent, and we'll decide which colors to use to reflect the activation ourselves.

The default handler for the WM_NCPAINT message will paint the Window's non-client area features for us, which includes the title bar. To get the effect of painting our own title bar, the easiest thing to do is wait until Windows has completed its own painting of the title bar before repainting the area according to your own needs. You can, if you're doing a more difficult task, look at the region that was passed with the WM_NCPAINT message, to see for yourself the area that Windows needs to repaint.

Unfortunately, the OnNcPaint() handler doesn't take a parameter for the region passed in the message. If you need to handle this part of the message, you can create your own handler by putting an ON_MESSAGE() invocation in your message map and using the wParam value as the region.

You'll notice that the function shown above makes a call to the Windows API `::SystemParametersInfo()`, which provides information about a wealth of things. On this occasion, it's used to find the exact font used in window captions. You can pass this API a variety of different parameters to get or set most of the configurable aspects of Windows. Note that you shouldn't cache these settings, because the user can change them during the lifetime of your application. If the user changes one of the settings, your application will be sent a `WM_SETTINGCHANGE` message.

Small Title Bars

In previous versions of Windows, a fairly common application for non-client painting techniques was the development of a window with very small borders and a very small caption area. You might have seen many applications that display windows like this one:

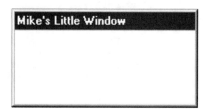

The window is an instance of `CMiniFrameWnd`, which is ideal for a frame around any property pages, toolbars or floating tool palettes that you might develop. `CMiniFrameWnd` is a drop-in replacement for `CFrameWnd`, except that it does not support minimize or maximize buttons. Like `CFrameWnd`, `CMiniFrameWnd` can be its own pop-up and doesn't have to be a child window. `CMiniFrameWnd` is actually derived from `CFrameWnd` and, with the exception of its constructor and its `Create()` member function, it has almost the same functionality as `CFrameWnd`.

In these versions of Windows, that is, 95/98 and NT 4.0/2000, implementing non-client painting to build a smaller caption isn't necessary because the appropriate use of the `WS_EX_TOOLWINDOW` style will have Windows handling the small caption for you. You can still use `CMiniFrameWnd`; it's just that MFC ignores the specialized painting code.

Creating CWnd Objects

As yet, we've not described any direct creation of `CWnd`-style objects, so now is as good a time as any. When you call the `Create()` function of a `CWnd` derived object like `CFrameWnd` or `CMiniFrameWnd`, you'll need first to register the information about the actual window class with MFC, which then registers the class with Windows. This is necessary to allow MFC to manage any windows created through this class. Note that `CDialog`-based windows don't make use of this mechanism, as the dialog box definition inherently provides all the information necessary to create the window.

To register the window class you need with MFC, call `AfxRegisterWndClass()`. As its first parameter, this function takes the combination of flags you'd normally use in the `style` member of a `WNDCLASS` structure with the Windows `RegisterClass()` API. These **class style** bits actually affect *all* windows created from the class, not just a particular window instance. Allowed class styles include `CS_HREDRAW` and `CS_VREDRAW`, which we'll examine in a moment. Other interesting class styles are `CS_DBLCLKS`, which allows windows of the class to receive `WM_LBUTTONDBLCLK` and `WM_RBUTTONDBLCLK` messages when the user double-clicks the mouse, and `CS_BYTEALIGNCLIENT` that can be used on frame windows to improve drawing speed.

The three subsequent parameters to the function are optional. They default to zero, but can be handles to the cursor, background brush or icon you wish the class to use. The prototype for the function looks like this:

```
LPCTSTR AFXAPI AfxRegisterWndClass(UINT     nClassStyle,
                                   HCURSOR hCursor = 0,
                                   HBRUSH  hbrBackground = 0,
                                   HICON   hIcon = 0);
```

The CS_HREDRAW and CS_VREDRAW bits cause windows created with the style to be redrawn any time the size is changed, whether horizontally or vertically. Since this means your entire window will repaint for a resize operation, you may wish to register a class which doesn't feature these bits – or at least knock these bits out of the window style that is used when you handle PreCreateWindow() – if your window has to perform a long, complicated painting operation.

Successful Registration

If the registration is successful, the function will return a pointer to a string. This pointer will contain MFC's special version of the class name for Windows to use when it's creating the window. You'll need to make a copy of this result before going on, since MFC uses a single static buffer (localized for each thread running against the library) to hold the return value from this string. A CString object is ideal for your copy of the string.

To throw together a simple mini-frame window quickly, you might write code like this:

```
CMiniFrameWnd wndMini;

CString strClass = AfxRegisterWndClass(
                        CS_VREDRAW | CS_HREDRAW,
                        ::LoadCursor(NULL, IDC_ARROW),
                        static_cast<HBRUSH>(::GetStockObject(WHITE_BRUSH)),
                        ::LoadIcon(NULL, IDI_APPLICATION) );

wndMini.Create(strClass, _T("Mike's Little Window"), MFS_MOVEFRAME,
                                        CRect(50, 50, 200, 130));
wndMini.ShowWindow(SW_NORMAL);
```

For clarity, we've declared the CMiniFrameWnd object in our code fragment as a local variable. Of course, since the mini-frame C++ object must outlive the Windows object, you would never declare the CMiniFrameWnd object within the function where you initialize the window. The C++ object would be destroyed and MFC would get sick, since it would be trying to process messages belonging to a dead object. More realistically, you might put the wndMini object in the CWinApp object or the CMainFrame object, whichever has the more appropriate life span.

CMiniFrameWnd's Create() function takes the class string from AfxRegisterWndClass() as its first parameter. The function assumes the title for the window as its second parameter, and a set of flags for the window class that dictate how it will perform as the third parameter. The final parameter is a reference to a CRect that dictates the initial size and position of the window. The icon will be shown when the window is minimized.

We have allowed the user to move the window by specifying MFS_MOVEFRAME. You could use MFS_4THICKFRAME to disallow sizing of the mini-frame, or use MFS_THICKFRAME to create a window that can be sized at will. MFS_SYNCACTIVE will cause the miniature pop-up to activate itself at the same time its parent window becomes active. Of course, having two windows active is impossible, but this just means that the mini-frame window will be painted and look active whenever its parent becomes active.

For other CWnd-derivative classes, the style parameter can be a combination of the normal Window styles like WS_POPUP or WS_CHILD. For the CMiniFrameWnd class, you can combine these WS_ styles with the MFS_ styles outlined above. You should beware of using styles that are incompatible with the mini-frame window. You must have a WS_CAPTION, and a mini-frame window is always a WS_POPUP.

Dynamic and Pop-up Menus

After all this talk about message maps and command dispatch mechanisms, it's probably obvious that message handling in MFC is designed to be rather static. This fact isn't very disturbing until you realize that you might like to alter your menus dynamically via some user-accessible setting. If your application has to be compiled with the menu items connected to functions via a message map, how can you write a program which lets the user change the content of a menu at run time?

It's becoming increasingly common for applications to provide some special floating pop-up menus. These menus, usually called **context menus**, allow the user to conveniently perform some special operation that's associated with the area of the screen where they created the menu. If you use Visual C++ 6.0, or any other modern, robust Windows program, then you've probably already come across numerous context menus – the project window, class browser, documentation viewer and toolbar area all have their own context-menu area. Such a menu usually shows up right where the user's clicked the mouse to activate it. Such a Visual C++ 6.0 menu looks like this:

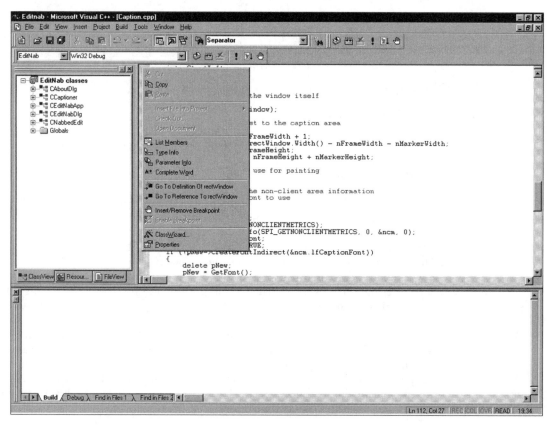

Of course, I gratuitously showed the Visual C++ 6.0 IDE, but lots of other applications implement this feature. For example, Microsoft Word, where I'm writing right now, offers a context menu to let me get at formatting commands quickly.

These context menus are sometimes user-configurable. So, let me address these two issues with one sample: `CtxtMenu`. This has a dialog box to allow you to alter information that constructs a context menu for the user at runtime. That dialog box is shown here:

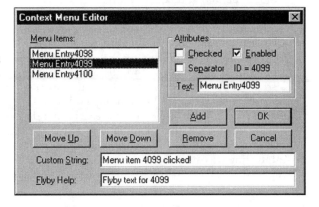

The dialog box presents a crafty user interface for managing a list of `CMenuEntry` items. The application declares the `CMenuEntry` class in `MenuEntr.h` and implements it in `MenuEntr.cpp` – if you really call it an implementation. `CMenuEntry` objects are very simple – just data structures which grow up to be objects. I implemented them this way to make it easier to use a `CArray` template collection class to kick them around. Aside from the purpose of this chapter, it might be interesting to review the sample to investigate the way the `CMenuEditorDlg` works with the rest of the application in manipulating the arrays of menu entry objects.

The most interesting part of this work is probably the code in the `CCtxtMenuView::OnEditMenu()` function:

```
void CCtxtMenuView::OnEditMenu()
{
   CCtxtMenuDoc* pDoc = static_cast<CCtxtMenuDoc*>(GetDocument());
   ASSERT(pDoc != NULL);
   ASSERT_VALID(pDoc);

   // Create the dialog object
   CMenuEditorDialog dlg(pDoc, this);

   // Copy the document array into it
   CopyArray(dlg.m_arMenuEntries, pDoc->m_arMenuEntries);

   // Display the dialog. If the user liked their changes,
   // copy them back into the document
   if (dlg.DoModal() == IDOK)
      CopyArray(pDoc->m_arMenuEntries, dlg.m_arMenuEntries);
   dlg.m_arMenuEntries.RemoveAll();
}
```

The `OnEditMenu()` function copies the object array list from the document object in the application to the dialog that allows the user to view or edit the array. This mechanism makes rolling back the changes a simple matter of not copying them to the document's copy of the array when the user cancels the dialog box.

You might have noticed that I store an array of the `CMenuEntry` items in the `CDocument`-derived `CCtxtMenuDoc` class in my application. This is a bit convoluted, but the sample is designed to demonstrate an interesting technique using menus, not the proper design of a full-blown application. In real life, I'd probably store the array in the application object, rather than in the document. I'd also probably be interested in doing the processing for the Edit | Menu Content command in the document or in the application object. I'd make these changes simply because the application only ever needs to have one copy of the data that describes the menu. In this sample, however, the document really *is* the menu data. Moving the data from the document to the application object makes more architectural sense in a real application, but it also means that you'll need to find some interesting way to make that data persistent for the application, perhaps by storing it in the system registry.

Dynamically Creating a Menu

The problem of implementing a context menu with dynamic elements essentially falls into three parts. The first is handled by the `CMenuEditorDialog` and the mechanisms I mentioned above, which let the user create, modify and view the custom menu in the application. I solved this by creating a user interface for managing the menus themselves and their purpose in the application. Your own solution will more than likely be different to mine; I allow the user to show a string of their choice as a reaction to each menu item. You might be interested in having some code begin to execute a macro or command within your own application for your own purpose.

The second part of the problem is actually constructing the menu, while the third part is reacting to the menu choices and supporting the functions necessary for MFC's management of the menus. Let's first examine the problem of dynamically creating a menu.

In the sample application, I decided to hook the context menu to a right-click in the client area. I just used ClassWizard to add a handler for the `WM_CONTEXTMENU` message to the message map in the view. `WM_CONTEXTMENU` was introduced in Windows 95 and Windows NT 3.51; this message is sent when the user presses the *Shift+F10* key combination, or when they press the context menu key on a keyboard that has the extra Windows-specific keys.

The `WM_RBUTTONDOWN` message tells us where the cursor was when the user put the right mouse button down. This is convenient because it tells us where we can create the floating menu. The floating context menu, also known as a **pop-up menu** in Windows parlance, can be displayed with the `CMenu::TrackPopupMenu()` function.

`TrackPopupMenu()` displays the menu and returns when the user makes a selection, or dismisses the menu without actually making a selection. The function returns *before* the `WM_COMMAND` message corresponding to the user's menu selection is sent. Since `TrackPopupMenu()` is a member of the `Cmenu` class, you can guess that the menu that the function displays is actually that associated with the `CMenu` object.

The code that displays the menu looks like this in the sample:

```
if (!PopMenu.TrackPopupMenu(TPM_LEFTALIGN,
    ClientPoint.x, ClientPoint.y, GetParent()))
    AfxThrowUserException();
```

`TrackPopupMenu()` takes several parameters. The first is a flag that describes where the menu will be positioned. I used `TPM_LEFTALIGN`, which means that the left edge of the menu will line up with the point I specify. I could have used `TPM_RIGHTALIGN` or `TPM_CENTERALIGN` to achieve similar affects in different directions. The second and third parameters give the point relative to which the menu will be displayed. These are screen coordinates, by the way. I had to convert the client-relative mouse coordinates received in the message to screen coordinates to make the menu appear where the user would expect it to. That process is simple, since there's a `ClientToScreen()` member function in `CWnd`. Stripped to its birthday suit, all I need to do is this:

```
// point is a CPoint passed by the message
CPoint ClientPoint = point;
ClientToScreen(&ClientPoint);

// Now, ClientPoint is the same point as point(!),
// but is actually screen-relative
```

The fourth parameter just lets the menu know which window owns it – which window will receive the `WM_COMMAND` message generated by any selections that the user makes in the menu. Since this menu is being displayed from a function within the application's view, I call `GetParent()` to have Windows associate the menu with the frame window of my application.

If my call to `TrackPopupMenu()` fails, by the way, I call `AfxThrowUserException()` to trigger the error handling code I wrote in my function. I just catch any `CUserExceptions` to process errors and clean up anything that might have been created before the error was encountered. You'll find the `CCtxtMenuView::OnRButtonDown()` function a *slightly* pedantic example of error handling with exceptions in your own functions.

As I'll point out in Chapter 9, MFC's `CUserException` class isn't for user-defined exceptions but is intended to reflect an exception caused by the `USER` module within Windows. This case constitutes an appropriate use of the class – something went wrong with creating a menu, and that's handled by `USER`.

Building Menus out of CMenuEntrys

`CMenu::TrackPopupMenu()` takes care of displaying the pop-up menu and waiting for the user's response to it. It doesn't actually create the `CMenu` object or its content, but that's easy enough; I just allocate a `CMenu` object on the stack and add menu items to it.

First, I call `CMenu::CreatePopupMenu()` to get Windows to give me a handle to a valid menu object. Then I start adding menu items to that menu by calling `CMenu::AppendMenu()` repeatedly, for each menu item I want to modify. In the sample, the code picks apart the different `CMenuEntry` items in the document's array. To make things clear, let's examine a fictitious call to `CMenu::AppendMenu()` that looks something like this:

```
if (!PopMenu.AppendMenu(MF_ENABLED | MF_UNCHECKED | MF_STRING,
    ID_FILE_OPEN, _T("Open &File")))
    AfxThrowUserException();
```

`AppendMenu()` takes as its first parameter a set of flags which describe the menu to be added. In the above call, I use `MF_ENABLED` to indicate the menu is enabled, `MF_UNCHECKED` to indicate the menu doesn't have a check mark, and `MF_STRING` to show that the menu is really a string and not a bitmap. The second parameter is the ID that's associated with the new menu item, while the third is the string that the menu item will display.

You'll notice that the string I pass for the third parameter contains an ampersand (&). This character indicates to Windows that the letter following it should be the mnemonic for the menu item. As a clue to the user, the mnemonic character shows up with an underline. So, the above call generates a menu entry that looks like this on the screen:

Open <u>F</u>ile

The user can get at it immediately, without scrolling a selection through the menu, by using the *F* key. If you'd like to have an ampersand in your menu text without having anything underlined, just place two ampersands side by side. The string,

```
_T("Standard && &Poors")
```

ends up like this on the screen:

Standard & <u>P</u>oors

You can make a menu of bitmap objects using `MF_BITMAP`. Such menus are often *huge*, though, and are usually avoided because they're not very pleasant to view. If you wanted to create such a menu, however, the third parameter to `AppendMenu()` would actually be a pointer to the `CBitmap` object you wanted to display, rather than a pointer to the string for the menu's text.

There are lots of other interesting ways to manipulate menus. For example, you can use `InsertMenu()` to add a new menu item in the middle of an existing menu. Since I'm building my own menu from scratch, `AppendMenu()` is far more appropriate. You may also use `DeleteMenu()` to remove an entry from a menu. `DeleteMenu()` has a pretty simple prototype:

```
BOOL DeleteMenu(UINT nPosition,
                UINT nFlags);
```

The second parameter, `nFlags`, determines what the first parameter means. If `nFlags` is `MF_BYCOMMAND`, the first parameter specifies the command ID of the menu item you wish to delete. If `nFlags` is `MF_BYPOSITION`, the `nPosition` parameter specifies the position of the menu item you wish to delete in a scheme which identifies the first menu item as zero, the second item as one, and so on. If you'll be deleting more than one menu item using `MF_BYPOSITION`, remember that removing a menu item renumbers all of the higher numbered menu items. To avoid confusion, personal embarrassment, and the stinging ridicule of your peers, it's best to remove items with `MF_BYPOSITION` in descending order of their position.

If I was interested in modifying an existing menu, I wouldn't call `CreatePopupMenu()`, either. Instead, I'd use a function like `CWnd::GetMenu()` to retrieve the existing menu object associated with a window. By calling the functions I needed to modify the menu appropriately, and then calling `CWnd::DrawMenuBar()`, I might be able to modify and refresh the menu of an existing window.

Now, whacking together the menu in the `CtxtMenu` sample is pretty straightforward – I just zip through the array of menu items and build the menu. The real work is in this short loop, built into the `ShowContextMenu()` function in my view, which is called from `OnRButtonDown()`:

```
for (nIndex = 0; nIndex <= nBound; nIndex++)
{
    CMenuEntry* pThisOne = &(pDoc->m_arMenuEntries.ElementAt(nIndex));
    if (!PopMenu.AppendMenu(pThisOne->m_nAttributes,
                            pThisOne->m_nID, pThisOne->m_strCaption))
        AfxThrowUserException();
}
```

Once the menu is built call its `TrackPopupMenu()` method, which brings us back to where we started. The call displays the menu and has Windows give it focus. If the user presses arrow keys or mnemonic keys associated with the menu, Windows will respond properly. Windows will dismiss the menu if the user presses the *Esc* key or clicks outside of the window that owns the menu.

Letting MFC Know About Your Menu

The third of the three pillars of dynamic menu enlightenment is tricking MFC into acknowledging your menu. This, again, really isn't that hard, though it would be prudent to be concerned about performance. This time, the challenge is to make something that is normally static actually behave as if dynamically. MFC doesn't have much of a problem with this, but it certainly isn't as easy as the normal, run-of-the-mill implementation.

If you're in a rush, or at least not in such a demanding mood, you can take a very simple approach to working the message map. You could reserve a range of command IDs for the possible dynamic items that your application might add. By coding, say:

```
#define FIRST_DYNAMIC_COMMAND   2000
#define LAST_DYNAMIC_COMMAND    2999
```

you can remind yourself that no static menu or button should ever have an ID between 2000 and 2999, and that your dynamic menu items will all fall within this range. You can then add to your message map the `ON_COMMAND_RANGE()` and `ON_UPDATE_COMMAND_UI_RANGE()` macros like this:

```
ON_COMMAND_RANGE(FIRST_DYNAMIC_COMMAND, LAST_DYNAMIC_COMMAND,
                                        OnDynamicMenuSelection)
ON_UPDATE_COMMAND_UI_RANGE(FIRST_DYNAMIC_COMMAND, LAST_DYNAMIC_COMMAND,
                                        OnDynamicMenuUIUpdate)
```

Given that code, you'll be charged with implementing two functions that will figure out which menu item was clicked or which menu item MFC is asking you to update. The problem with this approach is very subtle; you're not able to provide fly-by help, that is MFC won't be able to find a string in your application's resources that can be used to display a description of the menu item in your application's status bar. However, there is a solution to this – you can override `GetMessageString()` in your frame window. This function takes a `UINT` and a reference to a `CString` as a parameter. You'll need to populate the string with the fly-by help that describes the command with the `UINT` you've been given.

A more complete implementation involves overriding the `OnCmdMsg()` function in your window. This function allows you to hook some code into MFC's command message dispatch mechanism, which will take care of both updating your dynamic menu's user interface and invoking any functionality associated with the dynamic menu choices.

The function prototype looks like this:

```
BOOL CCmdTarget:OnCmdMsg(UINT              nID,
                         int               nCode,
                         void*             pExtra,
                         AFX_CMDHANDLERINFO* pHandlerInfo)
```

The first parameter is the ID of the menu item that's being handled. `nCode` is either `CN_COMMAND` or `CN_UPDATE_COMMAND_UI`. This value dictates the use of the other two parameters, `pExtra` and `pHandlerInfo`.

Inside MFC, the `OnCmdMsg()` function is very busy dispatching calls to the `ON_COMMAND()` and `ON_UPDATE_COMMAND_UI()` handlers in your application. And, as if that wasn't enough, `OnCmdMsg()` also handles events fired by ActiveX controls and a couple of other sundry communication mechanisms between objects.

Normally, MFC will dynamically disable menu items for which no command handler is available. This feature is designed to help you when you're first writing your application; if you've not coded the handler, MFC will indicate that to you and your users by disabling the item. You can see that a menu item isn't enabled at a glance – that is it is grayed out and unselectable, which shows that you have work to do. If MFC *can* find a handler for your menu entry, though, it will enable the menu choice and then call `OnCmdMsg()` normally. If you don't want MFC to disable unhandled menu items automatically, you can set the `m_bAutoMenuEnable` member of your `CFrameWnd` to `FALSE`.

Normal calls to `OnCmdMsg()` come in two flavors – first, when MFC is sniffing out the command user interface, and second where some command event (like the user pressing a button or poking around with a menu item) has occurred and your application needs to respond to it. These calls normally propagate to the `ON_UPDATE_COMMAND_UI()` handlers for your application. In the `CtxtMenu` sample, since I have no such hard-coded handlers, I override `OnCmdMsg()` to see if I'm receiving the call for any of the dynamic menu items that are owned. The framework will call `OnCmdMsg()` in this way just before the menu is displayed. For normal pop-up menus on the frame of the application, this is when the user clicks on the menu or presses *Alt* or *F10* to activate the menu. For context menus, like those produced by the `CtxtMenu` application, `OnCmdMsg()` is displayed just after the call to `TrackPopupMenu()` is made – but before it returns!

My implementation of `OnCmdMsg()` in my application's view works by calling a member of the document class to see if the command ID we've received is of interest to the application. If it is in the range of command handlers for the menu items contained in the context menu, I'll consider doing some processing for it. If it isn't, I'll immediately call the base class implementation. Since `OnCmdMsg()` is called repeatedly – once for every menu item on each of the menus that could be displayed by the user – it's imperative that the function executes quickly.

To optimize it, I try to short-circuit the work it does by making sure it's worth checking the remainder of the parameters. So, the function starts out like this:

```
BOOL CCtxtMenuView::OnCmdMsg(UINT nID, int nCode, void* pExtra,
                                    AFX_CMDHANDLERINFO* pHandlerInfo)
{
    CCtxtMenuDoc* pDoc = static_cast<CCtxtMenuDoc*>(GetDocument());
    ASSERT_VALID(pDoc);

    if (!pDoc->MenuIDInCustomRange(nID))
        return CView::OnCmdMsg(nID, nCode, pExtra, pHandlerInfo);
```

If, for example, the document knows that the IDs on it range from 1001 to 1009, and I've been handed 303 as the ID to check, I'll call the CView implement of OnCmdMsg() straight away. If, however, I was handed 1005, I'd call the document again to ask it for a pointer to the CMenuEntry identified by the ID I received. The function continues with this code:

```
    CMenuEntry* pEntry = pDoc->GetEntryFromID(nID);
    if (pEntry == NULL)
        return CView::OnCmdMsg(nID, nCode, pExtra, pHandlerInfo);
```

Note that I check to see if the returned pointer is NULL. If it is, I know that the command ID denotes a menu entry that is in my range but was deleted. Maybe the user added item 1005, deleted it, and then continued to add items up to 1009. The first check would pass, since 1005 is in the range of 1001 to 1009, but this second check would fail as we don't know anything about a menu item named 1005 because it was deleted. Isn't it nice to know that in this age of 500 MHz Pentium III machines, someone still cares about saving a few cycles?

In the meantime, getting these calls to work properly is crucial to the functioning of the application. If I avoided calling the base class implementation, other items in the application would never become enabled, and they would never generate calls to their ON_COMMAND handlers. The application would be completely inoperable!

If execution makes it past these two if statements, I know the pEntry value I have is something with which I need to concern myself. If the nCode passed to me is CN_COMMAND, it means the user has activated that command. It would be at this point where I'd implement whatever handler I needed to for my application. Since this is just an illustrative example, I'll pop up a message box to show whatever text the user entered and associated with the menu item. That's easy:

```
    if (nCode == CN_COMMAND && pHandlerInfo == NULL)
    {
        MessageBox(pEntry->m_strText);
        return TRUE;
    }
```

I have to check pHandlerInfo too, to make sure that it's NULL; this value indicates that the framework is placing the call because the user actually clicked on the menu item. The Foundation Classes will call OnCmdMsg() with CN_COMMAND as its second parameter, and pHandlerInfo pointing to an initialized structure, if the framework is trying to find a handler before displaying the menu. In other words, pHandlerInfo isn't NULL if MFC is searching for a handler for the particular command ID, but is NULL if the user actually activated the choice.

In the sample, I'm not at all interested in handling the 'sniffing around' case, so I only test for the 'activated' case. Frankly, I can't really think of a reason why you'd ever be interested in handling the handler detection. If you've set up a system where you're dynamically managing a source of command messages, such as a menu or a control bar, enabling the items with the ON_UPDATE_COMMAND_UI() handler is quite enough. Of course, you need to know how that side of the function works. That's simple too:

```
    else if (nCode == CN_UPDATE_COMMAND_UI && pExtra != NULL)
    {
        CCmdUI* pUI = static_cast<CCmdUI*>(pExtra);

        pUI->Enable(pEntry->IsEnabled());
        pUI->SetCheck(pEntry->IsChecked());

        return TRUE;
    }
}
```

If nCode is CN_UPDATE_COMMAND_UI, pHandlerInfo will always be NULL, but the pExtra parameter will be interesting as it will point to a CCmdUI object that describes our menu item.

You can see that I cast pExtra – a pointer to a void – to a pointer to a CCmdUI without any hesitation. I don't even check to see that it's a pointer to a CCmdUI object with a call to IsKindOf(). There are two reasons for this apparent devil-may-care approach. The first is that CCmdUI doesn't have run-time type information – even if I felt like being safe, I couldn't. The second is that I *know* this will be a pointer to a CCmdUI because of the way the command handler works. It can't be anything else. I can only suppose it's defined as a pointer to a void, rather than a pointer to a CCmdUI object, because of the possibility of expansion of the command routing mechanism later in the life of MFC.

Once I have that CCmdUI object, I can call Enable() or SetCheck() on the object to enable or check the menu item. I do that based on the settings in the CMenuEntry object I found before; I just set the menu item to fulfill the user's request.

That's it! With the OnCmdMsg() implementation we reviewed here, the menu will work fine. But it will be lacking one thing – fly-by help.

Fly-By-Night

Implementing fly-by help takes one more step – overriding the GetMessageString() function of the frame window. This function lives in the frame window because it's the frame that owns the status bar where fly-by help messages are displayed. The prototype for the function looks like this:

```
void CMainFrame::GetMessageString(UINT nID, CString& rMessage) const;
```

All the function needs to do is to get a string for the command ID passed by MFC. If it gets such a string, it should copy it to rMessage. If it can't, it should set rMessage to an empty string. (It can call rMessage.Empty(), or set rMessage = "", whichever is more convenient.) Inside MFC, the default implementation of this function runs off and tries to load the string resource of the same ID. If it's successful, it tries to parse it, since the command string will have both the fly-by help and the tooltip help, and put the correct half of the string into rMessage – that is, the half of the string before the newline character that marks the tooltip text.

In the sample, my override for this function has some of the same structure as the OnCmdMsg() handler, in that it has to decide quickly whether it should be handling the message or not. If it should, I get the fly-by string the user wanted from the CMenuEntry object. If not, I just call the base-class implementation. The implementation is only a couple of lines long:

```
if (pDoc->MenuIDInCustomRange(nID))
    pDoc->GetMenuStr(nID, rMessage);
else
    CFrameWnd::GetMessageString(nID, rMessage);
```

Once it has the string, MFC does all of the work to display it. Our job is done.

Go Forth and Apply

Remember that command routing applies to other things besides menus; toolbars are the most obvious additional applications. MFC also calls OnCmdMsg() for these features, which means what you've learned about OnCmdMsg() in this section applies to toolbars, dialog bars and chocolate bars.

Also, OnCmdMsg() is a member of CCmdTarget. That means *every* window, as well as things like CWinThread and CWinApp objects, gets an OnCmdMsg() implementation. You can hang these handlers anywhere you like. In the sample, I chose to implement my OnCmdMsg() override in my application's CView-derived class. I did this because the view is exactly where the menu will be popped up. If I later implement a different view, I'll need to change the way the menu items are handled. This makes sense – read on to understand why.

Another thing I should do is reiterate what I said before about the implementation of this application. Throughout this book, I've tried to make the samples reasonable and concise, but the CtxtMenu sample tested my mettle in two ways. First, it quickly became complicated. The code in the document to manage templated arrays of CMenuEntry objects and the code in CMenuEditorDialog to provide a user interface to edit that array are both rather elaborate. The source code for this sample is a good place to look if you're interested in looking at how to use templated collection classes for more realistic applications.

The other issue is that, if you take it too seriously, this application can confuse you about how to design document/view applications. I mentioned earlier that the array of CMenuEntrys lives in the document. Putting the entries into the document may not be an idea applicable to a real project, but it is a *very* realistic approach for getting the handlers for the context menu into the view. After all, the view defines how the user sees data. If the user is working with one representation of data, they'll be interested in a certain set of commands to manipulate that particular representation of that data. If the user is working with a different representation, they'll be interested in a slightly different set of commands. In fact, that's why it's called a **context menu** – the content and meaning of the menu is dependent on the context in which the menu was requested.

If my application demands very similar menus, or I find a cool way to explain to the application which view was active and which menu should be displayed, I might move the OnCmdMsg() override to a 'higher' point in the hierarchy. That is, I might implement the override in the frame window so that I only need to implement it once, but I'd also need to provide a more complicated implementation that was aware of all the different views supported by my application.

The Gentle Art of Subclassing

So back to the topic of subclassing, which was introduced earlier in the chapter. As you design your application, you'll naturally try to reuse as much existing code as possible. That code comes from any number of libraries included with Visual C++, and maybe even some special-purpose libraries that you've purchased and added to your toolkit. At the procedure level, you may be interested in reusing a single function. You'll do this a thousand times a day, reusing code to copy strings, display messages, or write data to a disk file. The C run-time libraries are probably the biggest source of such routines, providing programming mainstays like `sprintf()` and `strcat()`.

You might not realize that the Windows API itself is also a reusable library. The Windows libraries which you link with your program connect it to the dynamic-link libraries which make up Windows itself; by calling the `::MessageBox()` API, you're just reusing some existing code that's built into Windows.

This sort of reuse is simple, but not very potent. It isn't very powerful because it only allows you to reuse one function at a time. If you don't like one little nuance of `printf()`'s formatting rules, you're on your own to find some other way to format your strings – you can't steal most of a function's capabilities and change just a few aspects of how it works unless you can come up with some crafty way of faking a second call to the function.

Functions, then, aren't built to be very big. Once, I woke up and found myself in the middle of a room with a bunch of people listening to some guy at the front who was blathering on about functions and procedures and subroutines. The leader seemed surprised to make eye contact with me, so I surmised this must be some sort of computer science course.

The leader was suggesting that functions should never be more than fifty or sixty lines long – no longer than a printed page, in other words. That's what makes reusing code in functions so simple; functions generally don't have much code underneath them, and don't often have complicated side effects. The leader went on about how shorter functions are easier to write, understand, debug and, therefore, easier to maintain. But I knew the real reason that functions should be short – nobody who writes functions for reuse wants to bake so much into one function that decisions about its implementation will affect its efficacy in situations for which it wasn't originally designed.

Like School in the Summertime: No Class

That's where all of this object-oriented stuff comes in. As a software designer, you can carefully engineer classes as definitions for objects. The objects can be cleanly reused throughout your code, but you can also inherit parts of the definition and override others to customize them gently for what you need.

When you're writing C++ software for Windows, the concept of inheritance has two meanings. One is the C++ meaning; we can take a class we've defined and subclass it. This lets us reuse the functionality implemented in that class, replacing functionality we don't like or don't need in objects of our new class. The other meaning is the Windows-specific definition; in MFC, Windows identifies its windows by classes, and you can perform something called subclassing on those classes, too. While the words 'subclassing' and 'class' come up in both descriptions, the techniques and their semantics are quite different.

There will come a time, sooner or later, when you'll realize that your needs are greater than the functionality Windows provides for you. (Maybe you could argue that this day has already come and gone – that's why you're writing a new Windows application.) As you browse through the different features implemented by the control and window objects you can use for free, you'll probably find you'd like something a little extra.

You may, for example, want to have a list box which allows the user to select from a bunch of different graphical images, instead of words that just *describe* some graphical image. You might want the user to see the way a color looks before he or she selects it, or to have some mnemonic by which to remember a choice. Your goal may not be so tangible or grandiose – you may wish you could have a chance at doing something to a window just before it paints, or just after the user lets go of the mouse on the menu.

Windows Subclassing

As you'll have gathered by now, Windows applications work by waiting around for messages. Those messages are sent to a **window procedure**, which the application registers for a particular type of window class – even the control classes that Windows implicitly registers for you. While you're probably nodding your head and saying, "That's obvious, Mike, give me my money back," there's a lot of meaning in that sentence. Let me pick it apart a little.

First, the notion of 'messages being sent to a window' implies that the window is interested in the messages, and that's true up to a point – a window wouldn't even be able to paint itself properly if it didn't receive *any* messages. But the vast majority of messages sent to a window are absolutely uninteresting – they're passed on to the **default window procedure** for the window's class.

When you write a program, you nab a few of these messages and react to them to make your application behave differently than the window would by default. You might paint a drawing in the middle of the window, if it was a pop-up, or you may react to command messages sent by controls on the window. If you didn't step in and execute some code of your own, the window wouldn't paint anything, or react to any of the menus or push buttons you had set up.

Of course, the beauty of the default window procedure is it gives you something to do when you don't want to handle a Windows message, but instead wish to do whatever any other healthy, red-blooded window does. By calling the default window procedure, you let the window do what a normal window does.

All of the messages sent to a window are handed to the window procedure; there, they are either handled directly or passed on to the default window procedure. The idea behind subclassing a window, then, is to place your own function in between Windows and the normal window procedure. You can watch for messages that interest you and react appropriately, while ignoring messages which don't interest you at all.

You won't need to subclass most windows. When you write your application, you'll handle messages on behalf of the window because your message handling function is wired directly to the window. In an MFC application, the window procedure is shared by all windows. MFC walks through the permanent window map to find the C++ CWnd-derived object whose handle matches the target of the message being processed. If a matching window handle isn't found, MFC lets Windows process the message. If MFC *does* find a matching window handle, it tries to find a C++ member function that will handle the message. It does this by walking the message maps for the window class, as I outlined back in Chapter 3. The real meaning of these maps is actually quite interesting, but let's resume our subclassing discussion before we have a detailed examination of the maps.

Subclassing the Win32 Way

To subclass a window, you'll need to get Windows to call your own message handling function instead of calling the window procedure originally associated with the window. If you're doing plain Win32 programming without MFC, subclassing is usually accomplished by using the Windows ::GetWindowLong() API. The ::GetWindowLong() function allows you to retrieve a pointer to the window procedure – a pointer to a function – for the window you were interested in subclassing. You could squirrel away the pointer you receive from ::GetWindowLong() with code like this:

```
FARPROC pfnOldProc;
pfnOldProc = (FARPROC)::GetWindowLong(hWnd, GWL_WNDPROC);
```

The first parameter to ::GetWindowLong() is the handle for the window which you'd like to subclass. The second is a constant, defined by the Windows headers, which identifies the attribute of the internal data for the window you wish to change. The GWL_WNDPROC constant identifies the window procedure. There are half a dozen other constants, but they're beyond the scope of this discussion.

Now you have a copy of the old pointer for safekeeping, you can wire up your new procedure. The new procedure needs to be defined with the appropriate parameters and return values so that Windows can both pass it the message data it needs and obtain the return value it expects. If you get warnings when trying to use your function, *don't* randomly cast the pointer to the function – you'll just mask the problem. Your new procedure should have a function prototype which looks like this:

```
LRESULT CALLBACK MySubClasser(HWND    hWnd,
                              UINT    msg,
                              WPARAM  wParam,
                              LPARAM  lParam);
```

You can set things up so that MySubClasser() is called for messages to the window by making a call to ::SetWindowLong(), like this:

```
::SetWindowLong(hWnd, GWL_WNDPROC, reinterpret_cast<LONG>(MySubClasser));
```

After this call, any time Windows wants to dispatch a message to the subclassed window, the identified MySubClasser function will be called. Of course, you don't need to call your function MySubClasser – any name will do. You might have dozens of different names for dozens of different subclassed Windows.

::SetWindowLong(), by the way, neatly returns the old value while you're setting the new value. This fact lets you write the code in shorthand, without calling ::GetWindowLong() first:

```
pfnOldProc = (FARPROC)::SetWindowLong(hWnd, GWL_WNDPROC, MyFunction);
```

Note that a cast is necessary to make the LONG return type of the function acceptable to the assignment operator and the FARPROC variable. This kind of cast is acceptable, since we know the value coming back from SetWindowLong() is a LONG that really represents a pointer to the exact function type we expect.

The Subclassing Function

As I've been saying, the subclassing function can do anything it needs to with the messages it receives. Most developers take the strategy that the function will only actually react to one or two messages to gently tweak the behavior of the underlying window. Then, any message that isn't handled can be dished off to the old procedure.

It might work like this:

```
LRESULT CALLBACK MySubclasser(HWND hwnd, UINT msg, WPARAM wParam, LPARAM lParam)
{
    switch (msg)
    {
    case WM_PAINT:
        // painting code here
        break;

    default:
        return (*pfnOldProc)(hwnd, msg, wParam, lParam);
    }

    return 0L;
}
```

When this function receives a WM_PAINT message for a window, it will react to it by executing some painting which is somehow different from the code the window would normally execute. That's the code I would write; it would show up where the painting code here comment is. Any other message handled by this function is shoved through the default case where I dereference the pointer to the old function and call the old window procedure. Note that I return the value which the old function returns to me. If I discarded it or returned my own value, I wouldn't let Windows know about the outcome of the previous function. In the WM_PAINT case, I end up returning my own value because my painting code is running the show, not the normal window procedures.

Since the callback will invoke the old procedure via the pfnOldProc pointer, your pfnOldProc pointer must have global scope or be available through a function call. Both the code setting up the callback and the callback itself need to be able to see the value.

It's easy to reuse functionality in the old window function too. If I wanted the normal window painting to happen first – which I might, so that I could erase it instead of letting it erase what I've drawn – I could call the old code first, like this:

```
LRESULT CALLBACK MySubclasser(HWND hwnd, UINT msg, UINT wParam, LONG lParam)
{
    LRESULT dwRetValue;

    switch (msg)
    {
    case WM_PAINT:
        dwRetValue = (*pfnOldProc)(hwnd, msg, wParam, lParam);
        if (dwRetValue == 0)
        {
            // painting code here
        }
        return dwRetValue;
```

Continued on following page

```
      default:
          return (*pfnOldProc)(hwnd, msg, wParam, lParam);
      }

      return 0L;
  }
```

You can see that I use `dwRetValue` to nab the return value from the normal painting code, and then execute my own code, only if that code returned zero. Paint message handlers always return zero unless something goes really wrong, in which case I should probably reflect this problem back to the caller. I choose to skip my code if the normal window procedure doesn't work. For `WM_PAINT`, this logic is almost inconsequential, but I'm bringing it up here because it's important to understand that, for many other messages, this mechanism is extremely important. It's the only way Windows is able to know what you did with a message.

More Lies

You may have suddenly realized I was talking about sub*classing* windows, but the code above uses `::SetWindowLong()`. Since `::SetWindowLong()` sets the window procedure for only one window instance, the subclassing function is called only for a particular instance of the window, not for all windows of that class. That is, the above code snatches messages for only one object of a window class.

It's unfortunate but true that words which really describe one concept are sometimes bent around by common (and perhaps careless) usage to describe other ideas. Pedantically, what I've described above isn't really subclassing, but it's what most non-MFC Win32 programmers mean when they say they've subclassed a window.

You can, on the other hand, *really* subclass things by using `::SetClassLong()` in place of `::SetWindowLong()`. `::SetClassLong()` uses `GCL_WNDPROC` instead of `GWL_WNDPROC` to identify the window procedure pointer. Using this function means every window of the class you've identified will have its behavior modified.

Whatever the quirks of the language, the semantics of using `::SetClassLong()` are still slightly different from the C++ definition of subclassing. In C++, subclassing means you've created a class which can be reused by any other part of your code. Windows SDK subclassing using `::SetWindowLong()` or `::SetClassLong()` still means you're changing a window or an existing class – not basing a new class on an existing one.

The great side effect, however, is that you can achieve results which affect all windows of a given class in your process. For instance, you might use `::SetClassLong()` to change the way all list boxes work throughout your application. That is obviously undesireable; the result would be worse than working at Microsoft – your customers would question your sanity, education, and upbringing. Changing the class once does it all!

Unsubclassing

When the window you've subclassed is destroyed, your subclass function won't be called anymore. It should be able to perform its duty throughout the life of the window. If you've used `::SetClassLong()`, your function will be called when *any* window of the subclassed type is called. This means your function must live forever – someone, somewhere, may yet create such a window. If you can't figure out how to code a function which lives forever, you'll need to **unsubclass** the object with another call to `::SetClassLong()`. It's as simple as undoing what you did with `::SetClassLong()` in the first place:

```
::SetClassLong(hWnd, GWL_WNDPROC, (LONG)pfnOldProc);
```

Just stuff the old value back into the class information for the window. Windows will call the old function directly and forget completely about your new window procedure. You *will* need to do this; if your function goes away when Windows is still calling it, you'll be in big trouble.

Subclassing MFC Objects

Given your knowledge of subclassing, you'll soon be eager to do it in your favorite MFC applications. In most situations, subclassing a window in MFC is very simple – far easier than juggling the pointers to procedures like those in the SDK code snippets I presented above.

The `OwnDraw` sample shows how to subclass a list box with your own code. I used a subclassed list box in this example to implement an **owner-draw list box**. List boxes, combo boxes, buttons and menus can all be owner-dawn, if their corresponding style is set. The owner-draw feature allows you to be responsible for drawing the elements within the UI feature instead of letting Windows do the work for you. When Windows does the painting in the box, your life is easy; you just stuff the element full of text and let Windows do the dirty work. However, sometimes it's nice to have boxes (buttons or menus) which contain things Windows won't paint for you: text with icons, colors, or different fonts. For now, let's concentrate on how the MFC code handles the messages sent to the list box rather than what they really mean.

In `OwnDraw`, I use an owner-draw list box to show the different fonts on the system. The box needs to respond to three different messages in order to work: `WM_DELETEITEM`, `WM_MEASUREITEM`, and `WM_DRAWITEM`. The problem is that these messages are sent to the dialog box itself, and not the control within the dialog.

Handling messages is no problem in the dialog – we've done it throughout this book. Since the dialog is an MFC window, MFC knows about it inherently. Handlers for different messages in the window are hooked up in the message map and that's that. To subclass the list box, we'll need to let MFC know about it. The list box isn't already an MFC window because MFC didn't explicitly create it – it was created for the dialog template by Windows indirectly, without MFC's direct knowledge.

But what is an MFC window? Which windows does MFC know about? Let's have a look at the windows which MFC creates directly and those that MFC is only aware of temporarily.

About MFC Objects

By now, you know that MFC wraps the Windows API with C++ objects and interfaces that allow you to write software for Windows more effectively. I've previously mentioned that the C++ objects supplied by MFC must be created before and destroyed after the underlying Windows object, but the underlying MFC mechanisms which make this whole process work still remain a mystery.

The most common examples of this object-wrapping mechanism are windows themselves. Your application has several window classes which you define – your CView-derived and CFrameWnd-derived windows are the most obvious examples. But the mechanism is in place for *any* object which might be created by Windows outside of MFC, and then used within an MFC application.

By the way, if you're a student of any object-oriented design methodologies, you may be familiar with the *'has-a'* relationship. This means that a given object actually includes a different object (or a pointer to one) as an instance variable in its definition. This relationship exists between all of the Windows objects wrapped by MFC objects, i.e. the MFC object *has a* Windows object.

The problem is that MFC programmers are interested in dealing with Windows in a way they understand – that is, by dealing with the C++ objects directly. It would be annoying at best to have to memorize rules for the use of direct Windows API functions *and* CWnd-object functions. It turns out that you can, with very few exceptions, use direct Windows API window handle-based calls interchangeably with MFC C++ window object functions.

Blew Myself Right off the Map

The mechanism in MFC which makes this all work is the **permanent object map**. MFC manages an internal data structure which relates window handles with MFC CWnd objects. This allows MFC to know which object should receive messages and which should be manipulated by the various wrappers which MFC implements.

The permanent object map isn't really anything you need to worry about, but it's useful to understand how it works so it doesn't bite you later. Of course, if there's a permanent window map, then by implication there must be a temporary one too, but for now let's have a look at the former.

Most of the windows your application deals with are MFC windows, i.e. they're windows MFC inherently knows about and was responsible for creating. Your main CFrameWnd and all of your views are examples of MFC windows. They're created by building a C++ class first, then calling the Create() (or CreateEx()) member on that object. CWnd::Create(), of course, ends up calling the Windows ::CreateWindow() API.

The creation code in MFC gets the window handle for the window and stores it in the m_hWnd member of the C++ object. But there are many messages sent to the window before the Windows API returns – what if you need to trap those messages and handle them in your CWnd derived class? If the class isn't yet initialized (since the MFC CWnd::Create() function hasn't returned) it cannot process messages.

To work in this situation, MFC has a trick up its sleeve. While it creates the window, it installs a **window hook** which lets it know about all window messages. Window hooks allow MFC to hear about any message which is sent to your system. MFC sets up the hook just before creating the window and disconnects it as soon as it has finished. The hook lets MFC easily nab the first few messages the window receives in its lifetime, therefore initializing the CWnd object right away. You may want to browse Wincore.cpp to learn exactly how MFC handles the creation of a window.

Temporary Mappings

The initialization which takes place beyond setting the m_hWnd member of the corresponding CWnd object involves adding that newly created CWnd object to the permanent object map. MFC carries the object in the permanent object map throughout the lifetime of the window. When it dies, MFC will kick it out of the permanent map. This is ideal for windows which are a major part of the application. MFC won't spend much time managing the map and will be able to route the most frequently-sent messages to the important windows quickly by finding their CWnd objects in the map.

Of course, for windows that aren't quite so transient, aggressive management would be more of a nuisance than a necessity. Remember that *every* window ends up receiving messages. If MFC managed the permanent map for all the controls in a dialog box you created, for example, it would spend a great deal of time shoving around CWnd objects. Those objects are pretty expensive – they take up memory, have a great big vtable, and get in the way of sending messages to more popular windows.

And so, enter the **temporary map**. MFC allows you to create a temporarily valid CWnd object to represent any window that was created by your process but not directly created by a single call that you made. If you need to use an API not wrapped by MFC, for example, that API may return a window handle that you'll need to use. Since the window wasn't created for your application outside of MFC, you might need to attach to the window before using it. Windows in the temporary map can also come from calls that create more than one window at once.

For example, when you create a dialog, you immediately have the handle to the dialog window. But many windows are created under the dialog box from the template you've supplied – the controls are all windows you're likely to be interested in, but your code isn't directly notified of their creation. A prime example of code which uses a temporary map is the CWnd::GetDlgItem() function I mentioned in Chapter 5 on dialogs and controls. The implementation of this function is trivial. It makes sure you've given it a valid window handle and then calls CWnd::FromHandle() – this function is the real workhorse.

As it turns out, CWnd::FromHandle() isn't really that complicated, but its effects are far-reaching. It tries to find a CWnd object resembling the HWND you've provided in the permanent map, and then in the temporary map – MFC manages both of these maps for your currently running thread. If it *can't* find a match in either thread, it allocates a new CWnd object and returns a pointer to it. If it *can* find a match, it returns the pointer for the existing object from the map. After calling GetDlgItem(), or after calling FromHandle() directly, you obtain a pointer to a CWnd object which you can play with to your heart's content. You can use the pointer to shoot the underlying window full of strings, kick it around the block, or mail it home in a cardboard box, but you can only consider the pointer valid during the processing of the current Windows message, period.

The reason for this dire warning is that MFC will destroy the temporary `CWnd` object later on. It's interested in being tidy, you know, so it will free up those objects when it can. MFC assumes you won't keep the pointer and invites you to ask for a new one any time you like. There are a couple of salient ramifications of this rule.

> **1** Never, ever, get a pointer to a temporarily mapped MFC object and squirrel it away in a global variable or in member data. That implies you're planning on using it later. You shouldn't — it probably won't be valid.
>
> **2** Never, ever, compare pointers to `CWnd`s to see if they refer to the same window. MFC might allocate one, have it land at some address and then allocate another one later and have it land at another address. Instead, compare the `m_hWnd` members for equality.

By the way, MFC cleans up the temporary map when it handles **idle time**. This is MFC's way of saying your application has nothing more interesting to do right now, and that it looked around for another message for your application to handle, but there were no more messages pending. It's quite possible you'll find situations where a pointer to a `CWnd` object *is* valid across two messages. Maybe the message you're handling is necessarily associated with some other message and you'll not have any idle time between the two. But don't count on it – as Windows evolves, these things will change. Your approach might work on Windows NT, but not on Windows 95/98, or it may work on both Windows NT and Windows 95/98, but not on Windows 2000.

All of this idle time processing happens in a function called `CWinThread::OnIdle()`. `OnIdle()` calls a couple of undocumented helper functions, named `AfxLockTempMaps()` and `AfxUnlockTempMaps()` to force the cleanup. You do not need to call these functions directly.

You Are Here

I've explicitly mentioned the way that dialog controls can be temporarily mapped using `CWnd::GetDlgItem()`. There are other ways that your windows can find themselves on the permanent map. One is via the `SubclassWindow()` function, which I'll explain further in the next section when I finally get back to the notion of subclassing windows.

Another way for a window to become mapped by MFC is via the `Attach()` function. This member function of `CWnd` accepts a window handle and initializes the given `CWnd` object to represent that window. The window is entered in the permanent map and can be used any way you wish. The process, given some existing handle of a window in hWnd, is pretty simple. It looks like this:

```
CWnd wnd;
if (!wnd.Attach(hWnd))
{
    // Something is really wrong,
    // e.g. hWnd is a bogus handle
}
else
{
    // Party on wnd!
}
```

The resulting `wnd` object can be a member of another class, or you might switch the syntax of this example around a little to dynamically allocate a `CWnd` object. You can tuck away the pointer in your member data and then use it, after you've called `Attach()` on it to get it initialized.

If you're no longer interested in maintaining a mapping to a given window, you can just call `Detach()`. This will force MFC to unmap the window object. Only after MFC forgets about the mapping will it be safe to `delete` the `CWnd` object if you've dynamically allocated it, or let it go out of scope if you've allocated it automatically.

`Attach()` is the function to use if you want to get a handle to some window and begin using MFC to play with it. For example, you might call an API that creates a window. Since that API wasn't written using MFC, the framework has no notion of the window's existence. If you can get a handle to the window, you can work with it by calling Windows APIs directly, but it's far more flexible to use `Attach()` to gain a real C++ object for the Windows object. That C++ object might be of a special class which will do all sorts of work for you, and it might encapsulate some important data which will make it more convenient to use the wrapped object.

Remember, though, that calling `Detach()` is usually required before destroying the object. Calling `Detach()` does *not* destroy the underlying Windows object; it only removes the MFC mapping to it. If you don't call `Detach()` and the window is destroyed by Windows, the C++ object isn't destroyed – it's simply left lying about with an invalid `m_hWnd` member. At this point, of course, it's safe to destroy the C++ object if you wish. On the other hand, if you don't call `Detach()`, then the destruction of the C++ object will also cause the destruction of the involved window.

And so, now we know three ways to get MFC to work with a given window. We can create a `CWnd`-derived object and then have it create a window for us. This is the most direct approach, especially when you're planning to fully implement the window. Members of your `CWnd` class will be called in response to messages received by the window.

If you find a window handle that you're interested in, create a `CWnd`-derived window, and then call `Attach()` to associate that object with the window that already exists. Using `Attach()`, you are able to call `CWnd` members to alter the window or send it messages. But, after using `Attach()`, you can't override anything in your `CWnd`-derived class – or expect any of the mapped functions be called in response to messages the window receives. If you need to execute message handlers in a C++ object created separately from the Windows object, you'll need to call `SubclassWindow()` or `SubclassDlgItem()`.

Back to Subclassing

Let's get back to the application with the owner-draw list box. To implement the list box, you'll find that I had to create a `CListBox`-derived class in my application. I did this simply by adding a new class with the **Add Class...** button in ClassWizard and making sure that `CListBox` was selected in the **Base Class:** drop-down list box.

With the class set up, I can use ClassWizard to add handlers for any messages or overrides for functions that interest me. I did just that; you can see all of the work in the `FontList.cpp` and `FontList.h` files.

> *There's a list box that shows colored text, too – it's in the* ClrList.cpp *and*
> ClrList.h *files in the* OwnDraw *sample. The techniques are exactly the same, but the*
> *user interface in the colors list box is slightly different. It just means some of the*
> *messages the box handles are a little different, or are handled a little differently. Again,*
> *that was fodder for Chapter 5.*

However, creating and hooking up the messages in these classes isn't enough. I've defined the
CColorListBox and CFontListBox classes, but no code makes an instance of it and nothing tells
MFC about it. Up to this point, we've always used CWnd::GetDlgItem() to gain a pointer to the
CWnd object associated with a control, but since I want these classes to subclass the windows in
question, I'll end up using a slightly different technique.

First, I'll need to add actual instances of the CColorListBox and CFontListBox classes to my
COwnDrawDlg. This happens in OwnDlg.h like this:

```
// Implementation
protected:
    HICON m_hIcon;
    CColorListBox m_ColorList;
    CFontListBox m_FontList;
```

So, whenever my COwnDrawDlg class is instantiated, MFC will implicitly create CColorListBox
and CFontListBox instances, but they're not yet connected to actual Windows objects. To make
that connection, I'll have to use the CWnd::SubclassDlgItem() function. The best place for that
is right in the OnInitDialog() function, called when the dialog is started. I do both calls in one if
statement, just because I'm slick. It looks like this:

```
BOOL COwnDrawDlg::OnInitDialog()
{
    CDialog::OnInitDialog();

    // More initialization

    if (!m_ColorList.SubclassDlgItem(IDC_COLORBOX, this) ||
        !m_FontList.SubclassDlgItem(IDC_FONTBOX, this))
    {
        EndDialog(IDCANCEL);
        return FALSE;
    }

    // Yet more initialization
```

If SubclassDlgItem() fails, it will return FALSE. If either call fails, I bail out of the dialog
immediately by calling EndDialog(). The return value I use after the call to EndDialog() is
irrelevant, since the dialog won't be shown to the user when EndDialog() is called in the
OnInitDialog() handler.

The first SubclassDlgItem() parameter is the ID of the control I want to subclass. Make sure you
get this right; there's no way for MFC to know of the type of the control you want to play with. If you
hook a CListBox-based class to a push button, for instance, things will quietly go nuts. You don't
need to undo SubclassDlgItem(); as the subclassing is disconnected by MFC as the involved
Windows object is destroyed.

The second parameter is a pointer to the CWnd object, which acts as the parent of the window that you're subclassing. Since both controls are children of this very dialog box, I can just use the this pointer from my COwnDrawDlg to set their parent.

That's all there is to it. Once these two calls are done, the CColorListBox and CFontListBox objects will start receiving messages dispatched by MFC. Since you've created the box before subclassing it, though, you won't receive some of the messages a window gets very early in its lifetime. Most notably, since the window has already been created, it's too late to expect WM_CREATE and WM_NCCREATE messages.

Subclassed windows will react to messages they receive however they see fit. As in the SDK example I gave earlier, I'll often need to let the code in the normal message handler for the window perform some work for me. In the handler for DeleteItem(), for example, I need to delete some data that I tucked away in the item data for the entry in the box. But I also need to make sure the list box can also delete the item it is managing. The handler I wrote accomplishes this with the code here:

```
void CFontListBox::DeleteItem(LPDELETEITEMSTRUCT lpDeleteItemStruct)
{
    LOGFONT* pFont = reinterpret_cast<LOGFONT*>(lpDeleteItemStruct->itemData);
    delete pFont;
    CListBox::DeleteItem(lpDeleteItemStruct);
}
```

I don't need to call the base class implementation after my work is done. Not making the call is the appropriate choice in this case; I can't get the item data from the list box if it's already been deleted, so I can't call the base class implementation first. It doesn't make sense to call the base class DeleteItem() implementation in the middle or at the end of the function either, so the above solution is the most natural. Besides, the CListBox version of DeleteItem() doesn't do anything. You may or may not have knowledge of what the base class does – but it is better to know it. This is why MFC ships with source code. You can check the MFC sources to see what MFC would do if it were in your shoes.

In fact, there are quite a lot of instances where you won't want or need to call the base class implementation at all. Often, you won't need to call it when you're implementing painting code – if I need to paint something myself, why have the base class repaint it? The DrawItem() override in the CFontListBox code is a perfect example of this situation. Unless you're augmenting what the base class is already painting, you'll not need to call the base class from any of your paint handlers.

Be very careful when you're writing these handlers. You should probably test your code just after you've got the handler hooked up to make sure that it's working right. (And "working right" means that it works fine in both debug and release builds!) Then, incrementally implement code in your handler to make sure you know which part of the routine is having what effect on your application. When you are writing a subclassing handler, it's very easy to make your application react in ways you've never seen *any* application behave before.

About Object-Oriented Design

I've prattled on about subclassing Windows objects, but I've not said much about how you should approach subclassing C++ objects while you're writing programs with MFC. Back in Chapter 3, I explained some benefits of using MFC's CObject class as a base class for your own classes. If you need any of those benefits, go right ahead and get them by deriving your new class from CObject.

There are, though, some situations where having a CObject isn't a good idea. CObject introduces a few virtual functions, which adds a bit of overhead to objects of any CObject-derived class. For some applications where performance is the key, this overhead is intolerable. A great example is MFC's own CString class, which is very much its own dog. It's not derived from CObject, and hence is designed with no dependency on CObject, because even the slight per-instance increase in size that CObject derivation would add to CString would make CString unusable for many applications.

Another reason to avoid CObject as a base class is the desire to have a very specific layout for your object. It's a design goal that the size of a CString is exactly equal to the size of a normal string pointer, for example. Other classes, like CRect and CPoint, don't derive from CObject either, so that they're guaranteed to have the same memory footprint as their underlying base types. That is, a CRect sits in memory and looks exactly like a RECT structure from the Win32 headers.

On the other hand, many other sundry MFC classes *are* CObject-based. GDI objects like CPen and CBrush are created frequently, but never in the numbers that make classes like CString famous. Those GDI classes are also expensive system resources; it is imperative that you know when one is allocated and when it is correctly released. The diagnostic features of CObject are absolutely necessary in this circumstance, so a CObject base is the obvious choice.

If you're aggressive about using object-oriented techniques carefully when building your application (and you should be – within the realms of practicality of course) you'll undoubtedly be concerned about reusing other, more interesting classes in your application. This is the kind of work we've been doing throughout the book – your application, frame window, document and views, along with all of your dialog boxes, are all based on MFC objects.

But things get a little more exciting when you start to reuse classes at a slightly lower level. You might, for example, design a special list box class which subclasses CListBox, as I did in the OwnDraw sample. The CFontListBox class uses item data in the list box to manage information about each item. There will be a bit of a problem though, if someone reuses this class and calls AddString() directly, without managing the item data properly. The item data will be touched by other functions in the class; since it wasn't set up properly, all hell will break loose as the code works with uninitialized data or a null pointer.

If I carefully designed this class to make it easier to reuse, I might think about a way to make sure any user of the class could use AddString() (and other CListBox functions, too, but I'll pick on AddString() as an example) without causing problems. One obvious approach would be to write my own AddFontString() function which users of the class should call instead of using the regular AddString() function.

This would work, as long as the users remembered to use my special AddFontString() function instead of the familiar AddString() function. It's inevitable that bugs will arise, sooner or later, as the result of a developer forgetting to call the right function. I may even cause such a bug myself, if I began using the class after having put it on the shelf for a while. Since this is C++, I should have some way to conveniently reuse things, hiding the implementation inside CFontListBox from other developers who need to steal my carefully crafted functionality.

Overriding CListBox::AddString() is an obvious alternative, but a quick check of the documentation will reveal that AddString() isn't virtual. That means code which manages a pointer to a CListBox object, points it at a CFontListBox object and calls AddString() through that pointer, will end up calling the CListBox implementation of AddString() instead of CFontListBox::AddString(). That stinks.

To avoid problems with performance, MFC doesn't make every function it implements virtual; sucking extra memory for a virtual table in each and every class would be very wasteful. However, it often seems necessary to override functions for which MFC hasn't provided virtual implementations. The trick is actually to write a handler for the LB_ADDSTRING message which the list box receives. The handler for this function *is* virtual, and is hooked up using the normal message map mechanism that all MFC windows have. Letting the messaging architecture of Windows carry the approach has a couple of extra benefits:

> It doesn't force the issue of having an entry in a virtual function table. If there are overrides, they're not carried to every single class – just the ones which are actually used.

> It also allows your derived class to handle messages sent to it by non-MFC or non-C++ code. This is pretty important if the list box instance ends up in a .dll where it might be reused by the outside world.

As I mentioned briefly above, I've been using AddString() as an example. It's likely that other functions will need overrides; you'll need to figure out which message will be the right one to handle in reaction to the appropriate functions in your control and in your application. Override anything you need to; react appropriately, and go forth and build a new world.

Can You See My House from Here?

Now, I've gone on and on about playing with CWnd objects and their maps, but I've been lazy in not describing a couple of other factors that come into play. Since I'm done (and thank goodness, too – I'm out of bad cartography puns!), let's clear up those issues.

First, throughout this section, whenever I said, "CWnd," I really meant, "CWnd or any derivative class". So, if you want to Attach() a dialog box, go ahead. But you should probably call Attach() on the CDialog object instead of a plain CWnd. It's in situations like this where the slumbering giant of object-oriented programming wakes up and enables some formidable functionality.

Second, earlier in this section I talked about MFC's mapping of CWnd objects. As you might expect, MFC maps other objects too – it maps GDI objects, for instance, and some user objects, like menus. You'll find that CGdiObject and CMenu classes have Attach() and FromHandle() functions just like CWnd does. Unfortunately, there's not much in the way of subclassing for these guys, but it's very important to remember that a pointer to one of these object types is just as likely – if not more likely – to be temporary as a pointer to a CWnd is. You'll need to follow the same rules I outlined for CWnd – avoid comparisons and avoid keeping the pointer around.

Third, you need to realize you can't create C++ objects to resemble Windows objects in one thread and then use the C++ object in another. The reason for this is that MFC manages both the permanent map and the temporary map in storage that's local to each thread. If you need to do this kind of thing, you should first make sure your design is really as sane as you think it should be – do many threads really need to be playing with a single window? If you're sure that's the way to go, you must pass the handle to the window from one thread to another and Attach() it in both threads separately. You can read more about this kind of thing in Chapter 10, which talks all about multithreaded programming with MFC.

Writing Programs for the Windows Shell

Even if you don't work in Redmond, you still probably regard the release of Windows 95 as one of the more significant landmarks of the PC industry in the 1990s. The user interface provided by Windows 95, that is the **Shell**, was the first visual facelift to hit the Windows operating system since the release of Windows 3.0 back in 1992. In 1996, Microsoft added the same user interface to Windows NT 4.0, making the operating systems more compatible than ever before. Further improvements to the user interface came with Windows 98 and Windows 2000; the shell is now a ubiquitous part of the entire Windows family. Though you may be unaware of the fact, you are constantly using the shell, whether saving a file to disk or moving files around or logging in at startup.

As a developer, you get access to most aspects of the Windows user interface for free, but other features of the shell will require you to work at them. It's those features that we'll be looking at in the rest of this chapter; we'll cover:

> Shell file handling

> Folders and the shell

> The Windows taskbar

Working With the Shell

The most substantial difference in the Windows shell compared to the pre-95 versions of Windows is given away by the very name of the technology; the shell provides the basic interface between the user and the operating system. The user will use the shell to ask the operating system to run new programs and to perform other system management features. By letting your program interact more readily with the shell and by allowing it to appear as if it were an intrinsic part of the shell, the user will be able to concentrate more readily on their work – their documents, spreadsheets and databases – without being distracted by the system or applications they're using.

The features of the new shell can be accessed in two different ways – through COM interfaces, or through a few Windows API functions. MFC doesn't wrap these areas of the API at this time, but it's still important to know how to use them.

If you're new to COM, you can find out more about it in Chapter 13.

Shell APIs

The shell APIs allow you to perform a variety of tasks, from notifying the user about progress while they are moving some files around, to getting information about file types registered with the system. Let's examine each of these functions in more detail.

Manipulating Files

Windows likes to give the user progress information about file operations. It's important that your applications do this, in order to give the user the feeling that they've been carefully integrated into the system. Unfortunately, writing file manipulation routines is a bit of a nightmare – it's a task which always becomes more complicated as you get closer to finishing it. Writing the routines themselves is tedious enough, but giving useful feedback and good support for error conditions is unamusing at best.

The Windows shell implements a function called ::SHFileOperation(). This returns an integer – zero if it was successful and nonzero if there was a problem. The function takes a single parameter: a pointer to a SHFILEOPSTRUCT structure. While you can do lots of neat things with files, you'll find that the structure is really quite simple to use. Here's what it looks like:

```
typedef struct _SHFILEOPSTRUCT {
    HWND           hwnd;
    UINT           wFunc;
    LPCTSTR        pFrom;
    LPCTSTR        pTo;
    FILEOP_FLAGS   fFlags;
    BOOL           fAnyOperationsAborted;
    LPVOID         hNameMappings;
    LPCTSTR        lpszProgressTitle;
} SHFILEOPSTRUCT, FAR *LPSHFILEOPSTRUCT;
```

The beautiful aspect of the ::SHFileOperation() API is that it provides the user with feedback as the operation progresses. If you've copied lots of files or done an install with the Windows shell, you've undoubtedly seen the file progress dialog box – it features a cute animation that shows paperwork being copied from one folder to another. The API takes complete control of drawing the animation, updating the progress dialog and reacting to the user if the operation is to be cancelled. The box will even prompt for help if there are file naming collisions or directories that need to be created!

You can, of course, ask the function not to display these progress dialogs or provide the prompts – more on that later. However, if you *do* elect to allow the API to display messages, you'll need to fill in the hwnd member of this structure so that the API knows which window to use as a parent for the prompting or confirmation dialogs it generates.

You'll need to use the wFunc member to specify exactly what operation you'd like to perform. This member can be one of several constants. If you specify FO_COPY, the API will copy files specified by the pFrom member to the location specified by the pTo member. The pFrom member may be a single file name, a file name with wildcards, or a bunch of file names in a list.

The strings referenced by both pFrom and pTo must each be terminated by *two* NULL characters. So, if I wanted to copy a file named Wahoo.dat from my Windows directory to my A: drive, I would initialize a SHFILEOPSTRUCT like this:

```
SHFILEOPSTRUCT sfo;
memset(&sfo, 0, sizeof(sfo));
sfo.wFunc = FO_COPY;
sfo.pFrom = _T("C:\\WINDOWS\\WAHOO.DAT\0");
sfo.pTo = _T("A:\\\0");
SHFileOperation(&sfo);
```

> **Note that I only actually code one \0 in the strings, since I know the language will add one more.**

The FO_DELETE constant makes the function delete the file or files specified by pFrom, while pTo is ignored. The FO_MOVE constant causes the function to move files from pFrom to the location specified by pTo, optionally renaming them along the way. You can perform an in-place rename using FO_RENAME.

Once you have the SHFILEOPSTRUCT set up, just call ::SHFileOperation() and the work will be done. If you allow the function to display a progress box or make prompts, and the user presses the Cancel button at any time, the SHFILEOPSTRUCT will come back with its fAnyOperationsAborted flag set to TRUE.

The pFrom and pTo members should be initialized to point at strings which specify the source and target files, although you don't need to specify a target for a delete operation, of course. Usually, the pTo string will contain a simple target that identifies the target file, or a wildcard to identify a group. If you're performing a rename, move, or copy operation, then you might want to provide a list of targets instead of an individual one, in order to combine a set of different operations in the same call. Your approach will be dictated by the pattern of the operation you desire. For example, if you need to rename all the *.dat files in the current directory to *.inf, you could make a call like this:

```
SHFILEOPSTRUCT sfo;
memset(&sfo, 0, sizeof(sfo));
sfo.wFunc = FO_RENAME;
sfo.pFrom = _T("*.DAT\0");
sfo.pTo = _T("*.INF\0");
SHFileOperation(&sfo);
```

If you have a discontinuous bunch of files, though, you might not be able to use wildcards to express the operation you desire. Instead of making multiple calls, you can specify a list of files in your pTo string which will correspond to one in your pFrom string. This call, for example:

```
SHFILEOPSTRUCT sfo;
memset(&sfo, 0, sizeof(sfo));
sfo.wFunc = FO_RENAME;
sfo.fFlags = FOF_MULTIDESTFILES;
sfo.pFrom = _T("ONE.DAT\0TWO.DAT\0THREE.DAT\0");
sfo.pTo = _T("ICHI.DAT\0NI.DAT\0SAN.DAT\0");
SHFileOperation(&sfo);
```

renames the file One.dat to Ichi.dat, Two.dat to Ni.dat, and Three.dat to San.dat. To make this feature work, you'll need to make sure you set the FOF_MULTIDESTFILES flag.

If you specify wildcards in your pFrom string, the function will traverse any subdirectories it finds which match the wildcard specification. If you use a pFrom string of "C:\\WINDOWS*.*", for example, the function will copy files from Windows and all its subdirectories. It will create directories at the destination and place files where they were in the source path. If you don't want to copy subdirectories and their files, you should make sure you set the FOF_FILESONLY flag.

Making Progress

As Windows works through your call to ::SHFileOperation(), it will show the user an animation to indicate that it is making progress. The dialog that shows the animation will also include information about what file names are being copied. You can see a sample of the dialog here:

The call to ::SHFileOperation() will show a progress dialog if Windows expects the operation to take an appreciable amount of time. If the file operation ends quickly because of cache hits or because of the size of the involved files, don't be surprised when Windows doesn't show a box. If you're sure you don't want the call to present a progress dialog, you should set the FOF_SILENT flag in the fFlags member of the SHFILEOPSTRUCT you pass. If you're copying temporary files or other files which won't have names that interest the user, you can set the FOF_SIMPLEPROGRESS flag and the resulting dialog box won't show the file names as they're processed.

If you've asked for a simple progress dialog box with the FOF_SIMPLEPROGRESS flag, you can get the ::SHFileOperation() function to display whatever title string you'd like by initializing the lpszProgressTitle member of your SHFILEOPSTRUCT.

Prompting

If you specify a directory or folder that doesn't exist, the function will ask the user whether they wish to create it. If this request is declined, the function will return without an error or any indication that the operation failed – you'll need to check to see if the target was created for you to make sure the function did something. If you don't want the function to prompt before it creates the directory, set the FOF_NOCONFIRMMKDIR flag.

The FOF_NOCONFIRMATION flag can be used to turn off *all* confirmations that the function might generate. Aside from creating directories, the function might also ask if you wish to overwrite existing files.

If you're copying or moving files and the function finds that a target name collides with an existing file, it will overwrite the target files without warning. If you set the FOF_RENAMEONCOLLISION flag, you'll cause the function to rename the file before placing it in the target directory. If, for example, you copy Extra.dat to a directory where Extra.dat already exists, the function will name the target file "Copy of Extra.dat".

The Shell Namespace

The Windows shell interface is centered around a desktop which contains folders and shortcuts instead of simply holding the opened windows of running applications. Folders allow the user to collect other files, folders, and shortcuts in a convenient user interface. Shortcuts provide the ability to create a link to another file, folder, computer or object somewhere else.

The Windows shell manages the desktop and all the folders that are stored on it, and provides developers with the ability to manipulate this information. The shell calls this its **namespace** because the folders, shortcuts and other objects are all identified by names known to the shell and to the user. This set of names provides the heart of the interface, even for the programmer.

The functions in this group make great use of a common notion – a data structure called a **PIDL**, which is short for '**p**ointer to an **id**entifier list'. You can run off and ask Windows for a PIDL by calling the ::SHGetSpecialFolderLocation() API, which takes three parameters and has this prototype:

```
HRESULT WINAPI SHGetSpecialFolderLocation(HWND        hwndOwner,
                                          int         nFolder,
                                          LPITEMIDLIST *ppidl);
```

The last parameter is a pointer to a pointer to an item ID list, and it's where the function will store its resulting value for you. If the function needs to display a dialog box to prompt the user, it will use the hwndOwner parameter as the parent for that dialog. The second parameter is a constant that indicates which special shell folder you want to start enumerating. You can ask for any one of these special folders:

Constant	Special Folder	Meaning
CSIDL_BITBUCKET	Recycle Bin	References a directory that contains the files and objects in the user's Recycle Bin. This is normally C:\Recycle, but may be moved by the user.
CSIDL_COMMON_DESKTOP		File system directory that contains files and folders that appear on the desktop for all users.
CSIDL_COMMON_PROGRAMS		File system directory that contains the directories for the common program groups that appear on the Start menu for all users.
CSIDL_COMMON_STARTMENU		File system directory that contains the programs and folders that appear on the Start menu for all users.
CSIDL_COMMON_STARTUP		File system directory that contains the programs that appear in the Startup folder for all users. The system starts these programs whenever any user logs on to Windows NT or starts up Windows 95/98.
CSIDL_CONTROLS	Control Panel	References a virtual folder that contains everything that you'd see in the Control Panel.
CSIDL_DESKTOP	Windows Desktop	References a virtual folder that contains *all* names, starting at the desktop itself.
CSIDL_DESKTOPDIRECTORY		References a folder used physically to store file objects on the desktop. This is *not* the same as CSIDL_DESKTOP because this folder only contains files and not links or other namespaces.

Constant	Special Folder	Meaning
CSIDL_DRIVES	My Computer	References a virtual folder containing everything on the local computer – storage devices, printers and the Control Panel. The folder may also contain mapped network drives.
CSIDL_FONTS	Fonts folder	References a virtual folder containing all fonts installed on this computer.
CSIDL_NETHOOD	Network Neighborhood	References a file system directory containing objects that appear in the Network Neighborhood icon, i.e. an enumeration of all other computers in this workgroup (or domain in NT).
CSIDL_NETWORK	Network Neighborhood	Virtual folder representing the top level of the network hierarchy. The content of this folder is the same as the Entire Network folder under the Network Neighborhood icon.
CSIDL_PERSONAL		File system directory that serves as a common repository for system-wide, documents.
CSIDL_PRINTERS	Printers Folder	References a virtual folder containing installed printers.
CSIDL_PROGRAMS		References a file system directory that contains the user's program groups (which are also file system directories).
CSIDL_RECENT		References a file system directory that contains the user's most recently used documents.
CSIDL_SENDTO		References a file system directory that contains Send To menu items.
CSIDL_STARTMENU		References a file system directory containing all Start menu items.
CSIDL_STARTUP		References a file system directory that corresponds to the user's Startup program group.
CSIDL_TEMPLATES		References a file system directory that serves as a common repository for document templates.

If the function fails, it will provide a COM-like error return via the function's HRESULT type. If things work okay, the function will return a success code and populate the pointer you passed to refer to a list of IDs of the items that you requested.

By the way, the item list that you get back from the `::SHGetSpecialFolderLocation()` call includes only the top-level item that you've requested. For example, if you call to retrieve the `CSIDL_DESKTOP`, the returned PIDL has only one entry – for the desktop. It turns out that the shell namespace is a hierarchy. You'll need to enumerate the items within the desktop in a separate operation. The list of IDs identifies items within the particular high-level folder you've requested.

The IShellFolder Interface

All the work you'll need to do with a folder is done via the folder's `IShellFolder` interface. This *is* a COM interface, but it's not something you'd ever call `QueryInterface()` to find. Instead, you can call a couple of special APIs to get the folders.

Since (for now) the shell namespace is the only one in town, and it's rooted by the desktop, you can get an `IShellFolder` interface referring to the root of the known universe by calling `::SHGetDesktopFolder()`. This function takes only a single parameter – a pointer to the `IShellFolder` you'd like to initialize.

To make it clear, the Windows shell uses `IShellFolder` to work with a particular folder. If you need to, you can enumerate items within the folder by requesting a list of IDs from the folder. The IDs might refer to files, links, shortcuts, or other folders. Let's have a look at what you can get done with folders – starting with their names and attributes and ending with how to enumerate their contents.

Folder Names

Now that you have a pointer to the desktop folder object, you can move around wherever you'd like. If you have an item ID, you can get the name of the item by using the `GetDisplayNameOf()` method of the `IShellFolder` interface. The method has this prototype:

```
HRESULT IShellFolder::GetDisplayNameOf(LPCITEMIDLIST pidl,
                                       DWORD         uFlags,
                                       LPSTRRET      lpName);
```

The `pidl` points to an interface ID list that has only one entry – that entry should identify the item that you'd like the name of. The `lpName` pointer references a `STRRET` structure that lets you know where the string you need is stored. `STRRET` has this format:

```
typedef struct _STRRET {
   UINT uType;
   union
   {
      LPWSTR pOleStr;
      UINT   uOffset;
      char   cStr[MAX_PATH];
   } DUMMYUNIONNAME;
} STRRET, *LPSTRRET;
```

When GetDisplayNameOf() returns successfully, it will have populated the STRRET structure you provided with the display name. The uType field of the structure indicates where the string may be found and how it will live out its life; if uType is set to STRRET_CSTR, the cStr buffer contains the string and you can use it as long as you have your STRRET structure handy. If the name is actually embedded in the identifier list which was passed to the call to GetDisplayNameOf(), uType will be set to STRRET_OFFSET, and uOffset will indicate an offset, in bytes, from the pidl passed to GetDisplayNameOf(). So, if uType is set to STRRET_OFFSET, the returned display name can be found starting at the byte at pidl+sName.uOffset, for example. If uType is STRRET_WSTR, the string is at pOleStr but is actually a zero-terminated wide character string.

You have no control over what uType value GetDisplayNameOf() will return to you – you can't even really accurately predict how the string will be returned. As such, the first thing you'll probably want to do after GetDisplayNameOf() returns is to create a CString object to hold the content – a format that is certainly more appealing to you. The AllFiles sample shows how to do this in its STRRETToCString() function.

Folders are named using a few different conventions. You can request a normal name, which is a displayable name that users might see in the shell. For example, if the item you're referring to is actually a UNC path to another computer, like \\Thumper\Droppoint, GetDisplayNameOf() would return "droppoint on thumper" if you passed SHGDN_NORMAL as the second parameter. If the item was a file, you'd get a short representation of the file name; for instance, C:\Windows\File.txt would translate to file. If you specify SHGDN_INFOLDER, the names returned by GetDisplayNameOf() are actually a bit terser, since you may have to do a bit more work to understand the folder's context. Printers, for example, are very different from items you may find in the Fonts folder. Finally, you can pass SHGDN_FORPARSING to get the raw name of the string – where an item referring to \\Thumper\Droppoint would really return that same UNC path, for example.

If you've got a STRRET which has a raw name, you can always use the ParseDisplayName() method of the IShellFolder interface to get an item identifier list for the name.

You can change a folder's name by using the SetNameOf() method. It accepts any of the parsed SHGDN_-type names we've just seen the GetDisplayNameOf() method produce, and uses the name to set the identified folder. The method takes these parameters:

```
HRESULT IShellFolder::SetNameOf(HWND            hwndOwner,
                                LPCITEMIDLIST   pidl,
                                LPCOLESTR       lpszName,
                                DWORD           uFlags,
                                LPITEMIDLIST*   ppidlOut);
```

The pidl parameter references a single-element list of IDs. The single element identifies the item that you'd like to rename. The lpszName parameter references the new name; you don't have to pass it using a STRRET, but note that the pointer is to an OLESTR, which is always a wide-character string in 32-bit Windows. uFlags can contain the same flags we saw for the uFlags member of GetDisplayNameOf(). The ppidlOut parameter is a pointer to an ITEMIDLIST that the function will populate with the newly named object's ID.

If you need the physical path of a particular item, you can send a list with a single ID in it to the `::SHGetPathFromIDList()` API. The function accepts a pointer to the pointer list and a pointer to a buffer which it will fill with the path. You must make sure the buffer you offer has at least `MAX_PATH` characters in it. The function will return `TRUE` if it worked, or `FALSE` if it couldn't get a path name for the object in question; for example, if the object isn't actually a file, the function will fail.

Other Folder Attributes

Folders, of course, have more than names to make them special. You can call the `GetAttributesOf()` method of `IShellInterface` to learn more about a particular item within a folder. `GetAttributesOf()` has this prototype:

```
HRESULT IShellFolder::GetAttributesOf(UINT         cidl,
                                      LPCITEMIDLIST* apidl,
                                      ULONG*        rgfInOut);
```

The `cidl` parameter indicates the number of items for which you'd like to retrieve attributes. The `LPCITEMIDLIST` points to a list of pointers to IDs of items that you'd like to query. The `rgfInOut` parameter points at an array of `ULONG` values, which will be filled with flags that describe the object you're interrogating. This parameter is unique because, before you make the call, you need to initialize the storage with flags that you're interested in interrogating. The `Shlobj.h` header defines masks that you can use to query items easily.

The group of flags in the following table pertains to the capabilities of the queried object or objects. They might be combined to indicate the availability of a combination of features:

Flag	Description
SFGAO_CANCOPY	The objects can be copied – this is synonymous with the DROPEFFECT_COPY value.
SFGAO_CANDELETE	The objects can be deleted, i.e. they are not read-only.
SFGAO_CANLINK	The objects can be made into a shortcut – synonymous with the DROPEFFECT_LINK value.
SFGAO_CANMOVE	The objects can be moved – synonymous with the DROPEFFECT_MOVE value.
SFGAO_CANRENAME	The objects may be renamed. Many system folders do not allow renaming.
SFGAO_CAPABILITYMASK	A mask that covers all capability flag values.
SFGAO_DROPTARGET	The objects can be used as drop targets.
SFGAO_HASPROPSHEET	The objects queried have property sheets.

If you're interested in all of these flags, you can initialize the corresponding ULONG you pass to the GetAttributesOf() method with SFGAO_CAPABILITYMASK. Alternatively, you can use particular SFGAO_ flags glued together with the binary OR operator (|). On the way into the GetAttributesOf() method, if a bit in the ULONG is set, the method will try to query that attribute; if the bit is clear, the attribute won't be queried. After the function returns, the same ULONG has the corresponding bits set if the attribute was requested and the attribute is applicable to the target object. Otherwise, the bit is reset.

This next set of flags applies to the group of attributes that represent how objects are displayed – they reflect how Windows displays the item in the shell. To get all of the following attributes, use the SFGAO_DISPLAYATTRMASK mask:

Flag	Description
SFGAO_GHOSTED	The queried objects should be displayed using a ghosted icon
SFGAO_LINK	The queried objects are shortcuts
SFGAO_READONLY	The queried objects are read-only
SFGAO_SHARE	The queried objects are shared

You can use SFGAO_CONTENTSMASK to cover all the contents attributes for the object. In fact, there's only one content attribute, so this might seem a little like overkill. However, the SFGAO_CONTENTSMASK constant is valuable because, some day, there might be more. Here's the one flag:

Flag	Description
SFGAO_HASSUBFOLDER	The queried folders themselves contain folders (and are, therefore, expandable in the left pane of Windows Explorer)

These miscellaneous bits have no corresponding mask and must be queried individually:

Flag	Description
SFGAO_FILESYSANCESTOR	The queried folders contain one or more file system folders
SFGAO_FILESYSTEM	The queried folders or file objects are part of the file system (that is, they are files, directories, or root directories)
SFGAO_FOLDER	The queried objects are folders
SFGAO_REMOVABLE	The queried objects are on removable media
SFGAO_VALIDATE	Forces cached information to be invalidated and refreshed

The last flag, SFGAO_VALIDATE, isn't an attribute at all — it instructs the method that any cached information relating to the object be refreshed before the query is completed.

Enumerating Folder Contents

You can plow through each item in a folder by using the folder's IEnumIDList interface, to which you can get a pointer by calling the EnumObjects() method of the IShellFolder interface. The EnumObjects() method takes these parameters:

```
HRESULT IShellFolder::EnumObjects(HWND           hwndOwner,
                                  DWORD          grfFlags,
                                  LPENUMIDLIST*  ppenumIDList);
```

The first parameter is a handle to a window that will be used as a parent for any prompts the enumeration needs to offer the user. The grfFlags parameter can be any combination of three flags: SHCONTF_FOLDERS, to include folders in the enumeration; SHCONTF_INCLUDEHIDDEN, to include hidden objects in the enumeration; and SHCONTF_NONFOLDERS, to include non-folder (i.e. file) objects in the enumeration. The ppenumIDList parameter points to your pointer to an IEnumIDList interface. You can use the LPENUMIDLIST type to declare such a pointer.

The Allfiles sample calls EnumObjects() from its own Traverse() function to recursively enumerate folder and non-folder items in the shell namespace, whether the items are hidden or not.

If the EnumObjects() method returns successfully, it will initialize the pointer you supply with a pointer to the interface. If the function fails, it will return an error code. The function will return successfully even if the object you'd like to enumerate is empty.

Once you have a pointer to an IEnumIDList, you can call any of its members to do the enumeration. Since looking through a list is pretty simple, the interface has only four members: Next(), Reset(), Skip() and Clone().

Next() returns the next group of items from the interface. The function takes the count of elements you'd like to request: a pointer to a list of pointers to their IDs, and a pointer to a ULONG which indicates exactly how many were retrieved. If you ask for more than there are available, the function will only return those that it has; like reading past the end of a file. Trying to retrieve too many items from the enumeration isn't considered a serious error condition.

The Traverse() function in the Allfiles sample simply calls Next() again and again to read all of the items the enumeration has to offer. Allfiles calls GetDisplayNameOf() to get a printable name for each item, and then decides if the item is worth printing or not by examining some of its attributes. The program doesn't print out the name for every single file, for example — instead, it only prints the names of folders to keep the generated output reasonable.

Reset() doesn't take any parameters and pops the context for the enumeration back to the beginning of the list.

The Skip() member of IEnumIDList takes a single ULONG parameter which indicates how many elements of the list should be skipped. It pushes the context of the enumeration up by just that many entries.

You can use the Clone() method to copy the enumeration object. The function takes a pointer to an LPENUMIDLIST, which will be populated with a pointer to the new IEnumIDList interface for the new enumeration. The new enumeration has *exactly* the same content and status as the original list.

When you're using the IEnumIDList interface, remember that it derives from IUnknown like all other COM interfaces. When you're done using the interface, be sure to call its Release() method to let go of the object! The Allfiles sample releases the enumerator after it knows it has retrieved all of the items in the enumerator.

Navigating Folders

The previous sections have discussed everything we can do with a folder once we've found it, but I've not said much about moving from one folder to another. When you call
::SHGetDesktopFolder(), you get a pointer to the IShellFolder interface on the granddaddy of all folders on your system. If you've also called ::SHGetSpecialFolderLocation(), you'll have a list of the IDs of a certain type of item within that folder. Alternatively, you could enumerate the contents of a folder by working with the IEnumIDList interface we've just discussed.

You can get an IShellFolder interface for a folder other than the Desktop folder by using the BindToObject() method on an existing IShellFolder interface. The function takes these parameters:

```
HRESULT IShellFolder::BindToObject(LPCITEMIDLIST pidl,
                                   LPBC          pbcReserved,
                                   REFIID        riid,
                                   LPVOID*       ppvOut);
```

The pidl parameter is a pointer to an ITEMIDLIST list that has but one entry, which identifies the item to which you'd like to attach. pdcReserved is reserved; it must be zero. The riid parameter must be IID_IShellFolder for now – maybe in a future version of Windows, you'll be able to query for a different interface on shell objects. The ppvOut parameter is a pointer to the pointer you'll use to reference the interface.

You can see all of these navigation functions in great, real-life action by examining the Allfiles sample. It's a console application which recursively finds objects in the shell namespace and prints out information about them. When it visits a folder, it uses IEnumIDList to examine each of the items in a particular folder. It then prints out the name and attributes for the item. If the item is a folder itself, the code continues by binding to it and repeating the print and query operations until it has traversed through every object in town.

Memory and ID Lists

Many of the interfaces and a couple of the APIs we talked about in this section return new ID lists for your program to use. These lists are stored in memory allocated by the shell. As such, you must carefully return that memory to the shell when you're done using the list.

The shell offers its memory manager implementation via the COM IMalloc interface which has two important members: Alloc() and Free(). The two functions work just like malloc() and free() from the C standard library, except they allocate or free memory actually owned by the process which supports the interface – in this case, the system itself.

In the `AllFiles` sample, you'll note that we call the `::SHGetMalloc()` API to get a pointer to the `IMalloc` interface. After we're finished using the interface and before the program ends, we'll call its `Release()` method to make sure the shell knows we're done with it. More importantly, we'll use its `Free()` method to let go of any memory lists which the shell has provided us. For example, the `::SHGetSpecialFolderLocation()` which makes the whole program go, will return a quite lengthy memory block. At the very end of the program, just before releasing the `IMalloc` interface itself, we'll call `Free()` on this block of memory so that the system can have it back.

You'll also note that some of the interfaces we described want to have a list of only one item. To facilitate calling such functions, the `AllFiles` sample has a routine that copies a list, but only provides the list's first entry in the target list. This makes it very easy to pass one element of a large list to functions that require a single-entry list. The function that does this for us is called `CopyItemID()`.

About the Microsoft Documentation

Before you read much of the documentation for the shell object interfaces, you should know that it's written for C programmers. The sample code is also written to be compiled as C, not C++, code. There is quite a difference – it's a lot easier to write COM code in C++ because the C++ language understands the vtables in the underlying interfaces and automatically passes the `this` pointer to members of the interface. So, code stolen from the online documentation written for C might look like this:

```
// Bind to the subfolder.
if (!SUCCEEDED(pFolder->lpVtbl->BindToObject(
            pFolder, pidlCopy, NULL, IID_IShellFolder, &pSubFolder)))
{
    g_pMalloc->lpVtbl->Free(g_pMalloc, pidlCopy);
    break;
}
```

But as a C++ programmer, you can write something a little clearer:

```
// Bind to the subfolder.
if (!SUCCEEDED(pFolder->BindToObject(
                pidlCopy, NULL, IID_IShellFolder, (void**)&pSubFolder)))
{
    g_pMalloc->Free(pidlCopy);
    break;
}
```

Note that there's no need to reference an explicit `lpVtbl` pointer, because C++ does it for you. Neither do you have to explicitly pass the pointer to the object to members that it implements, since C++ helps you with that, too. The parameter types are a little different as well – since C++ offers much stronger type checking, you might have to add an explicit cast to get the code to compile.

You can't combine techniques that use the C-style interfaces to the objects with C++ code. The `Shlobj.h` header file, where all of these little beasts are actually defined, looks to see if you're building a C++ or a C file. Depending on the presence or absence of the predefined `__cplusplus` preprocessor symbol, the header changes the way the interfaces and macros are set up to your needs. You can, if you absolutely need to, compile separate `.c` files in your project and link them to the balance of your C++ code.

There are a number of other shell functions that you may want to make use of such as ::SHAddToRecentDocs(), ::SHChangeNotify(), *and* ::SHGetFileInfo(). *You can find out more about these functions by searching the online help.*

The Taskbar Notification Area

The Windows shell manages an area at the bottom of the screen called the taskbar. This provides users with the ability to launch applications quickly by using the Start button, or to change focus to a running application quickly by clicking on the area of the taskbar that contains a button-like control for each running program. At the far right of the taskbar, there's an area called the taskbar notification area, shown here:

The taskbar notification area is a place where users can go to check on system-wide settings. The Windows shell normally displays the time of day here, and you can also find some applications that add an icon to enable you to change their settings, activate them or get their status easily. Many Windows device drivers add icons here. My system at home, for example, has an icon for the display driver and sound driver.

If you're writing an application that works in the background, it's more than likely that you'll be interested in adding a taskbar notification icon. If you're writing a more complicated application, you might want to offer a taskbar notification icon so that users can access a settings dialog in your application quickly, or so that they can change the state of your application.

You can manage taskbar icons rather trivially – just call the ::Shell_NotifyIcon() API. This function takes two parameters: a command code and a pointer to a NOTIFYICONDATA structure that will describe your icon.

The command codes are so simple that they're almost self-explanatory: NIM_ADD adds a new icon, NIM_DELETE removes an existing icon and NIM_MODIFY changes the attributes of an icon. The Windows shell will always use a small, 16-by-16 pixel icon for the taskbar notification area; if you supply a large, 32-by-32 pixel icon, the shell will shrink it automatically.

The NOTIFYICONDATA structure has only a few members. It looks like this:

```
typedef struct _NOTIFYICONDATA {
    DWORD cbSize;
    HWND hWnd;
    UINT uID;
    UINT uFlags;
    UINT uCallbackMessage;
    HICON hIcon;
    char szTip[64];
} NOTIFYICONDATA, *PNOTIFYICONDATA;
```

Like most structures used by the Win32 API, NOTIFYICONDATA has a cbSize element that you should initialize to the number of bytes in your structure, so that Windows can validate it.

The szTip member allows you to specify text for a tool tip – if the user lets their mouse pointer hang around for a little while on the icon that you've added, Windows will display this text in a tool tip to explain what your icon is all about. You can use this text to provide status; for example, the laptop computer I'm using to write this has a taskbar icon when the modem is running. The tool tip text for the icon is actually a string that lets me know how much data the modem has sent or received during the communications session (a good use for NIM_MODIFY). If you want to specify tool tip text, you need to make sure the uFlags member has the NIF_TIP flag set. If you don't, make sure it isn't.

Your application should always set the NIF_ICON flag and put a handle to the icon you want to use in the hIcon member of the structure. If you don't specify an icon, Windows will leave a gaping hole in the notification area. You can't easily write code to paint something in there.

uID identifies the notification area you've created. You don't need to worry about this item being unique among other notification areas in other applications because Windows also uses the window handle you supply in the hWnd field to identify the application owning the area. Windows will include the uID you supply in messages it sends you if the user moves around or clicks in the area of your icon. Windows won't send messages if you don't specify a valid message *and* set the NIF_MESSAGE flag in the uFlags member. You *do*, though, need to make sure that your uID value is unique within your application so that you can tell the icons apart when Windows sends a notification to you.

The sample application, named TBar, is a dialog-based program that doesn't use the notification area for anything meaningful. Instead, it allows you to add and remove taskbar notification icons at will. You can view the messages sent back from Windows when you prod at the taskbar notification area with your mouse.

The program registers its own message ID with a call to ::RegisterWindowMessage(). The application then tells Windows that the dialog acting as the main window of the application should be notified when the user manipulates the taskbar message. When a notification message is received, the application formats a string to explain the message and immediately adds it to a list box labeled Notifications. In a more serious application, you might want to call ActivateWindow() or some similar function to get focus to the window in the application you want to use to help get some work done. You can even create a new window in response to mouse messages (such as a click or double-click) so that the user can work with a different part of your program.

When the application terminates, or when the Remove button in the sample is pressed, the application calls ::Shell_NotifyIcon() to remove the icon. If you don't remove the icon when your application is terminated, Windows *will* figure out that you've orphaned the icon and clean up. Unfortunately, this doesn't happen very quickly and the delay is noticeable to the user – you should carefully clean up your notification icon so the user doesn't have to watch the clean up on the taskbar while they're busy trying to get some work done.

You'll notice that the application manages a copy of the NOTIFYICONDATA structure it uses to add the icons to the taskbar. This isn't strictly necessary – I coded the sample this way just to make it easy to look up information about the items in response to messages. It's important to note, however, that Windows manages a copy of the NOTIFYICONDATA structure after you call ::Shell_NotifyIcon(). There's no reason to keep your copy of the structure around; you can even delete the icon handle that you passed in the structure.

Summary

In this chapter, I hoped to provide some food for thought when questions arise about your application's user interface. So,

> - if you're brainstorming to improve a user interface
> - if you need to alert service technicians about a box of raisins blocking the cooling water flow from the core of a nuclear reactor
> - if you want a cool way for an untrained user to pick from 57,000 different reptiles in a pet store

then remember what you saw here and decide which method would be the best fit. However, the material we've covered is more likely to be the catalyst for one of your own ideas.

The key point to remember is that you, as the author of the software, will know exactly how the interface is supposed to be used. Your users, however, are a different kettle of fish. Design for them!

Much of the functionality we covered in the last part of this chapter isn't directly managed by MFC classes or functions; almost everything we talked about here is done through calls made directly to the Windows API. Future versions of MFC will offer built-in functionality to support your work with the Windows shell. In situations where working with the shell is easy, such as using the `::Shell_NotifyIcon()` API, there's no value that MFC can really add. However, for the more advanced shell interfaces, MFC should eventually be improved to facilitate this kind of programming.

8

Using the Windows Common Controls

Your applications will need to display controls – that is, the special windows with which the user interacts directly via the mouse and keyboard – to make life easier for the user. In Chapter 5, we examined lots of simple controls, most of which have been built into Windows since Version 1.0 of that venerable operating system. With the introduction of Windows 95 and Windows NT 3.51, Microsoft added several new controls to the operating system, called the **Windows common controls**. In Windows 98, and on older systems with updated versions of Internet Explorer installed, the controls have been updated considerably. Knowing how to apply these enhanced controls appropriately in your application can save you a great deal of work. In this chapter, we'll examine the enhanced controls, as well as a few interesting controls that are implemented by MFC but are *not* part of the common controls implemented by Windows.

Overview

There are a whole flock of common controls, most of which are implemented by Windows in a DLL called Comctl32.dll. The granddaddy of all controls, the rich-text edit control, is implemented in a separate DLL because it is so complex and can create dependencies on other expensive system services, such as OLE.

Having the rich edit control in a separate DLL makes it easier to keep your application as skinny as possible. We'll discuss the rich edit control at great length in this chapter, as well. The rich edit control is revised on a slightly different schedule than the remaining common controls are, since it lives in a separate DLL. The original control is called *Rich Edit Version 1.0* and lives in Riched32.dll. The revised control is called *Rich Edit Version 2.0* and is supported by Riched20.dll. The latter DLL has a few extra formatting features and far better support for localization. Unfortunately, MFC doesn't yet support Version 2.0 of the control.

Comctl32.dll has been updated, as well. The most up-to-date version of the library is installed with Windows 98 and Windows 2000. On Windows 95 and Windows NT 4.0 installations you will have to make sure the latest version of Internet Explorer is installed on the system before using some of the newest features. Throughout this chapter, I'll explicitly indicate that a given feature is available only in the newer DLL. If you see no such admonition, you can assume that the feature is always at your disposal.

You can create the Windows common controls like ordinary windows, or use them like regular controls in your application's dialog box templates.

As we saw in Chapter 4, MFC features CView-derived classes to help you create applications that have common controls in their frame windows or in panes in their splitter windows. MFC also provides direct wrappers for all of the common controls. The following table shows the names of the common controls, as well as the MFC class that wraps them:

Common Control Name	MFC Class
Animation Control	CAnimateCtrl
Date Time Picker Control	CDateTimeCtrl
Header Control	CHeaderCtrl
Hot Key Control	CHotKeyCtrl
Image List	CImageList
IP Address Control	CIPAddressCtrl
List View Control	CListCtrl
Month Calendar Control	CMonthCalCtrl
Progress Bar	CProgressCtrl
Property Sheet	CPropertySheet, CPropertyPage
ReBar Control	CReBar (also CReBarCtrl)
Rich Edit Control	CRichEditCtrl
Slider Control	CSliderCtrl
Spin Button Control	CSpinButtonCtrl
Status Window	CStatusBar (also CStatusBarCtrl)
Tab Control	CTabCtrl
Toolbar	CToolBar (also CToolBarCtrl)
Tool Tip	CToolTipCtrl
Tree View Control	CTreeCtrl

Of these controls several are new to MFC 6.0, including `CMonthCalCtrl`, `CDateTimeCtrl` and `CIPAddressCtrl`. The first displays a simple calendar interface that allows the selection of a date. `CDateTimeCtrl` is very similar to `CMonthCalCtrl` only it allows the selection of a time value as well as a date value. It also has the additional option of displaying dates and times in the form of an extended edit control. `CIPAddressCtrl` allows the manipulation of IP addresses. These new controls are discussed in more detail later in this chapter.

The `CRebar` class is also new and represents an Internet Explorer-type toolbar that can contain child windows as various controls, such as list boxes and edit boxes. This class is further explained in chapter 4.

You'll notice that a few of the controls (that is, the rebar, the toolbar, and the status window) are represented by two different MFC classes. The `CReBarCtrl`, `CToolBarCtrl`, and `CStatusBarCtrl` classes wrap rebar, tool bar and status bar controls directly, so if you're working on adding a toolbar or a status bar to a dialog box or pop-up window in your application, you should use these classes. However, if you need to put one of these controls inside an MFC-managed frame window, you should use the `CReBar`, `CToolBar` or `CStatusBar` classes. These classes work at a higher level to provide the ability to manage the sizing and layout of the controls within a frame window.

In 16-bit versions of MFC, as well as in the oldest 32-bit versions of MFC, `CToolBar` and `CStatusBar` contained code to do the painting for the controls. From MFC 3.0 onwards, these controls are actually painted by Windows, since MFC uses the Windows implementation of the controls provided by the `Comct132.dll` library. The difference between `CToolBarCtrl` and `CToolBar`, for example, is that the classes with shorter names are MFC inventions that own instances of the classes with longer names, or in other words, `CToolBar` owns an instance of `CToolBarCtrl`. Additional features mean that `CToolBar` and `CStatusBar` know how to work with `CFrameWnd` to lay themselves out within the frame window. The window type represented by `CReBar`, that is a toolbar that can contain child windows in the form of controls, is new to MFC 6.0, so it only appears in the most up-to-date versions of the library.

In our investigation of the common controls, we'll first cover some basics about the controls and their inclusion into your favorite project, before having a peek at the MFC support for each of the controls in turn to see what they're all about. Before we embark on our journey, remember that the Windows common controls are just that: *Windows* common controls. They aren't implemented by MFC; they're just wrapped by it. When Windows changes, the controls will change. Updates to MFC won't affect the way that the controls behave. Just as it is with the regular Windows controls, like push buttons and edit controls, the responsibility of implementing them is entirely up to Windows.

By the way, if you try to run the example applications under a version of Windows NT that doesn't support common controls, you'll be rewarded with an error like this one:

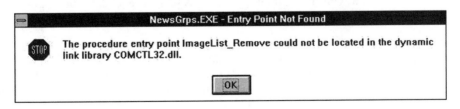

The error message indicates that a particular entry point in the library could not be found – MFC is trying to find a function to support one of the controls but can't, since your version of the library doesn't support it.

The Common Controls and Versioning

This chapter discusses all the features currently available in the common control DLL version that ships with Windows 98 and Internet Explorer 4.0, and Windows NT 2000. Of course, it's quite possible that your target system doesn't have the newest file installed. So, what do you do?

Well, you have a few choices. You can try to find the `InitCommonControlsEx()` entry point in the `Comct132.dll` you have loaded. Just call `AfxLoadLibrary()` and then call `GetProcAddress()` on the name `"InitCommonControlsEx"`. If the entry point is found, then you know you have at least version 4.70 – the version that comes with Windows 98 before Internet Explorer is installed. You'll have access to most of these controls, but only some of the functions that these controls implement.

If you want to use everything you've read here, though, you'll need at least Version 4.71 of the library. This version of the library comes with Internet Explorer 4.0. Unfortunately, I know of no other legal way of installing the DLL than installing the minimal version of Internet Explorer 4.0. There's a yet newer version of the library, which ships with (at least) Internet Explorer 5.0. The controls library has been only slightly updated with this release.

If you need to test for a newer version of `Comct132.dll` at runtime, you'll have to get the version information from the library at runtime and make a direct comparison. The `GetFileVersionInfo()` makes it pretty easy to get the information you need from the file.

The documentation that ships with Visual C++ is very careful to point out which version of the library supports which particular features. If you're thinking of using any of the features I've described here, I encourage you to check with the documentation. Providing the information here would be far too invasive – and, I'm afraid, I cannot vouch for the accuracy of the documentation. Furthermore, I regret that there's not a better redistribution story for the API and controls. The common controls have been one of the most aggressively grown areas of the Windows API, but I regret to say that their reuse has not been very carefully planned.

Common Control Basics

With the exception of the rich-text edit control, all of the Windows common controls use functions, structures and constants from the `Commctrl.h` file in the `Microsoft Visual Studio\Vc98\Include` directory. `Commctrl.h` provides the SDK-level interface for the controls. The header defines the structures and messages applications use to communicate with them. There are a few flat APIs, as well. The rich-text edit control has its API-level definition in the `Richedit.h` header.

For MFC apps, you'll want a C++ interface. When you bring in the headers for the MFC classes that wrap the controls, you'll also get the necessary Windows common control header files. To get the MFC wrappers provided for these controls, you'll need to include `Afxcmn.h` from the `Microsoft Visual Studio\Vc98\MFC\Include` directory during the compilation of the mainstream controls, and `Afxrich.h` for the rich-text edit control.

While the common controls provide exciting new functionality, writing code for them has relatively few surprises. Just like other controls, you'll be able to obtain a pointer to the MFC object representing a control by casting the result of GetDlgItem() to the right MFC class type. For example, if you have a tree view control in your dialog box identified by IDC_PARTSLIST, you can use the following familiar trick to gain a pointer to an initialized MFC CTreeViewCtrl object, which can be used to access the control with which you want to work:

```
CTreeViewCtrl* pTreeControl;
pTreeControl = static_cast<CTreeViewCtrl*>(GetDlgItem(IDC_PARTSLIST));
ASSERT(pTreeControl != NULL);
```

ClassWizard supports programming with the new controls and it knows about all of their notification and command messages. Since most of the new controls represent far more information than is conveyed in a simple data type, there is no real dialog data exchange support for them. The lack of DDX_ support means that although you can declare control member variables for your dialogs, ClassWizard doesn't support the transfer of information back and forth between member variables and the new controls. For some of the controls, where it is really interesting to move data about, I'll show you how to augment the code in your DoDataExchange() routine to achieve this.

The Visual C++ dialog box editor allows you to draw animation, tab, tree view, list view, hot key, slider, progress and spin controls. You can't draw header controls in the resource editor because, as we'll see, they're almost always coupled at runtime with another control and invade that control's client area. You can, however, create them dynamically and have them draw in a location of your choosing. It's up to you to effect a user interface by reacting to messages the control sends when the user touches it.

In the Visual C++ 6 IDE, you can use the dialog editor to draw a rich edit control on your dialog box resource. As with the other controls, you must make sure that you've initialized the control library before using the control.

Initializing the Common Controls Library

If you review the SDK documentation for the common controls library, you'll find that most of the functions warn you to call the ::InitCommonControls() API to get the library loaded and initialized. For all new applications you should use the alternative API function ::InitCommonControlsEx(). In an MFC application, explicitly calling these functions is unnecessary as the foundation classes will automatically initialize the common control library when you're about to create a dialog box, or when you're about to create a view style that uses one of the common controls for its client area, or when you're about to directly create a control itself. By deferring the initialization of the controls, MFC assures that your application initializes and loads as quickly as possible.

If you need to use a rich edit control, MFC will only initialize the rich edit control library if you use the CRichEditView or CRichEditCtrl classes to create the window. If, however, you draw a rich edit control on the dialog box template that your application creates, you must call the AfxInitRichEditCtrl() function to initialize the library *before* creating the dialog box window.

Notifications

While you, as an MFC programmer, will write simple functions to handle notifications from controls, Windows is really passing those notifications to the owners of the controls as messages. Since the introduction of Windows, notification messages have come from controls in the form of specially coded WM_COMMAND messages. These messages are currently used for controls, menus, and a few other sources as well.

WM_COMMAND messages have become overloaded, as they're used in so many different situations. But their popularity soars in spite of these flaws; they carry no information about the detailed cause of the notification, and they don't provide any mechanism for the application to indicate that it actually has processed the message.

Since the more aggressively designed common controls provide a rich user interface, they need to provide information about the exact cause of a notification to the owner window. The common controls dispatch information in the form of WM_NOTIFY messages instead of using WM_COMMAND messages. Since the WM_NOTIFY notification mechanism is prevalent in all common controls, let's examine that mechanism before we cover the controls themselves.

A WM_NOTIFY message carries a pointer to an NMHDR structure message in its lParam parameter. The NMHDR structure looks like this:

```
typedef struct tagNMHDR {
    HWND hwndFrom;
    UINT idFrom;
    UINT code;
} NMHDR;
```

The hwndFrom and idFrom members let us know which control sent the message. hwndFrom contains the window handle to the control, while idFrom contains the control's ID. The cause of the notification message is sent in the code member. Each common control has a number of values specific to that control that can be supplied in the code parameter. However, there is a subset of values for the code parameter that apply to all the controls. You can see this subset in the following table:

code Value	Description
NM_CLICK	The user clicked the primary mouse button inside the control
NM_DBLCLK	The user double-clicked the primary mouse button inside the control
NM_KILLFOCUS	The control lost the input focus
NM_SETFOCUS	The control received the input focus
NM_RETURN	The user pressed the *Enter* key while the control had focus

code Value	Description
NM_OUTOFMEMORY	The control couldn't complete the most recent operation asked of it – either programmatically or by the user – because the control ran out of memory or resources
NM_RCLICK	The user clicked the secondary mouse button within the control
NM_RDBLCLK	The user double-clicked the secondary mouse button within the control

These common notifications are not very explicit; you'll note that some of them deal with mouse clicks, yet the NMHDR structure doesn't contain coordinates or a keyboard state element to let you know where the user clicked the mouse. Neither does it indicate which keys might have been held down as the mouse was clicked. If you need this information, you're probably more interested in one of the control-specific notification messages. For example, if the user clicks on a list view control to change the selection, the control will send an NM_CLICK notification, but also an LVN_ITEMCHANGED message to tell you that the selection has changed.

On the other hand, if you aren't able to process a more specific message, then you'll need to get the additional information from the Windows API. You can call the ::GetKeyboardState() function to get information about the keyboard's state when the message was sent, or ::GetAsyncKeyState() to get the state of the keyboard as you actually process the message. The ::GetCursorPos() function will return the position of the mouse cursor.

If the notification message being sent is a message common to all the Windows common controls (in other words, one from the table above), the pointer supplied as the message's lParam parameter is to an NMHDR structure and nothing more. However, if the message is specific to a particular control, the pointer is actually to a different structure that has the NMHDR structure as its first member, and then subsequently contains information specific to the control. The precise form of this structure will depend on what notification is being sent. You'll see how this packaging mechanism is used as we come to look at the individual controls and the messages they send.

Of course, since you're an MFC programmer, you'll not be so directly concerned with WM_NOTIFY messages. Instead, you'll just write a member function and hook it up as a handler for a particular notification from a specific control. Most of these handlers can be added with the ClassWizard. However, if you do need to manually add the ON_NOTIFY macro to your message map, the macro will come in a form that looks like this:

```
ON_NOTIFY(notification code, id, member function)
```

The notification code is the specific notification you wish to trap, the id is the ID of the control that will send it, and the member function identifies the handling function in your class. The actual handling function will always have the same prototype, regardless of the actual notification or control that generates the message. The prototype for a notification handler looks like this:

```
void CClassName::MemberFunction(NMHDR*    pNMHDR,
                                LRESULT* pResult);
```

Of course, pNMHDR may not really be a pointer to a NMHDR structure, as we just described, so you may need to cast it to the appropriate type in the body of the function to get at the extended information for control-specific notifications. We'll see this process in action throughout the chapter.

For WM_COMMAND messages, you're probably used to returning TRUE or FALSE to indicate your success or failure at handling the message. However, WM_NOTIFY messages follow a different protocol; they'll pass you a pointer to an LRESULT. You should populate the referenced LRESULT to indicate your success (or lack of it) in handling the message. By default, you should set the value to zero with code like this:

```
*pResult = 0;
```

Some notifications will require other behavior or information returned in the area identified by pResult, but a value of zero means that you've handled the message and nothing else needs to happen. As it completes the addition of a notification handler for you, the ClassWizard will add the appropriate code to your application. You'll just need to modify it to carry out whatever operation you need.

Finally, I should point out that these notification messages are common across all controls in the sense that they don't include any control-specific information. Nevertheless, not all common control types fire all of these message types. These tables show which controls fire which messages:

	NM_CLICK	NM_DBLCLK	NM_KILLFOCUS	NM_SETFOCUS
Hot Key Control				
List View Control	X	X	X	X
Rich Edit Control				
Status Bar	X	X		
Tab Control	X			
Toolbar	X	X		
Tree View Control	X		X	X

	NM_RETURN	NM_OUTOFMEMORY	NM_RCLICK	NM_RDBLCLK
Hot Key Control	X			
List View Control	X	X	X	X
Rich Edit Control		X		
Status Bar			X	X
Tab Control				
Toolbar			X	X
Tree View Control	X	X	X	

There are a few controls that we've described that don't appear in these tables – because they don't send *any* of the stock notification messages. Animation controls, for example, don't let you know when they're clicked upon or when they receive focus. Controls that aren't present in this chart still may send control-specific notifications.

Image Lists

Many of the controls we'll discuss in this chapter manage graphical images. It can be a real chore to do image manipulation without causing memory leaks, and remembering subtle differences in the formats of bitmaps or icons is difficult at best. Further, keeping lots of images alive in memory at one time can significantly tax Windows' resources, and managing those resources so Windows runs as smoothly as possible is not enjoyable. To put an end to such strife in the life of Windows programmers, the common control library provides a collection called an **image list**.

Image lists aren't really controls, but they have some control-like features. They're actually a lot more like collection classes because they provide a place for your application to store and retrieve blocks of data, in this case bitmap images. As we'll see in the rest of the chapter, you can use image lists in conjunction with most of the other common controls. (We'll be covering collection classes in detail in Chapter 9.)

As with most other MFC classes that wrap system objects, you'll need to create a CImageList object before you call its Create() member to generate the Windows object. You call DeleteImageList() to destroy the Windows image list object before you destroy the C++ CImageList object. (Of course, you don't *have* to call DeleteImageList() – the destructor of the CImageList class will delete the image list object so Windows won't get sick.)

CImageLists are unlike controls because they don't directly create a window, but they *are* often used in association with CTreeCtrl, CListCtrl and CComboBoxEx instances. You'll never need to do data exchange with a CImageList, since it doesn't really hold any end user-accessible data. When you create an image list, you must let it know what type of images you'll be storing, by specifying a bitmap together with its size in pixels. The images in the list must all be the same size – there's no way around this.

The CImageList::Create() member has several overloads; here's one of them:

```
BOOL CImageList::Create(int  cx,
                        int  cy,
                        UINT nFlags,
                        int  nInitial,
                        int  nGrow);
```

The first two parameters specify the size in pixels for the images in your list. The nInitial parameter gives the object an initial count for the number of images you expect to store, while the nGrow parameter specifies the number of images by which the reserved space in the image list should grow when the space specified by nInitial is exhausted. Just as when you're using the MFC collection classes, you should try to tune these numbers carefully to grow the container appropriately without wasting memory or growing in steps that are too small. The CImageList class can't discard memory that it isn't actually using, so it's particularly important to use reasonable values for nGrow and nInitial.

Here you can see how to create and then initialize a `CImageList`:

```
CImageList m_ImageList;

m_ImageList.Create(::GetSystemMetrics(SM_CXICON),
            ::GetSystemMetrics(SM_CYICON), ILC_COLOR4 | ILC_MASK, 20, 3);
```

It's important to realize the significance of the size parameters; as you have to specify them when you create an image list, you can't keep images of different sizes in your image list. In the Doodads sample application from which this code is taken, I want to keep icons in the image list. I can find the size of icons on the system by calling the `::GetSystemMetrics()` API, providing `SM_CYICON` and `SM_CXICON` to retrieve the height and width, respectively. Note that the sample never calls `DeleteImageList()` on any of its image list objects; instead it relies on the destructor to tear down the image list implicitly.

`CImageList` objects also support the generation of images for drag-and-drop operations. In such circumstances, it's common to use a black-and-white version of the image that is being manipulated.

Image Masks

By specifying `ILC_MASK` for the `nFlags` parameter, you can ensure that the image list will keep a mask bitmap along with any bitmaps you insert into the control. If you pass `ILC_MASK` for the `nFlags` parameter, the control can produce masked bitmaps when requested by a control or your application. The generated bitmap mask can be used to paint the true bitmap as a shape with a transparent background rather than a complete rectangle of pixels.

The mask shape is determined by looking for pixels with the **screen color** in the original bitmap's image. The screen color can be set with the image editor in Microsoft Visual Studio. The mask will be present wherever the screen color is present – allowing the background to show through wherever the bitmap is drawn.

The upshot of the screen color is that if you *don't* specify that the image has a mask, you'll find that when the item is selected, your images won't have any 'see-through' areas where you drew with the screen color. If you *do* use a mask in the image list, the rendered image will let the background show through in areas of the image where you've drawn with the screen color.

`nFlags` also specifies the bit-depth of the image list control. By default, the control uses four bits per pixel, resulting in images that have up to sixteen colors. You can make a deeper or shallower image list by specifying an explicit `ILC_` value from this table:

Constant	Bits per Pixel	Colors
ILC_COLOR4	four	16
ILC_COLOR8	eight	256
ILC_COLOR16	sixteen	65536
ILC_COLOR24	twenty-four	16777218
ILC_COLOR32	thirty-two	4294967296
ILC_COLORDDB	–	–

The `IDC_COLORDDB` parameter is largely obsolete. It causes the image list to manage a **device-dependent bitmap**. Device-dependent bitmaps are available to maintain compatibility with older display and printer drivers, and aren't recommended for use in modern applications. If you'd like to have a mask for any of these color depths, you can bit-wise OR the `ILC_` constant with `ILC_MASK`, so the expression:

```
ILC_COLOR4 | ILC_MASK
```

results in a 16-color image list which manages a mask.

To drive the point home, you can see the difference in these two renderings. I've artificially captured the Masked Image List Demo dialog from the `Doodads` sample with both controls showing a selection. The icon in the box on the left is drawn with a mask, while the same icon is shown in the box on the right without a mask.

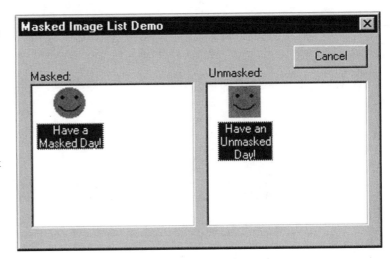

The effect of the mask is obvious on the page here as it is in the runtime application; you can bring up all the dialogs associated with the `Doodads` example by choosing the desired option from the View menu. The masking effect isn't quite so shocking, though, since the background of the list control doesn't contain anything pretty that you'd *want* to see shining through. On the other hand, if the image were to be used as the drag cursor for a drag-and-drop operation, you'd certainly want a masked image!

List Views and Image Lists

The `Doodads` example application features a dialog called Addresses that is implemented by the class `CAddressDialog` in `Address.cpp`. When you first open it, the dialog displays icons for the logos of most North American professional hockey, basketball, baseball, and football teams. You can select your favorite team and display its mailing address using the Info button, or by double-clicking on the control. (Unfortunately, since even my favorite players always ignore my letters, some of the information might be a bit outdated.)

The example uses a list view control to display the icons and to let you make selections, but the list view is actually dependent on an image list to manage the icons. The code from the dialog's `LoadList()` function looks like this:

```
void CAddressDialog::LoadList(CListCtrl* pList, int* pnArray, const int nSize)
{
    CWinApp* pApp = AfxGetApp();

    int nIndex;
    for (nIndex = 0; nIndex < nSize; nIndex++)
    {
        HICON hIcon;
        int nImage = 0;
        hIcon = pApp->LoadIcon(pnArray[nIndex]);

        if (hIcon == NULL)
        {
            TRACE1("Warning: Couldn't get icon %d\n", pnArray[nIndex]);
        }
        else
        {
            nImage = m_ImageList.Add(hIcon);
            ::DestroyIcon(hIcon);
        }

        LVITEM itemAdder;
        CString strTeamInfo;
        CString strTeamName;
        int nOffset;

        if (!strTeamInfo.LoadString(pnArray[nIndex]))
            TRACE1("Warning: LoadString() failed for %d\n", pnArray[nIndex]);
        else
        {
            nOffset = strTeamInfo.Find(_T("\n"));

            if (nOffset == -1)
            {
                TRACE1("Warning: Couldn't parse %d\n", pnArray[nIndex]);
            }
            else
            {
                strTeamName = strTeamInfo.Left(nOffset);
                strTeamInfo = strTeamInfo.Mid(nOffset+1);
            }

            itemAdder.mask = LVIF_TEXT | LVIF_IMAGE | LVIF_PARAM;
            itemAdder.pszText = strTeamName.GetBuffer(0);
            itemAdder.iSubItem = 0;
            itemAdder.iImage = nImage;
            itemAdder.lParam = reinterpret_cast<LPARAM>(new CString(strTeamInfo));
            pList->InsertItem(&itemAdder);
        }
    }
}
```

If you check the header file, you'll see that I've added a `CImageList` object to the member data for the `CAddressDialog` class. This object, named `m_ImageList`, provides the image list for the application throughout the lifetime of the dialog.

By repeatedly calling m_ImageList.Add() for each icon we wish to add, the image list is slowly built up, one by one. By this point in the proceedings we've already associated the image list with the list view control using this call in the OnInitDialog() handler for the CAddressDialog:

```
pHockeyCtrl->SetImageList(&m_ImageList, LVSIL_NORMAL);
```

The flag LVSIL_NORMAL lets the list view pointed to by pHockeyCtrl know that the image list object contains 'normal' icons. This flag could be LVSIL_SMALL if small icons were in the list, or LVSIL_STATE if the image list contained state images to describe the control's different editing states in a report application. Any common control class that is interested in images will have a SetImageList() member function that you can use to set the image list for the given control. Controls that work with image lists will accept an index into that image list to specify which image you're interested in, adding to a given item in the control.

Manipulating the Image List after Creation

Once an image has been copied into the image list, you don't need to worry about it anymore. The bits in the image are held in the image list and they can be retrieved as needed. You can even call DestroyIcon() on the handle if you no longer need it directly after it's added to the image list. Note that in the code above, we call the ::DestroyObject() API to make sure that the original icon object was killed once it had been copied to the list; this is just fine, as Windows will use the copy maintained inside the image list for as long as the list is around.

If you want, you can remove images from the list by calling the Remove() member of your CImageList object. This doesn't free any memory or destroy any objects; it just frees the slot within the image list so that it may be used by another item.

The List View Control

In the previous section, the introduction to CImageList offered us a couple of quick glimpses at some of the CListCtrl class' member functions. To implement the rest of the functionality required by the **Addresses** dialog box, I needed to write a few more functions. The **Addresses** dialog is shown here:

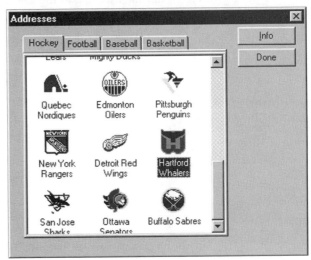

The box contains a list view control with the LVS_ICON style showing full-size icons. You can create a list view that shows smaller icons by using the LVS_SMALLICON style and associating the image list with such a box by using the LVSIL_SMALL flag in your call to CListCtrl::SetImageList(). I've also used the LVS_AUTOARRANGE style here to make sure the icons stay neatly spaced in the view — you can set these styles in the Styles tab of the list view's property sheet in the dialog editor. If you're so inclined, you can make the icons align themselves near the left-hand side of the box by specifying the LVS_ALIGNLEFT style, or make them align along the top of the box with the LVS_ALIGNTOP style.

If you want to change the style of the list box at runtime (like Windows Explorer does when you use the settings in the View menu), you can call the CWnd::ModifyStyle() function to remove the old style bit and use the new one.

The first function that we'll look at, CAddressDialog::OnItemchangedTeams(), handles the LVN_ITEMCHANGED notification. If the user is selecting an item in the list view control, the dialog's Info button (which has the ID IDOK) is enabled. If the user has deselected the item and ends up leaving the box with no selection, we ensure that the Info button is disabled. The code for handling item changes in the dialog is very simple:

```
void CAddressDialog::OnItemchangedTeams(NMHDR* pNMHDR, LRESULT* pResult)
{
    NMLISTVIEW* pNMListView = reinterpret_cast<NMLISTVIEW*>(pNMHDR;
    if (pNMListView->uNewState & LVIS_SELECTED)
        GetDlgItem(IDOK)->EnableWindow(TRUE);
    else
        GetDlgItem(IDOK)->EnableWindow(FALSE);

    *pResult = 0;
}
```

The notification passes a pointer in pNMHDR to an NMLISTVIEW structure, which is the notification structure for the list view control. You can see that it's cast to the appropriate type in the body of the function. The field we're interested in is uNewState, which tells us the new state of the item identified in this structure after the user makes the selection. The NMLISTVIEW structure looks like this:

```
typedef struct tagNMLISTVIEW
{
    NMHDR   hdr;
    int     iItem;
    int     iSubItem;
    UINT    uNewState;
    UINT    uOldState;
    UINT    uChanged;
    POINT   ptAction;
    LPARAM  lParam;
} NMLISTVIEW, FAR *LPNMLISTVIEW;
```

The hdr member is the generic NMHDR structure we've discussed before. iItem indicates the item that is the cause or focus of the notification, while iSubItem indicates any involved subitem. (We'll define and investigate subitems in the next section.) uNewState reflects the state the item has assumed, while uOldState shows the state the item had before the action causing the notification took place. ptAction shows where the mouse was when the event occurred, but is only used for the LVN_BEGINDRAG and LVN_BEGINRDRAG notifications. uChanged lets you know which attributes of the item have changed; uChanged uses the same flags as the mask member of LVITEM does to identify different attributes of the item.

If the item we've been notified of (indicated by the value of iItem) has the LVIS_SELECTED flag set in uNewState, it is selected. When the user already has an item in the control selected and then selects another, OnItemchangedTeams() is called twice – once to deselect the previous item and once to select the new one. Since the new selection message will be sent after the previous selection is removed, no extra logic is required to make sure that everything works correctly.

We also have to implement some code under the Info button. Here you can see how to cheat when you're designing the dialog; change the caption on the editor-supplied OK button to Info and use it for what you want. It will still have an ID of IDOK. You don't have to add a function to handle the button – and if you type as slow as my boss does, that will save you about an hour! In OnOK(), the button's handler, write some code to get the lParam, cast it to a CString and toss up the message box with the team's address. The end result looks like this:

```
void CAddressDialog::OnOK()
{
    CListCtrl* pList;
    pList = static_cast<CListCtrl*>(GetDlgItem(m_nActiveTab));
    ASSERT(pList != NULL);

    LVITEM itemSelected;
    int nSelected = pList->GetNextItem(-1, LVNI_SELECTED);
    if (nSelected == -1)
        return;

    TCHAR szTeamName[80];

    itemSelected.iItem = nSelected;
    itemSelected.iSubItem = 0;
    itemSelected.mask = LVIF_PARAM | LVIF_TEXT;
    itemSelected.pszText = szTeamName;
    itemSelected.cchTextMax = ELEMENTS(szTeamName);
    pList->GetItem(&itemSelected);

    CString* pMessage = reinterpret_cast<CString*>(itemSelected.lParam);
    MessageBox(*pMessage, szTeamName);
}
```

When we ask for the selected item, we request the text and the lParam data from it so that we can get the name and address of the team the user clicked on in one call. To make sure we get the data we need, we specify both the LVIF_PARAM and LVIF_TEXT flags in the mask member on the way into the GetItem() call.

The interesting function here is GetNextItem(). If you use -1 as the first parameter, this function finds the first item matching the description mentioned in the second parameter. We've used LVNI_SELECTED as the second parameter to get the first selected item. You could alter the first parameter to start your search from an item other than the first in the list, or you could alter the second parameter to change the search criteria. You can use LVNI_ALL to get every item in the list (if you write a loop that repeatedly calls GetNextItem()), or LVNI_TOLEFT and LVNI_TORIGHT to get the items immediately to the left and right of the currently selected item. There are a handful of other flags; you can check the GetNextItem() documentation to see their descriptions.

GetNextItem() is very flexible, but MFC makes things just a tad easier for the frequent situations when you're just interested in finding the selected item, or items, in a multiple-selection list view control. MFC has a couple of extra CListView member functions to do this. GetFirstSelectedItemPosition() will return a POSITION that can be used in subsequent calls to GetNextSelectedItem() to enumerate the items in the control. The above function might be rewritten like this; the highlighted code is the difference:

```
void CAddressDialog::OnOK()
{
    CListCtrl* pList;
    pList = static_cast<CListCtrl*>(GetDlgItem(m_nActiveTab));
    ASSERT(pList != NULL);


    LVITEM itemSelected;
    POSITION pos = pList->GetFirstSelectedItemPosition();
    if (pos == NULL)
        return;
    int nSelected = pList->GetNextSelectedItem(pos);

    TCHAR szTeamName[80];

    itemSelected.iItem = nSelected;
    itemSelected.iSubItem = 0;
    itemSelected.mask = LVIF_PARAM | LVIF_TEXT;
    itemSelected.pszText = szTeamName;
    itemSelected.cchTextMax = ELEMENTS(szTeamName);
    pList->GetItem(&itemSelected);

    CString* pMessage = reinterpret_cast<CString*>(itemSelected.lParam);
    MessageBox(*pMessage, szTeamName);
}
```

You could, if the list allowed multiple selections, continue calling GetNextSelectedItem() until pos became NULL. You'll see that enumerations in MFC work with this paradigm when we examine the C++-based collection classes in Chapter 9.

Note that the population code called in OnInitDialog() and implemented in LoadList() allocates a copy of the team's address and stuffs it in the lParam of the item. When the window is destroyed, you'll need to tear through the items in the box to make sure the extra memory is properly freed when the dialog is destroyed. If you don't, you'll leak memory like a beer cup at a hockey game. This listing of the FreeStrings() member of the CAddressDialog dialog class (which gets called by OnDestroy()) shows how we can delete all the extra memory by repeatedly calling GetItem() to walk through all the elements in the list:

```
void CAddressDialog::FreeStrings(int nID)
{
    CListCtrl* pList;
    pList = static_cast<CListCtrl*>(GetDlgItem(nID));
    ASSERT(pList != NULL);

    LVITEM itemVisit;
    int nCount;
    int nIndex;
    CString* pItem;

    nCount = pList->GetItemCount();

    for (nIndex = 0; nIndex < nCount; nIndex++)
    {
        itemVisit.mask = LVIF_PARAM;
        itemVisit.iSubItem = 0;
        itemVisit.iItem = nIndex;
        pList->GetItem(&itemVisit);

        pItem = reinterpret_cast<CString*>(itemVisit.lParam);
        delete pItem;

        itemVisit.lParam = NULL;
        itemVisit.mask = LVIF_PARAM;
        itemVisit.iSubItem = 0;
        itemVisit.iItem = nIndex;
        pList->SetItem(&itemVisit);
    }
}
```

`GetItemCount()` returns just that – the count of items in the list. In the loop, we call `GetItem()` to populate the `itemVisit` structure for each item in the list. We only need the `lParam` value for the item, so just use the `LVIF_PARAM` flag in the mask member of the structure. Given the `lParam`, we can cast it to a `CString*` which we then delete. This step is more important than it looks; if we don't cast the pointer appropriately, `delete` won't execute the proper `CString` destructor.

To be overly conservative, the `lParam` is set back to `NULL` with an extra call to `SetItem()`. The loop continues in a similar manner for each item in the list box.

Other List View Control Styles

The list view we used in this example was a simple list; it didn't do anything special. If you had small icons for the teams, you could have used those in the dialog by setting the appropriate style bit in the dialog editor. You could also have developed a list view control that used the report style, which has the ability to display **subitems**. A control with subitems will build a very simple hierarchy. In report style, the user sees all of the items along the left edge of the control – in the first column – and subitems are shown in subsequent columns. The Windows Explorer's Details view is implemented using a list control with subitems.

We'll take a look at all of the nuances of report style here, but also remember there are several extended list view styles. Those extended styles are *not* set with the resource editor – but instead are set by your code at runtime. Those extended styles are examined in the following section.

The Report Style

The report style, identified by the LVS_REPORT style bit, is a very interesting mechanism for conveying lots of columnar data to the user. You can see a report-style list view control in action within the Wordfreq sample application that is covered in Chapter 10. The application uses a CListView class as its main user interface. This class encapsulates a list view control within a CView-derived class appropriate for inclusion in any document\view application.

How exactly the list view control is used within that view is very interesting. Since the control has the LVS_REPORT style, it will actually have a **header control** in the top of its window. You can see a shot of such a control here:

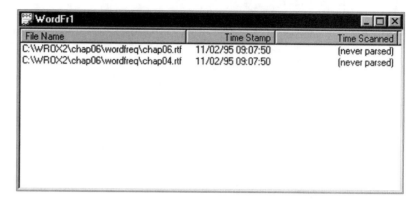

The header usually serves three functions in the user interface of such a control. First, it lets the user size the columns in the view. Depending on how interested they are in the values of one column, they can arrange the columns appropriately by dragging the border between two columns to force the control's layout to suit their liking. Second, the user can click on the control header block itself to indicate a request to sort the data in the control by that column, or to select the data in that column for some other operation. Finally, the column header serves to identify the meaning of the data in the column.

The header control is really a separate control – an instance of the Windows common header control that we'll investigate in more detail later. The header control is a child of the list view control that owns it, and the list view control in turn, is a child of the dialog or window that owns it. The header control sends messages to the list view, but the list view control is *not* obligated to pass them to its owner.

You can develop a pointer to the header control using the GetDlgItem() function. While the list view control obviously isn't a dialog, the same relationship exists between any window and the controls within that window as would exist between a dialog and its controls. That is, the list control is the parent of the header control inside it and can retrieve it using its ID. The header control will always have ID zero within the list view. Given a pointer to the list view control in question, we can find a pointer to the header using this code:

```
CHeaderCtrl* pCtrl = pListView->GetDlgItem(0);
if (pCtrl == NULL)
{
    TRACE0("This control isn't a report list view.\n");
    ASSERT(FALSE);
    return;
}
else
{
    // Party!
}
```

Of course, if you haven't initialized the list view with anything interesting, then you won't have much need to play with the header control. That is, you should do most of the work using the interfaces to the list view control and only resort to manipulating the header control directly when there's no other way to get the job done. Direct manipulation of the header control is not that uncommon; you might want to ask the header to see how many columns it has, or get a handle to it, subclass it and enhance its painting.

On the other hand, if you don't *need* to go hunting for the header control, don't touch it at all! You can, for example, insert and remove columns using the CListCtrl::InsertColumn() and CListCtrl::DeleteColumn() items; in this way you avoid manipulating the header control directly.

Adding Report View Columns

After drawing a report-mode list view on your dialog, or creating it dynamically, the first thing you'll want to do is add some columns to it. You can add a column by calling the InsertColumn() member of CListCtrl. This function has a couple of interesting overloads. One of them has this prototype:

```
int InsertColumn(int      nCol,
              LPCTSTR lpszColumnHeading,
              int      nFormat = LVCFMT_LEFT,
              int      nWidth = -1,
              int      nSubItem = -1);
```

The first parameter is the index of the column you'll be using, where the leftmost column is column zero. The second parameter is a pointer to a string that names the column, and the third indicates how the text in the column header should be justified. LVCFMT_LEFT, which is the default value for this parameter, makes the text flush left in the control. LVCFMT_RIGHT makes the text flush right, while the LVCFMT_CENTER centers the text. No surprises there. Note that these parameters affect both the text in the header and any text that might appear as data in the column within the control.

The nWidth parameter is -1 by default, which causes the control *not* to set the width of the column. You'll always want to specify some value here, since a control that's initially sized with the default width just looks terrible.

GetColumnWidth() takes a single parameter; the index of the column in question. It returns the width of the columns in pixels. The inverse function, SetColumnWidth(), returns a BOOL and accepts the index of the column to be set and the new width in pixels as two separate parameters. You can pass the LVSCW_AUTOSIZE constant to SetColumnWidth() as the width so that the control sizes the column to fit the data in the column exactly. You can use LVSCW_AUTOSIZE_USEHEADER to have the control use the header text instead of the maximum width of the data text.

If you're interested in carefully sizing the control's columns yourself, you can call
`CListCtrl::GetStringWidth()`. This function takes a pointer to a string and returns a width
that lets you know how wide a column needs to be to hold the string. Note that this value does *not*
include any compensation for an image that might be associated with the text.

The other version of the `InsertColumn()` function provides slightly more control, because it
accepts a pointer to an `LVCOLUMN` structure, which is directly used by the control. The function's
prototype is slightly similar:

```
BOOL InsertColumn(int    nCol,
                  const LVCOLUMN* pColumn);
```

The content of the `LVCOLUMN` structure is this:

```
typedef struct _LVCOLUMN
{
    UINT mask;
    int fmt;
    int cx;
    LPSTR pszText;
    int cchTextMax;
    int iSubItem;
#if (_WIN32_IE >= 0x0300)
    int iImage;
    int iOrder;
#endif
} LV_COLUMN;FAR *LPLVCOLUMN
```

You can guess that many of these fields are similar to the parameters of the more verbose
`InsertColumn()` overload we saw before. The `iSubItem` field, for example, specifies the subitem
that the column represents, while the `pszText` field contains a pointer to the title for the column.
The `cx` field holds the width for the new column, while the `fmt` field should be set to one of the
`LVCFMT_` constants we saw before.

> *By the way,* `LVCFMT_` *stands for List View Column ForMaT; impress your friends with
> this little mnemonic at the next cocktail party you attend. Most of the other constant
> prefixes follow a similar kind of logic so, with a bit of effort, you'll soon have enough
> party conversation to last the rest of the year.*

So, to use the `LVCOLUMN` version of `InsertColumn()` you simply need to create an `LVCOLUMN`
structure, initialize it, and then make the call. That initialization, though, needs to set up the `mask`
member of the structure properly. The `mask` contains bits that will indicate which other values in the
structure are to be considered when you are inserting the new field. If, for example, you wish to
insert a new column named 'Hometown' and you don't care how wide it is, you could indicate that
without setting a value for the `cx` field by just keeping the appropriate bit of the `mask` field clear. The
different bits you can specify in the mask are identified by these constants:

mask bit	Description
LVCF_FMT	The fmt member is valid
LVCF_IMAGE	The iImage member is valid
LVCF_ORDER	The iOrder member is valid
LVCF_SUBITEM	The iSubItem member is valid
LVCF_TEXT	The pszText member is valid
LVCF_WIDTH	The cx member is valid

So, the 'Hometown' example above would really come to be in these lines of code:

```
LVCOLUMN lvcol;
lvcol.mask = LVCF_TEXT | LVCF_FMT;
lvcol.fmt = LVCFMT_LEFT;
lvcol.pszText = _T("Hometown");
```

The version of the InsertColumn() function which accepts a LVCOLUMN structure is no more efficient than the simpler overload, though you'll find that the overload with more parameters is often more convenient. You should feel free to pick whichever suits your fancy.

It's important to understand the LVCOLUMN structure just the same, though, since it's also used by the CListCtrl::GetColumn() function. Plus, if you understand the meaning of the LVCOLUMN members, you'll understand what all the extra function parameters *really* mean. You can call this function to get information about any column that makes you curious. The function has this prototype:

```
BOOL CListCtrl::GetColumn(int      nCol,
                   LVCOLUMN*  pColumn) const;
```

It populates the referenced structure with information about the column that you specify. This function will only populate fields within the structure that you identify with bits in the mask field on the way into the call. If you need to find the width of the second column, you can write some code like this:

```
LVCOLUMN lvcol;
lvcol.mask = LVCF_WIDTH;
if (pList->GetColumn(1, &lvcol))  // second column has index 1
{
    // Got it!  It's in lvcol.cx
}
```

The mask field lets Windows answer your query as efficiently as possible; if you don't have any interest in the text, there's no need to force Windows to copy it. (By the way, you can just as easily retrieve the width of a column with the CListCtrl::GetColumnWidth() function. Unfortunately, there's not a direct accessor function for each of the individual column attributes.)

If you've specified LVCF_TEXT, to retrieve information from the control, you'll need to provide your own buffer. You can indicate the size of that buffer using the cchTextMax field in the LVCOLUMN structure. If you're supplying text data to the control, you don't need to keep a value in cchTextMax because the control will assume that your string is null-terminated.

List View Subitems

The iSubItem parameter is very interesting. If you leave it at -1, the column won't be associated with a subitem. You can associate the column with a subitem by passing the index of that subitem in this parameter; subitem zero is the item's text in the list control itself. You can use subsequent subitem indexes to identify items for columns further to the right.

As the name indicates, subitems are not items. If you have a list control in its regular icon or small icon view mode, you will only see items in the box. If you use report mode, the leftmost column of the box will contain items. **Subitems** are the items further to the right. You can use subitems to express detail about the items, but you can't rely on them always being there. As you know from using the Windows Explorer, there's value in allowing the user to switch from one view type to another to offer varying views of data.

As we saw in a previous code fragment, you can insert items into the control by calling InsertItem(). There are four overloads for the function; the simplest takes only a pointer to an LVITEM structure, which has this layout:

```
typedef struct _LVITEM
{
    UINT    mask;
    int     iItem;
    int     iSubItem;
    UINT    state;
    UINT    stateMask;
    LPSTR   pszText;
    int     cchTextMax;
    int     iImage;
    LPARAM  lParam;
#if (_WIN32_IE >= 0x0300)
    int iIndent;
#endif
} LVITEM, FAR *LPLVITEM;
```

The iItem member indicates where you'd like the insertion to take place; it specifies the index of the item before which you'd like the new item to appear. The iItem parameter is meaningless if the list view has LVS_AUTOARRANGE, as the new insertion will be moved immediately. The pszText element points at the string you'd like to show in the item. Like the list box column structure's mask field, the mask field here is used to indicate which fields are valid. When you insert an item into the box, you'll almost always want to provide either a string or an image identifier; the iImage field indicates an index into the image list associated with the control.

The lParam provides a 32-bit variable where you can tuck away user-defined data; it's essentially the same as item data in combo boxes or list boxes. You can call CListCtrl::SetItemData() to set the data, and CListCtrl::GetItemData() to retrieve it.

Inserting Subitems

When you insert an item, the iSubItem field *must* be zero. However, if you want to insert a subitem, the iSubItem field should be the index of the column where you want to insert the item. Subitems only apply to report view mode, where you'll find the subitems appearing in columns progressively further to the right. Although it's a rather inefficient way of doing things, this is quite easy to code and we'll look at how to do so in a moment. From a procedural point of view, it's actually easier to provide subitems to the control when the control calls you back for them. More on this in the next section!

Subitems can't be inserted directly. We saw how InsertItem() was used when we touched on how the list view control was loaded. For example, the **Addresses** dialog box called InsertItem() against LVITEM structures that were initialized with the names of sports teams and image list indexes for the logos of those teams.

When you insert an item, you also inserted all the subitems for that item. Instead of inserting subitems, then, you simply set them. If that image list is in report view mode, we might want to provide more data in columns to express some detail about each team that appeared in a particular row. Once the item is inserted, you can use SetItem() to provide more information about it. Given a list control pointed to by pList, we might insert an item with this code:

```
int nItem;
nItem = pList->InsertItem(0, "This Item");
```

Then, we can set text into the additional subitems by calling SetItem(). We could add some text for the first subitem with this call:

```
pList->SetItem(nItem, 1, LVIF_TEXT, "Column Text", 0, 0, 0, 0);
```

The first parameter is the item number that we're working with – essentially, the zero-based index of the row that the item of interest is in. The second parameter, which I've passed as a one here, is actually the subitem number. Subitems are numbered starting from one. The item itself always shows up in the leftmost column of the list, while subitems show up in the column that you specified when you created the column. A given subitem index is associated with a given column by the iSubItem field of the LVCOLUMN structure used when the column is created. In other words, columns are always numbered starting with zero at the left and incrementing monotonically. Subitems of a particular index are associated with a particular column at the time the column is created – that's why InsertColumn() accepts both a column index and a subitem index.

In order to load a list view control with columns, you can implement code for this algorithm:

```
Loop for each item to insert
   Insert the item
   Loop for each column with data to be set
      Set the data for that column
   Keep looping
Keep looping
```

The rest of the parameters to SetItem() specify information about the item. The prototype looks like this:

```
BOOL SetItem(int     nItem,
             int     nSubItem,
             UINT    nMask,
             LPCTSTR lpszItem,
             int     nImage,
             UINT    nState,
             UINT    nStateMask,
             LPARAM  lParam);
```

The nMask parameter can be any of the mask parameters we learned about previously. Instead of specifying flags for the members of the LVITEM structure, you'll just specify the flags for the parameters you'll provide to the call. If you don't provide a particular flag, the corresponding parameter will be ignored – as with the structure. In fact, MFC is internally initializing a structure and passing it to Windows when you make this call. In fact, MFC provides an override of the SetItem() function which accepts a pointer to an LVITEM structure.

If you specify LVIF_STATE, the nState parameter can be used to provide the state for the item, but be aware that the state is *only* valid for the item, and not for subitems. When setting the state, you must use the nStateMask parameter to indicate which state flags are to be set. lParam can be used to set the user data for the item. Note that only items themselves have lParam values and states – subitems do not.

While the approach of using InsertItem() and SetItem() to populate a box is simple, it takes forever. It'll work fine for controls with small content. However, for controls with larger data sets, you'll almost certainly prefer to use the callback mechanism that we'll investigate later on. In the meantime, the state field of the LVITEM structure lets you dictate the visual attributes of the control to indicate its current state. You can use any of these constants in the state field:

state value	Description
LVIS_SELECTED	This item is selected
LVIS_CUT	The item is selected for effect by a cut and paste operation
LVIS_DROPHILITED	The item is highlighted for the target of a drag-and-drop operation
LVIS_FOCUSED	The item has focus
LVIS_OVERLAYMASK	The application stores the index of the overlay mask for the item in the image list associated with the control
LVIS_STATEIMAGEMASK	The application stores the index of the state image mask for the item in the image list associated with the control
LVIS_LIVES	The King is not dead

By the way, LVIS *is usually pronounced 'Elvis', and stands for List View Item State.*

The `stateMask` field has the same effect for the `state` field as the `mask` field does for the whole structure. That is, you will use the `stateMask` field to indicate which values you're actually setting without first requesting the current state of the item. Note that the `LVIS_OVERLAYMASK` and `LVIS_STATEIMAGEMASK` flags preclude the use of other flags; since the index for these flags is returned in the `state` field of the item, the `state` field isn't capable of setting other flags to indicate the other conditions.

List View Item Management

Now that you know how to insert items in a list view, you'll need to know how to find and remove them.

You can completely empty a list view control of its content by calling `DeleteAllItems()`, which takes no parameters. To delete an individual item, you can call `DeleteItem()`, but you'll need to pass it the index of that particular item.

You can paw through the content of the list in a few different ways. At the simplest level, you can call `GetItem()` to retrieve information about a particular item. The function takes only a pointer to an `LVITEM` structure; you must initialize the `mask` and `iItem` fields of the structure to reflect what you want to know about the item. If you want the `LVITEM` structure to be populated with the state and text from the item with index 6, you might code:

```
LVITEM lvi;
CString strText;
lvi.mask = LVIF_TEXT | LVIF_STATE;
lvi.iItem = 6;
lvi.cchMaxLen = 255;
lvi.pszText = strText.GetBuffer(lvi.cchTextMax);
pList->GetItem(&lvi);
strText.ReleaseBuffer();
```

Note the use of the `GetBuffer()` and `ReleaseBuffer()` calls on the `CString` object to ensure we have enough memory for the data from the item.

You don't have to use `GetItem()` to retrieve individual pieces of information about an item; you can call `GetItemState()` or `GetItemText()` to get individual facts about one.

If you need to find an item of particular interest, you can do so by calling `CListCtrl::GetNextItem()`. Though the name of the function implies that it *continues* searching items in the control, it can actually be used to start a search. The function takes two parameters; the first is the index of the item after which the search should start and the second is a set of flags indicating the attributes of items that will fulfill your search. You can search for items that are in a particular geometric relationship with the starting item using these flags:

Flag	Description
LVNI_ABOVE	Searches for an item that is above the specified item
LVNI_ALL	Searches for a subsequent item by index (the default value)

Table Continued on Following Page

Flag	Description
LVNI_BELOW	Searches for an item that is below the specified item
LVNI_TOLEFT	Searches for an item to the left of the specified item
LVNI_TORIGHT	Searches for an item to the right of the specified item

With the four directional search flags, you can navigate items in the control in two axes. In report mode, only the below and above directions will be meaningful. But in the small and large icon views, all of the directions can be useful.

You can use these flags to find items that have a particular state:

Search Mask Flag	Corresponding Item Flag
LVNI_DROPHILITED	LVIS_DROPHILITED
LVNI_CUT	LVIS_CUT
LVNI_FOCUSED	LVIS_FOCUSED
LVNI_HIDDEN	LVIS_HIDDEN
LVNI_MARKED	LVIS_MARKED
LVNI_SELECTED	LVIS_SELECTED

GetNextItem() returns an integer indicating the item that matched the query. If no item matches the request, the function returns -1. A loop that would pull through the list and find out what items were selected might look like this:

```
CListCtrl* pCtrl = GetDlgItem(IDC_YOURLIST);
ASSERT(pCtrl != NULL);
int nItem = pCtrl->GetNextItem(-1, LVNI_FOCUSED);

while (nItem != -1)
{
    // Do something with nItem!
    nItem = pCtrl->GetNextItem(nItem, LVNI_FOCUSED);
}
```

Notice how we pass nItem to the call to GetNextItem(), which starts the next search at the element following the one we just found; that prevents us from searching through the list again and again. There's no need to increment nItem each time through the loop, since GetNextItem() doesn't consider the item that was passed as the search anchor.

Sorting Contents

You can cause a list view to sort itself by specifying ascending or descending sort styles on the box. The box will sort items as you add them to the list. The control will carefully place each new item according to the sort rules, which means that it's essentially using an insertion sort to handle your data. If you have a great deal of unordered data, you'll find that relying on the box to do your sorting is not going to be very efficient. Instead, you should sort it yourself before insertion.

If you leave the list box unsorted, you can implement your own sorting callback routines to make any sort mechanism possible. If you call the `CListView::SortItems()` member of the box, you can force the box to reorder its content.

`SortItems()` takes two parameters. The first is a pointer to a comparison callback function, and the second is a `DWORD` of user-defined data that Windows will use when calling back the function in question. The comparison function takes three parameters. The first is the `lParam` value for the first item within the comparison, while the second is the `lParam` value for the second item involved in the comparison. The third parameter of the function is the user-specified value. The prototype for the callback looks like this:

```
int CALLBACK CompareFunc(LPARAM lParam1,
                         LPARAM lParam2,
                         LPARAM lParamSort);
```

Note that the function is a global and bears the `CALLBACK` modifier. This function should be coded as a global in one of your modules, although you could also make the function work by declaring it as a `static` member of one of your classes. When Windows makes a callback into a function, it has no way to set up a `this` pointer for the function to use because it is unaware of the object context where the call should be executed. You could find a way to 'fake' a `this` using the user-defined parameter, but it usually isn't necessary. Instead, you should stick with a global function or a `static` member function.

You can see this function in action when it responds to user clicks on the header control in the view in the main window of Chapter 10's `Wordfreq` sample (in the `WordView.cpp` file). The code there uses the user-defined parameter to pass around a pointer to the active document. The comparison uses that pointer to query the document for the active sort order.

Callback Functions

The `CALLBACK` attribute identifies a function that you need to implement in your application. The function is called when Windows needs you to implement some behavior you'll define for Windows – in this case, you'll use the function to define the exact rules for comparing two items in your list view control.

The function returns an integer indicating the result of the comparison; if the items are equal, the routine should return 0. If the first item is the greater, the function should return a positive value, or a negative value if the second item is greater. After calling `SortItems()`, Windows will call your comparison functions many times before the control is finally repainted, so the callback function should be as efficient as possible.

Providing Callback Text

Part of the beauty of list view controls is that you don't *have* to bloat the memory requirements of your application by forcing all of your nasty little strings on the list control. You can certainly insert the strings directly into the control if you want to – it will simplify your development task – but you can also use a technique to provide text for items in the control on an on-demand basis.

Such an approach will have the control call your application back to request the content of the strings. Windows doesn't use a callback function for this, but instead sends a LVN_GETDISPINFO notification. The notification includes a pointer to a LV_DISPINFO structure. This structure in turn simply contains a LVITEM structure, which the control uses to request the information it needs to display the item for you. The iItem member notes the item that the control needs to display, while the iSubItem contains the index of the subitem that the control is requesting.

You can provide the text for the item by putting a pointer to the text into the pszText item of the structure. The control *doesn't* make a copy of this data; it will request it again and again as it is needed through the painting of the control. As a matter of fact, the buffer in which you hold the data must be active through the next two LVN_GETDISPINFO notifications because of the way Windows manages the text you pass – Windows doesn't make a copy of the string immediately, but it doesn't need it forever either. Of course, if the control is destroyed, the buffer can be destroyed even if a couple more LVN_GETDISPINFO messages haven't yet been processed.

That Windows needs to have the strings remain available sounds pretty goofy, but it *is* true, and it will affect the way your application works. If you have a collection of all the strings in memory, you can just return a pointer to them if you don't expect the strings to move around in the collection. Elements in an MFC collection won't move in memory unless you're adding or removing elements from the collection, and the collection is an array. Elements in a CList- or CMap-derived MFC collection never move unless you delete them.

If, on the other hand, you're reading data from a file, you're likely to read each line into a separate buffer and use the same buffer for subsequent lines of the file. Such an access pattern is going to force the issue of making sure strings continue to live without moving. To build suspense in an otherwise predictable book, I'll describe a technique for handling this problem in the next section.

In the meantime, you'll remember that I said item text normally 'sticks' in the control when you use InsertItem() to place the item. Since we're not actually inserting subitems, we'll need to implement an OnGetdispinfo() handler for our list view controls that have subitems. If you want, you can let the actual item text be supplied by the OnGetdispinfo() function, if you specify the constant LPSTR_TEXTCALLBACK as the pszText element of the LVITEM structure when you create the item. This is specially recognized by the control as a flag that it should use the OnGetdispInfo() mechanism to retrieve the text.

An Inconspicuous Resource

Everyone knows that the online help files are an incredible resource for finding information about the thousands of functions implemented by the Win32 API, but few people have ever heard of the Win32api.csv file. You can find this file in your Microsoft Visual Studio\vc98\Lib directory. The file is made up of comma-separated fields that describe all the different Windows API functions, including many which are no longer supported by the operating system. The first line of the file explains what each field means. There's a lot of information in here, including character set compatibility and the names of the header file and library file where the function is declared and defined.

You can use your favorite spreadsheet or database program to import the file and browse it, or search it at your leisure. However, while it's certainly effective, this won't teach you anything about the way list view controls can be used without just letting the control manage all the strings you have.

You can study the `APIBrow` application in the samples from the Wrox web site to see a great way to read a file and show it with a `CListCtrl` control. The program can work with any old comma-separated variable file; just specify the name of the file in the File Open dialog box when you get the application running.

The crux of the sample is a list view control that lives in the application's main `CListView`-derived window. The program reads the first line of the file and parses it to find titles for the columns in the list box. It then proceeds to read the remaining lines of the file and stores them in a `CStringArray`. The program isn't very efficient because it stores the raw, unparsed lines in the array. This inefficiency allows me to show off the workings of the callbacks, though, so it isn't really a bug.

When the list view control sends its `LVN_GETDISPINFO` message, `CApiBrowView::OnGetdispinfo()` is called by the framework. That function gains a pointer to the document and retrieves the whole line from the array in the document. It then parses the actual field from the line based on the subitem requested by the control. The whole procedure is relatively straightforward, but the twist comes in the way it reacts to the requirement that the string continues to live for at least two more `LVN_GETDISPINFO` notifications. Windows maintains the data longevity requirement because it doesn't cache the strings itself (assuming, rightly or wrongly, that you're able to do it more efficiently). Windows hangs on to the pointer you give it for a couple more messages, though, so you must make sure you don't delete or move the memory between subsequent calls.

To implement the smooth caching of the strings, I coded a function called `AddPool()` which hangs on to two `CString` objects. If the function is provided with a third, it discards the older of the first two. With this simple algorithm, I can ensure that each `CString` object won't move and won't be deleted until the `OnGetdispinfo()` function has handled two more callbacks.

The two string objects I use are simply members of the `CApiBrowView` class I implemented. In the constructor, I make them empty. Whenever I handle an `OnGetdispinfo()`, I make sure I rotate the pool to get the oldest string out and put the newest string in. The actual code to do it looks like this:

```
LPTSTR CAPIBrowView::AddPool(CString* pstr)
{
    LPTSTR pstrRetVal;
    int nOldest = m_nNextFree;

    m_strCPool[m_nNextFree] = *pstr;
    pstrRetVal = m_strCPool[m_nNextFree].LockBuffer();
    m_pstrPool[m_nNextFree++] = pstrRetVal;
    m_strCPool[nOldest].ReleaseBuffer();

    if (m_nNextFree == 3)
        m_nNextFree = 0;
    return pstrRetVal;
}
```

The real trick that's going on here is the careful use of `LockBuffer()` to make sure the `CString` objects aren't copied and reallocated. I'm not doing this for efficiency – I'm doing it because I can't let the strings move within memory while Windows still thinks it has a valid pointer to the string.

Editable List Views

Another cool feature of list view controls worth investigation is the editing of labels in the control. If you've specified the 'edit labels' style and the user clicks on the text of a label that already has focus, an edit control will appear over the label and the user will be allowed to change the text in the label. The application can also bring up the edit control for a particular item by calling EditLabel() and passing the index of the item you'd like to edit.

Label editing works for all items in list view controls that have the LVS_ICON, LVS_SMALLICON, or LVS_LIST style. However, label editing *only* works on items in the leftmost column of LVS_REPORT-style list view controls – you can't edit the labels on subitems in controls of this style, although it's a simple matter to create an edit control with the subitem's rectangle.

When the edit box for an item appears, the control fires an LVN_BEGINLABELEDIT message at the application. The message carries a pointer to an LV_DISPINFO structure that contains the current state of the item. If you receive an LVN_BEGINLABELEDIT notification and realize that you don't want to allow the user to perform the edit, you can return TRUE from the notification handler. Returning FALSE from the handler, or not handling the message at all, allows the user to perform the editing freely.

If the user presses *Enter* or clicks outside of the item once editing is underway, the changes are accepted by the application. The function will receive a new LV_DISPINFO via an LVN_ENDLABELEDIT notification. This LV_DISPINFO structure contains the new text for the item. If the user presses *Esc* or clicks outside of the item before any editing has taken place, the editing is canceled. In this case, the LVN_ENDLABELEDIT notification that is sent contains a pszText member that is NULL. You can test the pszText to see if it is acceptable to you; if it is, you can allow the edit by returning TRUE from the notification. Otherwise, return FALSE from the notification to revert to the field's previous content.

List View Extended Styles

List views also support numerous extended styles. Even though it features a tab that is labeled Extended Styles, the list view extended styles are *not* exposed to you in the Properties dialog of the Resource Editor. The Resource Editor allows you to modify extended Windows styles – that is, window styles applicable to most window types. The list view extended styles are specific to list views and must be sent to the control at runtime and can't be created on the control from the dialog template.

The extended style bits, the regular windows style bits, and the list view extended style bits are all separate. That is, you'll retrieve them and set them with three different sets of functions. Their separate treatment certainly seems odd, and it is – what you're noticing is the aging design of Windows.

To set those styles, you'll call CListCtrl::SetExtendedStyle(). This function accepts a DWORD for the new extended style bits you wish to assign the control, and returns the old style bits in a DWORD, as well. The function simply sets the bits – it doesn't add the bits you provide to the existing bits. If you want to set only a single bit, you'll want to call CListCtrl::GetExtendedStyle(), bit-wise OR the new bit or bits you want, and then call SetExtendedStyle() with the result of your computation. It might look something like this:

```
DWORD dwOldBits;
dwOldBits = pMyCtrl->GetExtendedStyle();
dwOldBits |= LVS_EX_FULLROWSELECT;
pMyCtrl->SetExtendedStyle(dwOldBits);
```

And that conveniently brings us to our first extended style: LVS_EX_FULLROWSELECT, one of the features of the newer Comctl32.dll versions. This style has your report-mode list view control draw its selection highlight across the complete width of the control. Furthermore, if the user clicks anywhere in the width of the control, the selection will change. Without this style, the control only highlights the text of the first column and you must click on the first column to change selections. Before this style became available, you had to subclass the control, make it owner-drawn, and do all the painting yourself. The ROWLIST sample, which is included in the Visual C++ product, shows how to get all that done – but the LVS_EX_FULLROWSELECT style has made it all moot.

If full-row selection isn't enough, you might wish to add grid lines using the LVS_EX_GRIDLINES extended style. This has the control draw both horizontal and vertical gridlines through the client area of a report-view control.

Another extended style that does nothing but affect the visual appearance of the control is LVS_EX_FLATSB. This extended style has the control use flat-style scroll bars. Flat-style scrollbars are just what they sound like – scroll bars that don't have a three-dimensional appearance and look, well, flat.

If your control has the LVS_EX_HEADERDRAGDROP extended style, the user can use the mouse to reorder columns simply by clicking and dragging them to a new position. Of course, this style is only available on report-mode boxes. You can retrieve the column ordering information by calling CListCtrl::GetColumnOrderArray() on a box. That function initializes an array indicating the visible order of columns for each of the logical columns in the control. Consider this code:

```
int nColumns = pMyCtrl->GetHeaderCtrl()->GetItemCount();
int* pOrderArray = new int[nColumns];
pMyCtrl->GetColumnOrderArray(pOrderArray, nColumns);
// use the array here,
// and when we're done...
delete [] pOrderArray;
```

To read the ordering array, we'll first get the count of columns from the control and allocate an array of integers so we'll have one integer for each column in the control. Then, we'll pass the array (and its count) off to GetColumnOrderArray(). The array, upon return, indicates the visible position of the given logical column. That is, the value at pOrderArray[2] indicates the visible location of the third logical column in the control. And if a control hasn't had its columns reordered, the visible column location is the same as the logical index. That is, pOrderArray[2] would be 2 if the third logical column is still the third visible column.

In the code above, to be a nice guy, I delete the array so we don't leak memory.

You can similarly set the order of the visible columns by calling SetColumnOrderArray(). It also takes a pointer to an array of integers and a count indicating the length of the array.

The LVS_EX_CHECKBOXES style is very exciting. It conveniently allows you to have the control display a checkbox with each item. The checkbox can be set or cleared – tri-state boxes aren't supported. You can see if a given item is set by using this code:

```
if (pMyCtrl->GetItemState(nItem, LVIS_STATEIMAGEMASK) >> 12) - 1)
{
    // it's checked
}
else
{
    // it's not checked
}
```

As you can see, we're just querying the image mask of the item and looking for a particular bit to be set or cleared. Internally, a list view control with the LVS_EX_CHECKBOXES style is just managing a special image list to simulate the checkboxes! Given that information, you can guess that you can check a particular item by coding:

```
pMyCtrl->SetItemState(nItem, 2, LVIS_STATEIMAGEMASK);
```

and clearing a checkmark with:

```
pMyCtrl->SetItemState(nItem, 1, LVIS_STATEIMAGEMASK);
```

It's that simple! Unfortunately, you'll just have to remember the constants 1 and 2 (and the 12 in the GetItemState() code fragment, above) as there's as yet no predefined constant with a nice name to use in their place. Maybe, eventually, Commctrl.h will toe the line and have some coding sense!

Normally, a report-mode control shows an image only with each item – essentially leaving your control with an icon on items in the first column. If you want to have an icon in each and every column, you can set LVS_EX_SUBITEMIMAGES. Then you just set iImage for the subitems (as well as the items) to get their images set.

A few extended styles can interact to change the way selection happens in the control. If you turn on LVS_EX_TRACKSELECT, the control will watch the mouse and automatically select items under the mouse position. Remember that this kind of selection only highlights the item – the control doesn't react as if the item has been double-clicked. You can adjust the reaction to the mouse hovering by calling SetHoverTime() to provide the number of milliseconds the control will wait for the mouse to be still before making an item the current selection.

LVS_EX_ONECLICKACTIVATE will send an LVN_ITEMACTIVATE notification if you click an item a single time. If you've set LVS_EX_TWOCLICKACTIVATE, you'll need to double-click the item before an activation notification is sent. A list view control without either of these styles will show the selected item with a highlight. But any control with either of these styles will end up previewing the item before it's clicked. A previewed item shows a highlighted text color, while an item that's actually activated also shows the selected text background color.

Certainly, the activation states now available in the control seem to be nothing more than eye candy. And, at the surface, they certainly are. But using one-click activation can make your application behave with the user-interface look and feel of a web browser – which is growing in importance as the initial interface experience of newer users.

The last interesting extended list view control style we'll discuss is `LVS_EX_INFOTIP`. When you have an icon-view control (that is, one with the `LVS_ICON` style) and `LVS_EX_INFOTIP` on the control, the control will display a tool tip when the user parks their cursor near an icon. Before the control displays the tip, it sends an `LVN_GETINFOTIP` notification, which carries an `NMLVGETINFOTIP` structure:

```
typedef struct tagNMLVGETINFOTIP
{
    NMHDR hdr;
    DWORD dwFlags;
    LPTSTR pszText;
    int cchTextMax;
    int iItem;
    int iSubItem;
    LPARAM lParam;
} NMLVGETINFOTIP, *LPNMLVGETINFOTIP;
```

The structure has the regular `NMHDR` structure as its first member. You can copy the text you want into the buffer referenced by `pszText`, as long as it isn't any longer than the number in `cchTextMax`.

Spin Button Control

The **spin button** control is used to provide your application with an interface for adjusting numeric values without having to actually retype them. The spin button control, which is also called an **up/down control**, can increase or decrease the value of an associated control without the user retyping the data in the control.

The control associated with the spin button is referred to as the spin button's **buddy**. You can let a spin button control adopt a buddy automatically. When automatically choosing a buddy, the spin control will take the first editable control before it in the tab order of the dialog box where it lives. Be careful with this setting; if your dialog has a bad tab order, you'll find the control buddying with the wrong control, often with some pretty curious results! If you like, you can explicitly define the auto-buddy setting, specified by the `UDS_AUTOBUDDY` style, in the control's property page while you are adding the control to a dialog box.

When the control finds its buddy, it will display its user interface inside its buddy's rectangle. You can have the control add itself to the left or to the right of its buddy, or let the control live a solitary life as a buddyless, unattached control. Without a buddy, the up/down control will have its own window rectangle and can be placed anywhere.

Should you wish to set the buddy manually, you can do so with the `SetBuddy()` method. This function takes only a `CWnd*`, referencing the window you wish to use as a buddy.

In this dialog box, the controls are aligned to the right side of their buddy because the controls have the UDS_ALIGNRIGHT style. If you wanted to have the spin button controls show up at the left of their buddy, you could use the UDS_ALIGNLEFT style.

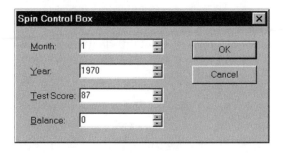

If a spin button control isn't associated with another control, you'll certainly need to trap its notification messages to make any use of it. The UDN_DELTAPOS notification lets you know that the control is about to change its position, and you can write code to react appropriately. If the spin button control *is* paired with another control, the control will still send UDN_DELTAPOS notifications, but it can also directly set the text of the paired control to reflect the scrolled position of the spin button control. The control will behave this way if it has the UDS_SETBUDDYINT style. (By the way, *position* here means the logical scrolled position of the control, *not* its physical position on the screen.)

If the control does have a buddy, you can still handle its notification messages. But a control that has a buddy will almost always have the "Set buddy integer" style – and that causes the control to automatically update its buddy – allowing you to get away with almost no work in most cases.

The control can be aligned either vertically or horizontally with its buddy. By convention, you should use a vertical control buddied with an edit control, while horizontally aligned spin button controls are for special scrolling applications – I'll come back to these near the end of this section.

In the Doodads example, you can use a dialog that contains spin button controls by selecting the Spinner command in the example's View menu. This dialog is implemented in the Spinner.cpp file. The dialog is really quite simple, since the controls do the tough work of allowing the user to adjust the control values; we used dialog data exchange routines on the edit controls to get and set values for the fields. You don't need to use dialog data exchange directly against the spin controls because they don't handle any information of their own; they just doctor the values of their buddy controls.

Data Validation

The Spinner dialog uses dialog data validation to enforce limits on the data entered in the controls. This is necessary because the user is welcome to circumvent the spinner controls and enter data directly into the control. The spinner and the control's validation code must cooperate to enforce the limits. In the OnInitDialog() function for the spinner box, you can call the SetRange() member of each of the controls to make sure that they're limited to valid values for the controls in use:

```
CSpinButtonCtrl* pMonth;
pMonth = static_cast<CSpinButtonCtrl*>(GetDlgItem(IDC_MONTHSPIN));
ASSERT(pMonth != NULL);

pMonth->SetRange(1, 12);
```

Without calling SetRange(), the control's range will default to being between 100 and 0, and that ordering is significant. Since the default 'lower' limit is actually a bigger value than the 'upper' limit, the control will seem to work backwards – that is, the control will increment its value if you press the ▼ button and decrease it if you press the ▲ button. You could use this to your advantage, I suppose, by purposefully setting the lower range higher than the upper range in a call to SetRange(). Maybe it would be appropriate for an application to be used in submarines or deep in mineral mines?

Using SetRange(), a spin button control can only represent a range of values corresponding to a small integer. The range must be between UD_MINVAL and UD_MAXVAL; at the time of writing, these values are -32767 and 32767 – they're defined in Commctrl.h.

If you call SetRange32(), however, you can exceed these ranges and use any 32-bit integer values you'd like. There's no need to use different functions to get values from a control with a wide range, as all of the get- and set-value functions for the control accept and return 32-bit integers.

The spin button control will automatically include a thousands separator if you don't actively request otherwise. This feature is controlled by the **No thousands** check box in the control's property sheet. In code, you'll see this style expressed with the UDS_NOTHOUSANDS symbol.

Each time the user clicks on one of the arrows on the spin button control, the control will send a UDN_DELTAPOS and update the value of the control's buddy (if you've specified the UDS_SETBUDDYINT style). If the user keeps the mouse down on one of the buttons, the control will continue to update but, after a period, it may be set to accelerate so that it updates by a larger count.

You can change the acceleration behavior by building an array of UDACCEL structures to define the acceleration you wish the control to have, before informing the control of the UDACCEL array you wish to use. The structure contains two UINTs; the first is the number of seconds to wait before using the acceleration number and the second is that acceleration count. Since the values in the **Balance** field of the dialog in the Doodads example are so large, I used the following code to enable faster acceleration:

```
static UDACCEL aAccelerationTable[] ={
    { 2,  100},         // immediately use 100's
    { 5,  500},         // 500's after 5 seconds
    {10, 1000},         // 1000's after 10 seconds
};
```

The thing to note here is that the first number in the first element is ignored; the acceleration number is used immediately. After that, the numbers of seconds you supply are absolute, not cumulative. In the OnInitDialog() function, you can use this call to set up the **Balance** field:

```
pBalance->SetRange(0, UD_MAXVAL-1);
```

```
pBalance->SetAccel(3, aAccelerationTable);
```

`SetAccel()` takes as its first parameter an integer that indicates the size, in entries, of the acceleration array. The second parameter is a pointer to that array. There's no need to disconnect the acceleration or undo it before the control is killed; since the array is copied into the control's data space, there's no need to manage it.

If you're writing a more systems-oriented application, you might see value in calling `SetBase()` to change the radix used by the control to 16, or back to 10. These are the only two base systems supported by the control. If you forget which you're using, you can always call `GetBase()`.

Stand-alone Spin Controls

As I've said, spin controls are normally used with an edit control – the edit control will serve as the spin control's buddy. Sometimes, though, you might be interested in using a spin control on its own. They're useful for paging through lists or states within a form. For example, if you have a dialog box that shows one database record, you might consider using a spin control to allow the user to move from the current record to subsequent or previous records. In such an application, the spin control takes up less space and might appear more natural than would an ordinary scroll bar. On the other hand, a scroll bar would convey the size of the scrollable set of data, but it could be difficult to position the control in such a way that the user would know that it's to be used for scrolling the data and not the dialog box itself.

Spin controls are normally aligned vertically. If you'd like to align the control horizontally, use the `UDS_HORZ` style.

Slider Control

You may have used a scroll bar to allow the user to choose a value from a valid range. Scroll bars have a very intuitive user interface for this kind of situation and are great when the selection can be made from any number in a large continuous range. However, scroll bars aren't very easy for users to understand when the selection is for a small number of acceptable values over a large range. The visual appearance of a scroll bar also leaves more than a little to be desired.

In the `Doodads` example application, we've implemented a dialog box that might be used to collect some of the parameters describing a photographic exposure. Using a **slider control** (also known as a **track bar**) for the exposure duration and *f*-stop, the box shows how this control might be used. The range of values for the shutter speed on a camera is immense; on our camera, it ranges from one two-thousandth of a second to thirty seconds!

However, only sixteen values from this huge range are valid, making a slider control the perfect tool for collecting this information from the user. Aperture settings work on the same principles, so we used a slider control to collect this information as well. The Exposure Settings dialog from the `Doodads` example is shown below:

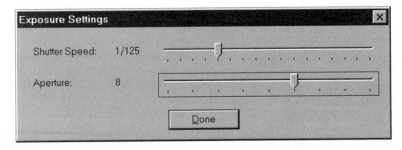

The slider controls shown in the dialog are both horizontal and both have tick marks below them, but you can alter these configurations as you require. These settings are all related to the style of control, so you would actually make these changes in the dialog editor as you add the control to your dialog box.

My Mouse Has Ticks

Normally, you'll create your slider control with the Autotick style enabled. The control will automatically format its tick marks, drawing a reasonable number at a comfortable frequency over the range of the control's motion. But if you don't specify the Autotick style, you can draw the tick marks yourself by calling the SetTic() member of the CSliderCtrl object which represents the control.

Unfortunately, there's no way to make tick marks and slider positions exist at non-linear steps through the width of the control. You can't, for example, create a slider that has five stops on the left half of its range and only two stops over the right half.

A slider's range is set using the SetRange() function, which can be used as soon as the control is first created. If you need to change the range of the control during its lifetime, you can use the SetRangeMax() and SetRangeMin() functions to set the upper and lower boundaries of the control respectively. However, if (like me) you're not paid for each and every line of code you write, you might want to call SetRange() to set both ends of the range at the same time.

In the Doodads application's Exposure.cpp file, we initialized the controls in the dialog based on two arrays. In the first array, pstrAperture[], the various aperture settings used on our camera are stored, while the second array, pstrShutter[], holds the different settings for the shutter speed. To make the controls return a range which can index this array, you make these SetRange() calls:

```
BOOL CExposureDialog::OnInitDialog()
{
    CSliderCtrl* pAperture = static_cast<CSliderCtrl*>(GetDlgItem(IDC_APERTURE));
    CSliderCtrl* pShutter = static_cast<CSliderCtrl*>(GetDlgItem(IDC_SHUTTER));

    pAperture->SetRange(0, ELEMENTS(pstrAperture)-1);
    pShutter->SetRange(0, ELEMENTS(pstrShutter)-1);

    // Rest of the function...
}
```

Note that 1 is subtracted from the number of elements in each array, so that the range is sized correctly for use as an index to an array.

The shutter control has the Autotick style; you don't need to do anything else with it. If you didn't like the layout, you could call the `SetTicFreq()` function and pass a number which would indicate the frequency of tick marks in the control. For example, `SetTicFreq(2)` would ensure that every other position in the control's range would have a tick.

To initialize the control, which doesn't have the Autotick style, I first call `ClearTics()` to clear any existing ticks, before repeatedly calling `SetTic()` to turn on the ticks at individual positions through the control's range. `SetTic()` takes the position within the control's range where you'd like to make a tick mark. Here's the code from the `Doodads` sample that does just this:

```
pAperture->ClearTics(TRUE);
int nIndex;
for (nIndex = 0; nIndex < ELEMENTS(pstrAperture); nIndex++)
    pAperture->SetTic(nIndex);
```

Note that the slider will stop at any valid position in the control's range, whether the position is actually marked with a tick or not.

Since we'd like to display the numeric values for the settings of the controls as feedback to the user, we're interested in being notified each time the user touches the slider. The control sends `WM_HSCROLL` messages to the parent window (or `WM_VSCROLL` messages if the control is aligned vertically). It's easy to trap the `WM_HSCROLL` message in your dialog; just use the ClassWizard to add a handler. There's only one fly in the ointment; the function receives a pointer to a `CScrollBar` object, and not a pointer to a `CSliderCtrl` object.

If I weren't running for Man Of The Year, I would simply cast the `CScrollBar` pointer to a `CSliderCtrl` pointer; but I can't compromise my image, even though this philosophy is sick, demented and should be considered as dangerous behavior. I'd land on some television talk show and people would phone up to ridicule me. Casting like this will work, but it's ugly, bad and unsafe. The sane way to get this done is to get the dialog ID of the `pScrollBar` object before you call `GetDlgItem()` on that ID. The code in the `CExposureDialog`'s `OnHScroll()` handler looks like this:

```
void CExposureDialog::OnHScroll(UINT nSBCode, UINT nPos, CScrollBar* pScrollBar)
{
    int nPosition;
    int nControl = pScrollBar->GetDlgCtrlID();
    CSliderCtrl* pControl = static_cast<CSliderCtrl*>(GetDlgItem(nControl));

    switch (nControl)
    {
        case IDC_APERTURE:
            ASSERT(pControl != NULL);
            nPosition = pControl->GetPos();
            GetDlgItem(IDC_FSTOP)->SetWindowText(pstrAperture[nPosition]);
            break;

        // And the remainder of the switch...
}
```

Once we have a safe, real pointer to the CSliderCtrl, we can call GetPos() to figure out where it has been moved to. This value is an index to the pstrAperture[] array, so we can simply extract the text and set it into the appropriate control.

Data Exchange with Sliders

The ClassWizard doesn't directly support data exchange with sliders, but it's easy enough to implement the exchange yourself. We've added m_nShutter and m_nAperture integers to the public member data of the CExposureDialog so that it's easy to look up the settings from outside of the dialog, back in the main application.

To implement the data exchange function, just check the m_bSaveAndValidate member of the pDX object passed to the function. If it's TRUE, call GetPos() on the CSliderCtrl objects to retrieve their positions and jam them into the member variables. If it's FALSE, use the values to initialize the controls with calls to the SetPos() member of the control objects. It all ends up looking like this:

```
void CExposureDialog::DoDataExchange(CDataExchange* pDX)
{
    CDialog::DoDataExchange(pDX);
    //{{AFX_DATA_MAP(CExposureDialog)
        // NOTE: the ClassWizard will add DDX and DDV calls here
    //}}AFX_DATA_MAP

    CSliderCtrl* pAperture = static_cast<CSliderCtrl*>(GetDlgItem(IDC_APERTURE));
    CSliderCtrl* pShutter = static_cast<CSliderCtrl*>(GetDlgItem(IDC_SHUTTER));

    if (pDX->m_bSaveAndValidate)
    {
        m_nShutter = pShutter->GetPos();
        m_nAperture = pAperture->GetPos();
    }
    else
    {
        pShutter->SetPos(m_nShutter);
        pAperture ->SetPos(m_nAperture);
    }
}
```

By the way, I could have coded this part of the program using DDX_ calls to swap the text back and forth but, just for variety, I decided to code the routine without DDX_. And, as usual, you should place the code clear of the ClassWizard comments, so that the ClassWizard won't mush the code at a later date.

Progress Control

Many time-consuming tasks that the computer performs have no visible effect, which makes the user suppose that the machine has crashed, leading to frantic actions. To this end, most applications have evolved different ways to indicate to the user that something *is* actually happening. To standardize on a nifty, graphical method for doing this, the Windows common controls library provides a **progress bar** control, which the MFC wraps with the CProgressCtrl class.

The progress control is easily the simplest common control that has been added to Windows, and consequently CProgressCtrl is a very simple class. Once you've drawn the progress control in your dialog, you can use CProgressCtrl::SetRange() to set its range. By default, without a call to SetRange(), the control will use a range from 0 to 100.

Contrived example of contrived examples, the CProgressDialog code in Doodads doesn't do any work. When you bring up the dialog shown above (click the **Progress** item in the **View** menu) and press the **Go!** button, the code will create a Windows timer that fires off every 500 milliseconds. In response to the timer message, the dialog calls StepIt() on the control class to increment the progress bar. We set the range for the control to be 0 to 90 during the OnInitDialog() function, and then use SetStep(1) to pump up the control by a notch each time StepIt() is called. The control will take about 45 seconds to crawl from left to right, since 500 milliseconds multiplied by 90 is 45 seconds.

There really is nothing to the progress control, but there is one interesting style you can apply. You can specify PBS_SMOOTH to have the control draw a single full rectangle for the progressed portion instead of drawing several regular, small rectangles to fill the area, and you can make the control have a border by using the **Border** style if you like. For an added novelty, you can specify PBS_VERTICAL which will display a vertical progress bar which fills from bottom to top, but it doesn't get much more exciting than that.

Animation Control

Most Windows users have machines that are at least partially capable of multimedia playback. The **animation control**, wrapped by the CAnimateCtrl class, can be used to play back simple .avi files. Normally, you'd need to write some code to call the Windows multimedia API directly, but the animation control can be used in a few situations to avoid getting your hands dirty.

You can create the control with the dialog editor window in the Visual C++ IDE. By positioning it appropriately, you can make sure the control shows the animation where you want it. The control's most important and unique style is **Centered**; if this style is set, the control will play the video clip at the recorded size and center the image within its rectangle, whether the image is larger or smaller than the control. If this style isn't set, the control will stretch or shrink itself to fit the image in its client area. The dynamic resizing is quite aggressive, so you should be careful when you are using it.

The control also features a Transparent style, which if set, will make the control understand 'screen' colors in the image. This means that if regions in the image are marked as being transparent, they will be rendered as such. The control will draw these parts of the image as if they were clear, letting whatever is in the dialog background show through them.

You can have the control open an image if you call the CAnimateCtrl::Open() function – just pass the name of the .avi file you'd like to play. Unfortunately, the animation control is very limited in the type of .avi files that it can handle; the file you pass must contain uncompressed data (or data compressed only with Windows' native RLE8 format) and must not manipulate the palette. If the file contains sound, it must only contain one stream of sound data (which will be ignored anyway).

Because of these limitations, you might have a very hard time finding .avi files that you *can* use with the animation control. Most available .avi files use very aggressive compression algorithms to ensure that they take up as little disk space as possible and have excellent performance. Open() will return FALSE if the file isn't found, or if the file has an unacceptable format. If you can find a copy of the Video for Windows SDK at http://www.microsoft.com/, you can use its AVIEdit tool to create your own drawings. Using the proper settings on any other commercial multimedia editing software should do just fine, too.

Playing a File

Once the file is open, you can call Play() to make the control play the file. The Play() function takes three parameters, each of which must be a UINT. The first parameter is the frame within the file that should be played first. The second is the last frame in the file that should be played. If the starting frame number is 0, the file will play from the beginning, and if the ending frame number is – 1, the file will play to the end. The third parameter is a count indicating how many times the file will be played.

> The play code runs in a separate thread, so the **Play()** function will return immediately. If it couldn't start the playback, it will return **FALSE**, otherwise it will return **TRUE**.

You can call Stop() on the control to make it stop playing at any time, which means that the control will continue to display the frame which was previously playing; you need to call Close() to make the control clear its display. You may ask the control to move within the file by calling the Seek() member function of the control's wrapper class.

Animation Control Notification

The animation control will throw back notifications to your parent window. If you're interested, you can trap these to get information about what the control is doing, or what the user is doing to the control. The two most interesting notifications are ACN_START and ACN_STOP. ACN_START is sent when the control begins playing the video file, while ACN_STOP is sent when you reach the end of the file. The control also sends the usual compliment of NM_ notifications to indicate when, among other things, the user clicks or double-clicks on the control.

In the Doodads example application, we've provided an Animation command in the View menu, which is hooked up to a dialog that allows you to supply a file name (or browse for one) and will attempt to play the file you request. The Open() function will fail and display an appropriate error message if the file was of a bad format and, because of the limitations of the control, you should expect to see this message quite often! (In fact, I couldn't find a suitable .avi file anywhere!) If you need to play high-quality images that change or manipulate colors on the palette, you'll be better off investigating the Windows multimedia APIs.

The Tree View Control

In many ways, the tree view control behaves just like a list box, except that it provides inherent support for the display of hierarchical information. Lots of things can be represented in a hierarchy – information from the 'parts explosion' problems often encountered when working with databases, or a directory structure, for example.

In the example application Newsgrps, which can be downloaded from the Wrox web site, I've developed a simple application that shows a tree view of the different Usenet newsgroups available on an Internet access provider that I sometimes use.

ReadList()

The box is populated by the ReadList() function, which is called during the special function FakeInitialUpdate(). FakeInitialUpdate() is called from the paint handler in the dialog box; it's named FakeInitialUpdate() because it's not the real OnInitialUpdate() function that other windows receive from MFC. I invented this mechanism to populate the box because I wanted the box to paint before spending a lot of time reading the data file and getting information into the box. This way, when the box comes up, the user can see that the machine is still working and not out to lunch. We couldn't use the real OnInitialUpdate() call because dialog boxes don't have that notification function – only CView-derived classes do. I didn't use OnInitDialog() for loading the control because WM_INITDIALOG is sent before the dialog is shown or has had a chance to paint.

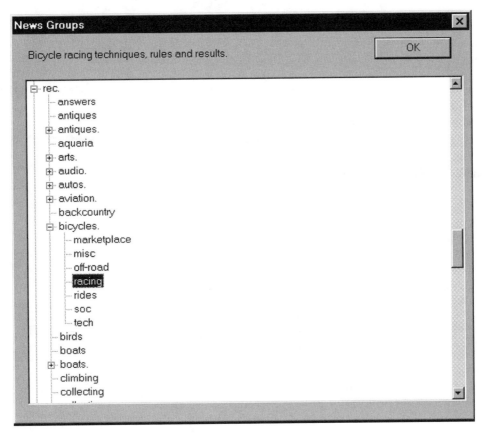

Anyway, `ReadList()` opens the `Newsgrou` file using the constructor of a `CStdioFile` object. As the file is read line-by-line, each line is picked into two parts; the first part is the name of the newsgroup and the second part is a description of it. You can then use the function `GetField()` to retrieve each dot-element of the newsgroup name.

For example, if you `GetField()` on the newsgroup comp.lang.c++, the function will return comp. if passed 1, lang. if passed 2, or c++ if passed 3. An empty string is returned if an index value higher than 3 is passed to `GetField()`.

> *If you're not familiar with Usenet newsgroups, you should know that they're the hierarchy that allows you to find postings in Usenet – a collection of systems on the Internet which act like a large, distributed bulletin-board, sharing postings about different interesting topics.* comp.lang... *is full of different discussions about different computer languages:* comp.lang.pascal, comp.lang.c++ *and so on. Computer languages have nothing to do with ice hockey, so discussions about that sport are over in* rec.sport.hockey; *other* rec.sport... *groups include* rec.sport.soccer *and* rec.sport.motorcycle, *for example. In the meantime, my dad is afraid that I'll* wreck.sport.motorcycle.

There are many thousands of newsgroups, and their number increases day by day; the data file included with this example contains a mere 3900 or so. Still, you can imagine that a hierarchical list like this one might make the basis for a part of the user interface of a program that lets you post or view Usenet messages. The Newsgrou file has this basic format:

```
<newsgroup name><whitespace><description>
```

Note that some newsgroups have a description of *??*; the news provider from which I stole this file doesn't have complete information for every newsgroup it carries.

Adding New Information

If new information appears in the newsgroup name as the file is dismantled, that item is then added to the tree view. Since the list only contains complete newsgroup names, the code must carefully add the section names as well. For instance, when the ReadList() routine first sees the comp component of a newsgroup name, it has to add that name to the tree control and remember that the item could possibly be a parent to other items.

comp.admin.policies is the first newsgroup in the comp structure. When the code sees comp.admin.policies, it adds comp to the tree control, remembers that comp is there, and then uses information about comp's position in the tree control to make sure admin is added as a child. Subsequently, policies is added as a child of admin. There might be some other admin entry in the hierarchy, but that entry is different to the one that we've made a child of comp.

The code that does this parsing uses an array of ten pointers to compare each field in the newsgroup name. So, after the name comp.admin.policies has been read, the first three elements of the array look like this:

```
m_szPrevious[0] = "comp";
m_szPrevious[1] = "admin";
m_szPrevious[2] = "policies";
```

Because there are only three fields in this particular name, array elements m_szPrevious[3] through m_szPrevious[9] contain empty strings.

When the next string is read, it is split into individual fields as well. As each field is removed, it's compared with the same field index in the m_szPrevious array. If there's a match, the comparison carries on. If the strings in a particular field don't match, we know that the newly-read newsgroup fits into the hierarchy at that level of indentation.

Tree View Styles

The tree view control supports a few style bits which affect its appearance and function. Like the list view control, you're allowed to click on items in the box to edit their labels if the box has the TVS_EDITLABELS style. The tree view control will notify you with TVN_BEGINLABELEDIT and TVN_ENDLABELEDIT notifications when the user starts and finishes editing.

The Newsgrps sample shows a tree control that features all three visible styles: TVS_HASLINES, TVS_HASBUTTONS, and TVS_LINESATROOT. The TVS_HASBUTTONS style causes the control to show a tiny button to the left of the item. If the item has children and can be expanded, the button has a plus sign in it. If the item has children and is already expanded, the button has a minus sign in it, and if the item has no children, the button won't be shown.

If you specify the TVS_HASLINES style, the control will show a faint line to the left of the items. This style helps users navigate the control, because it shows them how deep the items are. The TVS_LINESATROOT style also causes the control to show lines (and buttons, if specified) at the root level of the control. The name TVS_LINESATROOT implies that the style only works with tree views that have TVS_HASLINES set, but this isn't true; the style also controls the appearance of buttons at the root level.

CTreeCtrl

MFC wraps the tree view control with the CTreeCtrl class. You can gain a pointer to the class by using the very same GetDlgItem() technique we've seen for regular dialog box controls – there's no extra mystery here. Since the tree view control is considerably more complicated than a regular list box, you can imagine that building a hierarchy isn't quite as simple as just doing a bunch of AddString() calls. To build a structure, you must tell the control exactly how you want the new item to appear in the list.

Items in the box are identified by handles rather than by indexes. Indexes imply a linear structure, so they're not useful for tree views; an index of 4, referring to the fifth element in the list, really has no meaning when the fifth item might be a parent of other items in the box or a child of some. Conversely, handles can readily identify any object without implying relationships to the different items in the box.

Consequently, it shouldn't come as a surprise that the structure needed to insert objects into the box contains two handles to describe items that might affect the insertion operation. The structure in question is called TVINSERTSTRUCT; you can see a declaration of a variable of this structure early on in the ReadList() function. The structure has only three members, and is shown here in its entirety:

```
typedef struct _TVINSERTSTRUCT {
   HTREEITEM hParent;
   HTREEITEM hInsertAfter;
#if (_WIN32_IE >= 0x0400)
   union
   {
       TVITEMEX itemex;
       TVITEM item;
   } DUMMYUNIONNAME;
#else
   TVITEM item;
#endif
} TVINSERTSTRUCT, FAR *LPTVINSERTSTRUCT;
```

The hParent member identifies a handle to the item that will act as the parent for the newly inserted item. The hInsertAfter field specifies a handle to the item that precedes the new item. The item member turns out to be a TVITEM structure that describes the new item itself, and it's in a union along with the larger TVITEMEX structure which has the extra iIntegral field, which allows controls using custom draw to have some items that are taller than others.

Inserting Child Items

If you're inserting an item as a child, you indicate which entry you want to be its parent by placing a handle to it in the hParent member of your TVINSERTSTRUCT variable. The code that inserts objects into the newsgroups list does this whenever an item is added, since all items will be children. The exceptions, of course, are items which are used to denote the parent of a whole substructure in the Usenet hierarchy: alt., comp., rec., and so on. These are inserted as top-level items by adding them with an hParent of NULL.

You can use the hInsertAfter field in the TVINSERTSTRUCT to dictate where the new node will be placed in relationship to its siblings. You can use one of three special values here as well. TVI_FIRST forces the item to be the first in its level, while TVI_LAST forces the item to be the last at its level. TVI_SORT will let the control use the local sorting rules to sort the item and insert it in the appropriate spot.

Since a child item in the tree view control is always shown after its parent, it is never necessary to make the hInsertAfter handle equal to the hParent field. If you want to insert a child item, simply set hParent to the parent handle and set hInsertAfter to arrange the new item appropriately in relation to its siblings.

However, it's in the TVINSERTSTRUCT's item member where all the structure's action occurs. This structure, nested in TVINSERTSTRUCT, is a TVITEM type. When you're working with the tree control, you'll toss around these structures as complete descriptions of individual elements in the box.

Since TVITEM is itself a structure, it contains a few different fields, the most important of which is mask. When the control finally sees the TVITEM structure, mask tells it which fields in the structure are expected to be returned, or which fields (as provided from the caller) are valid. This is extremely similar to what we've seen before when we were looking at the list view. When an item is added to the tree control in the example, the code looks like this:

```
itemNew.item.mask = TVIF_TEXT | TVIF_PARAM;
itemNew.item.pszText = pstr;
itemNew.item.lParam = reinterpret_cast<long>(_tcsdup(pstrDescription));

m_hPrevParent[n] = pControl->InsertItem(&itemNew);
```

The InsertItem() member of the CTreeCtrl class does the insertion and accepts a pointer to the TVITEM structure which describes the item I want to insert. The insertion mask is created by bit-wise ORing the two constants TVIF_TEXT and TVIF_PARAM. These flags tell the control code that the lParam and the pszText members of the structure will be valid.

As you might guess, `pszText` is the actual text of the item and `lParam` is an extra value that is associated with each element in the list. In this code, it is used as a pointer to a string that has a description of the newsgroup. The `lParam` item is very similar to the item data we talked about when we described standard combo boxes and list boxes. That is, you can use it for whatever data you'd like – as long as you can fit that data into 32-bits.

The TVITEM Flags

This table shows the different fields of `TVITEM` and their corresponding meanings, as well as the `TVIF_` flags which indicate their validity:

Field	Meaning	TVIF_ flag
pszText	pszText contains a pointer to the text of the control. At insertion, the control makes a copy of the text for its own use. When you are retrieving an object, ensure this points to memory that's big enough to hold text; express the size of your buffer in cchTextMax.	TVIF_TEXT
lParam	An arbitrary parameter that you can use for anything you want.	TVIF_PARAM
cchTextMax	Used to set the maximum size for the text buffer referenced by pszText when the control is requested to provide text to the caller.	TVIF_TEXT
iImage	Index of the image to be used with this item. The index refers to the image list control associated with the control.	TVIF_IMAGE
iSelectedImage	Index of the image to be used when this item is selected. The index refers to the image list control associated with the control.	TVIF_SELECTEDIMAGE
cChildren	A count of the children this item owns; it's zero if the item is not a parent of any items.	TVIF_CHILDREN
hItem	Handle to the item in question.	TVIF_HANDLE
state	Flags indicating the state of the item; includes selected, overlaid, focused and disabled.	TVIF_STATE

Table Continued on Following Page

Field	Meaning	**TVIF_ flag**
StateMask	A mask indicating which flags are applicable.	TVIF_STATE
mask	Holder for TVIF_ flags.	(none)

Study the code in the Newsgrps sample program very carefully; it's not too hard to see where the actual insertions to the list box take place. A call to the InsertItem() of the control is made to load each of its elements in ReadList(). You might want to put a breakpoint on this line so you can see exactly how the box is loaded with real data.

Notifications

In the Newsgrps sample, I use the lParam member of the TV_ITEM to hang on to the description field of the newsgroup. As the newsgroup item is added, the string is duplicated by calling _tcsdup() and setting the resulting pointer to the lParam in the item. I then used ClassWizard to add a handler for the TVN_SELCHANGED notification message. This message is sent when the user selects a different item in the list. Here's the code from the example:

```
void CNewsGrpsDlg::OnSelchangedGroups(NMHDR* pNMHDR, LRESULT* pResult)
{
    NMTREEVIEW* pNMTreeView = reinterpret_cast<NMTREEVIEW*>(pNMHDR);

    if (!m_bClosing)
    {
        CTreeCtrl* pControl;
        pControl = static_cast<CTreeCtrl*>(GetDlgItem(IDC_GROUPS));

        LPTSTR pstr = reinterpret_cast<LPTSTR>(pNMTreeView->itemNew.lParam);
        if (pstr == NULL)
            SetDlgItemText(IDC_STATUS, _T(""));
        else
            SetDlgItemText(IDC_STATUS, pstr);
    }
    else
        free(reinterpret_cast<LPTSTR>(pNMTreeView->itemNew.lParam));

    *pResult = 0;
}
```

The very first line of the function, which builds a pointer to an NM_TREEVIEW structure, was provided by the ClassWizard, as was the very last line, which returns a status code for the function back to Windows. As I've mentioned before, notification message handlers for common controls are a little different to the WM_COMMAND notification handlers you might be used to writing. The code supplied by the ClassWizard, to cast the pointers around and return a result via the pResult pointer, is the bulk of the difference.

The NMTREEVIEW Structure

The NMTREEVIEW structure contains the notification information for the message. While you're handling this notification, two TVITEM structures are of some importance: itemOld and itemNew. These members of the NMTREEVIEW structure describe the previously selected and newly selected item, respectively. If no item was previously selected, the hItem of the respective structure will be NULL.

You should be aware that the user can significantly change the way the control looks without adding or deleting an entry. This is because the user can expand or contract a branch by:

> An appropriate mouse click

> The plus key and minus key, to expand or contract the branches respectively

> A press of the asterisk key, to expand all branches below the current selection

> A press of the right arrow to expand, or the left arrow to contract a single level.

However the selection changes, we obtain the lParam member of the itemNew structure, which should point at the string that describes the newly selected newsgroup. If the pointer is really NULL, the text in the IDC_STATUS control at the top of the window is blanked out. Otherwise, the text referenced by the pointer is used to set the content of the status control, so updating the description when the user clicks on it.

Other Population Methods

The newsgroups list in the sample populates pretty quickly, but you could conceivably have a complicated hierarchy, which takes forever to populate, or which might be of some arbitrary depth and size. In such applications, it might literally take hours to fully populate a big tree.

If the data is coming from some server over the network, the communication might overwhelm the network or your machine. If the server is far away, such a transaction might bog down transatlantic communication routes, upsetting the global economy. Such troubles might make it difficult for the folks at NHL headquarters to transmit hockey statistics to the rest of the world. Oh, the calamity!

While we didn't employ this method in the example, you could populate a tree view by writing code that carefully interacts with the user as the contents of the box change. Such an application would populate only the top-level items in the box, and then wait around for the view control to send a TVN_ITEMEXPANDING notification message.

In response to this message, you can offer the control information about the child items of the entry being expanded by the user. This minimizes the amount of communication you'll need to do with the data source for the control, and will also dramatically speed up the presentation of your user interface, as only the necessary data is retrieved and added to the control. Unfortunately, it also means that the code to populate and drive the box will be even more complicated than the hierarchical unrolling code written for the NEWSGRPS sample.

Fooling with Entries

A side-effect of the algorithm used in `ReadList()` is that it gives descriptive data to all the entries in the tree control. This isn't correct; only the nodes in the box without children, that is, nodes in the box that describe a group and not a branch of the hierarchy, should have a description. (This isn't a limitation of the control – it's a design decision for the sample based on the fact that we don't have a description for branches, just for specific groups.) Rather than jumping through hoops to fix the `ReadList()` algorithm, I wrote another function, called `CleanParents()`, to traverse the tree control and find parent nodes.

The code from `CleanParents()` retrieves a `TVITEM` structure for the item it is currently visiting. It requests the handle, child count and `lParam` value from the box for that item by setting the appropriate flags in the mask member of the `TVITEM` structure, before calling `GetItem()` on the control. The code fragment looks like this:

```
void CNewsGroupsDlg::CleanParents(CTreeCtrl* pControl, HTREEITEM hItem)
{
    static TVITEM itemVisiting;

    itemVisiting.mask = TVIF_HANDLE | TVIF_CHILDREN | TVIF_PARAM;
    itemVisiting.hItem = hItem;

    pControl->GetItem(&itemVisiting);
    if (itemVisiting.cChildren > 0)
    {

    // And more to follow...
}
```

If the item in question actually has children, the `lParam` pointer is freed and `NULL` is put back in its place. That step looks like this:

```
LPTSTR strFreeMe;

strFreeMe = reinterpret_cast<LPTSTR>(temVisiting.lParam);
free(strFreeMe);
itemVisiting.lParam = NULL;
pControl->SetItem(&itemVisiting);
```

Note that this function is recursive. The loop that drives it, and the function itself, uses the `GetNextItem()`, `GetRootItem()` and `GetChildItem()` members of the `CTreeCtrl` class to navigate the list of items in the box. When a parent item is detected, the function is called once more for each of the child nodes in the control. If we use recursion in this way, we can write a tidy routine to clean up the content of the tree.

Recursion is a tricky little beast; while absolutely essential for handling tree structures, it can be hard to understand. I hope you can groove on my usage of these important members of `CTreeCtrl`, even if you think the recursive code is confusing.

Smooth Scrolling

The newest incarnation of the tree view control supports smooth scrolling. That is, as an item expands or contracts, the control slowly redraws itself to show the extra items growing into the visible area of the control. That's really a nice feature — it helps users understand where the new elements really came from.

But for a control populated with parent nodes that have many children, you might notice that the smooth expansion just takes way too long. You can adjust the maximum time the control will spend smooth scrolling by calling `CTreeCtrl::SetScrollTime()`. This function takes only a single integer, which indicates the maximum scroll time in milliseconds. If a scrolling operation is about to take longer than the limit you've set with a call to this function, the scroll will paint itself immediately and forgo the smooth scrolling feature.

To make sure your user interface stays professional, remember that you can use the `CWnd::SetRedraw()` method to temporarily stop the control from painting as you insert items into it or remove items from it. Once you're done, remember to turn the redraw back on and invalidate the control so it repaints itself with your newest content.

CMonthCalCtrl

Since computers are such wonderful tools for the manipulation of information, and lots of information in our lives is time-related, the entry and display of dates is a very common requirement of most applications. Finally, Windows includes a control that allows users to pick a date from a very natural control that appears just as a calendar would look.

The month-calendar control shows as many calendar pages as will fit in its client area — up to a whole year. If you draw the control in the dialog editor, it will paint as many pages as fit. You can call the control's `SizeMinReq()` member to immediately size the control to hold just a single page, if you so desire.

No matter how many pages are displayed, the control can be scrolled back and forth to show dates in the future or past. The allowable range of dates to be selected can be set using the `SetRange()` member, and that range can later be retrieved using the `GetRange()` function. `SetRange()` accepts two pointers; one to the minimum allowable date and the other to the maximum allowable date.

For maximum flexibility, all the control's date handling functions have overrides that accept `COleDateTime` or `CTime` types, as well as the `SYSTEMTIME` structure that the Win32 API itself uses.

`SetRange()` and `GetRange()` are no exceptions. If you pass `NULL` for either pointer, you'll set the control to have no bound at the respective extreme — or that you're not interested in one of the ranges being returned to you. `SetRange()` returns a `BOOL` for success or failure, while `GetRange()` returns a `DWORD` with a number of flags. The value might have `GDTR_MAX` if there was a maximum limit, or `GDTR_MIN` if there was a minimum limit. Obviously these two flags can be ORed together to specify a range of dates.

The control can accept any range that `SYSTEMTIME` supports. The control works with dates as late as 9999 AD and as early as 250 AD; more than enough to meet our needs!

The control has only a few interesting styles. MCS_NOTODAY has the control withhold displaying a line below the date for today. MCS_NOTODAYCIRCLE has the control draw a red ring around the current date. The control's definition of today is settable and doesn't always follow the current system time even though it starts there by default. You can call the SetToday() or GetToday() functions to set or get the value.

MCS_MULTISELECT allows you to have the control select more than one value; without the style, the function allows only one selection. But even with the MCS_MULTISELECT style, the function only allows contiguous selections. You can set the number of days selectable using SetMaxSelCount(), while GetMaxSelCount() returns that value to you.

With a multiple selection control, you can call SetSelRange() to set the range of selected dates, and using GetSelRange(), you can retrieve the range of the selection. In a single-selection control, GetCurSel() and SetCurSel() perform the same work.

If you give the control MCS_WEEKNUMBERS, it will draw an extra column on the left. There, the control will indicate the week of the year for the week shown in the control.

Another interesting feature of the control is the MCS_DAYSTATE style. If the control has this style, it will send MCN_GETDAYSTATE notifications back to its owner. The owner can respond to the notifications and set a bit field that marks some days in the control with a bold font. The idea is that the bold dates in the calendar will indicate something special about the days in question – that they have an appointment booked, or that the shop is open, or that the President is coming to town, and so on. The real meaning of the state is completely up to you and your application.

When you receive MCN_GETDAYSTATE, you'll find that lParam points to an NMDAYSTATE structure. The members are pretty simple:

```
typedef struct tagNMDAYSTATE
{
    NMHDR nmhdr;
    SYSTEMTIME stStart;
    int cDayState;
    LPMONTHDAYSTATE prgDayState;
} NMDAYSTATE, FAR * LPNMDAYSTATE;
```

The ubiquitous NMHDR member starts of the list, of course. stStart is a SYSTEMTIME that lets you know which date is represented by the first bit of the day states requested. cDayState indicates how many MONTHDAYSTATE values are stored at prgDayState. It turns out that MONTHDAYSTATE is just a DWORD. And that's convenient; since DWORDs weigh in at 32-bits, there's one bit for each possible day in a month with one bit left over.

It's as if there was some sort of cosmic design behind all this.

When you receive the notification, it's up to you to set a 0 in the corresponding bit at prgDayState for each day you don't want shown in bold, and a 1 in the bits where you do want the date shown in bold. You shouldn't claim to be an engineer, if a macro to help you doesn't jump to mind. Something like this is quite adequate:

```
#define BOLDDAY(ds, iDay) \
    if ((iDay) > 0 && (iDay) < 32)\
        (ds) |= (1 << ((iDay) - 1))
```

If you receive a notification and stStart refers to June 1st, 1992, and cDayState is set to 1, you can set the 3rd and the 5th and the 17th to bold by coding:

```
pDayState->prgDayState[0] = 0;
BOLDDAY(pDayState->prgDayState[0], 3);
BOLDDAY(pDayState->prgDayState[0], 5);
BOLDDAY(pDayState->prgDayState[0], 17);
```

and be done with it. But it's quite possible that cDayState isn't set to 1, even if you show only one month in your calendar page. The notification may decide to send you an array big enough to hold dates that are visible at the end of the previous month or at the very beginning of the next month! As such, you might have to compute an offset relative to the end of the start date in stDate before running off and setting a bit in the array.

It's worth pointing out that the month-calendar control is fully localized. The formats for the date, the day names, and even the first day of the week adhere to the rules set up in the locale for the thread that created the control. All of the settings used by the control can be retrieved from the GetLocaleInfo() API.

The Doodads sample features a dialog box that lets you play a bit with the month calendar control. The Monthcal.cpp file contains all of its source code. The dialog lets you change the style bits and interact with the selection limit and the settings for today. It also handles the day state notification.

Special versions of the DDX_ routines exist for this control – they can store a single-selection control's chosen date into a COleDateTime or a CTime member. Calling the DDV_ routine for this control implicitly sets the ranges of the control.

CDateTimeCtrl

The date time control is an edit control that allows you to input a date value or a time value. You can't input both a date and a time into the same control, unfortunately – so some might say the control is poorly named. What the control displays is determined by it's style bits; DTS_LONGDATEFORMAT uses the locale-specific setting for the long date format, while DTS_SHORTDATEFORMAT has the control show a short date format. DTS_TIMEFORMAT uses the locale's time format.

The control can be made to show a check box beside the date or time it contains. If the checkbox is present and unchecked, the control operates as normal. If the checkbox is marked, the control disables itself (except for the check box) and indicates via it's API that no date is selected. If you have a situation where you need a date or time to be entered, but it's possible that the event referred to by the date or time might not happen, or might not have yet occurred, the DTS_SHOWNONE style is ideal.

Normally, when providing a date format, the control, when pressed, will show a drop-down button that will reveal a single-page month calendar control. The user can either enter the date by typing or use the dropdown to select the date from a calendar. If you add the DTS_UPDOWN style to the control, the control will present an up/down button that allows you to spin through the values of each field in the control.

The control, otherwise, is very simple. Like the month calendar control, all of the date-related functions in the control have overrides to work with a CTime, a COleDateTime, and SYSTEMTIME. And just like the month calendar control, the date time picker has a range for the selections valid in the control. The range can be set with SetRange() and retrieved with GetRange().

The current selection is retrieved with GetTime() and SetTime(). These functions work on the control even if the control is set to work with dates. In either case, the unused part of the control's data is *not* set in the returned value. So, if you call GetTime() on a control with the DTS_TIMEFORMAT style set, SYSTEMTIME won't change the date values in the structure.

Since it's possible that the date time picker is showing a month calendar control, the CDateTimeCtrl class features several functions to manipulate the month calendar control. They only work, however, when the control is being shown – you'll have to override CDateTimeCtrl and subclass the window to get the notification that the control is about to drop down. Then, you can call the month-calendar manipulators.

GetMonthCalCtrl() is the most important manipulator, as it returns a pointer to the CMonthCalCtrl object in use at the time. You can call GetMonthCalColor() or SetMonthCalColor() to customize the month-calendar control, or GetMonthCalFont or SetMonthCalFont() to change the font in the month calendar control.

Finally, this control too has overrides for DDX_ and DDV_ that accept either COleDateTime or CTime values.

CIPAddressCtrl

The services of the Internet have moved from the inside of Universities and military installations to everywhere else in the world. As such, it's quite surprising to learn of the applications that need to know about the configuration of network cards or the addresses of remote machines or devices. Recently, the delivery of my new car was delayed because the car wasn't reliably receiving packets from the DHCP server!

If you need to write an application that takes an IP address from the user, you can do so using the CIPAddressCtrl. The control shows a field of four entry points separated by three dots; just like an IP address – such as 128.0.0.1 or 207.46.130.14. Aside from a couple of extra interfaces, the control is suspiciously similar to an edit control.

You can call GetAddress() on the control to retrieve the address entered into the control. GetAddress() has two forms – one that takes references to four BYTEs, and one that takes a reference to a DWORD. The four-byte version sets each byte to the value entered in the corresponding field. The DWORD version ends up taking the same information packed into the DWORD.

And given the DWORD, you can use one of four macros to touch the individual fields: FIRST_IPADDRESS(), SECOND_IPADDRESS(), THIRD_IPADDRESS(), and FOURTH_IPADDRESS(). The macros work both as l-values and r-values.

Alternatively, you can call SetAddress() to put an address into the control. It, too, has an override that takes a single DWORD and one that takes four BYTE parameters.

You can call SetFieldRange() to set the range of a given field. The function takes an integer indicating the field – zero for the leftmost field, three for the rightmost – and a BYTE each to indicate the low range and the high range for that field. Each of the fields has an independent range, so you can use this function to set ranges to match most of the subnet masks you'll ever need.

The CIPAddressCtrl::SetFieldFocus() member allows you to drop focus into a particular field of the control. IsBlank() allows you to test the control to see if it has no address entered, and ClearAddress() allows you to completely reset the control to have no address at all.

Hot Key Control

Many applications use hot keys as a shortcut for different functions. In Visual C++, you might tap *F5* to start the execution of your program, for example. If you want to allow your user to configure the hot key assigned to a particular function, you might approach the problem by developing a user interface that allows the user to select their hot key from a list. Writing such a user interface from scratch is quite an undertaking, as there are tens of dozens of hot key combinations, and it's difficult to enumerate them all correctly.

For such applications, the common control library provides a hot key control that allows you to get the key name and the virtual key ID directly from the user in a very user-friendly interface. The Hot Key item in the View menu of the Doodads example brings up a hot key dialog shown here:

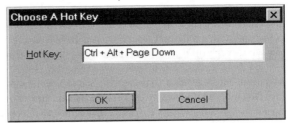

In the dialog, a hot key control accepts the user's hot key choice. The CHotKeyCtrl MFC class wraps the control, allowing you to get whatever keystroke the user makes. You can request the hot key's virtual key code and modifiers by calling GetHotKey() against the control, while you can initialize the hot key's control by calling the SetHotKey() member function.

In the example, I've wired these functions up in the CSetHotKey dialog box, which I built purely to hold a hot key control. During the data exchange, we check the m_bSaveAndValidate flag in the passed CDataExchange context, which is TRUE if MFC wants to copy data from the control to the member variables of the dialog class. Therefore, if it's TRUE, call GetHotKey(); otherwise call SetHotKey(). The code looks like this:

```
void CSetHotKey::DoDataExchange(CDataExchange* pDX)
{
    CDialog::DoDataExchange(pDX);
    //{{AFX_DATA_MAP(CSetHotKey)
        // NOTE: the ClassWizard will add DDX and DDV calls here
    //}}AFX_DATA_MAP

    CHotKeyCtrl* pCtrl;
    pCtrl = static_cast<CHotKeyCtrl*>(GetDlgItem(IDC_HOTKEY));
    if (pDX->m_bSaveAndValidate)
        pCtrl->GetHotKey(m_wVirtKeyCode, m_wModifiers);
    else
        pCtrl->SetHotKey(m_wVirtKeyCode, m_wModifiers);
}
```

I've put the code outside of the ClassWizard comments because the ClassWizard doesn't handle the hot key control. If we need to add regular controls to the dialog later, we can do so and any additional code won't interfere with the ClassWizard.

Virtual Key Codes

After the above call to GetHotKey(), and before the call to SetHotKey(), m_wVirtKeyCode holds the **virtual key code** for the hot key control. The virtual key code is a code that Windows uses to identify keystrokes uniquely. For most keys, this is the ASCII value associated with the key. Since many keys on IBM keyboards don't have ASCII values, the possible virtual key code values also include special variations.

The virtual key code information is useful for associating the hot key value with your main window. We could associate the hot key with the main window of the application with the WM_SETHOTKEY message; then, if the user presses the application's hot key at any time while the application is running, Windows will send your application a WM_SYSCOMMAND message with the SC_HOTKEY parameter. If you don't handle this message, Windows will make the application that owns the window (and, obviously, the window itself) active. If you do write a handler for the message, you can do whatever you'd like in response.

If you're interested in making the hot key activate some feature in your application, you could test for the hot key in the OnKeyUp() handler in your application's view, or you could use the ::RegisterHotKey() API to get Windows to send your application the appropriate WM_HOTKEY message when the user presses the designated hot key. While you still have a little footwork to do, the hot key control does the real grunt work for you by providing the most difficult part of such a configurable user interface.

Restricting Choices

Incidentally, you can call the SetRules() member of your CHotKeyCtrl to make sure the user is limited to appropriate choices. By default, hot key controls will accept any possible keystroke, but it's likely that you won't want a very common keystroke to cause any activity in your application other than what you'd expect.

The user shouldn't be able to bring up a dialog by just pressing the *A* key, for instance. During the `OnInitDialog()` handler of the dialog where your hot key lives, call `SetRules()` and pass it the appropriate `HKCOMB_` constant to avoid the appropriate type of keystroke which should be disallowed. Here are the `HKCOMB_` constants and their meaning:

Constant	Disallowed Combination
HKCOMB_A	*Alt* keystrokes
HKCOMB_C	*Ctrl* keystrokes
HKCOMB_CA	*Ctrl+Alt* keystrokes
HKCOMB_NONE	Unmodified keystrokes, keystrokes with no *Alt*, *Shift* or *Ctrl* key down
HKCOMB_S	*Shift* keystrokes
HKCOMB_SA	*Shift+Alt* keystrokes
HKCOMB_SC	*Shift+Ctrl* keystrokes
HKCOMB_SCA	*Shift+Ctrl+Alt* keystrokes

So, to make sure the user can't specify plain keystrokes, you might call:

```
pMyHotKeyControl->SetRules(HKCOMB_NONE, HOTKEYF_ALT);
```

You should be aware that this will still allow the user to specify relatively plain keystrokes, like *Shift+S*. To be sure that the user isn't allowed to specify shifted keys or plain keys, use:

```
pMyHotKeyControl->SetRules(HKCOMB_NONE | HKCOMB_S, HOTKEYF_ALT);
```

In both of these examples, the code for the key that is struck will be substituted with the same keystroke with *Alt*. If the user presses the *S* key, for example, then the control will register *Alt+S*. For different behavior, you can use a different `HOTKEYF_` flag (i.e. `HOTKEYF_CONTROL`, `HOTKEYF_SHIFT` and `HOTKEYF_EXT`, which represent the *Ctrl*, *Shift* and extended keys respectively).

Header Control

Many programs have the need to display lists of information. Frequently, each element in those lists is actually a row, consisting of several columns. Using a list box control that has tab stops for each of the columns is one solution, but it frequently leaves the user wanting to see more. Your tab stops might not allow the most convenient view of the information, which may be wider than you anticipated. You may also wish to allow the user to widen fields that they find more interesting, and narrow some fields which they don't.

Making the tab stops movable is one solution to this problem, but building a user interface to allow that kind of change is a very ambitious project. Enter the header control. It allows you to create a header bar for any window; you can label each block in the control to show what the column under the box might contain, and allow the control to do the grunt work of accepting the user's changes.

The Doodads example has a Statistics command in its View menu. Choosing this command brings up a CStatsDialog dialog, which is nothing more than a dialog class created with the dialog editor and added to the project with the ClassWizard. You can see this dialog box below:

The header control is *only* the block at the top of the dialog, showing the names of the different statistics. When the dialog is displayed, the user can use the mouse to manipulate the borders between the different columns of information to have them drawn at different widths. You'll need your own code to draw the text. Setting up the header control buys you tracking and measurement information for the table of statistics, while pleasantly providing labels for the data in the table.

In the example, I drew a group box to mark off an area where I wanted the list to appear. The WM_INITDIALOG handler for the CStatsDialog dialog measures this control and then destroys it. This technique is quite common and very useful; by drawing a dummy control in the dialog, you can visually lay out the dialog box. If you delete the control after measuring it, the user never sees it, but the code can learn the exact coordinates where another visual element of the application could be drawn. In the OnInitDialog() handler, the work looks like this:

```
BOOL CStatsDialog::OnInitDialog()
{
    CDialog::OnInitDialog();

    // Measure and destroy the placemarker window

    CWnd* pWindow = GetDlgItem(IDC_HEADER);
    pWindow->GetWindowRect(m_rect);
    pWindow->DestroyWindow();

    // and so on
}
```

The `m_rect` variable is a member of the `CStatsDialog` dialog class. In the rest of the
`OnInitDialog()` function, you can create the header control by measuring the font in the dialog to
determine the height and width required for the control. Since the dialog editor in the Visual C++
IDE doesn't support header controls, you need to create a `CHeaderCtrl` object yourself. The code
to do that looks like this:

```
CHeaderCtrl* m_pHeader;

m_pHeader = new CHeaderCtrl;

if (!m_pHeader->Create(HDS_BUTTONS | HDS_HORZ | WS_VISIBLE |
        CCS_TOP | WS_CHILD | WS_TABSTOP | WS_BORDER, rect, this, IDC_HEADER))
{
    TRACE0("Creation failed!\n");
    EndDialog(IDCANCEL);
}
```

Remember that you need to create the MFC `CHeaderCtrl` object before creating the control's
window by calling the `Create()` member of the class. The `Create()` function takes style bits; the
`WS_` bits are familiar to us from other windows, while the `CCS_TOP` bit is new for the common
controls. Here, it's used to indicate that the control should be aligned with the top of the rectangle
that we're creating. We give the control the `HDS_HORZ` style, since we want the control to put its
column markers at the top of the group box that used to be in the dialog.

A header control with the `HDS_BUTTONS` style will look like a row of buttons. That is, the controls
will feature beveled, three-dimensional edges, and will depress when the user clicks them with the
mouse. Without the style, the column headers will look flat and won't depress when the user activates
them.

Once we've created the control, we use an `HDITEM` structure to add the different header blocks to it
and to measure each of the items in the box into an appropriate space. You can see that I added three
to the length of the string, so that there is some border space around the word in the header. The
`HDITEM` structure definition looks like this:

```
typedef struct _HDITEM {
    UINT     mask;
    int      cxy;
    LPTSTR   pszText;
    HBITMAP  hbm;
    int      cchTextMax;
    int      fmt;
    LPARAM   lParam;
#if (_WIN32_IE >= 0x0300)
    int      iImage;
    int      iOrder;
#endif
} HDITEM, FAR * LPHDITEM;
```

The width ends up in the HDITEM's cxy field, and we point to the string that contains the title for the pszText field, while the cchTextMax field contains the length of that string. The fmt member of the structure can be a variety of bits; I used HDF_LEFT to justify the text in the header to the left, but I could have chosen HDF_CENTER or HDF_RIGHT to get the other text effects. I also used a HDF_STRING flag to indicate that I wanted to show a string; if I wanted to show a picture, I'd have used HDF_BITMAP.

The loop that does all of this work is here, for your reference:

```
HD_ITEM hdi;
TCAR szHeader[] = _T("Team\tPlayer\tPosition\tGoals\tPIM");
LPTSTR pstrToken = _tcstok(szHeader, _T("\t"));
int nIndex = 0;

while (pstrToken != NULL)
{
    hdi.mask = HDI_TEXT | HDI_FORMAT | HDI_WIDTH;
    hdi.pszText = pstrToken;
    hdi.cxy = (lstrlen(pstrToken)+3)*tm.tmAveCharWidth;
    hdi.cchTextMax = lstrlen(hdi.pszText);
    hdi.fmt = HDF_LEFT | HDF_STRING;

    m_pHeader->InsertItem(nIndex, &hdi);
    nIndex++;
    pstrToken = _tcstok(NULL, _T("\t"));
}
```

The HDITEM's mask field, like that for other controls (such as the tree control), tells the control which fields in the structure are valid, while the InsertItem() member does the work of inserting the item into the control.

Now that the control has been created, the user can interact with it. If they select one of the borders and begin dragging, the application will receive a WM_NOTIFY message with the HDN_BEGINTRACK notification, for example. Since the Statistics dialog in the sample wants to draw its own content, it needs to repaint when the user has finished adjusting the column size. The control will send a HDN_ENDTRACK notification when the user is finished dragging, so the sample contains a handler for that notification. Named OnEndTrack(), the handler for this message simply calls Invalidate() to force the dialog window to repaint. This handler was added manually, since the ClassWizard doesn't support the CHeaderCtrl class.

The code in OnPaint() measures the fields in the header control again before it redraws the content of the window. If you were using the header control over a list box, you might use this notification handler to build a new list of tab stops for the control, before setting them into the control with a call to the list box's SetTabStops() member function.

Painting

The painting code in the dialog isn't very complicated but it does look rather elaborate, as it performs a great deal of math to measure the items we're drawing correctly. We use the m_rect member of the dialog here to make sure that we paint within the bounds laid out in the dialog template for the group box control. The painting code builds two arrays dynamically: pWidth and pLeft. These two arrays manage the width and leftmost point of each column of the dialog, as dictated by the borders in the header control. We measure these borders each time the dialog paints, using this loop:

```
for (nColumn = 0; nColumn < nCount; nColumn++)
{
    HDITEM hd;
    hd.mask = HDI_WIDTH;
    m_pHeader->GetItem(nColumn, &hd);

    pWidth[nColumn] = hd.cxy;
    if (nColumn == 0)
        pLeft[0] = m_rect.left;
    else
        pLeft[nColumn] = pLeft[nColumn-1] + pWidth[nColumn-1];
}
```

The call to GetItem() allows us to retrieve any information we want from the item in the header. All we want here is the width, so we set only the HDI_WIDTH flag in the HDITEM structure, before calculating the correct value for the pLeft member, which we'll use later when drawing the content of the dialog.

The loop that does the painting isn't very exciting; it just shows static data. You might use very similar code to display information you've retrieved from a database, although of course you'd need to get subsequent records during the loop instead of just fabricating the string to be shown.

Freeing Memory

Since we create the header control in this application using the new operator, we have a real object floating around on the heap. We need to take care of this object, so I've added code to the dialog's destructor in order to delete the C++ object created during OnInitDialog(). If I hadn't performed this step, the application would leak the memory used for the CHeaderCtrl.

You could, of course, make your life a little easier by using a member variable that's automatically destroyed. I'm just showing off. In fact, you may feel that the whole example is just a little contrived, since with the report view of the list control available to us, you'll never really need to do this sort of construction with a header control. However, if you want to know a little more about the controls you're using, then maybe this discussion has helped.

Header Controls and List View Controls

If you've created a list-view control and added LVS_REPORT to engage report mode, you're already using a header control. The list view control will create a header control as a child window inside its own client area. You can call CListCtrl::GetHeader() to gain a pointer to the header control in use by the windows control.

Given CHeaderCtrl object, you're free to call any of the members you'd like. You can find the number of columns in the control, for example, by calling GetItemCount(). You might modify the images associated with the items by calling SetImageList() on the header, and then calling SetItem() to adjust the features of each column.

Tooltip, Toolbar and Status Bar Controls

These controls replace functionality provided by the older MFC user interface objects, CStatusBar and CToolBar. Currently, MFC still supports these classes – take a look at the Oldbars sample on the Visual C++ CD for more on this topic. The classes now use the common controls internally to realize backward-compatible functionality for older applications. However, MFC also wraps the common controls more directly. The tool tips control is covered by CToolTipCtrl, while toolbar controls are covered with CToolBarCtrl; CStatusBarCtrl wraps the status bar common control.

In fact, now you can get the best of both worlds; if you're using a CStatusBar, you can get a reference to the underlying CStatusBarCtrl using CStatusBar::GetStatusBarCtrl(). Similarly, if you're using a CToolBar, you can make a call to CToolBar::GetToolBarCtrl().

The CStatusBar and CToolBar classes are designed to be used in an MFC frame window – any window derived from CFrameWnd. The classes are written to work closely with the frame window to perform layout and alignment operations. If you're trying to add a tool bar or a status bar to another type of window, like a dialog box, you'll want to use CStatusBarCtrl or CToolBarCtrl. Unfortunately, you'll need to size and layout the controls yourself in such applications.

Tab Controls

The Windows common tab control is very similar to the property page dialogs that you see in MFC. Even though the tab control is used as a control, it doesn't imply the same dialog box semantics as the CPropertyPage and CPropertySheet classes. That is, the tab control is just a tab control; it only draws the tabs that you're used to seeing at the top of a property page, whereas the property page adds all of the logic to move around the dialog boxes underneath the control. If you use a tab control yourself, you'll only get the tabs – you'll need to react to the notification messages sent to the control in order to get any real work done.

In the Doodads sample, for instance, the **Addresses** dialog box uses four different list view controls with a tab control. The tab control in the sample has four tabs – each with the name of a different sport. When the user selects a different tab, I hide the visible list view control and show the one related to the tab they've selected. The **Addresses** dialog box looks like this:

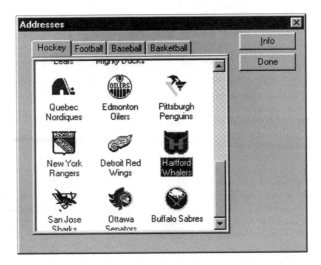

Tab controls are very simple. They're wrapped by the `CTabCtrl` class, and can be created via the `Create()` member of this class, or by drawing the control on the dialog box in the resource editor. If you examine the `IDD_ADDRESSES` resource in the sample, you'll see that I drew one list view control and carefully positioned the tab control immediately above it. In the `OnInitDialog()` handler for the dialog, I get the style and position of the existing list control and create three others in exactly the same spot. The actual code to perform this control replication is in the `CopyList()` function.

The `OnInitDialog()` handler gains a pointer to the tab control in the dialog and calls a function (`AddTab()`) which eventually calls the object's `InsertItem()` member to insert tabs for the control. This last function takes two parameters. The first is the index where you'd like to insert the new item, while the second parameter is a pointer to a `TCITEM` structure, which looks like this:

```
typedef struct tagTCITEM {
    UINT mask;
#if (_WIN32_IE >= 0x0300)
    DWORD dwState;
    DWORD dwStateMask;
#else
    UINT lpReserved1;
    UINT lpReserved2;
#endif
    LPTSTR pszText;
    int cchTextMax;
    int iImage;
    LPARAM lParam;
} TCITEM, FAR *LPTCITEM;
```

The first thing you'll probably notice about this declaration is that there's a big conditional directive. Here, the conditional just assures that the structure stays the same size even if the header is being compiled to assume an older version of `Comctl32.dll` at runtime.

The `mask` member is like the masks for the other common controls – you'll need to use it to indicate which fields in the structure are valid. The structure has a `pszText` member that you'll use to set or get the text in a particular tab. If you're receiving text from the control, you'll need to make sure `cchTextMax` lets the control know how many characters to expect to find at `pszText`. You can indicate that the `pszText` and `cchTextMax` values are valid if you use the `TCIF_TEXT` flag in the `mask` field.

The `lParam` is a user-defined member. Like all the other `lParam` fields we've seen, you can use it to store any `DWORD`-sized value you'd like. To get or set the `lParam` field, you'll need to make sure the `TCIF_PARAM` flag in `mask` is set.

The `iImage` member specifies an index into the image list associated with the control. The control will use the image at that index on the tab. You'll need to make sure `TCIF_IMAGE` is set in `mask` if you want to specify or request an image index from the control. You'll also need to make sure that the control knows about the image list by calling `CTabCtrl::SetImageList()`.

Once an item is inserted, you can call `GetItem()` to retrieve the `TCITEM` structure describing the item. If you'd like, you can tweak the structure and set it again using `SetItem()`. Both of these functions take an integer, indicating the index of the item you'd like to handle, and a pointer to the `TCITEM` structure with which you're working. If you get bored with a particular item in the control, you can call `DeleteItem()` to remove it. If all the items disgust you, you can quickly rid yourself of them by calling `DeleteAllItems()`.

`GetItem()`, `DeleteItem()`, and `SetItem()` each accept an integer that identifies the index of the item you're interested in manipulating. The index is zero-based, so the first tab in the control is numbered zero.

Handling Selections

You can find out which item is selected in a tab control by calling `GetCurSel()`. The function simply returns the index of the active tab as an integer. You can set the active tab by calling `SetCurSel()`.

When the user clicks a tab to change it, the control fires off a `TCN_SELCHANGING` notification. If you trap this notification, you can decide if you want to allow the change or not. If you *don't* want to allow the change, you can return TRUE (that is, set *pResult to a non-zero value) to prevent the selection from changing, while returning FALSE allows the selection change to occur. If you allow the selection to change, it's a good idea to use the `TCN_SELCHANGING` notification to save any changes the user has made to the controls you're associating with the page.

If the selection change is approved – that is, if you don't handle `TCN_SELCHANGING`, or if you return FALSE (that is, set *pResult to zero) from your `TCN_SELCHANGING` handler – the control will send a `TCN_SELCHANGE` notification. It is here that you'll probably play some switcheroo to reflect the change to the selected tab in your user interface. In the sample application, it is where I hide the inactive list control and show the newly activated one.

You'll note that the list view and the tree view controls throw similar notifications, but with subtly different names. It's the direct result of a plot to keep people buying computer books.

Tab controls send only TCN_SELCHANGE, TCN_SELCHANGING, TCN_KEYDOWN and TCN_GETOBJECT notifications, the last one supporting drag and drop. There is no tab control-specific message structure, so you're on your own to find information about the cause of the notification. If you call GetCurSel() while handling TCN_SELCHANGE, you'll find the freshly selected tab. If you call GetCurSel() from the handler for TCN_SELCHANGING, you'll find that the tab which still has focus hasn't yet changed to the tab that the user activated.

Setting Drawing Parameters

The bulk of the remaining member functions in the CTabCtrl class deal with the positioning, layout and sizing of images on the tab. You can call SetItemSize() to artificially inflate the size of tabs, or call SetPadding() to change the size allotted within the item to the image.

You'll note that tab controls put their tabs in one row, left-to-right by default. If you want to have multiple rows of tabs, you should make sure your tab control has the TCS_MULTILINE style.

With the updated comct132.dll that ships with Internet Explorer 4.0 (and comes stock in Windows 98 and Windows NT 4.0), it is finally possible to make tab controls draw in any orientation. That is, you can now put a Windows common tab control on the right, left, or bottom edge of a window and have the control draw with its tabs and text facing the correct way.

Customizing Control Appearance

Common controls are nice, for all the reasons we've already discussed. But some applications demand something extra. For example, you might need to use a different font or color to show something about the state of an item (or items, of course) in a control. The controls don't inherently handle these decorations, so it's up to you to customize the controls' drawing code and do the extra painting yourself.

The technique of drawing a control yourself is called owner-draw. You can create owner-draw header controls, list view controls, tab controls, or status bar controls. Unfortunately, the remaining common controls don't support owner-draw. However, some of the controls support custom draw, which is a simplified technique we'll examine in the next section. This table shows which controls support which customized drawing mechanism:

Control	Owner Draw	Custom Draw
Header	X	X
List View	X	X
Status Bar	X	

Table Continued on Following Page

Control	Owner Draw	Custom Draw
Rebar		X
Tab	X	
Toolbar		X
Tooltip		X
Trackbar		X
Tree View		X

To make an owner-draw control, you'll want to first add the appropriate style to your control. For a list view control, that's `LVS_OWNERDRAWFIXED`, while `HDF_OWNERDRAW` allows you to set the style for a header control column. `SBT_OWNERDRAW` is for a scrollbar, and `TCS_OWNERDRAWFIXED` is for a tab control. You can add the style programmatically when the control is created (by adding it to the styles you pass the `Create()` member) or by calling `ModifyStyle()` on the control after it has been created. Or, you can mark the appropriate box on the **More Styles** tab of the property page for the control in the dialog editor. For a list view control, that's the **Owner draw fixed** box.

Once the control is marked owner draw, it will send a `WM_DRAWITEM` message whenever it wants to draw an item. Of course, since the control is owner-draw, it's up to you to paint the requested item in response to this message. The message carries a pointer to a `DRAWITEMSTRUCT` structure, which describes the item to be painted.

The two most important members of `DRAWITEMSTRUCT` are the `hDC`, which is a handle to a device context where you'll draw the item; and the `rcItem`, which is a rectangle within that DC where you'll draw your item. Then, the `itemID` member references the item you're being asked to draw — the value of that member is just an item ID.

In response to the draw request, the first thing you'll want to do is request information about the item — you can turn around and call `GetItem()` to request the item you want. Your call to `GetItem()` can provide you with the text of the item, as well as any other attributes of the item which interest you.

If the control supports selection — like a list view control does, you'll probably want to get the state flags for the item — again, since you're owner-draw, it's also up to you to reflect the selection or preview state of the item.

You can query the colors to be used for painting by calling `GetSystemColor()`. You can discover the system-wide highlighted text color, for example, by passing the constant `COLOR_HIGHLIGHTTEXT` for the foreground, and `COLOR_HIGHLIGHT` for the background. By using the resulting values in calls to `SetTextColor()` and `SetBkColor()` on your device context, you'll be able to paint with the colors that the user expects.

If you're painting a list view control, where an item might have subitems, you'll quickly notice that you don't receive `WM_DRAWITEM` notifications for each subitem in the control. If your control is in `LVS_REPORT` mode, you'll need to iterate all the subitems and draw them yourself — just keep calling `CListCtrl::GetItemText()` for each item. Then, call `GetColumn()` to find the width (and cumulative offset) of the column.

You can call `ImageList_DrawEx()` to draw any image associated with a given item. This function should have been wrapped by `CImageList`, but wasn't!

My description of owner-draw controls has been without code. That's because I feel you can't beat the product's own ROWLIST sample for an example of `DrawItem()` implementation. For a list view control, this sample shows how to paint icons, handle the text and focus rectangles, and does all those things correctly. Handling the message for the other controls is only slightly different – mainly in the measurement of subordinate items. If you want to draw text using your own font or by changing colors, just modify the sample by adding a `SelectObject()` call or by changing the color settings in the handler after you copy the code to your application.

The big disadvantage to owner-draw controls is their complexity. If you need to draw your own features within the control, owner-draw really is the only way to go. But if you only want to change a color or a font, you'll find that owner-draw is really too awkward. You have to implement code to paint the complete item, even if you're just interested in changing just one feature of the control! The code to do the rest of the painting already exists in the Windows-supplied implementation of the control, so if you can, why not use what Windows already provides?

Well, the newest version of `Comct132.dll` provides a solution: custom draw. Custom draw is supported by many different controls, including the list view control. For switching around simple visual aspects of the control, it's really the preferred technique.

Custom-Draw Controls

Custom draw works a little bit differently than owner-draw does. Custom draw allows you to modify only parts of the procedure by which a control normally paints itself. This way, you can make use of code already built into the control to do as much painting, or as little, as you need. It's up to you to implement the remaining parts of the painting to suit your requirements. You'll be able to do this by responding to notifications from the control, at which time you can alter the device context the control will use to paint the relevant parts.

While the approach of painting only what you need sounds like it would find a great home in a C++-oriented implementation that relies on subclassing, it's actually implemented using notification messages. When the control is created, it will send a NM_CUSTOMDRAW notification. How you respond to this notification determines how you'll end up painting items in the control.

When the control wants to paint something, it will send a NM_CUSTOMDRAW notification that indicates the drawing stage that the control is entering. When this happens, the notification points at an NMCUSTOMDRAW structure and this describes the stage that's about to start in its `dwDrawStage` member. These are the stages:

dwDrawStage	Meaning
CDDS_PREPAINT	Before the paint cycle begins.
CDDS_POSTPAINT	After the paint cycle is complete.
CDDS_PREERASE	Before the erase cycle begins.
CDDS_POSTERASE	After the erase cycle is complete.

The CDDS_PREPAINT notification means that the control is about to begin a full painting cycle – the control is about to paint all of its visible items, while CDDS_POSTPAINT means the control has finished painting its visible items. You can respond to CDDS_PREPAINT with one of five codes:

> ➤ CDRF_DODEFAULT. This response means that the control should just paint itself the way it normally does. Return this code if you don't want to hear about any other painting notifications from the control.

> ➤ CDRF_NOTIFYITEMDRAW. This response indicates that you're interested in getting NM_CUSTOMDRAW notifications for each item within the control. You'll want to return this to get your custom draw control working; handling the individual item notifications is exactly how you'll affect their painting process.

> ➤ CDRF_NOTIFYPOSTPAINT. If you return CDRF_NOTIFYPOSTPAINT, the control will send an NM_CUSTOMDRAW notification when the painting cycle for the entire control is complete.

> ➤ CDRF_SKIPDEFAULT. The control will not perform any painting at all. This return value means that you'll do *all* of the painting yourself, or that you don't want the control to do any painting for itself.

> ➤ CDRF_NOTIFYSUBITEMDRAW. This can be returned if you're handling custom draw for a list view control. It will cause notifications to be sent for each subitem of the controlas opposed to the individual items.

Obviously, the most interesting response here is CDRF_NOTIFYITEMDRAW. That tells the control you're going to modify the way it draws. Once you return this response, the control will send you notification messages for each item – and you can respond by changing colors and fonts for each of those items. The subsequent notifications you receive then describe the state of each item's painting process, rather than the state of the entire control's painting process. The state notifications are similar, though:

Code	Meaning
CDDS_ITEMPOSTERASE	After an item has been erased.
CDDS_ITEMPOSTPAINT	After an item has been drawn.
CDDS_ITEMPREERASE	Before an item is erased.
CDDS_ITEMPREPAINT	Before an item is drawn.
CDDS_SUBITEM	Flag combined with CDDS_ITEMPREPAINT or CDDS_ITEMPOSTPAINT if a subitem is being drawn. This will only be set if CDRF_NOTIFYSUBITEMDRAW is returned from CDDS_PREPAINT.

When any of these notifications are sent, you'll receive a pointer to a control-specific notification structure. The structure describes the data that you need to paint items for each control, and they vary greatly from control to control. The NMLVCUSTOMDRAW structure is used for list view controls, and has this structure definition:

```
typedef struct tagNMLVCUSTOMDRAW {
    NMCUSTOMDRAW nmcd;
    COLORREF clrText;
    COLORREF clrTextBk;
    int iSubItem;
} NMLVCUSTOMDRAW, *LPNMLVCUSTOMDRAW;
```

The `clrText` and `clrTextBk` members are `COLORREF` items you can change to enforce a different color. This deviates a little from the other controls, which don't have such members and instead have you call `SetBkColor()` and `SetTextColor()` on the provided DC.

The `nmcd` member is a nested structure, which contains the custom draw notification. We've talked about the `dwDrawStage` member of this fellow, but we haven't mentioned the other members. Here's what the structure looks like:

```
typedef struct tagNMCUSTOMDRAWINFO {
    NMHDR   hdr;
    DWORD   dwDrawStage;
    HDC     hdc;
    RECT    rc;
    DWORD   dwItemSpec;
    UINT    uItemState;
    LPARAM  lItemlParam;
} NMCUSTOMDRAW, FAR * LPNMCUSTOMDRAW;
```

`dwItemSpec` tells you which item you're drawing. This might be an index, but it could be a handle, too. In the case of a tree view control, for example, the value is actually a `HTREEITEM`. You might need to cast it in order to use it the way you would expect.

The rectangle member, named `rc`, gives you the bounding rectangle for the item. Unfortunately, this member exposes the greatest limitation of custom draw; you can't change the bounding rectangle. If you want to draw a different font, the font needs to fit within the bounding rectangle. So, if you select a different font that's taller, you might end up with clipping!

`hdc` is the device context used for the painting. If you're going to select a new font or otherwise alter the drawing capabilities of the control, you'll do so by selecting an object into this member. As usual, you'll need to keep the font (or any other objects) active throughout the life of the control as the control's implementation may reuse them at any time.

The `hdr` member, of course, is a plain old `NMHDR` member. It contains the basic notification we know is sent with every single notification message.

Let's look at a minimal custom draw notification handler; here, we'll handle notifications for a list view control:

```
void CCustListDlg::OnCustomDrawList1(NMHDR* pNMHDR, LRESULT* pResult)
{
    LPNMLVCUSTOMDRAW  lplvcd = reinterpret_cast<LPNMLVCUSTOMDRAW>(NMHDR);

    if (lplvcd->nmcd.dwDrawStage == CDDS_PREPAINT)
        *pResult = CDRF_NOTIFYITEMDRAW;
    else
```

Continued on Following Page

```
    if (lplvcd->nmcd.dwDrawStage == CDDS_ITEMPREPAINT)
    {
        if (lplvcd->nmcd.dwItemSpec & 1)
        {
            lplvcd->clrText = RGB(255, 255, 0);
            lplvcd->clrTextBk = RGB(0, 0, 255);
            *pResult = CDRF_NEWFONT;
        }
        else
            *pResult = CDRF_DODEFAULT;
    }
    else
        *pResult = 0;
}
```

In this fragment, we first check to see if we're receiving a notification for the global repaint stage. If so, we'll respond with CDRF_NOTIFYITEMDRAW to indicate that we want to be notified each time something happens to a particular item. Otherwise, we'll check to see if we actually are receiving an item-specific notification.

For item-specific notifications, we'll check the actual item number being painted. If it's odd, we'll change the foreground and background colors of the item and return CDRF_NEWFONT to show that we've made a change the control needs to pay attention to. The control will continue by using the features of the DC you modified, as well as the changes you've made to the notification structure itself, to paint the item. Otherwise, we'll return CDRF_DODEFAULT to tell the control that it should paint the way it normally paints. Alternatively, you can return CDRF_SKIPDEFAULT if you've completely painted the items yourself and you don't want the control to perform *any* action.

In the above example, I change only the color using the members of the list-view-specific notification structure. If I wanted to change the font, or if this were for any other type of control, I'd use the device context at lplvcd->hdc to effect the change. And certainly, for any other control, the cast at the first line of the function would be to that control's notification structure type.

If we find that none of the notifications are interesting, we'll return zero in order to tell the control that we didn't process this notification.

Unfortunately, you can't use ClassWizard to add such a handler; NM_CUSTOMDRAW just isn't in the list of notifications that you can add! Instead, you'll need to manually add the function (and its prototype) to your code.

Control-based Views

Back in Chapter 4, I described the CEditView class and made mention of control-based view classes. This class creates a view based on the stock Windows edit control. The CEditView class is based on the CCtrlView class, which I also described in that chapter.

CRichEditView, CTreeView, and CListView all make core use of the common control classes that I've explained here. The Wordfreq sample from Chapter 10 is an example of an application that is based on such a view, as it uses a CListView object to produce its user interface.

Remember that you'll probably need to override the `PreCreateWindow()` function for your `CCtrlView`-derived view class in order to set the style bits on the control you're about to create; there's also a sample of this in Chapter 4.

The Rich Text Edit Control

You might have noticed that up to this point I've neglected one of the most interesting common controls: the **rich text edit control**. I did this because the other common controls are interesting by themselves and comparatively simple. By contrast, the rich text edit control is a very complicated tool used to address a huge collection of problems and provide a great many features. It is a massive beast whose size and strength is only eclipsed by the Pittsburgh Penguins defensemen. That is to say, without fully understanding how controls can be embedded in views, it would be hard to understand how the rich text edit control can be best made to work with your applications. With a description of the `CCtrlView` class under our belt (back in Chapter 4, you'll remember), we should feel confident in going on to discuss the `CRichEditCtrl` class and all of its friends.

You could, if you really wanted to, work directly with a `CRichEditCtrl`. You can simply draw the control in your dialog box and create the dialog to realize the control. (Versions of Visual C++ previous to 6.0 didn't allow you to draw the rich edit control directly.) In this situation, you'll usually treat the control as a fancy edit control and ignore its impressive OLE containment features and drag-and-drop support. Before you create such a dialog box, you'll need to call `AfxInitRichEdit()` to have MFC initialize its support for the control.

The `CRichEditCtrl`class allows you to directly manipulate the control and its contents. Should you want to format characters, set tab stops, and so on, you can do so. Conversely, and true to its `CCtrlView` heritage, a `CRichEditView` expands the implementation of the `CRichEditCtrl` class by providing the same features as the control class, within a class that also supports interaction with a frame window. The `CRichEditView` class offers the normal `CView`-derived interfaces, and if you want to use the `CRichEditCtrl` interfaces, you can gain a reference to the control by calling `CRichEditView::GetRichEditCtrl()`. Once you've gained access to the control, you can do all sorts of cool things, which we'll examine here.

There's no need to call `AfxInitRichEdit()` when using a `CRichEditView` because it will automatically be done for you when the window is created. MFC knows that a `CRichEditView` will wrap a `CRichEditCtrl`, but it can't always make that assumption about a dialog box.

You can use the rich edit control to control the font, paragraph layout and color of text that you want to show the user. The control can also accommodate embedded OLE objects. The rich text edit control has a few shortcomings, though; it doesn't understand top and bottom margins, and therefore can't handle footnotes or page numbering.

Because of the robust support for OLE in the control, you'll need to construct your rich edit view application around a document derived from MFC's `CRichEditDoc` class. The document object you've associated with your `CRichEditDoc` will work with `CRichEditCntrItem` objects. These objects are derived from the `COleClientItem` class, which we'll discuss in Chapter 13. Suffice to say, for now, that the object acts as an agent to communicate with any object that is embedded in the edit control.

CRichEditDocs are unique because you can't let one CRichEditDoc be served by more than one view. The main reason for this is that the CRichEditDoc doesn't maintain any of the text – the control does. As such, multiple rich edit control views are no different to multiple rich edit control documents. If you ask AppWizard to use CRichEditView as your view class without having compound document support in your application, you'll receive an error message like this one:

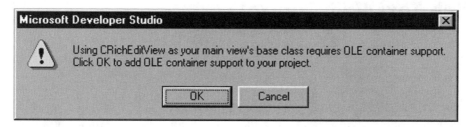

In the remainder of this section, I'll examine both functions directly available in the CRichEditCtrl class, and the functions that the CRichEditView class makes available to you. There are dozens of CRichEditCtrl functions, and they give you great control over the control (but little control over repetition). The functions in CRichEditView are a little less precise than those in CRichEditCtrl, but they're also a shade easier to use. If you ever find yourself needing extra command over the control, remember that you can always call CRichEditView::GetRichEditCtrl() to get a reference to the CRichEditCtrl object.

Possibly the best example you'll find of advanced CRichEditView use ships in the Visual C++ box; you get the source code to the WordPad program which ships with Windows itself! Just look up Wordpad in Visual C++ Help to install the sample. The application is very complicated since it handles all sorts of file conversions and robust compound document support, so it would be beneficial for us to examine some of the simpler CRichEditView features.

Before we get started, you might want to look through the Microsoft Knowledge Base to find the article on the **Rich Text Format**. (Searching for "RTF and specification" should do it.) The article explains the exact format and keywords that RTF uses to express the added features in text files. You *don't* need to memorize the document or even deeply understand it, but if you review the overviews, you should be in great shape. The point is that you'll need to understand the basic way that RTF works; since the rich text control deals with rich text, its interfaces have a lot to do with the inherent architecture of the format.

As we proceed, we'll see that the rich text control approaches text formatting at both the character and paragraph levels. The idea is that some text attributes, like the font name or underlining, relate only to characters. Others, such as line spacing or indentation, apply only to entire paragraphs. Yet another class of attributes pertains only to the document as a whole – paper and margin sizes, for example. By reviewing the RTF specification, you can make more sense of the approach that the rich text edit control takes to holding, selecting, and formatting text.

Character formatting can be applied to a given selection, or be made the default format for new text entered by the user. Paragraph formatting can be applied to any paragraph within your control. Let's take a look at the specifics of both formatting types here, as we start to investigate the broader features of the control. As you read along, you might want to work with the Rtf sample (again available form the Wrox web site), as some of the code fragments in this section of the book are showcased in that sample.

Character Formatting

No matter what character formatting function you call, you'll end up working with a CHARFORMAT structure. This structure has lots of members that describe how characters are formatted, or allow you to explain to the control how you would like some characters to be formatted. If you were a piece of information describing a character in a rich text control, here's where you'd hide:

```
typedef struct _charformat {
    UINT      cbSize;
    _WPAD     _wPad1;
    DWORD     dwMask;
    DWORD     dwEffects;
    LONG      yHeight;
    LONG      yOffset;
    COLORREF  crTextColor;
    BYTE      bCharSet;
    BYTE      bPitchAndFamily;
    CHAR      szFaceName[LF_FACESIZE];
    _WPAD     _wPad2;
} CHARFORMAT;
```

The most important member of this structure is cbSize, which identifies the size of the structure as it's passed to the Windows code that actually implements the control. By checking the exact size in cbSize, Windows can react appropriately when older programs send along structures that are different than the control implementation is actually expecting. Also, the implementation of the control can assume the pointer to the CHARFORMAT it received is completely invalid when a completely invalid cbSize is detected.

You *must* (that is to say, it is imperative to) initialize cbSize before Windows sees the structure. Thankfully, all of the MFC functions that handle a CHARFORMAT will initialize it for you before they send it to the control. But if you ever find yourself in the situation where you need to send a message to the control directly, you'll need to be positive that you initialize the structure.

The members of type _WPAD are in the structure, just to even out the size of the structure, to make word boundaries compatible with all platforms where Windows runs. They're not important to users of the structure.

The second most important member of the structure is dwMask. The mask is used to communicate which fields in the structure are important to you. If you're only making a bunch of characters bold, for example, you will only care about the dwEffects member. You can indicate that focused concern by setting the appropriate flag in dwMask. Here's a table that shows you which fields are reflected by which flags in dwMask:

dwMask Flag	Effect
CFM_BOLD	The boldness setting of the dwEffects field is valid
CFM_COLOR	The crTextColor member and the CFE_AUTOCOLOR value of the dwEffects member are valid
CFM_FACE	The szFaceName member is valid

Table Continued on Following Page

dwMask Flag	Effect
CFM_ITALIC	The italic setting of the dwEffects member is valid
CFM_OFFSET	The yOffset member is valid
CFM_PROTECTED	The protected setting of the dwEffects member is valid
CFM_SIZE	The yHeight member is valid
CFM_STRIKEOUT	The strikeout setting of the dwEffects member is valid
CFM_UNDERLINE	The underline setting of the dwEffects member is valid

The CFM_OFFSET flag indicates that the yOffset field is used to indicate that characters will be offset from the baseline of the line where they appear. For normal characters, this value is zero. For characters that are superscripts (like the letter n in the expression $2^n + 1$), the number is positive. For characters that are subscripts (like the letter D in the definition $C_D = 0.91$), the value is negative.

The CFM_SIZE flag tells Windows that the yHeight field is used to indicate the height of the characters. The values of yHeight and yOffset are both in **twips**. Twips are $1/20^{th}$ of a point, and since a **point** is $1/72^{nd}$ of an inch, a twip is therefore $1/1440^{th}$ of an inch.

If you specify CFM_FACE, you can use the szFaceName buffer to indicate the face name of the font you'd like to use. You can copy a string like "Arial" or "Lucida Blackletter" into the member if you'd like to use one of those fonts. You can use bCharSet and bPitchAndFamily to more stringently specify the font you'd like to use. These fields are only obeyed if the CFM_FACE flag is set.

By combining the CFM_STRIKEOUT, CFM_UNDERLINE, CFM_ITALIC, and CFM_BOLD flags for dwMask, you can specify which flags in dwEffects have meaning. You can use the CFE_STRIKEOUT, CFE_UNDERLINE, CFE_ITALIC, and CFE_BOLD flags in dwEffects in any combination. The dwEffects field can also be set to zero to indicate characters that have none of these features.

The CFM_COLOR mask bit directs the control to heed the crTextColor and CFE_AUTOCOLOR bit in the dwEffect field. If the CFE_AUTOCOLOR bit is present, the control will set the text color to 'auto' and always use the default window text color defined in Control Panel. If the CFE_AUTOCOLOR bit is cleared, the crTextColor field should specify the foreground color for text in the control.

The color is specified as a COLORREF, which you can get from the RGB() macro or from an API like ::GetSysColor(). The control displays text on a background color which can be set by calling CRichEditCtrl::SetBackgroundColor(). Note that the background color is an attribute of the control, and not of the text in the control. The foreground text attribute can be applied to individual characters in the control.

Character Management Functions

Initially, by default, a rich text edit control will use the variable-width system font. This is a miserable font, since it supports no styles like bold or underline. These shortcomings make it a boring font to use within the rich text edit control. You can use the CRichEditCtrl::SetDefaultCharFormat() call to set the default character formatting for any new characters entered into the control. If you make such a call during the OnInitialUpdate() of your view, you can get a cool font into the control before the user starts doing any work. Something like this, for example, would do quite nicely:

```
void CRTFView::OnInitialUpdate()
{
    CRichEditCtrl& theCtrl = GetRichEditCtrl();
    CRichEditView::OnInitialUpdate();

    CHARFORMAT cfm;
    cfm.cbSize = sizeof(cfm);
    cfm.dwMask = CFM_FACE | CFM_BOLD;
    cfm.dwEffects = 0;
    _tcscpy(cfm.szFaceName, _T("Arial"));
    theCtrl.SetDefaultCharFormat(cfm);
}
```

You can use the CRichEditCtrl::GetDefaultCharFormat() function to retrieve the default character format. It accepts a reference to a CHARFORMAT structure, which it will populate according to the dwMask that you've used to initialize it.

Managing a Selection

Selecting text in the rich edit control is very important. You can use the CRichEditCtrl::GetSel() function to retrieve the selection. This function takes reference to a CHARRANGE structure, which is nothing more than two LONGs laid out like this:

```
typedef struct _charrange {
    LONG cpMin;
    LONG cpMax;
} CHARRANGE;
```

The two members, cpMin and cpMax, specify the index of the first and last selected character, respectively. I think that the names are poorly chosen, since cpMax might quite naturally be less than cpMin. If the user made a selection by moving toward the beginning of the control, for example, then the cpMax field will be less than cpMin and will indicate where the cursor was left.

You can retrieve the text inside the current selection by calling CRichEditCtrl::GetSelText(). The function offers a couple of overloads. One can be passed a LPTSTR which points at a buffer and will return a long indicating the number of characters stored in the buffer. Another overload accepts no parameters and returns a CString with the text held in the control. The buffer must be long enough to receive the selection – no check is made by Windows on the length. This function returns plain text; it doesn't give you access to the RTF stream inside the control.

You can set the selection by creating a CHARRANGE structure and passing it off to the CRichEditCtrl::SetSel() function.

The reason the selection is so important is that you can use other functions to change the formatting of the current selection. If you're writing an application that will behave as a word processor, you'll find that the commands you implement to let the user perform formatting against the text they enter will just call the formatting functions. Since the user has already made the selection, they've supplied the recipient of the command they're about to issue.

On the other hand, if you want to place text in the control and format it yourself, you'll need to manage the selection *after* inserting the text, but before you can make a call to change the formatting. You'll want to call `CRichEditCtrl::HideSelection()` to make sure the selection doesn't 'flash' as the user is watching the control. Letting the control forgo repainting the selection will also speed the updates to the control. That is, calling `SetRedraw()` on the control to stop automatic updating while you're reformatting selections in the control, possibly in addition to calling `HideSelection()`, will significantly help your application's performance.

`HideSelection()` takes two `BOOL`s. The first is `TRUE` if you want selections to be hidden, or `FALSE` if you'd like the selections to be shown again. The second parameter determines whether the selections continue to be shown even when the control loses focus – if the second parameter is `TRUE`, selected characters will be highlighted even when the control loses focus. `FALSE` resets this behavior to remove the highlight when the control loses focus.

By uniting all of these concepts, we can write code that will efficiently inject some formatted text into the control. If I want to have this text, for example:

You could be the owner of a beautiful machine
Buy this new Vahagoga ST-3500 today!

You might start by getting a reference to the control, hiding the selection and retrieving the current selection so that we can restore it later:

```
void CRTFView::OnAutotext()
{
    CRichEditCtrl& theCtrl = GetRichEditCtrl();
    CHARRANGE crOldSel;

    theCtrl.HideSelection(TRUE, FALSE);
    theCtrl.GetSel(crOldSel);
```

The next step is to figure out where we want to insert the new selection. Since we have the old selection, we can insert our text after it:

```
    CHARRANGE crInsertSel;
    crInsertSel.cpMin = crOldSel.cpMax;
    crInsertSel.cpMax = crOldSel.cpMax;
    theCtrl.SetSel(crInsertSel);
```

We'll want to set the format for our text, so our bold formatting is there:

```
    CHARFORMAT cfm;
    cfm.cbSize = sizeof(cfm);
    cfm.dwMask = CFM_BOLD;
```

```
cfm.dwEffects = CFE_BOLD;

SetCharFormat(cfm);
```

Then, we'll construct a `CString` that has our text and get it inserted:

```
theCtrl.ReplaceSel("You could be the owner of a beautiful machine\n");
```

We can then tweak the format. Note that I have to make the text format mask include the `CFM_BOLD` style so that the control turns *off* the bold format:

```
cfm.dwMask = CFM_BOLD | CFM_ITALIC;
cfm.dwEffects = CFE_ITALIC;

SetCharFormat(cfm);
```

We can then add the text, like this:

```
theCtrl.ReplaceSel("Buy this new Vahagoga ST-3500 today!\n");
```

Since everything is done, we can put the selection back where it used to be and make the selection visible once again:

```
theCtrl.SetSel(crOldSel);
theCtrl.HideSelection(FALSE, FALSE);
}
```

Programmatically adding text to the control and formatting it is a matter of correctly predicting where the selection will be, and moving to the spot where you want to add more text.

With the rich edit control, you're really doing a lot of work in order to get the formatting done! The Rich Edit control is often misapplied by users who want to have the ability to do syntax coloring, like the editor in the IDE itself does. You certainly can get this kind of painting done, but you'll find that it is *very* hard to make performance adequate, since you'll need to do so many calls to set the formatting. And since you're doing this work for each and every keystroke, the user is really going to notice even the slightest flaws.

Finding Characters

You can map out where you are within the control, line-by-line, using functions like `CRichEditCtrl::LineFromChar()`. The function takes the index of a character in the control and returns the line number where that character appears. If you pass −1 for the character index, the function will return the line number where the selection is currently. Conversely, if you call `CRichEditCtrl::LineIndex()`, you can find the character offset of a line number that you pass the function. Remember that both character indexes and line indexes are zero-based.

You can get the text for a particular line by calling `CRichEditCtrl::GetLine()`. This function accepts an `LPTSTR` pointer, which points to an area in memory you'd like filled with the text from a particular line. The function has an overload which accepts an integer indicating the length of the available buffer.

Complex Selections

The `GetDefaultCharFormat()` and `SetDefaultCharFormat()` functions we talked about in a previous section work on the default character format setting. If the user types new characters to be inserted in the control, the default character formatting will take effect. If the user types new characters into the control to replace existing characters, then the new characters will take the format of the old characters. This means that if the user is just typing, their newly added text will have the default format. If the user has highlighted some text and types to replace it, they'll be replacing the text but keeping the format that affected the replaced text.

It's easy to imagine that the selection might involve characters that are formatted with different attributes. If this is the case, `GetCharFormatSelection()` will indicate the discontinuous selection in the `dwMask` member. This table shows the content of the `dwMask` member and the `dwEffects` member for different selections.

Selection Content	dwMask	dwEffects
All normal characters	CFM_BOLD	0
All bold characters	CFM_BOLD	CFE_BOLD
Some bold, some normal characters	0	0

Of course, the table neglects other effects and flags – my intent is to clearly show the flags pertinent to the content of this example. You can test the content of the selection in a little more detail by calling `CRichEditCtrl::GetSelectionType()`. This function will return a group of flags that includes some or all of those shown here:

Flag	Meaning
SEL_EMPTY	The selection is only an insertion point
SEL_TEXT	The selection contains only text
SEL_OBJECT	The selection contains at least one OLE object
SEL_MULTICHAR	The selection contains more than one character
SEL_MULTIOBJECT	The selection contains more than one OLE object

Some of these flags are mutually exclusive; `SEL_EMPTY` will never be combined with any other flag, of course, but if the user has a complex selection, you might find `SEL_OBJECT`, `SEL_MULTICHAR` and `SEL_MULTIOBJECT` combined in various ways.

If you offer the user feedback in your user interface to show what formatting is applied to the section, you'll need to analyze very carefully the information returned from the control, so you can accurately give the user what they expect when they issue commands.

Formatting with the View

You might have noticed that most of the functions I've mentioned here are members of the control class (which is CRichEditCtrl) and not the view class (which is CRichEditView). You could also make some simpler calls against the view class to get your formatting done; one of the most notable is OnCharEffect(). This function takes two DWORD parameters; the first is the mask and the second is the effect you wish to enforce. The call changes the formatting of the current selection.

To make characters bold, you might code:

```
OnCharEffect(CFM_BOLD, CFE_BOLD);
```

You can make a single call to hook up multiple effects, if you'd like – just use the bit-wise OR operator. You could turn on italic and bold attributes, for example, by making this call:

```
OnCharEffect(CFM_BOLD | CFM_ITALIC, CFE_BOLD | CFE_ITALIC);
```

The OnCharEffect() function is used heavily by CRichEditView from a slew of undocumented functions which are designed to handle commands from menus or toolbar buttons in an editor-style application. The class has these undocumented command-handler functions:

CRichEditView member	Parameter(s)	Effect
OnCharBold()	none	Makes text bold
OnCharItalic()	none	Makes text italic
OnCharUnderline()	none	Makes text underlined
OnParaCenter()	none	Makes paragraph centered
OnParaRight()	none	Right-aligns paragraph
OnParaLeft()	none	Left-aligns paragraph
OnBullet()	none	Adds bullets to paragraph
OnColorPick()	COLORREF	Changes foreground color for text

Furthermore, the class features UPDATE_COMMAND_UI() handlers for these functions as well. There are no IDs defined for these handlers by MFC, but it's easy enough to hook them up. You'll need to manually insert an ON_COMMAND() handler into your window's map. Just make sure the map references the member you want scoped to CRichEditView directly, like this:

```
ON_COMMAND(ID_INSERT_BULLET, CRichEditView::OnBullet)
```

Again, since MFC doesn't provide them for you, you'll want to define IDs like ID_INSERT_BULLET yourself so that it matches a menu item or command button in your application.

The CRichEditView class also implements the cut, copy, paste, find, and replace functions that the normal CEditView class does. Additionally, it supports an OnEditPasteSpecial() function that will allow the user to perform operations normally associated with the **Paste Special** menu item.

Paragraph Formatting

Formatting paragraphs in a rich text edit control is similar to formatting characters. The major difference is that paragraphs in the control don't get a default format. That is, you can't set a paragraph format to apply to characters newly added to the control. You can call CRichEditCtrl::SetParaFormat() and pass it a reference to a PARAFORMAT structure to set the format of a paragraph. The SetParaFormat() function will return TRUE if the function worked and FALSE if it didn't.

Here's what the structure looks like:

```
typedef struct _paraformat {
    UINT  cbSize;
    _WPAD _wPad1;
    DWORD dwMask;
    WORD  wNumbering;
    WORD  wReserved;
    LONG  dxStartIndent;
    LONG  dxRightIndent;
    LONG  dxOffset;
    WORD  wAlignment;
    SHORT cTabCount;
    LONG  rgxTabs[MAX_TAB_STOPS];
} PARAFORMAT;
```

The _WPAD member is just to space members of the structure so that it lays out in memory in a fashion acceptable to all platforms where Windows runs. You shouldn't fool with either the _wPad1 field or the wReserved member.

cbSize must indicate the correct size of the structure in bytes so Windows might validate the structure when it's received. MFC will always initialize the member for you if you make a call to an MFC function, but if you ever pass a pointer to the structure to Windows directly yourself, you'll need to make sure that the member is initialized.

The dwMask member contains flags that let Windows know which fields in the structure are to be considered for use by functions you call. This table shows the flags for dwMask, noting what fields in the structure they represent.

dwMask **Flag**	**Meaning**
PFM_ALIGNMENT	The wAlignment member is valid
PFM_NUMBERING	The wNumbering member is valid

dwMask Flag	Meaning
PFM_OFFSET	The dxOffset member is valid
PFM_OFFSETINDENT	The dxStartIndent member is valid and specifies a relative value
PFM_RIGHTINDENT	The dxRightIndent member is valid
PFM_STARTINDENT	The dxStartIndent member is valid
PFM_TABSTOPS	The cTabStobs and rgxTabStops members are valid

The wNumbering field lets you specify whether or not you'd like to have the paragraph participate in a bulleted list. Presumably, the wNumbering field is so named because, some day, it will allow a paragraph to participate in numbered lists, but for now, the control only supports bulleted lists. The field can have the value 0 for no bullets, or PFN_BULLET to indicate that the paragraph should have bullets.

The dxStartIndent is used to indent the paragraph's first line. If the PFM_OFFSETINDENT flag is specified, dxStartIndent will be relative to the existing start indent for the paragraph. If PFM_STARTINDENT flag is set, the dxStartIndent value is an absolute distance from the left margin. In either case, the value is in twips. The dxRightIndent field specifies an indent relative to the right margin for the paragraph. The value is also in twips.

You can affect the rest of the indentation in the paragraph using the dxOffset field. The body of the paragraph will be indented if this value is positive; that will make the first line appear to have a hanging indentation. If this value is negative, the first line will appear to be indented relative to the rest of the paragraph.

The wAlignment value specifies alignment for the affected paragraphs. The value can be PFA_LEFT, PFA_RIGHT, or PFA_CENTER, for left, right, or centered alignment, respectively.

The cTabCount and rgxTabs fields work together to specify the tab stops for the paragraph. cTabCount indicates the number of entries in the rgxTabs array that contain valid tab stops. The entries in rgxTabs, from index zero to index cTabCount-1 inclusive, provide the position of the tab stop.

Once you've prepared a PARAFORMAT structure, you can call SetParaFormat() against the view or against the control. These functions both take a reference to your PARAFORMAT structure and apply the formatting to the selected paragraphs.

You can retrieve the formatting for a paragraph by calling GetParaFormatSelection() against the view, or GetParaFormat() against the control. Either of these functions will populate a PARAFORMAT for you, so that the structure reflects the formatting of the selected text.

Serializing a Rich Edit Control

If you're using a CRichEditView in your application, AppWizard will have already coupled it with a CRichEditDoc object. CRichEditDoc has all the code you need to perform serialization for the control, and for all the OLE objects it might contain.

After you call Serialize() to throw the content of the control into an archive, you cannot serialize any other data to the same archive. You *must* serialize the members of your document first, *then* serialize the content of the edit control to the archive. If you do it the other way round, you'll find that you'll get lots of messy assertions about invalid data forms. The reason for this is that the control writes plain text to the archive; the control can't know when the textual serialization data ends. When the control reads its data, it simply reads until the end of the file.

> The simple rule is this; make sure you serialize any extra data elements in your CRichEditDoc class *before* you call the Serialize() implementation in the base class.

The content of the control is available to you directly *only* as plain, unformatted text. You can use the GetWindowText() or GetSelText() members of CRichEditCtrl to retrieve the text. If you're interested in adding formatted text to the control, you can use techniques like the ones we examined before to format the information dynamically by calling SetSelectionCharFormat().

You can also get the control to render its data to you as a stream, which you can later send to whatever storage or transmission mechanism you'd like. If you want to store data from the control somewhere else, call CRichEditCtrl::StreamOut(). The function's prototype looks like this:

```
long CRichEditCtrl::StreamOut(int nFormat, EDITSTREAM& es);
```

The first parameter takes a set of flags that indicate what kind of data you'd like to serialize. If you'd like the control to provide a stream of plain text, you can specify SF_TEXT. The control will put formatted rich text in the stream if you use SF_RTF, and you can make the control produce rich text *without* in-line binary representations of any OLE objects by using SF_RTFNOOBJS. You'll find that the plain text serialized by SF_TEXT contains no formatting information besides paragraph breaks. If you want the control to generate line breaks and 'fake' formatting for other features (such as using spaces to simulate indentation), you can use SF_TEXTIZED.

The control will produce all of its content for the stream unless you specify the SFF_SELECTION flag, in which case it will just output the selected text.

The second parameter is a reference to an EDITSTREAM structure. The EDITSTREAM structure lets the application give the control enough information to get a streaming operation going. The structure is used both for reading (with the StreamIn() function) or writing (with the StreamOut() function), and has this layout:

```
typedef struct _editstream {
    DWORD dwCookie;
    DWORD dwError;
    EDITSTREAMCALLBACK pfnCallback;
} EDITSTREAM;
```

`dwCookie` is a user-defined value – you can jam anything you like in here. `dwError` is used to express an error to the control, or by the control to tell the caller about an error. It will contain an error code like those you might receive from the `::GetLastError()` API.

The `pfnCallback` function, though, is where all the fun lies. This member is a pointer to the function that will actually perform the reading or writing for the application. The callback function must either be global or a static member of a class. Either way, it won't know what instance of the object it relates to. You could get around this limitation by passing your `this` pointer through the `dwCookie` member, though. The prototype for your `EDITSTREAMCALLBACK` function looks like this:

```
DWORD CALLBACK EditStreamCallBack(DWORD  dwCookie,
                                  LPBYTE pbBuff,
                                  LONG   cb,
                                  LONG   *pcb);
```

The callback function receives as its first parameter the same `dwCookie` value you passed in the `EDITSTREAM` structure. The `pbBuff` parameter points to an area of memory where the control expects to receive or has provided information to be read into or written from the control. The `cb` parameter indicates how much memory is available there. The `pcb` parameter is a pointer to a `LONG` which lets your function tell the control how many bytes were actually read or written. If your callback function is successful, it should return a non-zero value. If it fails, it should return zero.

Let's drive this whole idea home with an example. If I'd like to do my own storage in a `CRichEditCtrl`, I might create a `CFile` object to store my data. Then, I can call `StreamOut()` against the control after I've prepared an `EDITSTREAM` object. That half of the operation might look something like this:

```
void CRTFView::OnStream()
{
    CRichEditCtrl& theCtrl = GetRichEditCtrl();

    CFile fWrite("C:\\Test.rtf",
                 CFile::modeCreate | CFile::modeWrite | CFile::typeBinary);

    EDITSTREAM strm;
    strm.dwCookie = reinterpret_cast<DWORD>(fWrite);
    strm.pfnCallback = WriteEditData;

    theCtrl.StreamOut(SF_RTF, strm);

    fWrite.Close();
}
```

I don't check it here for reasons of clarity, but if `StreamOut()` is successful, it will return the number of characters written to the file in total. You can see that I use the `dwCookie` value to pass a pointer to the opened `CFile` to the callback routine via the `EDITSTREAM` structure. I have to cast it explicitly to a `DWORD` so that I don't get an error message from the compiler.

The `WriteEditData()` function I wrote looks like this:

```
DWORD CALLBACK WriteEditData(DWORD dwCookie, LPBYTE pbBuff,
                                           LONG cb, LONG FAR *pcb)
{
    CFile* pFile = reinterpret_cast<CFile*>(dwCookie);

    try
    {
        pFile->Write(pbBuff, cb);
    }
    catch (CFileException* pEx)
    {
        pEx->Delete();
        *pcb = 0;
        return 0;
    };

    *pcb = cb;
    return 1;
}
```

Making sure that you have the function prototype down correctly is imperative. If you don't, you'll either get a warning when you assign the address of the function to the `pfnCallback` field of the `EDITSTREAM`, or your application will crash as the control tries to make the callback. Don't use random casts in attempts to guess what's wrong with the function – you'll just cloud the issue!

You can see that my function is pretty simple. First of all, I have to cast the `dwCookie` parameter back to a pointer to a `CFile` object. That done, I can ask the `CFile` object to write the data specified by `pbBuff` for length `cb`. If the call to `CFile::Write()` throws an exception, I set the number of bytes written to zero and let the control know that I can't write anymore by returning a zero. If things go well, though, I assume that the function wrote all of the characters asked and returned that information to the caller.

You'll note that I'm using a `CFile` object, and that I opened it as `typeBinary`. This doesn't seem intuitive; since I know the control will be writing only text to the file, why would we need a binary file? Well this way, I don't need the file to do any translation for me. The control will provide carriage return and linefeed pairs; I don't need the file to translate lonely linefeeds into carriage return-linefeed pairs. As such, I'm eager to get the slight performance gain offered by a binary-mode file.

Uncommon Controls

The classes we've talked about here simply wrap controls that are implemented in Windows as normal window classes. MFC doesn't do much, other than instantiating the classes and making many of the API calls you will need to work with the controls easier to use. Nevertheless, MFC does add a few control classes of its own. While these classes aren't truly common controls, they are controls that you can use in your applications to realize some neat functionality without doing too much of the boring work. Let's take a look at two of them now. The first is `CCheckListBox`, which allows you to display a check box for each item in your list box. The second is `CDragListBox`, which adds some MFC code to a Windows common control implementation to realize a list box with moveable items.

Checked List Boxes

List boxes are traditionally employed to let users make a selection of one item from a list of items. You can use a multiple-select list box to allow the user more than one choice, but with such a control the selection is difficult; the user needs to knowthat they have to hold down the *Shift* key or the *Ctrl* key to get the selection they want efficiently. Far more intuitive is the **checked list box**. An example is shown below:

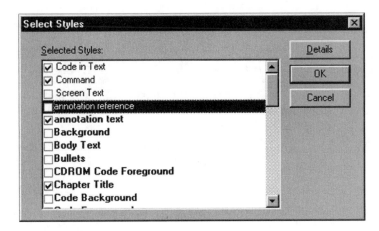

You can see that the control *does* allow a single item to be selected, but the user can also choose to mark or unmark the checkbox associated with each item. You might have used this control in the setup of Windows 95/98 or Visual C++ itself, for example, to decide what components you wanted to install. There's a subtle aspect of the control that's very interesting; it allows the user to have a very obvious, primary selection by highlighting a particular item – but it also allows them to select or deselect other items persistently.

Let's drive this point home by comparing it to a similar dialog that allows multiple selections. If a setup program provided you with a list of installation options in a multiple-selection list box, you'd still be able to select all of the features you wanted to install at the same time. But if the options were complicated – as they are in most setup programs – you might be tempted to add a Details push button to allow the user to get more information about a particular option. But the problem is that the Details push button doesn't make much sense when coupled with a multiple-selected box. What if the user has three components selected? What should the dialog box opened by the Details button show then? With a checked list box, on the other hand, the user can check the boxes of the items they fancy but still maintain only a single selection – the object of the Details button's activity.

Style Council

Since `CCheckListBox` will subclass the control it manages, you need to make sure the control you work with meets some simple criteria. First off, the control must be an owner-draw control; that is, it must have the `LBS_OWNERDRAWFIXED` or `LBS_OWNERDRAWVARIABLE` style. If it doesn't, MFC will assert as it attaches to the control. You'll normally want to fill the control with lines of text, so you'll probably choose `LBS_OWNERDRAWFIXED`. If each item in the control might be of a different height, you'll need to use `LBS_OWNERDRAWVARIABLE`.

In many cases, you'll be able to use the `CCheckListBox` class directly, but if the list box has the `LBS_SORT` or the `LBS_OWNERDRAWVARIABLE` style, you *must* derive your own class from `CCheckListBox` to write handlers for messages the list box receives to implement these styles. If the box has `LBS_SORT`, you'll need to write a handler for `CompareItem()`; for `LBS_OWNERDRAWVARIABLE`, you'll need to put a handler in for `MeasureItem()`. If the box doesn't have `LBS_SORT`, `CCheckListBox` also requires that the list box manage the strings. That means that, if you don't have `LBS_SORT`, you *must* have `LBS_HASSTRINGS`.

This is all twisted like a kitty-cat playing with a ball of yarn, so let's make a little chart to see what really happens:

List Box Style	If Present	If Absent
`LBS_SORT`	You must derive your own class and implement `CompareItem()`	You must add the `LBS_HASSTRINGS` style
`LBS_OWNERDRAWVARIABLE`	You must derive your own class and implement `DrawItem()` and `MeasureItem()`	You must have `LBS_OWNERDRAWFIXED`
`LBS_OWNERDRAWFIXED`	You're fine	You must have `LBS_OWNERDRAWVARIABLE`

Sorted list boxes are pretty common, so you might want to invoke a tiny bit of trickery to avoid having to make your own class when you're working with a checked list box. First, you should carefully decide if you really need a sorted box; if the strings for the box are always known, just use the `InsertString()` function to add them to the box in the proper order yourself. They'll stay in the order you used, and you can turn off `LBS_SORT`. If you really need the strings to be sorted on your behalf, though, you'll have to make your own class and hook up a `CompareItem()` function.

The Creation

The `CCheckListBox` class is a little different than the other control classes we've talked about. Instead of dynamically allocating a control pointer with a call like this,

```
// Wrong!
CCheckListBox* pItem;
pItem = static_cast<CCheckListBox*>(GetDlgItem(IDC_MYLIST));
```

you'll need to keep an instance of the class in your dialog box member data. During the execution of `OnInitDialog()`, you'll need to call `SubclassDlgItem()` on the member to make sure it is initialized before the box needs to paint. So, the code looks like this:

```
m_checkedList.SubclassDlgItem(IDC_MYLIST, this);
```

We talked about the exact duty that `SubclassDlgItem()` performs back in Chapter 7, but I can let you in on another secret here; you can actually use a `DDX_` function to realize the same effect. Specifically, you can call `DDX_Control()` to set up the subclassing instead. This means that you can use ClassWizard to add the member variable and hook up the exchange if you're not interested in fooling with `SubclassDlgItem()`.

For this situation, the `DoDataExchange()` function will simply call `DDX_` against a member variable of the type `CCheckListBox`:

```
DDX_Control(pDX, IDC_MYLIST, m_checkedList);
```

If you choose to use `DDX_Control()` and a `DoDataExchange()` function, you'll need to make sure that the `DoDataExchange()` function has been called at least once before you work with the control in question. You can force a call to `DoDataExchange()` if you call `UpdateData()` and pass `TRUE` as its only parameter.

Actually Using CCheckListBox

Once you have the correct style bits in place and all of the subclassing hooked up, you can begin using your `CCheckListBox`. You can use `AddString()` or `InsertString()` to add strings to it, just as you would with any normal box. You can implement the same notification handlers, too.

Before you populate the box, though, you might want to call `CCheckListBox::SetCheckStyle()` to dictate what style you want check boxes in the list box to have. The function takes a single integer, which is just one of the `BS_` styles to indicate what kind of check box you want. The default is `BS_AUTOCHECKBOX`; this results in a check box that is either checked or not, and automatically responds to the user changing the state with the mouse or keyboard. You can also pass `BS_AUTO3STATE` to have a box that features **tri-state check boxes**. Tri-state check boxes are either checked, not checked, or in an indeterminate grayed state. These styles are exactly as explained in Chapter 5 where I described plain old check box controls.

The documentation tells you that you can also use `BS_CHECKBOX` and `BS_3STATE` as parameters to this function, which indeed you can. If you do, though, you'll be responsible for marking and unmarking the boxes yourself. No message is sent to you when the user clicks on the boxes; you'll have to trap the `WM_LBUTTONDOWN` and `WM_KEYDOWN` messages to react appropriately. You can see what an appropriate reaction might be if you look at the MFC source in `Microsoft Visual Studio\vc98\Mfc\Src\Winctrl3.cpp`.

You can set the state of check boxes in the list with `CCheckListBox::SetCheck()`. The function takes two integers: the first is the zero-based index of the item whose check box you want to set, and the second is the desired state. You can pass `BST_UNCHECKED` to remove the check or `BST_CHECKED` to set the check. If you have a list box with `BS_AUTO3STATE` buttons, you can pass `BST_INDETERMINATE` for the second parameter to make the button go to the indeterminate state. A new `CCheckListBox` has buttons with the `BS_AUTOCHECK` style by default.

You can query the state of an item using `CCheckListBox::GetCheck()`. It accepts one integer, which is the index of the item you'd like to query. It will return an integer with the same meaning as the second parameter to `SetCheck()`. Items inserted into the box are not checked by default.

As an added bonus, you can individually enable or disable items in the box with a call to `CCheckListBox::Enable()`. If an item is disabled, it appears gray and the user can't select it or change its checked state. This function takes the index of the item of your desire. A second parameter is optional; if it is not specified, or if it is TRUE, the call will enable the specified item. You can disable the item by passing FALSE for the second parameter. Items added to the box are enabled by default.

You can check to see if an item is enabled by calling `IsEnabled()`. This function takes the index of the item that so fascinates you; it returns a BOOL that indicates the state of the item. If you pass an item that is out of bounds – that is, an index that is larger than highest index in the control – you'll get TRUE back anyway.

The `Wordfreq` *sample shows one way to use the* `CCheckListBox` *class.*

CDragListBox

You'll often encounter situations where you might wish to allow your user the opportunity to choose an order for items within a list box. Traditionally, this has been done by associating a couple of push buttons with the list box and then hooking up code to let the buttons move the selected item up or down. This is effective, but awkward; it requires the user to move the mouse from the list control to the buttons, and takes up some extra space in the dialog box for the buttons.

Unfortunately, list boxes that support dragging don't offer any visual hint to the user that the items in the box may be rearranged by dragging. You might want to include information in your online help, or a bit of text on the dialog itself, to let the user know they can rearrange items within the box simply by moving them.

MFC provides a class called `CDragListBox` that you can use in these situations. It isn't a common control, but it is largely implemented by Windows. You can create a drag list box by drawing a normal list box control in your dialog box template, or by calling `CDragListBox::Create()` to create the control directly. If you create the control using `Create()`, you won't need to subclass the control explicitly. If you create a list box control on a dialog box template, you'll want to subclass the control to get it to behave like a drag list box.

Note that a list box that you use to make a drag list box cannot have the sort or multiple select styles.

You might, for example, add a `CDragListBox` member to your dialog box. If you called that member `m_listDragger`, you could make calls like this from your `OnInitDialog()` handler in order to get the control set up:

```
m_listDragger.SubclassDlgItem(IDC_YOURBOX, this);
m_listDragger.AddString(_T("String one"));
m_listDragger.AddString(_T("String two"));
m_listDragger.AddString(_T("String three"));
```

When you perform the subclassing, MFC will make a call to the Windows `::MakeDragList()` API. This function resides in `Comct132.dll`, but the drag list implementation there only works to let the control's owner know that the user has begun or has finished dragging an item. It's the MFC-supplied code that completes the control's user interface.

If the user clicks on an item and begins dragging it, the control will send a notification message to its owner to indicate what's happening. The notification is sent via a registered Windows message which MFC has picked up during its initialization; the message identifier is held in CWnd::m_nMsgDragList. The CDragListBox class implements an OnChildNotify() handler to detect the message.

If CDragListBox receives a DL_BEGINDRAG notification, then the class will react by calling its BeginDrag() member. This function in turn draws the bar that indicates where the selection will be dropped. CDragListBox::BeginDrag() receives a CPoint that indicates exactly where the cursor was when the drag operation began.

When the class receives a DL_ENDDRAG notification, it calls its Dropped() member to move the item. It does the move by calling DeleteString() and InsertString() – there's no black magic going on. Dropped() accepts an integer which provides the original index of the item being dragged. The function also accepts a CPoint that indicates the position of the cursor where the item was finally dropped.

CDragListBox maps the DL_DRAGGING notification to the Dragging() member function. The DL_DRAGGING notification is sent whenever the user moves the mouse as they're dragging an item in the box. The function receives a CPoint indicating the present position of the mouse pointer. The function needs to return a constant to provide feedback to the user during the drag operation. If the function returns DL_COPYCURSOR, the control will show a cursor with a plus sign that would indicate the item is to be copied. If the function returns DL_MOVECURSOR, the control displays a cursor to indicate that the item is simply moving. If the provided point is not a good place to drop something, the function can return DL_STOPCURSOR to indicate this to the user.

The default implementation of Dragging() will check to see if the point is past the end of the box. If it is, the function will return DL_STOPCURSOR. Otherwise, the function always returns DL_MOVECURSOR. The default implementation of dragging in the class, therefore, doesn't support copying items.

Dropped(), BeginDrag(), CancelDrag(), and Dragging() are all virtual functions. You can override them as you see fit to do any interesting handling you like.

Summary

In this chapter, we've examined the MFC classes that wrap the Windows common controls, and we've also taken a peek at some MFC classes that implement functionality above and beyond the regular Windows controls. Though the common controls are relatively new to Windows, you owe it to yourself to learn to use them, because they vastly extend your user-interface arsenal. Further, by using these controls, your application implements an interface that's comfortable and familiar to the user.

> At the time of writing, the **CBreakfastBar**, **CPubBar**, **CFernBar** and **CPianoBar** classes were not complete. I've been researching **CPoolBar** and **CDartBar** carefully, and should have a proposal for their implementation soon. I had expected to see them in the product by now, but testing is taking a longer time than anticipated.

Utility and Exception Classes

Throughout this book, we've stressed that MFC is more than just a class library. It provides a strong framework with many application-level classes and lets you step over the tiny implementation details of your program and jump into the real work at hand. However, the libraries also contain the classes you normally see in a typical class library – classes which play a supporting role to the rest of the framework. These support classes are the classes we'll be looking at in this chapter.

For example, MFC provides its own string manipulation class, as well as several classes which can serve as containers for other types of data. The container classes come in two flavors: bland, type-unsafe implementations, and template-oriented type-safe implementations.

In this chapter, we'll cover:

> ➢ CString
> ➢ MFC's CException class
> ➢ MFC's classes for file input and output
> ➢ MFC's collection classes
> ➢ Data structures in MFC

CString

MFC provides for the encapsulation of strings with its CString class. As an experienced C programmer, you're certainly used to tossing around char arrays and doing pointer math to find different characters or search for substrings. Although this kind of work is amusing for a while, it can quickly get very tedious.

You're always allocating memory and copying things around. You don't get much help if you make errors like forgetting to free a block of memory or overstepping the range of memory that you've allocated.

You may need to get the text from a window, for example. Some programmers just assume their window's text isn't any bigger than a certain amount and code that assumption into their program:

```
TCHAR szText[255];
::GetWindowText(hWnd, szText, 255);
```

This might work, if you can guarantee the window doesn't have more than 254 characters in it. But the moment there's more text in there, you're in trouble. You could (and should, really) work a little harder and write some code which finds the length of the text first, allocates a buffer, and then stores the text in the newly allocated buffer:

```
int nLength = ::GetWindowTextLength(hWnd);
LPTSTR pstr = new TCHAR[nLength + 1];
::GetWindowText(hWnd, pstrText, nLength);
```

This code works great, but it isn't a lot of fun; you might forget to either allocate an extra character for the string's terminator or forget to free this memory later.

CString provides for this kind of management – for the most part, if you use CString, you won't need to spend time worrying about how long a string you receive from an API call will be. If you're using MFC, you'll have a pointer to a CWnd instead of a window handle like we had above. Given that, you can make use of MFC's code to measure the length of the window's title and manage it in the CString:

```
CString str;
pWnd->GetWindowText(str);
```

And that's all there is to it! The implementation of CWnd's GetWindowText() member function actually has the smarts that finds the length of the string, asks the passed CString to allocate that much memory (exactly) and then retrieves the text. CWnd, like many other classes in MFC, cooperates with CString to gain an advantage that's greater than the sum of their parts.

Of course, CWnd also provides an override of GetWindowText() which works on a regular character buffer. The regular function allows you to pull the text of a window back into an array of regular characters, and that's fine for the situations where you're content to do your own memory management or are prepared to deal with known-length strings.

Before we delve into the CString features and practices, let me point out that I won't often refer to any particular sample in this chapter. The utility classes tend to be ubiquitous throughout code written in MFC. It's best that you try searching all of the sample code on disk when you're interested in finding a particular usage of a given utility class, as the applications are too numerous or diverse to catalog. Looking through the MFC source code, itself, is a great idea, too. Not only will use see proper usages of MFC's own classes, but you'll also gain invaluable knowledge of MFC's implementation.

Constructing CString Objects

The code fragment just demonstrated in the last section creates a `CString` object the simplest way — using the default constructor to create a string that's blank. Our call to MFC's `CWnd::GetWindowText()` function fills the string with some characters. The data will be in the string and taking up memory until we decide to destroy the string object or it goes out of scope.

`CString` has a variety of constructors that allow it to attach itself to many different sources of string data. You can initialize a `CString` to contain a string constant, like this:

```
CString strTeam(_T("Pittsburgh Penguins"));
```

or you can initialize it to contain a single character:

```
CString strCharacter(_T('x'));
```

Some people prefer to use the equals sign in initializations, but that's really nothing more than a matter of style — it doesn't change the generated code at all. You might code, for example:

```
CString strSport   = _T("Hockey");
CString strCharacter = _T('x');
```

You'll notice that, throughout this book, I'll protect my string constants with a macro named `_T()`. `_T()` is the same macro as `_TEXT()` — both macros have the exact same effect, but one is (obviously) a lot easier to type and a bit less invasive to read. The `_T()` macro does nothing more than make code easier to port to Unicode builds. The Unicode character set is deeply involved in some solutions for international programming. Care for Unicode now saves lots of time later, so I'll also use the Unicode-ready `TCHAR` type instead of the plain `char` type; and pointers to `TCHAR` objects are represented by `LPTSTR` and `LPCTSTR` types. You can read more about the macro, all of its friends, and its real effect and meaning in Appendix B. In the meantime, I'm going to use it everywhere to help you get used to it.

`CString` has a couple of novel constructors. You can create a `CString` which replicates a particular character a given number of times. If you want to have a string which consists of the letter 'x' repeated 16384 times (I'm not so sure what practical reason you might have for doing that), you might construct it like this:

```
CString strLetterX(_T('x'), 16384);
```

You can also construct a `CString` by forcing the string to load from a string resource in your application. To get this to work, you'll need to cast the ID you have for a string to an `LPCSTR`; probably the most readable way of doing this is to use the `MAKEINTRESOURCE()` macro. MFC will notice the passed pointer isn't a valid string pointer and will try to call the appropriate API for you. If you have a string resource with the ID of `ID_FILE_NEW`, say, you can code:

```
CString strPrompt(MAKEINTRESOURCE(ID_FILE_NEW));
```

to get `strPrompt` to contain the string's text. `CString` also, of course, supports copying from another `CString`, like this code:

```
CString str1 = _T("My string");
CString str2(str1);
CString str3;
str3 = str1;
```

which leaves `str1`, `str2`, and `str3` containing the same data.

You can also pass a pointer to an array of characters as the first parameter and an integer as the second parameter to indicate the length of the array. In this case, the array need not be null-terminated. This isn't a very popular constructor, but is useful for some special situations — such as picking data out of some of the less friendly Win32 data structures.

While I've used string constants in most of my examples showing the construction of `CString` objects, there's nothing wrong with using pointers to plain old strings:

```
TCHAR* pstr = _T("My name");
CString strVerb = _T("is");
TCHAR szName[] = _T("Mike");
CString strSentence;

strSentence = pstr;
strSentence += _T(" ") + strVerb + _T(" "); // temp object!
strSentence += szName;
```

Note that all but the default `CString` constructors can throw a `CMemoryException` if they run out of memory while they are trying to initialize an object. If you create many strings (in a loop while reading a file, for instance), it's best to `catch` those exceptions so your application doesn't halt. Of course, you may run out of memory at any moment, but you're certainly more likely to do so while processing large amounts of string data. There's a lot more information about MFC's relationship with exceptions later in this chapter.

CString Operators

Above, you can see I've coded a couple of extra lines using some simple operators to further manipulate the `CString` object I've constructed. After the code fragment in the previous section executes, the string `strSentence` has the content `"My name is Mike"`.

`CString` supports these operators:

Operator	Effect
+	`_tcscat()`, `_tcscpy()`
+=	`_tcscat()`
>	`_tcscmp()`

Operator	Effect
<	_tcscmp()
==	_tcscmp()
=	_tcscpy()
[]	read-only character indexing

The operators that can change the length of the string also do the necessary memory management. You'll see I pointed out a difference between operator+= and operator+ because they are different – one copies the string, while one modifies the string itself. That is, operator+ concatenates two strings and forms a new string. operator+= adds one string to the end of another, modifying the target string in the process.

Using the += operator is particularly useful for formatting text and putting together large strings. While this method is a convenient way to get work done quickly, you'll find it lacks a little in performance. Semantically, the middle statement in the above example (the one marked // temp object!) is equivalent to:

```
strSentence += CString(_T(" ") + strVerb + _T(" "));
```

The statement causes Visual C++ to generate code which concatenates the string literals to the CString objects. The statement also copies the temporary CString from the right side of the assignment operator to the left. This mechanism is a bit wasteful; each CString copy results in a memory allocation and two memcpy() calls.

The rules surrounding temporary objects in the C++ language are a bit involved, and I think they're best left to a book which focuses on the language. The situation I invented above is only one of very, very many ways to make a temporary object appear; some of the other important situations where they crop up will be described in a section or two. But your favorite C++ language reference will help you understand all of the situations where they might appear.

CStrings and String Resources

String literals are annoying. They make your application difficult to localize and it's sometimes difficult to find strings that generate messages or other output once you've hard-coded them into your application. Windows provides **string resources** to help you solve some of these issues.

As we described briefly in Chapter 1, string resources can be edited with the string table editor. That string resource table becomes a part of your application's executable file and the strings in it are available to you any time you need them.

You can use the CString::LoadString() function to load a string from your application's resource table. LoadString() takes the ID of the string resource you want to load and returns TRUE if the string was loaded, FALSE if not. The function might also throw a CMemoryException if real estate is tight when you ask for the string.

Back in Win16 days, it was advantageous to use string resources just because it helped Windows more efficiently manage your executable image as it was loaded in the memory. By putting string constants into resources, you slightly improved Windows' ability to perform well in low-memory situations. Since the Win32 memory manager has improved (and since Win32 manages resources differently to Win16), you'll find this isn't such a compelling reason anymore – but there are still enough good reasons to use string resources instead of string literals. Check out Appendix B if you're still not convinced.

Comparing Strings

The CString class features a full complement of comparison operators. You can use:

Greater than	>
Less than	<
Less than or equal to	<=
Greater than or equal to	>=
Equal to	==
Not equal to	!=

Each of these operators can be used to compare CStrings with each other. The operators are also appropriately overloaded to allow you to compare a CString with an LPCTSR. These operators enable convenient constructs like this:

```
CString str1 = _T("Money");
CString str2 = _T("Pride");
CString strAnswer;
CString strHigher;

if (str1 > str2)
{
    strHigher = str1;
}
else
{
    strHigher = str2;
}
strAnswer = strHigher + _T(" is more important");
AfxMessageBox(strAnswer);
```

If you're interested in a more explicit notation, or reacting to the different possible results of a comparison in different ways, you can use the Compare() function. Compare() works just like strcmp(). The following if statement is equivalent to the one shown immediately above:

```
if (str1.Compare(str2) > 0)
{
    strHigher = str1;
}
else
```

```
        {
            strHigher = str2;
        }
```

Since you know `Compare()` will return a value greater than zero if the compared string is "higher", zero if the strings are equal, or a negative value if the compared string is "lower", you can squirrel away the result and use it to avoid re-testing the strings.

`CString::CompareNoCase()` is also available to compare strings without regard to case, just like `strcmp()`. The function works exactly like `CString::Compare()`, but doesn't pay attention to case.

`CString` also features the ability to do comparisons using collation rules. `Compare()` and `CompareNoCase()` end up doing strict value comparisons between the strings. `Collate()` and `CollateNoCase()`, however, compare the values of the strings using the rules of the currently selected codepage. Collation is important in applications that are to be localized, as users will expect their native-language rules to apply to any sorting the application does. For example, in France, words beginning with an accented E should be sorted with the same weight as words not having an accent on their E. `Compare()` would sort such words differently because the strict character values of the strings are very different. But the slower `Collate()` functions know the extra rules and will react appropriately.

Searching CStrings

You'll often need to find the index of a given character in a string. `CString` provides three functions to help you search a `CString`. You can call the `Find()` member to match any substring; this function is similar to the `strstr()` function in the C run-time libraries. The function returns the index of the first instance of the passed string that's found, working from the left of the target string. Both of the following `Find()` invocations return 4:

```
    int nIndex;
    CString strTarget = _T("The Pittsburgh Penguins");

    nIndex = strTarget.Find(_T("Pitt"));
    nIndex = strTarget.Find(_T('P'));
```

You can also go through the string starting from the right, using the `ReverseFind()` member function. This `ReverseFind()` invocation returns 7:

```
    int nIndex;
    CString strTarget = _T("The Pittsburgh Penguins");
    nIndex = strTarget.ReverseFind(_T('P'));
```

If you want to search for any one of a group of characters, you can use the `FindOneOf()` member of `CString`. This function accepts a pointer to a string which contains characters you're searching for. You may want to write a function to see whether a string has any whitespace by doing something like this:

```
BOOL HasWhitespace(CString* pString)
{
    int nIndex;
    nIndex = pString->FindOneOf(_T("\n\r\t "));
    return (nIndex != -1);
}
```

All 'find' functions return −1 if no match is found in the target string; we take advantage of this return value. Unfortunately, case-insensitive versions of these functions don't exist.

Modifying a CString

Of course, most of the fun in handling strings is modifying the content of the string in one way or another. CString provides a swath of functions for such efforts, and they deserve our attention. Again, the primary advantage for using CString to handle your parsing chores are the same as the core benefits as any other use of CString. That is, you don't have to worry about any memory management issues no matter how your strings grow.

CStrings provide a variety of conversion functions; you can convert a CString to upper or lower case by calling the object's MakeUpper() or MakeLower(), while MakeReverse() reverses the content of the string. These functions all work on the string in-place, and affect the entire string.

You can perform a variety of replacements on the characters and substrings in your CString objects. Just use the Replace() function, which has two overrides to cover both characters and strings. You can use this override:

```
int Replace(TCHAR chOld, TCHAR chNew);
```

to replace any occurrence of chOld with chNew. The string-based version looks like this:

```
int Replace(LPCTSTR lpszOld, LPCTSTR lpszNew);
```

and replaces occurrences of the substring lpszOld with lpszNew. Both of the functions return a count indicating how many matching instances were actually replaced.

These are pretty simple functions which make their substitutions as they go from left to right. You might start out with a string that has some odd characters, and replace them with something more meaningful:

```
CString str(_T("Fizzsburgh Fenguins"));
str.Replace(_T('F'), _T('P'));
str.Replace(_T('z'), _T('t'));
```

You'll note that the two character replacements above here are just the same as these two string replacements:

```
str.Replace(_T("F"), _T("P"));
str.Replace(_T("z"), _T("t"));
```

because a substring of one character is just the same as a character. If you're replacing content character-by-character, though, you'll find using the character-based overrides is just a little faster.

Of course, the substring overrides replace whole substrings at a time. After the above code executes, we'll have changed sports:

```
str.Replace(_T("Penguins"), _T("Steelers"));
```

You can also provide a null lpszNew to effectively remove the substring identified by lpszOld. Since you can't provide a null character to the override which accepts characters, MFC provides a Remove() member which will delete any occurrences of a particular character.

CString users have long requested the ability to insert and remove characters based on their index within the string. And, in Visual C++ 6.0, MFC has finally granted their wishes. You can call Insert() to insert a particular string or substring at a given index. And the Delete() member works similarly – you can delete any number of characters starting at a particular index within the string.

Extracting the Contents of CString

Aside from using GetBuffer() and to get to the directly modifiable data of the CString object (which we'll discuss a little later), the class provides numerous functions which allow you to get at some or all of the data held by the string.

Two handy functions that allow you to use the CString as if it were a character array are GetAt() and SetAt(). You can use the GetAt() member of CString to get a character at a given index in the string and you can use SetAt() to set the character at an index in the string. In both cases, the index is passed as a parameter to the function. SetAt() takes the character to be set as the function's second parameter.

In debug versions, both functions test the index to make sure that it's inside the string, but release versions of the function don't perform this index check. The string won't be grown if you try to reference a character past the length of the string; you'll just step on memory which you don't own, possibly raising an access violation exception.

As a shorthand for the GetAt() function, MFC implements an operator[] for the CString class. This allows you to treat the CString data as if it was an array, using array syntax. You can retrieve characters from the CString using this syntax, but you can't set them. You can use the familiar syntax to get any single character within the string. For example:

```
CString str = _T("Vancouver Canucks");
TCHAR ch = str[2];
```

sets ch to 'n'. CString's operator[] does not return an l-value. So, you *can't* code:

```
str[2] = 'x';
```

as the operator returns a TCHAR, not modifiable reference to a TCHAR.

The CString class also offers convenient, BASIC-like Right(), Left() and Mid() functions. Left() allows you to pull off a specified number of characters from the left of the string, while Right() and Mid() do the same for the right or middle of the string respectively.

The great thing about these functions is they return a new `CString` object containing the substring you've requested. Once again, you don't need to guess at a size for a buffer; the `CString` bases its own buffer on the size of the returned string.

You can use `CString::SpanExcluding()` to return a substring which doesn't have any characters from a set you provide to the function. The function accepts a string which contains the characters in the set to avoid; it returns a new `CString`, which contains characters from the original string, up to the one before the first character that appears in the parameter set which was passed:

```
CString str = _T("All of these characters will be there, up to the comma");
CString& strShorter = str.SpanExcluding(_T(","));

// str is now == "All of these characters will be there"
```

`SpanIncluding()` is a similar function, which returns a substring of all characters that are in the set of characters passed to the function. You might use the function to do some parsing, like this:

```
CString str = _T("444-555-1212 is my phone number.");
CString& strNumber = str.SpanIncluding(_T("1234567890-()"));

// str is now == "444-555-1212"
```

`CString` members like `Right()` and `SpanExcluding()` continue to lift the burden of string manipulation from your shoulders by making it easy to allocate and free memory associated with the string. This is no more evident than when you need to pass the resulting string as a parameter to another function; you can simply reference the call in the function invocation, like this:

```
CString strName = "Geddy Lee";
SetBassPlayer.FirstName(strName.SpanExcluding(_T(" ")));
SetBassPlayer.LastName(strName.Mid(6, 3));
```

The code that's generated creates a temporary string object to be passed to the called function, and then destroys the temporary object when the function returns.

CString Formatting

Since there's a pretty common need to format a message of unknown length and to then create a string out of it, `CString` features the `printf`-like `Format()` member function. You can pass `Format()` a `printf`-style control string with a variable argument list.

Internally, `Format()` uses a parsing algorithm which is the same as `printf()`, but doesn't copy any characters. Instead, it just counts the characters which would be generated by `printf()`. Before calling `vsprintf()` in the C run-time libraries, it takes this total and makes sure enough characters are allocated in the string.

The `Format()` code passes all of the arguments, including the control string, to `vsprintf()` and has the function drop its output in the data area owned by the `CString`. A `CString::Format()` call is, therefore, only slightly more expensive than a `vsprintf()` call in terms of speed.

However, the beauty of the call is you don't have to guess how much memory to allocate when you want to format a message into a buffer. For instance, if you started out with code like this:

```
TCHAR szMessage[192];      // some arbitrarily large size
DWORD dwErrorCode;
int nCause, nLine;

GetErrorCode(&dwErrorCode, &nCause, &nLine);
wsprintf(szMessage,
    _T("Fatal error #%ld: Cause code 0x%4.4d on line %d",
    dwErrorCode, nCause, nLine));
```

you'd be wasting a lot of memory on the stack and you wouldn't be able to sleep nights, thinking that there could some time be an error message which eventually nets more than 192 characters when it's coupled with a long bunch of integers. (The GetErrorCode() function is completely fictitious, by the way.) The far more robust and concise solution involves Format(), like this:

```
CString strMessage;
DWORD dwErrorCode;
int nCause, nLine;

GetErrorCode(&dwErrorCode, &nCause, &nLine);
strMessage.Format(_T("Fatal error #%ld:"
    " Cause code 0x%4.4d on line %d"), dwErrorCode,
    nCause, nLine);
```

During the Format() call, the CString will be set to the correct length automatically.

CString in the newest versions of MFC also exposes a variable-arguments version of Format(). You can collect a va_args-style parameter list in a function of your own, and then send off the va_args parameters to FormatV(). You might use this technique to do your own formatting with a routine that takes variable parameters, something like this:

```
void WriteErrorLog(CStdioFile& refFile, int nError, LPCTSTR pstrFormat, ...)
{
    CTime timeWrite;
    timeWrite = CTime::GetCurrentTime();
    CString str = timeWrite.Format("%d %b %y %H:%M:%S - ");

    // write a timestamp
    refFile.Write(str, str.GetLength());

    // then the error code
    str.Format("Error %4.4d - ", nError);
    refFile.Write(str, str.GetLength());

    // properly format whatever else the caller gave us
    va_list args;
    va_start(args, pstrFormat);
    str.FormatV(pstrFormat, args);

    // write it!
    refFile.WriteString(str, str.GetLength());
    return;
}
```

This code fragment allows callers to write a string to a file. The function will format a timestamp before the data is written, and then format the balance of the arguments. So, you can make simple calls, like this one:

```
WriteErrorLog(fileLog, 53, "no more memory");
```

and the function might write:

```
13 Feb 99 20:22:11 - Error 0053 - no more memory
```

depending on the time, of course. That code really does nothing that we haven't learned about – formatting time and the integer are quite simple tasks. But since `WriteErrorLog()` is declared to take variable arguments, more aggressive calls are quite possible. You can include your own formatting escapes, which will later be passed to `FormatV()` to be implemented. This call, for instance:

```
WriteErrorLog(fileLog, 53, "Can't get %d bytes", 8192);
```

nets us this output:

```
13 Feb 99 20:22:12 - Error 0053 - Can't get 8192 bytes
```

Anything can happen on the parameter list, even strings. The only curveball in the bag is that you can't format a self-referential string. That is:

```
CString str;
str.FormatV("%s", str);
```

is a real no-no, for both `Format()` and `FormatV()`.

Working Directly with the Buffer

One of the easiest ways to make your work with `CString`s a little more efficient is to consider doing the work directly against the buffer that the `CString` manipulates. Directly touching the buffer also grants you the ability to use functions that can't work with `CString`, but instead take a pointer to a character array.

You can get a modifiable pointer to the buffer in a `CString` by calling the `GetBuffer()` member of the object, which accepts an integer indicating the minimum number of characters you expect to be available in the buffer.

You'll want to make sure any space your modifications will require can fit in the space you ask for.

`GetBufferSetLength()` can also be used to gain direct access to the buffer. `GetBufferSetLength()` is different than `GetBuffer()` in that `GetBufferSetLength()` specifies the length of the string contained by the `CString` object instead of just the buffer. `GetBufferSetLength()` will supply a zero terminator in the data owned by the `CString` object at the length you specify. Both functions allocate the space you ask for, but `GetBufferSetLength()` will drop a null character at the length you've specified.

`GetBufferSetLength()` is the function to use if you know you'll end up with a specific length before you do your manipulation of the buffer. If you don't know, and need to stick with a maximum known length, `GetBuffer()` is the way to go.

Remember that if the `CString` is newly created, it will have no length. Code like this will result in disaster:

```
CString str;
LPTSTR pChars = str.GetBuffer(0);
strcpy(pChars, _T("Hockey"));
```

(Your machine won't crash, but you'll have to terminate the application that used this code. It's not like your significant other will leave you, but the reduced productivity might jeopardize the lock you have on the department's hockey tickets.) However, it's useful to pass a zero to `GetBuffer()` when you already know that the buffer is long enough to suit your needs; it's often useful to modify the content of the buffer in-place.

By the way, you can get the length of a `CString` object by calling the `GetLength()` member of the object to get the current length of the string. You know that the `CString` object always has at least as much memory as `GetLength()` returns.

Improving Efficiency with the ReleaseBuffer()

If it weren't for the repeating constructor, we might fill a massive `CString` like this:

```
CString str;
LPTSTR pWork;
int nCount;

pWork = str.GetBuffer(16384);
for (nCount = 0; nCount < 16384; nCount++)
    *pWork++ = _T('x');
str.ReleaseBuffer(16384);
```

The call to `ReleaseBuffer()` lets the `CString` object regain ownership of its buffer, so after the call to `ReleaseBuffer()`, you should assume that the pointer you received from `GetBuffer()` is invalid.

This silly example points at a more serious interest, though; the above loop, rewritten to use `operator+` to concatenate each individual character, would cause `CString` to abuse the memory manager. The loop would take a really long time to run, and be quite an embarrassment.

If you're writing code that must concatenate globs of data into a single CString, do try to pay attention to the performance ramifications of your code.

Note that the lengths we pass *don't* include an extra count for the terminating null, and that this code fragment doesn't add a null terminator character to the string. The length of the string is maintained by the CString and is reset when we pass the new length to the ReleaseBuffer() function. If you can't conveniently manage the length of the string while you're using a pointer returned from GetBuffer(), you can add a null terminator and then pass –1 to ReleaseBuffer() to allow the CString to calculate the length of the string itself.

Running Out of Buffer

Remember you're not allowed to add more to the string than you've allocated space for. Running off the edge of the buffer will get you into trouble, just like it would if you ran off the end of a buffer that you'd allocated yourself. Note that MFC doesn't prevent you from modifying a CString when you have a buffer pointer to it. If you call GetBuffer() and then perform any other operation on the string which changes its length, CString will reallocate the buffer to gain more space, and the pointer you've been retaining from GetBuffer() will become invalid. You shouldn't use any other CString member functions until you've called ReleaseBuffer().

The most efficient approach to string intensive work with MFC involves using CString objects to hold your strings. Whenever you need to dynamically construct strings, particularly when you're concatenating strings together, your best bet is to build the string with regular character arrays or dynamically allocated buffers, before turning those arrays or buffers over to a CString object for safe keeping.

Unfortunately, this sort of approach compromises how easy CStrings are to use, which is what made them so appealing in the first place. We wouldn't recommend you do all concatenations within a normal TCHAR array, but it's a very good way to shave time off code that you often re-execute.

Using Normal String Functions

As you get used to CStrings, you'll be tempted to use your favorite string functions from the C run-time libraries. Although you've already seen some of the cooler CString functions that help you to get work done faster, there are some operations that you might need to perform that are only available as C run-time library functions. For instance, you might need to find some tokens in a string. Since CString has no such functionality, you'll need to call the _tcstok() function in the C run-time library.

There are many other instances when you might need to retrieve a read-only pointer to the content of a CString. For example, you might need to pass the content of a CString off to wsprintf(). You'll need to cast the CString to an LPCSTR, which might go something like this:

```
CString strName = _T("Charles Bukowski");
int nCount = 10401834;
TCHAR szOutput[80];

wsprintf(szOutput, _T("For the %ldth time, clean your room, %s!"),
    nCount, (LPCTSTR)strName);
```

Of course, since `wsprintf()` only reads from the CString, we can get a pointer to the contents without any further problems. The CString class implements the (LPCTSTR) cast operator, so the cast will return a pointer to the CString's buffer. If we had coded the `wsprintf()` call without this cast, we'd have ended up passing the whole strName object rather than its data content! The same rules about the life of a pointer returned from a GetBuffer() call apply here, i.e. the pointer can become invalid if the CString object needs to reallocate its memory in order to gain more storage.

The notion of explicitly casting a CString is important only when the C++ language can't otherwise figure out what to do. Functions that take strings usually have very appropriate declarations. You might declare a SetUserName() function like this:

```
void SetUserName(int nJerseyNumber, LPCTSTR pstrPlayer);
```

The formal parameter type in this declaration lets the language know the second parameter should be a LPCTSTR. If you made the following call, you wouldn't need to perform any explicit casting:

```
CString strPlayer("Wayne Gretzky");
SetUserName(99, strPlayer);
```

However, many functions don't have such explicit prototypes: functions like `wsprintf()`, `CString::Format()`, and MFC's `TRACE()` function, for example. These functions can't provide types for their variable argument lists because the argument lists are (get this) variable! The compiler can't know that you want to invoke the cast operator unless you explicitly invoke it yourself.

Parsing

Since the standard library `_tcstok()` function modifies the string that it parses, you'll need some way to get a non-const pointer from a CString. To use `_tcstok()` against a CString, you'll have to call GetBuffer() to realize a pointer to the string. Code to rip up a string using `_tcstok()` might look like this:

```
CString str = _T("First\tSecond Third,Fourth\t    Fifth");
LPTSTR pstr;
LPTSTR pstrToken;
TCHAR seps[] = _T("\t, ");

pstr = str.GetBuffer(0);

pstrToken = _tcstok(pstr, seps);
while (pstrToken != NULL)
{
    AfxMessageBox(pstrToken, MB_OK);
    pstrToken = _tcstok(NULL, seps);
}
str.ReleaseBuffer(-1);

AfxMessageBox(pstr, MB_OK);
```

Note that the loop ends with a call to ReleaseBuffer() with -1 as a parameter. This is the default value for this parameter and should only be used with null-terminated strings. This allows the str object to recalculate its length, which was changed by the `_tcstok()` routine.

The final `AfxMessageBox()` call only displays First, as you would expect, since `_tcstok()` inserts a null terminator after parsing to that point in the string.

Don't panic: `_tcstok()` is very similar to the `strtok()` function you've been using for years. See Appendix B for more information.

Empty Strings

You should note that when you create a CString, it is empty. In MFC 6.0, this state of emptiness is the same as holding a null string; an empty CString is just an empty CString with no length and no string storage memory associated with it. Earlier versions of MFC made a distinction between strings which were empty and strings that were really containing a null string. The change that made completely empty CString objects the same as CString objects that owned an empty string was made in the interest of efficiency.

You can empty (by which I mean free completely) the memory associated with a CString by calling the CString::Empty() function on the CString object. Note that a CString will also free its memory automatically when it's destroyed; you don't need to worry about explicitly requesting that before you delete it.

Usually, strings aren't empty. You can get their length by calling GetLength(), and you can find out if they're empty or not by calling IsEmpty(). GetLength(), like the `_tcslen()` function which you've used against C-style strings, doesn't return a count which includes the terminating character of zeros. So, here:

```
CString str = _T("Hockey");
int nLength = str.GetLength();
```

nLength ends up with the value 6.

The Empty() function is now less useful than it once was. Originally, it was intended to be used in exception handling code in very old versions of Visual C++, which featured compilers that didn't unroll temporary objects while exiting an exception handling function. In handling the exception, your code would have to manually Empty() each CString which was active at the time of the exception.

Since all versions of Visual C++ later than 4.0 feature a compiler which performs true standard C++ exceptions (and some slightly older versions have almost complete standard exception handling), the exception handling code that's emitted by the compiler itself will call the destructors for the CString objects which are in scope when the exception is handled, so you no longer need to call Empty() against your objects.

Empty() is still useful when you're aware of a memory-intensive CString object that contains unwanted data. Of course, in many such circumstances, it might be more natural to just destroy the object, or call FreeExtra().

You can realize such a situation when you release the buffer of an empty string:

```
CString strTest;
CString strEmpty;
LPTSTR pstr = strTest.GetBuffer(100);
*pstr = '\0';
strTest.ReleaseBuffer();
```

`strTest` ends up containing zero characters, but still internally manages at least 100 bytes of memory, which increases to least 200 bytes in a _UNICODE build. And it might allocate even more, if it's using a fancy allocator that trades coarse granularity for great speed. `strEmpty`, on the other hand, is truly empty; it isn't managing any memory whatsoever. Both strings, after the above code executes, would return TRUE for `IsEmpty()`. If you've manipulated the content of a string with `ReleaseBuffer()` and have previously made a very aggressive length assumption in your call to `GetBuffer()`, you might want to call `CString::FreeExtra()` to let `CString` release any fat it has lying around. If you're planning on continuing to alter the string, the call to `FreeExtra()` really isn't worth it – and actually can suck a little bit of performance from your code.

CStrings and COM

We haven't talked much about COM, OLE, or ActiveX – it'll come in later chapters. If you've done any COM programming, or if you've come back here after reading the ActiveX chapters, you know the biggest principle behind COM is that applications should have interesting ways to interact. "Interacting", as far as COM is concerned, means applications have convenient ways to share windows and data and input and output – and that necessarily means the applications in question will share memory.

Since COM will place itself in between different running objects, it may need to take ownership of blocks of memory to be exchanged between one object and another. This is the only reasonable way that COM can, for example, allow an object to load, give some data to another object, and then have the first object die. If the object itself allocated that memory, the object would end up automatically freeing the memory as it died – so it is necessary that COM own the memory.

`CString` inherently supports conversion between an OLE string, represented by an instance of the data type `BSTR`, and the data in a `CString`. You can call `CString::AllocSysString()` to have MFC allocate a `BSTR` and copy the `CString`'s data to the `BSTR`. The function returns the `BSTR` and throws an exception if the conversion doesn't go well. If you're working against an ANSI build of MFC, MFC will first convert the string data to Unicode before copying it; if you're compiling against a Unicode build of MFC, then MFC doesn't need to convert the string.

If you find yourself with a `BSTR` given to you as a result of a COM call, you can convert it to a `CString` by using a special `CString` constructor that accepts a `BSTR`: just pass the `BSTR` to the constructor, and that's that. The constructor makes a copy of the data represented by the `BSTR`, so changes you make to the string are *not* made to the data previously owned by OLE.

Conversion Functions

`CString` is a very handy class because its implementation allows you to implicitly pass a `const` pointer to the underlying buffer, to any function that accepts a pointer to a `const` string. In both the C Runtime libraries and the Windows API, such functions are very common.

MFC supports `CString` itself aggressively (obviously!), which adds even more value to the class.

If you do any COM programming, though, you'll find that COM has its own idea of how strings are represented. If you're calling a method on a COM interface that accepts a string for input, you'll end up passing a `BSTR`. A `BSTR` is a string whose length is stored as an integer before the actual text and is terminated by a trailing zero. By convention, `BSTR`s always contain double-byte Unicode characters – but a very few heathens have desecrated this standard and packed plain ANSI characters into the strings.

If you have a `CString` and need a `BSTR` from it, you can call `CString::AllocSysString()`. This function accepts no parameters and doesn't change the `CString` object upon which it is called. It copies the current content of the `CString`, converting it to Unicode, if necessary, and allocates a `BSTR` for it. The function returns that `BSTR`.

When you pass a `BSTR` to a COM method as an input parameter, it is then owned by the receiving method. You shouldn't free it yourself, and the `BSTR` is independent of the `CString` that bore it.

On the other hand, if you receive a `BSTR` from a COM function, you can turn it into a `CString` just by assigning it, like this:

```
bstrFoo = GetABSTRFromSomeoneElse();
CString strFoo = bstrFoo;
```

MFC will copy the `BSTR` into the `CString` object, converting it if necessary. It might be necessary for you to call `SysFreeString()` on the `BSTR` if the COM rules dictate that you, as the recipient of the string, are the owner. (Here's a hint: you'll almost always need to free the `BSTR` yourself.)

There are a few situations where conveniently converting from ANSI to Unicode character sets and back is handy, and as such, MFC provides a few macros that can help you. Those macros are most often used with OLE as well, though, so I've covered them in Chapter 13 on OLE Containers.

Binary Data in CString

While it is a bit tricky, you *can* use `CString` to contain binary data. You're truly better off using a class more suitable for the task, like `CLongBinary` (described in the database chapter) or `CByteArray` (described later in this chapter), but it's really up to you. `CString` can be quite an adequate container of any arbitrary binary data. But it's even more important to realize that `CString` will work if you ask it to contain more than one NULL character.

To set some binary data into a `CString`, get the buffer and `memcpy()` the data into it. Then, release the buffer by calling `ReleaseBuffer()`. You *must* pass `ReleaseBuffer()` the length of the data you set; otherwise, `ReleaseBuffer()` will truncate the data where it finds the first zero character. You can get the binary data out again by calling `GetBuffer()`. You can retrieve the length of the data by calling `GetLength()`. `GetAt()` and `SetAt()` allow you to get and set bytes (or words) at any point in the string.

Alternatively, you can use the length-known constructor for your object. That is, given a pointer to a bunch of bytes and the length of the array, invoke:

```
CString str(pstr, nLength);
```

and the string will copy all of the data up to the given length – even if it contains more than one null.

No other functions are guaranteed to work properly; Find(), for example, will stop searching once it hits the first null character. It's trivial to call GetAt() to implement your own find routine, and you'll have to, since the normal Find() member can't possibly know what you really mean with the extra nulls.

Dynamically Allocating CString Objects

Of course, in addition to creating static or automatic CString objects, you're also likely to dynamically create CStrings using the new operator. You can make a pointer to a CString object behave like a pointer to a string in normal C++. For instance, you could code:

```
CString* pMyName;
pMyName = new CString(_T("Mike Blaszczak"));
```

Of course, this is similar to getting things done with a static object and the same constructor parameter:

```
CString MyName(_T("Mike Blaszczak"));
```

This is less error-prone and therefore a lot easier to handle than the following. (Can you find the error in the next three lines?):

```
TCHAR* pstrMyString;
pstrMyString = reinterpret_cast<TCHAR*>(malloc(_tcslen(_T("Mike Blaszczak"))))
                                                * sizeof(TCHAR));
_tcscpy(pstrMyString, _T("Mike Blaszczak"));
```

The best part of a CString object is that it owns the memory, so is responsible for cleaning it up once it is gone. When you assign a new value to a CString object, it will grow the amount of memory it owns as appropriate to accommodate the longer text. While CString will grow its memory allocation, it will not shrink it until the string is emptied completely. This means that once the following code has been executed, str still owns about eighty bytes of memory, not nine:

```
CString str;
str = _T("Ask not what your country can do for you, "
            "ask what you can do for your country!");
str = _T("Smaller.");
```

When you destroy a CString object, either by letting the object fall out of scope or by using delete against a dynamically created object, the object will automatically free the memory associated with the string for you.

Designing with CStrings

Using CStrings in your application improves the robustness of your code in a few different ways. Due to the inherent protections of the debug builds in MFC, your testing will very rapidly uncover problems with array bounds. By using CString objects, you can frequently avoid the need to allocate memory yourself, eliminating mistakes in memory allocation code and in code that references arrays. MFC's careful support for its own string class lets your code do less work and MFC's code do more work – and this means you're getting more return on your investment in the library.

Despite the many considerable advantages of using CString, the class has a few pitfalls. Unfortunately, some of them can affect your performance. While some object-oriented pundits insist that you shouldn't need to worry about the implementation of a class when using it, this isn't a realistically obtainable goal at all times. While it might be possible to implement high-level classes that hide implementation details from their user, smaller classes – particularly data storage classes – are actually defined by access patterns and their implementation. For a class like CString, it's especially foolish to expect this level of opacity; it's just impossible to realize algorithms that have completely flat performance characteristics.

You should carefully consider what your use of CString will cause. As I implied, when I discussed the memory allocation patterns of CString objects, there are a few traps you can fall into when you use them. It's possible, for example, to beat the daylights out of the memory manager and make the CString class nearly overheat by doing lots and lots of concatenation. For those situations, you should either pre-allocate a long CString, or do your work in traditional C/C++ character arrays before copying the finished string to a CString object.

If you coded:

```
CString str;
int n;
for (n = 0; n < 16384;n++)
    str += _T('x');
```

you'd end up with a string that held the letter 'x' 16384 times. But you'd waste lots of time; this tiny loop takes over seven seconds to execute on a 90 MHz Pentium system. (And older versions of MFC take more than twice as long to execute it!)

OK, so my example is somewhat unrealistic; you'd be far better off using the constructor that allows you to prepare the string right off the bat – CString will be able to efficiently set all of the characters in one call. But you might be writing a loop that tries to build a string from 16384 database records than from single characters and the same point applies – you can cause CString to waste lots of time by doing concatenation. CString doesn't know how big you intend to let the string become, so it has to grow the string little by little each time you add a character. If it assumed the string was going to become very big, it might be able to skip some reallocations, but it would also be wasting memory... and that would be a problem if you had lots and lots and lots of CString objects.

Efficiency

We've examined the situations which leave you needing to perform special stunts during your use of `CString` objects: the most notable is the use of functions like `GetBuffer()` and `GetBufferSetLength()` to alter the internal size of the buffer and retrieve a pointer to the string's memory. I've covered that material for two reasons. First, so that you have a feel for the way `CString` works – and that insight will help you diagnose problems that you otherwise might not have been able to understand. The second reason is that you'll certainly spend more of your time as a developer figuring out how to fix strange situations. Since any code-monkey can see that:

```
CString str = _T("Hockey is Best");
CString sport = str.Left(6);
```

sets `sport` to `"Hockey"`, it's not really a good investment to spend time on explaining it. (And that part of `CString` is certainly pleasing to object-oriented purists; who cares where the bytes are stored?) But as you use `CString` more and more seriously in all of your programs, there are a couple of things you might need to understand first. One is quite technical, and the other is just a bit religious and intangible. Let's take the technical one, first.

CString Reference Counting

For MFC 4.0, Microsoft did some work to help improve the performance of code that uses `CString` objects. The technique employed is called **reference counting**. Reference counting lets MFC keep only one copy of a `CString`'s data in memory. The most important ramification of this technique is that a `CString`'s data isn't copied every time you use the assignment operator or pass a `CString` as a by-value parameter. In old versions of MFC, the following code would result in two copies of the string in memory:

```
CString strHomeTown = _T("Pittsburgh");
CString strFavoriteTeam = strHomeTown;
strHomeTown = strFavoriteTeam;
```

> *Pedantically, of course, there are* three *copies of the string: one in the application's initialized data segment and two more in the heap, created by the `CString` instances. For this discussion, I'm counting the number of dynamically allocated strings in use by MFC.*

In MFC Version 4.0 and later, `strHomeTown` actually bears a special flag indicating that it references the same string as `strFavoriteTeam`. This makes the assignment statement much faster than before. In old versions of MFC, the assignment does a memory allocation and a memory copy of all the bytes in the string. This is wasteful, particularly in the situations we investigated before: where the string is repeatedly changing size, or where the string exists only temporarily.

In the latest release of MFC, `strHomeTown` doesn't get its own copy of the string's data until `strFavoriteTeam` or `strHomeTown` are independently changed. That is, the class has code in it to minimize the number of allocations and reallocations that happen when you use the class to manage data.

Reference counting in CString is actually handled by a hidden implementation structure named CStringData. When a CString object is initialized, a new CStringData object is allocated. When a CString is copied, the new string finds out about the existing CStringData object instead of allocating its own. After the code fragment above executes, the reference management done by CString precludes the copy from happening. Instead, strHomeTown and strFavoriteTeam both point at the same CStringData object.

Outwardly, this really has no bearing on the way you'll perceive the string – again, thrilling the object-oriented pundits. You can still display strHomeTown; you can still pump strFavoriteTeam to the printer. You can still use either string in any way you want. If you change strFavoriteTeam, the implementation of CString will realize that the string data it's using is also being used by another string, so it will reallocate the data for you before performing the work on the new copy of the string data. After the two lines above execute, strFavoriteTeam simply references strHomeTown and doesn't have any data of its own. If we subsequently execute this code:

```
strFavoriteTeam += _T(" Penguins");
```

MFC immediately allocates strFavoriteTeam its own buffer because it is about to modify the string. It doesn't have its own string, and it would be unacceptable to change the data actually owned by another object. strFavoriteTeam quits referencing the CStringData object used by strHomeTown, and marks that CStringData object to reflect that fact – only then will MFC allocate an additional copy of the data before performing the concatenation. After the above statement executes, strFavoriteTeam and strHomeTown are back to the 'normal' state of being the sole CStrings with a reference to their data.

If we examine another example, we can see that CString can also change the state of a string if we alter the referenced string. Maybe I'll start with:

```
CString strHomeTown = _T("Pittsburgh");
CString strFavoriteTeam = strHomeTown;
```

and then code:

```
strHomeTown = _T("Seattle");
```

I'd find that strHomeTown would realize that the memory it was holding for the content of the string was no longer needed for itself, but it would know that some other string object is referencing the memory. strHomeTown, then, would not free the memory it originally allocated when we constructed it. Instead, it would just make a note of the fact that the memory was no longer being referenced. Effectively, strHomeTown would pass the ownership of that internal memory to strFavoriteTeam. strHomeTown would allocate its own buffer and toss the string "Seattle" into it.

While the exact details of CString's implementation are not important, it's certainly interesting to know that CString does this sort of management. Those details become particularly interesting as you decide how to craft functions that accept, return, and manipulate CString objects.

You might, for example, write a function that returns the name of your favorite team:

```
CString GetTeam()
{
    CString strTeam = _T("Pittsburgh Penguins");
    return strTeam;
}
```

If you call this function, you're likely to assign its result to another CString object:

```
CString strMyTeam = GetTeam();
```

In older versions of MFC, this code would cause a temporary CString object to be created. The temporary CString would allocate some memory for the string data within the function. The function would return that temporary object, and create another object named strMyTeam. strMyTeam would allocate its own memory, and then copy the string data from the temporary object to itself. The temporary object would be destroyed and its memory freed.

Since CString objects are passed about in programs very frequently, it was decided to tune MFC so that it didn't free and release this memory. Modern versions of MFC still create the temporary object for the return value of the function, have it allocate memory and initialize that memory with the string we've coded in the function, and then return that temporary object. But when the assignment happens, the new strMyTeam object simply references the data in the temporary object – it doesn't allocate its own memory. The temporary CString object is destroyed, but doesn't take the CStringData object it carries with it since that object knows that the strMyTeam object is reliant on it. So, in this situation, MFC is only doing as much memory management as is absolutely necessary.

When passing CString objects to a function, you'll need to select from one of three choices: you can use a reference to a CString, you can pass a CString object by value, or you can pass a pointer to a character array. Let's discuss what each of these choices means, so that we can understand which one's best for each of your functions.

CStrings as Replacements for String Constants

It's important to remember that using a CString allocates memory. As a result, you'll not want to use a CString when a plain old initialized C-type string will do just as well. I'd think this admonition would go without saying, but I've seen lots of code that uses CString when it really doesn't need to.

For instance, consider this declaration, at global scope:

```
const static CString strMyRegKey(_T("MyRegKey"));
```

If you're doing nothing with strMyRegKey(), other than passing it off to the registry functions in Win32, you're wasting your time. The compiler emits the string "MyRegKey" into the executable image. Then, at initialization time, MFC has to allocate some memory and copy that string – which is a string constant anyway! – into the memory MFC's allocated. The constant nature of the string means that you're quite unlikely to get any benefit of CString.

I've met many other developers who use CStrings in similarly questionable ways, but this is probably the most unforgivable example I've seen.

Especially since the authors of this code posted their source on the Internet after complaining loud and hard about how much MFC hurt their performance! If you don't write good code, a library will just let you make bigger mistakes faster.

CString Arguments by Value

When coding a function that manipulates a string, the simplest approach would seem to be passing a CString by value: maybe you'd code your function prototype as:

```
void Example(CString str);
```

This function receives a copy of any CString that you pass. This isn't as expensive as it sounds, because the reference semantics still apply; the passed string will initialize the function's local copy by causing it to reference the same data; while a temporary CString object will be created, it won't have to reallocate the data in the string. (And since a CString is only four bytes, even copying the whole thing wouldn't be so bad.) The function can alter the local CString, but if it does change the string, the data *will* be reallocated.

You can certainly use this function to pass plain CString objects:

```
CString str(_T("Something here"));
Example(str);
```

but you *can* also use the same prototype to pass regular pointers to strings, like this:

```
Example(_T("Something else"));
Example(pstrMyString);
```

The use of regular string pointers, or a string literal, works because CString has a constructor that takes a pointer to a string. The rules of the C++ language specify that it is acceptable to go hunting for a constructor that could be used to perform a conversion in this case, and that behavior is handy. But it's also inefficient; you're constructing a temporary CString object each time you call the function with a pointer to a plain string! If you need to receive a pointer to a string, you'll find it makes more sense to declare, instead, a function that accepts a pointer to a C-style array of characters using the LPCTSTR or LPTSTR types.

CString Arguments by Reference

You can, if you'd like, pass CString objects by reference. A function declared in such a way might look like this:

```
void Referencer(CString& str)
{
    str += _T("Hockey!");
}
```

The code within this function can manipulate the passed string directly, but such manipulations will actually change the string owned by the calling function. So, this code:

```
CString str(_T("My favorite is "));
Referencer(str);
```

```
printf(_T("%s\n"), (LPCTSTR)str);
```

will print the string My favorite is Hockey! to the standard output device. (While such a program might seem pointless, it's actually quite soothing.)

In some situations, this is just unacceptable; you'll want the calling function to have its own copy of the string so it might change it and do something interesting with the results. But, in cases where you're just referencing its content, the best way to introduce a CString into your function is by using a reference to a CString object. That way, you'll do *no* copying whatsoever – you won't even invoke the efficient reference copying semantics built into CString. Instead, you'll work on the CString object you were passed directly.

An interesting twist on the notion of passing a reference involves using the const modifier keyword to dictate that the object will not be changed by the function. That prototype would look like this:

```
void NoChange(const CString& str);
```

The body of the NoChange() function can't change the contents of the str string parameter. The addition of the const modifier causes a couple of interesting effects. First, the compiler knows the function can't change the object. This may help the compiler perform optimizations, particularly if this function turns out to be inline. Unfortunately, the compiler may not be as aggressive with the optimizations as you might expect because the C++ language allows developers to cast away constness.

More importantly, the C++ language *does* afford the compiler leeway in implicitly casting parameters to the function, now that the parameter is declared const. The previous example function, Referencer(), could not accept a string literal or a pointer to a string. In code, this means that you might be limited at how you call the function. If your parameter is a const reference, however, you can pass a string literal or a pointer to a string. Words of this language fail me; since I learned C++ before English, let's spell the facts out in their native tongue:

```
CString str(_T("The best is "));
Referencer(str);    // this is okay
Referencer(_T("Let's watch some ")); // this won't compile!
LPTSTR pstr = _T("These tickets are for ");
Referencer(pstr);   // this won't compile either!
NoChange(str);      // all of these are okay
NoChange(pstr);
NoChange(_T("In my house, it's "));
```

It should go without saying that reaching the goal of having your code do everything it should is far more important than any concern of style or efficiency; you don't have to be Howard Roark to understand that form follows function. As such, you should choose the parameter passing method that suits your program the best; serve the goals of your function, not the insecurities of your critics.

How To Decide

To summarize all of this, let's make a table that shows which string-type arguments grant our functions which features. The reasons for all of the answers this table provides are in the previous three sections – if you need more information or are concerned with one of my parenthetical little remarks, please do refer back a page or two to get the details.

In the meantime, here's mud in your eye:

Parameter Type	Accepts `CString`	Accepts pointer to string	Function Can Use `CString` member functions	Creates Temporary `CString`	Modified parameter modifies Caller's Data
`CString`	Yes	Yes	Yes	Yes	Yes
`CString&`	Yes	No	Yes	No	Yes
const `CString&`	Yes	Yes	Yes	Yes (if pointer)	Not modifiable!
`LPCTSTR`	Yes	Yes	No	No	Not modifiable!
`LPTSTR`	No	Yes	No	No	Yes

By deciding which parameter types developers who call your function are likely to pass, and by reaching a compromise between how you'll implement your function and your efficiency concerns, you should be able to choose a clear winner.

In some situations, you might not find the application of your function so clearly predictable – that's certainly true for developers on the MFC team. We must assume, in good faith, that the developer calling the function knows what they're doing best.

In anticipation of flexible usage, MFC usually provides two overloads of each function that accepts a `CString`: one implementation takes a `CString` reference, and the other takes an `LPCTSTR`. This covers all the bases as efficiently as possible; the C++ language won't force the construction of a temporary object when the caller passes a pointer to a string because the `LPCTSTR` overload is more appropriate. The `CString&` overload allows MFC to manipulate or copy the `CString` object as efficiently as possible.

Of course, the previous paragraph describes a generalization in the design of MFC – some functions are affected by mitigating circumstances and, certainly, the correct operation of the function is far more important than simply making the function efficient. My intent is not to rationalize the whole design of MFC, but to provide enough information so that you can make sense of some of the techniques used. Besides, I provide plenty of rationalization in the next section.

Why Not Standard string Objects?

Since 1992 (or so) authors have written that, by the time their readers see these words, the ANSI Standard Committee for the C++ language will have formally ratified its standard. I might be one of the first authors (of a book, at least) to say that the standard has finally been ratified. It's only taken since 1992, but it's finally with us!

The language standard defines a `string` class. `string` turns out to be a specialization of another class (also specified by the standard) called `basic_string<>`, but the two classes are really not that different: `basic_string<>` uses whatever type you'd like for its individual characters, while `string` uses `char`. This class is really actually nothing more than a collection of `char` type data – which fits the most abstract definition of a string that you can think of. The standard says the `string` class will implement the management and storage and retrieval of strings in a very specific way.

Unfortunately, that very specific way falls short for what many real programmers – and almost all Windows programmers – really need. The standard doesn't support the notion of casting string data from one format to another, and it doesn't address the issues presented specifically by Windows – such as loading a string resource from your application's binary resource table, converting string data to OLE and ANSI character sets and back. The standard string may not even necessarily be implemented with any of the cool reference counting features in `CString`.

To add further insult to injury, the ANSI-standard `string` class doesn't provide any implicit conversion operators. That is, you can't convert a string object to a pointer useful for passing data to an API or to a function that was written before the ANSI class became standard.

These terrible shortcomings make it easy to see why MFC doesn't adopt the standard `string` class in lieu of its own, `CString` class – which has been heavily tailored for Windows and is flexible enough to be compatible with existing data management techniques. The second best approach, which would have MFC derive its own class from the ANSI-standard `string` class, would simply be futile; you can't have the benefits of the standard and have the features you need in your own custom-derived class. Instead of expanding MFC by creating an MFC-specific string class, or by letting MFC derive its own class from the ANSI-standard class, expanding all MFC string-handling member functions to support both, and calling it the next version, you can expect to see MFC stick with its own string class – that makes the most sense for Windows programmers and MFC programmers alike.

In the meantime, you may wonder how to use the insertion and extraction operators with the standard C++ stream classes. It's quite possible, but it involves an understanding of how these operators really work and what types they use. If you dredge up the definition for one of the stream insertion operators, you'll find that it looks a little like this:

```
ostream& ostream::operator<<(const char* s);
```

So, if you code:

```
CString str(_T("When does the puck drop?"));
cout << str;
```

the language can implicitly cast your `CString` object to a `const char` pointer without further delay. However, reading a string isn't such a simple matter. You can't just code:

```
cin >> str;
```

because the C++ standard I/O streams don't know how to handle CString. CString, after all, needs to allocate memory for the string that's being read and doesn't know an appropriate way to make that happen. As such, you'll need to do it yourself. Perhaps the easiest way to do so would be to code a global implementation of the operator>>() function to work with CString, like this:

```
istream& operator>>(istream& stream, CString& str)
{
    LPTSTR pstr = str.GetBuffer(1024);
    stream >> pstr;
    str.ReleaseBuffer(-1);
    return stream;
}
```

Of course, we use istream instead of ostream here, because this is an input stream and not an output stream. You'll recognize the call to CString::GetBuffer() from our treatment of the CString buffer from earlier in the chapter. The limitation to this function is the same as any code that uses operator>> to do input – you can't control how much data will be placed into the string. If the call to the ostream::output>>() reads more than 1024 characters, we'll be in trouble. There's nothing you can do, though – istream doesn't know how to limit the amount of input that it will read.

Data Structure Wrappers

Developers with any experience of using the Windows SDK outside of a C++ development environment know there are lots of chores involving the management and conversion of data types. Being an operating system with a graphical user interface, Windows is quite fond of geometric primitives like points and rectangles, coded something like this:

```
RECT rectClient;
// get the client area of my window
GetWindowRect(hWnd, &rectClient);
int nMiddleX = (rectClient.right — rectClient.left)/2;
int nMiddleY = (rectClient.bottom — rectClient.top)/2;
```

Not only is this kind of coding tedious, it's error prone. As so much Windows code juggles data structures like this, it only makes sense that the Microsoft Foundation Classes would provide some assistance. Let's take a look at the data structures available to ease this pain.

Points

The most basic of the coordinate data types managed by Windows is the POINT struct, which, as you might guess, simply manages the x and y coordinates of one specific location. The structure has both coordinate values in one data type, which simplifies the manipulation of the data when you compare it to manipulating two integers separately.

The CPoint class in MFC completely wraps the POINT data type from the Windows SDK. A CPoint object has the same member variables as a POINT: integers named x and y. You can construct a new CPoint by passing the constructor the x and y values to initialize the point.

You can also pass a POINT or a SIZE, from which the x and y coordinates can be copied. Some Windows messages send points as two small integers packed into a DWORD value, so the CPoint constructor will also accept a DWORD.

The CPoint class is not based on CObject, but actually derives from the tagPoint structure used by the Windows SDK headers to make the POINT data type. As such, you can transparently pass a pointer to a CPoint object to any function or Windows API that normally takes a pointer to a POINT structure.

Comparing CPoints

MFC supports the comparison of CPoint objects using == or != operators. You can also use the -= or += operators to add a SIZE or CSize to a point in order to offset it by a given value. Binary + and − operators are also supported to assign a CPoint with a value offset from a second CPoint by a CSize or SIZE. The + operator is augmented by the Offset() function which allows you to separately manipulate the members of the function. These three code fragments are semantically identical:

Example 1	Example 2	Example 3
| ```
POINT pt;
pt.x = 10;
pt.y = 15;
pt.y += 22;
pt.x += 35;
``` | ```
CPoint pt(10, 15);
CSize sz;
sz.cx = 35;
sz.cy = 22;
pt += sz;
``` | ```
CPoint pt(10, 15);
pt.Offset(35, 22);
``` |

Each results with the point (45,37) in pt.

By providing these versatile extensions to a data type with which all Windows programmers work, MFC aids developer productivity. You don't have to worry about compatibility, since the CPoint has a cast operator to let you freely move between CPoint objects and POINT structures.

By the way, one of the side effects of these constructs is that you can avoid explicitly creating POINT structures when you only temporarily need one for a function call. You might be writing code like this when you call an API that accepts a point:

```
POINT pt;
pt.x = 35;
pt.y = 93;
PointOverThere(&pt);
```

Instead, you can cut this to one more readable line and minimize the length of time the extra memory is used:

```
PointOverThere(CPoint(35, 93));
```
```

The temporary CPoint object drops away as soon as the function returns. Temporary CPoint objects don't have the potential to be nearly as expensive as CString objects simply because CPoint objects are self-contained and CString objects need to allocate memory and potentially copy a large, variable-length block of data.

Sizes

MFC's CSize class wraps the Windows SDK SIZE structure. This structure is identical in content to the POINT structure; it contains two integers, but they're named cx and cy instead of x and y. As you might suspect, the main difference between SIZE and POINT (and therefore between CSize and CPoint) is purely conceptual. A CSize is used to indicate the size of an object, while a CPoint is used to indicate a location.

CSize doesn't feature an Offset() function like CPoint does, but it does feature a comparable set of operators. You can compare sizes by using == and !=. You can use the + operator to add one CSize to another, or the − operator to subtract. You can also use += and −= operators to increment or decrement one CSize by another.

The sparks really fly when you combine two points to make a rectangle. It's as if Pythagoras himself has grabbed you up and whipped you into another axis of freedom!

Rectangles

The Windows RECT structure is covered by MFC's CRect class. This class can be constructed without any parameters, or with four integers that describe the top, left, right and bottom edges of a rectangle. Of course, CRect also sports a copy constructor that will initialize it from another CRect. To calculate the dimensions of your rectangle, you can use the CRect::Height() function to compute the height, and CRect::Width() to find the rectangle's width.

You can also call IsRectEmpty() to see if the rectangle has height or width less than or equal to zero, and IsRectNull() to see if all four coordinates of the rectangle are 0.

You can use the CenterPoint() member of CRect to find a CPoint which marks the center of the rectangle. You can reference the top left point with TopLeft(), or the bottom right point with BottomRight().

You can always access the elements of a CRect class like you would the members of a RECT − the names of the members are even the same. CRect.left is the left-hand edge of the rectangle, CRect.right the right, CRect.bottom the bottom, and CRect.top the top. Fortunately, you can call SetRect(), to conveniently re-initialize all of the points in the rectangle in one statement. You can also zero a rectangle by using SetRectEmpty(). Note that this last function is inappropriately named, as it actually makes a null rectangle, not an empty one.

Many of my MFC samples use the CRect class for different calculations. Few use the class more aggressively than the Hexview sample, though. In its view, the OnDraw() and OnPreparePrinting() use both CRect and CPoint classes to calculate sizes and layout pages for all the rendering the application performs.

Normalizing Your Rectangle

One of the handiest aspects of CRect is the ability to normalize the rectangle. Most Windows APIs (and, as a result, some CRect functions) won't work if the rectangle's bottom and right edges are less than the top and left edges. You can call NormalizeRect() on the rectangle object to assure that it is normalized.

Often, you'll find that you don't have a CRect, you'll have the point at the top left or bottom right of the rectangle. The TopLeft() and BottomRight() functions (respectively) return a reference to such a CPoint object. Since these functions return a reference, you can use the function return as an l-value to make an assignment to the top left point:

```
CRect rect;
CPoint pt1(125, 129);
rect.TopLeft() = pt1;    // sets rect.left = 125 and rect.top = 129
```

Try to remember the TopLeft() and BottomRight() functions whenever you need a point. Their judicious use will make your code a lot more readable!

Moving and Resizing Your Rectangle

You can readily add area to a rectangle by using InflateRect(). This function takes a POINT, a SIZE or a pair of integers and adds the value to expand the rectangle's size by subtracting the passed width from the .left member, adding the passed width to the .right member, adding the passed height to the .bottom member and subtracting the passed height from the .top member. If a negative value is passed, the rectangle will shrink in size along the corresponding axis using the same rules.

You can move the rectangle by calling OffsetRect(). It also takes a POINT, a SIZE or a pair of integers, but instead of making the rectangle bigger, it effectively moves it by adding the same value to each of the rectangle's members. You can move the rectangle in either direction along each axis by using positive and negative values as appropriate. The OffsetRect() function is complemented by the slightly less verbose operator-= and operator+= functions, which have the same effect but only work with POINT data types.

You can get MFC to find the intersection of two rectangles using the IntersectRect() member or the & and &= operators. The intersection of the two rectangles is the largest contained by both rectangles passed to the function or used against the operator. The CRect class can similarly find the union of two rectangles (the smallest encompassing both rectangles) using the UnionRect() member function, or the |= and | operators. While these esoteric operators have some appeal, they can make for some rather unreadable code.

CRect also has equality (==) and inequality (!=) operators, allowing you to test two rectangles to see whether they cover the exact same space.

Handling Time Values

Because computers are rapid calculation and data management tools, they frequently need to compare something against time. The archiving of lab records, analysis of data over well-marked periods, or just the stamping of a file with the current date and time are all applications where some help with the management of time data types would be very helpful.

While the Visual C++ C run-time libraries provide the time_t type and the tm structure, MFC offers a far friendlier set of functions to help manipulate time-based values. The CTime class encapsulates these functions for your use.

CTime

CTime contains a variable of type time_t to maintain both time and date information internally. The raw time_t in the class is protected; you can access a copy of the value by calling GetTime(), but the original data isn't directly accessible. CTime can be constructed to initialize a time from time_t, or from DOS and Win32 time data structures. The two latter constructors are handy if you want to build a CTime for use against the time and date information on a file.

Thus, the range of a CTime object is predicted by the available range of time_t. For current versions of Visual C++, that means that CTime works from January 1st, 1970, until January 18th, 2038. time_t is presently a 32-bit quantity, and the range of the object is just 2^{32} seconds – nearly a lifetime, for most!

You can also construct a CTime from individual time components; this constructor takes six integers as parameters: the year, the month, the day of the month, the hour, the minute and the second value you wish to initialize.

Once the time value is initialized, you can call GetHour(), GetMinute() or GetSecond() to retrieve any time component of the value. The date components are retrieved by calling GetYear(), GetDay() or GetMonth().

Note that the CTime structure in current versions of MFC is limited to dates from 1970 to 2038. The values passed to the six-integer constructor of CTime are not range-checked in release builds of MFC, but out-of-bounds values for these functions will cause ASSERT() messages in debug builds. If you need better precision or a wider range of dates, keep reading until you get to the COleDateTime section in this chapter.

To add to the convenience of using CTime, MFC includes operators for the CTime class. You can perform a full compliment of comparisons with the normal comparison operators, or you can use an assignment operator to assign a CTime or a time_t to an existing CTime object.

You can convert a CTime value into a printable string using the Format() member of the CTime class. The function allows you to specify a string which contains percent-sign (%) formatting commands, similar to the way the run-time library printf() function works. These formatting commands, though, are tuned to the needs of time and date information.

This table shows which formatting commands you can use and what effect they'll have:

Formatting Command	Description
%a	An abbreviated form of the weekday name (*Sun* or *Thu*, for example)
%A	The full weekday name (that is, *Thursday* or *Sunday*)
%b	An abbreviated month name (for example, *May* or *Apr*)
%B	The full name of the month (such as *September* or *May*)
%c	The complete date and time representation appropriate for locale; this is dependent on the settings in the Control Panel
%d	The day of the month as an unpadded decimal number (for example *3* or *23*)
%H	The hour in 24-hour format (00 through 23)
%I	The hour in 12-hour format (01 through 12)
%j	The day of the year as a padded number (001 through 365, and sometimes 366)
%m	The month as a decimal number (01 – 12)
%M	The minute as a decimal number (00 – 59)
%p	The current locale's AM/PM indicator for 12-hour clock
%S	The second as a decimal number (00 – 59)
%U	The week of the year as a decimal number, with Sunday as the first day of the week (00 – 51)
%w	The weekday as a decimal number (0 – 6; Sunday is 0)
%W	The week of the year as a decimal number, with Monday as the first day of the week (00 – 51)
%x	The date representation for current locale
%X	The time representation for current locale
%y	The year without the century as a decimal number (for example, 03 or 93)
%Y	The year with the century as a decimal number (for example, 2003 or 1993)
%z	Lowercase version of %Z
%Z	The time-zone name or abbreviation; no characters if the time zone is unknown

If you're experienced with C, you probably recognize these commands as being the same as those for the standard strftime() function. And, in fact, MFC is calling strftime() to do the formatting for it. That has the side effect of automatically localizing the output of the routine. If you ask for a month or a day name, for example, the name is given in the language that matches the current locale.

Performing Time Math

By introducing another class together with addition and subtraction operators to the CTime class, MFC enables the application of date math to CTime objects. You can use the minus operator to subtract one CTime object from the other. The result is a CTimeSpan object, which can later be added to a CTime object using the plus operator.

CTimeSpan can:

> record differences about as large as sixty-seven years with a resolution of one second

> be compared with other CTimeSpan objects using the normal comparison operators

> support addition and subtraction operators forming other CTimeSpan objects

> be used to add or remove time from a CTime object

You can examine the content of a CTimeSpan by calling its GetDays(), GetHours(), GetMinutes() and GetSeconds() members. Taken as a whole, these values represent the quantity of time in the CTimeSpan.

You can call GetTotalHours(), GetTotalMinutes() or GetTotalSeconds() to return the integral time in the span expressed in the units specified by the function.

You can also create CTimeSpan objects by directly constructing them. The CTimeSpan constructors can accept time_t types or a reference to another CTimeSpan to perform a copy. You may also pass the individual components of the time span to the constructor, specifying a LONG number of days and integers for the number of hours, minutes and seconds you wish to initialize in the time span.

CTimeSpan has a Format() member which is similar to, but not quite as comprehensive as, the Format() function in CTime.

Daylight Saving Time

As you work with CTimeSpan, you must remember that the results you get from CTimeSpan, and the continuity of CTime itself, will be affected by daylight saving time. If you live in an area where daylight saving time isn't used, it's up to you to make sure the machine knows about it. The C run-time documentation includes information about how daylight saving time and normal time zone information is kept in the library. Since the CTime class is based on the time routines in the C run-time library, the documentation also applies to MFC.

The C run-time library gains information about your machine's time zone from the TZ environment variable. If there is no TZ environment variable in effect when your program initializes, the C run-time libraries look for information from the operating system – settings that you can manipulate using the Control Panel. Look for information on the _daylight, _timezone, and _tzname variables in the C run-time documentation for the exact rules that affect you.

MFC's other date/time management class, `COleDateTime`, treats time as a pile of seconds — it doesn't pay attention to daylight saving rules.

COleDateTime

While `CTime` is a great general-purpose date/time management class, it has several limitations. Most notably, it's only useful for times that fall in between January 1, 1970, and January 18, 2038, and that don't need a resolution of more than one second. For many applications, this range is just fine — no program I write needs to care, even about those twenty-three days before I was born, but I couldn't talk the rest of the team into changing the `CTime` epoch. On the other hand, if you're writing a program which tracks the Kennedy family and the consequences of their actions, you'll not only need a huge hard drive but also a better time management class.

MFC implements a class called `COleDateTime`. The purpose of this class is to wrap the OLE `DATE` and `TIME` data types. You'll find that these data types (and therefore the `COleDateTime` class) is capable of near-millisecond precision from the first of January in year 100 of the common era to the thirty-first of December in year 9999 of the common era — or whatever era we'll be using at that time!

`COleDateTime` looks a lot like the `CTime` class, so I won't describe its individual functions here. There are two really important differences, though, which are appropriate to examine. The first is that, as its name implies, `COleDateTime` relies on the OLE (COM) subsystem in Windows. This means that using `COleDateTime` requires that you add the `Afxdisp.h` header file to your application. Doing so will bring in a little bit more of MFC, and will also make your application dependent on a few additional system DLLs. This means that your application will take more memory. If it uses OLE anyway, you won't even notice the difference, but if you otherwise have no interest in OLE support in your application, you might want to think about inventing your own date-time management class.

The other interesting difference between `COleDateTime` and `CTime` is that `COleDateTime` features a much more interesting `Format()` member function. As you'll recall, the `CTime::Format()` function is roughly similar to the `strftime()` function of the C run-time library. The `COleDateTime` class implements a `Format()` function which can do all this, but can also format time according to the settings that the user has made in the **Internationalization** or **Regional Settings** dialog of **Control Panel** on their machine. The `Format()` function in `CTime` only makes the standardized locale available.

As `CTimeSpan` is to `CTime`, so is `COleDateTimeSpan` to `COleDateTime`. That is, you can calculate and format differences between events identified by two `COleDateTime` objects using `COleDateTimeSpan`. Again, `COleDateTimeSpan` is similar enough that it doesn't warrant extra coverage here. It's enough to say, though, that `COleDateTimeSpan` is capable of handling the vaster differences in the range encompassed by `COleDateTime` objects.

The Year 2000

Many people in the computer world are alarmed about the year 2000. The turn of the millennium will bring problems only to those who've asked for it; if you've stored information in a format which needs to be read by a computer, you'll find you need to ensure the data is inclusive of information about the century. Starting on January First, 2000, the string "00" won't be readily identifiable as a specific year; it might refer to the year 2000, or it might designate the year 1900.

Some systems already have this problem: my driver's license expires in the year "01". Those coppers will *never* catch me!

If you feed the string "00" to one of the conversion functions, you might or might not get the year 2000 back. This behavior is a cross between a bug and a feature: some code in OLE translates "00" to 2000 depending on which locale you're running in, and some doesn't. Maybe it'll be stable by the year 2000, but the only real solution is for you to fix the bug in your code. You need to ask for less ambiguous things. The string "2000" means a date in the year 2000 no matter *what* locale you're in or what version of the OLE system DLLs you have installed. If that's what you mean, that's what you should ask for.

In the year 2000, I'll turn thirty. Thankfully, I already have a sports car and a motorcycle, so I won't need to do any shopping to get my mid-life crisis started.

Exception Handling

Professionally written code always checks the result of any function called to make sure that it doesn't run into an error. Software should be robust; maybe it can't run in every situation, but it should be able to detect those situations and do something useful about them. Unfortunately, this means that code often has to include if statements, which nest very, very deeply as you touch more and more things that might fail. For example, let's write the name of a president to a file:

```
LPTSTR pstrName = NULL;
FILE* fOutput = NULL;
BOOL bSuccess = FALSE;

fOutput = _tfopen(_T("PREZ.DAT"), _T("w"));
if (fOutput != NULL)
{
   pstrName = _tcsdup(_T("John Fitzgerald Kennedy"));
   if (pstrName != NULL)
   {
      if (_fputts(pstrName, fOutput) == _tcslen(pstrName))
         bSuccess = TRUE;
      free(pstrName);
   }
   fclose(fOutput);
}
```

Even for this simple example, we're already indenting three levels to handle all of the possible errors. Adding to this, implementing a more complicated (and more realistic) example would show the real weakness behind this way of programming: you'd indent forever, you'd forget about uninitializing other things after unrelated error conditions, and your code wouldn't be very maintainable.

To address the code quality, readability and maintainability issues that if-else-based checking raises, the C++ language introduces the concept of exceptions. The idea is that you can readily implement constructs that clean up the errors and release resources, avoiding the need to check return values from functions and the implied need for callers to know how their functions work internally.

The code example we discussed before is slightly more readable if we use exception handling mechanisms:

```
LPTSTR pstrName = NULL;
FILE* fOutput = NULL;
BOOL bSuccess = FALSE;

try
{
    fOutput = _tfopen(_T("PREZ.DAT"), _T("w"));
    if  (fOutput == NULL)
        throw _T("Failed to open file!");

    pstrName = _tcsdup(_T("John Fitzgerald Kennedy"));
    if (pstrName == NULL)
        throw _T("Failed to allocate memory!");

    if (_fputts(pstrName, fOutput) == _tcslen(pstrName))
        throw _T("Failed to write data!");

    bSuccess = TRUE;
}
catch(LPCTSTR pstr)
{
    PostErrorMessage(pstr); // fictitious function
}

if (fOutput != NULL)
    fclose(fOutput);
free(pstrName);
return bSuccess;
```

The second code fragment is cooler than the first in lots of ways. First, it doesn't indent all over the place and leave lots of questions about what will happen when an error is handled. This might not seem so intuitive if you're not well-weathered by the C++ winds, but you'll quickly learn to let your eyes hop down to the catch() block to see what's going to happen. The catch() block and all of its contents are known as the **exception handler**. This fragment also allows us to naturally clean up from the work that we were doing. With a little careful coding, you can do all of the tidying for both error and non-error conditions in one place.

Hiding the Error Handling Mechanism

The other interesting thing is a bit hidden, but is probably the most important. If you want to, you could code throws in any function, expecting that the caller of the function is making the call from within a try block to later catch the exception. This completely hides the error handling mechanism, which would be some sort of return-value setup. If you had used real C++ operators (like calling new instead of strdup() or _tcsdup()), you would have been able to benefit from the exceptions that the standard implementation of the functions would throw, simplifying the code.

In the meantime, let's look closer at how the second example really works. The throw statements cause a jump to the appropriate exception handler, and also unwinds the stack. The throw keyword expects an expression, the type of which determines the exception handler which will be invoked.

Multiple Catch Statements

A `try/catch` block might have more than one `catch` statement to handle different types of exceptions. You can just concatenate the extra `catch()` code to the end of the block. Maybe we want to handle the memory allocation error a little differently:

```
try
{
    // ... other code ...

    pstrName = _tcsdup(_T("John Fitzgerald Kennedy"));
    if (pstrName == NULL)
        throw _tcslen(_T("John Fitzgerald Kennedy"));

    // ... other code ...
}
catch(LPCTSTR pstr)
{
    // ... throw string handler ...
}
catch(const size_t& n)
{
    _tprintf(_T("ERROR!  Couldn't get %d bytes\n"), n);
}

// ... uninitialization code ...
```

The new `throw` statement takes a `size_t` expression which will result from the call to `_tcslen()` to see how much memory wasn't available. The additional `catch` statement accepts that `size_t` and formats a nice error message with it. Note that, even though `size_t` is an integer underneath, we don't catch an integer because it's always a good idea to catch a type which is as unique as possible. In real life, you'll probably want to make your own data type or class for your custom exception situations. You might consider deriving your exception class from MFC's `CException`.

> Note that **CUserException** (which we'll investigate in a few pages) is not designed to be a user-defined exception type. Here, *'user'* refers to the **USER** module, one of the core components of Windows, and not the user of the class library. It may, however, refer to something the user of the resulting program has done.

Since the `catch` statement isn't limited to simple types, you have the ability to wrap almost any kind of functionality around the data surrounding the error. You can use the class to hold more information about the error, or to provide more functions to clean up or reset the state of the device that caused the error for example. MFC offers several such error reporting classes. Let's take a look at them in the remainder of this section.

Exceptions and MFC

Microsoft's first C++ compiler, Microsoft C/C++ version 7.0, didn't support the C++ exception syntax. At the time, the syntax was just in its final stages of ratification. Unfortunately, subsequent compilers didn't implement exceptions either. Version 8.0 of the compiler was shipped in Visual C++ 1.0, while a 32-bit version of the compiler was made available in Visual C++ 1.1, but the public had to wait until version 2.0 for exception handling support to appear in the compiler.

However, MFC started supported exception handling in MFC 2.0, which was bundled with Visual C++ 1.0. MFC provided this support using a set of macros, even though the underlying compiler didn't support exceptions. The idea was that MFC was a class library and wouldn't make much of an impact on the world if it avoided the use of a C++ idiom that was, at the time, gaining lots of popularity. Without the compiler's support for exceptions under it, the Microsoft Foundation Class library had to implement its own exception handling macros and classes.

The macros which MFC defines to be used for exception handling are defined with the same names as the C++ keywords. They are differentiated from the standard C++ keywords by being all uppercase. Since the macro implementation for exception handling keywords couldn't provide exactly the same functionality with the same set of keywords, there are a few extra macros for special situations. In modern versions of MFC, the macros map directly to real C++ exception keywords. The macros and keywords compare like this:

MFC Macro	Standard C++ Construct
TRY	try
CATCH	catch
AND_CATCH	catch
END_TRY	catch(CException* pEx) {...
THROW	throw *expr*;
THROW_LAST	throw;
CATCH_ALL	catch(CException* pEx) {...

Note that the MFC CATCH() and AND_CATCH() macros take two parameters: the type of catch and a data item in which to store that type of exception; the normal C++ catch keyword accepts a data declaration there. You'll also note there's a special MFC macro, named AND_CATCH, which you can use when you need to catch another exception in the same exception handler.

The MFC CATCH_ALL macro and the END_TRY macro both resolve to catching pointers to CException objects. CATCH_ALL does not resolve to catch(...) as you may originally guess, and END_TRY was originally designed to be a backstop for unhandled exceptions in a TRY block. The table above doesn't list all of the MFC macros – the ones not shown simply provide syntactic sugar. END_CATCH, for example, closes all of the extra brackets that the CATCH macro put into your program.

One thing the macros do hide is the management of CException objects which have already been thrown. If you catch a pointer to a CException-derived object, it is your responsibility to delete the object once you've handled it. This means your code will probably be of the form:

```
try
{
    pFile->Open(/* params */);
}
catch (CFileException* pEx)
{
    pEx->ReportError();
    pEx->Delete();
}
```

The `Hexview` sample has code exactly of this form in an `OnOpenDocument()` override in `CHexViewDoc`. As we learned back in Chapter 4, this override allows us to directly read the file without letting any extra data from MFC's serialization get in the way. For `Hexview`, which dumps hexidecimal data from any file, reading the raw file is of paramount importance! Once the file is opened, the sample hangs on to the `CFile` object in the document object and other members of the document class can read from it as needed by the view.

Note that you must not invoke `operator delete` on the exception pointer. Instead, you need to call the `CException::Delete()` member on the object. Some exceptions which MFC throws are raised in low-resource conditions, which means MFC has to throw a pointer to an exception object which was preallocated in MFC's static data area, long before the exception was actually caused. (Think of the alternative – if MFC was going to throw an exception for a low memory condition, it certainly couldn't allocate a new `CMemoryException` object on the heap!) Since such an exception object is really a static object, you can't blindly call `operator delete` against it. Instead, you should call the `Delete()` member of `CException` – which knows how to handle the exception appropriately.

CException

The MFC exception macros revolve around the `CException` class. This class doesn't contain any very interesting member variables or functionality beyond the backbone of exception handling and cleanup. When a `CException`-derived class is thrown, `CException` prints a message to the trace device to show that the exception has been thrown. However, the real functionality comes as MFC uses various classes which are declared for each type of exception which may be thrown. MFC implements these exception types:

```
CArchiveException
CDaoException
CDBException
CFileException
CInternetException
CMemoryException
CNotSupportedException
COleDispatchException
COleException
CResourceException
CUserException
```

We can't list all the MFC functions which might throw an exception here, but you can get a good idea of what a given MFC function may do if you have a look at that function's documentation. If the declaration of the function shows a `throw()` specifier, the call is capable of throwing that type of exception. In the meantime, let's take a quick peek at each `CException` type to see what it can do for us. Some of the `CException`-derived classes get coverage in other parts of the book; `CInternetException`, for example, is covered in Chapter 17, which discusses Internet Client Programming with MFC.

CMemoryException

The `CMemoryException` class is thrown by any Microsoft Foundation Class or library function which allocates memory. Most often, these little monsters come flying out of MFC's OLE classes when your application is handed a defective transfer buffer or interface from another application. Several other classes also generate them; a `CEditView` can throw one when the edit control in the view runs out of memory, for example.

Most memory exceptions are thrown when you call `new` to get some memory. If the operating system can't satisfy your request, the exception will be thrown and you'll need to handle it if you don't want your application to die in a fiery crash. Note that Windows NT is a beast of an operating system; you'll have to completely exhaust physical, paged and committed memory before `new` finally fails.

Of course, your code may be destined for some other 32-bit platform, like Windows 95/98 and Windows NT/2000, so it's always a good idea to ensure your application has something reasonable to do when `new` fails.

CUserException

The `CUserException` class is a thin derivation of the `CException` class. A `CUserException` is thrown by MFC whenever a user-interface related problem arises. In the dialog data exchange routines, for example, a `CUserException` is thrown by calling `AfxThrowUserException()` when validation fails against one of the fields involved in the data exchange operation – MFC uses `CUserException` for this situation since that exception type denotes something in the application's interaction with the user has gone wrong. `CUserExceptions` have no accessible member variables, so `AfxThrowUserException()` takes no parameters.

The MFC-supplied code in `CWnd::DoDataExchange()`, `CDocument::ReportSaveLoadException()` and `CWndProc::ProcessUserException()` all have backstops which do nothing when handling a `CUserException`, but react and/or complain appropriately when handling other, more serious exceptions. As a result, you can throw a `CUserException` without causing your application to halt, but it still signals the exception and lets you out of the function or loop you're running.

CNotSupportedException

There are a few functions in MFC which are implemented without support. You can't call `Duplicate()` on a `CMemFile`, for instance. There are also some actions or option flags which are not supported. For example, you can't subclass a window more than once using MFC, and you can't specify a versionable serialization when you are *writing* data to a serialization object – versionable schemas only work when reading. In these circumstances, MFC will throw a `CNotSupportedException`.

This exception is unlike others in MFC, because it's designed never to be caught in release builds – it's for debugging purposes only. If, in testing, your debug code ever nets this exception, you should check to find out what silly thing you've done in your code.

CDBException

In a later chapter, we'll discuss some special MFC classes designed to aid access to database files and servers.

The database classes rely on some pretty complicated mechanisms to pass data around. In the simplest case, things are at least as complicated as getting data from, or putting data to, a file. In the most elaborate case, the database object is helping your program communicate with a far off machine which is running powerful and complicated database server software.

The CDBException class encapsulates the error information that database errors generate. Since the MFC database classes lie upon ODBC (Microsoft's Open Database Connectivity API), the most important error code contained in CDBException mimics the RETCODE which all ODBC APIs return. This value is stored in m_nRetCode. The string associated with that error is stored in m_strError. Since not all ODBC drivers share the same capabilities, some m_nRetCodes will have no corresponding error string; m_strError may be empty.

CDBException also contains information about the error that comes directly from the database software and isn't standardized to conform to ODBC's error code conventions. The m_strStateNativeOrigin member contains a string of the form "State: %s, Native: %ld, Origin %s". The state value describes the state that caused the error; it's a five character alphanumeric string, the meaning of which is defined by ODBC. (See Appendix A of the *Programmers' Reference* book in the ODBC SDK.)

The number following the word Native in the string is the native error number from the data source. This number isn't touched by ODBC; it comes directly from the database software serving the query that failed.

The final substring in m_strStateNativeOrigin is an indicator of the error's source. Each component in the multi-tiered ODBC architecture tacks on an extra string here, so the exact source for the error code can be readily identified. If something chokes on SQL Server, you might get "[Microsoft][ODBC SQL Server Driver][SQL Server]" as the error origin string. However, if the error was raised by the SQL Server driver and not by the database itself, the string would only contain "[Microsoft][ODBC SQL Server Driver]".

While CDBExceptions can be thrown with the AfxThrowDBException() function, they aren't constructed like other MFC exceptions. The parameters to AfxThrowDBException() provide the exception with the RETCODE which caused the exception, a pointer to the CDatabase and the HSTMT context which caused the error; this function then constructs the CDBException. The constructing code will determine the string and source information from the database software and ODBC database driver before returning.

CDaoException

Starting with Version 4.0, MFC provides classes which facilitate data access with DAO, or **Data Access Objects**. Data access objects are Automation objects served by the system which allow your application to work with databases managed by the Jet database engine. The Jet Engine, besides being named to be easily marketed, is the database engine which is also shipped with Microsoft Access and Visual Basic.

When you use the DAO-related classes, which we'll examine in Chapter 12, error conditions will throw CDaoException objects. The exact error code is returned as an SCODE in the m_scode member of the exception object. SCODE is a special data type used by COM to convey error conditions, and is entirely equivalent to the more widely known HRESULT in 32-bit Windows. In fact, as fate has it, the SCODE has been deprecated as a datatype in favor of the HRESULT.

Unfortunately, MFC was written before that deprecation happened. Rather than break all users of CDaoException, MFC is sticking with the equivalent (but older) datatype.

The CDaoException object references some DAO-specific error information via its m_pErrorInfo member. This member points to information about the specific error which caused the exception to be thrown. Usually, the data access objects will report only one error at a time. However, in some circumstances, they will throw more than one at a shot. You can find out how much error information is available by calling CDaoException::GetErrorCount().

You can find information about each specific error with a call to GetErrorInfo(). This function takes an integer which identifies the index of the error information of your desire. The error information isn't returned from the function – it causes the m_pErrorInfo pointer to point to the error information.

CFileException

File I/O is one of the greatest source of exceptions, next to memory allocation. Sometimes, it seems like almost anything can go wrong while you're working with a file: lack of disk space, network volumes going off-line, protection problems, file locking issues and so on, all make file I/O a risky business. MFC will throw a CFileException from any of its file I/O classes: CFile, CStdioFile, CMemFile and COleStreamFile are all suspects when a CFileException shows up. Some other related classes, which depend on classes from the CFile tree, are also potential perpetrators when a CFileException is thrown.

Saving a CFileException

When you catch a CFileException, you can examine its member variable to see exactly what went wrong. The object contains two data members: m_cause and m_lOsError. The latter code can be used to retrieve an error from the system's _sys_errlist[] array. Code to get an error message from the operating system might go something like this:

```
catch(CFileException* e)
{
   CString str;
   if (e->m_lOsError == -1)
      str.Format(_T("Can't: %d, %ld (%s)\n"), e->m_cause, e->m_lOsError,
            _sys_errlist[e->m_lOsError]);
   else
      str.Format(_T("Can't: %d, %ld (%s)\n"), e->m_cause, e->m_lOsError,
            _sys_errlist[e->m_lOsError]);
   MessageBox(str, _T("File Open Error"));
}
```

The declaration for _sys_errlist[] comes from Stdlib.h, so you must be sure to #include this file when you build your project. The Stdlib.h header also provides many constants which equate to the different possible values for m_lOsError. You can test against these values to react to specific errors in specific ways.

On the other hand, m_cause is set to one of several MFC-defined constants. The possible values are given here:

MFC-defined constants	Description
CFileException::none	No error was detected.
CFileException::generic	Some error occurred that MFC couldn't identify. You'll need to check m_lOsError to find out what really happened.
CFileException::fileNotFound	The filename which was specified to an opening operation couldn't be found.
CFileException::badPath	Some part of the path is invalid – maybe an incorrect drive letter.
CFileException::tooManyOpenFiles	There weren't enough open file buffers or handles to satisfy the file open request.
CFileException::accessDenied	The operating system or network blocked access to the file for security or file attribute reasons.
CFileException::invalidFile	The file handle used was bad. Either the file handle was closed or it was never opened.
CFileException::removeCurrentDir	You tried to remove the current working directory.
CFileException::directoryFull	You tried to add a file to the root directory of a volume, but there are no more file entries in that directory.
CFileException::badSeek	The file read/write pointer couldn't be set.
CFileException::hardIO	There was a hardware error during an I/O operation.
CFileException::sharingViolation	You wanted to share a file which wasn't available to you because of sharing protection.
CFileException::lockViolation	There was an attempt to lock a region which was already locked.
CFileException::diskFull	The device where the file resides has no more free space.
CFileException::endOfFile	A request was made to read past the end of file.

Purposefully Throwing a CFileException

By the way, you can throw an error by creating a new CFileException object and setting its m_lOsError and/or m_cause members in the constructor. The CFileException constructor takes both of these values, but also provides defaults for both of them.

The `CFileException` class constructor has this prototype:

```
CFileException(int cause = CFileException::none, LONG lOsError = -1);
```

You can also throw a `CFileException` by calling `CFileException::ThrowOsError()` and passing an operating system error number – any of the error number constants from `Stdlib.h` will do. MFC will automatically fill in the appropriate `m_cause` code as the exception is constructed. You can translate an operating system error code to an `m_cause` code at any time by calling `CFileException::OsErrorToException()`.

> `OsErrorToException()` and **ThrowOsError()** are both **static** members of `CFileException`, so you don't even need a **CFileException** object to use the functions.

If you don't have an applicable `m_lOsError` value, you can call `ThrowErrno()` to throw the exception. Again, this member of `CFileException` is `static`, so you can use it at any time. `CFileExceptions`, which have an `m_cause` value but no `m_lOsError`, keep `-1` in the `m_lOsError` member; you should make sure your code is able to deal with this eventuality.

`AfxThrowFileException()` is always available to create and throw `CFileException` objects as well, but it only provides a default parameter for `m_lOsError` – you must specify a value for the `m_cause` member.

CArchiveException

As we discussed in previous chapters, MFC's `CArchive` class is used to serialize data to or from persistent classes. The class may need to report an error if the object that's being recreated from serialization can't be created before its member data is read. This limitation is caused by the use of a `CMap` object to track the location of objects in the file.

CResourceException

MFC will throw a resource exception whenever it needs to find a resource but can't. This most often occurs when it's looking for a string resource. You can throw a resource exception by coding:

```
AfxThrowResourceException();
```

Resource exceptions don't provide any information about the exception. Most `CResourceExceptions` are thrown from `CDialog`, `CToolBar` and `CControlBar` and their derivatives. Note that MFC will also throw a resource exception in instances where a resource doesn't seem to be directly involved, particularly when trying to attach a C++ GDI object to a `NULL` or an unloadable Windows GDI object.

Common Exception Features

All CException-derived exceptions feature a couple of interesting functions: GetErrorMessage() and ReportError(). GetErrorMessage() has a prototype that looks like this:

```
BOOL GetErrorMessage(LPTSTR lpszError, UINT nMaxError, PUINT pnHelpContext = NULL);
```

For the lpszError parameter, you'll need to provide a pointer to a buffer which you own. You can specify the size of that buffer with the nMaxError parameter. When you call GetErrorMessage() on a CException or CException-derived object that you've caught, the function will populate your buffer with an error message which describes the exact error condition. If the function can successfully describe the error message, it returns TRUE. If it can't, it returns FALSE.

You have the option of providing the address of a UINT for the third parameter. If you do, your UINT will be populated with a help context ID which describes the error message. For most error messages which come from MFC, the UINT will be exactly equal to the identifier for the string resource where the error message was stored. Error messages from CFileExceptions, CDBExceptions, COleExceptions and CDaoExceptions are formatted dynamically and will not have a help context ID with them. You can learn how MFC gets the text for these errors by reading up on ::FormatMessage() later in (well, darn near the end of) this chapter.

Most GetErrorMessage() calls don't deal with CStrings, by the way, because there might not be enough memory to *get* a CString.

If you decide to make your own CException-derived classes to help you deal with problems in your application, you should make sure you implement an override for GetErrorMessage() in that class so that you can report errors easily.

MFC Macros vs. Standard Exception Handling

Although you can still use the MFC exception handling macros, you really should use standard C++ exception handling in all modern code. You can use C++ exception handling against the standard C++ types, plus any primitive or compound data type you can think of. The disadvantage to the macros is they can only catch CException-derived exceptions. Older versions of MFC used stock C++ code without the exception keywords to implement the exception handling macros but, starting with version 3.0, the macros equate to some compatibility code plus constructs which use the real C++ exception keywords. This means that real C++ exceptions are more compatible, and they are used internally by MFC anyway.

Note that there's a huge difference between MFC exceptions in previous versions of the compiler and standard C++ exceptions in new versions. In old versions, you would find that temporary objects weren't destroyed when you used MFC exceptions to escape a function. Of course, the objects were removed from the stack, but data they might reference wasn't cleaned up because their destructors were never called. This could result in memory leaks, particularly if the objects contained dynamically allocated information, as CStrings do.

As mentioned earlier, this was the reason behind CString's Empty() member function. You'd have to call this member for any CStrings which would go out of scope when you handled an exception. Otherwise, when the function died, all of the memory owned by the CStrings wouldn't be freed and you'd be left with a large memory leak.

The Visual C++ 6.0 Solution

Thankfully, this awkwardness has been done away with. Visual C++ now supports the normal semantics implied by standard C++ exceptions: the generated code will correctly call the destructors on local objects, allowing them to free their memory and resources. Visual C++ has featured such exception handling semantics since Version 2.0.

However, this functionality is only enabled when you use the /GX command line switch on the compiler; by default, this functionality is off, but the AppWizard-produced project files have the switch on. You can find the setting for your project by looking at the C++ tab in the Project Settings dialog. Check for the Enable Exception Handling check box when you have C++ Language selected in the Category: drop-down. The dialog and page you're after are shown below:

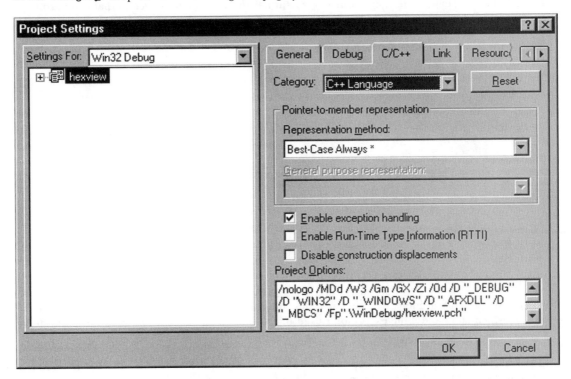

If you write programs which work with MFC, you should *always* use the /GX option. If you don't, your application can leak memory in rare circumstances. Unfortunately, those circumstances are exactly when it's most dangerous to leak memory – while handling error conditions. Never compile a program which uses MFC without the /GX option. You may find it tempting to not use /GX, especially if you find out that programs built without /GX don't have code to unwind exceptions and can be, in extreme cases, fifteen to twenty percent smaller than the same code with the /GX option. But just don't do it – it's not worth it.

Note that after defining the _AFX_OLD_EXCEPTIONS flag, you can rebuild MFC to cause it to use the old, non-unwinding exception code. You should never need to do this; if you do, the code in question is broken and should be fixed. If there's something else pressing you, you can rebuild MFC while carefully making sure _AFX_OLD_EXCEPTIONS is defined; this will make MFC revert to the old exception code.

You should try to use standard C++ exception syntax when you can because it's slightly faster and results in a code image that's ever so slightly smaller.

Win32 Structured Exception Handling

There is another type of exception which can be caught by applications running under Windows NT/2000 and Windows 95/98; these are exceptions generated by the operating system. These exceptions are raised when your application does something which is trapped at the system level, such as divide by zero.

The syntax for catching the exceptions is very similar to the try/catch code that standard C++ code uses, but instead, you'll need to use the __try/__except keywords.

A typical exception trap might look something like this:

```
int CarefulDivide(int n, int d, int nNotANumber)
{
    int nResult;

    __try
    {
        nResult = n/d;
    }
    __except(GetExceptionCode() == EXCEPTION_FLT_DIVIDE_BY_ZERO)
    {
        TRACE(_T("Bogus divide trapped!\n"));
        return nNotANumber;
    }

    return nResult;
}
```

As with standard C++ exception handling, the __try statement opens the block of code to watch for exceptions. When that block of code ends, the compiler expects to see one or more __except blocks, which can handle the exception raised in the __try block. The statement in parentheses governs the type of action which the exception handler will take.

Most exception handlers will be coded as the above example, with a comparison between a defined constant and a call to the GetExceptionCode() function. If the values are equal, the exception handler is executed and all other handlers are ignored. You can code any number of GetExceptionCode() handlers to trap any variety of errors.

EXCEPTION_EXECUTE_HANDLER

Unfortunately, the way __except() really works is slightly hidden by this technique. The expression inside __except() must evaluate to one of three values. The first value, 1, is represented by the constant EXCEPTION_EXECUTE_HANDLER (defined in Excpt.h) and causes the handler to be executed. Since the C++ equality operator evaluates to 1 when both sides of the operator are equal, the test that we used in the example evaluates to EXCEPTION_EXECUTE_HANDLER when the return from GetExceptionCode() equals the constant being tested.

EXCEPTION_CONTINUE_SEARCH

If both sides of the operator are not equal, the == operator evaluates to a zero. This value is equal to EXCEPTION_CONTINUE_SEARCH; the code will continue to search through the handlers for an appropriate contender, and then up the stack for another block of handlers which might take care of the exception.

EXCEPTION_CONTINUE_EXECUTION

Finally, you can use __except(EXCEPTION_CONTINUE_EXECUTION) to force the code to continue executing where the exception occurred. Some exceptions can't be continued, invalid instruction traps, in particular. If you try to continue after such an exception, you'll throw a new exception with a code of EXCEPTION_NONCONTINUABLE_EXCEPTION.

The following table shows all of the exceptions that you can trap. These values are #defines from the Winbase.h header which in turn uses information from the Winnt.h header, and match possible return values from GetExceptionCode(). The rest of the definitions you'll need for the GetExceptionCode() function (which is a macro in a function's clothing) and some other structures used when you throw your own operating system-level constructions are from Excpt.h:

Exceptions	Description
EXCEPTION_ACCESS_VIOLATION	The thread tried to read from or write to a virtual address for which it doesn't have the appropriate access.
EXCEPTION_BREAKPOINT	A breakpoint was encountered.
EXCEPTION_DATA_TYPE_MISALIGNMENT	The thread tried to read or write data which was misaligned on hardware which doesn't provide alignment. For example, 16-bit values must be aligned on 2-byte boundaries, 32-bit values on 4-byte boundaries, and so on.
EXCEPTION_SINGLE_STEP	A trace trap or other single-instruction mechanism signaled that one instruction has been executed.
EXCEPTION_ARRAY_BOUNDS_EXCEEDED	The thread tried to access an array element which was out-of-bounds and the underlying hardware supports bounds checking.

Table Continued on Following Page

Exceptions	Description
EXCEPTION_FLT_DENORMAL_OPERAND	One of the operands in a floating point operation is denormal. A denormal value is one which is too small to be represented as a standard floating point value.
EXCEPTION_FLT_DIVIDE_BY_ZERO	The thread tried to divide a floating point value by a floating point divisor of zero.
EXCEPTION_FLT_INEXACT_RESULT	The result of a floating point operation can't be exactly represented as a decimal fraction.
EXCEPTION_FLT_INVALID_OPERATION	This exception represents any floating point exception not included in this list.
EXCEPTION_FLT_OVERFLOW	The exponent of a floating point operation is greater than the magnitude allowed by the corresponding type.
EXCEPTION_FLT_STACK_CHECK	The stack overflowed or underflowed as the result of a floating point operation.
EXCEPTION_FLT_UNDERFLOW	The exponent of a floating point operation is less than the magnitude allowed by the corresponding type.
EXCEPTION_INT_DIVIDE_BY_ZERO	The thread tried to divide an integer value by an integer divisor of zero.
EXCEPTION_INT_OVERFLOW	The result of an integer operation caused a carry or borrow out of the most significant bit of the result.
EXCEPTION_PRIV_INSTRUCTION	The thread tried to execute an instruction whose operation isn't allowed in the current machine mode.
EXCEPTION_NONCONTINUABLE_EXCEPTION	The thread tried to continue execution after a non-continuable exception occurred.

Note that many of these exceptions have very different meanings; their exact meaning will depend on the architecture of the machine hosting Windows. The quantity which exactly constitutes a division underflow, and which instructions are protected in which modes, varies between the Power PC, Alpha, MIPS and Intel machines – and the operating system and tools are still available for some of those platforms. Any operating system exception handling code you write is likely to be machine-specific.

Of course, you may only be trying to trap math errors. Since they're effectively the same on every machine, you can trap them with the same code, but using the EXCEPTION_SINGLE_STEP value to try to write a debugger for all platforms would be difficult at best!

Now, here's the other side of the coin – you can't mix operating system exception handling code and C++ structured exception handling code in the same function, i.e. one function can't have both `__try` and `try` blocks. This limitation might disappear in subsequent releases of Visual C++, but, for the time being, you'll have to code around it by putting your operating system trap-sensitive code in a function separate from any code which needs standard C++ exception handling.

Exception Messages

The 'operating system' exceptions that we've been talking about, by the way, are actually that – exceptions which the processor throws at the lowest possible hardware level in order to get the operating system's attention.

Windows 95/98 and Windows NT/2000 react to these processor exceptions because they've installed low-level handlers for them. If you're using an Intel processor, it turns out the exception being thrown by the hardware isn't really much different than a non-maskable interrupt. If you're using a different processor, the mechanism is much the same but information describing the exception is probably described to the exception handler code in a more reasonable fashion than it is for Intel processors.

The upshot of this is Visual C++ provides support for trapping those exceptions without you needing to get your hands dirty with assembly language programming. We've outlined those mechanisms here. But they deserve a couple of extra notes because seeing evidence of the way exceptions work just might surprise you.

Exceptions thrown during the execution of your application will *always* be noticed by the debugger. When the debugger is loaded, things are different for your process – the operating system knows your application is being debugged, and notifies the debugger of certain operations which your program might otherwise keep between itself and the operating system.

One such operation is the case of an exception being thrown; the kernel tells the debugger about the exception only when a debugger is running – otherwise, the operating system expects that the program itself will handle the exception. The notification of the debugger is called a **first-chance notification**, but you often see the text "First-chance exception" in the debugger's output window. The debugger is telling you it received information about the exception so that you know it happened. The debugger usually lets the exception pass, and the operating system and the C Runtime Libraries will try to work together to find an exception handler for the error.

Assuming the debugger doesn't handle the exception, the search begins for a handler. If a handler for the exception is found, execution continues at that handler. If a handler is not found, the debugger is again notified and told there has been some trouble. This second notification is called a "last-chance notification". If the debugger doesn't accept this notification, the operating system automatically terminates the process which was being debugged.

All exceptions pass through the same mechanism. If the hardware in your system reacts to a divide-by zero or a memory access violation in your code, it ends up asking the operating system to start performing the steps we've outlined above. If your application has code that executes a `throw`, the compiler emits code which asks the runtime library to – eventually – call the `::RaiseException()` API to ask the operating system to get the exception process started.

Exceptions, at this level, are identified by a numeric code and receive a bunch of arguments. The runtime library uses the same numeric code every time: `0xE06D7363`.

(I don't know what 0xE0 means, but I can tell you that 0x6D7363 turns out to be the ASCII characters "MSC" – short for "Microsoft C".) Other exceptions, most notably, the ones thrown by the operating system, have other identifiers. You may have previously seen, for example, 0xC0000005, which is an **access violation**. Access violations are raised by the hardware if an application tries to read memory it doesn't own or write to memory to which it's not allowed to write.

Let's consider this simple C++ program:

```
#include <iostream.h>    // line one

void main()
{
    cout << "Hello" << endl;

    try
    {
        cout << "About to throw\n" << endl;
        throw 35;  // line 10
        cout << "Never reached!\n" << endl;
    }
    catch (int n)
    {
        cout << "Caught integer " << n << endl;
    }
    return;
}
```

The program starts out by printing Hello. Since other books have done a better job with this much of a program, we'll quickly get into what matters – a try/catch block. The try block prints out another message saying that it's just about to throw an integer, which we catch later. If you ran this program in the debugger, the throw line would cause this message to show up in the debug output window:

First-chance exception in Thatfile.exe 0xE06D7363: Microsoft C++ Exception.

This message is entirely benign; it's just the first-chance mechanism we talked about a couple of paragraphs before. The debugger doesn't stop on its own exceptions, so the mechanism which lets the operating system find a handler for this exception begins to run. This puts us in the first statement of the catch block right away. However, if you throw an exception of a type which isn't matched by a handler – that is, isn't caught by a catch block with an appropriate type, then the debugger will stop in its tracks with a message very much like this one:

The message identifies the fact that a "Microsoft C++ Exception" actually caused the problem. So, if you're debugging an application that causes the debugger to generate this message box, you know that someplace a throw statement threw an exception of a type that wasn't handled.

Finding that throw statement might be another matter altogether. The debugger is still on your side, though, because it lets you configure the way it responds to the first-chance notification.

If you use the Exceptions... command, available in the Debug menu when you're in a debugging session, you'll get a dialog box like this one:

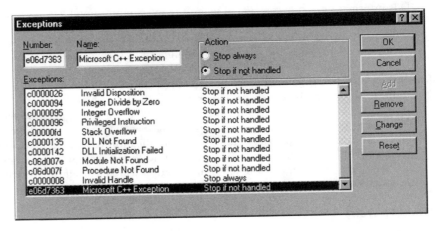

In this box, I've clicked on the Microsoft C++ Exception in the Exceptions: list box. With that entry highlighted, the Action group box describes what will happen when the debugger receives the first-chance notification. Stop if not handled means the debugger will halt execution at the last-chance notification – i.e., just before the operating system would throw the process being debugged out of memory. If we change the line:

```
throw 35;
```

in our above program to throw a data type for which we don't have a matching catch block, such as a double, like this:

```
throw 35.0;
```

we can end up exercising this mechanism. Running the code ends up showing us the same first-chance message in the debugger output window, but will end up halting execution after the runtime libraries realize no appropriate catch block exists. Unfortunately, the execution stops deep within the kernel and you'll end up staring at some assembler code. It makes me pretty excited, but I understand it may not be fun for everyone.

You'll note, though, that the stack window in the debugger shows you from where the exception was thrown. For the above exercise on an Intel machine, you'll end up with this stack trace:

```
KERNEL32! 77f1ccc7()
_CxxThrowException@8 + 57 bytes
main() line 11
mainCRTStartup() line 255 + 25 bytes
KERNEL32! 77f1b26b()
```

By double-clicking on these lines in the debugger, you'll eventually find your way to the line which threw the exception in question. If the exception was a Microsoft C++ Exception, it'll turn out to be the code which called the function _CxxThrowException, a function provided as an implementation detail by the C++ runtime library. The line before this item in the stack trace will be the caller – the exact line which caused the exception. From the stack trace above, you can see that line 11 of my program's main() function is the culprit.

This information is only presented when the executables involved have been loaded with debugging information. When reading such a stack trace, remember the line number is relative to the beginning of the file, and not the named function – the code which caused the exception in this example appears at the eleventh line of the source code file which contains `main()`.

If we use the Exceptions dialog box to change the way the debugger reacts to the first-chance notification, we can make the debugger halt on the line which throws the exception just as it is being thrown. With the Stop always radio button checked, the debugger will always halt execution in response to the particular execution type being thrown. Since this is done in response to the first-chance notification, it doesn't matter if your application has a handler for the exception or not. The debugger will stop at the code which tries to find the exception handler – you can step through it if you want, or you can make a note of the situation which caused the exception before you let the program continue.

When To Worry

We've investigated a couple of features of the debugger and seen how they work with the operating system. You can alter settings for exceptions your application might generate so you have a better shot at debugging them – few errors in a C++ program are worse than failing to handle exceptions that might be thrown.

By understanding the way exceptions work, and in particular having some insight into the messages the debugger will generate as they're being processed, you can learn when it's appropriate to panic and when it's not. If you're calling code in someone else's library, for example, you might see first-chance exception error messages go by in the debugger as that other code executes. If that's all you see, fine – the other code is handling the exception itself. There's really nothing wrong with that, though lots and lots of first-chance exception messages might mean the other code is using exceptions inappropriately. Throwing exceptions is expensive, since it requires the operating system get involved with finding an appropriate handler.

But if you see a first-chance exception message and then immediately see another message indicating an MFC exception was constructed or a warning indicating the exception wasn't handled, you know something really is wrong. If there is such a pressing issue, the debugger will be activated and you'll have a chance to examine the code which caused the problem.

One of the most famous examples of benign first-chance exception messages lies within Windows itself. If you write code which brings up a modal property sheet, even with `CPropertySheet`, you'll find that during the execution of the `PropertySheet()` API a first-chance message is generated. Many people jump to the conclusion there's a bug in MFC or a bug in Windows – and that's not a reasonable conclusion. (Ironically, most of these people also ask "What's a first-chance exception?" when reporting the bug they're sure they've found.) It turns out Windows is modifying the style bits on the dialog templates which were supplied to the sheet as pages. Since the templates are usually provided in memory that's write-protected (since they're loaded from resources in an executable image) writing to them causes an exception.

Duly, the debugger drops the exception message and then lets the operating system find the exception handler. The exception handler rights the wrong and makes a copy of the sheet and changes the styles there. Since the system expects this situation and handles it quite adequately, there's nothing really wrong with the code. You'd have cause to worry if the exception *wasn't* handled by the operating system and the debugger actually trapped the situation.

That situation is made obvious by the debugger; it will pop up a message box naming the exception and will drop you at an appropriate spot in your code showing the exception. Because you might have caused Windows (or some other piece of software) to cause an exception by passing bad values to it, you may need to look at the stack trace to decide who called who with what parameters before the cause of the exception becomes evident.

Collection Classes

As they take their first programming steps, most programmers learn about different **data structures**. A data structure makes weak or strong relationships between different pieces of data. Most often, a data structure allows you to conveniently find one piece of information if you're given another.

MFC provides inherent support for three different data structures: lists, arrays and maps. These structures allow you to squirrel away data in a variety of ways, each with its own advantages and disadvantages when it comes to memory use, speed and convenience of retrieval, as well as speed and convenience of storage.

Further to this, MFC also offers two different flavors of its three different data structures. The first flavor uses traditional C++ classes. The structures support standard C++ data types without any additional intervention. When you use these classes to build collections, you don't need to worry about any type information; the classes enforce type safety by not letting into the collection objects which are not directly derived from the class you used to declare the type.

The other flavor of classes MFC provides are type-safe, as well, but require that you derive your class from CObject. The classes will do a bit more work for you since they know you've used CObject's dynamic creation and serialization capabilities. When retrieving pointers, you'll also retrieve a CObject* from the functions in the collection class.

For some applications, CObject-derivation might be unacceptable. You may often need to manage lists of objects which aren't CObject-derivatives and the casting of data types to and from CObject types is often costly. To address these situations, you can use type-safe collection classes that were introduced with Visual C++ 2.0 and MFC 3.0.

The Type-safe Collection Classes

The type-safe collection classes are based on C++ templates. Your code will use the MFC-supplied collection template to build a collection class which can handle the exact type you need to collect. The drawback to template-based collections is the template generates new code for each type against which it is instantiated, potentially bloating the size of the executable code in your application.

The real reason there are two flavors of collection classes in MFC relates to the history of the C++ compiler. Before Visual C++ 2.0, the Visual C++ compiler didn't support C++ template classes, so the only alternative was to offer collection classes that manipulated CObjects.

Lists

A list is an ordered collection which isn't indexed. This means elements in the list appear wherever they are inserted, whether at the beginning, the middle, or the end of the list. Due to the implementation of the list collections, insertions anywhere in the list are very fast, no matter how large the list is.

Unfortunately, searching for a particular element within a list requires you consecutively test all the elements, as this structure doesn't offer direct access to an arbitrary member. For large lists, searching is an incredibly expensive proposal since the code in MFC must visit each element in the list and test it – so the time you spend finding a particular item grows in direct proportion to the size of the list.

Lists are great candidates for storing data elements in your program when you are concerned about the order in which you're storing them, but when you don't often need to find one element in particular.

Don't assume that you'll need a list in your application just because you hear the word *list* in the English description of your problem. It would be silly to use a list-based collection class to hold a list of your customers because you'd waste lots of time trying to find one particular customer. The order in which you have your customers stored is completely unimportant to you, so the well-ordered feature of lists is irrelevant to this application.

On the other hand, it made sense to use a list-based collection for the list of objects which were managed in the drawing program from Chapter 4. We did care about the drawing order, since we wanted to let certain objects appear as if they were on top of others. The drawing program frequently plays with all objects and doesn't often need to find a particular object. If the program was handling thousands of objects, it might slow down as it tried to decide which object was under a mouse click for selection, but the program doesn't support mouse-based selection.

To use a list in MFC, you should first choose the list class which handles the data type your application needs to list. This table shows the MFC list classes appropriate for each data type:

MFC Class	List Element Type
CObList	CObject*
CPtrList	void*
CStringList	LPCTSTR

When any MFC list container object is constructed, the list is always empty. After populating a list, you can reset it to being empty by calling the parameterless RemoveAll() member of the class.

Living with Lists

You may add items at the beginning of the list by calling AddHead(), or at the end of the list by calling AddTail(). These functions take a pointer to the item to be added. There are two versions of these functions; one takes a pointer to a single element and returns a POSITION structure which points at the head or tail of the list, where the item was added.

The other takes a pointer to another CList-type collection object and adds all of the items in that other list to the list. This version of the function doesn't return a value.

By the way, the POSITION structure allows you to cycle through the elements in the list. You can call GetHeadPosition() or GetTailPosition() on a list container object to get POSITIONs which reference the head or the tail of the list respectively. You can get the next element of the list by calling GetNext() or GetPrev(). These functions take a reference to the POSITION you've previously retrieved and return the value of the list at the position passed.

You can begin creating a list of professional hockey teams by constructing a CStringList object and calling AddHead() or AddTail() to add their names to the list. Since you don't care about the list of the teams (perhaps they're in order of wins last season), you can choose where to add them. The code might look like this:

```
CStringList    listTeams;

listTeams.AddHead(_T("Pittsburgh Penguins"));
listTeams.AddHead(_T("New York Rangers"));
// ... more teams ...
listTeams.AddTail(_T("Carolina Hurricanes"));
listTeams.AddTail(_T("San Jose Sharks"));


LPCTSTR pstrFirst;
LPCTSTR pstrSecond;

POSITION pos;
pos = listTeams.GetHeadPosition();

pstrFirst = listTeams.GetNext(pos);
pstrSecond = listTeams.GetNext(pos);

ASSERT(pos != NULL);
```

When you add a team to the head of the list, you should expect it to be displaced by the next team added to the head. To avoid confusion, you could add all of the elements in order by calling AddTail() all of the time, adding new teams to the end of the list with each call.

If you have a POSITION structure which references a given element of the list, you can call InsertBefore() or InsertAfter() to add an element just before or just after the element referenced by the POSITION. InsertBefore() and InsertAfter() both take references to a POSITION, and use the position to decide where to insert the item.

Finding Items in a List

You can find a given element of the list by calling Find() on your list. Find() walks the list to test pointer values of data elements in the list against other elements in the list; it doesn't compare the values represented by the elements. You can only use Find() to secure a POSITION for an element in the list if you already have the address of the block of data associated with the element in the list.

Using CObList

CObList is the type-safe version of MFC's list management classes. It contains instances of your own CObject-derived data. And so, you'll need to create your own CObject-derived class to hold the data you're interested in. Me, I want to know about hockey teams and their players – so my class might look like this:

```
class CHockeyTeam : public CObject
{
public:
    CString m_strCoachName;
    CString m_strOwnerName;
    CString m_strAdminAddress;
    int m_nGamesWon;
    int m_nGamesLost;
    int m_nGamesTied;

    CObList m_listPlayer;
};
```

Now you can create CHockeyTeam objects and build them into a list which describes last season. The only real trick we've used here is to nest another CObList in the class, so that each element in the teams list will contain its own list of players; exactly what you need to keep track of everything going on in the league.

Code for the destructor of the CHockeyTeam class should take care of cleaning up the memory used by m_listPlayer, while code for the constructor can load the list if nothing else does. Glossing over the details of how CHockeyPlayer is created, you might start a table for the Philadelphia Flyers with code like this:

```
CHockeyTeam cFlyers;
cFlyers.m_strCoachName = _T("Bill Dineen");
cFlyers.m_strOwnerName = _T("Some Rich Guy");
cFlyers.m_strAdminAddress =
                _T("Broad Street, Philadelphia, Pennsylvania 12031");

CHockeyPlayer* pTemp;
pTemp = new CHockeyPlayer(_T("Kevin Dineen"), 35, 58, -2, 79);
cFlyers.m_listPlayer.AddTail(pTemp);
pTemp = new CHockeyPlayer(_T("Eric Lindros"), 42, 39, 5, 62);
cFlyers.m_listPlayer.AddTail(pTemp);
pTemp = new CHockeyPlayer(_T("Peter Tanglianetti"), 10, 58, -2, 71);
cFlyers.m_listPlayer.AddTail(pTemp);
```

Some of the players in the example above are retired; MFC doesn't validate this information. The example above also has one other problem – the CHockeyTeam class you see, and the CHockeyPlayer class you don't see, aren't declared to be serializable. If they were, you'd be able to serialize the whole list with one call. The Serialize() implementation for CHockeyTeam should call Serialize() on its m_listPlayer member in order to effectively serialize all the data in the compound data structure.

Memory Ownership

It's important to concern yourself with the exact ownership of the memory handled in the collection classes. The CObList and CPtrList class manages pointers to data rather than the actual objects, while the CStringList class manages a list of actual objects and takes ownership of the actual data. Each node in a CPtrList list contains a pointer; it doesn't contain the actual object itself. When you add an element to a CPtrList class, you're only adding the pointer to the list rather than the data to which the pointer references. That is, CStringList copies the object before it is inserted into the collection, while the CObList and CPtrList classes only maintain a pointer to the added item within the list.

So, code like this,

```
CStringList list;
TCHAR sz[] = _T("Pittsburgh Penguins");

list.AddTail(sz);
CString strList = list.GetTail();

TRACE1("sz        = %s\n", sz);
TRACE1("pstrList  = %s\n", (LPCTSTR)strList);

sz[0] = _T('x');
CString strList2 = list.GetTail();

TRACE1("sz        = %s\n", sz);
TRACE1("pstrList2 = %s\n", (LPCTSTR)strList2);
```

produces trace output which looks like this:

```
sz          = Pittsburgh Penguins
pstrList    = Pittsburgh Penguins
sz          = xittsburgh Penguins
pstrList2   = Pittsburgh Penguins
```

When we called AddTail(), the list class copied the string into its own memory. You can use the template version of the collection classes, including CList, to build collections which allow you to manage the memory involved in the collection *or* build templates which manage actual objects.

CPtrList and Memory Responsibilities

The assignment to sz in the above example only changes the original string and not the copies managed in the list; the strings which subsequently come from the list always remain the same. If you use a CPtrList instead of a CStringList, the pointers stored in the array will all point at the original buffer and, therefore, the alteration effectively changes all of the strings. Here's the different version of the code:

```
CPtrList list;
TCHAR sz[] = _T("Pittsburgh Penguins");

list.AddTail(sz);
CString* pstrList = reinterpret_cast<CString*>(list.GetTail());
```

Continued on Following Page

```
TRACE1("sz          = %s\n", sz);
TRACE1("pstrList    = %s\n", (LPCTSTR)pstrList);

sz[0] = _T('x');
CString* pstrList2 = reinterpret_cast<CString*>(list.GetTail());

TRACE1("sz          = %s\n", sz);
TRACE1("pstrList    = %s\n", (LPCTSTR)pstrList);
TRACE1("pstrList2   = %s\n", (LPCTSTR)pstrList2);
```

The output of this code fragment reflects the change to the common buffer:

```
sz          = Pittsburgh Penguins
pstrList    = Pittsburgh Penguins
sz          = xittsburgh Penguins
pstrList    = xittsburgh Penguins
pstrList2   = xittsburgh Penguins
```

What the output from the sample really means is that the use of a CPtrList makes you responsible for managing the memory your objects use; the pointer-based class *doesn't* copy the data and simply uses the pointer. When you are adding an element, you need to allocate extra memory and then free it when you are removing individual elements or destroying the array. As we review the other container classes (maps and arrays), you'll note this feature is true for them as well.

GetHeadPosition() and GetTailPosition() are useful if you plan to cycle through the content of the list, but if you're interested in looking at the head or tail element directly, you should call GetTail() or GetHead().

When considering CStringList objects, both of these functions return a reference to a CString. For the other classes, they return the data type appropriate to the collection; CObList returns CObject pointers and CPtrList returns void pointers.

You can find the number of elements in your list by calling GetCount() against the list object. GetCount() takes no parameters and returns the number of elements in the list as an integer. You can test the list for emptiness by calling IsEmpty(), which returns a BOOL.

You can search through your list for a particular value by calling the Find() member of your list collection. The function takes a reference to the value you're interested in finding and a POSITION. The POSITION should describe the first item in the list to be checked. Searching will progress towards the end of the list and will stop when a match is found, returning the POSITION of the matching element. The POSITION is equal to NULL if the element couldn't be found.

> *The position parameter to the function isn't required; a default value of NULL is passed if the parameter isn't present. The NULL position means that the list will be searched from the beginning.*

Note that Find() searches for a match by comparing values. For CStringList objects, the values are actually compared, but when CPtrList and CObList objects are involved, only pointers to the objects are compared.

To search by comparing values, you can cycle through the list yourself, performing whichever comparison you'd like to. If your list is named `listYours`, the search might work something like this:

```
POSITION posCurrent;
posCurrent = listYours.GetHeadPosition();
while (posCurrent != NULL)
{
    CObject* pCurrent;
    pCurrent = listYours.GetNext(posCurrent);
    // cast pCurrent to your object's type
    // compare appropriately
    if (/* equal */)
    {
        break;
    }
}

// at this point, if posCurrent == NULL, the match
// wasn't found. If posCurrent != NULL, it marks
// the matching element
```

An alternative to this method is to make a type-safe list and supply your own `CompareElements()` function to compare elements of the list with a key element as appropriate.

Templated Lists

The problem with `CObList` is it will accept pointers to any `CObject`-derived class. When you think about how `CObject` is used, you'll realize this means `CObList` will accept pointers to almost any MFC class in your application. If, through some coding error or some data error, a `CHockeyTeam` object was added to the `m_listPlayer` list, all hell would break loose. But `CObList` doesn't mind, since it thinks it's collecting `CObject`-derived objects. And both of those classes derive from `CObject`, so there's no compile-time error.

Through defensive programming, you should be able to avoid type-mismatch problems. Any code which manipulates `m_listPlayer` should check that its pointer is to the proper class, which is easy if you use the run-time type information built into `CObject`. A function which adds a player to the list could have this code in it:

```
void CHockeyTeam::AddPlayer(CHockeyPlayer* pNewPlayer)
{
    ASSERT(pNewPlayer->IsKindOf(RUNTIME_CLASS(CHockeyPlayer)));
    // ...more code...
```

Ideally, such type checking should be done by the collection class itself. MFC uses C++ templates to develop type-safe code for a heterogeneous collection of objects, but you'll have to do a lot more work to develop such a list; you'll need to instantiate an MFC `CList` template:

```
CList<CHockeyPlayer, CHockeyPlayer> m_listPlayer;
```

Note that, in order for this declaration to work correctly, you'll need to include `Afxtempl.h` while compiling. If you use templates in more than one of your program files, it's a great idea to place the `#include` directive for this file in your `Stdafx.h` file.

The two instantiation parameters which are accepted by the template (usually referred to as TYPE and ARG_TYPE respectively) indicate which type the collection will maintain and which data type will be used to reference the elements, in that order. The list in our example will contain CHockeyPlayer objects and when we call functions like AddTail() to add items or retrieve items with GetNext(), the type returned will be CHockeyPlayer. Retrieving an element from the list nets a copy of the element, so code which gets the object and tweaks it will not alter the object which lives in the list. The ASSERT() in the following code fragment is never tripped because it's the name of the player held in Player that is changed, not the name of the player stored in the list:

```
CHockeyPlayer Player;
Player = m_listPlayer.GetHead();

Player.m_strName = _T("Some other guy");

CHockeyPlayer Original;
Original = m_listPlayer.GetHead();
ASSERT(Original.m_strName != Player.m_strName);
```

Using the template forms of CList requires you have a copy constructor on your managed class. You'll also want to implement an assignment operator for your class, unless the default assignment operator developed by the language is adequate for you – and it almost never is.

If you need to, you can store pointers in the list instead of real data. Then, you'd need to add a new element for every player and that changing the object referenced by the pointer changes that element for all others. You'll also actually need to manage the memory for those objects. The declaration of such a type-safe list collection would look like this – the declaration simply declares pointers instead of references to be the data type of choice:

```
CList<CHockeyPlayer*, CHockeyPlayer*> m_ListPlayer;
```

Usually, you'd let the collection class maintain the actual stored objects because that relieves you from writing any memory allocation code for each new object you add to the list. You can get the best of both worlds by collecting objects and specifying a reference type for the collection interrogation functions. Such a declaration for the CHockeyPlayer classes would look like this:

```
template CList<CHockeyPlayer, CHockeyPlayer&> m_ListPlayer;
```

With this mixed declaration, you may add an object just as before:

```
CHockeyPlayer Player;
m_ListPlayer.AddHead(Player);
```

But remember that the interrogation functions return a reference to an object which is in the list:

```
CHockeyPlayer playerForward;
playerForward = m_ListPlayer.GetHead();
```

The code above calls GetHead(), which returns a reference to the CHockeyPlayer object in the list. The assignment operator accepts that as an r-value, and copies from the referenced object to the playerForward object.

You must be able to freely convert from one type to the other, since the collection class will accept references to new items or items retrieved from the list. Your class (in this example, the CHockeyPlayer class) must provide a copy constructor and a default constructor in addition to operator=(), to be used when assigning new elements to nodes within the collection.

The documentation for MFC implies that you can use any types you wish for the collection's instantiation parameters. That turns out not to be the case. Here's a list of possible combinations:

CList Declaration	Notes
CList <CHockeyPlayer, CHockeyPlayer>	Works, but is inefficient, since all functions will always pass everything by object.
CList <CHockeyPlayer*, CHockeyPlayer>	Unusable.
CList <CHockeyPlayer, CHockeyPlayer*>	Unusable.
CList <CHockeyPlayer, CHockeyPlayer&>	Works, and is commonly used. The collection owns the memory and calls are quite efficient since you'll only pass references.
CList <CHockeyPlayer*, CHockeyPlayer&>	Unusable.
CList <CHockeyPlayer*, CHockeyPlayer*>	Works. Your collection manages pointers, though, and not the memory that objects in the collection will occupy.
CList <CHockeyPlayer*, CHockeyPlayer&*>	Works. Ditto.

The rule governing the allowable types runs like this. For a collection declared with a given TYPE and ARG_TYPE, you must be able to implicitly convert from an object of TYPE to an object of ARG_TYPE. There's no way to *implicitly* convert from a CHockeyPlayer* to a CHockeyPlayer&, so this kind of collection is unusable. On the other hand, it's possible to convert from a CHockeyPlayer to a CHockeyPlayer& so that manifestation of the collection is acceptable.

Different variations of the templates above will require different operators and constructors to be built into your collected class and you may need to implement slightly different helper functions for each type of template. For more information on what might be required, read on!

Template List Helper Functions

The type-safe classes use helper functions to assist with the creation and destruction of elements. There are seven different helper functions:

> ConstructElements()
> DestructElements()
> SerializeElements()
> DumpElements()
> CompareElements()
> CopyElements()

➤ HashKey()

These functions provide the code in the template collections with a type-safe way to manage or manipulate elements they're containing. If you have other classes in the classes you'll be using with your type-safe classes, or if objects in your collections will own their own memory, you'll want to write implementations of the appropriate helper functions for your application. The template helper functions are global; they are not members of any particular class or templated class. We'll describe each of the seven helpers here, except for HashKey(). Since HashKey() is used only by CMap, we'll discuss that function when we come to describe CMap later in this chapter.

ConstructElements()

The CList template class calls ConstructElements() when elements are added by AddHead(), AddTail(), InsertBefore() or InsertAfter(). The default implementation of ConstructElements() doesn't call the constructor for elements which it will be adding. Instead, it just fills the allocated memory with zeros.

Flooding the memory with zeros is fine for simple data types. If you need to have your objects initialized by their constructors, you should write a ConstructElements() function which takes two parameters. The first parameter is a pointer to the first element MFC wants you to initialize, while the second should be an integer illustrating how many elements MFC needs you to create. You should construct the elements so they're consecutively located in memory. However, you should *not* use the vector operators if you need to allocate memory during ConstructElements() – that is, you should only use the new and delete forms which don't require square brackets.

To beat the hockey player example into the ice, we can declare a ConstructElements() function for the CHockeyPlayer class, which calls the constructor on each of the objects to be initialized, like this:

```
void AFXAPI ConstructElements(CHockeyPlayer* pElements, int nCount)
{
    int nWorker;
    for (nWorker = 0; nWorker < nCount; nWorker++, pElements++)
        pElements->CHockeyPlayer::CHockeyPlayer();
}
```

The explicit call to the constructor is necessary to initialize the object which the template class is planning to use. It looks pretty goofy, but you really can perform this call – it only takes the memory referenced by pElements and runs the CHockeyPlayer constructor on it. This effectively initializes the memory at pElements to be a CHockeyPlayer object – from now on, that memory is a real player.

Some assert that the explicit constructor call is illegal, and depending on which revision of the ANSI draft you read, it is. Unfortunately, ANSI has changed its collective mind on this issue a couple of times, but the compiler that ships with Visual C++ had already assumed the proposal was a lot closer to being a standard than it truly was. If you think the explicit call is too garish, and especially if you're worried about portability, you can use placement syntax operator new to achieve the same effect:

```
void AFXAPI ConstructElements(CHockeyPlayer* pElements, int nCount)
{
```

```
        int nWorker;
        for (nWorker = 0; nWorker < nCount; nWorker++, pElements++)
            new(pElements) CHockeyPlayer;
    }
```

Should you choose to use placement new syntax, you'll need to be sure to include the header file `new` for the proper declaration of placement new for your application. Further, you may find this use of new collides with the DEBUG_NEW macro which ClassWizard often provides for your source files. Since the macro replaces calls to plain `operator new()` with calls to a special placement-syntax `operator new()` that helps with tracking debug-time information, the DEBUG_NEW macro is incompatible with explicit use of the placement new operator. You'll need to decide between using DEBUG_NEW and the placement syntax.

Both of the above `ConstructElements()` function implementations are appropriate for lists of players declared in either of these ways:

```
    CList <CHockeyPlayer, CHockeyPlayer> m_listPlayers;
    CList <CHockeyPlayer, CHockeyPlayer&> m_listPlayers;
```

The above `ConstructElements()` implementation works just fine on lists where the list actually owns the object. On the other hand, if you're using a template class with a TYPE which is a pointer, you'll need to write a `ConstructElements()` function which allocates memory on behalf of the collection. Since the `new` operator allocates memory *and* calls the constructor for that memory, it's ideal for use in this type of `ConstructElements()` function.

```
    void AFXAPI ConstructElements(CHockeyPlayer** pElements, int nCount)
    {
        int nWorker;
        for (nWorker = 0; nWorker < nCount; nWorker++, pElements++)
            *pElements = new CHockeyPlayer;
    }
```

Note that the parameter accepted by `ConstructElements()` is a pointer to a pointer. Since the collection manages pointers, the `ConstructElements()` function will be asked to initialize an array of pointers.

DestructElements()

To complement the `ConstructElements()` function, there is a `DestructElements()` function which is called by `RemoveAll()`, `RemoveHead()`, `RemoveTail()` and `RemoveAt()` and has the same parameter list as `ConstructElements()`.

By default, this function doesn't perform any work. If the objects in your collection need to be destroyed (to free the memory they own, for example) you'll need to implement a `DestructElements()` function to take care of this. For CHockeyPlayer, such a function looks like this:

```
    void AFXAPI DestructElements(CHockeyPlayer* pElements, int nCount)
    {
        int nWorker;
        for (nWorker = 0; nWorker < nCount; nWorker++, pElements++)

        pElements->CHockeyPlayer::~CHockeyPlayer();
    }
```

The exception for ConstructElements() also applies to DestructElements(). If you want to create a collection class which manages a collection of pointers, you'll need a DestructElements() implementation that releases the memory allocated by the ConstructElements() call. So, for a list declared like this:

```
CList <CHockeyPlayer*, CHockeyPlayer*> m_listPlayers;
```

you'll want a DestructElements() implementation such as this:

```
void AFXAPI DestructElements(CHockeyPlayer** pElements, int nCount)
{
    int nWorker;
    for (nWorker = 0; nWorker < nCount; nWorker++, pElements++)
        delete *pElements;
}
```

MFC does provide implementations of DestructElements() and ConstructElements() for CString based template collections, but doesn't provide an implementation for any other class.

SerializeElements()

To store your collection or reinitialize it from a stored copy, you can call the Serialize() member of the collection object. This will call a SerializeElements() helper function which serializes the specific type the collection holds. If your class is CObject-based like the CHockeyPlayer class, you can just call the Serialize() member function of the class like this:

```
void AFXAPI SerializeElements(CArchive& ar, CHockeyPlayer* pElements, int nCount)
{
    int nWorker;
    for (nWorker = 0; nWorker < nCount; nWorker++, pElements++)
        pElements->Serialize(ar);
}
```

If the collected class isn't CObject-based, you'll need to write code which is appropriate for the data serialization. Since SerializeElements() is a global function, it's not a member of any class; you'll need to either implement a function with the same effect as CObject::Serialize() or you should make the SerializeElements() function a friend of your class.

DumpElements()

For debug builds, you may also wish to provide a DumpElements() call which can dump the elements of your function. It's only called when the collection object needs to complain about unreleased memory in a debug build, and the dump depth is greater than zero. This function should dump information about the objects it is called against.

The first parameter to the DumpElements() function is a reference to a CDumpContext, which is used to display the diagnostic information. Like the other helpers, the function also takes a pointer to the first object to be dumped and a count of the objects to dump.

A typical `DumpElements()` function might look like this:

```
#ifdef _DEBUG
void AFXAPI DumpElements(CDumpContext& dc, const CHockeyPlayer* pElements, int
nCount)
{
    int nWorker;
    for (nCount = 0; nWorker < nCount; nWorker++, pElements++)
        pElements->Dump(dc);
}
#endif
```

To save space in release builds, you'll want to encase your `DumpElement()` declarations and implementations in conditional directives to prevent their compilation into release builds.

CompareElements()

Two of the templated collection classes, `CList` and `CMap`, care about the equality of elements which you insert into them. Of course, they need a way to perform comparisons between two different items in the collection. The default implementation of `CompareElements()` only compares the value of the pointer to the two elements, which is not useful in most cases. You should provide a customized version of `CompareElements()` for your class if you wish to perform another comparison method.

The prototype for the `CompareElements()` function you write should look something like this:

```
BOOL AFXAPI CompareElements(const TYPE* pElement, const ARG_TYPE* pElement2);
```

Note that the function returns a `BOOL`. The templates only care about the equality of the elements; they don't care about their relative value. So, you just need to return `TRUE` if the two items are equal, or `FALSE` if they're not. Also note the parameter types shown above as `TYPE` and `ARG_TYPE` should match your template's `TYPE` and `ARG_TYPE` expansion parameters for your own collections. I didn't use the normal syntax for the expansion above to avoid confusion. To keep roughing the hockey example, let's assume we still have a collection declared like this:

```
CList <CHockeyPlayer*, CHockeyPlayer*> m_listPlayers;
```

An appropriate `CompareElements()` helper function would look like this:

```
BOOL AFXAPI CompareElements(const CHockeyPlayer* pElement,
                            const CHockeyPlayer* pElement2)
{
    if (pElement1->m_strName== pElement2->m_strName)
        return TRUE;
    else
        return FALSE;
}
```

The core of the function just uses the `CString` comparison function. If the strings are equal, we know the two objects represent the same player. Even though we care only about equality of the players' name, in real life you might need to make a deeper comparison; two fellows named Ron Smith, for example, might be in the league but not be the same player. So you may also wish to compare the jersey numbers and team names of the players before returning `TRUE`.

The comparison function can do whatever you need to — it's up to you to decide what makes each of your objects unique. Even though you may eventually sort players in the list by their plus/minus statistic, you need to use CompareElements() to help the implementation of the collection classes.

You can get away without having a CompareElements() function if you're using a CList, because CList only uses the function to make comparisons when you call the CList::Find() function. If you're using a CMap class, on the other hand, CompareElements() is absolutely essential, because the hash algorithm needs it to resolve collisions.

CopyElements()

A CArray object (which we'll discuss in a few pages time) will manage a block of memory containing the elements you've asked the object to contain. When you call CArray::Append() or CArray::Copy() to move lots of items from one array object to another, CArray will want to copy those elements as quickly as possible. However, it will need to have you supply a function which will recreate the items at their home in the new array and, as such, it will call CopyElements() to get the job done. CopyElements() has a prototype which looks like this:

```
void AFXAPI CopyElements(TYPE* pDest, const ARG_TYPE* pSrc, int nCount);
```

Your implementation should copy nCount consecutive elements starting at pSrc and going to pDest. The default implementation of CopyElements() just uses memcpy(), which makes it unusable for objects that can't be bit-wise copied. If you need CopyElements(), you'll probably want to make sure that you have an assignment operator defined for your class. If we did so for the CHockeyPlayer class, we could do something like this:

```
void AFXAPI CopyElements(TYPE* pDest, const ARG_TYPE* pSrc, int nCount)
{
    while (nCount-- > 0)
        *pDest++ = *pSrc++;
}
```

CopyElements() is pretty simple, but, like the other helper functions, it's essential when you're working with objects which own other objects or memory. CArray is the only class which needs the CopyElements() helper.

Debugging Helper Functions

When you're working with the template-based collection classes, your biggest challenge will be to make sure you have proper helper function implementations. If your code doesn't behave as you expect, the odds are that your helper functions are not being called — the default implementations of the functions won't initialize your classes, serialize your data, or free your memory correctly.

If you think you're suffering from these problems, there are a couple of easy things to check. First, place a breakpoint in your helper functions to be sure they're being called. If they are, there's something wrong with your actual helper function implementation. If they're not, you should try to figure out why.

The two reasons why MFC won't call your function are really C++ language issues. Your helper functions won't be called if they don't have the correct prototype. If you really need:

```
void AFXAPI ConstructElements(CHockeyPlayer** pElement, int nCount)
```

but you've actually coded:

```
void AFXAPI ConstructElements(CHockeyPlayer* pElement, int nCount)
```

you won't get an error message. Instead, the compiler will (quite rightly) decide the default implementation of ConstructElements() is a closer match for the function call inside the template and will call that default implementation instead.

The other reason a helper function might not be called is because it isn't known to the compiler at the time the template is instantiated. The function prototype needs to appear *before* the template class is ever instantiated. In other words, you shouldn't declare a template-based collection until the compiler has seen **formal prototypes** for the helper functions. (In case you're not a language lawyer, a formal prototype is a prototype for a function which includes type information for the function's return and all of its parameters.)

I like to declare formal prototypes for the helpers in the same header file where I declare any class that may be collected; so I might declare my CHockeyPlayer class in a file called HockeyPlayer.h. The file might have content that, from thirty thousand feet, looks like this:

```
class CHockeyPlayer : public CObject
{
// implementation details
};

void AFXAPI ConstructElements(CHockeyPlayer** pElement, int nCount);
void AFXAPI DestructElements(CHockeyPlayer** pElement, int nCount);
void AFXAPI SerializeElements(CArchive& ar, CHockeyPlayer** pElement, int nCount);
#ifdef _DEBUG
void AFXAPI DumpElements(CHockeyPlayer** pElement, int nCount);
#endif
```

Keeping prototypes of the helper functions with the declaration of the class guarantees me that other classes which might hold collections of CHockeyPlayers will get the function prototypes at the same time they get the definition for the class. You can see this technique in action in the Wordfreq sample from Chapter 10.

Messy Declarations

You may notice declarations for templated classes can be pretty messy – they're surprisingly lengthy and often loaded with lots of the symbolic type modifiers that C and C++ have made infamous. When I'm interested in keeping my sanity or impressing my boss, I like to use a typedef to make the declaration of a template-based collection a little tamer. I'm likely to add the typedef to the end of the header file where I declare the class I want to collect. So, at the end of Hockeyplayer.h, I might add a line like this:

```
typedef CList <CHockeyPlayer, CHockeyPlayer&> CHockeyPlayerList;
```

Instead of fooling around with a noisy error-magnet declaration like this:

```
CList <CHockeyPlayer, CHockeyPlayer&> m_PlayerList;
```

I can use the less error-prone and more pleasing:

```
CHockeyPlayerList m_PlayerList;
```

whenever I want to have a catalogue of stick-carrying, puck-hogging skaters.

> *By the way, all of the advice I shared about template class helper function applies equally to all of the different types of templates: they all use* ConstructElements(), DumpElements(), SerializeElements(), *and* DestructElements(). *Only the* CList *and* CMap *classes will ever call* CompareElements(). *Only* CMap *uses the* HashKey() *function.*

Arrays

For instances when you need immediate access to a random element in your collection, you may use an array-based collection class. Each element contained in the array is accessible by referencing a particular integer – the element's index. The array has an inherent size beyond which index integers are invalid.

One of the most expensive operations that you can conduct against an array is adding or removing an element from any position, other than from the end. Compared to a list, this is one of an array's major disadvantages. All array elements past the insertion or deletion point must be moved to make room for an added element or to fill up the space left when an element is removed.

At first, it might not seem completely intuitive that MFC arrays are useful; after all, you can get the same effect by using a normal C++ array. While this is true, C++ arrays (even those which are dynamically allocated with new []) are less dynamic than those based on MFC's array class.

MFC freely controls the size of the array for you, as elements are added or removed from it. Writing and debugging code to dynamically resize the array is a pain, so you'll save yourself some time by using MFC's implementations.

Unfortunately, MFC's array class isn't a sparse array. In other words, unused array elements still take up space, so be warned about 'oversizing' your array. For example, having a CUIntArray where only elements 3 and 100 have data in them takes up just as much memory as an array where all 100 elements are in use. If you need a sparse array, consider using a CMap collection.

This table shows the MFC array classes appropriate for each data type:

MFC Class	Array Element Type
CUIntArray	unsigned int
CWordArray	WORD

MFC Class	Array Element Type
CStringArray	Cstring
CDWordArray	DWORD
CByteArray	BYTE
CObArray	CObject

This code builds a list of the first 100 prime numbers:

```
BOOL IsPrime(int nNumber)
{
    // ... detect primeness of number ...
}

void BuildPrimeList()
{
    // build list in CUIntArray m_PrimeArray;
    int nCandidate = 2;
    int nFound = 0;

    m_PrimeArray.RemoveAll();
    m_PrimeArray.SetSize(100);
    while (nFound < 100)
    {
        if (IsPrime(nCandidate))
        {
            m_PrimeArray.SetAt(nFound, nCandidate);
            nFound++;
        }
        nCandidate++;
    }
}
```

Remember that inserting or deleting an element at the end of an array is efficient; performing the same action at any other position on the array is quite expensive if the array has any elements. The more elements that need to be moved, the greater the expense.

You can find the number of elements in an array by calling the GetUpperBound() member of the array object. You can call GetAt() to return an element at a given index of the array and you can change that value by calling SetAt(). The Foundation Classes also provide the operator[] for the array classes as a shorthand for calls to GetAt().

InsertAt()

InsertAt() can be used to insert an element into the array, displacing subsequent array elements to the next higher index value. This function accepts the index for the new item, the value for the new item and the number of copies to be inserted. This final parameter has a default of 1, so it can be omitted in most calls.

An overridden version of `InsertAt()` can take an index and a pointer to an array of a similar type. The function adds the new array at the specified index all in one shot, moving all of the subsequent indexes towards the end of the array.

DeleteAt()

`DeleteAt()` allows you to remove elements from the array, compressing the array to fill the void created by the removed elements. This function takes two parameters; the first is the index of the element to be removed and the second is the count of any subsequent elements that should also be removed. The second parameter defaults to 1, so may be omitted for most calls.

RemoveAt()

`RemoveAt()` removes the element at the index passed, while `RemoveAll()` clears all elements from the array.

The array will always have enough memory to hold the elements it contains and will sometimes claim more memory as required. This memory is used to handle new elements as they're added to the list. Rather than resizing the array as every element is added, the array code anticipates that more elements will be added.

You can call `SetSize()` to dictate how memory will be handled by the array. This function's first parameter sets the opening size that the array should be built to, while the second parameter indicates how many elements should be added to the array when the array runs out of space. The second parameter defaults to -1, which tells the array code to try to pick a reasonable growth size, which will result in a minimal amount of reallocations.

Heuristically, MFC will try to grow the array by four elements at a time while the array is 32 elements or less in length. If it grows anymore afterwards, it will grow the array by one eighth of its size at each increment until it is at least 8192 elements in length, at which point, the array will be grown by 1024 elements at each increment.

If you're adding a lot of elements to a new array collection object, you should call `SetSize()` beforehand so the array will not continually reallocate and move memory as you go. Setting the grow-by parameter to a higher value will significantly increase the performance of the array, but will cause the array to waste a great deal of memory. You can trim any excess from the array's memory pool at any time by calling `FreeExtra()` upon it.

Template Arrays

MFC's array classes and list classes share the same data typing problems; MFC arrays only accept the data types which have been predefined. If you have your own memory buffers which you wish to store in an array or you need to store user-defined object types in your array, you should consider a type-safe array.

Template arrays can be declared using the `CArray` and `CTypedPtrArray` template classes. For example, if you'd like to store an array of beverages and their costs in preparation for the development of a point-of-sale application, you'll usually declare elements of a custom `CBeverage` class and, to make use of the functionality which is made available by `CObject`, derive `CBeverage` from that class.

Maybe the definition of the class will look like this:

```
class CBeverage : public CObject
{
    // drink name, eg, "Manhattan", or "Mike's Lager"
    CString    m_strBeverageName;

    // cost in cents, eg, 350 == $3.50
    int    m_nCost;
}
```

The `CArray` class is a reasonable choice for the beverage list; we want to be able to enumerate the beverages and randomly access any given one after the user has made a selection from a list. The element entry in the list will probably equal the element entry in the array; this one-to-one correspondence is possible with a `CList` collection, but accessing an arbitrary element of the `CList` class takes much more time than getting to a given `CArray` element.

We can declare an array of beverages called `DrinkList` using the `CArray` template, like this:

```
CArray<CBeverage, CBeverage&>  DrinkList;
```

Like the other MFC template classes, you'll need to reference `Afxtempl.h` to get the declarations necessary to use this class.

Implementing Template Array Functions

You'll need to consider implementing the `ConstructElements()` and `DestructElements()` helper functions which we discussed when treating the `CList` template class in the previous section. `CArray` calls `ConstructElements()` when `SetSize()` or `InsertAt()` are called, while `CArray` calls `DestructElements()` as a result of calls to `SetSize()` or `RemoveAt()`. Since `CArray` has no searching functions, it doesn't need a `CompareElements()` function.

Maps

While lists provide ordered collections of elements, and arrays provide a way to reference an element by index, maps provide a method to develop a logical relationship between two arbitrary data items. Maps are associative containers. This is appropriate when you need to retrieve information associated with a given data item, but the items in question fall in a very wide range of possible values.

Maps exceed arrays and lists when it comes to their search capabilities; the primary feature of a map is its ability to find the data associated with a key and map it to its associated value. You can choose from any one of seven MFC map types once you've decided which data types you're interested in mapping. This table shows the MFC map class that's appropriate for each data type:

MFC Class	Map Key Type	Map Value Type
CMapPtrToPtr	void*	void*
CMapStringToOb	CString	CObject*

Table Continued on Following Page

MFC Class	Map Key Type	Map Value Type
CmapStringToPtr	CString	void*
CMapStringToString	CString	CString
CMapWordToOb	WORD	CObject*
CMapWordToPtr	WORD	void*
CMapPtrToWord	void*	WORD

For example, CMapStringToOb allows you to map the plain string name of something to a pointer that actually represents it. The CMapStringToOb class will provide the functions necessary to build the map, as well as ones to look up values.

The Advantage of MFC Maps

You could simulate the functionality built into this class by creating a list which has elements including strings and CObject pointers. You'd have to write code to rip through the list and compare each element in the list to the string, returning the CObject pointer in the matching element. The Microsoft Foundation Classes maps have an advantage over this method because they build a hash table so the matching entry can be found without a linear (or binary!) search of the map's keys. This makes maps the container of choice for lookup-intensive applications.

Adding elements or removing elements from a map is relatively inexpensive. These performance characteristics make maps appealing for almost all data storage applications. If, by the nature of your data you can shoehorn the key values for your lookups into a contiguous range of integers, you should use an array collection, since it will be even faster than using a map; however, for many realistic applications where the key values are almost random or over a very broad range, the map collection excels when asked for rapid data retrieval and diverse data type management.

When you construct a map object using one of the classes we've named here, you can choose whether to pass the constructor a number that will affect the granularity of memory management throughout the life of the map object. The value, which defaults to 10, is the increment at which new memory blocks are allocated for storage in the map, by which we mean that, by default, the collection will always allocate enough memory to hold the next multiple of ten elements. If you are adding a great many elements to your collection, you should increase this number to cause the class to allocate memory a little less frequently.

InitHashTable()

The hash table size will also directly affect the performance of your map collections. By default, the map will contain a hash table with seventeen elements. If you plan on storing more than twenty or so objects in your map, you should consider calling the InitHashTable() function. The function takes two parameters: an integer, which indicates the new hash table size, and a flag, which, if TRUE, will cause the function to allocate memory for the new hash table right away. If the parameter is FALSE, the memory will not be allocated until the next time an item is inserted into the map.

You can add elements to the map by calling its SetAt() member function. The actual type of this function's parameters depends upon the type of mapping you're using. The first parameter is always the key for the mapping, and the second is always the value for the mapping.

Lookup()

The Lookup() member of your map object allows you to retrieve a value based on its key value. Like SetAt(), the types of the parameters are dependent on the exact type of map you're working with. The first parameter to this function is the key which you're using, while the second is a pointer to a reference for the returned value. The function returns TRUE if the value was found and FALSE if it wasn't.

The map classes support operator[], allowing you to set a mapping using a slightly shorter and more readable set of instructions. The two statements:

```
mapAges[_T("Dick Clark")] = 72;
mapAges.SetAt(_T("Dick Clark"), 72);
```

are exactly equivalent.

You can remove one element from the map by calling RemoveKey(). This function accepts the key value whose entry should be removed. You can remove all of the elements from the map in one go by calling RemoveAll() on the map.

You can cycle through all of the elements in a map by calling GetStartPosition(); this function returns a POSITION which identifies the first item in the mapping. You can call GetNextAssoc() with the POSITION you receive from GetStartPosition() to get subsequent items in the mapping.

A POSITION indicates a position within an enumeration. Within both CMap and CList classes, you may disrupt your loop by altering the list while hanging on to a POSITION because the POSITION may become invalid after certain operations. You shouldn't remove the object referenced by the POSITION you have from the list and expect to continue iterating with that POSITION, for example. If you modify items after the POSITION you're currently using, you'll shorten or lengthen your iteration process. A POSITION does not indicate a complete snapshot of the items to be enumerated; if the underlying collection changes, so will the semantics of the POSITION object.

GetNextAssoc() takes the POSITION as its first parameter and accepts references to the key type and value as its second and third parameters, respectively. This code cycles through all the mappings in a CMapStringToOb object named mapCountries:

```
POSITION pos;
pos = mapCountries.GetStartPosition();
while (pos != NULL)
{
    CObject objCountries;
    CString strCountryName;

    mapCountries.GetNextAssoc(pos, strCountryName, objCountries);
}
```

Note that maps aren't well-ordered, so the order of elements returned by each iteration of the map isn't well-defined and, in some cases, may not be repeatable.

The number of elements in the mapping can be found by calling GetCount(). This function returns an integer indicating the number of mapped items, while IsEmpty() returns a BOOL informing you whether or not the map is empty.

Template Maps

The same typing problems we mentioned about the other collections also exist for maps. Of course, MFC provides a template-based map class which you can use to work around these problems by creating a map class specifically tailored to each of the types you want to collect.

If you include `Afxtempl.h`, you can reference the `CMap` template class. A template instantiation for `CMap` might look like this:

```
CMap<CString, CString&, CPlayer, CPlayer&>  mapAgents;
```

Note that the `CMap` template has four parameters, while the `CArray` and `CList` templates only have two. `CMap` has four because it needs type information for the storage and reference of the keys and the values held by the template. The first parameter to the template dictates the data type the class will use for storing keys in the map, while the second parameter indicates what data type the class will use when referencing those elements with functions like `SetAt()` or `Lookup()`. The third parameter dictates the data type to be used when the map stores a value, while the fourth dictates the data type used when the class references a value.

So, the above declaration creates a `CMap` which relates a `CString` to a `CPlayer`. All the parameters to member functions of `mapAgents` will take references to those types.

Like the other template collection classes, `CMap` can make use of helper functions. It will call `CreateElements()` in response to `SetAt()` and `DestroyElements()` in response to calls to `RemoveAt()` or `RemoveAll()`.

You should also consider providing a `SerializeElements()` implementation if you need serialization of the map class. You might also want to add a `DumpElements()` for debug builds.

HashKey()

Beyond these regular helpers, `CMap` can also call `HashKey()` to develop a hash key for a given item. This function accepts a key element and should return an integer hash value that should identify the input as uniquely as possible. If the function can return the same value for two different inputs, this is okay, but it should happen as infrequently as possible. If the function can return a unique value, the lookup in the map will score a direct hit. If the function returns a value that was previously used by another item in the mapping, MFC will resort to a very small linear search of all the matching elements.

Remember that your `HashKey()` function will be called once for every element added to the mapping; if your `HashKey()` function isn't reasonably efficient, the efficiency with which you populate your map will also suffer.

MFC doesn't provide a default implementation for `HashKey()`, unless the collection is referencing a `CString` type. The `CString HashKey()` function can be found in `Strex.cpp` in the `\Vc98\Mfc\Src` directory, and looks like this:

```
UINT AFXAPI HashKey(LPCSTR key)
{
    UINT nHash = 0;
    while (*key)
```

```
            nHash = (nHash<<5) + nHash + *key++;
      return nHash;
   }
```

The function steps through the string, adding the character value of each key to a total and then shifting that total five bits left through each iteration. This is effective because the shift makes the least significant bits of each character in the string more meaningful by jumping them to the left. Of course, you might need to provide your own for a variety of reasons – for example, this algorithm is pretty bad for very short strings.

Note that all helper functions are of the same signature, no matter which collection class they're supporting. You only need to code one version of a given helper function for each class, even if you're using more than one type of collection for that type. CList, CMap and CArray collections of the same type all share the same implementation of SerializeElements(), DumpElements(), CreateElements() and DestroyElements().

Another Path to Type Safety

If you're writing a new application, you should consider using the template classes to contain any objects you're manipulating. The use of template classes is most appropriate when you're manipulating a number of collections of different data types, or when you need to manage a collection of objects or data values which are not already supported by a built-in MFC collection class.

If you're working to migrate old code from MFC classes towards truly type-safe versions, you might consider using CTypedPtrList, CTypedPtrArray or CTypedPtrMap. These class templates wrap the conventional MFC collection classes, allowing you to avoid most of the type casting inherent when you use templates. The templates are very simple; they just force the parameters of the regular MFC classes to be of a specific CObject-derived type.

And that's also the rub in MFC's type-safe collection classes; they can collect only pointers to CObject-derived objects. If you need to make a collection of structures or even just plain old integers, you need to use one of the real template types.

Files

If you're like me, you have a pretty big disk drive on your development machine. On those bigger drives, files grow like weeds. There are literally thousands and thousands of them, taking up acres of space. Almost all programs read or write some kind of file; they may let the user decide to save their work in a given file, or the program might need to read some data from disk for lookup information. Saved NETHACK dungeons and SimCity 3000 games also account for a huge amount of drive use.

You can always use standard C or C++ run-time library functions to access files in your MFC application. But by using MFC's classes, you can enlist MFC's help to manage the objects and data structures associated with your files. MFC's file management classes implicitly understand CStrings, for example. The true beauty of using MFC file access methods is you can derive your own classes. While it's amusing to use a CStdioFile object to read and write text files, it's downright exhilarating to derive your own class that implements member functions to do parsing or formatting work specific to your particular application.

CFile

The base class for all the MFC file classes is CFile. CFile wraps itself around file primitives from the Windows APIs, using Windows file handles to perform its operations. CFile operations are unbuffered, so every call to any of its members that perform file I/O necessitates a call to the Windows API.

A call to the Windows API can be bad; Windows may (or may not) translate each and every one of those calls to a physical disk read. If you read a few bytes at a time, you're wasting an incredible amount of time in the operating system. It's much faster to read 512 bytes by calling the operating system once to fill a buffer before doing the pointer math yourself than it is to read 512 bytes by calling the operating system 32 times getting 16 bytes with each call. The operating system tries to compensate by buffering the data itself, but that buffering can almost never compete with well-planned file access patterns implemented in your own code.

Tuning File Access

You can avoid problems with file I/O performance by using any one of several techniques. By swapping CFile for CStdioFile, you can gain some buffering for free. You could continue to use CFile, but tune or buffer your own file accesses, making CFile I/O calls, and therefore calls to the underlying operating system, as sparingly as possible.

Truly tuned applications will also avoid reads which span logical disk sectors by making sure that data stored in files is aligned on pages, which can be read without forcing the read of more than one physical sector. CFile adds a negligible overhead to the Windows file API calls, so if your application uses CFiles and seems inefficient, the cause is almost certainly nothing to do with what CFile is doing.

Working with CFiles

CFile has three constructors so you can construct a CFile object in three different ways:

➢ A parameterless CFile constructor exists which creates a CFile object, but doesn't associate it with a particular file.

➢ You can provide a file handle previously returned from the Windows ::OpenFile() API.

➢ A CFile constructor can take a filename and file mode flags to indicate how the file should be opened. The file is opened as the object is created.

After building a CFile *object with the default constructor, you can open the file using* CFile::Open()*; it takes the same parameters as the opening constructor.*

The first parameter that CFile::Open() and the opening constructor accept is a pointer to the filename. The second parameter, the mode flags, can be a combination of these values:

Mode Flag	Description
CFile::modeCreate	Forces the file to be created. If the file already exists, the file will be truncated to have no length.

Mode Flag	Description
`CFile::modeRead`	Opens the file for reading only.
`CFile::modeReadWrite`	Opens the file for reading and writing.
`CFile::modeWrite`	Opens the file for writing only.
`CFile::modeNoTruncate`	Combines with `modeCreate` to open a file for append.
`CFile::modeNoInherit`	Prevents the file from being inherited by child processes. If this flag is present, any process created by opening the file will not gain the pre-opened file handle.
`CFile::shareDenyNone`	Opens the file without locking read or write access to the file. If the file is opened for compatibility mode by any other process, the file open will fail for this process.
`CFile::shareDenyRead`	Opens the file and locks read access to the file. The file open will fail if another process has opened the file in compatibility mode or has locked the file for read access.
`CFile::shareDenyWrite`	Opens the file and locks write access to the file. The file open will fail if the file is opened in compatibility mode or for write access by any other process.
`CFile::shareExclusive`	Opens the file for exclusive access. If any other process has the file opened in compatibility mode or if the file is opened with read locks or write locks by any other process, the file open will fail.
`CFile::shareCompat`	Opens the file with compatibility mode, allowing any process on a given machine to open the file any number of times. The file open operation will fail if the file has been opened with any of the other sharing modes.
`CFile::typeText`	Sets text mode with special processing for carriage return/linefeed pairs (used in derived classes only).
`CFile::typeBinary`	Sets binary mode (used in derived classes only).

Note that this last version of the constructor, which opens the file for you, can throw a `CFileException` if the file open fails for any reason. When you open a file, you should avoid using `shareCompat`; you should decide what your application will do to the file and code your application to react appropriately. It's difficult to design a file format which can be read from and written to by different processes, so most of the time you can use `shareDenyWrite` to force other applications to fail when they attempt to write to the file.

Read()

Once the CFile object has been constructed and the file opened, you can use the Read() function to read information from the file, if the file was opened with the modeRead or modeReadWrite flags. Read() takes two parameters. The first is an LPVOID providing an address where the data will be read. The second is a UINT and dictates the number of bytes to be read from the file. The function returns the number of bytes actually read; this number may be less than the number of bytes requested if the end of the file is reached before the requested number of bytes are returned.

If the Read() function detects an error during the read operation, it will throw a CFileException to report the error. When you code a call to Read(), you should be certain to place the call within a try/catch block to trap any exception which may be raised by it. This code fragment shows how to trap the exception and present an error message. Remember that sometimes you'll want to read past the end of file and that an EOF error isn't something that you'll want to handle as an error:

```
int nRead;
TCHAR szBuffer[80];
try
{
    nRead = fMyFile.Read(szBuffer, 80);
}
catch (CException* e)
{
    CString strMessage;

    strMessage.Format(_T("Error during file read: %d", e->m_lOsError));
    MessageBox(strMessage);
    e->Delete();
}
```

Remember MFC makes GetErrorMessage() and ReportError() functions available, so you might want to write error reporting code which is smoother than in this example. In the above code frament, I'm pulling a fast one – the code in the try block will probably throw a CFileException*. But I know that CException* is a base class of CFileException*, and therefore can use it as the target of my catch block. Since I'm doing nothing specific to CFileException* in my catch implementation, my code is quite adequate – and has the side-effect of also catching any other CException-derived exception.

Write()

If the file was opened with modeWrite or modeReadWrite, you can call Write() to write data to the file.

Both Read() and Write() do their work at the current file pointer. While Read() and Write() always implicitly move the file position forward by the number of the bytes that have been read or written, you can also move the file pointer by calling Seek() against the CFile object.

Seek()

Seek() accepts two parameters: an offset, and a set of flags. The first parameter, a LONG, is the offset for your seek. The second parameter you can pass can be one of these:

Flag	Description
CFile::begin	Seeks relative to the beginning of the file, effectively making the offset an absolute position
CFile::end	Seeks relative to the end of the file, allowing negative offsets to seek into the existing file data
CFile::current	Seeks relative to the current file position

You can retrieve the current file pointer by calling GetPosition(). This parameterless function returns a LONG indicating the current file position. You can return to that position by calling Seek() with the returned value. SeekToBegin() brings the file position to the very beginning of the file, while SeekToEnd() moves the file position to the end of the file.

The Hexview sample uses Seek() and Read() to get information from the header, byte by byte. In the CHexViewDoc::ReadLine() function, the code seeks to a position at a mulitple of 16-bytes and reads 16 more bytes. It then formats the bytes into a buffer and returns it to the caller, the view, for display.

Remove(), Rename() and Duplicate()

Without creating or opening the file to begin with, you can call Remove() with a filename to delete it. Similarly, you can call Rename() with the name of an existing file and a new filename with which to rename it. Both of these functions are static, each will throw a CFileException if an error occurs, and neither can accept a name that contains wildcards. Remove() and Rename() quietly go about their business. If you'd like to have cute animations to show the user what progress your application is making, you can use SHFileOperation(), which I described in Chapter 7.

You can generate duplicate handles for an opened file by calling the Duplicate() member function of an existing and opened CFile object. Don't confuse this operation with copying a file; duplicating file handles is a technique used to read or write to the same file using different handles. This is appropriate if you wish to pass the handle to another process; the child process should use the duplicated handle to avoid putting the file into a state which will hinder the progress of the parent process as it works with the same file handle.

GetStatus()

The GetStatus() member function of CFile has two overloads. The first takes a reference to a CFileStatus structure, while a special static version takes a pointer to the filename in a string and a CFileStatus reference. These functions populate the CFileStatus structure with status information about the file associated with the CFile object or the file which is named in the static version's first parameter.

The CFileStatus structure includes several member variables. CFileStatus::m_mtime is a CTime which shows when the file was last modified, while m_atime is a CTime showing when the file was last accessed. Note that the file must exist on a volume which supports the update of file access times for the information to be valid, otherwise m_atime is equal to m_mtime.

A LONG containing the file's length can be found in CFileStatus::m_size, while the file's attributes are stored as flags in m_attribute. You can compare m_attribute against the flags in the following table to look for the presence or absence of a given attribute:

Flag	Description
CFile::Attribute::normal	The file is normal
CFile::Attribute::readOnly	The file can't be deleted or written to by any user or process
CFile::Attribute::hidden	The file is hidden and doesn't appear in normal directory searches
CFile::Attribute::archive	The file has been changed since the last backup
CFile::Attribute::directory	The file in question is actually a subdirectory
CFile::Attribute::volume	The file is actually the volume label
CFile::Attribute::system	The file is a system file and is excluded from normal directory searches

CFileStatus also contains m_szFullName[], which is a null-terminated string containing the file's name. These members may not always be populated; if the file was created by opening it, CFile knows the actual file name and path associated with the open file object. However, if you've created the CFile object by using the constructor that takes an active file handle or a pointer to a runtime library-style FILE structure, you'll find that the name might be empty.

Unfortunately, Windows NT and Windows 95/98 introduced extra attribute values that can mark a file as being compressed or archived off line. MFC stores the file attribute in a BYTE, and a BYTE is simply too narrow to hold those new flags. It wasn't possible to fix this problem in the version of MFC which shipped with Visual C++ 6.0, so you'll need to be aware of the problem until a fix can be applied

You can use the SetStatus() function to set the status of a file. The m_szFullName member of the CFileStatus that's passed to SetStatus() is ignored; you can't rename a file by changing its status, so use Rename() instead. SetStatus() only exists in a static version; you can't change the status information for a CFile object.

File Handles

Though a CFile object (and objects of CFile-derived classes) features its own method to open and close files, under the covers MFC is actually using the Win32 API to manage files. If you ever need to call a function that uses a file handle, you can retrieve the open file handle from the file object's m_hFile member. If the CFile object isn't open, the m_hFile member is NULL.

If you receive a file handle which you'd like to wrap with a CFile or CFile-derived object, you can pass the file handle to the appropriate constructor of CFile.

File Names

You'll often need the name of a file you're working with. Even though you can get the operating-system handle from the `m_hFile` member, you won't impress the user if you use this number in error messages or status displays. You can get the file name from an opened `CFile` member by calling `GetFileName()`. The name is just the file's name; i.e. if the opened file is really `C:\Hockey\Nhl\Scores.dat`, calling `GetFileName()` will result only in `Scores.dat`. If you need the full path, you can call `GetFilePath()`. If you need only the file's title (which, for this example, would be `Scores`), you could call `GetFileTitle()`. Each of these functions returns a `CString`.

These functions will always return correct information reflecting the state of the file. However, they will return an empty string if you used the handle constructor of `CFile`. This is because if it's given only the file's handle, there's no way for MFC to determine the name of a file.

CStdioFile

The `CStdioFile` class derives from the `CFile` class to provide buffered I/O routines, so the class can efficiently look ahead to find line delimiters. To this end, you can call `ReadString()` to read a line of text to the file.

The `ReadString()` function takes a pointer to a string buffer and a maximum number of characters to read. The function returns a pointer to the string in question, unless it reads past the end of file, in which case, it returns a `NULL`.

> **No error return is given if the function reads more than the specified maximum number of characters before finding a newline character.**

`WriteString()` will write a line to the file. It stops at the first null character and doesn't write that character to the file. The written string can contain any number of newlines, which are translated to carriage-return newline pairs as the string is written.

Both `ReadString()` and `WriteString()` can throw exceptions, so be prepared to catch them by using the appropriate `try`/`catch` blocks.

CMemFile

Windows NT/2000, Windows 98, and Windows 95 developers are often interested in the use of memory files as a way of speeding up their code or simplifying memory access. The idea is to write to a block of memory as if it was a file, allowing you to conveniently dump structured information.

`CMemFile` derives from `CFile` and replaces the file access primitives used for files with code that works against memory files. `CMemFile` is fast because the file is actually just a block of memory and can be readily accessed without a physical operation.

The `m_hFile` member of a `CMemFile` is always `CFile::hFileNull`, since there isn't an operating system file handle associated with the memory block managed by MFC.

You can't call `LockRange()`, `UnlockRange()` or `Duplicate()` against a `CMemFile`, since any of these calls result in the class throwing a `CNotSupportedException`.

`CMemFile`s don't have an associated name. You can't pass a reference to a `CMemFile` object to another process to share the data in the file. `CMemFile` has `Open()` and `Close()` functions, but they aren't useful because there isn't a physical disk file associated with `CMemFile`; perhaps it's a bug why these functions don't throw `CNotSupportedException`. However, `CMemFile` does support `Read()` and `Write()` calls.

Note that `CMemFile` is not a Win32 memory mapped file. Real memory mapped files provided by the operating system normally *do* have names, but certainly take up disk space. A Win32 memory mapped file is a file that exists on disk and has been mapped into memory, while a `CMemFile` is a block of memory which you can pretend is actually a file, but won't be stored on the disk.

When you work with `CMemFile`, you should ensure the calling code can catch both `CFileException` and `CMemoryException` exceptions. You should be prepared to react to both situations in your application. Again, if you end up calling a function that's not supported by the object (such as `Duplicate()`), you'll get a `CNotSupportedException`. You should only get `CNotSupportedException` exceptions when you're debugging, as they indicate that you've coded something that can't be done no matter what is happening at runtime – they *don't* indicate a transitive error condition that might not exist later.

MFC and File Security

In Windows NT, applications can completely secure themselves. To receive a respectable security rating from the United States Department of Defense rating system, NT has features to ensure that every **securable object** is associated with an owner. For example, the owner of a file is responsible for setting security levels for the file and can allow or disallow any individuals or groups of people the normal privileges associated with file access: read, write, delete or list access.

The owner of any securable object can set up auditing, so that events that constitute possible breaches of security can be recorded. An object's owner can even assign ownership to another user of the system.

Windows NT identifies users by their **username** and secures the user's access to the system using a **password**. Only once a user has been validated by a machine's login process can they use the resources of that machine. A user can't use shared resources on a machine over a network unless the network's domain controller has validated their account, or if the other machine knows their account information.

The NT File System

In Windows NT, the set of securable objects includes disk files, but, because of compatibility constraints, only disk files stored on Windows NT's native **NT File System** (NTFS) can maintain security information for files.

This may change, however; since Windows NT provides extensible, installable file systems, someone may someday provide a driver which allows Windows NT to use files stored by another operating system on another computer on a different network.

Since operating systems like VMS on Digital VAX machines have security features comparable to Windows NT, such a mapping would be very reasonable and quite probably all encompassing.

Alas, the Microsoft Foundation Classes don't provide classes that facilitate access to the Windows security APIs; but using a CFile-derived object doesn't preclude the use of them. The security APIs which are designed to work with files are relatively easy to understand, but, once you figure them out, I would encourage you to write several one-off test applications to make sure they do exactly what you think they do.

Most file security work will start with a call to the ::GetFileSecurity() API. This API's prototype is shown here for your reference:

```
BOOL GetFileSecurity(
    LPCTSTR lpszFile,
    SECURITY_INFORMATION si,
    PSECURITY_DESCRIPTOR psd,
    DWORD cbsd,
    LPDWORD lpcbsdRequired);
```

The first parameter is a pointer to the filename for which security information should be received. This filename can include a full path, but may not include wild cards. Note that this API also accepts directory names, since directories can have security records as well.

The second parameter is of the SECURITY_INFORMATION type which is set to one or more flags, indicating which type of security information should be retrieved:

> OWNER_SECURITY_INFORMATION only retrieves information about the owner or owners of the file.

> GROUP_SECURITY_INFORMATION requests that the primary group identifier for the object be returned. Only group information is returned; no user-level information is returned.

> DACL_SECURITY_INFORMATION is used to return the **discretionary access control list**, or DACL. This is the real 'security descriptor' that most users are interested in.

The DACL can be picked apart by other APIs, like ::GetAclInformation() and ::GetAce(), allowing you to find out exactly which users have what kinds of access to the subject of the list.

Have a peek at the Check_Sd example, which comes with the Win32 SDK, to see a complete example of file related security programming. As you review the code, remember you can retrieve the handle to an MFC CFile object by checking its m_hFile member.

Most security APIs, like ::GetFileSecurity(), take the name of the file instead of the actual handle. You can always get the file name from a call to CFile::GetFilePath().

Sundry Stuff

In the minutes I spent planning the organization of this book, I realized there are a few MFC features that can't be hung elsewhere. Since this chapter is devoted to the utilitarian nature of MFC, let's take a look at a couple of things that make writing programs a little easier but don't really fit well anywhere else in the organization of the book.

Wait Cursors

Your application will undoubtedly need to spend at least *some* processing time on actually getting work done. If your application doesn't need to do any work, you should carefully re-evaluate the reason that you're spending time writing it.

But for the bulk of you who are interested in doing something with your CPU cycles will find you'll need to give the user some clue you've wandered off and gotten busy with something that isn't obvious. Nobody likes to use an application that starts working, doesn't respond to the user and doesn't even bother to tell the user that something interesting is happening inside the machine.

According to the Windows Interface Guidelines for Software Design (which you can find in the online references and that you really should read if you're in any way responsible for deciding what applications look like), a good way to let the user know your application is busy is to turn on the **wait cursor**. This is the familiar hourglass-shaped cursor that tells the user you're not ready to work with him or her just yet – you're getting something done, you won't respond, but you haven't crashed.

You can turn on the wait cursor by calling the `BeginWaitCursor()` member of the nearest `CCmdTarget`-derived object. (Remember any `CWnd`-derived object is also a `CCmdTarget`-derived object – your application object is also a `CCmdTarget`-derived object.) This function takes no parameters; it simply turns on the wait cursor. If you call `EndWaitCursor()`, you'll take away the wait cursor. MFC implements a reference count internally so that calls to `BeginWaitCursor()` and `EndWaitCursor()` can be nested.

If you implement one function to do some work for you and bracket its work with calls to `BeginWaitCursor()` and `EndWaitCursor()` like this:

```
void CYourView::OnGetBusy()
{
    BeginWaitCursor();
    for (int nCounter = 0; nCounter < MAX_WORKLOAD; nCounter++)
    {
        // do something lengthy
    }
    EndWaitCursor();
}
```

you won't have to worry about the `EndWaitCursor()` call in this function, even if you bracket the function with another `BeginWaitCursor()` and `EndWaitCursor()` pair. So, another function, like this one:

```
void CYourView::OnGetReallyReallyBusy()
{
    BeginWaitCursor();

    for (int nCounter = 0; nCounter < 5; nCounter++)
        OnGetBusy(); // nested call!

    EndWaitCursor();
}
```

won't turn off the wait cursor until the outermost nested `EndWaitCursor()` call is completed.

Waiting Through Dialogs

If you make a call to a function which produces a modal dialog, though, you'll need to restore the state of the wait cursor. For instance, if you did something like this:

```
void CWaiterDlg::OnOK()
{
    BeginWaitCursor();

    // ...some huge amount of work...

    if (AfxMessageBox(_T("Do you really want to?"), MB_YESNO) == IDYES)
    {
        RestoreWaitCursor();
        // some huge amount of continuing work...
    }
    // maybe not here!
    EndWaitCursor();
}
```

you'd need the call to `RestoreWaitCursor()` to bring the wait cursor back after it was automatically pre-empted for the call to `AfxMessageBox()`. You would need to do the same call if you had brought up your own `CDialog`-based window. I structured the code above in such a way to show that the `RestoreWaitCursor()` call isn't necessary if you are going to take away the wait cursor anyway. The comment marked *some huge amount of work* is a good place to get more done. After the `RestoreWaitCursor()` call, the wait cursor will be back up. If the user presses No in the box, though, the `RestoreWaitCursor()` call would be skipped and the wait cursor *won't* be up at the line marked *maybe not here!*

An Easier Way

Of course, there's a slightly easier way to manage the wait cursor. It's appropriate to use if you've been up all night after driving home from a hockey game in a distant city, for example, and have come to work tired and are afraid of forgetting to call `EndWaitCursor()`.

The idea is to create a `CWaitCursor` object instead of using the explicit calls. The constructor and destructor of `CWaitCursor` call `BeginWaitCursor()` and `EndWaitCursor()`, appropriately. The last example, above, would look like this if it were coded with `CWaitCursor`:

```
void CWaiterDlg::OnOK()
{
    CWaitCursor waiter;

    // ...some huge amount of work...

    if (AfxMessageBox(_T("Do you really want to?"), MB_YESNO) == IDYES)
    {
        waiter.Restore();
        // some huge amount of continuing work...
    }
    // maybe not here!
}
```

Note you don't have to call `EndWaitCursor()` at all – not impressive in this snippet, but quite handy when your function has several paths of execution. You *do* have to call `CWaitCursor::Restore()` after the dialog box, though.

Error Messages

Error messages are terribly difficult things to write. There are lots of shipping, shrink-wrapped, commercial programs which have error messages like 'File save failed' or 'Bad error encountered!'. That is, many programmers are too reluctant to make a real, meaningful sentence that might help their users actually *diagnose* a problem – not just become aware of some symptom.

The Win32 API quite neatly comes to the rescue with the `::FormatMessage()` API. The function allows you to (among a lot of other things) get an error message from the system to describe a problem – in the user's native language, to boot!

If something fails, you can call the `::GetLastError()` API to first get an error code for the problem at hand. The system will return a `DWORD` describing the problem. The `Winerror.h` header file from the `\vc98\Include` directory has lots of handy preprocessor symbols that can help you test for particular errors in your code. But that doesn't get you much closer to finding an error message. Code like this, on the other hand, would:

```
if (!::SomeAPI()) // your function call here
{
    // it failed, be reasonable:
    DWORD dwError = ::GetLastError();

    LPTSTR lpBuffer;

    if (::FormatMessage(FORMAT_MESSAGE_FROM_SYSTEM |
        FORMAT_MESSAGE_ALLOCATE_BUFFER,
        NULL, dwError,
        MAKELANGID(LANG_NEUTRAL, SUBLANG_SYS_DEFAULT),
                        reinterpret_cast<LPTSTR>(&lpBuffer, 0, NULL) != 0))
    {
        AfxMessageBox(lpBuffer);
        ::LocalFree(lpBuffer);
    }
    else
        AfxMessageBox(_T("Unknown error!\n"));
    return;
}
```

If the API in question fails, we can immediately call `::GetLastError()` to get the related error code. Then, we can call the `::FormatMessage()` API with the flags `FORMAT_MESSAGE_FROM_SYSTEM` and `FORMAT_MESSAGE_ALLOCATE_BUFFER` to ask the system to provide us with an error message and to allocate the buffer for it. The function will populate the `lpBuffer` pointer with a pointer to the error message. We use that pointer directly in a call to `AfxMessageBox()` to show the error string. Since the system gave us the memory, it's our responsibility to free it, so we must call `::LocalFree()` to give the memory back when we're done.

`::FormatMessage()` takes a bunch of other parameters and is capable of using lots of different flags, but I'll skip describing those because they're not necessary for reporting errors.

One that is interesting, though, is the fourth parameter — where I used the `MAKELANGID()` macro to specify a **language identifier** for the function. It turns out that a language identifier identifies a language — you don't need to be a Zamboni driver to understand that. But an appropriately selected language ID, like the one above, lets us make an error message that is localized by the system automatically. You can read more about language IDs and localization issues in Appendix B.

This function, by the way, is the underlying mechanism in lots of the `GetErrorMessage()` and `ReportError()` implementations in the `CException`-derived classes.

Summary

This chapter has covered the important utility classes that MFC has to offer, in addition to some of the more significant constructs that Visual C++ can help you with when you're busy programming. Using the code MFC provides can mean you'll never have to write a linked list again, which can greatly reduce your workload when it comes to carefully parsing files or chopping up information from a database record.

10

Writing Multithreaded Applications with MFC

Earlier in the book, in the chapter on MFC application architecture, I mentioned that `CWinApp` was a derivative of the MFC `CWinThread` class. I left `CWinThread` largely unexplained, to keep the ground clear for this chapter, where I shall have enough room to properly explain threading without muddying the `CWinApp` issues which I want to discuss.

If you're not interested in writing multithreaded applications, you can get through your life without reading this chapter. The `CWinThread` information from Chapter 3 is quite adequate to fight your single-threaded battles. However, even if you aren't of a multithreaded disposition, you may still want to read the introductory sections in this chapter and skip the details later on. Threads are an important part of the Win32 API and a crucial part of the system's operation as a whole. Understanding them can bring you one step closer to Super Windows Guru Enlightenment.

So let's get right down to it. This chapter will explain:

> ➢ How threading is perceived by a programmer using Win32
> ➢ The details of `CWinThread`
> ➢ How MFC and the Win32 API work together
> ➢ How to write a for-real MFC application that does interesting stuff with threads

Threads and synchronization objects are implemented on Win32 platforms like Windows 95/98 and Windows NT, but they're not available on Win32s. If you're planning a Win32s application, you won't be able to use threads or synchronization objects in your application.

What's a Thread, Anyway?

The term **thread** is shorthand for 'a thread of execution', and it represents the most fundamental information a running program needs while it is executing: a user-mode stack to hold temporary variables and return addresses for subroutines, a kernel-mode stack to hold addresses for interrupt service returns, and a set of processor registers. This information is collectively referred to as the **thread context**.

The information that the CPU needs to keep track of everything is largely stored in the CPU's registers; the registers themselves either contain information or flags, indicating the machine's current status, or they contain pointers to that information in memory. Two important examples of such pointers are the **instruction pointer**, which lets the CPU know where in memory it will find its next instruction, and the **stack pointer**, which lets the CPU know where it can store or retrieve temporary values, such as local variables or the address of the routine that called the currently-executing routine.

The job of the CPU is simply to execute the instructions that we, as programmers, provide. It gets the next instruction and executes it. That instruction will change some part of memory or one of the registers. It might even change the instruction pointer, so that the instruction called isn't the next one in sequence, but an instruction that actually resides somewhere else in memory – perhaps the beginning of a subroutine, or on the other side of an `if` statement.

The operating system knows it needs to remember everything in the thread state to enable it to switch between threads. That state is collected into a thread context. The thread context, therefore, is everything the CPU knows about on its own, without relying on any memory to help it out.

A CPU doesn't know anything about switching threads, so once given a thread to execute, it will continue until the thread says, "I've finished!" or you pull the plug. The thread context is simply used by the CPU – but it is handled by the operating system. It's the operating system that makes things seem as if there are multiple threads. It occasionally stops the CPU from working at one thread and makes it start working on another. This process is handled by a set of code collectively known as the scheduler, buried in the bowels of the operating system.

Thread Priorities

The scheduler knows which threads take precedence over others; it knows to give those threads all the time they need at the expense of the less important ones. This hierarchy determines the **thread priority**.

How much time the scheduler actually gives a thread is determined by a combination of the thread priority and the process priority (we'll cover the differences between threads and processes a little later). Process priorities always fall into these four categories:

Process Priority Class	Base Priority Score
REALTIME_PRIORITY_CLASS	24
HIGH_PRIORITY_CLASS	13
NORMAL_PRIORITY_CLASS	9 if the thread has a window in the foreground, or 7 if it has a window in the background
IDLE_PRIORITY_CLASS	4

Thread priorities, meanwhile, come in seven different flavors:

Thread Priority	Priority Score Adjustment
THREAD_PRIORITY_TIME_CRITICAL	Indicates a score of 15 for IDLE_PRIORITY_CLASS, NORMAL_PRIORITY_CLASS, or HIGH_PRIORITY_CLASS processes, and a base priority level of 31 for REALTIME_PRIORITY_CLASS processes
THREAD_PRIORITY_HIGHEST	Two above the base priority for the process
THREAD_PRIORITY_ABOVE_NORMAL	One more than the base priority for the process
THREAD_PRIORITY_NORMAL	Exactly the base priority score
THREAD_PRIORITY_BELOW_NORMAL	One less than the base priority for the process
THREAD_PRIORITY_LOWEST	Two points below the normal priority for the priority class
THREAD_PRIORITY_IDLE	A score of 1 for IDLE_PRIORITY_CLASS, NORMAL_PRIORITY_CLASS, or HIGH_PRIORITY_CLASS processes, and a score of 16 for REALTIME_PRIORITY_CLASS processes

A thread always exists in the context of a process, and a thread cannot span more than one process. (We'll cover more detail regarding the semantics of threads and their relationship to processes a bit later on.) Windows uses information about the process and the thread to make sure the thread gets time based both on its own needs and on the needs of the process it serves. Windows determines the overall thread priority, on a scale of 1 to 31 (where a higher number means a higher priority), by assessing the thread priority relative to the process priority. The second column in the tables above explains the rules Windows uses.

You can see that a process with IDLE_PRIORITY_CLASS and a thread with THREAD_PRIORITY_IDLE will score a 1. It will be scheduled when the operating system doesn't want to do anything else at all. This is not to say that the thread will never run; if the system (or the specific processor, if the program is running on a multiprocessor system) isn't very busy, the thread will be scheduled to run quite often; it's just that any other thread with a higher priority will run more often.

At the other extreme, your process might be running with REALTIME_PRIORITY_CLASS and your thread will have THREAD_PRIORITY_TIME_CRITICAL. This nets you a priority score of 31. Windows will try to schedule your thread as often as possible, to the point of starving other threads of time, and note that setting thread priorities to TIME_CRITICAL really isn't a good idea.

It's quite important to understand that thread priorities are designed to be used *temporarily*. For example, you might create a thread that opens a few windows in response to the user; it would be quite reasonable to use the CWinThread::SetThreadPriority() call to change the priority of the thread to something higher, so that the response to the user commands seems instantaneous. After doing this, though, you should be absolutely sure to drop down the thread priority – even (or especially!) in error conditions.

If your application needs to create a couple of pop-up windows in response to a menu command, you might code a handler for that menu like this:

```
void CMyFrame::OnOpenWindows()
{
    CWinThread* pThisThread = AfxGetThread();
    pThisThread->SetThreadPriority(THREAD_PRIORITY_HIGHEST);

    m_pPopupOne = new CPopupTypeOne(this);
    m_pPopupTwo = new CPopupTypeTwo(this);
    if (m_pPopupOne->Create(/* params */) == NULL ||
                            m_pPopupTwo->Create(/* params */) == NULL)
    {
        delete m_pPopupOne;
        delete m_pPopupTwo;
        m_pPopupOne = NULL;
        m_pPopupTwo = NULL;
    }
    else
    {
        m_pPopupOne->UpdateWindow();
        m_pPopupTwo->UpdateWindow();
    }

    pThisThread->SetThreadPriority(THREAD_PRIORITY_NORMAL);
    return;
}
```

As you can see, I use the `AfxGetThread()` function to get a pointer to the currently running `CWinThread` object. By calling that object's `SetThreadPriority()` member, I can raise the priority of the thread to `THREAD_PRIORITY_HIGHEST`. I *don't* use `THREAD_PRIORITY_TIME_CRITICAL` because I'm just trying to make my application respond quickly to the user – I respect the fact that there might be threads around which really *do* need to respond to time-critical events, like heart monitors or transmissions from a satellite, not to mention some critical parts of Windows NT!

We can assume that the two windows I want to create are managed by the member variables `m_pPopupOne` and `m_pPopupTwo`. The code above allocates the window objects and then creates them. If the creation of either window fails, the windows are deleted and the `m_pPopupOne` and `m_pPopupTwo` members are reset to `NULL` so we know the windows aren't available.

After all this work, I call `SetThreadPriority()` again to make the priority return to `THREAD_PRIORITY_NORMAL`. If there's a chance that the thread's priority wasn't `THREAD_PRIORITY_NORMAL` in the first place, I might instead want to code a call to `GetThreadPriority()` to save the initial priority before changing it. While it might seem as if this function does almost no work, it *does* ensure that the initial update of the window happens at a higher priority than normal. The effects of this code won't be drastic on a system where there's not much happening, but on a system which is heavily loaded with threads which aren't operating at a very high priority, the code will make the application's response to the user seem somewhat crisper.

If you're writing an application which responds to hardware, or some other external event input, you might consider raising the thread priority permanently, but do this as sparingly as possible – you'll be starving other threads of attention. After all, *every* interactive Windows application is busy responding to external events as they're input – your users will attack your program with mice and keyboards.

Even if your computer isn't informing the world about the ailing health of a world leader, it's still connected to enough devices to ruin your day. If you've created an application with such a high priority that the machine starts to ignore other needs, you'll find that things won't stay stable for long. It's a common mistake to give one busy thread a very high priority; it's a mistake because the code that's needed to control your user interface won't run. Note that Windows NT dynamically adjusts thread priorities, which makes it even less of a good idea to play with the priorities of your threads except temporarily, as shown here.

Switching Contexts

When operating systems developers talk about **context switching**, they're referring to the act of moving an operating system's execution focus from one thread to the next. The operating system must completely preserve the state of the current thread context when it wants to stop executing that thread and start another one.

Throughout its lifetime, each thread runs for a while and then is pre-empted by the system to let another one run. This starting and stopping could happen hundreds of times a second. Just as the many frames of still pictures per second in a motion picture make it seem as if you're really watching continuous action, these fast state transitions make it seem as if the threads are all running continuously and concurrently. Many newer processors are capable of helping the operating system by switching contexts very, very efficiently. The operating system needs to switch threads continually so it can serve all of the demands of the software running on it.

Processes vs. Threads

Beyond threads, the operating system also enforces another arbitrary division between concurrently executing units of code – **processes**. At any given time, your Windows machine might be running several processes. You might be compiling a C++ program, playing Minesweeper, and printing a report from your checkbook, while two users are connected to a SQL database on your machine, running queries or performing updates. Since they're all separate applications, each is executing on your machine as a separate process.

However, each one of these processes may consist of several threads. A good example of a multithreaded process is the SQL database system I mentioned. One thread in the database manager process may be servicing a user's request by reading or writing the database file while the other may be waiting for an I/O operation over the network. The process – what the user perceives as the SQL database server – owns both of these threads.

A given thread can dynamically create and destroy other threads, or a thread can decide for itself that its work is done and terminate of its own accord. A thread must be owned by a process, even if the process in question is a part of the operating system. A thread can't be owned by more than one process.

Processes are big. They're whole programs. They have their own private memory space, which they don't share with anyone. By contrast, a thread is usually used to implement just a single task, like printing. It might not even be something the user can discern as a identifiable task – one thread in Visual Studio, for example, has nothing to do all day but sit and wait for files that you've opened in the editor to change and ask you if you want to load the new version of the file.

Every process has at least one thread – the **primary thread**. It's created by the system when the process is loaded into memory and begins executing. This makes perfect sense; a process alone is just a memory image, but a thread is something that actually breathes life into that memory image and gets it to do some work. This structure is also the natural reason that CWinApp is a derivative of CWinThread.

A thread is smaller than a process because a process includes a range of logical address space that's completely dedicated to loading and running the program. One program, which might consist of several executable images including one .exe file and any number of .dll files, owns a range of memory. It's that memory range which defines the process that's running. A thread, on the other hand, doesn't own any memory besides some stack space.

As it's injected into the process, the primary thread brings with it all of the things it needs: a stack, an instruction pointer, and an initial state for all of the registers in the CPU. Then it starts running. The first thread will start executing at main(), or at WinMain(), or whatever symbol you've specified in the Entry-point symbol option under the Output Category on the Link tab of your Project Settings dialog when you built the application.

The thread might subsequently decide to create more threads that similarly need entry points. The Windows ::CreateThread() API is the function used to create a new thread and get it running. It takes, among its other parameters, an address for a function which will control that thread. When that function returns, the thread ends.

While the threads are running, Windows is starting and stopping them to give the illusion that they're running at the same time. If a thread is stopped, it's said to be **suspended**. Some people refer to the act of making a suspended thread run again as **releasing** the thread. If you have more than one CPU in your machine, the illusion fades and the threads really *are* running at the same time. One CPU might run thread A, while the other might run thread B. Windows might decide to suspend thread A for a moment, to let thread C run on CPU number one, but can still let thread B continue to run on the second CPU.

From your perspective, your thread and all the others will get execution time almost arbitrarily from the operating system. They'll get time as often as their priority warrants when compared to other running threads, but there's very little way to predict exactly *when* your thread will execute. If you start reading about thread APIs, you'll notice that phrases like 'at least' and 'at most' and 'no earlier than' are used very frequently. Those words are important – they mean exactly what they say, and you need to understand fully the particulars of the effects of the functions you call if you want your programs to work safely.

To stop executing, a thread can call the ::Sleep() API if it realizes it has no useful work to do and wishes to relinquish the rest of its time slice to other threads on the system. This API takes a single parameter: an integer that specifies the minimum number of milliseconds that the thread will rest. Again, remember that the number specifies a *minimum* number of milliseconds; the operating system might not necessarily schedule your thread to run again in exactly one second if you code ::Sleep(1000).

Applications for Multithreading

If you think about it for a bit, you might wonder what the point is of having multiple threads. After all, it's not like two things are *really* happening at once, and going through these hoops to let the operating system pretend that two things can happen at once is more trouble than it's worth, isn't it?

Largely, you're right – it *is* more trouble than it's worth. There's usually no real reason to write a multithreaded application. Some marketing guys hear that 'multithreaded' is a cool buzz word and harass the developers to implement many threads, like some nightmarish Dilbert cartoon, or some developer gets it into their head that they won't be cool unless they use multiple threads. So, in order to look good in front of their friends, they scamper off and write an application which creates threads that create threads that create threads.

In fact, what you get are performance bottlenecks. The operating system has to take some amount of time to switch from thread to thread – you can't get away from that. There are also a few things to worry about when you're trying to communicate between threads – more on that later. So, unless you absolutely need the threads, there's really no point. You're slowing down your application and making work for yourself when you should be out watching ice hockey games or playing with your motorcycle.

Times When You Shouldn't

When you're adding threads to your application, there are lots of issues that crop up that might not immediately spring to mind. For instance, you should be aware that threads often stall because of Windows APIs. If you were to think about the function of the API, you'd realize the problem immediately, but nobody, particularly not experienced Windows programmers, is too caught up in thinking about problems from this angle.

There are several unfortunate sample applications around (such as `Mtmdi` in the advanced MFC samples, for instance) which imply that it's a great idea to create one thread per window for your applications. This can be good in a few select cases but, in the sample, it's actually a pretty bad idea. MDI applications manage a frame window, a client area window and a child window for each opened document. These windows frequently send messages between one another. The `::SendMessage()` API, which these windows use internally, causes the thread sending the message to stall until the receiving thread can get the message, process it and return.

This adds a great deal of extra processing. The sending window must stop executing, and the scheduler must get around to starting up the receiving thread before the application can continue. How terrible! This architecture introduces extra overheads just because it uses multiple threads. It would be a better idea to let the windows all run with one thread.

Times When You Should

I've outlined some situations where using threads is a false economy but, on the other hand, there are times when using a thread to help you with your work is a smashing idea. For example, a *great* time to consider using a thread is when you have lots of work to do, but you also need to keep an eye on some external event, a piece of hardware, or the user.

If you're writing a communications program, for example, you would have a few potential applications for threads. You might let the primary thread for your application act as a traffic cop, having it handle the user interface. It might also coordinate communications between other threads in your application. It would then be a great idea to create another thread for handling the communications port. If there was something waiting at the port, the communications thread could nab it and tuck it away in a private buffer. If there isn't anything at the port, the thread could relinquish the rest of its time slice, giving the CPU back to other threads in the application or in the system.

The primary thread could query the subordinate thread for characters it has received. If the subordinate thread has any new characters, it could provide them to the user interface thread to draw them on the screen.

This is a good architecture for two reasons. First, the extra code you'll write to manage the two tasks is very logically separated. You're not using a thread for the sake of starting another thread, you're actually gaining benefit from it. If you *didn't* use two threads, you'd have to design your application carefully to keep it peeking at the communications port when it wasn't doing other work. The other work would stall while your application fooled with the communications port. On the other hand, with the threads in place, your application can make simple checks for the other thread quite naturally. You could even set up a mechanism where the communications thread actively notifies the user interface thread. That makes responding to information on the communications port almost as easy as handling a message!

Second, the use of threads is pretty natural too. You're not constructing a dependency between the two threads where one *consistently* needs information from another before it can get work done. Some threaded applications stall because one thread actually spends all of its time waiting around for another. In this hypothetical application, this wouldn't be true; the traffic-cop thread has plenty of work to do in interacting with the user. When it has time, it can get information from the communications thread to digest later, but the threads can execute independently without much waiting.

This notion of independent execution is something you should strive for. You'll find that good multithreaded applications have two very definite roles for threads. One is where the thread is always running, independent of other threads, and includes some mechanism for providing results or data back to the original thread. The other is a thread that almost never runs; it sleeps, or waits for an event to happen. When it happens (the event *triggers* the thread), the thread does some work quickly and then falls asleep again, or maybe just terminates.

Threads and Message Loops

If you programmed Win16 for a long time, you probably tried at one time or another to make 'fake' threads by doing extra processing inside your message loop. Even if you haven't had this kind of experience, you still need to realize there are some very important relationships between a thread and a message loop.

A message loop is a loop that retrieves messages from the thread's message queue and dispatches them to the appropriate function. MFC replaces much of that mechanism with code that efficiently dispatches the messages to the appropriate C++ object's member function for handling.

Don't be misled by the jargon. The message loop is just code. It's just a loop. It runs. It needs a thread to be running. Each thread that has its own message queue must have its own message loop. If the thread stalls, no messages for that thread get retrieved or processed. They keep piling up until the message queue overflows (which can take a long time under Win32). If you have a worker thread that doesn't have any windows, it might not be sent any messages, so it's quite normal not to endow the thread with a message loop. However, if you have a user interface thread, you will certainly give it a message loop so that it can handle messages sent or posted to windows that it has created.

This introduces a very important concept – any window that's created is owned by a particular thread. Thinking about it, this is obvious; you can't execute a code outside of a thread, and you must execute code to create a window. *Only* the creating thread can retrieve messages for a window; it might ask another thread to do work in response to the message, but no thread can retrieve messages sent to a window that it doesn't own. It turns out, though, that threads can also receive messages directly. We'll examine that topic in a section called 'Thread Messages' later on. (I'm really a whiz at naming these things. Please don't let any of the editors tell you that they had a hand in it.)

Applying Threads

Programming with threads seems simple at first; just decide which execution bottlenecks make your application slow and throw some threads at them. In reality, especially a reality colored by experience, it's much more important to approach the application design carefully, with threads in mind all along.

Almost all good multithreaded programs are attempts at maximizing the time for which a process is allowed to execute. If your application ever spends time waiting for input, output, or other events outside the direct context of the process itself, it can probably benefit from a multithreaded architecture. The time your application spends waiting for network I/O to complete could be used to update the user interface, perform more processing, or even begin another I/O operation. The idea of having multiple threads here is that one thread waits on the I/O while another gets some real work done.

If these blocking conditions exist in your application, then the workload should be split amongst many threads, getting more work done at the same time. If you've written a program that performs some unit of computation, writes the results of that computation to a disk file and then loops to perform the same task again, you could benefit by allowing the I/O to take place in one thread and the computation to take place in another. The time spent waiting for the operating system to perform writes will block the I/O thread, but the computational thread will be free to continue processing.

On the other hand, if your program performs some computations, writes the results to disk and then exits, it's a waste of time to implement threads. Your application will have to wait for the I/O operation to complete before returning to the user anyway, so why use another thread? You gain nothing from the preemptive multitasking afforded while your I/O work completes.

In the Windows environment, I/O operations happen a lot more often than when you're just writing a file to disk. You may wish to use additional threads to maintain the user interface of your application while the primary thread processes data. This technique is most applicable to situations where output is extremely slow – printing, for example.

Unfortunately, it's beyond the scope of this book to explain how to apply threads correctly in every circumstance and, perhaps even more unfortunately, that means I can't really completely describe when not to apply them either. I can't paint every painting that could be painted just to show the difference between the bad paintings and the good ones. (I *am*, however, working on seeing every hockey game ever played, and I'll soon be able to write something up.) Instead, I can outline situations that are certainly good and situations that are certainly bad; it's up to you, as a developer, to make a decision that will work for you and meet your specific needs.

If you can't prove that additional threads will benefit your application, don't use them. Sorting out the mess may be more complicated than justifying to your customers, your users, your boss or your spouse why your program appears to be so slow. If you've misapplied threads and your customer *is* your spouse, your situation might be considered completely hopeless.

Creating Threads

There are two ways to create threads in MFC applications. The first way is very MFC-centric and is particularly applicable to situations where you need to have a thread running to service a particular window and the processing associated with it. The second approach involves creating a thread in an MFC application which follows the Win32 thread management APIs more closely, so offering you more control over the behavior of the thread, but making it a tad more difficult to associate a thread with a window in your application directly.

The MFC technique for creating a thread is very much the same as the method for creating any other Windows object. MFC objects have a longer lifetime than their related Windows counterparts, being created before and destroyed after the existence of the Windows object. If you wish to create another thread for your process, you must first create an instance of the CWinThread class. The CWinThread's constructor simply initializes the CWinThread object; it doesn't actually create a thread.

Your Own Threads

The implementation of CWinThread is complete, in that it wraps the Windows threading API for you; you needn't be concerned with the functions that Windows itself uses when it is creating, executing or destroying threads. However, CWinThread's implementation is incomplete in that it does no work for you; you must derive a class in your application from CWinThread and override some functions to make sure you gain the functionality you need.

The only member function of CWinThread that you *must* override is InitInstance(). This function is similar to the InitInstance() function of CWinApp, in that it's called each time you create the thread that is wrapped by the instance of the thread class (i.e. it is called from CreateThread(), not the constructor). You should perform any initialization your thread needs in the InitInstance() member of your CWinThread-derived class. CWinThread has a corresponding ExitInstance() function which is called when your thread terminates. This function is the appropriate place for any destruction code required by your thread.

Once your `CWinThread`-derived object is created, creating the actual Windows thread is only one step away; simply call the `CreateThread()` member function of `CWinThread`. The MFC approach to creating a thread may therefore look something like this:

```
CMyThread* pWinThread;                          // derives from CWinThread

pWinThread = new CMyThread;                      // _not_ CWinThread!
if (pWinThread->CreateThread() == FALSE)
{
    MessageBox("Couldn't Create Thread");
    delete pWinThread;
    pWinThread = NULL;
}
```

The MFC thread object, pointed to by the `pWinThread` pointer, is created by the `new` operator, but the actual Windows thread isn't created until the call to `CreateThread()` returns.

Thread Messages

Threads can receive messages directly. In Win16 applications, you could only send messages to a window, but in Win32 applications you can post messages either to a window or directly to a thread, even if that thread doesn't have any windows. You can do this using the `::PostThreadMessage()` API, or the `PostThreadMessage()` member function of `CWinThread`.

In addition to the regular message parameters (that is, the message number and its `WPARAM` and `LPARAM` parameters), the API takes the ID of the thread to which you're posting the message (instead of the handle of the destination window). The `CWinThread` member function, of course, doesn't take a thread ID parameter – it posts the message to the thread represented by the `CWinThread` object. A message posted in this way – directly to a thread and not to a window – is appropriately called a **thread message**.

In the message pump that MFC uses, MFC picks out thread-targeted messages because the `MSG` structure returned by Windows in the message loop for thread messages always has an `hWnd` of `NULL`.

Note there is no function named `SendThreadMessage()` in either MFC or the Win32 API. That's because thread messages are always posted and never sent; it makes no sense to send a thread message, since it would block the sending thread. Why bother making a call across threads when the thread initiating the message has to wait for the message to be processed anyway? This underscores the fact that sending (as compared to posting) a message from a given thread to a window owned by a different thread isn't very efficient. It's not a design flaw – sometimes, waiting for the response to the message is simply necessary – but blocking on the message processing of another thread certainly isn't the kind of thing you should do frequently in your applications.

If you've written your own class based on `CWinThread`, you can use message maps in the class to catch thread messages. The message map entry macro named `ON_THREAD_MESSAGE()` lets you nab any old message, while `ON_REGISTERED_THREAD_MESSAGE()` lets you catch registered messages. You might catch a couple of messages sent to instances of your thread class named `CWorkThread` using a message map like this:

```
BEGIN_MESSAGE_MAP(CWorkThread, CWinThread)
    ON_THREAD_MESSAGE(ID_MSG_TERMINATE, OnTerminate)
    ON_REGISTERED_THREAD_MESSAGE(nSequenceStartMsg, OnStartSequence)
END_MESSAGE_MAP(CWorkThread)
```

Threads are a little different from windows in the way they process messages. They don't receive messages which are normally destined for windows, so pretty much any message identifier you'd like to use is just fine. Even if the message ID you use is exactly equal to some other message the thread processes, the thread can tell the difference between messages passed to it and messages it is processing on behalf of a window. When the thread gets a message for itself, the target hWnd of the window is NULL, while a message sent to a particular window identifies that window in the hWnd of the message information. As the message pump buried in CWinThread pumps messages, it receives information about each message in the form of an MSG structure. The discrimination between thread-destined messages and window-destined messages is made during the same dispatch mechanism that we talked about back in Chapter 3.

A thread-destined message is never sent to anything other than the thread. In MFC, the message is offered to the CWinThread-derived class which was to receive the message, and then is offered up the class hierarchy until it reaches the CWinThread class in MFC itself, and finally to the CCmdTarget class (which is the base class for CWinThread). In MFC 6.0, neither of these classes has any message handlers of its own.

The ON_THREAD_MESSAGE() macro takes the identifier of a message which you'll be handling as its first parameter, and the name of the function which handles your message as its second parameter. ON_REGISTERED_THREAD_MESSAGE() takes the name of a handler function as its second parameter too, but the first parameter must identify a variable which contains a value returned from the ::RegisterWindowMessage() API provided by Windows. MFC will throw an assertion if the message number isn't in the expected range of values for such a message.

If you were to code the above message map, you might initialize the nSequenceStartMsg variable at the global scope within your module, like this:

```
UINT nSequenceStartMsg = ::RegisterWindowMessage(_T("My very own message!"));
```

If you're an old-time C programmer, you might gasp audibly at the notion of calling a function to initialize a global variable – but C++ allows it quite happily.

You won't often need to register a message for your thread-to-thread communications pleasure, since you can use any old message ID without fear of doing something that Windows would normally do for you. Windows never sends messages directly to threads. The ID_MSG_TERMINATE message I used in the code fragment a few paragraphs ago is something I made up all by myself. I'm very creative.

If you need to send a message from a thread in your application to a thread that lives in another application, it behooves you to be very cautious. You shouldn't go around assuming that some other application knows which message identifiers you mean it to respond to if you haven't already let it know about them. The ::RegisterWindowMessage() function solves this problem. You pass it a string that serves as the name of your message. The API then invents a message ID that's guaranteed unique, but repeatably identifiable. In other words, if two applications call ::RegisterWindowMessage() with the same string, they'll always get the same message ID.

Thread Messages in Days of Yore

The information about thread messages I've presented so far applies only to MFC version 4.2b and above. Before that, CWinThread didn't support message maps. If you find yourself using or maintaining code produced for a version of MFC prior to 4.2b, you'll come across a rather different technique for handling thread messages. This technique is still supported, and while you shouldn't implement it from scratch – the new way is much preferred – you should still be aware of it.

You can override the PreTranslateMessage() function in your class to have a crack at messages the thread will process before they're grabbed by the normal Windows TranslateMessage() and DispatchMessage() APIs. You need to do this because those APIs simply discard thread-bound messages.

CWinThread::PreTranslateMessage() takes a pointer to an MSG structure which contains information about the message sent. When a message is sent to a thread, the hWnd member of the MSG structure will be NULL. Since a thread can receive a message without having a window, and since thread messages are sent directly to threads and not to a window, the lack of a window handle lets you know without a doubt that the message is thread-specific. So, your PreTranslateMessage() routine can be very simple:

```
BOOL CYourThread::PreTranslateMessage(MSG* pMsg)
{
    if (pMsg->hWnd == NULL)
    {
        // It's yours! do something interesting
        // pMsg->message is the message id
        // pMsg->wParam and ->lParam are params
        return TRUE;
    }
    else
        return CWinThread::PreTranslateMessage()
}
```

If the message has a NULL hWnd, you know it's aimed squarely at your thread and that you can handle it. You can pick apart the MSG structure passed to you to get the juicy marrow inside. Otherwise, you should call the base-class implementation of PreTranslateMessage() to let the message dispatch proceed normally. You should handle the message in the PreTranslateMessage() override. Thread messages are always posted, so there's no need for you to return anything to the code which originally posted the message. On the other hand, you must return TRUE to the dispatch code which called PreTranslateMessage() so that code knows you ate the message and that it doesn't need to be dispatched to anyone else.

Again, versions of MFC from 4.2b onwards thankfully make it unnecessary to do this PreTranslateMessage() work when handling messages posted directly to a thread.

Benefits of MFC Thread Creation

The MFC technique has some benefits. Most notably, if you create a thread in this way, it's very easy to make the thread responsible for a particular window. Associating a thread with a window allows your application to process user input and output using an individual, separate thread, while others perform independent work in other portions of your program. The most appropriate way to realize this functionality is to have your InitInstance() function create the window it will be managing. Once the window is created, you should make the m_pMainWnd member variable of CWinThread be a pointer to the window you've created. This causes the message dispatch code built into CWinThread to manage the window exclusively.

> Because the thread can only retrieve messages addressed to windows it owns, you can't create a window before you create the thread you wish to use for it.

Aside from m_pMainWnd, CWinThread has some other interesting member variables. You can get the Win32 handle to the thread represented by a given CWinThread object by examining the m_hThread member variable. This variable is NULL if the CWinThread instance has yet to actually create the thread. The 'sandwich creation' paradigm we've seen with most other MFC objects is at work here again: create the C++ object first, then create the Windows object, then destroy the Windows object, then destroy the C++ object.

The m_bAutoDelete member variable is TRUE by default. This means the CWinThread object wrapping the thread object will be destroyed by MFC when the Windows thread terminates. Having this variable set to TRUE can makes managing threads a bit more convenient, since it causes MFC to delete the CWinThread object as the thread terminates.

These member variables bring to light another advantage to the MFC method for creating threads; the member variables can be directly set before the thread is actually created. You can make these settings in the constructor for the thread, or directly on the thread object after it's created but before calling the CreateThread() member.

When your Windows thread is finally created, the first thing it does is execute the InitInstance() member of the thread class. Just like CWinApp::InitInstance(), CWinThread::InitInstance() can return FALSE if the initialization of the thread has failed. If, for example, the window creation for the thread fails, it would be a good idea to return FALSE so that work on it stops and the unused thread is destroyed.

In addition, you can also override the CWinThread::Run() function to have the thread do some work for you. If you do your own work here, *don't* call the base class implementation of the function because it will just enter a message loop and won't return until it has received a WM_QUIT message.

Worker Threads

The MFC method for creating threads readily lends itself to the application of threads for handling a given window's events. However, this technique is not always appropriate, because sometimes you may wish to use a thread for a task that doesn't involve a window. For instance, you might want to create a thread to perform a task in the background, such as a long recalculation, complex database activity, or a slow printing operation.

Starting a Thread

To provide for these circumstances, MFC also implements the AfxBeginThread() function, which allows you to create threads without deriving your own version of CWinThread. You can also use the API to manage threads based around your own derivative of CWinThread. To this end, the function is implemented with two overrides.

The first overloaded version takes a pointer to a function that will control the thread. It looks like this:

```
CWinThread* AfxBeginThread(
            AFX_THREADPROC          pfnThreadProc,
            LPVOID                  pParam,
            int                     nPriority = THREAD_PRIORITY_NORMAL,
            UINT                    nStackSize = 0,
            DWORD                   dwCreateFlags = 0,
            LPSECURITY_ATTRIBUTES lpSecurityAttrs = NULL);
```

This version also takes a LPVOID parameter which is handed to the controlling function as a parameter; you can use it to pass a pointer to a structure of information to the controlling function. We'll see a great example of this (just ask me how great it is!) in a couple of sections' time.

The other version of the function takes a pointer to a RUNTIME_CLASS information object which is defined by the CWinThread-derived class you'll be using to control the thread. We discussed the run-time type information used by MFC earlier in the book. The prototype for this overload of AfxBeginThread() looks like this:

```
CWinThread* AfxBeginThread(
            CRuntimeClass*          pThreadClass,
            int                     nPriority = THREAD_PRIORITY_NORMAL,
            UINT                    nStackSize = 0,
            DWORD                   dwCreateFlags = 0,
            LPSECURITY_ATTRIBUTES   lpSecurityAttrs = NULL);
```

As you can see, the majority of the parameters are the same as those for the other overload. Since they're common, let's discuss them first; they're used to control exactly how MFC will perform its ultimate, internal Win32 CreateThread() call.

nPriority can be used to set the initial priority of the thread; values like THREAD_PRIORITY_HIGHEST and THREAD_PRIORITY_ABOVE_NORMAL can be used to allow Windows to schedule time for the thread more readily, while THREAD_PRIORITY_BELOW_NORMAL and THREAD_PRIORITY_LOWEST cause Windows to schedule time for the thread less often. The default value of THREAD_PRIORITY_NORMAL is adequate for almost all uses. You can find a discussion of all these parameters earlier in this chapter.

The nStackSize parameter dictates the initial size of the thread's stack; remember that each thread has its own stack. The default value of zero for this parameter causes Windows to allocate the same amount of stack space for the new thread as for the spawning thread. Although Windows will dynamically grow the stack, setting this value to gain more stack space can result in a slight performance improvement for the thread, as Windows won't have to allocate additional stack space for the process, little by little, as it executes and demands more space.

dwCreateFlags can either be zero or CREATE_SUSPENDED. If it's zero, which it is by default, the thread is created and immediately allowed to run. If the parameter is CREATE_SUSPENDED, the thread is suspended and doesn't run until the Win32 API ::ResumeThread() is called against the thread.

The lpSecurityAttrs parameter accepts a pointer to a security attributes structure. You'll almost never need to use this parameter, as threads almost never need anything more than the default security. If you *do* need to provide some security, you can allocate a SECURITY_ATTRIBUTES structure yourself and use the ::InitializeSecurityDescriptor() call in the Win32 API to initialize the lpSecurityDescriptor field in that structure.

> *The security functions are not part of the Windows 95/98 or Win32s API. All of the security functions return the failure code appropriate to the specific function and set the last error (visible with a call to the ::GetLastError() API) to ERROR_CALL_NOT_IMPLEMENTED.*

`AfxBeginThread()` returns the address of the new object immediately after the new thread is created, and the thread calling `AfxBeginThread()` runs concurrently with it. Since `AfxBeginThread()` always returns a pointer to a `CWinThread`, you may need to cast it to a pointer to the derived thread class which you actually wish to implement if you use the runtime class overload.

The Controlling Function

If you're using the `AFX_THREADPROC` version of `AfxBeginThread()`, you'll need to provide a pointer to a function to control the thread. This is called the thread's **controlling function**.

The controlling function of a thread implements that thread. It's called to start the thread, and when it returns the thread is terminated. The function doesn't need to do any work to start or terminate the thread, as this is handled by the operating system, but it does do all of the preparatory work for the thread's initialization. You may find this one of the most intuitive ways to implement a thread, since no extra work is required. The controlling function runs in the context of the thread.

The function which creates the thread can communicate with the controlling function using the second parameter to `AfxBeginThread()`. Neither MFC nor Windows make use of this parameter's value; they just send it along as a parameter to the controlling thread. As such, you can use it to send a number or a pointer to the newly running thread, or just set it to `NULL` if you don't need it. Of course, you may have to cast the parameter you wish to send to `LPVOID` if it isn't a pointer.

The prototype you should use for your controlling function is:

```
UINT SomeControllingFunction(LPVOID pParam);
```

More often than not, the controlling function for a thread will be a global function not associated with a class. Your controlling function *can* be a member function of a class, but only if it's a `static` member. Semantically, this means that you can't make use of the `this` pointer, explicitly or implicitly, in the implementation of your controlling function. As a strategy to avoid this shortcoming, it's a very common practice to pass a pointer to any object the thread might use during execution.

The other option is to make the function a `friend` of the class.

There are also some rules about exactly which objects you can pass safely and successfully from thread to thread. I'll talk about these in a section called 'Threads and MFC', closer to the end of the chapter. That section also includes some suggestions for how you can easily work within the rules.

When you're designing your thread class, keep in mind the implications of the C++ language. Unless your controlling function is a member or `friend` of the `CWinThread`-derived class you're using, you can't access any variables or functions that are not declared as `public`.

The Runtime Way

I need to make good on my promise to describe the other thread creation mechanism presented by the second overload of the AfxBeginThread() function. To save you looking back, here it is again:

```
CWinThread* AfxBeginThread(
            CRuntimeClass*        pThreadClass,
            int                   nPriority = THREAD_PRIORITY_NORMAL,
            UINT                  nStackSize = 0,
            DWORD                 dwCreateFlags = 0,
            LPSECURITY_ATTRIBUTES lpSecurityAttrs = NULL);
```

We already described all of the other parameters, so the real mystery is the pThreadClass parameter. This lets you offer the function runtime type information to identify the particular class you'd like to use to create your thread object. We've already discussed the specifics of this MFC mechanism in detail when we examined the CObject class in Chapter 3, so I can get away here with saying that all you need to do is to slap the MFC-supplied RUNTIME_CLASS() macro around the name of your CWinThread-derived class.

If you wanted to use a class called CPrinterThread, which you've based on CWinThread, to control your thread, you could make your call like this:

```
pNewThread = (CPrinterThread*)AfxBeginThread(RUNTIME_CLASS(CPrinterThread));
```

The AfxBeginThread() function will create an object of the class you've specified by calling its default constructor; then it will start the thread and attach it to that object. Windows will use the newly constructed thread to enter your CPrinterThread::InitInstance() function. Your thread will run until it completes. For a thread created like this, 'completes' can mean that the InitInstance() call returns FALSE because the initialization failed and the thread couldn't even get started the way it wanted to. Alternatively, it can mean that initialization succeeded and the Run() member of your class finally returned and the thread is done.

Like all other MFC objects, a CWinThread-derived object used in this manner usually outlives the inner Windows object. Your CWinThread-derived class creates an object before the real Windows thread is created, but your object lives after the CWinThread-managed object terminates only if you've set the m_bAutoDelete member of the object to FALSE. Otherwise, MFC will take care of deleting the thread object just after the thread stops running.

If you have a thread which you're sure will run to termination before your creating thread dies, you might consider using m_bAutoDelete. Be careful, though – m_bAutoDelete removes all record of the thread. The pointer returned by AfxBeginThread() is no longer valid, so you can't use it to gain the handle to the thread from the m_hThread member. That member, as we'll see in the next section, is the key to getting the return code from the thread.

Normally, when you use the CRuntimeClass* overload of AfxBeginThread(), you'll use the dwCreateFlags parameter to the function to make the thread create as suspended. This will let the AfxBeginThread() function return with a pointer to the new thread object before that object is actually set into motion. You can use the opportunity to initialize member variables of the thread, so the code in the thread class can later have information about your exact request. Once your initialization is done, you can call ResumeThread() against the suspended thread to get it running. ResumeThread() offers you the ability to create a CWinThread object and get that object running with a different thread.

Terminating a Thread

Threads can terminate in one of two ways: either naturally or prematurely. A thread ends naturally when its controlling function returns. For worker threads, this means that the controlling function has simply finished its work and returned. For user interface threads, this means that the thread must call `PostQuitMessage()` to force the message loop in the MFC-supplied controlling function of the thread to exit. If the thread is managing an MFC window, MFC will automatically perform a `PostQuitMessage()` itself as the main window for the thread is destroyed.

In a worker thread, the controlling function can simply return, or it can call `AfxEndThread()`. `AfxEndThread()` accepts one parameter, a `UINT` which is the result code for the thread. This function terminates the thread.

I'll say that again. `AfxEndThread()` *terminates* the thread. That means the thread doesn't get to clean up after itself. MFC will clean up any internal stuff that it has done for you, and so will the C runtime library through a call to `_endthreadex()`. However, 'internal stuff' doesn't include any data structures or objects that you've created in that thread, and doesn't let the program destroy objects that it has temporarily created. Consider the class `CFoo`, which I've just invented:

```
class CFoo
{
    char* m_pFoo;
public:
    CFoo() { m_pFoo = new char[2048]; }
    ~CFoo() { delete [] m_pFoo; }
};
```

While `CFoo` is useless, it's certainly safe. If a `CFoo` object is constructed, it allocates a bunch of memory and hangs on to it. When it's destroyed, it turns around and releases that memory. It seems like there's no way to get in trouble with the `CFoo` class.

But `CFoo` coupled with `AfxEndThread()` is a disaster. Imagine if you coded this thread controlling function:

```
UINT CongressThreadFunc(LPVOID pParam)
{
    CFoo fooey;
    // Do some important work
    AfxEndThread(1);
    return 2;
}
```

I've called this function `CongressThreadFunc()` because it seems to leak resources without explanation, and doesn't do anything at all, even though it says that it's going to do some important work. But even without the aid of a subcommittee, we can figure out the reason that this function leaks memory.

`fooey` is constructed on the stack; it calls the `CFoo` constructor, which allocates two kilobytes of memory. We then do some important work (or, at least, we say we do). When we call `AfxEndThread()`, that's it — our thread is over. We don't go any further in the execution of this function, and we don't really go much further in the execution of the thread either. Inside of `AfxEndThread()`, MFC cleans up some stuff it needs to remember about each thread, and then asks the C Runtime library to do the same thing. MFC shuts down the thread, and that's all. There's nothing more.

The CFoo destructor would normally be called by this code; that's very true. The compiler emits code to call the destructor implicitly – that code is associated with the return statement. Functions that don't have an explicit return statement have the same code implicitly tucked into the function; you can imagine it being just inside the last closing brace. (In fact, if you open the disassembly window in the debugger, that's where you'll usually see the call to the destructor actually made. Assuming, of course, you can read assembler code!)

But because the call to AfxEndThread() is made and never, ever returns (because it ends the thread!), that CFoo object is never destroyed and therefore leaks memory. That also means the return statement never executes either. This thread function ends and gives the thread the return value 1 by virtue of its call to AfxEndThread(). It *does not* end up executing the return statement, and it *does not* return the value 2.

In other words, AfxEndThread() is a very, very dangerous function and should almost never be used. The times when it is safe to call AfxEndThread() are few and far between. Even if you have no local variables in the function you're executing, you don't truly know if the function that called your function within that thread has local variables and objects which could cause memory leaks if not properly destroyed or released.

Premature Termination

Prematurely terminating a thread is a little more complicated than simply returning from the controlling function, like you might do in normal circumstances. If code within the thread knows it needs to terminate, it can work on exiting the controlling function, exiting the Run() member function or finally leaving the InitInstance() member. In a completely catastrophic case, the thread code can call AfxEndThread() – but you'll need to deal with the consequences.

Yet another problem with this call is that it must be made from the thread which is to be terminated, but it's often the thread that created the secondary thread which wants to terminate it asynchronously. The primary thread can't call AfxEndThread() for the secondary thread, so it must set up some communication method with the secondary thread.

If, for example, you implement a secondary thread to take care of printing in your application, the primary thread will need to be able to shut down the secondary thread to give the user the opportunity to cancel printing. For user interface threads, the secondary thread may be able to trap a message to clean up any work currently in focus. The primary thread can then simply post that message to the window managed by the secondary thread to have it terminate.

Before a user-interface thread terminates, MFC calls the ExitInstance() function in the derived class, so some of the cleanup work can be placed there as well. Note that this is only true for user-interface threads; threads which don't have message loops, or threads which don't receive WM_QUIT before they're terminated *won't* call their ExitInstance() member.

For worker threads, the problem is a little more complicated. The controlling thread has no direct predefined method of communicating with the secondary thread, so you must provide your own communication mechanism. You can solve this problem by avoiding it; have your printing thread also manage the progress dialog box, for example. That way, the code that handles the Cancel button runs in the same thread that handles the printing and could cleanly use AfxEndThread(). On the other hand, if you're convinced you need two different threads, you might write some code which notifies one thread that the other needs some attention by posting a thread message or signaling a named event you created using ::CreateEvent().

Play it Safe!

Some developers like to use APIs like `TerminateThread()`, which initially seems quite handy – it will let you end a thread from outside that thread. If you decide you don't like the work the thread is doing you can just kill it with `TerminateThread()`.

However, you might notice that MFC's `CWinThread` class doesn't implement `TerminateThread()`. You could call it, if you had to, by using the `m_hThread` handle that's a member of the `CWinThread` object, but you shouldn't. `TerminateThread()` is far more dangerous than `AfxEndThread()` – and `AfxEndThread()` shouldn't be used. `TerminateThread()` is like radioactive nuclear waste from Planet X-1; under no circumstances should you ever think of putting it in your program!

MFC doesn't implement this function simply because it's too dangerous. `TerminateThread()` stops a thread, period. It doesn't let the thread clean itself up, or let it release memory or other resources that it might have. It just stops executing. This is just miserable; not only will you leak the files and memory you've already allocated, you run the risk of being in the middle of allocating one of those resources. If the resource is allocated and Windows hasn't yet assigned it to your thread, or if the C runtime libraries are in the middle of managing some pointers in the heap, or if GDI is in the middle of passing some data back and forth between the system and a device driver, the game is probably almost over. Windows NT will protect the rest of the system, but Windows 95/98 can't and there's nowhere to go but down. The next allocation, or the next paint, or the next file access can cause your application just to drop dead.

While `AfxEndThread()` has the same net effect as `TerminateThread()`, it does at least do the termination in an orderly fashion. That is, you can be sure you're not in the middle of managing some system-critical data structure when you call `AfxEndThread()`. `TerminateThread()` asynchronously shoots the thread in the head. Both functions are bound to cause memory leaks and other tragedies; `TerminateThread()` additionally causes heartache, hysteria, fatigue, unemployment, instability, and random crashes.

> *There are several other ways to cause a thread to be terminated, such as `ExitThread()`, or `ExitProcess()`, which terminates the process in which it is executing and all threads owned by that process. Calling `AfxEndThread()`, for example, eventually causes `ExitThread()` to be called to terminate the thread but also performs additional cleanup and uninitialization that would need to performed manually if calling these thread API functions directly.*

As I mentioned, there are a couple of good ways to make sure that a thread quits safely. One way is to post a message to it. Exactly what you'll do will depend on your threads. For user interface threads with an identifiable main window, it's a good idea just to close the window; your thread can clean up in `OnClose()` for that window. If you don't have an identifiable main window, or you're interested in terminating a worker thread, you can consider posting your thread a message directly. If your worker thread doesn't even process messages, you might consider setting up some synchronization object (see below) to let your thread know that it needs to quit.

Checking Return Codes

When your thread terminates, either by calling `AfxEndThread()` (which it really shouldn't) or by directly returning from the controlling function, it can offer a return value that will provide the primary thread with some information about the success or failure of the thread. By convention, most programmers use a return value of zero to indicate that the thread completed successfully, and use some non-zero value to indicate an error code. This allows the non-zero error return to provide more information, such as a code that indicates the exact cause of the failure. Of course, you're free to implement whatever return code semantics you wish.

To get the return code from a completed thread, you can call the Windows `GetExitCodeThread()` API. This API takes two parameters: a handle to the thread to be examined, and a pointer to a `DWORD` that will contain the return code from the thread. For instance, you might implement your controlling procedure like this:

```
UINT SomeThreadProcedure(LPVOID pParam)
{
    CMyThreadObject* pObject = (CMyThreadObject*) pParam;

    if (pObject == NULL ||
            pObject->IsKindOf(RUNTIME_CLASS(CMyThreadObject)) == FALSE)
    {
        return -1;
    }

    if (!pObject->DoSomeWork())
    {
        return 1;    // meaningful failure code
    }

    if (!pObject->DoSomeMoreWork())
    {
        return 2;    // meaningful failure code
    }

    return 0;
}
```

This thread controlling function anticipates that it will be passed a pointer to a `CMyThreadObject`. If that pointer is null, or if the pointer is not pointing to an instance of `CMyThreadObject`, the function will immediately terminate the thread with a return code of `-1`.

The function continues by calling some member functions of our thread object class to get the work done. If any one of them fails, the function exits early and returns a non-zero code, but if things go well, the function returns zero. We can check for the status code returned by a secondary thread from its primary thread when the execution of the secondary thread ends.

Your main thread might create and execute this secondary thread by running code like this:

```
LPVOID pNewMyThreadObject = (LPVOID)new CMyThreadObject;
CWinThread* pRunningThread = AfxBeginThread(SomeThreadProcedure,
                                            pNewMyThreadObject);
```

The `AfxBeginThread()` call kicks off the controlling function for the second thread, passing it a pointer to the thread object which would have been derived from `CWinThread`. Say, for instance, we wanted to see if the thread has terminated, we might use code like this:

```
DWORD dwRetCode;

if (!GetExitCodeThread(pRunningThread->m_hThread, &dwRetCode))
{
    // Catastrophic failure!
}

if (dwRetCode == STILL_ACTIVE)
{
    // Still running
}
else
{
    // Done running...
    // dwRetCode has return code from thread's controlling func
    // or AfxEndThread.
}
```

Believe it or not, `STILL_ACTIVE` turns out to be `0x103`, so you'll need to make sure you don't use that value as a status you want to return.

Another way of checking to see if the thread is still running is to use the `::WaitForSingleObject()` function against the handle to the thread; waiting on the thread object itself is a far (far!) more reliable and efficient way to wait for a thread to quit than calling `GetExitCodeThread()`. You might then call `GetExitCodeThread()` *after* a call to `WaitForSingleObject()` has indicated that the thread has stopped. You could test a thread without waiting using a call like this:

```
if (::WaitForSingleObject(pRunningThread->m_hThread, 0) == WAIT_OBJECT_0)
{
    // The thread is done running
}
else
{
    // The thread is still running
}
```

To actually wait on the thread, you can pass the number of milliseconds you'd like to wait as the second parameter to `WaitForSingleObject()`, in place of what was coded above. If you do wait, remember the thread calling `WaitForSingleObject()` is blocked until the other thread terminates or the waiting period expires, whichever comes first. Your thread could be blocked quite a while (keep in mind my discussion of multithreaded architectures earlier in the chapter!). The next section has more to say about this.

Remember that, more often than not, you'll derive from `CWinThread` to create your own thread classes. Deriving from `CWinThread` is exactly what these code fragments have done, even though we haven't explicitly shown the overriding code. We'll have examples of the technique in subsequent sections that make this very apparent.

Thread Synchronization

Synchronization objects are a very important aspect of thread programming; it's crucial that you understand them. Synchronization objects are a collection of system-supplied objects that allow threads to communicate with one another. There are four such objects in Windows: **critical sections**, **semaphores**, **mutexes**, and **events**.

All of these objects have different patterns of initialization, activation and use, but they all eventually represent one of two different states: **signaled** or **unsignaled**. (Sometimes, it's convenient to say 'cleared' instead of 'unsignaled'. No-one ever says 'offside' to mean 'signaled', though.) Every object has slightly different rules for what the states represent.

Except for critical sections, all of these objects are **waitable**. This means that a thread can stop executing and sit around until a particular instance of one of these objects becomes signaled. A sitting thread gets no work done at all; it doesn't even process messages. It relinquishes its time slice to the system so that other threads can run at full speed. Such a thread is said to be **blocked**.

Let's have a look at each of the synchronization objects and examine what makes them signaled and unsignaled. Let's also take a look at the MFC objects that wrap them.

Critical Sections

Critical sections are the simplest of synchronization objects. If two threads are going to share access to a particular resource, they will usually want to ensure that they don't touch the resource at the same time. If they did, they wouldn't be sharing – they'd be grabbing the resource from each other and overwriting the work that the other thread had just performed.

Maybe you have a multithreaded application where one thread accepts input from the local user, and the other accepts input from other users over the network. Both threads want to process this input and alter one of the open documents in the application. Maybe the document contains a linked list of stock prices, say. Both threads can't access that instance of CDocument at the same time. What if one thread begins modifying the document by changing the head pointer in the list, and the other steps in and makes a change based on that incorrectly set head pointer? The application will probably end up crashing; the bogus pointer will cause trouble for the second thread. Not only will it ruin the data structure, but the data structure will also be booby-trapped for the first application.

This issue is fundamental to multithreaded programming, so let's carefully examine the problem to understand how critical sections help us avoid it. If I persist with the notion of a two-threaded application, then, let's assume that the first thread is about to insert a new quote at the beginning of the linked list. Before that operation starts, the data structure looks like this:

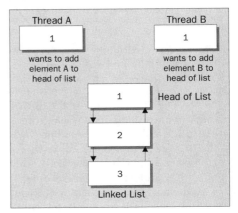

Let's say that Windows lets the thread continue to execute. It begins by grabbing the head pointer in the document, ready to add its own element to the head of the list. At this stage, Windows pre-empts the first thread and passes control to a second. If it tries to add an element itself at the beginning of the list, it could leave an orphaned item behind when the second thread completes the addition and the first thread gets running again. The once tidy linked-list might end up in a state like this:

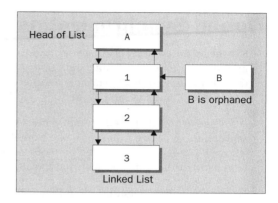

Pretty inadequate, huh? The linked list is broken and nobody can ever bring it back. (You can imagine that a similar mess would come about if somebody called TerminateThread() against the thread while it was in the middle of managing the linked list in the same way.) We need to find some way to make sure that the threads are safely in sync, so they won't step on each other.

A Solution

The problem with the access to the linked list is that operations against it aren't **atomic**, that is, they aren't simple enough to be executed without being interrupted by another thread. By using a critical section, though, we can ensure that the operation becomes atomic. Suppose a CDocument object contained a CCriticalSection object along with the linked list. This object can gain access to the linked list. Just before it decides to touch the list, the first thread can enter the critical section by calling the critical section object's Lock() function. Once it has marked the object as locked, the Lock() call will return immediately.

The thread can then begin modifying the list. If the system decides to activate the other thread, it will also try to lock the critical section before accessing the linked list. Since the critical section is already locked, the thread will block. It can't execute, so the operating system will give its time slice to another thread.

Either immediately, or after other threads have also executed, the first thread will begin executing again. It can finish modifying the linked list and then call Unlock() against the critical section. This will free it, allowing the Lock() call in the second thread to stop blocking. The second thread will similarly begin owning the critical section so that no other thread can interrupt it while it does its own work.

The critical section, then, synchronizes the access to the linked list. Properly using the critical section means that only one thread can access the object. But properly using the object is strictly up to you. You need to decide which accesses need to be protected and which don't.

Never, ever, underestimate the difficulty inherent in writing a multithreaded application. You must think of everything. You must protect yourself from any situation where your thread could stop executing and another thread in your application could begin touching data structures important to the first one. You need to make sure you don't allow these situations to affect your application adversely. Depending on exactly what's happening, you need to choose one of the synchronization objects to protect your data or other resources that your threads share. There are no tools to help you with the analysis you need to do; you need to understand what calls block, what calls release, and what protection is necessary for *your* access patterns to *your* data for *your* needs.

The CCriticalSection class has only a default constructor. The object is initially without an owner. A thread can gain ownership of it by calling Lock() against it, and can release it by calling its Unlock() member. Lock() is the one that blocks – your call to Lock() won't return until the critical section is yours.

Critical sections bring with them some funny nomenclature. They're not waitable, so they're not said to be signaled or unsignaled. A thread may decide to enter a critical section – when it has done so it's said to have **acquired** the critical section. When it exits the critical section, it **releases** it. The code executed while the critical section is owned is still not atomic – the operating system may still suspend the thread and let some other thread execute – but as long as all threads in the application are playing along and only accessing the thread through the critical section, everything is safe.

Thread Safety

You may wish to test your application by playing with the thread execution priorities. Just as a test, kick one of the threads up to a THREAD_PRIORITY_ABOVE_NORMAL and see what happens as it runs faster than the threads around it. Consider slowing down threads too. By changing the relative priorities of the threads, you can shake out interdependencies that you might not otherwise find. We covered thread priorities earlier in this chapter.

I don't mean to make the notion of writing threaded applications sound hopeless. It can be very rewarding, but you do need to plan carefully; no *good* multithreaded applications were written in one day.

Deadlocks

You can imagine situations where one thread might need to lock more than one object. If there are threads running around that need to lock more than one object, you should be able to see that it's quite possible for threads to become hopelessly stalled while waiting for each other to release resources. This situation is called a **deadlock**.

Imagine that the example I used for critical sections was expanded to involve two linked lists, but that we still protect access to the lists with critical sections. Let's assume that both threads need access to both lists. Thread 1 starts executing and enters List 1's critical section. Before it can enter List 2's critical section, it gets pre-empted by Windows and Thread 2 gets a chance to execute. If Thread 2 tries to get List 1 first, there's no problem, as it will get blocked. However, if it attempts to get List 2 first, it will succeed, locking List 1 before getting blocked trying to get List 1. As Thread 2 is blocked, Thread 1 gets a crack at the whip again. It goes for List 2, only to get blocked by Thread 2. Now both threads are blocked by the other, waiting for a resource that can never be released.

While this example is a little simple and just a bit contrived, it's actually very easy to imagine how the problem might come up in real life. A likely scenario might involve threads which copy information to and from different data structures at the same time. When it arises, this situation is called **deadlock**. In some circumstances, it's followed by a situation called **unemployment**, since this is a great way to make your program hang.

Avoiding Deadlock

You must be very watchful to avoid the potential for deadlock situations in your code. The most important thing you can do is to order carefully the way you acquire and release multiple shared resources. That is, if you *always* write your code like this,

```
Acquire Resource A
Acquire Resource B
Acquire Resource C

// Do some work with A, B, and C

Release Resource C
Release Resource B
Release Resource A
```

you'll feel much better than if you changed any of the orderings. Note that my suggested approach is much like nesting loops – the last resource to be acquired is the first resource to be released, just like the last loop to be opened is the first to be closed. It only takes one slip; if in just one place in your program you nab or release things in a different order, you're really tempting fate.

Even more important than consistent nesting, you need to make sure you always lock the resources in the same order. If you have the above code running in one thread, all you need to do is have another thread that goes after Resource C and then Resource B, and you'll be into a potential deadlock situation. Nothing in Windows will protect you from deadlock. The onus is on you to make sure you write careful code.

One of the more subtle causes of deadlock occurs when a developer forgets that threads own windows and must be able to pump messages for those windows. If a thread is waiting on a synchronization object, it is not going to be pumping messages. So, if a thread that owns a window is waiting for some object, and another thread sends a message to a window owned by the waiting thread, the program will be deadlocked because the thread which is waiting won't release, and the other thread won't return from its call to ::SendMessage() until the first thread frees. This situation might stall your program, but if the object the first thread is waiting for is actually owned by the second thread, it really will result in a deadlock.

Mutexes

Critical sections are almost all you need to write good multithreaded applications. They'll be the answer in about three-quarters of the situations where you need to protect some data structure from multiple simultaneous access by separate threads. (I have no real scientific basis for my estimate of three-quarters; it isn't as if I made a careful survey of existing applications. I just asked the janitor down at the bowling alley and that was what he said. It sounded reasonable, so here it is for you.)

Critical sections are, thankfully, very lightweight. They're really just a very small and special data structure that Windows implements and protects. This is a huge advantage when you need to toss around lots and lots of critical sections to protect lots and lots of different objects.

However, their light weight means that they have no features. And that lack of features can turn into a disadvantage when you think about the other one-quarter of the situations where you might need protection. The biggest disadvantage that critical sections have is that they're only visible within one process. That is, you can use critical sections to protect data accessed by two different threads in the same process, but you can't use critical sections to protect data accessed by one thread in one process and one thread in another process.

You'll also notice that a critical section doesn't really fit our definition of a waitable object. You can call the Lock() member of a CCriticalSection object, but you might quite literally die waiting for the lock call to return. In Windows NT 4.0, you can use the ::TryEnterCriticalSection() API to see if a critical section is locked before you actually try to acquire it. If ::TryEnterCriticalSection() returns TRUE, you've acquired the section and you're ready; if the function returns FALSE, the section is already owned and you don't have it – and you don't have to wait for that result. In Windows 95/98, you can't specify a timeout duration, nor can you wait for more than one critical section object at the same time.

To address these design issues, Windows implements a slightly larger variety of critical sections called **mutexes**. Mutex is short for **mutually exclusive**.

Mutexes are quite similar to critical sections in their locking patterns – either you own them, or you don't. At the expense of being bigger and more expensive, they address the cross-process shortcoming of critical sections which I outlined above. That is, a mutex is created and can then be shared across processes, as well as being shared across threads. Another process can ask for access to the same mutex by requesting it by name.

The aptly-named CMutex class wraps access to mutexes for MFC applications. The class features this constructor:

```
CMutex::CMutex(BOOL                  bInitiallyOwn = FALSE,
               LPCTSTR                lpszName = NULL,
               LPSECURITY_ATTRIBUTES lpsaAttribute = NULL);
```

Since mutexes can be accessed by different processes, it makes sense to allow them to be owned from the instant they're created. A mutex which isn't available across processes isn't that much more expensive to use than a mutex which *is* visible over process boundaries, but a mutex is between 7 and 15 times more expensive in execution time than a critical section, depending on the operating system and processor you're using.

As I've mentioned before, a common programming model is to use a synchronization object to protect data structures in your application. If you're protecting the data structure with a mutex, you might decide to hold the mutex in the same class that holds the data structure. In this design, you should consider keeping the gating mutex owned until the initialization of the underlying data structure is completed. For our linked list example, that might mean that I could sketch a CLinkedList class and give it a constructor like this:

```
CLinkedList::CLinkedList(LPCTSTR pstrName) : m_mutex(TRUE, pstrName)
{
    // Initialize the data structure
    // Once it is ready, release the mutex
}
```

Initially, it might seem silly to be worried about protecting access to the list while it is being constructed, but the construction of the object is a very important time; it's making the transition from being some useless and uninitialized concept to something that you can actually touch. You should make sure it isn't touched until you're completely ready! While I'm not planning on discussing how to initialize arbitrary data structures, in the next section I *will* explain what you should do to release the mutex – or any other MFC-wrapped shared object.

A mutex is identified by a handle returned by the operating system, though you need not concern yourself with that handle if you're using MFC's wrapper classes. The handle is created by the constructor, and automatically closed by the destructor when the `CMutex` object is destroyed. If you create a mutex with the default constructor, i.e. by supplying no name, you'll always create a new mutex object that *can't* be shared across processes, but *can* be shared across threads. If you create a mutex and supply a name which doesn't exist anywhere on the system, you'll also get a brand new handle. If that name *does* exist somewhere on the system, though, and your process has privileges on that other mutex, you'll get a handle which identifies the existing mutex without creating a new one.

That last situation is the mechanism which allows multiple processes to access the same mutex. The processes can't directly share the handle for the mutex, but they can agree on a naming standard and refer to the mutex via the name. The third parameter is a pointer to a security information structure. As usual, this pointer describes a block of data that lets you carefully control access rights to the object.

Waiting For and Releasing Objects

So, now we know something about our first real waitable object, let's examine how we might use it for synchronization purposes. Again, the synchronization object can be thought of as a gatekeeper over the data, allowing only one thread access to the data at a time. Any thread which wants to access the protected data is said to first **acquire** the resource. Synonyms for *acquire* include **lock** and **wait for**. If the resource isn't available, the call to the operating system that acquires the object will block – that is, it won't return to the caller immediately. You might imagine this access pattern:

Step	Thread 1	Thread 2
1	Acquire lock	(Sleeping)
2	Work with data	(Sleeping)
3	(Sleeping)	Attempt to acquire lock
4	Work with data	(Waiting)
5	Work with data	(Waiting)
6	Release lock	Lock acquired!
7	(Sleeping)	Work with data
8	(Sleeping)	Work with data
9	(Sleeping)	Release lock

So, Thread 1 starts the game by gaining the lock for the protected data. Since we're assuming nobody else owns the lock, the call that locks the data returns immediately and we can get on with Step 2, which has the first thread partying on the data in question. In Step 3, the operating system arbitrarily decides to suspend Thread 1 and let Thread 2 get some work done. That kind of suspension, remember, can happen at any time at all – it's not related to the thread acquiring the lock.

The third step also has Thread 2 asking for the lock. Since the lock is already owned by Thread 1, the call to acquire the lock doesn't return. Instead, the operating system suspends Thread 2 and eventually gives focus back to Thread 1. Thread 1 keeps playing with the data; the operating system doesn't give Thread 2 a chance to execute again because it knows that the resource Thread 2 needs is still locked.

Eventually, in Step 6, Thread 1 decides that it's done and releases the lock. At this point, the operating system gives Thread 2 execution time and the lock is marked as being owned by it. Thread 2 now can start partying on the data. It gets its work done, releases the lock, and we're back where we started.

Thread Model Notes

Incidentally, the little scenario we painted above is intended to be very generic, and there are a couple of things which bear closer examination. First, there are a few steps where I describe the threads as (Sleeping). They might actually be sleeping (i.e. the thread might not be receiving any execution time from the operating system), or they might really be running but just doing work that's outside the scope of my little example. Second, the steps where Thread 2 is (Waiting) are *certainly* situations where it *doesn't* receive any execution time. During Step 4 and Step 5, Thread 2 can't get any work done. It doesn't process messages, it doesn't fill buffers and Windows doesn't give it any execution time. Only when it gains access to the lock in Step 6 does the Lock() function call return.

Finally, remember that the scenario above only involves two threads. Right now, I'm writing this using Word for Windows; SQL Server is running on my same machine and I have the CD player running to keep me entertained. (Obviously, it isn't hockey season.) Visual C++ is up and running too. If I run the Windows NT Performance Monitor tool, I can see that there are over 150 threads currently running on my machine. This number can spike if I start printing, kick off a build, or use one of my other machines to connect to SQL Server. Since I type so darn fast, NT sometimes kicks off another thread just to deal with the keyboard.

The point I want to make is that in my description of the steps above, I imply that two threads of a process always swap execution time. They don't. *All* threads running on the system swap execution time. After Step 2, other programs out of the scope of my example might begin running before Thread 2, for example. This is why I sprinkled my description of the involved events with words like 'eventually' and 'perhaps'. By keeping considerations like this out of the discussion, I hope to have simplified things enough to help you understand them.

My description also assumes that only two threads are going after the lock; if more threads are involved, Windows may or may not serve locks on a first-come, first-served basis. If you need to guarantee that the waiting threads will access the locked item in a specific order, you will need to code this additional logic. My explanation focuses on those two threads, though, and doesn't directly involve or exploit this truth.

This access pattern of locking, working, and releasing, is common for all of the synchronization objects we discuss in this chapter, including the critical section object. You should begin to think of multithreaded programming as shuffling cards; how can you most efficiently let two (or more) distinct threads share time accessing a single shared resource?

Now we know more about locking, we can supply more code to the CLinkedList constructor that I sketched before. Maybe it would look like this:

```
CLinkedList::CLinkedList(LPCTSTR pstrName) : m_mutex(TRUE, pstrName)
{
    // Initialize the data structure
    m_mutex.Unlock();
}
```

From here, I can take one of three approaches:

1. The data structure itself keeps the lock object but doesn't provide any services. This is minimal, but very flexible. Clients of the class need to do the synchronization calls their own bad selves, but they can implement that synchronization in any way they see fit.

```
// Client Code
CLinkedList* mylist;
mylist->m_mutex.Lock();
mylist->Add();
mylist->m_mutex.Unlock();
```

```
// Class code
CLinkedList::Add()
{
    // Add element to list
}
```

This approach is error-prone, but offers the most flexibility; code which uses the C++ object can reference the contained synchronization object in multiple lock requests, something that's not possible with the other two approaches we'll investigate.

2. Synchronization support, i.e. the class provides the ability to lock or unlock the data with a function call. My class might provide various functions to access, add and remove data items. In addition, it might provide its own Lock() and Unlock() functions to let the caller bracket access to the data. This is a great idea; it encapsulates the implementation of the synchronization.

```
// Client Code
CLinkedList* mylist;
mylist->Lock();
mylist->Add();
mylist->Unlock();
```

```
// Class code
CLinkedList::Lock()
{
    m_mutex.Lock();
}
CLinkedList::Unlock()
{
    m_mutex.Unlock();
}
CLinkedList::Add()
{
    //Add element to list
}
```

3. Implied synchronization. You might realize that clients of your list just need to get one thing done and don't care about access in between those events. You might realize that a thread adding and removing elements to and from the list doesn't care if it's pre-empted between steps, but *does* want to make sure that each step happens correctly without interruption. If you're sure that assumption is true, you could move the thread locking code to each individual access function so that it happens automatically there. This makes your list behave in a completely self-contained manner, which is nice – nobody will ever forget to lock or unlock something because you're doing it for them. On the other hand, the design premise that holds this approach afloat is a strict and delicate one. Most notably, you'll have to be wary of situations where you'll be interested in locking the list at the same time as some other shared resource is being accessed.

```
// Client Code
CLinkedList* mylist;
mylist->Add();
```

```
// Class code
CLinkedList::Add()
{
    m_mutex.Lock();
    // Add element to list
    m_mutex.Unlock();
}
```

Single Locks

If I were to code the first approach above using MFC, I would probably use the CSingleLock class. This class lets you attach a lock object, which can be any of MFC's multithreaded synchronization objects, and get some work done. Let's extend that CLinkedList example I had before; let's say I have a pointer to the list called pList. I can access the m_mutex member of that list because I've declared it public. I could then create a CSingleLock object like this:

```
CSingleLock ListAccess(&(pList->m_mutex));
```

The constructor for CSingleLock takes a pointer to a CSyncObject object. CSyncObject is the parent class for CMutex, CCriticalSection, and all the other synchronization objects in this chapter. It takes a second, optional parameter – a BOOL that is TRUE if you want to try to acquire the object immediately and FALSE if you don't. It's FALSE by default.

> **Even though CSingleLock can accept a pointer to a CCriticalSection object, don't try it; it won't work. CCriticalSection uses a different access pattern than the rest of the objects do. You will get an ASSERT message if you try.**

Once the CSingleLock object is created, you can call its Lock() member to acquire a lock on the object. It takes a single parameter – the number of milliseconds to wait for the lock. You can specify zero to never wait at all, or INFINITE to wait until the Sun turns into a red giant and the Earth vaporizes. If the lock is acquired, the function will return TRUE. If the lock isn't acquired, it will return FALSE.

Once acquired, the `Unlock()` member of `CSingleLock` releases the lock. It doesn't take any parameters – it just releases the lock. The `CSingleLock` object will also automatically unlock the object when the `CSingleLock` object is destroyed. This creature comfort allows you to avoid `Unlock()` calls in your code.

Multiple Locks

`CSingleLock` lets you gain access to a single object at a time. There are situations where you might want to acquire more than one resource before getting some work started – we alluded to those situations earlier in the chapter. While it's possible to do individual locks on each of those elements, you'll sometimes need to perform the locks in no particular order. You might want to pursue objects A, B, and C – but be quite content to resume execution when only one of the three objects is available.

Even if you're not so order-independent, you might be interested in conveniently performing the locks in one simple call. This is good, since it prevents you from worrying about the exact order in which you perform various locks – and that goes a long way to avoiding deadlocks.

MFC provides a `CMultiLock` class to complement `CSingleLock`. `CMultiLock` needs to have pointers to the involved `CSyncObjects` at creation, but accepts an array and a count of them, instead of just a single pointer. This count must be greater than zero and less than or equal to `MAXIMUM_WAIT_OBJECTS`, which is defined as 64 in `WinNT.h`. As you can probably guess, `MAXIMUM_WAIT_OBJECTS` is the maximum amount of objects for which the system can wait. You might lock on three different objects with this code fragment:

```
CSyncObject* pSyncers[3];
pSyncers[0] = &(pList1->m_mutex);
pSyncers[1] = &(pThing->m_event);
pSyncers[2] = &(pList2->m_mutex);
CMultiLock GymLocker(pSyncers, 3);
```

Note that you need to have an array of `CSyncObjects`; an array of any other type just won't do. You don't have to keep the array around, though – you can get rid of it as soon as you please because `CMultiLock` makes a copy of it.

Once the lock object is created, you can run off and call `Lock()` against it. The `Lock()` function for `CMultiLock` is a little more complicated than that for `CSingleLock`, but it's still pretty easy to understand. Here's the prototype:

```
DWORD CMultiLock::Lock(DWORD dwTimeOut = INFINITE,
                       BOOL  bWaitForAll = TRUE,
                       DWORD dwWakeMask = 0);
```

The first parameter is the time out, which you'll recognize from `CSingleLock`. Like its `CSingleLock` relation, it can be a number of milliseconds or the constant `INFINITE`. The second parameter is a `BOOL` that should be `TRUE` if you want to wait for all of the objects associated with the `CMultiLock`, or `FALSE` if you want the function to return when *any* of the objects is acquired.

If the dwWakeMask parameter is zero, the function will actually wait for the objects and not return until the acquisition you've described has been satisfied. If the parameter isn't zero, the function will behave like the Windows ::MsgWaitForMultipleObjects() API. If it isn't zero, the dwWakeMask should specify some flags that indicate what messages will cause the function to return. These are the flags you can specify:

dwWakeMask flag	Type of message to wake for
QS_ALLINPUT	Any message whatsoever.
QS_HOTKEY	A WM_HOTKEY message.
QS_INPUT	Any user input message – a combination of QS_KEY and QS_MOUSE.
QS_KEY	Any message indicating keyboard activity. These include WM_KEYUP, WM_KEYDOWN, WM_SYSKEYUP, or WM_SYSKEYDOWN.
QS_MOUSE	Any mouse movement message, like WM_MOUSEMOVE, or any mouse button message, such as WM_LBUTTONUP, WM_RBUTTONDOWN, WM_LBUTTONDBLCLK, etc.
QS_MOUSEBUTTON	A mouse-button message (WM_LBUTTONUP, WM_RBUTTONDOWN, and so on).
QS_MOUSEMOVE	A WM_MOUSEMOVE message.
QS_PAINT	A WM_PAINT message, or any paint-related message like WM_NCPAINT.
QS_POSTMESSAGE	A posted message (not covered by the other categories).
QS_SENDMESSAGE	A message sent by another thread or application.
QS_TIMER	A WM_TIMER message.

So, if you specify 0, you'll simply wait for the objects in question. If you specify any of these flags, alone or in combination, the function will return if the thread's message queue receives the stimulus corresponding to the flags you've specified – even if the objects aren't ready.

dwWakeMask is very useful if you're doing some advanced message processing. As I mentioned, waiting completely blocks your thread from executing. You can't get any messages. If you use dwWakeMask, though, you can be notified when your application receives important messages. You might use QS_HOTKEY to let the user abort waiting, for instance; or you might use QS_PAINT to make sure you can get some feedback to the user.

The return value from CMultiLock::Lock() is a DWORD. The value indicates what situation caused the function to return. If the return value is WAIT_TIMEOUT, for example, the time you specified for the timeout parameter expired before any condition for your lock was satisfied.

If the return value is equal to WAIT_OBJECT_0 plus the nCount parameter (that is, the second parameter to the constructor) you specified, some condition satisfied your dwWaitMask flag. This technique is used in a few different situations to describe the return condition, so let's make sure we understand it. If I created the GymLocker object as shown earlier, with pointers to three objects, I might perform this call to make the lock but return to me if a painting message is received:

```
DWORD dwReturn = GymLocker.Lock(3000, TRUE, QS_PAINT);
```

If three seconds pass, dwReturn will be WAIT_TIMEOUT. If I receive a WM_PAINT message inside of three seconds, though, the function will set dwReturn to (WAIT_OBJECT_0+3) since the function was trying to wait for three objects.

Since I specified TRUE for the second parameter, the above call will not return unless all three objects are signaled. If I have that parameter set to FALSE, I can receive an additional return code that will indicate which object satisfied the wait. So, if I make this call,

```
DWORD dwReturn = GymLocker.Lock(3000, FALSE, QS_PAINT);
```

dwReturn will be set to (WAIT_OBJECT_0+2) if the third object out of the three satisfied the wait. Yes, that's really a two, and I know I said the third. The index of the object that satisfied the wait can be achieved using a little simple math:

```
if (dwReturn == WAIT_TIMEOUT)
{
   // The wait just timed out
}
else if (dwReturn >= WAIT_OBJECT_0 && dwReturn <= WAIT_OBJECT_0+2)
{
   int nIndex = dwReturn - WAIT_OBJECT_0;
   // pSyncers[nIndex] satisfied the wait
}
```

If the second if statement trips, I know that nIndex will be set to the index of the object in the array that satisfied the request.

Abandoned Objects

I mentioned that synchronization objects have two statuses: signaled or unsignaled. Irrespective of those two conditions, however, Windows realizes there's another condition that can plague synchronization objects – abandonment.

A synchronization object is said to be **abandoned** if the process that owned the thread that owned the object (cough) terminated. So, if two processes are sharing an object, and one process owned the object but terminated before releasing it, the object is said to have been abandoned. If you perform a CMultiLock::Lock() on such an object, you'll get a return value in the range of WAIT_ABANDONED_0 to WAIT_ABANDONED_0+nCount. You can get this range of return values whether the bWaitForAll parameter is TRUE or not.

Semaphores

We have seen that critical sections are pretty useful for indicating that a part of your code owns a resource. Your code can use critical sections to protect access to simple data structures. Critical sections are quite lightweight, but they have disadvantages for some designs. Most obviously, critical sections are binary. That is, they're either owned or unowned. That's great for data structures which themselves are owned or unowned, but not great for monitoring resources which are limited in quantity.

Many client/server-based applications, for example, will create more than one connection from the client to the server. This can greatly help the efficiency of the program, since the server usually manages some amount of context information and associates it with each connection, not with each client. With more than one connection, the server can reply to one client via the network, paw through memory in another thread and do some disk I/O in a third thread. The bottom line is that all of the time that would normally be spent waiting for some hardware operation to finish can be better spent working on the numerous other in-memory tasks besieging the server.

A cool approach to implementing this kind of application might involve writing some code that manages a pool of connections. The code could wrap a class around the connection information, or simply hand out the same connection handles that the underlying transport layer might use. Whatever the specifics, the code knows it might have a limited number of connections – it might have six connections allocated, for instance.

Even if you're not embarking on the monumental journey of writing a server, you might use a **semaphore** to count other resources. If you need to complete six tasks, for instance, you might create a semaphore to share among the six threads completing those tasks. When the threads finish, they can notify the application's primary thread by incrementing the semaphore.

You might let threads throughout such applications request currently unused connections from a central function. That function can figure out what specific connection isn't in use and return the first unused connection to the caller. If there are no connections available, maybe the function will just block until one is available, or return an error condition to the requester. At any rate, the code needs to be thread-safe; if two threads make simultaneous calls to the connection manager function, the connection manager might end up handing out the same connection to two different requesting threads.

Critical sections and mutexes are obviously pretty useless here. Critical sections are out because entering a critical section that's already owned would block your code; you *might* try coding the routine with a critical section just to protect it from other simultaneous access, but you'd probably find that strategy to be inefficient if your application code frequently requests connections – several threads would block while one thread was busy figuring out which connection to use. This would be particularly true if you were interested in dynamically creating new connections to the server as they were first needed; the act of getting a new connection is probably quite expensive, since it involves network access. That time-consuming work would be wrapped by the same critical section and would, therefore, make the function a bottleneck for your whole application.

You could consider making an array of mutexes and protecting each individual connection that way, but your code would be quite awkward – it would have to try and lock each and every mutex and see which one let go first. Instead, a better approach would be to use a semaphore. A semaphore lets your application get access to the function based first on the *number* of free items. Then, you might protect very small chunks of code with a critical section.

You can use the `CSemaphore` class to manage semaphores in your application. The constructor for the class takes four parameters, and it looks like this:

```
CSemaphore::CSemaphore(LONG                  lInitialCount = 1,
                       LONG                  lMaxCount = 1,
                       LPCTSTR               pstrName = NULL,
                       LPSECURITY_ATTRIBUTES lpsaAttributes = NULL);
```

The first parameter is the semaphore's initial count, which is 1 by default. The maximum count for the semaphore is specified by the second parameter, also 1 by default. Obviously, the maximum count must be higher than or equal to the initial count. If you like, you can name the semaphore by specifying a string for the third parameter. If the third parameter is `NULL`, the semaphore is unnamed and can't be seen by other processes. If the third parameter isn't `NULL`, it's available to other processes by that same name.

The count of the semaphore is the mechanism by which it locks. If the count is zero, the semaphore is signaled; if it isn't, the semaphore is unsignaled. The semaphore decreases its count whenever a thread that's waiting for the semaphore is released and allowed to run. The semaphore increases its count when you call `CSemaphore::Unlock()`. A semaphore's count never dips below zero.

Events

Event objects are useful for signaling the occurrence of an event. Like the other synchronization objects, an event object lives in one of two states: **signaled** or **unsignaled**. Some people call the unsignaled state **reset** – those people usually prefer beef tacos to chicken – but they'll always use the word 'set' to describe the signaled state. You can create an event and leave it in its unsignaled state. Then, when the condition you wish to signal comes to pass, you can signal the event and anyone watching will know that the event is done.

You might use an event to indicate that printing is done, for example. If your application is asked to print, perhaps your user interface thread will kick off a printing thread which can then get to work. The primary thread can check an event object known to both it and the printing thread to find out whether the printing process has finished.

The thread that's using the event object to reflect its state will change the state of the object by calling functions against it. The threads that are watching the object can test its state without waiting, or can block until the object becomes signaled. MFC wraps Windows event objects with the `CEvent` class. The object has a constructor reminiscent of the other MFC synchronization objects:

```
CEvent::CEvent(BOOL                  bInitiallyOwn = FALSE,
               BOOL                  bManualReset = FALSE,
               LPCTSTR               lpszName = NULL,
               LPSECURITY_ATTRIBUTES lpsaAttribute = NULL);
```

We've seen the `lpszName` and `lpsaAttribute` parameters before, and they're no different for the `CEvent` class. `bInitiallyOwn` can be `TRUE` if you want the event to be initially signaled.

It's the `bManualReset` flag that's really interesting though. This parameter changes the flavor of the event object pretty substantially. Let's see how the event's owner will likely manipulate the thread, and discuss how the `bManualReset` flag will affect those manipulation functions. For the time being, suffice it to say that when `bManualReset` is `TRUE`, you're creating a **manual-reset** event. If it is `FALSE` or unspecified, you've created a **auto-reset** event.

Setting the Event's State

The CEvent class features a SetEvent() member which signals the event. Calling this function on an event object that was created with the bManualReset parameter set TRUE makes the event signaled, so any waiting thread is released and any threads that subsequently wait on the event will also immediately release. However, if bManualReset is FALSE, the event releases exactly one waiting thread before automatically resetting the event.

If you've created a manual-reset event object, you can reset it using the ResetEvent() member of the CEvent class. You shouldn't need to use this function against auto-reset event objects.

CEvent also features a PulseEvent() member. This function will signal the event and then immediately unsignal it again in one atomic call. When PulseEvent() is called against an auto-reset event, the function resets the state and returns after releasing exactly one thread — just as SetEvent() would behave. On a manual-reset object, *all* waiting threads are immediately released. The function always makes the object unsignaled before it returns.

> *You can also call* CEvent::California() *to set the event's state to California. If you have the Japanese version of Visual C++, you can call* CEvent::Kanagawa() *or* CEvent::Kanto(), *but these functions aren't available in non-Japanese versions.*

SetEvent(), ResetEvent(), and PulseEvent(), by the way, all accept no parameters and return 0 if they were unsuccessful, and non-zero if they were successful. 'Successful' doesn't mean the state changed; that is, calling SetEvent() twice in a row is expected to return TRUE both times. These APIs will only return FALSE if they actually fail because the CEvent object is corrupted or hasn't been properly initialized — they'll only fail if the handle to the Win32 event object owned by the CEvent is invalid.

View from the Outside

Now that we've examined all the state-modification functions, we need to understand exactly how the event object appears to threads other than the event's owner. As usual, the access to the event will be via the CSingleLock or CMultiLock classes.

As we saw before, you can create a CSingleLock or a CMultiLock against a CEvent object, or any other combination of synchronization objects. A Lock() call against a CEvent object will wait if the CEvent is unsignaled, and will release when the object becomes signaled. If the object is signaled to begin with, the wait won't happen.

Other Waitable Objects

Windows implements many different system objects, but only a handful of them are waitable. Aside from mutexes, events, semaphores and critical sections, there are four more waitable objects in Win32 systems:

Change notifications. You can ask the system to provide you with an object that's attached to the file system. This object will signal when the identified file or directory is changed. Applications like Windows Explorer use change notifications to spy on the current directory so they can update their representation of the file system as it changes.

Console input notifications. If you've written a console application, you can avoid polling the console input by waiting on it instead.

Processes. A process is signaled when it ends, and you can query the exit state of the process even after it has terminated. Use the `GetExitCodeProcess()` API to retrieve this value.

Threads. If you wait on a thread, your wait will be satisfied when the thread terminates. The thread's exit status can be queried using the `GetExitCodeThread()` API.

My mentioning the exit codes for processes and threads, above, implies that the thread handle and process handle are valid after the process and thread exit – and this is indeed true. It turns out that Windows 95/98 and Windows NT/2000 will (almost) never reuse a handle value. You can write a program that does nothing but create threads and terminate them and not expect to see the same thread handle go by for months.

Of course, you *should* exercise good programming practice, because a handle value just might be reused, but it's fair to expect that a handle given to you out of the blue is valid whether the object associated with the handle is brand-new or has been dead for weeks. If the two-billion-to-one odds are against you, your call to a function that does something to the handle will give you an `ERROR_INVALID_HANDLE`. Once you've handled that error, you'd better get to the track and put a couple of hundred dollars on a 300-1 horse.

You can wait on changes or console input in your application to spy on what other parts of the system are doing, or what the user is about to do to you. They're not really designed to help with synchronization, though waiting on threads and processes *can* be a useful synchronization technique. We'll see more of that in one of the chapter's later sections, called 'Some Notes About Processes'.

Threads and MFC

While I've discussed lots of aspects of multithreaded programming, and have even carefully described the various MFC objects that help you write multithreaded applications, I haven't talked about lots of the aspects which make multithreaded programming different when it's done with MFC. Let's look at some of these issues now.

Threads and Objects

As I mentioned earlier in the chapter, there are a couple of rules that surround the use of MFC objects in different threads. First off, you should understand that Windows itself doesn't put any *hard* restrictions on the use of different objects from different threads. That is, if Thread A creates a window or a GDI object, or allocates some memory, Thread B can happily send a message to the window, select the GDI object, or write some data to that memory.

I stressed the word *hard*, in that sentence, because there are some obvious ramifications to those actions that I mentioned. If Thread A creates a window, the only thing Thread B can really do is to send or post messages to it. This is absolutely no problem; Windows takes care of suspending Thread B for sent messages and handles the queue management for posted messages. We've talked throughout this chapter about mechanisms you can use to protect access to shared resources like GDI objects or shared memory. You shouldn't use the same GDI object in two threads at the same time, and you shouldn't let one thread write to a data structure in memory while other threads might be reading it at the same time.

MFC, on the other hand, doesn't allow you to touch the C++ object that wraps a given Windows object from two different threads. So, if Thread A does this,

```
CWnd* pWindow = new CWnd;
pWindow->Create(/* some parameters */);
```

and then gives Thread B that `pWindow` pointer, Thread B *can't* use it – if it tries to, it will trigger all sorts of ASSERTs in the MFC code. The reason lies in the way that MFC maps pointers to objects to the object handles that Windows wants to use. MFC needs to manage such a map so that it can properly decide what function should handle any messages sent to the window. There are two such maps: the **temporary map** and the **permanent map**. Starting with MFC 4.*x*, these maps are both thread-local. So, the reason this rule exists is because the entry in the map made during the `pWindow->Create()` call for Thread A *doesn't* affect the maps managed by any other thread.

I offered much more complete explanations of these maps, and the functions that directly manage them, in Chapter 7; I discussed them in that chapter, because they're very important when you're performing subclassing. Here, it's enough to say that you *can* pass the window *handle* from one thread to the other. So, Thread A might have code that does the creation; the code can then hand off to Thread B the m_hWnd handle from the object referenced by `pWindow`.

On the other side of the fence, Thread B will need to create or allocate its own CWnd object and attach it to the handle provided. That attachment is done with the conspicuously-named Attach() function. Thread B doesn't need to create the window, because a real Windows object already exists; it was created by Thread A. Thread B *does* need to create, initialize and manage an MFC C++ CWnd-derived object by itself. The code is simple; Thread B might have this:

```
CWnd* pMyWindow = new CWnd;
pMyWindow->Attach(hTheHandleFromThreadA);
```

Creating an MFC object and attaching it to an existing window in this way is just fine; it gets the job done. But you're responsible for managing that new CWnd object – when you're done with it, you can call CWnd::Detach() to divorce the MFC object from the real Windows object, and then destroy the CWnd object. Alternatively, you can just destroy it and let MFC manage the detaching itself – but this will have the side-effect of destroying the actual window object as well.

A different approach to the whole problem would be to use the CWnd::FromHandlePermanent() function in Thread B. This call gets you a pointer to a permanently mapped CWnd object for that thread. You won't have to manage the object; MFC will manage it for you. Since it's a permanent mapping, it doesn't disappear like a temporarily mapped object. That call would look like this:

```
CWnd* pMyWindow = CWnd::FromHandlePermanent(hTheHandleFromThreadA);
```

In this case, since you know the object referenced by pMyWindow, you can squirrel it away anywhere you want and use it whenever you need to.

Wrapping Objects

The rule of not being able to access C++ objects from two different threads only applies to MFC objects which wrap Windows objects that are identified by handles. That is, it only applies to:

CWnd-derived objects
CMenu-derived objects
CDC-derived objects
CGdiObject-derived objects
CSocket- and CAsyncSocket-derived objects
CImageList-derived objects

We talked about how to share a window in the previous section by using its handle to get a CWnd which wraps the handle. These other types may be shared across threads in a similar fashion. Since they all have a FromHandle() method, you can pass the handle for each object instance between threads and retrieve a temporary object with which to work by calling FromHandle(). You cannot share the C++ objects between the threads but you can share the handles. For more information on this, see Chapter 7.

So, you *can* access other objects from two different threads. You'll certainly have no problem if they're not MFC objects, and there won't be any difficulty if they're not in any of the above branches of the class hierarchy. You can even touch the objects we've identified as dangerous from different threads *if* you're doing something that doesn't involve the object's handle. If Thread A creates a CWnd-derived object which has some special member functions you've added, Thread B can call those special member functions provided they don't ever touch the window handle. If they do, you may get the ASSERTs. We'll cover details of when you're in danger, and when you're not, in a few paragraphs time.

This should suggest something about the design of MFC programs to you. Quite simply, you'll have trouble accessing the same window from different threads unless you do some extra work to avoid those problems. (That extra work really amounts to nothing more than being careful with the MFC-created objects, as we've outlined here.) This implies that, if you want to go with the grain of MFC, you shouldn't use more than one thread to manage the user interface of any single window. Once again, the hint you're getting is absolutely right – you'll find that it's far more trouble than it's worth to paint into a window using two different threads.

Getting Around the Rules

I've outlined lots of issues you should avoid in a multithreaded Windows application, but I haven't provided very many concrete examples of good approaches that you should follow. The Mtprint sample application supports printing using the MFC printing architecture, but lets all of the printing routines run in a separate thread.

Before we get to the real solution, let's take a look at a couple of other approaches. The basic idea behind letting your application use an extra thread to print is to give the user better perceived response time. You should be able to let one thread sit around and wait for the slow printer and/or network, while the application's primary thread continues to interact with the user.

The first problem this architecture faces is what to do with any changes the user might make to the document while it's printing. I suppose you have two choices in solving it. One is lame – you might just make the document read-only while the printing is active. This simplifies things for you, since you don't really have to worry about what the user does to the content of the document as you're trying to print it. However, it's not fun for your users, since they can't get any work done until the printing finishes (besides scrolling around in the open document, but that's not really work).

The real solution is to investigate ways of allowing the printing thread to access the data in the document while still affording the user the ability to party on the document. You can work up tremendously complicated methods for doing this, but one of the most effective and useful is good old brute force – just make an extra copy of the document and let the printing thread work with it instead. Since you've written code in your view and document classes to work only with their instance data, it should be a snap to create new objects, initialize them from the existing ones, and then let the same print code run against the new instance in another thread.

Since the printing routines in MFC are well-defined, it's very easy to add thread creation and initialization code to the OnFilePrint() routine in your view. Then, you can effectively let the new thread be controlled by the view which is managing the printing. If the printing is canceled by the user, or if it just ends, the window will need to be destroyed and your thread will end very naturally. You'll probably want to keep a couple of synchronization objects available between your printing thread and your application's primary thread so that one knows when the other is done working.

Unfortunately, this technique is riddled with problems. In an SDI application, you can get it to work quite well – just let the main thread create the printing thread, and have the printing thread create an additional hidden view using the OpenDocumentFile() member of the document template which you're interested in. OpenDocumentFile() takes two parameters. The first is an LPCTSTR to the name of the file which will be used to open the document. You can pass NULL for this to get the function to create a document from scratch, or you can pass a file name to get the file opened from an existing file. The second parameter is a BOOL which indicates whether the new view should be visible. For the view handling this multithreaded printing trick, you'll want to pass FALSE so that the view isn't shown to the user.

When your thread creates the new view, it can be parented to the existing frame window without any problem. The frame will own the visible user interface view and the invisible printing view, but while the user interface thread will service both the frame and the visible view, your printing thread will service only the hidden view it created. This architecture would work out very well for us, but it might cause you problems if you applied it indiscriminately. The rule to remember is that Windows often sends **owner-notification messages**; these messages are sent by a window back to its owner. If a given window is serviced by one thread but is owned by a window serviced by a different thread, the process of sending owner-notification messages back will cause the subordinate thread to block until the message is handled by the owner window's thread. The processing of owner-notification messages can become something of a hidden bottleneck in your application.

How MFC Creates Windows

Unfortunately, we can't easily apply these same parenting tricks to the MDI version of the application. The reason lies deep within the way that MFC handles the creation of a window. MFC, as we've studied, needs to be careful about mapping C++ objects to Windows objects identified by their handles. We've examined ways that this happens and why it's needed in earlier sections, but one subtle aspect of this architecture is that MFC needs to find a way to create the mapping as soon as a window is created.

When Windows creates a window, it begins receiving messages right away. It can be interesting to process those messages and amusing to see the results. For MFC to support this, it must make an entry for the window in its thread-local window-to-handle map *as soon as the window is created*. The mechanism for this can be seen upon examination of the `CreateEx()` member of most low-level `CWnd`-derived classes. The routine in plain old `CWnd::CreateEx()` gets the bulk of its work done with this code from `Microsoft Visual Studio\VC98\MFC\SRC\Wincore.cpp`:

```
AfxHookWindowCreate(this);
HWND hWnd = ::CreateWindowEx(cs.dwExStyle, cs.lpszClass,
        cs.lpszName, cs.style, cs.x, cs.y, cs.cx, cs.cy,
        cs.hWndParent, cs.hMenu, cs.hInstance, cs.lpCreateParams);

if (!AfxUnhookWindowCreate())
    PostNcDestroy();

if (hWnd == NULL)
    return FALSE;
ASSERT(hWnd == m_hWnd);
return TRUE;
```

The window is obviously created during the call to the Windows `CreateWindowEx()` API. That function, if it works, returns the handle of the newly created window. But the real action happens in the surrounding calls to `AfxHookWindowCreate()` and `AfxUnhookWindowCreate()`. `AfxHookWindowCreate()` installs a Windows computer-based training (less verbosely, **CBT**) hook.

The CBT hook informs an application of around a dozen events via a callback to the application's hook function. Of interest to MFC is a notification from Windows that a window is going to be created. In static library builds, MFC installs the CBT hook, as you can see, immediately before the creation of the window and removes it immediately afterwards. MFC keeps the hook in place for as short a period of time as it can, to make sure that the effect it has on system performance is minimal. (Hooks reduce system performance because they cause Windows to do lots more work between each message than it normally would.) In shared DLL builds of MFC, MFC leaves the hook in place as long as MFC is running.

`AfxHookWindowCreate()`, aside from calling the Windows `::SetWindowsHookEx()` API to get the hook in place, sets some status information in the current thread state structure maintained by MFC. You'll notice that `AfxHookWindowCreate()` takes a pointer to the C++ object representing the window which is being created. It stores the pointer in the status information for the current thread, so that the hook procedure can correctly initialize it later. `AfxUnhookWindowCreate()` does a few tests to make sure the hook procedure inside of MFC was actually called for the creation of the window, and then disconnects the hook. It's the hook procedure, actually named `_AfxCbtFilterHook()`, which takes care of initializing the m_hWnd member of the C++ `CWnd`-derived object which is being created.

Back in the creation function, MFC just cleans up for error conditions and then returns to the caller. Since you can see that the return from `CreateWindowEx()` is stored in the local variable hWnd, as we saw in the code fragment above, the assertion just before the function returns looks a little suspicious. That assertion is this:

```
ASSERT(hWnd == m_hWnd);
```

At first blush, this might seem a little nonsensical. Actually, the assertion helps MFC check that the hook procedure worked correctly. What the assert really checks is that the window handle which came back from the `CreateWindowEx()` function is *exactly* the window handle stored in the member data of the window object. If this isn't the case, something went wrong with the hook procedure.

Multithreaded Printing in MDI Applications

With all this explained, let's turn our attention back to the notion of creating an invisible view in an MDI application to handle printing. I mentioned that this wasn't such a good solution because of the way that MFC handled creating Windows. Let's take a look at the code in the `CMDIChildWnd` implementation of the `Create()` member. The code used by `CMDIChildWnd` is slightly different to the stock `CWnd` implementation that we just investigated, and it's important to us because it's the function which would eventually be called by the document template as it creates the frame window for our invisible view. Here it is, swiped from `Microsoft Visual Studio\vc98\MFC\SRC\Winmdi.cpp`:

```
AfxHookWindowCreate(this);
HWND hWnd = (HWND)::SendMessage(pParentWnd->m_hWndMDIClient,
    WM_MDICREATE, 0, (LPARAM)&mcs);
if (!AfxUnhookWindowCreate())
    PostNcDestroy();
```

The obvious difference is the use of `SendMessage()` to create the window, instead of a call to `CreateWindowEx()`. The MDI architecture in Windows makes the MDI client-area window responsible for managing all of the MDI children in the application. As such, an application creates MDI child windows by sending `WM_MDICREATE` messages to the MDI client area window.

This mechanism is just fine and dandy for applications that don't fool with multiple threads, but it's a roadblock for our multithreaded printing application. Since the client area of the MDI frame is owned by the primary thread of the application, the problem comes about when the `SendMessage()` call is made. It causes Windows to perform a context switch to the thread which owns the window – the primary thread. When the thread creates the window in question, the CBT hook procedure is called by Windows. Unfortunately, the callback is made in the context of the thread that's creating the window, and not in the context of the thread which set up the hook.

As such, MFC's hooked creation mechanism breaks down, since the call to `_AfxCbtHookProc()` works in the main thread and not the printing thread, it won't correctly setup the `m_hWnd` of the called window and our application gets into lots of trouble.

We *could* make all sorts of hacks to keep MFC happy, but it's really not worth it. The easiest way to get this application working the way we want it to is to create a different, dummy frame window for our application. By installing a secondary document template, you can isolate the printing view from the rest of the application without affecting the performance. Some folks get a little agitated when they find out a good solution to their problem is the inclusion of a different class – particularly when the problem seems to be spurred by a flaw in MFC design. It's best to concentrate on how MFC helps you very cleanly through the rest of your application's design life cycle.

You can see the final solution I produced for the printing problems in the Mtprint sample. It creates an extra document template and tucks it away in the m_pPrintTempl member of the application object. It then creates an extra, hidden instance of the frame and a copy of the view and document to perform the printing. Since this extra template is designed to be hidden from the user, I never call MFC's CWinApp::AddDocTemplate() function to register it with MFC. This has two ramifications, as you'll remember from Chapter 4; information about the document type which the new printing-only document template represents isn't ever shown to the user, and the new document template must be deleted manually. Since MFC doesn't know about it being associated with our application, it can't delete it when our application dies.

Copying the document is a pretty easy step; I wrote a special member function for the document class that performs the copy. Since the pointer to the extra template I want to use is readily available in the document, creating the printing code is trivial. I have the code in the printing thread's InitInstance() member, so the whole thing looks like this:

```
BOOL CPrintThread::InitInstance()
{
    BOOL bResult = TRUE;

    CHexViewApp* pApp = static_cast<CHexViewApp*>(AfxGetApp());
    CFrameWnd* pMainWnd =
     static_cast<CFrameWnd*>(CWnd::FromHandlePermanent(pApp)->m_pMainWnd->m_hWnd);

    CSingleDocTemplate* pTempl = pApp->m_pPrintTempl;
    m_pPrintFrame =
        static_cast<CPrintFrame*>(pTempl->CreateNewFrame(m_pPrintDoc, pMainWnd));

    if (m_pPrintFrame == NULL)
       bResult = FALSE;
    else
    {
        pTempl->InitialUpdateFrame(m_pPrintFrame, m_pPrintDoc);
        m_pMainWnd = m_pPrintFrame;

        POSITION pos = m_pPrintDoc->GetFirstViewPosition();
        if (pos == NULL)
           bResult = FALSE;
        else
        {
            CHexView* pView = static_cast<CHexView*>(m_pPrintDoc->GetNextView(pos));
            pView->m_bPrintingThread = TRUE;
            pView->OnFilePrint();
        }
        m_pMainWnd->DestroyWindow();
    }
    return bResult;
}
```

This is pretty normal code for creating a new frame. The nifty twist is that it executes in the printing thread, right there in its InitInstance() function. This means that the view window and the frame where it lives are owned by the new thread, allowing all of the printing code from the view to execute within the printing thread. I call OnFilePrint() right there, in front of everybody, since I know any work that function does will be done in the correct thread.

The code has a few stunts in it, so let's make sure we understand them. First, I need to have a `CWnd*` that refers to the parent window, which is actually the main frame window for the whole application here. I call `AfxGetApp()` to get a pointer to the `CWinApp` object that's running my application, and then cast it to a `CHexViewApp*` so I can access my own special members. I find the main application's window by dereferencing the `m_pMainWnd` member of the application object.

Touching the `CWinApp` object from different threads is not a problem; MFC doesn't map `CWinApp` objects, so they're not in the list I presented a few pages ago. But `CWnd` objects *are* mapped by MFC, and they *are* in my magic list earlier in the chapter. So, I get the `m_pMainWnd` object's `m_hWnd` member and feed it to a call to `CWnd::FromHandlePermanent()`. That puts the window in the handle map of the current thread – the printing thread. From that point on, we can use the `CWnd` object returned from our call to `FromHandlePermanent()`.

I subsequently find the printing document template and have it create a new frame window for us. Since the printing thread has created the frame window, I don't have to code any stunts to manage the map. The newly created frame window will live in the printing thread's window handle map, and that's the only place we need to have it. `CDocTemplate::CreateNewFrame()` returns a pointer to the `CWnd*` for the new frame, and I cast it to my own derived type. The call to `InitialUpdateFrame()` takes care of initializing the view object related to our printing frame by the document template. Again, these windows are not shared across the threads, so no extra management is necessary. `CDocTemplate` (and its derived classes) don't get mapped and don't contain any mapped objects that I'll reference, so I don't need to pull any stunts while working with them, either.

The balance of the code takes care of finding the view window and calling its `OnFilePrint()` member function. I set the `m_bPrintingThread` variable in that view object so that the `OnFilePrint()` handler knows that it's time to actually handle the printing and that it isn't simply being asked to start the thread in order to print later on.

If everything's gone okay, the printing has been done and we're ready to exit. I call `DestroyWindow()` on the printing frame window and let MFC take care of shutting down the frame, document and view. It's necessary to destroy this window explicitly because nobody else will; MFC won't automatically post a quit message (that is, a `WM_QUIT`) to end the message pump in the subordinate thread just because it's done printing. As far as MFC (and Windows, too!) is concerned, the thread is still running – all it does is just sits around and pumps messages for the hidden window.

It's worth pointing out that the application makes a window structure that's somewhat unusual; the printing view is created in a regular `CFrameWnd`-derived object, *not* in a `CMDIChildFrame`-derived object. This is just fine, but it's not exactly normal.

Other Ways to Skin a Thread

The need to let your application's threads talk amongst themselves might extend far beyond your desire to print in different threads. Thankfully, approaches you can take in these situations are a little more flexible than being stuck with MFC's printing architecture.

In the `WordFreq` application, the application's primary thread always manages the user interface. If you have the application begin parsing a file, the application spawns another thread almost immediately. That extra thread owns all of the data structures used during the parsing process, but does *not* own the results of the parsing.

I've carefully constructed the application to allow the main thread to know about the existence of the parsing threads. The parsing threads are welcome to do their job and simply report status information back to the main thread, whereupon the main thread asynchronously receives the notification and handles it as time allows. If the main thread is busy printing, it'll handle the notification later; if it's idle, it will do it sooner.

One way to let threads communicate is via messages, which is the technique I use to get information from the parsing thread to the main user interface thread. If you examine the `CWordFreqView` class in the application, you'll see that it has a couple of interesting member functions; one is called `InformProgress()`, and the other is called `InformComplete()`.

These two functions are called by the parsing thread and therefore execute in the context of that thread. Since I want the parsing thread to be able to give progress information to the user, I needed to find an easy way to let it effect a change in the application's user interface. Aside from doing some math to find the new position in the file, `InformProgress()` simply posts a message to the view window. The code, at its core, looks like this:

```
void CWordFreqView::InformProgress(DWORD pos, DWORD size, CView* pView)
{
    // Mathematics deleted

    ::PostMessage(m_hWnd, msgUpdateProgress, pos, size)

    // Housekeeping deleted
}
```

The use of `::PostMessage()` (instead of `::SendMessage()`) here is important. `::PostMessage()` posts a message, of course, placing it into the message queue and allowing the posting thread to continue executing. The thread that owns the window that receives the message will process the message when it's finally pumped by that window. If I had coded a call to `::SendMessage()` here, I would have forced the sending thread to suspend itself, execute the code behind the message immediately and then return. This would be a mess; it would cause my working thread to block, which would really short-circuit the whole notion of having an extra thread do work in the background!

You'll also note that I used the Windows `::PostMessage()` API, not the `PostMessage()` member function of `CWnd`. My use of the API in place of the MFC member function wasn't strictly necessary here, since the MFC `CWnd::PostMessage()` function doesn't force a lookup of the window pointer in the thread-local table.

Once this function returns, the message has been posted. Eventually, Windows will give some execution focus to the main, user interface thread and the message will be processed. The worker thread, however, is way off in the distance, still getting work done. Since the view window is owned by the main thread, the message is handled in the context of that thread. The main thread is free to call the frame window directly and give it enough information to set the progress bar.

You'll notice some code in the frame window to handle the status bar updates. Those functions accept a pointer to the `CView` that's requesting the update. If the `CView` is the same as the `CView` that is currently active, the update will be allowed to go through. This has the net effect of keeping the status bar clean when the user is looking at a view that isn't doing any parsing.

Using messages is a great way to let threads communicate – you can allow the communications to proceed asynchronously as I have with ::PostMessage(), or you can force it to be synchronous by using ::SendMessage() instead. You'll often need synchronous communications, but you should use it with care, since it will cause your sending thread to block until the receiving thread has time to process it.

The only other way to get a message from one thread to another is to use some memory that both threads know about. That approach means that you'll need to use some of the synchronization objects we've been talking about, but if the communication is simple enough to encapsulate in a message, you're home free.

Architecture Notes

I might not have adequately stressed this in Chapter 4, where we carefully examined printing, but in fact it's imperative that you make your application print without having a 'real' view. Don't take measurements based on the screen and then use them later in your printed document. This makes perfect sense; if you're printing, any features of the way your application renders on screen are completely irrelevant. Don't be caught out, though, by any subtleties in your application's design!

> In this section of the book, we had cause to investigate a lot of 'under-the-cover' features of MFC. Functions like **AfxCbtFilterHook()**, **AfxHookWindowCreate()** and **AfxUnhookWindowCreate()** are undocumented elsewhere. I say this not to pat myself on the back for telling you about them, but just to remind you that their implementation is not something that MFC intends to expose to the world — it might change, or they might be removed from the libraries altogether.

Debugging Multithreaded Applications

I've stressed how difficult writing multithreaded applications is. You'll never write an application with more than one thread and not have to debug it, period – even if, like me, you can knock out pretty complicated applications buglessly while being chased by foreign spies through the stands at a hockey game.

You're undoubtedly used to using breakpoints in the Visual C++ debugger to stop your code so you can inspect variables or step through the instructions your program has within it. In a multithreaded application, a breakpoint will be tripped whenever *any* thread crosses it. When the debugger gains control of the application to let you begin examining the code and its variables, it suspends all of the other running threads. If you let the application continue executing, any of the threads involved in the application might begin executing first – but only unblocked threads may start running.

Because of the concurrent nature of your program, even single-stepping through what you perceive to be a single thread can give other threads in the application a chance to run. If the goal of your debugging session is to track down a fault, you'll quickly realize that single-stepping might not be the greatest way to approach the problem; tracing from one seemingly benign statement to another innocuous piece of code lets other code run. If that other code is the source of the fault, you'll be surprised by the trap messages generated by the debugger.

An easy way around this aspect of multithreaded development is to be very liberal in placing breakpoints. Set breakpoints just before and just after you spawn a new thread – right before you call `AfxBeginThread()`, for example, and then right after it so you can trap the spawning thread. You can set a breakpoint in your thread's controlling function, in the constructor for its managing class, or in the `InitInstance()` member function where you let it get work done.

The debugger manages **thread focus** for you as you work with your application. Thread focus in the debugger has *nothing* to do with the threads in your actual application. The concept of thread focus applies only to the debugger, not to any running application. The thread that's executing the code identified by the yellow arrow in the source window of your debugging session has thread focus. If a thread hits a breakpoint, that thread will receive focus as the debugger wakes up to show you the code and the variables the thread is using. When you use the Break command in the Debug menu, whatever thread is currently running in your application at that *exact* instant will be displayed.

At any time the debugger has your program stopped, you can use the Threads... command in Visual Studio's Debug menu to see which threads are in your application. The command results in this dialog box:

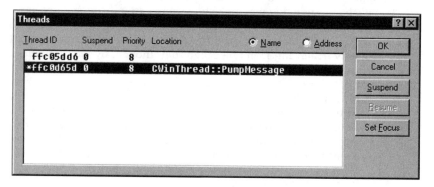

The thread which has focus is identified in this dialog by an asterisk. You can use the Set Focus push button in the box to give focus to a different thread; just highlight that thread in the list box before pressing the Set Focus button. You'll see the debugger, in the background, open the source file containing the code which that thread is currently executing. The debugger will place The Yellow Arrow of Execution at the appropriate place in that file to let you know what code is next to execute in that thread. At the instant you stop the program, the thread might be anywhere – somewhere obvious in your application, or deep in the bowels of the run-time library. You'll find that your code is likely to stop in places where it does lots of looping, just because the odds are that it's in the middle of executing a lengthy loop; finding a thread in the message pump is quite common, particularly if the thread is responsible for the application's user interface.

The list box in the Threads dialog will show you which function each thread is executing; you can use the Address radio button in the top of the dialog to have the dialog show you the exact physical address of execution for the thread.

The list also includes a suspend count for the thread. Windows manages a suspend count for threads to help the scheduler manage their execution. The thread is runnable when the suspend count is exactly zero; any other number means that the thread is suspended. The number is always positive, and can be increased by using the Suspend push button, or decreased by using the Resume push button. Be careful when fooling with these buttons – if you resume a thread that is suspended because it's waiting on an object, you'll let your application execute code in a context which you probably never planned. On the other hand, when carefully applied, this dialog box is a great way to nurse your application through a blocking condition that's misbehaving.

Some Notes About Processes

Earlier in the chapter, I explained that processes are bigger than threads. I then spent the rest of the chapter prattling on about threads and the way they can talk to each other. I didn't say much about processes, mainly because processes aren't quite as useful as threads.

As I mentioned, processes are whole, living, breathing applications. If you end up writing a program that's really a system of many smaller programs, you're really reading the wrong book and should be pretty bored by now. (And you probably should be writing a book for *me* to read.) It's quite common to need to run another program from your own, and when you do, you'll often need to be notified when the process ends, and to know *how* the process ended.

This problem is a real head-scratcher for Win16 programmers. Unfortunately, they're stuck with the `WinExec()` API, which isn't particularly powerful. Thankfully, although it's supported in Win32, it has been superseded. In Win32, you should use the `CreateProcess()` API. This API is very, very powerful. Like all other powerful Windows APIs, it takes about fifty parameters.

To solve our problem of creating an application and waiting until it's done, we can call `CreateProcess()` to get the process running and wait on the process handle we get back, which will signal when the process ends. The `WaitForSingleObject()` API is the key to waiting for that handle. Let's have a look at exactly how it's done.

The prototype for `CreateProcess()` looks like this:

```
BOOL CreateProcess(LPCTSTR            lpApplicationName,
                   LPTSTR             lpCommandLine,
                   LPSECURITY_ATTRIBUTES lpProcessAttributes,
                   LPSECURITY_ATTRIBUTES lpThreadAttributes,
                   BOOL               bInheritHandles,
                   DWORD              dwCreationFlags,
                   LPVOID             lpEnvironment,
                   LPCTSTR            lpCurrentDirectory,
                   LPSTARTUPINFO      lpStartupInfo,
                   LPPROCESS_INFORMATION lpProcessInformation);
```

There are lots of parameters here, like I promised. Thankfully, most of them can be NULL. The two most important are `lpApplicationName` and `lpCommandLine`. The former is a string that names the executable file. You must pass a full path name if the executable is not in the current directory; you can't just pass an executable name and expect Windows to find the file for you on the path. To lessen the sting of this work, I've written a function called `FindOnPath()` for the Spawner sample. It returns an empty string if the file couldn't be found on the path, and a full path if it was found. This function has nothing to do with MFC, so I won't describe it here. It chops up a `CString` a little bit and does some simple API calls.

`lpCommandLine`, meanwhile, has a pointer to the command line you'd like to send to the application. This command line is exactly what is passed to the running application, period.

The next two parameters, `lpProcessAttributes` and `lpThreadAttributes`, point to security attribute structures to control access to the newly created process and the thread object inside of it. If you're writing a program for Windows 95/98, these are obviously ignored, since Windows 95/98 doesn't do any security work outside of the network. But if your application is running under Windows NT/2000, these `SECURITY_ATTRIBUTE` blocks can describe who has what access to the process and thread respectively.

The `bInheritHandles` parameter is a flag which lets you decide if handles owned by the creating process (your application) are assumed by the created process (the program you're running). Normally, this parameter will be `FALSE`. That will save a bit of memory and time by not forcing the operating system to duplicate all of the handles to objects your application has opened. But you may wish to make it `TRUE` if you're planning on letting the applications communicate via files, some shared memory, a named pipe, or another mechanism.

Process Creation Flags

The `dwCreationFlags` parameter is usually 0, but you can combine a few interesting flags to get some advanced work done. Some of the more important flags include `CREATE_SUSPENDED`, which allows you to load and initialize the process and its primary thread, but not run the primary thread until you release it with `ResumeThread()` later. If there are timing issues or post-initialization things you need to take care of, this flag can be quite useful.

If you're using `CreateProcess()` to launch a Win16 or DOS application and you're running your application under Windows NT, you can specify the `CREATE_SEPARATE_WOW_VDM` flag to have Windows NT run the application in a separate virtual machine. That'll get you some additional protection from crashing applications, at a slight cost in resources. The flag has the exact same effect as the Run in Separate Memory Space check box in the Shortcut tab of an application's Shortcut property sheet:

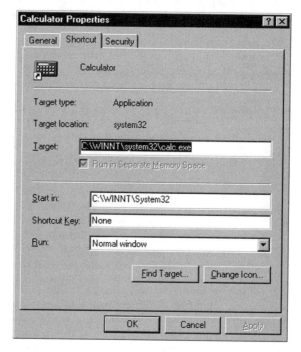

You might also specify `CREATE_NEW_CONSOLE` if you're running a console application. This will create a new console window, instead of letting the new application share the current application's console window. You might want to forgo this flag and run your application with the `DETACHED_PROCESS` flag so that the process runs *without* a console window. This is a great trick for processes that you need to run without a user interface. If the process needs a user interface later in its execution, it can dynamically create a console window with the `::AllocConsole()` API.

You'll also need to use the `dwCreationFlags` to specify the process priority for the new process. As usual, you can use `HIGH_PRIORITY_CLASS`, `IDLE_PRIORITY_CLASS`, `NORMAL_PRIORITY_CLASS`, and `REALTIME_PRIORITY_CLASS`.

The Process Execution Context

The next three parameters each specify some aspect of the execution context of the process. lpEnvironment has a pointer to the environment (that is, the SET variables) for the process, and lpCurrentDirectory specifies the initial current directory for the new process. The parameters can be NULL if you wish the new process to inherit a copy of the same environment or use the same current directory as the spawning process.

The lpStartupInfo parameter points at a STARTUPINFO structure. If you think the end of the big parameter list must be near, you're wrong. While lpStartupInfo is the penultimate parameter, the STARTUPINFO structure it points to has another eighteen values. Once again, we don't have a *real* issue because we can usually leave most of the fields NULL.

Still... the most important field is cb, which *must* be set. Like some of the other Windows API structures we've seen, this field contains a count of bytes in the whole structure so Windows can validate it. A great way to get going when you're about to use such a structure can be found in the Spawner sample. It looks like this:

```
STARTUPINFO suInfo;
memset(&suInfo, 0, sizeof(suInfo));
suInfo.cb = sizeof(suInfo);
```

With a couple of lines, the structure is ready to go. I just need to set the fields I'm interested in. Here are all of the fields in the structure:

```
typedef struct _STARTUPINFO {
    DWORD    cb;
    LPTSTR   lpReserved;
    LPTSTR   lpDesktop;
    LPTSTR   lpTitle;
    DWORD    dwX;
    DWORD    dwY;
    DWORD    dwXSize;
    DWORD    dwYSize;
    DWORD    dwXCountChars;
    DWORD    dwYCountChars;
    DWORD    dwFillAttribute;
    DWORD    dwFlags;
    WORD     wShowWindow;
    WORD     cbReserved2;
    LPBYTE   lpReserved2;
    HANDLE   hStdInput;
    HANDLE   hStdOutput;
    HANDLE   hStdError;
} STARTUPINFO, *LPSTARTUPINFO;
```

The fields you'll need to fill out depend on what flags you specify in the dwFlags field. You can specify no flags (like I did in the sample) if dwFlags is zero. This lets the operating system use the defaults for everything, and that's it. The flags can be accumulated with a bit-wise OR operator (|).

If you use the STARTF_USEPOSITION flag, you can give the main window of the spawned application an initial position by setting the dwX and dwY. If you have STARTF_USESIZE in the flags, you can provide a size by setting dwXSize and dwYSize. If you want to provide both an initial size and position then, logically, you'll need to provide STARTF_USEPOSITION | STARTF_USESIZE.

These initial positions and sizes are useful for exact positioning, but if you'd like to have the window shown as minimized or maximized, you need to use the `wShowWindow` field, activated by the `STARTF_USESHOWWINDOW` flag. This function takes the same constants as the `CWnd::ShowWindow()` function to set the initial state of the window. You would use `SW_SHOWMINIMIZED` or `SW_SHOWMAXIMIZED` for minimized and maximized, for example.

If you're starting a console process, you might want to use `STARTF_USECOUNTCHARS` or `STARTF_USEFILLATTRIBUTE`. The former activates `dwXCountChars` and `dwYCountChars`, which will specify the initial size of the console window in characters. The `dwFillAttribute` member specifies the background and foreground colors for the window if you've specified the `STARTF_USEFILLATTRIBUTE` flag. Then, the `dwFillAttribute` can be a combination of flags to indicate which colors you'd like to mix. Here are all the flags you can combine:

```
FOREGROUND_BLUE
FOREGROUND_GREEN
FOREGROUND_RED
FOREGROUND_INTENSITY
BACKGROUND_BLUE
BACKGROUND_GREEN
BACKGROUND_RED
BACKGROUND_INTENSITY
```

So, if you wanted gray text on a black background, you could use:

```
FOREGROUND_BLUE | FOREGROUND_GREEN | FOREGROUND_RED
```

If you wanted bright yellow text on a blue background, you could use:

```
FOREGROUND_GREEN | FOREGROUND_RED | FOREGROUND_INTENSITY | BACKGROUND_BLUE
```

These same flags are used by the `::SetConsoleTextAttribute()` API, by the way. Unfortunately, the constants are only useful for these APIs – they're not values that you can hand off to the functions you use to create brushes or pens.

As the exception to prove the rule, two of the fields are used regardless of the `dwFlags` field: `lpDesktop` and `lpTitle`. `lpTitle` is only referenced for console applicationsand specifies the title for the console window. It should be `NULL` for GUI applications; if it's `NULL` for a console application, the name of the executable is used instead. `lpDesktop` specifies the name of the desktop. This is useful for applications that need to indicate what user, or upon what system they're running. This parameter is ignored in Windows 95 applications. If you don't need it, use `NULL` to run the process on the same desktop as your parent process.

Some Additional Process Creation Notes

So, all of these parameters come together to actually create the process. If the creation fails, the function returns `FALSE` and you can call the `::GetLastError()` API to find out the exact cause of the failure. If the function returns `TRUE`, it will populate the `PROCESS_INFORMATION` structure that you passed as the last parameter of `CreateProcess()` with data that describes the created process. More on that in a second; let's tie up a loose end first.

With all due candor, if you *are* writing a system with many different programs, you can use the handle to the thread returned to you from CreateProcess() in the PROCESS_INFORMATION structure. You'll need to make sure you correctly create the process so that the primary thread is accessable by the processes that need access to it. The easiest way to ensure that is to make sure you provide NULL for the LPSECURITY_ATTRIBUTES parameter, but if you really need security between the processes, you'll need to make sure you hook up the correct attributes for the different accounts and groups running around in your system. You might have to call CreateProcessAsUser() to make the running process (or the system) think that the new process is running as a different user.

> *The* CreateProcess() *and* CreateProcessAsUser() *APIs are very powerful and flexible. I've only scratched the surface of that power here; there are lots of details that I've glossed over (particularly subtle variations between Windows 95/98 and Windows NT implementations of the function), and lots of aspects I have chosen to neglect altogether. I think I've described everything you'll need to know in most cases, though. Please read through the description of these functions in the Win32 API online documentation for more information before you use these functions.*

Process Information

The PROCESS_INFORMATION structure is populated by the CreateProcess() function only if it succeeds. The structure is pretty small (compared to these huge parameter lists):

```
typedef struct _PROCESS_INFORMATION {
    HANDLE hProcess;
    HANDLE hThread;
    DWORD dwProcessId;
    DWORD dwThreadId;
} PROCESS_INFORMATION;
```

The two HANDLEs can be used to identify the process and thread in later calls. If you created the process with CREATE_SUSPENDED, for example, you might call ResumeThread() on the hThread to get the primary thread running. The DWORDs are IDs; they're useful for keeping an eye on the process in a debugger, or as parameters to the PostThreadMessage() API, but that's about it.

Creating a Process

In the Spawner sample, the code to create a process is quite simple. It just uses the CreateProcess() API:

```
UINT SpawnAndWait(LPVOID pParam)
{
    // Other stuff...
    memset(&suInfo, 0, sizeof(suInfo));
    suInfo.cb = sizeof(suInfo);

    bWorked = ::CreateProcess(pInfo->m_strAppName,
                              _T(""),
                              NULL,
                              NULL,
                              FALSE,
                              NORMAL_PRIORITY_CLASS,
                              NULL,
                              NULL,
                              &suInfo,
                              &procInfo);
```

Continued on Following Page

```
        if (bWorked == FALSE)
            // Something's wrong
        else
            // Everything is just fine
    }
```

We can get away with almost all of the parameters being NULL. The call will return TRUE if the process was created and started, or FALSE if the process couldn't be initialized. The call can run any kind of process – a regular Win32 program, a Win16 program, or a DOS program. If you're running Windows NT, you can also start any application for the POSIX or OS/2 subsystems.

Waiting On a Process All Day Ain't the Latest Thing

With apologies to the Rolling Stones, the last step of getting the sample to work is writing some code to wait for the child process. Back in Win16 days, you had to cook up some wacky trick to call GetModuleHandle() again and again to see if your subprogram, launched with WinExec(), was done running. Alternatively, you could hook up a NotifyRegister() function which would let you know when any other application terminated. Unfortunately, Win32 changes the process model and doesn't make it quite as easy to do this without engaging expensive registry (or confusing process management) APIs.

In Win32, things aren't necessarily simpler, but they are nicer. Instead of cooking up some weird timer-using, GetModuleHandle()-calling hack from the east side of town, we can use real APIs and scientifically proven techniques. At the beginning of this section, I alluded to using WaitForSingleObject(). That would work quite nicely; you could wait for an INFINITE timeout and just sit there, unless of course, you didn't *want* to just sit there. That's easy to solve – just create another thread and have *it* wait instead. When it's done, it can signal the primary thread, which would be busy doing other things.

The addition of a thread to sit and wait is a big step in the right direction, but it has a problem; the waiting thread will block on the WaitForSingleObject() call forever. After all, INFINITE is one heck of a long time. What if the user shuts down the application? We can't abandon the thread; it will leak memory and resources. A smart alternative is to use WaitForMultipleObjects().

The primary thread can create a semaphore that's not signaled. The waiting thread can then wait on both the semaphore and the process. If either signals, it's done working. The waiting thread knows, then, that it is either time to quit and shut down, or time to quit and let the main thread know the subordinate application has finished. Phew!

So, my approach in Spawner was to give the thread a pointer to a semaphore. The primary thread clears that semaphore on creation, and will signal it as the user decides to leave the application. The waiting thread will wait both on that semaphore handle and the process handle for the spawned program. The code to do this is really pretty simple. From the Spawner sample's thread controlling function, the code looks like this:

```
HANDLE hArray[2];
hArray[0] = procInfo.hProcess;
hArray[1] = pInfo->m_psemClosing->m_hObject;

DWORD dwReturn = ::WaitForMultipleObjects(2, hArray, FALSE, INFINITE);
TRACE("Signaled with %d!\n", dwReturn);
```

The ::WaitForMultipleObjects() call returns when either the process handle or the semaphore signals. The API returns an index into the array to indicate which object signaled. If the return from the function is 0, we know that the spawned process has finished running. If the return value is 1, the function knows that the application is shutting down.

The spawned process will take care of signaling itself when you're done running it, but we need to manage the semaphore ourselves. In this case, the semaphore is created as a member of the CSpawnerDlg class. It's initialized with a count of zero, meaning that it's signaled. We can release it later as the window is dying, with a call to its Unlock() function. I could do just that in the PostNcDestroy() message handler in the application's dialog:

```
void CSpawnerDlg::PostNcDestroy()
{
    m_sfClosing.Unlock();
    CDialog::PostNcDestroy();
}
```

This code will work just fine — the wait in the thread will clear, and the thread's controlling function will exit and get the thread shut down. To be completely safe, though, I should use WaitForSingleObject() to make sure the thread exits. If the code in the thread procedure after the WaitForMultipleObjects() call does any real work, it would more than likely take a while to exit. But if I let the process terminate before that, it might not get to clean up after itself completely.

Solving the problem is quite easy — I just need to wait for the thread after unlocking the semaphore. One call does it all, like this:

```
void CSpawnerDlg::PostNcDestroy()
{
    m_sfClosing.Unlock();
    ::WaitForSingleObject(m_pThread->m_hThread, INFINITE);
    CDialog::PostNcDestroy();
}
```

By making sure that the thread has enough time to finish executing properly, I can ensure that my application will run (and stop running) cleanly.

One Instance at a Time

I mentioned, in Chapter 3, that the m_hPrevInstance member of your application's CWinApp object reflects the obsolete status of the hPrevInstance passed to MFC's WinMain() function. That is, m_hPrevInstance is always NULL, even though you might have other instances of your application running.

You might be interested in finding some other way to let your application know that it has been running previously. Back in Win16 days, if you didn't think it was appropriate to allow your users more than one instance of your application, you could always check m_hPrevInstance to see if it wasn't NULL. You could post an error message saying that only one instance was allowed, or you could do a little bit more work and find that other instance and activate its main window to bring it to the user's attention.

We can work around the obsolescence of m_hPrevInstance in Win32 by using threads and waitable objects. You might remember that I said you could specify a name when you created semaphores, events and mutexes in your application. This name would make the object visible to other applications that wanted to reference the object by that name. You can imagine then, that an easy way for an application to know if it's running somewhere else is to try and create a synchronization object using a given name. We can add some code like this to our application's InitInstance() function to do that:

```
m_hEvent = ::CreateEvent(NULL, FALSE, FALSE, _T("Hello"));
if (m_hEvent == NULL)
    // Something REALLY wrong
    return FALSE;

if (::GetLastError() == ERROR_ALREADY_EXISTS)
{
    // Some other instance is running!
    ::CloseHandle(m_hEvent);
    return FALSE;
}
// Remember to close the handle in this case, too
```

If the creation call returns a NULL, something is really, really wrong. Otherwise, we should get a handle to an event object called "Hello". If the event object is new, the handle identifies the new object. If the event object already exists, the CreateEvent() function will return a handle referencing that existing object. In that case, a subsequent call to ::GetLastError() will return ERROR_ALREADY_EXISTS. By checking for that condition, we'll know if the handle already exists. If it does, we'll know that some other instance of the application is running.

There are two things wrong with this implementation as it stands. The first problem is pretty easy to fix; it's a little silly to name such a shared object "Hello". If any other application does that, you'll run into trouble. Instead, we can just call AfxGetAppName() to return the name of our application. If you have an application with a common name, though (such as "ReportGenerator", or "Smith", or "Jones") that can still be a problem. You might want to code a more difficult name (such as "Investment Business Information System Reporting Module", or "Blaszczak", or "Koslowski") to help ensure your uniqueness. Your name can be up to _MAX_PATH characters long. (_MAX_PATH is a constant found in Stdlib.h; it's usually at least 255 characters.)

The second problem is that our implementation isn't finished; we need to find some way to signal the existing application so it can activate its main window for us. Solving this is going to take a little thought, because we need to make sure the event objects we create are killed too. We can address the issue of activating our window by creating a thread. When the application starts, it can try to create the named event object. If the object does exist, it can signal it and exit. If the object doesn't exist, it can begin running – but it should first create a thread that sits around and waits on the event object. If the object is signaled, the thread will react by activating our application's main window and letting it appear active to the user. The thread will then continue to wait for that one object.

If you've done hard time, like me, you're probably realizing that programming with threads is like smashing a rock full of problems into smaller, more manageable stony little issues. Adding this extra thread to our application is a case in point. The thread solves some big problems for us, but creates an extra issue — making sure the application correctly terminates the thread as the application dies. We can use a second, private event object to help the thread know when to exit as the application is dying. With these enhancements (and after rewriting the code to use the MFC `CEvent` class), the earlier `InitInstance()` code will look something like this:

```
BOOL COnlyOneApp::InitInstance()
{
    m_pInstanceEvent = new CEvent(FALSE, FALSE, AfxGetAppName());
    if (::GetLastError() == ERROR_ALREADY_EXISTS)
    {
        m_pInstanceEvent->SetEvent();
        return FALSE;
    }
    m_pShutdownEvent = new CEvent;

    // More stuff...
}
```

With that done, we have the two events we need squirreled away in the instance data of our `COnlyOneApp` object. If we note that the instance event already exists with the name of our application, we set the event and kill the current application.

We then need to invent a `CWinThread`-derived class to wait for the signaling of the shared instance event object. I called my class `CActivationWatcher`. It's really simple; we create the `CActivationWatcher` thread simply by calling the `AfxBeginThread()` function (as described earlier in the chapter), just after we create the shutdown event object, like this:

```
m_pActivationWatch = (CActivationWatcher*)
                        AfxBeginThread(RUNTIME_CLASS(CActivationWatcher));
```

The `OnlyOne` sample implements a simple application with all of this code hooked up properly. The application does nothing but protect itself from multiple instances — other than the code we've discussed here, it's just a default MDI application. In that application, I decided to make `CActivationWatcher` a `friend` class to `COnlyOneApp`. This lets `CActivationWatcher` get the protected `m_hShutdownEvent` and `m_hInstanceEvent` members directly from `COnlyOneApp`'s instance data.

This architecture has me on the run from object-oriented zealots everywhere; they're calling for my crucifixion. This architecture is really just a publicity stunt. I hope to get lots of free press for a boring book, but I can justify the decision in a couple of other ways too. Methods to get the handles would have married the two classes just as soundly, and making a nested class would have been more than a little confusing.

I could also have decided to make the variables `public` members of the `CActivationWatcher` object. In that situation, after making the above `AfxBeginThread()` call and requesting that the thread should start suspended, I could then initialize the members, and resume the thread. I thought that was too much extra fluff for *this* simple example. Still, taken in its most general form, this idea has merit for more reasons than its earthy disdain for object-oriented zealotry; it can be very useful if you have lots of complicated data or initialization work for a new thread, or if you can't gain global access to the class which has your initialization data.

Anyway, we need to code the body of the CActivationWatcher thread. It's a blind worker thread, i.e. it has no user interface and no message pump. As such, I code everything it does right in its InitInstance() override. The first thing that happens is the setup of an array so we can wait on the two objects. We also gain a pointer to the application (since that's where we'll find the handles upon which we need to party), and declare a couple of utility variables:

```
BOOL CActivationWatcher::InitInstance()
{
    COnlyOneApp* pApp = static_cast<COnlyOneApp*>(AfxGetApp());
    CSyncObject* pEvents[2];
    pEvents[1] = pApp->m_pInstanceEvent;
    pEvents[0] = pApp->m_pShutdownEvent;

    DWORD dwSignaled;

    // Other stuff...
}
```

The 'other stuff' is a simple loop that does a Lock() on a CMultiLock object over and over again until one of the two events is signaled. If the signaled event is the shutdown event, the loop exits so the InitInstance() function can return FALSE. Returning FALSE from InitInstance(), you'll remember, causes MFC to terminate the thread. If the signaled event is the instance event, we know that someone (besides our doctor, perhaps) wants to see us become more active. The code looks like this:

```
BOOL CActivationWatcher::InitInstance()
{
...

    CMultiLock Locker(pEvents, 2);

    while (1)
    {
        dwSignalled = Locker.Lock(INFINITE, FALSE);
        TRACE(_T("dwSignalled is %d\n"), dwSignalled);

        // Is it Shutdown?
        if ((dwSignalled-WAIT_OBJECT_0) == 0)
            break;

        // Is it Instance?
        if ((dwSignalled-WAIT_OBJECT_0) == 1)
        {
            CWnd MainWindow;
            if (MainWindow.Attach(pApp->m_pMainWnd->m_hWnd))
            {
                CWnd* pWnd = MainWindow.GetLastActivePopup();
                pWnd->SetForegroundWindow();
                MainWindow.Detach();
                OnIdle(0);
            }
            else
                ::MessageBeep(0);
        }
    }

    // Never do ExitInstance() or Run()
    return FALSE;
}
```

Each of the `if` statements tests the return value from the `Lock()`. These statements use the rules I described earlier in the chapter; by doing a little subtraction, I can tell which event in the array was signaled. The real important work happens if we've been asked to activate our application.

You'll remember the rule that I discussed earlier – MFC objects which wrap a mapped Windows object can't be used from different threads. The code above shows how to use `Attach()` and `Detach()` to avoid falling into that trap. If the window really does exist and we can successfully `Attach()` to it, I make calls against my own `CWnd` object instead of directly against that one. When I'm done, I can call `Detach()` against my `CWnd` object so that MFC can clean the map. If I don't call `Detach()`, the destructor of my local `CWnd` will throw an `ASSERT`. If I don't do the `Attach()` call, the `SetForegroundWindow()` call will not be able to find the `m_hWnd` of the main window in the thread's map and therefore also toss an `ASSERT`.

Note that the call to `GetLastActivePopup()` returns a pointer to a `CWnd` and we don't have to bother doing any `Attach()` or `Detach()` calls. This is because the pointer was created during the execution of our own thread, right here in the `InitInstance()` function. The temporary pointer lives right in `CActivationWatcher`'s own thread-local map and doesn't need to be managed explicitly by our code.

Since a new `CWnd` object will be created for my thread, and a new entry added to the temporary object map, the map could become congested. (The odds of the map getting so congested that you actually have a problem are about the same as finding an underweight fifth-term senator, but we need to be professional and write bulletproof code with public data members, even though we like to tell dumb jokes.) The key to relieving that congestion is to call the `OnIdle()` member of `CWinThread`.

In my earlier explanation of temporary maps, I indicated that this function is called when there are no other messages to be processed by the thread. Since our thread doesn't have a message loop, it will never realize that there are no more messages to process and will never clean out the map. It's a good idea to call it explicitly when you have no message loop, as we've done here – if you write a thread class that *does* have a message loop, don't worry about calling `OnIdle()` yourself.

In case you're wondering, `CWnd::GetLastActivePopup()` retrieves a pointer to the `CWnd` that was most recently popped up by the identified window. By calling `GetLastActivePopup()`, we can easily find the window owned by the application that's really active. If we called `SetForegroundWindow()` on the main window of the application, we would make that window active, even if the application had some modal dialog active! This would be awkward at best. `GetLastActivePopup()`, conveniently gives us a pointer to the real, active child window for the application. This lets us correctly reactivate the application, without disturbing activation within the application's window hierarchy.

Back in the application object, we need to signal the thread that we're shutting down. The best place to do this, for a worker thread with no user-interface, turns out to be the destructor of the application object. We're always guaranteed that the destructor will be called. If something in `InitInstance()` fails, `ExitInstance()` won't be called; therefore, since we created the thread and event objects at the very beginning of `InitInstance()`, we can't rely on `ExitInstance()` to do our cleanup.

```
COnlyOneApp::~COnlyOneApp()
{
    if (m_pShutdownEvent != NULL)
    {
        m_pShutdownEvent->SetEvent();
        if (m_pActivationWatch != NULL)
            ::WaitForSingleObject(m_pActivationWatch->m_hThread, INFINITE);
        delete m_pShutdownEvent;
        m_pShutdownEvent = NULL;
    }

    if (m_pInstanceEvent != NULL)
    {
        delete m_pInstanceEvent;
        m_pInstanceEvent = NULL;
    }
}
```

The only real trick here is that I've made sure the code will pause before the thread ends. The call to the ::WaitForSingleObject() against the m_hThread member of the activation thread makes sure we do so. The thread's handle becomes signaled when the thread ends. After cleaning up the CEvent objects allocated by InitInstance(), we're home free.

Everything I Needed to Know About Threads, I Learned in Kindergarten

Here's one last piece of advice about programming with threads (and processes, for that matter) – you need to be careful to remember that sharing is important. If you have your primary thread create other threads, it will need to be careful to shut them down correctly – don't resort to ::TerminateThread() hacks, for reasons I explained earlier.

If different threads in your application share different resources, you'll need to make sure that those resources are protected from being accessed in two different ways at the same time from two different threads. By using the synchronization objects we discussed in this chapter, you can ensure that you'll stay out of trouble.

By focusing your design around your code's careful sharing and management of resources, you'll always have less trouble when writing multithreaded applications.

Summary

This chapter has covered a great many details about the development of multithreaded applications. It's provided all of the insights I can muster for people who are interested in this kind of programming. By introducing extra threads to some applications, you can get a great performance benefit from your application, but you'll also increase its complexity tremendously. That means more work for you, the developer, as you track down tricky synchronization problems and worry about resource leaks.

The most important thing to do when you are writing a multithreaded application is to concentrate on the design of the application very, very carefully. Try to decide:

> Will threads really help the problem anyway?

> How will I deal with killing threads in error situations?

> How will the threads I create get information back to their parent?

> What unseen things could cause the threads I've created to block?

> How will my threads react when the user suddenly closes the application?

If you don't think about these things, you'll be asking for lots of trouble later!

Creating Dynamic-link Libraries

If you've been programming in C or C++ for more than a couple of days, you're already familiar with the notion of tossing your frequently used code into a library. Often reusable code is stored in a static library. The linker can retrieve code from a static library and add it to your executable image while it's built. But in a multitasking environment, there is some advantage to using a **dynamic-link library (DLL)** for the storage of frequently-used code and data.

In this chapter, we'll cover:

- ➤ The differences between static and dynamic-link libraries
- ➤ How to create dynamic-link libraries
- ➤ The different types of MFC architecture that can be applied to the libraries
- ➤ How to decide between the two architectures
- ➤ Tips for healthy linking

Libraries

When you reuse someone else's code, for example the `printf()` routine from the standard C run-time library, or indeed entire classes such as those found in the Microsoft Foundation Classes libraries, the linker will end up retrieving the routines and adding their image to your executable.

When the linker puts all the referenced routines together with your code into one executable, it's said to be **statically linking** your code. Statically linking code can save you a great deal of time; you don't have to rewrite (or debug!) routines like `printf()`, or whole classes like `CWinApp`, for every application where you'd like to use them. You are able to update your code by recompiling against the libraries you need, pulling in bug fixes and new features just by linking again.

When they became available, back in the stone age of software development, static libraries were looked upon as one of the state-of-the-art development techniques. However, aggressive modern use of static libraries has shown them to have a few shortcomings. One example is as follows. It is possible for many running applications to require the same code from a particular static library, and each application would have that code linked into its executable image, loaded into memory as a separate copy. Not only does loading multiple copies of code in these executables waste memory at runtime, it also wastes disk space as each executable image contains essentially the same code.

Let's take a look at the mechanism that Windows provides to address the problems of static linking, such as that outlined above, and discuss how, as C++ and MFC programmers, this facet of Windows applies to us.

Dynamic-link Libraries

The solution provided by Windows to help us reuse code more efficiently comes in the form of **dynamic-link libraries**. Dynamic-link libraries are blocks of code, and sometimes even resources and data, wrapped up into a special kind of executable module that can be loaded and discarded as necessary.

Because a dynamic-link library can be used by a number of applications at once, Windows imbues its loading and unloading mechanism with a level of intelligence. The loader ensures that only one copy of the library is loaded at any one time, and that it remains loaded for as long as it's needed – no matter how many programs are referencing it. Windows manages this with a **reference count** for each DLL.

Each time an application attempts to load a DLL, its reference count is increased, and each time an application attempts to unload a DLL, its reference count is decreased. Only the first attempt at loading a DLL results in Windows actually reading the image from disk and storing it in RAM, and it is only when the reference count for the DLL reaches zero that the DLL is actually unloaded from memory. The value of the reference count indicates the number of applications using the library. Using this protocol, it doesn't matter in what order applications attempt to load and unload the DLL. As long as its reference count is positive, Windows will not discard the library because it knows that it is still being used.

The DLL image is a program in itself. Any data in the DLL is local to the instance of the DLL as referenced by a particular client program. We'll show a special technique for enabling a block of memory to be shared among all instances of the programs that reference it, but such data is certainly the exception to the rule and not the practice.

As an interesting aside, you may think that we haven't been using dynamic-link libraries until this point in the book. But, of course, the architectural aspects of dynamic-link libraries are fundamental to Windows, and almost all of the Windows system files are really dynamic-link libraries! The graphics display interface code (that is code which handles user interface items like dialog boxes and edit controls) and many application extensions, such as the common dialogs, are implemented as a collection of DLLs. This helps Windows to manage memory efficiently for itself; if your applications aren't using COM, for example, there's no reason for the COM system code to be floating around in memory.

Most dynamic-link libraries live in files with the extension .dll, but you can give the library file any extension you wish. Some special DLLs might have extensions other than .dll; for example, ActiveX controls use the extension .ocx and many of the 16-bit Windows system DLLs were named with an .exe extension. You're free to choose any of these names for DLLs that your program will explicitly load – that is, DLLs which your program will ask for by name once it's running. However, if you implicitly load a DLL by linking to an import library, the file for that DLL must be named with a .dll or .exe extension. We'll look in more detail at implicit and explicit linking, and how DLLs are loaded, throughout this chapter.

Architectural Decisions

Before we spend time examining DLLs in greater detail, let's study the architectural differences between static and dynamic linking in a little more depth.

Static linking means that the linker resolves your code. When you build your program, the linker decides which functions and data you reference in other libraries and copies that data and code directly into your executable image. The linker goes through lots of gyrations to whittle down your executable image so that it contains as little code as possible – the linker tries not to include code or data that isn't actually referenced, and only makes your executable as big as it needs to be. There are some options that you can give the linker, and also the compiler, to fine-tune this process, but that's the way it works.

Dynamic linking means that the external needs of your code are resolved at runtime. At runtime, the operating system has no idea what specific routines you'll need – it can't perform the intensive analysis that the linker is able to perform while you're building your program. So, as the operating system loads your application, it decides which DLLs you need to run and loads them. Thus, if your application only uses one 200-byte function in a DLL that contains lots of other functions, and weighs in at one megabyte, then the whole megabyte of code is committed by the operating system to your process. Any code that supports the function you call is paged into memory and becomes part of your **working set**.

> If you've not heard the term before, a **working set** is the set of all memory pages which a program is currently using. Even if a program has a small executable image, it might have a huge working set if it asks for lots of memory from the operating system as it runs.

If you're not well-acquainted with the way Windows memory management works, this process sounds pretty harsh, and it is. When the code in the DLL becomes part of your working set, Windows **reserves** that memory for your process. It isn't actually in use – if other applications (or your own process itself) need the memory, it can still be very efficiently returned to your process. As code in the DLL starts executing, Windows loads that code into memory and actually **commits** the memory. Committed memory is worse than reserved memory in the sense that it's very difficult to release for other uses.

On the other hand, the DLL itself doesn't know which parts of the code you expect to use. It needs to assume the worst and initialize everything in sight in preparation for any calls that you might eventually make. That means that code throughout the DLL is running in preparation for calls that might never come – the runtime libraries initialize, MFC initializes, and static objects are constructed. Pages throughout the image will come into memory unless the application has been very carefully tuned to avoid it, and that means loading a DLL can be very expensive.

MFC 6.0 itself is available in two different forms – as a static library and as a dynamic link library. Applying what we know about the effects of the linking model to MFC applications reveals some interesting details. Your executable image – as a file on disk – will almost certainly be smaller if you dynamically link to MFC. However, the working set of your application is likely to be larger if you link your application with MFC's DLLs. On the other hand if you link statically, your executable file will be larger, but it will have a smaller working set.

It's easy to observe the statistics that support my assertions. Simply make a generic application with the AppWizard and run it while watching the working set statistics shown by the Performance Monitor tool under Windows NT. Unfortunately, the issues aren't quite as simple as these easily observable statistics.

If your application is a part of a system that includes other applications that use MFC, the impact of loading the MFC DLL is minimized because Windows can logically map memory to let each process share the same code. Since pages are shared across working sets, *your application's* total working set is larger, but the impact on the *system* isn't as pronounced as in a situation when you statically link MFC.

If you're not using the exact same version of MFC in the case where different applications are running concurrently, you'll probably find that it's better to link to the MFC DLL statically. However, if you're building several applications that will always execute together, you should dynamically link to MFC. Sometimes, you don't have a choice in the matter – for example, ActiveX controls built with MFC *always* dynamically link to the MFC DLL.

Above and beyond memory usage, there are other factors that must be taken into consideration when writing DLLs – particularly when you're considering the use of DLLs with MFC; these will be discussed later. Now, however, we will take a closer look at DLLs themselves. They have a few important features that should be explained before we investigate how things really work when MFC is added to the equation.

If you feel that you already understand how DLLs work, you can skip the next few pages and get to the crux of the matter by reading the section called 'Using and Writing DLLs with MFC' later in this chapter. If you want to know what makes DLLs go, then please read on.

Initializing a DLL

When a DLL loads, it will usually need to initialize itself before it can do any work. Whether the initialization is as simple as constructing static objects in the image, or if it involves actually going out and connecting to other computers or acquiring other resources, the initialization will happen and does take some amount of execution time.

Windows provides for initialization routines by allowing you to implement an entry point function which will be called just after your DLL is loaded and just before it is removed from memory by Windows. This entry point is usually given the name DllMain(), but this is only defined by convention. Give your DLL an entry point function and name it whatever you like; you'll just need to tell the linker about the name you've chosen using the /ENTRY: option.

Normally, the linker sets the entry point for your DLL to be _DllMainCRTStartup(). This function is defined by the C run-time (CRT) library, and offers the library a chance to initialize itself in the context of your application. If you do use the CRT entry point, there must be a pseudo-entry point in your own code called DllMain() that's called by the CRT once it's finished its initialization. In this case, you have no option but to call this function DllMain().

If you implement your own entry point (by specifying it with the /ENTRY parameter to Link on the command line, or with the Entry-point Symbol: field in the Link options tab of the Project Settings dialog) you should call _DllMainCRTStartup() just as soon as your own entry point function is called. If you don't make this call, you'll find that the C run-time library is in an uninitialized state, and that static C++ objects in your code might not have been created.

The prototype for your DllMain() should match the following:

```
BOOL WINAPI DllMain(HINSTANCE hinstDLL, DWORD dwReason, LPVOID lpvReserved);
```

The first parameter, hinstDLL, is a module handle for the dynamic-link library instance which is just being loaded. Your DllMain() function should squirrel this value away so that it can be used later, when you might want to load resources. Since the DLL file is a separate module, it can have its own resources, distinct from those in the calling application – so you should be careful to use the correct resource handle when you are doing a LoadString(), LoadCursor() or any other Windows API function that deals with resources.

While we described the DllMain() function as an entry point for your user-level code (after the *true* entry point of _DllMainCRTStartup() has been called), DllMain() is called both when your dynamic-link library is being loaded and being released. When the function is called during a load, dwReason is set to DLL_PROCESS_ATTACH. Once a process is finished with your DLL, dwReason will be set to DLL_PROCESS_DETACH.

You should also note that DllMain() is also called when the process in an application associated with a DLL creates or destroys a thread. For the creation of a thread, dwReason will be set to DLL_THREAD_ATTACH, while dwReason is set to DLL_THREAD_DETACH when a thread terminates.

DLL_THREAD_ATTACH and DLL_THREAD_DETACH calls are only made when the application creates or destroys additional threads; these call modes are not performed when the application creates or destroys its primary thread. The DllMain() notification calls are made for *every* thread in the process, since there's no way for anyone (not to mention Windows) to accurately and quickly predict whether the new thread will enter or leave the DLL. You can turn the notifications off by calling the DisableThreadLibraryCalls() API, but doing this can break MFC.

Only threads in the process which loaded the DLL call the entry point – that is to say, a thread created by Windows for Windows *won't* call your DllMain() unless Windows itself has loaded your DLL. So if you're interested in knowing when a thread is created or destroyed globally throughout the system, you'll need to find another way.

If you decide to perform some sort of management in reaction to DLL_THREAD_ATTACH and DLL_THREAD_DETACH notifications, you really should make sure that it doesn't take up too much time. Thread creation should be very inexpensive – you can raise the cost of threads by bloating your response to DLL_THREAD_ATTACH notifications.

The data to which the lpvReserved pointer points to is just that, reserved. Don't touch it; it's not yours. The pointer itself is set to NULL during DLL_PROCESS_ATTACH and DLL_PROCESS_DETACH calls which are being used for dynamic loads (explicit linking), and non-NULL for these calls during static loads (implicit linking). It's safe to test the lpvReserved pointer, but not the data to which it points. Don't worry about the distinction between static and dynamic loads, because we'll be covering them before the end of the chapter.

The DllApp sample application depends on an extra DLL called DynLib. DynLib has a DllMain() function which simply announces its execution to the debugger; you'll see it output a debug message when the library is first loaded, and another when the application terminates:

```
BOOL WINAPI DllMain(HINSTANCE hinstDLL, DWORD dwReason, LPVOID lpvReserved)
{
#ifdef _DEBUG
    TCHAR    szFormat[256];
    wsprintf(szFormat,
        _T("hInst = %8.8X, reason = %d, reserved %c= NULL \n"),
        hinstDLL, dwReason,
        (lpvReserved == NULL) ? _T('=') : _T('!'));
    ::OutputDebugString(szFormat);
#endif
    return TRUE;
}
```

Note that here, I call the ::OutputDebugString() API instead of using the MFC TRACE() macros. I use ::OutputDebugString() directly, because the sample isn't an MFC project! Even in an MFC-based DLL, during the execution of DllMain(), I cannot be sure that MFC has initialized. Thus so calls to MFC-based functions are not appropriate.

Now that we've seen what happens when a DLL loads or unloads, let's see how we actually initiate that loading or unloading process by examining how we can use a DLL in our own code.

Coding with DLLs

Clearly, you never have to do anything extra to load static libraries once you have added them to your application, but since a DLL is a separate module, you'll need some way to tell Windows that you want to load it. This is possibly the single weakest point of DLL architecture – it takes time to load and initialize the separate module.

When you are coding with DLLs, you'll want to make sure that the DLL can initialize quickly. Don't use lots of static objects in your DLL – they'll have their constructors run every time a new process (but not a new thread!) attaches to the DLL, which can really add up. If your DLL becomes bloated, you'll also find that it takes Windows a long time to get the code and data from the image into memory, particularly if your DLL isn't tuned to have as small a working set as possible.

Developers who complain that their applications load very slowly or cause trouble in the debugger sometimes approach me for help. When I ask them about their architecture, they describe their system and tell me that they load hundreds of DLLs. I blink in amazement – there's no reason, and certainly no fast way, to load 131 DLLs to get your application running. If you've found yourself with this kind of structure, you really do need to find a different way to architect your application!

Explicit Linking

In some instances, you won't be able to tell which library to load and run until your own application is actually running. For example, you might load an extension DLL that has been asked for by the user, or that's needed for a special operation. In these situations, you can use the Windows API to load the library directly and find the appropriate addresses of the functions within it.

The Windows ::LoadLibrary() API function takes a single parameter – the name of the DLL that you want to load. You can pass it any sort of file name you like. If you don't include an extension, Windows will assume you want a file with the .dll extension. If you don't name a specific path to the file, Windows will look for it in these places, in this order

1. The directory from which the application loaded. If the user ran Fooey.exe from the C:\Fooey directory, Windows will first look for your DLL in C:\Fooey.

2. The current directory for your process.

3. The 32-bit Windows system directory. Usually, this is Windows\System32 on NT, and Windows\System on Windows 95/98.

4. For Windows NT only, the 16-bit Windows system directory. Usually, this is Windows\System.

5. The Windows directory itself; usually Windows.

6. The directories in the system PATH environment variable.

Windows loads into memory the first DLL that it finds. It won't warn you if the DLL exists in more than one place; without any fanfare it just loads the first copy that it finds and stops looking. This is another possible downside to using dynamic-link libraries in your application. You have to carefully decide how to install your application, so you're certain to get the right versions of the DLLs you need.

Many developers put their DLLs into the Windows directory, centralizing the location of their dependent files and making it easy for subsequent versions to overwrite the files and update the installation of the application. However, users hate this. It means that deleting the program's directory won't remove everything that the program has installed. They have to wander over to the Windows directory and try to guess what other files the application used. And before they can delete the DLL, they have to assure themselves that the program they have just deleted is the only one that used it.

This isn't the kind of thing that most users feel comfortable doing. It's really a bad idea to install all the DLLs that your application needs in the Windows or Windows\System directories – you should use your application's own installation directory, since that's the first place Windows will look anyhow. While this means that you might end up with the same DLL in many places on your hard drive, you'll save on problems for your users. Drive space is far cheaper than support calls or lawsuits brought by self-anointed magazine gurus who think you've only erased a DLL to thwart your competition.

If Windows doesn't find the DLL, even after searching the PATH, the ::LoadLibrary() call will return NULL, you can get extended error information by calling GetLastError(). When it is successful, ::LoadLibrary() will return the instance handle for the library to be loaded.

Once you've loaded the library, you'll still need to find an address within the library to call the function you need. You can do this by calling ::GetProcAddress(). The only trick to using ::GetProcAddress() is in identifying the function which you'd like to call. You can do this in one of two ways; either via an **export ordinal** number, or by the actual name of the function. How you'll do this depends on the DLL with which you're working – let's take a look at exactly what exports are before we decide how we'll use them.

Exports

When it's compiled, a dynamic-link library module will be built just like any other code. The difference is the linking step; the DLL file has a layout very similar to an application file, but with one important difference – an **exports table**. The exports table, sometimes also called a **name table**, contains the name of every routine which the image exports and the address for the entry point of the routine. ::GetProcAddress() works by looking up entries in this table, either by the entry number (also known as the ordinal) or by the name of the entry.

When it's building your DLL, the linker will accept all of the modules and static libraries to generate the image. However, when it reads the module definition file, it will expect this file to have a list of exports. Module definition files traditionally have the extension .def. AppWizard will give you a default .def file which you must maintain as you continue to grow your library. Any application can also have a definition file, but its contents are normally used to describe the module to Windows itself, rather than provide any pertinent linkage information.

The exports list in the module definition file contains the names of the functions to be exported. Each name may optionally have an attribute or two, including an export ordinal number. A fragment from a typical module definition file might look like this:

```
LIBRARY    LinkList
DESCRIPTION    "My Amazing Linked List Library"

EXPORTS
    CreateList
    CreateNode

    InsertNode            @35
    SetCurrentNode        @36    NONAME
    SetCurrentNodeEx      @37    RESIDENTNAME
    GetCurrentNode        @38
    GetFirstNode          @39

    DllCanUnloadNow              PRIVATE
    DllRegisterServer            PRIVATE
    DllUnregisterSErver          PRIVATE
```

Line-by-line, the entries declare different functions that must be present in the executable image; the linker will generate an error if it can't resolve an address for any function you export. Any line can contain a semicolon, and text after that semicolon will be treated as a comment by the linker. Each entry must have a name, so that the linker knows which functions you want to export. You don't need to export every function in your DLL; you only need to export the functions that you want to allow to be directly accessed by a calling program.

As a matter of fact, you should export as little as possible. By hiding everything you don't need, you'll keep your implementation away from prying fingers and reduce your documentation burden. Further, smaller export tables are easier for Windows to manage, both when it's loading the DLL and, more importantly, when it's looking up functions with the `::GetProcAddress()` function.

The highlighted lines of code in the sample above feature an *at* symbol (@) together with an integer. This number is the export ordinal for the function in question. By explicitly naming an export ordinal, you force the linker to assign that ordinal to the function. In the above `.def` file, `InsertNode` would be assigned the ordinal of 35. We could retrieve a pointer to this function with this code:

```
void (*pfnInsertNode)();
HINSTANCE    hInstListLib;

hInstListLib = ::LoadLibrary("MyLists.dll");
ASSERT(hInstListLib != NULL);
pfnInsertNode = ::GetProcAddress(hInstListLib, "InsertNode");
ASSERT(pfnInsertNode != NULL);
```

Here, the `::GetProcAddress()` function is given the name of the function. Since the `.def` file also explicitly specifies an ordinal, we could pass the ordinal like this:

```
pfnInsertNode = ::GetProcAddress(hInstListLib, MAKEINTRESOURCE(35));
```

Note that .exe files have an exports table, but they're just not used as aggressively as they are in the case of a dynamic-link library. In Win32, Microsoft recommends that you don't use the exports table at all within your .exe module image – doing so would mean that you plan to allow other applications access to functions within your process, and such access isn't in keeping with the Win32 process model.

The linker will assign ordinals to each function that doesn't have one explicitly assigned in the .def file. There are rules for this, but they are a bit complicated, so the effect of not having an explicitly named ordinal is almost arbitrary; you shouldn't link to an export using its ordinal unless you know that the ordinal won't change.

As the linker builds the exports table for your executable image, it will create a temporary .exp file. The linker will write to and read from this file as it builds your import library. The linker leaves these files lying about, but they're not very interesting since the content of the .exp file isn't documented. However, the name of your .exp file will show up in error messages. If your .def file includes a function name that isn't defined anywhere in your executable image, for example, the linker will emit an error message saying that the symbol named in the .exp is an unresolved external.

Most people don't realize it, but the Microsoft Win32 linker is actually capable of spawning lots of other nifty little utilities to get its job done. If you're an old Win16 hand (like me), you certainly remember that there are separate Implib and Lib utilities to manage import libraries and libraries. The Win32 version of Link actually spawns Implib and Lib for you, so you don't have to fuss with it. Dumpbin, another utility that I'll mention near the end of this chapter, is also available through the Link command line.

Since ::GetProcAddress() retrieves an entry point in the code of a module, the function returns a pointer to a function. Syntax for declaring and using function pointers is a bit convoluted; you should take the time to refer to your favorite C or C++ language reference to make sure you understand how to declare and dereference function pointers.

The biggest caveat surrounding ::GetProcAddress() is that you need to be perfectly sure the pointer to the function you declare has an absolutely correct parameter list, calling convention and return value. If you make a mistake with any one of these, your code will probably step on the stack and cause a crash. Since ::GetProcAddress() returns a generic pointer, your code is responsible for casting that pointer to the correct type of function.

To provide a sample of using GetProcAddress() for finding the name of a function in a DLL, let's use GetProcAddress() to call MessageBox(). We all know the function prototype of MessageBox() goes like this:

```
int MessageBox(HWND, LPCTSTR, LPCTSTR, UINT);
```

so the first thing we'll do is declare a pointer to a function of that type. Function pointer syntax in C and C++ is really pretty gnarly; if you want to read more about it, check out section 4.6.9 of Stroustrup's *The C++ Programming Language*. Here's a pointer to a function that matches the prototype of MessageBox(); the pointer itself is named MBFunc:

```
int(*MBFunc)(HWND, LPCTSTR, LPCTSTR, UINT);
```

You certainly don't want to be using this kind of syntax for the rest of your program, so it's really convenient to write a `typedef` that we can use as shorthand. The `typedef` declaration itself isn't any easier on the eyes, but the ability to use a newly defined type without that messy syntax is really important. Here's the `typedef`; the new type is named `MBFuncPtr`.

```
typedef int (*MBFuncPtr)(HWND, LPCTSTR, LPCTSTR, UINT);
```

The `MessageBox()` API function is exposed from the Windows system DLL named `USER32.DLL`. Since we know it's on the path (otherwise, the user isn't running Windows in the first place!), we can just call `LoadLibrary()` to get it into memory, like in this code fragment:

```
#include <windows.h>
#include <stdio.h>

typedef int (*MBFuncPtr)(HWND, LPCTSTR, LPCTSTR, UINT);

void main()
{
    HINSTANCE hInst = LoadLibrary("USER32.DLL");
    if (hInst == NULL)
        printf("Couldn't load USER32.DLL!\n");
    else
    {
        MBFuncPtr pFunction = (MBFuncPtr)GetProcAddress(hInst, "MessageBoxA");
        if (pFunction == NULL)
            printf("Couldn't find MessageBox entry point!\n");
        else
        {
            int nRet = (*pFunction)(NULL, "Revolutionary Guide", "It worked!",
                                                                    MB_OK);

            printf("Returned %d\n", nRet);
        }

        FreeLibrary(hInst);
    }
}
```

We then call `GetProcAddress()` with the name `MessageBoxA`. The `MessageBox()` API that accepts Unicode strings is named `MessageBoxW`, but we want to pass ANSI strings – so we'll use `MessageBoxA`. You normally do not fuss with this detail, since the Windows system header files provide macros that rename the functions for you depending on which type of build you're doing. But those macros aren't useful when calling `GetProcAddress()`.

We have to cast the return value of `GetProcAddress()`, and our `typedef` comes in handy for this again. If the call works, we can dereference our new pointer and pass the parameters we want... and we're off to the races!

You can imagine that loading code this way for more than a few functions quickly grows incredibly tedious. The type management and data handling and all – it's a mess! As such, explicitly loading and calling DLLs is left for those very rare circumstances where the DLL name or the function called really isn't known until runtime.

More .DEF File Syntax

Some of the lines in the `.def` file have additional keywords, such as those highlighted below:

```
LIBRARY    LinkList
DESCRIPTION    "My Amazing Linked List Library"

EXPORTS
    CreateList
    CreateNode
    InsertNode           @35
    SetCurrentNode       @36    NONAME
    SetCurrentNodeEx     @37    RESIDENTNAME
    GetCurrentNode       @38
    GetFirstNode         @39
    DllCanUnloadNow             PRIVATE
    DllRegisterServer           PRIVATE
    DllUnregisterSErver         PRIVATE
```

NONAME means that the name of the function won't be placed in the export table in the resulting file. For huge DLLs, this can save an incredible amount of space. All but a few of the entry points in MFC are declared with NONAME, thus saving over 150 kilobytes of space in the image of the DLL!

When it's declared with NONAME, a symbol may not be the target of an explicit link using its name; you can only link to its ordinal because the name isn't stored in the executable. Since a client never explicitly links to the MFC libraries by name, with the exception of those few routines which aren't declared NONAME, this technique is acceptable for MFC. You'll need to decide how your DLL will be applied before you use NONAME to save some space. Implicitly linking to a DLL routine declared with NONAME is acceptable, since the import library only uses ordinals internally.

The RESIDENTNAME keyword is obsolete with Win32. In previous Windows versions, the keyword was used to indicate that the designated name would remain in a part of the name table kept in memory at all times. Since Win32 manages memory more efficiently, this keyword is meaningless to modern linkers and library utilities; Win32 can always keep the name table readily accessible without wasting memory space. You can still specify the keyword, but it will be ignored.

The PRIVATE modifier tells the linker that the given symbol is only for export from the DLL at runtime and not to be made available via the DLL's import library. This has an important effect. If you have a DLL which exports code that an application or another DLL might use, multiply defined entry points can cause many problems. For example, if you link one DLL to another, and both export DllRegisterServer(), you'll have great problems registering your DLL – you won't be able to predict which implementation of the function actually gets exported by the second DLL. The use of PRIVATE guarantees that you'll get the right one. (DllRegisterServer(), DllUnregisterServer(), and DllCanUnloadNow() are all functions commonly exported by ActiveX controls, which we examine in Chapter 15.)

The linker was modified in Visual C++ 5.0 to warn about the public export of those reserved symbols. This modification has been passed onto Visual C++ 6.0, so you'll want to make sure you retrofit any code that you have to avoid the warning messages so your friends don't mock you. Oh, and, of course, you'll want to avoid the problem that the warning is designed to help you notice!

DJ VC's .def Jam

You can avoid using a .def file by using __declspec(dllexport) in your function definitions. This technique isn't commonly used because you have no control over the export ordinals used for the functions. However, it is a much easier way to export functions from your code.

Control over exactly what function is associated with which export is important when lots of people are dependent on your DLL; if the exports shift every time you rebuild, you'll always have to relink any dependent programs. If you only add new exports, with ever increasing numbers, leaving the lower numbers assigned to same functions, then you'll reduce the need to relink all the time. It's a trade-off between how hard it would be to maintain the .def file yourself with your own explicit exports against how easy it is to add your own __declspec(dllexport) keywords and force everyone who uses your library to relink all of the time. Of course, this is only an issue for applications that *implicitly* link to the DLL.

Once you're done working with the library, you should call ::FreeLibrary() to let Windows know when to discard it. ::FreeLibrary() will decrement the library's reference count, since LoadLibrary() has incremented it. If this means that the library isn't in use, the library's reference count will go to zero and it will be discarded from memory. After you do a ::FreeLibrary() call, you should assume that any pointer that you've obtained from ::GetProcAddress() and still have lying about is invalid and shouldn't be used.

Implicit Linking

Implicit linking involves what's called an **import library**. An import library is a small static library that helps Windows resolve references to functions which appear in a DLL. The static library contains code to load the library and implements the call to the dynamic-link library for you.

When you use an import library, you call the functions in the DLL as if they were just there. You don't need to use ::LoadLibrary() or ::GetProcAddress() like we did in the code fragment above. But you do need to have the linker use the static .lib file which contains the import library. If you only have the DLL file, you're in trouble. If you're really determined to call the library by implicitly linking to it, you should have the header file available.

As we mentioned earlier, the Windows routines that you know and love are all implemented in DLLs. You implicitly link to these routines whenever you build a program for Windows. The various stub libraries can be found in the Microsoft Visual Studio\Vc98\Lib directory; they have names like Kernel32.lib and Gdi32.lib. We have quickly described all of the Windows libraries, as well as the other libraries shipped with VC++, in Appendix D.

> Note that implicitly linking to a given library means that your program will cause Windows to load that DLL immediately, right as your program loads. If you're using lots of DLLs, your application will delay its loading while Windows runs about initializing all of the required DLLs. If any of those DLLs fail to load, Windows will display an appropriate error message and your application will never begin executing.

By the way, if an implicit link fails, you'll get an error message like the one shown here. If your users report seeing such a message, it probably means that the wrong version of a DLL was loaded in place of the one you really wanted:

Implicitly linking your application to a dynamic-link library is clearly the way to go. It's also the way things work ninety-nine times out of a hundred. You can explicitly link to a library when you don't know which library you'll need until you load it, or when you don't know what function name you'll need until run time. Usually, these situations arise in the development of utility programs, macro languages or programming systems; in other words, don't expect to worry about explicit linking too often.

Therefore, a static load takes place when a dynamic-link library is loaded in response to an implicit link, while a dynamic load is the initialization of a dynamic-link library image in response to an explicit link.

> *Remember that you don't have to fool around with* `::LoadLibrary()` *or* `::FreeLibrary()` *or* `::GetProcAddress()` *when you are using implicit linking.*

Notes on Exports

You must remember to export some functions from your library; if you don't, the linker won't generate an import library to go along with your DLL. You can supply a `.def` file to export names from your library, or you can use the `__declspec(dllexport)` keyword in your function's definition. Such a declaration might look like this:

```
__declspec(dllexport)
long CountLines(LPCTSTR pFileName)
{
    // write some code here
}
```

> *In the* `DLLApp` *sample application, we didn't use this method for* `DynLib`*, the non-MFC DLL; we explicitly placed the name of the exported function in the* `DynLib.def` *file, so that you can see both approaches.*

MFC provides some convenient macros that you can use for a shortcut to this approach. You can use `AFX_CLASS_EXPORT` in your class declaration when you want to export your own class. This makes sure every function in your class, including functions hidden from your view, such as implicit constructors and destructors, are exported properly.

Many programmers declare functions without ever seeing their declaration line; when you use MFC's `DECLARE_DYNAMIC()` macro, you're declaring a function and some static data which MFC will need. `AFX_CLASS_EXPORT` ensures such functions are exported correctly.

Your DLLs can use other macros to export other things. AFX_DATA_EXPORT, for example, can indicate your DLL's desire to export data, while AFX_API_EXPORT will let you export a single function. In the DllApp sample, the BCDLib project implements a class that we'd like to export from the resulting Bcdlib.dll. To realize this, we used AFX_CLASS_EXPORT on the CBCDNumber class declaration in the Bcd.h header file, like this:

```
class AFX_CLASS_EXPORT CBCDNumber : public CObject
{
    // declaration here
};
```

The implementation of the CBCDNumber class will export all of its members. Any other application that includes the Bcd.h will see the class as importable. Similarly, I used the AFX_API_EXPORT() macro on the DDX_BCD() function, since it's just a function and not a class.

I've said in this chapter that you can use these macros if you want – but let me be a little stronger – you probably *should*. These macros all end up expanding to the same __declspec() modifiers, but for other platforms where MFC supports dynamic-link library-like constructs in the future, the macros might take on a new meaning.

DLL Coding Artifacts

Back in the days of Win16, coding with dynamic-link libraries was considerably more difficult than it is now with Win32. The most notable difference is that Win16 dynamic-link libraries don't run in the data space of the calling application. The most direct ramification of this architecture is that the Win16 DLL uses the stack space of the caller but has its own data space. It's important that the programmer understands this distinction, otherwise there will be no end of problems.

To circumvent any problems, most developers with Win16 experience carefully write their DLLs to make sure that they don't take the address of any data on the stack. Since any function's local data sits on the stack, you'll frequently see it declared as static to force it to reside in the DLL's data segment. This trick makes code that would normally be fine in an application have mysterious statics lying all over the place. Code written for a normal application like this,

```
void HoHoHo()
{
    char sz[50]; // no need to be static
    strcpy(sz, "Happy Holidays!");
}
```

suddenly looks like this when it's moved to a dynamic-link library:

```
void HoHoHo()
{
    static char sz[50]; // static just to be in DS
    strcpy(sz, "Happy Holidays!");
}
```

If you're porting code for DLLs from Win16 to Win32, you might be interested in getting rid of such declarations. Removing unnecessary junk from your data area will reduce your working set and improve the application's performance.

> *You'll note that, in the code fragments here, that I didn't stick with my convention of using the Unicode-friendly _T() macro. That's because your old Win16 code certainly wasn't Unicode compatible; after you've gotten rid of unneeded* static *declarations, you might wish to start making sure your code works okay for Unicode too.*

Win16 dynamic-link libraries are also significantly different from their Win32 cousins, because the Win32 DLLs are mapped into each process that uses them. This means that a Win32 DLL will get its own global data areas for every process that attaches to it. This certainly isn't true for Win16 DLLs. Once it is loaded, a Win16 DLL only gets one copy of its data segment. Some applications use this as a cheap interprocess communications mechanism – no such architecture will work in Win32. Normal global data for the 32-bit DLL is reinitialized for each process, but not for each thread.

We used the adjective *normal* in that sentence because you *can* get data from a DLL to be shared for all processes using the DLL by using some language extensions implemented by the Microsoft compilers. Executable files in Win32 are divided into **sections**. A section is a partition within an executable image that has its own set of attributes. For example, string constants in your program can be placed into a read-only section. Any code that tries to write to a protected, read-only section will generate an access violation exception and halt the program. A section is like a segment back in Win16 in that it logically and physically separates some code or data from other code or data. However, a section certainly isn't limited to 64 kilobytes in size!

Using the compiler's data_seg() pragma, you can force some of your data declarations to be emitted in a particular, named section. If you wanted to make a global variable called dwGlobal, and have it available to all instances of the same DLL, you could write code like this:

```
#pragma data_seg(".shared")
DWORD dwGlobal = 0;
// you may declare additional variables here...
#pragma data_seg()
```

The data_seg command in the pragma tells the linker to put subsequent data declarations in a segment of the executable named .shared. You can then make any data declarations you wish – as long as they're given initializers and you must close them up with pragmas that tell the linker to go back to the normal data segment.

Once that's done, compiling that module will result in an .obj file that puts all of its normal, private data in a normal, private section – and the extra data that you provided between the data_seg() pragmas in a section with the name you've provided. Above, I picked .shared, but you can use any old name you'd like – as long as it doesn't collide with one of the compiler's default names (.bss, .data, .idata, .rdata, .reloc, .rsrc, and .text). You can put these sections in many different source files if you like. If they each have the same name, the linker will coalesce them. If they have different names, the linker will keep them physically separate in the executable image.

There's one more step, though. Your library's `.def` file needs to have a SECTIONS tag in it that tells the linker to mark the section you've created as shared:

```
SECTIONS
    .shared READ WRITE SHARED
```

You need the SHARED tag to make the section shared. You need to have the READ and WRITE tags so the memory is marked readable and writeable. You can add more section names in this block of your `.def` file, if you choose.

With these tips in hand, your Win32 DLL should be a good deal cleaner than your 16-bit implementation. You need to pay a great deal of attention to the way you port old Win16 dynamic-link library code to Win32 – things are semantically different!

Building A DLL

You can build a dynamic-link library by selecting one of the DLL project types (Win32 Dynamic-Link Library or MFC AppWizard (dll)) from the new project list:

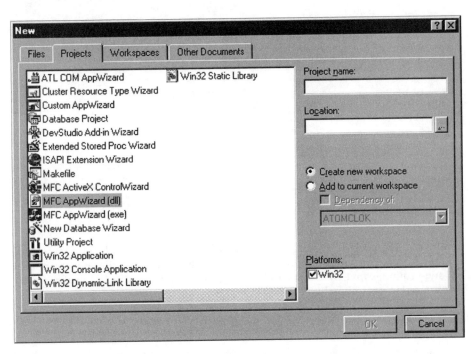

When you choose one of these project types, the resulting project will build using the appropriate `.def` file, as well as the correct compiler options, to produce a DLL executable image and an import library. Of course, you'll need to manage the `.def` file when you add or remove functions as you develop your application.

If you choose the Dynamic-Link Library project type, you'll be responsible for adding all of your own files to the project. If you use the MFC AppWizard (dll) project type, the wizard will create for you a project that builds to a DLL but includes references to the MFC libraries and source code files that declare and implement an application object. Such a project is extremely useful for getting advanced, application-level functionality into your DLL, such as document/view architecture support, or automation capabilities.

In the DLLApp sample, the BCDLib subproject is a normal AppWizard-generated MFC project. However, I used a subproject based on the Dynamic-Link Library project (rather than the MFC AppWizard(dll) project type) to build DynLib.dll. The code simply implements a single function called CountLines(); this function accepts the name of a text file and returns the number of lines in that file as an integer.

The CountLines() function looks like this:

```
long CountLines(LPCTSTR pFileName)
{
    int nFile;

    long lLines = 0L;
    int nRead;
    register int nIndex;
    const int nBufferSize = 4096;
    static szBuffer[nBufferSize];

    nFile = _topen(pFileName, _O_BINARY | _O_RDONLY);
    if (nFile == -1)
        return -1L;

    while ((nRead = _read(nFile, szBuffer, sizeof(_TCHAR)*BUFFER_SIZE)) > 0)
    {
        for (nIndex = 0; nIndex < nRead; nIndex++)
            if (szBuffer[nIndex] == '\n')
                lLines++;
    }

    _close(nFile);
    return lLines;
}
```

There's really nothing very interesting in the function – it just uses low-level disk I/O functions from the C run-time library to count the number of newline characters in a file. But the point is that you *can* call C-style routines in a DLL from a C++ program. The only trick lies in the header file, which declares the function prototype like this:

```
extern "C" long CountLines(LPCTSTR pFileName);
```

We use extern "C" to make sure the .cpp file, which pulls in this declaration, knows that the function uses the C (and not C++) calling convention, and accounts for name mangling – see later for an explanation of this. By the way, if you need to use extern "C" and __declspec() on the same function, extern "C" must appear first.

Easing the Build Process

If you're building a DLL, you're probably also building an application that uses it. Even if you're not interested in writing an application, you undoubtedly have an application that you'll use to test your DLL. Since your application will need to stay in lock-step with your DLL, you'll want to find a convenient way to build both simultaneously. In older versions of Visual C++, building a DLL at the same time as an application was quite a chore. However, nowadays, Visual C++ allows you to add your DLL project (or projects, if you have more than one DLL) to your application's project as a subproject. You'll probably want to maintain a project file for Visual C++ that builds your DLL by itself, so that you can redistribute that file with your source while keeping your test application to yourself.

Using Dynamic-link Libraries with C++

The linker's biggest responsibility is to match names and memory addresses. When the compiler sees that you want to call a given function, it sets up the parameters to that call, and makes a note in the object file that the linker should resolve the address of the target function in the assembly-code `call` instruction to point to the correct routine. This address isn't resolved until the linker gets its hands on all of the object files and libraries involved in your application, piles them up and decides where to place everything that is needed.

The compiler is what dictates the **calling convention** used to get from one routine to another. There are three primary aspects to any calling convention: the order in which parameters are passed to the function, the ownership of the cleanup tasks and the naming convention used for the functions declared and referenced.

In applications written with Microsoft Visual C++, the C++ calling conventions are used by default. C++ conventions dictate that the parameters will be placed on the stack from the right to the left. That is, the parameters closest to the right parenthesis in the function call are pushed first. The C++ calling convention also dictates that the caller will clean the parameters off the stack, and dictates that function names are decorated or mangled. **Decorated names** or **mangled names** provide each and every C++ function a completely unique name.

Name Mangling

The compiler generates the decorated name for a given function by taking into account the data types the function accepts, as well as the actual name of the function. Sometimes, the compiler steps in to provide its own name, since some functions, such as operator overloads and table initialization routines, have names that aren't easy to describe. The C++ language doesn't dictate a standard for name mangling, but all C++ compilers need to mangle names in order to implement overloaded functions. If the compiler simply took the name of the function without decoration, it would be impossible to have two functions with the same name and different parameter lists.

The C++ compiler generates the names based on a rather complicated set of rules. But, just as an example, you might find these translations if the relevant functions show up in an error message or in a dump of an object file:

Decorated Name	Function Declaration
?foo@@YAXH@Z	void __cdecl foo(int)
?foo@@YAXHM@Z	void __cdecl foo(int,float)
??0CBar@@QAE@XZ	public: __thiscall CBar::CBar(void)
??1CBar@@QAE@XZ	public: __thiscall CBar::~CBar(void)
?Fooey@Cbar@@QAEXH@Z	public: void __thiscall CBar::Fooey(int)

As you can see, not only does the mangled name help by providing a unique name for overridden functions, it provides an implicit resolution of name scopes, too. If you're interested in finding out the real declaration given a decorated name, you can use the undname utility. Use the -f option with the command, as it causes a full undecoration. You might enter this command:

    undname –f ??1CBar@@QAE@XZ

and you'll be rewarded with output like this:

    Microsoft® Windows NT(R) Operating System
    UNDNAME Version 5.00.1768.1Copyright © Microsoft Corp. 1981-1998

    >> ?? 1CBAR@@QAE@XZ == public: __thiscall CBar::~CBar(void)

while, without the -f option, you'd only get the function name and none of the parameters or return value.

Name mangling will affect you as you write a DLL because the client of that DLL will need to reference your functions by name in their code, but their linker run will need to see the decorated name produced by the compiler for them. You need to make these names line up – so you'll need to place them in your .def file. It will also be helpful to understand what's going on with the compiler and the way it calls other functions, just so you know what to do when you get a particular error message.

The C calling convention is exactly the same as its C++ counterpart, except that the function's name is not mangled. For this reason, C functions are slightly easier to put into a dynamic-link library, but you'll need to manage the names of your functions in the module definition file for the DLL. Since a C function's name is always just the name of the C function after an initial underline character, this matter is trivial.

For a C++ module, you'll have lots of hidden functions (like special names for constructors, destructors and overloaded operators), as well as names mangled with different decoration characters to describe the parameters and return value of the function.

Any old Win16 code that you might have lying about usually makes use of a PASCAL calling convention. This convention passes arguments left-to-right and forces the called function to clean up the stack frame. Further, the PASCAL calling convention maps all function names to upper case and doesn't prefix an underscore character to the function name. As it turns out, PASCAL was just a synonym for the __pascal keyword, which is now obsolete. Today, you should use the WINAPI macro instead. WINAPI maps to the __stdcall keyword to request the calling convention used by the Windows API functions.

Alternative Calling Conventions

What alternatives do you have to this name mangling business? Well, there are a few different ways to overcome this problem.

The C Calling Convention

The first is to simply use the C calling convention. You can only do this if your code can be used without any C++ constructs; that is, you're just exporting functions and not classes. To make sure your code uses the C calling convention, use the `extern "C"` modifier for your function prototype, like this:

```
extern "C" int Fooey(int nParameter);
```

You may then define your function with the same decoration:

```
extern "C" int Fooey (int nParameter)
{
    return nParameter * 2 + 3;
}
```

In either case, the function would be identified in the `.def` file by the name `_Fooey`. Of course, it's a little limiting to be restricted to C language functions – after all, we're interested in using C++ because we want to do object-oriented programming!

Exporting C++ Functions

It turns out that you can export your C++ functions and classes without much trouble (neglecting, of course, the pains caused by name mangling). As I suggested before, you have two approaches to exporting your functions – using export keywords on your functions, classes and data, or creating a `.def` file of your very own.

When you use a `.def` file for a C++-capable DLL, the biggest problem that you'll be facing is how to discover the decorated name that the compiler has produced for you. Perhaps the easiest way to get to this is to use the linker to generate a `.map` file. The `.map` file is a text file created by the linker as it builds your executable image. The `.map` file names each function in your image and identifies where the linker has placed it in the file. The linker identifies both the decorated and undecorated name in this file. A map is normally generated by the linker only for debug builds – you can examine the Generate mapfile checkbox on the Link page of the Project Settings dialog when you have the General category selected. Or, just look for the `/MAP` option on the linker. You can search for the symbols pertaining to the class you're trying to export in these listings. All of these symbols will contain the name of the class among some other characters. You'll need to find all of these and paste them into your `.def` file.

Of course, only C++ functions are ever subject to the C++ naming convention. Any function compiled in a file with the `.c` extension will result in a function that uses the C language convention. On the other hand, any file appearing in a `.cpp` or `.cxx` file will be treated with the C++ naming conventions. Header files follow the same rules as the source file that included them.

These rules aren't set in stone. On the `CL` command line, you can use the `/TC` option to compile a file as a C module, no matter what its extension is – or use the `/TP` option to compile a file as a C++ module, no matter what it is. Unfortunately, there's a bug in the IDE build system that prevents you from using these options in the IDE projects. Worse yet, there's no workaround besides building your program from `Nmake` at the command line. Maybe this will be fixed in a future version of Visual C++.

Testing Your Module Definition File

It's very good practice to find some way to test your module definition file, or even the dynamic-link library itself, to make sure that it has exported all of the functions you really meant to export. You can do this by simply creating a test application and linking it with your DLL. In any case, it's a good idea to have a test application. It's important to make sure that you test the integrity of your definition file by making sure everything you expect to be available in the DLL really is exported. The best way to do this is to pick through your `.def` file and make sure you touch all of those functions from your test application.

The MFC DLL Build

As we've mentioned before, MFC is built and distributed as a dynamic-link library. The library provides a shared implementation of MFC that multiple, concurrently running executables can share.

> If you dynamically link to MFC — either from a DLL or from an application — you should define the **_AFXDLL** preprocessor symbol. This will cause MFC's **Afx.h** header to automatically select the proper import library to snag the dynamically-linked MFC build.

You might be wondering why the DLL version of MFC is built the way it is; you certainly don't see MFC itself use the AFX_EXT_CLASS macro, or any of the __declspec() modifiers we've been talking about. The reason is that MFC is coded to be easily built into both static and dynamic libraries, without any modifications to the source code. MFC does need to sometimes do different housekeeping in its DLL version, and that code is encapsulated in #ifdef _AFXDLL preprocessor directives.

MFC exports all of its functions explicitly by using a .def file. Since we can't conveniently put modifiers in the source code, this is really the easiest way to get the MFC build done; in fact, MFC exports well over six thousand symbols from its .def file!

As a matter of fact, the master build process of MFC involves a tedious script that builds the libraries and dumps the map file from the linker. A batch file script is run against the map file to reformat it before it is massaged by a simple program that adds export ordinals to each function listed in the file; the library is then relinked with that new definition file. The Makefile on your CD in the Microsoft Visual Studio\vc98\Mfc\Src directory doesn't recreate this process the because the properly generated .def files are already supplied on the CD.

While either route sounds like a tedious and painstaking procedure, it really is the easiest way to manage the creation of the .def file. Otherwise, whenever a function was added, changed or removed from the library, you would need to fix the module definition file by hand.

Using and Writing DLLs with MFC

Up to this point, we've looked at how to use DLLs in Windows. What we've covered so far in the chapter applies to using C or C++ alone to write applications that use DLLs or are DLLs – but, in all combinations, I've neglected to describe what happens when you add MFC to the equation. There are a couple of added twists that will affect your approach to writing a DLL if you're planning on using MFC within that module. We've got lots of different situations to consider. We need to see what happens if we use a DLL from an MFC program, and we need to see what happens if we want to write a DLL which, itself, uses MFC.

It's trivial to use a DLL written in C from an MFC application. The DLL will expose a 'flat' function-level interface. Since it is written in C, it isn't capable of exporting C++ interfaces. That gives us the knowledge that all the functions exported from the DLL follow the C calling rules we talked about earlier.

You can include the header files in your modules and call the functions as you see fit, or as the documentation for the DLL prescribes. If the DLL is very old or wasn't very carefully written, you might have to use an extern "C" around the #include directive. Since you're building a C++ program, the compiler will assume that all function and data declarations it sees are to follow the C++ name mangling rules – even if they're not class member functions or member variables. On the other hand, since the DLL was built using C naming rules, it will always export symbols that are named using those C rules.

Since the compiler decides what symbol to reference based on the function's declaration, you'll need to make sure the declaration matches the definition. If the header file that declares the functions in your DLL is well-written, it will include the necessary `extern "C"` references so that the functions in the DLL will be properly available from both C and C++ programs. Older header files (or those that are just plain poorly written) can benefit from a trick using the `extern "C"` syntax. For example, you might have to pull a stunt like this:

```
extern "C" {
#include "somefile.h"
}
```

You'll know that you need to use this trick if you get lots of link errors stating that functions from the DLL you're using weren't found. Before you try it, make sure that you have told the linker about the import library you need; another way to get lots of link errors stating that functions from the DLL weren't found is to forget to link to the import library!

It's easy to use MFC to link to a C language DLL, or even to expose C language interfaces from your MFC DLL. You can use any of the tricks we've talked about so far to call your DLL and build the correct `.def` file. However, if you're writing a DLL with MFC, you'll usually want to provide more than a C language interface.

MFC DLL Models

If you're writing a DLL with MFC, you might decide to write a **regular DLL** or an **extension DLL**. We'll examine the difference between those approaches in a moment.

Back in the earliest versions of MFC, you had to choose between DLL architectures named _AFXDLL and _USRDLL. The architectures were named to denote the preprocessor symbols you had to define when you were building each type of library. Concisely: _USRDLL was ideal for situations where you'd be calling the DLL from non-MFC applications (this is, essentially, a regular DLL that statically links to MFC); the _AFXDLL architecture, on the other hand, was designed for applications specifically written for MFC, using DLLs that were also written for MFC (this is like an extension DLL). Although the preprocessor symbols are still in use, the terms _AFXDLL and _USRDLL, when applied to DLL architectures, are no longer used.

Regular MFC DLLs

A **regular MFC DLL** is one that uses MFC internally and can export C language functions and standard C++ classes. A regular MFC DLL can implement its own classes, and APIs, and export them to the application. However, it can't exchange pointers or references to MFC-derived classes with the application.

Let me stress that the code in the DLL simply can't move pointers to MFC-based objects across the boundary between the DLL and the application. If you need to implement a DLL that can do this, you'll need to write an MFC extension DLL, which we'll describe in a moment. The reason for this is that MFC maintains a lot of state information about its objects, and this information needs special handling if pointers are to be passed across DLL boundaries.

However, it turns out that there are a *few* MFC classes that can be safely passed across the boundaries of even a regular MFC DLL. I've coined the term **transferable object** to describe such an object.

A transferable object is an object of any class in MFC that meets these criteria:

> Does not derive from `CObject`

> Does not use static data within the MFC library

> Does not use state information within the MFC library

> Has no member functions which require the use of state information or static data from within MFC

> Has no members that are non-transferable MFC objects

I guess the term 'transferable' is a bit awkward, but it doesn't collide with other definitions and it does make some sort of sense. A transferable object is an object created from a class that you can throw over the border between one MFC DLL and another, or an MFC DLL and an MFC application, regardless of whether the DLL is an extension DLL or a regular DLL.

In MFC 6.0, the only classes that produce objects that meet the above criteria are the template-based collection classes and the MFC ISAPI classes (which we'll examine in Chapter 19). The collection classes only meet the criteria if they're containing objects that also meet those same criteria. By the way, my new term won't appear in the MFC documentation, I'm afraid, because the MFC documentation doesn't endeavor to describe what I'm trying to describe here!

When you build a regular MFC DLL, you can choose whether to statically or dynamically link it to MFC. The way your DLL uses MFC is independent of the way your application will use MFC, since the application and the library cannot exchange MFC objects. Of course, if you expect that applications that use your DLL will be likely to use MFC, you ought to link your DLL to MFC's DLL implementation, so that everyone can share the same MFC DLL instance and dilute its overhead.

Using MFC in your Regular DLL

MFC exists in your regular DLL independently of anything else. That's all there is to it. Your DLL needs to have a `CWinApp`-derived object in it so that MFC will properly initialize. Once loaded, your DLL can be called directly by any stock C or C++ program that doesn't use MFC. No extra initialization or protection is necessary.

Your regular DLL can also be called by any program that uses MFC. (Again, since you've written a regular DLL, you *can't* reliably pass non-transferable MFC objects across the boundary between the DLL and MFC.) It doesn't matter if your program is using MFC in a shared library or not.

However, if your DLL itself uses the DLL version of MFC, you'll need to protect any external entry point to your DLL by using the `AFX_MANAGE_STATE()` macro. MFC, as I've alluded to in various descriptions throughout the book, manages a tremendous amount of state information about your threads, processes, and executable modules. For MFC to properly keep that state information in the proper context, you'll need to invoke this macro as the very first line of your exported function. If you've written a function that pops up a dialog box, for example, you might code something like this:

```
extern "C" int ShowIt(HWND hwParent)
{
    AFX_MANAGE_STATE(AfxGetStaticModuleState());
    CWnd* pParent = CWnd::FromHandle(hwParent);

    CDialog dlg(IDD_DIALOG1, pParent);
    return dlg.DoModal();
}
```

The highlighted line invokes the `AFX_MANAGE_STATE()` macro to protect the rest of the function. In this situation where this macro is needed – that is, in implementing a dynamically linked regular MFC DLL, failing to provide this function will result in lots of failed assertions in debug builds at worst, and calls that just plain fail at best. Even the seemingly innocent function above absolutely requires the `AFX_MANAGE_STATE()` macro to work properly. If it's not there, the code won't find the `IDD_DIALOG1` resource when it needs to, and that means the dialog can't be displayed.

If you're building a DLL that doesn't use MFC in the DLL itself, you'll find that the `AFX_MANAGE_STATE()` macro resolves to nothing – the macro is declared to ignore its argument, and is not even seen by the compiler.

When you build your application to use a regular DLL, there's nothing special that you need to do to get it to work. Regular DLLs are very useful for situations in which you want to call your MFC-based routines from a C program, or even from a non-MFC C++ application. Regular DLLs are the architecture of choice when you want to write a DLL that is called from a different front-end development tool, such as Visual Basic or PowerBuilder. The other architecture, the MFC extension DLL, requires that both the calling program and the library be built to link dynamically to MFC.

MFC Extension DLLs

The MFC extension DLL architecture is the Cuban cigar of MFC dynamic-link libraries – it gives you a lot of things you really need, is somewhat expensive, and is illegal in some countries. It has one architectural disadvantage; a library built with the MFC extension DLL architecture must be called from MFC applications which were also built to link to the MFC libraries dynamically. It has one practical disadvantage; like anything else built against the DLL version of the MFC library, the `Mfc*.dll` files must be installed with your executables.

On the other hand, the advantages are clear – you can pass pointers and references to MFC objects happily between your DLL and applications that use it. This applies to non-transferable MFC classes too. Remember that the description of transferable versus non-transferable objects applied to regular DLLs only. With extension DLLs, all MFC objects can be passed across the DLL boundary.

If you'll recall from our discussions of `CWinApp`, MFC utilizes an incredible amount of information about the module in which it is running. Unlike the regular method of building DLLs, extension DLLs actually have code that manages the state information for each application that's running. This allows MFC to know which module is currently calling the library. Since the MFC library routines aren't statically linked, this method is necessary to allow MFC to reference the state information it needs for the application while running.

CDynLinkLibrary

The object that handles this is created from MFC's CDynLinkLibrary class. This object allows MFC to know that your DLL is a part of the application as a whole – the application can reference resources and classes in your DLL only if the CDynLinkLibrary class is present in your application. You'll create a CDynLinkLibrary object in your application, indirectly, by calling an MFC function named AfxInitExtensionModule().

You'll rarely need to play with a CDynLinkLibrary directly, so it isn't documented in the MFC manuals. The class is referenced, though, in a few of the tech notes. At any rate, the class has a constructor that takes two parameters; the first is a pointer to an AFX_EXTENSION_MODULE structure, and the second is a BOOL.

You'll need to make an AFX_EXTENSION_MODULE object in your application so that the CDynLinkLibrary object you have can initialize it. AFX_EXTENSION_MODULE holds that little chunk of internal information that MFC needs to know about your DLL. The CDynLinkLibrary initializes that information and adds it to a list of DLLs that MFC can handle. Your declaration of AFX_EXTENSION_MODULE is just as trivial as can be:

```
static AFX_EXTENSION_MODULE extMyExtension;
```

The second parameter to CDynLinkLibrary defaults to FALSE. MFC uses it to indicate that an extension module is a 'real' part of MFC. So, when your application loads Mfco42d.dll to gain OLE support, the CDynLinkLibrary in that module passes TRUE. You'll never have a good excuse to pass TRUE in your own DLLs, so don't.

If you're writing an extension DLL, you'll need to follow a few other rules. The DLL shouldn't have a CWinApp-derived class. This makes sense. As there's only one application in an application, so why would you want to have two applications in your application? Your DLL should also implement its own DllMain() function which calls the global MFC function AfxInitExtensionModule().

AfxInitExtensionModule() does exactly what the name says it does – it wakes up an instance of MFC's internal state information and lets the DLL work with MFC properly. If you call AfxInitExtensionModule() and the function returns FALSE, something is terribly wrong and you had better return zero from your DllMain() function. AfxInitExtensionModule() takes two parameters. The first is a reference to your AFX_EXTENSION_MODULE structure. The second is the handle to the instance of your DLL.

An acceptable DllMain() for an MFC extension might go something like this:

```
BOOL WINAPI DllMain(HMODULE hInst, ULONG uReason, LPVOID /* lpReserved */)
{
    if (uReason == DLL_PROCESS_ATTACH)
    {
        if (!AfxInitExtensionModule(extMyExtension, hInst))
            return 0; // big trouble — split!
    }

    return 1;    // oh happy day!
}
```

You'll note that I've commented-out the name of the unused `lpvReserved` parameter in this code fragment to avoid 'unused formal parameter' warnings.

Of course, you might have some other work to do in your `DllMain()` function. If so, you should do that work after your call to `AfxInitExtensionModule()`.

Dynamically Unlinking

Versions of MFC starting with 4.0 have the ability to dynamically load and discard extension DLLs. In the days prior to MFC 4.0, there was no way for MFC to correctly remove a DLL's information from the internal linked list of DLLs that it managed. As such, you just couldn't reliably load and unload extension DLLs – MFC would end up seeing the information for a DLL that was once loaded and then try to access it. Of course, accessing a DLL that isn't in memory is just not a good way to impress people!

Now you can do a tiny bit of extra legwork to let MFC know about the comings and goings of your DLL. First you'll need to add a call to a function named `AfxTermExtensionModule()` to your `DllMain()` function. Where you call `AfxInitExtensionModule()` in response to `DLL_PROCESS_ATTACH` in your `DllMain()`, you'll want to call `AfxTermExtensionModule()` in response to `DLL_PROCESS_DETACH` notifications in `DllMain()`. The whole thing comes out looking like this:

```
BOOL WINAPI DllMain(HMODULE hInst, ULONG uReason, LPVOID /* lpReserved */)
{
    if (uReason == DLL_PROCESS_ATTACH)
    {
        if (!AfxInitExtensionModule(extMyExtension, hInst))
            return 0; // big trouble — split!
    }
    else if (uReason == DLL_PROCESS_DETACH)
    {
        AfxTermExtensionModule(extMyExtension);
    }

    return 1;    // oh happy day!
}
```

Calling `AfxTermExtensionModule()` is optional, though I would strongly recommend it. If you don't call `AfxTermExtensionModule()`, information about your DLL will sit around in memory for the lifetime of your application. That's harmless, since most of the time your extension module's life span is exactly equal to the life span of the application using it. But you can bet a dollar that someday, someone, somewhere will try to dynamically discard your DLL when they call it from one of their applications. If they do this, they'll be in trouble if you didn't call `AfxTermExtensionModule()`.

With your `DllMain()` function suitably modified, you'll need to remember to use special MFC functions which load and discard MFC extension DLLs properly. In places where you'd normally call the `::LoadLibrary()` API, call `AfxLoadLibrary()` instead. In places where you'd normally call the `::FreeLibrary()` API, call the `AfxFreeLibrary()` function instead. MFC implementations of these functions work in the same way as the 'real' Win32 API implementations – internally, MFC is just doing a little extra work before and after the calls to the Windows APIs. `AfxLoadLibrary()` and `AfxFreeLibrary()` work just fine for DLLs that don't use MFC, so you might want to get into the habit of using them all of the time. They assure that MFC can properly manage the list of libraries, and the resource and class chains that are available in them. That is to say, if you don't carefully use these routines, you may find that operations such as loading resources or testing runtime type information in classes implemented by your subordinate DLLs don't quite work like they should.

Of course, you're allowed to use the `::LoadLibrary()` and `::FreeLibrary()` APIs to load and discard non-extension DLLs. The rules about MFC's special library management functions, and `AfxTermExtensionModule()` only apply to MFC extension DLLs.

Exporting Functions

Unfortunately, while MFC offers a couple of cool solutions to DLL developers, you'll still have to export the functions in your DLL yourself. Of course, the normal methods still apply; you can use the `__declspec(dllexport)` keyword to let the compiler do all of your work, or manually export what you want by writing your own `.def` file.

If you're writing an MFC extension, you can use the `AFX_EXT_CLASS` macro in your class definition to make sure everything is exported correctly. The `DllApp` sample application uses this declaration in its `Bcd.h` file – the code looks like this:

```
class AFX_EXT_CLASS CBCDNumber : public CObject
{
    DECLARE_DYNCREATE(CBCDNumber)
    // :
    // more stuff
```

When you're writing your own `.def` file, you should take great care to only export functions that you've defined yourself and that calling applications will need to use. Don't export any part of MFC, particularly if you've written a regular DLL. If you do so, the calling application might link with this version of MFC and get terribly, terribly sick as a result.

Loading Resources

I mentioned before that resources can be stored in DLLs. You can easily retrieve them providing you have the handle to the module that contains the resource. MFC makes things easier for you by providing the `AfxGetResourceHandle()` function, which is a function designed to return the handle your application should use to retrieve resources. If you're executing in the context of your DLL, MFC will return the handle of your DLL's module; otherwise, it will return the handle for the executing application.

If you need access to resources in your DLL or your executable, make sure that you use `AfxGetResourceHandle()` to get the module handle for the resource. This will ensure that you can use the appropriate `LoadResource()` call to retrieve the resource correctly.

Lots of Assertions?

Many developers who are taking their first shot at writing a DLL with MFC use the regular DLL model to build their project and then get lots of ASSERT messages from MFC when they try to run the code. In these cases, the ASSERTs are almost always at the beginning of some MFC function which is doing a check to see that a passed pointer is of the correct type. MFC defends itself from bad function calls by doing checks to make sure a pointer to an object is really an object of the type it should be; if not, then it throws out an ASSERT.

Because they were written before run-time type information was available in the Microsoft C++ compiler, the Microsoft Foundation Classes use a linked list of run-time type information structures to manage the relationship between inherited classes. This list is maintained separately for each executable module in normal builds of MFC applications and regular builds of dynamic-link libraries.

In extension builds, the information is a part of the data that MFC tracks for each module. On the other hand, if you use regular DLLs, each module maintains its own chunk of state information – including the lists of run-time type information for CObject-derived classes. That separation is what causes all the ASSERT messages, if you pass objects from one module to the other without using the right DLL architecture.

To illustrate, consider a regular DLL containing an implementation of the CDialog class. The DLL's CDialog run-time class information ends up having an entry in the linked list associated with the DLL, while the calling application has a semantically different CDialog run-time class tucked away in its own linked list. For this reason, the test on the run-time type of a pointer will fail when an attempt is made to pass it across the DLL/application boundary. Even though the object is really of the type that MFC is expecting, the test fails as MFC can't find the appropriate entry in the correct list. Of course, this isn't a problem if you're using the MFC extension architecture.

This is only one example of how the wrong set of application state information can cause trouble. The Microsoft Foundation Classes also maintains a great deal of information about the application's state. In particular, OLE support requires a vast amount of transient state information be kept up to date. If your application is asserting after crossing the line between the main line application code and any of its DLLs, it's very likely that the state information is not being properly communicated between these two halves of your code. Make sure that you have used the AFX_MANAGE_STATE() macro where necessary.

Summary of DLL Models

With the description of the two MFC DLL architectures out of the way, let's talk about how to build each one, and explain when you might want to use one or the other. Some of these paragraphs will concisely restate what has been discussed in the previous sections – I want to make sure you have a concise reference to use when you think you might have to write a DLL.

Let's start by looking at the preprocessor symbols involved. There are four that are related to the current discussion:

Symbol	Description
_AFXDLL	Define this symbol to dynamically link to MFC
_WINDLL	Define this symbol if you're building a Windows DLL
_USRDLL	Define this symbol to build a regular DLL
_AFXEXT	Define this symbol to build an extension DLL

Note that the _USRDLL and _AFXEXT symbols are mutually exclusive – if one is defined, the other should not be. These symbols are only relevant to DLLs and so should only be used when _WINDLL is defined. _AFXDLL can be used in both applications and dynamic-link libraries to tell the compiler to dynamically link to MFC. Of course, you will usually use Microsoft Visual Studio to set these symbols using the Project Settings dialog.

If you want to *statically* link MFC and write a DLL that uses MFC but doesn't expose MFC-derived classes to applications which use your DLL, you can do so by writing a regular DLL that statically links to MFC. To perform your build, you'll want to make sure the _USRDLL preprocessor symbol is defined when you include Afx.h, and you'll want to make sure that _AFXDLL is *not* defined.

If you want to *dynamically* link to MFC and write a DLL that uses MFC but doesn't expose MFC-derived classes to applications which use your DLL, you can do so by writing a regular DLL that dynamically links to MFC. You should make sure both the _USRDLL and _AFXDLL symbols are defined before you include Afx.h.

If you want to write a DLL which lets applications referencing the DLL use MFC-derived classes from the DLL, you can make an MFC extension DLL. You'll need to make sure that the _AFXDLL preprocessor symbol is defined, but the _USRDLL symbol is *not* defined. You'll also need to endow your application with a CDynLinkLibrary object as discussed previously.

Now that we have all of the different kinds of MFC projects out on the table, let's summarize which preprocessor symbols they use:

Project Type	_AFXDLL	_WINDLL	_USRDLL	_AFXEXT
Application without MFC				
Application using MFC static link				
Application using MFC dynamic link	✓			

Table Continued on Following Page

Project Type	_AFXDLL	_WINDLL	_USRDLL	_AFXEXT
Regular DLL using MFC static link		✓	✓	
Regular DLL using MFC dynamic link	✓	✓	✓	
Extension DLL	✓	✓		✓

Which Architecture Is Best?

I'm frequently asked: "Which DLL architecture is best?" It's a question I can't answer, simply because I'd need to be completely aware of the exact problems the questioner is trying to solve. You'll need to analyze what's happening in your system and decide for yourself what approach suits all of the needs you have and which approaches result in compromises that are acceptable.

If you're interested in writing a DLL and an application that exchange MFC-derived non-transferable objects, you will have to write an extension DLL. If you're writing an extension DLL, you'll need to write an application that's linked to the DLL version of MFC. This makes sense; if you can't change the application in question, you have no real reason to be passing MFC objects back to it.

When you need to reuse MFC code, the simplest approach is to write a regular DLL and wrap it with a C-style interface. This means that single functions will end up using real objects behind the scenes. You might have to design an API for your DLL that lets you return a context number or connection handle or something similar and then translate that identifier to the object for the particular context – using a CMap or CArray, for example.

The above table concisely spells out the differences among the different builds. The details of the differences between the builds have been explained throughout the chapter.

I must admit that, perhaps for only this subject within the book, I have not explained every possible workaround to the limitations that I've noted in MFC. I'm afraid that is entirely by choice. There are devious ways to get around the limitations that I've discussed in the various DLL models, but they're just too fragile (and too slimy) to write down on paper and tell people to use. Doing so would be irresponsible at best, since folks who followed that advice would probably end up with code that was broken by the next version of MFC.

About DLLApp

My DLLApp sample is dependent on the BCDLib dynamic-link library, which is an MFC extension DLL. The BCDLib.dll implements a CBCDNumber class which supports addition and subtraction on integers of unlimited size. The **Test BCD** command in the **View** menu brings up a dialog which has code that makes direct use of the CBCDNumber class. The code in this library just goes right ahead and uses the class; it doesn't need to perform any extra initialization or do any more work to make the DLL load or initialize as all of this is implicitly organized by MFC.

The BCDLib dynamic-link library makes use of lots of CString objects, but the library has no problem handing these objects back and forth across the boundary between the library and the application, because, as an MFC extension DLL, the application and the library are both aware of each other's classes. CBCDNumber is a derivative of CObject just because that's how we organized it; we could just as easily have made it into its own class. We wanted to have the debugging support provided by CObject, but more importantly, we wanted to make it easy to extend the CBCDNumber class by adding serialization later on. By basing the class on CObject, we have also made it relatively easy to put the class into MFC's non-typed collections, although it's just as easy to declare special template-based collections for the class.

You'll notice that there are lots of ASSERT_KINDOF() invocations in the DLLApp application. Almost all of these are unnecessary – they just let the sample show that the CBCDNumber class is a real class that MFC understands completely.

To get the DLLApp project running, you can just open the DLLApp.dsw project workspace file. Inside this workspace, you'll notice that there are actually three different projects – DLLApp itself, the BCDLib DLL and the DynLib DLL.

Troubleshooting DLL Projects

While DynLib and BCDLib in our example have no interdependencies, it's possible to create a DLL that makes use of another DLL. Of course, this happens behind the scenes for almost every DLL – when a DLL calls the Windows API, it is actually making a call into a DLL. There's nothing really wrong with having a DLL that uses another DLL. However, if your application uses two DLLs, with both drawing off a third, you may run into trouble as Windows tries to unload the DLLs as your application shuts down. Windows 95, in particular, doesn't robustly check for nearly-circular reference count situations and may unload one of the DLLs sooner than you'd expect, causing your application to fault when it tries to free a DLL that was prematurely discarded. This problem has been corrected in Windows 98.

This problem usually only occurs when your application does something as it's unloading – but that's very common for C++ applications, because they often make lots of calls while they are destroying static objects. If those calls are in one of the DLLs involved in your chain, it's very likely that Windows may have already removed the DLL and your call will fly into unused memory.

If you find problems related to the ordered unloading of DLLs plaguing your architecture, you can use ::LoadLibrary() and ::FreeLibrary() calls to explicitly force Windows to give the appropriate DLL the lifetime you require. Just falsely pin the DLL in question in memory using ::LoadLibrary(), and release it when you're perfectly sure you're ready by calling ::FreeLibrary().

Debugging DLL Projects

Since a dynamic-link library contains additional code, it will also contain additional debug information and routines. If you need to trace into this code, you'll need to tell Visual C++ where the code can be found. The executable file will contain information linking the code to the source, just like any other .exe file you debug has information connecting the object code to the source code. However, you'll still need to tell Visual C++ where the dynamic-link library resides before you begin your debugging session.

The libraries you want to debug should be named in the Additional DLLs box in the Debug tab of the Project Settings dialog, as shown below. If they are listed here, symbols from your DLL will be loaded by Visual C++ and you can reference them in the debugger. You can add a new row in the list for each DLL you'd like to debug, and note that you'll have to specify the absolute path and file name for each DLL unless it is on the path:

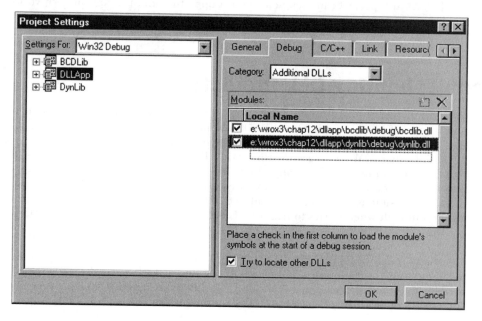

From the other side of the fence, you might have written a dynamic-link library and now need to debug it. If you don't have the source code for the calling application, or you're only interested in debugging the library and not the calling application, you may wish to open the dynamic-link library project and debug it directly. You'll need to specify the name of the calling program in the Executable for debug session in the Debug tab of the Project Settings dialog, shown for your reference here.

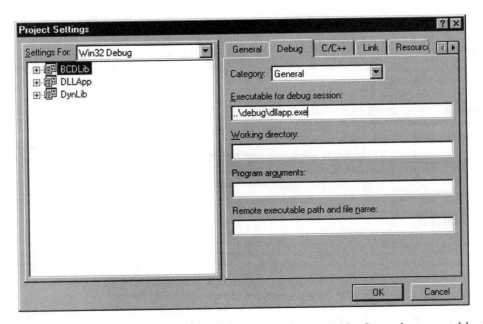

The debugger will begin by loading and running the named executable. Since the executable doesn't need to be associated with any source code, it's very likely that it will continue to run until it hits a breakpoint in your DLL. Of course, if you have the source for the calling application and it was built for debugging, you may place breakpoints in either the DLL or the calling application.

Debug Information

By the way, debugging information is huge. If the debug information is baked into the executable, Visual C++ must load all of the executable into memory when you're debugging it in order to gain access to all of the information. This means that an incredible amount of memory is devoted just to holding that data while your code is being debugged. If your application is complicated, you'll find that you might even begin to tax the memory management features of Windows NT or Windows 95/98. You may wish to consider building only certain modules with debug information to save space while they are working. Let's take a closer look at debugging information and learn when it resides safely on the hard drive and when it actually gets included in your real executable image.

Note that building a module with debug information is very different than making a debug build. You can arbitrarily turn debug information on and off for any module by modifying the setting in the Project Settings dialog. There's nothing wrong with building some modules with debugging information and other modules without it. On the other hand, you can't mix modules built with the _DEBUG symbol defined with others that do not have this symbol defined.

If you've built a default application, you've noticed that even a tiny SDI application with no OLE support takes up about 20K, while there's a file with the extension .pdb lurking around in your Debug directory. That file contains all of the debug information for any part of MFC which the application uses, as well as debug information for all of the Windows data structures MFC turns around and uses. That's a whole boatload of information – it's not unusual to see two or three-megabyte .pdb files.

In older versions of Visual C++, you could only place debug information within the executable file itself. Starting with Visual C++ 2.0, you could decide to put the debugging information in a separate file with the extension .pdb. The idea is just that it's more convenient for the debugger and, in particular, the operating system, to manage the debug information if it's in a separate file.

If, for example, you need to move a DLL to a different machine and you want to debug it, you need to make sure the .pdb file is available in the same directory where the DLL will be found by the applications that will use it. If you find this inconvenient, you can ask the compiler to use CodeView-style debugging information – that option will bake the debugging information into the executable image. You can expect the CodeView information option to bloat your executable size and slightly slow the response of the debugger and executable load time.

DLL Tools

Sometimes, you might be curious about the DLLs and imports a given DLL references. You can use the Dumpbin utility from the command line against any executable image you'd like. Dumpbin takes a variety of options and can even be used to look at the raw object code in your files.

You can find out which DLLs a program references by using the /IMPORTS option on Dumpbin. Dumpbin will display a list of the routines imported into a given module, showing in which executable image it expects to find those routines. Of course, most executables are dependent on more than one DLL. If you run Dumpbin on the DLLApp.exe, you'll see the routines it retrieves from BCDLib.dll and DynLib.dll, as well as the routines it needs from the Windows kernel, the C run-time library DLL implementation. This is an excerpt from Dumpbin /IMPORTS DLLApp.exe, showing the start and end of the output:

Microsoft (R) COFF Binary File Dumper Version 6.00.8133
Copyright (C) Microsoft Corp 1992-1998. All rights reserved.

Dump of file dllapp.exe

File Type: EXECUTABLE IMAGE

Section contains the following Imports

DYNLIB.dll
Ordinal   Name

bcdlib.dll
    4   ??0CBCDNumber@@QAE@XZ
    8   ??HCBCDNumber@@QAEAAV0@V0@@Z
    0   ??0CBCDNumber@@QAE@AAV0@@Z
    7   ??GCBCDNumber@@QAEAAV0@V0@@Z
    6   ??4CBCDNumber@@QAEAAV0@AAV0@@Z
   10   ?GetNumber@CBCDNumber@@QBE?AVCString@@XZ
    5   ??1CBCDNumber@@UAE@XZ
    3   ??0CBCDNumber@@QAE@PBD@Z

. (trimmed for space)
.
.

```
MSVCRT20.dll
    213  _controlfp
    3A6  exit
    1DE  __p__acmdln
    1C9  __CxxFrameHandler
    1CE  __dllonexit
    2D6  _onexit
    22E  _exit
    1C8  _XcptFilter
    225  _except_handler3
    262  _initterm
    1D1  __getmainargs
    1E0  __p__commode
    1E3  __p__fmode

KERNEL32.dll
    111  GetStartupInfoA
     ED  GetModuleHandleA
    132  GetVersion
    20B  Sleep

Summary

    1000 .bss
    1000 .data
    3000 .idata
    1000 .rdata
    1000 .reloc
    3000 .rsrc
    3000 .text
```

The output lists each DLL referenced, as well as the ordinal numbers (in hexadecimal) and names resolved by that DLL. The messy decorated (mangled) names that are retrieved from MFC are clearly visible, especially in comparison to the normal names that come from Kernel32.dll. (If your version of Dumpbin doesn't print the exact same version number, don't panic — you might not work at Microsoft and so would not have whatever random build of Dumpbin that I have lying around at the moment.)

The Summary section shows each of the sections in the executable format. The executable file format is well beyond the subject of this book, but these names represent the different blocks of code and data in the image; you'll remember my terse description of sections from my treatment of shared DLL data earlier in this chapter. Loosely, these translate to the segment groups you might remember from 16-bit programming days of old.

There are a couple of extra sections which really aren't executable or program data — .rsrc is the area in the executable which contains the resources in the executable image and the .reloc section is full of relocation information used by the loader. You can look up the Dumpbin program in the online help for more information, since it is capable of displaying many of these blocks in a readable format, or you can search Books Online for the names of specific sections of interest.

Dumpbin also has an /EXPORTS option, which, as you can guess, lists the functions and image exports. Each function shows its name and the export ordinal in the image. Dumpbin has a bunch of other options that you can read about in Books Online – I've described only the most salient here.

While it's always an educational exercise, you might find that running Dumpbin to find the imports required by an executable or a DLL is a valuable technique for diagnosing problems surrounding executables that refuse to load. You can use Dumpbin to make sure that you have all of the libraries and executables a program needs, or use it to investigate problems with routines being incorrectly exported. Since Dumpbin looks at the executable image directly, it reports the exact name of the function as it appears to the linker; this means that Dumpbin will provide decorated names to you when you dump a DLL or executable that contains C++ exports.

Visual C++ 6.0 still has Dumpbin, but now further includes the interactive Depends utility. Depends loads an executable image and recursively investigates which other files that executable needs. It checks each and every import as well, to see which have matches and which don't. So, you can quickly see which libraries are loaded and which functions are causing the dependencies. The tool also shows which DLLs are responsible for your application failing to load, if that is the case. Best of all, Dumpbin has no dependencies of its own so you can trivially move it to another system just by copying Dumpbin.exe over. Once copied, it's easy to find out why your program might work on your development machine but fail to load on another machine.

Getting Along with the Linker

This is as good a place as any, I suppose, to provide some extra information about the linker which ships with Visual C++. The points I'll make really are related to DLLs, but some of the information can be applied to anything that you'll ever link – which is, if you think about it, everything that you'll ever write.

The first point I need to make is that there are several different types of C run-time libraries, just as there are several different types of MFC libraries. You can statically link to the run-times, or you can choose the run-time libraries from one of several DLL implementations. The problem is that the type of C run-time library you use is very dependent on which version of MFC you choose to use.

Run-time Options

However, the exact version of the run-time libraries you get isn't specified by any option you give the linker – instead, it's actually set by an option that you give the *compiler*. In Microsoft Visual Studio, you can use the Use run-time library: drop-down list on the C/C++ tab when you have the Code Generation category selected in the Category: list box to select a particular run-time library. On the command line, the compiler accepts one of the options shown in this table:

Compiler Option	Description
/MD	Use a multithreaded, DLL version of the run-time libraries
/MDd	Use a debug, multithreaded, DLL version of the run-time libraries

Compiler Option	Description
/ML	Use static version of the run-time libraries
/MLd	Use a debug version of the static run-times
/MT	Use a static multithreaded version of the libraries
/MTd	Use a debug, static, multithreaded version of the libraries

As you can see, there's quite a myriad of options. Since your choices are really dictated by MFC, you're normally only interested in the 'multithreaded DLL' version, or the 'multithreaded DLL Debug' versions of the library when you're using MFC in a DLL. If you've statically linked to MFC, you may want to use the static version of the run-time libraries, but I would strongly recommend that you use the DLL implementation because it will very significantly reduce the load time of your application. Since the operating system itself uses the multithreaded DLL implementation of the run-time DLLs, you're guaranteed that Windows won't need to load the DLL. It will instead simply map a copy of it into the address space of your process.

In any case, you must *always* use a multithreaded version of the run-time libraries with your MFC applications. The multithreaded requirement is simply because MFC is multithread capable. Even if you end up writing a program that doesn't use threads, MFC needs to find certain thread management entry points in the run-time DLLs. If you don't use the right run-time library, the linker will present you with this message:

```
nafxcw.lib(thrdcore.obj) : error LNK2001: unresolved external symbol __endthreadex
nafxcw.lib(thrdcore.obj) : error LNK2001: unresolved external symbol __beginthreadex
```

You might find that the linker identifies a different library depending on how you've linked with MFC.

These error messages are very common for folks who have gone and created their own project or tried to compile an MFC program from the command line because the default run-time choice for the compiler *doesn't* select a multithreaded version of the library. If you do that, you'll find that the linker generates an error message because it can't find the entry points that MFC needed.

The /M-options accepted by the compiler are also the source of other embarrassing errors. If you specify one type of run-time library when you compile one module, then specify a different run-time library type when you link a second module, you'll find that the linker complains because it can't satisfy the request for the disparate library types. That error looks something like this:

```
LINK : warning LNK4098: defaultlib "LIBCMT" conflicts with use of other libs; use
/NODEFAULTLIB:library
```

One of the reasons I point out this specific error is that the advice built into the error message doesn't really fit the case when you're most likely to get it! If you follow the advice and specify /NODEFAULTLIB to the linker, the linker won't use any version of the C run-time libraries. Since no run-time libraries are available to your program, you'll end up drowning in a sea of unresolved external error messages – one for every single reference to *any* run-time library function! If you let the error slide, you'll soon find out that your executable image is badly flawed and quite unreliable.

To remedy this error, you'll need to find out what modules in your project were compiled with what run-time library options. Maybe the problem is as simple as a debug version of the libraries conflicting with a non-debug version. On the other hand, maybe you'll need to find out who built some other library you link to and ask them why they've given the library any particular preference for run-time library types.

If you yourself are building code which might be linked with debug or non-debug versions of the library, you'll want to investigate using the compiler's /Zl option which will ask the compiler not to specify any library preferences in the object files it produces. There's no way to set this option in the IDE other than to type it right into the compiler command-line edit control that's in the Project Settings dialog.

How the Linker Works

If you're building a library yourself, you'll also be interested to learn about the compiler's /Gy option. This option can be used to ensure that your linker will be able to process object files with as much granularity as possible. The /Gy option tells the compiler to put information about each function and data structure into a format the linker can use or discard as a unit. If the /Gy option is not present, the compiler will emit all functions in the object file so that the linker will be forced to take the entire contents of the object file, even if the executable image only needs one single function from the file. Obviously, this applies only to static linking situations – a DLL always loads everything into memory and dynamically resolves what it needs, even though everything still stays in memory. The /Gy option realizes the most potent gain for code that lands in a static library or code that is being built into an executable.

If, for example, I write a single module called MyFile.cpp and compile it into an object module named MyFile.obj without using the /Gy option, a high-level overview of the content of MyFile.obj would reveal a structure something like this:

```
BEGIN-CODE-BLOCK
    function1
    function2
    function3
END-CODE-BLOCK
```

If you wrote a program that needed only function2 and linked to MyFile.obj, you'd notice that the linker also brought in function1 and function3. It has to do this, since MyFile.obj only has a single code block. If, however, I recompiled MyFile.cpp with the /Gy option, the content of the object file would be something more like this:

```
BEGIN-CODE-BLOCK
    function1
END-CODE-BLOCK
BEGIN-CODE-BLOCK
    function2
END-CODE-BLOCK
BEGIN-CODE-BLOCK
    function3
END-CODE-BLOCK
```

The obvious difference is that each function is contained within its own code block, allowing the linker to perceive the module with much more granularity. As such, the linker knows that it can take each function from the object file separately. If you bake the object file into a static library or executable, the same rules apply — while it's linking an image, the linker can copy nothing smaller than an entire code block at a time. The linker, by the way, won't perform this aggressive analysis unless you give it the /OPT:NOREF option to remove unreferenced functions.

The use of /Gy can noticeably increase the size of your .obj files and static library files, and the /OPT:NOREF option (especially when used with /Gy) will slow down the linking process. As such, most people only build with /Gy and /OPT:NOREF when they're making their release builds, a practice which assures debug builds are still as fast as possible while release builds are as optimized as possible.

The benefit of using the /Gy option is that it will make your resulting executable images smaller. It's imperative that you use /Gy when you build static libraries, but its use is discretionary when you build applications or dynamic-link libraries. The option *can* make a small impact in the size of DLLs or applications and, as such, is the default for projects produced by the Visual C++ wizards. You'll note that wizard-produced projects use /Gy for release builds and don't use it for debug builds — for precisely the reasons outlined above.

By the way, the "BEGIN-CODE-BLOCK" notation I mentioned above is completely fictitious. .obj files are made of many different record types, and they're quite complicated. If you want to impress someone at a cocktail party, you can mention that these code blocks are actually called COMDAT records by folks who are *real* bit-heads, but you don't need to know much more than we've presented here to safely use the /Gy and /OPT:NOREF options.

You could, by the way, prove all of this to yourself by examining the .map file the linker optionally generates. Build a test case application using the /MAP option on the linker and not using the /Gy option on the compiler. Compare it to a .map file generated by the linker when you *do* build the source code with the /Gy option, and you'll notice that a lot less functions show up in the map.

Summary

This chapter has examined how MFC works with DLLs. When deciding whether to use a dynamic-link library in the design of your application, you'll first need to decide exactly why you want one. If your reasons are justified — you need to reuse code over different applications, or you want to provide code that other developers can use over and over again and is easily upgradeable — then you'll find that dynamic-link libraries are a wonderfully smooth path towards a rewarding implementation.

12

Writing Data Access Applications

Computers are great tools for storing and retrieving information. They're efficient at finding the facts that you're looking for, and make it convenient to cull summary information from that data. Most corporations use traditional database software (such as Microsoft Access, Microsoft SQL Server and Oracle) to keep track of their customers, their transactions and their assets. However data can be stored in a wide variety of other sources such as Excel spreadsheets, Web-based text files, ISAM (Indexed Sequential Access Method) data sources and emails. Many of the traditional data access technologies are highly suited to retrieving data from the type of source for which they were created, but are not suited to accessing data stored in other formats. With the problems of data being stored in such a variety of different ways, Microsoft developed the strategy of **Universal Data Access (UDA)**. This architecture has been designed from the onset to enable data, in whatever form it exists, to be available to any application that needs it.

Universal Data Access

UDA is a multi-layered architecture. Between the user application and the data source are up to three different layers of software that enable relatively easy access to data. These technologies interact together in such a way that the process of data retrieval is largely hidden from the user, saving him or her the time and trouble of physically having to sift through dozens of different sources to seek out that single piece of information they desperately need.

The main technologies that comprise UDA are listed below:

- ➤ **ODBC – Open Database Connectivity**
- ➤ **OLE DB**
- ➤ **ADO – ActiveX Data Objects**

This diagram illustrates how they interact:

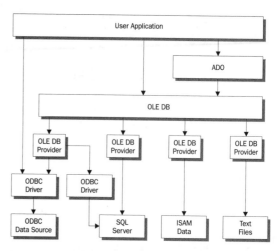

OLE DB forms the hub of UDA, and is based on Microsoft's COM (Component Object Model). It is the means by which selected records (or **recordsets**) are retrieved from the data source and passed back to the user. The task of getting the data is carried out by special software called **OLE DB providers**, which can specifically be written to access any data source. Many such providers are currently available, such as those for SQL Server 7.0 and Oracle 8. The list of providers is constantly growing as new ones are written to meet the data access needs of various developers. As well as retrieving data, OLE DB can be used to query a data source and process the recordsets so retrieved. The programs that achieve this are called **OLE DB consumers**. These applications enable standard database operations such as adding, deleting and sorting records.

Compared to ODBC and DAO, OLE DB is a relatively new technology. Also new is ADO, which is a set of COM objects that form a layer of abstraction between the data access application and OLE DB. The advantages of ADO lie in its ease of programming and the fact that it makes the power of OLE DB accessible to Visual Basic and scripting languages.

Finally I must introduce to you the most senior of these technologies, ODBC, which has for the best part of a decade been the means of accessing the vast majority of available data sources. It is still very popular, and as a result Microsoft have included it in their UDA strategy. For more details about UDA, look up www.microsoft.com/data/.

MFC Support for Universal Data Access

Because OLE DB is based on COM, the support for programming OLE DB data access applications from Visual C++ 6.0 is supplied by ATL – the Active Template Library – which was specifically developed for COM programming. Within Visual C++ 6.0 however, you can integrate ATL COM objects into MFC applications, allowing you to harness the power of both of these libraries. This is discussed further in Appendix F. Coverage of MFC's COM support starts in the next chapter.

> *ADO was developed primarily to allow Visual Basic and scripting programmers to access OLE DB, and is therefore harder to program from C++. Because of this, and the fact that there is no support for ADO in MFC, ADO will not be covered in this book. However, you can find an example of using ADO with Visual C++ 6 in Wendy Sarrett's* Visual C++ 6 Database Programming Tutorial *from Wrox Press (ISBN 1861002416).*

As this book is about MFC, there isn't the room to discuss ATL in any more detail, but you can find out more about it by looking up any of the following Wrox Press publications: *Professional ATL COM Programming* by Richard Grimes (ISBN 1861001401), *Professional COM Applications with ATL* by Sing Li and Panos Economopoulos (ISBN 1861001703), and *ATL COM Programmers Reference* also by Richard Grimes (ISBN 1861002491).

The `COleDBRecordView` class does bring a degree of native MFC support for OLE DB by wrapping both the OLE DB provider and consumer templates and presenting recordset data in a form view. An example using this class is presented towards the end of this chapter.

MFC and ODBC

MFC has full and comprehensive support for the most longstanding part of the UDA jigsaw – ODBC, and as you can see from the UDA diagram a few pages back, you can bypass OLE DB completely by using this technology. As I have said before, Microsoft have included ODBC in its data access strategy because its huge popularity and its widespread use. It is part and parcel of all the most up-to-date Windows operating systems. There is already an OLE DB provider for ODBC drivers which means that ODBC data sources can be accessed directly by ADO programmers; it is conceivable that one day OLE DB providers will be written that bypass ODBC altogether. However, for the foreseeable future, ODBC is alive and well, and for that reason, much of this chapter is devoted to explaining how to use MFC's ODBC classes.

In this chapter, I'll provide:

> An overview of ODBC

> A discussion of the ODBC API wrappers, `CDatabase` and `CRecordset`

> Notes on database development with MFC

> Some tricks and tips for designing client/server applications and database performance tuning

What about DAO?

Let me interject here, by mentioning another of Microsoft's data access technologies, **DAO**, that is **Data Access Objects**. These are a set of automation objects that allow communication with Microsoft's **Jet Database Engine**, which is the force behind Microsoft Access databases.

I bring DAO to your attention now, because as you can see from the chart on the previous page that DAO is *not* included as part of Universal Data Access, and consequently future support for the objects is not guaranteed. Indeed, OLE DB already bypasses DAO in that an OLE DB provider exists for data sources that are powered by the Jet Database Engine, thus enabling ADO programmers and the like, to get data held in Access databases.

Though DAO itself seems to be in decline, it is still fully supported by Visual C++ 6.0 and MFC 6.0, *and for that reason* it is discussed in this book. MFC wraps the DAO objects in three classes: `CDaoDatabase`, `CDaoRecordset` and `CDaoWorkspace`. The first two mirror the equivalent MFC ODBC wrapper classes.

Before we delve into the details about database programming using MFC, let me point out that ODBC and DAO, as you'll use them in MFC applications, share an incredible amount of common design. In fact, the similarities are so substantial, that I think it's appropriate to cover them both in one chapter. However, once you peel away the MFC skin around them, ODBC and DAO are very, very different. Taking this into account, I've included two almost completely separate overviews to cover each, as well as an additional section providing a comparison between them.

The rest of the chapter is written to allow you to understand how to write ODBC *or* DAO applications. In the few cases where an MFC user's perspective of one technology diverges from the other, I'll try to point that out as clearly as possible.

> **If you are uncertain which of these two technologies to employ for your data access applications, you should choose ODBC. As it is part of Universal Data Access, its future is pretty well assured. The same cannot be said for DAO.**

What is ODBC?

There are dozens of different vendors who offer relational database management software, each using a different library for accessing data in the database. Even when they do the same basic thing, various API functions exist for each platform, and sometimes even the vendor might not use the same file format over two of their own products!

Some applications may also have an interest in retrieving data from a format that isn't actually a relational database; they might want to read comma-delimited values from a text file, or need to get data from a portion of an Excel spreadsheet, for instance.

Learning each programming interface so that you can retrieve data from each of these platforms is tedious at best, and writing code for the other file formats is usually a complete project in itself. You'll soon be confused by the myriad of different nuances each vendor imposes on you, and your application will work only when one of your supported database systems is available. In the case of non-traditional database platforms, you'll have to write code from scratch to run off and read someone else's files.

Writing error-handling code is tiresome even when you're only considering text files; for complex file formats like those supported by Excel or dBase IV, you'll spend your afternoons wishing you had some other solution.

The ODBC Standard

ODBC is that solution. ODBC defines a standard set of functions for data access and carries a specification for which vendors can write drivers that grant your application access to almost any of the databases currently available. ODBC has a layered architecture. At the top, it starts with your application, which is written to call the ODBC APIs. Your application requests that a **data source** be opened by specifying a **data source name**, which identifies a particular data source configured by the user.

The data source name provides the next layer, the **driver manager**, with enough information to do its work. The manager loads the appropriate ODBC driver and initializes it for a connection to the data source you've named. The driver manager passes on any subsequent calls to the ODBC API, from your application to the driver. The driver actually implements the call, doing the work required to retrieve or accept data, or performing housekeeping chores.

The data source name represents a specific database or file that your ODBC application will access. The database may be comprised of many different tables, and once you're connected to the data source you can access any object within it.

A data source name really is just that – a name. When you ask the driver manager to connect you to a data source, it looks up the rest of the information it needs to get from your program on your machine to the data source. The driver manager finds the driver responsible for that data source, and the specific driver then opens the data source, wherever and on whatever machine the data it references actually lives.

Your applications can open a given data source more than once, and they can use more than one data source concurrently, even if they use different drivers to connect to different types of servers. You can implement your applications against the ODBC API directly, or you can use the interchangeable wrappers that the Microsoft Foundation Classes provide.

A Standard Set of Keywords

ODBC specifies that each driver must implement a standardized set of SQL keywords, settling on a very specific syntax for the SQL queries you'll send from your application to the database management system. By standardizing the syntax, ODBC allows you to learn one dialect of SQL. You can neglect the syntactic differences brought by vendors who have modified the standard SQL implementation with their own specific flavors.

> **SQL**, *which is usually pronounced 'sequel', stands for* **Structured Query Language** *and consists of a series of keywords that are used to carry out any operation involving data sources – creating and modifying databases; supplying queries; transaction management and manipulating data. Though SQL is covered by an ANSI standard, various 'dialects' of the language exist. Of course, since they're rooted in the standard, there is a subset of keywords common to all.*

Under the MFC covers, ODBC also standardizes the API used to access the database, which means that the driver interprets the SQL commands and the calls you use to express those commands in a common style. The whole puzzle, pieced together, looks something like this:

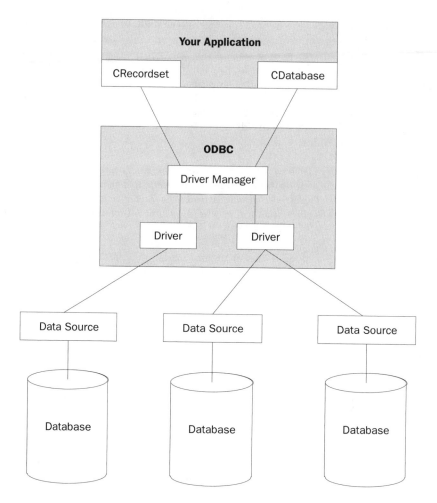

The driver manager, and any drivers it loads, will appear in the process that owns them. That's because the driver manager is implemented in a DLL which is mapped into the address space of each application that uses it. The actual database management engine might even be a DLL too. But it may also be an EXE that runs on the machine where your application lives, or it might be running on a completely different server machine. ODBC hides the implementation details of the back-end database management system for you. Once the data source is set up, you don't have to know where the database is stored or how it is configured.

What's ODBC For?

Having read this description of ODBC, you may be wondering why anyone would want to put this kind of insulation between their application and the source database. We alluded to some of the reasons at the very beginning of the chapter; the most compelling for you, as a software developer, is the notion that you'll only have to learn *one* dialect of SQL and *one* set of API functions to get at *any* kind of database for which you can find a driver.

However, there are several downsides. First, you probably will have restrict yourself to the standard dialect of SQL, i.e. that used by ODBC, which will preclude you from using some of the cool functionality that is implemented as a SQL extension in your database; very often, such extensions offer the only path to implementing a particular transaction efficiently.

ODBC doesn't actually prevent you from using any special extensions; it's quite easy to abort SQL commands which need vendor-specific extensions that ODBC doesn't understand. But, as soon as you do so, you lose the ability to move your application from one database back end to another.

You can ask ODBC to identify exactly what database is actually back there so that you can dynamically execute different SQL statements depending on the answer, but what fun is that? Even though it's a tedious job to examine the more aggressive queries in your application simply to make sure they work as quickly as possible against each database your application might use, you may find that this is the only way to guarantee your application provides the best possible performance against each of those back ends.

Let's tie this down with a more concrete example. Database developers are commonly troubled with the problem of a hierarchical parts list. The problem goes like this. A table in the database contains part numbers and descriptions. Each row in the table might be an individual part, like a nut, a bolt or a washer, but the row may also indicate that the item in question is really an element within a larger part.

For example, this table shows that we have three parts: a nut, a bolt and a washer. However, the IncludedPartNo column in each of those rows indicates that parts 1, 2 and 3 come together to make part 4, which turns out to be a fastener kit:

PartNo	IncludedPartNo	PartDesc
1	4	Nut
2	4	Bolt
3	4	Washer
4	9	Fastener Kit
5	9	Roller
6	9	Cable
7	9	Sensor
8	9	Plastic Case
9	*null*	Mouse Assembly

The problem can get even worse if one assembly of parts is, in turn, a subassembly of a greater part. Such **recursive relationships** are quite a tough nut for database programmers to crack. Efficiently getting any meaningful conclusions from this hierarchical information, like that in the parts table, can be problematic.

You may select some parts, and then construct a new SELECT statement for a further subquery, recursively exiting to the context of the previous statement after the inner statement has finished finding the parts required to build the greater part. (Phew!) This would work, but it would be terribly slow; you'd continually open new SELECT statements, reconnecting to the database for each deeper level.

You'll be limited by the number of open connections that your database and network will support, as well as by the amount of free memory on both your machine and the database server. Unfortunately, if you're sticking to the ODBC's SQL language dialect as strictly as you can, you have no other choice than to run against these limitations.

Oracle's CONNECT BY and SQL Server's Stored Procedures

It so happens that most Oracle implementations have an incredible feature; you can use CONNECT BY, a special clause in your SELECT statement, to have the database server perform the work of expanding the different levels of the hierarchy for you. Microsoft's SQL Server can achieve similar results if you use a stored procedure. Since these features are not implemented by every database server, and when they are implemented they can exist in radically different forms, you'll have to query ODBC to see which server is back there and find out what syntax it needs to achieve the result you want.

Beyond the restrictions for SQL syntax, ODBC injects some performance penalty. Since you're not calling the database API directly, but calling the driver manager and having it do the work, you're a couple of steps removed from the most efficient route to your data.

However, the performance penalty that is incurred by ODBC when compared to an application that is written directly against the API is rarely very significant. Unfortunately, while ODBC is quite mature, you might still encounter the occasional driver that has a dubious implementation. Hopefully, you can test with a different driver and see if the problem really involves the driver or not. And if it does, maybe it's appropriate to reevaluate your selection.

The single biggest benefit realized by ODBC's back-end independence applies to applications that are sold to a market which already has a database system. This fact almost always outweighs any slight performance issue. Most companies have already standardized all of their internal databases on some platform. They're probably not about to change it (and every application which depends on it!) to install your application. However, if you code your application to ODBC standards, you'll be able to pop in the correct driver and get moving straight away.

The single biggest benefit of ODBC comes to you as an MFC programmer; you can use MFC classes for database access to work with the back end. As usual, the Microsoft Foundation Classes are there to save time for you; you can use ClassWizard to hook up your different queries, allowing you to concentrate on the actual application rather than on the results you expect it to return.

Just Say DAO

DAO was first introduced in 1995 to provide an object-oriented means of accessing data sources, making use of the Jet Database Engine that had long been associated with Microsoft Access. This was meant to compete with the, even then, well-established ODBC protocol. The contrast between the two technologies could not have been more stark – DAO was a database programming model and ODBC, a system of low-level API calls. DAO gave a new lease of life to the Jet Engine (pardon the pun) by providing a programming interface which enabled more developers to get more work done with a platform that was easier to use. DAO was never intended to overtake ODBC as *the* means of programmatic access data, but to be a set of objects usable from a wide range of programming disciplines – a role that ADO has now inherited. DAO survives today as an efficient means of getting data from Access and other Jet-powered data sources. (You can, of course, do this using the ODBC driver for Access, but with reduced performance.) However, DAO's place in history is assured, as it can be seen as a forerunner to the ADO family of objects.

As far as MFC is concerned, the series of classes that wrap the DAO functionality were deliberately designed to mimic the corresponding ODBC wrapper classes as closely as possible and to hide the implementation of the DAO objects deep down inside MFC. The idea of writing the DAO classes to match closely classes which MFC developers already understand shouldn't be surprising to you – Microsoft is more interested in making progress than causing revolutions. The idea is that you can start writing with the DAO wrappers right now and not worry about anything complicated until you're ready to spend the time and effort to learn it – that motivation is usually caused by necessity more than any other external force. (When they finally figure out I don't do anything useful for a living, I'm not sure if they'll consider my termination as a cause for a revolution, or as a way to make progress, so maybe that outlook doesn't apply to everything...)

Jet Airliner, Don't Take Me Too Far Away

Even Steve Miller might realize that the Jet Engine provides an excellent way to access Jet's native database file format, the `.mdb` file, which you create whenever you create a Microsoft Access database. But since it's the Jet Engine we're working with, we can also access some additional databases that the Jet Engine can work with, given the proper drivers. (You could access any database in the world if you had a world-class driver, like Michael Schumacher.)

As it ships with Visual C++ 6.0, DAO grants you access to these database types:

- All version of Microsoft Access
- dBASE (Versions III, IV, and 5.0)
- Lotus Spreadsheets (files with `.wks`, `.wk1`, `.wk3`, and `.wk4` extensions)
- Excel Spreadsheets (Versions 3.0, 4.0, 5.0, and 7.0 (also known as Excel 95))
- FoxPro (Versions 2.0, 2.5, and 2.6)
- Paradox (Versions 3.0, 4.0, 5.0, and 7.0)
- Comma-separated text (`.csv` files)

You'll find that using DAO to work with native Microsoft Access databases provides the best performance, but you can use DAO to hit other database files if the need arises. You can use DAO to talk indirectly to a relational database, such as SQL Server, via the appropriate ODBC driver, but you will find that the performance in such an arrangement lacks luster.

You can, however, use DAO to **attach** to tables in another database. Attaching a table allows you to make a foreign table appear as if it was a real part of a database in Jet's native format. In this arrangement, you can use the table as if it were native. This is a terrible idea for just updating a record or two in a mammoth table, but it's a great way to perform updates to large subsets of your data if you're using DAO to access that data. The performance issues make table attachment a realistic option only if you're not working with data in one of the formats that DAO intrinsically supports.

Unfortunately, ODBC provides no similar attachment mechanism. ODBC connects you to a database, and that's that – you get the services of the database as-is.

Creating Data Sources

Now that we know what ODBC and DAO are really about, let's talk about data sources in a little more detail, so we can turn our attention to how ODBC works with MFC applications. I've saved the comparison between DAO and ODBC for the end of the chapter because it will reference lots of concepts that you'll read about before you get there. You could, I suppose, read the comparison without having made your way through the chapter, but you might find it a little confusing, since it will use lots of terms that you might not be particularly familiar with. On the other hand, reading the comparison both before *and* after you get through the technical details in this chapter might be a great way to completely cement your knowledge of DAO and ODBC.

When you start working with ODBC, you'll always get started by using a **data source**. You'll want to create a data source (or use an existing data source) any time you need your application to retrieve data through ODBC. If you don't have a data source that ODBC knows about, you can't ask ODBC to get any data for you because it doesn't know where your data is stored, or what driver to use to retrieve it.

When you create a data source in your application, you're really only creating a link between the actual data source and ODBC. (ODBC stores that link in the system registry – where angels fear to tread, where hackers are hackers and bugs are afraid.) ODBC will squirrel away some information so it knows how to find the data in question, but it doesn't actually create the data source for you. You'll have to use whatever mechanism you normally use in your database management software to initialize the data source. Some ODBC drivers do provide the ability to create a new data source through the driver, but, since there are some that don't, you shouldn't depend on this functionality.

DAO, on the other hand, doesn't care much about data sources. If you're planning on using DAO to get to an ODBC data source, you'll certainly be interested in learning how data sources are configured and what they're all about. However, as it turns out, DAO normally goes after database files by name. Since you're just using an MDB file, you just ask DAO to open the file and work with it. The file can be on a network server if you need to share the data (at the obvious expense of performance) or you can keep the file locally. DAO lets you do something that's not quite so easy to do with ODBC – you can use DAO to create new databases completely from scratch. If you don't have a file to open, you can ask DAO to create a database file for you, and you can begin adding tables and indexes to the blank file. We'll discuss exactly how this process works when we examine DAO's workspace object a little bit later in the chapter.

The first step in creating an ODBC data source, as viewed through the Control Panel, is to double-click on the ODBC icon. This will bring up the **ODBC Data Source Administrator** dialog box, as shown here:

To create a new data source, just click the **Add...** button. You'll be asked which driver you would like to use. You should select a driver appropriate for the database you're trying to access; if you're planning to create a data source for a FoxPro database, you'll need to use the FoxPro ODBC driver.

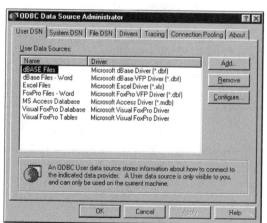

From this point onwards, the database driver will be loaded automatically when any program connects to this data source. This implies that the calling program doesn't need to know which driver to use when it opens the dialog. If you don't see a driver appropriate to the database system or format you wish to use, you'll need to install the driver itself.

System Data Sources

You might note that, as well as the plain ol' data sources we've discussed so far, ODBC also supports **system data sources**. The thing is, ODBC data sources are configured on a per-user basis, so if we were both at my house using my machine (and, I suppose, both drinking my beer), I might log in and see the data sources I've created, but if you logged in, you'd see only the data sources that you had created.

If we were interested in sharing a data source, we could both create the same data source under our user accounts and let it point at the same place. However, it's far more efficient to ask ODBC to create a system data source, i.e. a data source that's available to anyone using the system, rather than just to particular users.

You can see the available system data sources if you click on the System DSN tag on the ODBC control panel applet. You can then add, delete or set up existing data sources.

Locating and Installing ODBC Drivers

As a developer, you can install all the drivers you need by running the Visual C++ installation program; the distribution CD contains several drivers for different database platforms. If you don't see the driver listed in the Visual C++ setup, you'll need to contact third-party software vendors to find a suitable driver for their database.

If you are searching for a driver, a good place to start is the company whose database you're trying to access, as many database vendors provide ODBC drivers. Microsoft provides drivers for all of their database systems: SQL Server, Access and FoxPro, as well as some non-textual storage formats such as the one used by Excel databases. Microsoft also ships drivers for comma-delimited text files.

As a developer, you install the drivers and create a data source in a different way to your users; the ODBC setup will have to become a part of your installation process. We'll explain how this affects your setup code and how your user might perceive the setup process later in the chapter. Once you've chosen a driver, however, you'll be presented with the configuration dialog for that driver. An example of this configuration dialog, in this case for Microsoft's SQL Server driver, is shown here:

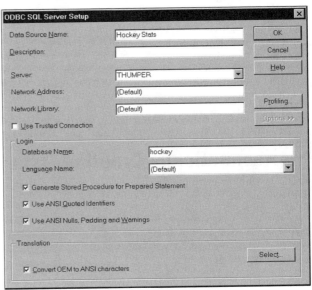

Almost all ODBC drivers will feature an Options>> button that expands the dialog to show additional options, but absolutely every driver must let you supply a data source name and a description. You can use any characters you'd like in your data source name or description – spaces are acceptable.

For the SQL Server driver, you can provide a server name and a database name to let the driver know where it should connect. The SQL Server driver also accepts the name of a network library, which allows you to specify that a particular transport layer should be employed when connecting to the server. You might need to fill in this option when you are connecting to a server over a special network bridge, or via a different transport protocol. Other controls in the dialog allow you to fine-tune the options used in your connection that are specific to SQL Server.

Some data sources have more options built into them. The figure shown here illustrates the options box for the Access driver:

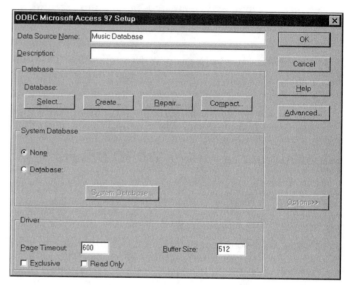

You can see that it has push buttons that allow you to repair damaged files, and to manipulate databases, create them from scratch and compact them to save disk space. You'll normally find that drivers which support database packages like Access or dBase have these extended features so that the user won't need to buy the full database package if something goes wrong.

Note that the data source name must be registered on your system if the database is to allow access from the applications running on your machine. Even if the database files physically reside on a different system, your machine must know how to access those files. ODBC doesn't provide a centralized naming service, so when you are installing the driver you must know exactly where the desired files are.

Programmatically Creating Data Sources

If you want to install your own data source programmatically, you'll have to call the ODBC API directly. The function that you need is called ::SQLConfigDataSource(), which takes four parameters; its prototype is shown here for your reference:

```
BOOL SQLConfigDataSource(HWND    hwndParent,
                         UINT    fRequest,
                         LPCSTR  lpszDriver,
                         LPCSTR  lpszAttributes);
```

The first parameter is a handle to a window that acts as the parent for any other windows that the installation requires. If you pass NULL for this parameter, ::SQLConfigDataSource() won't display any prompts as it adds the data source to your system. Like the other ODBC APIs, you'll probably want to pass NULL for this parameter and carefully check the value returned from the function to see whether the data source was correctly installed. As with the other dialogs that ODBC creates, you have little control over how it looks. Your users might not understand it, and it's difficult to hook appropriate help to it.

The fRequest parameter can be ODBC_ADD_DSN to add a new data source name, ODBC_CONFIG_DSN to change an existing data source, or ODBC_REMOVE_DSN to delete an existing one. Note that adding a data source which already exists won't cause the function to fail; you don't need to delete the configuration information before calling ::SQLConfigDataSource() with ODBC_ADD_DSN. The pre-existing data source will simply be replaced by the new data source. On the other hand, using ODBC_REMOVE_DSN against a data source that doesn't exist will cause an error to be returned from the function.

The final two parameters name the driver and the data source name setup string which you want for the data source. The lpszDriver string identifies the driver that the data source should use; this string should exactly match the text you normally see in the ODBC application. For example, you should use "Microsoft Access Driver (*.mdb)", if you're using Microsoft's Access driver – you should check your driver to find out exactly which string you need.

The configuration string describes the parameters that the data source name should have. Every data source needs a name, so this important parameter is usually specified first. Different drivers will require different parameters, so you'll need to check the documentation for your driver to see exactly what you'll need to supply in the configuration string. Each parameter is specified by its name and an equals sign. If there are more parameters in the list, you can specify a semicolon and immediately name the new parameter. You might create a new data source name for a CD collection with a call like this:

```
bRetCode = ::SQLConfigDataSource(NULL, ODBC_ADD_DSN,
    "SQL Server",
    "DSN=CD Collection;FastConnectOption=No\0"
    "UseProcForPrepare=Yes\0"
    "OEMTOANSI=NO;Server=(LOCAL)\0");
```

Note the lack of commas at the end of the middle two lines. We are using implicit string concatenation to join the three lines of options together to make things look neater.

The name for the new data source will be 'CD Collection', as specified by the DSN= key. The remaining options set the data source up in a way that we know will be compatible with the application. Again, you'll need to check your driver's documentation to make sure you specify all of the parameters you need with values that it will accept. If you omit a parameter which is crucial to the operation of the driver, the ::SQLConfigDataSource() function will fail.

Self-installing Applications

An application that uses ODBC correctly will always have some facility to install its data source. Letting the program install the data source gives you complete control over any configuration options which the data source provides, and lets you make absolutely sure things are ready to go when your program finally begins making ODBC calls. Getting to this state without user intervention increases your program's robustness and makes working with your application a lot more pleasant for your users.

A well-behaved DAO application will also try to get the database installed by itself, but faces much less of a challenge than would an ODBC application. DAO is easier for two reasons. First, installing a DAO database on a computer is simply a matter of copying your starter database file, in whichever format, to the location where you want it to live, or simply asking DAO to create the new blank file for you and writing code to create your database schema. Second, DAO allows you to work directly with the database to create and define database objects, i.e. DAO makes it easy to open a database and issue data definition language commands. I'll cover exactly how DAO does this in the section called 'Your Environment'.

Other Interesting Settings

One of the tabs you might have noticed on the ODBC Data Source Administrator dialog in the figure below is the one labeled Tracing. The tab reveals a property page that allows you to enable tracing for any ODBC transactions that occur. If you enable this option, a description of every ODBC call made by any application is sent to a file. You can select the name of the file with the Browse... button:

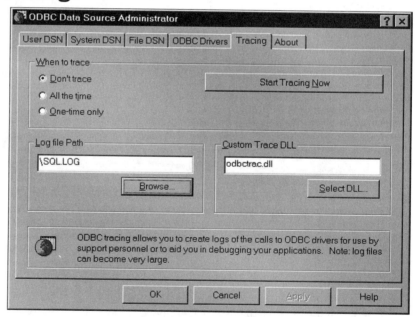

If you're suspicious your code isn't performing the calls you expect, or if you're curious about what SQL is being sent to the driver, you can turn on logging. By examining the log, you can see exactly what's happening and in what order. The disadvantage of this feature is that every application connected to every driver will write log records to the file. Even a single application can make tens of dozens of calls to its driver, and the log information for each of those calls quickly bloats the log file.

Your Environment

Now that we know about databases and data sources, we're ready to start learning about how to use them to get some work done. There's one more missing piece, though – understanding the environment where you'll get that work done.

In ODBC, there really is nothing to the environment. When you connect your application to a database, you're using that database and that's all there is to it. The rules surrounding that database are the rules that affect your connection. If you connect to a data source that's sponsored by Microsoft Access, for example, you'll connect directly to a database and won't have to worry that much about security. On the other hand, if you connect to SQL Server, you'll connect to the default database which the database administrator has set for your user account. You'll have to clear whatever security is set up for that server – depending on how the database server is configured, this security may be just a password the database knows goes along with your user name, or it might be a revalidation of your network account.

DAO enforces the notion of connecting to a database as an object. When you use DAO, you'll ask it to get connected to the database and use a **workspace** object to manipulate the database itself, i.e. the configuration of the database and its tables, indexes and other entities. If you want to, you can ask that database connection object to actually manipulate the data too. In contrast, when you use ODBC to connect to a database, you're connected direct to the database and you're ready to work with its data.

A workspace is DAO's notion of a connection between a user and a database. The workspace manages a list of databases that are active, and of individual users or groups of users who are known to use the workspace. DAO represents users, databases, and groups as objects within the database, and is capable of managing lots of interesting information on each of them. To do so, it uses a **system database**. The system database turns out to be a feature of Microsoft Access – it allows you to let your databases and users participate in a workgroup. You can read up on the system database and the security features it implements for you by checking in the Access documentation – all of the security features are in the Tools | Security menu of Microsoft Access. Wacky nuts, those Access folks.

The MFC `CDaoWorkspace` class wraps your access to DAO workspaces. You can create one using the default constructor – no parameters are necessary. Before you use the object, though, you'll need to call either its `Open()` method to get at an existing workspace, or its `Create()` method to work with a new workspace.

DAO supports the notion of a default workspace – an unnamed workspace where you log in as a guest. If the databases you want to access aren't protected by security that disallows guests, you can just work with the default workspace and not worry about anything else.

Beyond all this administrative mumbo-jumbo, a workspace allows you to manage transactions and handle databases. These are the neat features that distinguish DAO from ODBC. Since ODBC just runs off and connects to a database, DAO has quite an advantage when it comes to managing databases instead of just managing data. We'll see later that the ODBC classes perform transaction management and let you manage database parameters from the database connection object. DAO databases want you to perform this sort of work against the workspace object instead.

Data Definition Language Commands

Hardcore SQL users know that the SQL language is split into two functional groups: **data definition language** (or **DDL** for short) and **data manipulation language** (or **DML** for short). Just like water ballet means that you perform ballet in the water, data manipulation means that you manipulate data. DML includes all sorts of neat commands like SELECT, DELETE and UPDATE – commands that let you get, remove, or change data in your database.

Data definition language commands, however, are far more powerful. DDL commands allow you to add and remove tables, queries, indexes, users, views and other database-level objects. DAO lets you issue data definition language commands, while ODBC makes you send these commands directly to the database without becoming involved itself. Unfortunately, doing DDL against the database would mean that we'd have to play with some objects we haven't learned about yet – you can find some DDL sample code near the end of the chapter in the section called 'Other DAO Classes'.

CDatabase and CDaoDatabase

The first thing any database-oriented application does is connect to a database. For applications written for network servers, this really does mean connect; chat with the network card and get it to wake up the database server. For situations where the database is a just a file on your local machine, the process of connecting to the database simply means that you'll open the file and get ready to use it. In both cases, in the context of a database application that uses ODBC, you'll load the ODBC driver manager and begin a conversation through it to the ODBC driver you want to use.

When you program against a database management system's API, you'll usually open a connection to the database and receive a handle to the connection in return. Internally, this handle identifies the connection for the library; the library will manage all of the context information surrounding the connection for you. That contextual information might indicate whether or not a query is currently executing, whether your connection is using cursors, or if it's in a read-only mode.

The ODBC CDatabase object encapsulates the management of the connection and contexts. The CDatabase object represents your application's connection to the database, thus making everything that's in the context of that connection available through the CDatabase object. To initiate a connection, you can create a CDatabase object and then call its Open() function. CDatabase's default constructor does very little, so you'll need to create the object and then call Open() in two separate steps. The Open() function's parameter list looks like this:

```
virtual BOOL CDatabase::Open(LPCTSTR lpszDSN,
                        BOOL     bExclusive = FALSE,
                        BOOL     bReadOnly = FALSE,
                        LPCTSTR  lpszConnect = _T("ODBC;"),
                        BOOL     bUseCursorLib = TRUE);
```

The first parameter is the only one that's required; it's a pointer to the data source name you're opening. The data source name must have been previously installed and registered with ODBC. In development situations, you'll usually do this using the ODBC icon in the Control Panel or the ODBC Query application, installed with most Microsoft Office applications.

The Query application is a simple tool that allows you to test SELECT statements against an ODBC data source, but it can also be used to create a new data source.

So, you may open an ODBC database with some code like this:

```
CDatabase dbZIP;
dbZIP.Open("ZIP Codes");
```

Unfortunately, this only supplies ODBC with the name of the database you're opening. If the driver requires more information (such as a user name or password) in order to connect to the database, ODBC will prompt the user with a dialog box. Often, you'll want to have total control of your application and not wish any extra dialogs to be displayed. You can achieve this effect by supplying a **connection string** to the Open() call. The exact syntax of the connection string is dependent on your driver; the only standard contents for the string are DSN, PWD, UID and DRIVER. They have these meanings:

String Contents	Description
DSN	This names the data source. It can be used in place of the first parameter; if this parameter is specified, the first parameter is ignored and can be NULL
PWD	This provides the user's password. To specify an empty password, use PWD=;
UID	This supplies the user's login name for the database
DRIVER	This names the driver to be used for the connection

You can insert these into the connection string in any order. Each is followed by an equals sign, then the value you wish to set for the parameter, and the whole component finishes with a semicolon. To avoid the dialog when connecting to SQL Server, you can provide a connection string right in your data source name, like this:

```
CDatabase dbZIP;
dbZIP.Open(_T("ZIP Codes"), FALSE, FALSE, _T("ODBC;UID=MIKEBLAS;PWD=HOCKEY"));
```

You'll note that the connection string also includes the keyword ODBC (which was also the default value for this parameter). The keyword is actually meaningless, but you can't remove it – it must be supplied. Other connection modes may be available someday, and perhaps then the ODBC keyword will have real meaning. For now, you'll need to have ODBC; somewhere in your string.

> **CDatabase** doesn't try to open the data source and won't initialize the ODBC libraries until you actually call the **Open()** function. **Open()** is pretty expensive — prepare for a delay when you call it!

Opening DAO Databases

You should create a CDaoDatabase object and call Open() on it in two separate steps too. The Open() function for DAO databases is simple:

```
virtual void CDaoDatabase::Open(LPCTSTR lpszName,
                                BOOL    bExclusive = FALSE,
                                BOOL    bReadOnly = FALSE,
                                LPCTSTR lpszConnect = _T(""));
```

lpszName supplies the name of the database; remember that for DAO data sources, you'll want to go after a file name directly. You can specify a file name locally on your machine, like "C:\\MSOFFICE\\ACCESS\\ZIPCODE.MDB", or you can specify a UNC path name to a network machine. I could open a database on the bigger of my two development machines using "\\\\BUMPER\\DATABASES\\ZIPCODE.MDB". If you want to get to an ODBC data source through DAO, you'll need to make this parameter an empty string.

The bExclusive and bReadOnly parameters are just as they were with the CDatabase version of the function, and are described below. The lpszConnect string needs to point to an empty string if you want to connect to a DAO database, or it should point to an ODBC-style connection string if you want to go after an ODBC data source. Note that the syntax for this string is exactly the same as that for the CDatabase version of the function, but you'll always want to use the DSN keyword in the connect string you give to a CDaoDatabase object, because no other parameter to the function specifies the database name.

You'll remember that I said a DAO workspace makes the connection between a user and a database, and that DAO would specify a default workspace for you if you didn't ask for a particular one yourself. The CDaoDatabase object constructor accepts a pointer to the CDaoWorkspace object you'd like to use. If you don't specify such an object, the parameter defaults to NULL and that instructs MFC to ask DAO to use the default workspace.

Again, you can always access a pointer to the raw DAO object. With that pointer, you can directly query the underlying OLE object for any of the interfaces you can read about in the DAO SDK. The interfaces are the same ones MFC is using under the covers to get the job done. You can find a pointer to the CDaoWorkspace object your CDaoDatabase is using in the m_pWorkspace member. Note that this is a pointer to a real MFC object, not a pointer to a DAO SDK object. The m_pDAODatabase member of CDaoDatabase points at the raw DAO database object that is serving your requests.

Connection Settings

Let's return to CDatabase, at least for the time being. Once the database object has been opened, you can begin using it to work with your database. The CDatabase object by itself doesn't provide much in the way of movement of data from the database; you'll need to create a CRecordset object to be able to read through results returned from queries or stored procedures.

Since the CDatabase object encapsulates the connection to the database, it provides functions that manipulate the way your connection to the database will work. Therefore, before you run off and use a CRecordset object to get data, it's important to understand how the settings in the CDatabase object affect the way your recordset works.

Open()

Some of the most important settings are given to the Open() function. Aside from the data source name and the connection string, Open() also accepts a few flags. The first, bExclusive, must be FALSE; MFC will assert if this parameter is TRUE; further functionality may be added in a later version of MFC. bReadOnly, the third parameter to Open(), can be set to TRUE if you will only be reading from the database. This setting can give your database management software, or the driver, some leeway in optimizing access for your process, and protects the database from being accidentally modified by an errant program.

The fifth and final parameter, bUseCursorLib, controls the load of the ODBC **cursor library**. When this parameter is TRUE, which it is by default, MFC will request that ODBC always load its cursor library. If the parameter is FALSE, ODBC will rely on the driver for cursor support. If the driver has no cursor support, neither will your connection.

A **cursor** is just the notion of a position in a recordset. When you open the recordset, the cursor starts at the beginning of the set. You can always move the cursor through the recordset one record at a time – you'll do this implicitly as you fetch from one record to the next. But some database management software allows you to forward to the end of the set, rewind back to the beginning, or randomly jump to any row in the returned set. The ODBC cursor library inserts a layer between the driver and the data source to simulate the availability of cursors on the back-end. But this simulation comes at some runtime overhead (both in the size of your application's working set and the speed of your database connection) even if you don't use the services of the library.

Note that CDaoDatabase's Open() function doesn't have the bUseCursorLib parameter. DAO database connections *always* allow cursor operations, because they're an inherent feature of the Jet Engine – the cursor library for DAO is built into the DAO library.

When the cursor library is loaded, it steps in between the driver manager and the driver. It simulates the functionality of traditional cursors for databases and drivers that don't support cursors themselves. Cursors are primarily used to access rows in the result set returned by a given query dynamically.

If you need to examine different rows in the result set randomly, your application is a candidate for using cursors. If you don't need to work through your result set (other than getting the next row, row by row, to read all of your results), you are better off not using the cursor library. By eliminating the extra layer between you and the database, and by avoiding the load and management of an extra DLL and the buffers it creates, you can ensure that you enjoy the fastest possible throughput.

If the database back end or the loaded driver for it doesn't support cursors, ODBC simulates cursors by repeatedly calling the ODBC ::SQLFetch() API against the driver to access different rows. This technique only works when going forward through the result set, so the ODBC cursor library can't move backwards unless the back-end database supports it. If you open a static result set, the driver can make a copy of the result set and then dynamically seek through it. More information on result set types appears when we discuss CRecordset, later on in the chapter.

> The cursor library is named **Odbccurs.dll**, and if your application is reliant on cursors, it should redistribute and install this DLL. You can find a copy (and lots more information about setting up ODBC on your target system) in the ODBC SDK.

Timeouts

Before you call `Open()`, you may wish to set the amount of time that ODBC will wait around when trying to connect to the database. `SetLoginTimeout()` takes one parameter, which is the number of seconds to wait before timing out. ODBC connections support this member function in their `CDatabase` object, while DAO connections support this member function in their `CDaoWorkspace` object.

This setting is of particular interest when your data source exists somewhere over a network. Since the connection may take a long time to establish because of network traffic, you may wish to set a longer timeout to avoid extra 'connection timeout' or error messages in situations where communications with the database are slow but reliable.

Similarly, you can call `SetQueryTimeout()` to set the amount of time ODBC or DAO will wait before assuming that a query has timed out. Compared to connection times, query execution times are more dependent on query complexity and less dependent on network traffic. You should consider setting the timeout for queries to a larger value if you find that your queries are frequently timing out; setting the value too high means that users may completely lose control of your application if something really does go wrong with the database or the network. Both DAO and ODBC support `SetQueryTimeout()` as a member of their respective database connection types.

Once you've actually called `Open()` against your `CDatabase` object, you can call `GetConnect()` to retrieve the connection string, or `GetDatabaseName()` to retrieve the name of the database. You can also call `IsOpen()` against a `CDatabase` object to see whether it has been successfully opened. These functions are particularly useful when you're coding generic routines to work against any database. It's a good idea to make sure the database object you've been passed has been opened correctly, as in the next code fragment:

```
BOOL SetupTables(CDatabase* pDB)
{
    ASSERT_VALID(pDB);
    if (pDB->IsOpen() == FALSE)
        return FALSE;

    // More stuff...
}
```

You can also use functions like `CanUpdate()` or `CanTransact()` to see whether the database and drivers with which you've connected can accept updates or perform transaction management. These functions return `TRUE` if the associated capability is available, `FALSE` if it isn't.

`CDaoDatabase` doesn't support `GetDatabaseName()`, but it *does* support `GetConnect()` and `GetName()`. Of course, the former function is only useful if you've hooked your DAO database object to an ODBC data source.

SQL Commands Through CDatabase

Should you choose, you can use CDatabase to execute statements that don't return a result set. If you're about to perform a deletion or an update, you can call CDatabase::ExecuteSQL(), passing the SQL statement you wish to execute as the only parameter. Assuming you have a CDatabase object named dbZip open and ready, you might delete all rows in the ZIPCode table by calling ExecuteSQL() like this:

```
dbZip.ExecuteSQL(_T("DELETE FROM ZIPCode"));
```

Note that ExecuteSQL() doesn't return a value, but instead throws a CDBException if anything goes wrong. You must provide a try/catch construct for this exception at some level so that your application won't abnormally terminate if the exception goes unhandled. You might code such a trap like this:

```
try
{
    dbZip.ExecuteSQL(_T("DELETE FROM ZIPCode"));
}
catch(CDBException *pEx)
{
    AfxMessageBox(pEx->m_strError);
    pEx->Delete();
}
```

In this example, we simply throw an error message at the user when the exception is caught, but you might want to take some evasive action in your application based on the result, so that you can try to recover from the error.

Remember that errors are problems with the *execution* of a statement; if you try to perform an UPDATE or DELETE and don't affect any rows, then it isn't an error. If you misspell UPDATE, or the database went down between the time you connected to it and executed the UPDATE, you will get an error.

In the example given above, the ExecuteSQL() call uses a hard-coded statement to do its work. One of the common requirements is to create a SQL statement dynamically and send it to the database. At any point you need a SQL statement, including the ExecuteSQL() function, you can just put together a string with the information you need in it.

You could delete all of the zip codes for a particular state by using a function like this:

```
BOOL RemoveState(CDatabase* pDB, CString strStateCode)
{
    ASSERT(strStateCode != NULL);
    ASSERT(pDB != NULL);
    ASSERT(pDB->IsOpen());
    if (pDB == NULL || !pDB->IsOpen())
        return FALSE;
    CString str;
```

```
    str.Format(_T("DELETE FROM ZIPCode WHERE State = '%s'"),
                                        (LPCTSTR)strStateCode);
    try
    {
        pDB->ExecuteSQL(str);
    }
    catch (CDBException* pEx)
    {
        AfxMessageBox(pEx->m_strError);
        pEx->Delete();
        return FALSE;
    }
    return TRUE;
}
```

Notice how you can use `try/catch` blocks to handle errors defensively, and how we have used ASSERTs to help debug any problems that might crop up when the statement is called. The `if` statement at the beginning of the function might seem a bit redundant with the ASSERTs around it. Since ASSERTs disappear in a release build, the `if` statement will make sure that release builds of the program behave reasonably when something goes wrong. See how easily you can build a statement from the parameters given to the function!

This function will return TRUE even if there were no zip codes for the state passed; if you called the function with 'PA' as a parameter twice in a row, the function would return TRUE both times. If we drop the zip codes table from the database, on the other hand, `ExecuteSQL()` will throw an exception and the function will return FALSE.

`CDaoDatabase` has a function similar to `ExecuteSQL()` – it's simply called `Execute()`. It has a slightly different name to make sure you realize that it's different. It takes a pointer to your SQL string, but also takes an integer indicating what kind of options you'd like to affect on the results. You can use a combination of these flags for the options:

Flag	Description
dbDenyWrite	While this command is running, other users can't write to the tables involved in the query.
dbInconsistent	Perform inconsistent updates.
dbConsistent	Perform consistent updates.
dbSQLPassThrough	This option applies only to connections through DAO to an ODBC data source. The option causes DAO to pass the SQL statement directly through to the connected ODBC data source for immediate processing. Neither DAO nor the connected ODBC driver will preprocess the query.
dbFailOnError	Force the workspace to rollback if your command causes an error.
dbSeeChanges	Generate a run-time error (i.e. force MFC to throw an exception) if another user changes data that your connection is editing.

dbInconsistent is the default; if you specify neither dbInconsistent nor dbConsistent, DAO will assume you mean the former. dbInconsistent means that the database will allow your statement to update records resulting from a query that compiles data from more than one table. For example, you might open a recordset against a query that lists all the albums and artists in your music collection with a SELECT statement like this:

```
SELECT Artist.Artist_Name, Album.Album_Name
    FROM Artist, Album
    WHERE Artist.Artist_Number = Album.Album_Number
```

There's a one-to-many relationship between artists and albums, because one artist can have many albums. If you change records resulting from this query, you'll change data in the underlying tables. If you're not careful with your update, you can leave a particular artist without any albums, or destroy referential integrity relationships further down the line (for example, there might be some indirect relationship between artists, albums, and record companies).

By specifying dbInconsistent, DAO will allow you to update records in this kind of query – but it's up to you to make sure you don't ruin the integrity of your database.

Handling Transactions in ODBC

MFC's CDatabase class supports the notion of **transactions**, which are units of work that can be reversed in the event of an error. Note that a transaction isn't always just a single SQL statement; it may be a very large collection of statements which represent a logical unit of work within the meaning of the database. For example, to perform the simple task of giving someone a raise, you may select their current salary, add ten percent to it and then update it with the new amount. You might also go back to their personnel record and adjust their tax withholding information.

This is really just one transaction, even though it involves three SQL statements: one SELECT and two UPDATEs. If the SELECT works and the first UPDATE changes the person's salary, but the subsequent tax UPDATE fails, it's very convenient to be able to **rollback** the transaction, scratching out any changes since the transaction was started. If everything in the transaction works correctly, the transaction can be **committed**.

Rolling Back or Committing the Changes

You can rollback a transaction by calling Rollback() against the CDatabase object. If you successfully complete a transaction, you can call CommitTrans() on the CDatabase object to have the transaction permanently recorded by the database. For these calls to work, you must first call BeginTrans() against the database; the first statement executed after your call to BeginTrans() is the first statement which will be undone if you call Rollback(), or actually written if you call CommitTrans().

Note that the use of transactions has the added bonus of making all of the changes in the transaction become visible to other users all at once. In a multi-user database system, this is particularly important; one user might be querying the employee's salary before moving on to look at their tax information. If the update is only partially complete, the other process may see information that only represents part of the update transaction.

However, some database management systems change a great deal of the state information associated with the connection when performing a rollback. In particular, they often destroy the status associated with any open cursors, dropping whatever result set the connection may have had open at the time the transaction was committed.

You might implement the salary update code in MFC using a fragment like the one shown below. Assume, for this fragment, that the employee information is in a table called `Employee`, keyed by a column named `SSN`, while the actual salary resides in a column named `Salary`.

The `EmployeeTax` table, also keyed by social security number in a column named `SSN`, contains an integer representing the tax bracket in a column named `TaxBracket`. To prove that I'm clueless about taxes, I've hidden the implementation of the tax table lookup in a function called `FindTaxBracket()` that isn't shown here:

```cpp
BOOL UpdateEmployee(CString strSSN, int nPercent)
{
    CDatabase dbEmployees;
    try
    {
        // Try to open the database
        dbEmployees.Open(_T("My Employee Datasource"));
    }
    catch (CDBException* pEx)
    {
        AfxMessageBox(pEx->m_strError);
        pEx->Delete();
        return FALSE;
    }
    BOOL bInTransaction = FALSE;
    if (dbEmployees.CanTransact())
        bInTransaction = dbEmployees.BeginTrans();

    try
    {
        // Dynamically construct UPDATE statement
        CString str = _T("UPDATE Employee SET Salary = Salary * (");
        CString strValue;
        strValue.Format(_T(("%d/100) WHERE SSN = '"), nPercent);
        dbEmployees.ExecuteSQL(str + strValue + strSSN + _T("'"));

        // Dynamically update Tax table
        int nTaxBracket = FindTaxBracket(strSSN);
        str.Format(_T("UPDATE EmployeeTax SET TaxBracket = %d ")
            _T("WHERE SSN = '%s'"), nTaxBracket, (LPCTSTR)strSSN));
        dbEmployees.ExecuteSQL(str);
        if (dbEmployees.CanTransact())
            dbEmployees.CommitTrans();
    }
```

```
        catch (CDBException* pEx)
        {
            if (bInTransaction)
                dbEmployees.Rollback();
            AfxMessageBox(pEx->m_strError);
            pEx->Delete();
            return FALSE;
        }

        if (bInTransaction)
            dbEmployees.CommitTrans();
        return TRUE;
    }
```

MFC recordsets make use of cursors, so the `CDatabase::CanTransact()` function checks the database to see whether the data source in use supports transactions. The function returns `FALSE` if transactions are not supported and `TRUE` if they are. This return value is based on the `m_bTransactions` member of `CDatabase`, which is set during the execution of the `CDatabase::Open()` function.

If `TRUE` is returned from `CanTransact()`, the data source can accept a rollback or commit request and still keep its cursor context intact.

Problems with Transaction Processing

The problem with MFC's support for transactions is that not all databases have transaction capability. If you call `BeginTrans()`, `Rollback()` or `CommitTrans()` on a `CDatabase` object connected to a data source which can't handle transactions correctly, the function will return `FALSE` and be ignored. Relational database management systems that do support transactions include Oracle and Microsoft SQL Server.

The conservative code in `CDatabase` is idealistic, and there are few, if any, commercially available databases for PC platforms which will retain the cursor context over a transaction control command. When most database management systems commit or rollback a transaction, the context of any result sets the database was managing for the connection is lost. As such, the code in MFC that manages your travels through the recordset isn't able to synchronize with the reset state of the database again.

As a workaround, you can use `ExecuteSQL()` to issue whatever SQL command your back-end database uses to begin, end or abort a transaction. If you resort to this technique, you'll be throwing away part of ODBC's advantage – cross-platform portability for the back-end database. If you move your code to a different back-end database, you'll need to find out how to perform commits and rollbacks on that database. If you don't plan to move to a different database back end, you're all set; just use your `ExecuteSQL()` statements as they are.

Even if you get this workaround set up and working, remember that you'll invalidate any `CRecordset` objects that are active at the time of the commit or rollback. The code given below implements the `UpdateEmployee()` function that we have just discussed, using database-specific transaction management commands:

```
    BOOL UpdateEmployee(CString strSSN, int nPercent)
    {
        CDatabase dbEmployees;
```

```
try
{
    // Try to open the database
    dbEmployees.Open(_T("My Employee Datasource"));
}
catch (CDBException* pEx)
{
    AfxMessageBox(pEx->m_strError);
    pEx->Delete();
    return FALSE;
}

dbEmployees.ExecuteSQL(_T("BEGIN TRANSACTION"));
try
{
    // Dynamically construct UPDATE statement
    CString str = _T("UPDATE Employee SET Salary = Salary * (");
    CString strValue;
    strValue.Format(_T(("%d/100) WHERE SSN = '"), nPercent);
    dbEmployees.ExecuteSQL(str + strValue + strSSN + _T("'"));

    // Dynamically update Tax table
    int nTaxBracket = FindTaxBracket(strSSN);

    str.Format(_T("UPDATE EmployeeTax SET TaxBracket = %d ")
        _T("WHERE SSN = '%s'"), nTaxBracket, (LPCTSTR)strSSN);
    dbEmployees.ExecuteSQL(str);
}
catch (CDBException* pEx)
{
    dbEmployees.ExecuteSQL(_T("ROLLBACK TRANSACTION"));
    dbEmployees.Close();
    AfxMessageBox(pEx->m_strError);
    pEx->Delete();
    return FALSE;
}
dbEmployees.ExecuteSQL(_T("COMMIT TRANSACTION"));
return TRUE;
}
```

This function could be enhanced by providing additional try/catch blocks for the ExecuteSQL() calls which implement the transaction management. Even though these calls seem benign, they can create a variety of errors. You might wish to implement your own function for each of these routines; you could implement proper error reporting and save yourself some time.

Another workaround, and perhaps a cleaner solution, is to adjust the m_bTransactions member of your CDatabase object to TRUE manually. This will allow you to call the BeginTransaction(), Rollback() and CommitTrans() functions much more freely. The functions will work correctly, but might destroy the content of any result sets open against the database.

When the Open() function runs, it queries the data source to see what it does in response to transaction control commands, with the results of this interrogation being stored in two member variables in the CDatabase object. The data source's reaction to a commit command is stored in m_nCursorCommitBehavior, while its reaction to a rollback statement is stored in m_nCursorRollbackBehavior.

The value of each of these variables is equal to one of four constants defined by ODBC. If you attempt a rollback operation and m_nCursorRollbackBahavior is set to SQL_ERROR, or you try a commit operation and m_nCursorCommitBehavior is set to SQL_ERROR, the database object will throw an exception because the operation isn't supported.

This table shows the effect of a commit operation based on the m_nCursorCommitBehavior value, or the result of a rollback operation based on the m_nCursorRollbackBehavior value:

Flag	Description
SQL_CB_DELETE	Any CRecordset that is opened against this CDatabase object is lost and can't be retrieved. No further operations against any CRecordset for the CDatabase are valid. You should call Close() on each CRecordset to avoid any subsequent problems.
SQL_CB_CLOSE	Any CRecordset that is opened against this CDatabase object is lost, but can be immediately refreshed by calling CRecordset::Requery().
SQL_CB_PRESERVE	The operation is carried out normally, without affecting any open CRecordsets.

This means that if you tweak m_bTransactions to be TRUE after m_nCursorCommitBehavior was found to be SQL_CB_CLOSE, you can refresh any CRecordsets you have open by calling Requery() against them. The current position in the recordset will be lost, but you can revive the content with the Requery() call. On the other hand, if m_nCursorRollbackBehavior is SQL_CB_DELETE and you call Rollback(), you should Close() and re-Open() any CRecordset object which you have open against that data source.

Remember that m_nCursorCommitBehavior and m_nCursorRollbackBehavior show what reaction the database will have; they don't set that reaction. This means that changing these variables won't change the way your database behaves. They *reflect* rather than *affect* what is happening.

> Note that m_nCursorCommitBehavior *isn't necessarily equal to* m_nCursorRollbackBehavior *for all data sources.*

Transaction Processing in DAO

Transaction processing in DAO is appealing for the same reasons as it is in ODBC – it provides you with a convenient way to assure database integrity, even in the face of terrible errors. In DAO, though, you're usually talking to a Jet database. If that's the case, you'll find that using a transaction, even for the simplest of queries, will afford the database engine an opportunity to do a little bit of optimization. I might recode the above example with DAO like this:

```
BOOL UpdateEmployee(CString strSSN, int nPercent)
{
    CDaoDatabase dbEmployees;
```

```
    try
    {
        // Try to open the database
        dbEmployees.Open(_T("C:\\DATABASE\\EMPLOYEE.MDB"));
        if (dbEmployees.CanTransact())
            dbEmployees.m_pWorkspace->BeginTrans();
    }
    catch (CDaoException* pEx)
    {
        pEx->ReportError();
        pEx->Delete();
        return FALSE;
    }

    try
    {
        // Dynamically construct UPDATE statement
        CString str = _T("UPDATE Employee SET Salary = Salary * (");
        CString strValue;
        strValue.Format(_T(("%d/100) WHERE SSN = '"), nPercent);
        dbEmployees.Execute(str + strValue + strSSN + _T("'"));

        // Dynamically update Tax table
        int nTaxBracket = FindTaxBracket(strSSN);

        str.Format(_T("UPDATE EmployeeTax SET TaxBracket = %d ")
            _T("WHERE SSN = '%s'"), nTaxBracket, (LPCTSTR)strSSN);
        dbEmployees.Execute(str);
    }
    catch (CDBException* pEx)
    {
        if (dbEmployees.CanTransact())
            dbEmployees.m_pWorkspace->Rollback();
        dbEmployees.Close();
        pEx->ReportError();
        pEx->Delete();
        return FALSE;
    }
    if (dbEmployees.CanTransact())
        dbEmployees.m_pWorkspace->CommitTrans();
    return TRUE;
}
```

As you can see, the code isn't very different – I just used `Execute()` instead of `ExecuteSQL()`, and called the transaction management functions in the `CDaoWorkspace` object associated with my `CDaoDatabase`.

> Note that, whichever method you use (**CDatabase**, SQL or **CDaoWorkspace**), you *must* call **BeginTrans()** before any work is done. Otherwise, you'll never be able to rollback the transaction, and there wouldn't be any marked work to commit at the end.

Using the ODBC API Directly

I've already mentioned the Tracing tag in the data source administrator and, at that time, I discussed the fact that we could enable or disable ODBC statement tracing. Programmatically, you can enable or disable tracing by calling ::SQLSetConnectAttr() in the ODBC API.

You can use this function to set or change tracing options for your connection. The first parameter is a handle to the database connection you wish to modify. That handle, of the ODBC type HDBC, can be retrieved from the m_hdbc member of an open CDatabase, the database you wish to alter. The second parameter can be SQL_OPT_TRACE to turn tracing on or off, or SQL_OPT_TRACEFILE to set the name of the file for tracing. A third parameter supplies information to the call, depending on the attribute specified by the second parameter.

To turn tracing *off*, you can call ::SQLSetConnectAttr() like this:

```
::SQLSetConnectAttr(dbZip.m_hdbc, SQL_ATTR_TRACE,
                                  (SQLPOINTER)SQL_OPT_TRACE_OFF, 0);
```

Turn tracing *on* by passing SQL_OPT_TRACE_ON as the third parameter instead of SQL_OPT_TRACE_OFF. You can specify a name for the trace file using SQL_ATTR_TRACEFILE, like this:

```
::SQLSetConnectAttr(dbZip.m_hdbc, SQL_ATTR_TRACE,
                                  (SQLPOINTER)SQL_OPT_TRACE_ON, 0);
::SQLSetConnectAttr(dbZip.m_hdbc, SQL_ATTR_TRACEFILE,
                                  (SQLPOINTER)"C:\\MYLOG.TXT", 8);
```

When I described the tracing options earlier, I noted that the setting affects all drivers and data sources. Setting the trace file name with the ::SQLSetConnectAttr() API has the same global effect – in fact, the first parameter doesn't need to be a valid handle when you're setting SQL_ATTR_TRACEFILE. However, the setting you make for SQL_ATTR_TRACE is local to the handle where you make the setting and only affects calls that your application makes to the driver associated with the connection you've identified by its handle in the first parameter.

m_hdbc Outside of SQL Logging

Even if you're not interested in playing with SQL logging in your application, remember this technique. m_hdbc is available to you, and is important for almost every call you want to make directly against the ODBC API. m_hdbc identifies your connection, and the API will need to know about the connection to change it or get its status.

In the second call, we have carefully cast the third parameter to a SQLPOINTER, as this type is specified in the function's prototype; I need to coerce the string to match the function's prototype. ::SQLSetConnectAttr() accepts several other values as its second parameter, as it tries to change the different connection settings. To find out about the other parameters you can use, have a peek at the ODBC help file shipped with Visual C++, or the ODBC API Reference. There are a dozen different options, which are outlined overleaf:

Option Identifier	Description
SQL_ATTR_ACCESS_MODE	This sets the access mode for the database connection; the access mode can be either SQL_MODE_READ_ONLY or SQL_MODE_READ_WRITE. Normally, you'll get the net effect of this setting by changing the flags you send to CDatabase::Open().
SQL_ATTR_AUTOCOMMIT	This turns autocommit on or off. It affects transaction processing; if autocommit is off, you have control over transactions in your database and can use transaction management commands. If autocommit is on, every statement you send is committed automatically, immediately after it executes. autocommit may seem more convenient, but it is much slower, since the database can't batch its transaction housekeeping. The CDatabase class manages this setting around BeginTrans(), CommitTrans() and Rollback() calls. The parameter is automatically switched off outside of transactions defined with these calls, and turned back on once a CommitTrans() or Rollback() occurs.
SQL_ATTR_LOGIN_TIMEOUT	This sets the time allowed for the logon process before the client software times out and assumes the operation has failed. This may be set directly with the MFC CDatabase::SetLoginTimeout() function.
SQL_ATTR_ODBC_CURSORS	This controls the use of the cursor library. Normally, you'll use the cursors flag passed to your CDatabase object's Open() function instead of manipulating this parameter directly.
SQL_ATTR_TRACE	This turns diagnostic tracing on or off; see the example code and explanation above.
SQL_ATTR_TRACEFILE	This sets the filename for diagnostic tracing output. See the code fragment and background information above.
SQL_ATTR_PACKET_SIZE	This sets the network packet size for the database conversation. If your database is local, this parameter is meaningless. If your database is on the network somewhere, this parameter can be used to tune the size of packets your database server sends your workstation. You should choose a packet size that minimizes waste in network communications.

Option Identifier	Description
SQL_ATTR_QUIET_MODE	By default, the driver manager will use the application's main window to display error messages. If you wish to suppress all messages from the driver manager, you should tell SQL_QUIET_MODE to use a NULL handle. If you want an alternative window to parent messages from the driver, you can pass a handle for that window instead.
SQL_ATTR_TRANSLATE_LIB	This accepts a parameter naming a .dll that provides translation functions to the driver manager. The translation functions help the driver perform character-set translation. This setting is only useful if you're writing an advanced, internationalized application and your database back end doesn't support any translation mechanism for the target country.
SQL_ATTR_TRANSLATE_ OPTION	This is a user-defined option that is passed to the translation .dll you've specified with SQL_TRANSLATE_DLL. It can reflect state information to your .dll or set options; whatever your translation library needs.
SQL_ATTR_TXN_ISOLATION	This sets the isolation level for the database. It can't be set when a transaction is open against the database. The parameter can be SQL_TXN_READ_UNCOMMITTED, SQL_TXN_READ_COMMITTED, SQL_TXN_REPEATABLE_READ, SQL_TXN_SERIALIZABLE or SQL_TXN_VERSIONING. Some of these transaction levels may not be supported by your data base management system or your driver; you should consult the appropriate references to see how the vendors suggest you handle this setting.

Some of these settings are only supported by selected drivers, You'll need to check the documentation for your driver to make sure it supports the call you wish to make.

I have indicated some situations where you should use MFC-provided functions to set the option in question. As I have already explained, if you're interested in setting an option that MFC doesn't manage, you can directly tweak the setting using a call to ::SQLSetConnectAttr(). Note that you can also call ::SQLGetConnectAttr() to retrieve the setting's current value.

Using DAO Directly

I mentioned earlier that there are pointers in all MFC wrapper classes for the DAO programming interface to the underlying DAO objects. These objects are C++ objects, but they're *not* MFC objects. You can read up on these objects if you're interested in getting access to the nitty-gritty of the DAO mechanisms that make things go.

CRecordset and CDaoRecordset

As you saw in the previous section, the ODBC class CDatabase is often used with another class named CRecordset. While CDatabase encapsulates everything that happens between the database and the application, the CRecordset encapsulates everything that is handled for each statement the application might send to the database. The ExecuteSQL() function in CDatabase can't receive information returned from the database, except for error codes. CRecordset, on the other hand, only exists to manage the information associated with the execution of a statement. You can have any number of CRecordset objects (including none at all) open against a particular CDatabase object.

Similarly, when you're writing DAO applications, you can use CDaoDatabase with a CDaoRecordset object. Just like its ODBC counterpart, a CDaoDatabase handles everything you'd need to do once you're connected to a database, while CDaoRecordset lets you work with a particular record once you've executed a query.

Whatever kind of database you're using, remember that a recordset embodies the notion of a set of records. The CRecordset and CDaoRecordset classes encapsulate all of the records the database might have returned to you, but they only give you access to the values in one record at a time. If you need to sift through the data in the database, you're *usually* far better off asking the database to do it for you by providing a WHERE clause in your SQL statement. I emphasize 'usually' because there are a few situations when partying on all the data you got back from the database in an array might actually be more efficient – if you're rapidly looking something up over and over again in a list, for example. There are more optimization suggestions near the end of the chapter in the section called 'Notes About Performance Tuning'.

While you'll almost never derive your own class from CDatabase, you'll almost always use a derivative of CRecordset or CDaoRecordset when preparing a query in your application. This is because CRecordset and CDaoRecordset wrap each query, providing member variables for the temporary storage of values from each column of data returned from the query.

The most important functionality you'll need to add to your CRecordset class is support for the data that is returned from the query the CRecordset represents. You'll need to add a member variable of the appropriate type to your derived class for each column you expect back from your query. Each time MFC needs to fetch some data for the recordset, it will fill these members with the data from the appropriate row in the table.

MFC also needs to know how many fields to expect from the query; you'll need to set the m_nFields member of your CRecordset object to indicate how many fields you expect to return. It's easy to do this in the constructor of the object. It's also prudent to initialize the member variables to a benign setting to make sure you don't pollute your recordset at a later date.

This ODBC recordset constructor is stolen from the Music sample:

```
CArtistsSet::CArtistsSet(CDatabase* pdb)
    : CRecordset(pdb)
{
    //{{AFX_FIELD_INIT(CArtistsSet)
    m_Artist_Number = 0;
    m_Artist_Name = _T("");
    m_nFields = 2;
    //}}AFX_FIELD_INIT
    m_nDefaultType = CRecordset::snapshot;
}
```

A constructor for a DAO recordset would be almost identical, the only differences being that it would accept a pointer to a CDaoDatabase instead of a CDatabase, and be derived from CDaoRecordset rather than CRecordset.

The funny comments appear once again, a sure sign that this code came from ClassWizard. I created the Music application by selecting the **Header files only** support level for database code in AppWizard, before using ClassWizard to add the CRecordset objects I needed. ClassWizard prompted for the name of the data source and table that we wanted to connect to the new CRecordset, and then automatically added all this code to the application. Of course, you could have added it by hand, but the path of least resistance is easier to exploit.

The DaoView sample was written the same way, just asking CDaoRecordsets of ClassWizard. Note that when you ask AppWizard to **Header files only** for database support, it will hook up the Afxdb.h header for ODBC as well as the Afxdao.h file, because it doesn't know if you want to write an ODBC or DAO application. You might want to edit your Stdafx.h file to only include one of the two headers so you can compile just a bit faster. If you take any other level of database support (besides **None**, of course), AppWizard knows what kind of database support you want because it makes you pick a data source before proceeding.

Record Field Exchange

AppWizard also created the necessary DoFieldExchange() function for us. DoFieldExchange() is very similar to the CDialog::DoDataExchange() function that we talked about in Chapter 5, but DoFieldExchange() doesn't do any data validation; it just performs data exchange. The DoFieldExchange() function provided by AppWizard looks like this:

```
void CArtistsSet::DoFieldExchange(CFieldExchange* pFX)
{
    //{{AFX_FIELD_MAP(CArtistsSet)
    pFX->SetFieldType(CFieldExchange::outputColumn);
    RFX_Text(pFX, _T("[Artist_Name]"), m_Artist_Name);
    RFX_Long(pFX, _T("[Artist_Number]"), m_Artist_Number);
    //}}AFX_FIELD_MAP
}
```

Since the query represented by CArtistSet is pretty simple, there are only two RFX_ function calls – one for each column returned by the query. MFC makes RFX_ functions available for all major data types. You can use RFX_ functions for the appropriate data type when you're using a CRecordset, and use DFX_ functions for the appropriate data type when you're using a CDaoRecordset. This table shows the available functions and the data types that they manipulate. You'll notice that MFC doesn't always supply support for a given type against both DAO and ODBC recordsets; this is because DAO offers a richer (and stricter) set of types.

RFX_ Function	DFX_ Function	Data Type
RFX_Binary()	DFX_Binary()	CByteArray
RFX_Bool()	DFX_Bool()	BOOL

Table Continued on Following Page

RFX_ Function	DFX_ Function	Data Type
RFX_Byte()	DFX_Byte()	int
	DFX_Currency()	COleCurrency
RFX_Date()		CTime or TIMESTAMP_STRUCT
	DFX_DateTime()	COleDateTime
RFX_Double()	DFX_Double()	double
RFX_Int()		int
	DFX_Short()	short int
RFX_Long()	DFX_Long()	LONG
RFX_LongBinary()	DFX_LongBinary()	CLongBinary
RFX_Single()	DFX_Single()	float
RFX_Text()	DFX_Text()	CString

You'll notice a few interesting types in this table. We've seen CByteArray as one of the collection classes, and that CTime is used to manage date/time information. We also looked at COleDateTime back in the chapter on utility classes.

However, CLongBinary is new. This data type manages **binary long objects**, or **BLOB**s. It's often handy to store arbitrary runs of binary data in a database, like a picture, a fax image, or something similar. If you have such a column in your table, you can use CLongBinary to handle this kind of information.

CLongBinary is quite simple; you can get an HGLOBAL (which is a handle to the memory containing the binary data) for the object from the m_hData member, while the m_dwDataLength member shows how long that memory block is. You can use the regular Windows APIs for managing the data; for example, you can use GlobalReAlloc() to manipulate the size of the memory block associated with the CLongBinary object.

Opening a Recordset

Recordsets, like CDatabase (and, I suppose, most other objects in MFC), don't automatically open themselves when you construct an object. The constructor for CRecordset only has one optional parameter; a pointer to the CDatabase object that should be used when the recordset is opened. (Of course, CDaoRecordset takes a pointer to CDaoDatabase.)

If you don't specify a CDatabase object when you construct your CRecordset object, MFC will call GetDefaultConnect() when you try to open it. ClassWizard provides a GetDefaultConnect() function in your CRecordset-derivative class; this function takes no parameters but needs to return a CString containing the connection string that you want to use.

Similarly, if you don't offer your CDaoRecordset object a CDaoDatabase, MFC uses a function called GetDefaultDBName() to return the name of the database file you'd like to use.

In either architecture, the recordset object will run off and create the appropriate database object using the default parameters for the constructor.

What Light Through Yonder Recordset Breaks!

CRecordset, like CDatabase, has an Open() function. It accepts three parameters, all of which are optional. The first parameter is an integer indicating what type of recordset you wish to open. You can pass one of four constants as the first parameter: dynamic, dynaset, snapshot or forwardOnly. Each of these constants is a member of an enum in CRecordset, so you'll need to accordingly scope the constant you use – CRecordset::dynamic, for example.

When you open a DAO query with CDaoRecordset, you can choose from dbOpenDynaset, dbOpenTable, and dbOpenSnapshot. Like the constants for CDaoRecordset, these constants are values from an enum in CDaoRecordset and need similar scoping.

Before we examine the other parameters for these functions, let's take a look at each of the four recordset modes so we can understand them. After all, what good is an opened recordset if you don't know what it's doing?

Dynasets

CRecordset::dynaset and CDaoRecordset::dbOpenDynaset mean that you'll open a dynamic recordset which features bi-directional scrolling. A dynamic recordset (or **dynaset**) is a recordset that stays current with the underlying data. That means that if a record appears in a result set you've opened as a dynaset, and some other user of the database system changes that record, you'll know about the change immediately.

If the user updates the record, you see the change as soon as you select that record again. If the user deletes the record, your recordset skips over the record, but if someone else adds a record that falls into the criteria for your recordset, you won't see it until you requery the database.

You can refresh the recordset by calling its Requery() member. This re-executes the SQL statement associated with the recordset and returns the rows that fit the criteria at that time. If you're using an ODBC CRecordset, you'll find that dynasets don't work when you have the ODBC cursor library loaded; you must specify FALSE for the appropriate parameter when you open the database. A CDaoRecordset will always work correctly in dynaset mode if you're touching a local database file or using an attached table, but may not work if you're using DAO to get to ODBC.

No matter how you connect to the database when running your CRecordset, the m_pDatabase member of the object contains a pointer to the CDatabase object which is managing the connection to the database. The same holds true for the m_pDatabase member of the CDaoRecordset class; m_pDatabase points at a CDaoDatabase. CDaoRecordset also holds a pointer to the underlying DAO object in its m_pDAORecordset member.

Note that the online documentation makes a clear distinction between a dynaset and the type of recordset specified as CRecordSet::dynamic. The difference is that for a dynaset, you have to specifically call Requery() to update any changes made by other users to the database, whereas for the CRecordSet::dynamic recordset, you do not have to do this. Note that some ODBC drivers do not support the CRecordSet::dynamic type of recordset.

Snapshots

Alternatively, you can specify `CRecordset::snapshot` for your ODBC recordset, or `CDaoRecordset::dbOpenSnapshot` for your DAO recordset. Snapshot recordsets ask the database management software to prepare a static image of the database records that are returned from your query. Snapshots are cool because they let you work with a bunch of data that you know won't change. That's good if you're just looking a few things up or letting the user browse. Snapshots, for example, are perfect for windows where you let the user pick a particular record from the database, but where the user might leave the window open while they go play with the photocopier or gossip about the local hockey team.

On the other hand, if you're doing updates of records on the database server, and you need to be sure of the database's referential integrity as you go along, you shouldn't use a snapshot. Without special care, other users can change data in the records referenced by a snapshot without you noticing.

If a database actually resides on a server, i.e. away from your machine, snapshots are expensive because the network will have to get all the records from the query before you can start working with the snapshot. Also, whether the records have come from a remote server or from a local file on your machine, some software somewhere (be it a database driver or ODBC or DAO themselves) will be using some memory or some disk space to hang on to the snapshot records as you use the query. The upside, though, is that seeking through a snapshot (particularly in a random pattern) is very fast.

On the other side of the coin, you won't see any result set updates until you `Requery()` the data. Snapshots on ODBC data support bi-directional scrolling if and only if the underlying data source allows scrolling. Again, DAO always allows bi-directional scrolling if you're working with one of the native data sources, but is dependent on the ODBC rules if you're actually using ODBC to go get the data.

> In DAO, snapshots are always read-only, period. You can never update data through a DAO snapshot recordset. However, in ODBC, snapshots can be updateable depending on the driver used — check the driver documentation for more details. To enable updateable snapshots, make sure you load the cursor library when you create your **CDatabase** object.

forwardOnly

The cheapest connection type for an ODBC recordset is `CRecordset::forwardOnly`; MFC and ODBC don't perform any extra management. `forwardOnly` mode won't show you any result set updates unless you requery the database, that is it creates a read-only recordeset. However, `forwardOnly` mode instructs ODBC to avoid the bother and overhead of managing the complete recordset in a snapshot because the database management software knows you aren't able to scroll randomly or backward through the result set. Note that, to set up `forwardOnly` mode, you have to specify `CRecordset::readOnly` as the third parameter in the `CRecordset::Open()` function, in addition to specifying `CRecordset::forwardOnly` as the first parameter in the same function.

DAO recordsets don't support `forwardOnly` mode implicitly. You *can*, however, add the `dbForwardOnly` flag to a DAO snapshot to achieve the same effect. There's more information on these modifiers in the next section.

Table Mode

DAO supports a single additional recordset mode. You can have DAO open your recordset in table mode if and only if the query you're performing references exactly one table. If your query references a stored query, or if it references a view or more than one table, DAO won't allow table mode for the query.

Using table mode is exactly the same as using a dynaset – it supports random, forward and backward scrolling, and lets you update and delete records, scroll through the set or append records to the set at any time. The only difference between the two is that table mode is just a shade faster because DAO knows that you're only referencing a single table and can internally tune things to be more efficient.

Which Mode for Me?

Next to the wager you make on the Stanley Cup Playoffs, choosing the proper access mode for the recordsets in your application is one of the most important decisions that you'll make. An improper choice can paint you into a corner or make your application unnecessarily slow. Making the right choice can help you get the best of the database technology installed on your computer and make your job easy.

In general, you should try to avoid using read-only snapshots. Really, the only time that you should use one is if you're letting your user browse to make a choice. If you imagine a typical interactive database application, you might see a couple of places where using a snapshot is appropriate. One might be a pick list that the user brings up to fill in a field that's used somewhere else, or you could use a snapshot to populate that list – the list is always read-only and doesn't need to lock the database while it is being used.

Another spot where you might use a read-only snapshot is in the main query for the application, if it has one. If, for example, your application uses a huge query to find all the customers in the region of the salesperson who is using the application, a snapshot would allow them to browse the database without locking records. You would need, however, to make sure that the record they eventually select still exists, that it isn't living on the snapshot despite having been deleted from the database by another user. A great way to do this is simply to reselect the primary key for the records. In our example of a user browsing a bunch of customers, the primary key might be a customer number.

As I mentioned, a forward-only recordset is a read-only snapshot without the ability to scroll backwards or move to a random record. Such a recordset is more appropriate for populating a pop-up list than it might be for your application's main query. If there's a chance that your main query has more records than you'd comfortably like to fetch and then hold in memory, you'd probably be better off using a snapshot and only fetching records the user actually scrolls onto in your user interface.

So, essentially, a snapshot is good for short-duration lists or large queries that have a very long lifecycle. The latter application might not sound so intuitive, but it makes a lot of sense because snapshots lock the database very controllably.

For most other work against your database, you'll want to use a dynaset. This allows you the most stable referential integrity, as well as the most reasonable performance for quick database updates, which will undoubtedly prove to be the most frequent type of access you make through the duration of your application. Beyond a dynaset, DAO offers a special-case recordset called a **table**. As we learned above, a table is just like a dynaset, but is slightly more efficient because DAO knows all of the records are in a single table rather than in the result of a query. If you can, in your DAO applications, use a table-type set instead of a dynaset.

Opening ODBC Recordsets

Now that we understand the different kinds of recordsets, let's talk about actually getting one open and playing with it. You'll recall that I got distracted into describing recordsets when I mentioned that the Open() functions for the CDaoRecordset and CRecordset classes support different modes of record management.

So, as we discussed, the first parameter to the Open() function on an ODBC recordset indicates what mode you'll be using for the recordset. The second parameter to CRecordset::Open() is a pointer to a string. By passing the name of a table in this string, the recordset will query all the columns and rows from that table. You can also pass your own SQL SELECT statement using whatever limiters and qualifiers you need, or you can send a CALL statement to execute a stored procedure.

Open() also accepts NULL as a query parameter, which causes the MFC to call back the GetDefaultSQL() function in your CRecordset-derived class to retrieve information about the query. ClassWizard provides this for you, but you might want to implement your own, returning the query you'd like to execute as a CString. Ideally, you should only return the SELECT clause of your query statement from your GetDefaultSQL() function.

If you need to specify a WHERE clause, it should be in the m_strFilter member of your object before you call Open(). Similarly, you can provide any sorting clause you need, including a GROUP BY or an ORDER BY clause in your m_strSort member.

Whatever you pass to Open(), or however you specify the SQL to be executed by the recordset, you need to make sure that you have the appropriate member variables to handle the results, and that your DoFieldExchange() is hooked up correctly. MFC has many ASSERTs that will be tripped if the number of parameters and the number of fields that are associated with the query don't match the number of parameters and fields actually managed by your recordset. The third parameter dwOptions is used to specify miscellaneous recordset options, such as limiting activity to adding records but not editing or deleting records, and enabling to use of bookmarks. Note that, as specified earlier that this has to be set to readOnly before you can use forwardOnly mode.

Opening DAO Recordsets

DAO recordsets are far more interesting to open. You can choose one of three overloads. The first is fairly simple, but the other two will take a bit more explanation and we'll have to come back to them later. Here's the prototype for the first one:

```
virtual void CDaoRecordset::Open(
                int     nOpenType = AFX_DAO_USE_DEFAULT_TYPE,
                LPCTSTR lpszSQL = NULL,
                int     nOptions = 0);
```

The first parameter is a constant that indicates what kind of recordset you'd like to open: dbOpenDynaset, dbOpenTable, or dbOpenSnapshot. The second points at a SQL statement, a list of table names, or a list of query names. If you let it stay at its default, the recordset will call its GetDefaultSQL() member to retrieve a string to be used in the query to the database. The SQL statement must conform to the SQL syntax for DAO, which is documented in the DAO SDK. The syntax is described in great, gaping detail in the SDK section of the help contents in Visual C++.

The final, nOptions parameter is very interesting. It can take on some of the values we learned about when we examined the CDaoDatabase::Execute() function, but there are some even more interesting flags you can pass. Here's a table:

Flag	Applicable Recordset Types	Description
dbAppendOnly	Dynasets	This allows only the addition of new records. Existing records can't be changed or deleted.
dbDenyWrite	All	This prevents other users from writing to the tables involved in the query.
dbDenyRead	Tables	This prevents other users from reading the tables involved in your query.
dbInconsistent	Dynasets, Tables	This performs inconsistent updates.
dbConsistent	All	This performs consistent updates.
dbSQLPassThrough	Dynasets, Snapshots	This passes the SQL statement directly through to the connected ODBC data source for immediate processing. Neither DAO *nor* the connected ODBC driver will preprocess the query.
dbForwardOnly	Snapshots	This allows forward-scrolling only.
dbFailOnError	All	This forces the workspace to rollback if your command causes an error.
dbSeeChanges	Dynasets, Tables	This generates a run-time error (i.e. forces MFC to throw an exception) if another user changes data that your connection is editing.

The middle column of this table indicates what types of recordsets can be used with the flag in question. Remember that there's a description of dbInconsistent and dbConsistent earlier in the chapter.

You can also call Open() against CDaoTableDef *or* CDaoQueryDef *objects. We'll see what those objects do later in the chapter.*

Exception Handling

Opening a recordset may not always succeed. If it fails, MFC will throw `CDBException`. For this reason you should place the `Open()` code within a `try/catch` block. The code in the `Music` example shows how to do this. For example, the code around the open recordset call in preparation for the retrieval of artists looks like this:

```
try
{
    pSetArtist->Open();
}
catch (CDBException* pEx)
{
    CString strMessage(_T("Could not retrieve list of artists"));
    AfxMessageBox(strMessage);
    pEx->Delete();
    return;
}
```

Note that our above example produces a very generic error message. If you like, you can pick apart information in the `CDBException` object to explain the specifics of the error to the user, or you can use the `ReportError()` member of the exception object to have the system generate an error message to give your users.

Around the `CDatabase::Open()` call, you have code which actually creates an error message with the string returned from the exception:

```
try
{
    m_MusicBase.Open(pApp->m_strDataSource, FALSE, FALSE, strConnect);
}
catch (CDBException* pEx)
{
    CString strMessage(_T("Could not open database: "));
    strMessage += pEx->m_strError;
    AfxMessageBox(strMessage);
    pEx->Delete();
    return FALSE;
}
```

Of course, the problem with this approach is that the error message from the database management software is probably more interesting to a database administrator than it is to a user.

You Look Fetching!

The purpose of a recordset is to return data to the client application. A `CRecordset` or `CDaoRecordset` object only actually holds data from one record of the result set in the database at a time. This record is the current record for the set; you can alter the context of the set, changing the current record and having the set retrieve the corresponding record from the result set for you.

There are lots of different ways to move through the recordset. For example, you can call `CRecordset::MoveNext()` or `CDaoRecordset::MoveNext()` to get the next record into the set. This function calls the appropriate ODBC or DAO APIs to grab the next record, the data from the row is returned to the member variables within the object, and you can then do anything you want with them. `MoveNext()` doesn't return anything; it simply moves the focus of the current record onto the next in the set, and it will throw an exception if there is a problem – such as moving past the end of the recordset.

It's not uncommon to rip through a recordset as fast as possible, processing each record in some manner. You can use the `IsEOF()` function against the recordset to see when you reach the end, as if you were reading a file line-by-line. A code fragment that pulls through each record in a set named `CMyRecordSet` is shown here:

```
CMyRecordSet recSet;
recSet.Open(/* ...some parameters... */);
while (!recSet.IsEOF())
{
    // Do something with the current record
    recSet.MoveNext();
}
```

You'll note that there's no need to call `MoveNext()` after the recordset is opened. As soon as it's open, the first record is implicitly made available to the set. If you want to see if *no* records were returned, `IsEOF()` would return `TRUE` immediately upon returning from `CRecordset::Open()`. The notion of having a current item be the first item after a search or query option is completed is common to most of the iterators in MFC.

If your data source supports it, you can also move backwards through the recordset using `MovePrev()`. This function moves the current record one record closer to the beginning of the set. It can fall off the beginning of the set if you go too far, but `IsBOF()` is provided as a test to avoid such an occurrence.

> Note that both `IsEOF()` and `IsBOF()` only work once you have gone *past* the last or first record in the set respectively. They don't show if the current record *is* the last record, or the first record.

You can jump to the beginning of the recordset by calling `MoveFirst()`, or jump to the last by calling `MoveLast()`. Coupling the idea of `MoveLast()` with `MovePrev()` allows you to move backwards through a recordset, using code like that shown next:

```
CMyRecordSet recSet;
recSet.Open(/* ...some parameters... */);
recSet.MoveLast();
while (!IsBOF(recSet))
{
    // Do something with the current record
    recSet.MovePrev();
}
```

> `MoveFirst()` and `MoveLast()` are expensive functions, and are not always supported by the database.

You can use the `Move()` function to scroll through a number of rows relative to the current position. You can use a negative number to go backwards from the current position, or a positive number to go forwards. So, you can get the ninth record in a set with these two calls:

```
recSet.MoveFirst();
recSet.Move(8);
```

Once there, you can jump ahead to the thirteenth record by using:

```
recSet.Move(4);
```

`Move()`, and all of its friends, like `MoveNext()`, causes calls to the `DoFieldExchange()` member of the record to initiate the data exchange required to populate the member variables with their new data.

None of this scrolling will work if the underlying driver doesn't support scrolling. Remember that you can request the connection to the database to use the ODBC cursor library, making up for any drivers which don't inherently support scrolling; this makes it an alternative worth considering.

You should also be aware that repeatedly scrolling or randomly jumping through your result set is a very costly operation. To save on resources, you should try to process your recordset in one go.

Bookmarks

ODBC and DAO allow your application to manage **bookmarks** within the recordset. Bookmarks allow you to jump back to an arbitrary record within the recordset at a moment's notice – assuming, of course, that the recordset and the underlying data source support random scrolling and bookmarks. You can test for bookmark support at runtime by calling `CRecordset::CanBookmark()`.

If you're using DAO, you can create a bookmark by calling the `CDaoRecordset::GetBookmark()`. This function returns an OLE `VARIANT` data type that you'll need to tuck away yourself before you can return to the bookmark. You can use a `COleVariant` object to hold the data. Nabbing a bookmark against a DAO recordset is simple:

```
COleVariant varMarker;
varMarker = recSet.GetBookmark();
```

If you're using ODBC, you can execute the same function name in your `CRecordset`-derived object, but the function will initialize a `CDBVariant` object for you:

```
CDBVariant varMarker;
recSet.GetBookmark(varMarker);
```

The `COleVariant` (or `CDBVariant`, in the case of ODBC) object holds the bookmark. In either case, that bookmark object indicates an exact cursor position within the recordset. If you're interested in returning the cursor to that position, you can do so by calling `CDaoRecordset::SetBookmark()` if you're using DAO, or `CRecordset::SetBookmark()` if you're using ODBC. The call scrolls the recordset to the place you had previously marked. Again, the code is simple. Assuming you have the `varMarker` from your call to `GetBookmark()`, you can just do this:

```
recSet.SetBookmark(varMarker);
```

While ODBC doesn't support the call, DAO additionally has `SetAbsolutePosition()` and `GetAbsolutePosition()` members to let you jump to a specific record number in the query. This is different from the `Move()` function, of course, because `Move()` is relative to the current record. You can also use `GetPercentPosition()` and `SetPercentPosition()` to move a percentage of the way through the complete recordset.

Remember that you need to call `DoFieldExchange()` after moving the record position, so MFC has a chance to populate the member variables for the fields in your object.

Changing Your Recordset

While your `CRecordset` or `CDaoRecordset` object is open, you can add new records, delete old ones, or even update current records that appear in the set. Note that these operations don't always work on every result set. For example, you can't delete records that have come back from a stored procedure, and some database systems won't let you delete or update rows that were returned from a SQL view. A view is a database object that can be the source of a SELECT statement, but actually gathers its data from at least one other underlying table using a SELECT statement of its own. If the SELECT statement used to create the view joins more than one table, the database management system might not be able to accept insertions into the view. The ability to perform operations other than SELECT upon a view is implementation-dependent.

You can use `Delete()` to delete the current record from the database. Once you've done that, you must call one of the `Move()` functions (i.e. `Move()` itself or any of its friends, like `MoveNext()`) to get to the next record that you wish to work with.

Adding and Editing a Record

You can call `AddNew()` to begin the process of adding a new record to your set. Simply call `AddNew()` against the recordset, setting the member variables of the `CRecordset` object as appropriate, before calling `Update()` to actually complete the operation. To add a new album to our database, you might write code like this:

```
// Assuming that CAlbumsSet is already connected and open...

setAlbum.AddNew();
setAlbum.m_Album_Name = _T("Question The Authority");
setAlbum.m_nArtistNumber = 315;
setAlbum.Update();
```

In a similar way to the AddNew() function, you can call Edit() to begin the process of changing a given record. After executing the AddNew() code, you might fix the album name with some code like this:

```
// Assuming that CAlbumsSet is already connected and open...
// and that the new record is the current record
setAlbum.Edit();
setAlbum.m_Album_Name = _T("Question The Answers");
// Don't need to change setArtist.m_nArtistNumber...
setAlbum.Update();
```

Note that your database might not let you change the key column in the table. This will not only depend on your database software, but also upon the particular type of index and integrity rules you have applied. If there is a problem with updating or adding a row, the problem won't make itself evident until you call Update(). If there is an error, Update() will throw an exception to bring the problem to your attention.

To check that you're allowed to perform a particular change against a given recordset, you can call CanAppend() or CanUpdate(). CanAppend() will return TRUE if you can add rows and FALSE if you can't. CanUpdate() returns TRUE if you can add, delete and update rows and FALSE if you can't.

Passing Parameters

All of the uses of CRecordset and CDaoRecordset that we've discussed up to this point have accepted a string for the query; we've implied that the easiest way to put together the string is to use a function like CString::Format() to build it. This can be a cumbersome approach if you have a number of parameters to bind, or if you don't know the parameters until the query is actually run.

For these situations, you can use bound parameters in your recordset by simply substituting a question mark for each field in your query that you can later replace. A query that is written in this way is said to be **parameterized**. You might want to find all zip codes in a certain range, for example; you can do this with a parameterized query like this one:

```
SELECT ZIPCode, City, State
    FROM ZIPCodes
    WHERE ZIPCode BETWEEN ? AND ?
```

When you create a CDaoRecordset or CRecordset for this query, you'll want to have member variables for the three output values from the query: the zip code, the name of the city and the name of the state. You'll also want to specify two range parameters: one for the low limit, and one for the high limit.

Since these parameters are part of the recordset, and you'll need some mechanism to copy the data from the variables to the query when the query is executed, MFC will need to know about them. You can notify MFC that you have a parameterized recordset by setting the m_nParams value of your CRecordset or CDaoRecordset object to the number of parameters you have. m_nParams is zero by default. If it is zero when MFC runs your DoFieldExchange() function, it will assume you have no parameters to be bound.

You should set m_nParams in your constructor and initialize the representative member variables to benign values, just as you do with the output bind targets in your constructor. A constructor to support this statement might look like something like this:

```
CZIPSet::CZIPSet(CDatabase* pdb)
    : CRecordset(pdb)
{
    //{{AFX_FIELD_INIT(CZIPSet)
    m_ZIPCode = _T("");
    m_State = _T("");
    m_City = _T("");
    m_nFields = 3;
    //}}AFX_FIELD_INIT
    m_nParams = 2;
    m_LowerBound = _T("");
    m_UpperBound = _T("");
}
```

Note how we used a string for the zip code to preserve the formatting of the data in the database. This way, you don't have to get an integer and pad it with zeros every time you want to print it.

You'll also need to modify your `DoFieldExchange()` function so that you can use the same `RFX_` functions as normal to transfer data from columns to your record variables. However, you'll have to tweak the `CFieldExchange` context so that MFC knows you're specifying a parameter and not an address for the output of a column in the query.

You can do this using the `SetFieldType()` member of the `CFieldExchange` object passed to your `DoFieldExchange()` function. `SetFieldType()` takes one of two constants: `CFieldExchange::outputColumn` or `CFieldExchange::param`.

`outputColumn` means that any subsequent calls to `RFX_` functions will specify information output columns, while `param` means that subsequent `RFX_` calls provide data to the parameters in your query. The setting is sticky — call it to set the mode of the exchange and then make your subsequent `RFX_` calls. A `DoFieldExchange()` function for the zip code example might look like this:

```
void CZIPSet::DoFieldExchange(CFieldExchange* pFX)
{
    //{{AFX_FIELD_MAP(CZIPSet)
    pFX->SetFieldType(CFieldExchange::outputColumn);
    RFX_Text(pFX, _T("ZIPCode"), m_ZIPCode);
    RFX_Text(pFX, _T("City"), m_City);
    RFX_Text(pFX, _T("State"), m_State);
    //}}AFX_FIELD_MAP

    pFX->SetFieldType(CFieldExchange::param);
    RFX_Text(pFX, _T("LowerBound"), m_LowerBound);
    RFX_Text(pFX, _T("UpperBound"), m_UpperBound);
}
```

DAO applications perform data exchange in exactly the same way, except they use a `CDaoFieldExchange` object to manage the exchange. Since the OLE-based data types which DAO uses are different than the simple, cardinal data types which ODBC uses, you'll also need to use different functions to actually effect the data exchange. The functions all have the same names but begin with `DFX_` instead of `RFX_`. You might want to review the section 'Record Field Exchange' that was presented earlier in this chapter to refresh your memory of the interesting types handled by the `RFX_` and `DFX_` functions.

Note that although the second parameter is a string, MFC doesn't even look at it when you call for `param` mode, so it doesn't matter what you pass – just as long as it isn't NULL. The parameters are resolved in the order they are received in the statement, and you must carefully check your `DoFieldExchange()` code to make sure that you have the RFX_ calls in exactly the right order when compared to your source statement.

Alas, ClassWizard doesn't provide any support for the creation of parameterized recordsets. You'll need to hack in the support yourself. Get out your machete and pump the code you need right into the constructor and `DoFieldExchange()` function. As usual, stand clear of the {{//-style comments that ClassWizard uses to mark its territory.

Dynamic Recordsets

All of the `CRecordset` and `CDaoRecordset` objects we've talked about are static, i.e. they all contain member variables for every column they'll retrieve, and hard code a `DoFieldExchange()` function which exchanges data between the record and the member variables.

There are some situations when you might wish you could dynamically bind columns to variables in your program. If you're writing applications (rather than utilities), these situations aren't too common. As you write an application, you'll almost always know what rows you can expect to receive in reply to your query. If you're writing a utility, however, like the general Microsoft Query tool or the ISQL/W tool for SQL Server, you'll be accepting SQL statements from the user, and you'll have no clue what information will be coming back from the database.

In my opinion, managing recordsets with dynamic columns is more trouble than it's worth. To deal with your query, you'll have to run out to the database and request a list of the *columns* returned, and then you'll need to find some way to handle the *rows* you're getting back dynamically.

`CDaoRecordset` and `CRecordset` are inherently static. If you need to do work like this, you're probably better off working at the level of the ODBC API, since all of the code you'll need to write will work directly with the API to retrieve the information about the query and the data types it will generate. The DYNABIND sample that ships with Visual C++ is a good example of using the data dictionary to dynamically create queries using `CRecordset`. The DAO and ODBC SDK provide all the information you'll need to implement such queries yourself.

Other DAO Classes

MFC implements a handful of interesting classes for DAO which don't mimic any of the classes that are available for ODBC. DAO enjoys more coverage simply because it is richer. While ODBC is just a fancy way to talk to a database, DAO is actually an additional layer of interesting programming value between your application and the database.

The most interesting things you can do with DAO include something I mentioned at the beginning of the chapter; performing data definition language commands against your database. Before we have a look at the way DAO can be used to change the schema of your database, let's examine the classes we could use to retrieve information about the schema of your database.

The first family of classes we'll be interested in are the DAO object information structures: `CDaoTableDefInfo`, `CDaoIndexFieldInfo`, `CDaoQueryDefInfo`, `CDaoParameterInfo`, `CDaoRelationFieldInfo`, `CDaoRelationInfo`, and `CDaoFieldInfo`. Note that despite their names, these are actually structures, not classes!

These structures all provide information about particular DAO objects. Looking at their names, you can guess what they can tell you: `CDaoTableDefInfo`, for example, tells you about the structure of a table, while `CDaoQueryDefInfo` tells you about the definition of a query. A query, in this context, means a database query object, i.e. a query that the user (or some application) has defined and given to a database to have and hold. If you've used Microsoft Access, you're certainly familiar with queries – they're a great way to define a commonly-used database request and have it stored right there within your Access database. Since DAO's roots are in the Jet engine used by Access, it's only natural that DAO also has support for this kind of query.

I'm not going to spell out the meaning of each of these structures – they're easy enough to find in the online help if you decide you need them – but I *do* need to make a few points about how they work. Fortunately, those points are applicable to all of the structure types.

First, you'll almost always be able to get some information from one database object about other database objects. For example, a database object has lots of information about other objects – tables and queries. If you ask the database to tell you about a particular table, you can also find out about fields in that table or indexes in that table. This means exactly what it sounds like – DAO has a class hierarchy all its own!

Second, there are sometimes, but not always, real live MFC *classes* that mimic these structures. Once you've connected your database object to a usable database, you can use the database object to request one of the information structures the database knows about, *or* you can attach a `CDaoTableDef` object to your `CDaoDatabase` object and open it against a particular table in your database. Here's a list of the different information classes and information structures available to you:

MFC Structure	MFC Class	Description
CDaoDatabaseInfo	CDaoDatabase	Database
CDaoFieldInfo	*(none)*	Column from a table or query
CDaoIndexFieldInfo	*(none)*	Column involved in an index
CDaoIndexInfo	*(none)*	Index
CDaoParameterInfo	*(none)*	Parameter
CDaoQueryDefInfo	CDaoQueryDef	Stored query definition
CDaoRelationFieldInfo	*(none)*	Column involved in a relationship
CDaoRelationInfo	*(none)*	Relationship
CDaoTableDefInfo	CDaoTableDef	Database table or table-like object (e.g. a view)
CDaoWorkspaceInfo	CDaoWorkspace	Workspace

You might be wondering why there are both structures and classes. The reason is simple – efficiency. The structures are useful, lightweight objects that can be retrieved from DAO at a moment's notice when you need to know something. Using the structures is your best bet when you're just browsing around the database looking for information. On the other hand, if you're really doing work with the underlying object, you should use the MFC class object. You can't do any actions against relationships or indexes, so MFC doesn't provide objects. On the other hand, you'll certainly want to ask the *database* to do something, so you'll very likely create a CDaoDatabase object instead of a CDaoDatabaseInfo structure. Some objects are a closer call. If you want to create a new table, you'll need to use a CDaoTableDef object. If you just want to retrieve information about an existing table, though, you can work with a CDaoTableDefInfo structure. In the real world, you'll probably find yourself using both structures and classes to get things done.

While it doesn't sound like much work to populate a structure, it *is* a great deal of work for *these* particular structures. MFC has to ask DAO for the information, and has to do so through an Automation interface to the underlying data access object. That means that MFC must make a dispatch call for each and every value which you need, crossing over into the system DAO code via the bridge that COM built. The most expensive aspect of this transaction is the type conversion; members of the structures are always normal C++ or MFC data types, while DAO is busy returning VARIANT data to MFC. To save you effort, MFC converts the data for you.

The third point is that the information retrieval functions come in different flavors. Again, for efficiency, you can ask MFC to get only a few of the more commonly used fields from DAO, or all of the fields in the whole darned structure. If we look at the declaration for CDaoTableInfo, we'll see comments that are associated with each element to tell us when the field is populated:

```
struct CDaoTableDefInfo
{
    CString      m_strName;            // Primary
    BOOL         m_bUpdatable;         // Primary
    long         m_lAttributes;        // Primary
    COleDateTime m_dateCreated;        // Secondary
    COleDateTime m_dateLastUpdated;    // Secondary
    CString      m_strSrcTableName;    // Secondary
    CString      m_strConnect;         // Secondary
    CString      m_strValidationRule;  // All
    CString      m_strValidationText;  // All
    long         m_lRecordCount;       // All
};
```

You don't need to pick through the header file for this information – it is, of course, echoed in the online help.

As you can imagine, the attributes, the name and the 'updatable' flag are pretty essential pieces of information describing a given table, so they're always retrieved. Validation rules are rarely interesting, so those aren't retrieved until you actually retrieve all of the structure. To populate a CDaoTableDefInfo structure, you can call the GetTableDefInfo() member function of CDaoDatabase, which looks like this:

```
void GetTableDefInfo(
                int               nIndex,
                CDaoTableDefInfo& tabledefinfo,
                DWORD             dwInfoOptions = AFX_DAO_PRIMARY_INFO);
```

The `nIndex` parameter identifies the table you're interested in. Table indexes start at zero and continue to the number returned by `CDaoDatabase::GetTableDefCount()`, but don't include the number returned by that function. If there are six tables, they're numbered 0, 1, 2, 3, 4 and 5.

The second parameter is a reference to the `CDaoTableDefInfo` structure you'd like to populate. The third parameter, which is optional, indicates the level of information you'd like to populate in your structure. The value `AFX_DAO_PRIMARY_INFO` is the default, as you can see. For more information, you could pass `AFX_DAO_SECONDARY_INFO` or `AFX_DAO_ALL_INFO`.

Let's unite everything we've discussed and write some code which will print out the names of all the columns in all the tables in our database. We'll just use the `TRACE()` macro to generate the output, but you could just as easily imagine it heading for a list box. We'll assume that this code gets going after the db object was opened:

```
// CDaoDatabase db; - someone else created and connected it
CDaoTableDef defTable(&db);

int nTables = db.GetTableDefCount();
int nTableIndex;

for (nTableIndex = 0; nTableIndex < nTables; nTableIndex++)
{
    CDaoTableDefInfo infoTable;
    db.GetTableDefInfo(nTableIndex, infoTable);
    defTable.Open(infoTable.m_strName);
    TRACE1("%s\n", (LPCTSTR)defTable.GetName());

    int nColumns = defTable.GetFieldCount();
    int nColIndex;
    CDaoFieldInfo infoField;

    for (nColIndex = 0; nColIndex < nColumns; nColIndex++)
    {
        defTable.GetFieldInfo(nColIndex, infoField);
        TRACE1("    %s\n", (LPCTSTR)infoField.m_strName);
    }
    defTable.Close();
}
```

The inner loop doesn't touch any real objects and just uses a `CDaoFieldInfo` structure to get the name of each column. The outer loop, though, which enumerates the tables, actually creates a `CDaoTableDef` object which it must use to get the `CDaoFieldInfo` structure populated. I wrote the code to get the table name from a call to `CDaoDatabase::GetTableDefInfo()` first, and then use that name in a call to the `Open()` member of the `CDaoTableDef` object. Once the inner loop has enumerated all of the columns, we have to be sure and close the table definition object with a call to `CDaoTableDef::Close()`.

DAO Objects and DDL Operations

The extra DAO structures and objects I've mentioned are extremely useful when you're interested in creating tables or other database objects. The `CDaoTableDef` object, for example, has a `Create()` member as well as an `Open()` member. `Create()` is, as you might suspect, used to build a new `CDaoTableDef` instead of opening an existing one. Once the new table definition object is created, you can start adding columns or other attributes to it. The columns to be added are described using the `CDaoFieldInfo` structure, and passed along to the `CreateField()` member of `CDaoTableDef`. There's an overload of `CreateField()` that takes the appropriate parameters if you don't have a `CDaoFieldInfo` structure handy.

So, again assuming that someone has created and connected our db object for us, we could write some code like this to add a table named Players with three columns: a number named PlayerID, a string named Name and another number named Jersey:

```
// CDaoDatabase db; — someone else created and connected it
CDaoTableDef defTable(&db);

defTable.Create(_T("Players"));
defTable.CreateField(_T("PlayerID"), dbLong, 0);
defTable.CreateField(_T("Name"), dbText, 60);
defTable.CreateField(_T("Jersey"), dbByte, 0);
defTable.Append();
```

You'll notice that the second parameter to CreateField() is a constant identifying the data type of the new column. The online help lists all of these just as well as I could. More importantly, though, the third parameter indicates the length you'd like to reserve for the column. For ordinal types, the length parameter is ignored. For dbText types, though, the width defines the maximum width of the entry in the database. Here, I've used sixty characters because I can't think of a hockey player with a name longer than that.

Once you've created all the fields you want, you can call CDaoTableDef::Append() to get them added to the database. This function is named Append() because DAO views the process of your creating a table as adding a table definition to the collection of table definitions in the database. You are, indeed, doing just that — the new table will be in the collection, so if you were to run the code fragment we had earlier that enumerated tables, you'd note that the GetTableDefCount() function returned a count one higher than it used to.

Opening Recordsets

I mentioned earlier that CDaoRecordset::Open() had a couple of extra overloads, which worked against objects that we hadn't yet covered. Well, we've just examined them! If you have a CDaoTableDef or a CDaoQueryDef, you can call an overload of CDaoRecordset::Open() which accepts a reference to one of those objects. DAO will assume you want to select all of the columns in the table or the query and use them.

Error Handling in DAO

The last example brings up one last point I'll need to make about DAO before I put a sock in it, and that (the point, not the sock) is error handling. All DAO functions end up throwing exceptions if they run into a problem. They usually throw a CDaoException, but they may end up throwing a CMemoryException too. You *must* bracket all of your calls to DAO member functions with try/catch blocks if you expect to make it in life.

When a DAO exception is thrown, you can assume that the database is in the same state it was *before* the operation failed. If the operation was opening the database, you don't need to close the database when an exception is thrown because the database is never opened. However, if you receive an exception when executing a query against an opened database, you'll still need to close the database — it was the query that failed and not the connection to the database.

What About AppWizard?

As you've been creating your applications, you've probably noticed the database option page in AppWizard. The dialog offers you several choices for the kind of database support that you want in your code.

AppWizard is designed to produce simple browsing applications that are centered on one recordset. If you choose to add a **D**atabase view without file support, or a **D**atabase view **w**ith file support, AppWizard will produce an application that has a `CRecordView` in its main window. As it creates the application, AppWizard will wire this view to the frame window and to a recordset that accesses the named data source.

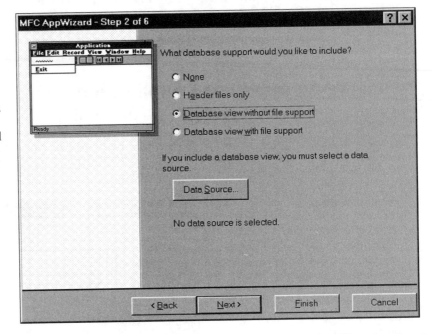

While some applications are designed to work with a single data set, most aren't. AppWizard makes it easy to create utility applications which maintain a single table or let the user browse through the records in a given database view or table. When you choose either **D**atabase view without file support or **D**atabase view **w**ith file support, AppWizard will produce such an application.

Depending on the architecture of your database application, you may or may not be interested in what AppWizard has to offer. For simple maintenance applications, AppWizard is an obvious choice, but if you want to create an application that doesn't have a view of the recordset in its main window, you have some decisions to make.

I usually write my database applications from scratch, starting with an AppWizard-produced application that is produced by selecting the None *or* Header files only *option. Since my applications don't often show any database information in their main windows, this makes sense, even though I do hook up my own code to log into the database.*

Whenever I need a `CRecordView` *in my application, I add it with the ClassWizard and hook it up manually. If you're at all nervous about how to get the* `CRecordView` *class wired into your application, you can start with AppWizard and work your way out, changing and adding the things that ClassWizard gave you in the new application.*

If you're having trouble, here are a few things to check:

> Obtain the ODBC database class prototypes and macros by using #include <afxdb.h> in your Stdafx.h file, or get the DAO prototypes by using #include <afxdao.h>. These headers include everything you need for the definitions of the database classes in MFC.

> Make sure that you're linking to Mfc42.lib, or a variant thereof, to get the MFC wrapper classes for ODBC or DAO.

Once you've created the application and arranged to get the correct headers and libraries into it, you can use ClassWizard to add CRecordset (or CDaoRecordset) classes wherever you see fit.

Tweaking an AppWizard Application

One of the most important things to remember about the database applications that you produce with AppWizard is that they're just a starting point. Of course, this is true of *every* application you produce with AppWizard, but it somehow seems like AppWizard database applications are fundamentally limited. This is because the application's architecture is so ingrained that it can seem impossible to change the features of the application.

When you use AppWizard to produce an application, you're allowed to select a data source from those installed when the application was first created. You'll see a message box like that in the figure here, with a list of all the data sources you've installed on your system:

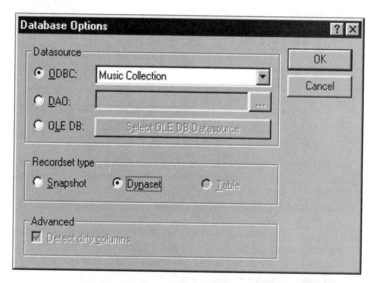

This dialog gives the first perception of the limitations of AppWizard-produced database applications – you can only connect a database application to one data source with the Wizard. After you select a data source in the dialog, AppWizard loads the driver and gathers any additional information it needs to connect to the data source. This information isn't stored in the application; it's used while AppWizard connects to the database to bring back a list of tables, like that shown here:

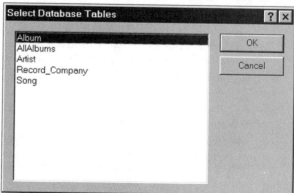

The Select Database Tables dialog won't be shown if your data source only supports one table — for example, if the driver for the selected data source reads text files. Once you select a table (or tables), AppWizard is ready to continue the creation of the application. It runs off to the database to examine the table you selected, brings back a list of columns in the table, and declares appropriate member variables in the CRecordset-derived or CDaoRecordset-derived class to store the information. If you select multiple tables, AppWizard will still collect the information, but will instead build a join that returns the Cartesian product of all the data in the tables. Unless you want that product, you'll want to edit the GetDefaultSQL() function provided by AppWizard to include a limiting WHERE clause, to perform a more reasonable join. AppWizard also uses the information it collects to implement data exchange with the record and the member information in the recordset's DoFieldExchange() function.

AppWizard only works this way to get you started. MFC applications are not limited to connecting to one data source, retrieving one table and using data sources which are only known at compile time. You can connect to any data source you need, and to as many as you require. If you'd like, you can add additional recordsets to your application using ClassWizard. When you ask ClassWizard to add a CRecordset- or CDaoRecordset-derived class, it will show you the same Database Options dialog and draw you through the process of selecting a database and objects within that data source to use in the new recordset.

MFC lets you use as many tables as you'd like, using any kind of SQL statement. You can prompt the user for a user name and password if it's needed, hard code a user name and password, or just let the driver do the talking when the application runs. You have very little control over the way the driver looks and acts, so this last approach isn't always very favorable.

When an AppWizard-based database application starts, it connects to the database during the OnInitialUpdate() of the CRecordView, which acts as the hub of the application. The CRecordset object that actually drives the query for the application is a member of the CDocument object in the application. The CRecordView object keeps a pointer to the same object, and it retrieves that pointer directly, since it is declared as a public member. The code, taken from the RecView sample, looks like this:

```
void CRecviewView::OnInitialUpdate()
{
    m_pSet = &GetDocument()->m_recviewSet;
    CRecordView::OnInitialUpdate();
}
```

As you know, the OnInitialUpdate() member of the CRecordView class will open the data source; it retrieves a pointer to the recordset by calling OnGetRecordset(). AppWizard also supplies an implementation of this function which simply returns the m_pSet variable from the CRecordView-derived class.

If you need to change the way this mechanism works, most of your attacks should be directed at the CRecordset-derived object that AppWizard created for you. AppWizard will create two functions that look like this:

```
CString CRecviewSet::GetDefaultConnect()
{
    return _T("ODBC;DSN=Music Collection");
}

CString CRecviewSet::GetDefaultSQL()
{
    return _T("dbo.Album");
}
```

The functions you'll actually get might be a bit different. Since you might have a different data source name, or might specify a username or password when accessing your data source, the string returned by GetDefaultContent() might be different. If you connect to a data source that scopes access to objects with the database name, you'll see that scoping in the string returned by GetDefaultSQL(). Otherwise, you'll see a command appropriate for the driver you're using.

You can change the way that AppWizard connects to a database by altering the connect string in GetDefaultConnect(). For this SQL Server database, you'll probably be interested in providing some username and password information for the connect string, which, by the way, could be dynamically created. You might pop up a dialog box that prompts the user for a username and password, and uses the strings that are returned from there.

The GetDefaultSQL() function returns the SQL statement to be executed, based on the table name which was specified when AppWizard built the program. ODBC accepts a shorthand syntax for simple SELECT statements; GetDefaultSQL() just returns the name of the table and ODBC will react as if you had sent the following statement:

```
SELECT * FROM dbo.Album
```

If you change the SELECT statement, you should be prepared to work with the record field exchange routine and member variables in the class. You'll also need to adjust the m_nFields setting in the constructor to make sure you tell MFC to expect the correct number of columns from the query. Back in the CRecordView-derived class, you might also need to change the dialog data exchange routine if you've altered the list of columns that were returned from the query.

The syntax I've used in these statements for the name of the table we're accessing, where the name of the table is separated from the name of the owner of the table by a dot, is specific to SQL Server. The ODBC driver for SQL Server knows what's going on, and passes all the necessary information along to the database. But if you sent that same SQL to another driver, the driver would most likely generate an error — you will not get away with using it against, say, an Access database.

What Are CRecordViews?

Most applications that deal with a database exist simply to provide a front end for manipulating records in that database. These applications invariably provide a user interface that resembles a form, and often that form is drawn on the screen to mimic exactly the paper form used before the database system and its supporting applications were created. For instance, a claims-processing application might present a user interface that resembles the paper claim form the insurance company uses. The technique of replicating the form on-screen makes the application very approachable for its users and relieves the application developer from working out a new layout for the form.

Applications that have this kind of user interface can use the CRecordView class from the Microsoft Foundation Classes. CRecordView is very much like CFormView, which we discussed in Chapter 4, but it's specifically designed to work with database recordsets. Above and beyond the capabilities of CFormView, CRecordView provides a mechanism to perform data exchange between a record in a database and the contents of the fields in the view. CRecordView is a subclass of CFormView that adds some extra code to handle data transfer from records.

The RecView sample application implements such a view. It runs off to the database to show a list of albums to the user, allowing them to scroll through the list and view what's available. The CRecordView object is created by the document template; since CRecordView is a child of CView, it is registered in the document template during CRecviewApp::InitInstance(), like this:

```
CSingleDocTemplate* pDocTemplate;
pDocTemplate = new CSingleDocTemplate(
    IDR_MAINFRAME,
    RUNTIME_CLASS(CRecviewDoc),
    RUNTIME_CLASS(CMainFrame),        // main SDI frame window
    RUNTIME_CLASS(CRecviewView));
AddDocTemplate(pDocTemplate);
```

In your application, you'll need to hook your CRecordView to a template of your own choosing for the view most appropriate to your application. The document/view relationship between a CRecordView and its supporting CDocument is normally very weak. The use of a CDocTemplate-derived class to let MFC know about your document/view relationship is something that we investigated back in Chapter 4.

In AppWizard-generated applications, you'll find that the view just uses the document as a convenient place to store a pointer to the opened recordset that is driving the view. The recordset is never persistent, i.e. you'll never want to save the CRecordset object to disk when the user saves a file. Of course, you might want to save information about the query or record currently being viewed, but even this exercise is rare.

The CRecordView's Dialog

If you create an application with AppWizard that has a CRecordView, AppWizard will generate an empty dialog box template for you. You'll need to lay out controls on the blank dialog template as you see fit, before hooking up the dialog data exchange to the recordset in the view.

If you're working on an application that you're already begun outside of AppWizard, or you want to add another CRecordView to any application, you should start by drawing your dialog first. Next, use ClassWizard to add a CRecordView object to your application, specifying the created template to ClassWizard so that it can correctly build a constructor for your CRecordView-derived class that will display the appropriate dialog box template.

To make the dialog display information from the CRecordset, you can have the dialog data exchange routine use m_pSet, the member added to the derivative of the CRecordView which points to the recordset driving the view. Your DoDataExchange() function might then look like this:

```
void CRecviewView::DoDataExchange(CDataExchange* pDX)
{
    CRecordView::DoDataExchange(pDX);
    //{{AFX_DATA_MAP(CRecviewView)
    DDX_FieldText(pDX, IDC_ALBUM, m_pSet->m_Album_Name, m_pSet);
    DDX_FieldText(pDX, IDC_ARTIST, m_pSet->m_Artist_Name, m_pSet);
    DDX_FieldText(pDX, IDC_CATALOGCODE, m_pSet->m_Catalog_Code, m_pSet);
    DDX_FieldText(pDX, IDC_RECORDCO, m_pSet->m_Record_Co_Name, m_pSet);
    //}}AFX_DATA_MAP
}
```

Notice the use of the **DDX_FieldText()** routine in lieu of the normal **DDX_** functions. **DDX_FieldText()** differs from the normal data exchange functions in that it knows how to set fields in the recordset to be a true database null value when the associated control is empty. If your database model requires that you provide an empty string for certain columns instead of an actual database null, you should avoid using the **DDX_FieldText()** function.

You can test for null in a given field by directly calling IsFieldNull() against the recordset. The IsFieldNull() function takes a pointer to the member you want to test; you can call it as we've shown in the following code fragment:

```
if (IsFieldNull(&m_Artist_Number))
{
    // It's null; do something!
}
```

You can use IsFieldNull() to see if *any* fields in the current record of a CRecordset object are null by passing NULL as the parameter to the function. If you need to set a field to null, you can use the CRecordset::SetFieldNull() function. It also takes a pointer to the member variable representing the field in the CRecordset's member data and will set that member to be a database null.

Applications that feature a CRecordView have an interesting user interface. They have a different menu, and a toolbar that allows the user to jump to the very beginning of the recordset, or to the very end. You can see this user interface in the following figure:

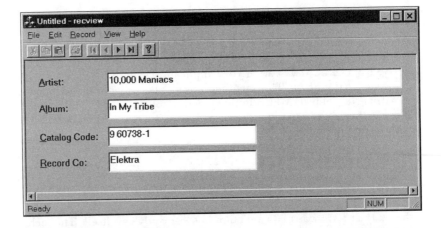

The user can use the arrow buttons on the toolbar or commands in the Record menu (shown here) to move from record to record, or to jump to the first or last record in the set:

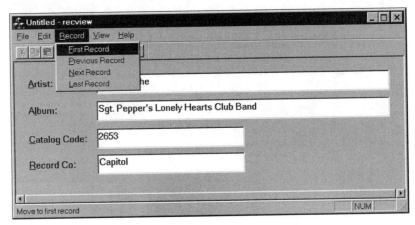

The CRecordView will disable the buttons and menu commands as appropriate. If it is at the end of the recordset, it will disable the forward button and menu command, while if at the beginning, it will disable the backward button and menu command.

When the user moves from record to record, the CRecordView::OnMove() function is called. The MFC implementation of this function writes out any changes that the user might have made to the data in the record. Once that is done, the function moves to the requested record and refreshes the data in both the view and the dialog by calling UpdateData().

Opening the Associated Recordset

While the code in CFormView handles the creation and display of the dialog box, the extra code that is added in CRecordView handles the initialization and connection of the data source. The class you derive from CRecordView in your application should provide a function called OnGetRecordset(). This member doesn't take any parameters, and returns a pointer to a CRecordset object. MFC's implementation of OnInitialUpdate() will call this function to retrieve the recordset, and if the recordset isn't already open, it will open the recordset using Open() without any parameters.

If you don't implement a GetDefaultSQL() override in your CRecordset, you'll want to make sure that your recordset is open before the OnInitialUpdate() routine is called, otherwise your recordset won't open correctly and will probably throw an assertion. You might open your own recordset by overriding OnInitialUpdate() in your CRecordView-derived class, before calling the OnInitialUpdate() function in CRecordView itself. The technique should look something like this:

```
void CRecviewView::OnInitialUpdate()
{
    m_pSet = &GetDocument()->m_recviewSet;
    m_pSet->Open(CRecordset::snapshot,
        "SELECT Artist_Name, Album_Name, Catalog_Code "
        "   FROM Artist, Album "
        "   WHERE Artist.Artist_Number = Album.Artist_Number"
        "   AND Album.Record_Co_Number = 35");
    CRecordView::OnInitialUpdate();
}
```

I used CRecordset::snapshot because the recordset that is provided must support scrolling in order for the view to function correctly, otherwise the user won't be able to scroll forward and backward through the result set.

If you build your application with a CRecordView using AppWizard, it will have provided a GetDefaultSQL() implementation for you, and you won't need to worry about making sure the CRecordset object for the view is open before OnInitialUpdate() runs. The CRecordView code will not Close() the recordset until just before the recordset window itself closes.

COleDBRecordView

Visual C++ 6.0 comes with a new class to support the viewing and manipulation of data made available through an OLE DB provider. It is very much like `CRecordView` except it allows you to specify an OLE DB provider as a data source. The MFC AppWizard walks you through generating an application that uses `COleDBRecordView`, and then generates ATL code for data access. This ATL code is based on the OLE DB consumer templates. Because all the code is generated for you by the wizard, you can use it without having to first learn all the technical nitty-gritty of OLE DB consumer templates.

> *If you do want to learn about these templates, you can refer to any good ATL book, like those listed at the beginning of this chapter. All cover OLE DB in far more detail that we are able to in this chapter.*

Lets see how you use `COleDBRecordView` to create a simple MFC based application that scrolls through the records in a table.

Creating the Shell

Start a new project using the MFC AppWizard. To keep things nice and simple create an SDI application with document/view architecture support. So in Step 1, select the Single Document option just like we have done before.

In Step 2, things get more interesting, as it is here that we specify that we want database support. The options available to you have already been discussed back in Chapter 2. For this example you can either choose Database view without file support or Database view with file support – either will do. The main difference between the two is that the latter supports serialization.

Note that the Data Source... button springs to life and we press it to get this dialog:

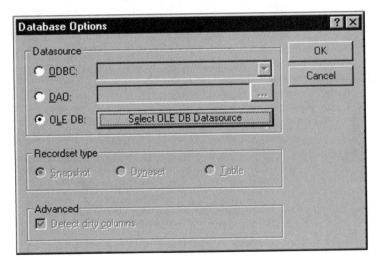

Then choose OLE DB as the data source and then click on the button to select an OLE DB provider from the list:

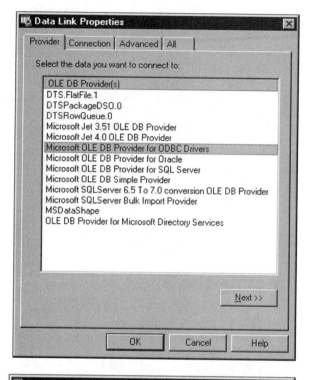

For this example I am going to use the OLE DB Provider for ODBC. I am going to allow you to have anther look through my music collection – well, not all of it, as it only included artists with names beginning with A to D and a few E's. Seeing as we already have our ODBC connection to my Music.mdb database, we shall take advantage of this. So press Next>> and either type in "Music Collection", in the Use data source name box as illustrated here:

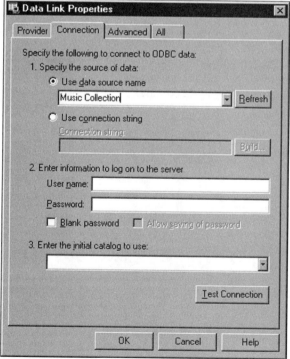

or select it from the list of available ODBC connections from the drop-down box. Note that in the lower right corner of this dialog box is an irresistible little button called <u>T</u>est Connection, which might as well have been called "Press Me". If you do, Windows checks to see if the ODBC connection indeed works, and in confirmation, this little box pops up:

This means that, as far as the data access part of our operation is concerned, we are up and running; the OLE DB provider to ODBC connection to Access data source line of communication is in order – we are ready to go.

However, there is still one more thing to do before AppWizard will allow us to continue; we have to specify which data we want from the data source, the final link in the chain. Press OK twice and you will get this new screen:

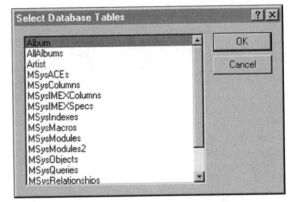

Note that there is a long list of options available to you to choose from. Don't worry about all the entries beginning with MSys – they don't really concern us. We are going to choose the very first option – the Album table of my music database, which will display the album title, its catalog number and other information. Press OK and you will be passed back to AppWizard. After all that work, we are still on Step 2! However we don't want to specify anything else out of the ordinary so we can skip the remaining steps and accept the default AppWizard settings by pressing Finish.

Explanation of OLE DB Consumer Code

You may notice that the creating of the project takes a little longer than usual – AppWizard is calling up the ATL libraries as well as the MFC ones to create this project. Now in Visual studio, you can expand the trees in FileView to see what we have got. Note that you have application, document and view header and source files as usual. However there are a couple of new files that deserve a little more attention.

If you named your project OLEDBSample, you will see a file called OLEDBSampleSet.h. This is where AppWizard wrote the code for your OLE DB consumer template classes. Open it up and you'll see some weird looking code, which we'll look at very shortly. Note that there is also a OLEDBSampleSet.cpp file but it doesn't do anything except include some header files. In the header file there will be a class declared and implemented called COLEDBSampleSet. It derives from CAccessor which is the OLE DB consumer template that is responsible for picking your rowset (the OLE DB term for recordset) from the data source:

```
class COLEDBSampleSet : public CCommand<CAccessor<CAlbum> >
```

Note that we have two class templates, CCommand<> and CAccessor<>, one nested inside the other. This is a common feature of ATL which may be unfamiliar to you as an MFC programmer.

The COLEDBSampleSet class's job is to bind a C++ class to the data source. As you can see, the class that is bound is CAlbum. AppWizard automatically created this class, naming it by just prefixing C to the name of the database table – clever stuff eh? It also created the definition of the class which looked up the table schema and generated member variables that correspond to each field.

```
class CAlbum
{
public:
    CAlbum()
    {
        memset( (void*)this, 0, sizeof(*this) );
    };

    int m_Album_Number;
    int m_Artist_Number;
    char m_Album_Name[193];
    int m_Record_Co_Number;
    char m_Catalog_Code[33];
    char m_Media_Type[33];
    BOOL m_Printed;

BEGIN_COLUMN_MAP(CAlbum)
    COLUMN_ENTRY_TYPE(1, DBTYPE_I4, m_Album_Number)
    COLUMN_ENTRY_TYPE(2, DBTYPE_I4, m_Artist_Number)
    COLUMN_ENTRY_TYPE(3, DBTYPE_STR, m_Album_Name)
    COLUMN_ENTRY_TYPE(4, DBTYPE_I4, m_Record_Co_Number)
    COLUMN_ENTRY_TYPE(5, DBTYPE_STR, m_Catalog_Code)
    COLUMN_ENTRY_TYPE(6, DBTYPE_STR, m_Media_Type)
    COLUMN_ENTRY_TYPE(7, DBTYPE_BOOL, m_Printed)
END_COLUMN_MAP()
};
```

Note how the wizard first assigns basic types to each of the fields mapped from the database, and then inserts them one at a time into a **column map**. This is where the actual data retrieved from the database is bound to the member variables. The COLUMN_ENTRY_TYPE() macro has the column number of the Access database table as its first parameter, and the member variable to contain the data from that column as its third parameter. The second parameter is a large enumeration that is used internally by OLE DB to convert the basic C++ data type supplied by AppWizard to something that OLE DB can work with. The types themselves are nothing fancy: DBTYPE_I4 specifies a 4-byte LONG integer; DBTYPE_STR a NULL-terminated ANSI string, and DBTYPE_BOOL is nothing more than a common or garden Boolean.

If you don't need all the fields, you should remove them from this class – from the place where they are initialized and the corresponding entry from the column map.

The other section of code generated in this file is the COLEDBSampleSet class itself. It contains but one method, Open(), which carries out all the dirty work of opening the connection and getting the data. Two OLE DB objects, instances of the ATL CDataSource and CSession classes, are necessary for this data access operation to work. Many of us drive cars and motorbikes, or both, but unless you really take time to poke around under the hood with the manual in your hand, you are not going to know that much about how the engine works and how each constituent part interrelates. It's the same with our OLE DB objects; trust me – these objects work.

```
HRESULT Open()
{
    CDataSource  db;
    CSession     session;
    HRESULT      hr;

    CDBPropSet   dbinit(DBPROPSET_DBINIT);
    dbinit.AddProperty(DBPROP_AUTH_PERSIST_SENSITIVE_AUTHINFO, false);
    dbinit.AddProperty(DBPROP_INIT_DATASOURCE, "Music Collection");
    dbinit.AddProperty(DBPROP_INIT_PROMPT, (short)4);
    dbinit.AddProperty(DBPROP_INIT_LCID, (long)2057);

    hr = db.OpenWithServiceComponents("MSDASQL.1", &dbinit);
    if (FAILED(hr))
        return hr;

    hr = session.Open(db);
    if (FAILED(hr))
        return hr;
```

Two CDBPropset objects are also created; the first, dbinit, is an array of properties passed as the second parameter to the OpenWithServiceComponents() method. Note that one of these properties specifies the data source: "Music Collection". Note also, in typical COM fashion, how we always test each operation for success or failure, passing the outcome to the HRESULT variable. For this data access operation to work, hr has to contain the value S_OK.

The second `CDBPropset` object, `propset`, contains an array of properties that determine how the rowset can be manipulated. The default, Wizard-generated properties allow forward and backward scrolling, and the ability to insert, delete and modify records:

```
CDBPropSet propset(DBPROPSET_ROWSET);
    propset.AddProperty(DBPROP_CANFETCHBACKWARDS, true);
    propset.AddProperty(DBPROP_IRowsetScroll, true);
    propset.AddProperty(DBPROP_IRowsetChange, true);
    propset.AddProperty(DBPROP_UPDATABILITY, DBPROPVAL_UP_CHANGE |
                            DBPROPVAL_UP_INSERT | DBPROPVAL_UP_DELETE );
```

The following function call is where the OLE DB consumer does the bulk of its work. This `Open()` method contains the SQL statement to obtain the data as its second parameter. The statement was inserted, based on your choice of database table back in AppWizard. Therefore, if you want to modify what is returned, you would do so here:

```
hr = CCommand<CAccessor<CAlbum> >::Open(session, "SELECT * FROM Album", &propset);
```

Alternatively, you can use the `DEFINE_COMMAND()` macro which immediately follows the column map in the `CAlbum` accessor class:

```
DEFINE_COMMAND(CAlbum, "SELECT * FROM Album")
```

If you use this macro, you would pass `NULL` as the second parameter in the `Open()` method above:

```
hr = CCommand<CAccessor<CAlbum> >::Open(session, NULL, &propset);
```

After assessing the success or otherwise of this operation, `COLEDBSampleSet::Open()` finishes by selecting the first entry in the returned rowset, with a call to `MoveNext()`.

Linking In To MFC

This class, `COleDBSampleSet` is hooked into the standard document/view architecture through the MFC-derived document class. You will notice in the document header file there is a member variable which is an instance of `COleDBSampleSet`.

```
class COLEDBSampleDoc : public CDocument
{
protected: // create from serialization only
    COLEDBSampleDoc();
    DECLARE_DYNCREATE(COLEDBSampleDoc)

// Attributes
public:
    COLEDBSampleSet m_oLEDBSampleSet;
```

The view class grabs a pointer to `COLEDBSampleSet` in its `OnInitialUpdate` method:

```
void COLEDBSampleView::OnInitialUpdate()
{
    m_pSet = &GetDocument()->m_oLEDBSampleSet;
```

You may also note that your view class is derived from `COleDBRecordView`:

```
class COLEDBSampleView : public COleDBRecordView
```

You didn't specify this – the Wizard did. Indeed all the code presented in this section has been Wizard-generated. However, your program won't show you anything. Run this code and you will get the rowset from the Music Collection, nicely stored in your `m_oLEDBSampleSet` member, but it will be completely invisible to you. You have to hook the data up to some controls on in your view class.

Populating the Form

Add a few fields to the blank resource form using the resource editor. You will probably want to include data such as "Album title" and "Catalog number", or "Artist ID", though the latter won't mean much to you unless you have a separate table with the IDs matching the artists themselves. You're the boss; how you build your resource dialog is up to you! Make sure you give the resource IDs meaningful names, though, like `ID_ALBUM_NAME` and `ID_CATALOG_NUMBER`, for example.

Now it gets fun; we have to connect the data to these controls.

Do Data Exchange

Normally you would be able to use ClassWizard to generate member variables for any of the controls on your form. However, in this case the variables already exist in the `CAlbum` class. Therefore you have to insert the `DDX_` macros by hand:

```
void COLEDBSampleView::DoDataExchange(CDataExchange* pDX)
{
    COleDBRecordView::DoDataExchange(pDX);
    //{{AFX_DATA_MAP(COLEDBSampleView)
        // NOTE: the ClassWizard will add DDX and DDV calls here
    //}}AFX_DATA_MAP

    DDX_Text(pDX, IDC_ALBUM_NAME, m_pSet->m_Album_Name, 193);
    DDX_Text(pDX, IDC_ALBUM_ID, m_pSet->m_Album_Number);
    DDX_Text(pDX, IDC_ARTIST_ID, m_pSet->m_Artist_Number);
    DDX_Text(pDX, IDC_RCODE, m_pSet->m_Record_Co_Number);
    DDX_Text(pDX, IDC_CATALOG_NUMBER, m_pSet->m_Catalog_Code, 33);
    DDX_Text(pDX, IDC_MEDIA, m_pSet->m_Media_Type, 33);
    DDX_Text(pDX, IDC_PRINT, m_pSet->m_Printed);
}
```

I recommend you put the DDX_ macros outside of the AFX_DATA_MAP macros otherwise ClassWizard will complain the data mappings are not valid; I have said before that anything between //{{ comments is jealously guarded by ClassWizard. You can, if you want, put DDV_ macros here as well if you wish to validate data the user enters. For example, it would be a good idea to limit the size of character strings that can be entered into the edit boxes; to do this you would use the DDV_MaxChars() macro:

```
DDX_Text(pDX, IDC_ALBUM_NAME, m_pSet->m_Album_Name, 193);
DDV_MaxChars(pDX, m_pSet->m_Album_Name, 193);
```

Now you can compile and run the program! You should see something like the following:

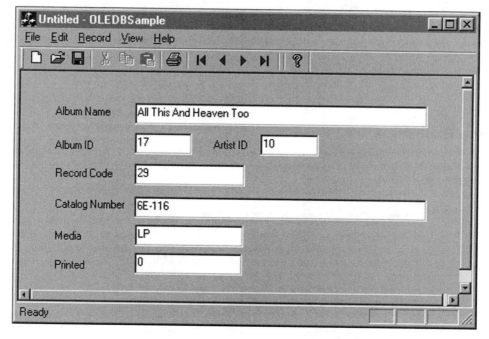

AppWizard generates menu items and buttons to navigate through the record set. Note that the code to implement the scrolling is buried deep within OLE DB and does not show up in ClassView. MFC assumes that all you want to do is move backwards and forwards through the rowset, or select the first or last records. If you want to do more fancy work, such as selecting a particular record or implementing a Search facility, you have to do that yourself.

By default AppWizard set properties in the propset array that allow the manipulation of the rowset itself; to change entries and then update the database itself. However no code is generated to achieve this, so if you want to go further and modify data, add or delete records, that code has to be added yourself.

Database Applications and Control Data

You might remember the GetItemData() and SetItemData() calls which we mentioned when we talked about dialog controls in Chapter 5. These functions, which exist in both the CListBox and CComboBox classes, allow you to associate a DWORD-sized value with entries in list and combo boxes, respectively. You can set this value with SetItemData(), and then use GetItemData() to retrieve the information. We have seen that the advanced common controls that are made available in Windows 95/98 also have similar functionality.

One of my favorite tricks is to use this data to carry extra information about items in the list box, and it proves to be an almost essential technique when working with databases. For example, your database might manage a list of hockey players, and the table that carries that information is probably organized so that it has three columns. The first column is a unique integer that acts as the key for the table, uniquely identifying each player numerically. The other two columns would then be used to hold each player's first name and surname.

When you present this information to the user, you'll only want to provide the name; the system-assigned player ID number is probably of little or no concern to the user. Unfortunately, the problem is that when the user selects a given player in the list box, the application will probably need the system-assigned player ID number to go off and work with any other tables in the database. Instead of requerying the players table to find the ID, it's far easier to tuck the key value for the player into the item data for the player's entry in the list box while populating the box.

When the user makes a selection from the box, call GetItemData() against the selected element and you'll have the data you need to work with the selected player throughout the rest of the database. In the Music sample, I use this technique for all of the combo box items. Code to do the population is quite simple:

```
while (!pSetAlbum->IsEOF())
{
    nAdded = pAlbumBox->AddString(pSetAlbum->m_Album_Name);
    if (nAdded != CB_ERR)
    {
        CRecord* pNewOne = new CRecord(pSetAlbum);
        pAlbumBox->SetItemDataPtr(nAdded, pNewOne);
    }
    else
        break;
    pSetAlbum->MoveNext();
}
```

If you have more than a DWORD's worth of data to store, consider building a structure or a simple class to hold all of your information, as I'm doing above using CRecord. Before you add the element to the list box, allocate that structure and populate it with the information you need, before calling SetItemData() and passing the pointer to that structure. Each element of the list box should have such a structure floating around in memory, which you'll have to clean up before the list box is destroyed.

However, at any time during the life of the list box, you can call `GetItemData()` to find that pointer and use it as you see fit. Of course, this information is completely invisible to the user, as they never see the extra item data.

When writing a database application, it's an interesting approach to store the primary key for a given record as the item data in a list box or combo box. Then, you're free to use the string in the combo box as the human-readable identification for the name of the item. When the user selects the item, you can nab the item data and use it in a subsequent query without first searching on the value that the user selected.

Notes About Performance Tuning

While computers have helped us to store and organize, search for, summarize and retrieve information faster than we could ever have hoped to do manually, most people are still not satisfied with the performance of their database applications.

Database management software faces an incredible challenge; to arbitrarily accept some data definition and begin storing data into it, allowing the user to arbitrarily retrieve that data based on a complicated set of rules. Such a general approach rarely results in an efficient solution.

If you had the time, you could sit around and code your own routines for storing the records you needed in your very own file format. Of course, if someone came along and said that you needed to store nine-digit zip codes instead of the five-digit variations, your hard work would be almost completely for nothing. You would have to reexamine all of your routines, and might be forced to change your file format completely.

You'll find that tuning your database is, in large part, about learning to find a comfortable compromise between hard-coding features and data structures, and leaving everything in your database up to the application, the user or the database management system. The classic tradeoff between speed and flexibility, evident throughout computer science, is no less relevant when applied to database programming.

With the pieces of the tuning puzzle that are under your control, you can manage several things that can help performance. What you are able to do will doubtless depend on millions of other parameters within your organization, ranging from minimum hardware specifications and network topology to senseless political issues and budget allocations.

The one parameter of database access that you should be able to understand, if not control, is the access pattern. Even within a given application, you'll sometimes go after data in your database and expect only one row in return, while other times you'll make a query against some data and expect tens of thousands of well-ordered rows to be available.

One-off queries are usually employed to validate some data the program has received from the user:

Is a city called 'Seattle' really in a state called 'Washington'?

or to test for the existence of some condition:

Does the account number 351435 actually have a floating balance payback interest accrual plan?

On the other hand, browsing queries are usually wide-open requests for information that offer the user a selection of choices:

Show me all accounts and let me select the one I like.
Help me find someone in Seattle with a name like 'Blasz-something'.
Which albums were produced by Alice Cooper?

Even when they are performed in a loop, one-off queries are usually slowed more by the act of communicating the request to the database server software than by any other bottleneck. Although it's certainly possible to write a terribly complicated SQL statement that takes days to execute and only returns one row, those cases should be relatively infrequent.

One-off queries rely on communications more than they rely on the speed of the back-end server. Even though you're only expecting one row, you're going through all of the overhead of sending the statement, allowing the back end to execute it and then letting it return the results to you. If the back-end database is right on your machine, this isn't a huge overhead, but it can still be quite considerable. If the back-end database is actually a database server located someplace away on a network, you're in trouble – the network transmission time alone can be monstrous!

On the other hand, database queries which allow the user to browse through many more rows are more often hampered by the ability of the database server to access all of the information referenced by the query first, before shipping it off to the client. If the database is a server, the running query has to compete with other users for a chance to access the data. The data is shipped off to the client, where it is compiled and held locally in some form of temporary storage to make it more efficient for the client to page back and forth over the result set. Compared to the transmission time, the time required to develop the result set and build the temporary database is very large.

While this certainly isn't a book on database programming, I think it's important to understand the issues affecting database performance, paying particular attention to how they affect the way an application based on MFC and ODBC works. Let's take a look at some different ways to make your applications work faster.

Tuning Your Database Machine

Depending on what kind of database server software you're using, you should carefully analyze the configuration and setup of your database server machine. Most database vendors can provide configuration guides that let you know how much memory each user connection and running query will take. If you can estimate how many processes will be connected to your system at any one time, and then multiply that by the vendor's numbers, you will be well on your way to estimating the amount of memory your server will need.

For example, Microsoft SQL Server for Windows NT takes about 50Kb per connection, plus memory for the operating system. If you assume that you'll have 100 users, you should make sure your machine has 5Mb of memory just for user connection context information! This memory is above and beyond the SQL Server cache space, and certainly doesn't include the minimum of 24 megabytes of RAM that NT Server needs.

If you're running your application against a local database, there isn't much you can do to improve performance, besides adding enough memory for all processes (and cache space) to co-exist peacefully. Make sure that you don't allocate so much disk cache space that you end up forcing the system to page memory around just to keep the application running.

If your server is a monster and you're planning on allowing dozens of users to connect to it, you should consider putting the machine on the network twice. You should consider installing two network cards so the machine can concurrently execute different network I/O requests to different legs of the network. Since, from the server's perspective, the ability to communicate with the network can be a big bottleneck, having more than one card will significantly improve your server's efficiency by increasing its ability to broadcast data over the net.

Tuning Your Database

Database application programmers face huge challenges, especially as computers are supposed to be so good at managing information. Most database applications are charged with immense information management and retrieval tasks.

Imagine the database system at your favorite credit card company. If the processing center takes care of three million accounts, it will have one table with three million records in it just to manage information about every cardholder. This table probably has the cardholder's address, name and account number.

If you estimate that each of those three million cardholders purchases an average of six things a month with their credit cards, we've already reached eighteen million database transactions per month. Actually, there are probably a lot more; the charge has to be approved before it is actually entered, and all of the reporting work that happens also has to be factored in. Interest needs to be charged and payments need to be processed as well. That's six million more transactions. New accounts need to be added, disputes need to be adjusted and cards need to be terminated.

By performing the math on these (very sketchy!) figures, you can imagine that their computer needs to process between ten and twelve transactions per second every day of the year. The number is considerably higher if you allow for the time the machine needs to be down for maintenance and backups! We could probably generalize that, if it takes more than a tenth of a second for this machine to find the basic card holder record in the accounts table, the system will quickly grind to a halt as transactions arrive faster than they can possibly be handled.

In this kind of system, an incredible amount of thought and planning goes into performance tuning. So much, in fact, that the database probably isn't even implemented on a generic SQL-oriented database management system. However, for the sake of argument, let's assume that the company has decided to use some mainframe SQL database implementation.

The `Accounts` table in this system will be accessed in several different ways. Easily the most common query against it will be by account number; almost every transaction handled by a machine will hit the account table to get something done. Undoubtedly, the `AccountNumber` of the `Accounts` table must be indexed, and it might be worthwhile to index the `Name` fields of the table too, even though comparatively few transactions will be initiated using the cardholder's name without their account number.

Each access path, as used in business transactions that the database needs to support, should be given this same type of careful examination. If the data is frequently searched, it should be indexed. If indexing the data helps the machine resolve joins or lookups, it is imperative that the machine should have the tools necessary to make the retrieval occur as quickly as possible. On the other hand, it's possible to have so many indexes that frequent updates or inserts force too many index updates and therefore become too expensive to use.

Most high-end database platforms, like Gupta's SQLBase, Oracle's System 7 and Microsoft's SQL Server, provide some way to examine the plan of execution that the database management system has chosen for the query at hand. You should examine the critical queries that your system uses and make sure that your application will run with reasonable execution plans in time-critical situations.

However, perhaps more importantly, the database itself needs to be logically arranged. Which tables will hold what information? In designing all but the simplest databases, you'll need to do a great deal of analysis to make sure the design of your database isn't laden with inherent inefficiencies. Here are some simple dos and don'ts:

> Don't store the same piece of information in more than one place

You can't update things efficiently if they're stored in too many places; if the balance of a credit card account is stored in six different places throughout the database, it will necessitate six updates to reset the balance. Worse yet, such a design causes a referential integrity problem. Setting the balance in only five places means that the balance is off in one place; how can a program know which balance is correct if some don't match?

> Store reference tables for all values

It is imperative that an application should be able to edit the information stored in it. Doing this by using `SELECT DISTINCT` on existing data is risky and slow. If you have a table from which you can do a simple `SELECT` to test for validity, you'll save an immense amount of time by performing edits and by coding other queries, particularly queries to drive reports.

> Work the server

If your server supports some operation, let the server do it. Transmitting data to the client, having the client perform the operation and having it react to that operation is a very expensive round-trip ticket. If you can have the server do work with data that it already has, your application will always be faster.

The only limit to this recommendation is that you may eventually give the server so much work to do that it is forced to ignore requests from other users. Don't select all of the data and allow the client machine to compute summary information; have the server do it. At the other extreme, don't send the server a request to add two integers together when the client machine is perfectly capable of doing it.

> ➤ Cache what you can

On the other hand, if the client machine owns some data and has everything it needs to process that data, then let it do so! There's nothing wrong with the client machine validating an entry against a list of states; this list isn't likely to change, and there's nothing wrong with coding it right into your program.

Frequently asking the database to do work that the client could easily accommodate clogs the network and pesters the server when it has a stack of other work to do. You might take this technique to the point where your application, at startup, retrieves some validation lists from the server and keeps them on the client to avoid using the server to do validation.

This is probably the line where the benefit of caching starts limiting return for the investment; if you keep lists locally, you'll either have to make sure the lists never change, or that your code checks both the list and the database. Remember that the database layer – that is, DAO or ODBC and the involved drivers themselves – might do some caching depending on what recordset type you're using in your application. And remember too that sometimes caching is worthless work if you're not frequently re-accessing the same data!

There are numerous methodologies for designing databases, and several references for dissecting database designs to see what's wrong with them. Investigate which one is the best fit for your design and your organization; but once you start with it, stick to it to make sure you benefit from it as much as possible!

About ODBC and Unicode

You'll note that very little MFC database code you encounter looks to have been written with Unicode in mind. Neither will it take into account any of the international programming issues that we examine in Appendix B. That's because ODBC only recently started supporting Unicode. ODBC version 3.0, which first shipped with Visual C++ 5.0, now features Unicode-friendly APIs. But it's only with the release of Microsoft SQL Server 7.0 that ODBC providers have become available which are able to access Unicode data.

However, MFC has not yet been updated to support Unicode. That's because there are, as of this writing, no ODBC drivers that support it! As it makes little sense to write software that cannot possibly be tested, such support is currently absent from MFC. As soon as some drivers start shipping, you can expect that MFC will be modified to embrace the newly available (and verifiable!) support.

Comparing DAO and ODBC

If you've read the whole chapter to this point, you should understand some of the differences between DAO and ODBC by your own recollection, so this section will thus serve as something of a review for you. On the other hand, maybe you've skipped to this section to gain an understanding of the different technologies in order to decide which would be more appropriate for your application. Either way, we'll spend a couple of pages here contrasting the differences between DAO and ODBC. You can compare some of the differences between simple DAO and ODBC objects with exactly the same functionality by having a look at the `RecView` and `DaoView` samples: `RecView` uses ODBC, while `DaoView` uses DAO.

Database Support

DAO is only capable of connecting directly to a particular set of PC-oriented databases – the list of DAO-compatible databases is given earlier in the chapter under the heading 'Jet Airliner, Don't Take Me Too Far Away'. ODBC, on the other hand, is a complete architecture for connecting to different databases no matter how big they are – from tiny text files to mammoth databases running on scary mainframes. You can, however, use DAO to get to ODBC (if you're willing to pay a bit of a performance hit) and therefore, given the right driver, you can use DAO to get anywhere ODBC can go.

Efficiency

You'll usually find that DAO is more efficient at accessing the native file formats it supports than ODBC when accessing the same data through the appropriate driver. Conversely, you'll find DAO to be less efficient than ODBC when trying to access a remote server that isn't available through DAO directly. If you know what kind of data you're going after, this fact can help you readily decide what database layer you should use.

Data Sources vs. Databases

DAO is only interested in connecting to databases, while ODBC connects to a data source. That is, a DAO program would have to be written to be configurable before you could change the database you were working with. On the other hand, users of an ODBC program can get to the Control Panel and reconfigure their data source list to point at a different database without any trouble at all. This fact makes ODBC somewhat more scaleable and far more manageable than DAO.

If you're writing a program to keep track of your video tape collection, where the data comes from doesn't matter quite so much. If you're writing a program that will be installed on tens of dozens of different classes of computers far-and-wide across your organization, you'd probably want to use ODBC just to make sure you were making life easier for the helpdesk folks. While it's easy to have DAO install and create a database, it's also possible to have an ODBC application create a data source and install it on the client machine.

Data Definition Language Support

DAO allows you to open a database and directly perform data definition language calls, while ODBC doesn't. ODBC requires that you issue data manipulation language commands outside of the scope of ODBC, so your code will be very database-dependent.

Object Oriented Interface

The ODBC classes in MFC only represent two classes: CDatabase and CRecordset. While DAO mimics these classes with CDaoDatabase and CDaoRecordset, it also offers CDaoWorkspace, CDaoQueryDef, and CDaoRecordView to allow you access to the different objects DAO uses. DAO also implements a few more objects that you don't normally see when using the MFC wrappers: groups, users, fields, indexes, relations, and database engines.

As an MFC programmer, you can go along using these plain old classes and pretend nothing's different. But, as soon as you're ready, you can peek under the covers and work with a more impressive object-oriented structure. If you have a gander through the DAO SDK documentation, you'll realize that DAO implements lots of collections which you can manipulate — as we saw with the CDaoDatabase object, DAO manages a collection of table definitions for the database.

Summary

In this chapter, we've had a good look at writing database applications using MFC. I've provided an overview of the Open Database Connectivity API as well as Data Access Objects, the technologies that hold up the database classes in MFC. I've also provided a few tips about performance tuning, making a few suggestions to squeeze extra performance from your database applications. We've also visited each of the database-oriented MFC classes, giving you an in-depth look at what makes them tick, so you should feel confident using them yourself.

With an understanding of these features, you're armed to go out into the world and write your own database applications. Be careful when designing your own database application, and you'll quickly be able to write efficient programs.

13

Writing OLE Containers

Windows is designed around the notion of multitasking – the idea being that you can start one process and turn your attention to another while the machine takes care of the first. One of the more interesting facets of multitasking is the user interface that Windows provides, allowing us to move from process to process with the click of a button.

The next logical step is to have the processes talk to one another. One of Microsoft's solutions to the issue of process interoperability is **COM** (the **Component Object Model**), which provides a system dedicated to sharing functionality between applications. COM encourages developers to break an application into a series of objects that can be passed around and used by any other application.

COM is the technology underlying **OLE** (**Object Linking and Embedding**), which allows data from a number of different applications to appear in the same document.

In this chapter, we'll look at:

> ➢ How you can write an application using MFC to take advantage of OLE object functionality
> ➢ The ideas behind an **OLE client** and an **OLE server**
> ➢ The basic structure of the OLE architecture through MFC-tinted glasses
> ➢ In-place activation

Understanding OLE

It's unlikely that you're interested in writing your own word processor or spreadsheet package, but sometimes developers want to get hold of some of the functionality with which these types of commercial packages are graced. If the application you wish to pillage supports OLE, you're free (once you understand how to use OLE, of course) to bring borrowed functionality into your own programs. If the application doesn't support OLE, you're just out of luck – you have to hope that the application has some other programmable interface that you can learn and then use.

Before we embark on how to use OLE, let's take a closer look at its basic architecture. The 'spreadsheet chart in a word processing document' example can serve as a basis for this expedition. That is, we'll examine the typical situation of a user wanting to place a chart (drawn by their spreadsheet program) into a word processing document (maintained, obviously, by their word processing program).

Typically, when a user chooses to embed an object into their word processor document, they will see a list of embeddable OLE object types. When the user selects a particular object type (a Chart in our example), the word processor requests that COM provides it with a Chart object. The COM subsystem processes this request and discovers that it needs to launch the spreadsheet program to **serve** that object. COM provides information about the server's interfaces to the **container** application (in this example, the word processor), which is then responsible for positioning and sizing the object in the container's user interface. The server is responsible for painting the Chart object in the word processor.

Object, Object and Object

Unfortunately, COM and OLE use some very confusing terminology. COM objects differ when compared to C++ objects, even though you might use a C++ object to represent a COM object in your code. COM objects are known to the system; by contrast, the system never knows exactly what C++ objects you might have floating around. The operating system certainly doesn't provide any standard way for one application to ask another what C++ objects it has active at any time.

To make matters worse, the term **object** means something different to users and developers. OLE users call the material embedded in a document an object. While the embedded 'object' is certainly at least one COM object from the programmer's point of view, it might consist of several, and those COM objects almost always comprise of more than one C++ object.

The word **method** is similarly overloaded. To a C++ developer, the term means a member function of a class. In COM, however, a method is a given function in an interface. This isn't perfectly compatible with the C++ definition, because a given object may have many interfaces and each of those interfaces has many methods. In C++, some people refer to interfaces and methods interchangeably. In COM, an interface is a collection of methods and an individual method is strictly a function.

What Kind of Applications Can I Write with OLE?

When you're interested in writing a program that can contain OLE objects, you'll have more decisions to make than when you're creating a normal Windows application. If you're reading this chapter, you're probably already interested in writing an application that uses OLE, but what sorts of applications use OLE?

Typically, OLE containers fall into two different types (we'll be looking at other types of OLE applications in the next three chapters):

General purpose OLE Containers	You might want to write an application that lets the user edit some type of document, picture, list or other type of file, like Excel, Word or Ami Pro. Your application provides users with anything they could want in the way of editing tools for this kind of document, but you also want to give users the ability to create **compound documents**. By letting users drop OLE objects into your document, you enable them to extend the functionality of your application by including drawings, charts and other visual aspects of your document that your product doesn't support out of the box.
Special purpose OLE Integrators	On the other hand, you might have a very specific idea in mind for an OLE object in your application. You may want to steal the graphing capabilities of a spreadsheet package, or you may be interested in having a word processor display documents with a little more integration (and control!) than just spawning a copy of the word processor. This kind of application doesn't rely on the traditional user intervention that a general-purpose container might; it probably runs off and creates the OLE objects it needs by itself, showing them to the user when necessary.

The difference between these two approaches is simply the extent to which the user will be involved in creating and placing the type of OLE objects that the application uses. General-purpose containers will always allow the user to insert any kind of OLE object at any time. They'll probably use the Insert Object dialog that we can see here:

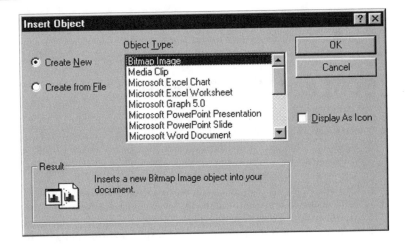

OLE Applications and AppWizard

The easiest way to approach the task of writing an OLE container is to start with AppWizard. When AppWizard asks you what level of support you'd like in your application, you can select one of the OLE options shown in the table below:

Level of Support	File Support	Container Support	Server Support
None	✓		
Container	✓	✓	
Mini-Server			✓
Full-Server	✓		✓
Both Container and Server	✓	✓	✓
Adding Active Document Containment Support	✓	✓	
Adding Active Document Server Support	✓		✓

You may remember we looked briefly at each of these options in Chapter 2. In this chapter, we're going to focus on exactly what container support means.

As usual, AppWizard just provides a starting point for your coding. You can create an application with container support very easily using AppWizard and build from there. If you have an existing application, you'll need to understand the features that AppWizard offers and how you can replicate them in your application.

Before we start touring the different features of an AppWizard-generated program, let's continue our peek at how OLE works under the covers.

COM and Your System

At its most abstract level, COM provides a basis for running programs to share objects. These objects are often some visible doodad which one application wants to borrow from another: a graph, an equation from the Word Equation Editor or a drawing of a heat exchanger in an oil refinery, complete with temperatures and pressures for all of the pipes going in and out.

Of course, the object isn't obliged to provide a user interface; you might use some object to provide a connection to a special database, or encapsulate code that implements all of the business rules your organization needs to process insurance claims or quote prices on building supplies. Such an object may run without a user interface, simply accepting calls to the COM interfaces that it uses internally.

What COM does is to provide a standard for these different objects, no matter what level of support they provide for their clients. COM demands that any application wishing to expose functionality via OLE objects requires those objects to implement a specific set of **interfaces**. The interfaces specified by OLE group together different methods that perform specific tasks. An application wishing to use OLE to work with objects provided by other modules must use those interfaces, following COM's guidelines to see if they exist, to gain access to them and meter how they are being used.

Waking Up COM

Of course, before we can go play with OLE objects, we need to make sure that COM is ready and willing to help us out. In an MFC application, you can call the `AfxOleInit()` function that ties some code in the MFC library to COM. As the COM system runs, it will load other modules on behalf of your application. You need to occasionally poll COM to offer it the ability to free these modules if they're no longer in use.

Within `AfxOleInit()`, MFC calls the `::OleInitialize()` API to get COM to set itself up. This call loads the necessary OLE libraries and lets COM know that you'll be coming round later to do some real work. COM loads several DLLs, depending on what you want to do with your application.

MFC's `AfxOleInit()` function calls `::OleInitialize()` because it's all MFC needs. MFC doesn't directly support DCOM, nor does it support multithreaded apartment COM objects. However, you *can* graft objects that support these features onto your MFC application, but you won't have any support for MFC in doing so. If you need to call a more aggressive initialization function, you can do so directly.

When your application dies, MFC will automatically call an internal routine to cut off its links with COM. This routine ends by disconnecting anything that was started by COM, followed by a call to the `::OleUninitialize()` API to clean things up, free memory and to discard the OLE DLLs.

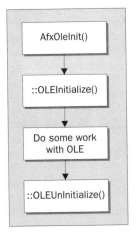

One important thing to remember is that you should only call `AfxOleInit()` once during your application's lifetime – if your application loads several DLLs, don't call `AfxOleInit()` in each one. Instead, you should depend on the application to intialize OLE for each of the DLLs. An AppWizard-produced application will already have a call to `AfxOleInit()` call hooked-up for you. The code AppWizard generates looks like this, for your `CWinApp::InitInstance()` override:

```
// Initialize OLE libraries
if (!AfxOleInit())
{
   AfxMessageBox(IDP_OLE_INIT_FAILED);
   return FALSE;
}
```

As you can see, the initialization is terribly simple – if it fails, `AfxMessageBox()` pops up an error and we return `FALSE` from the `InitInstance()` function to stop the initialization of app.

Identification

Once OLE is initialized, you'll want to start working with objects and their interfaces. It turns out that you generally won't have to get your fingers dirty with this level of detail if you're just writing a document container or server or both. But if you need to debug any code, or need to enhance your container to work directly with any sort of object, you'll need to know how OLE identifies objects and interfaces.

The identification mechanism OLE uses has a few different parts – and all of those parts are available (and cross-referenced) in the registry. Broadly speaking, OLE uses the notion of a **globally unique identifier**, or a **GUID**, for short. GUIDs are 128-bits long, and are usually represented by a few groups of numbers in curly brackets.

GUIDs are easily generated, and are essentially guaranteed to be unique by the mechanism that generates them. Of the 128 bits, some come from your machines physical network address – which itself is asserted to be unique by the network card manufacturer. Another bunch of the bits come from a representation of time on the machine where the GUID is actually generated. You can generate a few GUIDs and look for a pattern using the `Guidgen` utility. It's installed with Visual C++, but unfortunately not on any menu. However, you can execute it from the Run command on the Start menu, though. They're free – don't worry about it.

A **class ID** (abbreviated **CLSID**) is stored in the registry as the main method of accessing an OLE server. The CLSID is no different from a GUID – it's another 128-bit identifier. The GUID for the Windows 98 version of Microsoft Paint, for example, is `{D3E34B21-9D75-101A-8C3D-00AA001A1652}`. And so we know that we can find the OLE information for the program at `HKEY_CLASSES_ROOT\CLSID\{D3E34B21-9D75-101A-8C3D-00AA001A1652}` in the registry.

Within that key, there are several subkeys; the most important is the name of the server executable, which tells OLE where to find and how to load the executable that offers objects of the class identified by the GUID.

The default key in the key named for the CLSID is the simplest identification mechanism is that used in the Insert Object dialog, which we saw a few pages ago. Under the CLSID key for the server's class, the default key contains the application's long name. This is the same name that you set with the File type name (long name) field in the tab of the Advanced Options dialog in the fourth step of the AppWizard when generating a server application.

OLE objects are also known by a **program ID**, which is an actual plain-text string. For Microsoft Paint, one such string is `Paint.Picture`. The program ID (sometimes called a **ProgID**) can be found in `HKEY_CLASSES_ROOT`, too; for Microsoft Paint, the full path to the key is `HKEY_CLASSES_ROOT\CLSID\Paint.Picture`.

You can ask OLE to create an instance of a class using either the program ID or the CLSID. Once you've done that, you can start asking that instance for particular interface, and you'll also do that using a GUID. Each interface defined in the OLE objects by your machine will be identified by a particular **IID**, or **interface ID**. The IID provides an identity for the interface, so the IID used for a particular interface is the same on every class in your system.

We'll learn that `IUnknown`, for example, is a very important interface implemented by every object. It's IID is `{00000000-0000-0000-C000-000000000046}`. Fortunately, you'll never need to type the actual IID; you can just reference the predefined symbol `IID_IUnknown`.

What's the Registry for?

GUIDs, which identify the interfaces and objects themselves, are terribly hard to remember. You would never suddenly decide that you wanted to play with an equation object and ask your object to insert one by specifying `00021700-0000-0000-C000-000000000046`, the class identifier (`CLSID`) for the object. Instead, when you use the insert object command in most applications, you see a dialog box (like we saw in the first couple pages of this chapter) listing the insertable objects installed on your system.

It's a lot easier to select the object by name in the dialog than to enter that big scary `CLSID`. The application brings up this dialog box by reading the **system registry**. The registry, among other things, contains information about all COM objects registered on the system. Any application that can act as a server for a COM object must register that object by making the appropriate changes to the registry. The following figure shows some of the registry details for the objects on my system:

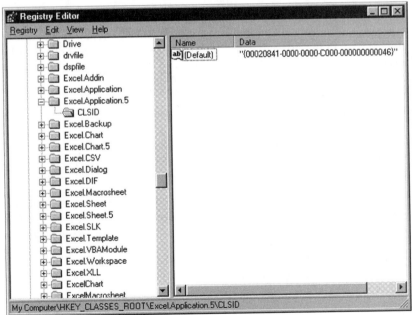

Note that a few entries that appear in the registry aren't around in the Insert Object dialog box. The missing objects don't have an `Insertable` key under their entry – and that's exactly why they're not listed. Some COM objects are designed to be used in a stand-alone situation: created, manipulated and then discarded. We'll examine such objects in our chapter on OLE Controls.

The definition of an insertable object is an object that can be inserted into another application's document – an object that is embeddable. Such objects can save themselves to become persistent, so that the application, which owns the document holding the object, can reinitialize the object when the user loads the document again.

Here's where the idea of reusability becomes a little more solid; a COM object is nothing by itself. The interfaces it expresses and the intelligence that it brings along with it only apply to the most rudimentary functions; the object can save, load and render itself in a couple of different ways. The object may also give its clients direct access to its data, in addition to being able to write it and read the data to or from a storage mechanism. However, most COM objects don't expose any other interfaces; it's the client which is responsible for getting all of the work done, deciding where the server should sit, hooking up persistent storage for the object and asking the object to perform as it sees fit.

For the application to make use of the object, that object must implement the required standard COM interfaces in the expected way, otherwise the container won't be able to control it properly. As you learn to write containers in this chapter, we'll explain the different interfaces to which MFC can grant us access.

You'll also see how to use them to your advantage while working with the object, and how to smoothly integrate the functionality won by using COM into your container application. We'll come to understand how COM works through MFC's eyes.

The registry is updated by your application when it first runs. This happens automatically because MFC manages a linked list of the `COleClassFactory` objects in your application. MFC visits each class factory in the list and asks them to register themselves. AppWizard, if you used it to create your application, also writes a `.reg` file which can be merged with the content of your registry if you'd like to set up your application without running it.

Interfaces

Every COM object must implement at least one COM interface, called `IUnknown`. `IUnknown` specifies three methods: `AddRef()`, `Release()` and `QueryInterface()`. These functions make up the most rudimentary interface that every COM object will have.

`IUnknown`'s `QueryInterface()` method allows a client, such as your container application, to see if a given COM object supports a particular interface. If `QueryInterface()` works, it brings back a `void` pointer to the interface you requested. If it failed, it lets you know why – the most common reason for failure is that the queried object simply doesn't support the requested interface. Whenever a container works with an object from some other server, it will need to call `QueryInterface()` to gain pointers to the interfaces that object implements before it runs off and calls them.

A client can't assume that a server implements any interface except the very IUnknown interface that the client first encounters. Given that IUnknown interface, you can call its QueryInterface() method to obtain other interfaces. The normal QueryInterface() prototype looks like this:

```
HRESULT QueryInterface(REFIID riid, void** ppvObject);
```

The first parameter is a reference to the interface ID, or **IID**, of the specific interface you'd like to find. The second parameter is a pointer to a pointer where receive the address of the new interface. Using the above prototype of QueryInterface(), you'll always need to cast the pointer to the type of interface pointer that you'd like to find. For example, you might try to find the IOleObject interface on an object you've already created and are referencing using a pointer named pMyObject by writing this code:

```
LPOLEOBJECT lpOleObject;
if (SUCCEEDED(pMyObject->QueryInterface(IID_IOleObject,
                            reinterpret_cast<LPVOID*>(&lpOleObject))))
{
    // it worked!
}
```

If the call fails, it will return a failure HRESULT which will trigger the SUCCEEDED() macro into failing. The failed call will also set lpOleObject to NULL.

Visual C++ 6.0, though, introduces some impressive compiler support for COM. Some of that support allows you to write more convenient (and no less efficient) code to query for a particular interface using a different override of QueryInterface(). That implementation deduces the IID of the interface given the type of the pointer you provide! This neat feat of programming simplifies the above code considerably by eliminating the cast and the direct reference to the IID symbol:

```
LPOLEOBJECT lpOleObject;
if (SUCCEEDED(pMyObject->QueryInterface(lpOleObject)))
{
    // it worked!
}
```

Pretty neat, huh?

When QueryInterface() *does* succeed, it returns a pointer to some interface. You are responsible for letting that interface know when you've finished with it. The object will manage a **reference count** so that it knows when its useful life has finished and it can free itself from memory. This count is automatically incremented when the QueryInterface() implementation for the object successfully retrieves an interface and gives it back to you. The reference count is maintained privately by the object itself; you can't request it.

The count is decremented when you inform the interface that you've finished with it by calling `Release()` against it. `Release()` doesn't take any parameters. After you call `Release()`, the object implementing the interface may or may not remain in memory. The code may stay in memory if someone else is referencing it, but it will soon drop out of sight if the object is no longer being referenced. Somewhere, maybe deep inside MFC, or in the implementation of a COM API, the first call made against a COM object locks one of its interfaces. The last call made against the object, whether directly by your application, indirectly through MFC, or via a COM API, will release an interface and let it remove itself from memory.

After the object entrusts you with a pointer to one of its interfaces, you're responsible for carefully managing of that interface. If you make a copy of the pointer to the interface you got back from `QueryInterface()`, you should call the `AddRef()` member of the interface so that the interface knows it really has two clients: yourself and the code to which you passed the reference. (Of course, it might have more clients than you – but the point is that the server needs to accurately count your multiple references.) Like `Release()`, `AddRef()` doesn't take any parameters – and it turns out they don't return HRESULTs either. These methods are simple enough that they can't possibly fail.

When the count returns to zero, the object knows that it can be freed. The code implementing the interface isn't allowed to remove itself from memory while it is still being referenced, so this count is very important. If you call `AddRef()` more than you call `Release()`, you'll find that the object never removes itself from memory. If you call `Release()` more than you call `AddRef()`, you'll find that the object might disappear from out of under your calls through the pointers you think are still valid.

In theory, once you've implemented `IUnknown` for your objects, you could run off and implement all sorts of your own interfaces on the client side of the equation. Unfortunately, this approach denies the object and your client application any hope of being used again. Other applications won't know which interfaces you've implemented, and certainly won't be able to figure them out on the fly.

However, the approach of writing your own custom interfaces is sometimes quite appropriate. You might have to provide data back to your application in real time, or you might have a design that closely relates your application to its objects, but if you are interested in maximum reusability, you should adhere to the standard COM interfaces as carefully as you can. We discuss custom interfaces a little more at the end of the next chapter.

Creating the Interfaces

Interfaces exist on objects, by the way; they're not off floating in the air. Before you can call any interface, you'll need to call `::CoCreateInstance()` to actually build the object which carries it. While `::CoCreateInstance()` is a COM API, you'll still need to use it within your MFC applications. MFC doesn't provide a wrapper for the actual act of creating a COM object.

A typical call to `::CoCreateInstance()` might look like this:

```
HRESULT hResult;
LPUNKNOWN lpUnknown;
hResult = ::CoCreateInstance(CLSID_MYSPREADSHEETAPP, NULL, CLSCTX_LOCAL_SERVER,
    IID_IUnknown, &lpUnkown);
```

The function passes useful data back in two ways. One of these is the HRESULT return value. All COM APIs use the HRESULT data type to express success, failure and the error condition. (Nearly all methods do, too – except for AddRef() and Release(), which we investigated before). You can look at an HRESULT to detect success or failure by testing the value with the SUCCEDED() or FAILED() macros; an HRESULT of zero means that there was no problem, non-zero means that something went wrong. You can also test non-zero values against various constants defined in Winerror.h to see exactly what the error was. CoCreateInstance(), for example, will return S_OK if everything worked, REGDB_E_CLASSNOTREG if the class couldn't be found in the registry, or CLASS_E_NOAGGREGATION if you've passed a non-NULL second parameter (to indicate that you'd like to aggregate the newly created object) and the object doesn't support aggregation. Winerror.h defines several hundred different error codes, so I'm not about to regurgitate them here – you should check the documentation to find the error codes generated by the particular function you're using.

The function returns its second item of data by reference in the last parameter, which is a pointer to a void pointer. Above, we passed the address of an LPUNKNOWN pointer. If the ::CoCreateInstance() function was successful, it will put a pointer to the requested interface into the referenced pointer (lpUnknown). You can then use that pointer to perform anything else you need. The ::CoCreateInstance() API has already called AddRef() once on the object for you, so you have ownership of that pointer and need to call Release() whenever you're done.

The first parameter is a class ID, like we examined back in the 'Identification' section near the beginning of the chapter. The parameter I used above is just made up; normally you will be able to find the CLSID in a header file or a type library for an OLE server.

The second parameter to CoCreateInstance() introduces a complicated topic that we won't discuss deeply in this book: **aggregation**. *This involves writing a COM object that has other COM objects in it. The outer object intercepts calls to the inner object and changes the way it works – COM's answer to inheritance, if you will.*

The third parameter describes what kind of server you'd like to run; the same object may be implemented by a .dll or a .exe. .dlls are certainly faster and are usually smaller, but .exes are sometimes more robust. Anyway, this function describes exactly which version of the object's server will be loaded, since there might be more than one implementation on your system. The values in this table are for your reference:

Constant	Description
CLSCTX_INPROC_SERVER	The server should be a DLL, which runs in the same process space as the client.
CLSCTX_INPROC_HANDLER	A DLL should be loaded into the client's process space to serve this object. The DLL may actually load another image and communicate with it and that image may actually implement the server.

Table Continued on Following Page

Constant	Description
CLSCTX_LOCAL_SERVER	The server is an executable application, which will run out-of-process, but on the same machine as the client.
CLSCTX_REMOTE_SERVER	The server will run on a remote machine. This type of creation is only useful if you've installed and enabled DCOM – for notes on that, see our discussion of AfxInitOle() a few pages ago.
CLSCTX_INPROC	The server must run in the same process space as the client (either as an inproc server or an inproc handler).
CLSCTX_SERVER	The loaded server must be the direct server, not just a handler.
CLSCTX_ALL	The server can be any of the types and in any of the locations previously listed.

Again, this is really just background information to help you understand COM in a little more detail; when you are writing OLE support into your MFC application, you will almost never have to get your hands dirty with this level of information.

The fourth parameter to CoCreateInstance() also refers to a GUID, but actually identifies the interface we're requesting from the object, not the object we're interested in creating. If an object or application implements custom interfaces, the application's development kit should provide you with a header or type library that defines the interfaces that the program may declare. If you're working with a standard COM interface, you'll find the IID_ declaration you need in the Oleidl.h header.

The IID_ definitions identify an interface ID. The one you'll most commonly see is IID_IUnknown, which gets the IUnknown interface. Other IID_ definitions declare interface IDs for other well-known OLE interfaces, such as IOleObject or IDataObject. Just append the interface name to the IID_ prefix to get the right definition.

> *By the way, the inclusion of Afxole.h in your application gets you all of the COM/OLE headers from the system, as well as from MFC.*

Creating Objects

When you ask COM to instantiate an object, it doesn't really do very much work. COM finds and then loads the code that serves the object. The server's executable module is then allowed to initialize itself. If the object is held in a DLL, Windows steps in and calls the DLL's DllMain() function to get it going. If the object has come from a .exe server, it is offered special flags on its command line, which indicate it's being run to serve an OLE object. The executable will receive the option /Embedding on its command line. AppWizard provides servers with code to detect this option and react appropriately. The important point is, as a client, you don't have to worry about explicitly loading and/or running the dynamic link library or .exe yourself – you just ask COM for it.

Once the server is loaded, we're ready to run. COM will allow calls against the server and we can ask for any interface the server implements. The ::CoCreateInstance() function is really shorthand for a common idiom in COM development.

COM objects implement an IClassFactory interface that's responsible for creating objects that the server supports. Creating an object really involves getting the standard IClassFactory interface and asking it to create an instance of the object that you need to use. The ::CoCreateInstance() function within COM might be implemented something like this:

```
HRESULT CoCreateInstance(REFCLSID rclsid, LPUNKNOWN pUnkOuter,
                         DWORD dwClsContext, REFIID riid, LPVOID* ppv)
{
    LPCLASSFACTORY pCF;
    HRESULT hResult;
    hResult = CoGetClassObject(rclsid, dwClsContext, NULL,
                                           IID_IClassFactory, &pCF);

    if (SUCCEEDED(hResult) && pCF != NULL)
    {
        hResult = pCF->CreateInstance(pUnkOuter, riid, ppv);
        pCF->Release();
    }

    return hResult;
}
```

Calling ::CoGetClassObject() in this implementation returns a pointer to the class factory interface in the object. If that works, the function continues by calling the CreateInstance() interface on the class factory. If the call works, we'll return the resulting interface and a successful result handle, otherwise the function will return an error code.

Note the call to the Release() method of the class factory interface; just like any other interface, the class factory must be released so the object can correctly manage its reference counts. You'll also have to eventually release the interface you received from the ::CoCreateInstance() API.

Workin' At The Factory

Warren Zevon probably doesn't know it, but COM doesn't implement the IClassFactory::CreateInstance() function. The implementation of the class factory is the responsibility of the object itself. MFC COM objects are managed by a class factory built into the COleObjectFactory class in MFC. This class is often instantiated as a member of another class that really implements the object you need to create.

The COleObjectFactory instance is added to classes which need to be created by COM with the DECLARE_OLECREATE() and IMPLEMENT_OLECREATE() macros. These macros are very similar to the DECLARE_DYNCREATE() and IMPLEMENT_DYNCREATE() macros which we learned were attached to CObject back in Chapter 3.

COleObjectFactory ends up implementing the IClassFactory and IClassFactory2 interfaces defined by COM. These standard COM interfaces are needed in every server, so MFC uses a single C++ class to implement them. The notion of using an 'inner' class one of the ways to skin the C++ implementation of COM cat. It makes sense, since COM expects to see the interface as a table of pointers to functions and C++ programmers can use a class to get it for free because each of the functions in the interface is just declared virtual in the implementing class. The **vtable** of the object ends up being maintained by the language, and is also available to COM as the interface. We'll see some details on this in just a bit. It's worth noting that ATL, the COM-focused class library in the Visual C++ box, takes a very different approach to inherently providing COM interfaces (and their stock implementations) from C++ classes.

If you pick through a class that supplies an interface to COM on behalf of MFC, you'll find a few more macros that establish the virtual functions and their parameters. For the IClassFactory interface, for example, you'll see this structure right in the middle of the declaration of the class.

```
BEGIN_INTERFACE_PART(ClassFactory, IClassFactory)
    INIT_INTERFACE_PART(COleObjectFactory, ClassFactory)
    STDMETHOD(CreateInstance)(LPUNKNOWN, REFIID, LPVOID*);
    STDMETHOD(LockServer)(BOOL);
END_INTERFACE_PART(ClassFactory)
```

The BEGIN_INTERFACE_PART() names the interface class and the interface itself. In the above example, the class member ends up being named m_xIClassFactory.

MFC will also use a DECLARE_INTERFACE_MAP() macro to create an interface map that provides a way to connect particular interface IDs to the member functions that handle them. MFC uses the interface map to decide which function in a hierarchy of classes will actually handle the implementation of an interface that a client has requested via COM. MFC uses the interface map while it's handling a call from a client to the QueryInterface() method against an object implemented by MFC.

DECLARE_INTERFACE_MAP() is a declaration to the compiler of the structures and members used by BEGIN_INTERFACE_MAP() and END_INTERFACE_MAP() macros which will later define each of the interfaces handled by the class. Interface maps are very similar to message maps both in function and in content. We'll look at these macros again in the next chapter when we discuss creating OLE servers.

You'll almost never need to monkey around with COleClassFactory, but the details of the implementation of the class, as well as the concepts it represents, will prove quite important to understand. You can take comfort in knowing the details under the covers, just like you know your pet moose is waiting for you when you get home.

What are Interfaces, Really?

During the OLE chapters in this book, we'll mention some of the different interfaces used in OLE. As an MFC programmer, you don't often have to worry about the exact implementation of an interface, but it's helpful to know what an interface really is, since it is so germane to the way COM and OLE work.

As we have already discussed, you can ask an object to give a pointer to one of its interfaces, but we also said an interface wasn't anything in particular – just a collection of different, related functions, supported by an object for some purpose. This makes it seem as if the actual interfaces to which you have a pointer are really just little clouds of data that make no sense.

Well, they are – but you should know what's going on inside them. The pointer to an interface is really a pointer to a virtual function table, sometimes called a **vtable**. This table is managed (by most C++ implementations) for classes that have virtual functions. The vtable lets the compiler resolve calls to a virtual function through a pointer to the class. Suppose you have a construct that uses a virtual function, like this:

```
CWnd* pWindow;
pWindow = new CDialog;
pWindow->Create( /* some parameters */ );
```

The dereference operator (->) actually looks up the address of the Create() function in the vtable of the object before calling it. The vtable is initialized at the object's construction time, in plain old C++, without a hint of COM in sight. This is what makes the code call the correct (CDialog rather than CWnd) implementation of the function.

It turns out this vtable is what makes up an interface. Both vtables and COM interfaces are just tables of function pointers. In C, COM programming is tough because you have to find some way to build these tables of function pointers, but, in C++, it's easy – you just use constructs in the language which you know will produce the proper table of pointers for your interface. C++'s virtual functions are just perfect for that kind of action.

In MFC, declaring an interface means using a class that defines the interface as a member of that class. This just adds a class member whose virtual functions match the corresponding interface methods layout, so the class has the function table it needs to implement the interface. Many of the classes we'll talk about in our COM/OLE discussions will implement an interface, while all of them will use other object's interfaces. Once again, MFC is helping you by providing some insulation between you and the complexities of the interfaces, which you'd otherwise have to code yourself.

About Embedded Objects

The examples of adding objects to a document which I've been tossing around here all describe the act of embedding an object – placing one object inside of another. Such an object is referred to as being **embedded** since it generally behaves as if it were embedded within the application's own native document.

Embedded objects are always used in general-purpose containers; the user will expect the object to be inserted with the Insert Object... command. Special-purpose containers may or may not use embedded objects, or they may use some combination of embedded and non-embedded objects.

MFC's OLE code uses a simple API called ::OleCreate() to allow OLE to do all of the extra housekeeping that makes embedding possible. ::OleCreate() builds an object in much the same way as ::CoGetClassObject(), even though it also requires an embedding storage mechanism. Like most other COM APIs, you'll never need to call ::OleCreate() directly, as MFC will do it for you (for example, when the user calls the Insert New Object dialog to place a new object in their application's document).

Much of the user interface for MFC's OLE implementation (such as the Insert New Object dialog, as well as several other sundry dialogs that OLE requires for data conversions and when one OLE application is too busy to talk with another) actually comes from code that is part of the operating system. The code lives in a DLL called Mfcuia32.dll. Previously, code for the DLL was one of the sample applications that shipped with Visual C++, but unfortunately the source code isn't included in the product any more.

Up to this point in the chapter, we've examined some of the inner workings of COM and come to understand what some special COM object scenarios are all about. Let's move ahead to see how MFC encapsulates that functionality and makes it easy for you, as a C++ programmer, to use it.

A New CDocument

OLE is like Tokyo; it's an incredibly big place and absolutely fascinating, but you need to understand some of the language and culture before you can begin to get the most out of it. To get started, let's have a peek at a stock OLE application created by AppWizard and look at what it's doing. Once we understand some of the moving pieces, the whole picture won't seem quite so overwhelming.

If you want to follow along with the narrative, you can use AppWizard to create a container application of your own and plug in the extra code and changes described here. The finished product, called Cntnr, can be found on the Wrox web site.

If you create an OLE container using AppWizard, you can compile and build this application and begin using it immediately. You'll notice you can use the Insert New Object... command in the Edit menu to add any sort of object you like to the application. By embedding objects like this, you'll find that your document can contain almost anything!

You can work with the objects as they live in your document by double-clicking on them. After that double-click, the object is said to be **activated** or in-place activated. The container (your application) and the contained object negotiate which menus and toolbars will be shown. They decide how much of the client area is available for UI presentation, and the active object gets first crack at any input messages from the keyboard and mouse.

If you embed an object into the document and the object is selected, you can also examine the Edit menu. There, you should see new choices in the menu pertaining to the object that is selected within your document.

The biggest difference between this application and the others we've examined in the book so far is OLE support. That OLE support mostly originates from the use of MFC's COleDocument class in place of CDocument. COleDocument lets your application support OLE embedding and in-place editing (in addition to all of the other CDocument features).

In-place Editing

MFC-based OLE containers inherently support **in-place editing**. In-place editing means an active, embedded object can be altered where it sits in the containing application. This gives the user the impression your application is itself capable of managing that type of object, offering almost seamless integration for all the data which he or she may place into your document.

For in-place editing to work, both your application and the object's server must be able to support in-place editing. As MFC already provides that support, applications you write using MFC are inherently ready to go. Unfortunately, all servers don't necessarily support in-place editing.

If you were running Windows NT 3.51, you could demonstrate an embeddable OLE object that doesn't support in-place editing by inserting a Paintbrush Picture into your MFC application. You'd find that Paintbrush would actually run and would show you its full user interface when you tried to activate the object, almost as if you had run your application and Paintbrush separately. You have that impression because that's effectively what would be happening! Since that old version of Paintbrush didn't support in-place editing, you couldn't change the way your Paintbrush picture looks without actually seeing the Paintbrush program.

Nearly all modern OLE applications now support in-place editing. Although it's a bit more cumbersome than direct in-place editing, you can still go ahead and use a server that doesn't support in-place activation to edit an embedded object. In the out-of-place context, you'll have noticed the server changes its File menu. Whilst it is editing an embedded object, the server won't allow you to save the object to a file; you can either exit the server, discarding your changes, or exit the server and have it write your changes back to the host document.

Editing with In-place Support

When you are working on an object that does support in-place editing, you'll find working with the embedded object is a lot more convenient for the user. The object enters a state known as **in-place active**. It negotiates with the container to add some of its own menus and buys some real-estate from the container to show its own toolbars. The user can edit the document as if it was displayed in its native host.

Microsoft Excel supports in-place activation and, as you can see below, the simple `Cntnr` application has an Excel Chart object that can be activated:

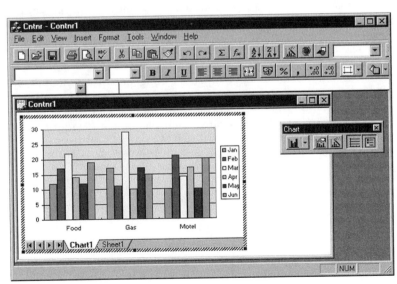

You can see that the toolbars from Excel have replaced the application's toolbar, while some of the menus from the application live on, they are augmented by the menus from Excel. The container and the activating object engage in two processes known as **toolbar negotiation** and **menu negotiation** to decide whose menus live on and in which positions.

Container Templates

As it is produced by AppWizard, your `CWinApp`-derived class will have a slightly more elaborate `InitInstance()` function than we've seen before. After creating the document template and just before registering that template, `InitInstance()` executes this call:

```
pDocTemplate->SetContainerInfo(IDR_CONTNRTYPE_CNTR_IP);
```

`SetContainerInfo()` takes a resource ID which identifies a **mergeable menu** and an accelerator table that the application will use while an object within it is in-place active. The resources you identify with this function's only parameter are normally provided for you by AppWizard. The menu is described as mergeable because of a special format that MFC can use to construct the menu with elements from both the container and the server.

This special format just uses two consecutive menu separators to indicate where the menus from the server should be added to the menus in the container. Below, you can see the way the special in-place menu looks in the Resource Editor:

When this application lets a server go in-place active, MFC will request the server's in-place active menu and add it to the current menu bar. Essentially, our application will keep its Window and File menus, while the server will be free to modify the menu in whichever way it sees fit.

Note that menu negotiation might be reinitiated by the in-place active object if you somehow change its context. For example, if you have a Microsoft Excel workbook that has gone in-place active, Excel will ask that the menus be re-established as you move from spreadsheets to charts within the in-place active object. Excel normally shows these with different menus when a workbook is active in an independent Excel application, so Excel will try to enforce the same user interface even while in-place active.

If you use different document templates throughout your container, you'll need to make sure they're fully initialized, using an appropriate menu for merging and a call to `SetContainerInfo()`. You only need to do this for documents in your application that will be OLE aware; if you have other documents which aren't OLE-aware, you'll want to use `CDocument` to build them, not `COleDocument`.

Keeping Track of Objects in a Container

As you might have guessed, `COleDocument` adds special support for OLE containment. The most important feature of `COleDocument` is a list, maintained by a `COleDocument` instance, which contains a pointer to information about each OLE object that is inserted into the document. The list contains pointers to objects based on the `COleClientItem` class. AppWizard will produce a derivative of this class for your application; in the Cntnr example, the client item information class is named `CCntrCntrItem`.

This list is just a regular `CObList` that we discussed in Chapter 9. We can cycle through the list by getting a `POSITION` context from `COleDocument::GetStartPosition()`, using that `POSITION` to find each item by repeatedly calling `COleDocument::GetNextClientItem()`. While we're painting or trying to figure out the target of different mouse clicks, we'll often rip through this list.

When you use the Insert <u>N</u>ew Object... dialog to add an object to the document, code like this runs:

```
void CCntrView::OnInsertObject()
{
    COleInsertDialog dlg;
    if (dlg.DoModal() != IDOK)
        return;
    CWaitCursor waiter;

    CCntrCntrItem* pItem = NULL;
    TRY
    {
        CCntrDoc* pDoc = GetDocument();
        ASSERT_VALID(pDoc);
        pItem = new CCntrCntrItem(pDoc);
        ASSERT_VALID(pItem);

        if (!dlg.CreateItem(pItem))
            AfxThrowMemoryException();
        ASSERT_VALID(pItem);

        if (dlg.GetSelectionType() == COleInsertDialog::createNewItem)
            pItem->DoVerb(OLEIVERB_SHOW, this);
        ASSERT_VALID(pItem);

        m_pSelection = pItem;
        pDoc->UpdateAllViews(NULL);
    }
    CATCH(CException, e)
    {
        // handle the exception
    }
    END_CATCH
}
```

You'll note that the code above doesn't call `CDocument::SetModifiedFlag()` on the document. That's because MFC leaves the state of the document as a choice for yourself; if you think that the insertion of an object doesn't modify the state of your document, you're free to leave the document unmodified. Normally, you'll call `SetModifiedFlag()` yourself to indicate that the extra object is a part of your document and its insertion reflects a change to the content of your document. We'll see how an object, once inserted, can reflect its changes back to the document containing it when we examine the `OnChange()` member in a couple of pages.

All the action happens after the user responds to the `COleInsertDialog`. If the user responds in a negative way, the function ends. But if the user responds positively, the function creates a new `CCntrCntrItem` object associated with the document with which we're working. You can see that the `CCntrCntrItem` constructor takes a pointer to the `COleDocument` that owns the list of contained OLE objects. `CCntrCntrItem` passes this pointer on to the `COleClientItem` constructor, which takes care of adding this `COleClientItem` to the list of items managed by the document.

We call the `CreateItem()` member of the `COleInsertDialog`, which finishes the creation of the object by (eventually) calling the `::OleCreate()` API. `CCntrCntrItem` needs to know about the document with which it is used to serve two different purposes; the storage mechanism that the new object needs is encapsulated in the `COleDocument` object and the `CCntrCntrItem` will need to add itself to the list of objects that document maintains.

AppWizard modifies the view in an OLE container application by managing a special variable called `m_pSelection`. This is a pointer to a `COleClientItem`-derived object type, which AppWizard provides for your application. If it is NULL, this pointer indicates that no object in the container is selected; otherwise the pointer references the currently selected item. Note that `m_pSelection` is explicitly initialized to NULL in the `OnInitialUpdate()` member of the view.

As the above code fragment shows, the selection is set before a call to `UpdateAllViews()` is made. This allows the selection to be reflected in the user interface of the application when it draws itself.

Activation Patterns

We've discussed objects going in-place active and what that means for the container. Some servers (like Excel) go in-place active as soon as they're inserted. If you don't want to see this behavior, you can tweak the handler for the Insert **N**ew Object... menu item.

The `COleDocument` class provides a `GetInPlaceActiveItem()` function which returns a pointer to the `COleClientItem` which is currently in-place active. If there isn't an in-place active item, the function returns NULL, otherwise you'll receive a pointer to its `COleClientItem`.

You can make an item active by calling `COleClientItem::Activate()`, or make one inactive by calling `COleClientItem::Deactivate()`. `Deactivate()` simply performs its work and returns, but `Activate()` is a little more complicated. Here's its function prototype:

```
void Activate(LONG nVerb, CView* pView, LPMSG lpMsg = NULL);
```

The important parameter here is the first one; the verb that you wish to execute in the server. You have a smattering of choices, enumerated below for your reference:

Verb	Description
OLEIVERB_PRIMARY	Simulates the user double-clicking on the object. The object can do whatever it wants in response to the verb. If the object supports in-place activation, the primary verb usually activates the object in-place.
OLEIVERB_SHOW	Indicates that the object is to be shown to the user for editing or viewing. This verb is normally executed when the object has just been inserted, as it readies the object for initial editing.
OLEIVERB_OPEN	Causes the object to be open-edited in a separate window. If the object doesn't support open-editing, this verb has the same effect as OLEIVERB_SHOW.
OLEIVERB_HIDE	Causes the object to remove its user interface from the user's view. The object goes away as if it was closed, but doesn't actually shut down.
OLEIVERB_UIACTIVATE	Used to activate the object in-place and show any user interface tools that it needs, such as menus or toolbars. If the object doesn't support in-place activation, it will return E_NOTIMPL.

The second parameter, the pointer to the view, does just that; points at your view. The Activate() function needs to know about the view associated with the object so that it can properly negotiate the features of the window and get everyone to repaint at the right time.

If, during your program's execution, you want to programmatically activate or deactivate an object, you'll need to call Activate() or Deactivate(). If you want to change the activation pattern, you need to tweak the insertion code in the menu handler just before you UpdateAllViews(). After tweaking the code, it might look like this:

```
m_pSelection = pItem;    // set selection to last inserted item
if (pItem ==
        static_cast<COleClientItem*>(GetDocument()->GetInPlaceActiveItem(this)))
    pItem->Deactivate();
pDoc->UpdateAllViews(NULL);
```

If you're sure that the item you've just inserted has gone in-place active, you can undo the effect by calling Deactivate() immediately. If you deactivate the object, do what you can to avoid repainting when you call UpdateAllViews().

Painting in an OLE Container

After that `UpdateAllViews()` call, `CCntrView::OnDraw()` will be called and the information in the view updated. The default code that AppWizard produces is a little weird. It does everything it can to find an object embedded in the document and, if it finds one, it asks the object to paint itself by calling the object's own `Draw()` member. Out of the box, the AppWizard code looks like this:

```
void CCntrView::OnDraw(CDC* pDC)
{
    CCntrDoc* pDoc = GetDocument();
    ASSERT_VALID(pDoc);

    if (m_pSelection == NULL)
    {
        POSITION pos = pDoc->GetStartPosition();
        m_pSelection = (CCntrCntrItem*)pDoc->GetNextClientItem(pos);
    }
    if (m_pSelection != NULL)
        m_pSelection->Draw(pDC, CRect(10, 10, 210, 210));
}
```

Even though the function we're calling here is named `Draw()`, remember that it is the special implementation of `Draw()` which lives in the `CCntrCntrItem` object. The default `COleClientItem` code runs off to the `IViewObject` interface on the object it represents, which has a method called `Draw()`. This interface allows the container to request any object to draw itself in a variety of modes.

These modes, called **aspects** in OLE, allow the object to express itself in a variety of different circumstances. For example, you can request that the object render itself as an icon, or as a thumbnail representation of the object's real content.

It is appropriate to show an object, which might be inactive, or which is not yet placed within the document, as an icon. The thumbnail is great for situations when you want to browse through different OLE objects, seeing what they're about, without getting the object in full detail. It chokes down resolution and detail, so the object won't need that much space; ideally thumbnails should be 120 pixels square and only use 16 colors.

`COleClientItem::Draw()` takes an optional third parameter which isn't used in the code fragment above. This parameter specifies the aspect that you'd like to draw. The aspect can be any one of these constants as defined by the OLE headers:

```
DVASPECT_ICON
DVASPECT_CONTENT
DVASPECT_THUMBNAIL
DVASPECT_DOCPRINT
```

In the `Cntr` example application, there are three extra menu choices, each of which allows you to request a different aspect of the selected object. These commands are evident in the <u>V</u>iew menu and work by using the `SetDrawAspect()` and `GetDrawAspect()` members of the `COleClientItem` class.

By default, the draw aspect is DVASPECT_CONTENT, so that the full content of the object will be drawn. By calling SetDrawAspect() in response to each of the menu items, we change this to a different behavior. Since Draw() is still called from CCntnrView::OnDraw() with no third parameter, the object will always draw itself in the default aspect specified by the last SetDrawAspect() call, while GetDrawAspect() returns the current default aspect for the object.

For your reference, you can see the icon style here:

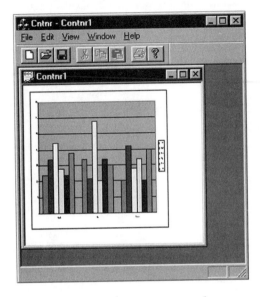

The icon view is appropriate when you don't want to spend time painting the content, or when you feel layout around the object isn't important.

Unfortunately, even though it's a powerful server, Excel doesn't support a thumbnail view. It isn't hard to find servers that are missing some of the basic OLE functionality. If you select an aspect that the object doesn't implement, it just won't draw. The Draw() call will return FALSE to indicate this failure.

Positioning, Moving and Sizing an Object

AppWizard sometimes generates code that's a little odd, at least at first glance. It forces your inserted OLE objects to be a particular size at a particular place – you saw the hard-coded rectangle in the view's Draw() code earlier. The object will always be placed there, since the rectangle is always as it is in the code. AppWizard also generated some code in the container item override, which looks like this:

```
void CCntnrCntrItem::OnGetItemPosition(CRect& rPosition)
{
    ASSERT_VALID(this);
    rPosition.SetRect(10, 10, 210, 210);
}
```

`OnGetItemPosition()` is called through the framework against the object based on a request from the container whenever its current position needs to be known; for example, when the server goes in-place active. You'll need to provide a slightly better implementation of this function, but we'll need to do a little homework first. We can pick a size and position for the container, and then return that information to the server when it's requested – as generated by AppWizard; we end up returning a square of constant size 200, offset just a bit from the top left of the container.

The easy part of realistically solving the positioning problem is adding a `CRect` object to the member data of the `CCntrCntrItem` object. You should also add code to serialize this item with the rest of the container item's member data. The extra code for the `Serialize()` function isn't anything too shocking:

```
void CCntrCntrItem::Serialize(CArchive& ar)
{
    ASSERT_VALID(this);
    COleClientItem::Serialize(ar);
    // now store/retrieve data specific to CCntrCntrItem
    if (ar.IsStoring())
        ar << m_rectPosition;
    else
        ar >> m_rectPosition;
}
```

Now that we've laid down the basic infrastructure for handling the rectangle, we'll need to run about and tweak the `CCntrCntrItem` code so that it manages the value in the `m_rectPosition`, using it and updating it as needed.

As the item becomes in-place active, the container item's `OnChangeItemPosition()` function is called. This function accepts a reference to a `CRect`. We can just call the base-class implementation of the function, and copy the rectangle it discovers into our own rectangle in our member data. `OnChangeItemPosition()` is called when the object has gone in-place active and the user changes its size or position. The returned coordinates should indicate where, relative to the container's client area, the object is shown. We can update `OnChangeItemPosition()` to look like this:

```
BOOL CCntrCntrItem::OnChangeItemPosition(const CRect& rectPos)
{
    ASSERT_VALID(this);
    if (!COleClientItem::OnChangeItemPosition(rectPos))
        return FALSE;

    m_rectPosition = rectPos;
    return TRUE;
}
```

The implementation of `OnChangeItemPosition()` supplied by MFC in `COleClientItem` does nothing more than arrange for clipping of the object – it intersects the passed rectangle with the clipping rectangle managed by the container view.

If the user changes the position of our object, we'll record the new position in our m_rectPosition member for later use. OnGetItemPosition() reports the position and size of the object to any server that requests the information. The AppWizard code for OnGetItemPosition() uses a hard-coded rectangle, as we saw earlier. To fix the OnGetItemPosition() function, we can get it to assign the m_rectPosition rectangle to the object that is maintaining the reference passed to the function. The finished work looks like this:

```
void CCntnrCntrItem::OnGetItemPosition(CRect& rPosition)
{
    ASSERT_VALID(this);
    rPosition = m_rectPosition;
}
```

Now the only problem is getting information back from the server to see exactly how big it's likely to be. Sizing information is available from the server, but it's not in the exact format we'd like to see. All of these coordinates we've so far been tracking in our rectangle member have been in pixels, relative to the client area of our container, but when we request the bounds of the object through OLE, it dictates that the information be returned in a HIMETRIC mapping mode. This means that we'll have to do a conversion.

Here's a little function, called RefreshSize(), to request the size from the server, convert the coordinates to pixels and then update the rectangle:

```
void CCntnrCntrItem::RefreshSize()
{
    CSize size;
    if (GetExtent(&size))
    {
        CClientDC dc(NULL);
        dc.HIMETRICtoDP(&size);

        m_rectPosition.bottom = m_rectPosition.top + size.cy;
        m_rectPosition.right = m_rectPosition.left + size.cx;

        CDocument* pDoc = GetDocument();
        ASSERT(pDoc != NULL);
        pDoc->SetModifiedFlag();
        pDoc->UpdateAllViews(NULL);
    }
}
```

In the above code, I use the m_rectPosition member of the CCntnrCntrItem. This CRect member of the item is initialized by the constructor to some arbitrary values in the constructor for objects that are inserted into the document from scratch. For objects that were previously stored in the document, of course, the value of the rectangle is serialized as the document is loaded.

The function above works by calling GetExtent(), a member of COleClientItem. It accepts a pointer to a CSize and fills that size with the extent of the object in HIMETRIC units. If the function was successful, i.e. if the OLE object isn't empty, the size is converted by retrieving the system device context after passing NULL to the CClientDC constructor. This lets us call HIMETRICtoDP() against a device context which will use the size returned from GetExtent().

The net result is the size of the object in pixels. If we were using a different mapping mode in our view, to be certain, we should make sure to get the device context from the view.

It's appropriate for us to call `RefreshSize()` just after the object has been inserted, which means that we can run off to the `OnInsertObject()` function in our view and make sure that we retrieve the size just after the object is added. The code fragment from the `OnInsertObject()` function looks like this:

```
if (!dlg.CreateItem(pItem))
    AfxThrowMemoryException();   // any exception will do
ASSERT_VALID(pItem);
pItem->UpdateLink();
pItem->RefreshSize();
```

You'll note that, before we make the call to `RefreshSize()`, we call `UpdateLink()`. This function causes the object to update its user interface, doing all the math necessary to measure and repaint its content, before informing the server of its size. If we called `RefreshSize()` without calling `UpdateLink()` first, the object may not have been ready to tell us about its size because the object, itself, wouldn't know where it should be sized.

The value returned from `OnGetItemPosition()` constitutes only a request. If the container decides that it wants to crop the server's image, it has the final say. Again, the roles in the relationship between an OLE server and an OLE client are very strict. If the client wants the server to perform some action, the server performs it. The server is expected to be completely submissive and do nothing more than serve the wishes of the client. (The customer is **always** right!)

Through the whole sizing and activation operation, it's important to remember that the object only reports its size. The math in `RefreshSize()` is to update the rectangle with the right size, and we assume that the rectangle has the correct position. Our `OnChangeItemPosition()` function is called when the user moves the object while it is in-place active, but in all other cases, the server has no say about where it resides within the container. Instead, the rectangle occupied by the object can be set by the client.

Tracking Changes

When the object goes in-place active, it's usually because the user is about to change it. Changes to the object will be reported back to your application via a call to the `OnChange()` member of the `COleClientItem`-based object associated with the OLE object. `OnChange()` is called with two parameters: nCode of type `OLE_NOTIFICATION`, and dwParam, a `DWORD` parameter.

We'll need to write an override for the `OnChange()` function. AppWizard has already provided an implementation, but it doesn't do much – it just calls the base class implementation and then `UpdateAllViews()` to get the application to repaint.

The implementation of `OnChange()` that AppWizard provides looks like this:

```
void CCntnrCntrItem::OnChange(OLE_NOTIFICATION nCode, DWORD dwParam)
{
    ASSERT_VALID(this);
    COleClientItem::OnChange(nCode, dwParam);
    GetDocument()->UpdateAllViews(NULL);
}
```

The call to the base class version of OnChange() is very important; it sets the modified flag in the document associated with the view. This lets the document know that one of the document's components has been changed, even if the document itself hasn't. Since the document in your container application is responsible for storing and loading the objects as well as the document's own content, you'll need to be completely sure that the document's modified flag is managed correctly.

A State of the Object Address

The nCode parameter indicates what type of change took place. nCode might be set to OLE_SAVED if the item was just saved, or OLE_CLOSED if the item was just closed. The OnChange() function can also be called with nCode set to OLE_CHANGED_STATE, to indicate that the object has changed its state. The states in an OLE control's lifetime describe how far it is through its initialization and how it is presented. If the nCode is OLE_CHANGED_STATE, dwParam will include extra information indicating the state of the object. A variety of constants are defined by the OLE headers for this purpose:

dwParam	Description
emptyState	Means that the object is empty
loadedState	Means that the object has just loaded and has connected itself to the document
activeState	The server has been activated in-place but hasn't yet merged its menus, toolbars, and other user-interface components with those of the container
openState	Means that the server has opened its own window to allow the user to edit it, but it isn't in-place active
activeUIState	Means that the server has gone in-place active with all its user-interface components displayed

Note that an object going in-place active will pass briefly through activeState before it reaches activeUIState. Note also that dwParam has no meaning for nCodes of OLE_SAVED and OLE_CLOSED.

You can use the state change notification to react to the user as the user changes the state of your object. You might want to have code that caches more information or perform extra computation only while the object is actually active – or, you might actually change the way that your object renders data depending on which mode it is in. At any time, you can find the state of your object by calling GetItemState(). It'll return one of the constants from the table above. It's quite normal to use a call to GetItemState() to decide how to render yourself in your OnDraw() implementation.

Change Notifications

In addition to the above values we discuss, nCode might be set to OLE_CHANGED. This indicates the object has changed its content rather than any part of its user interface. This is your cue to make sure the change is recorded, which is exactly why we call the base-class implementation of the function to ensure that the document is marked as dirty and unsaved. If you receive an nCode of OLE_CHANGED, the dwParam reflects the aspect of the OLE object that has changed.

The code that AppWizard generates by default forces an update of all views of the object no matter what state or change has occurred.

Picture This

Finally, we need to change the painting code in `CCntnrView::OnDraw()` to use the rectangle we've been busy cooking up. The beauty of C++ is that we only have to code handlers for the update work once. After that function is implemented, it's available for any `COleClientItem` in the house.

Now is as good a time as any to add some proper painting code to the view. The real difference between this code and what we had before is that we need to work with all of the views, not just the active one:

```
CCntnrCntrItem* pCurrent;
POSITION pos = pDoc->GetStartPosition();
while (pos != NULL)
{
    pCurrent = static_cast<CCntnrCntrItem*>(pDoc->GetNextClientItem(pos));
    pCurrent->Draw(pDC, pCurrent->m_rectPosition);
}
```

This code ensures that every embedded object gets painted. It's terribly inefficient, but here are some ways to speed it up:

Paint only what's visible	During the loop, we could compare the position of the object to the client rectangle of the window. This would allow us to avoid all of the OLE overhead involved in the call to `Draw()` against objects which aren't visible anyway.
Paint only what's active	Through a given iteration of the loop, you might want to write code to draw a gray rectangle, or some similar placeholder, instead of spending time rendering the OLE objects that aren't active. When you see the effect it has on your OLE interface, you might decide this isn't so pleasing, as users have to activate objects to see what they're all about. This technique can, though, save you an incredible amount of time when you are drawing your application.
Paint only what's invalid	You should also consider checking the rectangle owned by each object before you ask the object to paint. If the object isn't in the invalid rectangle of the window, don't bother painting it.

Make sure you choose a painting method that's appropriate for your application; utilizing these suggestions to some degree will help you ensure that you paint just as quickly as you can. You might want to leave the slow painting code for now so that you can study the way painting and drawing works in the container before you run off and optimize the code without completely understanding what's going on.

A COleRose is a CRose

It's important to remember that, even though we're concentrating on these extra OLE-enabling shenanigans, COleDocument performs all of the things that you're used to a CDocument doing. You'll still use it to store your application's data and to manage any files that your application needs, but as an OLE container, your application will also need to maintain information about the OLE objects that it contains.

In your serialization code, you should be positive that you've called the base-class implementation of Serialize() once you're done with your own code. If you don't, MFC won't be offered the opportunity to serialize information about the objects you're using, and your users won't be able to get the objects back into memory when they load data files from your application.

When you serialize the document from an OLE container, your application will read or write to a normal data file, but you might find it more efficient, or even necessary, to read or write data into an OLE-formatted storage. You can call the EnableCompoundFile() member of your COleDocument object during your document's constructor to change it to work with structured OLE compound files rather than flat files. If you ask for any OLE document support from AppWizard, you'll have a call to EnableCompoundFile() in your constructor of your CDocument-derived class.

You should call this function during your constructor because both your document and MFC will get sick if you change the setting during your document's lifetime. The function takes a single Boolean parameter (TRUE, by default), which enables compound files if it is TRUE and disables them if FALSE.

Compound file support is faster for documents stored on a hard disk drive because, even though it involves a lot of seeking, your application and the OLE objects in it can incrementally access their own data very rapidly within the file.

Storing the file directly on a floppy will be much slower than a traditional 'flat' document because of the larger amount of index and format data, and the increased seeking which the format mandates. Users rarely save files directly to floppies – they're more likely to save to the hard drive and then copy the file to a floppy, which implies that turning compound file support on in your document will be a safe optimization.

Building a User Interface

When an OLE object isn't in-place active, the user still may be interested in positioning it or changing its size. Since our container is now aware of the size and position of all of the objects it contains, we can go ahead and start looking at how the user might manipulate the position and size of the object, even when it isn't in-place active. Not all programs will need to implement such code, since not all applications are interested in letting the user manipulate and move contained objects within the client area presented by the container application.

But for applications that are interested in implementing a mechanism for the user to place objects in the container, we'll have to write code to react to the mouse. For example, we'll write handlers for WM_LBUTTONDOWN to learn where the user has pressed the mouse button and react accordingly.

As we mentioned before, mouse-handling code is a real pain in the ankle. The math is a nightmare and the code is tough to debug because you can't always switch to the debugger without the mouse context changing. In addition, the way that Windows handles mouse messages requires that you have to maintain a lot of status information to effectively implement a state machine that allows your code to handle the transitions inherent in beginning and ending moving and sizing operations.

As usual, MFC has a class to help us avoid some of this tedium: CRectTracker. This class can help us in a few different ways; it allows us to draw a tracking rectangle in our application, framing the active OLE object with a line and boxes that indicate to the user that the object is sizable. CRectTracker, when active, also helps us by providing code to handle the mouse moves and redrawing of the tracker. We need to call the tracker to notify it of moves as they happen, but we needn't worry about actually implementing the redrawing – it's all built-into CRectTracker.

CRectTracker doesn't help us when the user actually moves the object, since it's only useful for resizing it. Fortunately, allowing the user to move the object is pretty easy.

We'll need to write code that provides the standard user interface for OLE objects. Basic features that users will expect to perform with their mouse include: clicking the mouse to select OLE objects, using the mouse to drag OLE objects, dragging the border of an OLE object to resize it, and double-clicking to open an OLE object.

As a consequence of these features, we must make sure that the currently selected object is framed with a border so that the user can easily identify it.

Most of the activity happens when we add a handler for the left mouse button. After visiting the ClassWizard to get the WM_LBUTTONDOWN handler in our application, we code it to look like this:

```
void CCntrView::OnLButtonDown(UINT nFlags, CPoint point)
{
    POSITION         pos;
    CCntrCntrItem*   pCurrent;
    CCntrDoc*        pDoc = GetDocument();
    BOOL             bHit = FALSE;

    pos = pDoc->GetStartPosition();

    CCntrCntrItem* pLastFound = NULL;
    while (pos != NULL)
    {
        pCurrent = static_cast<CCntrCntrItem*>(pDoc->GetNextItem(pos));
        if (pCurrent->m_rectPosition.PtInRect(point))
        {
            bHit = TRUE;
            pLastFound = pCurrent;
        }
    }
    // more later...
```

As soon as the user presses the left mouse button, we'll enter a loop to see where the button was pressed. The loop takes a peek at each object to see if the point where the mouse was clicked is in the rectangle owned by any object. We'll keep searching through the list, though, even if we think we've found a hit. That's because we want to find the object that's highest in the z-order of the list. Since OnDraw() draws the list in order, we need to find the *last* object in the list to find the object closest to the top of the z-order of the drawn objects.

The PtInRect() member of the CRect class makes such a test pretty simple. Once the loop has been all the way round and has not found a hit, we know the user has clicked on something that's not an OLE object. We can change the current selection to NULL, like this and deactivate anything that's currently active. That'll look like this:

```
if (!bHit)
{
    if (m_pSelection != NULL)
    {
        if (m_pSelection->IsInPlaceActive())
            m_pSelection->Deactivate();
        m_pSelection = NULL;
        pDoc->UpdateAllViews(NULL);
    }
}
```

Since m_pSelection is set to NULL when the user hasn't selected any particular object, we'll know that the selection has moved away from focusing on any one particular object in the container. So we might need to handle the mouse-down event in some other way when m_pSelection is NULL. For example, the user might be selecting an object that the application should draw, or they could be selecting a section of text. Whatever happens is completely up to the application, but, if there isn't a visually selected object (again, since m_pSelection is NULL), the OLE code we're writing needs to make sure that we won't draw the rectangle around the object when it's painted. You'll see the enhanced Draw() function for the view later.

On the other hand, if our loop detects that we did in fact hit an object, we'll need to set up the tracker, which is illustrated here:

```
void CCntnrView::OnLButtonDown(UINT nFlags, CPoint point)
{
    //... stuff from before ...
    if (!bHit)
    {
        if (m_pSelection != NULL)
        {
            if (m_pSelection->IsInPlaceActive())
                m_pSelection->Deactivate();
            m_pSelection = NULL;
            pDoc->UpdateAllViews(NULL);
        }
    }
    else
    {
        CRectTracker tracker(m_pSelection->m_rectPosition,
            CRectTracker::resizeInside | CRectTracker::solidLine);
        if (tracker.Track(this, point))
        {
            m_pSelection->m_rectPosition = tracker.m_rect;
            pDoc->SetModifiedFlag();
            pDoc->UpdateAllViews(NULL);
        }
        return;
    }
```

Continued on Following Page

```
    // here, we could perform other mouse click processing
    // because we know the user clicked outside of all OLE objects
}
```

The CRectTracker constructor takes a pointer to the object's rectangle, as well as some style bits, which describe the tracker that we want to show. The first style bit we specify is CRectTracker::resizeInside. This means that the resize blocks in the tracker will be drawn on the inside of the rectangle bordering the object, but we could have specified CRectTracker::resizeOutside, forcing the tracker to draw the blocks on the outside of the object.

The other style bit we gave is CRectTracker::solidLine. This makes the rectangle a solid line. We could have specified CRectTracker::dottedLine to make the tracker use a dotted line or CRectTracker::hatchedBorder to give the object a thicker, hatched border with a fuzzy appearance. These decisions are superficial; do whatever you or your users like.

Whatever you decide, it's important for you to have a border around the objects to denote the selected objects from other, unselected ones. You might, for example, use a solidLine around all objects and a hatchedBorder around selected objects.

With the tracker created, we call its Track() member function, passing it a pointer to the current view and the point at which the mouse went down. This enables the tracker to draw the rectangle on the window as it's being moved, and handle the movement relative to the point where the mouse first went down, exactly as the user expects.

The Track() function doesn't return until the user lets go of the mouse button, which is useful because it relieves us of handling mouse move messages and worrying about border calculations.

The Track() function takes a couple of extra, optional parameters which aren't used in this example. The first optional parameter (the third actual parameter) is a BOOL which, when TRUE, allows the user to invert the rectangle while they're sizing it. Effectively, this means that if the CRectTracker is actually sizing the object, you can make the left edge of the object become the right edge, giving the rectangle a negative, inverted width. By default, the parameter is FALSE.

The second optional parameter to Track() can be a pointer to a window. If the parameter isn't supplied, the first parameter is used and so the current view's size will be used to limit how the rectangle grows and moves. Otherwise, the rectangle describing the window referenced by the fourth parameter will be used to govern the size of the tracker.

Once Track() does return, we copy the rectangle member of the CRectTracker object back to its correct position, and force the document to refresh our window and any other associated views, allowing the object to be seen in that new position.

Paint a Happy Face

The finally tweaked `OnDraw()` function has code in its inner loop which looks like this:

```
void CCntnrView::OnDraw(CDC* pDC)
{
    // ... other initialization code ...
    while (pos != NULL)
    {
        pCurrent = static_cast<CCntnrCntrItem*>(pDoc->GetNextClientItem(pos));
        pCurrent->Draw(pDC, pCurrent->m_rectPosition);

        if (pCurrent == m_pSelection)
        {
            CRectTracker tracker(pCurrent->m_rectPosition,
                CRectTracker::resizeInside | CRectTracker::solidLine);
            if (pCurrent->GetItemState() == COleClientItem::openState ||
                pCurrent->GetItemState() == COleClientItem::activeState)
                tracker.m_nStyle |= CRectTracker::hatchInside;
            tracker.Draw(pDC);
        }
    }
}
```

The important addition to this section of code is the test to see whether the current item is active or opened. If it is, we draw the rectangle with hatching inside it, making the object appear disabled in the window. This gives the user feedback that they have already opened the object and cannot manipulate it further.

The Size of It All

As the mouse moves through your window, it generates `WM_SETCURSOR` messages. `WM_SETCURSOR` is Windows' way of asking your application to change the cursor. By default, the `WM_SETCURSOR` message causes your window to use the cursor registered with the window class. For most windows, that message is the normal arrow (or whatever customized cursor the user has supplied in its place). You can respond to `WM_SETCURSOR` to have your application display a different cursor depending on the mouse position. Responding to `WM_SETCURSOR` is a great way to offer feedback for different 'hot' places on your window, as well as a great way for us to change the cursor depending on how the user has dragged or sized an object.

If we add a handler for `WM_SETCURSOR`, we'll be able to take some action each time the mouse takes a new position in our window. Since we want the mouse to be able to move the selected object in the window, we'll process this message to see when the mouse is over the active object. The handler looks like this:

```
BOOL CCntnrView::OnSetCursor(CWnd* pWnd, UINT nHitTest, UINT message)
{
    if (m_pSelection != NULL)
    {
        CRectTracker track;
        track.m_rect = m_pSelection->m_rectPosition;
        if (track.SetCursor(this, nHitTest))
            return TRUE;
```

Continued on Following Page

```
    }
    return CView::OnSetCursor(pWnd, nHitTest, message);
}
```

If there is an active selection, we create a tracker and initialize it so it uses the rectangle for the selected object, before we call the SetCursor() member of the object, passing it a pointer to the current view and the hit testing information received from the message. The SetCursor() function decides if the mouse is within the rectangle handled by the tracker and if it is, the function sets the appropriate cursor and returns TRUE.

If the cursor is within the body of the object, the stock Windows four-arrows cursor is shown. This gives the user the feedback they need to know that the object can be dragged and moved. If the cursor is near the edges of the object, the function sets the appropriate two-arrow cursor to indicate that the user can resize the object using the mouse.

If track.SetCursor() returns TRUE, we get the application to return TRUE immediately. This prevents Windows from processing the cursor message and resetting it to the stock cursor as defined by the window's class, which in the case of our standard CView, is just the normal arrow cursor. If the function didn't change the cursor, we do indeed return to Windows and allow it to change the cursor to an arrow.

The tracker in the OnLButtonDown() function realizes that the user has pressed the mouse button to do some resizing because it tests to see if the mouse hit any of the sizing handles on the tracking rectangle. If it did, it goes into a mode that allows the user to drag the object to a new size. Otherwise, it processes the click as we discussed before when we presented our implementation of the OnLButtonDown() function.

Activation

The only task that is left is to make sure we can activate the object by using the mouse. This is relatively very simple; just handle WM_LBUTTONDBLCLK by implementing an OnLButtonDblClk handler. If there's an active object, we can activate the object by sending it the appropriate OLEIVERB. Here's the function:

```
void CCntnrView::OnLButtonDblClk(UINT nFlags, CPoint point)
{
    if (m_pSelection != NULL)
    {
        CCntnrCntrItem* pItem = static_cast<CCntnrCntrItem*>(m_pSelection);
        if (nFlags & MK_CONTROL)
            pItem->DoVerb(OLEIVERB_OPEN, this);
        else
            pItem->DoVerb(OLEIVERB_PRIMARY, this);
    }

    CView::OnLButtonDblClk(nFlags, point);
}
```

The standard is that the user should be able to hold down the *Ctrl* key to open the server fully, while simply double-clicking should bring the object in-place active. To serve this need, we test the nFlags variable passed with the message. If the user has the *Ctrl* key down, the test for the MK_CONTROL mask will be TRUE and we'll execute the OLEIVERB_OPEN verb, otherwise the OLEIVERB_PRIMARY verb is sent.

Note that the OLEIVERB_PRIMARY verb, used to make the server go in-place active, will have the same effect as OLEIVERB_OPEN on servers that don't support in-place activation. Also note that MFC provides inherent support for tapping *Esc* to kill the in-place activation of the open object, so we don't need to write any special code to make sure that the server can leave the active state.

The Edit Menu

You've probably noticed that the Edit menu of our example is still a little bare. The default implementations of Paste and Paste Link don't do anything for OLE objects, so we'll need to correct that. Fortunately, the fix is pretty easy; the code we need to write isn't much more complicated than what we saw in the Insert New Object... handler.

To get the Paste command to work, we'll need to implement a handler for it. We can then insert code like this:

```
void CCntnrView::OnEditPaste()
{
    CCntnrCntrItem*    pItem = NULL;
    CCntnrDoc*         pDoc = GetDocument();
    ASSERT_VALID(pDoc);

    ...

    CWaitCursor waiter;
    try
    {
        pItem = new CCntnrCntrItem(pDoc);
        if (!pItem->CreateFromClipboard())
            AfxThrowMemoryException();

        pItem->UpdateLink();
        pItem->RefreshSize();

        m_pSelection = pItem;
    }
    catch (CException* pEx)
    {
        // ... error handling stuff ...
        pEx->Delete();
    }
}
```

In this case, the important code is all inside the try block and is essentially the same as the Insert New Object... code. The most obvious difference is that this code isn't driven by a dialog box. Information about the object is on the clipboard, so after creating a new CCntnrCntrItem object, we simply call the CreateFromClipboard() member of that object for it to be created and added to the document.

Note that this code is unaware of the clipboard's power. While the code is just fine for pasting in OLE objects, you might not always want this. As it stands, pasting some text from Word results in an OLE object being pasted into the document, and is a remarkably inefficient way to reuse text from one application to another.

There are a few solutions to this problem, one of which is to use the <u>P</u>aste command strictly to paste 'flat' clipboard data, like text. The other solution is to add some intelligence to our code – we can use an MFC class called `COleDataObject` to pick apart the data that appears on the clipboard.

OLE and the Clipboard

The clipboard is far more robust when transferring an OLE object than it is when just pasting 'flat' formats. Normally, you add data to the clipboard by putting it in some global memory and passing a handle to that global memory. The block of memory must be specially marked as being safe to use between processes so that Windows can do some magic between the producer and the consumer.

When we're using OLE, things are a little more robust – the producing application just places information on the clipboard, indicating that data is available. It's not until the data is actually consumed that the source application needs to supply actual data. In the beginning of our paste handler, we might build a `COleDataObject` from the data on the clipboard to investigate exactly what's available to us. This code might make a good preamble to that showcased above:

```
void CCntnrView::OnEditPaste()
{
    CCntnrCntrItem*   pItem = NULL;
    CCntnrDoc*        pDoc = GetDocument();
    ASSERT_VALID(pDoc);

    COleDataObject   Obj;
    Obj.AttachClipboard();
    if (Obj.IsDataAvailable(CF_TEXT))
    {
        STGMEDIUM myStg;

        if (!Obj.GetData(CF_TEXT, &myStg))
            MessageBox(_T("Failed!"));
        else if (!(myStg.tymed & TYMED_HGLOBAL))
            MessageBox(_T("Unrecognized format"));
        else
        {
            LPSTR lpstr = (LPSTR)::GlobalLock(myStg.hGlobal);
            MessageBox(lpstr);
            ::ReleaseStgMedium(&myStg);
        }
    }
    // can't get data in a CF_TEXT format.
    // we should just paste the object the way we were going to
    Obj.Detach();

    ...
}
```

The `AttachClipboard()` member of `COleDataObject` populates the object from the OLE data which is expected to be available on the clipboard. We can test for any registered clipboard format by calling `IsDataAvailable()` and passing it the appropriate clipboard format identifier. This could either be one of the `CF_` formats from the table below, or a custom format which was previously registered using the `::RegisterClipboardFormat()` API.

Clipboard Format	Description
CF_TEXT	Plain text.
CF_BITMAP	Bitmap graphics.
CF_METAFILEPICT	A picture stored as a Windows GDI metafile.
CF_SYLK	SYLK format.
CF_DIF	Data Interchange Format. This is used by some spreadsheets.
CF_TIFF	Tagged Image File Format. This is used by some imaging programs and particularly popular with fax receiver programs.
CF_OEMTEXT	OEM text. Like CF_TEXT, but uses the OEM character set.
CF_DIB	Device independent bitmap graphic.
CF_PALETTE	Palette information. This is often sent in conjunction with CF_DIB.
CF_PENDATA	Data captured by Windows for Pen Computing, including stroke and ink information.
CF_RIFF	RIFF sound format.
CF_WAVE	WAVE sound format.
CF_UNICODETEXT	Like CF_TEXT, but allows characters from the Unicode set.
CF_ENHMETAFILE	Enhanced Windows Metafile.
CF_HDROP	A global memory object that contains a DROPFILES structure. Used to handle multi-file drag-and-drop across applications (and from the Window shell). This format only works on operating systems with the new shell.
CF_LOCALE	A global memory object that contains information about the locale for the data on the clipboard. You can provide data of this format in conjunction with the CF_TEXT format to let the recipient of the clipboard know what locale you used to format the data.

Since CF_TEXT is just regular text, we can pick it apart by calling GetData() on the object, but beware; CF_TEXT doesn't mean what you might think. CF_TEXT is available from almost every paste operation, because most providers can tweak their data into this format very easily, but the CF_TEXT version of an object often isn't even close to what the user might expect. The CF_TEXT data produced when an Excel chart is on the clipboard is a purely textual, tabular representation of the data used to make the chart. So, the tabbed data that is returned might look like this:

```
841.25\t77.56\t158996\n\856.77\t79.41\t162786\n866.73\t80.75\t165545\n
```

At the data source, the actual table looks a lot more like this:

841.25	77.56	158996
856.77	79.41	162786
866.73	80.75	165545

and the chart is really some graphical representation of that same information.

At any rate, the call to COleDataObject::GetData() requests that the STGMEDIUM which we declared should be populated with information from the CF_TEXT data on the clipboard. STGMEDIUM is an OLE-defined data structure essentially used to abstract the exact data type received from OLE data handling calls. STGMEDIUM is a union of lots of common data types (HGLOBAL, HBITMAPS and so on), each one pertaining to a different clipboard data type.

If the call to GetData() is successful, we use ::GlobalLock() to gain a pointer to the data on the clipboard and display the string using a simple MessageBox() call, just for demonstration. For a real application, we might perform whatever insertion we need to get the plain text data into our document.

Paste Special

One way to solve the problem of getting the right data representation (and therefore the right format) is to offer the user control over what data format is used to perform the paste operation. Most applications expose this via a Paste Special... command in the Edit menu. This command shows the user a dialog before it executes the paste operation; the user can choose any one of the available representations for the data on the clipboard. Such a dialog is shown here:

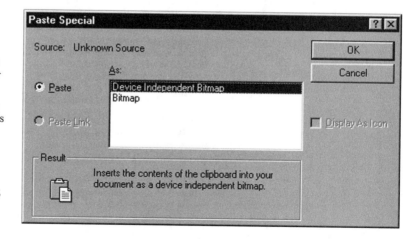

The Paste Special dialog is implemented by the MFC class `COlePasteSpecialDialog`. You can create an instance of this class, tell it what formats you're interested in offering, optionally turn on linking and get it to display the dialog.

Once the dialog has been initialized and created, you can call the object's `DoModal()` function to show it to the user and get their reaction. If the user accepts the dialog, the function will return `IDOK`. If they dismiss it with the intent of aborting the paste operation, you should take note of this and perform no further actions. Code from the example that implements a Paste Special dialog looks like this:

```
COlePasteSpecialDialog dlg;
dlg.AddStandardFormats();
if (dlg.DoModal() != IDOK)
    return;
```

The `AddStandardFormats()` call tells the dialog to display any standard formats which are acceptable for pasting into your application. Note that this call, as written, will also let the user paste a **link** to the data in question (we haven't talked about links yet, but it's coming up in a section or two). If you don't want to let the user paste links, you can pass `FALSE` as a parameter to `AddStandardFormats()`.

If your application implements its own format, having used `::RegisterClipboardFormat()` to tell Windows and OLE about it as the application started, you should use the `AddFormat()` member of `COlePasteSpecialDialog` to get the dialog to display your format. You'll need to pass `AddFormat()` some information which describes your format.

The `::RegisterClipboardFormat()` API accepts, as its only parameter, the plain text name of your clipboard format. This format name will be given to the user in situations where they need to see it, so keep it terse, descriptive and clean. The function returns a `UINT`, which uniquely identifies the format. If some other application has registered the same format, the function returns the same `UINT`. This is the function that is used by all the applications that want to be users of a format; they register the name and get a `UINT` that matches everyone else's.

On the other hand, `AddFormat()` can take that `UINT` and organize any future pasting using that format. The function also accepts the ID of a string resource that names and describes the format. The resource is split in half by a newline character. The string before the newline character names the format for the user, while the text after it describes the result of a paste operation.

`COlePasteSpecialDialog::AddFormat()`'s prototype looks like this:

```
void AddFormat(UINT ClipboardFormat, DWORD tymed,
               UINT nFormatID, BOOL bEnableIcon, BOOL bLink);
```

The function also accepts a flag, indicating whether the D<u>i</u>splay as Icon check box in the dialog is shown or not, and another flag that controls the display of the Paste <u>L</u>ink checkbox in the dialog.

The `tymed` parameter is a `DWORD`, which indicates how the data will be exchanged by your application. `TYMED`, which stands for *type of media*, is an OLE type that specifically describes how data is conveyed. The various formats are given in this table. These values can be combined with the bitwise OR operator if more than one format is available.

TYMED Formats	Description
TYMED_HGLOBAL	A handle to global memory.
TYMED_FILE	In a file. The exchanged data simply names the file.
TYMED_ISTREAM	An OLE stream.
TYMED_ISTORAGE	An OLE storage.
TYMED_GDI	Passes a GDI object – either a handle to a device-independent bitmap or a handle to a palette.
TYMED_MFPICT	A metafile.
TYMED_ENHMF	An enhanced metafile.
TYMED_NULL	No data is to be passed.

When you're pasting, all you're really interested in is a simple and convenient way to get at the data. You'll also need to check the TYMED used so that you know how to free the data that was given to you; for instance, TYMED_FILE means that you're responsible for deleting a file. If you received data via TYMED_HGLOBAL, you'll need to call ::GlobalFree() on the handle to release the memory.

If you're an experienced OLE programmer, you can use an override of AddFormat() which accepts a pointer to a FORMATETC structure. This structure is used by OLE to manage information describing data formats. The AddFormat() version we've just discussed works just like the FORMATETC version – it just helps you by translating the parameters you supply into a FORMATETC before using them later.

Once the list of formats is set, you can use the dialog to insert the object in much the same way the Insert New Object... dialog worked. Please refer to the code in the example to see exactly what it does. It's quite similar to the code in the handler for the new object command. You can find all of the code in the example's Cntrvw.cpp file. Look for the CCntrView::OnEditPasteSpecial() function.

Copying and Cutting OLE Objects

Back to the clipboard! We haven't yet implemented Copy and Cut commands for our own menu. We should do this so that users cut and paste objects to move them from one container to another, or copy and paste objects in order to replicate them.

Implementing cut and copy commands is trivial because the COleClientItem class gives us functions that do all of the dirty work with the object's data and the clipboard. The Copy implementation looks like this:

```
void CCntrView::OnEditCopy()
{
    ASSERT(m_pSelection != NULL);
    if (m_pSelection != NULL)
        m_pSelection->CopyToClipboard();
}
```

The Cut implementation is just a little bit more complicated because it actually updates the document. We need to mark the document as 'dirty' and then have it repaint, which means that our Cut implementation looks like this:

```
void CCntnrView::OnEditCut()
{
    ASSERT(m_pSelection != NULL);
    if (m_pSelection != NULL)
    {
        CCntnrDoc* pDoc = GetDocument();
        m_pSelection->CopyToClipboard();
        m_pSelection->Delete();
        m_pSelection = NULL;
        pDoc->SetModifiedFlag();
        pDoc->UpdateAllViews(NULL);
    }
}
```

By the way, the example application also has implementations for the various UPDATE_COMMAND_UI functions associated with the menu commands. The calls to do this are pretty obvious; we just handle the UI update function by checking to see whether m_pSelected is NULL. The only tricky UI update comes when we need to see if pasting is possible in order to update the Paste command. Here's the code:

```
void CCntnrView::OnUpdateEditPaste(CCmdUI* pCmdUI)
{
    if (COleClientItem::CanPaste())
        pCmdUI->Enable(TRUE);
    else
        pCmdUI->Enable(FALSE);
}
```

The only trick is that CanPaste() is a static function of the COleClientItem class. We don't need to have a COleClientItem floating around to be able to use the function, but we'll need to carefully qualify the invocation of the function in order to make the call – that is, we'll call COleClientItem::CanPaste() and not just CanPaste(). Very similar code appears in the UI update handler for the Paste Link command, which we'll implement in the next section. You might not often see this kind of syntax, but it's useful when you need it!

Links

You might also want to implement a command that sends you out golfing. You'll need to allocate a few CIron, CWedge, and CDriver objects before you get them collected in a CGolfBag collection.

Oh, wait a minute, *OLE* links. All of the objects we've talked about have been embedded, but OLE stands for Object *Linking* and Embedding, so we'll have to take a look at that too. Inserting a link means that the object doesn't really live inside of the container's document. Instead, the document includes a much less substantial object that requests data from its source. The primary difference between a linked and an embedded object is that the linked object will update itself when data in the source document changes, while an embedded object is a separate copy of the source data.

Pasting a linked object involves some very different architectural components of MFC, but, as far as we're concerned, it's almost the same as pasting an object directly. Essentially, to paste a link, we'll have to call a different member of the `COleClientItem` class. Where we called `CreateFromClipboard()` before, we'll now have to call `CreateLinkFromClipboard()`.

The whole trick looks like this:

```
void CCntnrView::OnEditPasteLink()
{
    BeginWaitCursor();

    CCntnrDoc* pDoc = GetDocument();
    CCntnrCntrItem* pItem = new CCntnrCntrItem(pDoc);
    if (!pItem->CreateLinkFromClipboard())
    {
        pItem->Delete();
        EndWaitCursor();
        MessageBox(_T("Could not create link from clipboard!"));
    }
    else
    {
        m_pSelection = pItem;
        pItem->RefreshSize();
        pDoc->UpdateAllViews(NULL);
        EndWaitCursor();
    }
}
```

As this construction is a bit simpler than the other applications, we haven't used `try/catch` error handling. Instead, we just check the return value from the `CreateLinkFromClipboard()` function directly.

Drag-and-drop

Drag-and-drop allows users to move objects from one application to another without using the keyboard or any menus. You might select a chart in Excel and then drag it to your container to embed it, rather than selecting it in Excel, using the menu to copy the item, transferring focus to the container and then using the container's menu to paste the object.

The drag-and-drop protocol provides a convenience to users. You may not be interested in implementing it if you're going to write a special-purpose container, but if you're writing a general-purpose one, your users will expect to see this kind of support. Remember – almost every other similar application in the market offers it.

Getting Started with Drag-and-drop

The drag-and-drop protocol works with three different entities: the object that's being dragged, the **drop source** and the **drop target**. The drop source is the application that originally had the object, while the drop target is the application that accepts the object once the drop is completed. The drop source could be an OLE container or an OLE server.

The dragged object is just that – an object. The manager of the data, which is sometimes the drag source, is what orchestrates all the work behind the scenes. This implies that, in order to handle every kind of object, our container must also be a drag source; even though it doesn't serve any objects, someone may insert an object within our container, before dragging it off to some other.

For now, to implement the drop target code, you'll need to identify the view in your application as a drop target. First, you'll need to add a `COleDropTarget` object to the member data of the `CView` object in the application. To ensure the information is available throughout our application, make sure the object is declared in the `public` part of the view class, then use ClassWizard to add a handler for the `WM_CREATE` message in your view. Your finished code will look like this:

```
int CCntnrView::OnCreate(LPCREATESTRUCT lpCreateStruct)
{
    if (!m_dropTarget.Register(this))
        MessageBox("Could not register as drag/drop target");

    if (CView::OnCreate(lpCreateStruct) == -1)
        return -1;
    return 0;
}
```

Calling `Register()` lets OLE know that we'll support an `IDropTarget` implementation under the covers. Of course, MFC does most of the work for us, but it's still important to declare our intentions before we get started with the rest of the code.

Take a Drag

In the example so far, you have almost every thing you need to make drag-and-drop work. There's an additional function to be called, `DoDragDrop()`, which is a member of the `COleClientItem` class. We'll call the function when the user presses the mouse button over an object within our container. The `DoDragDrop()`'s prototype looks like this:

```
DROPEFFECT DoDragDrop(LPCRECT lpItemRect,
    CPoint ptOffset,
    BOOL bIncludeLink = FALSE,
    DWORD dwEffects = DROPEFFECT_COPY | DROPEFFECT_MOVE,
    LPCRECT lpRectStartDrag = NULL);
```

The first parameter is the item's rectangle, while the second is the point where the mouse went down inside the object. This point is relative to the object. That is, the point should be nearly (0,0) if the user put the mouse down near the top left corner of the object. This point shouldn't be relative to the container's client area.

The third parameter, `bIncludeLink`, should be `TRUE` if your application is prepared to offer and support the linking of this object. If your application is strictly a container and can't serve objects, you should always pass `FALSE` for the `bIncludeLink` parameter. Containers can't support objects, period. If you've written a combination server/container, you should make sure you only offer links for objects that you actually serve.

The dwEffects parameter indicates the functions that the drag operation will support. DROPEFFECT_COPY means that the item will be duplicated when it is dropped, while DROPEFFECT_MOVE means that the item will be copied and then deleted from the drop source when it is created in the drop target.

The lpRectStartDrag rectangle tells the dragging code where the process will actually start. If the parameter is NULL, the process starts when the mouse moves one pixel from where it started. If the parameter isn't NULL, the mouse cursor has to be dragged outside of the rectangle specified before the dragging operation starts.

Note that all of these coordinates are screen coordinates. They aren't relative to the client area of the window where the operation is taking place. So, we need to tweak the code in the OnLButtonDown() to make sure that we can handle the drag operation. We'll start with the CRectTracker, which you create once you know the user has clicked on an object.

As we have seen before, CRectTracker has a HitTest() function. We'll use it here to see if the user clicked on the object itself and not actually on one of the sizing grabbers on the tracking rectangle.

If you perform the hit test and discover that the user has indeed clicked in the heart of the object, you'll need to call the DoDragDrop() member of the CCntnrCntrItem object. In the implementation, we use a flag named m_bDragMode to make sure that we know when we're dragging an object from our application.

If any of the drag-and-drop functions (in particular, OnDrop()) are called when m_bDragMode is FALSE, the code knows that the drag-and-drop operation originated outside of our container application. We'll also test the flag here, so we know if we need to do any clean-up work after an internal drag operation. Dropping an object within an application is often used to just move it; dropping an object from another application is shorthand for cutting and pasting it.

This is the new code fragment from OnLButtonDown(). You can find the whole thing in the Cntnrvw.cpp file in the example:

```
if (tracker.HitTest(point) == CRectTracker::hitMiddle)
{
    CRect rectScreenObject = pCurrent->m_rectPosition;
    CPoint ptClickOffset(point.x - rectScreenObject.left,
        point.y - rectScreenObject.top);

    CRect rectAwake = rectScreenObject;
    rectAwake.InflateRect(1, 1);

    ClientToScreen(&rectScreenObject);
    ClientToScreen(&rectAwake);

    m_bDragMode = TRUE;
    DROPEFFECT dropResult = pCurrent->DoDragDrop(rectScreenObject,
        ptClickOffset, TRUE, DROPEFFECT_COPY | DROPEFFECT_MOVE, &rectAwake);
    if (m_bDragMode == FALSE)
        return;
```

```
    if (dropResult == DROPEFFECT_MOVE)
    {
        pCurrent->Delete();
        pDoc->SetModifiedFlag();
        pDoc->UpdateAllViews(NULL);
    }
}
else if (tracker.Track(this, point))
{
    // ... old code here ...
}
```

When the `DoDragDrop()` call returns, it provides a `DROPEFFECT` value which describes the result of the drag-and-drop operation. By testing this value, you can decide what needs to be done in response to the result. In the example application, we've deleted the dragged object if the drag-and-drop operation resulted in a move. This is all that's required of your application, although you might be interested in displaying a status message, or, in other cases, marking the document as dirty.

Our drag code is by no means complete. We need to handle several different notification functions, each called during different parts of the drag-and-drop process. These functions are all members of view objects that are registered as a drag source; they're not actually called unless the object has registered itself as supporting OLE drag operations.

The biggest difficulty with handling drag-and-drop operations is that we don't know anything at all about the incoming object, so the handling functions have to be written in a generic fashion. Even if the object came from our own application, we need to treat it abstractly. Of course, we don't normally know much about an object when it is embedded in our application. But, for drag-and-drop, we have to provide some amount of user interface to make sure that the user has a grip on what's going on; more specifically, we need to know how big the object is.

On the Clipboard

The OLE object will be given to us using clipboard data formats. OLE will notify us that a drag-and-drop operation has been initiated, but we can get the object's actual information from the pointers provided to us using the different clipboard data formats that OLE provides for every object.

Of particular interest to us is the Object Descriptor, which gets us an `OBJECTDESCRIPTOR` structure. This has two members that we'll make use of: a size and a point. These members are used to describe the object's size and the position of the mouse when the drag started.

The online help documents all of the other format information that is available during the transfer of an object. You can look these up if you're interested – the most pertinent one is a Link Source Descriptor, which can uncover information about the source of a linked object.

In order to use this clipboard format, we have to call the Windows
`::RegisterClipboardFormat()` API. This function returns a clipboard format identifier, which can be used to get the information in that format back from OLE. We wrote this code to register the format in the `CCntrView` constructor:

```
CCntrView::CCntrView()
{
    if (m_cfObjectDescriptor == NULL)
    {
        m_cfObjectDescriptor = (CLIPFORMAT)
            ::RegisterClipboardFormat(_T("Object Descriptor"));
    }
}
```

`m_cfObjectDescriptor` is a static member of the `CCntrView` class. Since it's static, it has to be added to the class definition in the header and it should be declared in the `Cntrvw.cpp` file. The declaration looks like this:

```
CLIPFORMAT CCntrView::m_cfObjectDescriptor = NULL;
```

You'll note that I take the conservative approach of initializing `m_cfObjectDescriptor` in the constructor. I could call `::RegisterClipboardFormat()` in the initializer list above but that would induce a dependency on the initialization order of objects in my application – which I might not be able to manage effectively.

Anyway, we'll need to code a function to get the information about the object we're passing around. It can be a member of our `CCntrView` class, and will look like this:

```
BOOL CCntrView::GetSizeInfo(COleDataObject* pObject, CSize& szSize, CSize& szPlace)
{
    HGLOBAL hDesc = pObject->GetGlobalData(m_cfObjectDescriptor);
    if (hDesc == NULL)
        return FALSE;

    LPOBJECTDESCRIPTOR pDesc =
                    static_cast<LPOBJECTDESCRIPTOR>(::GlobalLock(hDesc));
    if (pDesc == NULL)
        return FALSE;

    szSize.cx = static_cast<int>(pDesc->sizel.cx);
    szSize.cy = static_cast<int>(pDesc->sizel.cy);

    szPlace.cx = static_cast<int>(pDesc->pointl.x);
    szPlace.cy = static_cast<int>(pDesc->pointl.y);

    ::GlobalUnlock(hDesc);
    ::GlobalFree(hDesc);
    return TRUE;
}
```

The trick in `GetSizeInfo()` is to call `GetGlobalData()` on the `COleDataObject` passed to it. This function returns an aspect of the data which we request in the first parameter; the return value is a handle to a global block of memory, which you can lock down using the `::GlobalLock()` API.

As we designed this code, it was tempting to put the `GetSizeInfo()` function in the `CCntrCntrItem` class. We couldn't do this because the drag-and-drop routines will need the sizing information before a `CCntrCntrItem` object has been created from the object data dragged into the application during the drag operation.

Now, at various points in the drag operation, you'll need to call this function to get size and positioning information about the object you're dragging around.

OnDragEnter()

`Cview's` `OnDragEnter()` member function is called when the user is about to drag-and-drop a selection into the window. The return value from this function indicates to Windows what will happen if the user drops the files into the window. The default implementation of this function returns `DROPEFFECT_NONE`, which means the drop will not be allowed. If you wish to allow the drop, you should override this function and return some other code.

This is the first function that's called during a drag operation and is also called as soon as the drag operation begins. You'll need to use the ClassWizard to make a handler for this function before you code it to get some information from the object that is being dragged. `OnDragEnter()` receives a pointer to the `COleDataObject` being manipulated, as well as to the point where the mouse is residing when the button was finally released to complete the drop operation.

The function needs to return a `DROPEFFECT` code, which describes what would happen if the user released the mouse button to drop the object. Since we also need to return that same state information from `OnDragOver()`, the function which is called when an object is dragged with the mouse, `DROPEFFECT`, simply delegates the decision to `OnDragOver()`.

So, the whole thing comes together like this:

```
DROPEFFECT CCntrView::OnDragEnter(COleDataObject* pDataObject,
    DWORD dwKeyState, CPoint point)
{
    if (!GetSizeInfo(pDataObject, m_szObjectSize, m_szPreviousOffset))
        return DROPEFFECT_NONE;

    CClientDC dc(NULL);
    dc.HIMETRICtoDP(&m_szObjectSize);
    dc.HIMETRICtoDP(&m_szPreviousOffset);

    return OnDragOver(pDataObject, dwKeyState, point);
}
```

If finding the drag acceptance is an expensive operation – for example, if you've got to look through a long list of items and compare positions as part of your hit testing; you might want to find a way to cache the results so that you can efficiently respond to drag queries.

The warts on the face of this code are the calls to `HIMETRICtoDP()`, as OLE (almost) always reports coordinates in a `HIMETRIC` scale. After getting the sizes from `GetSizeInfo()` into `m_szObjectSize` and `m_szPreviousOffset`, they have to be tweaked into device pixels because it's more convenient for us to draw with device coordinates when working with the mouse – unless you're already using `HIMETRIC` in your application's main window! `m_szObjectSize` contains the size of the object, while `m_szPreviousOffset` contains the offset of the mouse when the drag-and-drop operation was initiated. `m_szPreviousObject` is relative to the object's rectangle.

OnDragOver()

`OnDragOver()` is called each time the user moves the mouse to position the dragged object. You can add a prototype and shell for the function with ClassWizard. The function is passed a pointer to the object being dragged, information about the keyboard state, and the point where the mouse cursor resides.

`OnDragOver()` has a number of responsibilities; providing the user with visual feedback about the operation taking place, so they know where the object will be dropped, and how the operation will be performed, if it is allowed. The function also uses its return value to indicate to OLE what the mouse cursor looks like during the drag operation. Normally, the function returns `DROPEFFECT_NONE`, which indicates that the drop operation will be denied. This causes the mouse cursor to appear like the international 'don't do it' sign; a circle with a diagonal stroke through it. This return value is brought back, through MFC and OLE, to become the return value of `DoDragDrop()`.

If the function returns `DROPEFFECT_MOVE`, the standard mouse cursor will appear, while `DROPEFFECT_COPY` displays a standard mouse cursor with a small plus sign (+) next to it.

DROPEFFECT code	Cursor
DROPEFFECT_NONE	🚫
DROPEFFECT_MOVE	▶
DROPEFFECT_COPY	▶ ⊞

`OnDragOver()` can draw the rectangle outlining the target of the drop using the `DrawFocusRect()` member function of the CDC class. The implementation looks like this:

```
DROPEFFECT CCntnrView::OnDragOver(COleDataObject* pDataObject,
   DWORD dwKeyState, CPoint point)
{
   point -= m_szPreviousOffset;

   DROPEFFECT retval;
   if (dwKeyState & MK_CONTROL)
      retval = DROPEFFECT_COPY;
   else
      retval = DROPEFFECT_MOVE;
```

```
    if (point != m_ptDragPoint)
    {
        CClientDC dc(this);
        dc.DrawFocusRect(CRect(m_ptDragPoint, m_szObjectSize));
        m_ptDragPoint = point;
        dc.DrawFocusRect(CRect(m_ptDragPoint, m_szObjectSize));
    }
    return retval;
}
```

The code features a small optimization; if the current point is exactly equal to the last point we drew for our rectangle, the drawing code is skipped. The current point is held in `point`, while `m_ptDragPoint` holds the previous drawing point for the object. `m_ptDragPoint` is initialized to (-1, -1) in the object's constructor and reset to (-1, -1) in `OnDrop()`. The value of (-1, -1) safely indicates that the point is invalid – and will force this comparison to fail whenever the drag operation is just getting started. Note that there are two calls to the rectangle drawing function. One redraws the old rectangle to erase it, while the other draws the rectangle in the new position.

OnDragLeave()

`OnDragLeave()` is called if the user has selected an object in our application and then dragged it off to some other application. `OnDragLeave()` is the last we'll hear of the action. To close the drag operation, we'll just erase the tracking rectangle by drawing it just one more time. Since the member variables in our view object are still in shape from the last call to `OnDragOver()`, we can just run off and draw the focus rectangle. It's easy:

```
void CCntnrView::OnDragLeave()
{
    CClientDC dc(this);
    dc.DrawFocusRect(CRect(m_ptDragPoint, m_szObjectSize));
}
```

There's nothing to clean up at this point because the user has moved out of our window. Some other application (or the system itself) will have to free the object and clean up any internal state information that's floating around. `OnDragLeave()` doesn't even return a value. The drag isn't our problem anymore.

Don't Bogart that Object

When the user finally finishes with their drag, OLE gets MFC to call the `OnDrop()` function of your view. This function finalizes the drag-and-drop operation. It cleans up any activation rectangle lying about from the object being dragged through the view's client area, and then decides what needs to be done to finish the drag-and-drop operation based on the flags we've set throughout the operation.

In any case, the function starts by doing some math to see where the dragged object landed:

```
if (!GetSizeInfo(pDataObject, m_szObjectSize, m_szPreviousOffset))
    return FALSE;

CClientDC dc(NULL);
```

Continued on Following Page

```
dc.HIMETRICtoDP(&m_szObjectSize);
dc.HIMETRICtoDP(&m_szPreviousOffset);
point -= m_szPreviousOffset;
```

You've seen essentially the same code in OnDragEnter(). We just get the size information from the data object and convert all of the coordinates to fit our client area, then we have to decide if we're moving from our own application or not. If we are, we'll execute this code:

```
if ((dropEffect & DROPEFFECT_MOVE) && m_bDragMode && m_pSelection != NULL)
{
    m_bDragMode = FALSE;
    if (m_pSelection->m_rectPosition.TopLeft() != point)
    {
        m_pSelection->m_rectPosition =
                        CRect(point, m_pSelection->m_rectPosition.Size());
        pDoc->SetModifiedFlag();
        pDoc->UpdateAllViews(NULL);
    }
    return TRUE;
}
```

It's also important that we reset the m_bDragMode flag. We take care of finalizing the drag operation here, so the code back in LButtonDown() can be avoided. It will test m_bDragMode, see that it is FALSE and exit early.

On the other hand, if we were dragging some new OLE object into our application, we would need to create the object from data provided in the data object passed to OnDrop(). That process is similar to the other object creation work we've done before. It'll look like this:

```
else
{
    CWaitCursor waiter;
    CCntnrCntrItem* pItem = NULL;
    try
    {
        pItem = new CCntnrCntrItem(pDoc);
        if (!pItem->CreateFromData(pDataObject))
            AfxThrowMemoryException();
        if (!GetSizeInfo(pDataObject, m_szObjectSize, m_szPreviousOffset))
            AfxThrowMemoryException();

        CClientDC dc(NULL);
        dc.HIMETRICtoDP(&m_szObjectSize);
        pItem->m_rectPosition = CRect(point, m_szObjectSize);
        m_pSelection = pItem;
        pDoc->SetModifiedFlag();
        pDoc->UpdateAllViews(NULL);

        return TRUE;
    }
    catch(CException* pEx)
    {
        // error handler...
        pEx->Delete()
    }
```

The basic difference between this code and what we've seen previously for inserting a new OLE object is that it positions the object carefully, based on the point and size information the object gave us after the drag operation. Apart from this, the creation code here is very much like that we've seen for the Paste or Insert New Object... menu choices.

Stunts with Drag-and-drop

Drag-and-drop is pretty simple, once you get through all of the math and data gathering that has to happen. It's important to note that the functions for drag-and-drop support shown here (OnDrop(), OnDragEnter(), OnDragLeave() and OnDragOver()) were all members of the CView used in the example. These functions also exist in the COleDropTarget class. We added an object of this class as a member to the CView in the example. If you wanted to, you could have different subclasses of COleDropTarget to handle different types of inserted objects, allowing them to behave with very different rules as the user dragged and dropped objects.

You might wish to offer help to your user by placing informative text in the status bar during your handling of the different drag-and-drop messages. You can do this by looking at the dwFullUserTypeName of the OBJECTDESCRIPTOR structure returned from the object's descriptor. You might want to write a GetObjectType() function similar to GetSizeInfo() implemented in the example for retrieving the display size of the object.

Perhaps the most deceiving of all stunts is optimization. To keep things clear and simple, none of the code in the chapter has been optimized to paint reasonably. Any time the activity requires a repaint, we trundle off and call UpdateAllViews() and pass NULL. This is bad! Everything will repaint in every view, and that can be expensive. In most cases, it would be pretty easy to use the m_rectPosition member of the invalidating object to make only the appropriate part of the view repaint. Back when we discussed how OnDraw() works for an OLE container, we also discussed some appropriate optimizations generally applicable to drawing the objects in the container.

Incidentally, all of the drag-and-drop functions shown here wrap up the IDropSource and IDropTarget interfaces on OLE objects. If you're curious about other tricks you can try with OLE drag-and-drop, you can read up on these interfaces in the Platform SDK references.

Other Kinds of Containment

We've reviewed plain OLE Embedding in this chapter, and shown how MFC can act as a client for embedded OLE objects. There are a couple of other kinds of OLE containment, though, and they deserve our attention. One other kind of containment is for OLE Controls. We'll discuss that kind of containment in Chapter 16. Another interesting kind of containment involves **OLE Document Objects**.

DocObjects, for short, are a variant of regular OLE Embedded objects. They differ from regular OLE embedded objects in only a couple of ways. First, a DocObject becomes active in the complete client area of the container – not just in a small rectangle. The DocObject is free to present whatever user interface it wants, and generally won't interact with the user as if it was an intrinsic part of the user's document. The user, in fact, normally sees a DocObject as a completely separate object rather than an object that's a part of the original document.

Since a DocObject takes over the entire client area, it uses slightly different rules to negotiate menu space with its container. And it will also be allowed to span more than one page – unlike a regular embedded object, which can't be bigger than a page.

Typically, DocObject container applications will let the user feel as if they've embedded another application rather than just an object of the application. The container application might collect the documents of different applications into one compound file, like the Microsoft Office Binder application does. In your own applications, you might have a different application appear as a different view type. For example, you might let the user edit your native data in one view while you show Excel or PhotoShop as a different view. You can have your application store all the data – both your own native data and the hosted application's data – on a single file.

DocObjects are essentially always activated; they *don't* ever go to a selected state, like embedded objects do. Such a limitation makes sense, as the selected state does nothing more than let the user resize and position the embedded object. As a DocObject is always as large as its container window, it needs no user interface for sizing or moving.

You can add DocObject containment support (or server support – which we'll cover in the next chapter) by marking the appropriate box in AppWizard's third step, shown here.

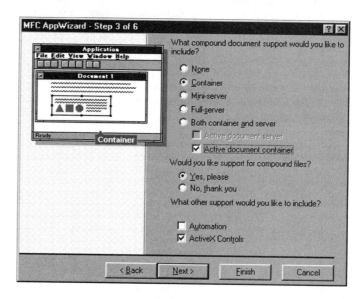

You'll need to have some sort of containment step already enabled, since MFC uses the regular embedding code as a basis for the extended, DocObject containment support. Since the user model for a DocObject container is different than that for a regular embedded object container, the code provided by AppWizard is just a little different.

First off, AppWizard provides a slightly modified `OnInitialUpdate()` handler for your view. The view needs to activate a DocObject item after serialization, so the initial update handler of the view finds the first DocObject item associated with MFC document and activates it. If you write an application that stores more than one DocObject per document instance, you may want to revise the code to activate a particular view. Otherwise, the code is just fine as it stands – it gets a loaded object activated as it is displayed for the first time.

The view also features some extra code (in `OnCancelEditCntr()` and `OnSetFocus()`, specifically) to handle those DocObject-specific activation patterns. The container item is also different – it'll have extra overrides to handle the activation, too.

In your DocObject-compatible application, your application's document class still derives from `COleDocument` if you're writing a container. All the rules for serialization are the same for your own data, but it's even more crucial that you give the base class serialization code a call when you're ready to write data to a file. Otherwise, you won't serialize the data associated with the contained object. You'll notice, though, that the constructor for the document calls `EnableCompoundFile()`. That's essential because the contained DocObjects *must* serialize into a compound file.

DocObject Command Targets

The DocObject model also introduces an interesting way for the containing application and contained application to communicate. This mechanism is the **OLE command target** feature. It borrows strongly from MFC's normal `CCmdTarget`-based implementation, but the beauty is that it crosses the client-server line.

Under the covers, the process of sending a command down to the server object uses the `IOleCommandTarget` interface. The interface is really simple – it just requires a command ID and a target. The process is so similar, in fact, to regular MFC command routing, MFC features a few macros to directly connect MFC command handlers to OLE-based command handlers.

Of course, the connection mechanism is a map. You can add a `DECLARE_OLECMD_MAP()` macro to the declaration of your view or your document. Then, add a command map to the implementation of your class. A simple map with a couple of entries looks like this:

```
BEGIN_OLECMD_MAP(CYourDoc, COleDocument)
    ON_OLECMD_PRINT()
    ON_OLECMD(NULL, OLECMDID_MYOLECOMMAND, ID_MYCOMMAND)
END_OLECMD_MAP()
```

The first entry attaches a predefined MFC command to a well-known OLE command. Here, the OLE print command is being attached to the stock `ID_FILE_PRINT` command MFC applications handle. Whenever the client receives an OLE print command from the server, it'll be redirected to the `ID_FILE_PRINT` command handler – just as if the regular menu item had been clicked.

The second entry attaches the `OLECMDID_MYOLECOMMAND` command from OLE to the `ID_MYCOMMAND`. The macro accepts three parameters – the second is the command ID for OLE, and the third is the command ID for the menu handler you're attaching. The first parameter is a GUID indicating the group of command IDs that are being considered. `NULL` means that the command ID is of the standard group – any other GUID value can be used as you define your own groups.

Here are the standard commands and the stock MFC commands to which they map:

`ON_OLECMD_CLEARSELECTION()`	`ID_EDIT_CLEAR`
`ON_OLECMD_COPY()`	`ID_EDIT_COPY`
`ON_OLECMD_CUT()`	`ID_EDIT_CUT`
`ON_OLECMD_NEW()`	`ID_EDIT_NEW`
`ON_OLECMD_OPEN()`	`ID_FILE_OPEN`
`ON_OLECMD_PAGESETUP()`	`ID_FILE_PAGE_SETUP`
`ON_OLECMD_PASTE()`	`ID_EDIT_PASTE`
`ON_OLECMD_PASTESPECIAL()`	`ID_EDIT_PASTE_SPECIAL`
`ON_OLECMD_PRINT()`	`ID_FILE_PRINT`
`ON_OLECMD_PRINTPREVIEW()`	`ID_FILE_PRINT_PREVIEW`
`ON_OLECMD_REDO()`	`ID_EDIT_REDO`
`ON_OLECMD_SAVE()`	`ID_FILE_SAVE`
`ON_OLECMD_SAVE_AS()`	`ID_FILE_SAVE_AS`
`ON_OLECMD_SAVE_COPY_AS()`	`ID_FILE_SAVE_COPY_AS`
`ON_OLECMD_SELECTALL()`	`ID_EDIT_SELECT_ALL`
`ON_OLECMD_UNDO()`	`ID_EDIT_UNDO`

You'll note that there's support for printing and print preview. MFC hooks up these responses to work correctly in the document object environment whenever they're issued.

Let me stress that OLE commands can be sent both from the client to the server and from the server to the client.

DocObject Downside

Unfortunately, as appealing as the DocObject paradigm seems, it's a very weak standard. Different application developers have interpreted the specification differently, and Microsoft's own applications use extensions to the specifications that aren't documented. As such, achieving full compatibility is very, very difficult. You'll find that most of the Office applications work fine with MFC's DocObject containment, as long as you stick to their simplest features. Third-party applications may or may not work. A particular pitfall to avoid is nested containment – that is, containing a DocObject that, in turn, contains another DocObject or another plain OLE Embedded object.

Unless you're certain to stick to the most conservative features, you will probably want to avoid DocObject containment in your applications. DocObject servers, on the other hand, are a little safer to use because the server side of the specification is subject to a little less interpretation. I've covered this aspect of OLE here mainly for completeness – hopefully, in future versions of the product, the specification will become clearer and stricter and the feature will shape up.

Automation

Up to this point, the container application perceives the OLE objects it contains as lifeless little blobs. You can glue them up in your window and hope they look nice, but once that's done, they're just like me; a good-looking management problem.

Automation provides a way for you to invoke **methods** or get or set any **properties** that an object might expose. The idea is that the container may have created the OLE object for more than just looks; in the case of automation, the object might not even have a user interface.

Automation is designed around COM's `IDispatch` interface. This interface features a method called `Invoke()`, which defines an elaborate but relatively straightforward protocol for objects. A COM object can listen to the `IDispatch` interface or interfaces it provides and react accordingly. The `Invoke()` protocol allows the caller to provide parameters to the invoked method or understand different data types that the server object might manage.

You can imagine that Automation is terribly useful when coupled with robust components that are exposed as automated objects from other applications. The use of Excel as an embedded object has often been referred to in this chapter, but think of how much more power the container application might have if we could ask Excel to update, change, reformat, or populate that spreadsheet!

The popularity of Automation received a real nudge when Microsoft began promoting Visual Basic for Applications (VBA). The idea was that even those with little programming experience could use VBA to increase the flexibility of different applications by combining them with other applications. Imagine writing an Excel macro (with a Basic-like syntax) that automates the process of developing reports that are Word documents built from boilerplate text and graphs drawn by Excel.

VBA is good for applications built informally on the desktop, but Automation is also applicable to more serious applications written in C++. You might need to use C++ for performance or compatibility reasons; if those Excel charts come from the complex summarization of tens of thousands of database records, you could probably get the job done using Excel's VBA implementation, but performance would be prohibitively slow.

How Does It Work?

The `Xdriver` example application shows how to write a simple MFC program to talk to Excel. Instead of putting automation code in to the container example, we've created a separate example. The example is quite simple; it creates the Excel application object and allows you to perform a couple of different operations against it.

Dispatch Driver Eight Takes a Break

The rock group REM didn't realize it when they wrote that song, but calling the `Invoke` method of the `IDispatch` interface is often a nightmare. You have to build a list of parameter values in an array then accompany it with an array of parameter types, before looking up the dispatch ID of the method you want to invoke. If you have some named parameters, you're in even worse trouble because those have to be added to a different set of arrays.

MFC has a class to take away some of this tedium, of course. Once you have the `LPDISPATCH` you wish to use, you can create a `COleDispatchDriver` object and use its members to set and get properties or invoke methods in the object. Even if you don't have the `LPDISPATCH` you want, you can use the `COleDispatchDriver` class to load the associated COM server if you know the Program ID of the server you want to build.

We could, for example, build a `COleDispatchDriver` by just constructing it:

```
COleDispatchDriver myDisper;
```

Then, we could call `myDisper.AttachDispatch()` to tell the dispatch class what `LPDISPATCH` interface, exactly, we want to call. If we use this method, we'll need to call `ReleaseDispatch()` to make sure the dispatch interface is properly released when we're done. We'll then need to call `DetachDispatch()` to shut down the `COleDispatchDriver` object. Calling `DetachDispatch()` doesn't destroy the `COleDispatchDriver` object, it just makes it ready to be used against another dispatch interface.

The `AttachDispatch()` and `DetachDispatch()` functions assume that we've already gained a `LPDISPATCH`. If we haven't created the COM object yet, we can call the `CreateDispatch()` member of `COleDispatchDriver`, which loads the object, performs a `QueryInterface()` call for the `IID_IDispatch` interface, and then initializes the `COleDispatchDriver` from there.

The neatest thing about `CreateDispatch()` is that it has two overrides. One is for when we don't know the `CLSID` of the object we're after in the first place and want to use the program ID string. The other override takes the `CLSID` and tries to hook up the interface itself.

Invoking a Method

Once you've created the `COleDispatchDriver` and attached it to a dispatch interface, you can invoke any method in the dispatch you'd like. The `InvokeHelper()` function takes an interesting variable list of parameters:

```
void COleDispatchDriver::InvokeHelper( DISPID dwDispID,
                                       WORD wFlags,
                                       VARTYPE vtRet,
                                       void* pvRet,
                                       const BYTE FAR* pbParamInfo,
                                       ...);
```

The first parameter is the dispatch ID for the exact method you wish to invoke. The second is a set of flags that designates the type of dispatch you're performing. Normally, this parameter is `DISPATCH_METHOD`, since you usually use the `InvokeHelper()` function to execute a method in the object attached to the dispatch helper.

You could, however, also supply DISPATCH_PROPERTYGET or DISPATCH_PROPERTYPUT to indicate that you were setting or getting a property value using InvokeHelper(). COM objects use their IDispatch interface for both properties and methods, so this isn't really as strange as it sounds, but it does make the meaning of your code a little cloudy. Just for style, it's good to use InvokeHelper() for methods and SetProperty() and GetProperty() for tweaking properties.

The third parameter to InvokeHelper() specifies the type of return value that the method being invoked will provide and the fourth is the address of the variable that will receive the property value or return value. Of course, it must be the same type as specified in the previous parameter.

Data types handled by Invoke are pretty much always VARIANTs. A VARIANT is a union that allows Invoke to easily pass values around without much regard to their type. If you were using Automation interfaces directly, you'd have to create, initialize, set and destroy VARIANTs for each parameter type you pass. InvokeHelper() takes care of this for you.

However, the naming convention of VT_ lives on in the type identifiers which InvokeHelper() lets us use. This means that the third parameter for InvokeHelper() can be any one of these identifiers:

Symbol	Return Type
VT_EMPTY	void
VT_UI1	BYTE
VT_I2	short
VT_I4	long
VT_R4	float
VT_R8	double
VT_CY	CY
VT_DATE	DATE
VT_BSTR	BSTR
VT_BSTRA	BSTRA
VT_DISPATCH	LPDISPATCH
VT_ERROR	SCODE
VT_BOOL	BOOL
VT_VARIANT	VARIANT
VT_UNKNOWN	LPUNKNOWN

You'll notice that there are a few more VT_ types offered in the system headers. Unfortunately, InvokeHelper() is limited to supporting the types listed here.

The last parameter before the ellipsis, `pbParamInfo`, specifies the types of the parameters passed to the function as subsequent arguments. These are represented by an ellipsis because the number of parameters can vary.

Rather than forcing us to build an array of VT_ values to describe the parameters we'll be passing to the invoked function, MFC resorts to a little trickery. If you're not much of a C or C++ language lawyer, you might not know that adjacent string literals are concatenated if nothing appears between them. So, if we code:

```
CString strName =  "Mark " "Messier";
```

you might think it was a syntax error, but, in fact, the statement is exactly equivalent to:

```
CString strName =  "Mark Messier";
```

MFC uses this trick by defining a group of VT-like preprocessor symbols (prefixed with VTS_ rather than VT_) to allow us to build argument lists for passing to the interface. So, the idea is that:

```
#define    FIRST   "Mark "
#define    LAST    "Messier"

CString strName = FIRST LAST;
const char szName[] = FIRST LAST; // same thing — not a feature of CString
```

is equivalent to both of the statements above. Given preprocessor symbols that uniquely identify each of the possible parameter data types as string constants, we can simply string together the different type names and let them expand to one large string.

The `InvokeHelper()` function can then pick apart the string, character-by-character, to figure out what parameter types to expect. The remaining parameters to the function make up a variable-length argument list; they actually provide the values of the parameters in question. While there's quite an elaborate process underneath the covers, we're left with an incredibly simple method for specifying parameter lists for the `InvokeHelper()` function.

Here's a list of the types that can comprise the fifth argument to the function:

Symbol	Parameter Type
VTS_I2	short
VTS_I4	long
VTS_R4	float
VTS_R8	double
VTS_CY	const CY*
VTS_DATE	DATE

Symbol	Parameter Type
VTS_BSTR	const char*
VTS_DISPATCH	LPDISPATCH
VTS_SCODE	SCODE
VTS_BOOL	BOOL
VTS_VARIANT	const VARIANT*
VTS_UNKNOWN	LPUNKNOWN
VST_UI1	BYTE*
VTS_PI2	short*
VTS_PI4	long*
VTS_PR4	float*
VTS_PR8	double*
VTS_PCY	CY*
VTS_PDATE	DATE*
VTS_PBSTR	BSTR*
VTS_PBSTRA	BSTRA*
VTS_PBSTRT	BSTRT*
VTS_PDISPATCH	LPDISPATCH*
VTS_PSCODE	SCODE*
VTS_PBOOL	BOOL*
VTS_PVARIANT	VARIANT*
VTS_PUNKNOWN	LPUNKNOWN*

So let's take a look at a couple of `InvokeHelper()` examples. If we want to call a method, which takes two short integers and returns a Boolean, we might do so like this:

```
short int nParam1;
short int nParam2;
BOOL bRetValue;

myDisp.InvokeHelper(DISPID_SAMPLE, DISPATCH_METHOD, VT_BOOL,
    &bRetValue, VTS_I2 VTS_I2, nParam1, nParam2);
```

Again, remember that we use a space and not a comma between the two `VTS_I2` specifiers. We want to specify one string that is built by concatenating together the two distinct strings each `VTS_I2` macro represents.

If we have another method that takes a double and two long integers and returns nothing, we could call `InvokeHelper()` in this way:

```
double dParam1;
long int lParam2;
long int lParam3;

myDisp.InvokeHelper(DISPID_SAMPLE, DISPATCH_METHOD, VT_EMPTY,
                    NULL, VTS_R8 VTS_I4 VTS_I4, dParam1, nParam2, nParam3);
```

Since there's no return value, the address for the return variable (the fourth parameter) is NULL.

Setting and Getting Properties

You can set and get properties using the `GetProperty()` and `SetProperty()` members of `COleDispatchDriver`. `GetProperty()` takes the dispatch ID of the property in question, a `VT_` to indicate the type of variable in question, and the address of the target variable in your program. You could query a Boolean property with code like that in the fragment below:

```
COleDispatchDriver myDisp;
myDisp.CreateDispatch(_T("MyAmazingServer"));
BOOL bValue;

myDisp.GetProperty(DISPID_FONT_ITALIC, VT_BOOL, &bValue);
```

The `VT_` type used in the second parameter can be any one of those used by the `COleDispatchDriver::InvokeHelper()`. In the above hypothetical code fragment, we're assuming that someplace we have brought in a header file that defines the dispatch ID named `DISPID_FONT_ITALIC`.

`SetProperty()` is amazingly similar. With the same context as the `GetProperty()` call above, we could set the font to be italic by calling:

```
myDisp.SetProperty(DISPID_FONT_ITALIC, VT_BOOL, TRUE);
```

Be careful that `SetProperty()`, `GetProperty()` and `InvokeHelper()` don't return error codes; they throw exceptions. After a call to any of these, you might find yourself facing down a `COleException` or a `COleDispatchException`.

Looking Up Dispatch IDs

In the `GetProperty()` example fragment, we used a constant which we assumed was available to us. If the server with which you work has a header with such definitions, you're in wonderful shape, but if it doesn't, you'll need to find a way to get the dispatch IDs for each of the properties or methods you wish to use.

To solve this problem in the `Xdriver` example, we've included a function called `GetDispID()`. This function accepts the name of a method or property as a string and retrieves the dispatch ID from the application's **type library**. The type library is used for exactly this purpose, to let callers dynamically interrogate the interfaces that a program provides.

The GetDispID() function uses the GetIDsOfNames() method of the IDispatch interface. This call is relatively straightforward; but to make it work, we had to resort to something of a trick. Since we're using a COleDispatchDriver throughout the rest of the code, we don't always have an actual pointer to the dispatch interface. Fortunately, it turns out that COleDispatchDriver has the pointer as a public member variable named m_lpDispatch.

On the other hand, we might not always want a dispID from the main application object dispatch; for example, while handling the **New Book** button, we need to get the IDispatch interface of the application's Workbooks object, then we need to find the dispID of the Add method in that interface. If we don't pass a third parameter to our own GetDispID() function, it tries to find the named method on the application object's dispatch interface. If a pointer to a dispatch interface is provided as the third parameter, we'll use that interface to find the requested method.

The code for GetDispID() looks like this:

```
BOOL CXDriverDlg::GetDispID(LPTSTR pstrName, DISPID* pdisp,
                                      LPDISPATCH lpDisp /* = NULL */)
{
    HRESULT hr;

    if (lpDisp == NULL)
        hr = m_Dispatch.m_lpDispatch->GetIDsOfNames(IID_NULL,
            &pstrName, 1, LOCALE_SYSTEM_DEFAULT, pdisp);
    else
        hr = lpDisp->GetIDsOfNames(IID_NULL, &pstrName,
            1, LOCALE_SYSTEM_DEFAULT, pdisp);

    if (FAILED(hr))
    {
        CString str;
        str.Format(_T("Could not find DISPID for %s"), pstrName);
        MessageBox(str);
        return FALSE;
    }

    return TRUE;
}
```

m_Dispatch is a member of the dialog class that we've added. It gets initialized in the OnConnect() member using CreateDispatch().

Note the way that we handle the result from GetIDsOfNames(). Since we're calling COM directly, we'll need to carefully handle the result and act accordingly.

You can refer to the online help included with Excel to learn more about the different objects that Excel supports. There are over two dozen different objects, each with its own dispatch interface, and therefore its own set of properties and methods!

Automatic for the People

Even with the `COleDispatchDriver` trick up our sleeve, it can be tedious to set up `COleDispatchDriver` objects and the according calls to different invocation, set, and get functions. Of course, this approach wasn't so bad when we wrote the `Xdriver` example, since it makes relatively few calls, but if we were really to kick Excel around the block, we'd be interested in any of the dozens (and dozens!) of different calls and properties of the various objects that Excel exposes. This problem isn't unique to Excel either; you're likely to have a great time with almost any robust Automation server.

If we have access to the type library for the application, the ClassWizard can help out, since it features an **Add Class...** button leading to a menu with **From a type library...** on it. Selecting this will bring you to a dialog allowing you to create a wrapper class for interfaces defined in the type library. This dialog is shown here:

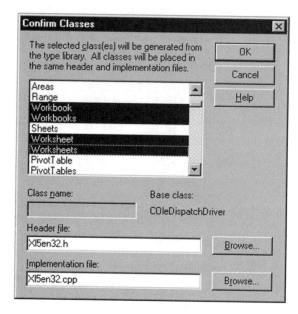

Once you've wrapped the interfaces supported by your server, you can make function calls directly to objects of the C++ classes produced by AppWizard; you need do nothing else.

This method is much less tedious than that used in the `Xdriver` example, but note that the type libraries for many applications are huge. Even creating classes for one or two interfaces is an incredible addition in code size. All of those types and interfaces would dwarf the mainline code in `Xdriver` itself! On the other hand, accessing the type library through calls to `IDispatch::GetIDsOfNames()` is a rather expensive operation. The code we wrote does it for each call, but these calls are not very frequent.

If you were to use this sort of approach when shoving data into your target very rapidly, you probably wouldn't be happy with its performance. On the other hand, having the ClassWizard generate the code with all of the dispIDs hard-coded into the function avoids the dynamic type library hit and will give you better results.

Unfortunately, it's not always easy to dig up the type library for an application as they occasionally have strange file extensions or can be baked right into an executable as a custom resource.

Handling Character Types in OLE Applications

Applications you write that deal with OLE are likely to call methods in COM interfaces or COM APIs directly. Interfaces that accept strings, whether they're interfaces that are wrapped by or implemented by MFC, will accept Unicode parameters.

Put simply, the rules are these; if you're writing an ANSI-only application, you'll need to convert every string you give to OLE, or get back from OLE because those strings will be in Unicode. If you have a Unicode application, you won't need to worry about the conversions. If you're writing an application that can be compiled for Unicode or for ANSI, you'll need to write your code so that it conditionally converts strings from ANSI to Unicode if the string is an ANSI string, i.e. if the build is an ANSI build.

But, for the vast majority of applications, you *will* need to convert from ANSI in your application to Unicode in OLE. You'll need to do this even in Windows 95 and Windows 98; even though the rest of Windows 95 (and Windows 98) doesn't support Unicode, OLE under Windows 95 and Windows 98 *does*.

In MFC 3.x, Microsoft provided a library called `Mfcans32.dll`. This dynamic link library could be used by your ANSI applications to automatically convert parameters to Unicode and make return values become ANSI. The great thing about `Mfcans32` is that it quietly replaced the APIs and interfaces that it knew about. If `Mfcans32` didn't know about a custom interface you were using, you'd need to do the conversion yourself anyway. The bad thing about `Mfcans32` was that it slowed things down. If you made a call to a particular method and that method populated a structure with four strings and two integers, `Mfcans32` would take care of converting those strings every time you made the call to the method. That's great if you're using those strings, but if you care only about the integers, the automatic conversion turns out to be a waste of time. (Not doing work you don't need to do is a great way to save time. Maybe, someday, I'll write a self-help book.)

In MFC 4.0 and newer, Microsoft addressed the expense of the conversion at the unfortunate sacrifice of the convenience. MFC 4.0 got rid of the `Mfcans32` library and replaced it with a fistful of macros that can be used to do the conversions on an as-needed basis. This isn't as nifty as `Mfcans32`, but it certainly is lots more efficient. If you're not interested in the strings, you just don't convert them and you can play with your integers at will.

MFC actually steals code code to handle these conversions from ATL. The implementation is in `Atlconv.h`, which you'll find in `Microsoft Visual Studio\Vc98\ATL\Include` with the rest of the ATL headers.

If you're writing a function that will call a COM interface and you need to handle conversions, you'll need to invoke the `USES_CONVERSION` macro in your function. This macro declares a variable which is used by the macros which actually perform the conversion, so it is important that you declare it at the largest scope within your function as possible – that will let the conversion functions perform with the best efficiency.

Once you've invoked USES_CONVERSION, you're free to use any of the following macros to get some conversions done. The macros all have neat names, like this:

Macro Name	Function
T2A	Converts a string from a TCHAR type to an ANSI string
A2T	Converts from an ANSI string to a TCHAR string
T2W	Converts from a TCHAR string to a Unicode string
W2T	Converts from a Unicode string to a TCHAR string
OLE2T	Converts from an OLE string to a TCHAR string
OLE2CT	Converts from an OLE string to a const TCHAR string
T2OLE	Converts from a TCHAR string to an OLE string
T2COLE	Converts from a TCHAR string to a const OLE string

The macros accept a pointer to a string of the given type and return a pointer to the converted string. The macros are smart enough to do nothing if they don't need to. For example, if you are building for Unicode, a TCHAR string *is* a Unicode string. Since a Unicode string is the same as an OLE string, the T2OLE and OLE2T macros don't do anything in such a build. However, if you're building for ANSI, these functions will make the appropriate conversion because an ANSI string isn't acceptable as an OLE string without conversion.

The const versions of the above macros are appropriate for situations where the strings will be unchanged or passed directly to a function which requires a const string pointer.

You can find code that looks a little like this in the Xdriver sample's Xdrivdlg.cpp file. It works in response to the Connect button. Here's the function:

```
void CXDriverDlg::OnConnect()
{
    USES_CONVERSION;

    try
    {
        HRESULT hr = ::CLSIDFromProgID(L"Excel.Application.5", &m_XLclsid);
        if (FAILED(hr))
            AfxThrowOleException(hr);
        m_Dispatch.CreateDispatch(m_XLclsid);
    }
    catch(COleException* pEx)
    {
        // the function does clean up work here
    }
    // the function does more work here …
```

First things first, of course – this function *doesn't* use any of the conversion macros. Since I've got a string constant, I can just ask the compiler to hold a Unicode representation of that constant directly. That's what the L prefix before the string means. If I had an arbitrary string, I might want to use the macros so that the conversion could be done:

```
BOOL CreateSomeProgID(LPCTSTR pstrProgID)
{
    USES_CONVERSION;

    try
    {
        HRESULT hr = ::CLSIDFromProgID(T2OLE(pstrProgID), &m_XLclsid);
        if (FAILED(hr))
            AfxThrowOleException(hr);
        m_Dispatch.CreateDispatch(m_XLclsid);
    }
    catch(COleException* pEx)
    {
        // ... and so on
```

This version of the function uses the USES_CONVERSION macro to set up for conversions to be done later. Later comes pretty quickly; in the first statement in the try block, you can see I convert the passed parameter to an OLE string pleasing to the OLE ::CLSIDFromProgID() API. Again, if you build this sample for Unicode, the T2OLE macro won't do anything, but if you make an ANSI build, T2OLE will do the conversion for you. If you don't use USES_CONVERSION when you should, you'll probably end up with an error message like this:

YourFile.cpp(261) : error C2065: '_convert' : undeclared identifier

All of these macros work by allocating a buffer for the converted string on the stack using the _alloca() function from the C run-time library. The beauty of this is that the string dies automatically when the current language scope block ends. On the other hand, if you were to use this code in a loop, you'd be continually bloating the stack and if you're in a deep, deep loop, that can quickly cause problems.

If (for some crazy reason) I needed to call ::CLSIDFromProgID() in a loop that executed ten thousand times, I might be tempted to write this code:

```
void MyAmazingFunction(LPTSTR pstrProgID)
{
    USES_CONVERSION;

    for (int n = 0; n < 10000; n++)
    {
        LPOLESTR pstrOLE = T2A(pstrProgID);
        // do something with pstrOLE
    }
}
```

The strings will be allocated and allocated and allocated — they'll not be freed from the stack. This will cause your program to perform poorly because Windows will have to handle page faults to grow the committed size of your stack. You could avoid the problem by either not continually converting the string (since `pstrProgID` in this example never changes, there's no reason to convert it every time through the loop) or by placing the conversion and the actual work with the string in a separate function.

It's also possible to overflow the stack space that you have if you need to convert a massive string. Program ID's are normally short, less than 32 characters, so they're not dangerous candidates for the conversion macros. On the other hand, if you're tempted to use the macros to convert arbitrary buffers, some consideration is due. You might want to allocate your own buffer from the heap and directly use the conversion APIs (`::MultiByteToWideChar()` and `::WideCharToMultiByte()`, specifically).

There are a few more macros than I showed in the first table, by the way. Now that I've gotten through the explanation of what's really going on, let's examine them:

Macro Name	Function
DEVMODEOLE2T	Convert a DEVMODE structure with OLE strings to a DEVMODE structure with TCHAR strings.
DEVMODET2OLE	Convert a DEVMODE structure with TCHAR strings to a DEVMODE structure with OLE strings.
TEXTMETRICT2OLE	Convert a TEXTMETRIC structure with TCHAR strings to a TEXTMETRIC structure with OLE strings.
TEXTMETRICOLE2T	Convert a TEXTMETRIC structure with OLE strings to a TEXTMETRIC structure with TCHAR strings.
BSTR2TBSTR	Convert a BSTR to a TCHAR string.

Each of these macros actually converts all of the strings in popular OLE-related structures to usable forms. The TEXTMETRIC structure was the one I was thinking of when I was prattling on about converting strings you don't need. It's pretty common to grab a TEXTMETRIC just to see how big a font is — there's no need to convert the whole structure (and the two strings it contains) just because you need the size. This holds true for these macros, too — you can party on all the other aspects of the structure without a conversion if the strings don't interest you.

OLE Containers and the Document/View Architecture

There are many people who don't like using the document/view architecture; it causes them endless headaches, and forces them to conform to a programming style that they don't like. We showed how this doesn't have to be true back in Chapter 4; you can avoid or ignore the document/view architecture quite readily when writing simple MFC applications.

Things are a little bit trickier when you use OLE in your application, however. MFC OLE classes are, indeed, rooted firmly in documents. You'll find it very difficult to serialize data for embedded OLE documents in your application without using the `COleDocument` routines to do so.

If you really want to, you can continue with an architecture that uses `CDocument` for nothing but storing data, but you'll be stuck jumping through lots of hoops to make sure you're hooked up to the functionality MFC is trying to provide your view. It seems downright foolish to ignore the free OLE support offered by MFC. You might devise a method to trick the foundation classes into supporting you while you don't play along with their architecture, but that will become increasingly difficult, as you need to add more and more complex OLE support to your application.

Summary

Through this chapter, we've discussed all of the important things you need to know when you're writing an OLE container in MFC. We've seen how you can add useful facilities to your program by adding clipboard and drag-and-drop support, as well as how to create Automation clients. In the next chapter, we'll take a look at the other side of the COM equation: writing servers.

14

Writing OLE Servers

Most developers will be content to write OLE containers or clients, reusing the code provided by other applications or integrating those applications into a smooth, powerful solution for their problem. Some developers, though, will see a need to write their own reusable objects, implemented as OLE or COM servers. It's these noble but adventurous programmers that this chapter seeks to serve.

In this chapter we'll cover:

> Registering COM objects
> Serialization
> OLE's in-place frame
> Automation

OLE Servers

As we mentioned when we first investigated AppWizard, OLE servers that are generated by AppWizard can be either **mini servers** or **full servers**. Furthermore, a full server can also be an **Active Document Server**. A mini server lives only to serve an object; it often can't print by itself and certainly can't store or load its own file type without help. However, when it is running as an object embedded in some other application, it serves the containing application fully. If the containing application asks an object served by the mini server to print or save itself, then it must be able to do so. A full server, as we saw, can run either in the role of a mini server embedded in another application or as the source application its own right.

Technically, the Wizards can provide you with a couple of other server types. If you generate an ActiveX control using the ActiveX Control Wizard, you'll be generating a special type of OLE server. There's also an ATL COM Wizard, which produces tiny, lightweight objects which might act as servers. In this chapter, we'll examine mini servers and full servers; these aren't quite the same as ActiveX Controls because they're capable of serving full documents.

If you ask AppWizard for a full server, you might also ask AppWizard to provide code to implement an Active document. Active documents are a bit different than plain full servers, though it's very easy to write a program that provides both levels of service.

In this chapter, we'll take a look at these issues and get you on your way to writing a healthy OLE server. You'll notice that many of the issues exposed while you're writing a container are naturally reversed when you come to deal with servers, such as how you're providing data instead of using it, for instance.

Servers and Containers; Working in Perfect Harmony

The tango that your servers and containers will dance is documented fully in the online documentation provided with Visual C++. If you find your programs lack features or extensibility after reading my chapter, look through the MFC documentation to see what interfaces and features you could add to your code to make it more robust. Most of the extras you'd consider implementing are functions you can override in response to calls on the `IOleInPlaceActiveObject` interface.

Since we covered the basics of OLE in the previous chapter, we don't need to revisit them here. But there are a few additional issues that are specific to the server side of the equation. To provide a solid foundation, we should know about them before we embark on our mission to write an OLE server application using MFC.

Registration

In the previous chapter, we mentioned how OLE clients use the registry to look up the `CLSID` of an object they wish to create. It's the responsibility of the server to make sure it is properly registered. If it isn't, the server won't be visible to other applications that might want to make use of objects provided by the server.

OLE embedding servers written with MFC will actually expose document templates as the creatable object. By designing your MFC applications around the document/view architecture, you can assure that MFC is able to use the abstractions you've created for your data and its representations to work as an OLE server.

Any application that needs to create an embeddable OLE object from an MFC server must create the document, view and frame window required for support of that object. Thus, it's only logical that the template be exposed, since this template encapsulates the code that MFC will need to instantiate the document. Exposing the document template requires very little work on your part.

I feel compelled to point out that this architecture – the development of OLE servers from applications that implement the MFC document/view model – shows one of the fortes of the document/view model. Since your application can display itself to the user with code in the view, and also print itself with nearly the same code in the view class it implements, you've saved quite a bit of work. If you continue to architect your application with the same attention to the MFC-provided model for implementation, you'll find that having your application present itself in the special situations brought forward by activity as an OLE server won't really involve that much more code. Since MFC's document/view architecture relegates your application's rendering code to some specific rules, you'll find that following those rules provides you with a very simple method to fit into a very advanced and interesting architecture.

If you embrace the MFC architecture for OLE servers, your application will register the objects that your code exposes in one of two ways. One option is to have your installation program take the `.reg` script, produced by AppWizard and merge it into the registry. The code to do the merge is built into the `Regedt32.exe` tool shipped with Windows NT and the and `Regedit.exe` utility shipped with both Windows NT and Windows 95/98. Your installation program can spawn either of these Registry Editors and specify the file name of your `.reg` script in order to register your application's objects.

Application Self-Registration

If you don't have an installation program, or don't like the idea of spawning an extra application when setting up your program, you can avoid the process by letting your application register itself whenever it's run. Of course, self-registration is only effective for full servers. Since the user isn't at all likely to run your mini server in a stand-alone situation, you'll have to either force him or her to run your server or register the server by merging its `.reg` file.

By 'run' in this context we mean run the application wrapped around the objects, not instantiate the objects themselves. Of course, you can't instantiate your application's COM objects until you've registered them as a server.

COleTemplateServer

The code which registers your application lives in the `InitInstance()` function of your application object. As generated by AppWizard, this code first connects your document template to the `COleTemplateServer` object, which is automatically declared as a member of your `CWinApp`-derived class when generating an OLE project. That code looks like this:

```
m_server.ConnectTemplate(clsid, pDocTemplate, FALSE);
```

If you register other templates in your application, you should be sure to connect those to their own `COleTemplateServer` object. Each type of template you wish to expose to OLE must have its own unique `COleTemplateServer` instance.

ConnectTemplate()

The prototype for `ConnectTemplate()` is:

```
void COleTemplateServer::ConnectTemplate( REFCLSID clsid,
                                          CDocTemplate* pDocTemplate,
                                          BOOL bMultiInstance );
```

The call to ConnectTemplate() takes a reference to a CLSID as its first parameter. AppWizard produces a class identifier for you and includes a comment to allay your fears about its value not being unique. Here's what AppWizard produced for the sample application. You can find code like this in the primary module of your application, just before your InitInstance() override implementation.:

```
// This identifier was generated to be statistically unique
// for your app. You may change it if you prefer to choose
// a specific identifier.
// {75889AC0-46B2-11CE-8d47-8D4700AA0037DE94}
```

```
static const CLSID clsid =
    { 0x75889ac0, 0x46b2, 0x11ce,
    { 0x8d, 0x47, 0x0, 0xaa, 0x0, 0x37, 0xde, 0x94 } };
```

If you need to register other templates, you should use the Guidgen.exe application that's included in Visual C++, or the **GUID Generator** component in Component Gallery to add GUIDs to your application a little more directly. This tool can create new globally unique identifiers for any purpose and using this program to generate your GUIDs will ensure that they're unique.

The third Boolean parameter to ConnectTemplate() lets COM know if one instance of the server code can support multiple instances of the object. Passing FALSE tells COM that your server can handle multiple instances of the object with a single instance of the server code. If the parameter is TRUE, COM will try to instantiate a new copy of your server code each time an object is created.

MDI Applications

Generally, you can pass FALSE for the third parameter if you're writing an MDI application. Since an MDI application will inherently instantiate a new document and view for each instance of the application objects, you have no worries when it comes to managing data from different objects. MDI servers are a far more efficient implementation when you plan on supporting more than one concurrent instance of your object. SDI applications, on the other hand, can't handle managing more than one document/view pair without a new instance of the application as a whole – and, as such, they should pass TRUE.

The template servers, and any other class factories which your application offers, can be registered by calling the static RegisterAll() member of the COleTemplateServer class. This call registers all servers, so you can just perform one call to get your application's objects into the registry database. The call takes no parameters:

```
COleTemplateServer::RegisterAll();
```

When your application is linked to a debug build of the foundation classes, a call to RegisterAll() can produce a good amount of debug output if you've already registered the application. The warnings generated by the library are informational and you can safely ignore them.

What Gets Registered?

The information that `RegisterAll()` places in the registry is directly influenced by some of the choices you make when you use AppWizard. These choices show up in the Advanced Options dialog, which you can reach by pressing the Advanced push button on Step 4 of the wizard. We've visited this window a couple of times before.

As developers of OLE servers, the options that are of interest to us are on the Document Template Strings tab. You can see this dialog in all of its splendor here:

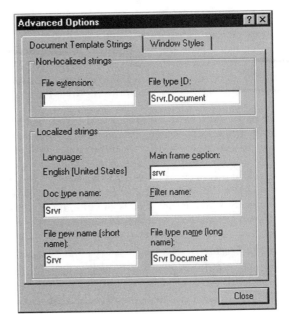

The Registration Database

The File Type ID field allows you to specify a file type for your application. This type identifies a 'short name' for your application to use, a name that will key your registration database entries. The registration information for the sample application `Srvr` is evident in the figure below, which shows the Registry Editor's view:

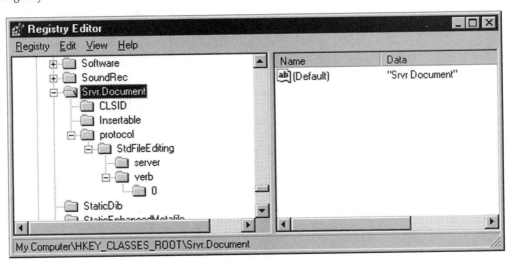

Neither Windows NT, Windows 95, nor Windows 98 installs an icon for the Registry Editor by default, but all operating systems install the program itself. Under Windows NT, you can find Regedt32.exe *and* Regedit.exe *in your 32-bit Windows system directory, usually called* \Winnt\System32. *If you're running Windows 95 or Windows 98, you'll find* Regedit.exe *in the* \Windows *directory. Under any operating system, the program should be found on your default executable path.*

Your file type ID can be anything you like, but it should be less than 39 characters long and can't contain spaces. By custom, the name should indicate the application that owns the entry. If the application has several different objects to be registered, they can be named after adding a period (.) to the file type ID. You'll notice, for example, that Excel registers both its Worksheet and Chart objects. If you've installed Excel, you can find entries for Excel.Worksheet and Excel.Chart under HKEY_CLASSES_ROOT in the registry, for example.

The use of a hierarchy of objects in more complicated OLE servers is quite common. Applications that can support their objects independently of each other will always do this to allow clients of the objects a maximum amount of flexibility in requesting functionality from the server. Remember that the COM objects you're registering may not necessarily correspond to only one C++ object. If you register a Chart object for your own spreadsheet program, for example, you'll probably relate the Chart object in the registry to the document template. This template may relate the Chart view in your application to an appropriate document type to support a chart as well as a frame window class (which manages all of the commands and resources a user editing a chart might want to have nearby).

Browsing the Registry

If you go hunting through the registry for the Microsoft Graph mini server which is shipped with Word and Access, you'll see that it exposes a couple of large objects: its Application object and its Chart object. It has a registry entry for each, one named MSGraph.Application and the other MSGraph.Chart.

If you browse the registry with Registry Editor, you can find these entries, but you should also note that there are two additional entries: MSGraph.Chart.5 and MSGraph.Application.5. The suffix 5 indicates the specific version of the server that is registered. The most recent version of the object is identified by requesting the file type without the version number; by naming the specific version number, you identify exactly which version you require, even if it isn't the newest.

The long file type name is used to identify your object in COM's various user interface elements. This is the string shown, for example, in the Insert New Object dialog. As such, you should use it to carefully identify the object to the user.

Altering Registration Database Entries

If you don't like the type names used when creating your application, you can change them by tweaking the .reg file and the string resources in your application. The string resource to change is identified by the document template registration. In the sample, the last and second-to-last substrings in the IDR_SRVRTYPE string are the ones that should be updated. Once you have changed this string, your alteration won't be registered until you run your application again. Changing the string won't unregister the old string, so you should tidy up the registry by deleting the old entries using the Registry Editor or by running your application with the /unregister command-line option *before* making your changes. Otherwise, you will be presented with a broken entry in Windows like the Insert New Object dialog, which can cause you confusion and heartache when you're debugging.

If you change the `.reg` file, you'll need to merge it with the registry before the change becomes effective. You'll need to change both the `.reg` file and the string resource file, otherwise the application will keep reregistering the name provided by the string resource.

Server Information

The `InitInstance()` code generated by AppWizard will also hook up some extra information for OLE server applications. In the last chapter, we indicated how AppWizard generated a call to `SetContainerInfo()`. As you might expect, the `CDocTemplate` classes also have a `SetServerInfo()` call in `InitInstance()`, which in the sample application, looks like this:

```
pDocTemplate->SetServerInfo(
        IDR_SRVRTYPE_SRVR_EMB, IDR_SRVRTYPE_SRVR_IP,
        RUNTIME_CLASS(CInPlaceFrame));
```

The first two parameters identify resources that are used when the application gains a user interface. The first parameter is the resource ID of the menu to be used when the server is opened, while the second identifies the resources to be used to build the in-place active menu.

The third parameter provides the run-time type information for the class that should be used to develop a frame for the application when it goes in-place active. The third parameter is optional, as is the fourth, which we don't supply in the code fragment. This missing parameter can be used to identify a view class that is to be used when the container goes in-place active.

When the third or fourth parameters are not specified, they default to NULL. As NULL, they mean that the server will use the frame or view associated with the template. You'll almost certainly want to specify a different frame for in-place activation, but you'll probably want to keep the same view.

Keeping Track of Server Items

Just as the container application we wrote in the last chapter used a linked list in the `COleDocument` class, MFC server applications will also create a list of objects that they are serving.

Server applications should use the `COleServerDoc` class as the base class for their documents. You can get the head of the linked list by calling `GetStartPosition()`; this returns the `POSITION` structure initialized to the top of the list. You can find the actual pointer to the first item by calling `GetNextServerItem()`.

Items in this list are of the type `COleServerItem` (or `COleDocObjectItem`, if you've written an Active Document Server), a class analogous to `COleClientItem`. AppWizard produces `Srvritem.h` and `Srvritem.cpp` files, which define and implement a derivative of the class that you can tailor to your needs. This class is different from the `COleClientItem` class because you're no longer using a COM object; you're providing one. There's a duality that exists between these two classes, since they're involved in a very close dance. Even if it's not an MFC application on the other side of the fence, you'll certainly see parallels between the two.

Essentially, everything that a COleClientItem can request is something that a COleServerItem should be able to provide. This only follows because one class is the client/server counterpart of the other. A COleClientItem has a GetExtent() function, for example, which we used in the previous chapter to find out exactly how big a COM object was. On the other hand, the COleServerItem has an OnGetExtent() function which you'll need to implement in order to return the size of your OLE object in HIMETRIC units.

The GetExtent() function doesn't directly call the OnGetExtent() function, but instead, requests that COM get the extent. In turn, COM asks the server code to provide that information; MFC receives this request and then calls the OnGetExtent() member of the appropriate COleServerItem. The functionality implemented by these interfaces exists whether or not your server or client were implemented using MFC.

The COleServerItem class implements code for the interfaces that a COM object implements normally. These interfaces include IOleObject and IDataObject in addition to IUnknown which we investigated before.

The IOleObject methods cover about two dozen different things that a client can ask a server to do in the normal course of every-day life. These interfaces are actually mapped by MFC to overridable handlers that you can modify. The most important functions deal with positioning and sizing the object; the container will expect to call these to notify the server that its size and position within the container have changed. COleServerItem::OnSetExtent() is called when the client positions the server – the function receives a reference to a size which it should remember for later, when it needs to draw. The default implementation of this function holds the extent in the COleServerItem member variable m_sizeExtent, which is of type CSize. MFC only handles this notification if the request is for the extent of the content is requested – that is, if the SetExtent() method is called with a request for DVASPECT_CONTENT, MFC will respond accordingly.

As we just mentioned, there's a corresponding COleServerItem::OnGetExtent() function. We saw in the last chapter how the client may or may not call it. Even if the client does call it, it doesn't need to pay attention to the result – the client has the final say over how the server's rendering is displayed. There's no reasonable way for *any* type of OLE server to dictate its positioning or size within the container – the container is completely at liberty to decide how it will display, manage, and resize items that it contains. The server can provide information about the size required to remember visual representation of the object it manages, but that information is provided to the client strictly on an advisory basis.

The drawing of the server item finally happens in response to the COleServerItem::OnDraw() call. You can implement drawing code in response to this function if you want the item to do things above and beyond what the view will do for the object. OnDraw() receives a CDC which is attached to a metafile.

What is Active When?

The trick to writing a good OLE server with MFC is to understand when each part of your MFC application is active. If you've implemented a full-server, you'll find that your server can be run as a stand-alone application and as such will have the normal document/view architecture you're used to seeing in your other MFC applications. But, when your server is active as a stand-alone application, your application won't have any COleServerItem instances floating around. Your application creates CDocument and CView instances all on its own and runs normally. If you try calling COleServerDoc::GetStartPosition() and COleServerDoc::GetNextServerItem(), you'll find that none are returned.

When someone embeds one of your application-supported objects in a container, MFC will create a `CDocument` and `CView` pair, but will associate those with your application's in-place frame instead of its main frame window. This creation is done via additional code that `COleTemplateServer` brings to the document template party. Your application is really running and supports your object fully, but it's providing a very limited user interface. Your view exists as a child window in the in-place frame window in the application that contains it if it is actually in-place active, or as a small rendering of your view window if your application is not in-place active. Your application can paint into this area and draw whatever it needs to, but in this state, it doesn't accept any direct input.

> In OLE parlance, your application has a *dead user interface*. If your user double-clicks on the object, OLE makes it *in-place active*. If they single-click on your object, they'll make it *active*.

It's important to remember that your application could possibly be running in any combination of these modes. A user might start your application and begin using it, only to have your application begin serving a COM object after the user starts a copy of Excel, loading in a spreadsheet that has one of the objects your application serves embedded in it. Of course, the same object instance isn't used to serve all of these clients, but if you write code in the implementation of your object that assumes the currently running instance of the object is the only running instance of the object, you'll get into lots of trouble.

In such a multiple-use circumstance, your application is only opened once if it's an MDI application. When the client (in this example, Excel) asks COM to create the object it needs, it does so by requesting services of the template server, as we mentioned in the previous section. That server reacts by creating document, view and frame instances for your object. Those additional object instances can live peacefully with the instances serving the rest of your application.

Remember your application may serve objects in different modes, but a given object is never in more than one mode at a given instant. OLE moves your object smoothly from one state to another as the user interacts with your object.

IsEmbedded()

Then, if your application is running as a stand-alone application and has a COM object embedded in a container, it will manage two document instances. One will be for the embedded object and the other will be for the interactive user. If the user has no documents open, the application will still have one opened internally to serve the embedded object. While you're processing, you can call the `IsEmbedded()` member of your `COleServerDoc` to see if it's embedded; the function returns non-zero when the document is associated with an embedded document, or zero when the document is running in the stand-alone application.

OnDraw()

Your application's COleServerItem instances are similar to views in that they are aware of which document they're working with. In fact, COleServerItems actually have OnDraw() functions which are called when the object needs to be drawn and OLE has marked the object as inactive. Since the inactive state doesn't allow the user to do any editing or to see any content, you can use the COleServerItem version of OnDraw() to give your object an alternate (and obviously inactive) representation. If you want your application to convey some information, such as a simplified view of its content, you might code an OnDraw() function which does that kind of drawing in your implementation of a COleServerItem-derived class associated with the server object in question. COleServerItems have a GetDocument() function which will return a pointer to the COleServerDoc-derived object which is associated with the server item object, so you can retrieve information from the document supporting your object.

The OnDraw() implementation in your COleServerItem implementation will only be called when the object is not in-place active. Your view's OnDraw() implementation will only be called when the object is in-place active.

In the Srvr sample, we've coded the OnDraw() function in the server item to display the text in the object and in the system font without any color. We did this to contrast with the object's in-place active representation, which does use the set foreground and background colors to draw the object's text in the active font.

When your server is in-place active, the drawing code in the view is called. When the server is *not* in-place active, your server item can do its drawing itself. It isn't uncommon to put code in your server item's OnDraw() that renders a faster, smaller, or less detailed version of your object than is available when your object actually goes in-place active. Remember, though, that the rendering your server object does in its OnDraw() is what the user will see when they work on a document which contains your object in their client application – including when they're printing!

Notes about Metafiles

The only drawback with the OnDraw() member of the COleServerItem is that it's called with a **metafile** device context, not a normal screen device context. You'll find that several GDI calls you're used to making against a regular device context are illegal against metafiles; specifically, any call which returns information from the device context, like GetTextMetrics(), GetDeviceCaps() or any function which relies on the device context actually being part of a window and being active in the window hierarchy. These functions include PtVisible() and RectVisible().

Since a metafile DC isn't associated with a particular device, you can't do anything which would depend on the exact device associated with the device context, which rules out things like EnumFonts() and EnumObjects(), as well as the Escape() function. Finally, you can't pretend the device context is a real DC by calling management functions like ReleaseDC(), DeleteDC() or CreateCompatibleDC(). It just won't work!

What Do Metafiles Mean to Me?

What do all of these awful-sounding restrictions mean to you as a programmer? Basically, that you'll need to be pretty careful when you're coding your rendering function in your server item. Any output function is valid: MoveTo(), LineTo(), TextOut(), DrawText() and so on. However, you might find that these functions are terribly difficult to use if the GetTextMetrics() function and all the other Get functions aren't available.

Fortunately, you're not completely painted into a corner just because you need to render to a metafile. There are a few ways out. One is to use MM_HIMETRIC coordinates in all of your painting, which means all the math you've done is the same, even when you're painting to the metafile for COM. You might need to keep around some parts of the computation, such as the height of your font in MM_HIMETRIC units, in order to redo the calculation while rendering to the metafile.

Since you're usually only interested in the height of a font, you can specify a negative value for the height of your font when calling CreateFont() or CreateFontIndirect(). This will cause Windows to match the font based on a relative size, rather than a size based on the logical coordinate system active in the device context where the font is being used.

An alternative is to convert coordinates back and forth from your other format to device pixels. You can use the HIMETRICtoDP() and DPtoHIMETRIC() functions in CDC to perform this work.

Transitions

As OLE asks MFC to make your application active, overridable functions in your object are called. By overriding these functions, you can do any interesting work you'd like in order to make sure your object does the right thing.

When the object is inserted into the container for the first time, the container can do nearly anything it chooses as it instantiates the new object. In our sample container in the previous chapter, we selected the object, and that was it. On the other hand, many other servers request that the object go in-place active as soon as it's inserted. If the server is capable of it (as your MFC server will be), it should go in-place active. Otherwise, it will be opened. When the user moves focus away from the object, it will deactivate and render itself in a rectangle.

OnOpen() and OnShow()

When the application is inactive, the user can ask it to open itself by double-clicking on the item. If the server is requested to go active, the OnShow() function is called in the server item object. On the other hand, if the user requests that object open itself fully, the OnOpen() member of your COleServerItem-derived class will be called.

The OnShow() and OnOpen() functions are called to reflect a very important change in the lifecycle of your object. Not only does the object's user interface change drastically as the object becomes shown or opened, the functions also indicate that the user is about to start working with the objects in question. You can override these functions to perform any such initializations you'd like. During these calls, it would be appropriate for the object to do any initialization it needs before changing modes, particularly if this is the first time the object is going active. Since they're a great place to initialize your application's drawing elements, you can think of these functions as having something in common with the OnInitialUpdate() function which the CView classes have.

If the user presses the *Esc* key to request the object to close, the server is actually responsible for reacting to the input. AppWizard hooks this up by default; it connects the *Esc* key to a function named OnCancelEditSrvr() in order to shut down the user interface of the object. The function just calls OnDeactivateUI() against the document and MFC takes care of the rest. This function isn't called if the container deactivates the object after the user performs some option specific to that container, such as clicking on the portion of the container's client area not occupied by the object's user interface.

Either way, MFC will eventually call the server's `OnHide()` function to shut down the server's active user interface. You can override this function if you want to undo anything you've done especially in `OnOpen()` or `OnShow()` to enhance your object.

The In-Place Frame

AppWizard will produce an in-place frame window for your application to use when you go in-place active. When your application runs in this mode, MFC will actually let the view float in the in-place frame as the client draws its user interface around the visible part of your view.

Of course, your view should draw itself in its `OnDraw()` function as it would normally. Relying on the in-place frame for your user interface while the user edits your object in-place means that you'll have very little extra work to do — you can just focus on the presentation and interaction of your object. If you implement extra menu items to your main frame, you should make sure that the code is also hooked up to your in-place frame. If it's not, these features will disappear.

Note that your in-place frame will also need to create whatever toolbars you might want to have in your in-place active user interface, but you need to create them in a slightly different way, compared to your regular frame window.

OnCreateControlBars()

Your in-place frame has a function called `OnCreateControlBars()`. In a standard AppWizard-produced application, the function is hooked up to create a standard dockable toolbar with tooltips but it won't create a status bar for your application. The `OnCreateControlBars()` function is called a little while after the application goes in-place active; MFC calls the function after the menu negotiation takes place and your server's user interface is merged with the user interface in the container.

Your in-place frame window uses the MFC `COleIPFrameWnd` class (or `COleDocIPFrame`, if you've built an Active Document server) as its base. This class has only one other overridable function, besides `Create()` and `OnCreateControlBars()`, and that is `RepositionFrame()`. `RepositionFrame()` isn't very interesting to override, unless you have done some work to provide very special toolbars or other non-client areas around your window.

If you do override this function, you'll probably want to call MFC's implementation in `COleIPFrameWnd`, so that any standard MFC toolbars you do have are still drawn and positioned correctly. The function takes two parameters, both pointers to `RECT` structures, which describe where the window will live. The first parameter is the rectangle where the in-place frame window should live, while the second is the clipping rectangle, which lets your frame know where it's allowed to draw.

However, the code uses different resources for the frame's menu and toolbars when they are in-place active, embedded or opened. The following list shows the menu resources available for the `Cntnr` sample, and the situations in which they're used:

Menu Resource ID	Usage
IDR_MAINFRAME	The server is running as a stand-alone application and doesn't have any opened documents
IDR_SRVRTYPE	The server is running as a stand-alone application and has an active, opened document
IDR_SRVRTYPE_SRVR_IP	Used in the in-place frame while an object is in-place active in the container
IDR_SRVRTYPE_SRVR_EMB	Used in the opened frame when the user has opened an embedded object

All of these menu resources are registered in the InitInstance() function of the sample's CWinApp-derived object. You're welcome to change them, but remember that you'll need to create additional items if you're interested in having a single server executable work for more than one object.

Extra Toolbars

The sample also has an extra toolbar resource named IDR_SRVRTYPE_SRVR_IP. This is set up in the in-place frame's creation function to be active when the function is run. The toolbar is different from the normal offering, because it hasn't got any file manipulation buttons.

At first, it might be a little confusing to understand how to code your application when all sorts of different menus and toolbars can be active. It's really simple – just implement all of the functions you could ever possibly want in your application's view class. If there's no menu item or toolbar button in the user interface for the corresponding function, it will never be called, but, if the menu item makes itself available at some point in the user interface, the user can access the functionality through the menu or toolbar. You can then carefully craft your menus and toolbars to only contain the commands appropriate for the context where the resource is used. For example, you shouldn't have file manipulation commands in your in-place active or open-embedded menus and toolbars; in these situations, the application doesn't manage any files, it only manages the object.

If you have any functions which need to behave differently depending on the activation state of the object, just use the GetItemState() member of COleServerItem to test the state of your object before carrying on.

Menu Negotiation

Of the four menu resources that the application contains, only the IDR_SRVRTYPE_SRVR_IP resource is subject to menu negotiation. Menu negotiation is performed between the container and server when the server's object goes in-place active.

Just as with the extra menu resource in the container, the IDR_SRVRTYPE_SRVR_IP contains extra separators to indicate where the client should place its merged items. If it is given this menu resource ID and its special format, MFC takes care of the menu negotiation for us when the server becomes in-place active.

Updates

The architecture of your server application also changes the way updates are performed. Through this book, we've collected user input via the application's view. If you want any user input, your OLE server can also do that. In the sample, we allow the user to type new text into the object by watching for the WM_CHAR message in the view. Normally, we would:

> ➤ Call Invalidate() to get the view to repaint
> ➤ Call UpdateAllViews() against the document so that other views would also update
> ➤ Let the document know it's been modified by calling the SetModifiedFlag() on it

However, for OLE documents, we also have to make sure that the server knows to tell the container it has changed. To do this, COM offers us a way to extend the container's document. Since an object in the container's document can change without the direct knowledge or action of the container, the server is responsible for letting the container know that the container's document is dirty.

UpdateAllItems()

So, in the same way that we call UpdateAllViews(), we also call UpdateAllItems() to make sure that each item associated with the document lets its container know that the data in the document has been updated. This normally causes the container to mark its document as dirty and refresh the image of the object. This technique is illustrated below:

```
void CSrvrView::OnChar(UINT nChar, UINT nRepCnt, UINT nFlags)
{
    CSrvrDoc* pDoc = GetDocument();

    if (nChar >= 32)
        pDoc->m_strText += nChar;
    else if (nChar == 8)
    {
        CString& str = pDoc->m_strText;
        int nLength = str.GetLength();
        if (nLength > 0)
            str = str.Left(nLength-1);
    }
    else
    {
        MessageBeep(0);
        return;
    }

    pDoc->UpdateAllViews(NULL);
    pDoc->UpdateAllItems(NULL);
    pDoc->NotifyChanged();
    pDoc->SetModifiedFlag();
    Invalidate();
}
```

Since the WM_CHAR handler is in the CSrvrView class, it is only responsive when the object is in-place active, or when the view is active in the application's frame when it's running as a stand-alone app. This means that, by design, the frame isn't responsive to keystrokes.

Verbs

In Chapter 13, we saw a few instances when the container might want to call DoVerb() against an object to have it perform some action. You saw the standard verbs that should perform one of the standard actions, such as in-place activating or hiding the objects, but you can use other verb numbers to initiate any type of activity in your server. When the client calls DoVerb() against the object, the server's OnDoVerb() function is called. You can check to see if the verb that was passed is one that you want to handle before calling the base class implementation of the function. Such an exercise might look like this:

```
void CSrvrSrvrItem::OnDoVerb(LONG iVerb)
{
   if (iVerb == 5)
   {
      // do your code for Verb #5
   }
   else if (iVerb == 4)
   {
      // do your code for Verb #4
   }
   else
      COleServerItem::OnDoVerb(iVerb);
}
```

The code above tests the iVerb parameter for different values to invoke the appropriate action we've specified. You should stick to positive verb identifiers greater than two; one, zero and all the negative integers are reserved for OLE itself. We hard-coded the integers in the fragment above; you will probably want to use preprocessor symbols that you can grab from an included file in both your server implementation and while developing your clients.

OLE verbs aren't quite as rich as those of Automation; you can neither pass parameters nor return values to indicate the success of the operation on the server side, but it can provide a simple interface for you to poke or prod your object in order to have it do simple tricks. For example, this is a great interface to use when you want your object to enter a different mode or state.

Serialization

Keeping in line with the document/view architecture, your server should use its document object to contain and manage any data that the object needs to hold. Since users will expect the content of your object to be persistent across invocations of the code, you should implement serialization in your document to make sure anything that should be is indeed persistent.

As an embedded object, serialization code in your object will write to the storage provided by your container. This allows the container to seamlessly store data from your server in the same file format as the container normally uses. The container may or may not be using a real OLE file format as its own, but that's not of interest to you, just serialize your data and be done with it.

Serialize()

By simply implementing a proper `Serialize()` function in your document, you'll be set:

```
void CSrvrDoc::Serialize(CArchive& ar)
{
   if (ar.IsStoring())
   {
      // write data to CArchive
   }
   else
   {
      // read data from CArchive
   }
}
```

In the `Srvr` sample, you'll see that we store and retrieve the colors, text and font information the object has active. The serialization code is in the application's `CDocument` implementation; we didn't need to do anything special. By the way, this code doubles as the application's saving and loading code for when the application runs stand-alone. There's no need to call the base class implementation of the function, as it doesn't do anything!

While the storage mechanism that your application uses is transparently implemented by your document's `Serialize()` function, it's important to remember that the underlying storage implementation may not be a plain flat file. If you've created a server application using AppWizard, you'll note that the constructor for your document calls `COleDocument::EnableCompoundFile()`. If compound files are enabled for a given document, the framework runs extra code as it creates the `CArchive` which the serialization routine will use. The extra code initializes an OLE compound file that will be attached to the `CArchive` object in lieu of a normal `CFile` object.

If you're writing your program from scratch, you'll want to be certain to call `EnableCompoundFile()` in the constructor of `COleDocument`-derived classes which you'll have participate in OLE embedding. By participating in OLE's compound file format mechanism, you'll allow your application tighter integration with the underlying operating system storage and management features. It's *not* appropriate to use `EnableCompoundFile()` if you expect to do anything but simple serialization – if you're interested in being able to carefully control the exact binary format your application reads or writes, you'll want to avoid the use of compound files.

Beyond OLE Documents

To keep things in perspective, let's take a look at some of the other ways that COM might be used to get some work done. What are OLE servers for, anyway?

In the land of cut-throat business deals and dollar profit, the big league business leaders want big league business applications. The problem with this type of application is that they have a tremendous amount of information built into the way they're coded.

You might need to perform some interest calculations. This may sound simple now, but when you get involved with the incredibly complicated rules that most organizations have, you may start to see the problems. They might be as easily fulfilled as taking a peek at your previous balance, or they might require you to look up lots of other facts surrounding your account history and payment schedule and get approval from an officer of the company!

Translating Business Rules

Translating these business rules into code is a terribly expensive process, not only because I charge seven to eight thousand dollars an hour for a consultation. (Exorbitant rates, sure, but they keep dumb questions to an absolute minimum.) Writing down business rules requires lots of people: a couple of programmers, a consultant, and a bunch of executives to make sure it gets approved. There needs to be some subject-matter experts around to express the rules of the business and a few analysts hanging around to make sure that the experts are completely emptied of the answers the developers require.

It would be delicious to reuse the code fragments that model a business process without rewriting the code each time. You can tuck some of this code into dynamic link libraries and redistribute it that way. Different applications could load the DLL and reuse the code in it. But a far more flexible solution would be to implement the rules in a COM object and use Automation to play with it. While just as effective as the DLL solution, this approach is much more conducive to repetition.

Why? Because Visual Basic for Applications is a lot easier to use than C or C++, and it's also easier to use than a macro plastered with wacky external function definitions. It also helps that COM objects have a little more infrastructure to facilitate their distribution and reuse.

The trend for the future of software is towards the implementation of reusable components; objects that can provide some amount of tangible functionality to someone who integrates them into a system. Such components will implement 'bite-size' objects, probably no bigger than a dialog box or a view. Maybe you'll be able to buy a copy of Excel 9.0 and just reuse its graphing object any time you need to. Or maybe a cottage industry will spring up around little COM objects that pull different printing stunts, from ID badges to postal bar codes.

What if I'm Not in Big Business, Smart Guy?

If you're not writing some stuffy application for a big industrial machine, you might be thrashing around trying to produce an application with some add-in functionality, or implementing some code that you know your users will want to have in lots of different applications. Servers you might want to write for embedded objects may include artwork managed in a proprietary format, or code that accesses and summarizes data in a way which most programs are incapable of performing themselves.

Even if you *are* writing such a custom object, you should seriously consider extending a programmatic interface to your software by adding support for Automation. This feature almost single-handedly enables serious reusability of your code.

Serving the Internet

Microsoft's plan for the future of COM and OLE involves things a lot more interesting than making one application's data available in the user interface of another application. Microsoft is working very hard to embrace the Internet and help developers write software which works naturally in the massively distributed heterogeneous computing environment embraced by large networks, like the Internet. As time goes by, you'll see that Microsoft's currently evolving plan for the Internet fully embraces COM. Today, these plans have become embodied in Microsoft's ActiveX technologies, and tomorrow will evolve into COM+.

Automation

With the exception of `DoVerb()`, we haven't said much about getting objects to directly perform your bidding. While it is interesting to use features of one application within another application – even if only to share data in a foreign application – it's also promising to make an application perform actions upon that data.

One of the features of COM is the capability of servers to expose **methods** and **properties** for the objects they manage. The mechanisms that COM provides to support the exposure of an object's methods and properties, together with the actual manipulation of an object's properties, is called **Automation**.

I think Automation is exciting because it lets COM objects evolve from being just wet fish, flopping around uncontrolled in your document, to the stage where they can actually interact with your program and do useful work. The term *Automation* is very appropriate; working with a particular COM server breathes life into objects that would otherwise be quite passive.

Automation uses the same client/server architecture as our other COM objects. The code that supports a given object is said to be a *server*, while the application making use of that object is said to be the *client*.

> In Automation, the client is sometimes called the automation *controller*. This term is synonymous with *client* in the context of Automation.

Prerequisites for Automation

For Automation to work, the server must expose automation interfaces. The client must know how to request that server interface, by which we mean that the client must know beforehand the extent of the work that the server can do and how to access the functions to get the work done.

Every standard automation server will implement at least one `IDispatch` interface to expose the objects and properties it can support. The `IDispatch` interface is relatively simple; it only contains four methods, above and beyond the normal `IUnknown` methods. As an MFC programmer, you'll rarely meddle with the interface directly, but an understanding of what the interface is doing for you under the covers can be a big help. Let's take a look at the different functions that `IDispatch` implements:

IDispatch::Invoke()

`Invoke()` is where all of the action takes place. Whether the controller is looking to set or get a property value, or to invoke a method, `Invoke()` is called to get the job done. `Invoke()` is passed eight parameters, but only a few are key to identifying a basic understanding of Automation.

```
HRESULT IDispatch::Invoke( DISPID dispidMember,
                           REFIID riid,
                           LCID lcid,
                           unsigned short wFlags,
                           DISPPARAMS FAR* pdispparams,
                           VARIANT FAR* pvarResult,
                           EXCEPINFO FAR* pexcepinfo,
                           unsigned int FAR* puArgErr );
```

The most important parameter is the dispatch ID, `dispidMember`. This parameter, of type `DISPID` (which is really just a long integer) indicates exactly which method or property is being referenced by the call to `Invoke()`. These identifiers, as you might guess, are almost always known by the developer at compile time. If the controlling program doesn't know about `DISPID`s that the server offers, it can query the server for a type library that will describe the methods and properties supported by the server. In the chapter on ActiveX Control containment, we'll examine this technique as we write a program that contains ActiveX controls and queries the automation interfaces of the controls for information about the methods and properties that they implement. ActiveX controls are one special case of Automation servers. While we'll have a few words in this chapter about the `GetIDsOfNames()` method, which is the gateway to the type information provided by the server, the code we provide for the Ocbench sample and describe in Chapter 16, demonstrates the use of the method, and the type information, quite soundly.

The `Invoke()` method also takes a flag, `wFlags`, indicating what sort of invocation is being requested. Essentially, this parameter dictates whether the invocation is to set the value of a property, retrieve the value of a property or execute a method.

COleDispatchDriver::InvokeHelper()

You might remember that we talked about the `InvokeHelper()` function in the previous chapter. On the client side, `InvokeHelper()` does some work to prepare a call through COM to the server's `IDispatch::Invoke()` method implementation. If your server is written with MFC, you never really need to implement `Invoke()` directly, as MFC's stock implementation takes care of everything. However, it's very important to realize that this mechanism is what is at work when your server object's exposed methods are called or its properties are changed.

`InvokeHelper()` hides many details of the type library and underlying parameter passing and translation mechanisms for the controller. Of the six parameters to the function, only two are terribly meaningful; one is reserved and unused and the others all describe parameter passing information or provide information for COM to propagate the return value to the caller.

IDispatch::GetTypeInfo( )

Information about the methods and properties that an object manages is stored in the object's **type library**, which, as we mentioned before, is related to `InvokeHelper()`. The type library is built into your application as a binary resource; when your application registers itself with COM, it lets COM know how to get to that resource. Your type library's content comes from an `.odl` file, which we'll examine later. `.odl` files are source code for type libraries; the data is converted to their binary representation by a tool called `Midl.exe`. This tool is a part of the OLE SDK and Visual C++ runs it for you as a part of your project's build process.

It's possible that the controller might want to pick apart the type information in the object in which it sits. For example, programming languages that support Automation will do this to check the syntax of the code they're interpreting to make sure the code is valid. Unless you need to dynamically adjust your code to handle absolutely any automation object, you won't need to call `GetTypeInfo()`. If you do call `GetTypeInfo()`, you will see that it nets a pointer to an `ITypeInfo` interface; you can call methods on that interface to get more information about the type data and the descriptions of the methods and properties supported by the server.

IDispatch::GetIDsOfNames( )

The `Invoke()` function will take a dispatch identifier as a parameter so the implementation of the method knows exactly which method or property you'd like to work with. Because the calling program might have the plain text name of the method or property it needs to invoke, it might not have the actual `DISPID` associated with that name. If this is the case, your application can use the `GetIDsOfNames()` method to look up the dispatch identifier for a given property or method name.

In an MFC automation server, the `CCmdTarget` takes care of handling the `IDispatch` interface for any object that you want to be automatable. We'll take a look at that implementation in a subsequent section, but for the meantime, let's review the differences between the way embeddable OLE objects and Automation objects work.

Differences from Embedding

Automation allows objects to run in a slightly different context. All of the objects we've talked about so far have had user interfaces; they draw something or take up space in the user's client. Nothing stops an embedded object from supporting Automation interfaces in addition to the embedding interfaces it needs.

It's also possible for a COM object to support Automation, without being embeddable or providing a user interface. The `Srvr` sample handles the first kind of object; it makes an embeddable object that also supports Automation. Before we pick apart the Automation features in the sample, let's take a look at the kind of designs Automation helps us consider.

Automation Techniques

If you've embraced the idea of providing OLE server support in your application, you should seriously consider adding support for Automation. If you have a simple application, you should be able to get away with a spartan Automation architecture; you won't have many properties to expose. On the other hand, if your application is complicated, you'll be interested in exposing many different objects, each with its own automation interface, properties and methods. Describing your application via Automation provides a simple and clean way for other applications to reuse the functionality your application provides.

As you work through such an aggressive design, as you control your automation interface, you should consider the needs your client applications will have. Aside from being able to manipulate the properties and documents that your application contains, you should also provide some programmatic ways to control your application itself.

The controller may want to hide, show, minimize or maximize your application, and you might even consider providing some way to let the controller request that your application doesn't update its user interface while Automation commands are being executed. This can greatly improve the performance of your application during automation situations, since it won't needlessly update its appearance when no user is watching anyway.

If your server provides the ability to manipulate multiple documents or views, you will need to make some mechanism that lets your controller select one of those available. Your controller might even want to gain a list of the opened documents.

Sizing the COM Objects

All of these approaches suggest that there might be COM objects in your application that are bigger than your application's documents. Often, this is actually the application object; after all, it's only natural to say your application needs to maximize or minimize itself. Selecting the active view or document can also be an operation that the application performs for the good of all the code inside of it. Maybe you'll want to give your application's main object some methods and properties, perhaps something like this:

Properties	Documents
	Views
	CurrentDocument
Methods	Maximize()
	Minimize()
	Open()
	Close()
	Hide()
	Show()

If you look carefully at this list, you may realize that many of the methods could be coded as properties, and some properties as methods. The `Maximize()` and `Minimize()` methods suggested here could become a `PresentationState` property, for example. You might set this property to 1 to indicate the application should be minimized, or 2 to indicate that the application should be maximized, and so on. A property which actually causes some action to be performed when the value of the property changes can be very versatile and terribly handy, since the controller can also use the property to request the current state of the application's user interface.

Your documents may also have similar interfaces. You can open a document as well as open an application. These are very different operations, but there's nothing wrong with identifying them using the same name, and using a different name is probably better than contriving some synonym just because similar naming will result in a sense of consistency. Without the benefit of that consistency, developers who encounter your objects will wonder if the Shut() method is for documents and the Close() method is for the application, or vice versa.

Object Hierarchies

Objects in your application will probably grow into a hierarchy. Each level of the hierarchy will need a way to find out information about individual objects in the next level of the hierarchy. In a spreadsheet program, the hierarchy might go like this:

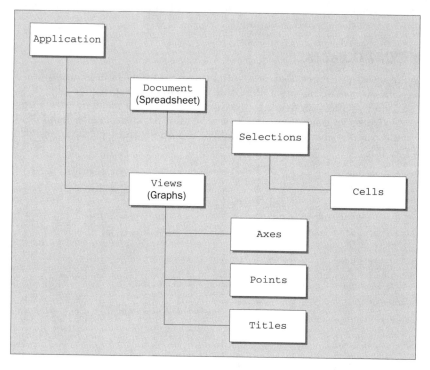

For most applications, it is appropriate for the document object to provide some method that allows you to change the selection. Once the selection is identified, you should be able to manipulate the individual cells it contains. Those cells provide properties and methods which manipulate their content; a cell might have a Contents property as well as a Format property and maybe a Recalculate() method. In this way, the controller can drill down through the contents of the spreadsheet application to get some work done. Of course, a more complicated spreadsheet will have a few more layers – workbooks containing a number of spreadsheets, for instance.

Implementing Automation in MFC

Once your server is running, any automation controller can get a pointer to its `IDispatch` interface and begin pestering the server with method invocations or property change requests. From this perspective, your application is receiving commands from some other application. MFC has infrastructure to handle these dispatch commands in much the same way as it handles messages sent to the application; it uses maps to describe which functions in an object handle which specific COM methods.

DECLARE_DISPATCH_MAP()

This whole mechanism is anchored in the `DECLARE_DISPATCH_MAP()` macro which you'll add to the definition of your classes when you want them to handle Automation. The dispatch map should be declared in one of your `.cpp` files using the `BEGIN_DISPATCH_MAP()` macro. You'll need to close the dispatch map with the `END_DISPATCH_MAP()` macro, just like you would a message map. Each dispatchable item in your interface will get a macro which gives MFC enough information to resolve the request from COM into the appropriate reaction, and, as we mentioned when we discussed the `Invoke()` method, COM could be asking us to get or set a property or actually invoke a method.

When an MFC object receives a dispatch request, it begins searching through the active dispatch maps for a given object. It performs this search in much the same way as it searches through the message maps of classes that handle windows. If a given class has an entry in its dispatch map, indicating that it can handle a particular sort of dispatch, the dispatch handling code in `CCmdTarget` will make sure the call is resolved against the appropriate handler.

Just like the message maps, the dispatch maps hold a link to the map in the parent class. If the searching code can't find appropriate dispatch information in a given class, the code will search the parent class in an effort to resolve the dispatch. This process is dissimilar from the message dispatch process in that MFC doesn't implement default handlers for any dispatched methods or properties, whereas most messages are handled in some way by MFC. Even if MFC can't find a handler for a message, it will call Windows, so the default message handler can be invoked and an error returned to the control that initiated the process. A further dissimilarity is revealed by the fact MFC doesn't perform any form of dispatch routing between views and documents and frames and applications in the way that it provides message routing for command messages.

After the Dispatch Map

Once a dispatch map entry that matches a dispatch call is found, MFC's job still isn't complete. If this were an ordinary message dispatch, MFC would simply put the appropriate parameters together and make the call. For OLE dispatches, the exact action depends on the exact sort of dispatch that has been invoked. If the dispatch is for a member variable property, MFC sets the member variable and then calls the notification function.

If the call is for a get/set property, MFC makes the call to the get or set function, as appropriate. If the dispatch is for a method, MFC takes care of unpacking all of the parameters, calling the function and wrapping up the return value. We'll describe the difference between the different property types in the 'Managing Properties' section.

In the meantime, the maps need to be appropriately laid out. The whole thing, as implemented in the `Srvr` sample application, boils down to this:

```
BEGIN_DISPATCH_MAP(CSrvrDoc, COleServerDoc)
    //{{AFX_DISPATCH_MAP(CSrvrDoc)
    DISP_PROPERTY_NOTIFY(CSrvrDoc, "ForegroundRedPart", m_FGRedPart,
        OnFGRedPartChanged, VT_I2)
    // :
    // : lots of other DISP_PROPERTY_NOTIFY macros omitted
// :
    DISP_PROPERTY_EX(CSrvrDoc, "Text", GetText, SetText, VT_BSTR)
    DISP_FUNCTION(CSrvrDoc, "Repaint", Repaint, VT_EMPTY, VTS_NONE)
//}}AFX_DISPATCH_MAP
END_DISPATCH_MAP()
```

As you might have guessed, the `BEGIN_DISPATCH_MAP()` function needs the name of the given class as well as the name of its parent class. The different `DISP_` macros are documented in the MFC references; look them up if curiosity makes your soul sting with desire, but remember that you don't have to really study these macros, as ClassWizard will help you to manage them in your application.

.ODLay Hee-Hoo!

Unfortunately, changing these macros and hooking up the appropriate member variables and member functions for the items you wish to expose isn't the only thing you need to do. COM also needs to know about your application's exposed methods and properties in case any controller asks about them.

As we mentioned before, the `IDispatch` interface is linked to a type library. The content of that type library is also a part of your application's source code. If you generated your program with AppWizard, you'll find a `.odl` file in your source directory. This file contains descriptions for the methods and properties your code implements. It's from here that the dispatches are associated with their own `GUID` and where COM gets the information on the necessary parameters for each method your object implements.

When you build a project that supports any amount of Automation, you'll see extra lines like these in your output window during the build:

```
Creating Type Library...
Srvr.odl
oaidl.idl
objidl.idl
unknwn.idl
wtypes.idl
```

The first file name identifies your project's actual `.odl` file being compiled; the subsequent lines are messages generated by the MIDL compiler as it processes common include files often referenced by `.odl` files. While the Wizards still generate `.odl` files, they're still capable of referencing the more modern `.idl` files provided to define the system-level interfaces.

Compiling the Type Library

The type library is compiled from a `.odl` file to its binary `.tlb` version, using a tool called MIDL installed with Visual C++. Starting with Visual C++ 5.0, the build system has been using MIDL in lieu of a tool called Mktyplib. MIDL can do everything that Mktyplib can do, and more.

If your project includes a `.odl` file, Visual C++ will use MIDL to create a type library from it. It's made available to COM whenever your server is around; information in the registry explains to COM where the type library can be found, and you need to do nothing else besides making sure that your application is properly registered and the type library is up to date.

Thus, if you want to properly implement an OLE server, you have to obsessively ensure that your `.odl` file, functions, dispatch maps and maybe even some member variables are all in sync. Even though this sounds terribly complicated, it's much simpler than fooling around with Automation at the API level. Although it can still be pretty tedious to perform this with MFC, ClassWizard can provide you with an immense amount of help.

Up until this point in the book, I've only skimmed the surface when discussing the usage of ClassWizard, because my aim has been to show you how MFC itself works. However, when it comes to Automation, ClassWizard really starts to come into its own; therefore, we're now going to spend a little time explaining how ClassWizard can be an asset when it helps you to write Automation servers with MFC.

Managing Properties

The Automation tab in ClassWizard (shown here) allows you to see the Automation features built into a selected class. The External names list box in the dialog shows all of the exposed Automation features; a gray letter M indicates a method, while the letter C denotes a custom property.

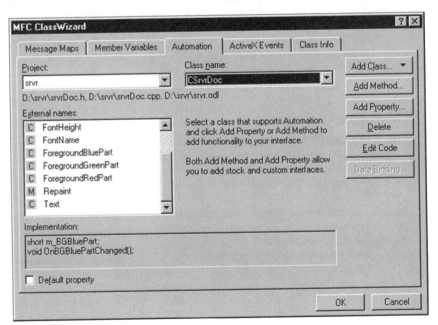

Obviously, you can use the Add Property... and Add Method... buttons to add a property or method. Both of these buttons lead to another dialog where you can specify the attributes of the item you're adding. Properties are simple – they just have an external name, a variable name and a data type. Here you can see the Add Property dialog:

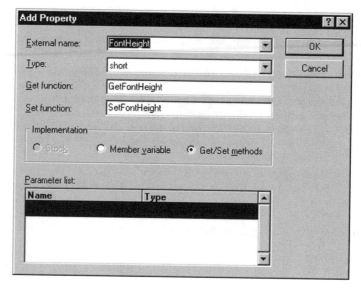

The External Name is the name that lands in the type library; it's the name that other applications will use when referring to your property. You should make this name reasonable, since other programmers will use it when writing code to exercise your object. You should note that the name can't contain spaces or other punctuation, aside from an underscore. You may also notice that this drop-down control is empty unless you're writing an ActiveX control; in the next chapter, we'll talk about some of the standardized properties and methods that are supported by ActiveX controls.

The Type indicates the data type for the property as exposed to COM. Some of the types in this field won't be familiar to you unless you have COM experience from previous work. We mentioned BSTRs back in Chapter 9. You'll also see some VARIANT types floating around in the box – you might remember our treatment of VARIANTs from the previous chapter.

MFC Property Support

Properties are supported by MFC in two basic flavors. The first is a simple property, where your class contains a member variable that represents the property. If an Automation controller calls your Invoke() method to change the value of the property, MFC will immediately effect the change and then call a notification function to let you know the change has taken place.

The change is already done by the time your function is called; you can't get the old value (unless you've squirreled it away somewhere). The change notification function is identified by the name in the Notification function box. This arrangement is called a **member variable property**, and is requested by the Member variable radio button in the Add Property dialog.

The Get and Set Methods

If you'd like a little more control, you can use a **get/set method**. This arrangement gets MFC to create two different functions. One is called to set your parameter and the other is called to retrieve the value of your parameter. Note that MFC won't manage a member variable for you. Instead, you need to implement the set and get functions to perform any management of the value that's required. The protocol established by the function pairs opens a new realm of possibilities for your application; you might expose a property which is actually the result of some operation or just the return value from some summary that you've performed on the object's private data. Such a property is called a **computed property**.

The set function takes a data type, appropriate for the parameter, and returns void. The function's prototype might look like this:

```
void CSrvrDoc::SetFontName(LPCTSTR lpszNewValue);
```

You should always use get and set properties when you want to limit, check, edit or block the values that clients might send. Since the function doesn't return a data type, you can deny the change without any repercussions. If controllers of your object absolutely must know that the change has been denied, you should use a true method to implement the option.

On the other side of the exchange operation, your get function doesn't take any parameters — it returns the data for the property. For simple data types, this is a no-brainer, but for more complex varieties, you'll need to take an extra step. The most notable of these data types is BSTR; as the fragment given below illustrates, you'll need to call the AllocSysString() member of CString:

```
BSTR CSrvrDoc::GetFontName()
{
    // TODO: Add your property handler here

    CString s;
    return s.AllocSysString();
}
```

AllocSysString() allocates a new BSTR and copies the CString's data to it. The allocated string becomes the property of the owner — in this case, the automation controller that caused the function call. The automation controller is also responsible for freeing the BSTR when it's done with the data.

AllocSysString() asks COM to use a shared memory allocator to acquire and initialize memory for the string. COM's allocator, coupled with the marshaling code that sits between processes, can handle the special case of getting memory in one process and passing the block of memory over to another process where it is freed. The memory manager provided by the C runtime library that ships with Visual C++, can't handle cross-process ownership of memory.

Methods

You can use ClassWizard to add methods as well as properties to your OLE server. Again, the big benefit of using ClassWizard is that you'll waste less time fooling with your .odl file. The syntax for methods in an .odl file is even messier than the syntax for properties; each method will be able to return a value and can take quite a few parameters. Here you can see ClassWizard's **Add Method** dialog box:

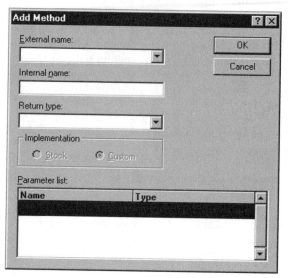

Methods have external names just like properties do. Again, this is the name that will be placed in the type library and will be used by any external user of the method to identify the method. The **Internal name** field is the name for your function and the **Return type** drop-down lets you choose the type of value that you'll return.

> Note you can make void methods but, unless your method is very simple, this isn't a great idea, because lots of things can go wrong between two applications. You should try to return as much descriptive information as possible in response to the call.

You can use the **Parameter** list box to describe the parameters your method will accept. The control allows you to name the parameters and their data type. Clicking on the control provides you with all the editing facilities that you'll ever need, including the ability to delete parameters that you don't want. Unfortunately, the dialog won't allow you to easily reorder the parameters, so make sure that you get the order right the first time. If your method doesn't require any parameters, just don't provide any entries in this box.

Controls in the **Implementation** group box will be disabled unless you're implementing an ActiveX custom control. It's only in the context of writing an ActiveX control in which there are any standard methods that you could select.

Once you've created your method function, you can code its implementation without further hesitation. MFC makes sure that everything is ready for you by the time your method receives execution focus, meaning that there's nothing else to do in your method implementation.

Automation and Privacy

You might notice that ClassWizard puts all of your properties in the `private` data of your document. This can be very annoying, since you might not be able to access the data from your view. You can safely re-declare this area as `public`, or you can move the declarations to a `public` area as we did in the sample application. Due to the simpler design, this is usually a better option than implementing set and get functions for your application. On the other hand, object-oriented pundits will balk at this solution and insist that it's a dangerous programming style that circumvents some of the benefits that C++, as a language, brings us.

And they're right! However, the academic way of doing things isn't always the most efficient. You might disagree with this way of thinking, in which case you can keep the data private and provide access functions – it's up to you.

About the Sample

The `Srvr` sample, which can be downloaded from the Wrox web site, exposes a bunch of different properties. The controller can change the foreground color of the text using the `ForegroundBluePart`, `ForegroundRedPart` and `ForegroundGreenPart` properties. These properties, which can range from 0 to 255, are combined to form a color reference used while painting. Similarly, the controller can modify the background using `BackgroundBluePart`, `BackgroundRedPart` and `BackgroundGreenPart`.

For all of these color attributes, we do absolutely no work besides clamping the value in the appropriate range in `OnFGRedPartChanged()` and similar functions. We don't even repaint the object, because we want the controller to be able to change more than one attribute without the object repainting over and over again. If we repainted automatically, changing more than one parameter would cause a great deal of flashing in the object as it redraws.

Exposing Repaint

As a part of the update strategy employed in the `Srvr` sample, we have also exposed a `Repaint` method. This method is rather unorthodox; a server can ask a COM object to repaint by calling the appropriate COM interface directly, but for an automation object, this isn't always possible. First, the automation object might not be embedded; if that's the case, the COM painting interfaces are probably not implemented for the object.

Secondly, even if the server object is embedded and also available via direct OLE SDK-level calls, the COM interface might not be available via high-level calls accessible through the implementation language. For example, Visual Basic for Applications doesn't support a method which forces an arbitrary object to redraw itself.

The overall idea is that the controller can make any necessary changes before it uses the `Repaint` method to force the object to change. An alternative strategy would involve having a flag built into the object; if the flag is `TRUE`, the object redraws itself automatically, and when the flag is `FALSE`, the object skips the redraw until the flag is returned to `TRUE`. This approach is very similar to the `SetRedraw()` method which Windows controls implement.

Of course, all of these painting worries only pertain to the automation objects that are concerned with presenting a user interface. If your object doesn't present a user interface, or doesn't allow the controller to directly manipulate it, you're probably not interested in a drawing strategy anyhow.

There is also a string property named `Text` in the object. This string can be queried to retrieve the current content of the object, or set to change the content of the object.

Other OLE Applications

The beauty of COM objects, blessed with the ability to perform Automation, is that they're controllable from lots of different platforms. After adding Automation support and carefully documenting it, you'll find that your users can call your application from almost any language, including VBA-capable applications like Access, Excel and Visual Basic, and scripting languages like JavaScript or VBScript. This makes your code incredibly reusable, even to people who don't have a great deal of programming experience.

Visual Basic for Applications is covered by many other books, but by taking a look at its syntax, you might deepen your understanding of how Automation objects are perceived from a controller. In Excel, you might create a new object and then work on it, using Visual Basic for Applications code that looks like this:

```
Dim MyEmbedded As Object
Dim MyObject As Object

Set MyEmbedded = ActiveSheet.OLEObjects.Add(classtype:="Srvr.Document")
Set MyObject = MyEmbedded.Object
```

Without getting too enthralled in the details of VBA, the code essentially asks COM to create a new `Srvr.Document` object. COM will run off to check the registry and find out that our beautiful little object is handled by `Srvr.exe`. After launching the executable and establishing the COM linkage to it, the `Srvr` object will live within Excel's currently active spreadsheet, but the VBA code will probably be interested in communicating with the object's `IDispatch` interface to get some work done.

Since the information about our Automation support is buried in our type library, Excel will have to dig it out – but it will and, by this point, already has. Consequently, you will write code to directly manipulate any property in the object, or call methods in the property. You might make the object red in the face by doing this:

```
Dim nOldRed As Integer
nOldRed = MyObject.ForegroundRedPart
MyObject.ForegroundRedPart = 255
MyObject.Repaint()
```

Debugging OLE Applications

When you're debugging OLE applications, you'll want to make sure that you have the OLE RPC Debugging check box set in the Debugging tab of the Options dialog. You'll need administrator-level privileges on your machine to set this check box, but once it's set, it allows you to trace across the boundary between the server and the client during an OLE call.

While this setting is very useful for diagnosing OLE problems, it's a bit intimidating to get things setup in the first place. You should load your OLE server or client code in the Visual C++ IDE, setting breakpoints as normal. If you're debugging a client, just go ahead, run the program and exercise it. If you're debugging a server, you'll also want to debug your application, but don't work with the user interface. Instead, start its client and use it to work your code. Insert or drag one of your server's objects into the client you're using and go from there – break points that you set in the server code will be tripped, even though you're really working with another process and only indirectly touching your server via OLE. OLE will be using your application, even if it's already loaded, to service the newly created object in the client application.

Sometimes, it's worthwhile to use two instances of the Microsoft Visual Studio if you're debugging both the server and client code. This is an ideal approach, as it's fast and extremely convenient, but it significantly taxes the available memory on your machine. Don't even consider it when running relatively substantial servers under Windows NT with less than 32 MB of physical RAM. If you have relatively simple servers, or are using Windows 95/98, your resource needs might be a little lower.

Automation and ActiveX Controls

In the next chapter, we'll explore ActiveX controls very carefully. I'll mention some things during that chapter that bear repeating here; there's a big difference between ActiveX controls and Automation.

Don't get me wrong; ActiveX controls are indeed based strongly in the foundations of Automation. But it turns out that ActiveX controls and ActiveX control containers subscribe to a very strict interpretation of what Automation does in the situations an ActiveX control usually faces. ActiveX controls *must* implement several COM interfaces that aren't part of the normal OLE 'shared-document' standard to be considered true ActiveX controls.

If you need to decide between ActiveX controls and Automation, you need to reflect on a few things. If you want to implement an object that has properties and methods and fires back events, ActiveX controls are a fine way to go if you want to play by the rules. In particular, if you don't mind making a COM object that is capable of creating a window and managing, however minimal, a user interface, an ActiveX control could be just the ticket. On the other hand, if you shudder at the notion of having a window (even if it's empty and even if you only use it to tell your container that you didn't really mean to create a window), you should consider using a raw Automation object implementation to solve your problem.

Custom COM Interfaces

As I implied near the beginning of this chapter, writing code that wants to grow up and be a COM object means that the code will need to support several interfaces. At a bare minimum, a COM object needs to support the IUnknown interface. To be able to provide a shared user interface and things like in-place activation, the OLE server needs to offer a lot more than just that IUnknown interface; it must also provide classes with appropriate implementations of the IOleObject and IClassFactory interfaces. If the server wants to render itself, or wants to be persistent, it should also expose an implementation of IDataObject.

It is possible that, some day, you'll want to write an object that breaks these rules. That is, you might want to write an object that simply exposes an IUnknown implementation and begins to offer other interfaces of which your client applications are expressly aware. Or, you might want to write a full-blown OLE document server that adds a few extra interfaces so you can expose some extra functionality of your own.

The of building **custom interfaces**, is quite like using a power tool. Of course, you shouldn't go about with power tools making holes in expensive speakers, load-bearing walls and water heaters just because you can – you need to have a good plan. And developing a good plan just might be the most difficult part of working with custom interfaces.

Custom interfaces are interesting; if you need to talk to other COM objects, or build a system that allows your own clients and servers to more aggressively communicate, you'll want to use a custom interface or two. If you're writing a special COM object which will talk with many programs which you (or your closest friends) are also writing, you can simply design the interfaces in much the same way you would design a C++ object. You'll want to write a header file that defines the interface so others can use it. That header file should also create a couple of #defines so that you can have a way to conveniently access the interface.

Maybe you'd like to create an interface called, say, IContents. This interface can be applied generically to anything that has contents – a magazine, a book, or a CD. So, maybe you would declare it to have a few different methods:

Method Name	Returns
GetUnit	The description of length and start units (e.g. "MM:SS", or "Page")
GetMaxEntries	The number of entries in the contents table
GetEntryName	The name of a specific entry
GetEntryStart	The starting point for a specific entry in the units given by GetUnit
GetEntryLength	The length or duration for a specific entry in the units given by GetUnit

Pretty simple, right? We can run off and make an implementation of this that MFC can understand, but we'll need the declaration for the server's interface as a class. I'll base that class on IUnknown, a class defined by COM itself, so it would go something a little like this:

```
interface IContents : public IUnknown
{
public:
    _stdcall virtual HRESULT GetUnit(LPOLESTR* pstr) = 0;
    _stdcall virtual HRESULT GetMaxEntries(LPINT pInt) = 0;
    _stdcall virtual HRESULT GetEntryName(LPOLESTR* pstr) = 0;
    _stdcall virtual HRESULT GetEntryStart(LPOLESTR* pstr) = 0;
    _stdcall virtual HRESULT GetEntryLength(LPOLESTR* pstr) = 0;
};
```

You'll note that I declared all of this in longhand, like I was writing my very own class, except I used the keyword interface instead of class up at the top. It turns out that interface is just a definition – it really maps to a struct. This is done so that you don't have to worry about constructors and destructors, and so that COM can be used from languages that don't even support constructors or destructors – like ALGOL. The _stdcall in each member function declaration simply makes sure that COM, the caller, and the implementer put the call stack together correctly.

I wrote the declaration this way just to make things appear pretty explicit. In fact, COM has a handful of helper macros (like DECLARE_INTERFACE()) which would help you pull some of the covers over the details in the implementation and others (like STDMETHOD()) which can help you avoid the slightly verbose syntax that pure virtual functions require.

If you wanted to declare the same interface as above using these macros, you could code this:

```
DECLARE_INTERFACE(IContents, IUnknown)
{
    STDMETHOD(GetUnit)(THIS_ LPOLESTR* pstr) PURE;
    STDMETHOD(GetMaxEntries)(THIS_ LPINT pInt) PURE;
    STDMETHOD(GetEntryName)(THIS_ LPOLESTR* pstr) PURE;
    STDMETHOD(GetEntryStart)(THIS_ LPOLESTR* pstr) PURE;
    STDMETHOD(GetEntryLength)(THIS_ LPOLESTR* pstr) PURE;
};
```

The DECLARE_INTERFACE() macro takes the name of your new interface as its first parameter and the name of the base interface as the second parameter. You can then make declarations for the methods in your interface. Here, I used the STDMETHOD() macro to get all of the proper decorations on each function. I also followed the function declaration with the PURE macro, which is a bit easier on the eyes than the formal =0 modifier.

You'll undoubtedly note that this class declares everything as a virtual function. The idea is that the class will *certainly* be an abstract base class, but the important part is that it will need a vtable so that COM can look at a table of pointers to functions rather than an actual pointer to a class object.

Again, this is a COM design idea that lets COM objects work with any language, instead of being tied to a vendor's specific implementation of a language – in this case, C++.

You should note that I stick to very COM-esque parameter passing conventions. That is, I let the object return OLE strings, and I always accept a pointer to a pointer to the string so that I can initialize it myself. Instead of actually returning a value, I always return an HRESULT and initialize the value by reference.

Loosely coded, the implementation of one of the functions might look something like this:

```
HRESULT CContents::XConts::GetMaxEntries(LPINT pInt)
{
    if (ObjectIsInitalized() == TRUE)
    {
        *pInt = GetEntryCount();
        return S_OK;
    }
    else
        return E_FAIL;
}
```

If the code above can provide the information the user needs, it does so and returns S_OK – which is a HRESULT that indicates to the caller that everything is just fine. If it runs into trouble, it returns E_FAIL as a generic failure code. You can paw through Winerror.h to learn about more appropriate codes. You might want to use E_OUTOFMEMORY if you can't remember why you failed, or E_INVALIDARG if the caller asked for something stupid.

Now that this is all said and done, I can actually write an MFC class that lets me get my work done. The compiler needs to see my declaration of interface IContents though, because it will be used in the macros I want for my class declaration. My actual MFC class would look like this:

```
class CContents : public CCmdTarget
{
public:
    // any other interesting stuff I have goes here
    // (like the normal, C++ implementation of my class)

protected:
    DECLARE_INTERFACE_MAP()

    BEGIN_INTERFACE_PART(Conts, IContents)
        STDMETHOD(GetUnit)(LPOLESTR*);
        STDMETHOD(GetMaxEntries)(LPINT);
        STDMETHOD(GetEntryName)(LPOLESTR*);
        STDMETHOD(GetEntryStart(LPOLESTR*);
        STDMETHOD(GetEntryLength)(LPOLESTR*);
    END_INTERFACE_PART(Conts)
};
```

You can see here that I use the STDMETHOD() macro to keep things more concise than in the previous example. STDMETHOD() makes a virtual function that returns an HRESULT. You can use the STDMETHOD_() macro if you want to return your own type instead of an HRESULT. For instance, the following macros each have the same effect:

```
STDMETHOD(GetUnit)(LPOLESTR*);
STDMETHOD_(HRESULT, GetUnit)(LPOLESTR*);
```

There are a few other nifty macros for making these declarations – you can check the COM references in the Win32 SDK documentation or the Objbase.h header file in the \Microsoft Visual Studio\Vc98\Include folder to learn about them.

The work I've done so far gets me a class called CContents, which implements a nested class called XConts. The nested class is also instantiated as a member: m_xConts. Since I based CContents on CCmdTarget, I get MFC's implementations of the AddRef() and Release() methods of IUnknown for free, in addition to MFC's support for letting my interface participate in aggregation.

Aggregation is, by the way, the ability of a COM object to effectively inherit functionality from another COM object. Aggregation involves an outer object which implements interfaces that are exposed via COM to other applications. The outer object contains – or aggregates – an inner object that implements some functionality that contributes to the features offered by the outer object. The only interface exposed to the world is that of the outer object. The inner object exposes an interface to the outer object, but doesn't expose an interface to the rest of the outside world. The outer object does, though, expose the interfaces of the inner object, indirectly. The outer object is responsible for maintaining the inner object – that is, the outer object creates the inner object when the outer object is created, and destroys the inner object just before the outer object itself dies.

The CContents class I created is a real, living and breathing MFC class. I need to implement the functions in it, and when I do so I'm welcome to add any members I want to make that implementation smoother. I might try and refrain from doing so, though, so that the class can remain as lightweight as possible. That would give anyone who uses the class as little baggage as possible in their implementations involving the class.

You'll need to hook CContents up to MFC's ability to dispatch queries for the object. To do so, just declare an interface map for MFC by using the appropriate macros:

```
BEGIN_INTERFACE_MAP(CContents, CCmdTarget)
    INTERFACE_PART(CContents, IID_IContents, Conts)
END_INTERFACE_MAP()
```

The INTERFACE_PART() macro invocation takes the name of my class, the IID for the interface that I've declared, and my name for the interface structure. An **IID**, by the way, is an 'interface ID'. It's just a special GUID that identifies an interface. Remember, IIDs are exactly like GUIDs because they have 128 bits and are globally unique. IIDs are just a subset of all available GUIDs; not all GUIDs are IIDs, but all IIDs are GUIDs.

If I decide that a CContents needs another interface, I can use another INTERFACE_PART() macro in the map above. I'd also want to add another INTERFACE_PART() block to my CContents class definition. If I wanted to, I could always derive another class, like CCollection, from CContents and have it implement the extra classes. It would naturally delegate the responsibility for interfaces it didn't implement back down to CContents – it could override them explicitly if it wanted to. Interface maps work just like message maps in this regard.

I can pick out an interface ID for my new interface, just by using the `Guidgen` tool that we've mentioned before. The important thing is that I supply a declaration for a friendly symbol like `IID_IContents` so that anyone else who wants to use my interface can easily do so. The declaration for `IID_IContents` should, then, go in the header that defines the rest of this stuff for any of my clients.

The Rubber Hits the Road

We've talked lots about declarations, but we haven't said much about the way they'll actually get *implemented.* Even though I've derived everything from `CCmdTarget`, I'll still need to actually write some code. There are a few things that just haven't been hooked up.

First, the `m_xConts` object inside of my `CContents` class doesn't know who its 'outer' parent is. I need to initialize it in my `CContents` constructor. It's simple – just do this:

```
CContents::CContents()
{
    m_xConts.m_pParent = this;
}
```

You'll also want to supply implementations of `AddRef()` and `Release()`. Those functions are almost trivial. As you probably know, they're responsible for making sure a class doesn't disappear while it's still being used. `CCmdTarget` has a member named `m_dwRef`, and initializes it in its constructor so you don't have to worry about it, except for implementing `AddRef()` and `Release()`. You don't really need to make `AddRef()` or `Release()` code – you can just call the base class implementation. Since your interface implementation class is based on `CCmdTarget`, you can just call the `InternalRelease()` and `InternalAddRef()` members of your base class to get the appropriate work done.

You'll need to also implement `QueryInterface()` to make sure you can expose interfaces to the people who care about them. `QueryInterface()` is very easy – it's just a shade less trivial than `AddRef()` and `Release()`. It could work like this:

```
HRESULT CContents::QueryInterface(REFIID iid, void** ppvObj)
{
    if (ppvObj == NULL)
        return E_POINTER;

    *ppvObj = NULL;
    if (iid == IID_IUnknown || iid == IID_IContents)
    {
        *ppvObj = &m_xConts;
        AddRef();
        return NOERROR;
    }
    return ResultFromScode(E_NOINTERFACE);
}
```

All the implementation does is check the interface ID requested. If it's `IID_IUnknown`, or `IID_IContents`, we give the caller a pointer to the interface class and increment our reference count. Otherwise, we return an error code indicating that we don't support the requested interface.

That's it. All that you need to do is implement the actual functions to handle the interface. Note that those functions are members of the inner class, so your declarations will look something like this:

```
HRESULT CContents::XConts::GetUnit(LPOLESTR* ppstr)
{
    METHOD_PROLOGUE(CContents, Cont);
    return pThis->DoTheWork(ppstr);
}
```

There are two important things to remember when writing these functions. First, you'll need to use an extra scope operator (the double colon : :) to make sure you reference the interface object which implements the class. This is the class that MFC will call in response to methods on the interface being invoked.

The other trick is the use of the METHOD_PROLOGUE() macro. Since the inner object is the one implementing the class, it has no natural way to access member data or member functions inside the CContents object. Since the language provides no provision for such access, MFC makes it easier by allowing you to use METHOD_PROLOGUE() to compute a pointer named pThis. pThis isn't the same as the normal this pointer; in the above function, this would point to CContents::XCont, while pThis would point to the CContents object.

Let me reiterate that you need to remember that you're going to implement a COM object, so you should use the COM-style data types; for example, I used LPOLESTR here instead of LPTSTR. This isn't a requirement for automation interfaces, because MFC will automatically convert from and to OLE strings to the string type appropriate for your application. But if you implement a raw custom COM interface, as I've been hypothetically proposing for the last few paragraphs, you'll need to make sure you're prepared to do the appropriate conversions.

The server or servers which implement this interface should be compiled for Unicode or built as ANSI and made to use the conversion macros we discussed in the previous chapter, unless you *know* that you'll *never* want to call the interface from a non-ANSI client. (And, if you are *completely sure* of this, I'd like to talk with you – maybe you can help me pick out the Stanley Cup winners for the next ten years and I can head to Las Vegas and quit writing books.)

Summary

We think you'll agree that MFC takes most of the edge off writing an OLE server. There are lots of OLE issues to worry about if you pick beneath MFC's veneer, but you'll probably find that the MFC implementation of almost every aspect of OLE is adequate for your programming needs. You can keep all of your program's architecture in the familiar document/view model, and let MFC perform all the work of fitting your views and user interface to the COM user interface model.

In the next chapter, we'll be taking another step into the world of COM with a look at creating ActiveX controls.

15

ActiveX Controls

In the years since Visual Basic custom controls, also known as **VBX**s, exploded onto the Windows programming scene, custom controls have advanced to the point where state-of-the-art controls are now based upon COM technology. Numerous programming environments – Visual Basic, Access, Visual FoxPro, Internet Explorer, FrontPage and, of course, Visual C++ itself now support the use of ActiveX controls (or **OCX**s) and demand and support for them is still growing. Of course, Visual C++ and MFC are well-suited to the design and creation of ActiveX controls, and those controls are precisely the subject of this chapter.

In this chapter, I'll explain:

- ➤ Applications for ActiveX Controls
- ➤ What ActiveX ControlWizard does when you create a custom control project
- ➤ How to add properties, methods and events to your control
- ➤ How to make your properties available through property pages
- ➤ Licensing your custom control
- ➤ The issues you'll face as an ActiveX control designer

Looking at the User Interface

As you well know, most Microsoft Windows applications live to interact with the user. They present the user with interfaces which can be manipulated with the mouse or keyboard to get things done. In this book, I've spent some time describing ways in which you might implement your user interface using stock Windows controls, as well as the newer 32-bit common controls.

However, there are times when the controls built into Windows just aren't enough. You might be interested in writing a control that lets you display a grid of information to the user like a spreadsheet, or you may decide that you need to use color, fonts or other graphics elements in your controls in a way which isn't compatible with the normal owner-draw techniques. Or you may simply want to wrap up your program's functionality and sell it as a separate commodity – a reusable component.

The Birth of Custom Controls

For situations where you want to pack some reusable code – especially code with a user interface – previous versions of Windows supported the notion of **custom controls**. In those days, custom controls were implemented in DLLs. The DLLs had to provide very specific entry points, each of which would implement some part of the control's life cycle. One entry point may register it, and another draw it on the screen. This architecture was fairly acceptable for the time, but the problem was that too many weird controls cropped up. They all had different (and strange) attributes and effects which needed to be spelled out to the developer in written documentation. Aside from the most basic of features, there really wasn't any standardization.

Visual Basic, which was only just becoming popular at the time, sparked a small cottage industry around Visual Basic custom controls. VBXs, so named because of their file extension, had a set of standardized ways to let the user get at the properties the control had to offer, as well as the events and methods the control also supported. Old custom controls didn't provide a formal way to do this.

And so, with the advent of VBXs, controls were discoverable. A program (such as Visual Basic itself) could approach an arbitrary control and discover its programmatic interface. Once the VBX was registered with Visual Basic, the programmer could touch it using its properties and methods. The VBX could hide all of those initialization calls and funky formatting issues underneath the veneer of the VBX's interface to the program. The programmer was alleviated from the external DLL declarations and didn't have to worry much about any of the implementation now hidden deep inside the DLL.

Soon, many different types of Visual Basic custom controls became available; everything from thermometers to little thumb-index tabs. Some of these controls didn't even have a user interface, but, instead, they provided a nifty way to encapsulate bits of functionality that Visual Basic (or other platforms) didn't have built-in.

Before the introduction of the VBX, a programmer who, for example, needed to access a database would have to get a DLL which would grant access to that database. They'd need to declare all of the DLL's functions in their VB program, before carefully calling each and every function. This worked just fine and, although the features of the DLL were realized at a very low level, the message got through and the programmer could get their job done.

But it isn't fun to program with such a model. Instead of making three or four initialization calls, putting the user's name and password in a special format and then making yet another function call, developers wanted to treat the database connection just like they'd treat any other object within Visual Basic. VBXs let them do this.

This was the first popular instance of component-oriented development in Windows. Instead of developing huge programs, you could develop simple little components, then collect a bunch of them and simply glue them together to get the required results.

However, although the VBX standard went through a couple of iterations, it didn't seem to gain much momentum in the marketplace outside of the Visual Basic programming community. Visual C++ began allowing developers to add Visual Basic-style custom controls to their projects, and many did. Unfortunately, the VBX standard isn't very easy to port to the Win32 architecture, and it's inherently dependent on a small part of the Visual Basic runtime, which also limited its lifespan. Thus, a new type of custom control was needed for the brave new world outside of 16-bit Visual Basic applications.

Custom Controls: The Next Generation

After much discussion, it was decided that OLE would be a good backbone for the next control architecture. There were many applications which already supported OLE, so it wouldn't be very hard to get some extension of that support to allow almost *any* application to use *any* OLE control thrown at it. These controls use many of the same mechanisms as the OLE objects we investigated in the last two chapters to express their desires and capabilities to their clients.

OLE controls were born when Visual C++ 2.0 shipped. That release of Visual C++ contained the OLE Control Development Kit, which offered the tools and MFC library extensions necessary to develop OLE controls. The world could begin to experiment with these new custom controls. (Believe it or not, I wrote the setup program for that part of Visual C++ and, as far as I know, no hard drives were inadvertently reformatted by my code.)

Since the release of Visual C++ 4.0, the OLE Control Development Kit has become a thing of the past. The controls still exist, of course, but the code to help you create OLE controls is now part of standard MFC. Since then, OLE Controls have also been renamed; they're now known as ActiveX controls. The ActiveX ControlWizard, which we'll describe in a few pages time, is now an integral part of the product, instead of an add-in which you may or may not have installed. (Unfortunately, that meant I had to find more subtle ways to make my contribution to the product. As far as I know, `CSyncObject` hasn't reformatted any drives, though.)

The Fundamentals of ActiveX Controls

Basically, ActiveX controls are just COM **in-process servers** with a few extensions thrown in. We haven't discussed in-process servers much, other than mentioning them in passing when we were describing other implementation styles. In-process servers are implemented as dynamic-link libraries and, as such, the code that serves an in-process object will always load in the same address space as the client. The server code can then run as a natural extension to the process, using its objects.

This contrasts with the various local server implementations we've seen, like those in Chapter 14, which all run as stand-alone executables. When the server runs as a stand-alone executable, a great deal of work – known as **marshaling** – has to be done between the server and the client, to make sure they're exchanging data compatibly and safely. This protection takes time for each and every call between the client and the server (since the COM subsystem has to dress up in a denim shirt and leather chaps, and strap on some revolvers).

However, when the server code runs in-process, it can run more efficiently since it often doesn't need marshaling. So, in-process servers were chosen to provide ActiveX controls with an efficient foundation. This means every ActiveX control you write with the MFC ActiveX ControlWizard will be a DLL.

Controls at Run Time

Obviously, ActiveX controls require COM when they run. Most ActiveX controls will require the run-time support found in the MFC DLLs. You *could* make your own implementation of the default methods and properties, and write your own control completely from scratch (you could even do it in plain old C instead of C++, if you wanted), but it's hard to do that. You'd be reinventing a pretty fancy wheel. Further, it's likely you'll want more than one control to be in memory at a time and unless you carefully architect the wheel you've reinvented, you're going to inefficiently load multiple instances of that same code.

> *You also can, however, use ATL to write OLE Controls. MFC produces controls that are notoriously full-featured. Additionally, they also carry the runtime weight of MFC with them. The MFC team has aggressively addressed these size issues, but ATL's innovative architecture allows it to produce ATL controls which are much smaller. From a fundamental level, ATL just takes a different approach to implementing the same structural features that MFC does. So the most basic aspects of controls which we discuss in this chapter apply both to ATL and MFC. But the actual implementation, and the Wizards used to cook up the controls, are substantially different. If you chose to pursue the size savings ATL offers, you should find a good book on ATL and review its discussion of control development.*

MFC contains a great deal of code to implement ActiveX controls and the various standards and interfaces they require, making things easier for you as a control developer. You just need to add the code for the unique features of your user interface, as well as the generic features you want your control to implement. This is in keeping with the whole MFC philosophy of wrapping popular parts of Windows while actually implementing generic functionality for the really ugly parts of the system, allowing you, as a developer, to run off and develop whatever gnarly features you want.

The Library

Back in Visual C++ 2.x, the OLE control run-time library was called `Oc30.dll` for ANSI controls and `Oc30u.dll` for Unicode controls. Nowadays, ActiveX controls are supported at run time by `Mfc42.dll` (or `Mfc42u.dll` if you're into Unicode).

> You can find notes on which files are necessary for what kinds of MFC applications in the `\ Microsoft Visual Studio\vc98\Redist\Redistrb.wri` file on your Visual C++ CD.

The `Oc30.dll` run-time support library used in previous versions of MFC wrapped a special version of MFC for use by custom controls. That build of the library was a cross between the _USRDLL and _AFXDLL versions of MFC – a control which linked with them could be used from programs that didn't link themselves with MFC, but the programs *could* use MFC themselves. However, `Oc30.dll` didn't implement some parts of MFC – like the document/view architecture!

Modern ActiveX controls – those built with MFC 4.0 or newer – are actually built with the extension library model of MFC. (For more information about what that means, check out Chapter 11 and the section towards the end of this chapter entitled 'The State of the Module Address'.) But it's sufficient to say for now that, because the full DLL supports control development, any ActiveX control you write with a current version of MFC can use any feature of MFC you wish. The MFC run-time also provides your control with two additional things.

First, `Mfc42.dll` code will help you by implementing the low-level interfaces that your control needs to support. Much like the server and container code described in Chapters 13 and 14, the run-time's code will call your control's code only when something special, something that defines your control's unique features, needs to be resolved.

Second, the run-time will provide you with implementations of actual tangible features that every control should have. We'll examine some of those features and see how we might apply them in a solution based on ActiveX controls later in the chapter. However, before you can fiddle with a control, you'll need to create a control project using the MFC ActiveX ControlWizard.

Creating a Control Project

You can find the MFC ActiveX ControlWizard as one of the entries in the Projects tab of the New dialog box. As I'm sure you'll recall, you can get there by using the New... command in the File menu. Once you pick a directory and a name for your control project, you'll get the first dialog of the wizard, which looks like this:

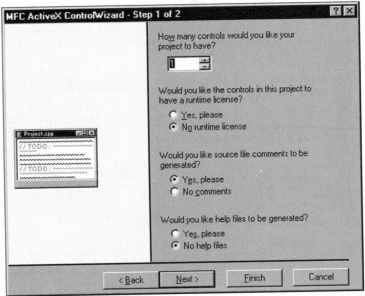

The above dialog, in addition to the dialog in the second and final step of the wizard, will allow you to set some interesting options that affect your control's operation. Read on to see what each of the options really mean.

How Many Controls Would You Like?

A single ActiveX control implementation file can support multiple ActiveX controls, so the wizard wants to know if you'd like to generate your project to have more than one control. If you pick a number larger than one here, the MFC ActiveX ControlWizard will emit multiple COleControl-derived classes in your project but will create only one project workspace file.

If you put more than one control in a project, you'll inherently require the user to load all of the controls, even when they only need one. This means that if there's a chance the user might not need all the controls you have to offer, you're probably better off putting them in separate projects.

If you have controls which will always, or at least usually, be used together, it's a great idea to make sure they live in the same project, as this will greatly improve the instantiation time for the controls. COM won't have to load a whole module, get it hooked up and initialize it, before other controls in the same module are available for use.

Would You Like a Run-time License?

This option adds support for **license validation**. This gives your control the framework it needs to implement a run-time test to ensure it's being run by a licensed user. We'll explain exactly how this works in a separate section nearer the end of the chapter.

Would You Like Source Comments?

If you request the affirmative side of this option, the files in your project will have source comments. These can help you follow the code produced by the MFC ActiveX ControlWizard. The familiar `// TODO:` comments will guide you through the implementation of your control.

Would you Like Help Files to be Generated?

If you respond affirmatively to this option, the wizard will produce context-sensitive help for your control. You'll get a rudimentary help file and the MFC ActiveX ControlWizard will make sure code lands in your project to make your control sensitive to the *F1* key when it's appropriate.

The second page of the MFC ActiveX ControlWizard, shown here, provides further options:

Let's examine those options, too.

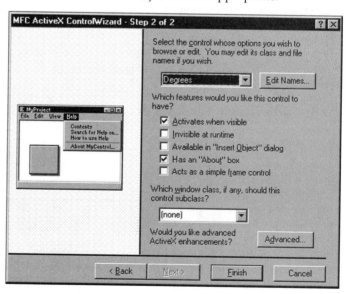

Activates When Visible

As you'll see later, ActiveX controls have activation rules similar to other in-place objects we've learned about. It turns out that ActiveX controls, though, won't create a window for the control until they're actually active (if at all). If you want your control to be active when visible, you should mark the Activates when visible box. Note the container may not support requests by controls to become activated when visible.

Invisible at Runtime

If you don't want your control to present a user interface when it is running, you can check the Invisible at runtime box. The option, when set, means the control will be visible when you're working with it at design time – that is, when you're placing it in the dialog editor or on a Visual Basic form – but not when the application runs. If the Invisible at runtime option isn't set, your control will have a window in which it can present its user interface.

If you've written a control that provides services but doesn't need a visible interface (such as a database connectivity service), this option is for you.

Run and Design Mode

Run mode and design mode are arbitrary states defined by the container. **Design mode** suggests a situation where the control is being positioned in a form or window, but that window isn't currently being used in a program. **Run mode** suggests the programmer has finished designing the application's user interface and the user is actually working with it. We say *suggests* because these modes are a protocol only; your container may or may not need to pay attention to them.

Available in "Insert Object" Dialog

If the Available in "Insert Object" dialog box is checked, the control will automatically register itself with COM as an insertable item. This means the control's registry entry will have the `Insertable` key. The presence or absence of this setting is really a design decision which is at your discretion. If you turn the option on, the user will be able to insert the control in any ActiveX control container. If you turn it off, the control can only be used in containers that search the registry specifically for ActiveX controls. Most developers leave this option off; your users will become confused (and maybe annoyed) if they insert your controls in applications that can't work with controls.

Has An "About" Box

As its name implies, this option allows you to give your control a simple About dialog. It will be hooked up to a method that will allow the control's container to display the box, which can be modified to your requirements. This option makes it easy to add this common feature to your control.

Acts as a Simple Frame Control

Even when they're in the same container, ActiveX controls are fundamentally disassociated, by which we mean that one control doesn't know anything about the existence of any other. However, it's conceivable you might want to implement some control that has influence over other controls, a common example being a group box. Such controls should be built with the Acts as a simple frame control option; they'll implement an `ISimpleFrameSite` interface for their container.

The container will listen to this interface and the control should use it to let the container preview any Windows messages the control receives. The container can react as it sees fit, even snatching the message away from the control in order to abort the processing of the message. That's the overview; the exact mechanisms are a little bit beyond the scope of this chapter, but you can find out about them by looking for `ISimpleFrameSite` in the online references.

Subclassing a Control

If you're so inclined, you can also use this wizard step to subclass a Windows control as a basis for your own ActiveX control. For example, if you want your ActiveX control to appear like a list box, but you want to avoid coding all of the basic features, you can choose the LISTBOX class in the Which window class, if any, should this control subclass? drop-down box. Later in this chapter, we'll cover some of the important issues you'll need to consider when you are subclassing a control.

You can change names used for the classes in your control by pressing the Edit names... button. The names are all up to you, but you can't change the classes that your control uses. We'll treat subclassing in detail in the second half of this chapter.

What's in the Project?

Once you've used the MFC ActiveX ControlWizard to create your project, you'll find it's a little different from most of the projects we've built so far. Your control project builds to a file with the `.ocx` extension; this file is really just a dynamic link library.

The DLL implements one or more `COleControl`-derived classes. This MFC class provides you with just about everything you need to implement an ActiveX control; you just need to plug in your own painting code and all the other bells and whistles. As you may guess, the rest of this chapter is about the different things you can (or need) to do with your `COleControl` implementation and how that code will interact with the container.

> The example code for this chapter is an ActiveX control called `Degrees`. The `Degrees` control draws a primitive bulb thermometer and offers the client the ability to set the range of the temperatures at the end of the control, as well as the currently indicated temperature. Amongst a few other interesting features, it supports the ability to change the color of the thermometer and its background area.

COleControl Module

`COleControl` is the backbone of each control in your project; you can have more than one `COleControl`-derived class if you have more than one control in your project, but your control module will only have a single instance of `COleControlModule`. The `COleControlModule`-derived object is declared in the main module of your control (`Degrees.cpp` in our example). It looks just like the `CWinApp` declaration we've seen for our other projects:

```
CDegreesApp NEAR theApp;
```

Believe it or not, the ActiveX Control Wizard for MFC still generates the NEAR modifier — it's meaningless these days. So, if you're too new to Windows, you can safely ignore it.

Just like applications, your control module has `InitInstance()` and `ExitInstance()` routines to do any extra initialization/clean-up for the control module.

Note that `InitInstance()` is called for each load of the DLL into a different process (corresponding to a `DLL_PROCESS_ATTACH` notification received by the `DllMain()` entry point of the DLL); `InitInstance()` will be called only once if a single container creates two instances of a control, but it would be called again against a new `COleControlModule`-derived object if the control is instantiated by a different container. The `DLL_PROCESS_DETACH` notification is called in response to `ExitInstance()`.

You'll only rarely add initialization code to your `InitInstance()` function. It's only worthwhile for things that you need to initialize once per application, no matter how many control instances are created. You can do setup work in your `COleControl`-derived constructor if you need the initialization to be done for every instance of the control, regardless of whether or not it appears in the same container as another instance of the control.

You'll note that MFC ActiveX ControlWizard no longer produces 16-bit and 32-bit project files for your new control. In any 2.x version of Visual C++, the OLE ControlWizard made both 16-bit and 32-bit projects, to ease porting. However, from version 4.0 onwards, you only get one project file and one module definition file.

Registration

You'll note there are two global functions in the main module of your control: `DllRegisterServer()` and `DllUnregisterServer()`. These functions must be exported by the DLL by name, so you'll find their fingerprints in the module definition file. As the names imply, `DllRegisterServer()` and `DllUnregisterServer()` are responsible for registering and unregistering the control.

You may remember we discussed self-registration for normal executable servers in the previous chapter. Since they are stored in dynamic-link libraries, controls can't register themselves this way, requiring you to either merge the `.reg` file with the registry, or to load the DLL and call the `DllRegisterServer()` function in the module. To unregister the control and clean the registry of its entries, you can call `DllUnregisterServer()`.

You'll note that the MFC ActiveX ControlWizard doesn't create a `.reg` file for an ActiveX control project; the registration functions are the only game in town when it comes to registering ActiveX controls.

While writing and testing your control, you can register it from the Visual C++ IDE by using the Register Control command in the Tools menu. If the registration is successful, you'll see a message like this:

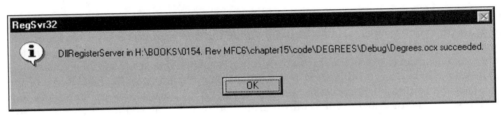

889

As you might guess, if the registry function fails, you'll get an error message that says so. The registration program is shipped with Visual C++; it's called `Regsvr32.exe`. The program is painlessly simple. You pass the name of your control's executable file on the `Regsvr32` command line and it calls the Windows `LoadLibrary()` API on that file name, followed by a call to the `DllRegisterServer()`. If the `DllRegisterServer()` function fails, the program reports the error.

Unregistering works in the same way, except you need to pass the `/U` option on the command line as well; the program reacts by calling `DllUnregisterServer()` instead. These options, and the commands, are hidden under the choices in the Tools menu commands.

You will need to re-register your control any time you make a change to its type library. The type library in the control will change whenever you add properties, methods or events to your control. If you're using a project generated by the MFC ActiveX ControlWizard, you'll note that the project has a Custom Build option that automatically runs `Regsvr32.exe` when it is necessary to do so and therefore automatically re-registers the control.

COleControl

As you know by now, any window in MFC is represented by `CWnd`, or a `CWnd`-derived class. If you're writing an OLE Control, however, you'll implement your control by deriving a class from `COleControl`. It's this class that provides the stock implementations of all the COM interfaces that make controls work.

Since most OLE Controls have windows, the class is derived from `CWnd`. Its heritage lets it do all the things windows do – most notably, paint and accept user input from the mouse and keyboard. But the additional features added in the more derived class make it interesting as a basis for the implementation of your controls. Let's investigate those features in detail to understand the major features of the controls you build and how they fit together.

Properties

Your ActiveX control can maintain any number of **properties** to serve its users. Your control's properties may describe some part of its user interface, such as the color it uses to draw or the font it uses in messages. In the `Degrees` sample, the control exposes properties for the upper and lower limits of the temperature, as well as the temperature itself.

Properties in ActiveX controls are, in many ways, exactly the same as the properties we saw in Automation objects earlier. You can add the properties using the ClassWizard and have them hooked up to notification functions or `Get/Set` functions, just like you could for Automation servers. Unlike the plain Automation server we saw before, you'll notice that the drop-down list for the external property name actually has entries. You'll probably call `Refresh()` from each of your control's Set functions after you change the member data in the control. The call to `Refresh()` gives your control the opportunity to update your user interface to reflect the change that was just made.

Stock Properties

The properties your control maintains can be divided into two groups: stock properties and custom properties. The entries you see in the External Name drop-down list in ClassWizard are the stock properties your control can maintain. These properties come almost for free – you have to hook them up, but you have to do very little work to maintain them. Once you've hooked up the property, your control accepts settings for it and maintains the request in its persistent data behind the scenes. You're responsible for drawing your control using that property as you feel it applies to your control.

When you add a stock property, you can use any one of the following:

External Name	Function Names	Purpose
Text	GetText() SetText()	The control's primary visible text content
Caption	GetText() SetText()	The control's primary visible text content
BackColor	GetBackColor() SetBackColor()	The background color for the control
BorderStyle	GetBorderStyle() SetBorderStyle()	The style of control's border
Enabled	GetEnabled() SetEnabled()	If non-zero, the control is enabled and will react to user input
Font	GetFont() SetFont()	Sets font for primary visible text in control
ForeColor	GetForeColor() SetForeColor()	The foreground color for the control's features
hWnd	GetHwnd()	This read-only property provides the Windows handle to the control's main window; only valid when control is active

If you don't think a stock property applies to your control, you don't have to implement it. It's reasonable for you to expect that containers will behave themselves if you don't implement a particular stock property. Stock properties are always managed by a Get/Set-style interface.

You may have noticed that both the Text and Caption properties call GetText() and SetText(). This is by convention; most controls will implement their caption and text with the same code, reflecting the same feature of their user interface. If you have text in your control, you may wish to hook it up to both the Text and Caption properties to be compatible with the expectations of the users of your control. Some controls treat these properties differently; for example, some might use the Caption property for static labels, while they use the Text property for text that is actually a part of the control's dynamic user interface.

You might have further noticed that there's no SetHwnd() function to complement GetHwnd(). That's because the control's hWnd property is read-only; you can't write it, so the Set side of the interface isn't present. The container can retrieve this property from your control if it wishes to manipulate your control's window directly.

The font style is interesting because it forces the control to process an LPFONTDISP as the parameter value. An LPFONTDISP is a pointer to the dispatch interface on the OLE font object managed by the control run-time and is intended to make efficient font management easy. In your control, instead of managing a font handle or all of the data required to dynamically create fonts, you can manage a CFontHolder object. The control's run-time implements this object and lets it get its fonts from those available; this way, if two controls are using the same font, the font is only actually created once, significantly lessening the strain on system resources.

Both color properties use the OLE_COLOR data type. The idea behind this data type is to provide some amount of portability for colors. Since OLE objects might need to render themselves against almost any device, the OLE_COLOR data type helps OLE to keep track of the palette, which will affect the way the control is rendered. You can convert from an OLE_COLOR to the COLORREF data type, used in device context calls, by calling the COleControl::TranslateColor() function.

The BorderStyle property indicates the type of border your control should draw. Your control should draw a border if the property is non-zero and not draw one if the style is 0. Right now, the value 1 for this property means the control should have a normal border. Your control, or containers for your control, may wish to define alternate border styles using different numbers; for example, you might draw a thick border if the BorderStyle property is 2.

Adding and Managing Properties

As you know, the easiest way to add properties to your control is to use the ClassWizard. The process is exactly the same as for adding a property to your Automation server, because that is exactly what you're doing. You can find instructions for this back in Chapter 14.

Controls differ from regular MFC Automation servers in that they can make your properties persistent. Your COleControl-derived class has a function called DoPropExchange() which implements the **property exchange** code for your control. Like the data exchange and record exchange functions we've seen in other MFC classes, DoPropExchange() takes a pointer to an exchange context and should therefore be coded to work in both saving and loading contexts. Your DoPropExchange() function is responsible for storing your control's properties between activations of the control.

A naked implementation of the DoPropExchange() function looks like this:

```
void CDegreesCtrl::DoPropExchange(CPropExchange* pPX)
{
    ExchangeVersion(pPX, MAKELONG(_wVerMinor, _wVerMajor));
    COleControl::DoPropExchange(pPX);
}
```

For a more detailed explanation of ExchangeVersion(), see the section called 'Control Versioning' later on in this chapter. In a nutshell, ExchangeVersion() helps you in a similar way to how the serialization schemas helped you with persistently storing the data for regular classes.

If you add a stock property, ClassWizard will add a stock property macro to the dispatch map for your control. The controls run-time library will pick through the dispatch map looking for the special stock property dispatch IDs it uses when performing the exchange after calling COleControl::DoPropExchange().

Once COleControl's implementation of DoPropExchange() returns, you can perform the exchange calls for the custom properties you have declared. If you don't think a property is important enough to be persistent between different activations of your control, just don't store it. You only need to store the properties you think are important; if you don't want some of the data made persistent, simply don't write it out.

Storing and Loading Properties

For the properties you do want to store or load, just use the appropriate PX_ function in your
DoPropExchange() function. In the example, we have used these exchange calls:

```
PX_Short(pPX, _T("LowerLimit"), m_nLowerLimit, 32);
PX_Short(pPX, _T("UpperLimit"), m_nUpperLimit, 212);
PX_Short(pPX, _T("Temperature"), m_nTemperature, 78);
```

Various versions of the PX_ functions exist to let you manipulate different data types. Here are the
different data types directly supported by MFC:

Property Exchange Functions	Purpose
PX_Blob()	Binary Large Object (BLOB) data
PX_Bool()	BOOL
PX_Color()	OLECOLOR type
PX_Currency()	OLE CY (currency)
PX_Double()	double
PX_Font()	OLE control font objects
PX_Float()	float
PX_IUnknown()	Pointer to an IUnknown interface
PX_Long()	long
PX_Picture()	OLE control picture objects
PX_Short()	short
PX_String()	CString data
PX_ULong()	unsigned long
PX_UShort()	unsigned short
PX_DataPath()	CDataPathProperty

All of the different PX_ functions take the same parameters. The first specifies the exchange context
you're handling. You can just pass the CPropExchange pointer which was passed to your
DoPropExchange() function here. The second parameter is the name of the property you're
manipulating, which must be passed as a string. The type of the third parameter is different for each
function as it reflects the data that needs to be serialized.

The fourth parameter indicates a default value for the parameter. This value is used when your
control is resetting itself to its natural state. The run-time will call OnResetState() in your control
as it initializes your control for the first time. The default implementation of OnResetState()
forces the property exchange code to use the default value to initialize the property. The default value
is also used when the value can't be read from the exchange object.

Persistent properties let your control retain its state between invocations, but you'll need to consider implementing some way for your users to manipulate your control's properties.

Bindable Properties

It's possible for an ActiveX control to expose a property a container will want to track. That is, a container may want to be notified the instant a particular property is changed within a control so that the container can react to the control appropriately. This sort of issue may come up if you were writing a control which did some data communications, for example. The control might have a `Connected` property to which its container could bind. If the connection was dropped, or if another computer wanted to establish a connection with your control, the control might change the `Connected` property – and the container would certainly want to react to the connection by performing some interesting operation, such as prompting the user for their password.

A control *must* implement a bindable property using `Get/Set` methods. MFC 'spies' on the `Get/Set` methods in the dispatch controller code it contains; if it notices that a bindable property is being changed, it will take care of firing off the appropriate notifications.

Bindable properties can be handled by the container in one of two ways – either using pessimistic or optimistic binding. **Optimistic data binding** has the control send a notification to the container after the property has changed. **Pessimistic data binding** has the control send a request to the container before it changes the property. The container is obliged to respond to this request – called `OnRequestEdit()` – with either TRUE or FALSE. TRUE means that the change is allowed, while FALSE means that it is denied. The actual property value only changes if the container returns TRUE.

If you pop into the ClassWizard, select a `Get/Set` property, and press the Data Binding... button, you'll be treated to a dialog box like this:

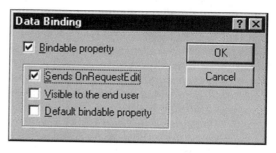

The box is very simple – it allows you to enable or disable data binding for a particular control. If you've chosen to allow data binding for the control, you can set three different attributes of the exposed bindable property. The first attribute is the most interesting – it tells the control whether or not it should send the `OnRequestEdit` notification I just mentioned when the property in question has changed.

`OnRequestEdit` turns out to be a raw OLE function – MFC makes it a little easier to call by providing the `BoundPropertyRequestEdit()` member of `COleControl`. As a control writer, you should generally call `BoundPropertyRequestEdit()` if you think containers will be interested in editing changes to your control. You shouldn't specify `BoundPropertyRequestEdit()` without good reason, though – if you have MFC send `BoundPropertyRequestEdit()` notifications for a particularly busy property (i.e. a property which changes often) you'll cause a performance hit at run time, as MFC fires off frequent notifications to the container. Depending on what the container does with those notifications, things can go slower than a herd of beetles in a cloud of turtle dust.

When a control implements bindable properties, it can follow one of two basic philosophies. It can either implement pessimistic data binding, or optimistic data binding. Pessimistic data binding means the control will assume it can't change the property without permission from the container. This means you can't accept a change unless you've called `BoundPropertyRequestEdit()` and been told by the container that the change is allowable.

Optimistic data binding has you simply notify the container via `BoundPropertyChanged()`. You should call this member of `COleControl` after you've changed the value of the property in your control. There's no way for the container to refuse the change if you're using optimistic data binding.

The other two settings in the dialog, <u>V</u>isible to the end user and <u>D</u>efault bindable property, are only interesting if you're writing a control which will be consumed by the public at large. So, if you're writing a control only you and your best friend will use, these settings don't matter much. But if you're planning on selling copies of your control to any Visual Basic programmer who asks, you'll probably want to make sure you have these bad boys set correctly.

<u>V</u>isible to the end user means the property will be shown to the end user if they browse through the list of properties supplied by the control. Of course, the property is still exposed even if this checkbox isn't set, but the container applications will not offer the property to the user. <u>D</u>efault bindable property means the property will be suggested to the user as a default when the user inquires about bindable properties. You can't have more than one default bindable property, but the one you have must be visible to the user.

As I mentioned, data binding is handled deep within MFC. You won't even see any code differences in your application. ClassWizard actually modifies the `.odl` file that defines your ActiveX control object to COM itself and to anyone who asks COM about your control. The `.odl` file contains a goofy language (and, I might even say, a little creepy) so we won't pay much attention to it. Suffice to say the `.odl` file is what makes your type library – it's compiled to a binary resource and tacked on to the executable image of your control so that COM (or anyone else nice enough to ask COM properly) can find it at run time. If you're writing real COM objects yourself from scratch, you'll probably want to spend some time with the MIDL compiler language reference in online help to learn some of the tricks you might need. But if you're just writing simple controls, you'll find it quite adequate to let ClassWizard manage the file's content for you.

Note that most folks assume data binding is a database-specific feature of ActiveX controls. It isn't – while it turns out to be a great way to get some behind-the-scenes data in the container side of the control updated just as soon as the control itself changes, the applications of data binding are *not* limited to database applications. Use data binding wherever you think it's a good idea! (Even some big-shot writers who put articles in national computer magazines get away with this fallacy. Then again, the same magazines claim things like "The PC is Dead" only a couple of months later.)

Default Properties

If you look closely at the Automation tab in the MFC ClassWizard dialog, you'll notice there's a checkbox labeled Default property. In case you have a headache and aren't quite up to the obvious, this check box allows you to mark a particular property in your control as a **default property**. The default property is assumed by COM to be the most important – or the most frequently accessed – property a control has.

By checking this box, you can later refer to your control from a language such as Visual Basic without specifying a particular property and VB will assume you mean to retrieve or set the default property. Obviously, there can be only one default property for your control. The default property will be identified in the control's dispatch map with the `DISP_DEFVALUE()` macro. This macro takes two parameters: the first is the name of your control class, and the second is a string that identifies the name of the default property. You must declare the default property elsewhere in the dispatch map for the class in question. If it is actually a base class which implements the property, the class in question doesn't need to repeat the entry – the default property can be a property of a base class.

Property Pages

Property pages provide your control with a way to let users conveniently review or modify the properties in your control. Internally, their implementation is similar to the `CPropertySheet` and `CPropertyPage` classes we reviewed in Chapter 6.

For stock properties, like the background and foreground colors supported by the `Degrees` sample, you can simply include a reference to the stock property page in your control. Your control will contain an invocation of the `BEGIN_PROPPAGEIDS()` macro supplied by the ActiveX controls run-time and, in combination with the `PROPPAGEID()` macros, will enumerate the property pages your control will support. The `Degrees` sample has code that looks like this in `Degctl.cpp`:

```
BEGIN_PROPPAGEIDS(CDegreesCtrl, 2)
    PROPPAGEID(CDegreesPropPage::guid)
    PROPPAGEID(CLSID_CColorPropPage)
END_PROPPAGEIDS(CDegreesCtrl)
```

Out of the gate, your control will have one property page. By default, this page supplied by the MFC ActiveX ControlWizard will be titled **General**, but you're welcome to change its name as you add controls to it. You can use this page to start offering a user interface for your control's custom properties, but if you decide to only offer stock properties, you can edit your `BEGIN_PROPPAGEIDS()` declaration so it contains only the property pages you require. The second parameter of the `BEGIN_PROPPAGEIDS()` macro indicates the number of pages that will be in the property sheet, and should equal the number of `PROPPAGEID()` macros that appear in the code between `BEGIN_` and `END_PROPPAGEIDS()`.

Life without Property Pages

By the way, your control should offer at least one property page. If you want to expose no pages at all, you'll have to pull a couple of stunts. First, you would need to remove the `DECLARE_PROPPAGEIDS()` macro from your function's class declaration. Then, get rid of `BEGIN_PROPPAGEIDS()`, `END_PROPPAGEIDS()` and everything in between from your control's source code implementation file. Your control will be a freak of nature if it has no property pages; exactly how any given container will react to this is completely unknown. The test container that ships with Visual C++ will complain and show a few benign error messages.

Adding Your Own Property Pages

It's quite possible you'll want to add more than one dialog's worth of properties to your control. If you do, you can add another property page to your application by drawing the page in the dialog editor and then using the ClassWizard to create a new C++ wrapper class for the dialog.

You'll note you can create new property pages by using the Resource... command in the Insert menu while your control project is open. In the Insert Resource dialog which results from using this command, you should expand the Dialog entry in the Resource type: tree control. This entry will reveal two interesting templates: IDD_OLE_PROPPAGE_LARGE and IDD_OLE_PROPPAGE_SMALL. You can insert these resources into your project and they'll be exactly the right size and have the correct styles and settings for a standard property sheet.

Just like we've done a thousand times before, just use the Add Class... push button in the ClassWizard to create the new class. In the Add Class dialog, make sure you use the COlePropertyPage class as a basis for your new class; don't use the CPropertyPage class!

Once the class is added, you'll need to adjust your BEGIN_PROPPAGEIDS() macro to include the GUID for the new property page. First, make sure you increment the second parameter of BEGIN_PROPPAGEIDS() so the run-time will know how many property pages you included in your project. Next, just add the PROPPAGEID() macro for your new property page instance to your code. The order of the PROPPAGEID() macros in your property page map will affect the order in which pages appear in your control's property sheet. You can add the new PROPPAGEID() anywhere you please to make the order pleasing.

The GUID for the new property page is created by the ClassWizard when you create the class, and hooked up in an IMPLEMENT_OLECREATE_EX() macro in the resulting implementation file. The property page GUID is also conveniently stored as a static member of your new property page class.

Therefore, if you added a class named CBoilerPropPage, your PROPPAGEID() line would look like this:

```
BEGIN_PROPPAGEIDS(CDegreesCtrl, 3)
    PROPPAGEID(CBoilerPropPage::guid)
    PROPPAGEID(CDegreesPropPage::guid)
    PROPPAGEID(CLSID_CColorPropPage)
END_PROPPAGEIDS(CDegreesCtrl)
```

The first PROPPAGEID() line in this fragment declares our new property page. The declaration simply identifies the class ID for the new property page object. When the user asks to see the property page, the container will be able to create the property page object using this class ID. The property page is generally serviced by the control's run-time; you don't have to do any work to get the page created or displayed. Of course, there is still some work to be done – you'll have to design the dialog resource used to display the page.

Like the CPropertyPage dialogs, you should create your property page dialog as a child dialog without a border, the Visible style or the Titlebar style. Unlike the regular CPropertyPage dialogs, ActiveX controls should stick to standard sized property pages. This will minimize the flashing and resizing of the pages caused by the user moving through the different tabs in the property page. The standard sizes which are currently used are 250 by 62 and 250 by 110 dialog units. (You won't have to worry about setting these options if you used one of the IDD_OLE_PROPPAGE templates.) If your dialog isn't exactly one of these sizes, it will work just fine, but the debug version of the controls run-time will show a warning message when the dialog is displayed.

Titling your Property Page

The title for your property page tab comes from your control's string resource table. Code in the constructor links the string with the page, like this:

```
CBoilerPropPage::CBoilerPropPage() :
    COlePropertyPage(IDD, IDS_DEGREES_PPG_CAPTION)
{
    // constructor code...
}
```

The COlePropertyPage class is implemented by the control's run-time providing the code for all of your property pages. The first parameter identifies the dialog template ID from your module's resources to be used to draw the template. The second parameter identifies a string resource to be used as the caption for the dialog tab.

After the ClassWizard

Finally, you'll need to make sure your shiny new property page is hooked up to the appropriate registration mechanism. The registration will add a GUID to the registry so your property page is creatable as an OLE object. That registration will require a name for your property page; most developers would use a string including 'Property Page', like 'Boiler Property Page', to describe the purpose of the GUID and related information in the registry. That title isn't the same as the title which will appear on the tab in the user interface. You should use the string resource table editor to add a string resource and assign it to an appropriate ID. The registry is updated with a call to the ClassWizard-generated override of the UpdateRegistry() function. In that override, you'll just pass along the ID you created to the runtimes.

The code that comes straight from the ClassWizard for UpdateRegistry() calls the AfxOleRegisterPropertyPageClass() to do the work, but has the third parameter set to zero. That third parameter carries the ID you want for the type name. ClassWizard doesn't hook up this ID, so you'll need to do it yourself. Otherwise, your new property page won't be created when the control is actually run.

> Remember that adding or removing property pages requires that you re-register your control to update the registry with information about the new pages. If you don't re-register, your new pages won't be visible.

Property Data Exchange

The property page is a dialog, just like many others we've seen before. Since the dialog is used to represent the control properties, as well as provide a way for the user to change them, you'll need to implement some code to exchange and validate the values provided by the user.

As you might expect, the COlePropertyPage class, which is the basis for each of your custom property page classes, has a DoDataExchange() function. Like its implementation in other dialogs, DoDataExchange() takes a pointer to a CDataExchange object which describes the data exchange. You can use the regular DDX_ and DDV_ macros we learned about in Chapter 5, to affect the exchange between the variables in the C++ dialog object and the controls in the dialog.

If you also want to exchange data between properties in your ActiveX control and the controls in your property dialog box, you can do this as extra steps in your DoDataExchange() function, using DDP_ functions to effect the exchange.

The DDP_ functions take four parameters, the first of which is a pointer to the data exchange object which is controlling the transfer. The second is the ID of a control on the property page, while the third is the variable you wish to exchange from or to. The fourth and final parameter is the name of the property; this name must exactly match the name you declared in your control's implementation.

The Relationship between Property and Control

You don't have to maintain a one-to-one relationship between your properties and your controls. You can create a property setting in the control based on a combination of settings in your control. The third parameter to your DDP_ function, which expresses the value you're interested in setting, doesn't have to be a member of the supporting dialog class.

The data exchange code in the Degrees sample looks like this:

```
void CDegreesPropPage::DoDataExchange(CDataExchange* pDX)
{
    //{{AFX_DATA_MAP(CDegreesPropPage)
    DDP_Text(pDX, IDC_TEMPERATURE, m_nTemperature, _T("Temperature") );
    DDX_Text(pDX, IDC_TEMPERATURE, m_nTemperature);
    DDP_Text(pDX, IDC_LOWER, m_nLower, _T("LowerLimit") );
    DDX_Text(pDX, IDC_LOWER, m_nLower);
    DDP_Text(pDX, IDC_UPPER, m_nUpper, _T("UpperLimit") );
    DDX_Text(pDX, IDC_UPPER, m_nUpper);
    //}}AFX_DATA_MAP
    DDP_PostProcessing(pDX);
}
```

The final line of the function makes a call to DDP_PostProcessing(). This is the function that performs the data exchange with the control properties. If you don't make this call, none of the values you've exchanged using the various DDP_ calls will make it to the properties in the control. The DDP_ functions take care of the exchange in only one direction; retrieving the value from the property in the control and placing it in the variable specified in your code.

Exchanging Data with the Control

So, when you're exchanging data from the control to the dialog, things work like this. To save space, I haven't included the parameters to these functions.

```
DDP_Text(...);      // put property from my ActiveX control into my
                    // member variable
DDX_Text(...);      // put data from member variable
                    // into the property dialog control
...                 // (maybe more DDP/DDX calls here)
DDP_PostProcessing(pDX);   // no operation
```

While exchanging data from the dialog to the control, the functions have these effects:

```
DDP_Text(...);      // remember to exchange the referenced
                    // property later
DDX_Text(...);      // put data from property dialog control
                    // into member variable
...                 // (maybe more DDP/DDX calls here)
DDP_PostProcessing(pDX);    // exchange all referenced properties
```

One of the net effects of the combined DDP_ and DDX_ processes is that you can't predict the order in which the properties will be reported back to the control. DDP_Text() calls build a list which isn't well-ordered. DDP_PostProcessing() then trundles through that list and effects the exchanges, but doesn't guarantee the exchanges will happen in any particular order.

A less obvious effect of the exchange process is that the variable with which you exchange DDP_ must remain in scope until DDP_PostProcessing() is called. If the variable doesn't remain in scope, you'll end up with a disaster. And so, code like this is a recipe for disaster:

```
if (m_bSomeMode)
{
    int n = 359;
    MaybeSomehowChangeThisValue(&n);
    DDP_Text(pDX,  IDC_MYCONTROL, n, _T("MyValue"));
}
DDP_PostProcessing();
```

because, by the time DDP_PostProcessing() is called in this miserable example, the variable n is long gone. Who knows what memory the exchange will actually reference when DDP_PostProcessing() tries to manipulate it!

Like regular dialogs, you can perform any extra data validation in the function without much extra work. For example, you can make sure the user has provided a lower value for LowerLimit than for UpperLimit, and the code looks like this:

```
// other stuff
//}}AFX_DATA_MAP

if (m_nLower >= m_nUpper)
{
    AfxMessageBox(IDS_BAD_LIMITS);
    pDX->Fail();
}
DDP_PostProcessing(pDX);
```

By the way, you have to perform the conditionals for your edits *before* the DDP_PostProcessing() call. If you don't, the control's properties will be updated by the exchange before the test is made, which certainly defeats the purpose of doing the check. And remember that CDataExchange::Fail() throws an exception which is trapped by MFC; any code after the call to that function won't execute.

Ambient Properties

Control containers also implement some standard properties, called **ambient properties** (or **ambients**, for short). Ambient properties are used to indicate the status quo of the container, in terms of font, foreground and background color, and language to use. To play along with all of the other controls in the container, your controls should adopt the value of the ambients as the initial values for the properties the control manages.

In fact, the standard properties (by way of some black magic in the implementation of the default `DoPropExchange()` function in `COleControl`) will all initialize to the ambient property value.

> As you design your control, remember ambient properties are suggestions; they're just a way to let the container let the control know about the status quo where it is being displayed. They tell the control that 'everyone around you has a green foreground' or 'all of the other controls in town are using Binkenbloom Narrow Gothic Plain', for example. If your control wants to play along, it should use the value granted by the ambient property. If, for any reason, it needs to use a different value for one of those properties, it should.

Retrieving Ambients

You can obtain the values of the ambient properties by calling `GetAmbientProperty()`.

```
BOOL COleControl::GetAmbientProperty(DISPID  dwDispid,
                                     VARTYPE vtProp,
                                     void*   pvProp);
```

As you can see, this function takes three parameters:

> ➤ The `DISPID` of the ambient in which you're interested
> ➤ The `VT_` type for that ambient
> ➤ The address of a variable to accept the ambient's value

A call to nab the ambient user mode looks like this:

```
BOOL bUserMode;
if (!GetAmbientProperty(DISPID_AMBIENT_USERMODE, VT_BOOL, &bUserMode))
   bUserMode = FALSE;
```

All of the `DISPID`s that refer to the standard ambient properties are defined in the `Olectl.h` header file. If you're not in the mood to interact so directly with the container, you can call the following helper functions in order to get ambients in a more user-friendly fashion:

Access Function	Property Meaning
`OLE_COLOR` `AmbientBackColor()`	The background color for your control.
`CString` `AmbientDisplayName()`	The name of the control to be used in error messages.
`LPFONTDISP AmbientFont()`	The primary font for your control.

Table Continued on Following Page

Access Function	Property Meaning
OLE_COLOR AmbientForeColor()	The foreground color for your control.
LCID AmbientLocaleID()	The locale ID for internationalization.
CString AmbientScaleUnits()	The name of the scale used by the container: e.g. 'millimeters' or 'inches'.
short AmbientTextAlign()	Justification: 0 = general alignment (numbers flush right, text flush left); 1 = left; 2 = center; 3 = right.
BOOL AmbientUserMode()	TRUE if your control is in user mode.
BOOL AmbientUIDead()	FALSE if the control shouldn't interact with the user – the control shouldn't change its cursor or react to input when this ambient is FALSE.
BOOL AmbientShowHatching()	TRUE if the container draws hatching around a selected control.
BOOL AmbientShowGrabHandles()	TRUE if container draws grab handles for the control when it may be resized.

The container is free to change the ambient property values at any time, using OnAmbientPropertyChange() to let you know which property has changed. You should react accordingly (and immediately) to the property change request before the opportunity is lost.

When the container notifies the foundation classes that an ambient property has changed, the foundation classes will call your OnAmbientPropertyChange() implementation. The function accepts a DISPID parameter that indicates which ambient has been changed. If the container doesn't specify a particular ambient as being changed, the parameter passed to OnAmbientPropertyChange() will be DISPID_UNKNOWN. You should react to this value by assuming that all ambients have changed.

Methods

If you wish, your control can also expose **methods**. As the name implies, a method is just a function which can be called on the control as an object. You should use methods to provide your users with the ability to get some action performed by the control. You might implement methods which activate or deactivate features, or cause your control to initiate some process.

If we dust off that hypothetical database control example we examined earlier, you'll be able to spot several situations where a method is ideal. You might design such a control so the name of the database you wish to connect with is a property. After setting that property, you might call a Connect() method to actually make the connection. You may have a similar Disconnect() method to shut down the connection, as well as Query(), Update() and Add() methods to perform other operations with the opened connection.

Methods are like functions – they can take parameters and offer return values. When you add a method to your control using the ClassWizard, you can specify the return value using the Return type drop-down, just as you would with an Automation server. You can also use the Parameter list grid box to specify the method's parameters and their types in a similar situation.

As you design your own controls, you'll realize there's a fine line between a method and a property. (And, in fact, you've already learned that properties can be implemented as two methods – one to set and one to get the value in question.) If we added a method to the Degrees control to flash the thermometer bulb, for example, how would we do it? If we added a method called FlashBulb it would work just fine. But what if we had a property called BulbFlashInterval? We could adopt a protocol insisting that BulbFlashInterval be set to zero for no flashing to occur. Otherwise, it has a value representing the flash interval in milliseconds. The choice is really yours; follow whatever advice you got from your favorite Object Oriented Programming Guru.

Since ActiveX controls are just a special flavor of Automation server, this should come as no surprise. The ClassWizard will add handlers to the declaration and implementation of your control's class to the DISPATCH_MAP() macro in your control's main module.

The only twist is that there are two stock methods: DoClick() and Refresh(). These are methods that are already implemented by COleControl. The DoClick() method calls your control's click method, OnClick(), whereas Refresh() forces your control to repaint its user interface. If you asked ActiveX ControlWizard to give your control an About box, you'll also have an AboutBox() method in your control. The AboutBox(), DoClick() and Refresh() methods take no parameters.

After these old favorites, it's completely up to you to expose the methods that make your control go. This can be tricky if your method contains more than one parameter; for instance Visual Basic reacts badly if you pass multiple parameters incorrectly.

Events

Events are what set ActiveX controls apart from regular Automation objects. They allow the control to inform the container that something has happened; the container will generally listen to the control and react appropriately to its events. Events serve the same functionality that notification messages serve for regular controls – they tell the owner of the control that something interesting has happened to the control and implicitly provide the owner a chance to react.

When your control wants to send an event off to its container, it's said to **fire** the event. Inside the workings of the machine, events are just invocations of methods by the control against the control's container. This makes sense, as events have parameters that can describe the event, even though they don't have return values. Just as methods allow the container to ask the control to get something done, events allow the control to tell the container that something has happened.

Adding Events

Your control will have an event map that describes which functions fire which events. You can add an event to this map using the ClassWizard. The map is really used for the housekeeping of the control during development, but the ClassWizard uses the table to understand the relationship between the events that are fired and the associated functions and their parameters. The declaration looks like this:

```
BEGIN_EVENT_MAP(CCommunicationsCtrl, COleControl)
    //{{AFX_EVENT_MAP(CDegreesCtrl)
    EVENT_CUSTOM("Terminated", FireTerminated, VTS_NONE)
    //}}AFX_EVENT_MAP
END_EVENT_MAP()
```

We've seen this style of map declaration in many different places around the MFC. `BEGIN_EVENT_MAP()` takes the name of our control class and the name of the base class for that control, while `END_EVENT_MAP()` closes up the definition. The map can contain one or more `EVENT_CUSTOM()` declarations to declare the custom events required by the control.

The first parameter to the `EVENT_CUSTOM()` macro is the external name of the event, the second is the function which fires the event and the third begins a variable list of parameter types which describe the parameters which the fire function accepts. You'll note I didn't use the `_T()` macro around the first parameter to the macro, even though it is a string literal. That's because the `EVENT_CUSTOM()` macro already has the `_T()` macro built-in.

The ClassWizard will declare a member function for the control, which actually fires the event to the container. The fire function just wraps up the dispatch ID for the event in a simple call so your mainline control implementation code can call it. The code appears in the definition of your control's class as an inline member function in your control's header file. This mechanism protects you from screwing up the parameters to the event firing. For our simple function, it looks like this:

```
// Event maps
    //{{AFX_EVENT(CCommunicationsCtrl)
    void FireTerminated()
        {FireEvent(eventidTerminated, EVENT_PARAM(VTS_NONE));}
    //}}AFX_EVENT
    DECLARE_EVENT_MAP()
```

`FireEvent()` kicks off the mechanism which reports the event back to the container. As the terminated event doesn't have any parameters, the second parameter to `FireEvent()` is set up to indicate the function needs no parameters. The `EVENT_PARAM()` macro accepts a list of macros to describe the parameters, working in exactly the same way as the `InvokeHelper()` member of `COleDispatchDriver`. You might want to refer to my review of that function back in Chapter 13 to refresh your memory on how macros are strings that the language concatenates together to describe the parameter list to the handling function.

Events with Parameters

If the event needs some parameters, the definition of the function would clearly have to reflect that; maybe you have a `NewData` event that tells the container the control has received some new data. Maybe the event notification takes the number of new characters received. So the container will know how many characters we've received, you can pass that along as a parameter to the event. The declaration would need to look something like this:

```
void FireNewData(int nCharacters)
    {FireEvent(eventidPoked, EVENT_PARAM(VTS_I2), nCharacters);}
```

You can fire the event just by calling the `FireNewData()` wrapper and passing the parameter for it. Call it whenever you need to; the framework will make sure the container finds out about the event as soon as possible.

The run-time supports a handful of stock events, which are described here:

Event	Firing Function	Purpose
Click	void FireClick()	Notifies the container that the user has clicked a mouse button on the control. Note that this message is fired when the button is released. Other mouse-related messages are fired before this one.
DblClick	void FireDblClick()	Notifies the container that the user has double-clicked a mouse button on the control.
Error	void FireError(SCODE scode, LPCSTR n, UINT nHelpID = 0)	Notifies the container that an error condition has arisen in the control. The SCODE is a COM status code and LPCSTR is a message to be associated with the error. The UINT parameter provides a help ID within the help file associated with the control's module. The container can use this number as a context ID to help the user.
KeyDown	void FireKeyDown(short nChar, short nShiftState)	Tells the container that the user has pressed a key. The first short indicates the key's code, while the second parameter indicates the keyboard's *Shift* state. Fired when WM_KEYDOWN is received by the control.
KeyPress	void FireKeyPress(short* pnChar)	Tells the container that a keystroke was received from the user. The parameter points to the key's code. This is fired when WM_CHAR is received by the control.
KeyUp	void FireKeyUp(short nChar, short nShiftState)	Lets the container know that a key was released. Like FireKeyDown(), this is fired with the key's code and the keyboard's *Shift* state. This is fired for WM_KEYUP.

Table Continued on Following Page

Event	Firing Function	Purpose
MouseDown	void FireMouseDown(short nButton, short nShiftState, float x, float y)	Tells the container that a mouse button has been pressed. The first parameter indicates which button was pressed, while the second indicates the keyboard's *Shift* state. The last two parameters provide the x and y coordinates of the incident, respectively. This is sent for the WM_*BUTTONDOWN messages.
MouseMove	void FireMouseMove(short nButton, short nShiftState, float x, float y)	Tells the container that the mouse is moving while a button is down. The first parameter identifies the button while the second parameter identifies the *Shift* state of the keyboard. The last two parameters provide the x and y coordinates of the incident, respectively. This is sent when the container receives a WM_MOUSEMOVE message.
MouseUp	void FireMouseUp(short nButton, short nShiftState, float x, float y)	Tells the container that the user has let go of the mouse button. The first parameter identifies the button while the second identifies the *Shift* state of the keyboard. The last two parameters provide the x and y coordinates of the incident, respectively. This is sent when the container receives a WM_*MOUSEUP message.

These events aren't fired unless you've declared them in your event map. If you have, they are sent automatically by the default implementation of the various message handlers in the COleControl class. If you implement a message handling function in your COleControl derived class, you should make sure you call the default implementation of the function if you expect the run-time to fire these messages for you.

Stock events can be added to your message map using the ClassWizard; just select the name of the stock event handler from the External name drop-down box in the Add Event window. Remember that adding or removing events means you need to re-register your control so its container can find the appropriate information in the registry.

Activations

Normal controls have activation modes which are very simple – they may or may not be visible, they may or may not have focus, and they may or may not be enabled. ActiveX controls have similar features. Of course, if your control is not visible due to clipping, or because some other window is on top of it, it won't need to paint. But an ActiveX control container can also request that a control go **UI dead**, which indicates the control shouldn't react to its user interface. We mentioned the AmbientUIDead() ambient property earlier in the chapter.

The UI dead state of your control is very similar to disabling the control. If your control is UI dead, it certainly shouldn't respond to mouse clicks or keystroke events, but you may also choose to paint your control in such a way that implies it isn't active.

If you chose the Activate When Visible box in the MFC ActiveX ControlWizard, your control will automatically enter an active state whenever it is visible. When your control is active, it could be either UI dead or not. When your control isn't active, it is absolutely disabled and not visible; it doesn't have a created window.

The `COleControl` class derives from `CWnd`. If your control is active, it has a window that you can use to express the control's user interface. The window might receive messages and you may wish to respond to them. You can handle that just like you might with any other window in MFC; just add an entry to your message map and hook up the appropriate function.

If your control is **inactive**, you won't have an active window. Instead, your control's `OnDraw()` function will be called when the container wants to retrieve the image of your control. `OnDraw()` renders your control's image to a metafile when your control is inactive. The same restrictions outlined in Chapter 14 for drawing in-place documents apply here – you need to be careful about which GDI functions you use.

Advanced Controls Issues

Believe it or not, we've already described just about everything that's essential for you to know when you are writing a control, so let's cruise through some more advanced issues in the rest of the chapter.

Three important issues remain:

> ➤ How to deal with writing subclassed controls
> ➤ How to protect your intellectual investment in your control code
> ➤ Versioning of the persistent property data which your control stores

You probably won't care about these things while you're still cutting your teeth on ActiveX controls, but once you get a few control projects running, you'll be glad you read about them here.

Writing Subclassed Controls

As we mentioned before, you can use the MFC ActiveX ControlWizard to create a project, which contains an ActiveX control that subclasses a Windows control. This might sound like a solution to all of life's little problems, but it isn't.

While it's a good way to get a control that behaves like some common Windows control, it's not as complete a solution as it first appears. The problem is that ActiveX controls commonly need to render themselves into device contexts which aren't really associated with devices; they're actually metafiles. Back in Chapter 14, we mentioned that many Windows device context functions are not designed to work in metafiles.

The metafile incompatibility of those drawing functions is very germane to the idea of using Windows controls as a basis for your ActiveX controls. Since the subclassed control will eventually receive a message to paint, the code produced by the MFC ActiveX ControlWizard will eventually send that message off to the control's base implementation within Windows. Unfortunately, the Windows code isn't designed to handle painting a control's image into a metafile and, as a result, any metafile-based rendering of your control is destined to cause problems.

There are a couple of interesting tricks to help with printing and rendering stock Windows controls, such as using the WM_PRINT message. WM_PRINT asks a control to render itself into an arbitrary DC – exactly what we would need a Windows control to do when implementing a subclassed ActiveX control. The problem is, though, that information from the device context in use still isn't available if that device context happens to describe a metafile. So, while WM_PRINT will work for printing and for some simpler controls, you'll find that it still isn't quite the solution required to get subclassed ActiveX controls properly painted in all circumstances.

In fact, your only real recourse is to do the drawing for the control yourself. For simple controls, like buttons, this really isn't hard at all, but for more complicated or elaborate controls, like list boxes or combo boxes, it's quite a serious undertaking. All this makes using a Windows control as a basis for your ActiveX control a lot less than it would at first seem.

You should carefully consider what the user will gain from your ActiveX-based control before you decide upon subclassing a Windows control. Writing the rendering code yourself can be quite tedious, adding weeks to an otherwise on-target project.

By the way, the metafile device context-related painting problem won't be evident in some containers. If the container asks the control to be active and draw itself, the control will appear to work. But if the container ever uses a metafile rendering of the control, the control will provide a bogus metafile and the container will blindly draw it, leaving the user with a gaping cavity in their application's user interface.

Handling Licensing in Your Control

The notion of ActiveX controls raises some very interesting marketing issues, particularly when used as a method for performing component-based development. The most fundamental question for any professional software developer is this:

Who can reuse a custom control, and when?

Your answer to this will probably come from some legal-minded employee at your company; it's impossible for us to guess exactly what your company will want to do with your code. We aren't purporting to give legal advice in this chapter; we just want to cover the technical, coding side of the issue so that you can understand exactly what options you have when you do get stuck in a room with the lawyers and they begin needling you for answers.

A Problem of Component Software

The benefit of component software is that you can reuse components you write. The problem with component software is someone else can reuse components that you write. Of course, this can also be a benefit if you are being rewarded for your work, but if you install an application that uses a very well-engineered control, what's stopping someone else from stealing your work by sucking the control into their program? This is the problem which licensing is charged with solving.

The licensing mechanisms supported by MFC allow you to check your control's license file is available before an instance of your control is created. Most controls that need to implement licensing will look for a file containing some string data to ensure that the control can be created correctly. You are certainly free to implement this in a different fashion, though. The MFC routines return Boolean values, so whatever implementation you choose will work fine, so long as you return the proper value.

Class Factories

As we saw in an earlier chapter, every COM object has a class factory. The class factory is the part of an object that manages the creation of the object; it creates the object when COM asks for it. The class factory is a part of your code – if you want to just create a new instance of your object and hand it off to COM without asking, you can, but if you want to implement a check to see if the user is allowed to create the control, you're allowed to do that too, which is where licensing comes in.

When an ActiveX control is created, the container has asked COM to create an instance of a certain class. COM deals with the request by calling the control's class factory to create the object. Normally, this is done using MFC's standard class factory implementation, buried well within the MFC libraries. However, if you enable licensing in your control's project, the COleObjectFactory class, which implements the class factory for ActiveX controls, works just a little differently.

> You may see the COleObjectFactoryEx class, rather than the COleObjectFactory. This is just a #define to ensure compatibility with the old Control Developers Kit.

GetLicenseKey()

Your control can implement a GetLicenseKey() function as an override for the class factory that manages access to the control, which returns a copy of the control's licensing information. The container can retain this information so that when it is run, the generated key can be compared to the retained key. If the two don't match, the control instance won't be created.

GetLicenseKey() returns a BOOL to indicate its success. Its first parameter is a DWORD which must be zero, since it is reserved for future use. The second parameter is a pointer to a BSTR. The BSTR will hold the new license key. In this chapter, we've not dealt with BSTRs directly because they simply manage a block of binary data – and are usually used to store strings. MFC can convert freely from a BSTR to a CString and back, so all of our OLE code examples to date used CStrings. You'll need to use a BSTR for license information, though, because the data might be a block of binary data – that is, it might not be a null-terminated string.

A BSTR points to the data it carries – you can cast BSTR to a LPCTSTR with no trouble. You can't, though, assume the data is null-terminated. Instead, you'll need to call SysStringByteLen() to find the length of the data in bytes. You could compare two BSTRs (one called bstrLeft and one called bstrRight) for equality using code like this:

```
int nLenLeft = SysStringByteLen(bstrLeft);
int nLenRight = SysStringByteLen(bstrRight);

if (nLenLeft != nLeftRight)
    // not equal — not the same length!
else if (memcmp(bstrLeft, bstrRight, nLenLeft) == 0)
    // they're equal!
```

You can see very similar code in the implementation of COleObjectFactory::VerifyLicenseKey() in the Olefact.cpp in the Microsoft Visual Studio\vc98\Mfc\Src directory.

You'll generally want to compare the license information returned by GetLicenseKey() with the license information embedded in the control's data. MFC does this for you whenever it creates a control for containment – either in a dialog box or using the CWnd::CreateControl() function, which we'll examine in the next chapter.

At design time, things are a little different. The container will ask the control to verify its license by calling VerifyUserLicense(), another override from the class factory. If the control doesn't implement the function, the default implementation will always return TRUE, effectively short-circuiting the licensing check.

VerifyLicenseKey() is called to verify that the key embedded in the container and the control's key are identical. This allows you to ensure that the control can be used by the container.

In design mode, the creation of the control is gated by the VerifyUserLicense() function. The implementation of this function, as produced by the MFC ActiveX ControlWizard, looks like this:

```
BOOL CDegreesCtrl::CDegreesCtrlFactory::VerifyUserLicense()
{
    return AfxVerifyLicFile(AfxGetInstanceHandle(),
            _szLicFileName, _szLicString);
}
```

AfxVerifyLicFile() is a helper function implemented by MFC to help test the validity of the license file. _szLicFileName and _szLicString are initialized strings which name the license file and its content. AfxVerifyLicFile() opens the license file in the same directory as the running module. If the first line of the file exactly matches the string in _szLicString, the AfxVerifyLicFile() function will return TRUE, allowing the creation to continue.

While these functions are implemented to read files and compare strings originally contained in those files, you can implement them in absolutely any way you like, as I mentioned a few pages back. You might run off and grab a code from your dongle or you might hit the network to make sure some validation server says it's okay to keep going, or you can hide something in the Registry. Just remember that whatever you do will be perceived as a delay in your application; if the users have to wait around for you to get something done, they won't be too happy.

Control Versioning

Earlier, we breezed over an important function call in your control class's DoPropExchange() function. This function is called whenever you want to initialize, load or store the persistent properties in your controls. One problem with any persistent data structure is that the serialized data might be out of sync with the code that reads it. If a user embeds your control in a document, saves it, updates your control code and then re-opens the document, you'll need to make sure your serialization code can handle the differences.

To help with this problem, the run-time offers the function which we skipped in our previous examination of the DoPropExchange() function. The call was to ExchangeVersion() and it looked like this:

```
ExchangeVersion(pPX, MAKELONG(_wVerMinor, _wVerMajor));
```

ExchangeVersion(), as you might have guessed, reads and writes versioning information from the property exchange context. The _wVerMinor and _wVerMajor are just short integers which are defined by the code produced by the ActiveX ControlWizard in your control's main implementation module. In Degrees.cpp, their definition looks like this:

```
const WORD _wVerMajor = 1;
const WORD _wVerMinor = 0;
```

ExchangeVersion() only writes the versions from these variables; that's why you can get away with defining them as const. ExchangeVersion() does read the versioning information from the file, but it maintains them within the CPropExchange object governing the exchange. You can later check the version returned by calling the GetVersion() member of that CPropExchange object. GetVersion() will return a DWORD which you can compare to constant version numbers.

Improving Degrees

Suppose we decided to improve the Degrees control by adding FreezingPoint and BoilingPoint properties to it. To make the control compatible with older data sets, we could add conditional code to intercept those cases. One solution would look like this:

```
if (pPX->GetVersion() >= MAKELONG(1, 1))
{
    PX_Short(pPX, "FreezingPoint", m_freezingPoint);
    PX_Short(pPX, "BoilingPoint", m_boilingPoint);
}
else if (pPX->IsLoading())
{   // reasonable defaults
    m_freezingPoint = 32;
    m_boilingPoint = 212;
}
// :
// : do the other properties regardless of version
```

If the program detects a new enough version number, it will try to read the FreezingPoint and BoilingPoint properties. If it doesn't, it will know the properties aren't in the persistent data stream. If the CPropExchange object says it is loading, you're still obligated to initialize the property values that aren't read. To get around this demand, just stuff reasonable values in them as we did in the code fragment above. It would also be acceptable to set some member data flag in the control's class and test the value later. Maybe it's completely impossible to think up reasonable values, and instead you'd like to have your control disable some of its features. Just watch that flag during the rest of your control's responses and you'll be just fine.

If you want to make sure your control is compatible with older versions, *never, under any circumstances*, remove a property in a newer version. If you find yourself in such a situation, you'll have to keep code to read the property and then do something reasonable with its value.

More on ExchangeVersion()

By the way, ExchangeVersion() takes an optional third BOOL parameter, which is TRUE, by default. As such, it will cause GetVersion() to return the new version numbers passed to ExchangeVersion() while writing. If the parameter passed is FALSE, GetVersion() returns the actual number read from the file. Passing FALSE means your code won't automatically convert from the older property streams to the newest version supported by the control. Since, while writing, GetVersion() will return the old version, the PX_ calls won't be made for the new properties in the given version.

The State of the Module Address

Earlier, we mentioned that ActiveX controls are implemented in modules which are a lot like _AFXDLLs, but not completely identical. The difference lies in the way MFC manages application state information for each of the architectures.

When MFC runs in a shared DLL, it needs to know which application is calling it. There are many pretty obvious reasons for this – for example, MFC needs to know the name of the application if it wants to post a message box for an error. If you stop to think about them, there are some state information items that are important – flags that indicate the activation status of the program or the help mode that the program might be using, for example.

If you make a call to MFC, that state information must be correct. It's automatically maintained in a plain old _AFXDLL by module state information associated with the thread handle, as well as in data that's instantiated by the DLL as it loads into each process. The MFC application can initialize that data for the DLL; since it was compiled with the _AFXDLL flag, it makes the appropriate initialization call.

However, controls don't have that luxury. They can't be real _AFXDLLs because they don't know if they're being called from a program that was written with MFC. There's no way for the control to make the correct initialization calls and make sure it has the right context information set up for MFC.

The way to get around this problem is pretty elaborate, if you look at its implementation deep within MFC. It only surfaces in a tiny macro which you'll need to use in some of your functions called AFX_MANAGE_STATE(). You'll find invocations of this macro in the sample controls and in any control produced by the MFC ActiveX ControlWizard. Here's an example:

```
STDAPI DllRegisterServer(void)
{
    AFX_MANAGE_STATE(_afxModuleAddrThis);
    // :
    // : rest of the code...
```

The ActiveX control header (namely, Afxctl.h) is endowed with a special macro called
_afxModuleAddrThis. This macro resolves to a function call which retrieves the state information
for your control stored by the MFC internal variable called afxModuleState and whose parent
class AFX_MODULE_STATE() is really interesting to study in Afxstat_.h. You could find how
MFC knows it is in a DLL or an EXE, or that MFC hides some memory allocation from you using the
CNoTrackObject internal class. The two macros work together to make sure the MFC DLL is
notified that your module is indeed the running code, and that any status information MFC needs to
change or retrieve remains associated with your module.

You'll need to put an AFX_MANAGE_STATE() macro invocation, just like the one above, in front of
any interface that your program exposes to the world. Code in the control run-time, which
implements your control's window procedure and COM interfaces, already has the wrapper, but if
you implement any message handling functions or OLE interfaces by yourself, you should protect
them with an AFX_MANAGE_STATE() macro.

My advice about the use of AFX_MANAGE_STATE() applies to additional Automation methods which
your control might expose directly, but doesn't apply to control methods which you've exposed using
ClassWizard. That is to say, if you implement an event or method for your ActiveX control and let
MFC call it, you've already been protected by the dispatching code in MFC. If you make your own
custom interfaces and those interfaces have methods, you'll need to worry about providing the
AFX_MANAGE_STATE() protection yourself.

If you've exposed an entry point in your control which you should have protected but didn't, you'll
notice a variety of problems. Most commonly, you'll cause assertions in MFC because of the incorrect
run-time type information lists. Your code might not be able to find its resources, and you might have
trouble getting any of MFC's window management functionality to work correctly.

Contracts and Obligations

If you've ever taken a course or read some books about object-oriented design, you've probably
heard about the notion of one class having a **contract** with another. This isn't to say that one class of
objects fancies itself the *capo di tutti cappi* of classes and wants to see the other classes rubbed out. It
means that in the design of a system the second class is expected to provide certain functionality or
features to the first. (Unless, of course, the second class implements the IMakeOfferUCantRefuse
interface.)

Since there are so many classes working together to provide functionality in an MFC application, and
particularly in an MFC application that supports COM, the behavior of the system as a whole is very
dependent on the contracts implemented between different objects.

These interdependencies are perhaps no more evident than in an ActiveX control. We've described a couple of tricks here, such as not offering property pages, which might fall short of the expectations of some containers. Containers of COM objects, whether they are controls or not, expect the object to provide certain levels of functionality, or in other words, that the objects will hold up their end of the contract.

If your control does do something the container doesn't expect, or indeed doesn't do something it does expect, you'll find the behavior of the system as a whole is not very predictable. The container is well within its rights to completely shut down or to display a list of error messages. Some containers might work differently to others in these borderline situations. If you need to embrace some marginal design by implementing your control or your COM object in a manner not quite in line with Hoyle, you should carefully test your solution to see how the various components react. Breaking these agreements is tantamount to using undocumented function calls – sometimes the technique is very useful and saves a lot of time, but in the long run you're just forcing a compatibility issue.

Note that some of the control attributes are not guaranteed to be implemented by all ActiveX control containers. This is particularly true of ambient properties, but is certainly true of some of the special flags, such as run-time mode and the semantics of <u>A</u>ctivates when visible.

The bottom line is that you should be careful about what you assume; make sure you know what contracts are supported by the object you're implementing, and make sure you know what will happen if you don't hold up your end of the bargain.

Caveat Creator

However, this advice about contracts also applies in the other direction as well. Some things which are implemented by ActiveX controls or ActiveX control containers are an absolute must if you wish to use them. One example is the way that ActiveX controls expect to start up; if an ActiveX control is created as a stand-alone Automation server, it will never fully initialize. Some controls will expect to do some initialization when they're created, but they'll also expect to do some initialization in response to the control being inserted into its container.

You don't know how a given control will be implemented unless you've found documentation which describes how the control will work. Therefore, you'll have to assume, somewhat defensively, that controls won't work unless they're embedded somewhere.

Where Should I Put this Control?

Unfortunately, versions of MFC before 4.0 didn't support containing ActiveX controls. But now MFC 6.0 is here, you can. ActiveX control containment will be investigated in the next chapter.

If you read through the ActiveX control references and are an advanced student of COM, you'll find you can write an ActiveX control container even without using MFC, but drawing ActiveX controls in dialog boxes and managing them is a non-trivial process.

Since ActiveX controls are just regular COM objects, it will seem as though you can just toss an ActiveX control into an OLE-aware program like Word for Windows and have it work. Actually inserting, saving and reloading the control should work just fine. But the problem is that your control can't fire events back to the application, since these Windows programs don't understand the interfaces that ActiveX controls use for such things.

Ever since Access 2.0 and Visual Basic Version 4.0, support for ActiveX control containment has been spreading to more and more products from many vendors. PowerBuilder from PowerSoft, Delphi from Borland, and Internet Explorer from Microsoft are just three of the many products that support ActiveX controls.

In the meantime, if you bump into me at the hotel bar during a conference, just ask – I'll be happy to tell you where to stick your control.

Testing your Controls

Microsoft Visual Studio has an ActiveX Control Test Container item in its Tools menu, which will start up a container that allows you to create any number of controls and fiddle with their properties and interfaces. You can also use some options in Test Container to make sure you're informed of notifications the controls send.

The test container is a great way to make sure your control is working, but it isn't very good for much more than smoke testing; it provides something of an ideal environment – it is very controllable, and also implements all of the standard ambient properties. If you're going to use your control in the real world, you should test it in the real world. Test your control to make sure it works in the container where you're likely to use it and in as many other containers as you can lay your hands on. If you're going to use your control in Visual Basic, you had better test it there to make sure it can deal with the ambients and interfaces that Visual Basic does and does not implement.

Summary

While ActiveX control technology is one of the younger children of the COM technologies, it's growing more and more versatile every day. Many development products and tools embrace the ActiveX control standard, and the near future will see Microsoft enhancing the ActiveX control specification to be both more robust and to provide better support for the use of controls in distributed containers.

In the next chapter, we'll look at putting ActiveX controls to work as we consider the creation of ActiveX control containers.

16

ActiveX Control Containers

There's absolutely no doubt in my mind that code to help with the containment of ActiveX controls (previously known as OLE controls or OCXs) was the most eagerly awaited feature of MFC 4. This feature is robust and complex; its implementation directly changed many parts of MFC. The containment also had effects that reached into the heart of Microsoft Developer Studio – changing the dialog editor and ClassWizard and influencing many features of the Components and Controls Gallery.

When we introduced MFC in the earlier chapters of the book, we examined the way an out-of-the-box AppWizard-generated program worked and discussed how we'd add features or change different aspects of the program. Since control containment is a very involved issue, we'll use a similar method in this chapter. We'll look at the code generated by the IDE when you add an ActiveX control to your project before delving into the real, technical issues of control containment. To that end, we'll do the following things in this chapter:

> Use the Components and Controls Gallery to add an ActiveX control to a project

> Examine the code which the Components and Controls Gallery generated

> Discuss the underlying MFC code and mechanism that make the whole scene work

> Look at the dynamic creation of controls

By the end of this chapter, you should be able to confidently approach the design decision of using ActiveX controls within your own applications.

Taking Credit for the Work of Others

Above all else, ActiveX controls promote the reuse of code predominantly involved in the user interface of applications. If you've gone through the trouble of writing your own ActiveX controls, you're undoubtedly dying to get them working with the new containment features of MFC. I promise this chapter will give you enough information to get off the ground with your own controls.

To get us started with our discussion, let's take an interesting control and add it to a standard Visual C++ project. You'll need to use AppWizard to create an MFC application. In the first step, ask for a dialog-based application so the code generated by the wizard will be minimal; this will also make it easier to understand what's going on in your application. In the second step, make sure you check the ActiveX Controls box to enable ActiveX control containment in your application. This checkbox doesn't add much code (we'll cover what it does, exactly, in a section named *Rules for Using Controls* later in the chapter), but it does tell MFC that you're interested in managing ActiveX controls in your application.

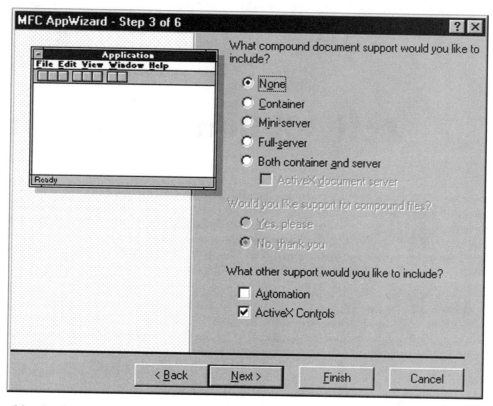

You should only check this box if you're really going to use ActiveX control containment; the corresponding code in MFC can slow down your application needlessly if you're not planning to use controls. The effect you'll notice is mainly that your program starts to take up more memory than you had wanted it to.

The rest of the settings in the wizard aren't pertinent to ActiveX controls — you can use whatever settings match your application most closely. If you choose to generate an SDI or MDI application, you'll find the same ActiveX Controls checkbox, which you can use to enable control containment.

Control Proxy Classes

When you compile and build this application, you won't notice anything special. To make use of MFC's ActiveX Control containment, you'll need to perform one more step. You'll need to use the Components and Controls Gallery to generate a proxy class for your control. It's very easy — just open your project and use the Components and Controls... command in the Add to Project tear-off in the Project menu. This will bring up the main Components and Controls Gallery window, shown next:

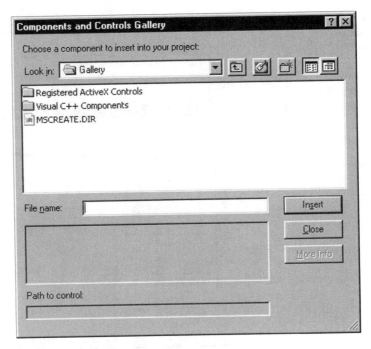

In this window, you can select the Registered ActiveX Controls folder, and then choose any ActiveX control (or any other component) you'd like to add to your project. Select the control and click on the Insert button. You'll be told the Components and Controls Gallery is going to create a proxy class in your project. The proxy class is a new class, generated by Components Gallery, based on information embedded in the ActiveX control and added to your project. The class wraps your program's access to the control, much like the COleDispatchDriver class we examined in Chapter 13 can wrap access to an automation server.

When you use the Components and Controls Gallery to hook up the control to your project, Visual C++ makes some notes about that fact in your project file. The information which links your project to the control is terribly important – it allows the wizards to know that your control exists, how to find it and what it means. If that link is damaged, you'll need to recreate your project file and reinsert the control in your project before any of the wizards will work again. As I mentioned, the wizards themselves make use of lots of information about the control too. You won't be able to do much work with the wizards and your control if you haven't used the Components and Controls Gallery to add the control to the project.

For the sake of our discussion, add the grid control to your project. Grid controls implement popular, nifty user interfaces – they look like spreadsheets, allowing your application to display tabular data. The user can often edit the data in-place and use the borders of the control to change the way the data is sized, ordered or organized. Depending on which version of the Visual C++ product you've installed, you might want to insert the DB Grid control or the FlexGrid control, both of which provide slightly different user interfaces or programmatic interfaces than the plain Grid control does. Happily, both controls are similar enough to the normal Grid control for the purposes of this discussion.

To get the grid control into your project, you can select the control and press the Insert button. Your request will result in a confirmation dialog box for the proxy classes to be generated by Components and Controls Gallery, as shown in this shot:

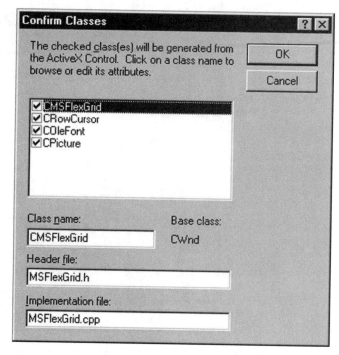

You'll see that the confirmation dialog for the Grid control is actually offering to generate four classes: CPicture, COleFont, CRowCursor and CMSFlexGrid.

CMSFlexGrid is the most interesting of the four – for now, anyway. It's the class that allows your containing application access to all of the events, methods and properties of the grid control. Components Gallery knows which functions to generate because it reads the information stored in the control's type library.

Conceptually, it's important to know the difference between events, methods and properties, even when you're writing a container and not writing a control. Methods and properties can be simply thought of as functions in the control which are called by the control's container. Events that the control fires can be thought of as functions in the container that are called by the control. With this abstraction in mind, you'll realize that all the Components and Controls Gallery does for information in the type library is to generate some simple functions to wrap each of the methods and properties. The exercise of reading an object's type library and building a wrapper class for the object is terribly similar to what ClassWizard does when you create a new class based on a type library for a normal automation server. If you're interested in more details about the differences between methods, properties and events, please check out the appropriate sections in Chapter 13. We'll describe these attributes in this chapter from the point of view of a control user rather than a control author.

For non-visual ActiveX controls (or, generically, any other Automation server), you could use the #import preprocessor directive to add the control to your project, allowing you the benefit of using smart pointers. You wouldn't really use #import with visual controls as this makes it harder to place the control in your dialogs or create them as the child of another window.

The type library contains information about each function the control implements for its properties, methods and events. The descriptive information in the type library contains the name of the function and describes the types of the parameters the function manages, as well as the return type for the function. The type library can even contain help strings for each of the functions, although Visual C++ doesn't provide an easy way of getting at that information. For a simple function, this isn't really an issue. If you have a look at the class generated for the grid control, you'll see a member of the `CMSFlexGrid` class that looks like this:

```
void CMSFlexGrid::SetText(LPCTSTR lpszNewValue)
{
    static BYTE parms[] = VTS_BSTR;
    InvokeHelper(0x0, DISPATCH_PROPERTYPUT, VT_EMPTY,
        NULL, parms, lpszNewValue);
}
```

You don't have to be Nostradamus to predict that this function is used to set some text in the control. You can't, however, be sure *what* text is being set – is it the text in the caption of the control, or in a particular cell, or somewhere else? If the function became only a little more complicated, you'd have a hard time guessing what the different parameters meant and how they were to be used, so you won't get very far without the documentation for your control. You can quickly get to the help file for a control through the <u>M</u>ore Info button on the Components and Controls Gallery dialog.

Now, the functions that make up a control's properties and methods aren't really the functions we're used to thinking of – they're actually methods in a dispatch interface. As such, calling the function isn't quite as simple as just running off and calling a function with some parameters tossed on the stack. We have to let COM do the work of providing access to and from the control's interface. Such a COM concept is familiar to the COM masters of the world; getting pointers to the functions and setting up their parameters is a trivial matter for such illuminati – particularly guys like John Elsbree. As the author of the original MFC ActiveX control classes, he's the *capo di tutti cappi* of such knowledge, but for average people like you and me, it's pretty hard.

The proxy class brought to you by the Components and Controls Gallery is just a class that sits between your application code and the code in the control and hides the details of those COM calls. The class helps you set up calls to the COM methods implemented by the control, which actually house the code that tweaks the control's properties or initiates its methods. The proxy class is set up in such a way that you can readily understand what's going on. It uses the same paradigm that Windows controls use while being poked and prodded from an MFC application – it's just a bunch of C++ functions attached to an instance of the control's class.

Let's pick apart the member functions of the proxy class in a little more detail.

Property Members

For properties, the proxy class will have two functions if the property can be read and written: one function will get the property, and the other will set it. If the property is read-only, the proxy class will have only a get function, or if it is write-only, the proxy class will have only a set function. A typical pair of get and set functions might look like this:

```
CString CMSFlexGrid::GetText()
{
    CString result;
    InvokeHelper(0x0, DISPATCH_PROPERTYGET, VT_BSTR,
        (void*)&result, NULL);
```

Continued on Following Page

```
    return result;
}

void CMSFlexGrid::SetText(LPCTSTR lpszNewValue)
{
    static BYTE parms[] = VTS_BSTR;
    InvokeHelper(0x0, DISPATCH_PROPERTYPUT, VT_EMPTY,
        NULL, parms, lpszNewValue);
}
```

These functions are pretty simple; they're just calls to helper functions in MFC which work with COM to ask the control to run one of its methods. The InvokeHelper() function's first parameter is an integer that identifies the DISPID of the property we're setting. The DISPID is an integer that COM uses to know which method in the function's dispatch interface to invoke — DISPID just stands for dispatch ID. The third parameter indicates the VARIANT type for the data which is being returned from the control. The GetText() function calls a get property method which returns a string, for example, while the SetText() function calls a function which offers no return value. The fourth parameter is a pointer to that return value — since SetText() doesn't have a return value, it passes NULL.

The function's fifth parameter points to an array of BYTEs that describe the parameter types the method accepts, in order. If the fifth parameter is NULL, the method takes no parameters. The remainder of the parameters are variable; they match each of the items in the array, and specify the actual values passed to the method for the given DISPID.

The members we examined above are actually for properties. But, as we learned back in Chapter 13, Automation objects (which include ActiveX Controls) actually implement properties via methods: one to set and one to retrieve the value of the property in question. If we had a method to call, we'd see that InvokeHelper() was used in exactly the same way — but we'd probably notice there were many more diverse parameters.

The InvokeHelper() function we use here is a member of CWnd. It's associated with the IDispatch interface. We used the InvokeHelper() member of COleDispatchDriver in Chapter 13 to use Automation interfaces in Excel from our MFC application.

Variant Parameters

From the documentation of the control, you should be able to figure out what each of the functions in the proxy class do for each of the properties in the ActiveX control. The proxy member names will have the same names as methods and properties in the documentation of the control. While you might expect there to be a perfect one-to-one correspondence between the parameters for events and their functions, or between the types of properties and their functions, this doesn't have to be the case.

If a property or parameter to a method is capable of accepting many different data types, the control's interface will probably be implemented with the VARIANT data type. You'll remember our discussion of this type from Chapter 13; VARIANTs are used frequently in COM to get data from one place to another in a way which is safe across different platforms, contexts and implementation languages.

They're also handy when you are writing code that might take different data types. COM doesn't support overloading of functions expressed in its automation interfaces. Instead of providing several different functions with different parameter types and then implementing some mechanism to discern between calls based on the parameter types, COM requires that only one function be implemented for each function name.

Many developers get around the lack of overrides in COM by using VARIANTs, though. If their function is capable of handling short integers, long integers and floating point types, for example, they'll just code it to accept a VARIANT. When the function is called, they'll examine the VARIANT to determine its data type and react accordingly. When ClassWizard develops the proxy class for such a control, it can't make any assumptions and generates a class that accepts a VARIANT parameter, too. Obviously, when you call the proxy calls, you'll have to pass a VARIANT, too!

The problem is that VARIANTs are pretty ugly. If you want to pass a six, you can't pass a six – you have to create a VARIANT, set it to hold a short integer, and then toss a six into it. That's slow and tedious. Unfortunately, it's largely unavoidable because ClassWizard just doesn't have enough information to make a more appropriate user interface. ActiveX controls are meant to be used in, or at the very least be compatible with, a scripting environment; therefore, the controls adhere to the limitations of the scripting interface, which is IDispatch and VARIANT data.

Fortunately, MFC can once again give some grace to the ugliness of Windows' implementation. You can create a COleVariant object and pass that instead. It's pretty simple. For example, if you want to call the grid control's AddItem() function (which accepts a VARIANT as its second parameter), you can just code:

```
AddItem("A new item for row two", COleVariant(static_cast<short>(2)));
```

Here, I have to explicitly cast the constant to a short integer. If I didn't, the COleVariant constructor wouldn't know exactly what kind of VARIANT to make, or more precisely, C++ doesn't know which overloaded constructor to use. 2 alone, of course, could be a short or a long. Since COleVariant has constructors to accept both, the call would be ambiguous. Some other data types handled by COleVariant don't have a chance of ambiguity, so you won't usually need to cast them.

Creating and passing a temporary object, as above, is just fine. C++ guarantees that the temporary object will last until the function returns, and that's plenty long enough for it to work in our application.

Since there's no way for the Components and Controls Gallery to know which C++ language data types are appropriate for a given VARIANT parameter to a function, it will only create a single function for you. However, you could, if you wanted to, add your own overloads as you need them. All you'd need to do is to fold up the appropriate type in a COleVariant on your way to the real function. So, I might take this code, supplied by the Components and Controls Gallery as part of the grid control's proxy class:

```
void CMSFlexGrid::AddItem(LPCTSTR Item, const VARIANT& Index)
{
    static BYTE parms[] =
        VTS_BSTR VTS_VARIANT;
    InvokeHelper(0x1d, DISPATCH_METHOD, VT_EMPTY, NULL, parms,
        Item, &Index);
}
```

and make my own overload, like this:

```
void CMSFlexGrid::AddItem(LPCTSTR Item, const int nIndex)
{
    static BYTE parms[] =
        VTS_BSTR VTS_VARIANT;
    InvokeHelper(0x1d, DISPATCH_METHOD, VT_EMPTY, NULL, parms,
        Item, COleVariant(nIndex));
}
```

Functionally, these functions are no different, but the second version is a bit more convenient than the first. As I mentioned earlier, you're more than welcome to add your own overloads and member functions to the proxy class, but remember that your changes will be overwritten should you decide to use the Components and Controls Gallery to refresh the proxy class (which you might want to do if the ActiveX control changes, for example).

If you do take the approach of writing your own overloads, you'll probably want to do your best to stay out of the way of the Gallery. Since ActiveX Controls are sometimes updated, you might find yourself in the position of regenerating the proxy class. If you change the Gallery-produced proxy class directly, like I did above, you'll be in trouble, since the Gallery will want to overwrite your changes. If, instead, you derive a second class and write the overloads in that class, then you'll be out of harm's way. Alternatively, you can create a second source file that implements more control class methods. Or, you can make a second `*.cpp` file that contains the extra implementations you want. Then, you'll just need to manage the fixes for the `*.h` files.

Setting the Machinery in Motion

We've seen how to use the Components and Controls Gallery to create a proxy class for an ActiveX control, but we haven't yet covered how an instance of the control is created, so we'll look into that now. MFC allows two ways to create ActiveX controls. One way is to create a control from a dialog template generated by the Microsoft Visual Studio dialog editor. The other is to dynamically create an instance of the control while your application runs. Of course, the actual mechanisms are a little more complicated than these two sentences imply, but that's what some of the sections in the rest of this chapter are about.

These two creation mechanisms, by the way, directly mirror the two ways you'd normally create a regular control. You can create a CButton, for example, by dynamically creating the C++ object and then creating the underlying window. Or, you could draw a button control on a dialog template and then ask MFC to create an instance of the template for you. Later, you can create a C++ CButton object from the control on the template.

It's important to understand that these two methods are *normally* applied to two very different kinds of applications. The first, dialog-based method represents the notion I like to call **static containment**. This method is appropriate if you just want to use a given control in a dialog and you always want to use that particular control in your application. In contrast, you could also choose to use **dynamic containment** for controls in your application. This approach *usually* means that you're going to let the user add controls to your application at run time. You won't know what controls are going to show up, so you can't make any assumptions about them in your application.

Of course, there's an exception that proves the rule. You can also create an OLE control dynamically and not place it on a dialog template, and still know a whole bunch about the control at compile time. Maybe you want to have a control inside of your view, but you don't want to use a CFormView-derived class. You can create an instance of the control's C++ wrapper class, then call the Create() member of the class to have the control created.

It's just that knowledge of the control at compile time is the only real difference between the two methods. And having that knowledge affects you, as a developer, more than it affects MFC. Whether you use static or dynamic containment, MFC is going to create the control and set up interfaces to the control as well as connect code to manage those interfaces.

If you draw the control on a dialog template, you can write code with knowledge of the control. You know that particular control will always be created on your dialog template, and you're sure it has certain methods and properties, and that it fires particular events in certain circumstances. If you know that a control with the ID IDC_STATES, for example, is a simple Windows list box, you would just write list box calls against it. You'd know that the control would have strings and you could access those with a particular message, and you would expect the control to send you a particular message when the user clicked on an item in the control.

Similarly, if you know that IDC_SALESSTAFF is an ActiveX grid control that contains information about members of your company's sales force, you can code grid control calls against it. You'll expect it to fire certain events when the user clicks on it or presses keys while the control has focus.

On the other hand, if you're doing dynamic containment and the user drops a control into a window, you won't be able to make very many assumptions about the control. Your code will need to dynamically find out what kind of control it is before it can do any work with it. We've certainly looked at lots of applications that use push buttons. We haven't looked at any applications that allow you, at run time, to decide if you want a push button or an edit control. Using static containment is very, very common. Dynamic containment is almost exclusively used in applications that allow some sort of software development, perhaps allowing the user to write macros or scripts to build simple applications or automate tedious tasks.

Both of these methods are appropriate for use at different times; you'll need to decide what to do, based on the requirements of your application. Either method can be used at any time, in conjunction with any other feature of your application. Most applications you'll write will use static containment; you'll probably just draw ActiveX controls on a dialog box template and then start writing code to interact with the control on the dialog just as you might use a regular Windows control. If you're writing a very programmable application, like your own communications package with an extensive macro language, or a program that automates software testing, you'll be quite interested in supporting dynamic containment. A developer writing a script within your application should be able to add ActiveX controls to it with ease.

Let's take a look at how MFC helps you when you want to use controls in either of these modes. In the meantime, don't try to find the terms *static containment* or *dynamic containment* in the Visual C++ documentation – I coined them myself.

Static Containment

Let's start with static containment first. Again, the idea here is to add a control to your project while building the project. If you've used the Components and Controls Gallery to add your control to your project, you'll see its icon in the dialog editor's **Controls** palette. The editor will allow you to place the control in a dialog template anywhere you'd like. If you bring up the properties for the control, you'll see the property sheets designed into the control.

The dialog editor lets you use the ActiveX control like you would any other control – just draw the control where you want it to be and set its initial properties. You can put more than one ActiveX control on a given dialog and you can use the dialog templates for normal dialogs, for dialog-based applications, or for CFormView-based objects. In the dialog editor, an ActiveX control will behave as if it is in design mode; it won't respond to any events you cause (like clicking on it), but you can bring up properties for the control and edit them to your heart's content.

When you or MFC instantiates the dialog, some extra code in MFC is invoked to create the ActiveX control. The most important part of that code is actually more closely associated with the dialog box – the code that sets up a spot for the control to get started with its layout and for it to communicate with the containing application.

Behind the scenes, though, the dialog editor is doing a lot of work to hold your application together. The dialog editor asks the control to serialize its persistent data after you've drawn the control in your dialog template. A binary image of that data is tucked into a special, user-defined resource type in your application's resource file. That resource has the same ID as your dialog box and the data in the resource identifies the control or controls in the dialog box directly. This peaceful, utopian control ID oneness is how MFC figures out that the control is an ActiveX control and that the control needs to be carefully created within the application. This mechanism lets more than one control be used in a dialog, and more than one dialog have controls.

When you save your dialog template in the dialog editor and the dialog contains an ActiveX control, a little extra work is done. Any normal controls, other resources and the dialog box itself will be there in the resource, but a bunch more data is required for MFC to instantiate the control. MFC obviously needs to know the control's CLSID to have OLE create it, for example. That information is tucked away right in the resource where the control is used.

If you pick apart the dialog resource in the application you've been using to follow along with our discussion, you might see some information like this in the **.rc** file:

```
IDD_DIALOG1 DIALOG DISCARDABLE  0, 0, 193, 92
STYLE DS_MODALFRAME | WS_POPUP | WS_CAPTION | WS_SYSMENU
CAPTION "Sample Dialog"
FONT 8, "MS Sans Serif"
BEGIN
    DEFPUSHBUTTON    "&Show Properties",ID_SHOW_PROPS,130,7,56,14
    PUSHBUTTON       "Cancel",IDCANCEL,130,24,56,14
    CONTROL          "",IDC_GRID1,"{A8C3B720-0B5A-101B-B22E-00AA0037B2FC}",
                     WS_TABSTOP,17,15,101,63
END
```

If you want to go digging in the .rc *file yourself, remember you'll need to set the* Open As: *drop-down in Microsoft Visual Studio's* Open *dialog box to* Text. *Otherwise, the Studio will get the file opened in the dialog editor and you won't be able to see the actual resource compiler script definition for yourself.*

You can see that the other controls in the box (the Show Properties push button, for example) use regular Windows resource script commands to state their type, title, ID, and location. The dialog editor has placed similar information about the ActiveX control there as well. Instead of specifying a valid Windows class name, the resource statement actually has the CLSID for the ActiveX control! The size and position values are used normally, as are the window flags.

On a Silver Template

When it comes time for MFC to create the dialog box or any other window that might contain a dialog box template, MFC finds this dialog resource and loads it into memory in its raw form. The framework then begins parsing the resource, reading through it to find any ActiveX controls. If it finds none, it lets Windows create the dialog box right out and that's the end. The CDialog or another CWnd-derived object gets initialized with the HWND of the created window and you're on your way.

However, in the far more entertaining world of dialogs decorated with ActiveX controls, MFC will begin parsing that resource to carefully ferret out any ActiveX controls. MFC will begin creating those controls and making them children of the dialog box, just like Windows would do internally with regular controls.

The process of creating an ActiveX control is quite a bit more complicated than creating a normal Windows control. MFC gets COM to create the object, which gets things rolling, but the control object also needs to be initialized with whatever persistent data it saved once it had been edited in the dialog editor. When the dialog editor saves an ActiveX control, it asks the control for a binary representation of its property data. The dialog editor adds the data provided by the control to the application's resource script in a custom resource called a DLGINIT. Here's what a typical one might look like:

```
IDD_DIALOG1 DLGINIT
BEGIN
    IDC_GRID1, 0x376, 163, 0
0x0024, 0x0000, 0x0041, 0x0036, 0x0044, 0x0041, 0x0038, 0x0035, 0x0038,
// :
// : lots more raw data deleted for brevity
// :
0x0002, 0x0002, 0x0001, 0x0001, 0x0003, 0x0101, 0x0000, 0x0100, 0x0000, "\377"
    0
END
```

Not too appetizing, huh? (It would be even worse if I didn't trim out some of the data; I'm not interested in filling these pages with gratuitous stacks of meaningless hexadecimal values. I just want to make my point. Plus, I'll have more room to talk about hockey if I don't.)

This resource type is defined and managed by the resource editor and MFC; it is *not* a normal Windows resource type. Windows treats it as a pile of binary data in the application; that's it. In fact, MFC itself doesn't do much more. The data is tagged so MFC knows the pile of binary data is associated with a particular ActiveX control, but MFC just loads the data from the resource and offers it to COM. COM, in turn, hands it to the control that knows how to manage it.

This pile of binary data is referred to by technicians as the **persistent property stream**. When you write an ActiveX control, exactly what ends up in the persistent property stream completely depends on what you've coded in your control's Serialize() function. If your control definitely needs to know something before it is created, it had better be a part of this stream.

Once the control initializes itself, that's it; MFC activates the control and you're done. If all the elements of the template are created successfully, the dialog will be created. There's nothing very magical about the dialog now that it is running. It has a HWND and is a real Windows dialog box. It just so happens to be very active with COM behind the scenes, but that's nothing which would preclude the use of any other functions that you're used to calling against a dialog box.

Breathing Life into the Proxy

So we've seen how MFC uses the resource information behind the scenes to create an ActiveX control, but how do you, as a programmer, connect a control from a dialog to the control's proxy class? After all, you'll need to instantiate the class and have it create a window if you want to get any work done!

The easiest way to get a proxy object associated with your control is to use dialog data exchange. If you've used ClassWizard to create a dialog class to be associated with your ActiveX control-bearing dialog template, you can use the Member Variables tab in ClassWizard to forge the connection.

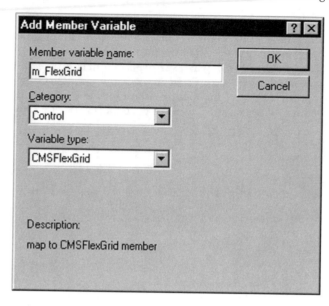

There, ClassWizard will add the appropriate DDX call to your dialog's DoDataExchange() function. Such an exchange is always done with a DDX_Control() invocation. So, for a simple dialog, you might see a DoDataExchange() implementation like this:

```
void COcxContDlg::DoDataExchange(CDataExchange* pDX)
{
    CDialog::DoDataExchange(pDX);
    //{{AFX_DATA_MAP(COcxContDlg)
    DDX_Control(pDX, IDC_GRID1, m_FlexGrid);
    //}}AFX_DATA_MAP
}
```

After DoDataExchange() has been called for the first time, you can assume that the m_FlexGrid variable has been initialized to refer to the IDC_GRID1 control. When MFC does a DDX_Control() call, it actually subclasses the control window so the control on the dialog is connected to the control object as a member of the dialog you're implementing.

This has two interesting effects. First, it makes the window class instance in your dialog permanently associated with the control window on the dialog box. Of course, the association is only as permanent as your dialog box – the subclassing is automatically disconnected when your dialog box dies. (We treated the use of control class members for subclassing in Chapter 7.)

The second interesting effect is that messages and other command routings, like events, are handled by code in the class that's used for the member. This means you can change any feature of that class to handle events fired by the control or to implement extra functionality to be associated with the control.

Remember that the framework doesn't call `DoDataExchange()` until *after* the default implementation of `OnInitDialog()` has run – so make sure your `OnInitDialog()` implementation calls the base class before it needs to use the control proxy.

Working with the Control

Once initialized, you can use the member class of your dialog to access features of the control. If your control has a text property, for example, the proxy class will have `SetText()` and `GetText()` functions. These functions do the COM work necessary to tell the control to change or retrieve the content of its text property.

You should feel free to review the header file that the Components and Controls Gallery produced so you understand the functions which were implemented for you. They should make sense. With all but a few exceptions, they should take convenient types and offer meaningful returns. If you're wrapping a control which you wrote, you should see a one-to-one correspondence between the properties and methods in your control and the functions in the proxy class.

If you need to change these functions, don't! As you develop your application, you might decide to upgrade the control by purchasing a new version from the vendor, or by improving the control's code and rebuilding the control. Any changes that the control vendors make to the parameters, types or properties in the event list, property list or methods of the control will make it desirable to have the Components and Controls Gallery refresh the proxy class. If you've sliced and diced the proxy class, your changes will be overwritten when the Gallery does its work. Since the Gallery is used to working with a whole class at a time, there's no way to hide your changes with special comments like you might with other wizards.

As we've said before, your only alternative for such a case is to create your own additional class, derived from the original control proxy class. Then, carefully use this class in situations where you might otherwise use the class provided by the Gallery. Unfortunately, this means that you'll need to write your own `DDX_Control()` statement outside of the ClassWizard comments in your `DoDataExchange()` function, but that's not hard at all.

You might, for example, use the Gallery to wrap up the grid control for your application. If you let the Gallery build a class named `CGridCtrl`, you might want to derive your own `CGridControl` class from `CGridCtrl`. In your application, you should use `CGridControl` instead of `CGridCtrl` because `CGridControl` insulates your application from any changes made to `CGridCtrl` by the Gallery when the interface supplied by the ActiveX control changes or in situations when you need to regenerate the control class.

Regardless of how you've hooked things up, once your proxy class is initialized, you'll need to learn how to actually *use* it. The class generated for you depends entirely upon the control you're using.

Event Notifications

When you compile and run your application, it might eventually create one of the dialogs involving the ActiveX control. The control, then, will be in run mode – the opposite of the design mode that had the control active in the dialog editor. In run mode, the control will react to events and fire them off to the container, but it won't allow the user to bring up its property pages.

When something amusing happens to your control, it will fire an event to let your container know. The grid control that we've been picking on fires twenty different events. Most of them indicate that the user did something to the control with the keyboard or mouse. If you're interested in reacting to the control as the user prods it, you can write handlers for these events. For example, if the user changes the selection, the control may fire RowColChange or SelChange events.

Events are very similar to the notification methods that normal controls send back to their owners. As an MFC programmer, as far as you're concerned handling an event from an OLE control is just the same as handling a notification from a regular control; set up a map entry, hook up a member function, and write some code. But an event from an OLE control isn't a message – it's sent back to its owner using **OLE connection points**. A connection point is something of a handshake between an automation object and its client that allows a notification to be sent from the server to the client in the form of a specialized IDispatch method invocation. MFC takes care of sinking those notifications, so it's really not necessary for you to make your hands dirty with the implementation if you're using MFC's containment code.

As such, you can wire up code to handle events, just like you might wire up code to handle messages. The easiest way, of course, is to use ClassWizard. If you've dropped the control in a dialog box, you can select the dialog's class in ClassWizard's **Class name:** drop-down and then select the control in the Object IDs: list. This all happens in ClassWizard's **Message Maps** tab – we've seen it several times before, but here it is again in case you're a little homesick:

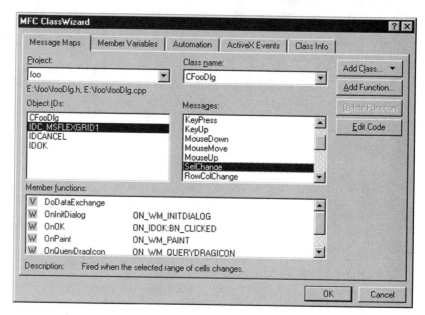

It's really that simple. Of course, you're probably interested in understanding a lot more than how to use ClassWizard, so let's have a look at exactly what mechanism is helping MFC dispatch events from controls back to your application.

Since I've let it slip already that the ActiveX control containment support is designed to fit MFC very closely, you might have guessed that events fired by ActiveX controls are handled by maps, just like the command messages sent by controls. If you've added a handler for the SelChange event to your dialog, you might end up with a map like this:

```
BEGIN_EVENTSINK_MAP(CFooDlg, CDialog)
    //{{AFX_EVENTSINK_MAP(CFooDlg)
    ON_EVENT(CFooDlg, IDC_GRID1, 2 /* SelChange */, OnSelChangeGrid1, VTS_NONE)
    //}}AFX_EVENTSINK_MAP
END_EVENTSINK_MAP()
```

The map is opened by a BEGIN_EVENTSINK_MAP() macro. That macro is analogous to the BEGIN_MESSAGE_MAP() macro – it even takes the same parameters. The first parameter to BEGIN_EVENTSINK_MAP() is the name of the class which contains the ActiveX control. In this example, the control lives in a class called CFooDlg, which is a CDialog derivative. We know it's a CDialog derivative, because it is supplied as the second parameter to the macro.

The body of the macro contains ON_EVENT() macros. One ON_EVENT() macro snags one event type for one control instance. In the above code fragment, the single map entry has CFooDlg as the first parameter. While this might seem redundant given the information already in the map's opening macro, it's necessary to make the macro work. The second parameter is the ID of the control that lives in the dialog template. The third parameter is the DISPID of the event that was fired. Again, this information is made available by the type library in the control's executable image. The fourth parameter to the macro indicates which CFooDlg member function will handle the notification.

The fifth parameter is a collection of VTS_ constants. As we learned back in Chapter 13, these can be strung together to describe the parameters used by the event to send information specific to the notification. In the above entry, VTS_NONE is supplied to indicate that there are no parameters. This means, directly, that the OnSelChangeGrid1 function won't take any parameters. Event handler functions never return a value – they're always of type void.

Of course, in a real application, you'll *always* have a more complicated EVENTSINK_MAP, because you'll be interested in lots of different events from your controls. There's only one event map for a particular parent window, but it contains information about all controls that might fire events in the parent window.

Using Normal CWnd Functions

The proxy class is a CWnd-derived class because it represents an object that has a window and we know its window handle. You can take some action on that window, such as calling MoveWindow() to move it or sending it messages with SendMessage(). However, many features of the window have a different semantic meaning when the window actually represents an ActiveX control.

When MFC creates an ActiveX control instance, it initializes a pointer to the control site. This pointer is NULL if the CWnd in question isn't an initialized ActiveX control. If the CWnd *does* represent an ActiveX control and the control has been created, the pointer, named m_pCtrlSite, points at a COleControlSite object.

Whenever you make a call to a CWnd member that would normally call a Windows API to directly manipulate the control, MFC first checks to see if m_pCtrlSite is NULL. If it is, MFC assumes the window is a regular Windows object and asks Windows to do the work. On the other hand, if m_pCtrlSite is actually a pointer to the site, MFC can use it to emulate the effect of the call with the proper ActiveX control call.

CWnd::SetWindowText(), for example, would normally just have MFC call the Windows ::SetWindowText() API. This call will work as normal for regular controls, but for ActiveX controls this will end up calling the SetWindowText() member of the COleControlSite object.

Unfortunately, COleControlSite is considered to be part of the MFC implementation and isn't documented. You can figure out how it works, though, by reading Occsite.cpp from your Microsoft Visual Studio\vc98\Mfc\Src directory. This file contains the code for all of the functions called from CWnd.

Here's a table of **CWnd** functions that will work correctly, even if the window in question is an ActiveX control.

Function	Effect / Notes
CheckDlgButton()	Sets or clears Value stock property.
CheckRadioButton()	Sets or clears Value stock property.
EnableWindow()	Enables or disables the control by querying and then setting its Enabled property.
GetDlgCtrlID()	Retrieves the m_nID member of the control site. This ID is held by MFC to provide the control with a child ID number. It is used in other calls involving IDs.
GetDlgItem()	Checks to see if the control ID is a real Windows control. If it isn't, it looks through the list of ActiveX controls on this window to find information about the identified control. The match is made against the m_nID in the control site. Used by all DlgItem-family functions.
GetDlgItemInt()	Calls GetDlgItem() to find the window. It then calls the control-safe implementation of GetWindowText() to retrieve a string which will be converted to an integer and returned.
GetDlgItemText()	Calls GetWindowText().
GetStyle()	Builds a style by checking to see if the control is enabled, visible and has a border. The control may implement its own style bits.
GetExStyle()	Builds an extended style word for the control by checking to see if the control has a client edge.
GetWindowText()	Retrieves the control's Caption property. If this fails, the function tries to retrieve the Text property from the control. This failure may cause a benign exception trace message in debug builds.
GetWindowTextLength()	Gets the text via a call to the control-safe implementation of GetWindowText() and returns its length.
IsDlgButtonChecked()	Calls the control-safe implementation of GetDlgItem() to find the control then gets the Value property of the control.
IsWindowEnabled()	Retrieves the control's DISPID_ENABLED property.
ModifyStyle()	Modifies styles after directly handling WS_BORDER and WS_DISABLED using stock Border and Enabled properties, respectively.
ModifyStyleEx()	Modifies style directly after directly handling WS_EX_CLIENTEDGE using stock Appearance property.

Function	Effect / Notes
MoveWindow()	Calls SetExtent() against the control's IOleObject interface, and SetObjectRects() on the control's IOleInPlaceObject interface to change the control's position.
SendDlgItemMessage()	Finds the window with a call to GetDlgItem() then uses the ::SendMessage() API to pass the message.
SetDlgCtrlID()	Changes the m_nID member of the control site.
SetDlgItemInt()	Converts to text and calls SetWindowText().
SetDlgItemText()	Calls SetWindowText() to set text.
SetFocus()	Calls DoVerb() with OLEIVERB_UIACTIVATE to activate the control.
SetWindowPos()	Uses the control-compatible implementations of ShowWindow(), MoveWindow() and EnableWindow() to implement the features of the SetWindowPos() Windows API. The function also calls the SetWindowPos() Windows API to change the z-order of the control.
SetWindowText()	Sets the control's Caption property. If that fails, it tries to set the control's Text property.
ShowWindow()	Calls DoVerb() with OLEIVERB_SHOW or OLEIVERB_HIDE against the control to show it or hide it.
ScrollWindowEx()	Calls ScrollWindowEx() on the window handle of the control, and follows up with a call to ScrollChildren() so the control can scroll any content to match the context.

You should feel free to use these functions, with two caveats. First, they may not make sense for some controls. For example, you can CheckDlgButton() on a control that isn't a button, but the results might not be what you expect. The CheckDlgButton() function tries to set the Value property of the ActiveX control. If the control isn't a button and uses the Value property for something other than expressing its checked state, the actual result of the call will be defined by the control.

The second caveat comes about if the control doesn't implement the property that corresponds to the function which wants to set that property. If the control doesn't even have a Value property, for instance, you'll notice that the debug build of your application emits a trace message expressing the fact that the property didn't even exist when you call CheckDlgButton(). (Specifically, it will be a warning that a DISP_E_MEMBERNOTFOUND exception was generated.)

A special note is in order about the child control ID of ActiveX controls that are managed by MFC. When you create an MFC-managed ActiveX control, the control window always has an ID of 0. The control, however, can be referenced by your calls to MFC applications using the dialog ID that you provided when creating it in the resource editor or while creating it dynamically. The actual control window is considered an implementation detail of the control, and is something that you shouldn't be fiddling with directly. The most tempting reason to alter or find the true child ID of the control is to send or trap messages from the control, and that practice is discouraged. Because the control is to be treated as a COM object, it is to be treated as a black box – that is, you shouldn't assume knowledge of the implementation of control. Since you don't know the implementation of control, the control implementation is free to change.

MFC and Ambient Properties

The ActiveX control architecture, as we described back in Chapter 15, provides for the availability of **ambient properties**. Usually just called ambients for short, these properties are actually implemented by the control container. They allow the container to prescribe defaults for certain properties for the control. The container will, for example, let all controls within the container know what language ID to use and what background color is appropriate for the controls. This allows the controls to show a user interface that meshes visually (and functionally) with the rest of the controls in the same window.

MFC provides a function in CWnd named OnAmbientProperty(). You can override this function in your container window (for example, in your CDialog-derived object) to provide whatever specialized value you'd like in response to control requests for particular ambients.

The default implementation of CWnd::OnAmbientProperty() calls a function in the container code which returns an appropriate value for the ambient property. If you're only interested in changing the value for one or two ambient properties, you're probably interested in calling the base-class implementation to handle the properties that don't interest you.

Your application may have some method of toggling user mode on and off. It might reflect the change to the control by using an OnAmbientProperty() function like this:

```
BOOL COCBenchView:OnAmbientProperty(COleControlSite* pSite, DISPID dispid,
VARIANT* pvar)
{
    if (dispid == DISPID_AMBIENT_USERMODE)
    {
        V_VT(pvar) = VT_BOOL;
        if (m_bAmbientMode)
            V_BOOL(pvar) = (VARIANT_BOOL)-1;
        else
            V_BOOL(pvar) = 0;
        return TRUE;
    }
    else
        return CView::OnAmbientProperty(pSite, dispid, pvar);
}
```

The code checks to see if the control is requesting the user mode ambient by comparing the passed DISPID with the well-known DISPID_AMBIENT_USERMODE symbol. (A list of ambient properties, their DISPIDs and brief descriptions appeared back in Chapter 15.) If the control is requesting the user mode ambient, we'll react by setting the type and value of the VARIANT referenced by pvar. Otherwise, we'll just delegate the response to MFC's implementation of the ambient properties. The actual code in the sample, by the way, is a little more complicated. We chose to store the ambient properties in the document object, so the document is queried in response to most of the requests.

Unfortunately, in VC++ 4.1 and newer, you'll need to manually enter a prototype and definition for OnAmbientProperty() – ClassWizard doesn't support the function.

If you handle a request for a particular ambient property, your function should return TRUE. Handling the request means you've either successfully figured out the ambient yourself, or you've successfully delegated the request to the base-class implementation and it was able to handle the request. With this logic, you should only return FALSE from a request for an ambient property if you've never heard of the ambient before, or if nobody you know has any reason to actually implement it.

Counter to what you might have assumed given our discussion of ambient properties so far, it *is* possible to change the value of an ambient property depending on what control is asking for it. You might want, for example, to force one control to think it's using a different locale than another, or have a control use a different ambient font.

Changing ambients on a per-control basis involves the first parameter to OnAmbientProperty(), which is a pointer to a COleControlSite. As I mentioned, COleControlSite isn't documented, though I am afraid I'm not prepared to defend exactly *why*. You can find the definition for COleControlSite in the Occimpl.h file in Microsoft Visual Studio\vc98\Mfc\Src. If you pick through the header, you can find a function named GetDlgCtrlId(). By calling this function, we can find the ID assigned to the control making the ambient property request. Alternatively, you can reference COleControlSite's m_hWnd member to compare against any window handle you might have lying around.

Of course, you should only use this method if you can't get the same task accomplished by simply setting the property for the control in question. If you need one control to have a different font, it would be just as easy to ask the control to use that font by setting that control's Font property.

Before you can use COleControlSite, you have to pull off a little stunt – to #include the header file in your source. Since this header resides in Microsoft Visual Studio\vc98\Mfc\Src, though, you can only reach the file if you've installed the MFC source code. (And being the kind of person who traces straight into the source code yourself, rather than ask questions of other people, you've done this, right?) You can use this #include directive to get the file:

```
#include "..\src\occimpl.h"
```

The trick is that Visual C++ is already set up to look at Microsoft Visual Studio\Vc98\Mfc\Include. By asking it to go a directory higher and then back down to the Src directory, you can be sure to find the file without having to update your configuration!

Of course, you could always copy the file into the Microsoft Visual Studio\Vc98\Mfc\Include *directory.*

Font Properties

Fonts are a special case for ActiveX controls. To keep font information safe across processes and correct across devices and rendering contexts, COM provides its own font object. It's pretty easy to convert from a windows HFONT or an MFC CFont to a COM font – you can just use the COM API named ::OleCreateFontIndirect(). This API initializes an LPFONTDISP – a special flavor of the IDispatch interface, but with a few extra methods to support use by COM font objects.

You can find code in the Ocbench sample that manages COM fonts and returns them as the ambient font for the container when queried by the control.

Plus ça Change, Plus c'est la Même Chose

The container is also responsible for letting the control know a particular ambient property has changed. This is necessary because controls are very likely to cache the values of ambient properties to improve their performance.

Unfortunately, MFC doesn't provide a function to take care of notifying your controls. Instead, you have to write some code that works against the IOleControl interface on the control. That interface has this definition:

```
interface IOleControl : public IUnknown
{
    HRESULT GetControlInfo(CONTROLINFO * pCI);
    HRESULT OnMnemonic(LPMSG pMsg);
    HRESULT OnAmbientPropertyChange(DISPID dispid);
    HRESULT FreezeEvents(BOOL fFreeze);
};
```

As you might guess, we're interested in calling the OnAmbientPropertyChange() function to let it know a particular ambient has changed. You can pass the DISPID of a particular property, or you can pass DISPID_UNKNOWN to force the control to assume that *all* ambient properties have changed. Given the CWnd that is associated with the control, it's pretty easy to call OnAmbientPropertyChange():

```
LPOLECONTROL pOleCtl = NULL;
if (SUCCEEDED(pWnd->m_pCtrlSite->m_pObject->
                 QueryInterface(IID_IOleControl, (LPVOID*)&pOleCtl)))
{
    ASSERT(pOleCtl != NULL);
    pOleCtl->OnAmbientPropertyChange(DISPID_AMBIENT_BACKCOLOR);
    pOleCtl->Release();
}
```

Having said it's easy, let's take a look at exactly what's happening. As you can see, the CWnd object has an m_pCtrlSite member. If the CWnd actually refers to a control, m_pCtrlSite won't be NULL and will refer to the IOleControlSite interface on the created control. MFC wraps IOleControlSite on the client side using the class COleControlSite, so m_pCtrlSite actually points at a COleControlSite instance.

936

COleControlSite ends up having a pointer to the actual IOleObject interface the control implements. This interface provides MFC with almost every method it needs to get ActiveX controls to behave like responsible embedded objects. Since we're interested in the IOleControl interface, we have to call QueryInterface() against IOleObject to gain a pointer to the IOleControl interface we need. The call to QueryInterface() is available because IOleControl, like all other sensible common object model interfaces, inherits from IUnknown to implement QueryInterface(), AddRef(), and Release(). You'll note that we call Release() in the code fragment above to let COM know we're done with the pointer we received.

And that's it. QueryInterface() will stuff the pointer to the interface we want into pOleCtl and we can run off and call OnAmbientPropertyChange(). You can, of course, use this same block of code to call other methods on that interface. For example, FreezeEvents() is useful to let your control know it should not fire events back to the container. You might want to use this method when your container enters a state where it isn't interested or isn't capable of processing events.

GetControlInfo() and OnMnemonic() work together to help the control and the container process keyboard events. The container can call GetControlInfo() to learn what mnemonics and keystrokes will interest the control, then it can call OnMnemonic() to inform the control that one of the keystrokes in which the control expressed an interest has been received.

The Control Site

The control site interface we neglected to describe above is a bit more impressive than the IOleControl interface. Here's the definition of the interface:

```
interface IOleControlSite : public IUnknown
{
    HRESULT OnControlInfoChanged(void);

    HRESULT LockInPlaceActive(BOOL fLock);
    HRESULT GetExtendedControl(IDispatch ** ppDisp);
    HRESULT TransformCoords(
        POINTL * pPtlHiMetric,
        POINTF * pPtfContainer,
        DWORD dwFlags);
    HRESULT TranslateAccelerator(MSG * lpmsg, DWORD grfModifiers);
    HRESULT OnFocus(BOOL fGotFocus);
    HRESULT ShowPropertyFrame();
};
```

Controls with a viable user-interface implement IOleControl, while containers actually implement IOleControlSite. MFC implements almost none of the methods of IOleControlSite site for you – if you or your controls want them, you'll need to provide your own implementation.

OnControlInfoChanged() is called by the control when it has changed the data contained in the CONTROLINFO structure. Again, this structure contains a list of mnemonics the control wants to handle – the control can change the list, but it won't need to do so very often. To save on processing speed, containers usually cache the structure and need to be notified if the control decides to handle a different set of mnemonics. The container should call the GetControlInfo() method on the control's IOleControl interface to get the new table.

ShowPropertyFrame() *is* implemented by MFC, even though the implementation does nothing. When a control wants to display a **property frame**, it should call the IOleControlSite::ShowPropertyFrame() method first to allow the container a chance at displaying its own property frame. A property frame is simply the frame window which holds all of the property pages a control will produce. Normally, a container will use the system property page. If the container returns E_NOTIMPL (as MFC does), the control should assume it needs to display the property frame itself; MFC-provided controls just use the stock system property page. On the other hand, if the container returns S_OK, the control should assume the container has taken care of showing the frame and that it doesn't need to do it itself. Some containers show a customized frame so that they can present the control's property pages in a more integrated user interface.

If the container implements extended properties, it needs to implement the GetExtendedControl() method on this interface. The interface should return a pointer to the IDispatch which implements extended properties. **Extended properties** are a way for a control to act as if it implements properties, but they are actually implemented by the container. Visible is an example of such a property – the container will generally administer the control's visibility, but the control may still want to offer a Boolean property to let onlookers know whether it is visible or not. Extended properties are a mechanism to such an end.

Selection

If your application is to support a design mode (that is, when not in user mode), it should allow the user to select the controls. This feature is only interesting in design mode because that's the only time you'd ever want users of your application to be able to select a control as an object itself, rather than as a target for subsequent input to the application.

The selection is really nothing interesting because it's handled by code in MFC itself. If a control knows it's in design mode and is clicked upon, MFC as the control container will draw a fuzzy rectangle around the control so the user can see that the control is selected. When the control is knocked out of user mode, it no longer requests that the container draw this selection box.

It's certainly nice of MFC to handle selection indication for us. However, MFC does *not* expose a way for our applications to detect what control is currently selected. You might then want to write a function as a member of the view class which looks like this:

```
BOOL CMyView::IsControlSelected() const
{
    CWnd* pFocus = GetFocus();
    if (pFocus == NULL)
        return FALSE;
    CWnd* pParent = pFocus->GetParent();
    if (pParent == NULL)
        return FALSE;
    if (pParent->m_hWnd != m_hWnd)
        return FALSE;
    return TRUE;
}
```

This function can then be called from a few different points in the rest of the view. It simply gets the window that has focus and tries to see if the parent of that window is the window associated with the view. Remember that I can't compare CWnd pointers to see if they refer to the same window; instead, I have to compare their m_hWnd members. If the window with focus doesn't have a parent, or if that parent isn't the view window, we'll return FALSE. Otherwise, we'll return TRUE. If this function returns TRUE, we know that one of the controls that is a child of the view has been selected.

Dynamic Containment

Dynamic containment, as I've described, is a rather different beast than static containment. You'll remember that the major difference is dynamic containment doesn't give you the luxury of knowing exactly what properties or methods the control is capable of throwing. However, this information *is* available to your application from the control's type library – you'll need to write code (just like the Components and Controls Gallery has) to pick apart the type library whenever you need to handle an event from the control. Most of the time, of course, the exact list of properties that a control manages isn't all that interesting.

Before you get that far, though, you'll need to do a little work to create the control in the first place. If you're going to offer the user the ability to select whatever control they're interested in, you'll probably want to write a dialog box which enumerates the controls found in the system registry. You can then let the control create itself at your whim. The obvious choice is to offer an Insert ActiveX control... choice on the Edit menu.

An Insert ActiveX control... option would have to invoke a dialog box that finds and lists the controls available to the application. The dialog has to rip through the system registry to find all of the controls. This isn't quite as hard as it sounds; the real issue is knowing where in the registry to have the code look for the stuff you want.

Let's write a COleInsertCtlDlg class to implement a way to drop a user-selectable control into a window at runtime. The class would have to call the RegOpenKey() during its handling of the WM_INITDIALOG message to get the HKEY_CLASSES_ROOT hive of the registry opened. It would then call RegEnumKey() to see which items in that hive of the registry have valid CLSID entries and Control values. If an entry in the registry has all of these keys, it's assumed it also has an InprocServer32 entry which points at the executable image of the control. If all of these entries are valid, the OnInitDialog() handler for the box proceeds by building a string for the list box in the dialog.

You can see all this code together in an application in the Ocbench sample. I want to point out some finer points, so I'll take the liberty of showing bits of it here:

```
BOOL COleInsertCtlDlg::OnInitDialog()
{

   // Code cut for brevity

   pszClass = reinterpret_cast<LPTSTR>(new TCHAR[_MAX_PATH*3]);
   if (NULL == pszClass)
   {
      EndDialog(IDCANCEL);
      return FALSE;
   }
   pszClsid = pszClass + _MAX_PATH;
   pszKey = pszClsid + _MAX_PATH;

   //Open up the root key.
   lRet = ::RegOpenKey(HKEY_CLASSES_ROOT, NULL, &hKey);
   if ((LONG)ERROR_SUCCESS != lRet)
   {
      delete pszClass;
      EndDialog(IDCANCEL);
      return FALSE;
   }
```

Continued on Following Page

```
      while (TRUE)
      {
          lRet = ::RegEnumKey(hKey, cStrings++, pszClass, _MAX_PATH);

          if ((LONG)ERROR_SUCCESS!=lRet)
              break;

  // Code cut for brevity

      }
```

The string inserted in the list box of the dialog contains the control's full name, a tab character and the CLSID of the control. This arrangement allows the list box to store both the name of the control – which the user of the application should recognize – as well as the CLSID that will be needed to create the control. (Relax! I'm getting there!) The tab lets me hide the CLSID in the actual list box text entry. To make the CLSID disappear, I call SetTabStops() on the list box to make the text after the tab appear impossibly far to the right.

```
  // got through all the conditions, add the string.
          lstrcat(pszKey, _T("\t"));

          // only add to listbox if not a duplicate
          if (LB_ERR == pBox->FindString(-1, pszKey))
          {
              lstrcat(pszKey, szID);
              pBox->AddString(pszKey);
          }
      }

      // set a tab stop to be off the right edge of the box

      CRect rectBox;
      int    nThird;
      pBox->GetWindowRect(rectBox);
      nThird = rectBox.Width();
      pBox->SetTabStops(nThird);

      //Select the first item by default
      pBox->SetCurSel(0);
      RegCloseKey(hKey);
      delete pszClass;

      return TRUE;   // return TRUE unless you set the focus to a control
                     // EXCEPTION: OCX Property Pages should return FALSE
  }
```

When the user finally selects an entry in the list, the dialog box object populates its m_strControlName and m_strControlCLSID members. This allows the dialog box to destroy itself and allows the caller to retrieve the CLSID of the control that's been created.

```
  void COleInsertCtlDlg::OnOK()
  {
      CString str;
      CListBox* pBox = (CListBox*) GetDlgItem(IDC_CONTROLS);
      int nSelected = pBox->GetCurSel();
      pBox->GetText(nSelected, str);
```

```
        int nTab = str.Find('\t');
        m_strControlName = str.Left(nTab);
        m_strControlCLSID = str.Mid(nTab+1);

    CDialog::OnOK();
}
```

At this point, we've initialized a couple of members of our dialog class with information about the ActiveX control that was selected – and that's enough information to actually get the control created.

The CreateControl() Function

Once your application has the control the user wants to insert, you need to get busy by creating a pointer to a CWnd object and calling its CWnd::CreateControl() member. CreateControl() has a couple of different overloads which look like this:

```
BOOL CWnd::CreateControl( LPCTSTR lpszClass,
                          LPCTSTR lpszWindowName,
                          DWORD dwStyle,
                          const RECT& rect,
                          CWnd* pParentWnd,
                          UINT nID,
                          CFile* pPersist = NULL,
                          BOOL bStorage = FALSE,
                          BSTR bstrLicKey = NULL );


BOOL CWnd::CreateControl( REFCLSID clsid,
                          LPCTSTR lpszWindowName,
                          DWORD dwStyle,
                          const RECT& rect,
                          CWnd* pParentWnd,
                          UINT nID,
                          CFile* pPersist = NULL,
                          BOOL bStorage = FALSE,
                          BSTR bstrLicKey = NULL );
```

As you can see, the overrides are identical except for the first parameter. The second version takes a reference to a **CLSID**, while the first takes a pointer to a string. In either version, the first parameter identifies the control to be created.

In the version of the function which takes a pointer to a string, you can supply the class name of the control (which might be something like "MSGrid.Grid", for example) or the string version of the CLSID for the control you need. The CLSID should be formatted "{A8C3B720-0B5A-101B-B22E-00AA0037B2FC}", for example, which is the format you'll find used in the registry.

If you have an actual CLSID data structure identifying the control you need, you can call the CreateControl() overload which accepts a reference to such a structure.

Note that the CreateControl() function is analogous to the Create() function CWnd normally uses to create a window, i.e. you'll first allocate a CWnd object and then call a function to get the window created. If you want to dynamically create a window in a dialog box, you could make a CWnd member and call CreateControl() on that member during the processing of the WM_INITDIALOG message for the dialog. In the Ocbench sample, I create a CWnd object on the heap using the new operator before calling CreateControl() to actually get the window created.

The balance of the parameters in the function simply describes how the window will work once it has been finally created. The second parameter, lpszWindowName, sets the Text or Caption property of the created control if it has such a property. If you pass NULL for this parameter, MFC won't try to set the caption of the control.

The dwStyle parameter can contain a few window style flags which will be applied to the newly created control. You can pass WS_VISIBLE, WS_BORDER, WS_DISABLED, WS_GROUP, or WS_TABSTOP to change the control's state as you see fit. Only these styles are honored because they're the only styles that make sense for ActiveX controls at large. Some of the styles are effectively ignored if the control doesn't support the style in question. For example, WS_BORDER only has an effect if the control supports a Border property. MFC adds a few flags to the ones you supply before actually creating the control. For example, MFC always adds WS_CHILD.

The rect parameter is a reference to a rectangle that bounds the new control. You can always move the control later with SetWindowPos() or MoveWindow(), as I mentioned earlier in the chapter. The pParentWnd parameter identifies the window that will act as the control's parent. This parameter can't be NULL – ActiveX controls can't be top-level windows.

You'll want to identify the control after it has been created. Since it's a control and a child window, you can supply it with an ID (in the aptly named nID parameter) that identifies the control. Once the control has been created, you can call GetDlgItem() against its parent window with the ID you specified to gain a pointer to the CWnd for the control. Note that the control may create a window which doesn't truly have the ID integer you've specified; that's an implementation detail of the control and, as I outlined earlier, it lets the control hide the way it works from prying fingers.

The last three parameters have default values. Together, all three defaults are set so the control won't store any of its persistent data. If you want the control to be able to store persistent data, you should supply a pointer to a CFile-derived object where you'll expect the control to store its data. This pointer can reference a regular binary file or a COleStreamFile class that wraps access to a compound file – or any other CFile-derived storage mechanism you have lying about. If your CFile does reference a structured storage, you should be sure to pass TRUE for the bStorage parameter. This will let your control store information in multiple streams within the storage if it wants to. Otherwise, you should pass FALSE so the control knows it shouldn't expect to use structured storage mechanisms.

The final parameter is a BSTR that contains the runtime license key for the control. This parameter is only important if you're working with controls which are licensed. The control will expect to have its licensing information in the BSTR you pass; otherwise it will fail the creation process.

Once you've received a successful return code from your call to CreateControl(), the CWnd object you used to make the call is valid. You shouldn't assume the CWnd actually owns a window because the control may not have created one – it might never create a window, or it might not create a window until it is actually activated. If CWnd *does* refer to a window, you can use all the regular CWnd member functions that we looked at before to kick the window around the block. Of course, the trick to seeing what a CWnd really means is to call ::IsWindow() on its m_hWnd member. If that function returns TRUE, you know you've got a live one.

You can't, by the way, expect to hook CreateControl() back to a CWnd-derived class which you've implemented. ActiveX controls handle their own messages – the messages they manage aren't reflected to the container. Events, on the other hand, are another matter.

Handling Control Events

You may want to derive your own class from CWnd in order to handle the events fired by ActiveX controls that you've dynamically created. The simple approach, applicable when you know what control you're creating, is to add an event sink map to your CWnd-derived class to handle the events that you know will come – stock events like mouse-down messages.

On the other hand, you could implement an override of our old friend CCmdTarget::OnCmdMsg(). You'll remember from Chapter 3, when we talked about dynamically handling command messages generated by a configurable menu, that this virtual function is called by the framework every time a message or command UI update is being handled. Well, it turns out that OnCmdMsg() is also called when an ActiveX control fires an event and no event map entry has handled it.

Your event-handling override of OnCmdMsg() will necessarily be pretty simple. This is what the OnCmdMsg() function looks like:

```
virtual BOOL CCmdTarget::OnCmdMsg( UINT nID,
                                   int nCode,
                                   void* pExtra,
                       AFX_CMDHANDLERINFO* pHandlerInfo );
```

The nID parameter is the ID of the control that generated the message. Since we set the ID in our call to CreateControl(), we should know what ID we're using. nCode identifies the type of command message which is being dispatched. For ActiveX control property requests, property change notifications, or events, nCode will be CN_EVENT – we discussed other popular values back in our examination of the Ctxtmenu sample. pHandlerInfo will be NULL when this function handles a control notification, but pExtra will be extremely interesting. It will point at an AFX_EVENT object.

Before I continue, I need to point out that AFX_EVENT is declared and defined in the Afxpriv2.h header file. If you've read other parts of this book before turning to this chapter, you know that Afxpriv.h and Afxpriv2.h are dangerous header files. Anyone on the MFC team (including, get this, *me!*) could stumble into the office one morning and completely change that file. Realistically, that won't happen; but if someone in the COM group insists they've come up with a radically different (and presumably better) way for ActiveX controls to work with their containers, you can bet they'll change Afxpriv.h every which way from Sunday (or even just subtly enough to be bad) to implement it. We'll *try* not to break compatibility with old code, but if you've used Afxpriv.h in your code, you're acknowledging that you're playing with MFC's implementation and that your code might break as the implementation changes.

With that said, AFX_EVENT has a structure like this:

```
struct AFX_EVENT
{
    enum
    {
        event,
        propRequest, propChanged,
        propDSCNotify
    };
```

Continued on Following Page

```
        AFX_EVENT(int eventKind);

        AFX_EVENT(int eventKind, DISPID dispid, DISPPARAMS* pDispParams = NULL,
            EXCEPINFO* pExcepInfo = NULL, UINT* puArgError = NULL);

        int m_eventKind;
        DISPID m_dispid;
        DISPPARAMS* m_pDispParams;
        EXCEPINFO* m_pExcepInfo;
        UINT* m_puArgError;
        BOOL m_bPropChanged;
        HRESULT m_hResult;
        DSCSTATE m_nDSCState;
        DSCREASON m_nDSCReason;
    };
```

So, if you've overridden OnCmdMsg() and identified the nID of a control you like, you can cast the pExtra parameter to an AFX_EVENT pointer. AFX_EVENT has a member that you'll most likely want to look at immediately – the m_eventKind member. The m_eventKind member reflects the nCode parameter to OnCmdMsg(). The values of these parameters *aren't* the same, but their meanings are.

The member is set to be equal to enumerated constants local to the AFX_EVENT structure. Those constants are event, propRequest, and propChanged. You can guess that these values correspond to the processing of an event, the response to a control asking for a property, and the notification that a property has changed.

If m_eventKind is event, you know that your control has fired off something interesting to you. The actual event is identified by the m_dispid member. Controls use DISPIDs to identify events (and properties) that they implement. m_dispid might be one of the standard events, such as DISPID_CLICK, or it might be a custom event which your control knows about. If the control is firing off a stock event, you already know what to expect for parameters. However, if the control is firing off its own event type, you'll need to ask the control about what parameters it has sent and what types those parameters bear.

Information about all the parameters is available in the AFX_EVENT structure. The m_pDispParams member points at a DISPPARAMS structure which identifies the number of parameters. That structure, in turn, points at a list of VARIANTs – the one-size-fits-all data type. In handling the OnCmdMsg() override in the sample, I wrote some code to format the VARIANTs in a human-readable form so that descriptions of events that go by can be added to a list box.

If you know that a DISPID is identifying a particular stock property, you can just get to work on the parameters themselves. Otherwise, you might want to look up the DISPID in the control's type library. This will allow you to find out which parameters the control passes with the event in question, which order those parameters appear in and how to handle any optional named parameters. Named parameters are parameters that COM might send across a dispatch interface to the client in a random order. Since they're named, they don't have to appear with every other parameter to be readily identifiable.

If you wanted to show events as they happen (for debugging and such like) then you might write something similar to the following code in the OnCmdMsg() handler:

```
AFX_EVENT* pEvent = (AFX_EVENT)pExtra;
if(pEvent->m_eventKind != AFX_EVENT::event)
    return CView::OnCmdMsg(nID, nCode, pExtra, pHandlerInfo);
CString str;

if (m_pEventDlg != NULL) // if Event log dialog showing
{
    UINT nIndex;
    for (nIndex = 0; nIndex < pEvent->m_pDispParams->cArgs; nIndex++)
    {
        str.Format("Parameter %d: Type %s, Value = %s",
            nIndex,
            GetVariantName(pEvent->m_pDispParams->rgvarg[nIndex].vt),
            GetVariantValue(pEvent->m_pDispParams->rgvarg[nIndex]));
    }
}
```

In AFX_EVENT, you'll find a pointer to a DISPPARAMS structure in m_pDispParams. DISPPARAMS has a count of arguments in cArgs, and information about each argument in the rgvarg[] array. You can read up on the GetVariantName() and GetVariantValue() functions in the Vtnames.cpp file. These functions convert the VARIANT information to readable types and values that are later added to the **Event Log** list box. MFC's COleVariant class couldn't help the sample with that kind of formatting. This is the case for most applications, so COleVariant concentrates on managing variant types and type conversions instead of value or type publication.

AFX_EVENT contains enough information to find out about the type of the parameters sent to your notification function, as well as the values of those parameters. If your container is only interested in handling well-known DISPIDs (like the DISPIDs for standard events), you're home free, but if you want to know more about the parameters and events (such as their names), you'll need to look through the type information stored in the control. To gain this information, you'll need to follow a simple algorithm:

1. Ask the control for its IProvideClassInfo interface

2. Call the GetClassInfo() method of the supplied IProvideClassInfo interface

3. Request the type attributes from the class information

4. For each type attribute, query to see if the type information describes events

5. Once you've found the event information, request the count of events

6. For each event, request the type information for the event

There are only six steps here, but you'll end up working with four different COM interfaces – right to the interface level! Fortunately, once our control has been inserted, we can steal some interfaces that MFC already has prepared for us. Steps 1, 2 and 3 above are all aimed at finding the interface on the control that supports browsing event type information. Unfortunately, the COleControlSite class that MFC created to hold your control site doesn't support any way to easily access the type information. It doesn't need to, since the event callback into the container simply uses the type information surrounding the dispatch call that transferred control there in the first place. That information is immediately packed up to form the AFX_EVENT structure your OnCmdMsg() function receives. So, if you want information on the specific parameter names that are flying around, you'll need to run off and find the type information yourself.

To implement the algorithm steps I outlined above, I decided to write a class, called CCtrlWrapper, derived from CWnd. To create the ActiveX control the user has requested, I would call its CreateControl() member function. The only *real* reason for creating this class is to have a more convenient place to hold all of the extra code which queries the event list, as well as to have a place to hold the data that the interrogation of the control generates.

In my CCtrlWrapper class (implemented in the Ctrlwrap.cpp file), the member function GetBrowseInfo() takes care of loading all the data the container could want. The algorithm above, however simple, is actually a little tricky to implement since it relies on so much contact with COM's various interfaces. The code in GetBrowseInfo() first gets the control's IUnknown interface from the CWnd::GetControlUnknown() member function. The code then requests the IProvideClassInfo interface from the control. The IProvideClassInfo interface is a seldom-used interface that allows a container to ask an Automation object about the attributes of the Automation server. In this case, that's the ActiveX control.

We're then ready to ask the control for a pointer to its type attribute structure. The TYPEATTR structure defines what sort of data types the control implements — we'll want to look at those type information databases because they'll contain information about the control and its events. The type information comes from the type library we baked into the ActiveX control's executable image back when we were writing controls in Chapter 15. So, to this point, the code we've written looks like this:

```
LPUNKNOWN lpUnk;
LPPROVIDECLASSINFO lpProvider;
lpUnk = GetControlUnknown();
if (SUCCEEDED(lpUnk->QueryInterface(IID_IProvideClassInfo,
                                    (void**) &lpProvider)))
{
    LPTYPEINFO lpClassInfo;
    if (SUCCEEDED(lpProvider->GetClassInfo(&lpClassInfo)))
    {
        LPTYPEATTR lpTypeAttrib;
        if (SUCCEEDED(lpClassInfo->GetTypeAttr(&lpTypeAttrib)))
        {
        // ... more work later!
```

We now need to step through the list of type attributes for the control to see what they're about. The control may implement many different type libraries, so we need to make sure we find the one that contains the events. The type library describing the control's events is always described with a couple of flags. The event-handling functions are implemented on the container side, so that means the type library will be flagged describing functions that are implemented in the container, not by the control. The IMPLTYPEFLAG_FSOURCE indicates that this is the case. The code we wrote also looks for the IMPLTYPEFLAG_FDEFAULT flag because the type library for the control's events will identify themselves as being the default to be used as the source of event calls. So, we've written a loop that picks apart the information available from the class' type attribute structure:

```
// what we had before, plus this...
UINT nCount;
int iFlags;
HREFTYPE hRefType;

for (nCount = 0; nCount < lpTypeAttrib->cImplTypes; nCount++)
{
    if (SUCCEEDED(lpClassInfo->GetImplTypeFlags(nCount, &iFlags)))
    {
```

```
LPTYPEINFO lpTypeInfo;
if ((iFlags & TYPE_MASK) == TYPE_DEFAULTSOURCE)
{
    if (SUCCEEDED(lpClassInfo->GetRefTypeOfImplType(nCount,
    &hRefType)) && SUCCEEDED(lpClassInfo->GetRefTypeInfo(hRefType,
    &lpTypeInfo)))
    {
```

We want to find the types that the functions implement, and the GetRefTypeOfImplType() method gets us a handle to the type data we want. We can populate a TYPEINFO structure using the GetRefTypeInfo() function. The "Ref" in this function name means COM will go digging around to find type information for any types the requested definitions ever reference. If controls always implemented their own types, we wouldn't need to make this additional call. Because controls actually use default types which COM itself implements, we need to make the GetRefTypeInfo() call to fluff-up the definition.

If we've gotten this far, the lpTypeInfo is ready to be used. Since there's more work to do, I implemented one more member function (called LoadEventTypes()) to actually do the work of getting the data and storing it in the application. Before I describe LoadEventTypes(), let me point out two important facts about the code we've been discussing.

First, all of this code is expensive. Picking apart the type library means COM has to find the executable image in question, get the type library, and pull it apart to find the information you're requesting. To find the library, COM has to read some information from the registry, too. Optimization is the reason why I went out of my way to write code (which we're about to examine) to keep information from the type library in memory while the user plays with the control. If you wrote your container to go hit the type library every time the user fired an event, your application would be slower than a boring date at a 7-to-2 hockey game.

Second, it's imperative that you properly release all of the memory and interfaces that this code gets. You can see that I used COM's SUCCEEDED() macro in a bunch of if statements to make sure all the calls I did work okay. If they don't work, or when the next block of work is done, I call the appropriate Release() function to let COM know that I don't need the interface or data structure anymore. If you don't do this, you'll get into big trouble. Either you'll leak memory (if you forget to release a data structure) or your program and its associated ActiveX controls will stay in memory forever. Nothing annoys users more than that.

Cold Hard Cache

Okay, now that we've found the type library that describes controls, we need to work on actually loading the information from the library. That's where the `LoadEventTypes()` function (also implemented in the `Ctrlwrap.cpp` file) comes in – it rips through the list of attributes on the appropriate branch of the type library to load all of the information describing the events. The core of the function is a loop which repeatedly calls `GetNames()` against the type info for each of the event entries.

The body of the loop looks like this:

```
LPFUNCDESC lpFuncDesc;
if (SUCCEEDED(lpTypeInfo->GetFuncDesc(nCount, &lpFuncDesc)))
{
    BSTR* pNames = new BSTR[lpFuncDesc->cParams+1];

    UINT cNames = lpFuncDesc->cParams;
    lpTypeInfo->GetNames(lpFuncDesc->memid, pNames,
                                  lpFuncDesc->cParams+1, &cNames);

    CEventInfo* pInfo = new CEventInfo(cNames, pNames,
            lpFuncDesc->elemdescFunc, lpFuncDesc->lprgelemdescParam);

    m_EventInfoMap.SetAt((WORD)lpFuncDesc->memid, pInfo);
    delete [] pNames;

    lpTypeInfo->ReleaseFuncDesc(lpFuncDesc);
}
```

`GetNames()` returns all of the names for an `IDispatch` interface member, i.e. it returns both the name of the function and the name of any parameters the function has. Since we're playing with COM directly, the information is returned in the form of `BSTR`s – COM's string object. To that end, I allocate an array of `BSTR`s so that `GetNames()` has a place to put its results. The `FUNCDESC` structure we got from COM also has arrays that describe the parameter list for the functions.

To keep all of this interesting stuff in memory, `LoadEventTypes()` creates a `CEventInfo` object. The `CEventInfo` class just manages all of the type and naming information. I use a `CMapWordToOb` collection in `CCtrlWrapper` to store the information for the lifetime of the `CCtrlWrapper`. (Note that my use of a `CMapWordToOb` collection is questionable – since `DISPID`s are really `DWORD`s, I'm sacrificing some precision. The truth is I'm really lazy, but I also know there are very few controls that actually use `DISPID`s outside of the range of a `WORD`.)

One type conversion I *can't* sneak around, though, is the use of `BSTR`s by COM to name the parameters and functions. `CEventInfo` takes care of converting the `BSTR` strings to more usable `CString`s during its constructor. The code uses the `USES_CONVERSION()` macros supplied by MFC which we examined back in Chapter 13.

During the handling of `OnCmdMsg()`, we would ask `CCtrlWrapper` to look up the event information based on the `DISPID`. There, it's a simple matter to just format some strings to be tucked into an event log dialog box.

Getting Information on Properties and Methods

Unfortunately, you'll have to go through almost the same exercise to get information from the control about its properties and methods. The code you'll need to use will be different, but not radically changed. The first difference is that you'll need to look for type libraries which don't have the IMPLTYPEFLAG_FSOURCE type identifier. Since properties and methods are implemented by the control, the type information won't be marked as being sourced by the control.

You'll also need to worry about the difference between three different kinds of functions; properties are implemented in COM by exposing 'get' and 'put' functions, while methods are just plain old functions. In the sample, I show how to use the invkind member of the FUNCDESC structure to do this. A property 'get' function has an invkind equal to the INVOKE_PROPERTYGET constant, while a property 'put' function has an invkind equal to the INVOKE_PROPERTYPUT constant. A generic method uses an invkind of INVOKE_FUNC. When I play my bass guitar, I like to INVOKE_FUNK.

You'll need to discern between these different types so you're sure you're invoking the correct method. There are no assumptions to make – just because you find a PROPERTYGET, you can't assume there will be a corresponding PROPERTYPUT function, since properties might be read-only. Conversely, you can't assume there will be a PROPERTYGET just because you've found a PROPERTYPUT. While it's uncommon, a control may expose a write-only property.

Aside from those two issues, though, there's really no difference between browsing for properties and methods and browsing for events.

By the way, you may have guessed that the code we've written here is the same sort of code that's at the heart of the Components and Controls Gallery. It is! When you ask the Gallery to insert an ActiveX control for you, it loads the type library for the ActiveX control you've identified and reads the exact same information. Instead of keeping it around in memory, it instead emits a header file and a .cpp file with the type and naming information it found. Similar code exists in lots of products – Visual Basic, for instance, might use similar code to populate its lists of properties and events when you're working with an ActiveX control. The OLE/COM Object Viewer sample (which ships in VC++ and is available from the Tools menu of the IDE) includes far more generalized versions of these routines.

In the sample, you'll find some code that allows you to browse the properties and methods of your favorite controls. We stopped short of implementing actual ways to change properties or invoke methods because that sort of functionality is available elsewhere.

Serializing Control Data

As you remember from our treatment of ActiveX controls from the control implementer's point of view (back in Chapter 15), ActiveX controls use their DoPropExchange() function to load or store information that they want to keep persistent across instantiations. It turns out the MFC implementation of the control run-time support library actually calls COleControl::Serialize() after preparing an archive object.

From the point of view of the container, the serialization is performed by the control's IPersistStorage interface. The interface supports a few methods, most notably Save() and Load(), which allow the container to request that the control serialize itself into a storage provided by the container.

If you're using an ActiveX control in a dialog box, you don't care about the control's ability to serialize its data. It will be created with the binary data found in the custom resource associated with your dialog. That binary data reflects the settings for the control properties you made in the dialog editor when you added the control to your dialog. We described how all this works earlier in the chapter – if you're allowing MFC to do the work, there's nothing to it.

On the other hand, if you're implementing your own container to support dynamic containment, you'll need to find a way to get to the control's `IPersistStorage` interface to load or store the control's data. Because COM provides helper functions, named `::OleSave()` and `::OleLoad()`, we really don't need to concern ourselves deeply with the way `IPersistStorage` really works. It's enough to say that we'll query the control for its `IPersistStorage` interface, call `OleSave()` or `OleLoad()` to get the control to do its thing. The real rub is getting at the information in a way that is convenient for us as container writers.

When `IPersistStorage` works with data, it writes the data to an object called a **structured storage**. Structured storage provides a way for COM objects to store information they contain in an efficient and portable way. COM helps objects represent their data in a way that is conveniently available no matter what kind of data the object needs to store.

For our container, though, the notion of a storage is a little bit much. A storage isn't compatible with any real file type because applications can't readily work with them. That is, without using COM to write your own data, you'd find it pretty hard to let your data coexist with the control's data in the same file.

One approach is to use the document/view architecture simply to manage the controls you're containing in the application. Assuming the rest of your application is using normal storage mechanisms and *not* using COM directly, you'll need to write a little code. On the other hand, if you're using MFC's OLE client support, you're a step ahead of the game. You can associate a `COleClientItem` with each control you've created. Then, you can use code built into `COleClientItem` to perform the serialization against a plain old `CArchive`.

On the other hand, if you haven't engaged compound document support in your application, you'll need to do some of the same things `COleClientItem` does. You'll need to create a storage in memory, ask the control to serialize its data into the storage and then attack the storage directly to get the data yourself. You can write the storage as an opaque block of binary data to your own archive without the data disturbing access to your application's own, non-control related data.

As I'll explain in great detail in the section at the end of the chapter called 'Restoring Controls from Serialization', you need to write all sorts of data to the document for each control. While serializing to store the controls, we'll write all of the details describing the control – its `CLSID`, its title and its position in the view, for example. The document then asks the control to write its persistent data to an in-memory structured storage and then finally to the archive.

The most interesting part of this whole mechanism is the code we stole from `ColeClientItem` — it uses some COM APIs to get the storage. The beginning of the function looks like this:

```
void CCtrlWrapper::WriteControl(CArchive& ar)
{
    LPUNKNOWN lpUnk = GetControlUnknown();
    LPLOCKBYTES lpLockBytes;
    LPSTORAGE lpStorage;

    SCODE sc = ::CreateILockBytesOnHGlobal(NULL, TRUE, &lpLockBytes);
    if (sc != S_OK)
        AfxThrowOleException(sc);
    ASSERT(lpLockBytes != NULL);
    ...
```

The `::CreateILockBytesOnHGlobal()` function is an COM API that creates COM's most basic storage object — a pile of bytes that COM can later use to store more complicated mechanisms, like a stream or, in this case, a storage. This work is done via the `ILockBytes` interface that COM returns to us in the `lpLockBytes` pointer. The first parameter to `::CreateILockBytesOnHGlobal()` is a handle to the global memory object which should be used for the actual storage. We pass NULL, since we want COM to supply a global memory object for us. The second parameter is a BOOL that tells COM it should delete the memory when we're done with the `ILockBytes` interface.

If the creation of the lock bytes works just fine, we'll continue by creating a storage on the lock bytes. Structured storages, as I noted earlier, are high-level persistent data storage mechanisms which COM uses for almost every large-scale object's data. The call looks like this:

```
    ...
    sc = ::StgCreateDocfileOnILockBytes(lpLockBytes,
        STGM_SHARE_EXCLUSIVE|STGM_CREATE|STGM_READWRITE, 0, &lpStorage);
    if (sc != S_OK)
    {
        VERIFY(lpLockBytes->Release() == 0);
        lpLockBytes = NULL;
        AfxThrowOleException(sc);
    }
    ...
```

COM's `::StgCreateDocfileOnILockBytes()` API does the real work for us. We provide it a pointer to a live `ILockBytes` interface as the first parameter and the function populates the `lpStorage` pointer passed as the last parameter with a pointer to an `IStorage` interface. The second parameter is a set of flags which dictate how we'll be accessing the storage and how we'd like the storage to be protected against access by other users. It's unlikely (well, so unlikely that others would say that it's impossible) that any other process would start working on our storage, but we set up things with the STGM_SHARE_EXCLUSIVE parameter to guarantee our access is our own. This flag isn't very important for us in this particular example, but if we were writing this code to go against a physical disk file instead of a global memory block, it would be very important. STGM_CREATE means that the storage will be created for us and STGM_READWRITE means that we'd like to both read and write it. The third parameter, which we've specified as zero, is reserved and *must* be zero.

Since the storage is created and we're ready to ask the control for its data, we'll do just that. The control is prepared to provide its data via its `IPersistStorage` interface. So, we'll call `QueryInterface()` against the `IUnknown` interface of the control to gain that interface, like this:

```
    ...
    LPPERSISTSTORAGE lpPersistStorage;

    if (!SUCCEEDED(lpUnk->QueryInterface(IID_IPersistStorage, (void**)
&lpPersistStorage)))
        ASSERT(FALSE);
    ...
```

With that done, we can call COM's appropriately named `::OleSave()` API to demand the control write its data. `::OleSave()` is a pretty simple API, if you take for granted all the complicated mechanisms which it uses to get its job done. It simply asks a COM object to write its data to a storage object and handles any error conditions that might come up. As such, the function takes a pointer to the `IPersistStorage` supplied by the object we want to serialize, a pointer to the storage we'll use to contain the data and a flag. That flag, supplied as the last parameter, is `TRUE` if the storage is the same used to load the object. Since our storage is brand new, we have to pass `FALSE` – our brand-new storage isn't the same as anything COM has seen before. If you use this API someplace else, though, you should set this flag to `TRUE` if you can. In that situation, COM can be a little more aggressive about using the storage, since it can make a few additional assumptions about it. In `Ctrlwrap.cpp`, the function does all this:

```
    ...
    sc = ::OleSave(lpPersistStorage, lpStorage, FALSE);
    lpPersistStorage->SaveCompleted(NULL);
    lpPersistStorage->Release();
    lpStorage->Commit(STGC_OVERWRITE);
    ASSERT(::StgIsStorageILockBytes(lpLockBytes) == S_OK);
    ...
```

Once the `::OleSave()` call returns, we run off and use a couple of methods on the `IPersistStorage` interface. (I've done tons of research, and I still can't find an interface called `ILikeHockey`.) `SaveCompleted()` tells the object we're done writing its data and `Release()` frees the interface. The `ASSERT()` I've coded above simply asks COM to verify that the block of memory we used is really a valid storage. An `ASSERT()` macro is just fine here as the call doesn't do anything we'd need in a release build.

Now that COM has written the data from the object for us, we'll pick apart the memory. We'll ask COM to supply us with the `HGLOBAL` used to store the data using the `::GetHGlobalFromILockBytes()` API:

```
    ...
    HGLOBAL hStorage;
    sc = ::GetHGlobalFromILockBytes(lpLockBytes, &hStorage);
    if (sc != S_OK)
        AfxThrowOleException(sc);
    ...
```

As you can surmise, `::GetHGlobalFromILockBytes()` is just the inverse of `::StgCreateDocfileOnILockBytes()`. That is, `::GetHGlobalFromILockBytes()` returns a handle to the global memory which is implementing a storage object.

Once we have the handle, we can continue with our quest by asking OLE to provide us status information for the lock bytes by using the `Stat()` method of the `ILockBytes` interface. That method populates a `STATSTG` structure which describes the storage. Among other things, it tells us how many bytes are actually in the storage:

```
   . . .
      STATSTG statstg;
      sc = lpLockBytes->Stat(&statstg, STATFLAG_NONAME);
      if (sc != S_OK)
         AfxThrowOleException(sc);
      ASSERT(statstg.cbSize.HighPart == 0);
      DWORD dwBytes = statstg.cbSize.LowPart;
      ar << dwBytes;
   . . .
```

So, finally, we write the data to the archive that got us here in the first place. Note that we `ASSERT()` against the `HighPart` of the size being non-zero. If the user has more than four gigabytes of persistent data in their control, they have problems much more serious than this author could solve. Then we'll lock the global memory handle to get all of the bytes themselves and pump them off to the archive:

```
   . . .
      LPVOID lpBuf = GlobalLock(hStorage);
      ASSERT(lpBuf != NULL);
      ar.Write(lpBuf, (UINT)dwBytes);
      lpLockBytes->Release();
      ::GlobalUnlock(hStorage);
   }
```

And that's the end. The control has been serialized to our own file.

Restoring Controls from Serialization

Now, though, that we have an arbitrary number of opaque data written to our stream, we'll need to find a way to get all that data back and do something with it. If the user loads a file that we've written, we would have to first populate an array so we know the details about the control – its `ID`, its `CLSID` and its position within the view.

Once those details have been read, we can zip through the array of controls and allocate new `CCtrlWrapper` objects for the new controls. To create the controls, we'll actually call `CWnd::CreateControl()` – but this time, we'll specify a lot more information than we did when the user created the control. The loop, placed in the `CDocument::Serialize()` function, might look like this:

```
   int nIndex;
   for (nIndex = 0; nIndex < m_arControls.GetSize(); nIndex++)
   {
      DWORD dwCtlDataSize;
      ar >> dwCtlDataSize;

      LPBYTE pBytes = new BYTE[dwCtlDataSize];
      ar.Read(pBytes, dwCtlDataSize);
```

Continued on Following Page

```
CMemFile fileCtlData(pBytes, dwCtlDataSize);

    CCtrlWrapper* pWrapper = new CCtrlWrapper;
    pWrapper->CreateControl(m_arControls[nIndex].m_strControlCLSID,
        _T(""), WS_VISIBLE, m_arControls[nIndex].m_rect,
        pFirstView, m_arControls[nIndex].m_nID,
        &fileCtlData, TRUE);
    delete [] pBytes;
}
```

You can see that our call to `CreateControl()`, as I promised, uses lots of information from the array to initialize the control like it was before we stored the file. The most interesting parameters, though, are the last two – we pass the address of a `CMemFile` and `TRUE`. This tells `CreateControl()` that we want to initialize the new control's persistent data from some information we have stored.

Earlier in the chapter, we described this seventh parameter as a pointer to a `CFile` object and the eighth parameter as a `BOOL` that is `TRUE` if the `CFile` represents an structured storage and `FALSE` if not. Since we picked the data from the control using `IPersistStorage` when we saved it, we can specify `TRUE` for this parameter.

The easiest way to supply a `CFile` to the function is to use a `CMemFile`, as I have above. I read the `DWORD` we wrote to indicate the length of the binary data in the file and allocate enough memory to hold that number of bytes. I then call the `CArchive::Read()` function to suck up that raw data. Using one of the `CMemFile` constructors, I initialize the `CMemFile` to build a memory file to hold the block of data I've allocated. Later, deep inside of MFC, when the implementation of `CreateControl()` needs to get that data, `CMemFile` provides it via a simple and speedy `memcpy()`.

We could have, if we wanted to, created a `CArchiveStream()` to hold native COM data, but that means we would have needed to use the less flexible stream storage from the control and actually spent more time and resources on loading the data. We can't, by the way, directly provide the `CFile` inside the `CArchive` object we're using, because `CreateControl()` expects that *all* the data in the file is to be used for initializing the control. Since our file contains lots more information and data than just those for this control, we need to create a `CFile` that contains only the information COM needs to reinitialize the control.

When a control container app writes out a file, you can imagine it having this format:

Control count
Control 1 information

...

Control *n* information
Control 1 persistent data length
Control 1 persistent data

...

Control *n* persistent data length
Control *n* persistent data

Only the shaded portion of the data is actually written using the normal MFC serialization code, i.e. using the insertion and extraction operators against a `CArchive` or by calling the `Serialize()` member of a `CObject`-derived class. The rest of the data at the end is blurted out by `CCtrlWrapper::WriteControl()` or read back in by `CWnd::CreateControl()`.

This file format is fine for my `Ocbench` sample; your application may require a more interesting or more substantial investment in the storage architecture.

Focus and ActiveX controls

A review of an AppWizard-generated control container will reveal that the code does only a little work to manage the tracking of focus among controls within the container.

The code needs to know what ActiveX control you're working with when you want to use control-specific commands (like the P<u>r</u>operty Page command in the <u>V</u>iew menu). The container relies only on `GetFocus()` and `SetFocus()`, the two `CWnd` member functions, to query the controls for focus or to change focus to another control.

Beyond this, the container isn't concerned with what control is showing activation status. It allows MFC to manage the design-time movement and sizing of ActiveX controls. You should note, though, that these features of the control containment are only available when the container is in design mode. If you change the ambient property to reflect that the control is in user mode, you'll find that your controls are immobile objects, that is, you can't move them, size them, select them, or get their property pages.

ActiveX Controls and the Document/View Architecture

ActiveX control containment and the MFC document/view architecture are completely unrelated. I mentioned using the document/view architecture because it's a convenient way to store information about the controls and their status while the user worked with the application. I also feel that such a design more accurately reflects situations where the user will actually be using dynamic creation of ActiveX controls. If you *do* decide to dynamically create ActiveX controls in some other way, though, you'll need to worry about the persistent data issues I described in the section *Serializing Control Data* earlier in this chapter. In other words, if you want your control to have the same properties and settings each time it is initialized, you should either allow the control a mechanism to serialize itself, or be prepared to set up all the properties for the control 'manually', the way you think they should be.

In my opinion, it's far more appropriate to provide the control with some storage mechanism. I reached this opinion because the control may want to serialize information that you don't know about, or can't understand. The control, also, might be updated between subsequent runs of your application. This means the control might add or remove properties, or change the way it stores the values associated with its different properties. If you're doing things the control should do for itself, you might run into compatibility problems. Finally, you'll find it faster to allow the control to manage its own data than for you to make repeated calls to the property set functions.

Showing Property Sheets

There are a couple more interesting things you can do with a control while you've got it contained in your application. If you're writing an application that does dynamic containment, you're probably interested in allowing your users to bring up the property pages of the control to directly edit the properties the control offers. This is quite a simple matter. With access to the `IUnknown` of the control, we can query for the `IOleObject` of the control. ActiveX controls always implement `DoVerb()` and handle the `OLEIVERB_PROPERTIES` verb by bringing up the property page for the control. Such code, minus the work to find the selected ActiveX control, looks like this:

```
LPUNKNOWN lpUnknown = pWnd->GetControlUnknown();
LPOLEOBJECT lpObject;

if (SUCCEEDED(lpUnknown->QueryInterface(IID_IOleObject,
                                        (void**) &lpObject)))
{
   CRect rect;
   GetWindowRect(rect);

   lpObject->DoVerb(OLEIVERB_PROPERTIES, NULL, NULL, 0, m_hWnd, rect);
   lpObject->Release();
}
```

We talked about the `DoVerb()` method in `IOleObject` back when we discussed using `COleClientItem` back in Chapter 13. You'll remember that `COleClientItem` simply wraps access to the `IOleObject` interface of objects living within a server. Here, we get the `IOleObject` interface of the control directly. ActiveX controls support all of the well-known `OLEIVERB_` constants, including `OLEIVERB_HIDE` and `OLEIVERB_SHOW`. Constants, besides `OLEIVERB_PROPERTIES`, aren't normally used by MFC containers, though, because the same functionality is exposed by normal `CWnd` member functions. Using `CWnd::ShowWindow()` is certainly easier than calling `DoVerb()` to hide or show the control window.

If you look up the documentation for `DoVerb()`, you'll note that we're avoiding most of the parameters for the function. The implementation of the `OLEIVERB_PROPERTIES` handler for ActiveX controls doesn't care about these parameters, so we just don't pass them. We *do* pass the parent window and a bounding rectangle, though – the parent window helps the application keep track of who should be active when, and the rectangle helps make sure the property page is displayed in a reasonable location on the screen.

Rules for Using Controls

Before rebuilding an application as a control container, you should make sure that your application object's `InitInstance()` member function calls `AfxEnableControlContainer()`. You'll also need to make sure you include `Afxdisp.h` in your project's `Stdafx.h` file. If you're creating a new project, you don't need to do these things; you just need to make sure you check the **ActiveX controls** checkbox in AppWizard. AppWizard will make those connections for you.

Your application does *not*, you'll note, need to enable any other sort of COM support if it uses ActiveX controls. You're free to decide on using Automation or implementing OLE container or server support on the merits of your application outside of its use of ActiveX controls. Aside from `Afxdisp.h`, you don't need to snag any other special header files to use ActiveX controls. The MFC team was very careful to try and make sure that ActiveX controls fit into the established MFC programming model relatively seamlessly.

Summary

ActiveX controls are a powerful vehicle for the reuse of code and user interface tools. Even if you weren't interested in the material in Chapter 15 and won't be writing your own ActiveX controls, the notion of using controls provided by other vendors or other developers can save you an immense amount of time in your development cycle.

17

Internet Client Programming

Over the 1990s, the computer industry has seen a surge in growth of computer-to-computer communications mechanisms. Such mechanisms are really nothing new in the industry as a whole, in that Unix computers have been operating over robust wide-area networks for tens of years. However, as more and more developers have sought to broaden this facility for the benefit of individuals and businesses alike, so this wide-area network has become global. This system of computers wired together, that is the Internet, is an autonomous network that connects the computers used by most major corporations, nearly all universities, and many individual users around the world. The Internet has actually existed, in various forms, since well before this recent commercial explosion, which has been fueled by the recent availability of cheaper high-speed connectivity. The real key to the Internet's popularity (and the reason that high-speed modems are important) is the creation of the World Wide Web. Before the web put a pretty (and somewhat easier to use) face on the Internet, normal folks didn't have much reason to care. Since the average consumer can now afford the equipment necessary to reach the Internet, numerous companies, known as Internet Service Providers (ISPs), have begun providing access to the Internet via stock telephone lines.

In today's market, many individuals gain access to the computing and data storage resources available at other sites by using a dial-up account to reach the Internet through a local ISP. The consumer makes a local phone call and connects to a bank of modems, computers and expensive high-capacity computer equipment, which allows them to reach other computers on the network in much the same way a billy goat might cross a bridge. Corporations that want to have a presence on the Internet are likely to buy the communications equipment and rent the communications lines themselves. This can afford their employees access to the resources of other companies or universities for research, product support, or peer interaction. Alternatively, the company may wish to publish information about their products and services on the Internet, so that consumers can see what is one offer and eventually be tempted to make a purchase – perhaps right online.

It turns out, though, that this onslaught of affordable hardware has made the Internet interesting to a lot more than the average consumer, or even to the marketing department of a company dying to do business with potential consumers. Since the Internet is a wide-area network that uses many well-documented standards and protocols, those protocols have become more interesting to the vendors of personal computer operating systems – companies such as Microsoft. Windows 95/98 and Windows NT all support the **TCP/IP** protocol right out of the box. TCP/IP, which stands for **Transmission Control Protocol/Internet Protocol**, provides a standardized way for computers to exchange data over a physical connection. This protocol, coupled with other mechanisms, makes it very easy for computers to share information by using the transaction-based protocols made popular by their use on the Internet. TCP/IP may also be augmented by a few **transport layer** protocols, which help it to work over non-traditional data communication layers – for instance, over a slow phone line instead of a fast Ethernet network connection.

A transport layer, by the way, is a part of a network protocol that allows your application to transmit data over the wire. Most operating systems – including Windows – implement their network connectivity with the concept of a protocol stack. The approach involves dividing the responsibilities for the implementation of the protocols the system supports among several layers. The topmost layer interfaces with the application, and provides very high-level functions. The lower layers are available to the application, but are primarily used by the higher layers to implement their own high-level functionality. One of the lowest layers of the protocol stack is the transport layer – the layer that we mentioned is the one responsible for getting bits out the network card and onto some other machine.

You can imagine that the layers are 'stacked' upon each other, and this is where the term **protocol stack** originates. Each level of the stack is independent of the implementation of the next level in the stack. The high-level protocols that we examine in this chapter are outside of the protocol stack; they are normally considered a part of the application implementation. But, since Windows provides `Wininet.dll` and MFC provides some wrapper classes, your use of the protocol enjoys a far more interesting and effective high-level interface to the protocol.

The additional high-level protocols allow users to transfer files (FTP), share authored and published formatted text and graphics (HTTP), and search for files and information (Gopher), with incredible ease. While these protocols are normally used by weekend surfers from the comforts of their homes, the rich standards allow corporate users to enjoy the benefits of the protocols. Corporate MIS departments are beginning to show a great interest in setting up **intranets** (networks that connect the computers within the organization) and using these same protocols to circulate information across the company without having to expose that information to the outside world. So, just as you might peruse the most recent hockey scores offered by your favorite sports channel, on the Internet you might, from your desk at work, connect to the corporate network and check out the latest reports from other parts of your company.

Until one of these well-known startups finally posts a few profitable quarters in a row, the corporate success of the public Internet is still a bit questionable. But the internal corporate application of these same technologies is very, very interesting. This chapter will investigate the support baked into newer versions of Microsoft Windows and MFC for these protocols. We'll discuss:

> The architecture underlying the use of Internet protocols

> The `WinInet` dynamic link-library and its supported protocols

The Smallest Pieces

Please note that it's beyond the scope of this book to discuss the actual low-level implementation and design of the protocols that are made available by these newer system features. We won't be discussing the actual bits over the wire, except where a passing knowledge of the protocol will help you write more efficient high-level code. On the upside, what we will be concentrating on is the high-level implementation, since the smallest details are actually managed for you by MFC and the Windows operating system itself.

Before we go any further, let's introduce these protocols, and frame them within our discussion. Later, we'll flesh out the details we need when we examine how to use them.

Internet connectivity for Windows applications is implemented in Windows 95/98 and Windows NT 4.0 by a DLL named `Wininet.dll`. This file implements an API that allows your machine to talk to other machines using three different Internet protocols: FTP, HTTP, and Gopher. All of these protocols have one thing in common; they follow a simple client-server model.

This flavor of client-server programming is pretty simple; it just means that a client machine, usually right in front of some fleshy human user, is asking some central machine, usually locked away in a special room, for answers to certain requests. The client machine doesn't necessarily have all the resources that the server machine does – the client machine probably has significantly less memory than the server machine, and generally doesn't have the disk space and network bandwidth that the server does. The server can concurrently answer requests from dozens or even thousands of different clients; it therefore centralizes data and/or software.

To implement any of these three protocols, the server must have the protocol software installed and running. The server software will sit about and listen to requests for information via the particular protocol, and respond to them as best it can. A given machine might be running server software for all of these protocols, just one of them, or none of them. The server machine can also be running additional server software; it's possible to have file services, printer services, database services, and all of these Internet services running on the same machine. (Of course, you might not want to do that in a production installation, because the machine will be just too busy.)

FTP

FTP stands for **F**ile **T**ransfer **P**rotocol. It's a simple protocol that allows a client machine to connect to a server machine and – you guessed it – transfer files. The administrator of the server machine has complete control over which files the client can retrieve, which directories can be saved to, and even which files the client can *see*. The protocol is secure, in the sense that the server can be configured to recognize users based on a password and user-name combination. The protocol can, however, be configured to allow anonymous communication; a user name and password need not be required for access.

As its name implies, FTP is very file-oriented. The client can send and receive entire files to or from the server, but it isn't necessarily able to perform searches, in-place writes, or appends to files that are on the server. FTP is great for *some* of the situations where you'd normally use a file server. While it's trivial to configure a file server to be accessible throughout your entire organization, it might be a little more difficult to publish that file server for the whole world (literally!) to see. It's these broad-reaching cases that make FTP appealing. On the other hand, a real file server supports seeking and locking and partial reads, while FTP doesn't.

HTTP

The World Wide Web is based on machines communicating using the **HTTP** protocol. HTTP, which stands for **HyperText Transfer Protocol**, allows client machines to easily request a single file from a server. The server provides the file and then hangs up the connection. Normally, the file that the client requests is a text file that's written in the HTML language – the **HyperText Markup Language**. This simple format allows machines to exchange formatted data, and even graphical data, very easily.

Gopher

Gopher is the most obscure of the 'big three' protocols. Gopher doesn't really stand for anything; it's not an acronym. It turns out, though, that the Gopher protocol provides an easy way to build menus of connections to different services, or different files full of data. Gopher, in a way, unites many different Internet protocols in a way that users can easily access them. The best attribute of Gophers is that they are easily searchable. Even though the user sees a hierarchical menu structure, machines that speak the Gopher protocol can traverse that hierarchy with ease.

All of these protocols are defined by **Requests for Comment** (**RFC**) documents. These documents are published on the Internet for the Internet; those interested in the technical growth of the Internet can comment on and debate the standard, and try to convince the authors that the standard should be changed. RFCs describe what really happens between two computers that speak these protocols to each other. The machines connect to each other by using some variant of the sockets protocol. Since you're using Windows, you'll end up using WinSock. We'll not examine the way sockets work specifically since they're just a part of the protocol stack which we're asking Windows to use to implement our requests. MFC asks `Wininet.dll` to handle a function, and WinInet asks WinSock to do the work. WinSock asks the operating system to have the TCP/IP protocol start talking to the wire. By the time we reach the WinSock level of the transaction, there are far too many uninteresting details; we'll ignore them, since it's more fun and more productive to rely on MFC for everything.

Usually, but not always, WinSock rides on the TCP/IP network protocol. So, by combining the rules of one of the three high-level protocols with the connection and conversation rules defined by WinSock, and the actual routing and communication rules defined by TCP/IP (or some other network transport protocol), you can actually get a request for information from Client Machine A to Server Machine B. Since all of these standards are well specified, and available on a wide variety of different platforms, it's a trivial matter to get lots of different machines hooked together on a network and cooperating.

Better still, `Wininet.dll` hides all of these details completely. By using the MFC wrappers for the features of `WinInet`, you can open something that looks very much like a `CStdioFile` but in fact represents a connection to an FTP server. You can then read from that file object as if it were a local file, even if it's actually coming from server that's amazingly remote.

The FTP and Gopher protocols supported by MFC aren't very robust or interesting. Of course, the protocols themselves aren't interesting – but they're very capable of solving problems, when applied correctly. The HTTP protocol, on the other hand, is rather robust and rather interesting; it affords more customizable, flexible and involved communication between the client and server machines. We can get away with shallow descriptions of the FTP and Gopher protocols in this chapter before we cover the MFC-provided support for each protocol in detail.

We'll also cover the MFC-provided support for HTTP-based communication in detail here – but our superficial treatment of the HTTP protocol in this chapter might not answer your questions about the proper application and extension of the protocol.

Okay, enough background. Let's have a look at some details.

The World Wide Web

Of these three protocols, the largest and most accessible is HTTP, which is the backbone of the World Wide Web. The most tangible advance in recent Internet technology, the World Wide Web has proved to be a catalyst for the Internet's explosive growth, fueled by cheaper computers and communications equipment. The Web, as it is called by authors who are paid per copy, and not per word, is simply a collection of autonomously published **pages** that contain interesting information. A web page can be as long as the author pleases, although most contain less than, say, ten kilobytes of data, but might reference much more data in the form of graphics and multimedia files.

As we learned earlier, web pages are written using a language called **Hypertext Markup Language**, or HTML for short. HTML is actually simpler than rich-text format, the Microsoft-invented format that allows word processors to exchange richly-formatted text data using a stream of plain ASCII characters. An HTML stream also contains plain-text characters and, similarly, uses **tags** to format particular blocks of that data. If I wanted some text on my web page to appear like this:

NHL: The Whalers *beat* The Bruins last night. <u>Box Score</u>

I might code this HTML:

```
<b>NHL</b>: The Whalers <I>beat</I> The Bruins last night. <a href="score.htm">Box
Score</a>
```

The tags are enclosed in angle brackets. Between the brackets lies the actual keywords or commands that make the formatting do what I want. You can guess that <b> stands for 'bold', while <I> stands for 'italic'. The real beauty of HTML, though, is not easily expressible using ink on this page – it's the provision in the language for links, indicated by the <a> tag. You can see the use of this tag in the example above. If the user were to click on the words 'Box Score' in the software they were using to read this HTML stream, then they would be 'jumped' or 'linked' to another file that's stored on the server Score.htm. Since that <a> tag doesn't contain any interesting decorations, we know that the new file resides on the same server that holds the file we're actually reading. It's quite possible, however, for the <a> tag to include both the name of a server and the name of a file on that server. You could also use slash or backslash characters to indicate that the file is stored in a different subdirectory on the same server. The target of the link might not even be an HTML page – it could be a command that has the user's browser request that the server where the page resides actually execute some program to do some very interesting work.

It's beyond the scope of this book to discuss all of the HTML tags and their uses – our examples will stick with those that are very basic. There are probably three dozen different tags, and they each can have several attributes. If you feel the urge to be very creative, you should have no problem finding a book on HTML, or even a reference made available online! I think that the actual interaction between the computers involved in retrieving and displaying a web page (the stripped-down client-server model that I mentioned before) is very pertinent to our treatment of the Internet in this chapter. With the web as our example, let's perform that examination with a little more attention than we did before.

Client-Server and the Internet

As it turns out, Internet applications are just a bold expansion of the client-server development paradigm (twenty cents). That is, when connected to the Internet, your computer acts like a client to any of tens of thousands of server computers scattered around the globe. By directing the software you're running on your client machine, you'll dictate what information you end up retrieving and what sort of searching you do.

I presented the above HTML text fragment as if it dropped out of the sky, but if you worked at Microsoft you'd be able to find that fragment of HTML on a server in my office, named rather appropriately MOOSEBOY. Now MOOSEBOY is running Windows 98, but it is also running a web server. So, if you worked at Microsoft, you could simply do plain old NET USE commands to see my server, as you would with any other computer hanging around on a network and running Microsoft software; *or*, you could use a special piece of software, called a **web browser**.

A web browser is a piece of software that the client machine runs. Generically, the software that a client computer uses to access other Internet servers is called a **client proxy**. It works on behalf of the actual human client to get some work done, so this name is quite appropriate. Specifically, though, a web browser is a program that knows how to retrieve and display HTML text. A web browser might use some snazzy graphical user interface to display formatted text, in which case the italics characters really are displayed *as italics*; but it could be running on a dumb terminal, in which case the italics characters are probably marked as flashing or inverse or underlined characters. A mixed blessing of HTML is its ability to be interpreted by the client in any way the client deems appropriate.

The web browser does its work with the server using HTTP, one of the high-level protocols I mentioned at the beginning of the chapter. HTTP rides on top of the TCP/IP protocol supported by Windows itself. HTTP specifies a way for one computer to connect arbitrarily to another machine and request information from it. The server software which, as I mentioned, runs on machines like MOOSEBOY, answers that request using the rules set up in the protocol.

HTTP is very simple – it's a text-based, targeted protocol. Your computer, when you ask it to connect to MOOSEBOY, opens a TCP/IP socket connection. MOOSEBOY then waits for your computer to make a request. Your computer can send a verb and an object – normally, a browser would send 'GET HOCKEY.HTML', for example, to get the content of a file named Hockey.html. If MOOSEBOY doesn't have a file named Hockey.html, it can return an error that's reported by your browser. The server is also likely to report the error to the user in HTML, and so it can be prettily formatted, and perhaps even contain links to places to get help with the error condition. If the server software on MOOSEBOY does find that file, on the other hand, and decides the client is allowed to receive it, then the file will be covered with a few descriptive headers and fired back to the client. The headers are also a part of the HTTP protocol, although the content of the body of that response is actually HTML.

Once your client receives that information, MOOSEBOY and your client will close their connection. Such short-lived connections are perhaps the biggest flaw of the worldwide web. If you request another page of information from MOOSEBOY, you'll have to ask your client to open another new connection, wake up MOOSEBOY, and request the information using the HTML protocol way from the beginning again.

Unfortunately, it's pretty likely that the user will make another request to the same server. The link that I mentioned, being to a file called Scores.htm in the HTML text fragment, means that the user might click on that word to retrieve another file from the same server. The client will have to resolve the address of the server again, and open the connection again — both are very expensive operations, even by themselves. If you aggressively code the client, and the server agrees to the protocol the client suggests, you can actually keep the connection open for all the repeated requests. That's by no means the default, and requires the client to go far out of its way.

The only issue left unexamined in this transaction is the actual location of MOOSEBOY and all of its files. If you worked at Microsoft, your computer would be able to find MOOSEBOY by asking a private **domain name server** to provide the network address for the machine after looking it up in a table. If you were really on the big, worldwide Internet, then you'd have to request the network address for MOOSEBOY from one of several public domain name servers. It would be my responsibility, as the administrator of MOOSEBOY, to make sure that my server was registered and available through those services. Of course, if MOOSEBOY were really on the true Internet, it would need a more interesting name; perhaps www.mooseboy.net would be good. The names given to machines within an organization only fall victim to the rules used within that organization. Rules used for naming servers on the Internet are actually governed by a bureaucratic body — and necessarily so, since machine names should be identifiable and meaningful, and certainly not allowed to collide. The server names that you're used to seeing, like www.microsoft.com or www.wrox.com, are completely interchangeable with my MOOSEBOY server for the purposes of this chapter. All the protocols work just the same whether you're on the Microsoft campus looking for hockey scores or in your living room trying to find the full text of a Shakespeare play.

No matter where you are, though, these different Internet protocols make use of a name known as a **Uniform Resource Locator**, or URL for short. A URL provides a way for you, as a user, to identify a very specific resource on some other machine. Those hockey scores, for example, might be identified by this URL:

```
http://mooseboy/boxscore.html
```

The first part of the URL, to the left of the colon, identifies the protocol to be used to retrieve the information. In this case, we're specifying HTTP; later in the chapter, we'll learn about FTP and Gopher URLs. After the double-slashes, you'll find the name of the server; and after that, you'll find a specific resource on the server. It's pretty common to see a URL without a resource name — just a server name, like this:

```
http://www.microsoft.com
```

This means that the server, when queried, is prepared to reveal the content of a default document. That default document is set by the system administrator. The server may or may not share with you the name of that document – but if you've been directed to such a URL, then you have to hope that it's going to be there!

God Is In the Details

So, we now understand that the HTTP protocol lets web browsers (or other client software) talk to web servers. The server is most likely to cough up a web page, which is usually nothing more than text formatted using the HTML language. The user asks the client to connect to a particular server, and to get a particular object from that server, using a URL.

This is how the web works – how people use HTTP. Saying that, HTTP does run a little bit deeper. The request that the client software sends to the server, and the server's response, both include headers that describe, or more accurately specify, that request or response. The real art of using HTTP lies in manipulating those details to fit exactly the situation that you're trying to solve. Let's investigate how HTTP works, so we can learn to understand its implementation – and, from there, let's work on the classes that MFC uses to let your application speak HTTP with the rest of the world.

See for Yourself

The HTTP protocol, and all the other protocols which we're discussing here, are text-based conversational protocols. This means that you can, if you want, start Telnet on your computer, and put yourself in the driver's seat. Normally, Telnet is used to work with another computer over the Internet as if you were connected to that machine with a dumb terminal. But, by asking Telnet to use a different **port number** on the server, you can wake up the server that answers a specific protocol. (Telnet comes with Windows 95/98 and all versions of Windows NT.)

You can try this out using Telnet yourself. The port number that HTTP servers use is normally 80; the administrator can configure the server software to use a different number – some use 8000, 88, or 8080. The most common reason for using a different port number is to separate the load of running the server software. If you connect to MOOSEBOY at port 80 to get real work done, you might connect to MOOSEBOY at port 8080 to play games or chat with other users. And maybe MOOSEBOY redirects requests for port 8080 to another physical machine that isn't quite as busy.

A port number is roughly analogous to a channel number. If the server named MOOSEBOY is running, it might have software that's listening for calls to come on a particular port number, for example. It might try to answer HTTP requests on port number 80, and HTTPS requests on port number 443. If MOOSEBOY doesn't have any FTP software running, it won't be listening to port 21 – so any client program that tries to start an FTP conversation on the standard FTP port won't receive an answer – and it'll be up to the client to realize that nobody's listening.

If you connect to your network (or to your Internet service provider), you might start Telnet and specify the port number you want at the appropriate place in the login dialog. Then, just type:

```
GET FILENAME.HTML HTTP/1.0
```

where `FILENAME.HTML` is really the name of an HTML file you know to exist on the server. You might not see any characters echoed back as you type; most servers don't provide this courtesy because they're used to talking to other machines rather than humans. The request is case sensitive — `GET` and `HTTP` must be in uppercase, and the name of the object you wish to receive must match the case as stored on the server. After the 0 at the end of the line, you'll need to press *Enter* twice so that the server knows your request consists only of this item. You'll see `TELNET` spit back the results of your request; it might be an error, if you incorrectly typed something. Or, it might be the HTTP-supplied header for your response followed by the actual content of the file. You could use the `HEAD` verb, if you wanted, in order to retrieve the headers that the server would normally use to describe the object.

The request you've typed has no headers in it, although you do get headers returned from the server. You can get more headers by claiming to specify a more advanced version of HTTP than 1.0; if you typed `HTTP/2.0` at the end of your request, the server might respond differently. If the server doesn't understand HTTP version 2.0, then you'll get an error message; if it *does* support HTTP 2.0, then you'll probably get some different headers.

All of this information flying back and forth is what's happening between the two machines when you use your browser to read the web. The headers, though, are very interesting.

In the reply, the server almost always tells you two important pieces of information; the length of the content that's about to follow, and the format of that content. The `Content-Length` header is simply followed by a number of bytes. The format of the content identifies the way the data is coming back to you. Normally, the `Content-Type` header will specify `text/html`, meaning that the data is plain text and is formatted as HTML. If you request an image, though, you might get `image/jpeg` back.

In the request, you can specify the content type that you want to receive. It makes no sense for the server to send you back a 400 kilobyte picture if your program isn't capable of handling pictures, right?

HTTP Transactions

Anything that happens on the web follows the transaction model that we've just examined. The client sends some request, which consists of a verb, an object, and some optional headers describing the request. The server sends back a response — which includes a result code to let the client know if the server was generally successful with the request or not. Let's take a look at some examples, just so you can be sure what we're talking about.

Within the book, it hasn't been the norm that we need to do this, but these HTTP fragments will include {cr} and {lf} to indicate that we're sending carriage returns and line feeds. With that in mind, say the client connects to a server and sends:

```
GET motorcycles.html HTTP/1.0{cr}{lf}
{cr}{lf}
```

but it turns out that the server's page about motorcycles is really spelled correctly. Since the server can't fulfill this request, it'll send back a pretty simple response to make sure the client knows that:

```
HTTP/1.0 404 Object Not Found{cr}{lf}
Content-Type: text/html{cr}{lf}
{cr}{lf}
<body><h1>HTTP/1.0 404 Object Not Found{cr}{lf}
</h1></body>{cr}{lf}
{cr}{lf}
```

And that's all. The header contains a response code: 404. That number indicates an error within the HTTP protocol; 404 means that the requested object was not found. The rest of the header is of the form:

```
<fieldname> : <value>{cr}{lf}
```

That is, there are one or more well-defined field-names followed by a colon and then a value for that field. When the value is completely specified, a carriage-return and line feed are added to the end the line. Here, the server has given us only one header – a field called Content-Type that tells us what sort of data the server will be sending in the body of the response. There are about fifteen different response header fields that are currently defined by HTTP, but only three are common and important. They are Content-Type, Content-Length, and Last-Modified.

Content-Type, as we described for the request, provides a syntax for describing what sort type and formats of data your client can accept from the server. Content-Type turns out to specify a format for the content – it identifies the type of the sent object. The tag might have the value text/html, for example, if the response was textual HTML. If the object were actually an image, the field might contain image/jpeg or image/gif. The receiving program needs to recognize and use this information to learn how to decode and use the response.

The client program can let the server know beforehand what it wants by sending an Accept: *field (we'll examine the* Accept: *request field a bit later in the chapter).*

The value for this field is a combination of type and format. Since you might accept more than one type, the header tells you which type and format were actually sent.

The values you can use in the content-type and accept – headers are all **MIME types**. MIME stands for Multipurpose Internet Mail Extension. As the name implies, the types were originally used to indicate the type of data that would accompany a bit of Internet mail if it contained binary data.

There are tens of dozens of MIME types, and more are being added all the time. The most common is, obviously, text/html, which means the content is just HTML text. You can send text/plain if you don't include any HTML tags. When you encounter a graphic, it'll probably be either image/jpeg or image/gif, depending on which of the two common formats was used to encode and compress it.

Content-Length can be present to indicate that the server will be sending a great deal of data. The value that follows this tag is simply an integer describing the number of bytes to be sent in the response. However, most servers simply send the data without this header and let the client know that the data is done when the stream ends.

`Last-Modified` lets the client know the last modification date and time of the object which was requested. The value here is just a date.

> *My description of these details is intentionally brief. The HTTP standard is a very deep subject, and it wouldn't be hard to write almost a whole book on HTTP itself. I think I've provided enough information to make you dangerous, but if you need more details, you can get them from the World Wide Web Consortium's web page at* `http://www.w3.org`. *Start off with the oldest, simplest version of the specification you can find. As you try to learn the standard, it's imperative that you don't overwhelm yourself with esoteric details that aren't implemented by most servers.*

The `HEAD` method is interesting because it returns headers that describe a particular object on the server without returning the whole object. If you go to the Microsoft web site, you can (at least, today, anyway) find the copyright message that covers the whole site at the URL `http://www.microsoft.com/MISC/CPYRIGHT.HTM`. You can imagine that three or four dozen of the company's best lawyers worked day and night on this, and it's pretty big. But you might not even know if you want to download the whole thing. You could connect to `www.microsoft.com` and issue this request:

```
HEAD /MISC/CPYRIGHT.HTM HTTP/1.0{cr}{lf}
{cr}{lf}
```

Note that there's nothing wrong with specifying the path to the object – since there's no sense of a current directory in HTTP, you'll have to specify all the path information every time you make a request. But my point is that we used the `HEAD` method this time, and that results in a very terse reply:

```
HTTP/1.0 200 OK{cr}{lf}
Date: Sun, 25 Jul 1999 01:23:24 GMT{cr}{lf}
Server: Microsoft-Internet-Information-Server/1.0{cr}{lf}
Content-Type: text/html{cr}{lf}
Last-Modified: Mon, 19 Jul 1999 20:20:26 GMT{cr}{lf}
Content-Length: 8853{cr}{lf}
```

This is just great – we've requested a lot of information about the copyright for the Microsoft web site, and we didn't have to read a lick of legalese! There are lots more header fields here than in our previous request, so let's examine them individually.

The big difference is that the object I requested this time really does exist. As a result, we got the status code of `200`, which means that the request was just fine and our data follows. The `Server:` field lets us know what server software is running over at `www.microsoft.com`; it shouldn't come as any surprise that the folks there are using Microsoft Internet Information Server. The content type of the page is `text/html`, which means we'd probably be able print it in this book and make sense of it as humans – assuming we understood at least a little bit of the HTML. If the response said the `Content-Type` was `image/jpeg`, for example, we'd expect that the object was a boatload of binary data that could be decompressed and eventually displayed to the user.

The `Date:` field tells us when the response was actually sent. (I guess you now know how I spend my Saturday evenings.) The presence of this field, which at first blush seems rather superfluous, brings us to an interesting point. I've been assuming through this chapter that the client is just walking up to the server and talking to it. That does happen, but far more often, the client actually asks a proxy server to go and perform its work. Servers are often hidden behind firewalls, as well. As a result, the flow of information (and the content of requests and responses) can sometimes change. The `Date:` header field seems like it might be useless for the typical client, unless you wanted to set the time on your machine based on the time at `microsoft.com`, I guess. But its presence is important for any of the stops along the way – the proxy might use that field to decide when to cache and when not to cache the response, and the firewall might parse the date for a similar reason.

The `Last-Modified:` field tells us the last time the object was actually changed. By comparing the above `Last-Modified:` field to the `Date:` field, you can surmise that the lawyers haven't done much in the past week. If this field is present, a browser might use it to avoid getting information from servers when it already has that information. With what we've learned about HTTP so far, you might assume that most browsers use an algorithm something like this to manage their cache:

```
if (we have this item in the cache)
   get headers for the item
   if (is there a Last-modified field?)
      if (is the Last-modified field newer than the cache?)
         actually get the whole item
      endif
   endif
else
   actually get the whole item
endif
```

The `Content-Length:` field says that there are 8853 bytes in the copyright message. We only retrieved the header, so the actual content of the copyright message would have to be retrieved with a second request using the `GET` method.

In the following section, we'll talk about the functions that MFC provides for you to create and populate requests, and to read and parse responses.

Internet Clients and MFC

The Internet is made up of lots of computers that talk to each other. As we've learned in the earlier section, one of the protocols which allow these computers to communicate is TCP/IP. Upon TCP/IP lie some more protocols – HTTP, FTP, and Gopher. These protocols let a client machine talk to server machines to send or receive information. All of these protocols are quite simple – they involve two computers using text-based commands to get and transfer information from one another.

While the text-based mechanism that enables this communication is quite simple, the underlying protocols are not, generally, very easy to implement. HTTP, as we've learned, is used to exchange web pages, and provides lots of surprisingly detailed semantics – many of which are required to provide even a remotely robust implementation of a browser or some other client software.

You might initially think that these protocols are only useful for interactive situations. You might use your computer to run the FTP program to send a file to your friend, for example, or use a browser program to 'surf' the web in order to find a bargain on a used sports car. But it turns out that programming these interfaces is very, very interesting. You might want to write a program which lets people search a database on your server of used cars that are for sale, or you might want to have one of your applications automatically transfer log files to a central server.

Since Microsoft realizes that many developers would love to make use of these protocols without reinventing the implementation of the underlying protocols, they've provided a DLL as an operating system extension to facilitate transfers with such protocols. The DLL, called `Wininet.dll`, is made available with Microsoft's Internet Explorer. Unfortunately, the only way to redistribute `Wininet.dll` is to have your customers install IE. Starting in MFC version 4.2, several classes have been provided to facilitate using the features of this DLL.

Using WinInet APIs with MFC

`Wininet.dll` forces the notion of a session on anyone who uses the DLL. A session is really nothing more than a connection between your application and the DLL. It provides your application with the ability to initialize and load the DLL, and affords the DLL a chance to get itself initialized and connected with the rest of the operating system. Your application, if it uses `Wininet.dll`, must manage at least one session.

In an MFC application, a `Wininet.dll` is represented by a `CInternetSession` object. That object can be constructed just before you need to start using the Internet protocols, or it can be constructed just as your application loads. `CInternetSession` lets you tell `Wininet.dll` exactly how you intend to connect to the Internet. If you need to connect to the Internet a couple of different ways from the same application, you'll need to create a couple of different `CInternetSession` objects and initialize them appropriately.

`CInternetSession` has a single, simple constructor:

```
CInternetSession( LPCTSTR pstrAgent = NULL,
                  DWORD dwContext = 1,
                  DWORD dwAccessType = INTERNET_OPEN_TYPE_PRECONFIG,
                  LPCTSTR pstrProxyName = NULL,
                  LPCTSTR pstrProxyBypass = NULL,
                  DWORD dwFlags = 0);
```

Since there are default values for all parameters, you can use a default constructor for your `CInternetSession` objects in many situations. The first parameter is a pointer to the name of your client-agent software. Many protocols – most notably, HTTP – send this string as a part of requests that identify your software to the machines you connect to. That name will show up in logs and maybe on the site administrator's desk some day, so you should make sure that you identify yourself responsibly. The default value of `NULL` will cause the constructor to run off and find your application's name via a call to `AfxGetAppName()`. The string that's returned from this API (that is, whatever string is in your `CWinApp` object's `m_pstrAppName` member) will be used to identify your software to the machines you talk to.

The dwAccessType parameter tells WinInet how you plan to connect to the Internet. The default value for this parameter, INTERNET_OPEN_TYPE_PRECONFIG, tells WinInet to look around in the registry for previously entered information on connecting to the Internet. The registry, on most machines, will contain information entered by the user via the Internet Setup Wizard or changed via the Internet icon in the Control Panel. If you know the machine is on the Internet directly – that is, the machine is connected via a physical, omnipresent link to an Internet backbone, then you can specify INTERENT_OPEN_TYPE_DIRECT. This setting is also appropriate if you'll be using an intranet, which is, as we outlined earlier, a collection of machines within an organization that uses the Internet protocols. You can specify GATEWAY_INTERNET_ACCESS if you need to bounce your Internet requests through a firewall, or INTERNET_OPEN_TYPE_PROXY if you are going to send your requests to the Internet via a proxy. GATEWAY_INTERNET_ACCESS causes the Windows Internet API to look for a gateway address in your TCP/IP configuration; you can adjust the list of gateways that you use by way of the network configuration dialog box in Control Panel.

CERN proxies require extra login information to make sure your connection works as you expect. If you don't specify INTERNET_OPEN_TYPE_PROXY, you can specify the pstrProxyName and pstrProxyBypass parameters as NULL. If you're using a CERN proxy, though, you'll certainly want to specify the name of the proxy with the pstrProxyName parameter. Additionally, you'll most likely want to specify a list of servers which you know are local. You can specify a pointer to a space-delimited list of dotted-quad addresses (that is, addresses of the form *m.n.k.j*, such as 127.0.0.1 or 157.101.103.155) as the pstrProxyBypass parameter. Connection requests to those addresses won't be made via the proxy; instead, they'll proceed directly to the address in question. If you do ask for INTERNET_OPEN_TYPE_PROXY, and pass a NULL for pstrProxyBypass, the WinINet API will try to use a list of bypassed addresses from the registry.

All the dwFlags which we've talked about are mutually exclusive. So, if your application needs to make some connections via a proxy and other connections directly, you shouldn't hesitate to create one CInternetSession object for each bunch of connections you plan to make. You can make multiple connections of the same flavor using a single CInternetSession; we'll investigate the creation of actual connections a bit later.

You can influence your connection in a few other ways by using the dwFlags parameter. These flags are, indeed, mutually inclusive, and they can be combined using the bitwise-OR operator. Here's the list of flags acceptable to the CInternetSession constructor, and what they mean to you:

Flag	Meaning
INTERNET_FLAG_ASYNC	This session will support asynchronous operations
INTERNET_FLAG_EXISTING_CONNECT	Try to reuse existing connections throughout the session

There are a few other flag values that can modify other objects in the MFC client-side Internet class hierarchy, and we'll describe them along with the functions to which they apply.

One issue that I should point out immediately. While MFC supports INTERNET_FLAG_ASYNC, you may not want to use it. Asynchronous downloads and connections, as implemented by WinInet, are asynchronous in *every* detail. If you request a connection to a server, the call that gets the connection actually returns to you long before the server has even been found on the network. You have to wait until WinInet calls you back to provide you with a handle before you can actually go and use that handle. And that's true for every level of the APIs. As such, the application of this technique is certainly nontrivial, and actually beneficial in only a few types of applications.

As usual, I've left the most involved parameter for last – dwContext. Talking to other computers on the Internet can take a long time. Some of the protocols induce a lot of overhead, and users of Internet applications often have connections over very slow links – like asynchronous analog modems over plain phone lines. As such, it's important in many applications to let the user know what progress you're making. The Windows Internet API provides for the use of callbacks to allow your application to know when some progress is made. The dwContext parameter simply allows you to identify each of the operations your application is working on, so that your progress handling function knows which operation is getting what work done.

MFC, of course, doesn't make you worry about anything as messy as a callback function; you can just derive your own class from CInternetSession and override the OnStatusCallback() function. You'll also need to let the system know that you want to receive status callbacks by calling the EnableStatusCallback() function on your CInternetSession-derived object. EnableStatusCallback() takes a single parameter, which defaults to TRUE. If TRUE, the parameter means the function will enable callbacks. If FALSE, the parameter will disable callbacks.

File Temple Pilots

The FTP protocol is probably the easiest Internet protocol to understand, so let's examine it first. (Meanwhile, the Stone Temple Pilots were a grunge rock band – you can examine their material on your own time.) 'FTP' stands for 'File Transfer Protocol'. This protocol allows any computer, as a client, to connect to any other computer that acts as a server of the FTP protocol. The client computer can request files – the server will send them to the client upon demand.

It's really not worth dissecting the inner workings of the FTP protocol, mainly because the protocol isn't at all extensible and, additionally, because it's pretty simple to begin with. Suffice to say the protocol is implemented by extra software for both the client and the server. The server must be running that software in order to answer requests from the client. The client software is provided by the Wininet.dll and is usable by the MFC classes we'll describe here – or by the Windows Internet API directly.

A server running the FTP protocol can implement any security it sees fit; if it doesn't like the user name and password sent by the client, it can deny the connection. It can also use the user name and password to decide which files the client is allowed to download – and the FTP server certainly doesn't have to expose all of the files it stores. MFC doesn't implement the server side of the FTP protocol, so the details of what goes on at the server are beyond the scope of this book; you should refer to the documentation for your server software or directly to the specification of the FTP protocol.

The FTP protocol is normally engaged by users who use a program named ftp from the command line. Usually, this program is found on Unix machines where the FTP protocol has its origins. However, Windows NT and Windows 95/98 also provide such a program. You can use the FTP protocol from your programs to exchange data between your programs and servers inside or outside of your company. Working with an FTP server is just like working with any other file system; there are files and directories. When you connect to an FTP server, you're at the server's root. You can change directories to go deeper, and you can enumerate files in any given directory. You can create and remove directories, and create, write to, read from, delete, or rename files.

The FTP protocol has *nothing* to do with the network operating system's ability to share files. FTP is its own protocol, and the beauty of it is that it is operating-system-independent; as such, FTP lets machines that are running very different operating systems move files around to each other. All of the Internet protocols we discuss in this chapter are implemented by a variety of machines using software from a large group of different vendors. I keep a machine running in my office that offers plain old Windows networking shares, publishes files via the FTP protocol, listens to, and responds to HTTP requests, and is even running a SQL Server. Aside from answering prompts (and, I guess, finding the darn CD in the first place), enlisting this machine into such diverse service didn't really involve any work at all.

Once you've opened your CInternetSession, you can create a CFtpConnection object by calling the GetFtpConnection() member of the CInternetSession object. GetFtpConnection() returns a pointer to that new CFtpConnection; you must use the delete operator on that pointer yourself when you're done with the FTP connection object.

The parameters for GetFtpConnection() look like this:

```
CFtpConnection* GetFtpConnection( LPCTSTR pstrServer,
                        LPCTSTR pstrUserName = NULL,
                        LPCTSTR pstrPassword = NULL,
                        INTERNET_PORT nPort = INTERNET_INVALID_PORT_NUMBER,
                        BOOL bPassive = FALSE );
```

The first parameter is the only one that's required; it specifies the name of the server you'd like to connect to. If you're surfing the net, you might specify "ftp.microsoft.com" to connect to a server at Microsoft that contains sample programs, updated drivers, technical specifications, and white papers. If you're on the intranet at the company where you work, you might name a server you've set up on your network. You can also specify a dotted-quad address if you don't know the normal name of the server; for example, you might specify the string "125.13.187.21" to connect to some server you've never tried to connect to and which probably doesn't actually exist.

The pstrUserName and pstrPassword parameters indicate what user name and password you'll use with your connection. If you pass the default value of NULL for these parameters, Windows will provide the server with the user name anonymous and an address equal to your mail address; for me, it would be mikeblas@msn.com. This is a very common way to get guest access to an FTP server. You're allowed to connect, but if you cause a problem at the site, the administrator of the site has your email address and can send you a note to ask just who the heck you think you are. If you're going to connect to a carefully secured server, you'll have to specify a real user name and password for these parameters to work on the target server.

A Friend in Every Port Number

The nPort parameter defaults to INTERNET_INVALID_PORT_NUMBER, which tells the system to use the default TCP/IP port number for this protocol. A server, no matter what protocol it's running, 'listens' for connections on certain port numbers. By convention, different protocols listen on different port numbers. This is a very convenient way to allow a single server to manage different protocols. This table shows the default port numbers for the various protocols supported by MFC and Windows. The port most typically assigned to a server of a particular protocol is called it's **well-known port**.

Protocol	Port number
HTTP	80
FTP	21
Gopher	70
HTTPS	443

If you specify INTERNET_INVALID_PORT_NUMBER, Windows will use the standard protocol number indicated in that table. If your server provides one of these protocols on another port number, you may wish to specify that number with the nPort parameter. (If you're familiar with the workings of the FTP protocol, you might be in a panic because you know that FTP actually uses two port numbers. One port is used to control the transfer of files and the other to transfer the data requested. nPort specifies the control port number, and Wininet.dll resolves the data port for itself.)

Taking Exception

Connecting to an FTP server is just as easy as asking your CInternetSession object to create a new CFtpConnection object for you. Your call to GetFtpConnection() may throw a CInternetException if something goes wrong, so you should bracket your call in a try/catch block. Generally, that might look like this:

```
CInternetSession sess;
CFtpConnection* pFTPSite = NULL;

try
{
    pFTPSite = sess.GetFtpConnection("ftp.microsoft.com");
    // work with the connection!
    pFTPSite->Close();
}
catch (CInternetException* pEx)
{
    pEx->ReportError(MB_ICONEXCLAMATION);
    pFTPSite = NULL;
    pEx->Delete();
}
delete pFTPSite;  // all done!
```

Remember that `CInternetException`, like all good `CException`-derived classes, has a way of retrieving error text from the operating system to describe the problem at hand. I used `ReportError()`, above, but `GetErrorMessage()` would also work. You can read up on these `CException` functions back in Chapter 9. The most important member of `CInternetException` is `m_dwError`; it is set to a code which you can compare against numerous constants defined in `Wininet.h` (and described in the online help) to decide exactly what happened and see if you can recover. Otherwise, you're probably best off telling the user or dumping the information to a log file.

I explicitly delete the pointer to my `CFtpConnection` object; this is safe because the C++ language assures us that calling `delete` against a `NULL` pointer is safe. If the connection *was* made and the object does exist, its destructor will run and shut down the connection. This scenario could come to pass, in the above fragment, if some code that actually works with the connection throws an exception. Explicitly closing the connection, though, shows good programming form.

Working with an FTP Connection

Given an FTP connection, you can perform lots of neat operations. `CFtpConnection` has several members that can do almost anything with the files on the other side of the connection.

You can call `CFtpConnection::GetCurrentDirectory()` to retrieve the current directory on the FTP machine, or call `CFtpConnection::SetCurrentDirectory()` to set the current directory on the other side of the connection. Obviously, these calls are useful for the navigation of the directory structure on the remote machine. If you don't like the directory structure on the remote machine, you can call `CreateDirectory()` to add a new directory, or call `RemoveDirectory()` to delete a directory from the remote machine, assuming you have the permission to do this.

You can directly copy a file from your machine to the FTP server, or from the FTP server to your machine, by using one of these functions:

```
CFtpConnection::GetFile( LPCTSTR pstrRemoteFile,
                         LPCTSTR pstrLocalFile,
                         BOOL bFailIfExists = TRUE,
                         DWORD dwAttributes = FILE_ATTRIBUTE_NORMAL,
                         DWORD dwFlags = FTP_TRANSFER_TYPE_BINARY,
                         DWORD dwContext = 1);

CFtpConnection::PutFile( LPCTSTR pstrLocalFile,
                         LPCTSTR pstrRemoteFile,
                         DWORD dwFlags = FTP_TRANSFER_TYPE_BINARY,
                         DWORD dwContext = 1);
```

The `pstrLocalFile` path that you specify to the function is relative to the current directory for your process. If you want, you can specify an absolute path in the parameter. Similar rules apply to the `pstrRemoteFile` parameter; the path you specify is relative to the current directory for this connection, but you're free to specify a relative or absolute path.

The `dwAttributes` parameter sent to `GetFile()` allows you to provide a set of file attributes for the file that's created on the local machine after the copy operation. You might specify `FILE_ATTRIBUTE_READONLY`, for example, if you want to make sure the file can't be erased. A full list of file attributes is available with our description of the `CFileFind` class.

The only truly interesting flags that can be given to both functions via their dwFlags parameters are FTP_TRANSFER_TYPE_BINARY and FTP_TRANSFER_TYPE_ASCII. These flags are necessary because they change the semantics used by the FTP protocol to correctly transmit out-of-bounds data over a connection that might not be capable of handling raw binary files. Note that the term 'binary' refers to 8-bit bytes and 'ASCII' to 7-bit bytes.

You can remove a file from the remote machine by calling Remove(); calling Rename() allows you to rename a file on the remote system.

By far the most interesting call you can make, however, is OpenFile(). The prototype for OpenFile() looks like this:

```
CInternetFile* OpenFile( LPCTSTR pstrFileName,
                         DWORD dwAccess = GENERIC_READ,
                         DWORD dwFlags = FTP_TRANSFER_TYPE_BINARY,
                         DWORD dwContext = 1 );
```

This function returns a pointer to a new CInternetFile object that allows you to read from or write to a file on the remote machine. If you need write access to the file, you can specify GENERIC_WRITE for the dwAccess parameter. dwFlags, as it did with the GetFile() and PutFile() functions, requires you to specify whether the file you're opening is binary or textual. For the sake of these APIs, "textual" just means that the data could be read line-by-line and doesn't contain any null characters.

If you know you'd like to call OpenFile(), but realize that you don't have a file name to open, you can use CFtpFileFind – which we examine a bit later in this chapter.

Since the CInternetFile object you receive derives from CStdioFile, you already know how to use it. You must remember, however, to call Close() on the file, and also to delete the newly allocated object that you received from the call.

Browsing the Web

CFtpConnection has two more siblings in the MFC hierarchy: CHttpConnection and CGopherConnection. CHttpConnection allows you to connect to a web server; that is, you can run off to a site and issue HTTP requests. I discussed HTTP and HTML back at the beginning of the chapter when I introduced the notion of writing a web server extension. This time, though, we're at the client end of the process.

CHttpConnection is very similar to CFtpConnection in that it allows you to connect to a server and get some work done. HTTP connections, though, generally enjoy a much shorter life than connections to FTP servers. HTTP is a transaction-oriented protocol, which means that the client will normally connect to the server, ask for something, and then close the connection. The request is for a method of a particular object – you might GET a file by name, for example; or POST a particular request. GET and POST are the two most common methods. Most servers support HEAD. The object of the request is simply the name of the object on the server that you're requesting. You'll notice that most Microsoft documentation refers to the method as a **verb**.

Normally, a web browser will make requests of a server by using the GET method. If you fire up your favorite browser and tell it to go to the web site at www.wrox.com, your client software will connect to the server and use the GET method to request an empty object name. That empty object name is special – the server sees that the request is empty and returns whatever default object the site administrator has defined. If you ask a browser to get a more detailed URL, say, www.wrox.com/professional.html, the object won't be empty; it will be the name professional.html.

GET asks the server to return the whole object and a bunch of headers describing it. On the other hand, the HEAD method (if the server supports it), asks the server to return only the headers describing that requested object – which we illustrated earlier on in this chapter. POST gets both the headers and an object, but it's usually used to give more information from the client to the server. While your favorite web browser will normally use GET to request pages you navigate to, it will usually use the POST method when, for instance, you return the content of a form to the server.

CHttpConnection is responsible for managing the connection between you and the server. You can open a new CHttpConnection by using the GetHttpConnection() member of CInternetSession. GetHttpConnection() takes several parameters:

```
CHttpConnection* GetHttpConnection( LPCTSTR pstrServer,
                    INTERNET_PORT nPort = INTERNET_INVALID_PORT_NUMBER,
                    LPCTSTR pstrUserName = NULL,
                    LPCTSTR pstrPassword = NULL);
```

The pstrServer parameter is simply a pointer to a string identifying the server where you'd like to go looking for web pages. The nPort parameter is similar to the nPort parameter for GetFtpConnection(); the default value of INTERNET_INVALID_PORT_NUMBER means that MFC will try to use the default port number for the HTTP protocol. pstrUserName and pstrPassword together provide a user name and password that you might need to gain access to the site if it is secured.

If the call works, you'll get a pointer to a useful CHttpConnection object. If something goes wrong, the function will throw a CInternetException object. Again, remember that the CInternetException object you get tells you what the problem really was; if you ask for a server that doesn't exist, you'll get error codes and error text in that CInternetException object, which will readily identify the problem. It's up to you to utilize that information appropriately in your application.

The connection object, just like CFtpConnection, is intended to resemble only your connection to the server. Given a valid CHttpConnection object, you're probably ready to fire off a request to that particular HTTP server. Doing so is a two-step process. First, you'll need to call OpenRequest() against that CHttpConnection object. This does nothing more than prepare the API for the request you want to make, but it does return you a new CHttpFile-derived object which can be used to access any object that you open on the other end of the connection.

You can tailor the request very carefully, or you can fire it off without any extra work, by calling the SendRequest() member of the CHttpFile object. Whichever path you take, though, the file will not retrieve any data and will not give meaningful results to Read() or ReadString() calls until you have successfully sent the request. CHttpFile derives from CStdioFile. Since, as an MFC programmer, you're already familiar with CStdioFile, you're ready to use CHttpFile to get some work done.

Stripped to its bare minimum (but leaving behind just a little error cleanup code), hitting a web server looks like this:

```
CInternetSession sess;
CHttpConnection* pHttpConenct = NULL;
CHttpFile* pFile = NULL;

try
{
    pHttpConnect = sess.GetHttpConnection("www.wrox.com");
    pFile = pHttpConnect->OpenRequest(CHttpConnection::HTTP_VERB_GET, "/");
    pFile->SendRequest();
    // ready to test for success
}
catch (CInternetException* pEx)
{
    pEx->ReportError();
    pEx->Delete();
}

if (pFile != NULL)
    delete pFile;
pFile = NULL;
if (pHttpConnect != NULL)
    delete pHttpConnect;
```

To keep the example simple, you can see that I've hardcoded the name of www.wrox.com for the name of the server. The second parameter to OpenRequest() is the name of the object on that server that I want to retrieve. Since the string I pass contains only a single forward slash, OpenRequest() knows that we just want to get the default page from www.wrox.com. The first parameter is a symbol defined in an enum inside CHttpConnection. That parameter specifies the verb that I want to use in the request. The above code fragment gets me to the same page where I would have arrived, had I walked up to my favorite browser and asked for http://www.wrox.com/. Parsing URLs is an art; to behave like a browser (or to simply get what it is you want) requires a surprisingly deep understanding of the protocol. For now, let's concentrate on how the protocol works. The details of URLs are described in the section on 'Addressing', later in this chapter.

You'll also notice that the example handles exceptions. Whether an exception is thrown or not, we'll end up deleting the objects we have. If an exception is thrown, the pointers to our objects are likely to not be initialized since it was likely the function that would've allocated them that threw the exception. If the object has actually been allocated, we can certainly call Close() on it.

As we explained earlier, you might use the methods GET, POST or HEAD when making a request. The code fragment above is all that's required to get a very minimal request sent off to the server. The verb you should choose depends on what you need to do:

Verb	Action
HTTP_VERB_GET	Request the full content of an object on the server
HTTP_VERB_POST	Post a new object linked to a particular object
HTTP_VERB_HEAD	Request only the header associated with an object on the server
HTTP_VERB_PUT	Put new content into an existing object on the server
HTTP_VERB_LINK	Associate a new response header with an object on the server
HTTP_VERB_DELETE	Remove an object from the server
HTTP_VERB_UNLINK	Remove additional response header information from an object on the server

By and large, most HTTP servers implement the POST, HEAD, and GET methods. They don't implement the other methods, because their standardization is weak. While most servers agree on the way to respond to these verbs when they don't implement them, servers that implement those other verbs do so in a very inconsistent manner! For example, the HTTP standard doesn't say much about which connections have permission to perform what verbs on what objects on the server. This ambiguity leads to great disarray. As such, if you think you need to use one of these extra verbs, you're probably best off investigating the documentation that came with your server to learn exactly how it is supported and exactly what it does.

If you're working against a custom or advanced server, you can specify a string as the first parameter to a different override of this function.

The code above doesn't send any extra header fields. It would be semantically equivalent to connecting to www.wrox.com and sending this request:

```
GET / HTTP/1.0{cr}{lf}
{cr}{lf}
```

The request is only sent with the call to CHttpFile::SendRequest(). If we wanted to add some headers before sending the request, we could call CHttpFile::AddHeaders() to do so. AddHeaders() accepts a string that identifies one single header or a list of headers. Therefore, coding the following:

```
pFile->AddRequestHeaders("Accept: text/*\r\nAccept-Language: en\r\n");
pFile->AddRequestHeaders("User-Agent: Mike's-Sample\r\n");
```

would result in three headers being sent in the request. The most commonly implemented version of HTTP, Version 1.0, defines about ten different headers. As with the headers on the response side, which we visited previously, I'm only going to describe a few of the more common and interesting headers. You can refer to the standards document, or the documentation for your server, to learn about the details.

`User-Agent:` is by no means required, but I would strongly encourage you to use it as you begin working with the `WinInet` classes. `User-Agent:` identifies your request as coming from a particular piece of software. If you make sure that your requests are decorated with this field, server administrators can see who you are and what you're doing. This is particularly important when you're doing development, since during this stage, your application is likely to go crazy and make the server sick. Even in production, having reliable `User-Agent:` information can help you with the diagnosis of server problems.

The `Accept:` field tells the server that we're only interested in accepting data of a certain form and format. We examined the `Content-Type:` response header earlier in the chapter, and `Accept:` is its request header counterpart. Here, I've specified `text/*`, which means I'll take anything as long as it's formatted as text. I might only be interested in pictures or sounds, or certain kinds of pictures and certain kinds of sounds; if so, I might specify `sound/*`. Your software can use the `Accept:` field to specify to the server what interests it. If the server has an object for the request, but can't meet the formatting request specified by the client's `Accept:` header, it will return a different error (`HTTP_STATUS_NONE_ACCEPTABLE`, which is 406) that's discernable from a plain old "not found" error (which would be `HTTP_STATUS_NOT_FOUND`, or 404).

The `Accept-Language:` field is very similar in format to `Accept:`. Since I got straight D's in French at high school, I specify `en` for English in the Accept-Language headers that I send. If I faired better in French, I might send `fr` to indicate that I wouldn't mind receiving the object in the French language. The HTTP standard explains that the formatting for this field is pretty robust. I can specify that I'd take French if nothing else was available, or specify an order of preference for different languages that *are* available. While most web page administrators won't translate their pages to different languages and make them available, the mechanism for doing so *is* available which can be put to good use by multinational corporations, for example.

Once you've created a `CHttpFile` object with a call to `OpenRequest()`, and called `AddRequestHeaders()` to adjust the headers to your liking, you can fire the request off with `SendRequest()`. This call pumps out the request and gets an answer from the server.

Handling Returned Information

`SendRequest()` returns `TRUE` if the request was sent and a response was successfully received, or it will throw an exception if the request could not be successfully dispatched. If this function returns without throwing an exception, your query was sent and answered by the server. But this doesn't necessarily mean that you get what you asked for. Your query could have crashed the server, which subsequently recovered and sent an error message back. If anything comes back to you, then your query was successful — even if it is a description of a server-side error.

You can actually get the status information from your query, for example the value of 200 for 'OK' status, that we saw before, or 404 for a 'not found' result. If the server really *did* crash on your request and then recovered itself to spit back an error message, you'll probably get a 500 code, which means that there was an internal server error. You can pop the return code out of the information that comes back into the CHttpFile object by calling CHttpFile::QueryInfoStatusCode(). It would look something like this:

```
CHttpFile* pFile = pHttpConnect->OpenRequest(/* some params */);
pFile->SendRequest();
DWORD dwStatusCode;
pFile->QueryInfoStatusCode(dwStatusCode);
```

After that, dwStatusCode would contain the integer reflecting the result of your request. It'll be one of the integers from this table:

Preprocessor Symbol	Status Code	Meaning
HTTP_STATUS_OK	200	Everything is just as you asked for.
HTTP_STATUS_CREATED	201	The resource you requested has been created.
HTTP_STATUS_ACCEPTED	202	Everything is going okay, but the processing of your request hasn't been completed. Used for queued requests.
HTTP_STATUS_PARTIAL	203	Only a partial result was available, so only a partial result was returned to you.
HTTP_STATUS_NO_CONTENT	204	The request was okay, but the object you requested or the action you initiated resulted in a response that had no content. *Not* sent for HEAD, because you did not request any content in the first place.
HTTP_STATUS_AMBIGUOUS	300	The object you requested was redirected, but the nature of your request resulted in the redirection being ambiguous.

Preprocessor Symbol	Status Code	Meaning
HTTP_STATUS_MOVED	301	The request was recognized, but the server administrator has permanently moved the object. The Location: header tag reflects the new location.
HTTP_STATUS_REDIRECT	302	The request was recognized, but the server administrator has *temporarily* moved the resource that you requested. Look for the Location: header tag in the response to find the location.
HTTP_STATUS_REDIRECT_METHOD	303	The request was recognized and the object was known, but the server is indicating that the object can't be accessed using the method, i.e. the verb, that you specified. You might be redirected to a new location, but you'll certainly be directed to use a different verb.
HTTP_STATUS_NOT_MODIFIED	304	The client requested an object if and only if the object has changed or has met some other criteria. This status code indicates that the condition wasn't met and the item will not be sent.
HTTP_STATUS_BAD_REQUEST	400	The request was ill-formed. That is, it contained a header completely unrecognized by the server or didn't include a properly identified verb and object.
HTTP_STATUS_DENIED	401	You asked for an object or method that requires authorization. You didn't provide that authorization, so you should resubmit your request with the appropriate authentication codes.
HTTP_STATUS_PAYMENT_REQ	402	You must provide payment for the resource your requested. You should specify a ChargeTo: header in your request. This mechanism (and therefore this error) is largely obsolete.

Table Continued on Following Page

Preprocessor Symbol	Status Code	Meaning
HTTP_STATUS_FORBIDDEN	403	You're not allowed to do what you asked to do. No mechanism of authorization will ever make it work; forget about it.
HTTP_STATUS_NOT_FOUND	404	What you asked for wasn't found. Maybe you misspelled something, maybe the server administrator moved it and didn't set up a redirect.
HTTP_STATUS_BAD_METHOD	405	You asked for a method that the server just doesn't support, or you asked for that method on an object that doesn't allow it.
HTTP_STATUS_NONE_ACCEPTABLE	406	The server can't respond to the request, because it can't present the item you re quested in a format compatible with the `Accept:` headers in the request.
HTTP_STATUS_PROXY_AUTH_REQ	407	The request went through a proxy, but the proxy didn't authenticate the request.
HTTP_STATUS_REQUEST_TIMEOUT	408	The client connected to the server and started making a request, but didn't complete the request before the server quit waiting.
HTTP_STATUS_CONFLICT	409	The requested resource isn't available because of a conflict in the state of the resource. This is usually a temporary situation. The object might have a sharing lock, for instance, which will eventually be released.
HTTP_STATUS_GONE	410	The object has been permanently removed. It has no new home.
HTTP_STATUS_AUTH_REFUSED	411	The request you made included an authorization, but that authorization was refused by the server.

Preprocessor Symbol	Status Code	Meaning
HTTP_STATUS_SERVER_ERROR	500	Something internal went wrong with the server. The server didn't crash, but it got so sick that it couldn't process your request. Usually, this indicates a configuration problem on the server.
HTTP_STATUS_NOT_SUPPORTED	501	The server doesn't support the method you demanded.
HTTP_STATUS_BAD_GATEWAY	502	The server that originally processed your request passed it on to a gateway or another server. It is *this* server which supplied an invalid response to the server you originally contacted.
HTTP_STATUS_SERVICE_UNAVAIL	503	The server couldn't process your request because the server is out of resources or is partially down for maintenance.
HTTP_STATUS_GATEWAY_TIMEOUT	504	The request made it to a gateway, but the gateway's communication with the server timed-out.

A couple of these error messages deserve a bit of closer examination. First, HTTP_STATUS_REDIRECT is automatically handled by WinInet unless you specify INTERNET_FLAG_NO_AUTO_REDIRECT in your session. If you really want to know about redirection responses, you can specify this flag and check out the return headers to see where to go. When you get the response, you can expect that a tag in the response headers, named Location:, will tell you where the document can be found. Otherwise, you'll not get the redirection response and WinInet will try to resolve the redirection. If you've not specified INTERNET_FLAG_NO_AUTO_REDIRECT, the response you'll receive is the result of the redirection attempt.

HTTP_STATUS_DENIED is a form of simple security offered by the HTTP protocol. It operates when you connect to a site and request a resource which has been protected by a user name and password. You'll get the HTTP_STATUS_DENIED status in your response. You'll need to resubmit your query using an Authorization: header that provides your user name and password. You can read the HTTP specification to find out exactly how to do that, but you'll undoubtedly find it more convenient to have MFC prompt the user on your behalf. You can do this by calling the CHttpFile::ErrorDlg() function, prototyped here:

```
DWORD CHttpFile::ErrorDlg( CWnd* pParent = NULL,
                    DWORD dwError = ERROR_INTERNET_INCORRECT_PASSWORD,
                    DWORD dwFlags = FLAGS_ERROR_UI_FLAGS_GENERATE_DATA
                        | FLAGS_ERROR_UI_FLAGS_CHANGE_OPTIONS,
                    LPVOID* lppvData = NULL);
```

ErrorDlg() provides a common user interface for things that can go wrong during the transaction. pParent provides a pointer to a parent window for the interface that the function will display. dwError specifies the error with which the function is to help you. Currently, ErrorDlg() can handle these status codes:

Status Code	When returned
ERROR_INTERNET_HTTP_TO_HTTPS_ON_REDIR	Notifies the user of the 'zone crossing' to and from a secure site. That is, the user is connected to a server that offered the user a secured connection, but the user has selected an unsecured resource from that same server.
ERROR_INTERNET_INCORRECT_PASSWORD	Displays a dialog box for obtaining the user's name and password. On Windows 95/98, the function attempts to use the network caching user interface and disk cache to retrieve the information before prompting.
ERROR_INTERNET_INVALID_CA	Notifies the user that the server does not have a certificate for this site which is using Secure Sockets Layer (SSL – see below). This means that the server is claiming to support security, but the licensing and authentication information covering the security protocol is invalid or nonexistent.
ERROR_INTERNET_POST_IS_NON_SECURE	Displays a warning about posting data to the server through a non-secure connection. The requested transaction would have the client send data to the server via the POST method, but the connection isn't using any security. The message warns the user about the dangers of this transaction.
ERROR_INTERNET_SEC_CERT_CN_INVALID	Displays an Invalid SSL Common Name dialog box, and lets the user view the incorrect certificate. Also allows the user to select a certificate in response to a server request.
ERROR_INTERNET_SEC_CERT_DATE_INVALID	SSL certificate has expired. The server is equipped to handle secure sockets, but the license for the key the server was using has expired.

As you'll note, almost all of these errors relate to security concerns for the data being sent between the server and the client. WinInet is capable of communicating over an enhancement to the normal sockets protocol used by the HTTP protocol. That enhancement is called the **Secure Sockets Layer**, or SSL for short. When you're using HTTP to talk to a server, you're using plain, unsecured sockets. When your client uses HTTPS to talk to a server, the server and your client use SSL to encrypt and decrypt all data that goes over the connection, making the transaction impervious to people who are trying to read over your shoulder. We'll treat HTTPS in more detail in the section entitled 'What is HTTPS?', but for now we'll focus on the ErrorDlg() member function.

The ErrorDlg() function allows you to display an error that requires a response from the user, or for which a *de facto* standard user interface has been established. Since most errors don't require user interaction, and don't have a user interface associated with them, you'll want to make sure that you still handle exceptions thrown by transactions that end up failing.

dwFlags lets you express what you'd like to happen to the information that the user provides in response to the user interface presented by the function. If dwFlags is set to its default value, which ORs together the FLAGS_ERROR_UI_FLAGS_GENERATE_DATA and FLAGS_ERROR_UI_FLAGS_CHANGE_OPTIONS flags, the user interface will request the needed information from the user, and return it indirectly to the caller by modifying the headers and options in the CHttpFile object against which the call was made. The CHANGE_OPTIONS flag affords you the luxury of not even getting your hands dirty with the information you're retrieving or setting for the query; it tells the function to get the user's response and make any necessary AddRequestHeader() or SetOption() calls to implement the user's request.

For current versions of Wininet.dll, the lppvData parameter is meaningless and unused.

The Tear sample that ships with the product shows a very typical application of the ErrorDlg() function. Tear sends its request, and then tests to see if the status code from the request states the request was denied for security reasons. The test looks like this:

```
DWORD dwRet;
pFile->QueryInfoStatusCode(dwRet);
if (dwRet == HTTP_STATUS_DENIED)
{
    // perform the call to ErrorDlg()
}
```

The call to ErrorDlg() requests a user name and password from the user and then allows the call to update the information provided by the user. In the if statement block above, the Tear sample has this code:

```
DWORD dwPrompt;
dwPrompt = pFile->ErrorDlg(NULL, ERROR_INTERNET_INCORRECT_PASSWORD,
        FLAGS_ERROR_UI_FLAGS_GENERATE_DATA | FLAGS_ERROR_UI_FLAGS_CHANGE);
if (dwPrompt != ERROR_INTERNET_FORCE_RETRY)
{
    cerr << _T("Access denied: Invalid password\n");
    ThrowTearException(1);
}
pFile->SendRequest();
pFile->QueryInfoStatusCode(dwRet);
```

If the user responds affirmatively to the ErrorDlg() user interface, the ErrorDlg() call will return ERROR_INTERNET_FORCE_RETRY. While this arrangement is a bit unintuitive, it turns out that the error message really states that the user entered data into the dialog and wants to retry the operation. Any other return value means that the user didn't respond to the request affirmatively and wants the request to be abandoned. So the above if statement checks for the force retry condition. If the condition isn't met, the code throws an exception that's caught later by some terminal error handling routines.

How Was Your Transaction, Dear?

Because it's quite common to try and query the status code from a transaction that's just completed, MFC provides the QueryInfoStatusCode() function to access status information from a CHttpFile object in a handy way. QueryInfoStatusCode() is a specialization of the QueryInfo() function. QueryInfo(), itself, has several overrides:

```
BOOL CHttpFile::QueryInfo( DWORD dwInfoLevel,
                           LPVOID lpvBuffer,
                           LPDWORD lpdwBufferLength,
                           LPDWORD lpdwIndex = NULL) const;
BOOL CHttpFile::QueryInfo( DWORD dwInfoLevel,
                           CString& str,
                           LPDWORD dwIndex = NULL) const;

BOOL CHttpFile::QueryInfo( DWORD dwInfoLevel,
                           SYSTEMTIME* pSysTime,
                           LPDWORD dwIndex = NULL) const;
```

The dwInfoLevel parameter can be any of the following flags:

Constant	HTTP Header	Description
HTTP_QUERY_MIME_VERSION	MIME-Version	Version of MIME used to encode the content of this response. MIME is protocol that allows binary data to be sent as ASCII text.
HTTP_QUERY_CONTENT_TYPE	Content-Type	This header describes the content of the body. It will match one of the Accept-Type representation types you mentioned in your request, but it won't include any wildcards and will instead describe a single specific type.
HTTP_QUERY_CONTENT_TRANSFER_ENCODING	Transfer-Encoding	Describes the encoding method used to format the message before it was sent. The recipient must use the same method to decode the message before its content is useful.

Constant	HTTP Header	Description
HTTP_QUERY_CONTENT_LENGTH	Content-Length	The length of the content of this message in bytes. The content is only the body of the response; it doesn't include the headers.
HTTP_QUERY_DATE	Date	This field indicates the date and time at which the response message was created; that is, the date and time the server responded to your request.
HTTP_QUERY_EXPIRES	Expires	The Expires field gives the date and time after which the response should be considered invalid. Normally, this is only interesting to caching software.
HTTP_QUERY_LAST_MODIFIED	Last-Modified	Date and time the object being sent was last modified on the server.
HTTP_QUERY_PRAGMA	Pragma	Allows the client and server to exchange implementation-defined header information.
HTTP_QUERY_STATUS_CODE	(intrinsic)	This flag returns the resulting status of the request. This will be one of the HTTP status codes we've discussed before, for example 200 for 'OK' or 500 for 'Internal Server Error'.
HTTP_QUERY_STATUS_TEXT	(intrinsic)	This flag returns the descriptive string for resulting status of the request. For example, the returned value will be 'OK' for a status code of 200, or 'Internal Server Error' for a status code of 500.

These flags can be ORed together with the following four flags which specify the type of information requested:

Flag	Meaning
HTTP_QUERY_CUSTOM	Finds the header name and returns it in lpvBuffer, or throws an exception.
HTTP_QUERY_FLAG_REQUEST_ HEADERS	Queries response or request headers.
HTTP_QUERY_FLAG_SYSTEMTIME	Returns the date/time string as a SYSTEMTIME structure.
HTTP_QUERY_FLAG_NUMBER	If the header has a value that is a number, this flag returns the data as a 32 bit number.

The first of the tables above does not give the full list of values that dwInfoLevel can take; this can be found in the MSDN library for Visual Studio 6.0. However two more values are worthy of further explanation: HTTP_QUERY_RAW_HEADERS and HTTP_QUERY_RAW_HEADERS_CRLF. If you request HTTP_QUERY_RAW_HEADERS, you'll get a buffer back that's populated with double-NULL terminated strings describing *all* of the headers. You'll need to parse them yourself. A double-NULL terminated buffer is actually a bunch of strings stored right after each other. Each string is separated by a NULL character, and the last string is followed by an extra NULL. If you received Content-Type: text/html and Content-Length: 2153 in the headers, HTTP_QUERY_RAW_HEADERS would actually give them back to you as:

```
Content-Type: text/html\0Content-Length: 2153\0\0
```

If you use HTTP_QUERY_RAW_HEADERS_CRLF, the individual strings will be returned in a format where they are separated by carriage-return/linefeed pairs. In regular C notation, that would look like this:

```
Content-Type: text/html\r\nContent-Length: 2153\r\n\r\n\0
```

Note that the last entry is followed by both an extra carriage-return/linefeed pair *and* a terminating null character.

If you need to look for a particular header that isn't represented by one of the constants above, you'll need to use HTTP_QUERY_RAW_HEADERS or HTTP_QUERY_RAW_HEADERS_CRLF and try to parse the headers yourself. That's that hard to achieve – the Tear sample that ships with the Visual C++ product includes some code that does exactly this.

Tear handles all of the redirection errors (such as HTTP_STATUS_MOVED and HTTP_STATUS_REDIRECT) by itself. It doesn't really need to, because the WinInet services will handle redirections automatically for you – unless you specifically ask to be notified of redirections by specifying the INTERNET_FLAG_NO_AUTO_REDIRECT flag – as Tear does in its initialization of its CInternetSession object.

If `Tear` notices that the request it issued results in a redirection error, it reacts by retrieving all of the headers with a call to `QueryInfo()`, like this:

```
CString strNewLocation;
pFile->QueryInfo(HTTP_QUERY_RAW_HEADERS_CRLF, strNewLocation);
```

and then using `CString::Find()` to search for the header text:

```
int nPlace = strNewLocation.Find(_T("Location: "));
if (nPlace == -1)
{
    cerr << _T("Error: Site redirects with no new location");
    cerr << endl;
    ThrowTearException(2);
}
```

If the header text isn't found (that is, if `Find()` returns `-1`), the sample throws an exception so that the sample will handle the error. In this case, it's quite appropriate to give up on the request we were making of the server. If we were told there was a redirection, and the redirection response didn't include the new location, then we're really in trouble, and there's nothing we can do to handle the redirection. In many circumstances, headers are optional and the server doesn't need to send them. As you write your application, you'll need to carefully consider the rules set forth by the HTTP specification to decide which headers are important and what they mean in the exact circumstances you've created.

If the header text *is* found, the sample's work isn't done; it has only found the index within the raw headers where the desired header actually lives. It also needs to snap the header off from the other headers, so that the new location text is available later. It's just a bit of string math — the sample skips over the `Location:` text, which is ten characters long. From that point on, the sample needs to find the first newline character, as that marks the end of the individual header. It looks like this:

```
strNewLocation = strNewLocation.Mid(nPlace + 10);
nPlace = strNewLocation.Find('\r');
if (nPlace > 0)
    strNewLocation = strNewLocation.Left(nPlace);
```

And, after all that, `strNewLocation` contains the value of the `Location:` header.

Releasing Resources

We've outlined the process of making an HTTP request using the appropriate MFC objects. In a nutshell, it looks like this:

1. Create a CHttpServer object, or use an existing one

2. Get an CHttpConnection object by calling CHttpServer::GetHttpConnection()

3. Get a CHttpFile object by calling CHttpConnection::OpenRequest()

4. Optionally, modify the request by calling CHttpFile::AddHeader()

5. Send the request by calling CHttpFile::SendRequest()

6. Use the data returned by the request

7. Close the request and delete the involved objects

So far, we've covered everything but steps six and seven. Step seven is the easiest, so let's nail it right now – the objects returned by the calls to the WinInet classes are dynamically allocated for you by MFC. You own them, though, and you must delete them when you're done. You can directly delete them without closing them first. This isn't great programming style, so MFC will emit a TRACE() message to the debugger if you delete an object that's still open. You can close the object using its Close() member function.

Remember that a CHttpFile is created as soon as you call OpenRequest(); this means that, even if you decide not to use SendRequest() to actually send the request, or if you end up getting an error response from the server, you still do need to delete the object. Failing to clean up after yourself will really drain system resources quickly. The memory leak you're causing isn't that bad, when compared to leaving the connection to the server open, which wastes network resources on your own machine *and* the server!

Step six is a little more involved. Once the request is successful, you can use any QueryInfo() call we've discussed to retrieve headers from the request. But if the request you've made returns content, you can use the Read() or ReadString() members of CHttpFile to retrieve that content.

Calls to Read() or ReadString() cause MFC to turn around and make requests directly to WinInet, which is receiving the response from the network. The receipt of the HTTP response doesn't happen immediately, so WinInet itself buffers received data as it arrives at your machine. If you use the Read() member function, you're asking MFC to fetch the exact bytes that were received. In other words, Read() is ideal for the receipt of binary data sent by the server. ReadString() can be used to read textual data, such as HTML.

Since CHttpFile is derived from CInternetFile, and CInternetFile is, in turn, derived from CStdioFile, you already know how to use the Read() and ReadString() functions; we've visited them before. It turns out, though, that CHttpFile does its own buffering of file data. You can call SetReadBufferSize() to set the buffer size used by a CHttpFile. If you call ReadString() without setting a buffer, a buffer will be set for you to improve efficiency.

If you're using Read() to read very small blocks of data, you really should set up a buffer so that MFC can provide data to your application with the greatest efficiency. Here, 'small blocks of data' means something less than a kilobyte at a time. It's a great idea to choose a buffer size that's several times larger than your read size but also an even multiple of your read size. So, if you're reading 768 bytes at a time, you might want to set a buffer size of 3072 bytes (which is four times 768 bytes) or 6144 bytes (which is eight times 768 bytes), for example.

You learn, elsewhere in this chapter, that CInternetFile buffering also supports buffering writes. That doesn't apply to CHttpFile, because you can't write to HTTP file objects. You'll also see that other protocols interact with the network and server in a different way, which means that they'll put new semantics on the concept of buffering.

Other Voices, Other Verbs

With apologies to Truman Capote, we've outlined how to send the most common of HTTP methods, which is a simple GET. This just asks the server to return the object you've requested. The HEAD and POST methods are very interesting, though, and appropriate for some other situations.

If you issue a HEAD request, you're doing the same work as a GET with the difference that you won't actually receive any content in the response. This is very valuable for sniffing around on the server to see whether, based on the headers that will describe the object, you want to do the work to actually receive the object from the server. We outlined the importance of this header earlier in the chapter, when we treated the basics of the HTTP protocol, and it doesn't deserve more treatment here since its use doesn't change the way you'll interact with CHttpConnection or CHttpFile.

A POST request is a little more complicated, because it *does* affect the way you'll work with CHttpConnection and CHttpFile. A POST request means that you'll be posting data to the server in a huge block outside of the request header. We've looked at GET requests throughout the chapter, so we know what they look like. A POST request might look like this:

```
POST /cgi-bin/process.exe HTTP/1.0{cr}{lf}
Content-Length: 21{cr}{lf}
{cr}{lf}
interest=bass-guitars{cr}{lf}
```

The difference is that the URL specified contains the item, while the extra data after the blank line contains the information that the client wants to provide the server. POST was originally intended to let clients machines send information to the server and have it stay there. Modern HTTP implementations have POST available to afford the client a method for sending data to the server *en masse*.

The object in the above POST request is an executable image, and as such, might need to receive a great deal of input from the user. Perhaps, the executable reads information off an HTML form and uses it to register the user's interest in a particular mailing list. We'll examine the server-side implementation of these applications in the next chapter.

For now, let's examine how you could use MFC's `CHttpFile` class to perform a POST operation. Obviously, we'll use the `HTTP_VERB_POST` verb instead of `HTTP_VERB_GET` when we call `OpenRequest()`. The big difference, here, is that we'll make use of the optional parameters that `SendRequest()` accepts to populate the body of the request with the data we'd like to post. Other than those differences, we'll follow the same seven steps we reviewed before. The raw request, above, would end up being coded like this in MFC:

```
CInternetSession sess;
try
{
    CHttpConnection* pHttpConnect =
                sess.GetHttpConnection("SomeServer");
    CHttpFile* pFile =
        pHttpConnect->OpenRequest(CHttpConnection::HTTP_VERB_POST,
                                        "/cgi-bin/process.exe");
    pFile->SendRequest(NULL, 0, "interest=bass-guitars", 21);
    // ready to test for success
}
catch (CInternetException* pEx)
{
    pEx->ReportError();
    pEx->Delete();
}
```

The use of these parameters has us passing all four optional parameters to `SendRequest()`. We've not seen the `SendRequest()` function prototype before, so let's have a peek at it here:

```
BOOL CHttpFile::SendRequest(LPCTSTR pstrHeaders = NULL,
                            DWORD dwHeadersLen = 0,
                            LPVOID lpOptional = NULL,
                            DWORD dwOptionalLen = 0);
```

The function's first two parameters specify headers for the request. You can supply headers via these parameters instead of using `AddHeader()` calls, if it suits you. Additional headers supplied by these parameters must be offered in one quick shot, however. You'll want to separate individual headers by a carriage-return and line-feed sequence, and pile them into one string, ending with an extra carriage-return and line-feed sequence.

The `lpOptional` parameter points at the data you'd like to send in the body of your POST request. You can send as much data as you'd like; you're limited only by the server-side software implementation. Microsoft Internet Information Server can accept up to four gigabytes of data, which is far more than you'd ever want to wait for! The length parameter must be supplied, because the data you POST can be of any format. Since the data might be binary, the function call can't rely on finding the first null byte to know where the string ends.

We don't have to specify a `Content-Length:` header, the library tacks it on to the request for us, based on what we pass in the `dwOptionalLen` parameter. Usually, `dwOptionalLen` ends up being the length of the string you give in the `lpOptional` parameter. The library will also provide a `User-Agent:` field, which is based on the application name we used to create the session object.

The Atomclok sample is a very simple console application that uses HTTP_VERB_POST to send a request to the atomic clock standard at the US Naval Observatory. The sample demonstrates a typical application of automated access to the web. The code retrieves the simple HTTP page; the clock's web page produces, parses, and then reports the results back to the user. If the program is invoked with the /S option on the command line, the program will set the system clock based on the retrieved time.

However, the Atomclok sample has a pretty big flaw, I'm afraid. It is very much dependent on the exact format of the data that the clock web site returns. Even a slight change could cause the program's parsing routines to fail. While the sample is fragile, it does demonstrate an important point – you'll find it far easier to work with the web if you have control over both the server and the client. Since I'm not in the Navy, I can't guarantee that the server will always return the time in a particular format. However, if I work on writing the server-side software, I can provide the time in whatever conveniently parsed format I wish.

HTML is a standard that makes it very easy for users to see nicely formatted text. Human beings aren't bothered by changes in font or color or layout – they can read the entire page and find the information they need. On the other hand, computers have no such reasoning and adaptation skills. It's very hard to write code which robustly parses a whole page just to find the time and date information that it contains, for example. If you *are* writing the server-side code, you'll find information in the second half of the sample invaluable. Unfortunately, the Atomclok sample demonstrates, rather painfully, how much parsing you'll need to do in order to rip information out of even the simplest of pages.

Finding Files

Whether you're connected to the Internet or not, there are situations when you'd like to enumerate files available in a particular place. You might want to collect a list of files to find out exactly how big they are before offering to copy them to a floppy for your user. Or, you might want to walk through a list of files out on an FTP site somewhere and present them to your user in a list control.

MFC 6.0 implements a nifty polymorphic class for these kinds of things: CFileFind. The CFileFind class has a default constructor, which will get you started. Once you've created the object, you can look for files that match a particular wildcard specification by calling the FileFind() member of the class. This fucntion starts searching, but doesn't actually go and find a file. If there are files to be found, this function returns TRUE. If there are no files to be found, this function returns FALSE. You can find each of the files by repeatedly calling FindNextFile() against your CFileFind object. Once you've called FindNextFile() successfully the first time, you can call any of a bunch of accessor functions on your CFileFind object to get information about the most recently found file. The accessor functions allow you to find information about the file, including its name, size, and time and date information. As long as FindNextFile() returns TRUE, there are more files to be found.

You can list the names of all the files in the current directory by using code like this:

```
CFileFind finder;
finder.FindFile("*.*");

BOOL bCountinue = TRUE;
while (bCountinue)
{
    bCountinue = finder.FindNextFile();
    CString str = finder.GetFileName();
    printf("%s\n", (LPCTSTR)str);
}
finder.Close();
```

You'll note (if you're astute) that I said `FindFile()` returns TRUE or FALSE if there are files to be found. I don't check this return value for two reasons. First, I'm a complete slob; second, I know that I can get away with it. If there are no files found, `FindNextFile()` will still return FALSE without complaint, and my loop will never execute. This code is more pedantic, but executes with the same results:

```
CFileFind finder;
BOOL bContinue;
if (bContinue = finder.FindFile("*.*"))
{
    while (bContinue)
    {
        bContinue = finder.FindNextFile();
        CString str = finder.GetFileName();
        printf("%s\n", (LPCTSTR)str);
    }
    finder.Close();
}
```

If you're planning something expensive before your loop gets going, like allocating a big array to hold your list, then you can check the return code from `FindFile()` to save yourself some time. If `FindFile()` has returned FALSE, you know there aren't going to be any files and that you probably won't need an array. On the other hand, you might want to check for failure before you start looping, complain to the user that they've entered a useless wildcard pattern, and return from your function early. I often return from functions early; last night, I got home from dinner around eight o'clock.

In the code fragment above, the `Close()` call I make on the finder object shuts down the find context managed by `CFileFind` and frees any memory the object was using. More importantly, it allows me to reuse the same object for a different search if I want this.

Once you've found a file, the usable accessor functions return information describing it. If you've found a file named `C:\Program Files\Microsoft Visual Studio\vc98\Mfc\Include\Afx.h`, here's what each of the accessor functions will return:

Accessor	String Value Returned
`GetFileName()`	`Afx.h`
`GetFilePath()`	`C:\Program Files\Microsoft Visual Studio\vc98\Mfc\Include\Afx.h`
`GetFileTitle()`	`Afx`
`GetFileURL()`	`file://C:\Program Files\Microsoft Visual Studio\vc98\Mfc\Include\Afx.h`

These functions are named just like functions with the same purpose in other classes, like `CFileDialog`. There's one `CFileFind` member that isn't in our table and that's `GetRoot()`. `GetRoot()` returns the directory used in the initial call to `FindFile()`. Passing a path, such as `c:\windows\system\*.dll`, for instance, to `FindFile()` results in `GetRoot()` returning `c:\windows\system\`.

You can call `GetCreationTime()`, `GetLastAccessTime()` or `GetLastWriteTime()` to retrieve the corresponding time stamp information from each file. These functions each have two overrides – one accepts a pointer to a `FILETIME` structure, and the other accepts a reference to a `CTime` object. They return `TRUE` if they're successful or `FALSE` if not. They'll also return `TRUE` if *no* call to `FindFirstFile()` is made.

In the code fragments, I ran off and searched for "`*.*`" to match everything in the current directory. You can adjust the current directory for your process using calls to the `::SetCurrentDirectory()` API. You can find the current directory for your process using the `::GetCurrentDirectory()` API. Or, if you don't want to change the current directory, you can just specify the path within the parameter you give to `FindFile()`. It's just fine to make the call with a drive letter, too; something like "`D:\\MSDEV\\MFC\\SRC\\*.H`", for example. Remember that backslashes are C++ string escape characters, so you'll need to double them up.

Message In a Bottle

If you need to find a resource remotely, you can use either one of two classes which are based upon `CFileFind`: `CFtpFileFind` or `CGopherFileFind`. `CFtpFileFind` works just as `CFileFind` does, but against remote directories on FTP servers. Since `CFtpFileFind` needs to know where you want to connect to find your files, the constructor takes two parameters – a pointer to the `CFtpConnection` for the server where you're looking for a match, and a `DWORD` to indicate which `dwContext` value you'd like to use to perform the operation. We described `dwContext` and its usage a couple of sections ago:

```
CFtpFindFile::CFtpFileFind( CFtpConnection* pConnection,
                            DWORD dwContext = 1);
```

After you've constructed the `CFtpFileFind` object, you can use it just as we described using `CFileFind` objects. There are a few important semantic differences. The most obvious involves file-naming conventions. `CFileFind` isn't case sensitive, ever. `CFtpFileFind` might be case-sensitive if you're using it to connect to a server that's case sensitive, and most FTP server implementations are. Something is funny about the way this works, though. If the FTP site you've connected to has never been touched by your machine, `WinInet` will run off to the machine and let the machine do the comparison for your file search. However, if the directory information from that server is cached on your machine, the search will be done by `WinInet` on your own machine, and the search will *not* be case-sensitive. Pretty wacky, huh?

File naming conventions are important to understand, even if you're not worried about case. On Unix systems, the forward slash is generally used to separate directory names. `CFileFind` takes care of checking for both, but if you connect to a machine that uses even goofier rules, you're on your own. Furthermore, most Unix machines think of a period as just another character in a file name, and don't use a period to separate extensions. On a `CFileFind` search, `"*.*"` will get you every file you can find. However, on a Unix machine, that wildcard specification will get you only the files that contain a period. Unix machines normally use a single star, as in `"*"`, to match all files. How the FTP server you've connected to implements particular aspects of the file attribute information is really up to that machine. Some will keep different times for last-access, last-change, and creation, just like Windows NT does. (If the FTP server is a Windows NT machine, it's pretty likely that it will expose all that information to the FTP client.) On the other hand, some Unix boxes don't carry all of these time stamps; the upshot is they will return the same time for each and every value.

Once the `CFtpFileFind` object has been constructed, it tastes just like a `CFileFind` object, with one obvious exception. If you're using a `CFileFind` object to find a directory, you can do so; just call `FindFile()` with the name of the directory. The object will let you enumerate a single file, which actually describes the directory. In the same circumstances, `CFtpFileFind` will actually return information describing the files *in* the directory. To retrieve information about the directory itself, you need to enumerate all the files in the directory where the subdirectory of interest lives. The `WinInet` API itself behaves this way, but this really has nothing to do with MFC. It turns out that `WinInet` is implemented this way because the connection to the FTP server behaves that way inherently, and if `WinInet` were to work around the FTP protocol, it could end up taking an incredible amount of time to weed through directories while trying to find information about a particular subdirectory entry.

Rodent Hunt

Gopher searches are completely different. Objects in the Gopher universe are actually identified either by their screen names or by locators. You can search for screen names using `CGopherFileFind`. From that file find object, you can request the `CGopherLocator` that identifies the object, or the screen name. The locator comes from `CGopherFileFind::GetLocator()`, while the screen name can be realized by calling `CGopherFileFind::GetScreenName()`.

> All the other accessor functions we discussed for **CFileFind** are unimplemented — they'll **ASSERT()** in debug builds and always throw a **CNotImplementedException**.

Since Gophers implement attributes, you can also query the attributes of the found object by calling `CGopherFileFind::GetAttributes()`.

Addressing

These days, you can't even see an advertisement for a hockey game without hearing about colons and slashes. These facts have nothing to do with penalties or aggressive play; they're used to provide the newest in marketing – uniform resource locators. We touched on URLs earlier in the chapter, back before we had any clue of what `WinInet` would really do for us. Let's take this opportunity to deepen our understanding of URLs and learn what they mean when we're working with the MFC Internet client classes.

Simpler URLs have a form like this:

```
scheme://server/object
```

`scheme` identifies the protocol or method to be used to retrieve the resource. Most of the URLs you'll see in today's advertising start with `http`, which means the HTTP protocol will be used to retrieve the resource. The `server` is the name of the machine which holds the resource. It's essential this machine is running the services necessary to answer the request you're making, regardless of the protocol you use to get it. The `object`, which may or may not be present as a part of the URL, will get you the specific resource that you'd like to have.

If you want to learn more about Wrox Press books, you might use the URL:

```
http://www.wrox.com/
```

to get the resource. Note that the URL ends in a slash and not an object; most browsers will accept HTTP URLs which don't end in a slash, but that's just a convenience. By the letter of the law, an HTTP URL without a trailing slash is actually erroneous; but, since so much software accepts it, it's become an almost reliable *de facto* standard. In the above URL, the server name is `www.wrox.com`, while the object name is simply `/`.

The slash at the end means that the server should get whatever default object is there. Here, we're asking for the default object at the root of the web server's published space. If you went to Microsoft's site and asked for:

```
http://msdn.microsoft.com/visualc/
```

you'd be asking for the default object in the directory `visualc`, which is in the root of the web space. That 'web space' is some directory on the server which acts as the server's repository for publishing web data. The server will almost certainly map requests in the root of the web space to some other directory than the root directory on the machine. The mapping allows the server administrator to make sure security stays tight. (After all, the world is just full of yahoos who would go play with `http://www.microsoft.com/windowsnt/system32/mfc42.dll` if that wasn't true.)

You might eventually stumble on a URL which has a real file identified in it, rather than just having you pick some file that the server sees as its default in a particular directory. This isn't common for HTTP URLs, but you can find them. A bunch of lawyers where I work actually believe that you'd care about what was in `http://www.microsoft.com/info/cpyright.htm`, for example. But the FTP protocol will almost always have you get to a particular file. Someone might direct you to look for a program you needed at `ftp://ftp.microsoft.com/softlib/mslfiles`, and that'll work with your browser. But they can also tell you to download a very specific file by using a more exact URL.

If you want to write a program that accepts a URL as input from the user, or reads URLs from other software and reacts to them, then you might try to think about one of two approaches. The first is very simple; it involves a member of `CInternetSession` called `OpenURL()`. Here's the prototype:

```
CStdioFile* CInternetSession::OpenURL( LPCTSTR pstrURL,
                                       DWORD dwContext = 1,
                                       DWORD dwFlags = 0,
                                       LPCTSTR pstrHeaders = NULL,
                                       DWORD dwHeadersLength = 0);
```

The function takes a pointer to the required URL as its first parameter. The second parameter is a `dwContext` value, which will identify the activity caused by this operation to your status callback function, if you have callbacks enabled. `dwFlags` can be any combination of the following flags:

Flag	Meaning
`INTERNET_FLAG_RELOAD`	Always retrieve this item, even if a fresh copy is in local cache.
`INTERNET_FLAG_RAW_DATA`	Receive the item as raw data, without applying any translations.
`INTERNET_FLAG_DONT_CACHE`	Don't add this item to the local cache after it has been downloaded.
`INTERNET_FLAG_MAKE_PERSISTENT`	Force this item to be added to the local cache after it has been downloaded.
`INTERNET_FLAG_TRANSFER_ASCII`	Expect the resulting resource to be an ASCII file. This option is irrelevant for protocol types other than FTP; for FTP resources, it affects the translation used by the connection.
`INTERNET_FLAG_PASSIVE`	Use passive FTP to retrieve the resource. If the URL doesn't refer to an object retrievable using FTP, this flag is meaningless.
`INTERNET_OPEN_FLAG_USE_EXISTING _CONNECT`	Don't create a new connection to the server holding the resource if one is already outstanding.

If you know you're firing off an HTTP request, you can use `pstrHeaders` and `dwHeadersLength` to specify headers for your request. These parameters have exactly the same meaning here as they do when you're using the `SendRequest()` member of `CHttpFile`.

The beauty of `OpenURL()`, however, is that it will parse the URL you've supplied, figure out what protocol it means, and open the resource it refers to. It will open that resource with the appropriate MFC class, and return a pointer to that file object to you. `OpenURL()` returns a `CStdioFile` pointer, which means that it might return a `CStdioFile`. It will do so if you pass it a URL that refers to the `file:` scheme, meaning that your URL actually identifies a local file. I might read my `Autoexec.bat` file using this URL:

```
file://c:\autoexec.bat
```

If you wanted to open a file on your network, using whatever networking operating system you've got installed, you might use this awkward syntax:

```
file://\\mooseboy\antlers\autoexec.bat
```

1001

This asks for the file `Autoexec.bat` from a share named `antlers` on a server named `mooseboy`. Please don't let the `file:` scheme cloud your understanding of the `ftp:` scheme. If you wanted to use your network operating system to get the file from `mooseboy`, you'd use the URL above. If you wanted to ask a server named `mooseboy`, which was running the FTP protocol, to get you a file named `Autoexec.bat` from a directory named `antlers`, you could do so with this URL:

```
ftp://mooseboy/antlers/autoexec.bat
```

You can certainly use forward slashes or backward slashes when using the `file:` scheme, but you should not expect backward slashes to work when you use the `ftp:` scheme.

So, given the first `file:` scheme URL, `OpenURL()` would return a pointer to a `CStdioFile` opened to the `Autoexec.bat` file on your local `C:` drive. The `ftp:` scheme would return a pointer to a `CInternetFile` object opened by the `antlers/autoexec.bat` file on the `mooseboy` server. These scenarios, of course, assume that the files and directories and servers involved exist and are healthy; if anything goes wrong, the `OpenURL()` will pitch a `CInternetException`.

If you pass one of the `http:` URLs we examined a couple of paragraphs ago, `OpenURL()` will return a `CHttpFile` object opened and ready to read. However, getting a file back in this case is only confirmation that you've successfully sent off your request. Remember, when you're using the HTTP protocol, an error response means that things were valid and successful; and as far as the protocol is concerned, you've successfully received a response. You can use the `IsKindOf()` member of `CObject` to test the runtime type of the object that's returned to you to see if it really is a `CHttpFile` object; if it is, you can then safely call `QueryInfoStatusCode()` to find out what *really* happened.

The `CStdioFile`, `CInternetFile`, and `CHttpFile` classes are polymorphic. That is, a pointer to the most derived class is usable as a pointer to an object of the base class or a pointer of a more derived class. In this case, polymorphism lets you indiscriminately use the `CStdioFile` member functions that you know and love – even if the function actually returned a `CHttpFile`. This is the beauty of `OpenURL()`; it returns a pointer to a `CStdioFile`, but that object might really contained in a more derived class that implements more extensive features than your ordinary standard input/output file.

You can use `OpenURL()` for simpler situations, but you'll probably be more interested in having complete control over your Internet client activities, and therefore you'll want to use the more discrete classes.

Breakin' Up Ain't Easy

`OpenURL()` is handy and very appropriate for some uses; any time you need to get a file, an HTTP page, or a gopher menu from a server, without worrying about complete control over exactly what happens, this member function is for you. There are other times when you need more control – you might want to restrict your application to handling only a certain specific type or a set of certain types of URLs, or you might want to carefully connect to the server before getting the object of your desire.

Parsing a URL seems like a trivial matter until you get into the nitty-gritty of the functions. MFC provides two functions to help. These are `::AfxParseURL()` and `::AfxParseURLEx()`. Both functions are global; they can be called at any time, even before you've created a `CInternetSession` object. `::AfxParseURL()` is appropriate for almost all applications; you can get the major component parts of a URL using a very simple call. Here's the function's prototype:

```
BOOL AFXAPI AfxParseURL( LPCTSTR pstrURL,
                         DWORD& dwServiceType,
                         CString& strServer,
                         CString& strObject,
                         INTERNET_PORT& nPort);
```

The input parameter for the function, `pstrURL`, points at a URL that you'd like to have parsed. The input URL can be of any form, as long as it's a full URL. It must include a scheme, and a server after that scheme. So, at a minimum, you can pass in URLs like:

```
gopher://latif.com
ftp://ftp.microsoft.com/
www://www.wrox.com
file://C:\autoexec.bat
```

Note that a trailing whack *isn't* required; `::AfxParseURL()` will assume one if it is necessary. You can pass more aggressively formulated URLs, such as these:

```
ftp://ftp.microsoft.com/ls-lR.txt
http://dir.yahoo.com/computers_and_internet/programming_languages/
file://C:\winnt\system32\mfc42d.pdb
```

If `AfxParseURL()` notices something wrong with the URL's syntax, it will return FALSE. The function doesn't check to see if the URL names a valid or available resource; nor does it test access rights of the particular item or its availability on the server; it just checks for syntax.

When `AfxParseURL()` can successfully parse the URL, it will populate the variables referenced by the `dwServiceType`, `strServer`, `strObject`, and `nPort` parameters. `dwServiceType` is the most discriminating of these parameters; it identifies exactly what type of scheme will be used to access the information stored at the URL. Popular return values include:

Scheme	Return Value
`ftp://`	AFX_INET_SERVICE_FTP
`http://`	AFX_INET_SERVICE_HTTP
`gopher://`	AFX_INET_SERVICE_GOPHER
`file://`	AFX_INET_SERVICE_FILE
`https://`	AFX_INET_SERVICE_HTTPS

If you examine the documentation for `AfxParseURL()`, you'll find that the function will recognize a couple dozen more schemes. They're not supported by `WinInet` so they're not really worth mentioning.

The `strServer` parameter refers to a `CString` object that will receive the name of the server which the URL refers to. The value returned will be stripped of other baggage. For the first of the URLs above, the parameter would receive `ftp.microsoft.com`. If the provided URL refers to a file, the `strServer` parameter will be left blank and the filename will be in the object parameter. This is true for local file names like `file://C:\winnt\system32\mfc42d.pdb`, as well as remote file URLs that use Microsoft's Universal Naming Convention, such as `file://\\mooseboy\antlers\winnt\system32\mfc42d.pdb`.

For non-file scheme URLs, strings referenced by the `strObject` parameter are populated with the object name. This is the object which you'd directly request from an HTTP server, or the path and file name which you'd request from an FTP server. The `nPort` parameter identifies the port which was specified in the URL. URLs which include port numbers can look like this:

`http://www.nwlink.com:80/~mikeblas/`

If no explicit port was named in the URL, `AfxParseURL()` will return the default port number associated with the protocol. We had a table of these presented earlier on in this chapter.

Extended Parsing Applications

The `::AfxParseURLEx()` function I mentioned earlier was added in MFC Version 4.21. It has a slightly more impressive prototype than its non-extended friend:

```
BOOL AFXAPI AfxParseURLEx( LPCTSTR pstrURL,
                           DWORD& dwServiceType,
                           CString& strServer,
                           CString& strObject,
                           INTERNET_PORT& nPort,
                           CString& strUsername,
                           CString& strPassword,
                           DWORD dwFlags = 0);
```

`AfxParseURLEx()` returns zero if it fails and returns non-zero if it was successful, just like `AfxParseURL()`. The `pstrURL` parameter still points to the URL to be parsed. However, the URLs which `AfxParseURLEx()` understands are a little more varied. We already know about the `dwServiceType`, `strServer`, `strObject`, and `nPort` parameters. Once again, they're no different to the lesser version of the function.

The new parameters, `strUsername` and `strPassword`, allow your code to pull user names and passwords from URLs. The URL syntax allows for user names and passwords to be a part of the URL, but that syntax isn't commonly used. An FTP URL for a user named `mikeblas` with a password of `antlers` at a server named `mooseboy` would look like this:

`ftp://mikeblas:antlers@mooseboy/testfile.txt`

If you fed this URL to `AfxParseURLEx()`, it would return with the password set to `antlers` and the user name set to `mikeblas`. The object would be `/testfile.txt`, while the server name would be `mooseboy`. At this time, `AfxParseURLEx()` only supports user name and password modifiers on URL specifications for `ftp` and `gopher` schemes; `http` schemes don't support those fields. This level of support probably won't change, since it's a matter of what's dictated by the URL Addressing specification, and not the whim of a Microsoft developer.

The `dwFlags` parameter to `AfxParseURLEx()` makes the function more interesting than simply being able to parse and return these extra fields. You can use a few different flag values to influence the way the function behaves. To understand what those flags really mean, we need to delve just a bit deeper into the interesting (yet strangely gentle) world of URLs.

Throughout this chapter, I've suggested that one great application of the world wide web, and the HTTP protocol that runs it, is the use of servers to provide user interfaces to server-side applications. You might be wondering how information actually makes it back and forth between the server and the client. It's really simple – the client fires off a request and the server sends back information formatted in a way the browser is expected to understand.

Normally, the user requests a URL that represents a particular HTTP file, and the server finds it and fires it back. The server doesn't do anything interesting; it just gets a file and pumps it across the network. But the server can be set up to expect more interesting information back from the client. For example, if the HTTP file tells the client software to draw a form on the user's screen, then the user might want to send the content of the form back to the server. This transaction could take place in a couple of different and interesting ways.

First, the client might send information to the server via some protocol that the server and the client have agreed upon themselves. Perhaps the server is extensible and allows for its own verbs beyond `POST` and `GET` and the others we examined. Maybe the server eschews HTTP altogether and opens a new socket port to listen to the client talk to it in a strange and unique language. A custom approach might be interesting for some very special applications, but the idea is limited by the fact that the user may not have a browser which supports your special extensions, or that the user may not have the time, means, or inclination to download your special software.

The other two methods rely on the same features of HTTP that we've been examining throughout the chapter: `POST` and `GET`. If you `POST` a form back to the server, the server will actually execute some extra code to parse the extra data sent along to the URL. The URL really only identifies a script or executable that will read that parsed data and do something with it (such as jam it into a database and get back to the user).

If your form sends data back to the server using the `POST` method, the URL isn't very interesting. If the client sends data back to the server using the `GET` verb, though, the URL will actually include information about what was on the form For example, if you've designed an HTML form with a single editable field called `Name` and hooked it to a script on your server called `Register.exe`, your server might see this URL:

```
http://mooseboy/register.exe?Name=Kevin+Dineen
```

Everything to the left of the question mark is a URL, and not at all different from what we're used to seeing. It identifies a file named `register.exe` on the server named `mooseboy`. The data to the right of the question mark can be thought of as parameters which are made available to the program `register.exe` when it runs. The program runs on the server, not on the client. It isn't downloaded; it's run right in-place on the server!

I'll explain these techniques and how you can even use MFC to write server-side Internet programs in the next chapter. But, for now, we're concentrating on this special URL syntax.

Since the user could type just about anything into a form, the URL has to be carefully formatted. URLs are not allowed to contain spaces, for instance, so any space must be translated to a plus sign (+), as we see above. The form in that example probably says Kevin Dineen, with a space and not a plus. The browser automatically translates the space to a plus, since it knows all the rules which govern URLs.

These rules are really quite simple. We already know one; spaces aren't allowed and are converted to plus signs. If a plus sign is intended, it has to be translated to an escape sequence which indicates that it really *is* a plus sign and not a space. The encoding is simple; the URL just contains a percent sign (%) followed by a two-digit hexadecimal code that indicates the ASCII character to be represented.

It turns out that a plus sign has the code 2E, so if our form had C++ in the name field, the URL it would send would look something like this:

```
http://mooseboy/register.exe?Name=C%2E%2E
```

Finally, if the URL needs to contain a percent sign, it can either be doubled or expressed as a hex value itself. So, either %25 or %% would indicate that a single percent sign was present in the URL.

While these rules are simple, you don't need to fool with them; the dwFlags parameter to AfxParseURLEx() can be used to dictate how they're interpreted. If you specify ICU_ENCODE, for example, the call to AfxParseURLEx() will decode any of the escape sequences present in the URL; otherwise, it will leave them unchanged. If you specify ICU_ENCODE_SPACES_ONLY, the call will convert spaces to plus signs, but do no other translation work at all.

Finally, if you specify ICU_BROWSER_MODE, the call will include information provided in the URL after a question mark or pound sign (which some servers use instead of a question mark) in the strObject result of the function call. If ICU_BROWSER_MODE isn't present, the call will discard anything after a question mark (or pound sign).

We've looked at some neat applications for URLs and Internet protocols here. In the next chapter, we'll examine lots of cool things that servers can do for us. This will be an opportune time to tie all the interesting features of URLs and HTTP together into a bundle of very usable knowledge!

Cookies

It's possible to associate just a bit of data with your request for a certain URL. Normally, the server sends you that data expecting you to return it when you make further requests from the same page. The idea is to make *some* persistence between successive connections to the same site. As you'll recall from our introduction, the HTTP protocol is normally stateless. People all over the world spend hours and hours of their time trying to find ways to work around that limitation.

Anyway, these bits of data are called **cookies**. You can find the cookie associated with a particular URL by calling CInternetSession::GetCookie(). The function takes three strings. The first is the name of the URL you're asking about, and the second is the name of the cookie. Since there can be more than one cookie per URL, you'll need to supply both. The third parameter is a reference to a CString that will receive the cookie's data, if it exists on the machine. There's also an overload for the CString-phobic; it takes a pointer to a buffer and a maximum length of that buffer for a total of four parameters.

If you want to associate a cookie with a particular resource, you can call `CInternetSession::SetCookie()` to do so. The function takes three parameters – the URL, the name of the cookie, and the cookie data.

What is HTTPS?

At the beginning of this chapter, I provided a brief overview of the main protocols involved in communicating over the Internet – HTTP, FTP and Gopher, before discussing MFC's extensive high-level support for these protocols. However, a fourth protocol, HTTPS, has only been mentioned in passing up until now. As you can tell from its name, HTTPS is based on HTTP and is functionally nearly the same as HTTP; the only difference is that HTTPS transactions are **secure** – which is why there's an 'S' in the name!

HTTPS is very secure, if properly installed. Unfortunately, as far as HTTP is concerned, any devious user can sniff out plain HTTP packets as they go by and read what they say, so they're not secure. HTTPS packets are encrypted before they're transmitted, and so casual thieves can't read the transmissions.

The differences between HTTPS and HTTP are really only noticeable on the wire. The bits going from your machine to the server are encrypted, that is they're encoded at one end and decoded at the other. The encryption and decryption is all completely transparent to you, the developer. Specifically, HTTP works over the normal TCP/IP sockets protocol, while HTTPS can use a protocol called **secure sockets layer**, which is sometimes abbreviated to **SSL**. This additional layer is already built into your client TCP/IP stack if you're using Microsoft's TCP/IP drivers, but may require some special software or licenses on your server machines if you need to set it up there.

If you're working with an HTTPS connection, the default port number on the server will be 443 instead of 80. Just as HTTP servers may request that you use a different port for your connection, some HTTPS servers might request that you use a different port as well. If you're using HTTPS, you need to specify the `INTERNET_FLAG_SECURE` flag in your call to `GetHttpConnection()` so that `WinInet` knows you'll be using secure connection mechanisms.

HTTPS connections are likely to request a password and user name before validating the connection, so you'll want to make sure you understand our earlier explanation of authentication before pursuing the use of HTTPS in your design.

Other Client Strategies

Internet technologies are changing the way computers work together, and new methods for that interaction are becoming available all the time. We've repeatedly described the protocols implemented in `WinInet` and made available by MFC as being 'low-level'. While that's true, it's important to remember that the DLL does all the intricate communication implementation for you. You might get an error out of one of the functions we've described here, and you may need to decide how to react to it appropriately. But you don't need to worry about negotiating connections, reacting to low-level error conditions, or implementing the subtleties of the protocols.

On the other hand, the libraries leave you with nothing more than a way to write data to and read data from other machines. You can't display that data very readily, nor do you get a cool user interface with which to browse files on other machines; you have to invent all that yourself.

There is an interesting way around the work involved in displaying HTML data. In Chapter 16, we described the use of ActiveX Controls in MFC applications. It turns out that Microsoft supplies its popular Internet Explorer as an ActiveX Control, which you can insert into any dialog, or into a CFormView for your application. Indeed, MFC 6.0 goes further by providing a CHtmlView class which draws Internet Explorer-type windows and allows for Web browsing from within an application. The CHtmlView class is described more fully in Chapter 4.

You can get started by using the Components and Controls... command in the Add to Project tear off in the Project menu; in the resulting dialog, select the Microsoft Web Browser control. The whole process of adding a control to your project is described in detail in Chapter 16, so I won't repeat it here. The process will add a class that wraps the ActiveX control for your use in your project; just reference a class named CWebBrowser2 and have it do your dirty work.

CWebBrowser2, as an ActiveX control, will work almost like any other control window. You can call Create(), for instance, to create it and get it drawn in your parent window. You can draw it with the dialog editor and place it in a dialog template in your resource file, and then use ClassWizard to manage events that it fires.

The control's user interface is similar to the user interface presented by the Internet Explorer application; the control presents a window which allows you to click on links to navigate to them, or highlight text or pictures and copy them to the clipboard. The control does not feature a place to type in URLs, or any menus or buttons. If you want them, you'll need to add those in to your application yourself.

By providing such a simple way to render HTML, your application can very readily show web pages. You probably won't want to let your users surf around randomly, but by having this control available as a tool to display retrieved or dynamically created HTML, you'll have a very handy way to make formatted information available.

The most important method which CWebBrowser2 exposes is Navigate(). The Navigate() method accepts a few parameters that let the control know where to go and how to get there. The prototype of the method, as wrapped by the Component and Controls Gallery, looks like this:

```
void CWebBrowser2::Navigate( LPCTSTR URL,
                             VARIANT* Flags,
                             VARIANT* TargetFrameName,
                             VARIANT* PostData,
                             VARIANT* Headers);
```

The first parameter is a pointer a string that indicates the URL that you'd like to browse to. The second parameter is a pointer to a `VARIANT` which will affect the way the browser handles the page once it's loaded. The value of the number can be any combination of the following flags:

Value	Meaning
1	Open the resource or file in a new window
2	Do not add the resource or file to the history list
4	Do not read from the disk cache for this navigation
8	Do not write the results of this navigation to the disk cache

If you need to use more than one of the flags, you can simply add them together; passing 6 (2+4) for `Flags`, for example, will cause the control to avoid adding the item to the History folder *and* to not use the Internet cache for the request.

The `PostData` parameter provides a string that will be posted with the request, and the `Headers` parameter allows you to specify headers for the request. We've covered posting data and request headers before, so these parameters don't need much more investigation.

Four of these parameters are pointers to `VARIANT`s, which makes them a bit annoying to use; they're specified as pointers, since they are optional. If you've created a navigator control and attached it to `m_Browser`, for example, you can simply call:

```
m_Browser.Navigate2(XE "http://www.wrox.com/", NULL, NULL, NULL, NULL);
```

to navigate to a prominent publisher's web site without further ado. You can use the `COleVariant` class we examined back in Chapter 16 to create objects to pass to the control. Our example of asking the control to not use the cache and not update the History folder would spell out like this:

```
COleVariant flags(2+4, VT_I2);
m_Browser.Navigate2(XE "http://www.wrox.com/", &flags, NULL, NULL, NULL);
```

There's no need to clean up the `COleVariant`s you create; their destructors will take care of themselves.

You'll notice that the method doesn't return any value; you get status information back from the control via any events that the control fires. The control lets you know all about the progress it's making. For example, as the control opens the site, it fires the `DownloadBegin` event, and fires the `NavigateComplete` event when everything is over.

The control which `CWebBrowser2` wraps is fully documented in the Platform SDK.

Summary

We've investigated ways to write applications that work as Internet clients. You're probably not interested in trying to win the browser war, but you can make great use of the different protocols we've discussed in order to allow your applications to exchange data with other machines on the Internet. You might enhance reporting tools in use by the field sales department at your company to throw sales information onto a central server so that it might be digested later.

Since the implementation exposed by MFC is offered at such a high level, you'll really have very little detailed work to get through before you can have your applications speaking to the rest of the world. It's possible to have your application work with custom protocols that you have enabled the server to understand. In the next chapter, we'll examine ways to alter the server's interpretation of the information you send it – and once you've mastered server-side use of the HTTP protocol, your applications can truly do absolutely anything with the network in between them.

Internet Server Programming

In the previous chapter, we examined some of the issues that relate to communication using the HTTP protocol from the perspective of the client in the transaction. However, there's a server on the other side of the transaction, and you could, conceivably, scratch-build a server yourself – and MFC would provide some degree of help. The `Httpsvr` sample on the product CD, shows how to write a low-bandwidth server using the `CAsyncSocket` class. But it turns out that such an endeavor could go on endlessly; you'd continuously extend and optimize the server, as you decided to add more and more features and more and more customized responses to the server's side of work.

On the other hand, you can buy prepackaged server software that has already been optimized and is full of interesting, robust features. But that software might not allow you to do everything you need to do on the server-side. Enter **ISAPI**, the Internet Server API. ISAPI provides a very simple mechanism for extending existing Internet server software to perform whatever tasks you need on the server's side of the transaction, using whatever resources the server has available.

In this chapter, we'll examine the two basic architectures for writing ISAPI code. While some of the details discussed are specific to Microsoft's Internet Information Server product, there are more than six commercial server packages that support ISAPI.

No Atmosphere, but Good Service

The web objects that we've talked about so far are all static (with the exception of the very brief discussion of the POST method in Chapter 17). In other words, you approach the server with your request, and it gets a file and sends the file back to you. There are many situations when it might be advantageous to provide information that's computed or customized on demand. Even if you don't provide some form of dynamic information, you may be interested in making a special log of requests, dynamically modifying data as it is sent or received, or simply storing information about users who have accessed your site.

While MFC doesn't provide support for extending FTP or Gopher servers, it does allow you to implement powerful extensions for HTTP servers. The idea is to make use of a simple extension to the URL naming mechanism; you can specify a server and an executable name to be run in response to your request. The server takes care of running the extension; it does *not* get sent to the client to be run. The server provides all the resources the program needs to run. Since the extension lives on the server, it might make use of the server's hardware and software resources, such as connecting to a database visible only to the server, or working with other machines on the server's private network.

You might decide to connect to a server named MOOSEBOY to retrieve hockey scores. The URL to do so might look something like this:

```
http://mooseboy/hockey_stats.dll?
```

This URL causes the client software to connect to MOOSEBOY and find the resource named hockey_stats.dll. The question mark (?), however, tells the server that it shouldn't retrieve the file and send it to the client. Instead, it means that the server should load the executable file and send whatever output it generates to the client machine. You could, if the server had its permission set up to allow it, retrieve the actual hockey_stats.dll executable file. The URL to do so would be subtly different:

```
http://mooseboy/hockey_stats.dll
```

The URL used to reference the actual DLL does not contain the question mark. Of course, the server would have to be configured to allow the download. It's possible to allow the execution of an image without allowing the download of that image; this option is available because the image executes on the server, and not on the client.

The whole premise of these more complicated URLs is simply that they allow the browser to convey extra information to the server with each request. When you connect to MOOSEBOY to execute hockey_stats.dll, you might want to supply some parameters or other data to the DLL so that it knows exactly what you want.

When attached to the URL, the parameters are limited in length. You can only reliably send about a kilobyte of parameter data to the server. If you need to send more data, you can do so by using the POST method. The idea behind the POST method is that the client tells the server that it wants to execute the DLL, and then follows that notification with the information the server-side code wants. We presented the exact format of a POST request back in the previous chapter.

Critical Government Interrogation

Historically, this sort of development has been done using an architecture known as **CGI**, which stands for **Common Gateway Interface**. Such extensions run as simple executables; if the server was asked to run the program, it would expect to spawn a whole new process and steal the results of the program by reading the data the program wrote to the standard output device. Of course, the standard output would actually be redirected to a pipe that would look, as far as the spawned program was concerned, no different than a file.

In most applications, the server would read the file and hold it just for a heartbeat before sending it off to the client machine. As soon as the spawned program was done, and the server's operating system was terminating the running process, the server would be ready to fire off the results to the client. This approach to writing server extensions was pretty easy to understand. Since the extension program was just that – a plain old program – the developer could write it using familiar tools and by doing very little work above and beyond writing a common command-line utility.

The downside to CGI development is that the server has to do an incredible amount of work to start and manage the spawned process. After all, spawning a process causes the operating system to allocate a ton of memory, read the executable image from a file, and then get the program running. While the program is running, the operating system has to facilitate the communication between the application and the server. In most operating systems, throwing data from one process to another in this kind of architecture isn't a very lightweight operation. Finally, once the program is done executing, all of the setup work has to be undone.

Servers based on the Microsoft Windows NT platform, however, have a few advantages in their favor. While such servers certainly can support CGI applications, the platform affords a much more efficient method for implementing extension applications. In Chapter 11, we learned some of the details behind the way Windows implemented DLLs (libraries of code that can be dynamically loaded and discarded by a running executable program).

For the application of server extension development, DLLs offer an architecture that's far preferable to that of separate executable images. DLLs actually load code into the requesting process; in this case, that's the server itself. This significantly cuts down on the amount of work the operating system needs to do to make the code in the DLL return information to, or accept information from, the server. Better yet, the server can keep the DLL loaded in memory as long as it is needed, instead of starting and stopping a full executable image over and over.

> *It isn't strictly true to say that the server keeps the DLL in memory indefinitely. The server is quite free to release a DLL if it's not in use. However, it is still true to say that loading a DLL is a lot less expensive than starting a new process. When writing an ISAPI DLL, you work with the assumption the server will load your extension and keep it loaded as long as the server is running.*

Finally, the server can carefully control what threads enter the DLL. On a busy web server, it is conceivable it may need to run the same executable multiple times to handle multiple concurrent requests. The use of a separate process to house the extension necessarily means that the server must create more than one instance of the module and let them run concurrently. This is a woefully expensive proposition; one that most web server administrators would hate to pay. The DLL architecture allows the server to simply enter the DLL with different threads of execution. The server can manage the threads in any way that it sees fit, and affords the designer of the server great flexibility in proper management of the operating environment.

While there are certainly performance advantages to using DLLs, there is a definite downside: stability. It's far easier to crash a server with a poorly written DLL than it is with an equivalent CGI program. DLLs are definitely a very useful tool for server-side development, but they're not appropriate for all circumstances.

Internet Server Application Programming Interface

One mechanism which uses DLLs to extend the computing capability of HTTP servers is **ISAPI**, which, as we said at the top of the chapter, stands for **Internet Server Application Programming Interface**. As you can see, the performance improvements that ISAPI offers can quickly be eaten up by spending hours saying a mouthful like 'Internet Server Application Programming Interface'; so it's really important to have a slippery little acronym like ISAPI.

ISAPI is a pretty simple architecture, but it makes you, as a programmer, think about some situations that you might not have considered before. This is a distinct disadvantage of ISAPI in comparison to CGI. Instead of writing simple programs, you'll need to carefully engineer DLLs.

The ISAPI architecture is implemented by several different server packages. I don't get out much, so I'm afraid the specific details I provide in this chapter will relate to Microsoft's Internet Information Server (IIS) product. IIS version 1.0 ships as an independent product, which may be installed on Windows NT 3.51 Server. IIS 2.0 ships as an intrinsic part of Windows NT 4.0 Server, though upgrades to versions 3.0 and 4.0 are available from Microsoft. Note that you *must* be running Windows NT 4.0 or Windows 2000 Server to use this software.

If you don't have access to Windows NT Server, then all is not lost. Oracle and Progress Software, among others, ship servers that support at least some part of the ISAPI specification; you can learn about these different packages by contacting the different vendors. Microsoft's own FrontPage package also allows you to test ISAPI applications using Windows 95/98 and Windows NT 4.0 Workstation.

Architecturally speaking, ISAPI DLLs can provide one or two different services. A DLL used via ISAPI on a server might be an extension, a filter, or both. In our discussion of the HTTP protocol in the last chapter, we discussed how a client machine packages a request and sends it to the server. The server processes the request and then sends the results back to the client. If you write a filter, your code will be executed at some or any of a variety of identifiable points during this process. Your filter tells the server which events it is interested in hearing about, and the server calls a function exported by the filter DLL to inform it of those events. Filters globally affect the operation of the server, and are notified about any connection made to the server if any task is carried out that would require their use. The client machine doesn't need to specifically ask the server to invoke a filter. In fact, the client is probably blissfully unaware of the existence of filters on your server.

If you write a server extension, the server calls you when the user provides a special URL, like the one on we saw on //mooseboy at the beginning of this section. The client can simply ask that the extension in the DLL be executed without further fuss, or the client can specify parameters for the execution of the server extension. Server extensions are useful for handling forms, generating dynamic reports from databases, or providing other dynamic content for the user on a per-request basis. Any online shopping you've done on the Internet has certainly involved some code that could have been implemented as a server extension.

You can put a filter and an extension in a given DLL, or you might separate everything into different pieces. You can't have more than one filter in a DLL, and you can't have more than one extension in a DLL. It's nice to have a filter and an extension in the same DLL when you've had reason to make the functionality of the filter and server extension mutually dependent.

Before we go much further, let me point out that ISAPI doesn't support Unicode. You can certainly write web filters and web extensions that deal with Unicode data, but how that works is up to you. All of the APIs, even the ones we know to pass references to strings around, are really architected as if they pass bunches of bytes around. Whether those bytes turn out to be a stream of single byte, multibyte, or double-byte characters (or binary data, or 12-bit packed tuples, or whatever!) is really up to the semantics established in the specific connection and not the programming interface itself.

Filters

As the server answers requests from client machines, it performs several very specific steps:

> Accepting the connection from the client

> Resolving any logical names in the reference to the resource

> Deciding if the resource the user has requested needs to be validated by some security mechanism (and then performing that validation)

> Formulating the response, in particular developing headers for the response

> Sending the response to the client

> Ending communication with the client

It's easy to imagine that it might be cool to write your own code to do any of these things. The 'out-of-the-box' server performs the most fundamental steps and gets things moving. There are always reasons for modifying default behavior, which is why we spend hours fooling around with languages like C++.

ISAPI Filter DLLs export two important entry points: `GetFilterVersion()` and `HttpFilterProc()`. When the server loads, it loads each of the filter DLLs it has been configured to use. It calls the `GetFilterVersion()` entry point on each DLL, and that function allows the DLL to initialize itself. If the DLL successfully initializes, the server will keep it in memory. The filter tells the server which notifications it's interested in receiving, and the server begins running. When the events actually occur, no matter which connection causes them to happen, the server calls the `HttpFilterProc()` entry point on each of the loaded filters until the notification has been successfully handled.

Microsoft's Internet Information Server lets you install filter DLLs by directly editing the registry. The order of the DLLs in that list dictates the order in which the filters will load. The filters are notified based on the notification priority they request; filters can request that they be notified in one of three orders: `SF_NOTIFY_ORDER_HIGH`, `SF_NOTIFY_ORDER_MEDIUM`, or `SF_NOTIFY_ORDER_LOW`. There's also `SF_NOTIFY_ORDER_DEFAULT`, which is equivalent to `SF_NOTIFY_ORDER_LOW`. If more than one filter loads and requests the same notification order, the server implementation dictates how the tie will be resolved. For those filters that request the same notification order, IIS will notify filters loaded earlier before notifying those filters loaded later.

When you write a filter with MFC, your DLL will include a single static instance of the MFC class CHttpFilter. You don't need to worry about implementing GetFilterVersion() and HttpFilterProc() because MFC implements them for you. However, you do need to make sure that the entry points which MFC has defined for you are properly exported from your DLL; just add them to your .def file. There's a Wizard included in Visual C++ that will set up your project for you, and I'll describe it later in this chapter. Suffice to say that the .def file for a typical MFC-based filter project could look something like this:

```
LIBRARY       YourFilter
EXPORTS
    HttpFilterProc
    GetFilterVersion
```

When the server loads your filter, the first thing it will do is find and call the ::GetFilterVersion() function. This function is really implemented by MFC, and MFC will go looking for an object of the class CHttpFilter, that single instance you declared in order to build your filter. You can think of the CHttpFilter-derived object in your module as being very similar to the CWinApp-derived object in your applications. Inside MFC, CHttpFilter implements the most fundamental features of a filter. You need to override certain members of CHttpFilter to augment that fundamental behavior and make your filter do something that you'll consider useful. CHttpFilter is markedly simpler than CWinApp, but like CWinApp it has functions that you almost always need to override, and others that you only need to override when you really need them.

The MFC implementation of the C-language, non-MFC ::GetFilterVersion() function, which is called by the server, ends up finding the global instance of that CHttpFilter-derived object you've created and calling its GetFilterVersion() member function. This function has a prototype like this:

```
BOOL GetFilterVersion(PHTTP_FILTER_VERSION pVer);
```

As I alluded to earlier, the function can return TRUE if your filter successfully initializes and FALSE if it can't initialize. Note that failing to load a filter doesn't necessarily mean that the server won't load; Internet Information Server, for example, just notes the problem in the server log and carries on. The single parameter is a pointer to an HTTP_FILTER_VERSION structure. This structure includes a couple of member variables that let you compare the version of the filter specification that your program was compiled to use with that of the filter specification which the server actually implements. The structure looks like this:

```
typedef struct _HTTP_FILTER_VERSION {
    DWORD   dwServerFilterVersion;
    DWORD   dwFilterVersion;
    CHAR    lpszFilterDesc[SF_MAX_FILTER_DESC_LEN+1];
    DWORD   dwFlags;
} HTTP_FILTER_VERSION, *PHTTP_FILTER_VERSION;
```

When your GetFilterVersion() override is called, dwServerFilterVersion will contain the filter's implementation version, packed up with the minor version of the spec in the low order word, and the major version of the spec in the high order word. For now, most servers (and MFC as well) implement Version 4.0 of the specification... so the DWORD will be equal to 0x00040000.

After returning to the server, that server expects to receive the version of the filter you support in the dwFilterVersion member. You don't need to do the comparison yourself; you can just set the member and walk away. If you want to, you can have a peek at the server version and respond in a way that you think is appropriate. You don't have to do anything, by the way; the base-class implementation sets up dwFilterVersion for you.

The lpszFilterDesc member has an unfortunate name; lpsz usually indicates a pointer to a zero-terminated string, but this member isn't a pointer. Instead, it's an array of 256 characters, not including the null terminator, which you can use to store a description for your server. MFC's implementation of CHttpFilter::GetFilterVersion() empties this string. You really should write some code that puts something meaningful into this string, because most servers use the string in log entries that involve the filter.

dwFlags is the really interesting member. I won't ruin the surprise by explaining that this member needs to be initialized with a bunch of flags that reflect how your server works and which notifications it is interested in receiving. It's here that you can set one of the SF_NOTIFY_ORDER_* flags which I mentioned one or two pages ago. You should try to use the lowest notification priority possible; HTTP servers are incredibly busy places, so you should try to minimize the work that the server needs to do. When the server calls your filter, it's spending time on you that it could be spending looking up accounts, pumping data off to the network, or opening files. By claiming the need for a lower priority, you can force the server to do less work. We'll see exactly why in a couple more paragraphs.

You'll also want to add one or both of SF_NOTIFY_SECURE_PORT and SF_NOTIFY_NONSECURE_PORT to the stew. If you specify SF_NOTIFY_SECURE_PORT, the server will only notify you about activity on connections which are using the Secure Sockets Layer, otherwise known as HTTPS. If you specify SF_NOTIFY_NONSECURE_PORT, you'll be notified about activity on connections that are made via regular HTTP – without the encryption that the Secure Sockets Layer brings. You can specify both, and you will receive notifications on any kind of connection. It is true that if you specify neither flag, then you will also receive notifications for both secure and non-secure connections; but it's better programming style to specify this explicitly.

Once you've combined a notification priority with a port type or two, you're about half done. You'll need to specify at least one flag that causes the server to call your filter when something happens. All of these notifications happen by means of the server calling the C-language, non-MFC exported function named ::HttpFilterProc(). Just like the MFC-supplied implementation of GetFilterVersion(), the MFC-supplied implementation of the exported function named HttpFilterProc() finds your CHttpFilter instance and calls its HttpFilterProc() member function. The default implementation of that function decides which notification the server is sending and passes it along to a member function of your class, where you can do whatever you think is appropriate.

You *can* override CHttpFilter::HttpFilterProc() if you want to, but it's not all that interesting to do so. This function has this prototype:

```
DWORD HttpFilterProc( PHTTP_FILTER_CONTEXT pfc,
                      DWORD NotificationType,
                      LPVOID pvNotification );
```

The NotificationType parameter receives a constant that indicates the type of notification you're receiving. It matches, exactly, a single notification type flag that you set in the dwFlags member of the HTTP_FILTER_VERSION structure, when you were handling the call to GetFilterVersion(). Even if you register to receive more than one notification, you'll only be notified of one notification for each call to HttpFilterProc(). The pvNotification points to some data that's specific to the notification. Some notifications pass a pointer to a structure of interesting data, while other notifications don't need to tell you anything interesting and so pass nothing of meaning here.

The MFC implementation of CHttpFilter::HttpFilterProc() is nothing but a big switch statement that calls a particular virtual member function of your CHttpFilter-derived class to let you handle the notification. MFC casts the pvNotification pointer to a type-safe pointer to the data which you're ready to receive, but that's all there is to it. If you want to do some work before and/or after every notification call, regardless of the notification type, then it's appropriate to write an override for CHttpFilter::HttpFilterProc(). You can call the base class implementation before or after you do some work to get the regular handler function executed.

The Chain of Command

HttpFilterProc(), like all of the overridable notification functions, returns a DWORD and accepts a pointer to an HTTP_FILTER_CONTEXT structure. To understand these features of the functions, we'll need to take a step back and examine the way filter notifications are handed out by the server.

If the server needs to send a notification, it will start by finding the filter with the highest SF_NOTIFY_ORDER_* setting. If you have a filter registered with SF_NOTIFY_ORDER_HIGH, it will be notified before any filter with SF_NOTIFY_ORDER_MEDIUM. Any filter with SF_NOTIFY_ORDER_MEDIUM will be notified before any filter with SF_NOTIFY_ORDER_LOW. With the highest priority filter in hand, the server makes HttpFilterProc() dish out the notification.

When the notification call returns, the server examines the return value. It expects to see one of these constants returned from the function:

SF_STATUS_REQ_FINISHED

SF_STATUS_REQ_FINISHED_KEEP_CONN

SF_STATUS_REQ_NEXT_NOTIFICATION

SF_STATUS_REQ_HANDLED_NOTIFICATION

SF_STATUS_REQ_ERROR

SF_STATUS_REQ_READ_NEXT

If a given notification handler function returns SF_STATUS_REQ_NEXT_NOTIFICATION, it is indicating to the server that it couldn't handle the notification, or that it didn't handle the notification and that it thinks there are other filters which may be interested in the notification. This response means that the filter didn't think anything was terribly wrong with the notification, and therefore that it doesn't think the server should discard it.

If the filter notification function thinks the request was completely bogus, or determined that the request could absolutely not be handled (or, for some reason, *shouldn't* be handled) by the server, it can return SF_STATUS_REQ_ERROR. This will cause the server to not pass on the notification to any other notification functions in other filters. The server calls the ::GetLastError() API to find your status code, fluffs up an appropriate response, and sends it to the client. You can use ::SetLastError() to set the value that the server will end up using.

If you return SF_STATUS_**REQ_ERROR** from OnSendRawData(), the server won't send any response to your client. This only follows if, say, there was an error while sending raw data; the server won't assume that it can successfully send data itself. The value you set with ::SetLastError() is an operating system error number; it is *not* an HTTP error number. Setting a last error of 401, for example, won't cause the server to generate a reply that indicates an Access Denied problem. Instead, the server will report a generic 'Server Error', which is HTTP error code number 501. The server may report the operating system error number you've set, or it may not – Internet Information Server 3.0 does. If you call ::SetLastError() and pass 12345 before returning SF_STATUS_REQ_ERROR from your handler, for instance, then the server will send this response back:

```
HTTP/1.0 500 Server Error (12345){cr}{lf}
content-type: text/html{cr}{lf}
{cr}{lf}
<body><h1>HTTP/1.0 500 Server Error (12345) {cr}{lf}
</h1></body>{cr}{lf}
```

Similar information will end-up in the log on the server. Of course, things might someday be brighter, and your notification function may successfully process a notification *and* decide no other filter needs to know about the request. In such a circumstance, you should return SF_STATUS_REQ_FINISHED from your notification handler. This will cause the server to close the connection with the client and that's that.

It's possible that, even though one HTTP transaction has finished, the server and the client will keep the connection open. This is a way around one of the biggest shortcomings of the HTTP protocol, which is based on repeatedly making connections from the client to the server. If you connect to my home page on the Web, for example, you'll download some HTML text. As your browser formats that text, it'll suddenly realize that it also needs to download a picture or two. It'll connect to the server again and get the picture of my motorcycle. Then, it'll disconnect, only to reconnect and get the picture of the hockey puck hitting the button-down yuppie twit *right* in the face. Then, it'll disconnect, and wait for your next command.

Disconnecting and reconnecting is terribly expensive. The client can't keep anything in cache itself; it has to go to the name server to figure out the exact network address of MOOSEBOY before connecting to it. Then, it has to actually connect to MOOSEBOY and get it to respond. This takes time; subsequent iterations through the process are probably faster than the first, but only because the other machines involved (e.g. the name server) probably have MOOSEBOY's address in cache, and the routers between your client and MOOSEBOY probably have the shortest path all worked out and in cache. But since HTML, by nature, often causes these sort of dense self-references, smarter browsers ask to keep the connection alive after the request has been fulfilled. That skips all of the lookup, translation, and connection steps to allow the server to continue responding to the client requests. This is a great optimization, since the protocol usually causes many requests to go to the same server in rapid succession.

While the exact mechanisms of such a negotiation are beyond the scope of this chapter, HTTP connections can be kept past the response from the server. You can enforce such a negotiation after a successful response by returning SF_STATUS_REQ_FINISHED_KEEP_CONN from your notification handler function. If the HTTP connection initiated by the browser asked for the connection to stay open, this return will honor the results of that negotiation. SF_STATUS_REQ_FINISHED and SF_STATUS_REQ_ERROR both cause the server to disconnect from the client after the response header is sent back to the client from the server.

Even on sunnier days, there's a difference between successfully handling a notification and being completely done with the request from the client. Notifications are smaller than HTTP transactions; that is, one HTTP transaction may cause several events about which the server will notify filters. SF_STATUS_REQ_FINISHED and SF_STATUS_REQ_FINISHED_KEEP_CONN relate to the latter; that is, the filter handles the notification and, in addition, realizes that the handling of the notification means that the currently pending request has been completed. A return value of SF_STATUS_REQ_HANDLED_NOTIFICATION, on the other hand, means your filter notification function has successfully handled the notification and it doesn't need to be passed on to other filters. If, however, you want other filters to also have a chance to play with this notification, then you should return SF_STATUS_REQ_NEXT_NOTIFICATION. If there are no other filters, then this is just the same as returning SF_STATUS_REQ_HANDLED_NOTIFICATION.

I've implied something, but not said it explicitly. So, with a fine point on it, none of these return values ask the server to do any extra work. The server will *not* send the client any information to indicate what's happened, unless you've returned SF_STATUS_REQ_ERROR from a function during the processing of a request. If you want to send back some error text, it's completely up to you to create it, format it and send it back to the server. Even in situations where SF_STATUS_REQ_ERROR does send back an error message, it might not be the error message you want. Generally speaking, if you want something to go back to the server, you should call CHttpFilterContext::WriteClient() and send it yourself. Then, you should return SF_STATUS_REQ_HANDLED_NOTIFICATION so the server knows you're done.

I've not introduced CHttpFilterContext::WriteClient(), or the other four member functions that CHttpFilterContext has. I guess it's about time we did. After all the groundwork is done, we'll learn exactly what notifications there are and what data is sent to them.

What to Do in Response

Each of the notification functions you can implement receives some parameters to describe the exact context of its call. The notification function might alter that data, record it, or supply it if it's missing; that behavior depends upon the exact functionality that you want your server to implement, and we'll learn about those parameters and their semantics in the next section.

For now, suffice to say that every one of these functions receives a pointer to a CHttpFilterContext object. That object has some interesting members, which we'll need to learn about if we mean to do any meaningful work in our notification handler.

As I described before, the server actually ends up calling functions exported by MFC when it sends your filter a notification. MFC finds your `CHttpFilter` instance and gives a call to the appropriate notification handler to get the notification dispatched. The server passes the filter procedure exported by MFC a pointer to an `HTTP_FILTER_CONTEXT` structure. The definition of this structure looks like this:

```
typedef struct _HTTP_FILTER_CONTEXT
{   // this is actually data
    DWORD     cbSize;
    DWORD     Revision;
    PVOID     ServerContext;
    DWORD     ulReserved;
    BOOL      fIsSecurePort;
    PVOID     pFilterContext;

    // these are pointer to functions
    BOOL (WINAPI * GetServerVariable)( struct _HTTP_FILTER_CONTEXT *pfc,
                                       LPSTR lpszVariableName,
                                       LPVOID lpvBuffer,
                                       LPDWORD lpdwSize );

    BOOL (WINAPI * AddResponseHeaders)( struct _HTTP_FILTER_CONTEXT *pfc,
                                        LPSTR lpszHeaders,
                                        DWORD dwReserved );

    BOOL (WINAPI * WriteClient)( struct _HTTP_FILTER_CONTEXT *pfc,
                                 LPVOID Buffer,
                                 LPDWORD lpdwBytes,
                                 DWORD dwReserved);

    VOID*(WINAPI * AllocMem)( struct _HTTP_FILTER_CONTEXT *pfc,
                              DWORD cbSize,
                              DWORD dwReserved);

    BOOL (WINAPI * ServerSupportFunction)( struct _HTTP_FILTER_CONTEXT *pfc,
                                           enum SF_REQ_TYPE sfReq,
                                           PVOID pData,
                                           DWORD ul1,
                                           DWORD ul2);
} HTTP_FILTER_CONTEXT, *PHTTP_FILTER_CONTEXT;
```

This structure is a little more complicated than most structures we've dealt with before, so let's spend a little bit of time with it before we discuss what it means. This structure does exactly what it says it will do; it keeps a context around for the server to communicate with the filter, and for the filter to communicate with the server. Filters (and extensions, as we'll see later) don't communicate with the client. Instead, they ask the server to communicate with the client on their behalf.

There are two distinct groups of members in the structure: one group of data members, and another group of pointers to functions. All right, they are all data members, but they're really things that you can use to call the server, because they're pointers to functions – actual, real-life executable code. That executable code lives in the server, so the server initializes the pointers before it hands the structure to the filter. The filter can then use those pointers to call code back in the server – to ask the server for more information, or to ask the server to communicate with the client, for example.

Pointer-to-function syntax in C and C++ is messy at best. It works, and you can learn it; I had to take three separate tests in pointer-to-function syntax before I was allowed to walk around at Microsoft without an escort. But it's just not fun to use since it's hard to read; just look at the declarations above!

Since MFC creates a `CHttpFilterContext` object for you, you have a fighting chance. The `CHttpFilterContext` object has a much more realistic definition:

```
class CHttpFilterContext
{
public:
    CHttpFilterContext(PHTTP_FILTER_CONTEXT pfc);
    ~CHttpFilterContext() { }

    BOOL GetServerVariable(LPTSTR lpszVariableName, LPVOID lpvBuffer,
        LPDWORD lpdwSize);
    BOOL AddResponseHeaders(LPTSTR lpszHeaders, DWORD dwReserved = 0);
    BOOL WriteClient(LPVOID lpvBuffer, LPDWORD lpdwBytes,
        DWORD dwReserved = 0);
    LPVOID AllocMem(DWORD cbSize, DWORD dwReserved = 0);
    BOOL ServerSupportFunction(enum SF_REQ_TYPE sfReq,
        LPVOID lpvBuffer, LPDWORD lpdwSize, LPDWORD lpdwDataType);

    PHTTP_FILTER_CONTEXT const m_pFC;
};
```

You can see that `CHttpFilterContext` maintains a copy of a pointer to the structure it was given by the server. But it also has member functions that bear the same names as the pointer-to-function names in the structure. Since MFC provides your notification handling functions with a pointer to a `CHttpFilterContext`, you can call back into the server simply by using the C++ member-call syntax with which you're accustomed.

Generating Output

`WriteClient()` is one of the more frequently used members. It takes a pointer to a buffer, a pointer to a number of bytes, and a reserved parameter. MFC's `CHttpFilterContext` defaults the `dwReserved` parameter to zero, so it's safely out of the way. The buffer you reference contains the bytes that you'd like to write to the client. You need to pass the address of a `DWORD` variable for the `lpdwBytes` parameter. This `DWORD` needs to be initialized with the number of bytes that you'd like to write. So, you might send a famous greeting to the client by making this call:

```
char sz[] = "Hello, world!\r\n";
DWORD dwLen = strlen(sz);
if (!pCtxt->WriteClient(sz, &dwLen))
    return SF_STATUS_REQ_ERROR;
```

It's important to note how I use `strlen()` to find the length of the string. Do not include the terminating null byte in the count that you pass to `WriteClient()`; the client doesn't care how you end strings, and thinks there might be more output on the way, anyhow. For the client, the end of the stream is marked by the connection being closed, not by any particular character sequence. `WriteClient()` returns non-zero if it works, but returns zero if it fails. I test for that failure, here. Like most other Win32 APIs, you can call `::GetLastError()` to figure out why the call failed.

`WriteClient()` does exactly what it says; it asks the server to pump the data you supplied back to the client. The server fulfills your request *right now*. If you write one byte, then the server builds up a whole packet, asks the network to send it, and gets it going to the client. This is expensive; if you write a million bytes by calling `WriteClient()` to send one byte at a time, you'll clog the whole Internet and bring down every server in the world. Worse yet, your application will be slow; lots slower than the pink slip your manager will bring you, anyhow. If you need to write something back to the client, build up a buffer using a `char` array or a `CString` and pump it out all at once.

Thanks for the Memory

The AllocMem() member is a neat way to get memory. It asks the server for some of its own memory, and the server manages that memory for you. That is, the server internally associates the memory with the connection that you're handling just now, and frees it for you automatically when that connection is terminated. You don't need to do anything extra!

However, AllocMem() can be the source of performance bottlenecks. General purpose memory routines, like malloc() (and its pal, new) from the C library, are good at handling diverse situations. AllocMem() isn't. If you use AllocMem() to allocate tens of dozens of little blocks of data, you're making lots of work for the server because it has to track and eventually free all of those memory blocks. If you need to grab some amount of memory just once or twice for each connection, it's appropriate to use AllocMem(). Using AllocMem() to hold tiny little pieces of memory which you use in formulating your response is bound to cause performance problems.

AllocMem() returns a void pointer to a buffer. It doesn't initialize any objects; it is not a replacement for new. You can cast the returned pointer to whatever type you need before using it.

Global Environment Consciousness

The HTTP protocol, by definition, is stateless. That is, the client connects to the server, does some work, and then disconnects. That's all; there's no state maintained between consecutive connections of the same server. It turns out that this is good for server designers because the server has only to reply to the request, without remembering anything.

There's plenty of information describing the connection as it arrives, though. All of the headers, which we've been talking about as being a part of the request, supply some contextual information; further information is available to the server inherently, because the server has a connection with the client.

Most of this information can be very useful, particularly while writing a filter. The information describing the connection is made available, via ISAPI, with calls to the GetServerVariable() function. The function has this prototype:

```
BOOL CHttpFilterContext::GetServerVariable( LPTSTR lpszVariableName,
                                            LPVOID lpvBuffer,
                                            LPDWORD lpdwSize);
```

The lpszVariableName points to a string that identifies the variable you're interested in receiving. You'll need to pass a pointer to a buffer that you own for the lpvBuffer, and lpdwSize will point at a DWORD. The DWORD should contain the size of the buffer, and when the function returns it will contain the number of bytes actually written to your buffer. This function is similar to the QueryValue() function made available in CHttpFile, but GetServerVariable() supports a few extra variables which aren't represented directly by headers. These variables correspond to information that the server makes available for you.

The MFC documentation provides a huge list of the variables that are available, so I won't reiterate them here. Let me point out, though, that one of the most useful variables is ALL_HTTP. This gets all of the headers in their raw form from the request and drops them in your buffer. You might code this, for example:

```
char sz[1024];
DWORD dw = 1024;
if (pCtxt->GetServerVariable("ALL_HTTP", sz, &dw)
{
    // do something with the headers
}
```

and then start parsing all of the headers which were returned to you.

Give Me a Call Sometime

Now we know what the notification function can return, let's look at why it would get called in the first place. There are seven different notifications for which the server will notify filters; we'll review each one and discuss its uses.

Reading Raw Data

As the server reads a block of data from the client, it can offer filters a chance to preprocess it. The raw data is just that; every byte the server has received from the client. The server sends this notification with the raw data as received from the client. The server may have called other filters if they were notified at a higher priority than you and those filters may have already translated the data. But you're certainly getting a crack at the data before the server has done absolutely anything else to it. The raw data really is the raw data; the data stream includes passwords, which may or may not have been encrypted, and includes headers that the client has sent as part of the request.

The applications for this notification should be apparent; you can do almost anything. This notification is incredibly expensive, however, since your filter will be notified for every single block of data that the server reads. You might be asked to process a single byte, but odds are you'll be passed several kilobytes of data. It's up to you to remember some context between each call that supplies coherent, semantic, continuous meaning to the data as it flows by.

You can receive these notifications if you specify SF_NOTIFY_READ_RAW_DATA in your GetFilterVersion() flags. CHttpFilter features a member named OnReadRawData() which has this prototype:

```
DWORD CHttpFilter::OnReadRawData( CHttpFilterContext* pfc,
                                  PHTTP_FILTER_RAW_DATA pRawData );
```

The HTTP_FILTER_RAW_DATA object pointed to by the pRawData parameter has this structure:

```
typedef struct _HTTP_FILTER_RAW_DATA
{
    PVOID pvInData;
    DWORD cbInData;
    DWORD cbInBuffer;
    DWORD dwReserved;
} HTTP_FILTER_RAW_DATA, *PHTTP_FILTER_RAW_DATA;
```

pvInData points at a buffer containing the data as it was read. cbInData is a count of bytes in that buffer, and cbInBuffer is a count of bytes in the buffer where cbInData sits. cbInData is less than or equal to cbInBuffer. If you need to do a translation that ends up expanding the data, you can do it in-place if you don't end up expanding to a total of more than cbInBuffer bytes. If you can't do it in-place, you'll need to split the work across two calls.

dwReserved holds my current bank balance multiplied by the odometer reading from my motorcycle. This field size *won't* expand in future versions of the ISAPI specification; the balance goes down and the mileage goes up, but the product remains practically constant.

Writing Raw Data

Similarly, your filter can be notified as the server starts writing data to the client. Again, your filter could be notified after other filters have been notified, but the server is completely done with the data and, other than giving each filter a crack at it, is ready to send it off.

This notification is sent if you register with the SF_NOTIFY_SEND_RAW_DATA flag. OnSendRawData() is the CHttpFilter member that is called for this type of notification. Its prototype is here:

```
DWORD CHttpFilter::OnSendRawData( CHttpFilterContext* pfc,
                                  PHTTP_FILTER_RAW_DATA pRawData );
```

This function also receives a pointer to the same HTTP_FILTER_RAW_DATA structure. The members have the same meaning here, but it's just that the data is going the other way.

Header Processing

The server will notify your filter, if you've set the SF_NOTIFY_PREPROC_HEADERS bit in your dwFlags return during the execution of GetFilterVersion() implementation of your filter, when the server has finished preprocessing the headers sent in the request to the server.

As we've discussed before, the client sends extra information in the header of the request to the server. Those headers can contain modifiers that will affect the way the server should interpret the request. When the request is received and read from the client, the raw data read notification is fired. The headers seen by the raw data read notification handler are just that – raw. The server sends the information in the headers directly along to the notification without any adjustments.

Once the raw data read notification returns, the server begins to preprocess the headers that were sent. The preprocessing simply means that any logical names, relative paths, or substitutable strings are parsed out from the headers and expanded appropriately. These processed headers are sent along to the OnPreprocHeaders() notification handler. Your override for this handler should have this prototype:

```
virtual DWORD OnPreprocHeaders( CHttpFilterContext* pfc,
                                PHTTP_FILTER_PREPROC_HEADERS pHeaders );
```

If you need to immediately respond to the request, you can use the context object pointed to by the pfc parameter to do so. The pHeaders parameter locates a structure that contains pointers to functions that allow you to do some additional work with the headers. The members look like this:

```
BOOL (WINAPI * GetHeader)( struct _HTTP_FILTER_CONTEXT *pfc,
                           LPSTR lpszName,
                           LPVOID lpvBuffer,
                           LPDWORD lpdwSize);

BOOL (WINAPI * SetHeader)( struct _HTTP_FILTER_CONTEXT *pfc,
                           LPSTR lpszName,
                           LPSTR lpszValue);

BOOL (WINAPI * AddHeader)( struct _HTTP_FILTER_CONTEXT *pfc,
                           LPSTR lpszName,
                           LPSTR lpszValue);
```

These members are all pointers to functions. You can dereference them to call back into the server to get a bit of work done. For example, your OnPreprocHeaders() function might add a header using this code:

```
DWORD CMyFilter::OnPreprocHeaders(CHttpFilterContext* pfc,
    PHTTP_FILTER_PREPROC_HEADERS pHeaders)
{
    pfc->AddHeader(pfc, "Accept", "Text/*");
    // ... more work ...
```

You can use AddHeader() to put a new header into the stream the server will use. You should pass the pfc parameter your notification originally received for the first parameter to AddHeader(), as we did in the code fragment above. The second parameter identifies the name of the header tag, and the third parameter identifies the value for that header tag. Above, we add the header "Accept: Text/*".

SetHeader() works as AddHeader() does – and also accepts analogous parameters. But AddHeader() is intended to add a new header, while SetHeader() changes the value of an existing header. If you call AddHeader() for a header that already exists, you'll find that you'll have duplicate tags with different values. SetHeader() can also be used to remove a header. Simply call SetHeader() with the header name and pass an empty string for the value of the header tag.

You can call GetHeader() to find the value of an existing header. All three functions return non-zero for success and zero for failure.

Authentication

The server will send a notification named SF_NOTIFY_AUTHENTICATION just before it tries to authenticate the connection. You can handle authentication requests by registering with this flag and writing an override for the OnAuthentication() member of CHttpFilter. You can implement this function if you're interested in doing your own authentication of users who show up at your server's doorstep.

Your OnAuthentication() function will receive a pointer to an HTTP_FILTER_AUTHENT structure, which has this content:

```
typedef struct _HTTP_FILTER_AUTHENT
{
    char* pszUser;
    DWORD cbUserBuff;
    char* pszPassword;
    DWORD cbPasswordBuff;
} HTTP_FILTER_AUTHENT;
```

The pszUser and pszPassword members point to the user name and password supplied by the user in the authentication request. You can perform your own authentication in your OnAuthentication() handler in one of two ways. Let look at these now.

The first authentication strategy is for you to simply check the password and user name using your own algorithm. If the user name and password are good, you can simply return SF_STATUS_REQ_HANDLED_NOTIFICATION. If you don't like the user name or password, you can pump back an error message with a call to WriteClient(), and return SF_STATUS_REQ_ERROR or SF_STATUS_REQ_FINISHED. The ERROR return is more appropriate for most cases, because it lets the server know that there was, indeed, an error; and that'll cause the server to write information to the log describing the problem. If you return FINISHED, the server will log the transaction as if there was no error.

The second authentication strategy involves a sneaky little switch. Normally, when a user hits your server, they're doing so anonymously, using the user account, which you configured when you set up the server. If you don't want users to make use of that particular account, you can force them into another account by altering the buffers referenced by the pszUser and pszPassword strings. Since the server software can enforce security rules when working with NTFS volumes, you can dynamically map anonymous requests to an account that you feel is appropriate based on the request. Making such changes can help you architect a more effective – and perhaps more easily maintained – security implementation. By altering the buffers and letting the request proceed to the server, the server will take care of allowing the request to execute in the context of the user account that you specify.

URL Mapping

When your GetFilterVersion() function tells the server you want to receive SF_NOTIFY_URL_MAP notifications, MFC will pass the notifications on to your filter's OnUrlMap() entry point. The function has this prototype:

```
virtual DWORD OnUrlMap( CHttpFilterContext* pfc,
                        PHTTP_FILTER_URL_MAP pUrlMap);
```

The URL Map override gives your filter the ability to map requests for a particular logical location to a physical location that might be different. If you're offering web space to the public, for example, you might decide that it is convenient to make directories accessible to your customers by building a tree that uses their customer ID number. Perhaps you have a customer with the user name mikeblas, and their ID number is 0031511.

If that customer actually stores their web pages in a directory named publicftp\0031511, but you want to point to that directory when the web server hits a URL like http://mooseboy/mikeblas/ you can perform URL mapping to resolve the address. When OnUrlMap() is called to map the URL, pUrlMap will point at a structure with these members:

```
const char* pszURL;
char* pszPhysicalPath;
DWORD cbPathBuff;
```

pszURL will point at the URL, and you can fill pszPhysicalPath with the physical location you want. You've only got as many characters in pszPhysicalPath as indicated by cbPathBuff, so you must make sure you don't write off the end of the buffer. If you perform the mapping, you should return SF_STATUS_REQ_HANDLED_NOTIFICATION. If you don't perform any mapping, there's no need to change pszPhysicalPath if you return SF_STATUS_REQ_NEXT_NOTIFICATION.

Modifying Log Writes

The server will occasionally decide to write information to the server's log file. Microsoft Internet Information Server may be configured to write a log of server activity to a SQL database, or to a plain comma-delimited text file.

If you've specified SF_NOTIFY_LOG in your dwFlags return from GetFilterVersion(), your filter can be notified whenever the server is about to write log information. Your filter can detect particular log writes and append information to them and/or write log information to a different location.

MFC will pass the log write notifications along to the OnLog() function of your CHttpFilter-derived object. OnLog() has this prototype:

```
virtual DWORD OnLog( CHttpFilterContext* pfc,
                     PHTTP_FILTER_LOG pLog);
```

As usual, the pfc parameter points at a CHttpFilterContext you can use to communicate with the client. The pLog parameter points at a structure that contains the information the server will record in the log. The structure has these members:

Type	Name	Meaning
const char*	pszClientHostName	Client's host name
const char*	pszClientUserName	Client's user name
const char*	pszServerName	Name of the server the client is connected to
const char*	pszOperation	HTTP command
const char*	pszTarget	Target of the HTTP command
const char*	pszParameters	Parameters passed to the HTTP command
DWORD	dwHttpStatus	HTTP return status
DWORD	dwWin32Status	Win32 error code

Any of the members of the structure may be empty. If you need to write alternate information, you can replace the pointers but you can't alter the memory that the pointers reference directly. If you allocate your own memory to hold a string to be returned, you'll need to make sure the pointer you hand off is valid until the next log notification call is made.

If you don't want to write the log entry, you can return SF_STATUS_REQ_HANDLED_NOTIFICATION from your notification handler without doing any work at all.

End of Session

When all that's left to do is reflect on what's been done, the server sends SF_NOTIFY_END_SESSION notifications. If your filter has registered to request this notification, it can clean up any data structure that it might have allocated to be stored in the pFilterContext structure, for instance, or it can release other data that it's kept around for the session.

As you architect your server, it's important to remember our discussion about 'keep alive' sessions earlier in the chapter. Since the client might want to have the session open, more than one request might pass through your server before the session is actually disconnected. Since such a session only disconnects once, this notification is only sent once, at that final disconnect, and not after each request has finished processing.

Putting it All Together

When someone connects to your server, you'll receive notifications about their activity in a reasonably deterministic order. Since the request from the client is sent to the server, the server will have to read it, which means that the first notification you'll receive (if you've requested to receive it) is given to OnReadRawData(). You can use this chance to party on the headers and request body directly, if you want.

The server itself will get to work on the headers, and then (if you've registered for it) call your OnPreprocHeaders() notification. Following this, the server will offer you an OnUrlMap() call. Now the server knows the user is ready to ask for some data, and it knows exactly what data they want to ask for, it's ready to provide that data. If it turns out that an authentication is necessary, the server will take care of sending the challenge and call OnAuthentication() when the response comes back.

Finally, if everything has gone swimmingly to this point, the server will be ready to write data back to your client. If you have requested to receive the notification, the server will end up calling your OnSendRawData() member. Here, you can make your own calls to WriteClient() to pump out some extra data or perform an in-place translation on the data in the buffer which was passed to you.

You'll receive a call to OnLog() because the server will want to write a record of the transaction to the log. You can usurp the log write if you don't think it's important enough; some people write filters that process only SF_NOTIFY_LOG to filter out 'noisy' logs or draw stronger attention to log entries that they feel are important, which can simplify their server management duties.

There's no guarantee you'll receive *all* of these notifications. An earlier error in processing one of the notifications could have stopped the transaction. Or another filter, with a higher priority than yours, could have requested that the notification not be propagated to your filter. The ISAPI specification does not, unfortunately, dictate the order in which notifications are sent, so some servers may change the order, depending on their own implementation details.

Furthermore, there are lots of subtle interactions between all of the notifications. If you fail the authentication request, for example, the server will notice and fire off an error message to the client. And, when it does, your `OnSendRawData()` function will be called because the error message is, after all, data that's going from the client to the server.

Certainly, if your server is busy, you won't receive calls in any particular order; the server is fulfilling requests from clients by using multiple threads. If two users are connected to your server almost simultaneously, you'll almost certainly receive two calls to `OnReadRawData()` in a row, as the server reads each of the requests from different threads. The balance of the calls for each of the requests will be similarly interposed as the server works on them.

Server Extensions

While filters are interesting for situations where you need to monitor everything coming from or going to your server, the more common application of ISAPI involves writing applications that can be run on demand.

ISAPI server extensions are the URL-activated applications that we've alluded to throughout the chapter. You can have the extension take absolutely no input information from the user, or your extension can interact heavily with the user. Let's first examine the architecture your server extension applications will use, and then move on to the actual semantics of implementing a server extension meaningfully on a server.

Your ISAPI server extension is implemented as a DLL, and that's what gives the ISAPI architecture a strong advantage over the traditional CGI architecture. CGI applications run as executables and work in a separate process from the server itself. The server writes data to the CGI extension, and reads from it by using redirected standard input and standard output handles. This means that the operating system, during the execution of a CGI extension, is heavily taxed; the server must spawn a new process to run the CGI extension, copy all the data which is to be sent to the server to the different process, and let the process run. The process then writes data back to the server via the same, slow interprocess mechanism. On a busy server, the CGI mechanism necessarily means that the server software is starting and stopping a new process for each CGI request. This, in turn, means the overhead in the architecture can begin to eat away at the horsepower that the server should be using for the needs of its many clients.

On the other hand, ISAPI server extensions load as a DLL. The server then has the code for the extension right within its own process, and can communicate with the code directly. Data passed from the server code to the extension DLL is simply given via a pointer in a function call, and doesn't need to be copied from a buffer in one process to a buffer in a separate process by special privileged operating system mechanisms. The server only pays the cost of loading the extension code once; it doesn't need to reinitialize the code for each and every execution of the extension.

These ISAPI-specific optimizations seem a bit minimal when taken at their face value, but add up very rapidly in aggressive server environments. Since a busy web server may be answering requests from hundreds (if not thousands!) of users, the server offers an environment that truly needs every iota of computing energy it can muster.

Your ISAPI server extension DLL must export two functions by name: GetExtensionVersion() and HttpExtensionProc(). The server software references these two symbols after the server loads the DLL. GetExtensionVersion() offers your server extension a chance to exchange version and descriptive information with the server, while the HttpExtensionProc() is called whenever your server DLL is asked by a user to perform some interesting action. These functions are C-level, plain functions; they're implemented for you by MFC and enhanced to provide a more interesting C++ oriented interface. Furthermore, since most server extensions traditionally provide very similar core features, MFC's code allows you to avoid some of the drudgery involved in implementing a useful extension.

Just as an application you write using MFC will have a single CWinApp-derived object, your server extension DLL will have a single CHttpServer-derived object. The code in MFC which implements the raw GetExtensionVersion() and HttpExtensionProc() functions exported from your DLL will find that single CHttpServer-derived object in your DLL and call some functions in it. The flow of control which MFC initiates by those calls can be overridden at any of a few interesting spots. There are also, of course, a couple of points where you're absolutely required to override the default behavior if you want your server extension to do anything interesting.

The Server Extension Life Cycle

Your server extension DLL is loaded upon demand. That is, unlike a filter DLL, your server extension DLL will be brought into memory when the server has been requested, by one of its users, to run the DLL. The server first tries to find the GetExtensionVersion() export in the DLL. If the server can't find that function, it will release the DLL and report an error back to the user. On the other hand, if the function is found, it is called. MFC answers the call by retrieving the CHttpServer object in your DLL and calling its CHttpServer::GetExtensionVersion() override.

If your override returns TRUE, the server then calls your DLL's HttpExtensionProc() export and passes to it all the information provided to the server when the user made the original query. If GetExtensionVersion() returns FALSE, the server knows the extension isn't able to load or initialize, so it terminates the extension DLL and returns an error message to the user.

If everything loads smoothly, however, the HttpExtensionProc() call is allowed to run. Much like the GetExtensionVersion() call, MFC calls the CHttpServer::HttpExtensionProc() override in your DLL. While you'll almost always override GetExtensionVersion(), you'll only override HttpExtensionProc() in very, very rare circumstances.

The HttpExtensionProc() function exported by the DLL can return success or failure. If the function returns failure, the server assumes that the DLL had a catastrophic failure and attempts to report an error to the client on behalf of the extension. If the DLL encounters an error that indicates a problem with the parameters to the function, or needs to return an error the user will understand, it should actually return that information to the user itself and then report success back to the server.

Whether the `HttpExtensionProc()` function returns success or failure, the server will keep the DLL in memory for further requests. Now that the DLL has been initialized and properly loaded, the server will never unload the DLL in the course of normal operation. If the server has been specifically set up for debugging, or if the server administrator chooses to take advantage of any advanced configuration management facilities available on the server, the DLL may be forced to unload. For example, Microsoft Internet Information Server provides a way to automatically unload DLLs after they have finished executing. This is a great idea for debugging and testing, since it means the DLL can always be replaced and will be reloaded the next time it is used. However, the repeated loading and unloading of the DLL will waste the server's resources, since the server should be working with the user instead of loading and killing DLLs for each and every request; a server in a production environment should never be configured this way.

When you write a server extension, you should place any module-wide initialization code you need to execute in your `GetExtensionVersion()` function. If that initialization fails, you can return `FALSE` from the function, and the server will fail the request the client has made. You can, of course, use the constructor of the class to initialize any member data you have in the class, but it's not a great idea to do anything very aggressive in the constructor. In particular, it's a bad idea to throw exceptions, since it's impossible to trap the exception and react safely. First, if there's a chance of failing the initialization in the constructor, there's no way to communicate the failure back to the server. Second, since the DLL has just loaded, MFC (if you've linked to it) isn't initialized.

The `InitInstance()` override of your server class will be called once for each execution of the server, but it doesn't receive any description of the activity which caused the extension to run. `HttpExtensionProc()` is finally called with all the information necessary to actually run the request.

Reacting to Commands

You could, if you wanted to, override `HttpExtensionProc()`. Its prototype looks like this:

```
virtual DWORD CHttpServer::HttpExtensionProc( EXTENSION_CONTROL_BLOCK *pECB );
```

The function returns a `DWORD`, as you can see, and accepts a pointer to a structure which contains information describing the call. The function returns one of four values to indicate its success or failure. `HSE_STATUS_ERROR` indicates the extension failed for some reason. `HSE_STATUS_SUCCESS` means the extension worked just fine. If your server extension encounters a problem, it should write error information back to the client and return `HSE_STATUS_SUCCESS`. `HSE_STATUS_ERROR` should be reserved for situations that are absolutely critical; they'll cause the server to write back a generic error message indicating a failure, and that won't offer your user (or the person who has to administer your server) much insight into what's really going on.

Your `HttpExtensionProc()` function can also return `HSE_STATUS_PENDING` or `HSE_STATUS_SUCCESS_AND_KEEP_CONN`. If `HSE_STATUS_PENDING` is returned it means your server extension has queued the request, will finish it at a later time, and will notify the server when the request has finally completed. (For more information on this mechanism, see our discussion of the `ServerSupportFunction()` a little later in the chapter.) `HSE_STATUS_SUCCESS_AND_KEEP_CONN` tells the server you've responded to the request successfully, but that you want to keep the connection open. Normally, HTTP connections are opened, a request is made, a response is received and the connection is closed. For reasons of efficiency, you may want to keep the connection open over several requests. If you know the client will make a request and immediately follow it up with further requests, for example, you can keep the connection open to avoid the overhead of reconnecting again and again. Some servers don't support keep-alive connections, and may ignore your request to keep the connection alive. Any server that supports ISAPI does support keep-alive connections, however, so you'll only have a problem with a keep-alive request when the connection between the client and the server has already been terminated at the request of the client.

The pointer parameter received by the function references an `EXTENSION_CONTROL_BLOCK` structure. (To make this part of the book easier on the eyes, I'll refer to this structure as an **ECB** for short.) The structure is initialized with lots of different and interesting members; here's what the structure definition looks like:

```
typedef struct _EXTENSION_CONTROL_BLOCK
{
    WORD    cbSize;
    DWORD   dwVersion;
    HCONN   ConnID;
    DWORD   dwHttpStatusCode;
    CHAR    lpszLogData[HSE_LOG_BUFFER_LEN];
    LPSTR   lpszMethod;
    LPSTR   lpszQueryString;           // QUERY_STRING
    LPSTR   lpszPathInfo;              // PATH_INFO
    LPSTR   lpszPathTranslated;
    DWORD   cbTotalBytes;             // Total bytes indicated from client
    DWORD   cbAvailable;             // Available number of bytes
    LPBYTE  lpbData;                 // pointer to cbAvailable bytes
    LPSTR   lpszContentType;         // Content type of client data

    BOOL (WINAPI *GetServerVariable)( HCONN hConn,
                                LPSTR lpszVariableName,
                                LPVOID lpvBuffer,
                                LPDWORD lpdwSize);

    BOOL (WINAPI *WriteClient)( HCONN ConnID,
                            LPVOID Buffer,
                            LPDWORD lpdwBytes,
                            DWORD dwReserved);

    BOOL (WINAPI *ReadClient)( HCONN ConnID,
                            LPVOID lpvBuffer,
                            LPDWORD lpdwSize );

    BOOL (WINAPI *ServerSupportFunction)( HCONN hConn,
                                    DWORD dwHSERRequest,
                                    LPVOID lpvBuffer,
                                    LPDWORD lpdwSize,
                                    LPDWORD lpdwDataType );
} EXTENSION_CONTROL_BLOCK, *LPEXTENSION_CONTROL_BLOCK;
```

The `cbSize` member should be initialized to the size of the structure when you receive the pointer, while the `dwVersion` member will have a value that indicates the version of the HTTP specification implemented by the server software. You can compare this value against `HSE_VERSION_MAJOR` and `HSE_VERSION_MINOR`, just as MFC does for you in the `CHttpServer::GetServerVersion()` implementation. Since this function has already made the comparison, you don't need to worry about doing it again each time you receive a command from the client.

I mentioned that the server extension function should return `HSE_STATUS_SUCCESS` even if it encounters an error. If your extension wants to communicate an error code back to the client, it should set the error code in the `dwHttpStatusCode` in this structure before returning. Even if your extension is successful, it'll need to set the success code of 200 in this member. I provided information about the different status codes and their meeting back in the section named *Handling Returned Information* in the previous chapter.

The connection between the server and the client is identified by the `ConnID` member. You'll be able to use this value to communicate with the client using some functions we're about to describe.

The HTTP verb used to send the request is provided in the `lpszMethod` member. The string points at `"POST"` for a request that was posted, for example. While this string normally points at only the standard verb strings that we outlined in the previous chapter, custom client software can pass user-defined verbs if it knows the server will handle them properly.

Information sent with the request is referenced by the `lpszQueryString` parameter. If the information provided to the server was relatively small, or was sent with a GET request, the data referenced by this member is all there is. If there's a larger amount of data, or if the client sent data with a POST request, the `lpbData` member might point at additional information. It's possible that the server wasn't able to read all of the data from the client in one gulp. The amount of data at `lpbData` is actually `cbAvailable` bytes; if `cbAvailable` is less than `cbTotalBytes`, `lpbData` only has a part of the request that was sent. In this case, you'll need to read the rest of the data from the client yourself using the `ReadClient()` callback function.

The `ReadClient()`, `WriteClient()`, `ServerSupportFunction()`, and `GetServerVariable()` members of this structure are actually pointers to functions which are implemented by the server software. You can call them to have the server perform various operations on your connection. Calling `ReadClient()`, for example, allows you to read more data from the server on the connection you've opened. When you're ready to send a response to the client, you can call `WriteClient()`. The hConn parameter accepted by these functions is simply the `ConnID` value from the ECB that initiated the request. The balance of the parameters to `WriteClient()` and `ReadClient()` are self-explanatory; they're a pointer to data that will be written and a count of bytes to be written, or a pointer to a buffer which will be filled with the read data and a count that shows how much data was to be read.

The `lpszPathTranslated` field points at a string that describes the physical, server-side location of the running script. As we mentioned earlier in the chapter, the web space published by the server isn't the same as the one physically present on the server. That is, the DLL invoked by this URL:

```
http://www.mooseboy.com/Extra.dll?test=1
```

isn't on the root drive of the server named `MOOSEBOY`. When the server is invoked, `lpszPathTranslated` will contain the path to the physical location of the DLL on the server.

I've pointed out the features of the extension block because they'll be interesting for you, but knowledge of them is *not* crucial. Let me reiterate that you won't often need to directly override `CHttpServer::HttpExtensionProc()`. MFC does lots of basic processing for you as it prepares for the call, and it even does most of the messy parsing work that you'd otherwise have to do for yourself. MFC will take care of reading the request data, parsing the request, and sending back standardized error message text for your application.

MFC Implementation of Server Extensions

We've examined the implementation of Windows applications throughout this book. We realized, pretty early on, that most people who write Windows applications have to implement the same things for almost any application they write; they need ways to parse the command line, ways to pump messages, and ways to display windows. Every part of MFC provides some way to conveniently implement those features.

While we've spent this chapter talking about DLLs that we can install on a server, the song remains the same. When you write a DLL that processes requests sent to a server by HTTP, you'll almost always end up performing the same familiar tasks as you breathe life into that DLL. You'll need to parse the query as it's arrived, and perhaps force the rest of it to arrive if it's really big. You'll need to formulate a response and carefully blast it back to the client. And you'll also need to worry about all sorts of error situations.

Once again, the MFC team has carefully applied the design philosophy that makes MFC tick to problems that lots of programmers will face to help them save time.

In the previous section, I've described how a raw ISAPI extension would be written. When MFC enters the picture, you have to worry about almost none of those issues and you can focus, instead, on exactly what your server extension needs to do.

When you write an MFC-based ISAPI extension, you'll normally start by asking the ISAPI Extension Wizard to produce your project for you. When you ask for the extension, you'll end up with a project that has a single `CHttpServer`-derived class. The project creates a DLL that instantiates that class just once as a static object within the module. MFC finds that object and communicates with it during the life cycle of the extension DLL.

So, you don't need to fool with messy exports and `.def` files, and you don't need to screw around with reading data from the client. When your server DLL first loads, MFC calls your `GetExtensionVersion()` override and returns its result to the server. If everything goes well, your server extension then gets a request from the user. MFC fully retrieves that request, cleans it up, and tries to parse it. The parsing means that it's actually MFC that has to work through the messy URL (or posted data) and deal with the screwy syntax that's found there. MFC breaks that information up into usable parameters and passes them along to a C++ function call. You only need to worry about defining the syntax of those parameters in a way that MFC can understand, and then implementing a response to the function call.

As I mentioned, MFC may call the `HttpServerExtension()` override in your class. At that point, it's done none of the parsing. In fact, it's the `CHttpServer::HttpServerExtension()` that runs off and fetches the query from the client machine. If `HttpServerExtension()` likes what's happened, it calls your `InitInstance()` override, and, if that's successful, it calls `CallFunction()`. `CallFunction()` tries to find the name of a command built into the information it got within the query, and, if it finds one, tries to match it to a command in your extension's **parse map**, which we'll examine in the upcoming section.

When your own server code finally gains control, you'll find that it does some very predictable work. First, it'll decide how to respond to the request. If the request is not valid, the server extension will write an error back to the client. This may be a simple HTML error, which could say nothing more than 'the request is invalid'. Or, it might be an aggressive error message that explains exactly what was wrong with the request and how the user might remedy the problem. On the other hand, if the request does work, you'll want to emit an HTTP header that describes your response, put out the body of your response, and then close the response. MFC provides three virtual functions that help you with managing the response you write, and you can override them to fit your specific needs. We'll describe the whole process after we have a look at how parse maps work.

Parse Maps

Parse maps are a little bit more complicated than message maps, which we've used throughout the book, but their use is *far* simpler than doing all of the parsing work yourself. The application produced for you by the ISAPI Extension Wizard has only a single entry, but it's structure demonstrates just about everything we need to know about how parse maps fit together. By default, you'll end up with a parse map with these entries:

```
BEGIN_PARSE_MAP(CSimpleExtension, CHttpServer)
    ON_PARSE_COMMAND(Default, CExtraExtension, ITS_EMPTY)
    DEFAULT_PARSE_COMMAND(Default)
END_PARSE_MAP(CSimpleExtension)
```

BEGIN_PARSE_MAP() is a macro which marks the beginning of the parse map, while END_PARSE_MAP() marks the end of the map. The entries between the two macros build the parse map, and therefore define the behavior of the extension. The first parameter to BEGIN_PARSE_MAP() is the name of the server extension class you've created; the example above gives away the fact my extension class is named CSimpleExtension. The second parameter identifies the base class for the server extension class; in the example above, the base class is simply CHttpServer.

If you need the capability, your server extension classes don't have to directly derive from CHttpServer. If MFC can't find a handler for the command your extension receives in the most derived class, it will start searching less derived classes for a handler, and will keep doing so until it reaches MFC's implementation of CHttpServer itself.

The ON_PARSE_COMMAND() macro is the most common of parse map entry macros. It identifies a member function of your server extension class that will handle a particular command sent to your server extension. In the above example, we've declared a function named Default(). The command sent to the server must also be named Default, and that's what you'll need to send to the server to have the code in the command handler executed.

If your server machine was named MOOSEBOY, and your extension was named Simple.dll, you could use this URL to execute the Default() member function:

http://mooseboy/simple.dll?Default

When this URL is given to a browser, it has the browser connect to the server. By providing the trailing question mark, the browser asks the server to *execute*, rather than retrieve, the file Simple.dll. The server loads that DLL and follows the rules for initializing an extension DLL. The server only passes what's to the right of the question mark (and the question mark itself) to the DLL, though code in the DLL can use function calls to retrieve the rest of the information. MFC parses the remaining information (which, in this case, is pretty trivial) and starts looking for the command in the parse map. The client request causes the Default() member function of the server extension class to be executed, and then control is returned to the server software.

The third parameter to the macro identifies the parameters which may be given to the function. The example above provides only ITS_EMPTY, which means that the function won't receive *any* parameters from the client software. You could use a handful of other types:

Macro	Type
ITS_I4	long int
ITS_I2	short int
ITS_R4	float
ITS_R8	double
ITS_PSTR	string

There's also ITS_RAW, which lets you skip MFC's parsing altogether. You get a pointer to the data sent and a count of bytes sent. But in the simple cases, the parameters are specified in the order they'll be offered in the URL, and that order also defines how they're sent to the handling function.

If we had a server extension which, in its parse map, had the entry:

```
ON_PARSE_COMMAND(Add, CExtraExtension, ITS_I4 ITS_I4)
```

then the function would take two long integers. A suitable URL for this function in the same DLL as our previous example on MOOSEBOY would look like this:

```
http://mooseboy/simple.dll?Add&35&1253
```

The first parameter would be 35, and the second would be 1253. MFC simply converts the value from the string passed to the server extension to the integer (or floating point) value required by the function by calling a conversion routine in the runtime library. If you tried to invoke Add using strings, like this:

```
http://mooseboy/simple.dll?Add&Hello&Goodbye
```

then both parameters would be passed to the function as 0, without warning or error. If you need to have careful control over the strings and their validation, you're forced to write a parse command that takes strings and does the validation for you. Such an approach is quite simple; just use the normal string manipulation routines to pick apart the string in the way you see fit.

Both of the previous examples show an ampersand between the command and the parameters for the command. MFC also accepts a question mark in that same position. MFC's parser would find this URL, for example:

```
http://mooseboy/simple.dll?Add?Hello&Goodbye
```

equivalent to the previous example.

> Note that not all clients support passing commands in the way I've outlined above, and could truncate the above to:
>
> `http://mooseboy/simple.dll?Hello&Goodbye`
>
> especially if this is the action for a fill-in form.

The examples I've thrown around so far are all URLs. If you're getting data from an HTTP form, you can have the form use a GET method to respond to the user, which will result in the browser putting all the information on the form into the URL and requesting that URL from the server. If you have lots of fields, or exceptionally wide data, then you'll need to use the POST method. This is because the HTTP protocol says that GET isn't guaranteed to work for blocks of data more than two kilobytes, and often fails for even narrower data. Whether you use GET or POST, everything we've written in these descriptions is applicable. MFC still sees the same data, with the same syntax, and reacts to it in the same way.

Writing Command Handlers

While we've examined the more common parse map macros, we've not said anything about the development of parse command handlers. The macros indicate that your class will necessarily have a particular handler that will be executed when the server receives a request for that command from one of the clients attached to it.

Such a function must adhere to a rather particular prototype. First, the function will always be marked as having no return value; it'll return void. Your function always works, and never needs to indicate failure directly to the caller. Instead, it reflects failure conditions back to the client, which means that it must know about the ECB, provided by the server, as a context for all the work that's going on in the extension. And this requirement dictates that the function must retrieve a pointer to that information.

In the previous section, we mentioned these two specific parse map entries:

```
ON_PARSE_COMMAND(Default, CExtraExtension, ITS_EMPTY)
ON_PARSE_COMMAND(Add, CExtraExtension, ITS_I4 ITS_I4)
```

The first one, for a command named Default, is the simplest. The function that handles its commands would have this prototype:

```
void CExtraExtension::Default(CHttpServerContext* pCtxt)
{
...
}
```

CHttpServerContext is a class which wraps the ECB structure passed directly to the raw HttpExtensionProc() function. The CHttpServerContext object allows you access to all the information we found in the ECB object before, simply because a CHttpServerContext object has an ECB structure right within it. You can access the dwStatusCode member of that ECB by dereferencing the m_pECB member of the CHttpServerContext, like this:

```
pCtxt->m_pECB->dwStatusCode = HTTP_STATUS_BAD_REQUEST;
```

All of the ECB members we discussed in the previous section can be accessed in this way. The `CHttpServerContext` class, though, makes access to the callback functions available in the ECB much easier; they're just member functions of the `CHttpServerContext` class.

If you want to, you can write data back to the client immediately by calling the `CHttpServerContext::WriteClient()` member, like this:

```
pCtxt->WriteClient("Hello!", 6);
```

Note that we're not required to pass the `ConnID` value, as the C++ version of the function provides that value automatically, based on the value stored in the context object.

If you've requested the `ITS_RAW` parameter type, you can only have one possible choice for prototyping your handler function – you'll accept a pointer to the context, a pointer to the data, and a `DWORD` count. It will look like this:

```
void CExtraExtension::Default(CHttpServerContext* pCtxt, LPBYTE pbData, DWORD
dwCount)
{
...
}
```

Remember the data you receive is exactly as sent from the server. You know the length, so don't expect a null-terminator!

Generating Output

`WriteClient()`, as we discussed, is a great way to send information back to the client. But it has its problems; if you're interested in sending a great deal of information back to the client, you might do so incrementally by making several calls to `WriteClient()`. That's not very efficient, since `WriteClient()` causes the server software to pump the data out to the network *immediately* each time the function is called. In other words, the function does no buffering. This is true whether you call the `WriteClient()` callback directly in your ECB or if you call `WriteClient()` as a member function of `CHttpServerContext`.

There are some situations where you may wish to fire data back to the client immediately. If you know your extension function will take a great deal of time to execute, you may wish to fire some data back to the client so that the client's browser can progressively render as much information as it has received and show it to the user. This technique, together with some of its variants, is known as a **server push**. Server pushes are simple to implement; just call `WriteClient()` to have the data written immediately to the client.

On the other hand, if you've written a loop that puts a little data back to the client each time, and doesn't necessarily take a long time to run, you may want to use the buffering scheme that's built into `CHttpServerContext`. When MFC creates the `CHttpServerContext` object it gives to your server extension command handler functions and it also creates a `CHtmlStream` object that's owned by that particular context. The `CHtmlStream` object, referenced by `CHttpServerContext`'s `m_pStream` data member, supports various overloaded versions of the insertion operator. Instead of putting the resulting output directly to the client, however, `CHtmlStream` grows a buffer which will finally be sent to the client if the server extension function completes successfully.

The overload operators supported by MFC 6.0's implementation of this class include these:

```
operator<<(long int dw);
operator<<(short int w);
operator<<(LPCTSTR pstr);
operator<<(const CHtmlStream& stream);
operator<<(double d);
operator<<(float f);
operator<<(const CLongBinary& blob);
operator<<(const CByteArray& array);
```

So, if you wanted to write a message to the client and have it buffered, you could write some pretty simple code:

```
*(pCtxt->m_pStream) << "Here are some numbers: ";
for (short int n = 1; n <= 10; n++)
    *(pCtxt->m_pStream) << n;
```

This syntax is somewhat ugly, but it's functional. To present an easier interface, MFC supports the insertion operator against the CHttpServerContext object directly, and implements it synonymously with the same operation against the inner m_pStream object. So, the above code could be rewritten a bit more easily as:

```
*pCtxt << "Here are some numbers: ";
for (short int n = 1; n <= 10; n++)
    *pCtxt << n;
```

To keep the baggage brought into your extension by MFC to an absolute minimum, the stream class doesn't support any formatting and will output values with no padding or tailoring. If you need to do that kind of thing, you'll need to use wsprintf() or CString::Format() yourself to get a string, and then pump the string out.

Since the operators return references to the object which they write to, you can stack them to avoid writing many lines of code for interesting output situations. For example, you might code:

```
*pCtxt << "Penguins: " << 4 << "<br>";
*pCtxt << "Flyers: " << 3 << "  (Overtime)<br>";
```

to show the final score. Note that we used HTML tags right in the text we printed; there's no carriage control, rich formatting, or other features here. This is because the output we write eventually goes to the client that initiated the request, and it is most likely a browser that can understand and display HTML. Since carriage control doesn't matter for the HTML stream the browser reads, the only real reason to add it would be to make the text more readable to any human who might come along and try to observe the HTML output directly, without using a browser.

Before it's Sent

When MFC flushes the stream back to the client, it just calls `CHttpServerContext::WriteClient()`. It'll do so all at once, if you haven't set a chunk size. If you do set a chunk size, MFC will write data in blocks no bigger than the chunk size over and over again until it is done. You can use the chunk size to throttle the data being sent – and that can be necessary if a proxy or firewall between you and the client has a limited capacity to accommodate large transfers. It's also necessary to pick a chunk size less than sixteen kilobytes if you're responding to a HTTPS request, as the encryption layer doesn't guarantee the ability to handle such large blocks of data.

The chunk size can be set using the `CHttpServerContext::SetChunkSize()` function. The function takes only one parameter – a `DWORD` indicating the new chunk size. The function returns the old size. You can retrieve the existing size at any time by calling `GetChunkSize()`.

The work of looping through the blocks in the chunks, or sending all the data at once happens in an overridable function of `CHttpServer` called `OnWriteBody()`. `OnWriteBody()` receives three parameters – a pointer to the `CHttpServerContext` object controlling the transaction, a pointer to the content, and a `DWORD` indicating the size of the content.

`OnWriteBody()` is provided simply for the ability to step in and write the data back to the client in absolutely any way you see fit. You can use the function to fluff-up server-side includes before sending, or to block the sending back to the client in any way you choose.

Writing Headers

You'll remember, from our treatment of the HTTP protocol elsewhere in this chapter, that headers are sent along with the request and, similarly, header information must be sent back from the server in the response. The headers you need, at a minimum, indicate the request was a success or a failure, and describe the type of data that you're sending back.

If you write a simple parse map handling function, you'll need to make sure you output the headers yourself. For the simplest of situations, the easiest way to do so is to call `StartContent()`, `WriteTitle()`, and `EndContent()` – three functions which are implemented by MFC to blurt out the appropriate data at the right time. If you consider our trivial `Add` example, you'll realize we can get a result back to the user in just a few lines of code:

```
void CSimpleExtension::Add(CHttpServerContext* pCtxt,
    short int n1, short int n2)
{
    StartContent(pCtxt);
    WriteTitle(pCtxt);
    *pCtxt << n1 << " + ";
    *pCtxt << n2 << " = ";
    *pCtxt << n1+n2;
    EndContent(pCtxt);
}
```

`StartContent()` sends a `content-type` header which indicates the format of the data in the body of the response to the client. The default implementation of `StartContent()` writes this header, and this header only; it also indicates that the content will be `text/html`. If you need to write out some other format, you'll need to override `StartContent()` in your extension; or, you'll need to refrain from calling it, and instead call the `AddHeader()` member of your `CHttpServerContext` object.

`AddHeader()` allows you to write any header you'd like. You need to append a carriage return and a new line to any information you add to the headers, though. That's how the client software tells one header from the next. `AddHeader()` takes a single `LPCTSTR` parameter that points at the header to be written.

`WriteTitle()` writes three HTML tags, calls `GetTitle()` to retrieve the name of the document's title, and then writes a few more tags. `WriteTitle()` expects `GetTitle()` to return a pointer to a string which identifies the title of the document. If your `GetTitle()` override returns 'Addition Sample', `WriteTitle()` will end up outputting this stream of characters:

`<HTML><HEAD><TITLE>Addition Sample</TITLE></HEAD><BODY>`

Again, if you're not going to be outputting an HTML page, you probably want to avoid calling `WriteTitle()`. You can override `GetTitle()` to return anything you'd like for the title of your document. While you can't have your `GetTitle()` implementation change what tags `WriteTitle()` will provide, you *are* free to use the function to provide different HTML tags that can fit in the `<HEAD>` block of your page.

Finally, `EndContent()` does nothing more than close HTML page by writing out:

`</BODY></HTML>`

to the stream.

MFC will take care of adding the status line to your headers. When your function returns, the value in the `dwStatusCode` field of ECB in your `CHttpServerContext` object is used to formulate the response to the user. That is, the value in `pCtxt->m_pECB->dwStatusCode` is what tells MFC (and your client!) that your function was successful or, if it failed, *how* it failed. The values you can place in this field are the same that you might expect in return when querying the status code from the client side of the operation, as we outlined in the section named *Handling Returned Information*.

If the value in `dwStatusCode` isn't `HTTP_STATUS_OK`, MFC will call `OnParseError()`. The function's prototype looks like this:

```
virtual BOOL CHttpServer::OnParseError( CHttpServerContext* pCtxt,
                                        int nCause);
```

As you can see, the function is virtual, so you can override it and provide any reaction to errors that you see fit. The `nCause` parameter can carry any of a few values:

nCause value	Description
callOK	The call worked, but had a logical failure
callParamRequired	A specific required parameter was missing
callBadParamCount	There were too many parameters supplied, or some required parameters were not supplied
callBadCommand	The command name was not found in any applicable parse map

nCause value	Description
callNoStackSpace	No stack space was available to prepare for the call to the command handler function
callNoStream	MFC called ConstructStream(), but the function failed to provide a new CHtmlStream-derived object
callMissingQuote	A parameter is missing a quote mark
callMissingParams	Some default parameter values were missing
callBadParam	A parameter had a bad format

If nCause is callOK, the error actually occurred because the extension failed, and an HTTP status code other than HTTP_STATUS_OK is expected to be at pCtxt->m_pECB->dwStatusCode. If you override OnParseError(), you should first call pCtxt->Reset() to flush the content of any data in the MFC-managed buffer between the server and the client before trying to write your data. If you can successfully handle the error condition, you should return TRUE; if not, you should return FALSE.

Once the error, if any, is handled, MFC will write back the status code as well as the headers you've previously specified. In some circumstances, you might not want MFC to handle writing out the headers – even the status code – for your application. If that's the case, you should set the m_bSendHeaders member of your CHttpServerContext object to FALSE. In this situation, MFC will only write what you've stuffed into the CHtmlStream object in your call context. You can, of course, write out extra data yourself using WriteClient(), and eschew CHtmlStream altogether; but you must also be prepared to properly write the headers and status code.

Advanced Parsing Situations

I only described two of the four parse map macros before the actual functions themselves distracted me. It's possible you may not know which values are going to come from the server, and you might not want to concern yourself with the order in which they'll be sent.

If the browser displays an order form, for example, you may want to allow the user to leave some fields blank, while other fields absolutely require a user response. MFC provides for these situations by allowing for default parameters. While the example of an address-entry form helps show the application of the concept, such a form is a bit long-winded. As such, I'll only treat (for the sake of discussion) three fields from a form like that: first name, middle name, and last name.

At first blush, we'll probably write a macro that requests three string parameters, like this:

```
ON_PARSE_COMMAND(GetName, CSimpleExtension, ITS_PSTR, ITS_PSTR, ITS_PSTR)
```

Such a macro would work just fine. If we coded an HTML form like this one:

```
<HTML>
<TITLE>Simple Form</TITLE>
<BODY>
<FORM METHOD=GET ACTION="http://mooseboy/reg.dll?GetName">
First: <INPUT Type="EDIT" Name="First">
Middle: <INPUT Type="EDIT" Name="Mid">
Last: <INPUT Type="EDIT" Name="Last">
<p><INPUT Type=Submit>
</FORM>
</BODY>
```

and had our favorite browser display it, we could fill it out and send it back to the server by pressing the Submit button. If we entered the name of a famous author, we'd find that the browser would run off in pursuit of this URL:

```
http://mooseboy/reg.dll?GetName?First=Edgar&Mid=Allan&Last=Poe
```

This is the ugly input that MFC is quite happy to deal with, thank goodness! We already know that everything to the left of the question mark shows us what server and executable file on the server will be run. And we've discussed enough to know that the first token to the right of the question mark will name the function to be run. You can see that the browser found this information in the ACTION= parameter to the FORM tag.

The rest of the information comes from the form itself. If you look carefully, you'll realize that the remaining part of the URL is simply made from pairs of:

```
field=value
```

each separated by an ampersand. This whole messy process is, unfortunately, the standard for exchanging information in forms using HTML. But the problem is that the user might not fill in a particular field, and some browsers won't send a blank field. The above parse map entry always requires the user to input a middle name, a last name, and a first name. Many people don't like to use their middle names, and many folks don't even *have* middle names. Since MFC will see the three required parameters in the parse map, it will respond with an error message to the user.

Sometimes, this isn't a problem; you might find yourself with:

```
http://mooseboy/reg.dll?GetName?First=Charles&Mid=&Last=Bukowski
```

or, equally:

```
http://mooseboy/reg.dll?GetName?First=Charles&Last=Bukowski
```

MFC can adequately handle the first case without us knowing anything more about parse maps. But it's the second case that's troublesome; MFC will recognize it as an error unless we change our parse map.

We could follow up this message map macro with an ON_PARSE_COMMAND_PARAMS() macro that allows us to tell MFC that some of the parameters have names. This will get us half way to our solution. We'd need to add the ON_PARSE_COMMAND_PARAMS() entry *immediately* after the ON_PARSE_COMMAND() entry in the map. Together, they might look like this:

```
ON_PARSE_COMMAND(GetName, CSimpleExtension, ITS_PSTR, ITS_PSTR, ITS_PSTR)
ON_PARSE_COMMAND_PARAMS("First Mid Last")
```

With an ON_PARSE_COMMAND_PARAMS() entry like this, MFC knows that the three parameters have names. This is good, because it means that MFC can find the parameters in the URL given to the server extension, regardless of the order in which they appear. With the above entry, then, all of these requests would work just fine:

```
http://mooseboy/reg.dll?GetName?First=Edgar&Last=Poe&Mid=Allen
http://mooseboy/reg.dll?GetName?Last=Poe&Mid=Allen&First=Edgar
http://mooseboy/reg.dll?GetName?Last=Poe&First=Edgar&Mid=Allen
```

And they would pass the parameters in the correct order your function expects, even if their order in the URL didn't match their order in the function.

But we'd still trip over the case where the submitted URL doesn't provide a Mid= entry at all. Fortunately, the ON_PARSE_COMMAND_PARAMS() string can also contain some default values, which allows us to work around the situation. You might add an entry that says:

```
ON_PARSE_COMMAND_PARAMS("First Last Mid=~")
```

The equals sign and tilde mean the middle initial parameter will default to a string that contains only a tilde. I arbitrarily chose this value; if I wanted to, I could provide a more meaningful string:

```
ON_PARSE_COMMAND_PARAMS("First Last Mid=Francis")
```

What I actually want to do, however, is provide an out-of-bounds condition that would be easy for my function to test for. That is, if I use a tilde as the default value, it's a trivial matter for my handler function to test the parameter it receives; if it's a tilde, then my function knows that no middle name was specified.

You can use defaults for values of any type. If you have a string that needs a space, you should use single quotes to delimit the string:

```
ON_PARSE_COMMAND_PARAMS("First Last Mid='Jean Paul'")
```

Even though the parameter information we provide here denotes a name for all of the parameters, the function will still work if it receives a request that doesn't have field names embedded in it. For example,

```
http://mooseboy/reg.dll?GetName?Charles&Bukowski
```

would have MFC matching the first parameter with the `First` field, the second parameter with the `Last` field, and relying on the default value for the `Mid` field. This arrangement provides just a shade more flexibility, but it does mean that all optional parameters must appear after all of the required parameters. This parse map entry and URL are unacceptable:

```
ON_PARSE_COMMAND_PARAMS("Mid='Jean Paul' First Last")
```

```
http://mooseboy/reg.dll?GetName?Mid=Allen&Edgar&Poe
```

because they don't abide by those rules.

Parsing Stunts

There are a couple of weak spots in MFC's parse map architecture. The first is that parse maps can become a little bit unruly, particularly if you have more than, say, two dozen fields in your command. You'll find the syntax starts to look a little ugly. At this point, you may want to investigate writing your own code to parse the information that comes in. Anyway, there's probably some way you can organize the data that's a great deal neater than having it passed to your handling function parameter-by-parameter.

The second is the current version of MFC can't handle multiple-select controls in HTML forms. If you have cause to use such a control, you'll also need to do your own parsing. Perhaps this situation will be remedied in a future version of MFC.

To do your own parsing, your best bet is to use the `ITS_RAW` type in your macro. Then, you can have a look at the raw data that's been received and do your own special case handling.

Notes on MFC and the ISAPI Architecture

I've not had much reason to mention this; I've just carried on like it didn't matter. But I guess it does, so I'll confess; your ISAPI DLL can be built to use MFC or not to use MFC. That is, you can link to the `CHttpFilter` or `CHttpServer` classes, and the code that implements them, while using other parts of MFC, or while using absolutely no other parts of MFC.

An even bigger aspect of ISAPI programming which I've only mentioned in passing is the Internet Extension Wizard. You can get to the Wizard by asking for a project type of Internet Server Extension from the AppWizard. The dialogs in the wizard will ask you if you want to have a `CHttpServer`, a `CHttpFilter`, or both, in your resulting project. If you request a `CHttpServer`, you don't get much; just the `CHttpServer` and a simple parse map that does nothing but handle a parameterless default command. The Wizard does, however, very kindly let you pick a name and description for your server extension.

If you ask for a `CHttpFilter`, the Wizard gives you a shot at naming the filter object and providing a description string, too. The Wizard will also grow an extra step which allows you to specify, in detail, which server extension notifications you'd like to receive and at which priority you should be notified. All of these settings correspond to flags and functions that we've already discussed.

Thread Safety

Another thing I've neglected to stress is that your ISAPI extension absolutely must be thread-safe across calls. The benefits of ISAPI, which I discussed at the beginning of this half of the chapter, strongly suggest that since the server itself is multithreaded, it could be responding to lots of different clients at any particular moment. If more than one of those clients requests information from the same extension at the same time, the server will enter the extension DLL with more than one thread concurrently.

This means a couple of important things for your extension DLL. First, **your code must be reentrant**. Reentrancy means that any given call to a function won't be adversely affected by any other concurrently running call to that same function. One of the most important aspects of writing reentrant code involves avoiding the use of global data for management of the state of the function. The function's state must be completely described by data that is local to that particular running instance of the function, not by data that can be shared by multiple running instances of the function. If you *do* need to share resources between instances of functions, you must protect those resources using some synchronization mechanism.

The Counter sample, which ships with the Visual C++ product, is a good example of a situation where careful planning about synchronization is necessary. Counter simply records the number of times it has been run in a text file. When run, it increments that count and then sends a bitmap containing an image of the numbers in the total count back to the client machine. If a couple of instances of Counter were run against the same file concurrently, it would not be able to reliably increment the count and send back accurate information to the client.

The author of Counter, though, realized that the text file itself could be used to block concurrent access to the file. If the file is opened in exclusive mode, other instances of the program can't open the file at all, and will have to keep retrying until they can. The program is guaranteed exclusive access to the file until the file is closed. By wrapping all of the critical code with access to the file, the problem is very simply solved.

The second issue is a little bit more involved; **anything you directly use must be thread-capable**. If your server extension runs off and creates a connection to a database, for example, in order to respond to a request from a user, then the underlying database technology must also be capable of running in multiple threads. Thread-capable is quite a different concept than thread-safe. Technologies you use in ISAPI extensions must meet both criteria.

Thread safety describes code that can be used safely from multiple threads at the same time. A class, for example, might be thread-safe, but a single object of that class may not be thread-safe. If a class manages static data that isn't protected for multiple cross-thread access, it will not be thread-safe. If an object doesn't manage its private instance data for safety across threads, objects won't be thread-safe. The first criterion listed above indicates that your command handler function must be thread-safe.

You can realize cheap thread safety, by the way, by simply making your function not execute when it's about to be entered by multiple threads. If we have a pair of oversimplified functions that increment and retrieve a counter value, for example:

```
LONG lCount = 0;
void IncrementCount()
{
    lCount++;
}
```

Continued on Following Page

```
LONG RetrieveCount()
{
    return lCount;
}
```

then there's a problem — what if one thread is trying to retrieve the count and another thread is trying to increment the count? The simple solution is to lock access to the lCount variable with a critical section. That'll work, and might look like this:

```
LONG lCount = 0;
CCriticalSection critsec;
void IncrementCount()
{
    critsec.Lock();
    lCount++;
    critsec.Unlock();
}

LONG RetrieveCount()
{
    critsec.Lock();
    LONG lReturn = lCount;
    critsec.Unlock();
    return lReturn;
}
```

This code works fine, and makes sense for the limited duration of our tiny functions. (Of course, if all we were doing was incrementing a variable, it would be a lot more efficient to use the ::InterlockedIncrement() API — my intention is to show the coarse implementation of thread safety with simple critical sections, since your own real applications will certainly do something more complicated than increment a variable.) But locking access for the entire duration of a much more expensive function is to be avoided. If you decide to avoid multithreading issues, for example, by having your command handler function lock a critical section and unlock it when it's done, you're drastically reducing the ability of your server to respond to requests in a very rapid manner. Pending requests will block on the acquisition of the critical section, and won't get *any* work done until other instances of the function have exited. You've essentially made the server single-threaded!

Going Further

Generally speaking, if you want to do anything above and beyond what MFC does for you when connecting to Internet-based servers, you have two remedies. The first is to just use the HINTERNET cast operator built into each of the Win32 Internet API support classes to get access to the handle you need to call the underlying WinInet API. At the time of writing, there's not much you can do with the API that you can't properly do through the classes themselves. However, MFC is challenged by WinInet because it's a moving target; WinInet continued to grow throughout the development of MFC 6.0, and will probably continue to embrace at least a little new functionality in the future. Running around with your own HINTERNETs might, therefore, be a necessary approach before the next MFC upgrade.

On the other hand, if you need to do something that's beyond the scope of what WinInet can help you with, you'll need to write your own implementation of the protocol in question. Since Windows Sockets let you talk to the TCP/IP machines scattered all over the network without worrying about the underlying protocol, you're not going to be in bad shape. The real rough spot is finding documentation on the protocols themselves. The beauty of the Internet is that many different people have worked together to figure out how all the protocols should work together peacefully on the same physical transport. These people have done a great job, because every day the Internet passes around packets for tens of dozens of different protocols and really doesn't do a bad job of getting them from here to there.

All of the high-level protocols used on the Internet, including the ones we've discussed here, are documented in one of two ways by the folks on the Internet itself. You can find **Requests For Comments**, or RFC's, that describe the way a protocol should work. You can generally find copies of a given RFC by browsing around at your favorite University FTP site. You can find repositories of RFC's all over the net – just try your favorite search engine. RFC's are identified by number; people who want to talk about the simple mail transfer protocol, or SMTP, are likely to refer to RFC-822, for example. So, the first thing you should snag from your FTP site is an index of all the RFCs, so you can find which one you're interested in. Many RFCs deal with protocols that only people who actually eat packets for lunch would want to learn; other RFCs are things that you actually use on your computer each and every day you decide to connect to the Internet.

The other set of specifications comes from best-of-practice documents. The most important best-of-practice document is that for HTML. It's continually evolving and being tugged in different directions by different vendors with their own agendas. You can get the latest version of the spec from `http://www.w3.org/`. Finding best-of-practice documents seems largely catch-as-catch-can because there doesn't seem to be a central repository for them, or even a central governing committee that approves, rejects, or moderates their development.

The only problem with these various standards is that they are ungoverned. Some vendors take the standards and extend them. Some vendors take the standards and ignore them. Some vendors adhere to the standards very carefully, and that means they break against anything that the other two groups of vendors have done. Since the Internet has no 'Sergeant at Arms', there's no enforcement of these standards. They're subject to lots of interpretation, and they don't always include a way for vendors to sniff out each implementation's extensions or even a fallback to some lowest common denominator. When you implement protocols based on these standards, you'll be torn between what will really work and what the standard actually specifies. You'll need to find a solution that is, unfortunately, based on a lot of empirical testing.

If you are interested in learning more about programming with ISAPI, then Wrox Press publishes a book that might interest you, Professional Visual C++ ISAPI Programming (ISBN 1-874416-66-4).

Summary

Through this chapter, we've learned a lot about the way computers on the Internet respond to the requests they're sent. More importantly, we've investigated a highly efficient mechanism to have those machines develop computed responses or perform work in response to the requests themselves.

The work done in MFC to support ISAPI is quite exciting. Since these MFC classes can be used without the presence of the rest of MFC, they provide a pleasingly light and efficient framework for servers. But combined with the rest of the power of MFC – particularly CDatabase and it's database connectivity support, they realize a great tool for developing server-side applications for the web.

As you write server extensions, make sure you concern yourself with performance. Otherwise, you'll have more problems with your users than with your code.

Installing Visual C++

If you're still considering whether to purchase Visual C++, if you haven't installed the product yet, or if you're just interested in finding out about some of the installation options that you may have missed when you did install it, then this appendix is for you. We'll be looking at all the requirements for the product, as well as some of the more obscure options that you can choose from when performing the installation. It should be note at this point that Visual C++ 6.0 is a big application, consuming a large amount of the registry, and you might have to uninstall programs before installing it.

Visual C++ 6.0

Before you begin to use Visual C++ 6.0, and even before installing it, the first thing you'll need to do is to make sure that your machine is endowed with the necessary gifts to run the product. To install the various configurations available, you'll need a varying amount of hard disk space. We'll discuss how much when we review the different installation options later in the appendix, but, for now, let's take a look at Visual C++ 6.0's basic hardware requirements.

A Computer

No kidding; you'll need a machine. This requirement (despite the aggressive efforts of our development team) can't be avoided. If you want to run Visual C++ on an Intel platform, you will need a 90MHz Intel Pentium processor or better. The faster your machine, the faster your builds will be. I'm a certifiable tough guy; I have a 450MHz Pentium II system as my primary development machine. However, using Visual C++ 6.0, you can enjoy quite adequate performance on a 120MHz or 133MHz Pentium system. In my opinion, the minimum configuration is not quite fast enough to use. You'll notice that the editor lags, and painting is slow – even if you turn off IntelliSense options. At about 120MHz you'll find that your machine responds quickly enough to edit efficiently, though you'll probably want to keep IntelliSense turned off. After this point, a faster processor just makes your programs build faster.

You can run Visual C++ on a Digital Alpha-based machine as well, but you'll need to make sure that you buy the version of Visual C++ appropriate to that processor. The Microsoft Foundation Classes, and all of the tools, are completely compatible with the support I describe for Windows NT throughout this book. You can use different Visual C++ releases to rebuild your code for each of these platforms and processors. Unless you use assembly language in your application, you can do this port with your eyes closed; provided you haven't written code that depends on the byte ordering of the processor, you shouldn't need to make any changes.

You can also buy a cross-platform development version of Visual C++ if you want to port your code to Apple Macintosh platforms. The Macintosh edition of the product hasn't been updated for a while – the current release is Visual C++ 4.2. As such, this tool provides only rudimentary compatibility with for code developed for the newest version of the product. There are several system services that Apple's operating system doesn't provide as mappings to the features in Win32. Unfortunately, porting code to the Macintosh is something that's beyond the scope of this book. Most of MFC will work just as it does on the Intel or Digital Alpha processors, but I *don't* point out areas of incompatibility.

24 Megabytes of Available Memory

Ideally, you'll need about twenty-four megabytes of free memory after you load your operating system, your network drivers, your cute screen saver, your anti-virus utility, an instance of your word processor, and all of the other stuff you keep in memory. Again, the more memory you have, the faster things will go and the happier you will be. I bought everything I could afford after I sold my grandmother's fine china, and I now have 128 megabytes of RAM. My machine is extreme; this memory might not even be truly necessary *except* for when I'm running SQL Server *and* Internet Information Server *and* Visual C++ on the machine while I'm doing development work. Certainly, for plain development work, you probably won't notice any great improvement with anything more than 32 megabytes of memory – unless you're building a very extreme project, or trying to win bragging rights from your brother.

That said, you'll find that you *can* run Visual C++ reasonably well on a machine with as little as 16 megabytes of memory – particularly if you're using Windows 95 or Windows 98 but *not* Windows NT. But adding just a few more megabytes of memory to such a system will result in an immediate and very noticeable performance gain – and since memory prices are always falling, you should seriously consider making the investment on your development machines.

A 32-bit Operating System

Visual C++ 6.0 doesn't run under Windows 3.x. You need to have a copy of Windows NT Version 4.0, Windows 95/98 or Windows 2000. (By the way, you *must* have Windows NT version 4.0 – versions 3.50 and 3.51 will *not* be adequate.) The programs in this book were all tested on Windows NT 4.0 and both Windows 95 and 98.

Visual C++ 6.0 isn't supported by OS/2.

A CD-ROM Drive

If you've opened the Visual C++ 6.0 box, you know that the product is provided on CD-ROM. More specifically, it's *only* provided on CD-ROM. You can't obtain the development environment on floppies at all, so you can't avoid the requirement of a CD-ROM drive.

A Hard Disk

You will need between 235 and 263 megabytes of disk space to complete a typical installation. As we'll see later in this section, you can get by with less, or you can install more of the product on your hard drive and be a magnetic media kingpin. Again, nobody can touch me; I have a pair of two gig drives on my primary machine, and a total of six gigs of space on my secondary, server machine. Since I have lots and lots of software installed, all this space is quite necessary – your storage needs might be smaller. Then again, if you're doing some very aggressive database work, maybe your needs are much larger. Realistically, it would be hard to imagine using a drive much smaller than a gigabyte for development. After you install Visual C++ and your operating system, you'll probably have more than half the drive left for your development (if you don't install anything else), and that should be plenty of room.

The machine I've described and said that I use for my own development work runs Visual C++ extraordinarily well; I don't have a lot of time to go and get coffee while I wait for small to medium-sized builds, but I'm quite happy to sit around and play Duke Nuk'em all afternoon. The typical system I've described which, significantly, is within the configuration range of most laptops, will do a great job as well. However, as with almost any piece of development software, the more hardware you throw at it, the better the performance will be. The machine described as my development machine for the book is very comfortable. I can't really complain, but I still do.

Such extremes are only necessary for two reasons. The first is that, like me, you have no self-esteem and you need to brag to your brother that your machine is more incredible than his is. The second is that, also like me, you can justify the expense for the machine and know that the better platform you have, the better your performance will be.

If you were buying a new machine, I would strongly recommend that you find the Windows NT Hardware Compatibility List. This document, available on the Microsoft web site, enumerates the CD-ROM drives, video display cards, tape drives, SCSI adapter cards and machines that Microsoft has tested and certified to be compatible with Windows NT Version 4.0. If you stick to that list, you should have no trouble getting support, updated drivers or performance enhancements from your investment. If you start deviating from the list, you might find that getting your hardware to work is somewhere between frustrating and impossible.

Now that you have a nice machine, pop the Visual C++ 6.0 CD-ROM into it and get Windows started.

Installation Options

After running the `Setup.exe` program from root directory of the CD-ROM, you'll be greeted with the dialog that initiates the installation of Microsoft Visual Studio and Visual C++. I won't waste your time describing each and every dialog box; I'm sure you can figure out how to supply your name, organization and product identification number.

This would be a good time to note, though, that 'Microsoft Visual Studio' is the name for what was once called the 'Integrated Development Environment' (**IDE**), and more recently 'Microsoft Developer Studio' or 'DevStudio', terms you will still see used. Visual Studio is so called because it's used for many different Microsoft development tools. Not only can you do all of your C++ work within one convenient environment, you can also write Microsoft Visual J++ code, develop Microsoft

Visual InterDev projects, and use the Microsoft Developer Network resources from a very similar environment.

Installing Microsoft Visual Studio can be like installing the IDE by itself. When you install Visual C++, you add the C++ libraries and compilers to the basic IDE setup. If, on a later occasion, you decide to purchase Microsoft Visual Basic, you won't need to reinstall Microsoft Visual Studio (even though the Visual Basic product includes it). Instead, you'll just add in the Visual Basic compilers and libraries, and make the existing Studio installation aware that these tools are available.

After you've agreed to the licensing page and entered your CD Product ID number, `Setup` may invite you to install some ancillary packages before it lets you continue with the real work at hand. Visual C++ forces you to install Internet Explorer and DCOM. If you're running Windows NT, setup will also check to see that you're using Version 4.0 – and will also assert that you have Service Pack 3 installed. If it isn't available, it will install it for you!

Internet Explorer is required for the development environment because the online help is formatted in HTML and designed to work with Internet Explorer. Programs that you write using the environment may or may not require the runtime services of Internet Explorer – the choice is entirely up to you. Service Pack 3 is required on NT machines primarily to repair bugs that adversely effect the operation of the environment while running the debugger. Setup may actually reboot your system two or three times to make sure all the updates are installed.

Installation Directories

Before you reach the main setup options dialog, you'll be asked for the installation folder you want to use for the "common" parts of Visual C++. Files and programs which land in this common area are shared among all products in the Visual Studio suite. If you're planning on installing other products from the suite, you'll want to make sure the drive where you place the common directory leaves you with room to grow.

After installation, Visual C++ will be quite content with the installed directories as configured. If you stick to writing standard C/C++ code or MFC applications, you will probably never care about the directories where Visual C++ installs files. However, if you ever need to write Custom AppWizards or use macros created by another user, then knowledge of the storage location will be required.

Installation Options

Things finally get interesting when you reach the Installation Options dialog, shown here:

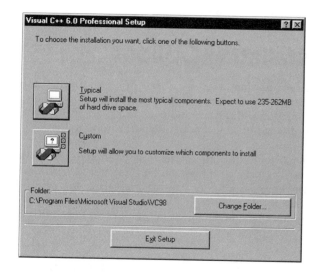

From this dialog, you can elect to create one of two different installations. Let's take a peek at exactly what each one means.

Typical Installation

The Typical Visual C++ installation option installs the development tools, C run-time libraries, C and C++ header files, system libraries and header files, MFC header files and MFC libraries to your machine. This setup choice also copies the Active Template Library and its related files. This installation does *not* copy Unicode MFC libraries or the source code for the C run-time and standard C++ libraries.

When you choose the Typical installation, Visual C++ Setup will whisk you away to the first installation progress dialog box.

Custom Installation

As its name implies, this option allows you to pick and choose exactly which files do and do not get installed on your system. You should use this option if you know you will need files that the typical installation option won't install, or if you're running the Visual C++ Setup for a second time to add files that you didn't install the first time. I would always recommend the custom installation option, and I'll be describing its specific options and features later in this chapter.

Unlike the Typical installation, selecting a Custom installation brings you to the beginning of the custom installation process. We'll discuss the options provided there in the next section. If you attempt an installation option and don't have enough space to complete it, Visual C++ Setup will notify you of the problem and offer you the ability to abort the installation or to continue after allowing you to clear some space on the target drive.

Once you've selected the appropriate option for your setup and completed it, you'll be ready to start writing programs for Visual C++.

A Note about Sample Source Code

Visual C++ 6.0 ships with several thousand lines of sample code to help you get started with your Windows programming tasks, and it keeps that information on the CD at all times. If you're interested in browsing a sample, make sure you have the CD handy. You can find and copy individual samples by using Help in Visual Studio, or you can copy them to your hard drive directly from the CD. However, but you *can't* copy the samples from the CD at setup time.

Custom Installations

Some special features aren't covered by the standard options offered in the Installation Options dialog. However, the Custom installation provides access to a series of dialogs allowing you to select or reject features for your installation specifically. The Custom installation has the added advantage of allowing you to see exactly what files will or will not be installed.

The Microsoft Visual C++ Setup dialog provides choices to include or exclude major parts of the development environment. The first two options (Microsoft Developer Studio and Microsoft Visual C++ Build Tools) should always remain checked, unless you are running setup after your initial installation to install additional files. The main dialog for a custom installation is shown here:

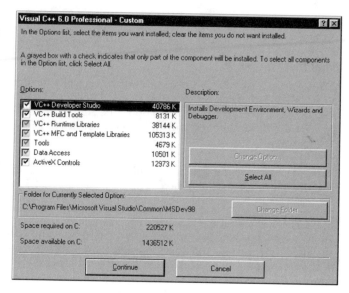

Let's investigate some of the more interesting installation options.

The Microsoft Foundation Classes and Template Libraries

The VC++ MFC & Template Libraries option allows you avoid installing MFC (and its sister library, ATL). Unless you have a very special installation need, you *will* want to install these files. If you don't plan on using MFC, you may remove the mark from this choice... and maybe find a more suitable book to read! With the MFC & Template Libraries item selected, the Change Option... button allows you to set a few extra options. Pressing it brings up a box that allows you to set details for the Microsoft Foundation Class Libraries or the Microsoft Active Template Libraries. If you select Microsoft Foundation Class Libraries and click Change Option...again, you'll see this dialog box:

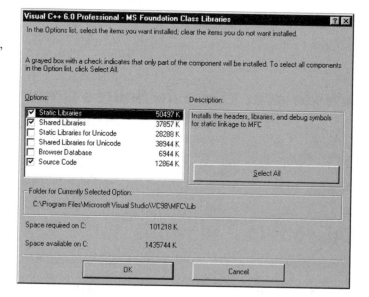

The most interesting options here are Source Code and the ...Unicode choices. Turning off the Source Code option can save more than twelve megabytes of drive space on your system by not copying the source code to the MFC libraries. However, having access to this source code is very handy when debugging, as well as when learning about the classes. Even though you didn't write the classes, the debugger will allow you to step into the MFC code so that you can learn how it works.

Internationalization

By default, only the ANSI versions of MFC are installed. If you're writing English-language applications for Windows NT/2000, Windows 95, or Windows 98, the ANSI libraries are quite adequate. However, if you're writing applications, which you plan to aggressively internationalize, you will certainly want to make sure the Unicode libraries are installed too.

The Unicode libraries options will provide you with widened versions of the MFC classes that are capable of working with the Unicode character set. Programming with MFC is largely the same no matter what character set you're using, as all of the subtler differences are absorbed by the MFC and the Win32 SDK. You can find a discussion on internationalization issues in Appendix B.

The Static and Shared versions of the libraries denote versions of MFC which are statically linked to your application, or dynamically linked to all running applications which use MFC. You should certainly install the shared version of MFC (it will be installed for you, since the Visual Studio uses it), and consider installing the static version too. We discuss the differences between these builds in Chapter 9.

Data Access

As MFC supports the use of Microsoft Open Database Connectivity (ODBC) drivers to access heterogeneous data sources, Visual C++ ships with a few 32-bit ODBC drivers which you may install at the same time as Visual C++. At the time of writing, only a few drivers are included with Visual C++. If your database isn't one of those supported, you should check with your database vendor to see if 32-bit ODBC drivers are available for their products.

MFC's database support in covered in great detail in Chapter 12.

Tools

Aside from the default development tools provided by Visual C++, by which I mean the C/C++ compiler, linker, the libraries and the resource management tools, **Setup.exe** is capable of installing a few important additional tools. The dialog shown below appears when you highlight the Tools option and press the Details... push button in the Microsoft Visual C++ Setup dialog:

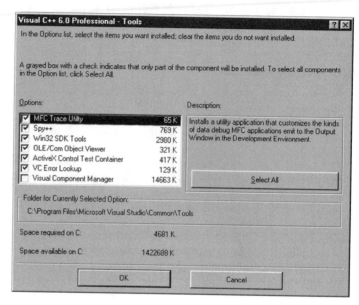

Spy++ is a tool that allows you to watch Windows messages as they are passed back and forth between active windows. Spy++ is also useful for finding the owner and children of a window, and can also be used to see what threads or processes are associated with a window, or vice versa.

The ActiveX Control Test Container is a tool covered in Chapters 15 and 16; it's used to test ActiveX Controls you've written yourself. The MFC Trace Utility is a relatively small tool to control the amount of diagnostic and informational output produced by an MFC application running under the debugger.

Win32 SDK Tools

When the Win32 SDK Tools option is checked, numerous tools from the Win32 SDK are installed by Visual C++. These tools include Pstat and PView for Windows NT (Windows 95/98 only has a version of the latter – PView95) which are used to monitor and modify processes running on your system. The handy WinDiff tool, which is a GUI version of the popular Diff file comparison utility popular on Unix systems, is also installed. WinDiff works on both Windows NT and Windows 95/98.

Online References

Once the setup of Visual C++ proper is completed, you'll be invited to install a copy of the Microsoft Developer Network. The true Microsoft Developer Network product is a subscription of CDs containing, at a minimum, an incredible amount of documentation and a browser to view that documentation. More expensive versions of the subscription provide dozens of CDs with each release and include beta versions of Microsoft operating systems, extensive development tools, loads of localized products for internationalized testing, and even BackOffice products!

The version that comes in the Visual C++ box is, of course, one of the most modest varieties. It's just a snapshot of the documentation release. The documentation will cover the development tools (including Visual C++ and all the SDK tools), as well as the libraries and the operating system APIs themselves. The samples for the products are all baked into this documentation, and you can use the interface provided by the documentation browser to copy the product samples to your hard drive.

Enough of an advertisement. The final step of your Visual C++ setup will allow you to install the MSDN CD that came with your package.

After Setup

Once you've run Setup, you'll notice that you've got a few new programs on your Start menu. Most notably, the Microsoft Visual C++ 6.0 product entry will be there. You can click on this choice to run the integrated development environment. Also, on your hard drive, are the discrete command-line tools: the C++ compiler itself, the linker, the library manager, Nmake (the program maintenance utility), and so on. You can run these tools from the command line at any time you like.

By default, everything installs in a directory under your Program Files directory. You'll end up with a Microsoft Visual Studio directory there; under that directory are lots of individual directories that hold the files used by the product.

In particular, you will notice that MFC has its own separate include directory. That means that any program using MFC will probably take header files from both Program Files\Microsoft Visual Studio\Vc98\mfc\include and Program Files\Microsoft Visual Studio\Vc98\include, where the standard C, C++, Windows, OLE and ODBC headers are stored.

The mfc\src directory has a few interesting subdirectories, the first of which is intel. This directory contains MFC source code files which are specific to builds of MFC that are targeted to Intel platforms. If you were to install MIPS or Alpha versions of Visual C++, you would end up with additional directories here. The intel directory only contains module definition files and function ordering files for the linker – you will only be interested in these files if you ever rebuild MFC for yourself.

The l.jpn, l.chs, l.ita, l.kor, l.fra, and l.deu directories contain localized versions of the MFC resources for Japanese-, Chinese-, Italian-, Korean-, French-, and German-speaking countries. Similar subdirectories exist under the mfc\include directory.

MFC also has its own special directory for libraries, called Program Files\Microsoft Visual Studio\Vc98\mfc\lib. These libraries are only used in projects that use MFC, so they are kept in a separate directory. Windows import libraries, additional object files and standard C and C++ run-time libraries are stored in Program Files\Microsoft Visual Studio\Vc98\lib.

System files, like the MFC DLLs, any OLE DLLs and the ODBC drivers you might have installed, are all set up in the System directory under your Windows installation directory. Alternatively, if you run Windows NT, this directory is called Winnt\System32. Note that if you have more than one operating system on your computer, you must run Setup under each operating system where you want Visual C++ to run. The first run is the beast because it copies everything; the second run will only update the files which need to be added or relocated, so it will proceed much faster.

Visual C++ Development Tools

All of the core development tools that Visual C++ installs on your hard disk drive land in the Program Files\Microsoft Visual Studio\Vc98\bin directory. If you're interested in using the individual command-line tools, you should make sure this directory appears in your PATH. The actual executable files are in this directory, along with the rest of the binary images that make up the development environment.

Note that the ...\Microsoft Visual Studio\Vc98\bin directory also includes executables that make up the development system. You'll find Cl.exe here, for example, which is the actual C/C++ compiler. You'll also find the linker (Link.exe) and the program maintenance utility (Nmake.exe). With this directory in your PATH, you can perform traditional development from the command prompt – just use the cl command (and the appropriate options) to get started compiling your code. If you've installed Visual C++ on Windows 95/98, you'll find a directory named ...\Microsoft Visual Studio\Common\Tools\win95. Visual C++ keeps this directory on the path so it can reach the special Windows 95/98 versions of PView (PView95) that I mentioned earlier.

Usually, you'll live in the Visual Studio and use the graphical program management tools to get your work done. In the meantime, you can use these tools from the command line while working with older projects or writing quick-and-dirty utilities that might make the development environment seem a little cumbersome.

Registry Entries

Visual C++ makes several changes to your registry after it completes a setup. Almost all of the necessary changes are localized under the HKEY_CURRENT_USER\Software\Microsoft\DevStudio key. Various subkeys contain information on the settings, defaults, fonts and toolbars you currently have configured in your Visual C++ environment.

Other settings are made to the HKEY_CURRENT_USER\Environment key (under Windows NT). Here, the Visual C++ Setup program will add the **Microsoft Visual Studio\vc98\bin** directory to the PATH, and it will also create Include and Lib entries so that the compiler can find its header and library files when run from a Windows NT Command Prompt or Windows 95/98 MS-DOS window.

> You should note that these settings affect only command-line builds; the integrated development environment uses a different list of directory names to find executables, header files and libraries when performing a compile.

Aside from changing the environment on your machine to correctly set up command-line compiles, you should *never* directly edit Visual C++ settings in the registry.

> If you ever need to customize Visual C++ or alter your installation, you should do so only using the **Tools** menu. It's too easy to make a mistake with the registry editor and render your installation useless.

International Programming

The importance of international markets for software is growing every day. This need is driven by the adoption of computers throughout the world marketplace and is augmented by the softening of trade barriers in the former Eastern Bloc countries. Markets that were formerly too volatile to consider for business commitments are becoming stable, and the use of computers in business is now spreading to those markets. Most developers have very little experience with internationalized development platforms, but the opportunity for worldwide software sales expands relentlessly, so localization issues like Far-Eastern character sets, right-to-left character sets for Middle Eastern nations, and European conventions for date formatting will soon be in every good programmer's arsenal.

Even if you don't localize your program, you'll still want to allow users in foreign markets to use their own native language — even in extended character sets — as data in your program. File names, directory names, and any text may be represented in ways you might not expect. Without minimal support for international languages, your program won't be usable for many users in the world.

Throughout this book, you certainly have noticed lots of funny macros (such as _T()) and routine names which might be strange to you. These constructs have appeared throughout code surrounding the use of strings, and in all the code fragments that deal with CString objects. This appendix will explain what those macros are for, and I will outline some of the steps that you'll need to take to make sure that your project can be readily adapted to overseas markets.

Internationalizing Your Project

Nearly everyone will develop different targets in their application's project for debug and release builds, mainly because those multiple targets are provided by AppWizard when you create the product. This will allow you to conveniently rebuild your application with the appropriate switches, depending on the results you require for that build. You should consider a similar approach when you embrace a plan to internationalize your project.

Normally, an MFC program is built to use a **multibyte character set** (MBCS) and will have the preprocessor symbol _MBCS defined. You can use the **Unicode character set** if you define the _UNICODE symbol while compiling your program. The _UNICODE and _MBCS preprocessor symbols are mutually exclusive – they shouldn't both be used in the same application.

If you didn't have anything better to do (if there isn't a hockey team in your town, for instance), you might have culled through the Windows header files and noticed that they refer to a symbol named UNICODE instead of the _UNICODE symbol mentioned here. They mean the same thing but you'll want both defined if you're making a Unicode application. MFC takes care of adding UNICODE for you if you've defined _UNICODE. However, if you mistakenly define UNICODE, nobody will come to your rescue. In a nutshell, there are two different symbols because someone lost an argument about strict ANSI compatibility.

Unicode is a character set introduced in the late 1980s to provide a global standard in character mappings for numerous languages. It also provides for non-alphabetic characters used internationally, such as Greek letters and technical symbols. The only disadvantage to Unicode is that each character is sixteen bits wide, effectively doubling the space your program will need for character data storage.

MBCS, on the other hand, is a much weaker standard than Unicode. It provides for character strings that are eight bits wide until a **lead byte** character is encountered in the string. The lead byte indicates that the next byte or bytes are actually part of the same character as the lead byte. The **trail byte** (or bytes), together with the lead byte, defines a character which is outside of the current application's commonly used character set. Immediately after the final trail byte is identified, the string continues with single-byte characters until another lead byte is found. You might want to refer to Appendix D, where all of the MFC libraries and their exact contents are listed, to determine which specific MFC library you'd use to gain support for a particular character set.

Having built both MBCS and Unicode versions of your application, you'll know that your application can be ported to any platform. By writing Unicode-compatible applications now, you can plan for future international support to your application. Even with only MBCS support in your application, you can expect to address a much greater market than you would with a less carefully written application.

Note that Unicode versions of the Windows APIs are available only in Windows NT – Windows 95/98 do not support Unicode calls; ::MessageBoxW() is implemented by Windows 95/98, though, but only to remind you of the limitations of these operating systems by supplying "Sorry Unicode not supported" types of messages. If you're targeting your application for the Windows 95 or Windows 98 platforms, your decision is easy – use the **multibyte character set support**. If you're targeting Windows NT exclusively, you'll find some advantage to using Unicode: it is slightly faster, because the Windows NT system is completely Unicode based. Unicode is easier to manipulate and completely covers all characters in almost all conceivable, commercially interesting languages.

If you call MBCS versions of the APIs under Windows NT, you're forcing the operating system to convert any strings you pass to Unicode before actually getting any work done. If the API returns string information, the string will also have to be converted back. Of course, the operating system is optimized to handle this efficiently, but it does slightly impact the performance of your application. Predictably, the strength of the impact has to do with the frequency of string-oriented calls in your application.

On the other hand, your application also has to work harder and use more memory because Unicode strings are almost always exactly twice as long as comparable MBCS strings. Of course, that two-to-one ratio changes, depending on the percentage of MBCS characters involving lead-byte sequences that your application actually handles. Since you're reading this in English, the odds are that the percentage will be pretty low, so you'll stick close to that two-to-one ratio.

Localizing Strings

A key decision when designing an internationalized application is the question of translation – when to do it, and when not to. Generally, you should translate your help file and all of the user-interface resources of your application. Menus, tool-tips, control captions, window captions and predefined contents for list controls should always be localized too.

On the other hand, programmatic interfaces to your application shouldn't be internationalized. If you implement Automation, you shouldn't translate the methods and properties your application exposes– this would break any code made up of words that also appear in a foreign language. If your application has a macro language, don't translate the keywords that the language uses. You *may* decide to localize the Automation interface names and keywords in your macro language if you can do so without breaking existing applications written against those interfaces or those names. That is, if you want to localize your Automation object names, you should register 'language neutral' versions as well as localized versions. You should make sure that the interpreter (or compiler) that your macro language uses can recognize keywords in all languages; otherwise, users who invest time and money in writing scripts in one language will be stuck when they try to use a differently-localized version of your program with the same macro code.

For most applications, building many languages into the product is just too much work. It is quite reasonable to avoid that work by providing programmability features in only one language.

The easiest way to make sure that your code can be translated is to put all the strings your program uses into string resources. If you take this approach, you can hand off the `.rc` file for your project to the translation team instead of having them pick through each and every line of your source code looking for things to translate.

International String Handling

If you're coding for MBCS, remember that your strings can contain multibyte characters. Conversions and 'pointer math' which depend on a particular width of the data in a string can go bad if the string turns out to contain rogue width data values. If you step through a string like the following in an MBCS build, your code will break badly:

```
char* pstr = "In Katakana, you would write タアガエ, however.";
char* pstrWorker;
for (pstrWorker = pstr; *pstrWorker != '\0'; pstrWorker++)
    DoSomethingTo(*pstrWorker);
```

Those Katakana characters are certainly multibyte characters, but the increment expression in your for statement only steps by the sizeof(char) at each iteration. You'll end up calling DoSomethingTo() on the Katakana characters twice; once for the lead byte and once for the trail byte. The code is broken! Even if you don't have string literals with Japanese (or other foreign language) characters in them, your users could input such data at any time, so this is something you truly need to worry about; see the section of this appendix called 'Pointer Manipulation' for a solution to this problem.

Another potential problem rears its ugly head if you're tempted to do a comparison on a couple of characters using an if statement like this:

```
char myChar;
if (myChar >= 'A' && myChar <= 'Z')
{
    // myChar is a letter; do something
}
```

This code will usually be okay in a Unicode application, but you shouldn't use it in certain circumstances. For instance, if a character has an accented, it would likely be out of the range and fail the test incorrectly; the rules for the language probably indicate that accented characters can be upper case. Also, many languages don't entertain the concept of upper case or lower case letters anyway – running this code in such countries is an invalid idea, plain and simple.

If you're doing such a comparison in an MBCS application, you'll need to worry about the code page the thread doing the comparison is using. The code page is a set of information which defines the way characters work within an application. We'll examine code pages, the routines that use them, and Unicode-compatible programming style through the remainder of this chapter.

In this example, where you're trying to decide if myChar is an uppercase letter, your code will not work if the text contains accented capital letters which don't fall in the range 'A' to 'Z'. Such accented letters can indeed be uppercase and the if statement needs to be able to test for them. So you should carefully use the appropriate C run-time library function or macro to test the data you're interested in. The C run-time libraries take care of implementing the rules to perform these tests appropriately. To bail us out of our upper case test problem, for example, the run-time libraries provide an isupper() macro which will check the passed character and return non-zero if the character is an upper case letter, or zero if it isn't.

Tchar.h

However, the isupper() function accepts a char; if you're working with Unicode characters, you should use the widened version of the function, named iswupper(), which accepts a wide character. Ideally, though, you should consider using the routines defined in the Tchar.h header. This file provides macros for all common string functions, as well as a data type that is dependent on your compile mode.

If you include Tchar.h and have the symbol _MBCS defined, Tchar.h will map all of its macros to functions that handle multibyte character sets. On the other hand, if you bring Tchar.h into your code and have the _UNICODE preprocessor symbol defined, the header will define functions that take Unicode strings or characters.

The table in the section 'Converting Existing Projects' indicates which Tchar.h macros map to which normal, standard C run-time library functions. By the way, this same chart does exist in the Visual C++ documentation, but we've reformatted and reordered it so that it's more convenient for knowledgeable developers. Undoubtedly, you'll have noticed these unfamiliar function names throughout most of the examples in this book.

New Data Types

Tchar.h also defines a few new data types. The TCHAR data type follows different rules, depending on the preprocessor symbols evident at the moment the file is included. TCHAR will become char for _MBCS and normal fixed-width character applications, or an unsigned short for _UNICODE applications. Tchar.h also defines pointers to strings of each of these types: LPCTSTR and LPTSTR.

So that you don't have to worry about your string literals, Tchar.h also provides a macro that can be used to change the data type of string literals in your source. Again, the effect of the macro is dependent on the preprocessor symbols that were defined when Tchar.h was included. Wrap all of your string literals in the _TEXT() macro:

```
puts(_TEXT("Hello, world!\n"));
```

You should note that the _TEXT() macro has a shorter equivalent: the _T() macro. It is identical to _TEXT(), differing in name only. So, this line of code is equivalent to the example above:

```
puts(_T("Hello, world!\n"));
```

The point of Tchar.h is to allow you to write one collection of source code that can be built in any character environment. This is ideal for code that you're writing now; you can continue to run it in a single-byte character environment. Later, you can flip a compiler switch and rebuild the same source code for use with multibyte character sets or as a Unicode application.

Practical Preparations

Remember that *everything* you do might have to end up in some other language someday. Cute little tricks, like the code below to add appropriate plural endings to text, are a real nightmare in other languages.

```
int nProcessed = ProcessOrders();
printf(_T("%d order%s processed!\n"),
    nProcessed,
    nProcessed == 1 ? _T("") : _T("s"));
```

In French, for instance, you'd need something like this:

```
int nProcessed = ProcessOrders();
printf(_T("%d commande%s traitée%s!\n"),
    nProcessed,
    nProcessed == 1 ? _T("") : _T("s"),
    nProcessed == 1 ? _T("") : _T("s"));
```

But in Japanese, the plural issue is a lot more complicated! This seemingly innocuous little feature can cost you lots of time when you port to other languages.

Adapting to local conventions for time and date representation can be just as horrifying. Study the countries and cultures that you're targeting. Try to secure beta testers in those countries and procure good feedback on the opinion of native users. Some things, like the practices of a different culture, can't be learned from books. Use the features of the operating system and libraries – for instance, you can use the Format() member of the COleDateTime class to help you format the date and time according to the local rules currently configured on the system where your code is running.

Converting Existing Projects

If you've already begun coding, the task of globalizing your product is a little more difficult, but certainly not insurmountable.

The first step is to switch to the appropriate MFC libraries and make sure the correct preprocessor symbol is defined for the character set you'd like to use. If you're planning an _MBCS build, you might not need to make any other changes to the project.

If you're planning on a _UNICODE build, you'll need to set the entry point for your executable by adjusting the linker options in your project. Get there by choosing the Settings... command in the Project menu and choosing the Link tab. Select Output in the list of categories and make sure the Entry-Point Symbol field is set to wWinMainCRTStartup. A correctly tweaked Link tab is shown below:

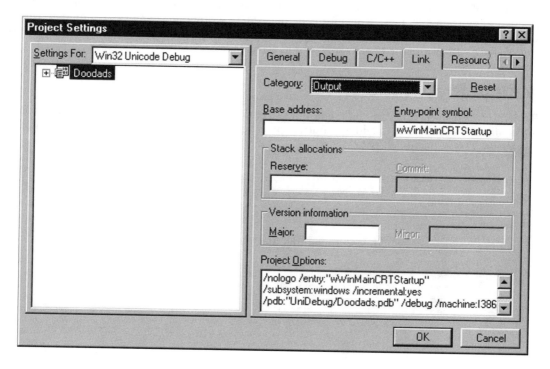

As your development work progresses, you should consider having regular code reviews to look for lingering language problems in your application. Appoint one member of your development staff to be the localization expert. Make sure your quality assurance team has access to computers configured for other languages – you can get the localized versions of Windows from the Developer Network CD Subscription, if you can't find them from your favorite retailer.

Building the Application

Once you've made all the necessary changes, try building your application. If everything goes okay, move along to testing it. If the build didn't work right, then as a first step, you can work through the compiler and linker errors that you have. If you've paid absolutely no attention to the internationalization rules we've described here, you'll find that your life will be miserable. For starters, you'll have to go through all of your code, carefully applying the _TEXT() macro to the strings in it. If your application has many diverse strings, you might want to move strings in your code out to string resource tables.

The trick behind the _T() (or _TEXT()) macro is that it expands to a Unicode string constant if _UNICODE is defined, but doesn't change the string otherwise. So, with _UNICODE defined,

```
TCHAR szPrompt[] = _T("Insert blank disk");
```

becomes:

```
unsigned short szPrompt[] = L"Insert blank disk";
```

Without _UNICODE defined, the same line of source code expands to:

```
char szPrompt[] = "Insert blank disk";
```

Now that all of your string literals are widened, make sure that your data types are too. Pointers to these strings should be of type LPTSTR, const pointers can be LPCTSTR and character arrays are defined with the TCHAR data type. The next trick is to make sure that you're using string functions that are appropriate for the character data type you're using. For code that uses the MFC's CString class, this is a non-issue: all CString functions have appropriate overloaded implementations that manipulate TCHAR strings just fine.

Single characters which appear in your source code don't need to make use of the _T() macro. If you use normal, single-byte ASCII characters, you *don't* need to hide them in a _T() macro because the compiler can promote them to the appropriate double-byte value without trouble. So, code like this:

```
CString str("Hockey is best");
str += '!';
```

is just fine. Note, also, that there's a few ways to take shortcuts. CString has constructors which take pointers to **wide** (that is, Unicode) strings, as well as **narrow** (that is, MBCS) strings. The constructor will automatically convert appropriately based on the type of build you're doing!

Now that you've changed all of these string data types, you should also begin using functions which accept those data types. Here is a full list:

SBCS (_UNICODE and _MBCS Not Defined)	Generic-Text Routine Name	_MBCS Defined	_UNICODE Defined
__isascii	_istascii	__isascii	iswascii
_access	_taccess	_access	_waccess
_chdir	_tchdir	_chdir	_wchdir
_chmod	_tchmod	_chmod	_wchmod
_creat	_tcreat	_creat	_wcreat
_execl	_texecl	_execl	_wexecl
_execle	_texecle	_execle	_wexecle
_execlp	_texeclp	_execlp	_wexeclp
_execlpe	_texeclpe	_execlpe	_wexeclpe
_execv	_texecv	_execv	_wexecv
_execve	_texecve	_execve	_wexecve
_execvp	_texecvp	_execvp	_wexecvp
_execvpe	_texecvpe	_execvpe	_wexecvpe
_fdopen	_tfdopen	_fdopen	_wfdopen
_findfirst	_tfindfirst	_findfirst	_wfindfirst
_findnext	_tfindnext	_findnext	_wfindnext
_fsopen	_tfsopen	_fsopen	_wfsopen
_fullpath	_tfullpath	_fullpath	_wfullpath
_getcwd	_tgetcwd	_getcwd	_wgetcwd
_itoa	_itot	_itoa	_itow
_ltoa	_ltot	_ltoa	_ltow
_makepath	_tmakepath	_makepath	_wmakepath
_mkdir	_tmkdir	_mkdir	_wmkdir
_mktemp	_tmktemp	_mktemp	_wmktemp
_open	_topen	_open	_wopen
_popen	_tpopen	_popen	_wpopen

SBCS (_UNICODE and _MBCS Not Defined)	Generic-Text Routine Name	_MBCS Defined	_UNICODE Defined
_rmdir	_trmdir	_rmdir	_wrmdir
_searchenv	_tsearchenv	_searchenv	_wsearchenv
_snprintf	_sntprintf	_snprintf	_snwprintf
_sopen	_tsopen	_sopen	_wsopen
_spawnl	_tspawnl	_spawnl	_wspawnl
_spawnle	_tspawnle	_spawnle	_wspawnle
_spawnlp	_tspawnlp	_spawnlp	_wspawnlp
_spawnlpe	_tspawnlpe	_spawnlpe	_wspawnlpe
_spawnv	_tspawnv	_spawnv	_wspawnv
_spawnve	_tspawnve	_spawnve	_wspawnve
_spawnvp	_tspawnvp	_spawnvp	_tspawnvp
_spawnvpe	_tspawnvpe	_spawnvpe	_tspawnvpe
_splitpath	_tsplitpath	_splitpath	_wsplitpath
_stat	_tstat	_stat	_wstat
_strdate	_tstrdate	_strdate	_wstrdate
_strdec	_tcsdec	_mbsdec	_wcsdec
_strdup	_tcsdup	_mbsdup	_wcsdup
_stricmp	_tcsicmp	_mbsicmp	_wcsicmp
_stricoll	_tcsicoll	_stricoll	_wcsicoll
_strinc	_tcsinc	_mbsinc	_wcsinc
_strlwr	_tcslwr	_mbslwr	_wcslwr
_strncnt	_tcsnbcnt	_mbsnbcnt	_wcnscnt
_strncnt	_tcsnccnt	_mbsnccnt	_wcsncnt
_strncnt	_tcsnccnt	_mbsnccnt	_wcsncnt
_strnextc	_tcsnextc	_mbsnextc	_wcsnextc
_strnicmp	_tcsncicmp	_mbsnicmp	_wcsnicmp
_strnicmp	_tcsnicmp	_mbsnicmp	_wcsnicmp

Table Continued on Following Page

SBCS (_UNICODE and _MBCS Not Defined)	Generic-Text Routine Name	_MBCS Defined	_UNICODE Defined
_strnicoll	_tcsnicoll	_strnicoll	_wcsnicoll
_strninc	_tcsninc	_mbsninc	_wcsninc
_strnset	_tcsncset	_mbsnset	_wcsnset
_strnset	_tcsnset	_mbsnbset	_wcsnset
_strrev	_tcsrev	_mbsrev	_wcsrev
_strset	_tcsset	_mbsset	_wcsset
_strspnp	_tcsspnp	_mbsspnp	_wcsspnp
_strtime	_tstrtime	_strtime	_wstrtime
_strupr	_tcsupr	_mbsupr	_wcsupr
_tempnam	_ttempnam	_tempnam	_wtempnam
_ultoa	_ultot	_ultoa	_ultow
_utime	_tutime	_utime	_wutime
_vsnprintf	_vsntprintf	_vsnprintf	_vsnwprintf
asctime	_tasctime	asctime	_wasctime
atoi	_ttoi	atoi	_wtoi
atol	_ttol	atol	_wtol
ctime	_tctime	ctime	_wctime
fgetc	_fgettc	fgetc	fgetwc
fgetchar	_fgettchar	fgetchar	_fgetwchar
fgets	_fgetts	fgets	fgetws
fopen	_tfopen	fopen	_wfopen
fprintf	_ftprintf	fprintf	fwprintf
fputc	_fputtc	fputc	fputwc
fputchar	_fputtchar	fputchar	_fputwchar
fputs	_fputts	fputs	fputws
freopen	_tfreopen	freopen	_wfreopen
fscanf	_ftscanf	fscanf	fwscanf
getc	_gettc	getc	getwc

SBCS (_UNICODE and _MBCS Not Defined)	Generic-Text Routine Name	_MBCS Defined	_UNICODE Defined
getchar	_gettchar	getchar	getwchar
getenv	_tgetenv	getenv	_wgetenv
gets	_getts	gets	getws
isalnum	_istalnum	_ismbcalnum	iswalnum
isalpha	_istalpha	_ismbcalpha	iswalpha
iscntrl	_istcntrl	iscntrl	iswcntrl
isdigit	_istdigit	_ismbcdigit	iswdigit
isgraph	_istgraph	_ismbcgraph	iswgraph
islower	_istlower	_ismbclower	iswlower
isprint	_istprint	_ismbcprint	iswprint
ispunct	_istpunct	_ismbcpunct	iswpunct
isspace	_istspace	_ismbcspace	iswspace
isupper	_istupper	_ismbcupper	iswupper
isxdigit	_istxdigit	isxdigit	iswxdigit
main	_tmain	main	wmain
main	_tmain	main	wmain
perror	_tperror	perror	_wperror
printf	_tprintf	printf	wprintf
putc	_puttc	putc	putwc
putchar	_puttchar	putchar	putwchar
puts	_putts	puts	putws
remove	_tremove	remove	_wremove
rename	_trename	rename	_wrename
scanf	_tscanf	scanf	wscanf
setlocale	_tsetlocale	setlocale	_wsetlocale
sprintf	_stprintf	sprintf	swprintf
sscanf	_stscanf	sscanf	swscanf

Table Continued on Following Page

SBCS (_UNICODE and _MBCS Not Defined)	Generic-Text Routine Name	_MBCS Defined	_UNICODE Defined
strcat	_tcscat	_mbscat	wcscat
strchr	_tcschr	_mbschr	wcschr
strcmp	_tcscmp	_mbscmp	wcscmp
strcoll	_tcscoll	strcoll	wcscoll
strcpy	_tcscpy	_mbscpy	wcscpy
strcspn	_tcscspn	_mbscspn	wcscspn
strftime	_tcsftime	strftime	wcsftime
strlen	_tcsclen	_mbslen	wcslen
strlen	_tcslen	_mbslen	wcslen
strncat	_tcsncat	_mbsnbcat	wcsncat
strncat	_tcsnccat	_mbsncat	wcsncat
strncmp	_tcsncmp	_mbsnbcmp	wcsncmp
strncmp	_tcsnccmp	_mbsncmp	wcsncmp
strncpy	_tcsnccpy	_mbsncpy	wcsncpy
strncpy	_tcsncpy	_mbsnbcpy	wcsncpy
strpbrk	_tcspbrk	_mbspbrk	wcspbrk
strrchr	_tcsrchr	_mbsrchr	wcsrchr
strspn	_tcsspn	_mbsspn	wcsspn
strstr	_tcsstr	_mbsstr	wcsstr
strtod	_tcstod	strtod	wcstod
strtok	_tcstok	_mbstok	wcstok
strtol	_tcstol	strtol	wcstol
strtoul	_tcstoul	strtoul	wcstoul
strxfrm	_tcsxfrm	strxfrm	wcsxfrm
system	_tsystem	system	_wsystem
tmpnam	_ttmpnam	tmpnam	_wtmpnam
tolower	_totlower	_mbctolower	towlower
toupper	_totupper	_mbctoupper	towupper

SBCS (_UNICODE and _MBCS Not Defined)	Generic-Text Routine Name	_MBCS Defined	_UNICODE Defined
ungetc	_ungettc	ungetc	ungetwc
vfprintf	_vftprintf	vfprintf	vfwprintf
vprintf	_vtprintf	vprintf	vwprintf
vsprintf	_vstprintf	vsprintf	vswprintf
WinMain	_tWinMain	WinMain	wWinMain

With all of these function call substitutions done, go and recompile your application. After you've sorted out all of these changes, you should have an application which can be localized quite readily.

Pointer Manipulation

The table on the previous few pages shows how Microsoft Visual C++ helps with internationalization by providing more appropriate functions than the normal Kernighan-and-Ritchie era string functions. To save work later, you should learn to use these functions – their names will become second nature to you after a bit of practice.

A cursory examination of the table will leave you thinking that the generic character manipulation functions are replacements for the normal string functions in the C run-time libraries. For the most part you're right, but there are a few other functions which help out in special circumstances. One of those circumstances is the pointer manipulation problem we discussed earlier in the appendix. The original code looked like this:

```
char* pstr = "In Katakana, you would write タアガエ, however.";
char* pstrWorker;
for (pstrWorker = pstr; *pstrWorker != '\0'; pstrWorker++)
    DoSomethingTo(*pstrWorker);
```

Rewriting this to use the features Tchar.h gives us, we can end up with something a lot more portable. Here's the rewrite:

```
LPTSTR pstr = _T("In Katakana, you would write タアガエ, however.");
LPTSTR pstrWorker;
for (pstrWorker = pstr; *pstrWorker != _T('\0');
                            pstrWorker += _tcsinc(pstrWorker))
    DoSomethingTo(*pstrWorker);
```

Instead of using the char* data type directly, I use the LPTSTR type. More importantly, instead of adding one to the character in question, I use the _tcsinc() function to step the pointer through the multibyte string properly. When _MBCS is defined, the _tcsinc() function resolves to a call to the C run-time's _mbsinc() function. Unlike the ++ operator, this function knows about the currently selected code page and can work with multibyte characters appropriately. There's a complementary _tcsdec() function, too.

Locale-specific Routines

As I mentioned earlier, some data handled by an application is actually affected by local custom. For example, some European countries use a comma as a decimal separator instead of the decimal point used in North America. Many put the components of a date/time string in a different order, and sometimes use different separators too. And certainly accented characters effect sorting orders and comparisons.

Programs that are aware of such customary differences are said to be aware of their **locale**. A program's locale defines the rules it will use to build strings of numbers, express percentages, place currency operators or format floating point numbers. The C run-time libraries implement the routines that set a program's locale and, since the Microsoft Foundation Classes also use routines from these libraries, the MFC is also aware of your program's locale.

The setlocale() Function

You can set your locale using the `setlocale()` function, found in the C run-time library. The function takes two parameters. The first is an integer indicating which part of the locale you are setting and the second is a string which sets the locale. The locale is logically split into several different components, as shown in this table:

Locale Identifier	Effect
LC_COLLATE	String collation – different rules for sorting order and alphabetization.
LC_CTYPE	Character semantics – rules governing what characters mean and how characters from the `Ctype.h` file work.
LC_MONETARY	Rules about currency markers and decimal places for small currency values. This is only used by the `localeconv()` function.
LC_NUMERIC	Conventions surrounding the use of numbers and separators between groups of numbers, as in decimal numbers and dates.
LC_TIME	Time formatting rules: format, military time, order of date parts and so on.
LC_ALL	Sets all facets of the locale.

These flags let you adjust individual portions of the locale. For example, you can use a European locale for time manipulation but leave the default locale for comparing strings.

The Code Page

The string argument can be a language name, a language name and a country, or a language name, a country, *and* a **code page**. Typical locale strings might be formatted like this:

```
"french"               // What it says!
"french_canada"        // French as spoken in Canada; Canadian number rules
"french_canada.1252"   // Same as above; exactingly specific
```

Note that both the language and country can be important; for example, the French language differs between France and eastern Canada. By providing both a country and a locale, you give the C run-time library enough information to format both strings and numbers correctly. While 'Monday' is 'lundi' in both Paris and Quebec, the countries use different date formats

Using the Code Page

The third locale string example given above includes a code page number. The code page defines the semantics of the locale exactly. Windows NT defines many code pages; your system may not have certain code pages loaded, and you may need to install them to do your testing. Versions of the Windows operating system released for that country will certainly include the code page. Since the code page specifically identifies information about the locale, you can specify *only* the code page, which means that you could use

```
".1252"
```

as a correct code page specification for the French language in Canada. The code page also contains the character set used by the locale.

Of course, not every country and language combination identifies a code page. While `"english_china"` might seem an ideal description of that whimsical little 'dim sum' place down on 148th Avenue, the C run-time libraries don't eat lunch there. The complete list of countries, languages and their abbreviations can be found in the Microsoft Visual C++ Run-Time Library Reference.

Identifying the Code Page

When you specify a code page, you can use the numeric value describing the code page as we've shown above, or you can use one of two special code page names. The first, `".ACP"`, names the ANSI default code page, while the other, `".OCP"`, specifies the OEM code page. By default, the code page loaded will be the ANSI code page specified by the system, but this setting can be changed via the controls in the International icon (Windows NT) or the Regional Settings icon (in Windows 98 and Windows 95) in the Windows Control Panel. If you change the code page, you can switch back by passing an empty string to the `setlocale()` function.

You can query for the current locale string by passing `setlocale()` with a NULL second parameter. The function will return the currently active localization string. Normally, `setlocale()` returns the string corresponding to the new setting.

In Conclusion

Without sounding like some kind of marketing monster from Planet X, with steel teeth, green skin and radioactive blood, I want to underscore the importance of using a multibyte character set to bring you a step closer to a wider international market. Choosing to support international users is something everyone responsible for the delivery of a product should consider. By adopting a policy that embraces Far-East markets alone, you will significantly increase your potential market base!

With a little forethought, this market can be yours for only the cost of the translation and some additional testing. If you botch the attempt then the returns will disappear because you'll have to spend lots of money re-engineering your application. Follow my advice, get lots of feedback from your target marketplaces and you'll reign supreme when the time comes to ship to far away lands.

Writing Console Applications

While the Windows graphical user interface (GUI) provides an interesting and effective interface for most programs that interact heavily with users, some applications aren't designed to work directly with the user. Simple utilities, which just need to run, will get the job done and get out. These programs, which run when there are no users around, are usually written as Windows **console applications**.

Console applications are just what their name implies; applications that work with the user as if they were connected to the computer via a dumb terminal. Unix systems, which do not use the X-Window system, of course, fall into this category. They are written to interact with the user through the classic C-style stdin/stdout routines. Windows provides some control over the console window as a graphical window, but the bulk of interaction you have with your user will be on the command line or via simple I/O operations.

In this appendix, we'll be discussing console applications, with and without MFC. For the first time in Visual C++ 6.0, AppWizard does support console applications built with MFC, but I'll explain all of the plumbing that goes into such an application whether you use AppWizard or not. The material in this chapter will shed some more light on the most fundamental architecture of an MFC application and may be beneficial to you even if you're not planning a console project.

The specific issues that we'll cover are:

- ➤ Building your console application project
- ➤ Performing I/O in console applications
- ➤ Using the console functions
- ➤ Caveats for writing console applications

Building Your Console Application Project

The first step to writing your console-based application is to build a project. Now that there's AppWizard support for building MFC-based console applications, this step is significantly simpler if you're using Visual C++ 6.0 or newer – just select the **Win32 Console Application** item in the **Projects** tab of the **New** dialog. You'll be offered the opportunity to select the basis for your application in the very first step of the dialog, shown here:

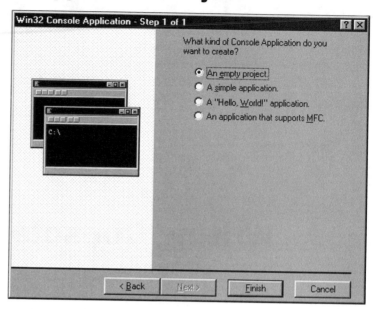

An **empty project** creates just that – an empty project. The build for the project will create a console application and won't use MFC. There will be no files in the project, initially, and that's that! You'll have to add your own files as you go. An **empty project** is a great choice for porting a text-based application from DOS or Unix.

The second choice, **A simple application**, gets you an application that does nothing – you get a `main()` function that just returns zero. You also get, though, a basic setup to use precompiled headers – `stdafx.h` and `stdafx.cpp` are hooked up for your project. A "Hello, World!" application gets the same code as the "simple application" choice, but it includes the headers for the standard C++ library stream routines and writes "Hello, World" to the console before terminating.

As far as this appendix is concerned, the real action doesn't start unless you choose **An application that supports MFC**. Before we talk about the specifics of an MFC-based console application, let's browse through some of the important settings that make a console application different from a normal, graphical application. The differences we examine are going to be common to all of the different application styles the Console Application Wizard can produce.

Preprocessor _WINDOWS Symbol Isn't Defined

For console applications, the symbol `_CONSOLE` is defined instead of the symbol `_WINDOWS`. Your application (or any headers you write) can look for the `_WINDOWS` symbol to be sure that they're being used in a graphical user interface application.

The project emitted by the AppWizard in the above steps is made to switch the executable type using these symbols on the compiler's command line. The `/D` option is given to the compiler to force it to predefine the specified preprocessor symbol. The `_WINDOWS` and `_CONSOLE` symbols are *not* used by the system headers or the MFC headers; they're there for your convenience.

The Compiler Doesn't Use Multithread Run-times

By default, the project emitted when you ask for a console application will not automatically use MFC. This implies something a little subtler – the project won't use the multithread-safe versions of the C run-time libraries. If you're going to use MFC (or, if you're going to write a multithreaded console application), you should make sure that you're using the multithread run-time libraries. You'll see how to fix this setting shortly.

The Compiler Uses Automatic Precompiled Headers

The compiler in a console application uses 'automatic' precompiled headers. This means that the compiler will try to save as much state information as it can between runs, but it also means that the compiler won't be as efficient as it could be when it builds your program. For an empty MFC application, the compiler parses around half a million lines of code, mainly because each module in the application wants to read Afx.h and Afxwin.h, and those files in turn want to read the gargantuan Windows headers. If you don't change the settings to use custom precompiled headers and you start using MFC, you'll be able to write your own book (not on MFC, please) before your first compile is done.

The Linker Looks Everywhere!

When you create a console application, the linker is told to get almost every import library for Windows that you can possibly name. It tries to get ones that you'll almost certainly need, like Kernel32.lib, and User32.lib if you want to use the MessageBox() API, for example, but it also gets libraries you probably don't care about, like Winspool.lib which lets you play with printers and print queues. You'll probably want to pare down this list to improve performance of the linker while building your application. (Remember that there's a list of libraries and their functions in Appendix D, and that you can always use the information in the file \Program Files\Microsoft Visual Studio\vc98\lib\Win32api.csv to find a particular function.) MFC applications don't use explicitly named libraries in the Linker option tab because the MFC headers use #pragma directives to instruct the compiler to ask the linker to get the libraries which are needed depending on what headers you use.

The Subsystem is Different

The linker accepts an option which you usually don't notice – the /subsystem option. This option tells the linker what kind of program you're about to link. Normally, for an MFC application, the /subsystem:windows option is present. This lets the linker mark the generated executable as being for Microsoft Windows (a nifty software offering from a tiny company in the Puget Sound area). However, since you actually want to write a console application, you need to change the way Windows perceives your executable image, so you must specify the /subsystem:console option.

The /subsystem option affects the way that the linker builds the executable image by changing the default entry point. For /subsystem:windows executables, the linker expects to have a WinMain() routine start the application. For /subsystem:console, the linker expects a main() routine.

Multithread-safe Applications

You don't need to worry about fixing the /subsystem option, since it will be set correctly for any console application that you create with the AppWizard. But if you're going to start using MFC with your application, you'll need to make sure that you link with the correct, multithread-safe version of the C run-time libraries. The easiest way to do this is just to select one of the Use MFC... options from the Microsoft Foundation Classes drop-down in the General tab of the Project Settings dialog. You can use MFC in a shared library or in a static library when you build a console application – either is fine. We covered the benefits of each approach earlier in the book. By selecting one of the MFC options, you'll let the IDE automatically choose the right run-time library.

If you're not using The Microsoft Visual Studio for your project, you need to make sure the compiler gets the appropriate /MT or /MD option. Choose /MT for statically linking to MFC and to the C run-time, or /MD to get a dynamically-linked version of the C run-times. If you're performing a debug build, you'll need to append a lower case d to these options so that you get a debug version of the library – /MTd to get a statically linked debug build, for example.

If you don't specify these options, you'll get errors from the linker (of all places!) about symbols like __beginthreadex and __endthreadex being undefined. This is simply because you've used MFC, which wants to find functions in the run-time which help with threads, but you've used a run-time which doesn't support threads. You never directly call these functions in your code, but MFC certainly does – and it won't link if it can't find them.

If you pick the wrong option, like using /MT when you should use /MD, or if you mix up debug and non-debug versions, you'll get a warning from the linker that says you've chosen incompatible libraries. All modules you compile with must have used the same options from the /M family.

I've slightly abused the term **thread-safe** *in this section. For the real scoop, you might want to review Chapter 10 on multi-threading.*

Precompiled Header Files

You'll find that the Wizard has created a file named StdAfx.cpp and had it include StdAfx.h. The StdAfx.cpp file won't contain anything else when produced by the AppWizard, and you shouldn't modify it to contain anything else, either.

In StdAfx.h, you need to add #include directives for all of the system header files that interest you. (We'll discuss exactly which files might interest you in the next section.) You'll find that your application's main source file, as supplied by the Console Application Wizard, will use a #include directive for your StdAfx.h file. This is just more of the same – we've done this for every application we've ever written with MFC in this book.

Any files that you add to the project will also be hooked up to use the StdAfx.h precompiled header file. When you build your project, the compiler will build StdAfx.cpp first. That file doesn't do anything but build the preprocessor's symbol table and then write it out to disk in one huge binary file. Subsequently, when you use the precompiled header file, the compiler *completely* ignores anything in your source file until it sees a reference to that header file.

And if it doesn't see a reference to that header, you'll get an error message:

fooey.cpp (1024) : fatal error C1010: unexpected end of file while looking for precompiled header directive

because the compiler knows it's supposed to find a reference to that header, but hasn't. If you want to have a source file or two not use the precompiled header information, you have an easy fix. Just switch to the C/C++ tab in the Project Settings dialog. There, make sure Precompiled Headers is selected in the Category drop-down so that you can see the settings that you'll need to fuss with. Here, you'll want to expand the view of the files at the left of the window, so that you can highlight only the source file you want to effect. With that file selected, make sure you have the radio button labeled Not using precompiled headers marked. The compiler won't then go looking for a reference to the precompiled header for that particular source file.

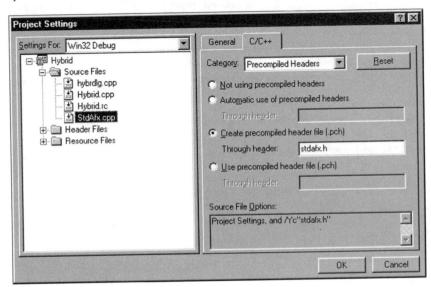

For the rest of the files in your project, whether you've already added them or whether you'll add them at some other time, you should make sure that the radio button labeled Use precompiled header file (.pch) is marked. The Through header edit control should still contain StdAfx.h.

When the compiler builds the StdAfx.cpp module, it will use the /Yc compiler option to make sure that a precompiled header file is created that is suitable for the rest of the project. The /Yc option corresponds to the Create precompiled header file (.pch) radio button in the Project Settings dialog. It is this option, in combination with the compiler running over the StdAfx.cpp source file, that actually creates your StdAfx.pch file. The other files, with the Use precompiled header file (.pch) option selected, will use the precompiled header file when you give the compiler the #include directive for the file named in the Through header edit control. The use of a particular precompiled header file is realized through the compiler's /Yu option.

You can, of course, substitute whatever name you'd like for your precompiled header files – I'm just using StdAfx.h and StdAfx.cpp by convention. Of course, if you don't use these names, you'll have to remember to change the names I've suggested as appropriate (that is, in all #include directives and in the dialog box, too).

You can also use more than one name – just set up more than one .cpp file to generate a .pch file, and then have your different groups of .cpp files reference the different precompiled headers. You'll only need to do this in very large projects.

The exception to all my precompiled header advice is the simplest program in town; if you can fit everything you need into one single source file, you probably won't want to worry about building the extra StdAfx.h and StdAfx.cpp files. If you do take a few minutes to build your StdAfx.h file when you set up your application, you'll save a little bit of time for each build, and that will quickly add up to the three-and-a-half hours it takes to attend a hockey game.

Choosing Header Files

The simplest possible StdAfx.h file will consist of just one #include directive – for Afx.h. This includes definitions for all of the MFC classes that wrap exceptions (like CException and CFileException), as well as neat classes like CFile and CString. Afx.h is good enough to write a console application, but it doesn't include anything that's even *remotely* Windows related. For example, it doesn't include functions that touch resources, like CString::LoadString() or CResourceException. And it certainly doesn't include CWnd or any CWnd-derived classes, most noticeably CWinApp.

You can, though, write small applications like the CToMFC and the FToMFC samples. (By the way, I almost called the sample application for this appendix Sorry because it's a *console* application.) With a thousand apologies to Brian Kernighan and Dennis Ritchie, and neglecting the actual ftoc() function that does the real conversion work, here's what the main part of the FToMFC application looks like:

```
#include <afx.h>
#include <afxwin.h>
#include <stdio.h>

CWinApp theApp;

void main()
{
    if (!AfxWinInit(GetModuleHandle(NULL), NULL, GetCommandLine(), 0))
    {
        return FALSE;   // Game over, man!
    }

    int nFahrenheit;
    CString strOut;

    for (nFahrenheit = 32; nFahrenheit < 220; nFahrenheit += 10)
    {
        strOut.Format("%d\t%d\n", nFahrenheit, ftoc(nFahrenheit));
        printf("%s", (LPCTSTR) strOut);
    }
    return;
}
```

Here, I go nab `Afx.h` and `AfxWin.h` but I also get `Stdio.h` from the C standard libraries! I can code with any libraries I want. Trust me on this, I really can – I've never met a library that I couldn't kick around the block. But the point of the example, perhaps the shortest MFC program ever written, is that MFC is really just a big pile of code. You can take what you need from that pile and leave the rest for any kind of application you'd like to write.

I use `printf()` to write to the standard output, which the C run-time libraries hooked to the console before my `main()` was even called. If I wanted to, I could use routines like `gets()` to read from the keyboard, which is also hooked to the console window and the normal C run-time standard input handle. If the user starts my program from a command line, the program will run within that existing command window. If the user starts CToMFC from the Explorer, the system will create a new console window where the application can run. Of course, if I wanted to, I could also use the standard C++ stream libraries and use `operator<<` to make my way to the standard output window.

> *Note that I used the* `(LPCTSTR)` *casting trick for sending the* `strOut` *string to* `printf()`, *as I described you should use with the* `TRACE()` *macros back in Chapter 3.*

The code above creates a `CWinApp` object directly without even deriving a new class. `CWinApp` isn't an abstract class and can be used directly, as above. MFC is dependent on having an initialized `CWinApp`-derived object hanging around. In other words, you've not written an MFC program unless you have a `CWinApp` object lying around. You can get away with using some subset of MFC without an initialized `CWinApp` object, but it's really a bad idea because the subset of MFC you try to use isn't necessarily predictable. For example, you can use most of `CString` without a `CWinApp`. But if `CString` throws a `CMemoryException`, the `CMemoryException` object will require a `CWinApp` object to load information about the error that occurred – even if you don't handle the exception yourself!

Other dependent routines, some as simple as `AfxMessageBox()`, want to be able to manage the application and its various states – the same states that we learned (in Chapter 3) are sometimes not shared from one thread to another.

Adding a CWinApp-derived Class

If you do want to derive a class from `CWinApp`, you'll find the process isn't as nasty as it sounds even though you're not directly supported by any of the Wizards. You have certainly seen a `CWinApp` object at work many times – they've been in all of our applications so far. The easiest way to get things moving is to steal some code from a scrap project you create with AppWizard; that'll get you all the proper definitions and overrides you want. You won't have a `main()` anymore, but you can do whatever you did in `main()` within `CWinApp::InitInstance()`. When you return from `InitInstance()`, your application will be terminated and the return code you made will be passed to the operating system – assuming you haven't created any windows.

The parameters you used to get in `main()` (like `argc` or `argv`) are available right there in the instance data of `CWinApp`. You can either reference the globals `_argc` and `_argv []`, or you can use the `m_pCommandLine` member variable.

The AfxWinInit() Function

Since a console application initializes via `main()` instead of `WinMain()`, MFC won't initialize itself in a console as it does in a regular Windows application. Initializing MFC in a console application will require you to use the global function `AfxWinInit()`, which is implemented in MFC but is not heavily documented. The function is normally called by MFC's implementation of `WinMain()`.

`AfxWinInit()`'s prototype looks like this:

```
BOOL AFXAPI AfxWinInit(HINSTANCE hInstance,
                       HINSTANCE hPrevInstance,
                       LPTSTR    lpCmdLine,
                       int       nCmdShow)
```

You should call `AfxWinInit()` before you try to do anything else with MFC – that is, you should call this function as the first thing you do in your `main()` implementation. The function returns `TRUE` if it is successful and `FALSE` if not. If the function returns `FALSE`, there's something terribly wrong; your machine is completely out of memory, or there's some serious instability inside Windows. You'll need to exit immediately.

Parameters to AfxWinInit()

The parameters this function takes are all things that are handed to your application when Windows calls your `WinMain()` function. Unfortunately, they're not passed to `main()` by the C runtime libraries, but their values are either readily available from Windows APIs, or else they're not needed at all.

The first parameter is the instance of your application, while `hPrevInstance` is a handle to your previous instance. Back in Chapter 3, and again in Chapter 10, we said that `hPrevInstance` is always `NULL` for Win32 applications. So, you can just pass `NULL` along for `hPrevInstance`. The `hInstance` parameter does need to be your current instance, though – and you can get that value from a call to `GetModuleHandle()`. While `GetModuleHandle()` is normally used to get the handle of a different module than your own, you can pass `NULL` as a parameter to `GetModuleHandle()` to get your own executable's handle.

Since your application's probably not going to display any windows, the `nCmdShow` parameter is meaningless. Normally, this parameter is given to a newly started program by the spawning program – usually, that's the Windows Shell itself. For example, if the shell wants the program to start minimized, it'll pass `SW_MINIMIZE` for this value. If you do decide to show any windows, you might want to reference this value to ensure that the windows are created with the program spawning as you expect.

Finally, the `lpCmdLine` parameter points to the command line for the application as a complete string – not as a parsed, changed, and tweaked version like you'd normally get from `argv[]` and `argc` in your `main()` function. In total, the complete initialization and use of MFC in a console application would look like this:

```
CWinApp theApp;   // Not required to derive our own

int main()
{
    if (!AfxWinInit(GetModuleHandle(NULL), NULL, GetCommandLine(), 0))
    {
        return FALSE;   // Game over, man!
    }

    // Do some work with MFC!

    return 1;   // Return an interesting code
}
```

I test the call to `AfxWinInit()` to make sure it was successful. If it isn't, I return immediately; returning from the `main()` function has the effect of stopping my program. Here, I return 1 if the program works and `FALSE` if it doesn't. Since this function lives in a console application, though, you're free to specify whatever error codes you want for whatever purpose you want. You'll likely do the exact opposite of what I did above, and return a non-zero value in the event of an error and a zero if your program works correctly. This makes the result of the program easy to test using the `IF ERRORLEVEL` construct in the batch file language built into the command interpreter.

It's only after the call to `AfxWinInit()` is done that MFC is ready to be used. The call initializes MFC and initializes your `CWinApp` object by setting up its members. If you're going to code everything you want to do right in `main()`, you're all set at this point. MFC knows where your resources are and can load strings and other resources from your module. When you shut down, everything will be just fine. If you derive your own class and use it in place of `CWinApp` in the example above, you can put code in the `CWinApp` constructor. Code you place in the constructor will run before `main()` is called and before MFC is initialized, however, so you'll need to be very careful what you include there.

A More Familiar Architecture

If you want to have the same architecture we've seen in our interactive Windows GUI-based programs – where `InitInstance()` sets up the application, `Run()` (believe it or not) runs it, and `ExitInstance()` is called as your application dies – you'll need to hook that up yourself within your `main()` implementation. That exercise might look something like this:

```
int main()
{
    if (!AfxWinInit(GetModuleHandle(NULL), NULL, GetCommandLine(), 0))
    {
        return 1;   // Game over, man!
    }
```

Continued on Following Page

```
CWinApp* pApp = AfxGetApp();
int nResult = 1;
if (pApp != NULL)
{
    if (pApp->InitInstance())
    {
        nResult = pApp->Run();
        pApp->ExitInstance();
    }
    else
        nResult = pApp->ExitInstance();
}
return nResult;  // Return an interesting code
}
```

After initializing MFC, I know that the MFC function `AfxGetApp()` is safe to use, and so I use it. It returns a pointer to my application's `CWinApp` object, which I use to call the `InitInstance()` function in that object. If that function returns successfully, I call the `Run()` member and save the return value of that function before calling `ExitInstance()` on the same object.

On the other hand, I might end up finding that `InitInstance()` failed – and if that's true, I just call `ExitInstance()` and get out of there. Note that the return value of the program comes from `ExitInstance()` if initialization failed, but from `Run()` if initialization was successful. I've made this design decision because it closely resembles what MFC itself would do in a GUI application.

Auxiliary MFC Initializations

There are some parts of MFC which might be bigger than even the mainline 'application framework' part of MFC. DAO is one such example – it relies on some OLE objects (and, therefore, on COM) to gain database access for your program. There are a few other components for which this is true, and you should make sure you initialize those components and shut them down correctly.

If you're going to use COM, you should call `AfxOleInit()` before you start working with COM via MFC in your console application. There's no corresponding shutdown function. `AfxOleInit()` returns a `BOOL`. If it returns `FALSE`, something is wrong with COM on your machine; your application couldn't initialize COM, and should terminate before it goes any further. The function doesn't take any parameters.

If you're going to use DAO, you should call `AfxDaoInit()` before you start using DAO, and call `AfxDaoTerm()` when your application is done. These functions neither accept parameters nor return anything.

If you forget to initialize some part of MFC, the best you can expect to get is a ton of assert messages from the libraries. Forgetting to terminate DAO before your application ends will similarly generate a few assertion messages as MFC realizes the libraries haven't been turned off correctly. This initialization of subordinate parts of MFC isn't unique to console applications – it's just that the code that does the work isn't normally something you write yourself. In GUI applications, it is placed in your application's `InitInstance()` override by AppWizard or ClassWizard.

Performing I/O in Console Applications

As I suggested when I pointed out my use of `printf()`, you can use any I/O routines that you would normally have in a real command-line operating system. If you've gone and stamped your console application with the `/subsystem:console` flag in the linker, you're really all set – the operating system will notice the subsystem setting and open a console window on your behalf. The run-time library will try to connect the normal standard I/O library handles to your console window: `stderr`, `stdout` and `stdin` will all be initialized to refer to the console window.

You can use `CFile` to write to or read from files, but you can also use the regular C library `FILE`-based stream routines, or the C++ library standard `stream` objects.

Windows, on the other hand, are a different matter. Since your console application doesn't have a message loop, you can get into trouble creating anything more than a message box or a dialog box. This is easily the strictest condition of writing a console application; we'll look more closely at what it means near the end of the appendix.

When a Console isn't a Console

The lack of architectural features in a true console application makes you wonder what's going on behind the scenes. Where's the framework for handling the window? In fact, the console is a text window created for you by the system.

The ownership of the console window seems more obvious when you realize that there's a **console API** built into Windows, which allows your application to create console windows for itself. Your application can use, destroy and modify those windows in any way it sees fit using those APIs. That's brought the carriage back around behind the horse, though – you're far more likely to code this as a real Windows application.

In other words, you'll be far more likely to implement an application that uses the console API by starting out with a normal, full-blooded, Windows-targeted MFC application, then adding console calls to it. You can minimize or even hide your application's graphical main window if you so choose, but you do get the benefit of a message pump and a window which lets you receive messages and carry on with some semblance of normality.

So, there are two approaches. You might consider writing a console application by using the Win32 Console Application choice when you create a new project and taking the console the system gives you. On the other hand, you might decide to write a Windows application as you normally do, and then create console windows dynamically for yourself.

The latter approach is very appealing if your application has to interact with the user by providing scads of text to them. You might normally show the text to the user in an edit control (or an edit view) if you want to keep a normal graphical look about your program. But there are times when lots of textual streaming data is just that; textual streaming data that you do not want displayed in your edit control. Your computer might be able to display the data faster if it is in a text-based window, and your users might feel more comfortable if the output stream is passed over to some other readily-identifiable window separate from your application. Since a console window can support copy and paste, you'll not have much problem with letting your users integrate such an application with other parts of the system.

A console window would be visually separated from the rest of a GUI application – your program has very little control over the console window, regardless of whether the application is a console application or a GUI application with a console. For example, your program *cannot* position the console window; neither can it gain a handle or a CWnd pointer to it. As such, you can't control the console's size or position with any real precision – we'll see what you *can* change later in this appendix. Furthermore, the system (and not your application) is the parent of the window. You can't make it a child of your frame and have it resemble other views or child frames. The window doesn't receive or send any messages that you can see or understand – there is no such class as a CConsoleView.

There are ways to pull these stunts, but I'm not about to explain them in this book. I'm not interested in explaining them because they're not very stable ways to play with Windows – they can break easily, and in doing so, they will cause more harm than good. There are some things you simply can't do, and you'll just have to find some other way to get the job done.

Using the Console Functions

In case you're interested in writing one of these hybrid applications, we'll take a look at some of the functions in the Windows API which handle console management. First things first – to use these functions, you'll need to make sure you explicitly include the wincon.h header. Since most applications don't use a console, you need to do this yourself – getting Afx.h or Afxwin.h won't include this header for you.

At the point in your application where you want to create a console, you can call the ::AllocConsole() API. This API creates the console window and returns TRUE if it is successful. You can only have one active console window per process. If you need to create more, you'll have to use the ::CreateProcess() function we talked about back in Chapter 10 to create a new process which you can communicate with, and let it drive a different console window for you. If you try to create two consoles at the same time, ::AllocConsole() will return FALSE. ::AllocConsole() doesn't take any parameters – it doesn't need them, because the console window will be displayed and sized to match the default parameters that Windows wants to use.

> Remember that you don't need to call ::AllocConsole() if your application was linked with the /subsystem:console flag — it got a console window for free from Windows as it started.

When you're done with your console window, you can call the ::FreeConsole() API to close the window associated with your process. ::FreeConsole() doesn't take any parameters and also returns a BOOL. If you don't have an active console window, ::FreeConsole() will return FALSE; otherwise, it returns TRUE to indicate success. While the console window is open, you can resize it, read from it (as the user types with it focused), write to it, or force it to scroll. You can also directly manipulate the buffer using some special calls.

The read and write calls all work against handles. Once the window is open, you can gain a handle to the console window by calling `::GetStdHandle()`. This function accepts a constant which indicates what kind of handle you want – you can pass `STD_INPUT_HANDLE` to get a handle from which you can read, or `STD_OUTPUT_HANDLE` to get a handle to which you can write. The function will accept `STD_ERROR_HANDLE` too. `STD_ERROR_HANDLE` can be used for input or output – but, unlike the other handles, it can't be redirected.

And, yes, Virginia, redirection *can* be done in your hybrid application. If you try running the Hybrid sample, you'll find that the output the application writes to the `STD_OUTPUT_HANDLE` when you click the Write button will go to the console window if you've created it with the Create Console button, and cause an error if the window isn't created because `::GetStdHandle()` can't open the handle. The same goes with the Read button. If you start Hybrid from the command line, however, using redirection just like you might with a plain old DOS program:

```
HYBRID >LOG.TXT
```

you'll find that the Write button in the sample always works; it will write to the file Log.txt whether or not there's a console window. If the Write button worked against `STD_ERROR_HANDLE`, it would always send information to the console, but since it uses `STD_OUTPUT_HANDLE`, the output may be redirected. The Read button still works with the console because it uses `STD_INPUT_HANDLE`. Note that this redirection works even though the sample application is marked `/subsystem:windows`!

> Note that redirection only works from the command line (or in the Program Arguments edit control in the Debug tab of the Project Settings dialog). You can't get redirection to work from the Run dialog under the Start button in Windows 95/98.

The sample uses the Windows `::WriteFile()` and `::ReadFile ()` APIs to write and read data to and from the console handles. `::WriteFile()` works by sending the textual data you give it to the console. Note that you have to use carriage return/newline pairs (that is, `"\r\n"` instead of just `"\r"`) to get to a new line. The run-time library isn't around to do the translation for you.

Pedantically, the sample is wrong – you should use `::ReadConsole()` and `::WriteConsole()` against the handle to the console window. You can only use these calls, though, if the console has *not* been redirected to some other place. If the user has run your program from the command line and used some form of redirection, the calls will fail. The benefit of `::ReadConsole()` and `::WriteConsole()`, though, is that they'll handle Unicode characters if you've built your application for Unicode. `::ReadFile()` and `::WriteFile()` won't properly handle Unicode.

By fooling with the sample, you can discover that during calls to `::ReadFile()`, what you type echoes. If you type to the console window while a read call isn't pending, Windows will queue the work up. If you don't want the console to echo as you type, and if you don't want the user to have to press *Enter* before their input is processed, you can use a call to `::SetConsoleMode()` to get the console to react the way you want it to. `::SetConsoleMode()` takes a combination of about a dozen different flags that let you turn echo on and off, and change the buffering rules. I won't regurgitate the flags here – you can find them in the online help for `::SetConsoleMode()`.

Console Limitations

You might have noticed that I haven't mentioned a few things that would seem obvious about console windows – I've not said much about changing their size or location, for example. This is because console windows are not real windows – you can't get a handle to the window itself, so you can't kick it around the block like you can with ordinary windows.

You do have a minimal amount of control over the window: you can call `::SetConsoleWindowInfo()`. The function takes a structure that lets you set the size of the console buffer and the size of the console window. You set these in character counts, not in pixels or device units. The console *window* size is actually the size of the console window, while the console *buffer* size is the size of 'rescroll' data that the console keeps around in memory.

There are routines to directly manipulate the console display buffers, but I haven't described them here. They will let you write directly, by position, within the console buffer. You can even set the display attributes for characters you display to add a little color to your boring textual output. See the Wrox publication *Beginning Windows NT Programming* by Julian Templeman (ISBN1861000170) for more about writing console applications.

Caveats for Writing Console Applications

I mentioned some of the pitfalls of writing console applications through the earlier parts of this appendix, but let's take a little time to spell them all out and make sure we understand them.

The most important difference between the Windows applications you've thought about writing before, and console applications like those we've discussed here, is the absence of a message loop. If you code your application with a simple `main()` function, you won't have a message loop unless you go well out of your way to create one. If you use a `CWinApp`-based application, you'll need to make sure you call the `Run()` function to get the message pump working.

If your application pumps messages, you won't have any problems. You can run off and use ODBC, DAO, or COM to your heart's content. That's all there is to it.

But if you *don't* have a message pump, you can expect trouble. You can use DAO, but you'll have problems in situations that involve DAO prompting the user for more information. There's lots of discussion about this in the Visual C++ 6 help files – check out the DAO SDK documentation to get the real scoop. If you're doing any work with COM objects, you'll require a message pump. If you ask the classes to do things which end up causing MFC to call `::CoInitialize()`, you'll end up crashing because when COM is initialized, it tries to create a hidden window for your application. If you never handle messages tossed around by this hidden window, you'll eventually make a COM call which hangs because it will wait forever to receive a message that doesn't come.

If you've written a minimal application, by the way, with just a `main()` entry point, you shouldn't even consider using ODBC, DAO, or COM via the classes provided in MFC. The classes that support all of these features of Windows require an application object – if you haven't provided an initialized application object, you'll eventually run into code in these classes which throws `ASSERT()` messages or downright crashes because the application object is unavailable or uninitialized. For classes like ODBC, you won't notice a problem until the classes try to pop up a message box, throw an exception to notify you of an error, or pop up an ODBC-supplied dialog box to prompt the user for something. On the other hand, you can expect that DAO and COM will get sick pretty quickly if they can't find your application object.

Summary

This appendix has investigated an interesting and often overlooked part of the Windows operating system: console applications. Again, even if it hasn't helped you write a specific application, I sincerely hope that it has given you some insight into the ways that MFC can be used in non-standard applications.

The Foundation Classes Headers and Libraries

Header Files

Here's a table that explains all of the MFC headers and their purpose, and makes some notes about which files can be included before which others. Note that most of the headers are included by other headers – you only ever directly include four or five in your code.

Header	Description
Afx.h	The main header file for MFC applications that don't use Windows. This header is all you need for console-based MFC applications. It defines all of the classes that work outside of Windows, including the collection classes and all of the application framework classes. You should include this file before other MFC files if you're writing a console application. If you're writing a Windows application, use Afxwin.h instead.
Afxadv.h	The definitions of some of MFC's more volatile classes are in here. Splitting these classes out into a separate header doesn't affect the use of MFC, but it helps indicate which classes in MFC are in a state of change. The classes here are documented in the section called 'Technical Notes' in the online documentation, so you can use them – at least for this version of the library. They might change in the future, or they might solidify and become a more stable, fully-documented part of the library. CRecentFileList, CDockState, and CSharedFile are all declared in this header, which is referenced by Afxpriv.h.

Table Continued on Following Page

Header	Description
Afxcmn.h	This file includes definitions for the Windows common controls. These controls are described in Chapter 8. You can't use this file unless you've already included Afxwin.h.
Afxcoll.h	This file contains the declarations for the MFC container classes, and is dependent on the content of Afx.h. Afxcoll.h contains definitions for the CObject-style and type-safe collections. The template collection classes are in Afxtempl.h.
Afxctl.h	This file contains declarations and classes used for writing ActiveX controls. You should include it in your control projects instead of including Afx.h or Afxwin.h.
Afxcview.h	This file contains definitions for CView-derivatives based on the tree and list common controls. This file is separated from Afxwin.h and Afxcmn.h to promote more granular and efficient linking, which then results in a smaller and faster executable. If you use the CTreeView or CListView classes, make sure you bring this header in after Afxwin.h.
Afxdao.h	This contains classes to support DAO-based database access. It defines the classes discussed in Chapter 12, including CDaoDatabase and CDaoRecordset. If you need this header, you should include it after Afxwin.h and Afxdisp.h.
Afxdb.h	Classes to support ODBC-based database application development. This file defines all of the classes we talked about in Chapter 12, including CDatabase and CRecordset. It also defines global functions that database applications use, such as the RFX_* record field exchange instructions. You should add a reference to this header file in your application when you use the database classes. You'll need to include Afx.h or Afxwin.h first.
Afxdb_.h	This file contains database support definitions and classes common to the ODBC and DAO database support routines. You never need to include this file – it comes in when you include Afxdb.h or Afxdao.h.
Afxdd_.h	This header contains declarations for the dialog data exchange functions. As with all header file names that end in an underscore, you'll not need to include this file directly. It is brought in by Afxwin.h.
Afxdisp.h	This file contains declarations and definitions for the COM dispatch interface. Essentially, it contains all of the extensions necessary to make CCmdTarget handle Automation, as well as all of the data types and wrapper classes that MFC provides to make COM programming easier. Only add this include file to your list if you're using COM, otherwise your program will be dependent on a bunch of run-time DLLs that you don't really need. That will needlessly slow your program's startup. You should include this file after you've included Afxwin.h. If you are using Afxcmn.h and you also need the OLE classes, you should include Afxdisp.h.

Header	Description
Afxdlgs.h	MFC's extended dialog classes are declared here; these classes include CPropertySheet and CPropertyPage as well as the MFC wrappers for the Windows common dialogs. This file is included for you when you include Afxext.h.
Afxdllx.h	This file actually turns out to contain source code which you may need to include in one of your source modules when writing an MFC extension DLL. The specifics of this technique and the exact purpose of the file are explained in Chapter 11, where we examine using and writing DLLs with MFC.
Afxdll_.h	This file declares classes that help MFC manage information about extension DLLs. The file is brought into your application by Afxwin.h if you're building your application with the _AFXDLL precompiler flag.
Afxdocob.h	All of MFC's classes for OLE DocObject support are in this header. You can reference this header directly whenever you need to use COleCmdUI, COleDocIPFrameWnd, or CDocObjectServer.
Afxdtctl.h	Definitions for the date-time common controls – CDateTimeCtrl and CMonthCalCtrl – are included in this header. If you don't need to use these controls, there's no need to reference this header. But you will need to get this header explicitly for the definitions of these control classes. MFC keeps these classes in a separate header to facilitate the granular building of the libraries.
Afxext.h	Afxext.h declares 'extended' MFC classes. These include the more advanced user-interface classes, such as CStatusBar and CToolBar. If you use these classes, make sure you get Afxwin.h first.
Afxhtml.h	This header includes the declaration for CHtmlView.
Afxinet.h	Classes like CHttpConnection, which allow you to write Internet client applications, are defined in this file.
Afxisapi.h	Classes that help with writing Internet server applications which use the ISAPI interface.
Afxmsg_.h	This file is indirectly referenced by Afxwin.h; you should never need to include it independently. It contains definitions for the declaration of message map entries.
Afxmt.h	Contains synchronization objects for multithreaded applications. These classes are described in Chapter 10. You can even use these classes in a console application, but you must always have included Afx.h first.
Afxodlgs.h	This file contains declarations for classes that provide MFC's implementation of OLE user interface dialogs. Some of these dialogs are discussed in Chapters 13 and 14. You'll need to include this file directly if you're making use of, or subclassing, MFC's implementations. You should include this file after you include Afxwin.h.

Table Continued on Following Page

Header	Description
Afxole.h	This file declares the classes necessary for core OLE support. These classes include the OLE-capable COleDocument-based classes and all of the OLE item and drag-and-drop support that goes with them. You'll need to add this after you've included Afxwin.h if your application makes use of OLE.
Afxoledb.h	Definitions for COleDbRecordView.
Afxplex_.h	This header implements the CPlex class, which is used by the implementation of MFC's CObject-based collection classes. The collection classes themselves are discussed in detail in Chapter 9, which treats the sundry utility classes in MFC.
Afxpriv.h	This file contains code required by MFC for its own implementation. If you browse it, you might find neat data structures or classes to help you in your work, but you should use them very carefully. Items in this file are perfect candidates for being changed as the implementation of MFC evolves. With that caveat, you can directly include this file.
Afxres.h	This header is used by resource scripts. .rc files for MFC applications include it directly. Your application will get the content of this file indirectly from Afxwin.h; you'll almost never need to reference it directly. It includes preprocessor symbol definitions for all predefined MFC resources.
Afxrich.h	This file contains definitions for the CRichEditCtrl class, as well as a few other related classes. If you use the rich edit control, you should bring this header in after including Afxcmn.h and Afxwin.h. The rich edit control is very powerful; it contains complete OLE support. You'll need to get the Afxole.h file, too.
Afxsock.h	Definitions for the CSocket and CAsyncSocket classes. These classes wrap access to the Windows Sockets API, a network-based communications API.
Afxstat_.h	This file defines the various structures of state information MFC manages for your running application. This state information is used by MFC to make sure it knows what your application is up to. It is never referenced by an application directly, but included by Afx.h.
Afxtempl.h	This file has the template-based implementations of the MFC collection classes. You should include it only after you've added Afx.h. The collection classes implemented by MFC are discussed in Chapter 9.
Afxtls_.h	Thread-local storage macros to assist MFC in managing per-application and per-thread status information. These macros are utilized by many of the structures in Afxstat_.h. This file is not directly referenced by applications, but is brought in by Afx.h.

Header	Description
Afxver_.h	This important header file manipulates lots of different preprocessor macros that configure certain aspects of MFC as it is built. When you build an MFC application, though, this header also adds some settings which ensure that your application correctly links to MFC. You'll never need to directly reference this file in your applications. In fact, you'll probably never even need to read this file – it's full of the finest implementation details and silliest low-level macros.
Afxv_cfg.h	This file does but one thing: it switches on a flag called _AFX_PORTABLE. If you're using a compiler which wasn't designed to build MFC (e.g. you're not using Visual C++, Watcom's compiler, or Symantec's compiler) you should make sure the preprocessor symbol _CUSTOM is defined so this file will be included. You can then amend it to make whatever tweaks and settings your build environment requires. It is never referenced by applications directly, and never used by MFC in normal situations.
Afxv_cpu.h	Referenced by Afxver_.h, this file makes some settings for Macintosh, Power PC, MIPS, and Alpha builds of MFC. This file is never referenced directly by an application.
Afxv_dll.h	This file is used to configure DLL-based builds of MFC. It defines many special symbols for the DLL builds to assure their segment layout is optimal. It is referenced by Afxver_.h and never touched directly by an application.
Afxv_mac.h	This file brings extra configuration tweaks for Macintosh builds of MFC. Another of the set of headers referenced by Afxver_.h and never referenced by applications directly.
Afxv_w32.h	This file configures MFC for Win32. It is always included, since MFC always runs on some variant of Win32. This file turns around to include the necessary system and standard C and C++ include files. That is, it's the file which brings Windows.h and all of its friends into your application, in addition to supporting headers like Tchar.h and String.h.
Afxwin.h	This is the primary header for MFC applications that will run under Windows. Use it after you've included Afx.h when you're going to build a Windows program. Don't use it if you want to make a console application. This file defines basic classes like CWnd and many of its descendants.
Winres.h	This file defines a subset of resource identifiers for use by MFC applications. It's referenced by Afxres.h, and simply provides a subset of the things the Windows headers would normally define. It is not directly referenced by MFC applications.

Run-time Libraries

This table enumerates the libraries and pre-compiled object files shipped with Visual C++ 6.0, and provides a short description of their function.

File	Description
Advapi32.lib	Import library for most advanced API services, such as registry operations and security APIs. Linking with this import library allows your application to access functions in the Windows Advapi32.dll.
Atl.lib	Support library for the Active Template Library.
Binmode.obj	Linking with this module will force files opened with the C run-time library to open in binary mode by default.
Cap.lib	Interface to the Call Attributed Profiler. This tool allows you to tune Win32 applications by analyzing their function call patterns.
Chkstk.obj	Run-time stack-depth checking probe. This object module helps your application check that it hasn't caused the stack to overflow by checking the depth of the stack before every function call. Since Windows NT carefully measures your application's stack segment and terminates the application gracefully in stack overflow conditions, this file is rarely necessary.
Comctl32.lib	Windows common controls. These are discussed in great detail in Chapter 8.
Comdlg32.lib	Windows common dialogs. This library provides interfaces to the standard file open, file save, font chooser, print and color chooser dialog boxes.
Commode.obj	(No, really.) Sets the global file commit mode flag to commit. Linking with this file sets all files to be opened in commit mode by default.
Compmgr.lib	Import library for comp.
Ctl3d32.lib	Three-dimensional control support. This library lets your program draw its dialogs and controls with a three-dimensional effect to enhance their appearance. This library is largely obsolete; it is provided to help with backward-compatibility issues.
Ctl3d32s.lib	The Ctl3d library for Win32s applications.
D3drm.lib	Direct3D rendering model APIs.
Daouuid.lib	UUIDs for DAO objects.
Ddraw.lib	DirectDraw APIs
Dflayout.lib	Import library for OLE functions that perform storage management on compound document files.

File	Description
Dlcapi.lib	Library for DLC 3270 connectivity.
Dplay.lib	DirectPlay APIs
Dsound.lib	DirectSound APIs
Fp10.obj	Linking with this library will force the application to use, by default, algorithms with 64-bit floating-point precision instead of 53-bit routines.
Gdi32.lib	Windows GDI import library. Linking with this library enables your application to call routines in the Windows graphic device interface to perform drawing on a display or printer. Such functions include SelectObject(), CreateFont() and LineTo().
Glaux.lib	OpenGL auxiliary functions; not used by most applications, but these extensions to OpenGL enhance the core library's functionality. Also see Opengl32.lib.
Glu32.lib	OpenGL Graphics core functions. Also see Opengl32.lib.
Hlink.lib	Support for IHlink and related interfaces. These interfaces help an ActiveX object implement generic hyperlink-style navigation.
Imagehlp.lib	Routines that allow system tools, such as debuggers, to retrieve debug information.
Imm32.lib	Routines for use of the input method editor (IME). The input method editor is a pop-up window that allows the convenient entry and assimilation of foreign-language characters in edit controls. With the IME the user can, for example, accept several Katakana characters, convert them to Kanji characters, and dump them into an edit control.
Kernel32.lib	Windows kernel import libraries. Linking with this library allows you to call routines in the Windows kernel. The Windows kernel implements functions such as CreateSemaphore() and GlobalAlloc().
Largeint.lib	Large integer math support routines. This library is provided for compatibility purposes only, as the compiler in Microsoft Visual C++ supports 64-bit integers.
Libc.lib	The standard C run-time library. This library implements functions from the standard C run-time library (like sprintf() and strcpy()) which will be statically linked to the calling program. Not safe for use in multithreaded or re-entrant applications.
Libcd.lib	A debug build of the standard C run-time library. Use this in your debug builds when you would otherwise use Libc.lib. This build statically links with your application.

Table Continued on Following Page

File	Description
Libci.lib	The standard C library. This library is similar to Libc.lib, but it implements a version of the standard iostream library that's compatible with the code in the standard libraries shipped with previous versions of Visual C++. This build statically links with your application.
Libcid.lib	Debug build of the standard C library with the standard iostream implementation. This build links statically with your application.
Libcimt.lib	Multithread-safe version of the C runtimes with the standard iostream implementation. This build statically links with your application.
Libcimtd.lib	Debug build of the multithread-safe version of the C run-times with the standard iostream implementation. This build statically links with your application.
Libcmt.lib	Multithread-safe statically linked C run-time library build. Contains code for standard C functions (like sprintf() and strcpy()) which are re-entrant and safe for use in multithreaded programs. This build statically links with your application.
Libcmtd.lib	Debug build of the multithread-safe statically linked C run-time library. Use this in your debug builds when you would have otherwise used Libcmt.lib. This build statically links with your application.
Libcp.lib	The standard C++ run-time library. This library implements functions from the standard C++ run-time library which will be statically linked to the calling program. Not safe for use in multithreaded or re-entrant applications.
Libcpd.lib	Debug version of the C++ standard library. This build statically links with your application.
Limcpmt.lib	Multithread-safe version of the C++ standard library. This build statically links with your application.
Libcpmtd.lib	Debug version of the multithread-safe version of the C++ standard library. This build statically links with your application.
Loadperf.lib	This import library provides access to routines that assist in the initialization of performance counter registry entries. The library is normally used by installation programs.
Lz32.lib	A library of Lempel-Ziv decompression routines. Usually used by installation programs. This library does *not* have routines to perform compression, only decompression.
Mapi32.lib	Microsoft Mail API library.
Mfcapwz.lib Mfcclwz.lib	Implement classes and functions which allow the development of custom Wizards.

File	Description
Mfcuia32.lib	Code that provides MFC's implementation of the OLE common user interface. Like Oledlg.lib, but provides ANSI interfaces instead of Unicode.
Mgmtapi.lib	SNMP Management APIs.
Mpr.lib	LAN Manager-style network APIs for connection management. These APIs can allow your program to connect and disconnect from Windows.
Msacm32.lib	Microsoft Audio Compression Manager API. Utilities to compress and decompress audio waveform data.
Msconf.lib	Import library for the Microsoft ActiveX Conferencing APIs.
Mslsp32.lib	License Service Application Programming Interface import library.
Msvcirt.lib	Import library for the DLL build of the standard C libraries with the standard iostream implementation. This import library is for the DLL version of the Libci.lib library.
Msvcirtd.lib	This import library is for the debug version of the Mscvirt.lib library.
Msvcprt.lib	Import library for the DLL build of the standard C++ libraries. This import library is for the DLL version of the Libcp.lib library.
Msvcprtd.lib	This import library is for the debug version of the Msvcprt.lib library.
Msvcrt.lib	Import library for the DLL build of the standard C libraries. This is for the DLL version of the Libc.lib library.
Msvcrtd.lib	A debug build of the DLL-friendly standard C run-time library. Use this in your debug builds when you would have used Msvcrt.lib for retail builds.
Mswsock.lib	Import library for Microsoft-specific extensions to the Windows Sockets 2 API.
Mtx.lib	Microsoft Transaction Server programming interface library.
Mtxguid.lib	GUIDs for objects supported by the Microsoft Transaction Server.
Nddeapi.lib	Network DDE API. Provides DDE-style services across systems via a network.
Netapi32.lib	LAN Manager API Interface. This library contains a function that allows you to make use of low-level features supported by Microsoft's network operating systems.

Table Continued on Following Page

File	Description
Newmode.obj	Causes your application to use the new operator error handling mechanism when calls to malloc() fail. By default, this won't happen; malloc() will fail, returning a NULL, and won't try to throw an exception. Linking with this object changes the behavior of the C run-time libraries to call the new operator's error handler on malloc() failures.
Ocx96.lib	UUIDs for interfaces specific to the OCX 96 specification.
Odbc32.lib	ODBC API. This library provides a back-end independent API for database applications. This library is further abstracted by MFC and we discuss how it is used in Chapter 12.
Odbccp32.lib	ODBC control panel applet interfaces.
Oldnames.lib	Kernighan and Ritchie C-compatible names for the standard C run-time library functions. This library maps 'old' standard names, such as execv() to their ANSI standard equivalents, such as _execv().
Ole32.lib	Core 32-bit OLE support.
Oleaut32.lib	32-bit Automation interfaces.
Oledlg.lib	System implementation of the OLE common user interface. Implements functions like OleUiEditLinks() and OleInsertObject().
Olepro32.lib	OLE property frame APIs. Also includes implementations of the OLE Font (IFont) and Picture (IPicture) properties.
Opengl32.lib	OpenGL core functionality. OpenGL is a graphics rendering language defined by Silicon Graphics Inc., and implemented for Win32 by Microsoft. Also see Glu32.lib and Glaux.lib.
Pdh.lib	Performance Data Helpers import library. This subset of the Win32 API provides easy interfaces for creating, querying and updating performance counters for your processes.
Penwin32.lib	Windows for Pen Computing extensions.
Pkpd32.lib	Pen Windows Kernel Functions.
Rasapi32.lib	Remote Access Services APIs for clients. Functions in this library allow you to perform calls to the system services that handle connections to a remote machine via a modem or other similar, comparatively low-speed data link.
Rasdlg.lib	Common user interface elements needed for RAS applications.
Rassapi.lib	RAS server-side APIs.
Rpcndr.lib	Remote Procedure Call helper function APIs.

File	Description
Rpcns4.lib	Remote Procedure Call name service functions.
Rpcrt4.lib	Remote Procedure Call Windows run-time functions.
Scrnsave.lib	Screen saver interfaces.
Setargv.obj	Linking with this module will cause your console application to expand wildcard filename command line parameters to matching real file names, each having its own entry in main()'s argv array parameter. Also see Wsetargv.obj for a version that works with Windows applications.
Setupapi.lib	File installation and removal routines – used for writing setup programs.
Shell32.lib	Windows interface shell APIs. These APIs provide functionality used by applications like Norton Desktop For Windows, extracting icons from executables or running another program with command line parameters, for example.
Snmpapi.lib	Primary Simple Network Management Protocol API functions. This protocol, for TCP/IP networks, is used to monitor gateways and the networks to which they're attached. Related to Mgmtapi.lib.
Svrapi.lib	Network APIs for inter-server communications.
Tapi32.lib	Microsoft Telephony API library. Implements telephony APIs like lineOpen().
Th32.lib	The 32-bit Toolhelp library. This library provides functions which are helpful when writing debuggers or other low-level tools. Routines from this library allow you to enumerate the processes and threads running in Windows, for example.
Thunk32.lib	Routines for run-time support of the thunk compiler.
Url.lib	This file defines routines used to parse URLs and translate MIME headers – these are Internet-related conventions for finding and defining the content of text data streams. The routines in this library are, for now, undocumented. They will be refined and more reasonably supported in a future version of the Win32 SDK – and, therefore, in a future version of Visual C++.
Urlmon.lib	Import library for URL monikers runtime support library.
User32.lib	Windows user import library. Linking with this library allows your application to make use of functions in the Windows user interface implementation. These functions include CreateDialog() and CreateWindow().
Uuid.lib	Standard UUIDs for stock OLE objects.

Table Continued on Following Page

File	Description
Vdmdbg.lib	Functions in this library provide access to functions related to debugging in an NT VDM.
Version.lib	Version checking APIs, such as GetFileVersion().
Vfw32.lib	Video for Windows APIs. Functions in this library allow you to play, record, edit or save multimedia video and audio.
Webpost.lib	WebPost API import library. This library makes it easy for client machines to post data to web sites hosted by an Internet service provider.
Win32spl.lib	The Win32 spooler API. Routines in this file provide access to print spooler status from other applications and computers.
Wininet.lib	Windows Internet Client APIs.
Winmm.lib	Windows Multimedia APIs. Includes multimedia device management, timer, wave file and multi-media I/O control functions, amongst others.
Winspool.lib	The Win32 spooler APIs. Routines presented by this library are for applications that need to use features of the Windows print spooler while printing.
Winstrm.lib	Windows NT TCP/IP interfaces. This file provides support for TCP/IP routing functions.
Wintrust.lib	Import library for APIs that implement trust verification of ActiveX Objects. This import provides access to functions such as WinVerifyTrust().
Wow32.lib	This library is used by the generic thunking mechanism to translate handles between 16-bit and 32-bit objects. The library also provides help with managing 32-bit memory from a 16-bit process.
Ws2_32.lib	Windows Sockets 2.0 API
Wsetargv.obj	Linking with this module will cause your Windows application to expand wildcard filename command line parameters to matching real file names, each having its own entry in main()'s argv array parameter. Also see Setargv.obj for console version.
Wsock32.lib	Windows Sockets APIs.
Wst.lib	Working Set Tuner DLL interface. The Working Set Tuner dynamic link library probes your application as it runs so that it will produce execution metrics which will help you minimize the working set of your application.

Always remember that a compendium of the major APIs, header files, and libraries is available in the Win32api.csv file in your Lib directory. This file is a comma separated variable file which can be imported by all popular spreadsheet programs.

A History of MFC

You Kids Have It Easy

If you're completely new to Visual C++, you might be wondering a bit about the history of Visual C++ and the Microsoft Foundation Classes.

Microsoft first began shipping a C++-capable compiler with version 7 of their C language package. This product ran under DOS and would produce code for DOS and 16-bit Windows; at the time, Windows 3.0 was still just making its way to market, and version 7 of Microsoft C/C++ was available three to six months before Windows 3.1 was released in May 1992.

MFC 1.0

This package also included version 1.0 of the Microsoft Foundation Classes. MFC 1.0 wasn't all that amazing (it had very few of the features covered in this book), but the product did provide a basic class library – simple classes that helped you with easy programming problems.

Although you could use this library with Windows applications, it didn't come equipped with any specialized advanced features for Windows. Neither did it provide the huge architectural classes (like CDocument and CView) which we see in today's MFC.

Microsoft C/C++ version 7 didn't hold a candle to the integrated development environments around currently. You would use a tool called Programmer's Workbench to edit and build your code; you could step through errors and fix your code without restarting the environment.

You could also get help on the libraries and the language right from the editor, but you had to leave the environment if you wanted to test your program, and certainly if you wanted to debug it. The

CodeView debugger was the tool of choice for debugging work. One version was available in the product for DOS-based applications, while another was available for Windows-based applications and the resources (among them dialogs) were edited using... Notepad.

MFC 2.0

After almost a year, Microsoft released Visual C++ 1.0 – a landmark release. You could now develop all of your code in a conveniently integrated environment, without reloading tools and changing user interfaces at each step of the development process. Visual C++ 1.0 included version 8.00 of the Microsoft C/C++ compiler, it still produced 16-bit code and could make applications for either Windows or DOS. Better yet, the system also included version 2.0 of the MFC libraries. With this release, MFC became a class library for Windows. Your applications started their lives with the AppWizard and you could use the ClassWizard to nurse your application into a healthy life.

As an interim measure for Windows programmers who were adopting Windows NT, Microsoft released Visual C++ 1.1. This version of the development environment contained the first 32-bit development tools released outside of the Windows SDK, and a special build of MFC to make it 32-bit compatible.

The end of the summer of 1993 found Microsoft releasing version 1.5 of Visual C++. Aside from widespread functional and performance improvements, this version of the toolkit also included MFC 2.5. The big additions for MFC 2.5 were formalized support for OLE and ODBC applications, which meant that you could now create a full OLE server with a few clicks in AppWizard!

The most recent version of this 16-bit compiler, Visual C++ 1.52, will more than likely be the last of its line from Microsoft, as the company has turned all its attention and resources towards the 32-bit development tool market. Visual C++ 2.0, released near the end of 1994, was the first big step in this direction, and an impressive development platform for 32-bit developers. It included the first version of the OLE Control Development Kit, as well as a compiler that supported C++ exceptions and templates.

MFC 3.0

These features then found their way into MFC, which had only emulated them up until this point. Version 3.0 of MFC was completely Unicode-aware, making it ideal for international development. It was also a *fully* 32-bit implementation, coded to work with the Macintosh, MIPS, Alpha and Intel versions of Visual C++, all of which were developed concurrently using Visual C++ 2.0!

Visual C++ 2.1, which was brought to the market at the beginning of February 1995, included a smattering of enhancements and several bug fixes.

MFC 4.0 and 4.1

Microsoft Visual C++ 4.0 began shipping in October 1995, and VC++ 4.1 was released to manufacture in March of 1996. It included classes to support the containment of OLE controls, wrappers for Windows multithreading objects, and represented a considerable advance in performance and efficiency. The database support in MFC was augmented with support for Data Access Objects, and many of the user-interface classes in the library were enhanced. This version of the library also finalized support for the Windows common controls. When compared to MFC 4.0, MFC 4.1 added little more than bug fixes and support for Internet Server Applications.

MFC 4.2

Early 1996 found the MFC team releasing Version 4.2 of MFC in the Visual C++ 4.2 product box. This version of MFC was compatible with the beta versions of the ActiveX and Win32 SDKs that were available around March and April of 1996. In hindsight, it was probably something of a mistake to release this version of MFC as it was. While MFC worked fine with the beta versions of the operating system components represented by those SDKs, the final release versions of those components had enough last-minute changes to break MFC badly, and cause problems for developers who were involved in applying the newer technologies those components represented. Unfortunately, that was a very large group of people; ActiveX is the cornerstone of Microsoft's Internet strategy.

This version of MFC enhanced MFC's OLE (or indeed, ActiveX) control support to include the OCX 96 specification, which focused primarily on performance enhancements for controls and the containers that used them. It also added several classes for client-side Internet applications.

MFC 4.2b

In late August of 1996, the MFC team released a patch that fixed the problems introduced by the final release versions of the system components I talked about in the last section. The 4.2b patch was provided as a massive eight-megabyte download from Microsoft's corporate web site, and installed over the existing files in a Visual C++ installation. While terribly inconvenient, the patch fixed dozens of bugs introduced by the last-minute changes to the ActiveX SDK and resulted in a far more stable build environment.

MFC 4.21

Visual C++ 5.0 began shipping in March of 1997. The product included MFC 4.21, which was so numbered because it offered few new features over its predecessor, MFC 4.2b. MFC 4.21 focused on stability and performance improvements, and fixed hundreds of bugs in the libraries, while also slightly adjusting the library to be compatible with the stricter adherence to the ANSI standard afforded by the newest of Microsoft's C++ compilers.

MFC 6.0

When Visual C++ 6.0 shipped in the Spring of 1998, it included MFC Version 6.0. The DLLs in this release are still named `Mfc42.dll` because they maintain backward binary compatibility with previous versions of MFC, though only for release builds. The MFC 6.0 release formalized the features that were previously available only in the Platform Preview Release, made available as an Alpha-quality release in late 1997; such features include more aggressive support for the newest common controls. In addition to adding new functionality to MFC, great effort was placed on making the MFC libraries a little more modular – so that common linking scenarios would result in smaller executable images and faster initialization.

Since the shipping of Visual Studio 6.0, service packs have also been released to further improve the functionality and performance of the application. As and when they appear, you should always install these service packs, as they contain the most up-to-date modifications and bug fixes for Visual C++ 6.0 and MFC 6.0, as well as other Visual Studio apps. At the time of writing, the latest service pack release is SP3.

So What's New In MFC 6.0?

Many of you reading this will be asking me "Why do I need to upgrade to MFC 6.0?" The changes from MFC 5.0 might be small, but they are significant. I've already mentioned the support for the new common controls in the previous section. Now I will present the new features in more detail:

Features Now Supported

The following table explains the new features:

Feature	Explanation
Active Document Containment	This alternative to the already well-established OLE technology allows the user to work with multiple documents within a single frame, rather than having to use different frames for each document type. So, from one application (say Word) you can activate another application (say Excel) and the menus and toolbars for that second application become available for use, all within the same frame. This contrasts with OLE, where only a part of the embedded object can be active and not the entire application. AppWizard creates all the necessary MFC code for Active Document Containment. This feature is implemented by the COleDocObjectItem class.
Dynamic HTML	You can host Dynamic HTML (DHTML) from within your MFC applications. HTML pages can be viewed in a specialized form view just as they would appear in a Web browser, complete with a history list, bookmarks and security features. The MFC class that implements these features is CHtmlView, which is covered in Chapter 4.
Internet Explorer 4.0 Common Controls	MFC classes now wrap the newest controls that came with Internet Explorer 4.0, which also appear in the Controls toolbar in the Dialog editor. CDateTimeCtrl wraps the date-time picker, CMonthCalCtrl the month calendar and CIPAddressCtrl the IP Address edit box. These classes are discussed in Chapter 8. Also new is the CComboBoxEx class that extends CComboBox by allowing image lists.
OLE DB Record View	A new MFC class COleDBRecordView has been included to wrap the OLE DB consumer templates and allow data accessed through an OLE DB provider to be displayed in a report view with forward and backwards scrolling enabled. This class is discussed in Chapter 12.
Wizard97 Style for Property Sheets	This is a brand new wizard style (Windows 98 and Windows 2000) which can be used to create property sheets and property pages with background bitmaps and wide title headers. The two MFC classes that implement the new functionality associated with this type of property sheet are CPropertySheetEx and CPropertyPageEx, which extend the already established CPropertySheet and CPropertyPage classes. The features of Wizard97 are discussed in Chapter 6.

In addition to this, MFC 6.0 has two new global functions: AfxCheckError() and AfxDumpStack(). The first tests the passed SCODE to see if it is an error. If so it throws a COleException, unless the code is E_OUTOFMEMORY where it throws a CMemoryException. The second creates an image of the dump stack – see the MSDN library for more details.

Finally the following classes are updated in MFC 6.0 with new functionality and styles:

Class	Explanation
CHeaderCtrl	Includes drag and drop support for reordering of header items and the inclusion of bitmaps in the header as well as text.
CHttpServer	Includes a function which passes data to the server.
CHttpServerContext	Includes two functions that control the size of chunks written to the server.
CImageList	Supports images used by other controls, e.g. header and list controls.
CInternetSession	Supports three functions for getting and setting cookies for a specified URL, and for getting the length of the cookie.
CListCrtl	Includes support for the grouping of items using working areas and virtual list views.
CMenu	Supports three functions for getting and setting the default menu item for a particular menu, and for getting the information on a menu item.
COleClientItem	Includes a function for getting the handle to an icon with a particular Class ID (CLSID).
COleDateTime	Allows the conversion of the information stored in a COleDateTime object to a Win32 SYSTEMTIME structure.
CProgressCtrl	Supports smooth and vertical styles for progress controls.
CPropertySheet	Supports stacked or scrolling tabs.
CReBar/CReBarCtrl	This brand new pair of classes implement an Internet Explorer 4.0 type toolbar. CReBarCtrl implements the internal control of the CReBar object. See chapter 4 for more details.
CSliderCtrl	Supports tooltips in slider controls and additional styles.
CSpinButtonCtrl	Supports 32-bit ranges.
CStatusBar/ CStatusBarCtrl	Supports tooltips, icons and background color n the status bar. CStatusBarCtrl implements the internal control of the CStatusBar object.
CString	Includes functionality to allow finding, replacing, removing, inserting, deleting and formatting. CString is discussed in Chapter 9.

Table Continued on Following Page

Class	Explanation
CTabCtrl	Supports new styles for tab appearance and focus, and inserting new tabs to an existing tab control.
CTime	Allows the conversion of the information stored in a CTime object to a Win32 SYSTEMTIME structure.
CToolBar/ CToolBarCtrl	Supports Internet Explorer 4.0 flat and transparent toolbar styles. CToolBarCtrl implements the internal control of the CToolBar object.
CToolTipCtrl	Allows the updating of tooltips.
CTreeCtrl	Supports check boxes and automatic single-node expansion in a tree control.

Integrating ATL and MFC

If you program COM objects as well as MFC applications you're probably familiar with the Active Template Library (ATL). It makes tremendous sense to use MFC for applications-level programming, but in many cases, ATL provides many tools that either exceed MFC's capability, or provide functionality MFC does not. As it happens, it is quite easy to marry the two technologies and use the best features of both.

There isn't the room in this Appendix to give anything more than a brief description of ATL. However, you can find out more about it by looking up any of the following Wrox Press publications: *Professional ATL COM Programming* by Richard Grimes (ISBN 1861001401), *Professional COM Applications with ATL* by Sing Li and Panos Economopoulos (ISBN 1861001703), and *ATL COM Programmers Reference* also by Richard Grimes (ISBN 1861002491).

Two Kinds of ATL Support

When we think about integrating ATL support into our MFC applications, we are really talking about two different kinds of integration. The first kind is a simple use of some of the ATL templates to make our COM programming life easier. The second kind of integration uses ATL to provide the COM server functionality, which corresponds roughly to the MFC ColeServer* classes that were covered in Chapter 14. The ATL code we integrate doesn't provide all of the functionality these classes provide, but if you're interested in a leaner, meaner COM server, perhaps the ATL approach is an easier mechanism to use. This is especially so, if you're used to working with ATL.

ATL Template Support

There are a myriad of details you must manage when working with COM objects, but arguably the most important is the object's lifetime management, i.e. reference counting. The examples I've used throughout the book have used simple pointer types to contain any COM object I instantiated. I had to call the object's `Release()` method when I completed my use of the object to allow the COM runtime to clean up. If you forget to release the object, it remains in memory, sucking up valuable resources. Or, you may have used some of MFC's COM support classes, like `COleVariant`, which make it easier to deal with variant data. And while `CString` provides some `BSTR` support, using `CComBSTR` is a dream when passing `BSTR`s around.

Smart COM Pointers

I mentioned COM object lifetime management and how difficult that can be at times. Do I `AddRef()` here or there? Did I remember to `Release()` this or that object? An elegant solution to this managerial dilemma is to use a **smart pointer** to contain the COM pointer. Essentially, you use a pointer class rather than a pointer variable and make the pointer class manage the details for you. If you assign a COM object's interface pointer to a smart pointer class, the smart pointer can release the object when its destructor is called or when its pointer is reassigned. The various rules for incrementing and decrementing the object's reference count can be coded in one place for reuse everywhere, making your code less bug-prone.

MFC has no smart pointer class, but ATL does (though you can use the Native Compiler COM support which provides smart pointers and a lot of other useful facilities, if you so wished). ATL uses the `CComPtr` template to create a class to manage any kind of COM interface pointer you may have. `CComPtr`'s template definition looks like this:

```
template< class T >class CComPtr
```

ATL also provides a related class for automatically obtaining a COM interface pointer through another pointer's `QueryInterface()` method:

```
template< class T, const IID* piid >class CComQIPtr
```

The template parameter `T` is the COM object's class, such as `IPersistStream` or `IStorage`. For `CComQIPtr`, the parameter `piid` is an existing COM interface pointer whose `QueryInterface()` method will be used to obtain the desired interface ID.

To use the templates, you first must include `atlbase.h` which declares the templates. A good place to do this is in `stdafx.h`, which makes the smart pointer templates available to all of your source files:

```
// Add support for ATL
#include <atlbase.h>
```

Once the templates are declared, you can create COM objects and assign their pointers. Here is an example where a compound document is opened and an `IStorage` interface pointer is returned. The `IStorage` pointer is then queried for its constituent `IPersistStorage` pointer. For this example, assume the file `SomeFile.doc` refers to an actual compound document:

```
// Declare the IStorage smart pointer
CComPtr<IStorage> pIStorage;
StgOpenStorage(L"SomeFile.doc",
            NULL,
            STGM_READ | STGM_SHARE_DENY_WRITE,
            NULL,
            NULL,
            &pIStorage);

// Declare the smart IPersistStorage pointer (note the QI)
CComQIPtr<IPersistStorage,&IID_IPersistStorage> pIPersistStorage(pIStorage);
```

If everything worked as planned, the `StgOpenStorage()` would open the `SomeFile.doc` file and return you a non-NULL `pIStorage` pointer. Then, you query the `pIStorage` pointer for its `IPersistStorage` interface. If this was successful, `pIPersistStorage` will also be non-NULL. The beauty of this is when the variables `pIStorage` and `pIPersistStorage` go out of scope, their `Release()` methods will be executed, which prevents the possibility of interface calls after the interface was released.

Once you have a non-NULL smart pointer, you use it just as you would a traditional pointer. For example, suppose the file `SomeFile.doc` contained a stream named `SomeStream`. You could open the stream using code such as this:

```
CComPtr<IStream> pIStream;
pIStorage->OpenStream(L"SomeStream",
            NULL,
            STGM_READ | STGM_SHARE_DENY_WRITE,
            0,
            &pIStream);
```

If you wanted to release the COM object before the smart pointer went out of scope (a common thing to do with storages and streams), you simply set the smart pointer to NULL:

```
// Close the stream
pIStream = NULL; // automatically calls Release()
```

If you didn't use any other ATL support when using COM objects with MFC, just being able to use the `CComPtr` smart pointer template is worth the effort. But luckily, ATL can help you with other COM programming chores, as we'll see.

Variants

When you think of scripting, and you're a COM programmer, you automatically think of IDispatch. And to make things easier on IDispatch, Microsoft defined a standard set of data that would be automatically marshaled. Collectively, this set of data is known as a VARIANT. A variant is really nothing more than a **discriminated union**, which is to say the union contains the set of all suitable variant data types (longs, pointers, etc.) and a discriminator, which is an enumeration that tells you what data is contained within the union. Given a variant, you first examine the discriminator, then interpret the data contained in the union as that data type. For example, if the discriminator was VT_LONG, you would expect 4 bytes of data in the union, and only the first 4 bytes would be used.

Using a wrapper for VARIANT data makes sense, as the wrapper class can easily manage the data and the discriminator. You'll often find it the case that a VARIANT must be initialized, and it would be nice to have some help when copying and moving variants around. Both MFC and ATL have such VARIANT wrappers, and in most cases, either will do when passing VARIANT data to IDispatch. The nice addition to the ATL VARIANT wrapper class is you have support for reading and writing the VARIANT data from a stream. If you have persisted the VARIANT data in a stream (including memory), you have an easy way to put that data into a CComVariant-based variable and pass that into IDispatch. There are times when this may be useful.

To use the CComVariant ATL class, you include atlbase.h just as you did for the ATL smart pointer templates.

COM's Binary Strings (BSTRs)

Just as IDispatch requires VARIANT data to automatically marshal parameters, IDispatch required a length-predicated string data type. (This is similar to a Pascal string for those of you familiar with Pascal.) The **binary string**, or BSTR, contains a wide-character string which has a 4-byte length value prefixed to the string. This allows the standard marshaler to easily determine how many characters the string contains and marshal the appropriate number. ATL provides wonderful BSTR support through its CComBSTR class. You also have an arsenal of ATL string conversion macros that allow you to easily convert a string in one form to a string in another.

If you refer back to my previous example where I opened the compound document, you'll see I passed in a hard-coded filename as a wide-character string. This is fine if you always want to open the same file. But in most cases you're more interested in allowing the user to select a file, which means you need some sort of wide-character string variable. This can be painful, unless you have CComBSTR. The same example could be written in this fashion:

```
// The user's desired filename is stored in strFilename,
// which can be a CString variable
CComBSTR bstrFilename(strFilename);

// Declare the IStorage smart pointer
CComPtr<IStorage> pIStorage;
StgOpenStorage(bstrFilename,
               NULL,
               STGM_READ | STGM_SHARE_DENY_WRITE,
               NULL,
               NULL,
               &pIStorage);
```

As it happens, BSTRs have a suite of special API calls to manage their creation and deletion. To create one, you must call SysAllocString(). To delete one, you pass the BSTR to SysFreeString(). To do anything else, you call another API method. CComBSTR, on the other hand, manages all of this for you. When a CComBSTR variable goes out of scope, the BSTR is released properly. If you reassign a BSTR variable, the old BSTR is released and the new BSTR is allocated as it should be. What could be easier?

As with smart pointers and VARIANTs, you must include atlbase.h somewhere in your code (preferably in stdafx.h to incorporate it in your precompiled header database). However, you also must include some of the ATL implementation code, in the form of atlimpl.cpp. If you bought my argument for including atlbase.h in your stdafx.h file, you might also buy into including the implementation file in stdafx.cpp:

```
// Include the ATL implementation
#include atlimpl.cpp
```

atlimpl.cpp is primarily concerned with memory management, as you might expect given you are working with strings and memory.

ATL COM Server Support

If your goal is to create a COM **local server**, which is an executable program versus a DLL, you can easily do so using MFC. But because ATL is so very COM-oriented, there are times you may wish to use ATL to manage the COM aspects of the application while using MFC to manage the other pertinent tasks. If you don't require the support MFC provides for local servers, perhaps to tune your application COM-wise to some specific design goal you may have, then you can skip MFC's local server classes in favor of ATL. In fact, the Microsoft Visual Studio team recognized this and added new support for ATL and MFC with version 6.0.

If you've worked with ATL previously, you know ATL uses the Workspace window in lieu of some sort of a ClassWizard. When you view your project in the Workspace window with its classes exposed, you right-click on parts of your project to invoke context menus with appropriate options. As it happens, this same mechanism is used to add ATL local server support to your MFC application.

> Note you should *not* create your MFC application with server support enabled. This is what you want ATL to provide. Simply create a generic MFC application and add the ATL support once the AppWizard has finished generating your application's initial code base.

Once you have a basic MFC application created, click on the ClassView button in the Workspace window. The topmost line of the tree control will contain your application's name. Right-click on this tree node and note the context menu you see:

If you select the New ATL Object... menu item and respond accordingly, Microsoft Visual Studio will generate ATL code for you and insert it into your MFC application's CWinApp-derived class source.

> **Note if Microsoft Visual Studio begins adding the ATL server code but returns with an error, the server code *was* actually inserted. Microsoft is currently reviewing this Microsoft Visual Studio bug.**

The first changes you'll note will be the addition of some included files:

```
#include <initguid.h>
#include "ATLTest_i.c"
```

These files are required to create your application's type library **GUID**. Just as MFC would do if you used the MFC COM server classes, Microsoft Visual Studio added code in InitInstance() to check the command line for registration/unregistration actions and to initialize the COM runtime. The code in InitInstance() actually calls a helper function, InitATL():

```
if (!InitATL())
    return FALSE;
```

As with any initialization code in InitInstance(), if InitATL() fails, it returns FALSE. In that case, InitInstance() returns FALSE which terminates the application.

If you further examine the code Microsoft Visual Studio added, you'll see you now have an instance of an ATL module declared, an object map created, and override code for CWinApp's ExitInstance() and CComModule's Lock() and Unlock() methods. There is also a CComModule helper function called FindOneOf() to help scan the command line for registration commands.

I'll leave the code in InitATL() for you to examine. Suffice to say the COM runtime is initialized, then the command line is scanned for UnregServer and RegServer commands; these indicate the application should unregister or register itself as a COM local server. If registration is desired, the registration takes place, the COM runtime is shut down, and InitATL() returns FALSE to InitInstance(). The application will now shut down, as is appropriate when simply registering. On the other hand, if the application is to be run instead, the class object for the module is registered, and if that is successful, the application continues executing.

You'll also see Microsoft Visual Studio added an IDL file and modified the project's settings to have the IDL file compiled, as you would expect. You can now add methods to the IDL file, as required, to provide the COM functionality you're looking for. There is one important thing to remember – MIDL will not only create the requisite COM implementation files for you, but it will also create the proxy/stub code you'll need to create the proxy/stub DLL your clients will require when using your local server. Don't forget to compile the proxy/stub DLL code and register that. You won't get far if you don't!

Greetings

This might seem an odd way to end the book, but I've included not one but two sample programs that illustrate ATL's capability is a very straightforward way – the `Greeter` and `GreeterTest` samples.

`Greeter` is a 100% pure ATL project, which I created with the ATL AppWizard. This compiles to form a DLL in which is stored some string resources containing various greetings – some moderately formal, others highly informal, but none rude! I can't go into much detail about the code for `Greeter` other than to invite you to peek in **ClassView** to see a very different class structure, and **FileView** that contains some unusual files. Note the COM interface `IGreeter` which contains the three methods contained in the DLL, is defined in the `Greeter.idl` file and implemented in the `GreeterImpl.cpp` file. The functions are:

> ➢ `GetSalutation()` – which pulls the string out the of string resource
> ➢ `GetMaxSalutationLength()` – which sets the maximum length for the string, 45 characters in this case
> ➢ `GetNumGreetings()` – which sets the maximum number of greetings on offer, that is 5

Obviously you can change these last two if you so wish. Of course, you can also add to the string resource using the resource editor.

Two other files are worthy of note: `Greeter.cpp` contains the standard functionality that make the DLLs work – including the essential `DllMain()` function. `Greeter.h` contains a long list of preprocessor directives and function definitions used by ATL behind the scenes, and doesn't make easy reading. However this file is needed if `Greeter` is to be used by MFC, which is where `GreeterTest` comes in.

`GreeterTest`'s name betrays its function. Its task is to extract greetings from the DLL and present them in a simple dialog box with additional functionality to allow scrolling between different greetings. As I just said, the header file for `Greeter` is required by `GreeterTest` for it to compile, so copy `Greeter.h` across to the `GreeterTest` directory. The outcome of this little exercise is the following:

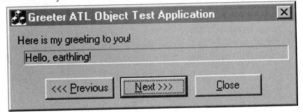

MFC Quick Index A

Functions and Macros in MFC

_afxModuleAddrThis, 913
AFX_API_EXPORT, 671
AFX_CLASS_EXPORT, 670
AFX_DATA_EXPORT, 671
AFX_MANAGE_STATE(), 681, 912, 913
AfxBeginThread(), 608, 616
AfxEnableControl Container(), 956
AfxEndThread(), 612
AfxFreeLibrary(), 685
AfxGetAppName(), 650, 971
AfxGetResourceHandle(), 363, 685
AfxHookWindowCreate() , 636
AfxInitExtensionModule() , 683
AfxInitRichEdit(), 258
AfxInitRichEditCtrl(), 419
AfxLoadLibrary(), 418, 685
AfxLockTempMaps(), 394
AfxMessageBox(), 242, 284, 285, 520
AfxOleRegisterProperty PageClass(), 898
AfxParseURL(), 1003
AfxParseURLEx(), 1003, 1004
AfxRegisterWndClass(), 373
AfxTermExtension Module(), 684

AfxThrowDBException(), 546
AfxThrowFileException(), 549
AfxThrowResource Exception(), 549
AfxThrowUser Exception(), 378, 545
AfxUnhookWindow Create(), 636
AfxUnlockTempMaps(), 394
AfxVerifyLicFile(), 910
AND_CATCH, 543
ASSERT, 686, 720
BEGIN_DISPATCH_ MAP(), 865
BEGIN_EVENT_MAP(), 904
BEGIN_EVENTSINK_ MAP(), 931
BEGIN_MESSAGE_ MAP(), 366
BEGIN_PARSE_MAP(), 1038
BEGIN_PROPPAGEIDS(), 896, 897
CATCH, 543
CATCH_ALL, 543
CompareElements(), 571
ConstructElements(), 577
CopyElements(), 572
CreateElements(), 580
DDP_, 899
DDP_PostProcessing(), 899, 900
DDV_, 898
DDX_, 898

DDX_Control(), 282, 501, 928
DDX_FieldText(), 754
DDX_HexText(), 277, 278
DDX_TextWithFormat(), 276
DECLARE_DISPATCH_ MAP(), 865
DECLARE_DYNAMIC(), 670
DECLARE_ PROPPAGEIDS(), 896
DestroyElements(), 580
DestructElements(), 577
DISP_, 866
DISPATCH_MAP(), 903
DumpElements(), 570, 580
END_DISPATCH_MAP(), 865
END_EVENT_MAP(), 904
END_PARSE_MAP(), 1038
END_PROPPAGEIDS(), 896
END_TRY, 543
EVENT_CUSTOM(), 904
EVENT_PARAM(), 904
IMPLEMENT_ OLECREATE_EX(), 897
ITS_EMPTY, 1039
ITS_RAW, 1039, 1048
MAKEINTRESOURCE, 507
ON_CBN_DBLCLK(), 262
ON_CBN_SELCHANGE() , 262
ON_COMMAND(), 382
ON_COMMAND_ RANGE(), 381

MFC Quick Index B

Classes, a list of the main references to MFC classes

Methods, a list of significant references to MFC methods

Index

Index

A